HISTORICAL DICTIONARY

The historical dictionaries present essential information on a broad range of subjects, including American and world history, art, business, cities, countries, cultures, customs, film, global conflicts, international relations, literature, music, philosophy, religion, sports, and theater. Written by experts, all contain highly informative introductory essays on the topic and detailed chronologies that, in some cases, cover vast historical time periods but still manage to heavily feature more recent events.

Brief A–Z entries describe the main people, events, politics, social issues, institutions, and policies that make the topic unique, and entries are cross-referenced for ease of browsing. Extensive bibliographies are divided into several general subject areas, providing excellent access points for students, researchers, and anyone wanting to know more. Additionally, maps, photographs, and appendixes of supplemental information aid high school and college students doing term papers or introductory research projects. In short, the historical dictionaries are the perfect starting point for anyone looking to research in these fields.

HISTORICAL DICTIONARIES OF THE AMERICAS

Jon Woronoff, Series Editor

Honduras, 2nd ed., by Harvey K. Meyer and Jessie H. Meyer. 1994.

Cuba, 2nd ed., by Jaime Suchlicki. 2001.

Mexico, 2nd ed., by Marvin Àlisky. 2008.

Haiti, by Michael R. Hall. 2012.

Colombia, by Harvey F. Kline. 2012.

Panama, by Thomas M. Leonard. 2015.

Dominican Republic, by Eric Paul Roorda. 2016.

El Salvador, by Orlando J. Perez. 2016.

Chile, 4th ed., by Salvatore Bizzarro. 2017.

Peru, by Peter F. Klarén. 2017.

Trinidad and Tobago New Ed., by Rita Pemberton, Debbie McCollin, Gelien Matthews, and Michael Toussaint. 2018.

Venezuela, 3rd ed., by Tomás Straka, Guillermo Guzmán Mirabal, and Alejandro E. Cáceres. 2018.

Guatemala, by Michael F. Fry. 2018.

Costa Rica, New ed., by David Díaz-Arias, Ronny Viales Hurtado, and Juan José Marín Hernández. 2019.

Argentina, New ed., by Bernardo A. Duggan and Colin M. Lewis. 2019.

Historical Dictionary of Argentina

New Edition

Bernardo A. Duggan and Colin M. Lewis

ROWMAN & LITTLEFIELD
Lanham • Boulder • New York • London

Published by Rowman & Littlefield
An imprint of The Rowman & Littlefield Publishing Group, Inc.
4501 Forbes Boulevard, Suite 200, Lanham, Maryland 20706
www.rowman.com

Unit A, Whitacre Mews, 26-34 Stannary Street, London SE11 4AB

British Library Cataloguing in Publication Information Available

Library of Congress Cataloging-in-Publication Data

Names: Duggan, Bernardo A., 1963- author. | Lewis, Colin M., author.
Title: Historical dictionary of Argentina / Bernardo A. Duggan, Colin M. Lewis.
Description: New edition. | Lanham, MD : Rowman & Littlefield, [2018] | Series: Historical dictionaries of the Americas | Includes bibliographical references.
Identifiers: LCCN 2018040419 (print) | LCCN 2018042858 (ebook) | ISBN 9781538119709 (Electronic) | ISBN 9781538119693 (cloth : alk. paper)
Subjects: LCSH: Argentina—History—Dictionaries. | Argentina—Biography—Dictionaries.
Classification: LCC F2804 (ebook) | LCC F2804 .D85 2018 (print) | DDC 982.003—dc23
LC record available at https://lccn.loc.gov/2018040419

∞ The paper used in this publication meets the minimum requirements of American National Standard for Information Sciences Permanence of Paper for Printed Library Materials, ANSI/NISO Z39.48-1992.

Printed in the United States of America.

Contents

Editor's Foreword

Argentina has always been a country of promise. It was about five centuries ago when it was carved out of South America by Spain, and much of its readily available wealth was harnessed to the needs of the metropolis. The country has also showed much promise since independence in 1810, becoming a republic and sometimes democracy, striving to become a modern and efficient nation. Alas, during this long trajectory it only came through on its promise periodically. Economically, it initially developed a very abundant agriculture thanks to the rich and fertile land, although it did not always manage its economy overly well, swinging back and forth between liberal and statist economic models, often spending more than it earned. Indeed, economic miracles faded, and political crises proliferated at times—this perhaps due to politics, which also kept swinging in different directions, from greater to lesser democracy, from elected leaders from the elite to others of a more populist bent to outright dictators, including military ones. Foreign policy sometimes made things worse, rarely better. Yet the country managed to maintain a vibrant culture—music, dance, art, literature, cinema, and theater—throughout, and somehow there was always a promise of better times to come.

It is not easy to write a historical dictionary about a country with such a long history, and especially so many twists and turns, but this volume has clearly succeeded. Just how complicated and uneven its trajectory was appears immediately in the chronology and is explained more cogently in the introduction. But the bulk of the information comes in the dictionary section, with dozens and dozens of entries on important geographic features and events, to say nothing of institutions, be they political, economic, or religious, and the many persons—initially only men but recently often women—who determined the country's direction. And yes, there are many entries on its culture as well, so that reading this book is far from dull, and one does come to an appreciation of why Argentina has often failed and yet come back again and will hopefully this time around fare better than before. That is for the reader to determine, as the authors stick mainly to facts and provide them in abundance.

The authors of this volume, Bernardo A. Duggan and Colin M. Lewis, have jointly filled what has been a long and regrettable gap in the series, given the importance of Argentina not only to the continent but on a global scale. The former was born and educated in Argentina, although he now lives in Australia. He studied at the London School of Economics, obtaining his doctorate with a dissertation on establishing iron and steel as a strategic industry in Argentina. His coauthor is professor emeritus of Latin American economic history at the London School of Economics. During a long career, Professor Lewis has been associated with various institutions in Britain and taught in Latin America; he has written several books on Argentina. These include *Argentina: A Short History* in 2002, *British Railways in Argentina* in 2015, and another on Argentina's business history coming along. Drs. Duggan and Lewis have gotten this crucial volume going and will hopefully keep it on track for a while.

Jon Woronoff
Series Editor

Acknowledgments

We are grateful to numerous colleagues and friends who have read material included in this historical dictionary. Their suggestions and thoughts—both direct and unwitting—have contributed to the scope and content of the project. We would also like to thank librarians and staff at the British Library of Political and Economic Sciences, London School of Economics and Political Science, Biblioteca Tornquist, Banco Central de la República Argentina, and the Library of the Universidad Torcuato Di Tella, Buenos Aires, for their help in identifying research material and data sources. Bernardo would particularly like to thank the Australian 18 Footers League, Double Bay, Sydney, for providing a wonderful "office" in which to work on the book, and its staff—especially Monika Gillespie, Riz Collins, Marc Desveaux, Maria-Elena dos Santos, and Jade Follett—for providing the necessary sustenance and keeping him cheerful. Colin owes a huge debt of gratitude to Elfair for her patience and tolerance, and for her love and unstinting moral support.

Reader's Note

Place names used in this book follow modern usage, with reference to earlier alternatives. Surnames follow current common usage.

In Argentina, as in several Spanish-speaking countries, two surnames are common, the father's surname preceding the mother's; at marriage, a wife may add the husband's surname to her own. For example, in the case of a marriage between John Doe and Jane Smith, the surname of children of the marriage would be Doe Smith, and Jane Smith might take the name Jane Smith de Doe. These conventions are not as common now as before the late 20th century. In the case of key figures, both names are listed and cross-referenced. (*See* indicates the name under which the entry appears.)

In order to facilitate rapid and efficient location of information and to make this book as useful a reference tool as possible, extensive cross-references have been provided within the dictionary section. Within individual dictionary entries, terms that have their own entries are in **boldface type** the first time they appear. Related terms that do not appear in the text are indicated in the *See also*. *See* refers to other entries that deal with the topic.

With a few exceptions, the information in this book ends in October 2017, the date of midterm congressional elections during the presidency of Mauricio Macri.

Acronyms and Abbreviations

AEA	Asociación Empresaria Argentina
ANE	Argentine North Eastern Railway Company
AR	Acción por la República
ARI	Afirmación para una República Igualitaria
AySA	Aguas y Saneamientos Argentinos SA
BAC	Buenos Aires Central Railway Company
BAGS	Buenos Ayres Great Southern Railway Company
BA&P	Buenos Ayres & Pacific Railway Company
BA&R	Buenos Ayres & Rosario Railway Company
BAW	Buenos Ayres Western Railway Company
BCRA	Banco Central de la República Argentina
CC	Coalición Cívica
CCR	Cordoba Central Railway Company
CEDES	Centro de Estudios del Estado y Sociedad
CEMA/ UCEMA	Centro de Estudios Macroeconómicos de Argentina
CEPAL	Comisión Económica para Amèrica Latina (y el Caribe)
CGE	Confederación General Económica
CGT	Confederación General del Trabajo
CGTA	Confederación General del Trabajo de los Argentinos
CONADE	Consejo Nacional de Desarrollo
CONADEP	Comisión Nacional sobre la Desaparición de Personas
DGF	Dirección General de Ferrocarriles
ECLA(C)	Economic Commission for Latin America (and the Caribbean)
ER	Entre Rios Railway Company
ERP	Ejército Revolucionario del Pueblo
ESMA	Escuela Superior de Mecánica de la Armada

EU	European Union
FAA	Federación Agraria Argentina
FAP	Fuerzas Armadas Peronistas
FAR	Fuerzas Armadas Revolucionárias
FAUNEN	Frente Amplio Unen
FFAA	Ferrocarriles Argentinos
FLACSO	Facultad Lainoamericana de Ciencias Sociales
FM	Fabricaciones Militares
FORJA	Fuerza de Orientación Radical de la Joven Argentina
FpV/PJ	Frente para la Victoria/Partido Justicialista
FREJULI	Frenta Justicialista de Liberación
FREPASO	Frente País Solidario
FR/PJ	Frente Renovador/Partido Justicialista
GB	Great Britain
GDP	gross domestic product
GOU	Grupo de Oficiales Unidos
IAME	Industrias Aeronáuticas y Mecánicas del Estado
IAPI	Instituto Argentino de Promoción del Intercambio
IKA	Industrias Kaiser Argentina
IMF	International Monetary Fund
JP	Juventud Peronista
MID	Movimiento de Integración y Desarrollo
MNT	Movimiento Nacionalista Tacuara
MPN	Movimiento Popular Neuquino
MRP	Movimiento Renovador Peronista
MSTM	Movimiento de Sacredotes para el Tercer Mundo
PAMI	Programa de Atención Médica Integrada
PCP	Partido Conserdador Popular
PDC	Partido Demócrata Cristiano
PDN	Partido Demócrata Nacional
PDP	Partido Demócrata Progresista
PI	Partido Intransigente

PJ	Partido Justicialista
PP	Partido Peronista
PPF	Partido Peronista Feminino
PRO	Propuesta Republicana
PS	Partido Socialista
SIAM Di Tella	Sección Industrial Amasadoras Mecánicas
SOEs	state-owned enterprises
SOMISA	Sociedad Mixta Siderúrgica Argentina
SRA	Sociedad Rural Argentina
TRIPLE A	Alianza Anticomunista Argentina
UADE	Universidad Argentina de la Empresa
UBA	Universidad de Buenos Aires
UC	Unidad/Unión Ciudadana
UCA	Universidad Católica Argentina
UCEDE/ UCeDé	Unión del Centro Democrático
UCEMA/ CEMA	Universidad del Centro de Estudios Macroeconómicos de Argentina *See* CEMA/UCEMA
UCR	Unión Cívica Radical
UCRI	Unión Cívica Radical Intransigente
UCRJR	Unión Cívica Radical Junta Renovadora
UCRP	Unión Cívica Radical del Pueblo
UD	Unión Democrática
UDESA	Universidad de San Andrés
UF	Unión Ferroviaria
UNA	Una Nación Avanzada
UNA	Unidos por una Nueva Alternativa
UNASUR	Unión de Naciones Sudamericanas
UNO	United Nations Organization
UP	Unión Popular
US	United States
UTDT	Universidad Torcuato Di Tella

YPF   Yacimientos Petrolíferos Fiscales

Map

Argentina.

Chronology

c. 11,000 BC and beyond Evidence of human settlement in southern Patagonia—Pehuenches and Puelches; Diaguita tribes along the eastern slopes of the central and northern Andes; Guaraní in northeast.

c. 1480 Parts of the northwest incorporated into the Inca Empire.

1500 Second expedition of Amerigo Vespucci sails along the east coast of South America, possibly entering the Río de la Plata, the first Europeans to do so.

1516 Juan Díaz de Solís, Spanish navigator, enters the Río de la Plata, which he names Mar Dulce (Sweet/Fresh Water). Landing on the east bank (present-day Uruguay), he and most of his crew are killed.

1520 Expedition headed by Ferdinand Magellan (Fernão Magalhaes) sails down the east coast of South America. He "discovers" Patagonia and Tierra del Fuego, passing the Straights. There he encounters the Tehuelche, the "giant" big-feet Indians from which the region takes its name.

1526 Following Solís's route, Sebastian Cabot, an Italian-born explorer employed by the Spanish Crown, surveys part of the River Plate delta, including sections of the rivers Paraná and Uruguay, trading with Guaraní Indians in the area of present-day Asunción. He acquired silver artifacts, subsequently referring to the river and the region as River of Silver (Río de la Plata).

1536 3 February: Having arrived in January with a party of approximately 1,500 sailors and soldiers, Pedro de Mendoza founds the city of Buenos Aires on the banks of the River Plate. He names the settlement the City of the Most Holy Trinity and Port of Our Lady of Good Air (Ciudad de la Santísima Trinidad y el Puerto de Nuestra Señora Santa María de Buen Aire). Within five years, after repeated attacks by Pampean Indians, the city is abandoned, the few survivors heading upriver to what is now Paraguay, leaving behind livestock and belongings.

c. 1540–1570 Explorers and settlers from present-day Peru and Chile begin to penetrate the northwest and west regions of Argentina, establishing towns and cities, along with civil, ecclesiastical, and military administrations in areas that will become the provinces of Tucumán, Salta, and Mendoza.

1573 Foundation of the cities of Córdoba and Santa Fe, which will subsequently become major centers, especially the former, where the first university in the country is established. First set up by the Jesuits as the Collegium Maximum de Córdoba in 1613, by 1622 the institution becomes a university with full degree-awarding rights.

1580 Successful refounding of the city of Buenos Aires by Juan de Garay, leading an expeditionary force from Asunción.

1582–1594 Establishment of La Rioja, Jujuy, and San Luis, cities that will later become capitals of provinces that take the same name.

1617 Creation of the colonial jurisdiction of Buenos Aires, centered on the city. Several other civic and ecclesiastical administrative units are founded in the littoral and center of the country.

1713 First licensed slave imports into Buenos Aires, a commercial monopoly granted to Great Britain under the terms of the Treaty of Utrecht—the Asiento de Negros.

1776 As part of a series of major colonial administrative reorganizations (the Bourbon Reforms), the Viceroyalty of the Río de la Plata is created. It included modern Bolivia, Paraguay, and Uruguay in addition to Argentina. Further organizational reforms follow between 1782 and 1785, resulting in the formation of legal and civil units and bodies, including eight *intendencias* (provinces) and an *audiencia* (superior law court) in Buenos Aires. Pedro de Cevallos Cortés y Calderón is named the first viceroy.

1778–1784 Juan José de Vértiz de Salcedo is second viceroy.

1784–1789 Nicolás Felipe Cristóbal del Campo y Rodríguez de Salamanca, Marquis of Loreto, is viceroy.

1789–1795 Nicolás Antonio Arredondo Pelegrín is viceroy.

1794 Consulado de Comercio (Merchant Guild) of Buenos Aires is set up, designed to order imperial "free trade" within the viceroyalty. Manuel Belgrano is appointed secretary of the Consulado.

1795 First meat-salting plant (*saladero*) is set up in Quilmes, southwest of the city of Buenos Aires.

1795–1797 Pedro Melo de Portugal y Villena is viceroy.

1797–1799 Antonio Olaguer Feliú is viceroy.

1799–1801 Gabriel de Avilés del Fierro, Marquis de Avilés, is viceroy.

1801–1804 Joaquín del Pinto Sánchez de Rozas Romero y Negrete is viceroy.

1804–1807 Rafael de Sobremonte y Núñez del Castillo, Marquis Sobremonte, is viceroy, the last Spaniard to hold the post. During the British invasion of 1806, he flees Buenos Aires with the colonial treasury, regarded by many contemporaries as an act of cowardice.

1806–1807 British invasions of the River Plate. **June 1806:** A British fleet commanded by Sir Home Riggs Popham, with land forces led by Sir William Carr Beresford, arrives off the coast of Buenos Aires, taking the town of Quilmes on **25 June**. Buenos Aires is occupied on **27 June** and Beresford designated vice governor. Santiago Liniers organizes a spirited defense and reconquest. **12 August:** Beresford surrenders. **3 February 1807:** An expeditionary force headed by Admiral Sir Charles Sterling and General Sir Samuel Auchmuty besieges and captures the city of Montevideo. **10 May:** Lieutenant General John Whitelocke arrives in Montevideo to take command of troops assigned the task of retaking Buenos Aires. **27 June:** Whitelocke lands on the coast of Buenos Aires, repulsing Liniers on **1 June** and marching on the city, parts of which are occupied by British forces on **3 and 4 July**. After several days of intense urban guerilla warfare, Whitelocke signs an armistice with Liniers on **6 July**, agreeing to an exchange of prisoners and the complete evacuation of the River Plate by British forces.

1807 10 February: Declaring Sobremonte to have abandoned his post, the City Council (Cabildo) of Buenos Aires appoints French-born Santiago Antonio Maríde Liniers y Bremond viceroy (1807–1809), the first viceroy to be appointed in such a manner. Subsequently, in recognition for his services to the Crown—repelling the first British invasion—Liniers is created first Count of Buenos Aires.

1809 May–July: Beginning of the independence movement in the Viceroyalty of the River Plate in Upper Peru (Bolivia).

1809–1810 Baltasar Hidalgo de Cisneros y de la Torre is viceroy. The last viceroy to serve in Buenos Aires, he declares the ports open to free trade with friendly and neutral powers, remaining in office until ousted during the May Revolution (Revolución de Mayo) of **25 May 1810**.

1810 22–25 May: City Council of Buenos Aires holds an "open meeting," Cabildo Abierto. Viceroy Cisneros is deposed on 25 May and the First Patriotic Junta (Primera Junta de Gobierno) formed, claiming authority over the whole of the former viceroyalty, encountering loyalist opposition in Montevideo and the northwest and secessionists elsewhere. **25–26 August:** Loyalists, including Liniers, are executed on the orders of the Primera Junta.

1810–1811 Partisan struggle in Buenos Aires and royalist successes at sea and in the north.

1811 Conservative collective presidency—First Triumvirate (Primer Triunvirato)—displaces liberal-leaning First Patriotic Junta.

1812 27 February: Modern Argentinian flag is flown for the first time at Rosario by Manuel Belgrano. **March:** José de San Martín and Carlos María de Alvear return from Europe, imparting leadership and impetus to the struggle for Independence. **8 October:** San Martín and Alvear, at the head of their respective regiments, demand the resignation of the First Triumvirate and form the Second Triumvirate. Abolition of the transatlantic slave trade.

1813 At the Assembly of the Year 13 (Asamblea del Año XIII), provincial representatives meet in Buenos Aires to establish representative forms of government and abolish hereditary titles. It takes the name of the Constitutional Assembly of the Provinces of the River Plate. San Martín and Belgrano achieve some initial notable victories over royalist armies, but the administration in Buenos Aires unable to prevent the separation of such former elements of the viceroyalty as Bolivia, Paraguay, and Uruguay take form. **November:** The defeat of Belgrano in Upper Peru leads to San Martín being appointed head of the patriotic forces.

1814 San Martín becomes governor of Mendoza and begins to organize the Army of the Andes to take the revolutionary struggle to Chile and Peru, subsequently becoming known as the Liberator.

1815 Alvear becomes supreme director (*director supremo*), heading the administration in Buenos Aires.

1816 24 March: Congress of Tucumán opens, leading to the formal declaration of independence on **9 July**. Juan Martín de Pueyrredón becomes supreme director.

1817 Congress moves from Tucumán to Buenos Aires, confirming the status of the city as the seat of the government of the new state. San Martín crosses the Andes and defeats royalist forces at the decisive battle of Chacabuco.

1818 2 April: San Martín's victory at the battle of Maipú reinforces the victory at Chacabuco, consolidating the independence of Chile and preparing the way to take the war to Peru, the remaining center of Spanish power in South America.

1819 25 May: Promulgation of the first national constitution (Constitución de la Provincias Unidas de Sudamérica), establishing a unitary system of government.

1820 Year of Anarchy: struggles between Federalists and Unitarians and conflict among various provinces. **20 August:** San Martín sets sail from Valparaiso, Chile, aiming to liberate Peru.

1821 Buenos Aires Cabildo abolished. Martín Rodríguez becomes governor of Buenos Aires, and Bernardino Rivadavia plans a series of liberal reforms, including the founding of the University of Buenos Aires, designed to modernize the administration and abolish remaining vestiges of colonial rule.

1822 United States recognizes the independence of Argentina. Rivadavia promulgates Amnesty Law (Ley de Olvido), which facilitates the return of political exiles.

1823 Publication of the *Gaceta Mercantil*, first modern newspaper designed to cover economic, political, and cultural affairs.

1824 Province of Buenos Aires signs a contract for a one-million-pound loan with Baring Brothers of London. Juan Gregorio de la Heras is appointed governor of Buenos Aires.

1825 Britain recognizes independence, signing the Treaty of Amity, Navigation, and Commerce. Brazilian forces enter Uruguay, leading to war between the Empire of Brazil and the Provincias Unidas. First imports of merino sheep arrive.

1826 Bernardino Rivadavia elected president of the United Provinces; new strongly centralist constitution is promulgated.

1826–1827 Brazilian–Argentine land conflict, with an outcome largely favorable to Argentina. **8 February 1827:** Admiral William Brown, in command of an Argentine squadron, defeats the Brazilian fleet off Juncal, capturing virtually all enemy vessels. **13 February:** Lavalle vanquishes Brazilian land forces at the battle of Bacacy.

1827 Rivadavia resigns as provinces oppose the centralist constitution. Vicente López y Planes is appointed caretaker president, but the national administration disintegrates. Manuel Dorrega is elected governor of Buenos Aires; Juan Manuel de Rosas is appointed to defend and extend the "Indian Frontier" of the province of Buenos Aires. International financial crisis, leading to default on the Baring Loan.

1828 The governments of Rio de Janeiro and Buenos Aires recognize the independence of Uruguay, nominally guaranteed by Great Britain. Juan Galo de Lavalle and veterans of the war opposed to the treaty with Brazil lead a rebellion against Dorrego, who is captured and executed.

1829 April–June: Lavelle's Unitarian forces are defeated by the Federalist Rosas, but subsequently, the Unitarist army led by José M. Paz secures a victory over Federalist general Facundo Quiroga. Stalemate is recognized by

Lavalle and Rosas in the Pact of Cañuelas, an effort to reestablish a civilian administration. **8 December:** Rosas becomes governor of Buenos Aires and is granted extraordinary powers. In effect, he rules until 1852.

1830–1831 Continuing hostilities between Unitarist League of the Interior and Federalist Pact of the Littoral. Federalist forces gradually secure the upper hand.

1832 Rosas is reelected governor of the province of Buenos Aires but is denied extension of extraordinary powers and steps down. Juan Ramón Balcarce becomes governor. The *Beagle*, a British Royal Navy scientific survey vessel captained by Robert FitzRoy with Charles Darwin on board, arrives in Argentine waters. Rosas leads expeditionary force against Pampean Indians, securing the southern frontier of Buenos Aires.

1833 Rosas's associates found the Popular Society for the Restoration (of Rosas as governor—Sociedad Popular Restauradora). **October:** Revolution of Restorers (Revolución de los Restauradores) leads to ouster of Balcarce as governor. Juan José Viamonte is elected governor but is forced to resign by Rosas a year later, facilitating his own return to power in 1835. Great Britain claims the Falkland Islands.

1834 Viamonte resigns, replaced by Manuel Vicente Maza.

1835 Rosas is reelected governor of Buenos Aires and granted "supreme and absolute" powers, approved by plebiscite.

1837 Diplomatic rupture with France.

1837–1838 War between the Argentine provinces, headed by Rosas, and the Bolivian–Peruvian Confederation.

1838 French warships blockade the port of Buenos Aires. *Estancieros* in the south of the province of Buenos Aires stage a revolt again Rosas.

1839 Hostilities between Uruguay and Rosas: Uruguayan forces and local allies invade the littoral provinces, anticipating an anti-Rosas uprising. Rosas defeats southern rebels, whose leaders are murdered in Chascomús, an act of retribution intended to discourage further uprisings.

1840 Anti-Rosas revolts in various interior and littoral provinces. End of the first French blockade.

1841 Defeat of most anti-Rosas forces in the interior, including those led by Lavalle, who is executed.

1841–1842 Roses instigates "reign of terror."

1842–1851 The "Great War" (Guerra Grande) in Uruguay, with Rosas intervening against Unitarian and pro-Liberal factions based in Montevideo, which is subject to the "great siege."

1845–1848 Anglo-French blockade of Buenos Aires, in part to secure the independence of Uruguay. Major clash of intervention occurs at the battle of Vuelta de Obligado in 1845, a victory for Anglo-French naval forces, though the conflict rapidly degenerates into a stalemate.

1847 Royal Navy abandons blockade of Buenos Aires

1849 Formal ending of hostilities between Buenos Aires and Great Britain.

1850 Rosas is reelected governor of Buenos Aires. Peace treaty between France and Buenos Aires. Brazil invades the interior of Uruguay in support of Liberal factions besieged in Montevideo. Rosas breaks relations with Brazil.

1851 Brazil and several Argentine provinces form an alliance against Rosas. Formation of the Grand Army, headed by Justo José Urquiza, governor of the province of Entre Ríos, hitherto a staunch ally of Rosas.

1852 3 February: Rosas's forces are defeated by Urquiza at the battle of Caseros. Rosas leaves for exile in Great Britain. **31 May:** Signing of the San Nicolás Accord by most provinces, reaffirming the 1831 Federal Pact, and the calling of a Constituent Assembly to draft a new constitution. Province of Buenos Aires rejects the accord, beginning a 10-year separation from the Confederation then headed by Urquiza.

1853 Promulgation of the Argentine Constitution, ratified by acceding provinces on 1 May. In view of the separation of the province of Buenos Aires, the city of Paraná, province of Entre Ríos, becomes the capital of the Confederation.

1854 Urquiza is elected first president of the Confederation.

1856 Establishment of Colonia La Esperanza in the province of Santa Fe, usually regarded as marking the beginning of modern European immigration.

1857 Inauguration of the first railway, Western Railway (Ferrocarril Oeste de Buenos Aires), financed by a group of prominent local and foreign merchants.

1859 War between Buenos Aires and the Confederation—the outcome is inconclusive but leads to the reincorporation of the province. Pact of San José de Flores.

1860 Bartolomé Mitre elected governor of the province of Buenos Aires. Santiago Derqui succeeds Urquiza as president of the Confederation, though Urquiza remains the dominant political influence. **8 October:** Derqui decrees the official name of the country to be La República Argentina.

1861 Renewed conflict between Buenos Aires and the Confederation. At the battle of Pavón, Mitre emerges victorious. Derqui goes into exile in Montevideo. Minor changes are made to the 1853 constitution in response to Buenos Aires demands. Buenos Aires becomes capital of the nation, as well as the province.

1862 Mitre elected new/first president of the Republic of Argentina under the slightly amended constitution.

1865 Outbreak of the War of the Triple Alliance (a.k.a. Paraguayan War)—Argentina, Brazil, and Uruguay against Paraguay. Mitre is named head of the land forces. Beginning of Welsh colonization in the Chubut Valley.

1866 Foundation of the Rural Society (Sociedad Rural Argentina), the premier association representing *estancieros*, particularly of the province of Buenos Aires.

1868 Domingo Faustino Sarmiento elected second president of the republic.

1869 First National Census. Publication of the influential daily newspaper *La Prensa* by José Clemente Paz.

1870 End of the Paraguayan War. Urquiza is assassinated by insurgents led by regional caudillo López Jordan. Foundation of the principal liberal newspaper *La Nación* by Mitre.

1871 López Jordan is defeated by federal forces commanded by general Julio Argentino Roca and forced into exile, an event often taken to mark the end of the "age of caudillos." Outbreak of yellow fever in Buenos Aires: the high death toll—possibly 15,000—prompts a campaign for improve public health. Promulgation of the Civil Code (Código Vélez Sarsfield).

1872 "Indian Wars" in the southwest of the province of Buenos Aires result in the extension and stabilization of the frontier. Publication of the epic poem *Martín Fierro* by José Fernández—a work that idealizes the free gaucho lifestyle. The main character in the poem, Fierro, becomes an iconic figure in national culture.

1874 Nicolás Avellaneda is elected president. Mitre, claiming to defend the interests of the province of Buenos Aires, stages an uprising but is defeated. Avellaneda seeks to consolidate the Indian frontier.

1875–1879 The Conquest of the Desert (Salidas de Roca), a series of campaigns against nomadic and bellicose tribes and discontented gauchos that results in the eradication of the "Indian menace," secures Argentine control of much of the western pampas and Patagonia and opens vast tracts of land to cattle raising and settlement. The planning and execution of the campaign is headed by Roca.

1876 Consolidation of immigration legislation and founding of the Immigration Department, charged with promoting migration and settlement.

1880 Roca is elected president. The defeated candidate, Carlos Tejedor, governor of Buenos Aires, revolts. With the defeat of Tejedor, the city of Buenos Aires is federalized, becoming exclusively the capital of the republic; work begins on the construction of the city of La Plata, the new capital of the province of Buenos Aires. The inauguration of Roca and the federalization of the city of Buenos Aires are taken to mark the definitive political formation of the nation-state and the consolidation of oligarchic rule by the National Autonomist Party (Partido Autonomista Nacional—PAN), a confederation of regional political and economic interests.

1881 Argentina joins the gold standard, introducing the first national currency.

1882 City of La Plata inaugurated by Buenos Aires Governor Dardo Rocha.

c. 1882–1885 Economic boom characterized by railway building, frontier consolidation, spread of cattle ranching and wheat farming, formation of banks and various public works companies, monetary reform, and massive foreign investment.

1884 Establishment of a system of national primary education, building on pioneering education reforms by Sarmiento in 1870.

1884–1885 Minor financial crisis, leading to the "temporary" suspension of the gold standard and the introduction of the national, inconvertible paper peso.

1886 Miguel Júarez Celman is elected president.

1887 Formation of the Argentine Industrial Union (Unión Industrial Argentina—UIA), the principal confederation representing nonrural business interests. Beginning of the modernization of the port of Buenos Aires, the Puerto Madero.

1888 Amendment to the Civil Code: civil marriage permitted.

1889 Creation of the Youth Civic Union (Unión Cívica de la Juventud). Founding of the National Historical Museum.

1889–1890 Beginning of the Baring Crisis, an economic crisis triggered by the ending of the investment boom (and capital flight), weakening commodity prices, profligate borrowing (and lending), and corruption, leading to inflation and default—and popular protest.

1890 Formation of the Civic Union (Unión Cívica), a splinter movement of the Youth Civic Union, which will later become the Radical Civic Union (Unión Cívica Radical—UCR), one of the principal political parties of the 20th century. The Civic Union issues a call to arms and establishes a camp in the center of Buenos Aires, triggering clashes with the army that lead to the resignation of Júarez Celman. Vice President Carlos Pellegrini assumes the presidency and serves out the Júarez Celman term of office.

1890–1892 Pellegrini administration stabilizes the economy and reaches agreement with foreign creditors. End of the Baring Crisis and the beginning of recovery.

1891 Beginning of Jewish colonization under the auspices of the Jewish Colonization Association set up by Baron Maurice de Hirsch. Banco de la Nación (official clearing bank) reconstituted in its modern format from an earlier entity that had closed in the Baring Crisis. UCR is formally established.

1892 Luis Sáenz Peña is elected president.

1893 UCR promotes revolts against the oligarchic system in the provinces of Buenos Aires, San Luis, and Santa Fe, pressing for political reform. Revolts put down by federal army.

1894 Modernization of the city of Buenos Aires begins with the inauguration of a Paris-style boulevard, Avenida de Mayo, which will ultimately link the Plaza de Mayo, location of presidential palace Casa Rosada, city hall, and cathedral, with the Plaza de Congreso. Publication of the socialist daily *La Vanguardia*.

1895 Luis Sáenz Peña resigns and is replaced by Vice President José E. Uriburu, who completes the term. Second National Census.

1896 Foundation of the socialist party, headed by Juan B. Justo. Leandro Alem, head of the UCR, commits suicide and is replaced by his nephew, Hipólito Yrigoyen.

1897 Inauguration of the Puerto Madero and first tramways commence operation in the city of Buenos Aires.

1898 Julio Argentino Roca elected president for second time. Launch of the satirical magazine *Caras y Caretas*, edited by José Álvarez.

1899 Gold standard is reestablished, and the Conversion Office (Caja de Conversión) is set up to manage the new monetary system.

1901 Compulsory military service is established. Argentine Workers Federation (Federación Obrera Argentina—FOA) is founded.

1902 Beginning of controls on immigration—Residency Law (Ley 4.144—Ley de Residencia), providing for the deportation of undesirable aliens. Border dispute with Chile resolved with British arbitration—Pacto de Mayo.

1904 Manuel Quintana is elected president. Alfredo Palacios becomes the first Socialist deputy elected to the federal congress.

1905 Radical uprising led by Hipólito Yrigoyen against the oligarchic system, taking Vice President José Figueroa Alcorta hostage. Although the revolt is suppressed, it is the last major violent challenge to the existing order and ultimately leads to political and electoral reform. Publication of the newspaper *La Razón* and magazine *El Hogar*. Labor legislation, limiting work on Sundays, sanctioned by federal congress.

1906 University of La Plata founded. Vice President Figueroa Alcorta assumes the presidency on the death of Manuel Quintana.

1907 Oil is discovered in Patagonia at Comodoro Rivadavia. Labor legislation regulating the hours of work of women and children is passed by Congress.

1908 Southern League (Liga del Sur) is founded in Rosario, province of Santa Fe, an organization representing tenant farmers. Inauguration of the Buenos Aires opera house, Teatro Colón.

1910 Celebration of the centenary of independence, the anniversary of the Revolución de Mayo. Roque Sáenz Peña becomes president. A general strike and mass street protest leads to further controls on immigration, the Social Defense Law (Ley 7.029—Ley de Defensa Social).

1912 Protest by farmers in the province of Santa Fe against terms of tenancies, rents, and commodity prices—El Grito de Alcorta. Sáenz Peña electoral reform law (Ley 8.871—Ley Nacional de Elecciones), providing for a secret ballot, compulsory voting, and "minority representation"—runner-up party receiving one-third of congressional seats contested. Radical candidates triumph in the city of Buenos Aires and province of Santa Fe in the first local elections held after the promulgation of the electoral reform law.

1913 Publication of the daily newspaper *Crítica*, edited by Natalio Botana. President Sáenz Peña hands power to Vice President Victorino de la Plaza due to ill health. First underground railway is opened in the city of Buenos Aires—the first in Latin America. Enrique del Valle Iterlucea is elected the first Socialist senator.

1914 Sáenz Peña dies. Progressive Democratic Party (Partido Democrática Progresista) is founded by Lisandro de la Torre. Third National Census. De la Plaza declares Argentine neutrality at the outbreak of the First World War. The outbreak of the war provokes a major commercial and financial crisis.

1915 System of retirement and invalidity pensions is set up for railway workers.

1916 First election held under electoral law of 1912. Hipólito Yrigoyen of the UCR is elected president. These are regarded as the first fair and free elections to be held in the country. The Radicals secure a majority in the lower house of the federal congress, the Chamber of Deputies.

1918 Federal interventions in conservative-controlled provinces result in the UCR obtaining a majority in the Chamber of Deputies but fail to deliver control of the Senate.

1922 Presidential election is won by UCR candidate Marcelo T. de Alvear.

1924 Differences between Yrigoyen and Alvear over matters of style and substance lead to the "antipersonalists" (anti-Yrigoyen faction) seceding from the UCR.

1928 Presidential election returns Yrigoyen to power.

1929–1930 Yrigoyen fails to deal with the consequences of the onset of the world economic crisis; he concentrates on the nationalization of oil and the federal interventions in the provinces necessary to achieve it.

1930 6 September: Military coup supported by political and economic interests opposed to Yrigoyen. General José Félix Uriburu becomes de facto president.

1931 Uriburu is forced out of office following his failure to impose a proto-fascist political project. **November:** Elections marred by fraud and the abstention of the UCR are won by General Agustín P. Justo, the candidate of the Concordancia coalition.

1932–1940 Regulating boards are created to provide price support and protect the interests of commodity producers.

1933 Controversial Roca–Runciman Agreement with Great Britain.

1935 January: UCR is reunited under the leadership of Alvear and decides to again participate in elections. **May:** Creation of the Banco Central de la República Argentina (BCRA).

1937 Elections marred by fraud return the Concordancia to power, with Roberto M. Ortiz becoming president.

1938–1940 Ortiz attempts to redemocratize the country.

1940 Ortiz is forced out of office by ill health and succeeded by Vice President Ramón S. Castillo, who reverses the redemocratization reforms.

1943 4 June: Lacking legitimacy and support, Castillo is ousted in a coup by the military freemason Grupo de Oficiales Unidos (GOU).

1943–1946 De facto presidencies of Generals Pedro Pablo Ramírez and Edelmiro J. Farrell. Real power increasingly lies with Colonel (later General) Juan Domingo Perón, and attempts to contain him fail.

1946 February: Perón is elected president. **May:** He dissolves the political parties that served as his vehicle to attain power.

1946–1952 Nationalization of the Banco Central, foreign trade, and public utilities; creation of a vast array of state-owned enterprises.

1947 Creation of the Partido Peronista. Law enabling women to vote is passed, but enactment is delayed.

1949 New constitution is adopted.

1951 Perón fails to place his wife Eva as the vice presidential candidate on his election ticket. **November:** Perón is reelected president.

1951–1955 Suspension of constitutional rights under a supposed state of internal warfare, stifling of the opposition, state takeover of nearly all the media, imprisonment of the most vociferous government critics, and severe repression of all dissenting voices.

1952 Death of Eva Perón, mainstay of the president's political support.

1954 April: Controversial election to replace deceased Vice-President Hortensio Quijano; mid-term Congressional elections rigged in favor of the Peronists.

1954–1955 Enactment of legislation establishing absolute divorce, equating legitimate and out-of-wedlock children, and enabling the opening and functioning of brothels pits the president against both the Catholic Church and his opponents.

1955 May: Call for constituent assembly to enact separation of church and state. **June:** Failure of both an attempted coup and efforts by Perón to find a compromise with the ruling classes and the opposition. **September:** The Revolución Libertadora overthrows Perón, who is driven to exile, and General Eduardo Lonardi is declared provisional president. **November:** General Pedro Eugenio Aramburu becomes provisional president after Lonardi is forced to resign; he pursues harsh de-Peronization policies.

1957 Constituent assembly declares the 1853 constitution the valid one, with the exclusion of all the 1949 reforms and the incorporation of article 14 bis (guarantees various basic social rights, including the one to strike).

1958 Elections are a contest between the two factions of a once again split UCR: the UCR Intransigente, headed by Arturo Frondizi and supported by the now proscribed Peronists, and the UCR del Pueblo, headed by Ricardo Balbín and supported by the outgoing military government. Unexpectedly for the latter, Frondizi is elected president.

1959–1962 Heavy pressure from the armed forces to keep Frondizi in line.

1962 18 March: Elections for provincial governors. In the hope of still channeling Peronist votes, Frondizi lifts the proscription on Peronist participation. The Frente Justicialista wins. **29 March:** Frondizi is overthrown by the military and replaced by José María Guido, the president of the Senate.

1963 Restricted presidential elections (proscription of Peronism and the left and restrictions on minor parties) result in Arturo Illia of the UCR del Pueblo being elected with 25 percent of the vote.

1964 Failure of attempt by Perón to return to Argentina from exile.

1965 Illia attempts to defeat Peronism electorally and not through proscription in legislative elections, but the Peronists win.

1966 The Revolución Argentina overthrows Illia and installs General Juan Carlos Onganía as de facto president.

1967 Creation of the left-wing armed group Fuerzas Armadas Peronistas (FAP).

1969 Creation of various Marxist armed groups, of which the most important is the Ejército Revolucionario del Pueblo (ERP). **29 May–3 June:** The Cordobazo—protesting worker and student organizations take over the city of Córdoba with popular support, and repressive military intervention is used to restore order.

1970 Peronist left-wing armed group the Montoneros bursts spectacularly onto the national stage with the kidnapping and assassination of former president General Aramburu. General Roberto M. Levingston replaces Onganía as de facto president.

1971 Levingston resigns, and General Alejandro A. Lanusse succeeds him.

1972 Lanusse paves the way for elections in 1973; he rules himself out of the contest, enables Peronism to participate, and introduces the ballotage system for electing the president and vice president. **November–December:** During a visit to Argentina, Perón co-opts the Peronists and an array of political parties into the Frente Justicialista de Liberación (Frejuli) and imposes the election ticket: Héctor J. Cámpora for president and Vicente Solano Lima for vice president.

1973 March: The Frejuli wins the election in the first round. **May:** Cámpora and Solano Lima take office. **June:** Perón makes his final return from exile in order to take charge of public affairs. **July:** Cámpora and Solano Lima resign, and Raúl Lastiri, president of the Chamber of Deputies, becomes the interim president. **September:** Perón wins the presidential election.

1974 May: Perón publicly breaks with the Peronist left. **1 July:** Perón dies and is succeeded by the vice president, his wife Isabel.

1974–1976 Isabel Perón's presidency. Characterized by the ever-bloodier internecine struggle within Peronism and the left, mounting economic problems, and a political vacuum, it lands the country in an unprecedented crisis.

1976 March: Isabel Perón is overthrown and replaced by a military junta headed by General Jorge Rafael Videla. The Proceso de Reorganización Nacional begins.

1976–1979 War to annihilate subversion, in which more than 10,000 people die or "disappear."

1978 Videla retires from active service and becomes head of state; he is replaced as head of the army and in the junta by General Roberto Eduardo Viola. Dispute with Chile over three islands in the Beagle Channel brings both countries to the brink of war.

1981 28 March: Viola (now retired) succeeds Videla as president and is replaced as head of the army and in the junta by General Leopoldo Fortunato Galtieri. **11 December:** Viola is forced out of office and replaced as president by Galtieri, who remains both in the junta and in command of the army.

1982 2 April: With government popularity at rock bottom, Galtieri launches an invasion of the disputed territory of the Falkland Islands. Mediation attempts to resolve the crisis fail. **May–June:** War between Argentina and

Great Britain, which ends with the British retaking the Falklands and Argentine surrender. **14 June:** Galtieri removed from office and prevented from nominating his successor. **1 July:** With the military junta falling apart, army-designated General Reynaldo B. Bignone becomes the final de facto president appointed by the armed forces.

1983 February: Trade Unions call for a general strike as the economic situation deteriorates. Military government passes an amnesty law (Ley 22.924—Ley de Autoamnestía), covering human rights abuses committed between May 1973 and June 1982. Election timetable agreed on by the military, who are desperate for a political way out. **September:** Nine election tickets, including a Peronist one, are confirmed for the presidential elections. **30 October:** Raúl Alfonsín of the UCR is elected president.

1984 Publication of the report about "disappearances" during the Dirty War—*Nunca Más*. Economic crisis deepens.

1985 "Shock" stabilization plan—Plan Austral—introduced on **14 June** by Economics Minister Juan V. Sourrouille to curb inflation and promote economic recovery. Measures include a wages and prices freeze, a promise to cease printing money to cover the fiscal deficit, and the introduction of a new currency (1 austral = 10,000 pesos). Federal commissions investigate military defeat in the Falklands War and arraign the military junta. Radicals triumph in midterm elections.

1986 Constitutional reform proposal to establish the post of prime minister, to make the political system less presidential, and to move the federal capital from Buenos Aires to Viedma, Patagonia. Military junta—Admiral Anaya, General Galtieri, and Air Force Brigadier Lami Dozo—is sentenced to terms in prison for conduct of the Falklands War. Punto Final Law sets a 60-day limit for registering claims of human rights abuses committed during the Dirty War. Brazil and Argentina sign a treaty to set up MERCOSUR, a trade agreement that subsequently leads to the formation of the South American Common Market.

1987 Barrack revolt by the "painted (camouflaged) faces" (*carapintadas*), military officers protesting against the treatment of the army. Alfonsín confronts protestors, who capitulate and are amnestied. Divorce law is approved. Minister Sourrouille seeks to renegotiate the foreign debt as the economy falters. Peronists (PJ) do well in the midterm congressional elections.

1988 Series of barrack revolts, which peter out. Formal establishment of MERCOSUR. Government begins to lose control of the economy; a new prices and wages free and revenue-sharing agreement between the federal and provincial governments is imposed—the so-called Spring Plan.

1989 Further barrack protests. Economic crisis deepens. Peronist Carlos Saúl Menem wins the **14 May** elections. Economic chaos threatens—hyperinflation and the looting of supermarkets, forcing Alfonsín to hand power to Menem on **8 July**, several weeks before the end of his term as prescribed by the constitution. Menem pardons approximately 300 individuals convicted of human rights abuses. Government starts to privatize state corporations, beginning with ENTel (telecommunications), railways, and television channels.

1990 Protests against the pardoning of those convicted of human rights abuses. Reestablishment of diplomatic relations with Great Britain. Macroeconomic instability and hyperinflation.

1991 1 April: Domingo Cavallo, minister of economy, introduces the Convertibility Plan—measures include laws requiring the government to balance the budget, the introduction of a new monetary unit (1 peso = 10,000 australes), which is equal to one US dollar, and a dual-currency arrangement with dollars and pesos circulating alongside each other and freely convertible. New currency is posted to enter circulation the following year.

1992 1 January: New dual currency system is effected. Privatization program is accelerated. Terrorist attack results in the destruction of the Embassy of Israel in Buenos Aires.

1993 Olivos Pact, signed by Menem and Alfonsín, paving the way for constitutional reform in 1994. Continuing privatization of public enterprises and the privatization of the pension system.

1994 18 July: Bomb explodes in the offices of the Jewish Mutual Association in Buenos Aires, killing 86. **22 August:** Constituent Assembly approves new constitutional reform: the presidential term is reduced from six to four years but immediate reelection of a sitting president permitted—hitherto, a sitting president could not stand for immediate reelection—the city of Buenos Aires is awarded similar status to the provinces, and the number of senators per province is increased from two to three.

1995 14 May: Carlos Menem is reelected under the amended constitution, becoming the first incumbent to serve two consecutive terms.

1996 27 July: Domingo Cavallo resigns as minister of economy—or is sacked, protesting against government corruption. Labor movement calls for strikes against the economic strategy.

1997 Protest against economic policy and corruption, with minor political parties capturing a larger share of votes in local elections.

1998 Efforts to reopen judicial proceedings against those charged with human rights abuses during the Dirty War are frustrated by Menem.

1999 Further corruption scandals rock the government. **24 October:** Fernando de la Rúa of the UCR wins the presidential elections for the Alliance Coalition.

2000 6 October: Vice President Carlos Álvarez of the minority FREPASO party in the governing coalition resigns in protest against corruption, notably the bribing of Senators by De la Rúa to secure the passage of legislation. Protests against government austerity measures increase.

2001 Emergency financial measures are introduced to balance the budget. **20 March:** Cavallo returns to the Economics Ministry, replacing Ricardo López Murphy, who had been appointed only two weeks before by De la Rúa. Midterm elections result in defeat for the Alliance Coalition. Cavallo introduces a freeze on bank accounts—cash withdrawals limited to a thousand pesos (or dollars) a month, the "corralito financiero." Virtual meltdown of share prices on the stock exchange. **December:** Street demonstrations—*cacerolazos*—looting of supermarkets and protests against the banks. Country risk rockets. **19 December:** Fernando De la Rúa declares a state of emergency and attempts to use the armed forces to quell discontent—the military demands that he seeks congressional approval for such action. **20 December:** Having failed to persuade Peronists to join a government of national unity, Fernando De la Rúa resigns and is helicoptered out of the presidential palace as demonstrations continue and the political class as a whole is held responsible for the crisis. Service on the foreign debt is suspended, triggering the largest ever default in world financial history. The government is a political vacuum.

2002 January: Approval of Economic Emergency Law signals the end of the Convertibility Plan. Congress enters an emergency session as a legislative assembly and finally nominates Eduardo Duhalde as president. Duhalde of the PJ, who was Menem's former vice president and had been defeated by De la Rúa in 1999, accepts the presidency. Emergency social assistance—Heads of Families Program—is established, providing a safety net for those most affected by the economic collapse.

2003 27 April: Ex-president Menem tops the poll in the first round of the presidential elections, narrowly ahead of Néstor Kirchner, also of the PJ. Both go forward to the second round, but Menem pulls out, possibly because opinion polls predict a massive defeat in the second round. By default, Kirchner becomes president. Reversal of privatization policy of 1990s begins as the government retakes control of the postal services. Menem is charged with fraud and takes up residence in Chile.

2004 Supreme Court overturns pardons for the Dirty War issued by Menem; further cases of human rights abuses are brought to court. María Julia Alsogaray, former Menem minister, is jailed for corruption.

2005 Supreme Court overturns time limit on human rights cases instituted by Alfonsín in 1986. Renegotiation of foreign debt—approximately 70 percent written down; technically, the country is no longer in default, though some bondholders—the "holdouts"—refused to accept settlement. Government repays debt to International Monetary Fund (IMF).

2006 More Dirty War human rights cases are brought to court, including those relating to the selling/adoption of children and babies born to "disappeared" parents—approximately 500 infants are reckoned to be involved, many given or sold to adoptive parents close to the regime. Conflict with Uruguay over siting of cellulose plant located on the east bank of the Uruguay River—Argentine protesters picket the international road bridge, blocking communications between the two countries.

2007 Government intervenes in the state National Statistical Agency, objecting to the publication inflation data. The team of statisticians is replaced and subsequent data massaged. **28 October:** Cristina Fernández de Kirchner is elected president, succeeding her husband. More pardons issued by Menem are overturned by Supreme Court. Administration is rocked by corruption scandals involving key ministers and associates of the Kirchners. Protesters continue to block international bridge to Uruguay.

2008 Conflict between the government and farm sector over commodity export taxes. Government pays off debt to members of the Paris Club as the economy is affected by the global crisis and the exchange rate deteriorates. Courts continue to review cases of human rights abuses. Restatization of private pensions schemes and of main airlines.

2009 28 June: Government is defeated in midterm elections, losing its majority in both houses of Congress, while various opposition groups capture control of key provinces. National system of family (child) allowances is set up. Political reform establishing compulsory, open primaries for all parties facilitates formation of electoral alliances among factions and groups. Claims to international waters and seabed in South Atlantic challenge British oil exploration in the region, restating claims to islands.

2010 Bicentenary of independence. Institutional creditors agree to a debt swop, extending repayment terms. Same-sex marriage legislation is passed by Congress in the face of considerable opposition from Roman Catholic hierarchy. **28 October:** Death of Néstor Kirchner.

2011 23 October: Following spectacular economic growth—the "China effect"—and possibly a sympathy vote, Cristina Fernández de Kirchner secures a record-breaking electoral victory and a second term in office.

2012 Protest against the UK militarizing the South Atlantic. **September:** IMF challenges official data on inflation and economic activity, threatening sanctions. **November:** New electoral law lowers voting age to 16 in advance of midterm elections in 2013. Former military junta heads are convicted of conspiring to kidnap babies and children of parents "disappeared" during the Dirty War.

2013 February: Argentina becomes the first country to be censured by the IMF. **10–11 March:** Falkland Island referendum shows overwhelming support to remain British—Buenos Aires rejects the poll and its result. **13 March:** Former Cardinal Archbishop of Buenos Aires Jorge Mário Bergoglio is elected pope. Agreement is reached with shareholders in restatized oil corporation REPSOL/YPF. **27 October:** Government loses midterm elections—including the critically important province of Buenos Aires—due to claims of corruption and poor economic management but retains majority in Congress. Economic crisis deepens—sharp decline in foreign exchange reserves, which fall by a third toward the end of the year, while rising inflation accelerates and living standards fall.

2014 Increasing economic instability—run on banks, sharp decline in exchange rate as international reserves continue to fall. Unpopularity of government reflected in growth of street protests and strikes. Court in United States adjudicates in favor of bondholders who had refused to accept the 2005 settlement—most of the bonds are now held by so-called vulture funds. Failure to meet the claims of the bondholders leads to a technical default in **July**.

2015 19 January: Special Prosecutor Alberto Nisman is found dead in mysterious circumstances—reputed to be about to publish report accusing Cristina Fernández de Kirchner of being involved in attempts to obstruct his investigation into the bombing of the Jewish Center in 1994. **25 October:** Presidential and congressional elections: with no presidential candidate gaining sufficient votes to be elected on first round, Danial Scioli (Mrs. Kirchner's designated successor) and Mauricio Macri go on to the second round on **22 November**. Macri wins. Elections mark the formal end of the reign of the Kirchners as Cristina Fernández de Kirchner completes her second term.

2016 March: Minister of the Economy Alfonso Prat Gay settles with the vulture funds, drawing a line under the 2002 default.

2017 22 October: Midterm congressional elections regarded as a victory for President Macri and a defeat for former president Fernández de Kirchner, despite Mrs. Kirchner gaining a seat in the National Senate. Although the governing Cambiemos coalition failed to secure an overall majority, it substantially increased representation in both houses, topping the polls in virtually all the major electoral districts contested. The result was an endorsement of Macri's economic and political reforms and strengthened his mandate. **25 October:** Former planning minister Julio De Vido, a close associated of Mrs. Kirchner, is jailed on charges of corruption when his parliamentary immunity from imprisonment is lifted. **3 November:** Amado Boudou, Mrs. Kirchner's former vice president, is seized by the police and jailed for convictions of illicit enrichment; he is released on a technicality several days later.

2018 Argentina heads the G20 and hosts the Leaders' Summit. **May:** President Macri makes a surprise announcement of a return to the IMF a few days after the BCRA raises base rates from 28 percent to 40 percent. With inflation touching 25 percent, the government seeks a standby credit of 30 billion US dollars in order to weather a currency crisis. The announcement triggers a protest from Mrs. Kirchner—her first public statement in several months. The fund offered 50 billion.

Introduction

THE COUNTRY AND THE PEOPLE

With an area of 2,789,400 square kilometers (1,073,518 square miles), Argentina is the eighth largest country in the world, and the second largest in South America. Located in the southeast corner of South America, to the north-northeast, the country shares a border with Bolivia, Paraguay, and Brazil, Uruguay to the east, and Chile to the west. Almost the whole of the republic is situated in the temperate zone of the Southern Hemisphere, although there are considerable variations in climate and topography, a variety matched only by the range and wealth of natural resources. The northwest and Patagonia developed rapidly as centers of mining and energy production, with known deposits of petroleum and natural gas in the region being the third largest in Latin America. Along the Andes, in addition to traditional activities such as sheep raising and wine production, new agricultural commodities are being developed and the region is beginning to realize fully its potential as a source of hydroelectric generation. The pampas, the agricultural heartland and defining feature of the country, now increasingly planted with soya, has the potential to produce high yields of arable, pastoral, and oleaginous commodities without the use of chemicals or artificial fertilizers, according Argentina a competitive advantage in the lucrative and expanding organic foods market, as well as an apparently limitless capacity to respond to surging global demand for more traditional temperate-region staples. New activities such as ecotourism and extreme sports are emerging in the far north and south of the country. The ability to harness Argentina's abundant natural wealth and utilize its topographical and climatic diversity has depended on several interrelated factors, such as an efficient infrastructure, a stable political environment, and an appropriate international trade regime.

Like Australia and the United States, Argentina is a country of immigrants. The period of mass immigration occurred between the 1870s and 1910s, though there were substantial inflows of people from Europe during the interwar decades and again in the late 1940s and early 1950s. Recent decades have witnessed migration from neighboring countries and, since around 2000, East Asia. About 40 percent of Argentines claim Italian descent, with approximately a further 35 percent Spanish origin. There are sizable German, French, Jewish, and Irish communities, with more modest immigration from the Levant—commonly referred to as *turcos* (Turks)—

present-day Lebanon and Syria. In the 1920s, the British community numbered around 250,000, supposedly the largest "outside the Empire," ignoring those who had emigrated from the British Isles to the United States.

Estimates in 2018 place the total population at around 44,700,000, making the country the fourth most populous in Latin America after Brazil, Mexico, and Colombia. Since 2000, the rate of population growth has averaged around 1 percent per annum, similar to that of advanced economies. Most social indicators also mirror those of the advanced economies. The current gender balance is 51 percent female and 49 percent male. About a quarter of the population is under 15 years of age, about two-thirds aged between 15 and 65, with around a tenth over 65. Average life expectancy is 77 years (80 for women and 74 for men), approximately a year less than in the United States. The fertility rate (average number of children per woman) in 2014 was 2.3; in the United States, 1.9. In 2018, the rate of infant mortality (number of death per 1,000 live births) was 8.9; 5.5 in the United States. The current literacy rate is 98 percent, one of the highest in the world, one percentage point behind that of the United States. In 2015, mean years of schooling for adults was 9.8 years, compared with 13.3 in the United States. The UN Human Development Index for 2016 placed Argentina in the top 50 countries, Chile being the only other Latin America country to feature in the list: Argentina is ranked 45 and Chile 38. The population is over 92 percent urban, making the country one of the most urbanized in the world. In Latin America, only Uruguay with some 95 percent has a higher rate of urbanization. The metropolitan area of greater Buenos Aires accounts for about half the total population. Other major cities include Córdoba, 1,500,000; Rosario, 1,400,000; and Mendoza, 1,100,000.

The official language is Spanish, though in the province of Chubut Welsh enjoys equal status with Spanish, as does Guaraní in the province of Corrientes. In terms of religious affiliation, the population is overwhelmingly Catholic, though only around 25 percent attend weekly religious services.

THE PRE-COLUMBIAN PERIOD

Regarded as the land of cattle and beef in the modern era, Argentina for paleontologists is the land of super dinosaurs (titanosaurs). Dinosaur Valley in the present-day province of Neuquén has yielded several massive fossilized remains. In 1993, the near perfect remains, 80 percent intact, of Giganotosaurus Carolini were found there. Dating from the Cretaceous period, it is the skeleton of the largest carnivorous super dinosaur yet to be discovered. Close by were fossils of plant-eating titanosaurs on which the creature may have fed. In 2012, the fossils of *Patagotitan mayorum* were found. Weighing in at 76 tons, this super herbivore is the largest titanosaur ever discovered—displacing *Argentinosaurus huinculensis*, previously held to be the biggest animal to have walked on earth. More discoveries are likely, possibly of even larger creatures.

Titanosaurs had disappeared long before the first peopling of Argentina. The grasslands of the pampas and Patagonia were probably among the last parts of the continent to be colonized by humans crossing the land bridge from Asia. There seems not to have been one single dominant culture. Archeological evidence points to human habitation in Andean valleys and Chaco forests toward the end of the Paleolithic period, around 11,000 BC. Virtually nothing is known about the social and economic organization of the earliest peoples; they are assumed to have been hunters and gatherers. In most areas, nomadic lifestyles probably prevailed from prehistory to near modern times, though sedentary maize-based cultures existed by the first century AD in the Andes, as semipermanent slash-and-burn cultures planting yuca and sweet potatoes arose in the north Paraná Basin. Although Argentina has nothing to compare with the densely populated urban societies of the Inca and Meso-America, at Cuevas de las Manos in Santa Cruz in southern Patagonia, caves have been found with images of spray-painted hands—hence the name of the location—representations of humans and animals, and depictions of hunting. The caves date from 7500 BC. Located in the Calchaquí valley system in Tucumán is the largest pre-Columbian settlement in Argentina—possibly one of the most significant of its kind in the region. Dating from around 850 AD, the settlement is thought to have been home to 5,000. At Pucará de Tilcara, Jujuy, is a 12th-century settlement, complete with fortress, necropolis, and reconstructed Inca-style pyramid. Predating the Incas, the site is thought to have been inhabited for several centuries. At its zenith, the population of Pucará was 2,000.

A 2004 inquiry recognized 35 indigenous groups, totaling approximately 600,000, or less than 1.5 percent of the total population, mainly distributed in the northwest, the northeast, the central pampas, and the center-north of Patagonia. This figure is double the pre-Colombian population peak, which is generally guesstimated at 300,000. There was a precipitous decline in the indigenous population after the arrival of Europeans due to conquest and exposure to diseases for which there was no natural immunity. Linguists and anthropologists identify three main language groups in Argentina: Quechua speakers in the northwest, Tupi–Guarani in the northeast, Araucanian–Mapuche in the center-west. Languages spoken by pampean tribes appear not to share a common root. The linguistic groupings broadly correspond with socioeconomic subdivisions. Agriculturalists of the Southern Andes whose economy was based on mixed farming and the herding of camelids—llamas, alpacas, and guanacos—characteristics shared with cultures of intermontane valleys of the altiplano. Low-land cultivators and hunt-er-gathers of the Chaco and northern littoral—groups who had probably reached the region from the Amazonia and farther north. Nomadic tribes of the pampas, Patagonia, and the archipelago to the far south—fishers, hunters, and gatherers who roamed the grassland in search of rhea and guanaco. At independence, the principal indigenous groups were the Guarani-speaking tribes of the northwest and the Mapuche (also known as Tehuelche) based in Patagonia and the western pampas. Crossing the passes from southern Chile (Araucania)—associated tribes inhabited territory on both sides of what would become the Chilean–Argentine frontier—the Tehuelche absorbed or displaced earlier indigenous groups. The Tehuelche, and the Guarani who refused to settle in the *reducciones* established by the Jesuits at the beginning of the 1600s, were never subdued during the Spanish colonial period. A loose confederation of bellicose tribes who shared a language and culture, by the 1860s the Tehuelche were a major force. They pushed back the frontier in the pampas from Buenos Aires to Santa Fe and Córdoba. There were repeated, coordinated raids on newly established agricultural colonies, as well as on cities considered free of the "Indian menace" since the 1840s: women and children were seized, hostages taken, and cattle rustled.

FROM SPANISH SETTLEMENT TO VICEROYALTY

The colonial period is conventionally dated from the early 16th century to the May Revolution of 1810, which marked the beginning of the end of Spanish control. European navigators began mapping the Atlantic coast of Argentina early in the 16th century—possibly as early as 1502, when a Portuguese expedition is recorded as sailing across the Río de la Plata. There were further expeditions along the southern coast and north up the Paraná in the coming decades, with a settlement being established on the east bank of the river by 1527. The main expeditions were headed by Juan Díaz de Solis (1516), Ferdinand Magellan (1520), and Sebastian Cabot (1526). The city of Buenos Aires was first founded in 1536, though subsequently abandoned following attack by pampean Indians. The city was successfully refounded in 1580, although it would be another decade or so before Buenos Aires was considered secure. Settlement was initially more successful in the north and west of present-day Argentina, as Spanish conquistadores from Chile and Peru crossed the Andes in search of the fabled city of silver and the realm of a mythical white king.

Several expeditions penetrated the northwest between the 1530s and the 1560s, leading to the formation of permanent settlements, including San Miguel de Tucumán, founded in 1565. The city would soon become the center of a major administrative region, part of the Viceroyalty of Peru.

Mendoza had been established a few years earlier by an expedition from Chile. Córdoba, destined to become an important city and administrative region in the center of the country, was founded in 1573. In addition to Tucumán, the other main administrative jurisdiction in the region were the Gobernación del Paraguay, centered on Asunción, and the Gobernación del Río de la Plata, Buenos Aires. Both were instituted in 1617 and, like the Gobernación del Tucumán, dependencies of Peru.

Hard on the heels of the conquistadores came the religious orders, notably the Dominicans and Franciscans—active in the north by the 1580s—yet arguably the Jesuits had a greater impact. The University of Córdoba was set up as a Jesuit institution in 1613—one of the first universities to be founded in the Americas. Other centers of learning organized by the order followed.

Through the 16th and 17th centuries, subsistence characterized the daily life of the vast mass of the population. Communities in the north were also required to supply drafts of forced labor conscripted to work in the silver mines of Upper Peru (Bolivia). The main market activities were stock raising and trade—particularly contraband—with centers of artisan textile production developing by 1700. Mules and cattle were raised on the grasslands to be herded north to supply the demands of the mines. During the early 18th century, cottage industries and sweatshops in the center and northwest were producing a broader range of "manufactures" for regional consumption and mining zones, but the fastest growing activity was the unofficial trade in imported cotton goods and luxuries from Europe, mainly Great Britain and France, and slaves shipped from Africa directly or via Brazil. This trade was financed by the illicit seepage of silver—bullion that should have been handled by the Crown. Contraband was mainly directed through Buenos Aires and upriver ports. Technically, Cadiz enjoyed a monopoly on trade between the region and the outside world. Silver was shipped via Peru, along the Pacific Coast, across the Isthmus of Panama, and through the Caribbean to the Iberian Peninsula, with imports flowing in the reverse direction. Goods smuggled directly though Buenos Aires enjoyed a massive price advantage.

Concerns about security and a desire better to regulate overseas trade led to the formation of the Viceroyalty of the River Plate in 1776. The creation of a new viceregal jurisdiction centered on Buenos Aires was one of several changes implemented by the government in Madrid to raise revenue to invest in imperial defense and to increase royal control. Related measures included the creation of other new viceroyalties, the formation of more subviceregal units, and the gradual implementation of "imperial free trade." Up to this point, Buenos Aires had been a backwater empire—neglected and loosely regulated. That changed in 1776. The rich mining district of Bolivia was detached from the Viceroyalty of Peru and transferred to Buenos Aires, which was also granted jurisdiction over what is now Paraguay and Uruguay. The bureaucratic and military establishments in the city were enhanced and made directly answerable to Madrid. Royal power was strengthened and centralized. The naval prefecture was enlarged and attention devoted to internal defense as well as the threat from overseas—forts were established along the Indian frontier. A merchant guild was formed, a new customs house built, the urban environment improved, and the status of Buenos Aires as a center of government, politics, education, and social life enhanced.

Administrative change brought economic progress. Bolivian silver remained the prime driver of the economy, funding government and stimulating economic marketization, and was the dominant export. Yet, in 1800, hides represented a quarter of all exports by value; bullion accounted for the remainder. Increases in the volume and value of trade fostered a demographic boom. By 1810, Buenos Aires was the fastest growing city in the Spanish world due to immigration—including the forced migration of slaves—and natural population growth. The stimulus was not confined to the area around Buenos Aires. Ranching and farming expanded in neighboring regions of Uruguay and Entre Ríos, and internal migrants were attracted to the littoral from the interior. Up-country "industries" were little benefited by prosperity in the littoral, which preferred legal imports, especially cotton textiles and silks, rather than artisanal woolens. The pronounced shift toward ranching in particular undermined other interior activities as capital and labor gravitated toward the production of cattle, hides, and tallow.

At the end of the colonial period, the population of the country was reckoned to be around 400,000. About 30 percent of this total was categorized as indigenous. By this time, Europeans—principally Spaniards—constituted the largest ethnic grouping. There was also a substantial mixed-race mestizo population. Particularly in the city of Buenos Aires, there was a large black population. The 1810 census enumerated the black population of the city as 9,615 out of 32,558, some 30 percent; the majority were African slaves. Growth created winners and losers—geographically and socially—as did administrative changes. Tensions associated with these processes were brought to a head by British invasions of the River Plate in 1806 and 1807 and the French invasion of the Iberian Peninsula. The collapse in royal authority in Spain, and "national" sentiment engendered by the expulsion of the British largely due to local efforts, inevitably led to a questioning of Spanish power and authority. Independence was in the cards.

INDEPENDENCE: MAKING THE STATE AND MAKING THE NATION (1810–1880)

The struggle for independence from Spain began on 25 May 1810, now taken as the formal date of independence, though the official declaration of independence did not occur until 9 July 1816. Portugal was the first country to recognize Argentina in 1821, followed by Brazil and the United States in 1822, Great Britain in 1823, and France in 1830. Spanish recognition did not occur until 1857. Although the revolutionary struggle against Spain concluded by the early 1820s, civil wars and regional conflict continued for much of the next 30 years. During the 1850s, the provinces that would become Argentina gradually came together. National consolidation is conventionally dated from the overthrow of the regime of Juan Manuel de Rosas in 1852, the promulgation of the Constitution of 1853, the reintegration of the province of Buenos Aires into the Argentine Confederation in 1859–1860, and the federalization of the city of Buenos Aires in 1880.

As early as the 1840s, immigration was beginning to pick up. Sheep raising in the north and west of the province of Buenos Aires attracted Scots, Irish, and Basque shepherds. The first railway was inaugurated in 1857. Gradually, in the 1860s and 1870s, regional networks radiated from the cities of Buenos Aires and Rosario. New lands were opened to settlement in the center-west as nomadic Indians were expelled from the pampas. Agricultural colonies and large cattle estates soon began supplying commodities to the world market. Port cities expanded, and the state was formed, largely due to the wealth created by overseas trade and a rising tide of foreign investment. Around the 1880s, Argentina was being projected as the country of the future—a new United States in South America.

GLOBALIZATION AND THE OLIGARCHIC STATE (1880–1930)

By the 1880s, mass immigration from Western Europe had made Argentina the third most populous country in Latin America after Brazil and Mexico. It was also the most urban: approximately one-half of the population lived in cities by 1914. Argentina was on course to becoming one of the wealthiest societies of the early 20th century. The result was the emergence of a civil society, enmeshed with the building of a state. The 1880s saw the development of the National Autonomist Party (Partido Autonomista Nacional—PAN), a coalition of regional oligarchies that came to monopolize national politics and eclipse other organizations. Because the PAN did not have a well-defined internal organization, factional confrontations proliferated and came to replace open electoral contests. Real politics was conducted inside the PAN, rather than the institutions of the state, an arrangement that facilitated order rather than democratic consolidation, and survived virtually unchanged until 1916.

Mass immigration, population growth, and urbanization transformed society and politics. That the PAN became more centralized, and possibly isolated, was suggested by popular protest triggered by the commercial and financial panic of 1889–1891 (the Baring Crisis), which provoked a series of events prefiguring those of 2001–2002. These protests in 1889 ultimately resulted in "reform from within." Managed elections required a more patriotic and democratic patina. Electoral reform, sponsored by President Roque Sáenz Peña (1910–1913) in 1912, led to the first free and fair elections in Argentine political history in 1916, the defeat of the PAN, and the ensuing Radical ascendancy of 1916–1930.

Mass and class politics did not necessarily imply ideology-based politics. Nevertheless, it was generally accepted that mass politics erupted into Argentine political life in the 1910s, and that the Unión Cívica Radical (UCR) was its initial beneficiary. The UCR successfully courted three distinct groups: dissident interior oligarchies; the growing urban, professional middle classes and small farmers; and sections of the enfranchised working class (in 1914, around 70 percent of the Buenos Aires working class had been born abroad and was therefore effectively disenfranchised, as rates of naturalization were very low). Two of these social classes were epitomized by UCR presidents of the period: Hipólito Yrigoyen (1916–1922 and 1928–1930), a teacher and minor public official, and Marcelo T. de Alvear (1922–1928), scion of an aristocratic family and prominent lawyer. After the 1950s, the party became more closely identified with the urban and rural middle class. Since around 2000, the UCR has maintained a significant, though declining presence in municipal and provincial government, despite the virtual decimation of its representation at the national level.

The first globalization—export-led growth and massive foreign investment—along with mass migration, made the oligarchic state. Factor endowments underpinned the liberal growth model of the so-called Belle Époque (1870s–1910s), an arrangement that facilitated the production of a broadening mix of commodities for global markets. During this period, the country became, successively, a major world supplier of wool, grains (principally wheat and maize), and with the development of refrigerated shipping, quality frozen and chilled meat, especially high-premium chilled beef. No other economy experienced such an exponential increase in the area under cultivation in such a short space of time or exhibited such a dynamic primary commodity export profile.

As reflected in the first Baring Crisis of 1889–1891, export-led growth was volatile. By the end of the 1880s, overseas investors doubted the capacity or willingness of the state to extract sufficient income to honor its obligations. The supply of new credits dried up, gold flowed abroad, and the government broke its bond with domestic and foreign creditors. Asset values declined, and the recession deepened. However, buoyant world demand for commodities soon facilitated a surge in export production. At the time, and notwithstanding the instability of the arrangement, recovery and growth were viewed as validating the liberal model of economic openness and global engagement based on comparative natural advantage.

The First World War, however, weakened the model. During the 1920s, world growth slowed and there was greater instability, not least in commodity prices. Hence, earlier economic stimulants such as trade expansion, foreign capital inflows, and immigration were less pronounced. The terms of trade were beginning to move against Argentina, and the scope for commodity diversification became increasingly limited as the frontier closed. Changes in the external commercial and financial context had an impact on the domestic political economy and prevailing economic ideology.

Broad movements in commodity production and export between the 1880s and 1920s would not have been possible without institutional flexibility, policy pragmatism, and macroeconomic efficiency. In the 1930s, there was a sharp contraction in the area of land under cultivation, which pointed to structural rigidity and a looming crisis of production and productivity. The transition from an extensive to an intensive growth model proved difficult. Between the 1930s and the 1980s, an increase in the production of one commodity tended to be accompanied by a contraction in the supply of another. Moreover, after the 1940s, the economy seemed incapable of increasing exports without constraining domestic consumption, or vice versa. Increased industrial production implied a contraction in resources available for agriculture, while generating inputs for agriculture meant curtailing resources available for manufacturing. Consequently, for much of the 1940s–1980s there was only modest growth in productivity and aggregate production.

The 1929 worldwide economic depression brought an end to the democratic experiment and the return of "oligarchic authoritarianism." Institutional and conjunctural explanations are offered for the collapse of Argentine democracy in the 1930s. For some, the UCR was too progressive, provoking an inevitable conservative backlash; for others, it was insufficiently radical and failed to restructure Argentine society and polity so as to secure democracy. Opponents certainly accused UCR administrations of corruption and protested against the "tyranny of democracy"—that is, its ability to manufacture electoral victories. The inertia of the administration in 1929–1930, as the country slipped into economic disorder, fostered disillusion, providing an opportunity for opponents of the regime. Consequently, the 1930 military coup attracted a fair measure of support: there was general antipathy toward an elected administration seen as failing the republic.

INSTABILITY, POPULISM, AND
RESTRICTED DEMOCRACY (1930–1976)

Political and economic instability were the overarching feature of the crisis years from the 1930s onward. Although originating in a military putsch, and dependent on the armed forces and police to contain opposition, the "Concordancia" administrations of the 1930s presented a largely civilian façade and were a disparate grouping of liberals, conservatives, and reformist socialists. Initially, the regime sought legitimacy in efficient macroeconomic management and, with the stabilization of the economy in the mid-1930s, in a measured return to democracy. Accident, in the form of the death of several consummate political operators, and the Second World War derailed the projected phased return to open politics. The regime lurched to the right, destroying the fragile party-political balance that had delivered stability in the executive and legislature. Concurrently, elements within the military railed against the subordinate role assigned to the armed forces and the pro-Allied stance of the administration, notwithstanding its formal declaration of neutrality.

In 1943 a group of officers, of whom Colonel Juan Domingo Perón was one, acted. The technocrats and oligarchs were removed, and a full military administration was installed. However, the armed forces were divided and ill prepared for government. Elections were called in 1946. To the surprise of many, the Democratic Union (Unión Democrática), the umbrella grouping established by existing political parties, was beaten decisively by Perón. Between 1943 and 1945, Perón had assiduously cultivated the support of organized labor. As a result, he became the presidential candidate of the Labor Party (Partido Laborista), the hastily constructed political wing of the General Confederation of Labor (Confederación General del Trabajo—CGT). Soon, independent trade union leaders were sidelined, and the Partido Laborista ultimately morphed into the Peronist Party (later the Partido Justicialista—PJ). In association with his charismatic wife, "Evita," Perón established a regime that would become increasingly centralist, statist, and antiliberal. Its main sources of support were organized labor, developmentalist military officers, nationalists, and at least in the early years, elements of the Catholic hierarchy attracted by the authoritarian, traditionalist, antisecularist, moralistic stance of the administration.

As with the UCR in the 1910s and 1920s, the PJ of the 1940s defied easy definition. In electoral terms, the overwhelming strength of the party lay with the working class, largely the urban working class. State-sector workers, too, were a major electoral bulwark. Nevertheless, the Peronists have not always enjoyed the unquestioning electoral support of labor, nor been exclusively dependent on it. As victories in elections in 1973, 1989, 1992, and 1995 indicated, the party often captured substantial support from the middle class; conversely, it failed to mobilize important elements of the working class in 1982 and 1999 (and possibly 2015). More a movement than a party, the PJ has proven to be the least institutionalized political organization in Argentina. Perhaps, too, the fragmentation of Peronism has mirrored the "deinstitutionalization" of party politics in general, as the role of (often ephemeral) electoral alliances became a more pronounced feature of political life. Peronism has become a contending alliance of factions headed by regional leaders. These features derived from, and conferred power on, a highly personalist leadership. This legacy of Carlos Saúl Menem (1989–1999), reinforced under the administrations of Néstor Carlos Kirchner (2003–2007) and Cristina Fernández de Kirchner (2007–2015), means that the PJ continues as a constellation of competing sectional and regional interests. Indeed, during the *kirchnerato*, various factions of the PJ virtually functioned as separate parties, contesting primaries and national elections. Only electoral defeat brings the contending elements of the movement/organization together.

The 1946–1955 Peronist administration, the *peronato*, can be divided into several distinct subperiods. The first, which lasted until around 1949, was characterized by high levels of popular support, rapid social progress, economic nationalism verging on autarchy, and increasing centralization. This was the "golden age" of Peronism, largely financed from windfall export earnings. The second phase ran from 1949 to about 1952 (when "Evita" died). During this period, high levels of mass support continued, but social tensions increased, and the regime became much more authoritarian as the economy faltered—possibly prefiguring the final years of Mrs. Kirchner's presidency. The final period of the *peronato* witnessed the fracturing of the "Peronist family": workers and nationalists were antagonized by a return to liberal orthodoxy reflected in wage cuts and the opening of the economy to foreign investment. The armed forces became alarmed at the threat of internal disorder. The Catholic Church was antagonized by proposed government interventions in education and family life, and by orchestrated demands for the canonization of "Evita."

It would be easy to blame these problems on populist strategies implemented by Peronist administrations between 1946 and 1955. Arguably, it was not these strategies per se that provoked a break in the national growth trajectory and divergence from other economies. Rather, the cause lay in the way these strategies were implemented. Proindustry ideas promulgated by the United Nation's Economic Commission for Latin America (as the Economic Commission for Latin America and the Caribbean—ECLAC—was then known) had broad appeal. Developmentalist ideology was widely embraced during the presidency of Arturo Frondizi (1958–1962). Targeting such sectors as steel and energy was designed to correct the bias toward "horizontal" industrial expansion, manifest during the Perón presidencies, when policy distortions had favored light industries. In its own terms, the Frondizi project was successful. Growth rates were high, if unpredictable. However, public-sector deficits grew, and despite an improvement in the terms of trade, soaring imports and erratic export performance soon caused balance-of-payments deficits.

Reconstructing society and polity, and reestablishing the international position of the country, exercised successive regimes in the 1950s and 1960s, but possibilities and outcomes remained confused. These were neatly illustrated by the coups of 1955. The first, headed by General Eduardo Lonardi, favoring the incorporation of Peronism (albeit without Perón) into the political mainstream and set about dismantling some of the agencies of economic intervention. The second coup of 1955 led to the installation of a hardline anti-Peronist, more internationalist regime, headed by General Pedro Eugenio Aramburu (1955–1958). He was responsible for instituting the proscription of Peronism, which undermined the legitimacy of subsequent elections. Deregulation and export promotion were applied with vigor, and Argentina submitted membership applications to the World Bank and the International Monetary Fund (IMF). In 1958, Aramburu's regime gave way to the elected presidency of Radical Arturo Frondizi (1958–1962). Although he had enjoyed a reputation as a radical nationalist, on assuming office Frondizi awarded risk concessions to foreign oil corporations. This was part of the so-called battle for oil. The second campaign, the "battle for healthy money," was based on an IMF adjustment package, a measure that also implied a prointernationalist position.

Partly for electoral purposes, Frondizi sought to balance a liberal, internationalist stance in economic and trade policy with a radical diplomatic program, courting communist Cuba and the Non-Aligned Movement. Frondizi's eventual removal from office was a result of adventurous intra-Americas relations, a failure to deliver on his promise to the military to defeat Peronism at the ballot box, and possibly domestic opposition to his economic policy. Successive civilian administrations of the 1960s, always closely scrutinized by the armed forces, were no more successful in restabilizing domestic politics or redefining the international position of the country.

By the mid-1960s, manufacturing accounted for around one-third of total economic activity, the composition of industrial output was more diverse than hitherto, and firms were larger. These phenomena were related to, and largely driven by, the "transnationalization" of business. However, while foreign-owned corporations tended to invest in the upgrading of technology, national firms invested less and kept productions costs low by recruiting cheap, unskilled labor. The presence of the state (mainly military-owned firms) in manufacturing grew. Across the manufacturing sector, a productivity gap was opening: all-round efficiency gains in sectors such as petrochem- icals, chemicals, and cellulose and (some) metallurgical sectors were offset by slow productivity growth in other branches.

The "bureaucratic-authoritarian" military regime installed in 1966 prom- ised to restore economic discipline. Foreign investment increased, precipitat- ing another cycle of transnational corporate expansion. The probusiness stance of the regime did not bring much relief to the agricultural sector, which continued to suffer pressure to generate resources (notably foreign exchange) essential for industrial development. The international oil crisis of 1973 prompted another policy shift, associated with the return from exile of Perón, who believed rising world commodity prices would end sluggish growth and finance fundamental structural change. As in the late 1940s, windfall taxes on agricultural exports supported an expansion in public ex- penditure. However, the boom could not last: after 1975, commodity prices and foreign reserves decreased sharply, inflation escalated, and there was another crisis in the balance of payments. Conditions were thus aligned for the 1976 coup, and for renewed efforts to restore order and stabilize the economy.

With the failure of the nominally developmentalist regime of General Juan Carlos Onganía (1966–1970) and the rise in mass protest characterized by urban uprisings, factory occupations, a spate of kidnappings directed against the heads of national and foreign corporations, and mounting guerrilla vio- lence, the public and military looked to the exiled Perón for salvation. After Onganía's administration, there followed the short-lived military presiden- cies of General Roberto Levingston (1970–1971) and General Alejandro Agustín Lanusse (1971–1973), under whose government Perón was permit- ted to return from exile in Madrid, Spain, where he had been sheltered by General Francisco Franco. Elected in March 1973, "Interim" President Héc- tor Cámpora of the PJ was a fervent loyalist who took office on 25 May and resigned in mid-July, triggering the need for new elections. Left leaning, as well as a loyalist, Cámpora's name was taken by the group of young activists who would later form the effective "youth militia" of the Néstor and Cristina Fernández de Kirchner regimes, La Cámpora. Returning in June, and elected in September, Perón arrived in a country that appeared to be falling apart. Standing for the presidency and vice presidency, respectively, Perón and his wife Isabel easily won the ballot. However, at 78 years of age, Perón was losing his touch and was demonstrably unable to contain conflict within the movement, as shown by gun battles at party gatherings and on the streets. Most rapidly alienated were the Montoneros, a radical anticapitalist Peronist youth organization committed to armed struggle. Initially regarding Perón as a potential ally, they later declared war on the regime of Mrs. Perón, who assumed the presidency on the death of her husband. Isabel proved particu- larly ineffective. Shifting to the right, she soon became beholden to sections of the labor movement and national business and shadowy criminal groups including armed gangs controlled by her minister of social welfare, José López Rega. The last days of her regime were marked by the open operation of official "death squads," near anarchy, and spiraling inflation. In this context, the military regime that took over in 1976 was almost welcomed.

EL PROCESO DE REORGANIZACIÓN NACIONAL (1976–1983)

Most had no idea what was to come during the bloody rule of the generals and admirals. The "Proceso de Reorganización Nacional" was a sinister descriptor for a project that sought to discipline society through the use of state violence and the systematic abuse of human rights in order to stabilize economy and polity. The confirmed number who "disappeared" during the Dirty War is 9,000, though some sources claim that the figure is nearer 30,000. For the regime, the defining moment occurred in 1982, when the domestic and international actions of the dictatorship descended into a tragicomedy of errors, culminating in the invasion of the Falkland Islands (Islas Malvinas) in April. These British-ruled islands in the South Atlantic had been claimed by Argentina since 1833. The events leading up to the invasion illustrated the arrogance and ignorance of the regime, which had completely misread both its influence abroad and the place of Argentina in the Americas and the wider world. Following the collapse of the liberal, debt-led program of Minister of the Economy José Alfredo Martínez de Hoz, as the stock market went into meltdown with a series of spectacular bank failures, the currency collapsed, and the country approached default. Fearful of a resurgence of street protest, the regime felt compelled to act. Deluded by his own rhetoric, misled by civilian foreign policy advisers and convinced of the capacity of the armed forces, General Leopoldo Fortunato Galtieri announced from the balcony of the presidential palace (the Casa Rosada) to an enthusiastic crowd on 2 April 1982 that Argentine forces had taken Port Stanley in the Falklands. The euphoria was short lived. The armed forces' ignominious defeat by the British followed on 14 June, the military lacking both the organizational capacity and the ability to resist the British task force dispatched to recover the islands.

The Falklands adventure, or debacle, was largely a function of the failure of efforts by the military to restructure the economy—implementing a revolution in productivity by authoritarian means, various sectors accepted the need for economic restructuring, though few accepted the social and political costs. The incoming military government of 1976 signaled a profound rupture with the previous promanufacturing regime. The collapse of the corporatist industrial alliance in the chaos of the last months of the administration of Isabel Perón (1974–1976), and the utter exhaustion of civil society, contributed to the new regime's autonomous power. Under the supervision of Martínez de Hoz, the economy was opened and wages reduced: foreign capital flowed in, and there was a near 40 percent contraction in real wages; exports grew, facilitated by the reduction in domestic consumption. Inflation was brought under control, subsidies were reduced, and by 1977 the primary deficit had decreased to one-quarter of its 1975 level. With the "depoliticization" of decision making, the junta's economic team enjoyed considerable protection from sectoral lobbying. Nonetheless, there were limits to "reform." Public expenditure was not brought fully under control, and the military refused to relinquish businesses, despite a supposed commitment to market economics. Furthermore, the armed forces exempted themselves from the discipline of the market and, in so doing, imposed greater fiscal pressure on other branches of public expenditure. As a share of the budget, military expenditure doubled in real terms during the second half of the decade.

The economic model combined incentives and penalties. Unfortunately, not all economic agents behaved as expected. Rising government and household demand for credit meant that the financial sector was the main beneficiary of the boom: those with liquid assets found it more profitable to lend to the banks than to invest in production. Moreover, by 1980, public expenditure was higher than in 1976, and the budget deficit even larger. Domestic and external indebtedness was becoming uncontrollable, just as international interest rates were on the increase. Yet another boom was proving unsustainable. It remains a matter of considerable debate how the military envisaged victory in the Falklands as solving these profound macroeconomic problems—including the debt burden they had created.

THE RETURN OF DEMOCRACY:
TRIALS AND TRIBULATIONS (1983–2003)

Democracy returned in 1983, but what kind of democracy—open and institutionalized, electoral and delegatory, or direct and participatory? There have been several crises since 1983, many of a similar order of magnitude to the institutional and economic crises experienced between 1930 and 1976 that triggered military intervention—the armed forces promising to clear up the mess caused by civilian politicians and to restore order, before returning a disciplined democratic order. Yet, since the military returned to the barracks in 1983, there have been no *golpes de estado*, though there have been profound political and economic shocks as the UCR and the PJ offered distinct approaches to rebuilding political institutions and healing society.

When the debt crisis and Falklands debacle resulted in the collapse of the Proceso regime in 1982, the scene was set for a heterodox solution to the "productivity crisis." Launched in 1985 during the administration of President Raúl Alfonsín (1983–1989), the Austral Plan was conceived of as a "war on inflation" by the democratically elected government that had taken office. Acknowledging the need for macroeconomic stability, it sought to stabilize through growth, rather than via a "corrective" recession. A new currency, the austral, was phased in. A freeze on wages and prices was similarly adjusted for residual inflation. The government committed itself to fiscal and monetary responsibility, and privatization was on the agenda. Together, echoing the European social-democratic economic model, these measures and promises were intended to promote cooperation among all major interest groups—labor, business, and the state—thereby ending the cycles of distributional conflict that had plagued the country since the 1940s.

Political optimism and economic crisis were the inheritance of the incoming Alfonsín administration in December 1983. A human rights lawyer who had consistently opposed the military and the war, Alfonsín was a committed democrat and constitutionalist. He represented the new face of Argentine politics. Perhaps this, as well as the association of some Peronists with the outgoing military regime, explained the electoral triumph of the UCR in the elections of 30 October. Alfonsín's victory was a watershed in Argentine political history: it was the first time that the PJ had been defeated in free elections.

The new government was confronted by an expectant electorate demanding that those responsible for human rights abuses during the Dirty War be brought to justice. For Alfonsín, the restoration of democracy was a moral and practical imperative, as was principled internationalism. Anticipating rewards for democratization from international institutions and foreign governments, the administration initially prioritized social spending and negotiations with the military over debt resolution. This was even more pressing, as the government had to confront several barrack protests. Although these hardly threatened a coup (being concerned with affronts to "military dignity" and spending cuts), they still represented a challenge to the government and democratic consolidation. Drift, rather than strategy, typified the early economic stance of the Alfonsín presidency. A standby loan was obtained from the IMF in 1984, and when this failed to stabilize the economy, the heterodox Austral Plan was launched in 1985. Initially popular, the plan could have succeeded, but it was sabotaged by debt overhang, some technical flaws, and principally, an electoral timetable that gave opponents ample opportunity to mobilize against it. The plan ended in hyperinflation that proved detrimental to the UCR in the 1989 elections and resulted in the transfer of power to incoming president Menem of the PJ, five months earlier than required by the constitution.

Economic agents had failed to cooperate, and the state appeared reluctant or unable to honor its side of the bargain. Although inflation remained under control and public confidence was maintained, investment did not increase. Crucially, the freezing of wages and prices was extended. A second round of shock treatment reduced the credibility of the administration. By 1989, central bank reserves were exhausted, the currency was in free fall, and hyperinflation had become inevitable. When elections were held in May, the monthly rate of price increases touched 150 percent, representing an annual inflation rate of 5,000 percent. The scene was set for another dose of liberal correction.

To its detractors, the legacy of democracy in 1989 was fiscal indiscipline and social disorder, manifest in the looting of supermarkets. Nevertheless, for the first time in Argentine political history, an administration of one political hue, which had gained office as the result of free, unrestricted elections, handed over the government of the country to another freely elected administration of a different political party. Although the transfer of power occurred earlier than provided for by the constitution, at a moment of profound crisis, there was no military intervention. Even if the Peronist victory in 1989 owed more to protest against the UCR than a vote of confidence in Menem, it was resounding. This, coupled with his skills as a coalition builder, gave incoming president Carlos Saúl Menem (1989–1999) considerable freedom of maneuver. He employed these advantages to construct a broad alliance within and outside the traditional ranks of Peronism and, indeed, the party.

Menem espoused "realism" in politics and international economic relations. Following currency stabilization in 1991—the so-called Convertibility Plan—foreign investment increased, as did the foreign debt. Internationalism also assumed a distinctly pro-US stance, reflected in positions taken in international forums and conflicts. The aspirations of the regime were signaled by the pledging of Argentine frigates to the international coalition involved in the Gulf War of 1991, the proposal to join the North Atlantic Treaty Organization (NATO), renewed commitment to the Common Market of the South (Mercado Común del Sur—MERCOSUR), which was gradually transformed from a free-trade zone into something approaching a common market, and efforts to foster close collaboration between MERCOSUR and the European Union. In contrast to PJ administrations of the 21st century, Menem was determined to secure allies abroad, notably in the United States and Europe.

The Convertibility Plan was devised and directed by Domingo Cavallo, minister of economy, and entailed the reform of the state: privatization, the liberalization of capital markets, and a renewed opening of the economy. Following a substantial devaluation, the domestic currency was to be completely underwritten by US dollars and foreign reserves held by the central bank, which was to be freed from political control and prohibited from printing money (that is, monetizing the fiscal deficit). The Convertibility Plan introduced a dual (or competitive) monetary system: pesos and US dollars circulated in parallel and were interchangeable. The central bank became, in effect, a currency board. Reform of the state meant removing the principal fiscal pressure points, specifically deficits generated by state-owned enterprises, provincial administrations, and social security funds. The balance of the federal budget was to be restored by, on the revenue side, tax reform and, on the expenditure side, the disposal of state enterprises, pension privatization, and imposing discipline on the provinces.

Ever the consummate populist politician, Menem reconfigured the PJ in his image and divided the opposition; he also secured constitutional reform enabling him to stand for a second consecutive presidential term. Constitutional change was prepared by the Olivos Pact, an agreement between Menem and former president Alfonsín. The principal modifications introduced by the Constitution of 1994 included an increase in provincial representation in the National Senate from two to three seats, the granting of province-style autonomy to the federal capital, a reduction in the length of the presidential term from six to four years, and a provision allowing a sitting president to seek immediate reelection (hitherto, a consecutive presidential term had been proscribed, incumbents being required to stand down for at least one term). The new constitution also established a complicated and unusual dual election threshold: to win in the first round, a presidential candidate was required to obtain 45 percent of the vote or more than 40 percent with a greater than 10-point margin over the runner-up. If any one candidate failed to meet these criteria, the two candidates receiving the most votes would go forward to a second round. Subsequently, two further significant modifications were introduced.

The 1994 settlement facilitated the reelection of Menem and secured the Convertibility Plan. The lessons of the PJ's midterm electoral victories during Menem's first term, and his second triumph in the 1995 presidential election, were that the electorate demanded economic stability and would not support political groupings deemed unlikely to deliver monetary order. Nevertheless, before and after 1995, Menem's political project represented a threat to democracy: he undermined accountability within the PJ, repeatedly changed the rules of the political game, and institutionalized corruption. Nonetheless, voters had few qualms about returning the PJ to office in 1995. Yet, by the late 1990s, the Menem administration had become a distributionist confederacy that preyed on the remnants of a failing state, conditions that contributed to an opposition victory in the 1999 elections and the installation of a new administration headed by President Fernando De la Rúa (1999–2001).

The opposition victory in the 1999 presidential and congressional elections can be viewed as a demand for economic stability and political transparency. The third consecutive constitutionally prescribed change of government since 1983, the 1999 elections appeared to confirm institutional stability and offer a distinct opportunity for democratic consolidation. That the UCR's Fernando De la Rúa was elected president suggested that the UCR had been forgiven by the electorate for the chaos of 1989. Carlos "Chacho" Álvarez of FrePaSo was elected vice president. However, initial confidence that corruption was on the wane and that democracy and stability could be saved was soon disappointed.

In retrospect, the Peronists were perhaps not as corrupt as popularly perceived, nor the Radicals as honest. The latter became clear in 2000 when it was revealed that De la Rúa had systematically bribed opposition senators to secure legislative majorities. Budget slippage (often a mask for illegal transfers of funds) and nepotism seemed to be as much a feature of the new administration as that of Menem and the PJ. Álvarez resigned in disgust. An apparent inability to resolve the spiraling political and economic crises became almost as much a feature of the De la Rúa administration in 2001 as of the Yrigoyen government in 1929–1930. Public anger was demonstrated in the October 2001 midterm elections: the tally of blank protest votes cast in such key areas as the gubernatorial contest in the province of Buenos Aires, and the senatorial contest in the city of Buenos Aires, were larger than the number of votes secured by the winning candidates. Less than two months later, with the imminent collapse of the Convertibility Plan, came street demonstrations and government paralysis. De la Rúa was forced to flee the Casa Rosada by helicopter amid violent antigovernment protests around the palace.

Ramón Puerta, president of the Senate, was sworn in as acting president of the republic in the absence of a vice president (the position had not been filled following the resignation of Álvarez) at the beginning of December 2001. Within two weeks, from 20 December 2001 to 1 January 2002, the presidency changed hands on five occasions as public protests continued. Ultimately, a joint session of both houses of the Congress elected Eduardo Duhalde president. A former governor of the province of Buenos Aires, Duhalde was the PJ candidate who had lost to De la Rúa in 1999. Duhalde managed to hold both the administration and the country together but was less successful in keeping the PJ united. Although Duhalde had been nominated to serve out only the remainder of De la Rúa's term, it soon became clear that he aspired to stand for a further full four-year term—in effect, engineering his own election. He was prevented from doing so by an anti–Buenos Aires alliance of PJ governors from interior provinces, fearful of the power amassed by the Buenos Aires faction of the party. Although there was no effective opposition, Peronist factions were unable to agree on a candidate for the 2003 election. Several Peronists indicated their willingness to stand, foremost among them being former president Menem and Néstor Kirchner, erstwhile governor of the sparsely populated Patagonian province of Santa Cruz. Kirchner was favored by Duhalde, who viewed his Santa Cruz colleague as malleable and able to defeat Menem, from whom Duhalde intended to wrest control of the PJ.

Duhalde miscalculated: Menem won the first round of the presidential election held in April 2003, obtaining a little more than 24 percent of the votes, a couple of points ahead of Kirchner; former UCR minister Ricardo López Murphy came in third with some 16 percent. In mid-May 2003, four days before the second-round runoff was scheduled, and with opinion polls showing that Kirchner was likely to win twice as many votes, Menem withdrew from the contest. He did so in order to claim that he had never been defeated in an election, though principally to deny Kirchner the legitimacy of a landslide victory—possibly envisaging a chaotic transition that would facilitate his comeback.

Between 1983 and 2001, there were many moments when the construction of a fully functioning democracy appeared feasible, and others when the democratic accountability of administrations was in doubt. Undeniably, electoral politics became the norm—citizens were able to vote freely—and did. Yet there were questions about what democracy delivered, and what kind of democracy was developing in the country, particularly as corruption and personalist politics were themselves virtually institutionalized—certainly systematic and functional to the system of governance.

THE REIGN OF THE KIRCHNERS: POPULISM AGAIN (2003–2015)

The *kirchnerato*—the 12-year reign of the husband-and-wife team Néstor Kirchner and Cristina Fernández de Kirchner—began so well. Kirchner appeared to offer a strategy for economic recovery and political stability. He continued the system of income support introduced by Duhalde and devised a strategy for government—*transversalismo*. At first sight, the construction of transversal alliances with factions of the UCR (the so-called K Radicals) and center-left, regional parties suggested a pluralistic, inclusive stance. The arrangement served as a system of patronage designed to capture and control. Yet it worked. The new president outmaneuvered Duhalde, and transversalism was soon delivering substantial electoral majorities that would become the hallmark of much of the Kirchner period.

By favoring particular candidates and groups in a succession of elections, for example, the mayoral contest in Buenos Aires and provincial governorship, and for the October 2005 midterm congressional elections, Kirchner created a loose confederation of individuals and interests who were beholden to him. This was not the politics of consensus, however, as Kirchner was suspicious of potential enemies. It was personality-driven leadership sustained by the granting (or withholding) of favors, a feature that was to become another hallmark of *kirchnerismo*. A further characteristic was orchestrated street protest encapsulated by the *piquetero* movement. "Picketing," organized road blockades, to draw attention to specific issues originated in the 1990s as a form of spontaneous popular protest. After 2002–2003, however, most factions of the PJ and parts of the labor movement organized their own *piquetero* groups, virtual mobs available for hire and answerable to political bosses. Increasingly, the most powerful of these was La Cámpora, nominally headed by Máximo, the playboy son of Néstor and Cristina.

The strategy was again successful. Economic recovery, underway by 2003, with growth later sustained by a boom in commodity prices and debt renegotiation—negotiations with the majority of foreign bondholders were concluded in February 2005—generated massive federal fiscal surpluses. A judicious disposal of these funds secured for Kirchner the support of many provincial administrators and the isolation of troublesome groups, including antagonistic segments of the PJ and the labor movement. Federal funds were deployed to divide a weak formal opposition, as well as to rule. Although Kirchner and his then minister of the economy, Roberto Lavagna, were not responsible for the economic recovery, their delivery of exchange rate stability and relatively low levels of inflation, as well as social assistance programs, were notable achievements. Family income subsidies, distributed by trade unions and other organizations affiliated with the regime, prevented social breakdown and served as a neo-Keynesian mechanism to reactivate the economy. Furthermore, a resolute stance in negotiations with the IMF and private foreign creditors generated confidence and domestic political capital: nationalist rhetoric and debt write-down yielded considerable electoral dividends. Nationalist hype was another characteristic of the *kirchnerato*. As the post-2005 commodity boom fueled a dramatic increase in fiscal resources, the rhetoric and action of the administration became even more populist and nationalist. Images of Perón and Evita were routinely included in Kirchner political propaganda.

The robust position of the fiscal and external account allowed the Kirchners to feather their own nest, and sustain their political ambitions, particularly the ascent of Mrs. Kirchner. She obtained a seat in the National Senate in October 2005, which proved to be the launching pad for a successful presidential campaign two years later. In 2007, as the wife ascended to the presidency, the husband assumed the leadership of the PJ. In the October 2007 presidential and congressional elections, voters were offered a choice of three Peronist factions and a plethora of opposition groupings. Although Mrs. Kirchner failed to take the three major cities (Buenos Aires, Córdoba, and Rosario), her Victory Front (Frente para la Victoria/Partido Justicialista—FpV/PJ) obtained 45 percent of the vote. Fernández's margin of victory over her nearest rival, Elisa Carrió of the center-left Civic Coalition (Coalición Cívica—CC), who obtained 23 percent, was well ahead of the 10 percentage points necessary to avoid a runoff. The other principal candidate, Kirchner's former minister of the economy, Lavagna, standing for the center-right An Advanced Nation (Una Nación Avanzada), won 17 percent of votes cast.

When Néstor Kirchner stepped down as president in 2007, conspiracy theorists argued that he was handing power to his wife to establish the Kirchner dynasty. Had he been elected in 2007, having served two consecutive terms, he would have been constitutionally barred from contesting the presidency at any point in the future. By allowing Cristina Fernández to assume power in 2007, he ensured his eligibility to stand for reelection in 2011, and would in turn facilitate her standing in 2015. The future promised an interminable tango of the Kirchners. If there was substance to this theory, the strategy was dealt a fatal blow in October 2010 with the death of Néstor.

Even before Kirchner's passing, the tango strategy seemed to be flawed. Some six months after the 2007 presidential elections, President Fernández de Kirchner's approval rating had fallen to around 20 percent, causing justifiable anxiety as the 2009 midterm elections approached. Despite bringing forward the elections from 25 October 2009 to 28 June, on the pretext that early elections would enable legislators to focus their efforts on resolving the negative effects of the global economic crisis, the government suffered major defeats. In the province of Buenos Aires, the list headed by businessman Francisco de Narváez of the center-right PRO came in at the top of the poll, beating the FpV/PJ list headed by Néstor Kirchner. Although Kirchner was defeated in an electoral district in which he was previously considered to be unassailable, he still obtained a congressional seat due to the proportional representation voting system. Nationally, the FpV/PJ gained the most votes, taking almost 31 percent, Carrió's CC/ARI came in second at almost 29 percent, with the PRO third on virtually 18 percent. In addition to the slap in the face administered by voters to Kirchner, the government lost its majority in both houses of Congress. CC/ARI made significant gains, particularly in the National Senate.

Administration losses were attributed to mismanagement of the economy, fears about inflation following official manipulation of the exchange rate and intervention in the state agency responsible for collecting and publishing macroeconomic data, and chaotic handling of farmer protests, a simmering dispute over taxation, and gross manipulation of prices that had united diverse rural and urban groups and caused an irreparable rupture between the president and her vice president, Julio Cobos, a so-called K Radical who had been expelled from the UCR when he agreed to join Mrs. Kirchner's ticket in

2007. In a refrain that would be echoed in coming years, the 2009 campaign was dominated by anxiety about crime and security, charges of corruption, and concern about the ways the Kirchners had undermined democratic accountability and manipulated the media—most notably in mid-2009, when tax inspectors raided the offices of a well-regarded newspaper that had become critical of the administration.

The electoral outcome in 2009, coupled with the death of Kirchner a year later, provoked fears of a weak administration in the run-up to presidential and congressional elections scheduled for October 2011. In the event, the widow confounded critics, retaining the presidency with 54 percent of the vote, 10 percentage points more than she had achieved in 2007, and a remarkable recovery from the low opinion poll ratings in 2007 and 2008. Hermes Binner, former Socialist governor of the province of Santa Fe, placed second with 17 percent. A well-respected regional political figure, he was the first Socialist Party candidate to gain such a significant share of the vote in federal elections. Again, and not to diminish what Binner had achieved, the poor performance in 2011 of groupings that had placed considerable expectations on building on what they had accomplished in 2009 demonstrated the fluidity and lack of permanence in political organizations and deinstitutionalization of national politics—perhaps something that the Kirchners had actively promoted in order to divide so as to rule. While they were in control of the purse strings, electoral volatility may have suited the Kirchners.

The reelection victory of Cristina can be attributed to the economic boom, and careful distribution of sweeteners. Some 60 percent of Argentine voters were better off in 2011 than they had been in 2005. And inequality, having risen dramatically during the first decade of the 21st century, was beginning to decline, gleaning further support for the government. In addition, the political reference point for most voters remained the economic and political meltdown of 2001–2002, since which the Kirchners had come to symbolize stability. Yet another explanation stems from a weak and divided opposition, which hardly offered a credible alternative to the incumbent administration. Furthermore, and despite views to the contrary expressed in 2010, the president was undoubtedly a consummate politician. By promoting the cult of personality, she sought to propel Néstor into the firmament of Peronist saviors of the country alongside Evita and Perón himself, while emphasizing their shared credentials as radicals and nationalists and as patrons of the poor. The language and stance of the regime had become increasingly populist. Most of the enterprises nationalized during the first Perón presidency and privatized by Menem had been taken back by the state, or passed to allies of the regime. Renewed radical rhetoric over the Falkland Islands also served to deflect attention from growing evidence of an impending crisis in state finances and productive sectors. Moreover, dissident Peronists, while they detested the Kirchners, had nowhere else to go. Many hardened Peronists could not bring themselves to vote for opposition candidates: the option was to vote for the FpV/PJ or not vote at all.

With the advantage of hindsight, 2011 can be regarded as the high point of Kirchnerism and the *kirchnerato*. Having obtained 54 percent of the votes in the presidential contest that year, in the 2013 midterms the administration could garner only 33 percent of the national vote, despite a reduction in the voting age to 16—a device that was expected to benefit the regime. In the province of Buenos Aires, the largest electoral district in the country, Cristina managed to secure only 32 percent of the vote, with the dissident Peronist Renewal Front (Frente Renovador—FR/PJ) headed by the president's erstwhile ally Sergio Massa, taking 44 percent. The political model of "direct democracy," involving popular mobilization and the use of state power to radicalize society to effect systemic change through the delivery of huge electoral majorities for the regime, had broken. A series of *cacerolazos* (street protests against corruption and scarcities) and large-scale anti-Kirchner demonstrations between 2012 and 2015 presaged defeat in the 2015 presidential elections and indicated that the government had no monopoly on mass popular mobilization.

Perhaps, too, by this stage, the electorate was bored with nationalistic posturing and anxious about the "Venezuelization" of Argentine politics and international relations—until Néstor's death, the Kirchners claimed kin with President Hugo Chávez of Venezuela. Many voters were aware that strident nationalism was not without cost. Bombastic language in international fora, and unilateral action against neighboring countries, such as restricting imports from Brazil and suspending energy supplies to Chile, gained few allies. More worrying still, Argentina's continued uncompromising opposition to the establishment of a modern Scandinavian-financed cellulose plant in Uruguay occasioned a sharp deterioration in diplomatic relations between the two countries. As a result, the country's closest allies in Latin America appeared to be Venezuela and Bolivia, joined subsequently by Ecuador and Cuba, and Iran, a "left-wing" association that irked other members of MERCOSUR and made few friends for Argentina overseas. Despite membership in the Group of 20 (G20) organization, and participation in such organizations as the left-of-center Summit of Progressive Leaders, Argentina witnessed a decline in its international standing.

ANOTHER NEW BEGINNING: RECRAFTING THE FUTURE, OR PERHAPS NOT? (2015–)

The 2013 midterm elections put pay to any possibility of constitutional change that would have allowed Cristina to stand for a third presidential term. In addition, the elections were, financially as well as politically, costly for the regime. Central bank reserves were depleted to fund political concessions in advance of the elections, limiting resources available to stabilize economy and polity in 2014 and 2015, and hemorrhaged thereafter. Capital flight, accelerating inflation, and exchange depreciation, coupled with political uncertainty, signaled the inevitable end of Kirchnerismo, although Mrs. Kirchner proved to be far from a "lame duck" president. There were, however, growing concerns about the president's increasing isolation, her health, and the influence of radical ideologues from La Cámpora, an overtly Marxist clique.

In late 2013, having first promised that the government would not change course, the president subsequently adopted a traditional Peronist stance when confronted by a crisis. She named Axel Kicillof, from La Cámpora, minister of economy (he had previously been number two at the ministry) and Jorge Capitanich, a successful businessman and politician from the province of Chaco on the right of the PJ, cabinet secretary. A classic Peronist strategy, appearing to favor contradictory positions, the ruse was designed to keep Cristina's options open. In this it failed. Resurfacing disagreement between Kicillof and Capitanich highlighted disunity within the administration, while Capitanich's efforts to control the economy and his colleagues appeared to exhaust him. The 2013–2015 period was one of intense upheaval and popular discontent. Although the street protests were provoked by a range of issues, their intensity and length showed the regime to be isolated. As the Kirchner era neared its end, important sections of the Peronist élite sought to ensure their own survival and were aware that, irrespective of the outcome of presidential, congressional, and provincial elections scheduled for October 2015, the incoming government would have the task of stabilizing the country.

"Nonsimultaneous" primaries held during the second quarter of 2015 brought disquieting news for Mrs. Kirchner. In three important provinces, the opposition won: in Santa Fe in April, an associate of the mayor of Buenos Aires, Mauricio Macri, topped the poll with 28 percent; in Mendoza, the opposition Front for Change (Frente para el Cambio) candidate secured almost 45 percent; in the city of Buenos Aires, the pro-Macri candidate obtained almost 50 percent of ballots cast. While the outcome in Buenos Aires may not have been unexpected, the result in Santa Fe was hailed as an indication that the right-of-center Macri was, for the first time, demonstrating an appeal beyond the Federal Capital and building a sequence of successes in advance of the national presidential campaign. Macri also attempted to enhance countrywide appeal by forging alliances with the UCR, which coalesced into the Cambiemos coalition. (Cambiemos has been translated as "Let's Change.") Dissident Peronists were headed by Sergio Massa of the FR/PJ, who performed well in the 2013 midterm elections, and subsequently formed alliances with other key figures. At various times, Massa sought to build alliances with Carlos Reutemann (mentioned as a possible vice presidential running mate)—the charismatic racing driver, former governor of the province of Santa Fe, and incumbent National Senator for that province, and Marco Lavagna, the son of the former minister of economy. It was assumed that a Massa–Reutemann–Lavagna formula might command substantial support across the political spectrum—within and beyond the PJ.

Although he had to wait until June 2015 to obtain the endorsement of the president, Daniel Scioli, sitting governor of the province of Buenos Aires, emerged as the candidate of the ruling FPV. The late endorsement, and the tortuous negotiations that must have been involved, would seem to indicate that Cristina secured a promise of protection from Scioli: she would be immune from criminal prosecution and retain a position of influence within the PJ. Scioli had a firm grasp on the local party machine in the largest electoral district in the country, although regarded with suspicion by factions on the left of the party, notably La Cámpora. Presenting himself as an ultraloyalist, despite several humiliating defeats by Mrs. Kirchner, Scioli always performed well in opinion polls and received the most votes in the open, simultaneous, and compulsory primary elections held in early August. A repeat of this result in October, with no candidate obtaining 45 percent of the vote (or 40 percent with a clear 10-point lead over the runner-up), would imply a second round in November. The question was whether the runoff would be between Scioli and Macri or Scioli and Massa.

In the final months before the October elections, voter opinion was shaped by the growing economic crisis and mounting charges of corruption against close associates of the president, namely Vice President Amado Boudou, while companies associated with the Kirchner family were under investigation in the United States, charged with money laundering. Further controversy surrounded the mysterious death of the prosecuting magistrate, Alberto Nisman, who was investigating the 1994 bombing of a Jewish cultural center in Buenos Aires (in which Iran was allegedly involved); it was rumored that Nisman had been about to publish evidence implicating Cristina in an alleged state cover-up. In retrospect, there may also have been a sense of voter fatigue with the Kirchners—it was indeed time for change. In the event, the results of the October round of the presidential contest gave Scioli a narrow lead over Macri. In the November runoff between them, Macri won with over 51 percent of the vote—an almost three-point lead over his opponent.

At the time of the second-round runoff in the presidential elections in November 2015, with the outgoing administration in control of the National Senate and holding the largest bloc of seats in the Chamber of Deputies, the parliamentary arithmetic raised doubts about whether the Macri administration would be able to delivery on election promises. There were fears about governability and the stability of the incoming government. Such concerns were reinforced by the behavior of Mrs. Kirchner shortly before the scheduled inaugural ceremony, traditionally held in the presidential palace, when the outgoing president would present the symbols of office to the incomer. In the event, she churlishly boycotted the ceremony and sought to pack state bodies with FpV/PJ loyalists in a flurry of last-minute appointments between the election and presidential handover. Yet even before the inauguration, it was clear that Macri would be able to form a working majority in the lower house. In the months immediately following the elections, there were a spate of defections from the FpV bloc, and several figures in the PJ indicated a willingness to "work with the government." This willingness acknowledged two factors: the importance of federal transfers for several provinces, and that the influence of governors on deputies could prevent electorally harmful obstructionism.

During the 2015 campaign, Macri declared that he would repair the damaged done during the *kirchnerato* to state institutions—notably, restoring independence to the Statistical Office—that he would adopted a developmentalist economic program—specifically that he would not adopt a neo-Menemist neoliberal strategy—and that social rights acquired under the Kirchners would be protected. In effect, Macri presented himself both as a candidate for change and as a moderate. Within days of taking office, many of the economic controls imposed in the final years of Cristina Fernández were removed, for example, interventions in the exchange market, and a deal done with those bondholders who had not settled in 2005. Autonomy was restored to the Statistical Office. Social indicators deteriorated during the first year of the new administration, though much of this could be blamed on the outgoing regime. International opinion of the country improved—as promised by Macri, "Argentina has returned to the world." The war against corruption was pursued, though the jury remains out as to whether the administration is delivering on the transparency front. Yet what had been delivered by the midterm congressional election in October 2017 was sufficient to give victory to Macri. The incumbent governing alliance topped the poll in 13 of the 24 electoral districts. Following the contest, commentators remarked on the "patience" and "maturity" of the electorate—declaring that voters are fed up with corruption and populism, arguing the beginning of a new dawn in Argentine politics. This is an extremely optimistic assessment.

Alluding to the desertions suffered following the presidential elections, Macri has declared that the FpV is finished. This may be so. That does not mean that Mrs. Fernández de Kirchner is finished. She stood for a seat in the National Senate in October 2017 for the province of Buenos Aires, having formed a new party, Unidad Ciudadana (UC), to support her campaign. In the event, UC secured for her the "minority" (third) seat; she had been expected to top the poll. This surprising "defeat" did little to dent her self-esteem. Although isolated by accusation of graft, while several of her close associates have been convicted of corruption and thwarted in her ambitions to unite and dominate the Peronist party, Cristina Fernández remains a force to be reckoned with. Exposing the peccadillos of associates of the former president and ensuring that she remains in the public eye will not harm the current government, while the political aspiration of Mrs. Kirchner will heighten divisions within the PJ. Yet the future of Cristina Fernández de Kirchner remains an enigma: paradoxically, the more charges of corruption brought against her, the more fervent her loyal supporters become, convinced that the government is playing dirty. Opinion polls suggest that she enjoys the support of about 30 percent of voters.

Rather than banking on Peronist electoral losses, the Macri administration needs to further strengthen its own mandate. It must also ensure discipline among the loose coalition of interests currently supporting it in Congress. These are not easy tasks for a relatively new political party such as Cambiemos and the disparate nature of the coalition. As during the Alfonsín and Menem presidencies, the first midterm elections held following success in the immediately preceding presidential election are a critical test. Macri passed that test. The subsequent fate of the Alfonsín and Menem administrations—and that of De la Rúa—is equally prescient. Only by delivering macroeconomic stability *and* (relatively) clean government can electoral success be achieved beyond the short term. Buoyed by the 2015 and 2017 election results, Macri and Cambiemos are looking to presidential and congressional elections slated for 2019. To gain a second presidential term, Macri will require a fair economic wind and political luck—a lot of it. This was demonstrated in May 2018 when President Macri announced that a standby line of credit was being sought from the IMF. The government negotiated a 50-billion-dollar loan to calm the markets after a sharp depreciation of the peso and the BCRA had raised base rates to 40 percent as inflation touched 25 percent. This was the first reconnection with the fund since President Néstor Kirchner had paid off the institutional debt in 2006 and "froze" relations with it.

With many Argentines still blaming the IMF for the economic and social meltdown that followed the 2001 default, this was an audacious and risky move. It signaled a change of strategy. Having targeted growth before macroeconomic stability during the early years of Macri's presidency, the government began to target inflation, shifting from a gradualist to a sharper program of adjustment. Growth had helped Cambiemos in the 2017 midterm elections—the trade-off between growth and instability worked electorally. Looking to the presidential and congressional elections scheduled for October 2019, the government is risking a short-term contraction in the economy in order to realize growth with stability in the medium term. This will depend on a good harvest (and rising export earning)—which looks uncertain—and confidence on the part of domestic and foreign investors. Much will depend on the strength of the export- and investment-led program of development and structural change that the government is banking on. The time frame is tight and the opposition on alert. Having remained remarkably silent for many months, Mrs. Fernández de Kirchner issued a highly critical statement following the return to the IMF, calling it a betrayal of the country. Peronism remains divided—not least by the divisive legacy of the Kirchner years; public qualms about the robustness of the economy and the conduct of the IMF may yet serve as the rallying point the PJ needs.

The Transparency International *2017 Corruption Perceptions Index*, available in February 2018, ranked Argentina 85 (out of 180 countries surveyed), as opposed to 106 (167) two years earlier; in 2001, the ranking was 57 (91). The World Economic Forum's *2017/18 Global Competitiveness Report* placed the republic 92 (137), a solid improvement on 104 (144) in 2014–2015; in 2001–2002, the Argentine position was 49 (75). The 2018 World Bank "Ease of Doing Business Ranking" placed Argentina at 117 (190), up from 124 (189) in 2015; in 2006 the country had been 85 (155). This data indicates what has been accomplished in the last year or so, and that much remains to be done.

A

ABAL MEDINA, FERNANDO LUIS (1947–1970). First leader of the **Montoneros**, of which he was one of the founders. He studied in the Colegio Nacional Buenos Aires, as did **Carlos Gustavo Ramus** and **Mario Firmenich**. As with many who took up arms as Montoneros in the late 1960s and early 1970s, Abal Medina had not begun his life as a Peronist and did not come from the left. In his teens, he had been a member of the violent right-wing **Movimiento Nacionalista Tacuara** (MNT). In 1964, Abal Medina joined the Juventud Estudiantil Católica (JEC) and met Father **Carlos Mugica**, a radicalized Catholic Peronist who advocated political violence as a response to repressive governments. Though Mugica eventually distanced himself from Abal Medina, he strongly influenced him; Abal Medina would subsequently become associated with the magazine *Cristianismo y Revolución* founded by **Juan García Elorrio** in September 1966. Later, he joined the Comando Camilo Torres (CCT), named after the Colombian Marxist Christian priest, set up by García Elorrio in early 1967.

The CCT aimed to set up a Cuban-style rural guerrilla movement in the province of **Santa Fe** or **Tucumán**, and from this *foco* carry out an anti-imperialist and antidictatorship struggle to deepen Peronist achievements and install socialism in Latin America. With this objective in mind, Abal Medina went for military training in **Cuba** in late 1967. On returning to Argentina, he questioned García Elorrio's leadership style and the delay in starting guerrilla operations. This led to a break between the two men and the formation of the Montoneros in 1968. Although the new organization headed by Abal Medina barely numbered a dozen people, it dedicated itself to preparatory training and the accumulation of resources. In late 1969 and early 1970, Abal Medina participated in robberies that generated cash and weapons for the Montoneros. The group then made its spectacular public debut in May 1970 with the **Aramburazo**. Abal Medina subsequently lost his life in a shoot-out with the police in September 1970.

ACCIÓN POR LA REPÚBLICA (AR). A right-of-center party founded by **Domingo Cavallo** in 1997, soon after leaving office as minister of economy, to promote Washington Consensus neoliberal ideas and policies that he had advanced when launching the **Convertibility Plan** in 1991. In the **presidential election of 1999**, Cavallo stood as party candidate, coming in a respectable third behind **Fernando de la Rúa** of the **Unión Cívica Radical** (UCR), who gained the presidency, and **Eduardo Duhalde** of the Peronist **Partido Justicialista** (PJ). This placing was attributed to the success of Cavallo as minister, and to his principled break with President **Carlos Saúl Menem**, whom he implicitly accused of **corruption**. With the economy in trouble, and Cavallo back at the **Ministry of Economy**, the AR was roundly trounced in the midterm **congressional elections of 2001**. The party virtually disintegrated on the collapse of the Convertibility Plan at the end of the year, most members joining (or rejoining) the PJ or splinter groups. In the **presidential election of 2003**, Cavallo endorsed Menem, adding further to the tribulations of AR. For years, the party was represented in the provincial legislature of **Córdoba** but has now disappeared.

ACOSTA, JORGE EDUARDO (1941–). Corvette captain directly implicated in crimes committed during the **War to Annihilate Subversion**; he was known as "El Tigre" (The Tiger). Acosta was in charge of the notorious secret detention and torture center at the **Escuela Superior de Mecánica de la Armada** (ESMA) and headed Task Force 3.3.2 based there. He is alleged to have taken the decisions concerning torture and assassinations at the ESMA and is accused of approximately 80 crimes. He was amnestied under the **Ley de Obediencia Debida** in 1986 but subsequently placed under preventive arrest for his role in the theft of babies of political detainees. In 1998, it was discovered that he had a secret Swiss bank account; it may have been used to keep property stolen from **Desaparecidos**. Following the repeal of the Ley de Obediencia Debida in 2005, the cases against Acosta were reopened. Together with **Alfredo Astiz** and other defendants linked to the ESMA, he was tried and convicted of crimes against humanity and sentenced to life imprisonment in 2011. One year later, he was sentenced to a further 30 years for the theft of babies. *See also* COMISIÓN NACIONAL SOBRE LA DESAPARACIÓN DE PERSONAS (CONADEP); DIRTY WAR; DISPOSICIÓN FINAL; HUMAN RIGHTS; *NUNCA MÁS.*

AEROLÍNEAS ARGENTINAS (AA). The company was formed by merging several lines operated by the military and mixed government–private enterprises, the largest of which were Aeroposta Argentina, Líneas Aéreas Dodero S.A. de Agencias y Representaciones (LADAR)—which also con-

trolled Sociedad Mixta de Aviación del Litoral Fluvial Argentino (ALFA)—
Sociedad Mixta Flota Aérea Mercante (FAMA), and Sociedad Mixta Zonas
Oeste y Notre de Aerolíneas (ZONDA).

One of several companies set up in the 1920s, the French-financed Aeroposta flew mainly to the south and provided international services to **Chile**
and **Paraguay**; the others organized in the mid-1940s, with private shareholders guaranteed a minimum 5 percent return on capital, to provide services to the interior and Paraguay and **Uruguay**. All were fully nationalized
in 1949, and Aerolíneas became the monopoly flag carrier in 1950.
Aerolíneas rapidly became the premier airline of Latin America. It pioneered
jet flights to and from the continent, buying British Comets in 1959—the
inaugural flight was from Buenos Aires to New York. In the early 1960s, the
company was also the first in Latin America to operate turboprop Avros and
French medium-range Caravelle jets, and acquired Boeing 707s in 1966. By
the mid-1970s, Aerolíneas had become the first South American carrier to
operate an all-jet fleet, and began flying Boeing 747s in 1977.

In 1971, the monopoly on international flights was reinstated, another
domestic carrier having been granted licenses in the 1960s, and 50 percent of
the internal market reserved for Aerolíneas. Labor disputes in the 1980s
meant that business was eroded by private domestic carriers, notwithstanding
the privileged position accorded Aerolíneas in 1971. By the mid-1980s,
mounting losses encouraged the government of the day to consider privatization—an outline arrangement with Scandinavian Airlines System was
mooted by President **Raúl Alfonsín** but successfully resisted by airline unions. In 1990, a consortium headed by the Spanish state airline, Iberia,
bought an 85 percent stake in Aerolíneas in exchange for cash and debt swap.
The government retained 5 percent of the company, and 10 percent of the
stock was allocated to employees. The national stakeholder was Cielos del
Sur S.A., which had taken over Austral, reprivatized in 1987. A year later,
Iberia bought out Cielos. When Iberia was privatized in 2001, its holding in
Aerolíneas was diluted by stock transfers and share sales to US banks and
American Airlines. In effect, management devolved on American Airlines
and the Spanish government holding company that had inherited Iberia's
remaining stock in Aerolíneas. Poorly managed and loaded with debt by its
US and Spanish proprietors, and subject to continuing labor and contract
disputes, bankruptcy loomed. Flights were suspended, passengers hemorrhaged, suppliers of goods and services went unpaid, and the greater part of
the fleet was mothballed. Marsans, a private Spanish air operator, bought
Aerolíneas for a knock-down price and the promise of a cash injection to
facilitate the resumption of flights. Costs were pruned, and the corner seemed
to be turned in 2003 when operating profits returned and market share began
to recover. But the political mood in Argentina shifted, and in 2008 Marsans
agreed with the government to reduce its stake in Aerolíneas, to make room

for local private investors. Negotiations stalled, and the government took the airline back into state ownership. When the renationalization bill came to Congress, it was ironic that former president **Carlos Saúl Menem**, who had promoted **privatization** in 1990 and was then a national senator, voted in favor of nationalization.

The reimposition of state control in 2008 did not bring an end to the crisis of the airline, despite a better operating position in part due to fleet modernization: labor disputes continued as workers maintained that their interests were being sacrificed for those of private investors and supply firms—friends of Presidents **Néstor Kirchner** and **Cristina Fernández de Kirchner**—at the same time as sweet deals were done with companies owned by the Kirchners themselves. In the final years of the *kirchnerato*, Aerolíneas became an important source of funding for **La Cámpora**, in effect the youth wing of the regime nominally headed by **Máximo Kirchner**, son of the presidents. Airline revenue was top-sliced, funds being transferred to finance La Campora projects and the life-styles of the leadership of the organization.

Having been mentored by **United States** carrier Delta since 2010, the airline joined the Sky Team Alliance in 2012. The future remains uncertain: it may be reprivatized or franchised, depending on a review of operations proposed by the government of President **Mauricio Macri**, elected in 2015. Aerolíneas is currently headed by Mário Agustín Dell'Acqua, an industrial engineer and businessman appointed by Macri in late 2016. *See also* ECONOMY; FOREIGN DEBT/FOREIGN INVESTMENT; STATE-OWNED ENTERPRISES (SOEs); TRANSPORTATION.

AFIRMACIÓN PARA UNA REPÚBLICA IGUALITARIA (ARI). An ephemeral political party that exerted significant influence at a crucial moment when the **Alianza** government headed by President **Fernando de la Rúa** of the **Unión Cívica Radical** (UCR) was disintegrating. Several key individuals associated with the formation of ARI had been members of the two parties that constituted the Alianza administration—the UCR and the **Frente País Solidario** (FREPASO). Originally established as a political movement in 2000 named Argentinos por una República de Iguales, it registered as a political party in 2002, adopting its current title—Affirmation for an Egalitarian Republic. Desertions from the Alianza administration were triggered by government responses to the impending economic chaos, charges of **corruption**, and what was seen as a lurch to the right by De la Rúa. ARI was itself subject to internal divisions—namely, a clash about ideology and electoral strategy between socialists and those who had previously been members of the UCR and dissident Peronist organizations. After 2002, ARI entered into an electoral agreement with the **Coalición Cívica** formed by **Elisa Carrió**, which soon became the dominant partner. Socialists who rejected the embrace of Carrió formed the rump ARI-Autónomo. Although the active, effective life of ARI was short, the history of the organization neatly reflected and foreshadowed the reconfiguration of Argentine politics at a time of crisis associated with the collapse of the **Convertibility Plan** in 2002 and efforts by left-of-center groups to form a viable political organization, as well as the increasing fragmentation of traditional party organizations at a time of economic crisis and political flux.

AGOSTI, ORLANDO RAMÓN (1924–1997). Commander-in-chief of the air force and member of the military junta headed by **Jorge Rafael Videla** in 1976–1979; Agosti was a graduate of the Escuela Militar de Aviación who quickly advanced in his career in the air force, becoming head of the service in January 1976 and participated in the coup that overthrew **Isabel Perón** in March of that year. In contrast to the army or the navy, the air force had a minor role in the **War to Annihilate Subversion** that became the notorious hallmark of the **Proceso de Reorganización Nacional**. Agosti was succeeded in January 1979 as air force commander and member of the junta by **Omar Graffigna**.

Following the restoration of democracy, Agosti was one of the defendants in the **trial of the military juntas** in 1985. Although accused of ordering 88 murders, 581 illegal arrests, 278 cases of torture (of which seven resulted in death), 11 abductions of minors, and 110 thefts in aggravated circumstances, he was found guilty of just eight specific counts of torture and sentenced to four and a half years in prison. The Supreme Court further reduced his sentence to three years and nine months. Agosti was the only member of the junta to complete his sentence and was released in May 1989. Although he was among the former top officers pardoned in 1990 by President **Carlos Saúl Menem**, he failed to have his military rank restored in an appeal to the courts in 1993.

AGRARIAN FEDERATION. *See* FEDERACIÓN AGRARIA ARGENTINA (FAA).

AGREEMENT BETWEEN ARGENTINA AND CHILE ACCEPTING PAPAL MEDIATION IN THE BEAGLE CHANNEL DISPUTE (1979). The agreement was signed in Montevideo on 8 January 1979 by the two parties to the **Beagle Channel Dispute** in the presence of Cardinal Antonio Samoré, the peace envoy of the Vatican. On his part, Pope John Paul II expressed a desire to obtain direct and concrete information on the positions of the two sides and to contribute to the achievement of a peaceful settlement to the dispute. The Argentine and Chilean governments committed themselves to settle the issue through mediation and would meet the pope's request of informing him of the terms of the dispute and of such background information and opinions as were deemed relevant for the negotiations. The Vatican imposed the additional condition that the request of papal mediation would only be accepted if Argentina and Chile did not resort to the use of force in mutual relations, returned to their military positions of 1977, and maintained the status quo. *See also* ALFONSÍN, RAÚL RICARDO (1927–2009); CHILE; FALKLANDS WAR (2 APRIL–14 JUNE 1982); PROCESO DE REORGANIZACIÓN NACIONAL; VIDELA, JORGE RAFAEL (1925–2013).

AGREEMENT BETWEEN ARGENTINA AND GREAT BRITAIN CONCERNING THE FALKLAND ISLANDS (1971). Although Argentina had a long-standing claim to the Falklands (a British colony since 1833), it was prepared to make practical arrangements for communications and supplies to the islands. As a result, this agreement did not deal with the question of sovereignty and betokened a readiness by both parties to seek a peaceful solution to the dispute. Argentina set up a regular weekly air service for passengers, cargo, and mail to the islands, while Britain established a regular shipping service for passengers, cargo, and mail to the mainland. Freedom of movement in both directions was facilitated, and postal, telegraphic, and telephone communications were established between Argentina and the Falklands. The agreement came into effect in 1972 and was terminated a decade later as a direct result of the **Falklands War.**

AGRICULTURAL COLONIZATION. Although **Bernardino Rivadavia** was the first statesman to promote colonization, the formation of agricultural colonies was central to the project of nation building advanced by liberal thinkers in Argentina from the mid-19th century. Influenced by the **United States** model of **immigration**, figures like **Juan Bautista Alberdi** and **Domingo Faustino Sarmiento** developed the thesis that the country was underpopulated and that the promotion of immigration was a responsibility of government. This sentiment found expression in the preamble of the **Constitution of 1853**. *Gobernar es poblar* (to govern is to populate) became the development slogan of the day, an approach that achieved concrete expression during the presidencies of Sarmiento and **Nicolás Avellaneda**, who as minister and president was largely responsible for drafting land laws intended to facilitate settlement.

Early colonization and immigration projects essayed by Rivadavia were compromised by the realities of the early national period: near constant civil wars, the insecure Indian frontier, and the interests of *estancieros*—the politically dominant cattle elite. It is no coincidence that settlement projects attempted in the 1820s were largely abandoned during the time of **Juan Manuel de Rosas**, notwithstanding a steady growth in the immigrant population associated with the takeoff of **wool** production in the 1840s. While most immigrants who arrived during the surge that started in the 1870s, and the boom of mass immigration in the decades around 1900, headed for the cities, these periods were also the heyday of agricultural colonization, notably after the stabilization of the Indian frontier in the 1870s. Most colonists came from northern Italy, France, Switzerland, and Germany. The main regions of settlement were **Santa Fe** and **Entre Ríos**, principally in areas that were regarded as unsuitable for ranching. There were significant zones of colonization in other provinces, for example, **Córdoba** and to a lesser extent **Buenos Aires**, **Misiones**, and **Corrientes**.

The first agricultural colonies were established in Santa Fe (in 1856, 1858, and 1859) with Swiss colonists installed at Esperanza, San Gerónimo, and San Carlos, respectively, and in 1857 at San José in the province of Entre Ríos. Large tracts of the provinces of Córdoba, Entre Rios, and Santa Fe— the *pampa gringa*—would be settled by European colonists. Four modes of colonization occurred in Santa Fe: "government colonies," formed by the provincial or federal government, with land being sold cheaply and directly to settlers; "official colonies," where land was sold at low prices to developers who were expected to prepare the ground for settlement and make it available for sale or rent under terms set by the government; "private colonies," which were speculative settlement ventures, the land obtained at market prices, though sometimes fiscal incentives were provided (developers were expected to mark out plots, provide roads, and set aside land for rural townships; in addition to selling land, the companies usually provided agricultural machinery and supplied technical and administrative assistance and commercialized crops; and "commercial colonies," where private firms largely engaged in leasing and exploiting land, with plots available to rent, and colonists were contracted to hire equipment from, and sell produce to, the landowner. The majority of colonies established between around 1870 and 1895 were "private colonies," typically colonization companies in the business of selling land to settlers. This also became the principal model elsewhere.

By the early 1890s, there were around 360 colonies in the province of Santa Fe, 220 in Entre Ríos, 130 in Córdoba, and possibly 60 in Buenos Aires. Initially, these settlements had been formed by individual *estancieros*, with colonization companies becoming increasingly active from the mid-1870s. Many early settlements were professionally administered and became prosperous. However, until the zones in which they were located had been linked to the railway network, most early foundations led a precarious existence. The main wave of agricultural colonization was over by the early 20th century, but there was a modest revival during the interwar period on the fringes of the **pampas**. The northeast, notably Misiones, was envisaged as a region of private European colonization. In the 1920s and 1930s, several

British, Danish, Polish, and German settlements were established. There were similar schemes in northern **Patagonia**, when new concessions awarded to British- and French-owned railway companies were connected to federal colonization schemes.

"Railway colonization" constituted possibly another model of colonization, and one that approximates the situation in the United States. The Central Argentine Land Company was organized as a subsidiary of the **Central Argentine Railway Company** to administer a land grant awarded by the federal government. The award envisaged the formation of colonies along the trunk line from **Rosario** to Córdoba. By 1870, colonies were being established along parts of the railway in Santa Fe, close to the port of Rosario. Within a couple of years, land was being sold off to the original colonists, with a second round of colonies being set up—followed by land disposal, occurring between 1879 and 1887. While the Central Argentine was unique in the scale of the land grant bestowed on it, during the railway mania of the 1880s "colonization railways" became a feature of the Santa Fe and Córdoba landscape. Largely provincially owned, they were financed through bonds placed in Paris. Many such companies collapsed after the **Baring Crisis**, their assets being turned over to bondholders, who assumed responsibility for the colonies, as well as the railways.

In spite of settlement elsewhere, the provinces of Santa Fe and Entre Ríos are most associated with agricultural colonization; they were the earliest and most active in the promotion of colonization. The most referenced colony is Esperanza, Santa Fe. Located in the center-east of the province, Esperanza was officially established in 1853 when a French entrepreneur signed a colonization contract with the provincial government. The first groups of families arrived in 1856 and 1858, about two-thirds of whom were Swiss. The colony struggled at first, but its future was assured with the arrival of the railway in 1885. Esperanza produced cereals for export, later diversifying into dairy production and market gardening for regional urban markets. Visited by Sarmiento in 1870, the region is today regarded as marking the beginning of successful agricultural colonization and the settlement of the interior.

Despite frequent allusions to homesteading in the United States and the granting of public land to support railway building, Argentine colonization differed from that farther north in that most colonies were commercial projects organized by land companies. Whether registered overseas or financed by local capitalists, the object of such companies was to sell land to settlers. There was no free disposal of public land to settlers. As farms became productive, settlers would repay loans and advances and purchase the land that they were largely instrumental in bringing into commercial use. *See also* AGRICULTURE; *ESTANCIA* COMPANIES.

AGRICULTURE. Ranching and farming were the mainstay of the economy from colonial times until the mid-20th century, when **industry** became the largest productive sector. Until the early 19th century, the main export staples were such **commodities** as hides, grease, tallow, and dried salted **meat**. Processed by *saladeros*, *tasajo* (jerked beef) was consumed mainly by slaves in **Brazil** and **Cuba**; the other items were sent to Europe. Fresh meat, largely a by-product of the production of hides, was consumed locally. Arable farming was little developed before the 1840s, and **grain** continued to be imported until the 1870s. Large-scale modern agricultural production dates from the **Conquest of the Desert** and the opening of the **pampas** to settlement, a process propelled by mass **immigration** and foreign investment in infrastructure. **Wool** became a major item of production and export after the 1840s. By the 1880s, newly opened frontier land was being planted with wheat and **maize**—and later linseed—as the result of **agricultural colonization**, mainly as a means of preparing land for seeding with European grasses and alfalfa to raise prime fat stock. Around 1900, the country had become one of the leading cereal and meat producers of the world—renowned by the 1920s for the quality of meat delivered to the European market by modern, capital intensive meatpacking plants, *frigoríficos*. The interwar decades also saw further development of oil-seed production (including sunflowers and cotton) and a boost to hard- and stone-fruit production, as well as the growing of citrus fruit. In the early decades of the 20th century, there were also efforts to revive the sugarcane and tobacco sectors. Like table grapes and wine, many of these products were significant elements of regional agricultural though were not substantial export items; wine did not emerge as an important export until the late 20th century. **Yerba mate** was another important regional staple, dating from the late colonial period, that was little exported other than to neighboring countries until its reputed medicinal qualities were widely promoted around the beginning of the 21st century. Yet soya is the outstanding commodity of the early 21st century.

Many commodities are produced across the country, though the principal agricultural regions are the pampas—cereals, soya, and animals, including dairy products; **Cuyo**—wine; **Mesopotamia** and northern **Patagonia**—fruit; **Tucumán**—sugar; and **Chaco**—cotton, tobacco, and tree products. Argentina ranks among the top 10 agricultural producing and exporting countries of the world. It is the third largest producer of soya, ranks fifth for wine, has the sixth largest cattle herd, and accounts for around a 10th of all meat produced globally. In terms of volume of production, the main commodities produced in Argentina are soya (accounting for about a third of total output) followed by maize (one-fifth), sugarcane (one-sixth), **grains** (other than maize; one-eighth), milk (a 15th); meat products account for little more than 3 percent of the volume of rural output, though clearly a much larger proportion of value.

Modern agriculture is capital intensive, a tendency that accelerated in the 1990s: while labor-intensive production of cereals on small- and medium-sized farms, and of cattle on vast *estancias*, was characteristic of the late 19th and early 20th centuries, present-day activities are highly mechanized. This can be seen in the production of such traditional commodities as wool, grains, and meat, and in "new" items like soya, vegetable cellulose, and biodiesel. There is a significant trend toward organic farming.

Taking the broadest possible estimate (export taxes, taxation on rural-sector incomes, value-added tax, fiscal contributions by the food-processing industries dependent on agrarian inputs, and social security contributions), the sector accounted for almost 13 percent of government tax receipts in 2014, around 20 percent of gross domestic product, and 16 percent of national employment. A similar broad definition of the rural commodity chains suggests that the sector accounts for something like 60 percent of exports, that is, including commodities and "manufactured goods of agricultural origin" (essentially, processed commodities like chilled and canned meat, vegetable oils, and packed food products).

Although agriculture is and was a crucial element of the economy, and export production was actively promoted until the early decades of the 20th century, **developmentalism** and import-substituting industrialization resulted in a policy shift in favor of manufacturing that had a detrimental impact on agriculture as credit and labor focused on urban activities. Politically, the ranching sector has not always enjoyed a good press, notably during the **Concordancia**, *kirchnerato*, and *peronato*. *See also* CRY OF ALCORTA; FARM PROTESTS; FOREIGN DEBT/FOREIGN INVESTMENT; FOREIGN TRADE; INSTITUTO ARGENTINO DE PROMOCIÓN DEL INTERCAMBIO (IAPI); KIRCHNER, CRISTINA ELISABET FERNÁNDEZ DE (1953–); KIRCHNER, NÉSTOR CARLOS (1950–2010); PERÓN, JUAN DOMINGO (1895–1974); *RETENCIONES*; SOCIEDAD RURAL ARGENTINA (SRA); *VENDEPATRIA(S)*.

AGUAS ARGENTINAS. Currently, Aguas y Saneamientos Argentinos S.A. (AySA) is a mixed state-owned corporation (90 percent of the capital is owned by the government, 10 percent by employees) providing water and sanitation services in the city of **Buenos Aires** and neighboring, mainly contiguous, districts of the province. AySA is the largest such enterprise in the country. Its history reflects that of other public utilities and, indeed, the financial and business history of the republic. The company started as a government enterprise; issued overseas loans was floated as a private, foreign-owned company; and was nationalized in the 1890s, privatized during the presidency of **Carlos Saúl Menem**, and renationalized by President **Néstor Kirchner**.

The company dates from 1869, when it was a pioneer of potable water supply in the Americas. It was part of the process of urban modernization that included the paving of roads, street lighting, and the opening of tramways, as well as water supply and drainage. Such infrastructure improvement was associated with civic pride and resources generated by the commodity boom of the period—and fear of yellow fever and cholera, killer diseases that were no respecter of rank or person. A further round of urban beautification followed during the investment and export boom of the 1880s, by which time operations were in the hands of the London-registered Buenos Aires Water Supply Company, established in 1888 with a nominal capital of £5 million (approximately US$20 million) to take over the 39-year concession awarded by the federal authorities to a local merchant house, Samuel P. Hale & Company. Charges were regulated, there was a cap on net income, and at the end of the concession, the enterprise would revert to the government without compensation. Nevertheless, although the company was to be loaded with debentures, and two-thirds of the equity capital consisted of 6 percent preference shares, the prospectus promised ordinary shareholders substantial dividends. **Baring Brothers** underwrote the share issue and later the £5 million debentures. Unable to place shares and bonds, Barings could not honor the call for capital due in late 1890, triggering the first **Baring Crisis**—the greatest of the 19th-century financial panics that almost brought down the Bank of England. When the Hale contract was rescinded in 1891, the provision of water and sanitation was taken over by the federal government. Organized as Obras Sanitarias de la Nación in 1912, it underwent a vigorous expansion program. By 1940, the state enterprise was one of the largest in the world, certainly the biggest in Latin America. Subsequent reorganizations ensured that the business remained firmly under government control.

By the 1950s, the company was experiencing difficulties due to underfunding and rapid urbanization, particularly in the Buenos Aires metropolitan area. At the end of the decade, water and sewage services were transferred from the federal government to the provinces, and water and sanitation provision was further decentralized in the **Proceso de Reorganización Nacional** period, supposedly to introduce market discipline. The near collapse of services in Buenos Aires paved the way for **privatization**. A 30-year operating concession for Aguas Argentinas S.A. (AASA), the successor entity, responsible for administering facilities in the greater Buenos Aires region, was granted to a consortium of foreign and local firms in 1993. French and Spanish businesses—water and sanitation companies and banks—were the principal shareholders, among whom Lyonnaise des Eaux, Sociedad General de Aguas Barcelona S.A., and the Compagnie Generales de Eaux S.A. were the most prominent. The privatization of AASA set an international record for such deals in the water supply and sanitation sector. Later, with the merger of Lyonnaise and the Compagnie de Suez, the Suez group assumed responsibility for AASA.

The 1993 contract was controversial: there were charges of a lack of transparency and poor regulation. Disputes over tariffs and service delivery—including claims of failure to extend and improve the supply and drainage network—became increasingly acrimonious after 1998, before economic meltdown in 2001. The renationalization of the company in 2006 became an international cause célèbre. While the state corporation had invested an average of US$25 million per annum between 1983 and 1993, Suez claimed to have spent US$200 million a year between 1993 and 2000 and to have effected a substantial reduction in operating costs and charges to consumers. As the concession provided for international arbitration, Suez instituted proceedings at the International Center for the Settlement of Investment Disputes (ICSID), claiming damages of US$1,200 million for the termination of its contract in 2006. Suez was not alone; in all, 20 claims were submitted to the court by water, energy, and telecommunications companies renationalized during the **Kirchner** presidencies. In April 2015, the ICSID awarded Suez damages of US$405 million. *See also* ECONOMIC CRISES; FOREIGN DEBT/FOREIGN INVESTMENT; STATE-OWNED ENTERPRISES (SOEs).

AGUIRRE LANARI, JUAN RAMÓN (1920–2017). Lawyer, career diplomat, and politician—elected to three terms as national senator for his native province of **Corrientes**. He is most remembered for serving as minister of foreign relations and religion under the last de facto president of the country, General **Reynaldo Bignone**. Appointed after the Falklands debacle, he had to cope with the mess left by outgoing president General **Leopoldo Galtieri** and his predecessor as minister, **Nicanor Costa Méndez**. Although clearly an interim appointee until elections were called—he held the post from early July 1982 until mid-December 1983—Aguirre Lanari made the best of a bad hand and gained some sympathy for his conduct of post–**Falklands War** negotiations at the United Nations. He was regarded as a principled individual, only agreeing to serve in the Bignone cabinet following firm assurances that there would be a speedy return to democracy, which probably explains his election as senator in the late 1980s. *See also* FALKLANDS DISPUTE.

ALBERDI, JUAN BAUTISTA (1810–1884). Lawyer, writer, diplomat, and public intellectual. He had a profound influence on the process of **national organization** and the **Constitution of 1853** and is sometimes called the

"Father of the Constitution." His main ideas were developed in a magisterial study whose short title is *Bases y puntos de partida para la organización política de la República Argentina*, first published in 1852.

A native of **Tucumán**—his father was Spanish and his mother from a prominent provincial family—Alberdi was orphaned at a young age. He began his education in the city of **Buenos Aires** before reading law at the **University of Córdoba**. He was already recognized by his peers as the most outstanding political thinker of his generation when in his twenties. His ideas were shaped by the civil wars of the period and by contemporary debates about constitutionalism and republicanism in Europe and the **United States**. A scathing critic of the regime of **Juan Manuel de Rosas** and **caudillo** politics, Alberdi spent much of his early adult life in exile in **Chile** and **Uruguay** and traveling in Europe. Opposed to the pretentions of the province of Buenos Aires to national leadership, he recognized **Justo José de Urquiza**, who had overthrown his erstwhile ally Rosas, as a force for national unity, views that brought him into conflict with another great political theorist, **Domingo Faustino Sarmiento**. For Sarmiento, there was little to choose between Rosas and Urquiza. Alberdi's opposition to the **War of the Triple Alliance** also antagonized yet another great writer-statesman of the period, **Bartolomé Mitre**. As president of the recently reunited country, Mitre was responsible for prosecuting the war against **Paraguay**. Alberdi strongly supported the **federalization of the city of Buenos Aires** and the national project advanced by General (later President) **Julio A. Roca**. As a diplomat, he served his country on missions to Chile, **Spain**, and **Great Britain**.

In *Bases y puntos*, Alberdi reviewed several constitutions, including those of most neighboring countries. His approach was also influenced by views on the links between political arrangements and economic progress. His principal arguments for the future governance of the country reflected an attempt to combine **Unitarian** and **Federalist** ideas, an effort to reconcile demands by interior provinces for autonomy with assumptions that national unity and modernization required a strong state. He coined the phrase "to govern is to populate," which became the leitmotif of liberal reformers, a project for national development based on constitutionalism and internationalism that recognized the importance of **immigration** and infrastructural development in building the new republic. *See also* CONQUEST OF THE DESERT/ DESERT CAMPAIGN; FOREIGN DEBT/FOREIGN INVESTMENT.

ALEM, LEANDRO NICEBRO (1842–1896). Important political leader and reformer of the late 19th century, founder of the **Unión Cívica Radical** (UCR). His family supported **Juan Manuel de Rosas**—Alem's father was a *mazorca* leader, one of those executed after the fall off Rosas, charged with murder and acts of terrorism. As a result, he changed his name from Alen to Alem, the Portuguese spelling: the execution and change of name reflected a shift in political philosophy from **Federalism** to liberalism. Described as the last liberal romantic, and an excellent legislator but a poor political leader, he devoted much of his life to campaigning against the moral bankruptcy and electoral manipulation of the political system associated with general and twice president of the republic **Julio A. Roca**, administered by the Partido Autonomista Nacional (PAN). Alem's approach to politics has been described as a mix of Federalism, liberalism, and **populism**. He became obsessed with the separation of power among the administrative, legislative, and judicial branches of government, a founding principle of the **Constitution of 1853**, though more honored in the breach.

Twice elected to the lower house of the **Buenos Aires** provincial assembly, Alem went on to represent the province as a national deputy and national senator. He objected to the **federalization of the city of Buenos Aires** in 1880, resigning his place in the National Congress. As the economic crisis of the presidency of **Miguel Júarez Celman** intensified, Alem formed what would become the UCR, along with his nephew, future president **Hipólito Yrigoyen**. He was one of the leaders of the **Revolution of 1890**, subsequently supporting uprisings against the system in the provinces. From the National Senate, he maintained his opposition to the regime and sought to advance the fortunes of the UCR. During his leadership, the party was divided among those who favored revolutionary struggle, abstentionism (not participating in elections until the government renounced fraud), and liberal parliamentarianism. Alem declared that the UCR contained some who were committed to establishing a liberal democracy, and those whom he described as socialists and anarchists. These controversies divided uncle and nephew. In 1896, he committed suicide, leaving a note accusing his associates of treachery—it was an event that shocked the political class.

ALEMANN, ROBERTO TEODORO (1922–). Trained as an economist and lawyer, minister of economy from December 1981 to June 1982. Appointed by de facto president General **Leopoldo Fortunato Galtieri**, he was adamant that the military project to reorganize Argentina had run aground not because the original plan was flawed but because policies had not been applied rigorously enough (presumably by **José Alfredo Martínez de Hoz** himself) and then were abandoned by **Lorenzo Sigaut**.

Advocating deflation, deregulation, and denationalization, Alemann appeared to be a rigid liberal ideologue. On taking office, he promised to start the immediate shutdown of "nonessential" public agencies and the sale of state enterprises. **Privatization** represented a return to the original post-1976 project but was also aimed at obtaining badly needed cash from the sell-off of assets and as a means of attracting foreign investors. Alemann's loyalty to the original principles of the **Proceso de Reorganización Nacional** was evident in his first package of measures. These comprised ending the two-tier exchange rate, introducing a general export tax, freezing public-sector wages, hiking taxes, and increasing public-sector prices. The basic outlines of the overall strategy were therefore very clear: correction through recession—drastic compression of domestic demand and radical cuts in public spending to reduce inflation and further open the economy to the international market. Traditional exports were to be stimulated through the exchange rate in an (ultimately failed) attempt to compensate for the heavy burden of servicing the **foreign debt**. The deep recession afflicting **industry** and commerce was to be prolonged deliberately to achieve the elusive goal of restructuring the industrial sector to make it more efficient and competitive, and on the premise that reducing domestic consumption would facilitate exports.

Echoing views held by General **Juan Carlos Onganía** as de facto president in the late 1960s and accepting that the Proceso had no specific time frame, Alemann admitted that political liberalization would be postponed into the distant future and await the recovery of the economy. However, everything changed radically when Argentina started the **Falklands War** on 2 April 1982. The international consequences for Argentina were estrangement from the **United States**, its main strategic ally, and enduring the imposition of economic sanctions by **Great Britain** and its European Economic Community partners. In domestic terms, the conflict subordinated all objectives to the requirements of running a war economy. Alemann had thereby no chance of implementing his economic plan, and the financial system suffered a highly significant loss of deposits. Massive amounts of cash were withdrawn to purchase US dollars in Montevideo, the capital of neighboring **Uruguay**. By May–June 1982, many banking institutions were forced to close their doors as they were unable to cope with both huge withdrawals of deposits and a steep increase in bank rate.

In mid-June 1982, the Falklands War culminated in disaster for Argentina: the military dictatorship was totally discredited. Galtieri was forced to resign, and the minister of economy stepped down; the project pursued by Martínez de Hoz and subsequently Alemann had become anathema to the majority of the population: it had failed to deliver, and the foreign debt accumulated since 1976 left the country on the verge of insolvency. *See also* CURRENCY; ECONOMY; FOREIGN TRADE; MINISTRY OF ECONOMY.

ALENDE, OSCAR EDUARDO (1909–1996). Politician and founder of the **Partido Intransigente** (PI). He was elected to the legislature of the province of **Buenos Aires** in 1948 and two years later became the head of its **Unión Cívica Radical** (UCR) bloc. Alende then served in the national Chamber of Deputies from 1952 until the **military coup of 1955**. He subsequently joined the breakaway **Unión Cívica Radical Intransigente** (UCRI) and was elected governor of the province of **Buenos Aires** in 1958. His tenure came to an end with the **military coup of 1962** that overthrew President **Arturo Frondizi**.

When Frondizi broke with the UCRI, Alende became head of the party and unsuccessfully stood as its candidate in the **presidential election of 1963**. He founded the PI in 1972 and was its unsuccessful presidential candidate in 1973 and 1983. However, he was again elected to the Chamber of Deputies in 1985 and served there until his death 11 years later.

ALFONSÍN, RAÚL RICARDO (1927–2009). Statesman, lawyer, and lifelong member of the **Unión Cívica Radical** (UCR); president of the republic (1983–1989) internationally applauded for his efforts to restore democracy after the collapse of the bloody regime of the **Proceso de Reorganización Nacional** that came to power following the **military coup of 1976**.

Known as Raúl Alfonsín, he was born to a middle-class family in the center-south of the province of **Buenos Aires** that epitomized modern immigrant Argentina; the family acknowledged Galician, German, and Welsh antecedents. He read law at the **University of Buenos Aires**. Awarded his diploma in 1950, he began to practice in his hometown of Chascomús, where he was also elected to the city council—political activity that led to imprisonment with the **military coup of 1955**. In the late 1950s and early 1960s, he was elected successively as deputy to the province of Buenos Aires assembly and as national deputy for the province. In the national chamber, he was elected vice president of the **Unión Cívica Radical del Pueblo** (UCRP) bloc, going on to head the Buenos Aires committee of the bloc. The **military coup of 1966** led to another period of incarceration. It was at this time that he developed political contacts within and beyond Radicalism, including among socialists and social Catholics, sectors that favored a constitutional path. While others embraced the concept of armed struggle during the de facto presidency of **Juan Carlos Onganía**, including the youth wing of the UCR, Alfonsín explicitly rejected such a course. His response to the slogan "Neither Military Coup, nor Elections: Revolution" was "Free Elections without Proscription"—a reference to the prohibition of Peronist groupings by the **military** during elections held in the late 1950s and 1960s.

With other like-minded Radicals, Alfonsín founded the **Movimiento de Renovación y Cambio** (MRC—Renovation and Change Movement) in 1972. This progressive, reformist association within the UCR questioned the conservative, traditional organization and ideology of the party typified by long-term leader **Ricardo Balbín**. The reformist strand was not widely supported within the party at this stage. In the **congressional** and **presidential elections of 1973**, Balbín led the party to a resounding defeat. The result led to heart searching and boosted the position advocated by the MRC. Alfonsín's national stature was furthered by his work for the **human rights** commission, established in 1975, investigating cases of murder and kidnapping laid at the door of the **Triple A**. Alfonsín courageously continued to represent the families of the disappeared after 1976, offering his services as a lawyer free of charge. He participated in international fora, laying bare the human rights violations of the post-1976 military regime. When in 1982 the military announced that elections would be held the following year, the MRC slate topped the UCR primaries: Alfonsín was nominated party presidential candidate.

The Radical electoral campaign focused on Alfonsín and stressed the need for transparency in politics and the importance of reconstructing civil society and democratic institutions. There was a stress on holding the military responsible for criminal acts and for reintegrating the armed forces into society. The UCR also denounced the so-called military–**trade union** pact, a reference to negotiations between the largely Peronist-dominated labor organizations and the armed forces to facilitate a return to the barracks. On 30 October 1983, the UCR obtained 52 percent of the vote and the Peronists 40 percent. The victory of the Radicals was unexpected and exceptional. It was the first time in recent Argentine political history that the Peronists had been defeated in fair and free elections and was testimony to the reputation that Alfonsín has established during the dark days of the Proceso.

On taking office, Alfonsín confronted a number of pressing problems: the economy was in free fall, burdened by **foreign debts** run up by the military regime and the accelerating inflation bequeathed by them; there were lingering doubts about the military and whether they would reintervene; public expectations were high and the social deficit acute. The government initially focused on social reform, abolishing all forms of censorship, making divorce legal, investing in **education** (including an emphasis on literacy), launching an inquiry into the disappearances (which resulted in the famous report *Nunca Más*), and beginning the process of prosecuting members of the military juntas. Leaders of the 1976 coup were sentenced and cases opened against torturers and murders. Continuing prosecutions alarmed middle-ranking officers, leading to claims of an attack on the military as an institution. To bring closure, Alfonsín promulgated the **Ley de Punto Final** in 1986, requiring that all charges against individual members of the military had to be registered within 60 days, and a year later the **Ley de Obediencia Debida**, designed to protect junior ranks from prosecution. This did not head off a series of barrack room revolts launched by the *carapintadas* (military protesters wearing camouflage paint on their faces) led by coronel **Aldo Rico**. The public reaction was instant and massive—street demonstrations in support of the government. As these political events were unfolding, the economy was unraveling. In early 1985, Alfonsín's first minister of economy, **Bernardo Grinspun**, was replaced by **Juan Vital Sourrouille**, who launch the heterodox **Austral Plan**, a neo-Keynesian growth package including a wages and prices freeze to stabilize and reactivate the economy. At first, the plan worked and delivered an electoral dividend in the midterm **congressional elections of 1985**, a result that recognized the political achievements of the government as well as confidence in the new minister. Soon, however, macroeconomic instability returned, in part due to an uncooperative political opposition, though mainly due to the actions of business and labor interests opposed to features of the plan. Furthermore, the government made the mistake of manipulating key measures for electoral purposes in 1987, that is, extending the plan beyond its natural shelf life and failing to implement the difficult, yet necessary, deregulation of prices and wages. The accelerating **economic crisis** ended in **hyperinflation**, debt default, electoral defeat for the UCR, and Alfonsín handing over power to his successor, **Carlos Saúl Menem** of the **Partido Justicialista** (PJ), five months before the end of his mandate.

The collapse of the Alfonsín administration made the UCR virtually unelectable for a decade. Yet the chaos of 1989 should not detract from his domestic political and cultural achievements, nor from advances in international relations. During Alfonsín's presidency, Argentina's standing in the world grew. The lingering territorial dispute with **Chile**, which was aggravated by the generals and admirals of the Proceso and almost ended in open war, was resolved: the treaty of peace and friendship between the two countries was submitted to referendum in Argentina and won overwhelming support. Alfonsín was also responsible for the formation of **MERCOSUR**, the South American Common Market, a project for economic integration specifically intended to promote growth that would reinforce democracy in the region. Regional efforts to seek a solution to the debt crisis—the so-called debtors' club of the **Cartagena Group**—were less successful. Relations with Great Britain improved, but there was little progress on the **Falkland Islands**, partly due to the position of Alfonsín's foreign minister, **Dante Caputo**, and despite the fact that Alfonsín had publicly and courageously spoken out against the **Falklands War**. During the Alfonsín presidency, the country reemerged as a positive, collaborative member of the community of nations, involved in the strengthening of multilateral institutions and participating constructively in international fora.

Whatever else, 1989 was positive and noteworthy because it was the first occasion in the history of Argentina that an administration of one political party that had come to office as the result of free, unrestricted elections handed control over to another democratically elected government of a different political party. Alfonsín may have regretted the much-derided proposal to transfer the national capital to **Viedma**—a project to stimulate regional development in the south—though not efforts to democratize the labor movement, a move that was frustrated by the Peronist opposition and the trade unions and consumed a great deal of political capital. Perhaps his biggest political mistakes were the agreement with his successor, Carlos Saúl Menem, to change the constitution to allow an incumbent president to stand for immediate reelection—the **Olivos Pact**—and his decision not to relinquish control of the party on leaving office, a move that frustrated generational renewal.

Alfonsín was an honorable, decent man and a committed democrat who valued human life. He left office no richer than when he began his presidency. The same could not be said of the four presidents who followed him. He supported the institutions necessary to rebuild democracy in the country—he was the only modern president not to pack the Supreme Court with friends of the regime. Tributes at home and overseas that followed the announcement of his death are testimony to his lasting reputation and esteem. Deservedly known as the father of modern Argentine democracy, he was a recipient of international awards.

ALFONSÍN, RICARDO LUIS (1951–). Lawyer and aspiring politician, born into the **Unión Cívica Radical** (UCR), though he did not enter politics until 1993, when he was a delegate at the UCR party convention that reelected his father, former president **Raúl Alfonsín**, head of the party. Alfonsín junior was first elected to office in 1996, becoming a provincial deputy in the **Buenos Aires** legislature and head of the party's foreign affairs committee. Following a family tragedy, he retired from public life. In 2007, he attempted—and failed—to secure election as governor of the province. Contesting the midterm **congressional elections of 2009**, he obtained a seat in the National Chamber of Deputies, going on to secure the UCR nomination in the **presidential elections of 2011**—he came in third. In recent years, he has steered the remnants of the UCR into largely center-right coalitions. A pale shadow of his father, he was the only one of Raúl Alfonsín's six children to have experienced a political calling.

ALIANZA. *See* ALIANZA PARA EL TRABAJO, LA JUSTICIA Y LA EDUCACIÓN.

ALIANZA PARA EL TRABAJO, LA JUSTICIA Y LA EDUCACIÓN. Commonly known as the Alianza (the Alliance), this political coalition was set up to contest the midterm **congressional elections of 1997**, looking toward the **presidential** and **congressional elections of 1999**. It was formed of the **Unión Cívica Radical** (UCR), a historic political party, and the **Frente País Solidario** (FREPASO), an organization composed of mainly dissident Peronists. Forging the coalition was not easy: there was considerable opposition within each of the two **political parties** and disagreement about who would stand for key electoral positions. Protracted negotiation prefigured the formation of subsequent electoral alliances in the early 21st century—alliances involving groups opposed to Peronism, as well as others made up of dissident Peronists. Many such coalitions proved to be ephemeral.

The Alianza signaled a realization by the UCR, which had been soundly beaten by sitting president **Carlos Saúl Menem** of the **Partido Justicialista** (PJ) in the 1995 elections, that it was unlikely to win in 1999 without support from other organizations. For its part, FREPASO recognized that the UCR possessed a nationwide electoral machine, while its base was largely confined to **Buenos Aires**. The principal founding figures were **Raúl Alfonsín, Fernando de la Rúa**, and **Rodolfo Terragno** of the UCR and **Carlos "Chacho" Álvarez** and **Graciela Fernández Meijide** of the center-left **Frente Grande**, forerunner of FREPASO. Convincing the electorate of unity and coherence was crucial—and initially well rewarded; in 1997, Álvarez won the mayoralty of the city of Buenos Aires and Fernández Meijide, standing for the Chamber of Deputies in the province of Buenos Aires, topped the poll. Her victory was a slap in the face for **Eduardo Duhalde**, PJ governor of the province, whose wife, **Hilda "Chiche" González de Duhalde**, headed the PJ list; there were similar congressional gains elsewhere in the country.

In 1989, it was decided that De la Rúa and Álvarez would compose the presidential/vice presidential ticket for the 1999 general elections: Fernández Meijide had been defeated by De la Rúa in the Alliance primaries and declined to serve as his running mate. She resigned her seat in the chamber in order to stand as coalition candidate for the governorship of the province of Buenos Aires. Agreeing to continue the Menem **Convertibility Plan** and competing on an anticorruption/transparency slate, the De la Rúa–Álvarez formula rapidly attracted support from other parties opposed to Menem, taking 48 percent of the popular vote in the presidential elections—10 percentage points ahead of PJ opponents Eduardo Duhalde and **Ramón "Palito" Ortega**. This was the high point of the Alianza.

As the 1997 economic crisis deepened, the Alianza could not deliver on manifesto promises and there were internal difficulties—De la Rúa found it difficult to govern collegiately. For Álvarez, the final straw was the discovery that the president had been bribing senators to secure the passage of legislation; he resigned in October 2000 after less than a year in office. De la Rúa survived barely another 12 months, forced out by mass protest in December 2001, when the alliance was formally dissolved. *See also* ECONOMIC CRISES; FRENTE AMPLIO UNEN (FAUNEN); FRENTE RENOVADOR (FR/PJ).

ALONSO, JOSÉ (1917–1970). Trade unionist leader of the **Confederación General del Trabajo** (CGT) during the 1960s. To counter the influence of the communist Federación Obrera del Vestido (FOV), in 1943 Alonso founded the Sindicato de la Industria del Vestido de la Capital Federal (SOI-

VA). The latter became one of the strongest **trade unions** in Argentina, supported by Secretary of Labor **Juan Domingo Perón**. Also, with government support, he created the Federación Obrera Nacional de la Industria del Vestido (FONIVA) two years later and became its vice secretary. Elected secretary of the SOIVA in 1946, Alonso became part of the Central Committee of the CGT and also assisted in the creation of the Unión Argentina de Trabajadores Rurales y Estibadores (UATRE). From 1952 to 1955, he was both a member of the directorship of the **Fundación Eva Perón** and an elected deputy for the federal capital.

The CGT was severely affected by the **Revolución Libertadora**, and to counter its impact a Peronist trade unions association, the 62 Organizaciones, was set up in 1957. Alonso became secretary general of the CGT following its legalization by President **Arturo Frondizi** in 1961, but the organization was not completely institutionally normalized until President **José Maria Guido** authorized a CGT Normalization Congress, which was held in February 1963. On that occasion, Alonso was formally elected secretary general with the backing of the 62 Organizaciones, which were by now the political arm of the CGT.

Although he initially supported the policies of President **Arturo Illia**, Alonso turned against them and led a struggle from March 1964 to July 1965. He broke with **Augusto Vandor**, the head of the 62 Organizaciones and major proponent of "**Peronism without Perón**," and was ousted by him in February 1966. The CGT then split over divisions about how to deal with the de facto regime of General **Juan Carlos Onganía**. In March 1968, with Perón's backing, **Raimundo Ongaro** was elected head of the CGT; the election was promptly annulled by the government. This led Ongaro to set up the splinter **Confederación General del Trabajo de los Argentinos** (CGTA), which was opposed to more pragmatic trade unionists or "participationists" such as Alonso and Vandor who sought to collaborate with the regime and, possibly, establish an independent labor movement. The CGTA was immediately outlawed, while the CGT itself was temporarily suspended. In July 1970, the CGT was once again normalized, with **José Ignacio Rucci** elected as its secretary general. The following month, Alonso was assassinated by the **Montoneros**.

ALSINA, ADOLFO (1829–1877). Prominent politician, a strong advocate of **Buenos Aires** provincial interests, sometime governor of the province, who served as vice president to **Domingo Faustino Sarmiento** in 1868–1874. Born into a prominent family, he spent much of his childhood and adolescence in Montevideo. Opposed to **Juan Manuel de Rosas**, his family had taken up residence there. With the fall of Rosas in 1852, Alsina returned to Buenos Aires and was immediately active in politics and the defense of provincial autonomy. During the presidency of **Justo José de**

Urquiza, who had ousted Rosas, Alsina campaigned for the independence of the province and was one of the key figures who brought about its detachment from the **Argentine Confederation** between 1852 and 1861 as the self-styled State of Buenos Aires. Gradually reconciled to the cause of national unity, Alsina continued to oppose the **federalization of the city of Buenos Aires**. Elected governor of the province in 1866, he developed national ambitions but realized that his autonomist inclinations meant that he had little support in the country at large and so agreed to become Sarmiento's running mate.

Alsina is best remembered for promoting economic modernization, which he associated with investment in railways and the telegraph and opening the **pampas** to **immigration** and settlement. To this end, as minister of war in the cabinet of **Nicolás Avellaneda**, he devised an effective means of defending and advancing the Indian frontier through the construction of a ditch and line of blockhouses-cum-cavalry posts linked by telegraph. Once the frontier had been stabilized, the line would be moved farther south and west, making highly productive land available for farming and grazing. This strategy prepared the way for the final stage of the **Conquest of the Desert**, completed by General **Julio A. Roca**. *See also* AGRICULTURAL COLONIZATION; AGRICULTURE; COMMODITIES; ECONOMY; GRAINS; MEAT; NATIONAL ORGANIZATION; TRANSPORTATION.

ALSOGARAY, ÁLVARO (1913–2005). Major proponent of economic conservatism in modern Argentina; minister of economy in 1959–1961 and June–December 1962; member of the Chamber of Deputies for the city of **Buenos Aires** in 1983–1999. Born in the province of **Santa Fe** to a prominent local **military** family, Alsogaray studied military engineering as well as civil and aeronautical engineering. He then entered business and, during the presidency of **Juan Domingo Perón**, was an important contractor for a number of **state-owned enterprises**. These included Flota Aérea Mercante Argentina (FAMA, the predecessor of carrier **Aerolíneas Argentinas**), of which he briefly served as director. Alsogaray's thinking increasingly became an anathema to Perón's politics and policies, and he supported the **military coup of 1955**. In 1956, he founded the Partido Cívico Independiente, which fared modestly in the elections held two years later. President **Arturo Frondizi** appointed him minister of economy in June 1959 in order to placate powerful agrarian interests and other conservatives. Alsogaray took tough economic measures, which made him deeply unpopular; he resigned in April 1961.

Following the **military coup of 1962**, Alsogaray used the influence of his brother General **Julio Alsogaray** to secure a post in the army-appointed government of **José María Guido**. He again served as minister of economy between June and December 1962 and during his tenure reintroduced most of his earlier policies. The military government that took charge in 1966 dispatched Alsogaray to Washington as ambassador; he held the post until 1968. Four years later he founded **Nueva Fuerza** to contest the 1973 elections. Although the party fared badly, it is noteworthy for an electoral agenda that was ahead of the times and ultimately implemented two decades later.

Alsogaray opposed the **military coup of 1976** but largely supported the **Proceso de Reorganización Nacional**. When the military was forced to relinquish power, he founded the **Unión del Centro Democrático** (UCEDE, sometimes UCeDé) to contest the 1983 elections. He and his daughter **María Julia Alsogaray** were elected to the Chamber of Deputies as the only two UCeDé members; he served until 1999. At Alsogaray's behest, in 1989 the UCEDE was co-opted into the newly elected Peronist government headed by promarket president **Carlos Saúl Menem**. Alsogaray supported the era's privatizations and served in numerous consultative posts. The most notorious of these involved preparing the feasibility study for the *aeroisla*, a preposterous and unrealized project for an artificial island in the **River Plate** where an airport would have been built as a replacement for the two existing ones serving the national capital.

Alsogaray retired from active politics in 1999 and died six years later. Ironically, he had lived to see his conservative economic proposals implemented by a Peronist government. However, this did not become a permanent legacy. In a throwback to a bygone era, the government of **Cristina Fernández de Kirchner** dismantled the key reforms introduced in the 1990s. *See also* ECONOMIC CRISES; ECONOMY; MINISTRY OF ECONOMY.

ALSOGARAY, JULIO RODOLFO (1918–1994). Career army officer and important **military** figure from the 1950s to the 1970s; younger brother of **Álvaro Alsogaray**. The two brothers were key players in efforts to "reposition" politics and economics during this period, projects for which Álvaro provided the intellectual input while Julio organized the military muscle. Julio was a serial *golpista*, instigating or involved in various uprisings and coups d'ètat. Although a relatively junior officer, he was an active participant and instigator of the 1951 attempted *golpe de estado* against President **Juan Domingo Perón**. Imprisoned for his involvement in the uprising, he was freed and reinstated in the army following the **military coup of 1955** and appointed director of the prestigious cavalry school. He went on to head the Army Staff College and the national gendarmerie and was ultimately appointed head of the army in 1966. Principal strategist of the **military coup of 1966** that ousted President **Arturo Illia**, whom he regarded as ineffectual and hesitant in curbing efforts by former President Perón to stage a comeback, Alsogaray nominated retired general **Juan Carlos Onganía** to head the regime of the **Revolución Argentina**. Alsogaray believed that Onganía and the

Revolución would take a hard line on Peronism and effect a return to liberal economics. He was disappointed on both counts. In 1971, Alsogaray narrowly escaped a kidnapping attempt by the **Ejército Revolucionario del Pueblo**. Had the attempt been successful, he would probably have met the same fate as de facto president **Pedro Eugenio Aramburu**, kidnapped by the **Montoneros**. Ironically, Alsogaray's younger son joined the Montoneros and was killed in a skirmish with an army patrol in the province of **Tucumán** in 1976. *See also* ARAMBURAZO (29 MAY–1 JUNE 1970); MILITARY COUP OF 1951 (FAILED).

ALSOGARAY, MARÍA JULIA (1942–). Politician who held various elected and administrative posts and read engineering at the **University of Buenos Aires**; daughter of **Álvaro Alsogaray**, most remembered for the **corruption** scandals in which she became mired around 2004. First elected to congress in 1985 on the **Unión del Centro Democrático** (UCEDE or UCeDé) ticket, the party headed by her father, she was an outspoken advocate of economic liberalism during the presidency of **Raúl Alfonsín**, a stance that would later bring her to the attention of **Carlos Saúl Menem**. When Menem and his minister of economy, **Domingo Cavallo**, launched the **Convertibility Plan**, which included a strong emphasis on **privatization**, it was unsurprising that Alsogaray was appointed head of several state enterprises. The UCEDE supported Menem in the **presidential election of 1989**, with key figures in the party becoming close to Menem. Named environment secretary in 1989—an agency later elevated to the status of a ministry—the following year she was appointed head of Empresa Nacional de Telecomunicaciones (ENTel), the state telecommunication monopoly, and in 1991 of **Sociedad Mixta Siderúrgica Argentina** (SOMISA), the government-owned steel company. She was charged with overseeing their disposal and, as environment secretary, assumed responsibility for a project to clean up and beautify the Riachuelo, the polluted river that marked the southern boundary of the federal capital. Rumor attributed this meteoric rise to a close personal relationship with the president.

Although little was delivered by the river cleanup project, most of the initial budget was spent on consultancy fees paid to agencies owned by friends of the minister, while a large loan obtained from the Inter-American Development Bank was diverted to social projects, incurring fines from the bank. More public opprobrium was triggered when investigative journalists disclosed that valuable real estate owned by ENTel had been transferred to private buyers, virtually for free, and that SOMISA had been sold for around 15 percent of its book value. During the *menemato*, her personal wealth is said to have grown from less than half a million US dollars to a figure almost five times that sum. In 2004, she was prosecuted on charges of misappropriating public funds. She was sentenced to three years in prison, barred from holding public office for six years, and required to surrender part of her property portfolio. Further charges of corruption followed: in 2013, she was arraigned in connection with contracts signed while environment secretary, and in 2014 she was accused of engaging in fraudulent activity detrimental to the interest of the state regarding the privatization of ENTel. She was jailed for six years in 2015 but served most of the term under house arrest due to her age.

Although Alsogaray may not have been the worst sinner during the *menemato*, and the crimes for which she was prosecuted did not involve charges of drug dealing or murder, her responses to public indignation reflected the sense of impunity that characterized many figures of the period, and later presidencies. To date, she is the only minister of the Menem presidencies to have served time in prison; no other official has yet been compelled to answer so many charges.

ÁLVAREZ, CARLOS ALBERTO "CHACHO" (1948–). Politician and regional figure who served as vice president for approximately 10 months in 1999–2000. Born to a **Buenos Aires** working-class family, Álvarez acquired a reputation as a principled democrat, a political reformer, and an effective administrator. Active in student politics, he read history at the **University of Buenos Aires**, where he was associated with the modernizing wing of the **Partido Justicialista** (PJ). He was a founding member of the **Movimiento Renovador Peronista** (MRP), which sought to make the party more transparent and accountable and was especially influential in the universities. Elected to the Chamber of Deputies in the **congressional** and **presidential elections of 1989**, he soon fell out with President **Carlos Saúl Menem**. Álvarez disagreed with Menem over the administration's lurch to the right—its embrace of neoliberal economics—and was frustrated by Menem's rejection of internal reform. Along with the likes of **Graciela Fernández Meijide**, he was a key figure in the formation of the Frente Grande, a loose left-of-center coalition that included dissident members of the PJ and which later morphed into **Frente País Solidario** (FREPASO). In the midterm **congressional elections of 1993**, he was reelected to the chamber, on this occasion representing the Frente. He also served as a member of the Constituent Convention that drew up the **Constitution of 1994**.

Having helped form the FREPASO in 1994 to contest the upcoming **congressional** and **presidential elections of 1995**, the first to be held under the new constitution, Álvarez was nominated for the vice presidency—**José Octavio Bordón** headed the party ticket. They came in second, winning 29 percent of the popular vote, but were roundly beaten by Menem, who was reelected president with virtually 50 percent. In 1997, Álvarez took the FREPASO into coalition with the **Unión Cívica Radical** (UCR), forming the **Alianza** to contest the 1999 elections. Álvarez again took the vice presidential slot, with **Fernando de la Rúa** (UCR) standing for president. They won with 48 percent of the vote, defeating **Eduardo Duhalde** and **Ramón Ortega** of the PJ, who gained 38 percent. Although the Alianza had a working majority in the lower house of **Congress**, the PJ held the whip hand in the National Senate. With a deepening recession, the new administration was confronted with mounting economic and political problems. Álvarez resigned from the vice presidency in October 2000 on discovering that De la Rúa had been bribing senators to secure the passage of legislation. Barely a year later, the Alianza government was turned out of office amid street protest and economic collapse.

After resigning, Álvarez retired from public life, retaining a reputation as a principled politician—perhaps he was fortunate in the timing of his resignation. In recent years, he has become a figure in Latin America, serving as president of the South American Common Market (**MERCOSUR**) and heading regional trade organizations. He has not yet returned to national political life. *See also* CAVALLO, DOMINGO FELIPE (1946–); CONVERTIBILITY PLAN; CORRUPTION; ECONOMIC CRISES; OLIVOS PACT.

ALVEAR, MARCELO TORCUATO DE (1868–1942). Lawyer, politician, statesman, diplomat, and member of an aristocratic land-owning family—his social status is reflected in his full name, Máximo Marcelo Torcuato de Alvear Pacheco. Democratically elected president of the republic (1922–1928), he was the second president to be elected after the passage of the **Sáenz Peña Law** and the second member of the **Unión Cívica Radical** (UCR) to hold that office. He was preceded and succeeded by **Hipólito Yrigoyen**.

One of the early activists of the UCR, along with **Leandro Alem**, Tomás Le Breton, and Yrigoyen, like them Alvear participated in the **Revolution of 1890**, which triggered the resignation of President **Miguel Ángel Juaréz Celman**. He and his associates gained a degree of notoriety as public agitators. However, Alvear's unconventionality did not derive from his political action, or membership in the UCR—this was not untypical of the age and his class—rather it was due to his marriage to a Portuguese opera singer, Regina Pacini. His pursuit of Pacini—she resisted his advances for several years—was a cause célèbre of the day. He was elected on the Radical ticket to the Chamber of Deputies, representing the province of **Buenos Aires** in 1912, the first midterm elections to be held after the reform of that year. In 1917, he was appointed ambassador in Paris, only returning to Argentina after his election as president. As the chosen successor of the incumbent president, Alvear's campaign had been organized by Yrigoyen, who anticipated total loyalty. Relations between the two soon soured as they came to represent two distinct strands of Radicalism: Alvear identified with the *antipersonalistas*, who favored a constitutionalist approach and a relatively orthodox stance in economic matters; supporters of Yrigoyen argued for a centralized, personalized (*yrigoyenistas* or *personalistas*) style of government focused on the leader and a more interventionist role for the state in politics and the economy. Relations deteriorated further when Yrigoyen was reelected in 1928. Alvear retired to Paris, where he had a house, and was there when the **military coup of 1930** occurred.

When Alvear returned to Argentina in 1931, it was to a rapturous reception, which alarmed the provisional government headed by de facto president **José Felix Uriburu**. He took control of the UCR—Yrigoyen had been imprisoned by the military—and organized opposition to the regime. Alvear was implicated in revolts in the interior, imprisoned on the island of Martín García (where he reencountered Yrigoyen), and later deported in 1932. He remained at his house in Paris until 1935, when he returned to Argentina, having obtained a pledge from **Concordancia** President **Agustín P. Justo** that the UCR would be allowed to participate in upcoming midterm elections in 1936—and that the elections would be free. Performing well in 1936, the UCR began to prepare for the 1938 presidential elections. Justo, however, reneged on the early promise and maintained the system of "patriotic fraud," which delivered the presidency to **Roberto Marcelino Ortiz**. Alvear's later years were spent protesting against **corruption**—there were several scandals about the awarding of contracts to foreign corporations—demanding the return of democracy, and preparing the UCR for that day. He remained a powerful political figure until his death, his reputation enhanced by his stand against the Concordancia. Alvear is remembered for his commitment to constitutional democracy, albeit within the parameters of the time.

Marcel T. de Alvear's period in office was characterized by prosperity and economic potential. By 1922, the **economy** had recovered from the impact of the First World War; investment and **immigration** picked up: it was a period of investment-led as much as debt-led growth. Commodity prices stabilized and agricultural output, particularly of cereals, increased, partly due to the movement of the frontier, though largely due to productivity-enhancing measures like the introduction of pedigree seeds. Rural productivity was also raised by investment in transport, port modernization, the construction of grain elevators, and upgrading of meatpacking plants. Manufacturing grew— General Motors and Ford opened assembly plants—and oil production expanded. Social protection was extended and funds applied to **education** and public health. There was social unrest, but real wages rose and the middle class grew. There was confidence in the country, the political system, and the future. In retrospect, the Alvear presidency marked the end of an era—the "golden" years of optimism in political life, social improvement, and economic buoyancy. Alvear remains the last democratically elected UCR president who completed his term. *See also* AGRICULTURE; ECONOMIC CRISES; FOREIGN DEBT/FOREIGN INVESTMENT; INDUSTRY.

ÁMBITO FINANCIERO. Well-regarded daily newspaper specializing in financial affairs founded in 1976. Launched shortly after the **military coup of 1976** (it had been planned for some time), the paper sought to promote economic liberalism, taking a probusiness and promarket line. Modeled on the *Financial Times* and the *Wall Street Journal* in terms of news coverage and style of reporting, its local model was the innovative *La Opinión*, owned and edited by **Jacobo Timerman**, which promised balanced reporting and embraced the then new print technology that facilitated high-quality production at low cost. Julio Ramos, the original proprietor of *Ámbito*, as the paper is generally known, maintained that coverage of economic and business affairs in mainstream newspapers was staid and parochial—insufficient attention was devoted to international business and finance, or trends in global markets. Like *La Opinión*, *Ámbito* developed a reputation for informed investigative journalism. Ramos recruited established economic journalists who felt constrained by the editorial policies of established newspapers. During the dictatorship, the paper was not uncritical of the government, particularly its economic program, yet it escaped the heavy censorship to which most newspapers were subject due to the focus on finance and business. For more than 30 years, *Ámbito* maintained a reputation for cutting-edge reporting in the field; it was the most widely read financial newspaper in the country. This reputation and position was eroded around 2010 following changes in ownership. In recent years, there have been further changes of ownership and in the journalistic and production teams, and its position has been overtaken by *El Cronista Comercial*. *Ámbito* is now part of the Grupo Indalo. *See also CLARÍN*; *LA NACIÓN*; *LA PRENSA*; MARTÍNEZ DE HOZ, JOSÉ ALFREDO (1925–2013); PROCESO DE REORGANIZACIÓN NACIONAL.

ANARCHO-SYNDICALISM. Anarchism, socialism, and syndicalism had a pronounced influence in Argentina during the period of mass **immigration**, especially from the 1880s until the First World War, and particularly on the labor movement. Influenced by political and world views brought to the country by Spanish and Italian immigrants, many **trade unions** and immigrant clubs were founded by anarchists and syndicalists. The fusion of the two ideologies found expression in political activism and the labor movement. Around 1900, anarcho-syndicalism was arguably the dominant force in such cities as **Buenos Aires** and **Rosario**, fueling strikes and demands for political reform in addition to better living and working conditions for workers. Such activism and action resulted first in a crackdown on popular demonstrations and later elite-inspired proposals for electoral reform. The strong influence of anarcho-syndicalism in Argentina may have been almost unique, possibly rivaled only by the fusion of challenges to the state mounted by anarchists and to capitalism spearheaded by socialists in Barcelona. By the

1920s, the influence of anarcho-syndicalism in Argentina was on the wane, displaced by reformist socialism, which placed greater emphasis on worker rights and favored a "compromise" with capitalism, and in the 1940s by the emergence of **Peronism**. *See also* CRY OF ALCORTA; LEY DE RESIDENCIA; PALACIOS, ALFREDO LORENZO RAMÓN (1880–1965); PARTIDO JUSTICIALISTA (PJ); PARTIDO SOCIALISTA (PS); SÁENZ PEÑA LAW; SEMANA TRÁGICA.

ANAYA, JORGE ISAAC (1926–2008). Commander-in-chief of the navy and member of the military juntas led by **Roberto Eduardo Viola** (1981) and **Leopoldo Fortunato Galtieri** (1981–1982); he was also the main architect and supporter of the **Falklands War**. In December 1981, Galtieri (commander-in-chief of the army) decided to oust President Viola in a palace coup. Anaya put a heavy price on his support: Galtieri would have to pursue a military solution to the dispute with **Great Britain** over the **Falkland Islands**. Based on severe miscalculations and badly mishandled, the Falklands War began in April 1982. Following the sinking of the battle cruiser **ARA *General Belgrano*** by a British nuclear submarine at the beginning of May 1982, which resulted in 323 deaths, the Argentine navy effectively withdrew from the conflict and left the army and air force to do the fighting. As is well known, the war ended in defeat for Argentina in June 1982.

Following the restoration of democracy, Anaya was acquitted on charges of **human rights** violations in the **trial of the military juntas** in 1985. Nevertheless, he was held to account for the Falklands debacle. The Rattenbach Report of 1983, an official inquiry into the conflict, found that Anaya had been the most determined of the three service chiefs to impose a military solution to the dispute and the least effective commander during the war. For these reasons, he received the heaviest sentence when the junta members were court-martialed by the Supreme Council of the Armed Forces in 1986. Anaya was given 14 years against only 12 for Galtieri and eight for **Basilio Lami Dozo**. But a civilian court of appeals later ruled that all three should serve 12 years, as they bore equal responsibility for the fiasco. In 1990, he was pardoned by President **Carlos Saúl Menem**, along with other former top officers who had led the **Proceso de Reorganización Nacional**.

ANCHORENA FAMILY. One of the great landed families of Argentina—arguably once the richest and most socially prominent oligarchic clan in the country; politically influential from the late 18th to the early 20th centuries; founded by Basque merchant Juan Esteban de Anchorena Zandueta (1734–1808), who married the daughter of an *estanciero*, Ramona Josefa López de Anaya Ruiz (1754–1822)—they had 10 children. The family was already significant when the **Viceroyalty of the River Plate** was formed in

1776. **Cattle**, land, **foreign trade**, and public office were the principal sources of their early wealth; the Anchorena came to own vast tracts of the province of **Buenos Aires** and new territory opened up by the **Conquest of the Desert**.

Tomás Manuel de Anchorena López de Anaya (1783–1847), the sixth child of Juan Esteban and Ramona Josefa, was prominent in local politics. A member of the **Cabildo Abierto**, later elected to the **Congress of Tucumán**, he was a keen advocate of **independence**. He accompanied **Manuel Belgrano** on his campaigns in the north and **Bolivia**. Alarmed by the centrist national project championed by figures like **Bernardino Rivadavia**, he broke with **Unitarians** and threw his weight—and considerable resources—behind his cousin, **Juan Manuel de Rosas**. Pressed to become governor of Buenos Aires, he rejected the post, deferring to Rosas, who offered him the **Ministry of Foreign Relations**, which he accepted. Mariano Nicolás de Anchorena López de Anaya (1785–1856), younger brother of Tomás Manuel, was an equally ardent **Federalist**: offered the governorship of the province after his brother had declined, he also deferred to Rosas but agreed to serve as Rosas's minister of finance. At this point, the Anchorena brothers were the wealthiest and most politically powerful figures in the province and the country. Initially inclined to support **Justo José de Urquiza**, who had ousted Rosas, Nicolás subsequently advocated the separation of the province from the **Argentine Confederation**. Tomás Severino de Anchorena García de Zuñiga (1827–1899), son of Tomás Manuel, served in the cabinet of constitutional president **Luiz Saénz Peña**, holding the foreign relations and interior portfolios jointly in 1892 and 1893 at a particularly sensitive moment in debt renegotiations with **Great Britain** after the **Baring Crisis**.

Around 1900, several members of the family were renowned for their contribution to rural modernization, notably the improvement of bloodstock and estate management. Tomás Esteban de Anchorena Riglos (1853–1916), son of Tomás Severino, established the most famous cattle stud in the country. By this stage, Juan Nepomuceno de Anchorena Arana (1829–1895), son of Mariano Nicolas Esteban de Anchorena Lopez de Anaya and great uncle of Tomás Esteban, had already founded the principal sheep stud in the republic. Responsible for the popularization of new, improved crossbreeds, he became the largest producer and exporter of **wool** in the country. By the 1920s, various branches of the clan owned almost 1,000,000 acres (c. 400,000 hectares), mainly located in the fertile **pampas**. Members of the family were elected to head the main commercial and business organizations of the country, for example, the **Bolsa de Comerico** (stock exchange) and the **Sociedad Rural Argentina** (SRA), and the Anchorena were related to most traditional oligarchic families, while some had married into the European aristocracy. With the **Alvear** and Alzaga families, the Anchorena constituted the "Three A's" of the rural elite of the province of Buenos Aires—

probably the most powerful of the three. The family is mentioned in the famous national epic poem *Martín Fierro* as the epitome of wealth and influence. Constructed at the beginning of the 20th century in beaux arts style, Palacio Anchorena was one of the grandest and most luxurious townhouses built by the land-owning oligarchy in the city of Buenos Aires, where it occupies almost a whole block on the north side of the Plaza San Martín.

Yet by this stage the family was losing prestige and influence as estates were subdivided; following in the fecund footsteps of Juan Esteban and Ramona Josefa, many later generations raised large families. In 1880, there were around a dozen main branches of the Anchorena; in 1920, some 40. Economic uncertainty undermined the prosperity of the rural sector, while changes in land tenancy and leasing law introduced following the **military coup of 1943** and strengthened during the first presidency of **Juan Domingo Perón** further reduced the wealth of the clan. These challenges had an impact on the fortunes of other great landed proprietors, but the Anchorena proved less resilient than many of their peers. The Palacio was sold to the government in 1936 and is now the **Ministry of Foreign Relations**. While the family name still remains emblematic of the rural oligarchy of the Belle Epoque, the current generation lives a more modest urban lifestyle than their opulent landed predecessors. *See also* AGRICULTURAL COLONIZATION; AGRICULTURE; CAUDILLO; *ESTANCIA*; FOREIGN TRADE; IMMIGRATION; NATIONAL ORGANIZATION.

ANDES. In Spanish, La Cordillera de los Andes, the mountain chain is the longest in the world, and one of the defining geographical features of the country, along with the **pampas** and major rivers. Geologically unstable, the mountains divide the Argentine lowlands to the east from the Chilean coastal plain and fjords to the west. The highest active volcanoes in the world are located along the Argentine–Chilean border, a border that has been much contested at various points in the 19th and 20th centuries. In Argentina, the mountain chains are narrowest in the south, where lakes and glaciers predominate, and wider in the north, where they constitute the dry altiplano, rich in minerals, and intermontane pampas. *See also* ARMY OF THE ANDES; BOLIVIA; CHILE; PATAGONIA; PERU.

ANGELOZ, EDUARDO CÉSAR (1931–2017). Career **Unión Cívica Radical** (UCR) politician and lawyer. He read law at the **University of Córdoba** in his home province, held various provincial and federal posts, and served three terms as governor of the province of **Córdoba**. His political career dates from 1953, when he became president of the youth wing of the UCR in the city of Córdoba, becoming president of the provincial branch 10 years later, when he was also elected to the provincial senate. In 1973, he was elected to the National Senate to represent the province, his tenure being cut short by the **military coup of 1976**. With the return of democracy in 1983, he was elected provincial governor by a historically large margin and reelected for a second term 1987. However, he stepped down from the governorship to contest the **presidential election of 1989** for the UCR. It was a mistake. As the government of President **Raúl Alfonsín** lost control of the economy, his chances of retaining the presidency for the UCR were dashed. As inflation tripped into **hyperinflation**, support for **Carlos Saúl Menem** of the **Partido Justicialista** (PJ) rose dramatically. In the election, Angeloz carried only two provinces in addition to his native Córdoba; Menem secured a 10 percentage point lead overall, topping the poll in all other 20 provinces and the city of **Buenos Aires**. Such a resounding defeat was thought likely to end Angeloz's political career, yet in 1991 he was once again elect governor of Córdoba and returned to the National Senate in 1995.

Regarded as a progressive governor, Angeloz during his third term had to confront major social problems in the principal cities of Córdoba: poverty, strikes, and violence—some of it politically motivated—were on the increase. This damaged his reputation, which also suffered as he became mired in **corruption** scandals. Although cleared of any wrongdoing himself, some of his closest associates were convicted. These events scarred his declining years. *See also* AUSTRAL PLAN; CONVERTIBILITY PLAN; ECONOMIC CRISES; ROSARIO.

ANGLO–ARGENTINE TRAMWAYS COMPANY. Once one of the largest tramway networks in the world, at its maximum extent the system was almost 550 route miles (c. 880 kilometers). The company dates from 1876, when several locally owned and London-registered tramways merged to form La Anglo, as the company was popularly known in Buenos Aires. This was something of a misnomer, though perhaps understandable given the original weight of British investment in the merged company and that the firm was registered in London and the Duke of Atholl chaired the board of directors for much of the interwar decades. In fact, the company was controlled by Belgian–German financial interests from the late 19th century, largely banks that had financed electricity generating and electrical equipment manufacturing conglomerates. Electric-powered tramways were major consumers of electricity and equipment.

The significance of the Anglo derives from the scale of its operations and historic location. Not only was it one of the latest networks in the world, epitomizing the mergers and backward and forward integration that took place within the sector, the company also pioneered the development of underground transport in Latin America, opening the first underground railway in 1913. The company was also involved in one of the great political scandals of the **Concordancia** period that owed its origins to the **Roca-**

Runciman Pact between **Great Britain** and Argentina signed in 1933— transport coordination in the city of **Buenos Aires**. This was depicted as a clash between a corporate monopoly back by a foreign government and local interests in the form of independent bus drivers, the owner-operators of *colectivos*, as well as a scheme to exploit consumers. Perhaps the Anglo was unfortunate in being at the center of a historic conjuncture (technological change associated with the rise of the internal combustion engine; the depression of the 1930s, which squeezed profits and wages; and the rise of economic nationalism among its principal clientele, middle-class passengers). The Anglo became the unacceptable face of foreign, oligopolistic capital and a venal *vendepatria* regime. Paradoxically, Atholl, who had quietly advocated nationalization for some time, found that the company faced virtual expropriation. The Anglo refused to accept the valuation placed on its assets when urban transport services in Buenos Aires were municipalized during the presidency of **Roberto M. Ortiz**, the penultimate Concordancia president in 1938, only to find its rights and assets transferred to the state in 1952. Further notoriety arose when the residual shell company pursued cases in Argentine courts and elsewhere for the return of assets or a settlement. Court cases began in the 1950s and continued until the 1980s; most were inconclusive or partial agreements, invariably with claims outstanding. As a result, during Argentina's not infrequent debt restructuring negotiations with foreign creditors during the 20th century, funds holding Anglo stock regularly pressed their case in international fora.

The company was formally wound down toward the end of the 20th century. It survived until then to press outstanding claims against the Argentine authorities and distribute the money received. Minor by comparison, convoluted, protracted negotiations to settle the demands of residual Anglo stockholders—by then largely speculative investors—prefigured that of the so-called holdouts, holders of Argentine debt after the collapse of the **Convertibility Plan** who did not settled in 2005 and pursued claims through US and European courts until 2016. *See also* ECONOMIC CRISES; FOREIGN DEBT/FOREIGN INVESTMENT; JUSTO, AGUSTÍN PEDRO (1876–1943); KIRCHNER, CRISTINA ELISABET FERNÁNDEZ DE (1953–); MACRI, MAURICIO (1959–); PERÓN, JUAN DOMINGO (1895–1974); STATE-OWNED ENTERPRISES (SOEs); TRANSPORTATION.

ARA *GENERAL BELGRANO*. Battle cruiser in service with the navy from 1951 to 1982, when it became arguably the most notorious Argentine casualty of the **Falklands War**. Originally built as the USS *Phoenix* and launched in 1938, it survived the Japanese attack on Pearl Harbor undamaged and saw service in the Pacific theater during the Second World War. It was decommissioned in 1946 and sold to Argentina five years later. Initially named the

17 de Octubre, it was renamed *General Belgrano* following the **military coup of 1955**. After Argentina invaded the **Falkland Islands** on 2 April 1982, **Great Britain** dispatched a task force to recover them and declared a maritime exclusion zone (MEZ) of 200 nautical miles around the archipelago within which any Argentine warship or naval auxiliary might be attacked by British nuclear-powered submarines. On 23 April, the British government clarified that any Argentine ship or aircraft deemed to pose a threat would be attacked. A week later, the MEZ was upgraded to a total exclusion zone. The purpose was to reduce the amount of time required to determine if any vessel in the zone was hostile or not, and not to confine military action by the British to the MEZ. By the end of April 1982, Argentina was reinforcing the islands and instructed naval units to take positions around the Falklands. On 1 May, all Argentine naval units were ordered to seek out the British task force and launch a "massive attack" the following day. The *General Belgrano* was detected near the exclusion zone by the nuclear-powered submarine HMS *Conqueror*. Britain decided it was a threat, and Prime Minister Margaret Thatcher, totally unaware that by this time the battle cruiser had changed course, authorized the attack. On 2 May, the *Conqueror* sank the *General Belgrano*: 323 crew members were killed in the attack, and 772 men were rescued over the next three days.

Following the sinking of the cruiser, the navy—which had pressed so hard for a military solution to the **Falklands Dispute**—simply withdrew back to bases on the mainland. Not only was this an act of cowardice, but it put the onus of the fighting on the army and the air force. Although the latter performed well, the land forces were ill prepared to face the British. By the middle of June 1982, the Falklands War was over.

ARA *SAN JUAN*. A TR-1700 German-built diesel-powered Argentine navy submarine the Armada República Argentina (ARA) *San Juan* entered service in 1985 and was lost at sea on 15 November 2017—the last day when the vessel was in contact. All 44 members of the crew are assumed to have died when the submarine plunged 700 meters to the seabed in the region of the San Jorge Gulf off the coast of Argentina. The cause of the catastrophe remains unclear, but the sinking sheds light on the financial situation of the armed forces, the quality of maintenance of equipment, and the reputation of the ministerial and military personnel responsible. *See also* CORRUPTION; GARRÉ, NILDA CECILIA (1945–); MILITARY.

ARAMBURAZO (29 MAY–1 JUNE 1970). Coinciding with the first anniversary of the **Cordobazo**, this was a high-stakes operation with which the left-wing Peronist armed group the **Montoneros** went public. Former de facto president **Pedro Eugenio Aramburu** was kidnapped in the city of

Buenos Aires on 29 May 1970 and taken to the farmstead "La Celma" near the small town of Timote in the west of Buenos Aires province, where he was murdered three days later.

The Aramburazo was perpetrated in order to achieve three aims, which were only partially attained. The first was for the Montoneros to make their public appearance with a spectacular action of national repercussions. It certainly made them known, but their political identity still remained unclear. The second objective was to subject Aramburu to "revolutionary justice" for two of his acts as president in 1956: the expatriation of the body of **Eva Perón**, and the illegal execution of 27 people following the failed insurrection of General Juan José Valle. Though "revolutionary justice" was definitely meted out by the kidnappers before executing their victim, its impact was limited by restrictions on freedom of the press. The final aim was purely political. Aramburu was involved in a conspiracy against then president General **Juan Carlos Onganía**, looking to extricate the armed forces from the government through an electoral solution. Aramburu had finally come to understand that moderate Peronists had to be incorporated in the democratic process. For the Montoneros, these plans were more dangerous than the continued proscription of Peronism. They believed the **military** would never allow elections, which would be won by the Peronists, unless the latter were divided.

The kidnapping and assassination of Aramburu undoubtedly destabilized the military regime but only delayed the attempts to give it a civilian alternative. Ten days after the Aramburazo, Onganía was replaced by General **Roberto M. Levingston**. He in turn was ousted in 1971 by General **Alejandro Agustín Lanusse**, who for the next two years pushed vigorously for an electoral exit strategy quite similar to that advocated by Aramburu.

ARAMBURU, PEDRO EUGENIO (1903–1970). Provisional president of Argentina from 1955 to 1958. A son of Spanish immigrants, he entered the Colegio Militar de la Nación in 1918; on graduating, he opted for a career in the infantry. Later, he enrolled in the Escuela Superior de Guerra.

Aramburu was posted to the province of **Santiago del Estero**, becoming interventor in a local commune following the **military coup of 1930**. He did not participate in the **military coup of 1943**, nor belong to the **Grupo de Oficiales Unidos** (GOU), although he acknowledged the need to break with the electoral fraud that had kept the **Concordancia** in power. Aramburu had no sympathy for the Peronist regime that emerged from the **presidential election of 1946** yet doubted a conspiracy against it could succeed, even when the confrontation between **Juan Domingo Perón** and the **Catholic Church** created the conditions for the **military coup of 1955** and the accession of General **Eduardo Lonardi** to the presidency. Perón's downfall exposed the squabbling within the **military** over how to deal with Peronism.

While Lonardi understood that Peronism was here to stay and would have to be accommodated somehow, Aramburu sought total de-Peronization. Backed by various minor democratic actors, anti-Peronist military hardliners forced Lonardi to resign, allowing Aramburu to become provisional president in November 1955.

The de-Peronization measures that followed included the intervention of the **Confederación General del Trabajo** and the **Confederación General Económica**, the dissolution of the Partido Peronista and a ban on Justicialista symbols, the expatriation of the body of **Eva Perón** so that it would not become a focal point of veneration, the dissolution of the **Fundación Eva Perón**, the setting up of committees to investigate economic mismanagement during the *peronato*, and a sheer act of vandalism—the demolition of the Palacio Unzué (the presidential residence in **Buenos Aires**) simply because Perón and the first lady had lived there. However, these policies had their limits owing to the resilience of the Peronist movement and indiscipline within the military. The latter resulted in a failed rebellion by Peronist officers, which culminated in the tragic **executions of June 1956**.

In terms of the **economy**, little was achieved as the government was unable to implement the proposals of the **Prebisch Plan**. Nevertheless, an agreement was reached with the so-called Paris Club (representatives from Austria, Belgium, Denmark, France, Germany, **Great Britain**, Italy, the Netherlands, Norway, Sweden, and Switzerland) establishing a multilateral trade and payments arrangement with Argentina that involved the consolidation of government debts totaling 500 million US dollars, including 10 years' unpaid interest, on which Argentina agreed to pay 3.5 percent per annum.

The uncomfortable truth was that Aramburu had a single mandate, to restore democracy, but by excluding Peronism that proved difficult. He allowed the setting up of neo-Peronist **political parties** in order to divide the movement, pinning his hopes on a victory by the **Union Cívica Radical del Pueblo** (UCRP) in the **presidential election of 1958**. From exile, Perón frustrated these ambitions with the **Caracas Pact**, which enabled the accession of **Arturo Frondizi** of the **Unión Cívica Radical Intransigente** (UCRI) to the presidency. Aramburu defended Frondizi when the latter was confronted with the threat of renewed military intervention, arguing that a civilian government with all its defects was preferable to a military government if it respected basic liberties. Nonetheless, he was unable to prevent the **military coup of 1962**. In the **presidential election of 1963**, he stood as candidate of the Unión del Pueblo Argentino (UDELPA), a minor party; he was unsuccessful.

Aramburu was not involved in the **military coup of 1966** and, having finally understood that Peronism had to be incorporated into the political mainstream and that the military had to extricate themselves from government, became part of the conspiracy to oust de facto president **Juan Carlos**

Onganía. But fate intervened—the **Aramburazo**. Aramburu was kidnapped and assassinated by the **Montoneros** in their spectacular public debut. The Montoneros stated that the execution of Aramburu was an act of revenge for the **Revolución Libertadora**. *See also* CONSTITUTIONAL CONVENTION ELECTION OF 1957; CONSTITUTIONAL CONVENTION OF 1957.

ARGENTINA (OR THE ARGENTINE). The name of the country sometimes causes confusion among English speakers. The official designation of the country in Spanish, adopted in 1860, is *La República Argentina*, which translates to "the Argentine Republic." Hence, the shortened version in Spanish is *La Argentina*, meaning that the correct rendering in English is "the Argentine," yielding the respective adjectives *Argentino/a* and *Argentinian*. Increasingly, the noun *Argentina* is used in English for the country and *Argentine* as the adjective. *See also* ARGENTINE CONFEDERATION; UNITED PROVINCES OF SOUTH AMERICA; UNITED PROVINCES OF THE RIVER PLATE.

ARGENTINE CONFEDERATION. The official name of the country from 1831 to 1852, the period roughly coterminous with the dominance of the **caudillo Juan Manuel de Rosas**, governor of the province of **Buenos Aires**. The name recognized the then dominant **Federalist** project that envisaged the country as a loose confederation of autonomous provinces—many provinces functioned as semi-independent states, simply delegating the conduct of foreign relations to the governor of Buenos Aires. The Confederation dates from the Federal Pact, a military agreement signed between the provinces of Buenos Aires and **Entre Ríos** on 4 January 1831. The pact was designed to overturn the **Unitarian** proposal for a unified, centralized state governed from the city of Buenos Aires. With the defeat of Unitarian forces in the interior, all the existing provinces acceded to the arrangement between 1831 and 1832. The Confederation years are sometimes known as the "Age of the Caudillos." The Confederation collapsed with the defeat of the Rosas in 1852, which facilitated the swearing of the **Constitution of 1853**, leading to the formation of the modern state. *See also* UNITED PROVINCES OF SOUTH AMERICA; UNITED PROVINCES OF THE RIVER PLATE.

ARGENTINE NORTH EASTERN RAILWAY COMPANY (ANE). In later years, the Argentine North Eastern–Entre Rios Railway; the group was a loose consortium of hitherto separate entities that operated the British-owned standard-gauge railway system in **Mesopotamia**. The other principal companies were the East Argentine Railway Company (EA) and Entre Rios Railway Company (ER). A late addition to the group was the **Buenos Aires**

Central Railway (sometimes the Buenos Ayres Central Railway Company). The ANE was formally constituted in 1889, absorbing provincial lines and concessions; the ER in 1892, acquiring federal lines and concessions, including the historic Primero Entrerriano formed in the 1860s.

Before the fusion, which was effected fitfully after around 1900, the most extensive, integrated network was that operated by the ER in the south of the province after which it was named, a system of approximately 390 miles in the 1890s. The EA operated a 70-mile route from Concordia in the province of **Entre Ríos** to Monte Caseros in the province of **Corrientes**, where it connected with the ANE, which ran on to the northeast and northwest of Corrientes. When these routes were completed, the ANE would operate the international rail service to **Paraguay** opened in 1911. In the late 19th century, some distance separated the ER and EA/ANE railheads. The region and the companies were badly hit by the **Baring Crisis**. As the regional economy picked up, so did the fortunes of the railways, which contributed to growth by embarking on modest programs of extension building—projects driven by sporadic competition and tentative collaboration. The ER and ANE struggled for regional rail hegemony, constructing branch lines and mainline extensions and developing river ports to improve connections with **Buenos Aires** and the **Littoral**. Concessions were obtained from provincial and federal authorities and capital raised in London. The two principal lines engaged in a tariff war designed to route traffic to their respective river ports and sought to "capture" the EA—the EA was taken over by the ANE in 1907. Schemes for joint administration alternated with bouts of competitive construction between 1910 and 1912 until the **United States**–based Farquhar syndicate promoted stock exchanges and shared directorships that resulted in effective integration. The rail companies operated as a single concern, although the ER and ANE maintained separate legal identities.

The last piece in the corporate jigsaw was the establishment of a working agreement with the Buenos Aires Central Railway (BAC). The BAC was a limited company registered in the city of Buenos Aires, largely owned by the entrepreneur Federico Lacroze, who later acquired a concession for what became the second line of the Buenos Aires underground railway. The BAC began as a standard-gauge rural tramway in 1888, operating from the Chacarita terminus in the outer suburbs of the city, running on to the delta at **Zárate**. In 1913, the BAC and the ER entered into an agreement to operate a ferry service across the **Paraná**, a facility that gave the Mesopotamian system direct rail access to the port of Buenos Aires. The BAC consisted of two legal entities, the Buenos Aires–registered company that held the equity and the Buenos Ayres Central Railway, a "shadow" corporation registered in London to service debenture stock secured on the assets of the Buenos Aires firm. The BAC issued bonds in London to extend and upgrade the system. The last coupons on the London bonds were honored in May 1931.

With rail nationalization in 1948, the ANE, BAC, and ER became the Ferrocarril Nacional General Urquiza (FCNGU), named for the former **caudillo** and onetime national president **Justo José de Urquiza**. *See also* BUENOS AYRES & PACIFIC RAILWAY COMPANY (BA&P); BUENOS AYRES WESTERN RAILWAY COMPANY (BAW); CENTRAL ARGENTINE RAILWAY COMPANY (CAR); CORDOBA CENTRAL RAILWAY COMPANY (CCR); ECONOMY; FERROCARRILES ARGENTINOS (FFAA); FOREIGN DEBT/FOREIGN INVESTMENT; GREAT BRITAIN; PRIVATIZATION; STATE-OWNED ENTERPRISES (SOEs); TRANSPORTATION.

ARMED FORCES. *See* MILITARY.

ARMY OF THE ANDES. Military force created in **Mendoza** at the time of **independence** by General **José de San Martín**, instrumental in the liberation of Argentina, **Chile**, and **Peru**. Set up in 1814, the army was initially a local force charged with defending the country from Royalist garrisons in Chile and farther north. The army became a truly national entity when Supreme Director of the **United Provinces of the River Plate** (sometimes **United Provinces of South America**) **Juan Martín de Pueyrredón** accepted the logic of San Martín's Continental Plan that the liberation of the country could only be secured if the struggle was taken to neighboring territories under Spanish control. Pueyrredón organized funds and supplies of men and matériel. In January 1817, at the head of force of around 6,500 composed of conscripted/liberated slaves, regular troops, local militia, and Chilean volunteers—Chile had declared independence in September 1810 but was reconquered a few years later—San Martín crossed the **Andes**. The Continental Plan envisaged two theaters of war, the west (Chile and **Cuyo**) and the north (the Argentine provinces of **Tucumán**, **Salta**, and **Jujuy** on the boundary with Peru and **Bolivia**). **Martín Miguel de Güemes** took charge of the northern forces. San Martín headed the western column. He demolished Spanish power in Chile and combined the Army of the Andes with a larger expeditionary force in 1820 to spearhead the liberation of Peru. Peru was finally liberated by Simón Bolivar and Antonio José de Sucre in 1824. *See also* MILITARY.

ARROSTITO, NORMA ESTER (1940–1978). A founder of the **Montoneros**, she was the only one without a Catholic or nationalist background: Arrostito began her activism as a communist militant. In 1967, she joined the Comando Camilo Torres, where she met **Mário Firmenich**, **Carlos Gustavo Ramus**, and **Fernando Abal Medina**. Although he was 10 years her junior, Arrostito fell in love with Medina. The four companions went on to found the

Montoneros in 1968. She participated in the **Aramburazo** two years later and, following the elections held in March 1973, became the staff supervisor of Oscar Bidegain (the governor of the province of **Buenos Aires** and a Montonero sympathizer). After President **Juan Domingo Perón** broke publicly with the Montoneros on May Day 1974, Arrostito and her guerrilla comrades went into hiding. Her fate was sealed with the **military coup of 1976**. She was captured in December of that year and was detained and tortured in the **Escuela Superior de Mecánica de la Armada** for over 12 months. She never betrayed her colleagues and was killed by lethal injection in January 1978. Arrostito's body has never been found.

ASOCIACIÓN EMPRESARIA ARGENTINA (AEA). Founded in 2002, this business association is the junior organization, standing alongside the Unión Industrial Argentina (UIA), which traces its origins back to the 1880s, and the **Confederación General Económica** (CGE), formally set up in 1952. While the UIA has traditionally represented big business and is viewed as an advocate of liberal economics, and the CGE champions small- and medium-sized enterprises, sometimes favoring government interventionism, the AEA presents itself as an advocate of entrepreneurship generally. Viewing entrepreneurial behavior as the motor of economic development, its stated mission is to advance the cause of private business and strengthen the institutional framework essential for successful business initiative. Rather than a conventional lobby, it seeks to promote entrepreneurial initiative and create a receptive climate for business. Accepting that business does not enjoy a good press in Argentina, the association attempts to counter negative public and official perspectives deriving from mid-20th-century statism (and the failure of state corporations) and the image of rapacious corporate behavior that emerged in the presidencies of **Carlos Saúl Menem**, which fueled an antibusiness stance by the state during the presidencies of **Néstor Kirchner** and **Cristina Fernández de Kirchner**. The fact that Argentine business is represented by three quite distinct bodies reflects the diversity of the community, as well as difficulties in fostering collaborative behavior. The mission to promote enterprise, and effect a change in public perceptions about business, also points to equivocal attitudes on the part of government and society to the private sector—do businesses generate jobs and wealth, or are firms exploiting consumers and dependent on official favors? *See also* CORRUPTION; PRIVATIZATION; STATE-OWNED ENTERPRISES (SOEs); YABRÁN CASE.

ASOCIACIÓN MADRES DE PLAZA DE MAYO. *See* BONAFINI, HEBE PASTOR DE (1928–); DIRTY WAR; FUNDACIÓN MADRES DE PLAZA DE MAYO; MADRES DE PLAZA DE MAYO; WAR TO ANNIHILATE SUBVERSION.

ASOCIACIÓN MUTUAL ISRAELITA ARGENTINA (AMIA). Widely attributed to agencies of the Iranian state or its proxies in Hezbollah, the bombing of the Israeli–Argentine Mutual Association headquarters and cultural center in downtown **Buenos Aires** is the worst international terrorist atrocity committed on Argentine soil. The bomb attack—a suicide bomber drove a van packed with explosives along the narrow street to the front of the building—took place on 18 June 1994. Some 85 individuals were murdered and several hundred injured—many experiencing life-changing injuries. So powerful was the bomb that virtually half a city block was destroyed. Unrebuilt, the site serves as a permanent reminder of the event. The outrage had domestic and international repercussions.

Two years before the attack on the AMIA, the Israeli embassy had been bombed, resulting in 29 deaths and 242 injuries. The second attack, on the AMIA, prompted complaints of negligence on the part of the Argentine authorities; the subsequent investigation charged incompetence or a cover-up. In 1999, Argentine arrest warrants were issued to apprehend members of Hezbollah, and in 2006 Argentine courts pointed the finger at the Iranian government—the president of the Islamic Republic and head of the Revolutionary Guard were cited. Several investigation have been held, the most recent led by **Alberto Nisman**, who died in mysterious circumstances in 2015. In 2006, Nisman accused the government of Iran of organizing the bombing and Hezbollah of carrying it out. Previously, President **Carlos Saúl Menem** was rumored to have accepted a bribe from Tehran to block an investigation—the attacks on the embassy and AMIA occurred during his administration. Menem vehemently denied the rumors, claiming that the bombings were aimed at him as he had authorized Argentine participation in the Frist Gulf War. In 2005, President **Néstor Kirchner** expressed indignation at the slow pace of the investigation, calling it a disgrace and an affront to the reputation of the country; he also acknowledged that there had been a cover-up. Years later, Menem was formally charged with obstructing the investigation into the AMIA bombing.

In a bizarre development in 2013, President **Cristina Fernández de Kirchner** announced that an understanding had been reach with the Iranian authorities to establish a truth commission, which would include representatives of Iran, to ascertain the facts. The memorandum was subsequently declared void by Argentine courts. At the time, when Argentina was experiencing an energy crisis and Iran suffering international embargoes, the deal initialed by Fernández de Kirchner was described as an oil-for-influence agreement, an oil for grain deal, an oil for nuclear technology deal (Argentina would share nuclear energy know-how with Iran)—or oil for blood. Before his death at the beginning of 2015, Nisman issued a report citing Mrs. Kirchner and other officials as involved in a cover-up and, possibly, seeking self-enrichment from a deal with Iran—the supporting evidence included leaked documents and transcripts of telephone conversation in which Argentine officials admitted that Iran was behind the bombings of the embassy and AMIA. Families of the dead and the injured still await justice and closure.

ASTIZ, ALFREDO IGNACIO (1951–). Commander, intelligence officer, and commando who served in the navy during the **Proceso de Reorganización Nacional** (1976–1983). Known as "El Ángel Rubio de la Muerte" (the Blond Angel of Death) for his role in the **War to Annihilate Subversion**, with a reputation as a notorious torturer, Astiz was a member of the Task Force 3.3.2 based at the **Escuela Superior de Mecánica de la Armada** (ESMA), a secret detention and torture center, and specialized in infiltrating **human rights** organizations. He was implicated in the December 1977 kidnapping of 12 activists, including three founders of the **Madres de la Plaza de Mayo** and two French nuns. None were seen alive again outside detention; the bodies of some of them were eventually discovered in a mass grave in a cemetery about 250 miles (400 kilometers) to the south of **Buenos Aires** in 2005.

In March 1982, days before the outbreak **Falklands War**, Astiz was appointed to lead a commando raid on the island of South Georgia, one of the Falkland dependencies. Astiz and his team were disguised as workers employed at the nearby Argentine-owned scrap metal firm. Astiz did little more than change into his uniform and raise the Argentine flag before surrendering to a force of Royal Marines sent to remove the commando group. Astiz was already in British hands before the Argentine invasion of the Falklands. The episode triggered rumors that Astiz had been sent on a death mission by his superiors, who had become alarmed by his international notoriety—French and Swedish courts had issued warrants for his arrest in connection with the abduction, torture, and murder of their citizens. He was taken to London, where the British authorities declined French and Swedish requests to hand him over, maintaining that Astiz was covered by the Geneva Convention relating to prisoners of war. It is ironic that, having denied others the right accorded by one international convention, Astiz enjoyed the protection of another.

With the restoration of democracy in 1983, Astiz was covered by the **Ley de Obediencia Debida** and the **Ley de Punto Final** (Pardon Laws) passed during the presidency of **Raúl Alfonsín** and which provided a kind of amnesty to **military** and security officers for crimes committed during the War to Annihilate Subversion. However, he was tried and sentenced to life imprisonment in absentia for the 1977 kidnapping of the nuns by a French court in 1990, and eight years later was dishonorably discharged from the military for defending his actions in a press interview. The Supreme Court declared the Pardon Laws unconstitutional in 2005; Astiz was detained on charges of kidnapping and torture. As a result of the discovery of the bodies of some of the December 1977 kidnapping victims, the prosecution of charges against him included murder. Together with numerous other defendants associated with the ESMA, Astiz was convicted and sentenced to life imprisonment for crimes against humanity in Argentina in 2011. *See also* ACOSTA, JORGE EDUARDO (1941–); COMISIÓN NACIONAL SOBRE LA DESAPARACIÓN DE PERSONAS (CONADEP); DESAPARECIDOS; DIRTY WAR; DISPOSICIÓN FINAL; *NUNCA MÁS*.

ATTEMPTED MILITARY COUP OF 1951. *See* MILITARY COUP OF 1951 (FAILED).

AUSTRAL PLAN. Crafted by his second minister of economy, **Juan Vital Sourrouille**, the plan was launched on 14 June 1985 by President **Raúl Alfonsín**. The symbolic feature was the introduction of a new **currency**, the austral, to replace the peso. More substantive measures included a sliding schedule for the conversion of peso accounts into austral accounts in order to avoid windfall gains/losses; a wages and price freeze, including utility charges; a pledge not to monetize the public deficit, which implied balancing the budget; proposals on liberalizing tariffs and interest rates; and a commitment to reduce the size of the state sector through **privatization**.

The innovative, heterodox plan was introduced because the country was close to bankruptcy and inflation on the rise. Sourrouille's predecessor, **Bernardo Grinspun**, had been unsuccessful in persuading the Washington agencies to adopt a sympathetic approach to the **economic crisis** that confronted the regime in 1983—including the massive debt run up by the outgoing military regime of the **Proceso de Reorganización Nacional**—or to convince the **trade unions** and business of the efficacy of his program to stabilize the economy and stave off default. The heterodox nature of the plan derived from a "shock" freeze on prices and wages—earlier orthodox stabilization strategies had focused only on wages, while freeing prices—notably, charges for services provided by **state-owned enterprises**. Given the fragile political situation, stabilization through recession and inflation was not an option. Sourrouille's strategy proposed stabilization through growth—a feasible Keynesian-style option given economic shrinkage since the **Falklands War** debacle.

The shock aspect of the arrangement, which had not been discussed in public to prevent economic agents from taking anticipatory action, was intended to kick-start the economy, squeezing residual inflation out of the system while lifting wages just as the freeze was announced. The plan was an immediate success: government revenue rose, inflation fell dramatically, and the economy began to recover, earning the government a political dividend in the midterm **congressional elections of 1985**. However, by 1986, the plan was in trouble. Export prices began to slip. Producers withheld goods from the market in the anticipation of future price improvement or the deregulation of prices. Businesses organized a tax strike. Labor pressed for wage increases and resisted privatization, supported by an uncooperative Peronist opposition in Congress. The government discovered that it was easier to freeze wages and prices than implement an orderly "thaw" but was also inclined to delay necessary adjustment for electoral purposes—another round of midterm congressional elections was due in 1987. When toward the end of 1986 the government began to print money, the writing was on the wall—electoral defeat in the **congressional elections of 1987** and **hyperinflation** in 1989. Carefully crafted, had the Austral Plan been effectively implemented and the domestic political and international economic climates been favorable, it might have succeeded. Aspects of the plan—monetary stability, privatization, curbing the fiscal deficit, deregulating the credit market—prefigured the **Convertibility Plan** that **Domingo Cavallo** implemented during the first presidency of **Carlos Saúl Menem**.

AVELLANEDA. Formerly known as Barracas al Sur, the county and town were renamed in honor of President **Nicolás Avellaneda** (1874–1880) in 1904. Located on the south bank of the estuary of the Riachuelo River (**La Boca**), immediately opposite the city of **Buenos Aires**, with a population of more than a third of a million recorded in the 2010 census, the municipality of Avellaneda is an important urban center in its own right, though now fully integrated into the sprawl of greater Buenos Aires. With the opening of the Southern Docks (Dock Sud) and associated railway development, the town rapidly eclipsed La Boca, on the north bank, as the principal southern port of the federal capital. By the early 20th century, a number of key industries had emerged, for example, meat packing, oil refining, chemicals and pharmaceuticals, paper production, electricity generation, industrial machinery and white goods, and shipbuilding. As the area emerged as a manufacturing center, there was a parallel growth in political and social activities, many associated with immigrants (Italians, Spaniards, and East Europeans) attracted by the burgeoning demand for labor, and who crowded into the slums that sprang up around the factories on low-lying waste ground. Trade unionism took root, as did radical politics—industrial workers, trade unionists, and residents from Avellaneda were prominent among the *descamisados* who occupied central Buenos Aires in October 1945 in support of then Colonel **Juan Domingo Perón**. The municipality also boasted two world-ranked soccer clubs and other popular sporting and cultural associations. The economic significance of the region was confirmed with the opening of the Avellaneda Transporter Bridge (Puente Avellaneda) in 1914, one of only three such structures in the world at the time, reckoned to be the most efficient system of providing road crossing in busy ports. Remodeled as a tourist attraction in 2010, the bridge is now regarded as a piece of industrial heritage of national and world significance. By the 1970s, with heavy industries in decline, Avellaneda witnessed increasing political agitation and, by the 1990s, was synonymous for urban decay, poverty, and squalor. Although not necessarily representative of the broader situation, the so-called **Avellaneda Massacre** of 2002, when police opened fire on picketers, killing two, came to symbolize the plight and desperation of many residents—the poor, the unemployed, and those who had barely benefited from the boom of the 1990s but were castigated by **economic crisis** triggered by the collapse of the **Convertibility Plan**. *See also* IMMIGRATION; INDUSTRY.

AVELLANEDA, NICOLÁS REMIGIO AURELIO (1836–1885). Statesman, lawyer, journalist, and economic modernizer who served as president of the republic from 1874 to 1879. Born in the city of **San Miguel de Tucumán** into a family that had been active in provincial politics since **independence**, Avellaneda's principal achievement was consolidating the project of nation building pioneered by his immediate predecessors **Bartolomé Mitre** and **Domingo Faustino Sarmiento**, notably in the areas of public works, **education**, and the promotion of **immigration**.

Before assuming the presidency, Avellaneda held several ministerial appointments in the **Buenos Aires** provincial government, as well as holding the federal portfolio for justice and education. As president and provincial official, he played an active role in frontier expansion, organizing **military** campaigns against nomadic Indians, financing the construction of military defensive and offensive positions, while writing a treatise on land distribution designed to stimulate settlement. These activities paved the way for the **Conquest of the Desert** (the final onslaught against **pampas** Indians and the opening up of **Patagonia**) by his successor as president, General **Julio A. Roca**. Avellaneda was instrumental in strengthening alliances among interior provincial elites that resulted in the **federalization of the city of Buenos Aires**, an arrangement that contributed to national political and institutional stability—the culmination of the project of **national organization** that had begun in the 1850s.

On assuming the presidency, Avellaneda was confronted by an acute **economic crisis** following the 1873 financial panic in European capital markets, which he tackled by implementing orthodox strategies—severe budget cuts, reducing the size of the public sector, and promoting exports. Arguably his main legacy was the Immigration and Colonization Law (Ley Avellaneda), which provided concrete incentives for migration and settlement, giving substance to those clauses in the **Constitution of 1853** designed to foster immigration. The Ley Avellaneda is credited with encouraging the development of agricultural colonies in various parts of the country and the ensuing boom in exports. The county and city of Avellaneda, located in greater Buenos Aires, was renamed in his honor. *See also* AGRICULTURAL COLONIZATION; AGRICULTURE; TRANSPORTATION.

AVELLANEDA MASSACRE. An event that occurred on 26 June 2002 at the **Avellaneda** railway station in the depressed industrial township of the same name in greater **Buenos Aires**. Two young adults, Maximiliano Kosteki and Darío Santillán, were killed as the result of what was described as police overreaction to a public protest. A demonstration had been organized by several *piquetero* groups, to blockade the Puente Pueyrredón, the main link between the town and the federal capital, campaigning against poverty and unemployment and neglect by the authorities. Avellaneda had witnessed a growth in unemployment as state firms were **privatized** during the 1990s as the result of the **Convertibility Plan** introduced by President **Carlos Saúl Menem** and his minister of economy, **Domingo Cavallo**. Poverty had increased dramatically during the **economic crisis** of 2001 that brought down the government headed by President **Fernando de la Rúa**. As events spiraled out of control, police fired into the crowd, causing a stampede. Kosteki was shot in the station; Santillán first tried to comfort Kosteki but then fled as the police charged. He was shot in the back running away. Both men died. In the preceding months, the government of interim president **Eduardo Duhalde** had begun to take an increasingly hard line with protesters blocking roads. On the day of the event, the police were accused of operating a shoot-to-kill policy in line with the government crackdown. Two police officers were subsequently convicted of murder, and several others of attempted homicide and obstructing the course of justice. Duhalde denied any responsibility for the police action and the deaths, but sections of the public held him morally culpable, and the events of June put pay to any future presidential ambitions that he may have harbored. Memories of state terror during the **Proceso de Reorganización Nacional** were still uppermost in the public mind, and Duhalde had acquired an unsavory reputation.

"AVIÓN NEGRO". Myth of the return of **Juan Domingo Perón** propagated during the period of the **Revolución Libertadora** (1955–1958). Its origins on the government side are explained by the extreme instability and multiple internal and external threats it faced, and in the Peronist camp by the limitations imposed on the mention of its leader's name. In the imagination of Perón and his supporters, such a desired return would overturn the break with legality after the **military coup of 1955**. He would certainly have to come back from exile by airplane, but why it should be black remains a mystery. In any case, Perón confirmed his exile: he went from imagining the restoration of his regime to sealing an electoral pact that enabled the election of **Arturo Frondizi** as president in 1958.

B

BAHÍA BLANCA. A major port complex located in the southwest of the province of **Buenos Aires**, about 350 miles (c. 500 kilometers) from the capital. In addition to Bahía Blanca itself, neighboring docks include Puerto Belgrano, Puerto Galván, and Ingeniero White. One of the best harbors in the country, it is composed of a series of wharfs, warehouses, a meatpacking plant, grain silos, electricity-generating stations, and shipping facilities, including a naval base—the largest deep-water port operated by the navy. Historically well served by an integrated network or railways and highways, it handles exports—cereals, **meat**, and **wool**, as well as minerals and manufactures. Little used in colonial times, the modern history of Bahía Blanca dates from the Indian campaigns of **Juan Manuel de Rosas** during the early stages of the **Conquest of the Desert**. He anchored the southern end of the frontier there in 1833; it served as a base for the final stages of the Indian wars between 1879 and 1883, initiated by General **Julio A. Roca** before he became president in 1880. Rapid economic development began after 1884, when the **Buenos Ayres Great Southern Railway Company** (BAGS) reached the city and following the construction of the Bahia Blanca & North-Western (BB&NW). Railway building by the Great Southern and BB&NW led to the development of the west of the province of Buenos Aires and the opening up of the then national territories of Pampa Central and **Neuquén**. European immigrants flooded in: ranching and farming took off. Later rail construction northward across the central **pampas** from Puerto Belgrano to **Rosario** was devised to promote the further development of the central pampas and reduce congestion at the port of Buenos Aires. With its complex of transport companies and agro-industrial complexes, as well as immigrant associations, Bahía Blanca has a strong tradition of radical politics and associational life. Nowadays, the area is an important center for the petrochemical and energy industries, as well as continuing as an important port—a major export point for oilseed, **grains**, and soya. Since the 1980s, the area has benefited from substantial investment, particularly to modernize infrastructure on which grain and soya exports depend, much of it from overseas—particularly the **United States** and **China**. A new free port is being set up to facilitate the export of manufactures and attract new industries to the area. *See also* FOREIGN DEBT/FOREIGN INVESTMENT; IMMIGRATION; INDUSTRY; TRANSPORTATION; UNIVERSIDAD DEL SUR.

BALBÍN, RICARDO (1904–1981). Lawyer and politician, and one of the most important figures of the **Unión Cívica Radical** (UCR); he joined the party in 1922 and worked on the campaign for the **presidential election of 1928**. **Hipólito Yrigoyen** was elected for a second term and named him district attorney during the federal intervention in **Mendoza** province.

Balbín was elected to the Chamber of Deputies in 1946, and he became the head deputy of the so-called Block of 44. His role as one of the opposition leaders to President **Juan Domingo Perón** brought him political and judicial persecution. Not only did Balbín suffer at the hands of Peronist goons, but in 1949 he was expelled from Congress and imprisoned. Once freed, he unsuccessfully contested the **presidential election of 1951** with **Arturo Frondizi** as his running mate. The overthrow of Perón in the **military coup of 1955** and the proscription of Peronism ought to have favored the UCR. Instead, the impossibility of Balbín and Frondizi collaborating led to the party splitting into the **Unión Cívica Radical del Pueblo** (UCRP) and the **Unión Cívica Radical Intransigente** (UCRI). Balbín unsuccessfully ran as the UCRP candidate in the **presidential election of 1958**, which was won by Frondizi of the UCRI as a result of the infamous **Caracas Pact**. Subsequently, **Arturo Illia** was chosen as the next presidential candidate of the UCRP; he won the **presidential election of 1963** but was overthrown in the **military coup of 1966**.

Balbín became one of the signatories of the **"La Hora del Pueblo"** declaration in 1970, which called for the restoration of democracy. When the outgoing de facto regime announced in 1972 that elections would be held the following year, he was able to use the UCR name once again; the UCRI had splintered into the **Movimiento de Integración y Desarrollo** (MID) and the **Partido Intransigente** (PI). Balbín and running mate Eduardo Gamond contested the **presidential election of March 1973**, which was won by **Héctor J. Cámpora** of the **Frente Justicialista de Liberación** (FREJULI). Perón returned definitively from exile and forced Cámpora and Vice President **Vicente Solano Lima** to resign so that he could call a snap election and take charge. The possibility of a joint ticket of the FREJULI and UCR headed by Perón with Balbín as running mate was mooted but proved unfeasible. The internal politics of both Peronism and Radicalism undermined this prospect. (There were doubts about the sincerity of the reconciliation of the two men— certainly about Perón's intentions.) Perón had to paper over the cracks in his Movimiento. Balbín and his running mate, **Fernando de la Rúa**, unsuccessfully contested the **presidential election of September 1973**, which Perón won resoundingly with his third wife, **Isabel Perón**, as his vice presidential running mate.

Balbín remained focused on avoiding yet another coup as the ruling Peronist movement imploded and the country careened toward the **military coup of 1976**. He did not live to see the **presidential election of 1983**, which **Raúl Alfonsín** of the UCR would unexpectedly win. His legacy includes an enduring commitment to democracy and efforts to create electoral space for the UCR; he is also remembered for an ideological commitment to the founding principles of the party that sometimes resulted in inflexibility and resistance to change, despite sincere attempts to tackle profound political crises confronting the country. *See also* ECONOMIC CRISES; MOVIMIENTO DE RENOVACIÓN Y CAMBIO.

BANCO CENTRAL DE LA REPÚBLICA ARGENTINA (BCRA). Established in 1935 by the **Concordancia** government, its Organic Charter was drawn up by **Raúl Prebisch**. The BCRA became the core agency of the Argentine banking and financial system and had three essential features. First, it combined certain functions previously exercised by several monetary and banking agencies, including the **Banco de la Nación Argentina**, the Finance Ministry (later **Ministry of Economy**), the Exchange Control Office, and the **Caja de Conversión** (the Gold Exchange Office). The gold standard remained suspended—"temporary" suspension was applied in 1928—and the BCRA was now free to adjust exchange rates and administer the system in order to manage the supply of money and credit and stabilize the peso. Second, it comprised a transitional Institute for the Liquidation of Bank Investments, which served as a mechanism for sanitizing bankrupt commercial banks by taking over their frozen assets in exchange for cash or redeemable bonds. And third, it was modeled on the Bank of England and created as a mixed enterprise, which resulted in an equilibrium between state power and the private sector as well as between public accountability and operational autonomy. In addition to serving as the financial agent of the government, regulating the operations of the financial system, administering the gold and foreign currency reserves, issuing the national **currency**, and facilitating the smooth functioning of capital markets, the bank was charged with managing and maintaining the exchange rate.

Argentina had never before possessed a comparable public-sector institution devoted entirely to excellence, with hiring completely determined by merit. As a result, the BCRA had the most cohesive and effective cadre of administrators in the country's history, which was able to coordinate policies with the Finance Ministry as well as other ministries. It was a truly national institution, above factions and dedicated only to the public good.

Following the **presidential election of 1946**, the original statutes were revised, and the bank's functions changed. In May of that year, all deposits were transferred from the banking system to the BCRA, which was nationalized and thereby ceased to be a mixed company. The charter was altered again in 1949: the BCRA was placed directly under the executive branch of government and was no longer required to have enough reserves in gold and foreign exchange to back the value of the peso; its exchange control functions were also incorporated into the charter. President **Juan Domingo Perón** had recast the bank from guardian of monetary stability to financial servant of the state: it was "democratized" rather than dismantled; it was required to support government macroeconomic strategy; it became an instrument to manufacture credit and money. Perón's downfall in the **military coup of 1955** led to the undoing of some of the changes imposed on the bank in 1946. The de facto regime of **Pedro Eugenio Aramburu** reformed the charter in December 1957. The nationalization of deposits was ended, on the understanding that the banking business should be left to the private sector and that the regulation of monetary policy could be done with stipulations regarding banks' minimum reserve requirements and the use of other instruments of monetary and credit regulations. The bank was once again charged with the regulation of the financial system, the promotion of capital market stability, and managing the exchange, rather than being an agent of monetary creation directly subservient to the government.

Just over two decades later, during the **Proceso de Reorganización Nacional**, the BCRA found itself in the eye of the storm caused by the unintended consequences of the financial reforms enacted by Minister of Economy **José Alfredo Martínez de Hoz**. In April 1980, it enacted a measure to shield the financial sector from the cost of receiving payments in suddenly devalued pesos. Thousands of businesses and home owners were bankrupted by the indexing of mortgages to the local value of the US dollar, until the measure was rescinded in July 1982. Moreover, in 1981, the BCRA had to introduce guarantees on all deposits as the free-for-all speculation known as "*la bicicleta*" destabilized many financial institutions. More turbulence followed with the **Austral Plan** during the administration of President **Raúl Alfonsín**.

In April 1991, during the presidency of **Carlos Saúl Menem**, a Convertibility Law was enacted that fixed the exchange rate between the peso and the US dollar at 1:1. The **Convertibility Plan** was devised by Economics Minister **Domingo Cavallo**, who instigated a revision of the Organic Charter of the BCRA in 1992: it was given administrative autonomy and specifically charged with "defending" the peso–dollar parity by managing foreign currency reserves—mainly a stock of US dollars and dollar-denominated securities—in order to keep the reserves in synch with the monetary base. Consciously modeled on the "self-regulating" 19th-century gold standard (save that the US dollar replaced gold), the Convertibility Plan had the bank functioned largely as a currency board, as had the Caja de Conversión in 1899–1913 and 1926–1928. In terms of managing the domestic economy, its principal policy instruments were confined to setting interest rates and open market operations—the bank also controlled a small contingency fund designed to ease adjustments in dollar stocks. When Cavallo returned to the Ministry of Economy in March 2001, he undermined the autonomy of the BCRA as part of a broad program of intervention in financial institutions in an unsuccessful last-ditch attempt to shore up the Convertibility Plan. Following the economic and political chaos that engulfed the country in late December 2001, the Law of Economic Emergency of 2002 repealed the Convertibility Law and removed constraints placed on the bank. Once again, the BCRA was charged with "managing" the exchange rate rather than defending it—basically precipitating a decline in the value of the peso (occasionally preventing the appreciation of the currency) and ensuring necessary supplies of credit to the market.

The advent of the *kirchnerato* brought echoes of Perón's attitude to the bank: in effect, the BCRA was subject to direct political control. In December 2005, President **Néstor Kirchner** announced the payment of the Argentine debt to the International Monetary Fund in a single disbursement. The latter was made in January 2006 and employed approximately US$9.8 billion from the BCRA, which thereby suffered a sharp fall in its reserves. Two years later, President **Cristina Fernández de Kirchner** found herself having to seek domestic financing for increasing public spending as well as **foreign debt** obligations. She used BCRA reserves to prop up government finances and support political goals and ordered a US$6.7 billion special account be created at the bank. This implied direct government access to the foreign exchange reserves of the bank, a move formalized by the approval of the reform of the Organic Charter of the BCRA by the National Senate in March 2012. Formally, the bank was now charged with promoting economic development and social equality, as well as preserving monetary stability and the integrity of the financial system. This was window dressing. In reality, the government was free to pay public debt using the bank's reserves and the BCRA was also enabled to expand its lending capacity to the Treasury, all of which effectively gave a boost to government finances, though monetizing government debt drove up inflation.

President **Mauricio Macri**, elected in November 2015, promised to restore the independence of the central bank, but the government has not yet prioritized legislation needed to deliver BCRA autonomy. Despite periods of political intervention, the bank has often been well served by highly qualified and technically competent staff who have sought to preserve the reputation of the institution at home and abroad, notwithstanding political interference. *See also* BANCO DE CRÉDITO INDUSTRIAL ARGENTINO (BCIA); DE-

VELOPMENTALISM/DEVELOPMENTALIST; ECONOMIC CRISES; ECONOMY; FOREIGN TRADE; HYPERINFLATION; ROCA–RUNCIMAN PACT (1933); RODRIGAZO; STATE-OWNED ENTERPRISES (SOEs).

BANCO DE CRÉDITO INDUSTRIAL ARGENTINO (BCIA). Established in April 1944 by the de facto government of **Edelmiro Farrell** as an autonomous government credit agency; it became one of the pillars of Peronist **economic policy**—especially during the period 1946–1949.

The key function of the BCIA was to provide the national economy with more circulating capital by underwriting long-term loans, and to finance investment of all kinds in the industrial sector. The bank would be funded by 50 million pesos supplied by the government and a long-term loan of 100 million pesos from the **Banco de la Nación Argentina**, with the interest to be agreed on (it could not exceed 4 percent). The BCIA had its charter modified in the Peronist five-year economic plan for 1947–1951: it was subject to oversight by the recently nationalized **Banco Central de la República Argentina** (BCRA) and was to coordinate its activities with the economic, financial, and social policy of the state.

Between June 1946 and December 1949, 51 percent of loans awarded by the BCIA went to "the public" and the remaining 49 percent to the **Instituto Argentino de Promoción del Intercambio** (IAPI). "Public" loans were awarded to both **state-owned enterprises** and the private sector, and mostly expended on the light industries that President **Juan Domingo Perón** and his "czar of the economy" **Miguel Miranda** were keen to promote. The loans granted to the IAPI were to an official institution that was basically engaged in commercial activities, and more than 20 percent of them were used in the purchase of foreign-owned railways. The BCIA also provided the IAPI with lines of credit so that it could make a wide range of purchases abroad, the aim being to supply the domestic market with capital goods for the development and diversification of national **industry**.

Owing to major economic difficulties stemming from Peronist policies in the late 1940s, after 1950 the BCIA had to restrict the amounts it provided in loans to "the public" and reduced its credits to an increasingly moribund IAPI. In October 1952, the government modified the bank's charter: it became the Banco Industrial de la República Argentina (BIRA), an autonomous agency independent of the BCRA, dependent on the Ministry of Finance, which was at the time struggling to bring order to the public accounts. *See also* ECONOMIC CRISES; ECONOMY; FERROCARRILES ARGENTINOS (FFAA); FOREIGN DEBT/FOREIGN INVESTMENT; FOREIGN TRADE; MINISTRY OF ECONOMY; MIRANDA–EADY AGREEMENT.

BANCO DE LA NACIÓN ARGENTINA. The origin of the present institution can be traced back to the bank established by the federal government in 1872 to challenge the influence of the **Banco de la Provincia de Buenos Aires**, regarded as the financial arm of an overmighty province that could be deployed to challenged central authority. Formed as a mixed entity (the government was to hold 10 percent of the equity), the Banco Nacional initially led a checkered existence. It remained a pale shadow of its provincial counterpart until the 1890s. Although the original capital was rapidly subscribed, its operations were limited by the established position of the Banco de la Provincia in Buenos Aires and by the status enjoyed by provincial banknotes from 1874 until 1881: when convertibility was suspended in 1874, only notes issued by the provincial bank enjoyed the status of legal tender in the province. The national bank suffered a further setback in 1876 when all notes other than those of the Banco de la Provincia were excluded from the province. These circumstances changed in 1881 with the **federalization of the city of Buenos Aires** and the introduction of the gold standard. Following the renewed suspension of convertibility in 1884, like most official and semiofficial banks, the Banco Nacional was encouraged to overissue, an expansion in currency supply and credit that contributed to the **Baring Crisis** and the collapse of the Banco Nacional.

After the crash, in 1891, the Banco Nacional was reorganized as the Banco de la Nación Argentina by acting president **Carlos Pellegrini**. Once again, it was constituted as a mixed corporation, supposedly to prevent political control. The bank did modest business until 1904, when its charter was modified—it became an exclusively state institution. As the principal official bank during the golden age of export-led growth, it grew in prestige and acquired an enviable reputation. Before 1914, it was already the dominant institution in the local market and gained in importance thereafter. On the eve of the First World War, the bank held almost half the reserves of the entire banking system. Given this position, it began to perform quasi-central-banking functions during the 1920s, following the suspension of the gold standard at the outbreak of the war. At one point, it appeared that the Banco de la Nación might indeed be reconstituted as a central bank. This was not to be. The **Banco Central de la República Argentina** began operations in 1935. Nevertheless, the Banco de la Nación remained by far the largest clearing bank in the country in terms of capital, share of deposits, and number of branches. The solidity of its reputation symbolized by the inauguration of a new headquarters, built in two stages and adjacent to the presidential palace, the **Casa Rosada**. Covering almost a whole city block, the neoclassical building contains the largest banking hall in the world. By the 1950s, the bank operated a near complete network of branches in the country and was opening outlets or affiliates in most of the principal American and West European capitals. The most recent overseas branch was opened in Beijing in 2015.

Now known as the Banco Nación, since the mid-20th century the history of the institution has mirrored that of the country. The bank served as an instrument for financing the pet projects of various regimes. During the **Proceso de Reorganización Nacional**, it engaged in several questionable domestic and foreign operations, basically functioning as the financial arm of the **military**. Perhaps the greatest damage to its reputation occurred in the 1990s. In 1996, news broke that bank directors had received bribes for the 1994 contract awarded to IBM to modernize IT hardware and software. It was the **corruption** scandal of the day. In 2006, the head of the bank maintained that its mission was to serve the broader community, particularly the credit needs of small- and medium-sized businesses—not speculators—yet a large part of its credit continues to be allocated to the state sector and large corporations, many of which are close to the government. *See also* ECONOMIC CRISES.

BANCO DE LA PROVINCIA DE BUENOS AIRES. Proceeded by several institutions—the Banco de Buenos Aires (1822–1826), the Banco de las Provincias Unidas de Río de la Plata (1826–1836), the Casa de la Moneda (1836–1853), and the Banco y Casa de Moneda (1859–1861)—the Banco de la Provincia de Buenos Aires was founded in 1863. As the name suggests, it was the **Buenos Aires** state bank. For the next three decades, it was the premier financial institution in the country. During the 1860s, the bank established a reputation as an expansionist institution that was well run, while financing the state—including assisting with railway projects and the provincial war during the civil wars of the period. By the early 1880s, the bank had established 24 branches in the city and province of Buenos Aires. It was responsible for the lion's share of capital invested locally in banking and held the greater part of total deposits. In 1884, the provincial bank accounted for 44 percent of total bank capital in the province and 68 percent of deposits; the federal government Banco Nacional (*see* BANCO DE LA NACIÓN ARGENTINA) held 28 percent of capital and 14 percent of deposits; the premier British banks held 17 percent of capital and 7.5 percent of deposits. This was the high point in the influence of the provincial bank. The **federalization of the city of Buenos Aires** in 1881 and loss of its note monopoly in the city and province reduced its business and status. Like all official banks, it failed during the **Baring Crisis**, brought down by overissue and incautious lending—postcrisis investigation revealed large advances to friends of the government, funds that financed land speculation. Only the Banco Nacional was more injudicious in advancing credit and creating money. Although the

corruption scandals surrounding the bank were little different from those afflicting other state banks, its size and influence in the market explain the intensity of the opprobrium heaped upon the directors and the institution.

Today usually referred to as Banco Provincia, the bank was reconstructed after the Baring Crisis and, having got into further difficulties, was reorganized again in 1906 as a mixed entity. It was nationalized in 1944, and partly reprivatized and renationalized several times since. It is currently wholly state owned. Despite these changes, it never regained its former predominant place in the sector, though it is the second largest banking group in the country. Like other state institutions since the mid-20th century, while developing a substantial conventional business—unsurprising given its location and status as the financial institution owned and operated by the largest and most prosperous province in the country—the bank has functioned to finance economic and social initiatives favored by governments of the day, as well as supporting friends of the regime. Over the last few decades, the bank has shown a dynamic image. It was among the first to embrace modern banking technology and pursued an aggressive strategy to increase market share, opening branches across the country and abroad.

Repeatedly, the bank has been accused of misusing funds to support electoral campaigns, mainly of dissident members of the Peronist Party and opposition groups such as the **Propuesta Republicana** (PRO). It has also been treated as a private money machine by governors of all political hues. In 2016, evidence came to light that former Peronist governor **Daniel Scioli** had made the largest ever cash withdrawal in the history of the bank from public accounts held at the **La Plata** branch, presumably to finance his unsuccessful campaign in the **presidential election of 2015**. Other recent scandals include activities in 2001: as the **economic crisis** of 2001 was maturing, the bank was rumored to be the conduit for illicit currency transfers to tax havens in anticipation of a devaluation. In 2015, following the appointment of Jorge Macri, cousin of current president **Mauricio Macri**, to head the bank, soft loans have been made to friends and associates of the Macri family and, indeed, to Macri enterprises. Substantial borrowing abroad in 2016, the first in the history of the bank, may also be viewed as supporting the macroeconomic strategy of the present administration. *See also* BANCO CENTRAL DE LA REPÚBLICA ARGENTINA (BCRA); BUENOS AIRES (PROVINCE); ECONOMY.

BANCO NACIÓN. *See* BANCO DE LA NACIÓN ARGENTINA.

BANCO TORNQUIST. *See* TORNQUIST, ERNESTO CARLOS (1842–1908).

BARAÑAO, LINO (1953–). Respected scientist and political figure. Trained in chemistry in Argentina—he took a first degree at the **University of Buenos Aires** and at prestigious universities in Germany and the **United States**—Barañao's main fields of research are in biology and experimental medicine. Among services to the scientific community, he has headed the national scientific research institute. His work has been recognized by several scientific bodies. In 2007, he was appointed to head the **Ministry of Science, Technology, and Productive Innovation** by President **Cristina Fernández de Kirchner**. He was retained in post by President **Mauricio Macri** following the **presidential election of 2015**—the only former minister to be reappointed.

BARING BROTHERS. One of the principal 19th-century merchant banks of the city of London, the house features prominently in the history of Argentina as the principal overseas financial agent of the province of **Buenos Aires** and the federal government.

The business was founded by a Bremen merchant John Baring, who settled in the west of England in the early 18th century. He soon became a leading **wool** merchant and textile manufacturer. In 1762, his sons established the London business John & Francis Baring & Company. The bank soon became known as Baring Brothers; finance rapidly dwarfed earlier commercial and industrial activities in importance. In the 19th century, the business diversified from financing commodity trades to underwriting government bonds and placing railway stocks. The firm was active in North America, Europe, and South America. Representing the governments of the **United States**, Canada, Russia, and Argentina, it rivaled (possibly displaced) Rothschilds as the leading London issuing house by the 1820s.

Barings' first major engagement with Argentina was as underwriter of the £1,000,000 loan floated in 1824 for the government of the province of Buenos Aires—the so-called London or Barings Loan. Its last was underwriting a loan for the Buenos Aires Water Supply & Drainage Company. In 1888, Barings contracted to place a $25,000,000 gold (c. £5,000,000) bond issue for the company. Reports reaching London in late 1890 of economic and political turmoil in Buenos Aires meant that Barings were unable to offload tranches of Water Supply & Drainage bonds and had to borrow to honor its agreement with the company. When rumors of the imminent failure of the house mounted in London, the Bank of England stepped in and, with the British government, launched a lifeboat to bail out Barings. City institutions, the government, and the bank established a fund to finance purchases of Barings paper, on the understanding that the house would be liquidated once the crisis passed. In modern terminology, although Barings was too big to fail in the immediacy of the crisis, contemporaries felt that it should not be allowed to survive or thrive once the panic was over. Yet Barings wriggled and survived, though its business and reputation were severely curtailed. The house was finally brought down by rogue trader Nick Leeson in 1995; he had engaged in illegal trading in derivatives from the Singapore office. The "second" **Baring Crisis** precipitated the sale of most of the business to Dutch bank ING for £1. Initially trading as ING Baring, the firm assumed responsibilities for debts run up by Leeson. Subsequently dropping "Barings," the company again trades as ING. *See also* AGUAS ARGENTINAS; ECONOMIC CRISES; ECONOMY; FOREIGN DEBT/FOREIGN INVESTMENT; FOREIGN TRADE.

BARING CRISIS. A near-perfect emerging market financial crisis and sovereign debt default, the greatest shock to the global financial system up to that point. The crisis was transmitted from Buenos Aires to London, then to other international financial centers like Paris and New York.

The immediate symptoms of the gathering storm were protests in Argentina in 1889–1890 over accelerating inflation and declining living standards; hardly secret insider knowledge that the **Banco de la Nación Argentina** was using gold intended to back the currency to defend the exchange rate—by December 1889 the bank's gold reserves were exhausted; a steady and then dramatic increase in the gold premium (the difference between the par rate for the paper peso and the market rate) in Buenos Aires—the premium average for the year was 35 percent in 1887, 47 percent in 1888, 94 percent in 1889, and 151 percent in 1890, peaking at 287 in 1891; private intimations made to Barings in Buenos Aires in May 1890 that the federal government was experiencing difficulty in meeting quarterly coupons due on the public debt; a virtual halt in **immigration** toward the end of 1890—there was no emigration in late 1890 and 1891; and the failure of **Baring Brothers** to place Buenos Aires Water Supply & Drainage Company bonds in London in Autumn 1890. In early November 1890, the directors of Barings stared into the abyss and asked the Bank of England for help. These events marked the ending of a period of debt-fueled expansion experienced over the preceding decade; the bubble was about to burst. Many components of the crisis prefigured those of later crashes and debt default.

Preceded by a "dress rehearsal" in 1884–1885 that resulted in the temporary suspension of convertibility, and an aborted austerity and debt conversion plan in late 1889 and early 1890, the crisis has been depicted as a crisis of development, a crisis of economic mismanagement, and a crisis of **corruption** and confidence. A crisis of development because considerable investment had been made in slow-gestation potentially productive sectors like railways that opened the **pampas** to settlement and the production of commodity exports. The problem? The time lag between the completion of lumpy capital projects and the equipping of farms and the generation of exports to service projects. Foreign borrowing and investment in infrastructure required near immediate servicing, while production and exports took several years to come on stream. In short, it was a crisis of liquidity, not necessarily insolvency. A crisis of mismanagement because of a sizeable chunk of productive investment related to railway companies benefiting from profit guarantees and others financed by debenture bond issues. Railways guarantees, most of which were denominated in gold or foreign currency, kicked in immediately—before traffic flows picked up to generate revenue that might reduce or minimize payments by the state. Similarly, bonds required immediate servicing. Had fewer railways been guaranteed or more capital raised by the issue of equity, this problem would have been considerably less—shareholders would have borne the risk rather than the state and Argentine taxpayers. It was also a crisis of mismanagement because the burden of financing profit guarantee fell on the state while the benefits of infrastructure investment were captured by the private sector—the owners of *estancias*. Only by taxing politically powerful *estancieros* or exporters could the government gain a share of the revenue and foreign exchange generated by agricultural production and exports. Most government revenue was derived from taxing imports—yet another "delay" in the fiscal loop. There was also substantial government investment in projects that were not directly productive—for example, the construction of the city of **La Plata** following the **federalization of the city of Buenos Aires**. A crisis of corruption because graft was involved in the allocation of many railway concessions (especially those of companies enjoying profit guarantees) and the illegal overissue of currency by official banks like the Banco de la Nación Argentina and the **Banco de la Provincia de Buenos Aires**. The main beneficiaries of the railway mania of the 1880s and virtually "free" credit created by the official banks were the political class—friends of the regime of President **Miguel Juárez Celman** and *estancieros*. The losers were creditors, those whose wages were paid in depreciating paper pesos, and any unable to protect themselves against inflation. At the peak of the crisis, the urban poor—those without "bread or work," to use a desperate contemporary observation—bore the brunt of the catastrophe. All these factors undermined the confidence of would-be investors (domestic and foreign) and unnerved financial markets.

Key statistics of the crisis are the growth in the monetary base, rising by an average of 18 percent a year between 1884 and 1890; that at the height of the crisis 40 percent of new borrowing was allocated to servicing the **foreign debt**; that in 1890 Argentine bonds in default represented 60 percent of the total stock of international debt in default. The fallout would be felt across Latin America, where there would be no new investment for virtually a decade, and in markets across the North Atlantic world and beyond, though to a lesser degree. The contagion effect in Latin America was immediate.

The market-average price of Latin American debt declined 25 percent in 1890–1891; in 1895, the average price of Latin American sovereign debt was down 40 percent.

A short-term solution with foreign creditors was reached at the beginning of 1891 brokered by the Rothschild Committee in London—a moratorium, a modest loan to enable Argentina to meet current obligations, and a token austerity package entailing a promise to overhaul the tax system, stabilize the banks, and reduce money supply. The deal was also intended to prop up the market for Argentine securities so that Barings could offload paper—it failed to do so. A long-term debt restructuring agreement was reached in 1893, the Arreglo Romero devised by Dr. Juan José Romero the *ministro de hacienda* (aka minister of economy) in Buenos Aires and signed in London by Lord Rothschild and the Argentine minister, Dr. Luis Domínguez, on 3 July. Bondholders accepted an average haircut of around 30 percent; interest rates on some securities were reduced by between 18 and 33 percent, and other interest payments deferred until 1898; amortization payments were deferred until 1901; the federal government agreed to assume responsibility for provincial debt contracted since 1884. In the event, Argentina resumed full interest payments a year ahead of schedule in 1897, and the flow of investment also picked up. Collateral arrangements led to the ending of railway profit guarantees; holders of *cédulas* were abandoned.

The immediate consequences of the crisis were a popular uprising in July 1890—the **Revolution of 1890**—and the resignation of Juárez Celman on 6 August of that year. Argentine gross domestic product contracted by 11 percent in 1891. In the longer term, a tighter fiscal regime, the retirement of paper currency, and debt rescheduling stabilized the economy—a process assisted by a recovery in export prices, a massive increase in the volume of exports, and a revival of **immigration**. Together, reform and recovery inaugurated almost half a century of relative **currency** stability—notwithstanding further international financial and commercial crises—macroeconomic growth and structural change, rising fiscal resources, and fairly impressive welfare gains. Associated consequences include action taken by the Bank of England to stem panic in the City of London. The bank launched a scheme to purchase Barings' paper. Intended to tie the house over until it could be liquidated, the project became a bailout. More importantly, the bank began to act as a lender of last resort for the first time in its history, indicating that it was well on the way to becoming a fully fledged central bank. In addition, the crisis fostered a degree of collaboration among financial institutions in the main European capital markets, notably, Berlin, London, Paris, and St. Petersburg, which could be regarded as establishing a precedent for future funding operations.

The Baring Crisis was the largest shock experienced by international financial markets up to that point. It was also the biggest banking, financial, and commercial crisis experienced by the country. In a number of respects, the crisis prefigured the collapse of the **Convertibility Plan** more than a century later, which triggered the largest ever sovereign debt default in the history of global finance. *See also* AGRICULTURAL COLONIZATION; AGUAS ARGENTINAS; BUENOS AYRES WESTERN RAILWAY COMPANY (BAW); CATTLE; COMMODITIES; CONQUEST OF THE DESERT/DESERT CAMPAIGN; CONVERTIBILITY PLAN; ECONOMIC CRISES; ECONOMY; FOREIGN TRADE; GRAINS; GREAT BRITAIN; HYPERINFLATION; SHEEP; TRANSPORTATION; WOOL.

BEAGLE CHANNEL DISPUTE. The key international relations problem of 1978 for the de facto government of **Jorge Rafael Videla**, it centered on the control of the territorial waters surrounding the islands of Picton, Lennox, and Nueva in the Beagle Channel opposite the city of **Ushuaia**, the capital of the Argentine territory of **Tierra del Fuego**.

British arbitration had awarded the islands to **Chile** in 1977. This was rejected by Argentina on 25 January 1978. The following day Videla met his Chilean counterpart, General Augusto Pinochet, and at the end of the summit signed the Acta de Puerto Montt. The declaration agreed to the formation of negotiating committees that, in three stages, would reach a solution for the "definitive delimitation of the jurisdictions corresponding to Argentina and Chile in the South." This unexpectedly brought the Magellan Strait, which had not been an issue in the arbitration, into the equation. When Videla went on a live national broadcast to explain that negotiations would be extremely difficult, everything pointed to war. On 29 September 1978, Santiago formally presented a diplomatic protest over the continuing Argentine "bellicose animus." This animus was part of the psychological warfare carried out by the Joint Chiefs of Staff. Nonetheless, the latter were clearly aware of Argentina's isolation in the event of war: **Brazil**, **Paraguay**, **Uruguay**, Ecuador, and **Peru** would not support Buenos Aires.

There was an unsuccessful Chilean bid on 18 October to arrange a meeting between Videla and Pinochet; the joint negotiating committees agreed on at Puerto Montt ceased to function as the two parties to the dispute could not find common ground. On 8 November, the Argentine head of state wrote to his counterpart hoping for renewed negotiations, but by then Chile was looking for a new mediator—the king of Spain or Pope John Paul II were the most likely ones. As a last chance, the governments of Argentina and Chile decided that their foreign ministers should meet to determine who would be the mediator and which of their differences would be submitted for arbitration. The Argentine **military** resolved to support and promote papal arbitration but was determined to initiate operations in the disputed area and its hinterland should arbitration fail to deliver an acceptable compromise.

The foreign ministers met on 12 December 1978 but failed to find common ground. The problem was not the mediator but the agenda to be presented to the pope. Chile wanted only the delimitation of the territorial waters since the issue of the islands had been resolved by the British arbitration, while Argentina wanted to include a fixed point on land on which to base the limits of the jurisdictions. On 14 December, Argentine Commander-in-Chief of the Army **Roberto Eduardo Viola** met with his top commanders and faced pressure from two of them, **Luciano Benjamín Menéndez** and **Carlos Guillermo Súarez Mason**, to set a date to initiate military operations as negotiations had failed.

The Brazilian, Chilean, and US governments received information to the effect that Argentina would invade the disputed area on 21 December 1978 and that the fleet was already at sea, though caught in very severe weather; the positions of Argentine land forces in the Andean region were already known in Santiago. On 21 December, Cardinal Antonio Samoré (who was handling the mediation issue on behalf of the Vatican) telephoned Videla, who at the time was meeting with Minister of Economy **José Alfredo Martínez de Hoz**. In his memoirs, the minister revealed that Videla requested his advice; Martínez de Hoz urged the president to prevent an outbreak of hostilities. Videla then burst into a meeting of the military junta and, with the support of Viola, stopped Argentina from going to war. That same night, both Videla and Pinochet informed the Vatican that they would accept papal arbitration.

The **Agreement between Argentina and Chile Accepting Papal Mediation in the Beagle Channel Dispute** was signed on 8 January 1979. On 12 December 1980, the papal proposal for a settlement of the dispute was issued. It confirmed Chilean sovereignty over the islands of Picton, Lennox, and Nueva, and Argentina was recognized as having maritime jurisdiction over waters in the Atlantic side of the Beagle Channel. After further diplomatic activity, the papal award provided a basis for agreement. On 23 January 1984, Argentina and Chile signed a preliminary treaty of peace and friendship, which the government of President **Raúl Alfonsín** successfully put to a plebiscite later that year. On 29 November 1984, a final treaty of peace and friendship was signed at the Vatican.

BEMBERG, MARÍA LUISA (1922–1995). Film director, writer, and actress born into the powerful Bemberg family—the founders of the **Cervecería y Maltería Quilmes**. One of the first Latin American **women** directors, she was a powerful presence in the intellectual life of Argentina between 1970–1990.

In 1970, Bemberg wrote the script for *Crónica de una señora*, a successful film on the Argentine upper class starring **Graciela Borges**. She grew increasingly disillusioned with how her scripts were interpreted by male directors and pursued a career directing. Bemberg's work specialized in portraying famous South American women and the Argentine upper class, and also focused on feminism. She wrote and directed *Camila* in 1984. Based on a true 19th-century story about the persecution and execution of a priest and his lover ordered by **Juan Manuel de Rosas**, it was a direct comment on **human rights** violations during the **Proceso de Reorganización Nacional** (1976–1983) and raised pressing issues such as patriarchy. *Camila* was an artistic and box office success: it became the Argentine film industry's most popular production of all time and was nominated for an Oscar for Best Foreign Language Film.

Among Bemberg's other films, those of noteworthiness are *Miss Mary* (1986) starring British actress Julie Christie, *Yo, la peor de todas* (1990), and her final film, *De eso no se habla* (1993), starring Italian actor Marcello Mastroianni. Arguably, Bemberg is Latin America's foremost female director.

BELGRANO. *See* ARA *GENERAL BELGRANO*.

BELGRANO, MANUEL JOSÉ JOAQUIN DEL CORAZÓN DE JESÚS (1770–1820). Intellectual, politician, military officer, diplomat, and hero of the **Independence** period who created the national flag; known as Manuel Belgrano. Reputedly descended from Spanish conquistadores on his mother's side and from an Italian merchant family on his father's, he studied law in **Buenos Aires** and at the Universities of Salamanca and Valladolid, where he was exposed to the Enlightenment and particularly influenced by the new economic thinking of the time. He was in Spain when the French Revolution started and was much influenced by debates about the rights of man and ideas about liberty, equality, and fraternity. On returning to the **River Plate**, he was appointed to the recently formed *consulado* (merchant guild), for which he produced treatises on rural and industrial improvement, infrastructure improvement (roads and ports), **education**, and commercial regulation, advocating free trade. Little came of these projects at the time. However, the **British invasions** proved transformative for his ideas and fortunes. Although lacking formal military training, he was valiant in the field and an effective strategist. Such qualities ensured that he was an active participant in the **May Revolution of 1810**. He was called upon to maintain the former **Viceroyalty of the River Plate** as a unified, centralized entity, seeing active service in **Paraguay**, activity that convinced him of the futility of such an exercise—these views were not well received in Buenos Aires. Perhaps his greatest contribution to the patriotic cause, certainly the most symbolic, was devising and unfurling in 1812 the banner that would become the blue-and-white national flag. (The official status of the flag was confirmed by the **Congress of Tucumán**, which declared independence, four years later.) His campaigns in the interior were crowned with stunning victories and strategic defeats, notably in Upper Peru (present-day **Bolivia**), defeats that reinforced his view that the territories of the viceroyalty could not be bound together as a unified entity. He was also unsuccessful in efforts to establish a constitutional monarchy in the River Plate, headed by a Bourbon or, more exotically, a descendant of Inca royalty. He advanced this proposal when on a diplomatic mission to **Great Britain** and **Spain** in 1814 and 1815. Although this project was supported by other key figures at the time, like **Juan Martín de Pueyrredón**, it was an idea that had passed by the time the Congress of Tucumán convened in 1816. By then, independence was equated with republicanism. Pleading the case for monarchy diminished Belgrano's status among radical patriots and reduced his influence among contemporaries. He ended his life in relative poverty and ill health. Later assessments, however, portray him as one of the key figures of the period. *See also* ROSARIO.

BELIZ, GUSTAVO (1962–). Politician, journalist, and academic; he read law at the **University of Buenos Aires**. A reformist member of the **Partido Justicialista** (PJ), he was appointed minister of interior by **Carlos Saúl Menem** during his first administration and minister of justice by **Néstor Kirchner**. On both occasions, his tenure of office was brief: from December 1992 to August 1993 under Menem and between May 2003 and July 2004 under Kirchner. He resigned as minister of interior after complaining of **corruption**. Having campaigned for greater transparency in the administration of justice, including nominations to the Supreme Court—he denounced some judges as corrupt—and accusing senior members of the security services of being involved in criminal activities, Kirchner demanded Beliz's resignation. Barely 30 years old when appointed interior minister, he is the youngest politician to have held the post in modern history. Having failed to promote democracy within the party, he resigned from the PJ in 1996, founding various new political groupings that enjoyed solid electoral support. He was elected to the city of Buenos Aires legislature in 1997 and in 2001 became national senator for the city. Another unrealized ambition was to serve as mayor of the city. In 2004, he reintegrated into the PJ, joining the **Frente para la Victoria**/Partido Justicialista (FpV/PJ) faction headed by Kirchner. Between 2005 and 2013, he worked at the Inter-American Development Bank in Washington, DC, and in 2014 assumed the directorship of the bank's regional integration agency. He continues to campaign against corruption and in favor of greater accountability in public life, writing books and contributing articles to the press on these subjects. *See also* MINISTRY

OF INTERIOR, PUBLIC WORKS, AND HOUSING; MINISTRY OF JUSTICE AND HUMAN RIGHTS; MOVIMIENTO RENOVADOR PERONISTA (MRP).

BER GELBARD, JOSÉ (1917–1977). Leader in Argentine business politics and minister of economy (1973–1974). Born in Poland, he immigrated to Argentina with his family in 1930. A Communist activist when young, he joined the **Unión Democrática** (UD) political alliance opposing **Juan Domingo Perón** in the **presidential election of 1946**.

Ber Gelbard was a leading figure in the Cámara de Comercio de Catamarca, advocating an alliance between business, the state, and labor behind a nationalist economic program. He helped to establish the **Confederación General Económica** (CGE), an organization representing mainly nationally owned small-scale industrial and commercial enterprises aiming to negotiate with the **trade unions** and government. Ber Gelbard became head of the organization in 1953. The following year, he was appointed by Perón as a minister without portfolio working on economic issues; after Perón's fall in 1955, Ber Gelbard was subsequently called upon to advise both civilian and de facto governments. Bel Gelbard became linked to businessman Manuel Madanes from 1965. They were first associated in the Fate tire factory and during the de facto presidency of General **Alejandro Agustín Lanusse** obtained the concession to manufacture aluminum at the Aluar plant in Puerto Madryn. The contract, whose technical aspects were the source of much controversy, was strongly backed by the air force.

The group associated with Ber Gelbard wanted to transform the national entrepreneurial structure, displacing the Unión Industrial Argentina (UIA) as the key business organization. Placing the CGE center stage would give the organization more political clout, allow member firms to lobby for state support for national business, and advance a protectionist agenda. This project dovetailed neatly with Peronist views, and following the **presidential election of March 1973**, under Perón's orders, President **Héctor J. Cámpora** appointed Ber Gelbard as "minister of economy, finance, public works and trade." He implemented a prices and salaries freeze (Pacto Social) and called for increased cooperation between business and government in economic planning. With the return of Perón to power in the **presidential election of September 1973**, he was confirmed in his powerful ministerial post.

In line with the Peronist **Tercera Posición**, Ber Gelbard increased trade with **Cuba** to the tune of one billion US dollars. Washington, DC, was infuriated but had no other choice than to accept as he threatened to close all US car manufacturing plants in Argentina. This may have been his only success, as the Pacto Social unraveled with the 1973 oil shock, the strains of rising labor wage demands, and the generalized chaos engulfing the country after Perón's death and the accession of his widow to the presidency. Ber Gelbard fell out of favor with President **Isabel Perón** and resigned in November 1974. His fall from grace was compounded by a congressional investigation into the Aluar contract. Everything indicated that it was designed with his company in mind. The government financed virtually the entire scheme, with private capital only supplying seven million US dollars for a project that ended up costing 140 million. Even worse, it did not achieve "independence" in aluminum production. The necessary technology was provided by foreign firms and turned out to be obsolete.

Having fled the country when the **military coup of 1976** became imminent, Ber Gelbard obtained political asylum in the **United States**. *See also* ECONOMIC CRISES; ECONOMY; FOREIGN DEBT/FOREIGN INVESTMENT; INDUSTRY;

BERGOGLIO, JORGE MÁRIO. *See* POPE FRANCIS (1936–).

BIGNONE, REYNALDO BENITO (1928–2018). The last de facto president of Argentina (1982–1983), he was involved in state terrorism during the **Proceso de Reorganización Nacional**. From December 1976, he was commander of the clandestine detention center "El Campito" in Campo de Mayo, the major garrison outside the city of **Buenos Aires**. It is believed that thousands of detainees passed through El Campito under the watch of Bignone.

Bignone succeeded **Leopoldo Fortunato Galtieri** as president on 1 July 1982 as a result of the political crisis triggered by defeat in the **Falklands War** and continuing economic difficulties. He oversaw the transition to democracy and tried to safeguard the **military** from prosecution for acts committed during the **War to Annihilate Subversion**. Bignone ordered the destruction of the list of **Desaparecidos** originally held by **Albano Harguindeguy**, minister of interior during the presidency of **Jorge Rafael Videla**, and then decreed an amnesty for the members of the armed forces for all acts undertaken during the struggle against subversion; this decree was later voided by **Congress**. Bignone benefited from the **Ley de Punto Final** and the **Ley de Obediencia Debida**, as well as from the pardons granted to senior military officers by President **Carlos Saúl Menem**. However, between 1999 and 2016, he faced seven trials and was convicted of **human rights** violations. He was jailed and later transferred to a military hospital, where he died. *See also* MILITARY JUNTAS, TRIALS OF THE; MINISTRY OF INTERIOR, PUBLIC WORKS, AND HOUSING.

BIOY CASARES, ADOLFO (1914–1999). Prominent fiction writer whose imaginary world consisted of fantasies and inexplicable events. Bioy Casares was a lifelong friend and frequent collaborator with fellow author **Jorge Luis**

Borges, whom he met in 1932 at Villa Ocampo, a house in San Isidro, province of **Buenos Aires**, belonging to **Victoria Ocampo**. The collaborative works of Bioy Casares and Borges are *Seis problemas para don Isidro Parodi* (1942), *Dos fantasías memorables* (1946), *Un modelo para la muerte* (1946), *Cuentos breves y extraordinarios* (1955), *Libro del cielo e infierno* (1960), *Crónicas de Bustos Domecq* (1967), and *Nuevos cuentos de Bustos Domecq* (1977). Nevertheless, Bioy Casares was an author in his own right. His best-known work is the novel *La invención de Morel* (1940), which mixes realism, fantasy, science fiction, and terror. It is the story of a fugitive writer from **Venezuela** who, avoiding justice, escapes to a deserted island in Polynesia. He sees tourists arriving and leaving the island and struggles to understand why everything seems to repeat itself. Eventually, the fugitive realizes that all the people he sees are actually recordings made by a special machine invented by Morel, which is able to record not only three-dimensional images but also voices and scents. Therefore, what the fugitive sees is undistinguishable from reality.

Bioy Casares wrote the following other novels and novellas: *El perjurio de la nieve* (1944), *Plan de evasión* (1945), *El sueño de los héroes* (1954), *Homenaje a Francisco Almeyra* (1954), *Diario de la guerra del cerdo* (1969), *Dormir al sol* (1973), *La aventura de un fotógrafo en La Plata* (1985), and *Un campeón desparejo* (1993). He also penned short story collections: *La trama celeste* (1948), *Las vísperas de Fausto* (1949), *Historia prodigiosa* (1956), *El lado de la sombra* (1962), *El gran serafín* (1967), *El héroe de las mujeres* (1978), *Historias desaforadas* (1986), *Una muñeca rusa* (1991), and *Una magia modesta* (1997). Further works include anthologies, essays, and the *Breve diccionario del argentino exquisito* (1971), a dictionary of Argentine slang.

BITTEL, DEOLINDO FELIPE (1922–1997). Prominent Peronist politician and a native of **Chaco**, a national territory that became a province in 1951. He served as its vice governor from 1953 until the **military coup of 1955** and subsequently two terms as governor. In 1963, Bittel successfully stood for the governorship as a candidate of the neo-Peronist Unión Popular del Chaco. His achievements were modest: he set up the Lotería Chaqueña and, following severe flooding in 1965, promoted the study of hydrological conditions in the area. He left office as a consequence of the **military coup of 1966**. Seven years later, Bittel was elected as the governor of Chaco once again, on this occasion for the **Frente Justicialista de Liberación** (FREJU-LI). Facing a crisis in the prices of cotton, a mainstay of the provincial economy, he attempted to ameliorate conditions in the province with a public works and regional development plan. Although Bittel was removed from office after the **military coup of 1976**, he remained one of the most visible Peronist faces during the **Proceso de Reorganización Nacional**. In 1979, he authored a harsh report to the Inter-American Human Rights Commission, which earned him a severe response from the de facto government. In the **presidential election of 1983**, Bittel was the running mate of unsuccessful Peronist candidate **Ítalo Luder**. That same year, he was elected to the National Senate, representing his home province, and served in that capacity until his death. *See also* CONGRESS; HUMAN RIGHTS.

"BLUE BOOK". *See* PRESIDENTIAL ELECTION OF 1946.

BOCA JUNIORS FOOTBALL CLUB (CABJ). In Spanish, Club Atlético Boca Juniors—always the English usage "Juniors." Formed in 1905 by Genoese immigrants—hence the nickname "Los Xeneizes," it is one of the premier national professional soccer teams. The others are Independiente, Racing Club, **River Plate**, and San Lorenzo de Almagro. River Plate is the famous rival—both were once located in the district of **La Boca**, where CABJ remains. A ticket for the Boca–River local derby, the *superclásico*, is one of the most sought after in South America.

Traditionally seen as a working-class team—La Boca and neighboring **Avellaneda** were once major centers of **industry** as well as **immigration**—the president of the club between 1995 and 2007 was **Mauricio Macri**. During this period, Boca achieved considerable success, winning the national championship six times as well as lifting international trophies. These successes played an important role in securing the mayorship of the city of **Buenos Aires** for Macri and, in 2015, the presidency of the nation. A successful businessman before pursuing a political career, Macri poured a great deal of money into the club. In terms of ranking, the team is second only to River Plate. Boca Juniors was the first Argentine club to tour in Europe in 1925, where it won 15 of the 19 games played to earn the title of Champion of Honor (Campéon de Honor) awarded that year by the Argentine Football Federation. Famous players include Sebastián Battaglia, Hugo Gatti, **Diego Maradona**, Martín Palermo, and Carlos Tevez.

The main stadium, La Bombonera, has a capacity of 49,000. There are two explanations for the name: the art deco style of the original building opened in 1940 resembles the chocolate box invariably carried by the architect when visiting the construction site; or it came from the "bombo," a large homemade steel drum favored by Peronists, beaten by fans on the terraces at intense moments during a match. The D shape of the stadium makes for excellent acoustics, and the stands shake when mass drumming and chanting reaches a fever pitch. There have been several schemes to redevelop the atmospheric site as the club is reluctant to move from La Boca. For home games, the team is kitted out in a dark blue and gold stripe, which gives it another popular nickname—"Azul y Oro." Boca claims to have the largest fan base in the country—twice that of River, and one which is more widely distributed across the provinces than any other club. Boca fans have a reputation for violence; La Bombonera has been closed several times following outbreaks of match violence. *See also* FRIGERIO, ROGELIO (1970–); PERÓN, JUAN DOMINGO (1895–1974).

BOLIVIA. Bordering the Argentine provinces of **Jujuy** and **Salta**, as Upper Peru, Bolivia once formed part of the **Viceroyalty of the River Plate**, having been transferred to the new viceroyalty from the Viceroyalty of Peru when the latter was created in 1776. Upper Peru was the first part of South America to declare **independence** from Spain—in 1809, anticipating **Buenos Aires** by a year. Anxious to preserve the territorial integrity of the former viceroyalty, insurgent Argentina advanced its claims, pretentions that were reinforced when Upper Peru was reconquered by royalist forces based in Lower Peru (present-day **Peru**). Although Buenos Aires accepted Bolivian independence in 1825, relations between the two countries deteriorated in the 1830s when opponents of **Juan Manuel de Rosas** were offered sanctuary there. An Argentine expeditionary force was repulsed in 1837. Subsequent minor boundary disputes were resolved amicably and at various points in the late 19th century, Argentina proposed rail connections to the Atlantic, in place of routes through **Chile**, after Bolivia lost Pacific provinces to Chile during the **War of the Pacific**. Through rail travel between Buenos Aires and La Paz became possible in 1925, with the completion of the section of track across the frontier, though scheduled services were not introduced for another year. A journey of 1,600 miles, taking five days, the route was operated by four different companies. As a travel magazine of the period observed, there was ample time for the traveler to enjoy the scenic beauties of the route. Although Argentina attempted to be an honest broker between Bolivia and **Paraguay** during the **Chaco War**, arguably, relations were closest between the two republics between 1946 and 1949, when president **Juan Domingo Perón** was successful in exporting his ideology of the **Tercera Posición** to La Paz—much to the annoyance of Washington. For years, until regime change in both countries, they cooperated closely on trade and labor matters.

The most notorious Argentine intervention in Bolivian domestic politics occurred in 1980. The **military** regimes of Argentina and Chile were complicit in what became the bloodiest and most brutal coup in the history of Bolivia when Hugo Banzer was ousted. Argentine death squads associated with the military governments of the **Proceso de Reorganización Nacional** cooperated directly with the Bolivian military to bring down Banzer, operating out of the office of the Argentine military attaché in La Paz. *See also* BELGRANO, MANUEL JOSÉ JOAQUIN DEL CORAZÓN DE JESÚS (1770–1820); CONGRESS OF TUCUMÁN; UNITED PROVINCES OF SOUTH AMERICA; UNITED PROVINCES OF THE RIVER PLATE.

BOLSA DE COMERCIO. Officially the Bolsa de Comercio de Buenos Aires (BCBA), the stock exchange was founded in 1854 and succeeded the ephemeral Bolsa Mercantil set up in 1822 by **Bernardino Rivadavia** to stimulate investment in **agriculture** and create a market for government debt. Dealing in company stock began in 1856; most of the early business remained confined to gold (in effect, fixing the exchange rate) and **commodities**. By the 1880s, dealings in stocks and shares in local businesses—banks and commercial and manufacturing enterprises—increased as the Bolsa registered companies and validated their prospectuses and capital accounts. Even so, the principal transactions were in mortgage bonds (*cédulas*), gold, and foreign currency certificates, and commercial paper. Activity grew and became more diverse during the 1920s; business in treasury bills and government bonds increased considerably. In 1937, the Securities Commission (later National Securities Commission) was established as a dependency of the recently formed **Banco Central de la República Argentina** (BCRA) to regulate flotations. The commission was represented on the board of the stock exchange, and the three institutions came to collaborate closely.

Economic crises and increasing government intervention in the economy in the middle third of the 20th century reduced and limited activity. Changes in the legal regime governing the financial, securities, and investment markets in 1968 began a process of liberalization, which increased further during the **Proceso de Reorganizacion Nacional**. Bolsa business grew exponentially in the 1990s with the **Convertibility Plan** and massive program of **privatization**. In addition to handling privatization issues, the BCBA attempted to develop the market for small- and medium-sized firms seeking capital, as well as to promote interest in the market among small, private savers. Such initiatives were brought to an abrupt end by the political and economic crisis of 2001 that ended the administration of President **Fernando de la Rúa**. Activity has since revived, notwithstanding restatization during the presidencies of **Néstor Kirchner** and **Cristina Fernández de Kirchner**. Indeed, there was something of a local stock market boom during the period of recovery and rapid growth, until around 2010. The BCBA anticipates a steady growth in activity because of market-friendly policies introduced by President **Mauricio Macri**, elected in 2015. There was a large increase in dealings in industrial stocks in 2016, and in the first half of the year the BCBA share index (MERVAL) outperformed all other stock market indexes in the world. Continued optimism, in part due to support shown for Macri in the midterm **congressional elections of 2017**, resulted in steady index growth until uncertainty returned with the currency crisis of 2018.

In the 1990s, the Bolsa signed agreements with the principal regional stock markets, plus an arrangement with the New York Stock Exchange in 1992 and the London Stock Exchange in 2000. The Bolsa is now regarded as one of the principal stock markets of Latin America. Since around 2008, the

MERVAL has proved less volatile than the economy at large and more robust than stock market indexes in some neighboring countries. The Bolsa is not to be confused with the acronym of the former Bank of London and South America, which was also known as BOLSA, though never La Bolsa. *See also* AGRICULTURE; AUSTRAL PLAN; ECONOMY; FOREIGN DEBT/FOREIGN INVESTMENT; FOREIGN TRADE; INDUSTRY; RODRIGAZO; STATE-OWNED ENTERPRISES (SOEs).

BONAFINI, HEBE PASTOR DE (1928–). Political activist and civil rights campaigner, best known as a founder member and sometime head of las **Madres de Plaza de Mayo** and of the **Fundación Madres de Plaza de Mayo**. During the **Proceso de Reorganización Nacional**, Bonafini lost two sons and a daughter-in-law, all of whom were "disappeared"—becoming **Desaparecidos**. Applauded for their courage and steadfastness in the face of a brutal regime, and antipathy from some sections of the public, the "Mothers" were held together by the resolve and leadership of Bonafini and erstwhile colleagues. Their efforts in search of information about their children and quest for justice brought international recognition. With the return of democracy in 1983 following the election of President **Raúl Alfonsín**, Bonafini expressed frustration with the government over the prosecution of those responsible for **human rights** violations and the apparent hesitant approach of the president himself. Others were more appreciative of the difficulties under which Alfonsín was laboring as he attempted to rebuild civil society, reestablish the rule of law, and embed democratic institutions in the face of a restive **military** and faltering **economy**. Bonafini's growing impatience with the **Unión Cívica Radical** (UCR) government of Alfonsín contributed to a rift in the organization.

After the split with former associates, who set up the Línea Fundadora de las Madres de Plaza de Mayo, Bonafini has espoused various radical causes and established something of a domestic and international role for herself. At home, she became increasingly close to the regimes of Presidents **Néstor Kirchner** and **Cristina Fernández de Kirchner**, particularly the latter, as they overturned legislation introduced by Alfonsín to place time limits on the legal processing of those accused of human rights abuses and pardons granted by his successor, President **Carlos Saúl Menem** of the **Partido Justicialista** (PJ), to members and associates of juntas established following the **military coup of 1976**. Bonafini and her organization received substantial sums of government money from the Kirchners, ostensibly for the provision of **education** facilities, health clinics, and social housing in poor districts. Internationally, Bonafini has expressed support for guerrilla groups and organizations that embraced violence as a political tool and has been critical of the **Catholic Church**.

Bonafini's increasingly erratic behavior caused mounting disquiet and further divided the movement she helped establish. And there were charges of financial malfeasance—at best mismanagement, at worst **corruption**—in the administration of funds for which she was responsible. On her watch, the Fundación illicitly used more than $1,500,000 pesos to cover the political campaign costs of **Amado Boudou**, a close associate of Mrs. Kirchner, and others. For some, the final straw came when Bonafini declared that the Mothers were no longer a civil rights campaign groups but a political body, "Las Cristinas," a women's group supporting Cristina Fernández de Kirchner. Fundación funds were used to pay the costs of political rallies and events sponsored by Las Cristinas. It transpired that Bonafini had an account in a Spanish savings bank from which she had withdrew amounts totaling 2,000,000 euros by 2009. The origin of the funds has never been fully explained. It is also recorded that she holds private foreign bank accounts in the Canary Islands, France, and Italy into which she made deposits from Fundación sources. She is currently charged with the misuse of public funds. Bonafini has protested her innocence and is inclined to ascribe criticism by former associates of Línea Fundadora and others as politically motivated and driven by jealousy at her fame and public profile. *See also* DIRTY WAR; DISPOSICIÓN FINAL; LEY DE OBEDIENCIA DEBIDA; LEY DE PUNTO FINAL; WAR TO ANNIHILATE SUBVERSION.

BORDÓN, JOSÉ OCTAVIO (1945–). Politician and academic who has held various public offices, including the governorship of the province of **Mendoza**, and served as national deputy and national senator for the province. In the province, particularly during his governorship, he was regarded as a modernizing figure. On the reformist wing of the **Partido Justicialista** (PJ), he fell out with President **Carlos Saúl Menem**, among other things, questioning the neoliberal economic strategies of the period while complaining of **corruption**. With other progressive, dissident members of the PJ, he formed the **Frente País Solidario** (FREPASO). He headed the party ticket in the **presidential election of 1995**, with **Carlos "Chacho" Álvarez** standing for the vice presidency. Although Bordón and Álvarez were defeated by Menem, the party performed well in the **congressional elections** of that year. Following disagreement with the other senior figures of the FREPASO, he resigned and joined the PJ, siding with the anti-Menem bloc. Between 1999 and 2003, he held various federal and provincial administrative posts. In 2003, he was nominated ambassador to Washington by President **Néstor Kirchner**, serving there until 2007. In 2015, he was appointed ambassador in Santiago de Chile by President **Mauricio Macri**. No longer active in political life, he enjoys a reputation as a personable, efficient administrator, largely free from the charges of corruption that stuck to many of his peers. *See also* MOVIMIENTO RENOVADOR PERONISTA (MRP).

BORGES, GRACIELA (1941–). Born Graciela Noemí Zabala, she is an acclaimed film and television actress. Her artistic surname was a courtesy of **Jorge Luis Borges** after her father barred her from using his surname when she began acting at age 14. Known for her talent and attractive looks, Borges epitomized Argentine beauty in the 1960s and became the most famous actress of national films of those days. Her successful career extends into the 21st century and comprises approximately 50 films and a range of television programs.

BORGES, JORGE LUIS (1899–1986). A key figure in Spanish-language literature, he was an Argentine short-story writer, essayist, poet, and translator. Sometime director of the National Library and professor of English at the **University of Buenos Aires**, Borges was a regular contributor from the first issue of *Sur*, the prominent literary magazine founded in 1931 by **Victoria Ocampo**. She introduced him to **Adolfo Bioy Casares**, another well-known literary figure who would become a frequent collaborator and close friend. Their collaborations are *Seis problemas para don Isidro Parodi* (1942), *Dos fantasías memorables* (1946), *Un modelo para la muerte* (1946), *Cuentos breves y extraordinarios* (1955), *Libro del cielo e infierno* (1960), *Crónicas de Bustos Domecq* (1967), and *Nuevos cuentos de Bustos Domecq* (1977).

Although Borges went blind, he was a prolific writer whose short stories bordered on the edge of the real and the fantastic—a style known as magical realism, of which the other major exponent was **Julio Cortázar**. Borges was described by the *New York Times* as the "Master of the Mystical." Two of his best-known collections of short stories are *Ficciones* (Fictions) (1944) and *El Aleph* (1949). They are connected by common motifs, including dreams, labyrinths, libraries, mirrors, fictional writers, philosophy, and religion. *Ficciones* is the most popular compilation of his short stories. The labyrinth is a recurring theme throughout and is used as a metaphor to represent a variety of things: the overwhelmingly complex nature of worlds and the systems that exist on them, human enterprises, the physical and mental aspects of humans, and abstract concepts such as time. The stories themselves can be seen as a type of labyrinth. *El Aleph*'s title work describes a point in space containing all other spaces at once. "Emma Zunz," one of the stories in this collection, was made into the film *Días de odio* (1954) by Argentine director **Leopoldo Torre Nilsson**.

Strongly anti-Communist and anti-Fascist, Borges got into trouble during the time of President **Juan Domingo Perón**. He was "promoted" from cultural posts to mundane jobs; his treatment by the government provoked outrage in intellectual and cultural circles. Alluding to Peronism, he famously remarked that dictatorships bred oppression, servility, and cruelty, which were contrary to the Argentine spirit of individualism. He was equally scathing of Perón's return to power in 1973. He accepted the directorship of the National

Library, which was offered to him shortly after the **military coup of 1955**, and was initially supportive of the **military coup of 1976**, but was later appalled by the excesses of the **Proceso de Reorganización Nacional**— against which he was vociferous. Regarded as an Anglophile, he also got into trouble with the authorities during the **Falklands War**.

Ficciones and *El Aleph*, together with other works by Borges, were translated into English. He lectured prolifically in Argentina and abroad—including the **United States**, where he held the Tinker Chair at the University of Texas at Austin. He was the recipient of major prizes. The award of the Formentor Prize in 1961, shared with Samuel Beckett, first brought him to international attention. He was shortlisted several times for the Nobel Prize for Literature but never won it—said by some to be the greatest literary figure of the 20th never to have been awarded the laureate. Other forms of international recognition came with the conferment of the title of Commendatore (Italy) and such honors as the Cervantes Prize (Spain) and Légion d'Honneur (France).

BORGES ACEVEDO, JORGE FRANCISCO ISIDORO LUIS. *See* BORGES, JORGE LUIS (1899–1986).

BORLENGHI, ÁNGEL GABRIEL (1906–1962). A leading trade unionist and socialist who became a significant Peronist figure; served as minister of interior (1946–1955) and sometime minister of justice. He began his political career in his teens and within a few years became the secretary general of the Confederación General de Empleados de Comercio, which had tens of thousands of members across Argentina. Under his leadership, the union became one of the most important nationally in the 1930s.

Borlenghi lobbied the National Congress for social legislation, which led to the enactment of the Ley del Sabado Inglés (which prohibited work on Saturdays afternoons) and the Ley de Indemnización por Despido (a severance pay law that among other things comprised advance notice of dismissal, paid vacation, sick leave, and compensation for industrial accidents). Nevertheless, he mostly concentrated on securing the passage of a retirement law for his union and finally achieved this in December 1943 after a meeting with Colonel **Juan Domingo Perón**, who was then secretary of labor and social welfare. Borlenghi rapidly became convinced that Perón provided a real opportunity for ameliorating the conditions of the working class and was always present at the colonel's meetings with union leaders throughout 1944. Pressed by Borlenghi and **Juan Atilio Bramuglia** of the all-powerful **Unión Ferroviaria** (UF), Perón issued a decree in October 1945 extending full legal status to the **trade unions**, including the right to participate in politics. This was a green light to set up the union-sponsored **Partido Laborista** (Labor

Party), which ultimately triumphed in the **presidential election of 1946**. Following the Peronist victory, Borlenghi was appointed to head the **Ministry of Interior**, an unprecedented move as the post was traditionally held by jurists.

Borlenghi wielded enormous power in his portfolio. He contributed to the incorporation of the **Partido Laborista** (Perón's 1946 election vehicle) into the Partido Peronista, which ultimately became the **Partido Justicialista** (PJ), as well as contributing to the president's effort to obtain political control of the **Confederación General del Trabajo**. In the aftermath of the failed **military coup of 1951**, the Interior Ministry was strengthened at the expense of the armed forces, conferring even more power on Borlenghi. A new internal security body, the Consejo Federal de Seguridad, was set up to coordinate the work of all provincial and national police forces. Borlenghi, who already controlled the 25,000 troops of the Policía Federal and now had even more men under his command, strove to Peronize the police forces. He assumed direct control of the Gendarmería Nacional, a militarized border guard previously supervised by the army, and of the Prefectura Naval, a river and port police force that had been commanded by the navy.

Unlike other leading Peronist figures such as Bramuglia and **José Figuerola**, Borlenghi somehow managed to retain his portfolio throughout the *peronato*. In fact, he remained minister of interior until three months before the **military coup of 1955**. The reasons for his longevity as a minister are that he did not threaten Perón's leadership and had good relations with the first lady. But he was deeply opposed to the conflict that Perón triggered with the **Catholic Church** in late 1954 and was forced to resign in the wake of the failed putsch of June 1955, which took place in the context of said confrontation. Borlenghi went immediately into exile, first in **Uruguay**, then in **Cuba**, and finally in Italy to receive medical treatment, which was ultimately unsuccessful. In Cuba, he is reported to have interviewed **Ernesto "Che" Guevara**, who expressed admiration for Perón. He died in Rome; his remains were reinterred in Argentina in 1996. *See also* MINISTRY OF JUSTICE AND HUMAN RIGHTS; REVOLUCIÓN LIBERTADORA (1955–1958).

BORN BROTHERS, KIDNAPPING OF THE (1974–1975). Together with the **Aramburazo**, this was one of the most notorious operations of the **Montoneros**. In September 1974, the Montoneros were experiencing financial difficulties. They decided to resolve them by acting against **Bunge & Born**, an Argentine multinational corporation that was considered the most powerful and influential in the country, adopting a tactic employed by similar groups during the period, kidnapping and ransoming business leaders.

Juan and Jorge Born, respectively the manager and director general of the company, were kidnapped on 19 September. Within hours, the Montoneros issued a "war communique" announcing that the brothers would be "judged" for their actions against the workers, the Argentine people, and the national interest. Held captive in a "people's prison," the two businessmen were interrogated about their activities and then "condemned" to a year's imprisonment; the sentence was reduced to nine months when the corporation yielded to the guerrillas' demands. The Montoneros demanded a ransom of 60 million US dollars, which was a world record. In addition, the group demanded that 1.2 million dollars in merchandise be distributed in *villas miseria*, the acceptance of worker claims for better wages and working conditions, and that Bunge & Born place busts of former president **Juan Domingo Perón** and the first lady in all their factories as punishment for its alleged participation in the **military coup of 1955**. The negotiations were long and arduous, and the Montoneros put on pressure by attacking the firm **Molinos Río de la Plata** (owned by Bunge & Born) and issuing death threats until the corporation finally yielded. Its representatives in France, Germany, **Great Britain**, and Italy met to make the necessary arrangements. Juan Born was released in March 1975 owing to ill health, and his brother Jorge was freed on 20 June 1975.

In a bizarre twist in the 1990s, Jorge Born became involved in a business with **Rodolfo Galimberti**, one of his kidnappers. Unsurprisingly, this caused severe strain among the shareholders of Bunge & Born. Furthermore, his dealings came under investigation for fraud. *See also* MILITARY COUP OF 1976; PERÓN, ISABEL (1931–); PROCESO DE REORGANIZACIÓN NACIONAL; WAR TO ANNIHILATE SUBVERSION.

BOUDOU, AMADO (1962–). Businessman, politician, and academic who read economics at the National University of Mar Del Plata, in his hometown, undertaking postgraduate studies at the **Centro de Estudios Macroeconómicos de Argentina**, a private university renowned for its free-market approach to economics; minister of economy in the first presidency of **Cristina Fernández de Kirchner** and vice president during her second.

Boudou's initial political party affiliation was to the right-of-center **Unión del Centro Demócratico** (UCEDE, sometimes UCeDé)—he was a member of the student wing of the party, which supported **Carlos Saúl Menem** in the **presidential election of 1999**; later, he joined **Partido Justicialista** (PJ). His early business career was as a student pop concert promoter; he was engaged by public works companies undertaking projects for the state and employed by the federal Social Insurance Agency, responsible for pensions and a wide range of social payments, including family allowance and child benefit. He became director of the agency in 2008 when **Sergio Massa**, the outgoing head, was appointed cabinet secretary by Fernández de Kirchner. He was at the head of the agency when the government controversially nationalized private pension funds, a measure for which he was largely responsible. A flamboyant individual, who cultivates a playboy-cum-popstar image, Boudou has had a stormy relationship with the **media**. He was romantically linked with Fernández de Kirchner, following the death of her husband, and faced multiple charges of bribery and **corruption**, both subjects generating considerable media interest.

As minister of economy between 2009 and 2011, he was responsible for unsuccessful efforts to strike a deal with the so-called holdouts, bondholders who refused to accept the terms of the 2005 debt default settlement following the economic crisis of 2001 that ended the **Convertibility Plan**. He has been charged with involvement in business deals incompatible with his office. For example, while at the **Ministry of Economy**, he ensured the awarding of a contract to the high-tech graphic company Ciccone for the printing of pesos. The affair became known as Boudougate. Other charges include illicit enrichment when vice president, the misappropriation of public funds, and shady property deals. In 2017, he was sentenced to three years in prison—the sentence was suspended—while facing several ongoing investigations. At the beginning of November, Boudou was arrested and jailed on three counts of illicit enrichment dating back to 2009. He was the second of Mrs. Kirchner's close associates to be jailed; **Julio De Vido** had been incarcerated in late October, three days after the midterm **congressional elections of 2017**. The convictions against Boudou were regarded as sound, yet the very public manner of his apprehension—images of his arrest at home, handcuffing, and bundling into a police car were widely broadcast—raised unease. There was an outcry against a politically motivated witch hunt, complaints made not only by his friends and close associates. Although the cases of embezzlement and money laundering were upheld, having spent over two months in jail Boudou was released in mid-January 2018 on a technicality. Other cases against him continue.

BRAMUGLIA, JUAN ATILIO (1903–1962). A leading Peronist figure; foreign minister (1946–1949) and an early proponent of **"Peronism without Perón."** A railroad worker who became a specialist in labor law, he was full-time advisor to the **Unión Ferroviaria** (UF) between 1930 and 1943. Following the **military coup of 1943**, which brought Colonel **Juan Domingo Perón** to prominence, Bramuglia successfully urged the UF to support Perón. At the time, the UF was the most powerful Argentine union, and the railroad workers were the first to join what became the Peronist movement. He helped establish the Secretariat of Labor and Social Welfare and, being its director general of social welfare, was extensively involved in the drafting and enactment of legislation. Bramuglia served as federal interventor in the province of **Buenos Aires** between December 1944 and October 1945. During the campaign for the **presidential election of 1946**, he headed the Junta

Nacional de Coordinación de los Partidos Políticos Revolucionarios, the body that coordinated the parties and organizations backing Perón's candidacy.

Elected president, Perón appointed Bramuglia foreign minister. Given his union background and role in shaping social policy, Perón feared that Bramuglia might challenge his leadership and seek to create an independent support base and acquire prestige within the movement. Mistakenly, Perón assumed that placing Bramuglia in charge of foreign affairs would keep him busy and isolated from domestic concerns. Bramuglia turned out to be Perón's ablest minister and achieved his greatest success as president of the Security Council of the **United Nations** (UN) between October and December 1948, at the height of the Berlin Crisis. His efforts at mediation were so well received internationally that they ultimately led to his downfall. As foreign minister, Bramuglia not only made Perón feel threatened, but he had also riled First Lady **Eva Perón** (Evita). Though working within the confines of the Peronist **Tercera Posición** in foreign policy, Bramuglia was far from happy with the close ties that Perón developed with the Franco dictatorship in **Spain**, not least because they hindered efforts to improve the international image of Argentina.

When Perón accepted an invitation for the first lady to visit Spain in 1947, Bramuglia opposed the trip from the start. His objection stemmed from disapproval of Evita's meddling in politics and the administration of foreign policy; he convinced the president that his wife should stick to noncommittal remarks when overseas. The initial trip was extended to include other European countries, becoming known in Argentina as the "rainbow tour." **Great Britain** was a country that the first lady became especially keen to visit: the official invitation from Buckingham Palace failed to materialize. So when Bramuglia, at the end of his stint at the UN Security Council, went on a five-day visit to London at the invitation of the British government in recognition of his attempt to solve the Berlin Crisis, Evita took it as a slap in the face. Not only did he meet his counterpart and the prime minister, but he was also received in Buckingham Palace with pomp and circumstance by King George VI. With both Perón and Evita bearing grudges, Bramuglia was systematically undermined; he resigned in August 1949.

Following the **military coup of 1955** that ousted Perón, Bramuglia went into exile, yet he was clearly aware that Peronism was there to stay and had to be brought into the political mainstream. Hoping to establish a "Peronism without Perón," he founded the neo-Peronist **Unión Popular** (UP) in December 1955. In exile, Perón continued to interfere in domestic politics and successfully thwarted Bramuglia's ambitions. Perón requested that supporters cast blank ballots in the **constitutional convention election of 1957**, even though the UP had been legalized. Perón further stymied the chances of the UP performing successfully in the **presidential election of 1958** when he made public the notorious **Caracas Pact**, the election deal that enabled **Arturo Frondizi** of the **Unión Cívica Radical Intransigente** (UCRI) to become president. Toward the end of Bramuglia's life, when Frondizi allowed Peronism to contest the provincial and **congressional elections of 1962** in various guises, Perón imposed his own candidates on the UP, marginalizing Bramuglia. Perón needed the party's legal status and powerful machine to win the elections but was unforgiving toward attempts at independence by the party leadership. *See also* MINISTRY OF FOREIGN RELATIONS AND RELIGION; MINISTRY OF LABOR; MINISTRY OF SOCIAL DEVELOPMENT.

BRAZIL. Since **independence**, relations with Brazil have been shaped by rivalry for control of the east bank of the **River Plate** dating from Portuguese and Spanish clashes in the colonial period, and by a quest for hegemony in South America. Yet notwithstanding such geopolitical antagonism, relations between the two countries have been largely peaceful, and by the early 21st century they had become close commercial partners.

It was probably inevitable that the struggles for independence, the crafting of new national identities, and the settlement of ill-defined, porous frontiers should lead to conflict. As the **United Provinces of South America**, a fledgling Argentina aspired to retain control of **Paraguay** and **Uruguay**, which had formed part of the **Viceroyalty of the River Plate** centered on **Buenos Aires**. The east bank of the River Plate, the scene of Spanish and Portuguese military action in the 18th century, proved to be an especially sensitive border region as the newly independent Empire of Brazil pressed for free navigation of the **Paraná** in order to secure access to interior provinces and the government in Buenos Aires sought to maintain the territorial integrity of the former viceroyalty and preserve its commercial dominance of the delta. The Cisplatine War or 1825–1828 led to a Brazilian invasion of present-day Uruguay and the incorporation of the region into the empire as the Província Cisplatina. The incorporation was never recognized by Argentina, which encouraged patriotic resistance. Although governments in Buenos Aires and Rio de Janeiro continued to meddle in the internal affairs of the country, the beginning of the end of this boundary dispute was engineered with British assistance in 1828 and the formal recognition of Uruguay as a sovereign republic. It was supposedly in defense of Uruguayan independence that both Argentina and Brazil allied against Paraguay in the **War of the Triple Alliance**—Paraguay claimed to be similarly acting in support of Uruguay against Brazilian interference.

One of the outcomes of the war, and the defeat of Paraguay, was Brazilian ascendance in the region, just as Argentina was completing the task of **national organization** and concluding the **Conquest of the Desert**, processes that deflected attention toward domestic development and securing the western frontier with **Chile**. During the final decades of the 19th century, both countries were preoccupied with internal development. Rapid growth around 1900 in Argentina also ensured the economic gravitation of Paraguay and Uruguay toward Buenos Aires, just as political instability in Brazil provided a distraction in Rio de Janeiro. Despite the threat of a naval arms race in the 1920s, basking in its status as one of the top 10 economies in the international system, Argentina was confident in its leadership of Spanish-speaking South America and dominance in the region. This self-confidence in regional diplomatic outreach and influence on the part of Buenos Aires intensified during the administrations of President **Juan Domingo Perón**.

Yet it was precisely at this time that the regional balance of power was beginning to shift. Alarmed at the clear military superiority of Argentina by the 1930s, Rio de Janeiro sought closer relations with the **United States**. Washington, DC, may have welcomed approaches by Brazil because Argentina was viewed from the United States as too close to Great Britain, hence Washington was content to promote Brazil as a regional partner and counter. This sentiment would be strengthened by Perón's fascist leanings and antagonism to the United States and by Argentine neutrality during the Second World War while Brazil afforded military bases to the United States, joined the Allies, and sent an expeditionary force, under US command, to the European theater. Brazil received substantial military assistance from the United States as a result and later financial aid for its industrialization project. By the 1960s, Brazil was pulling ahead of Argentina economically. Faster growth and structural change would soon ensure that Brazil was the larger and more dynamic economy, compounded by the Argentine experience of a succession of **economic crises**. The growing gap in **military** and industrial leadership, coupled with Brazil–Paraguay projects to develop hydroelectricity generation capacity in the upper Paraná, particularly exercised de facto regimes headed by the armed forces in Buenos Aires—even during the 1970s, when Brazilian and Argentine military administrations were collaborating in **Operación Condor**. Indeed, suspicion about the other seems to have been especially pronounced when the militaries were in power in both countries. In the late 1970s and early 1980s, the countries appeared to be on the cusp of a nuclear arms race.

A sustained improvement in relations between the countries dates from the return of democracy in both in the 1980s. In 1985, President **Raúl Alfonsín** met his Brazilian counterpart, President José Sarnay, to promote better relations based on economic cooperation and mutual support. At a time when the external environment was clouded by debt crisis and financial instability, Alfonsín saw economic integration as a means of sustaining growth that would reinforce democratization and political stability. The result was **MERCOSUR**, the South American Common Market, formally established in 1991. The trade bloc includes Uruguay and Paraguay; several other South

American countries are associate members (the membership of Venezuela was suspended in 2016). Macroeconomic synchronization is a long way off, yet the economic partnership has grown and often flourished, notwithstanding several commercial and tariff disputes, which became particularly pronounced during the presidency of **Cristina Fernández de Kirchner**; the Brazilian **currency** crisis of 1999, which precipitated a sharp devaluation that disadvantaged Argentine exporters, the collapse of the **Convertibility Plan**, and political disagreement; and Argentine sensitivity to such issues as recurrent projects to accord Brazil a permanent seat on the **United Nations** Security Council. In addition to cultural initiatives and education-related exchanges, motor vehicle production in the two countries is closely integrated, there is considerable cross-border exchange by medium-sized firms, and the militaries are collaborating in the production of equipment. Since the early 21st century, Brazil has become Argentina's principal **foreign trade** partner—the main market for exports and the principal supplier of imports; for Brazil, Argentina is usually its third or fourth most important trade partner. *See also* CHINA; ITAIPÚ DAM; MILITARY COUP OF 1966; MILITARY COUP OF 1976.

BRITISH INVASIONS. Sometimes known as the "English Invasions" (*las invasiones inglesas*), which took place in 1806 and 1807; instrumental in the process of **independence** and forging of the identity of the new nation. There had been illicit commercial interests in the **River Plate** for some time, but formal commercial relations between **Great Britain** and what became Argentina are usually dated from 1713, when the Treaty of Utrecht granted British merchants a monopoly over the slave trade to **Buenos Aires**, along with the right to send one trading vessel a year. With the Bourbon dynasty inheriting the throne of Spain after the War of Spanish Succession, closer relations between France and Spain triggered further British political and military interest in the area. This interest intensified at the end of the 18th century with the French Revolutionary and Napoleonic Wars, and the beginning of independence movements in Spanish America. Patriots from **Venezuela** were particularly active in London, convincing merchants that South America was ripe for revolution and that vast markets existed for direct trade. British merchants and proponents of independence peddled these views in official circles—several schemes for invading, and possibly settling, parts of southern Latin America were advanced in the late 18th century. Commodore Sir Home Popham, an enterprising naval officer with close links to the City of London, was among those convinced of these views.

In 1806, having taken Cape Town from the Dutch—the Dutch Republic was allied with France at the time—and with considerable military and naval forces at his disposal, Popham set his sights on Buenos Aires. Accounts differ as to whether Popham acted largely on his own initiative or in response to direct orders from London, or whether Popham interpreted his instructions imaginatively. It is also unclear what was intended by the assault on Buenos Aires—to take the city and settled a new colony, or only to maintain a British presence in the city, developing it as a trading entrepôt for the region along the lines of the Crown Colony of Singapore founded several years later. The facts are obvious. Having landed at Quilmes two days earlier, British forces took Buenos Aires on 27 June 1806, raising the union flag above the fort, and held the city for more than six weeks. A few days earlier, the Viceroy **Rafael de Sobremonte** has abandoned the city. Despite the wishful thinking of Venezuelan patriots, there was no popular uprising, perhaps because those favoring independence were in a minority and any assumed pro-British sentiment evaporated when it became known that the British intended to hold at least the city. Within days, opposition was being organized by **Santiago de Liniers**; reinforced from Montevideo, Liniers took the fort, liberated the city, and accepted the unconditional surrender of British forces, who were interned in the interior.

Popham had already left the River Plate before the reconquest began. He arrived to a tumultuous reception in London, enthusiasm for his enterprise and the prospects of developing trade with the River Plate intensified by the display of Sobremonte's treasure—20 carts containing bullion and precious artifacts were paraded through the city. The official reaction to Popham's adventure was cool. It is possible that without the display of treasure and city fervor, Popham might have faced a court-martial. When news of surrender in Buenos Aires reached London, public sentiment ensured that an expeditionary force would be assembled to reassert British control. The expeditionary force took Montevideo on 13 February 1807, waited for reinforcements, and headed for Buenos Aires in June. The second invasion was less successful than the first. The expeditionary force failed to retake the city, surrendered to Liniers, agreed to the return of Montevideo to Spanish rule, and accepted safe conduct to return to Britain, where the commander was court-martialed. With the French invasion of the Iberian Peninsula the following year, Britain and Spain would find themselves allies.

The immediate consequences of the invasions and the patriotic defense and liberation of the city were the acclamation of Liniers as viceroy and the reorganization of the administration at a *cabildo abierto*—and preparation for an anticipated second British invasion. In the longer term, the successful defense and reconquest by local forces, coupled with the flight of Sobremonte, generated a sense of patriotism and self-confidence, as well as weakening the authority of Spain. The symbols of resistance to Britain would soon become the emblems of independence. In addition, although the first invasion resulted in a British occupation of only a few weeks, during that time the freeing of trade and the publication of newspapers and pamphlets engendered a new worldview that capitalized on sentiments for freer trade and administrative changes that were already circulating. Indeed, many British prisoners captured in 1806 remained in Argentina. Several individuals who would later become prominent in the revolutionary struggle against Spain dealt with the occupying forces or were involved in the recapture of the city, including **Manuel Belgrano, Mariano Moreno, Juan Martín de Pueyrredón**, and **Cornelio Saavedra**. The events of 1806 and 1807 contributed directly to the **May Revolution of 1810** and ultimately independence.

BUENOS AIRES (CITY). Capital of the country, known variously as Santa María del Buen Aire, City of the Holy Trinity and Port of Buenos Aires, Most Noble and Most Loyal City of Buenos Aires, the Federal Capital of Buenos Aires, and the Autonomous City of Buenos Aires. The current status of the city derives from the **Constitution of 1994**, which granted Buenos Aires the near equivalent of provincial status; the title Autonomous City of Buenos Aires was officially adopted in 1996—the Spanish acronym is CABA. An earlier significant change in the modern administrative organization of Buenos Aires occurred more than a century before in 1880 with the **federalization of the city of Buenos Aires**. Located in the northeast of the province of Buenos Aires, the formal city limits enclose an area of 77 square miles (c. 200 square kilometers); to the north and east bounded by the **River Plate**, to the south by the Riachuelo River, and to the west by the province. The city is divided into 48 administrative districts (*barrios*), grouped into 15 communities (*comunas*).

First settled in 1536 by Pedro de Mendoza, the core of the town was based in the present-day district of **La Boca** at the mouth of the Riachuelo. Subject to repeated attacks by nomadic pampean Indians, by 1541 the original township had been abandoned. The settlers moved to **Paraguay**, from which an expedition was dispatched to reestablish Buenos Aires: Juan de Garay successfully refounded the city in 1580. For the next two centuries, the settlement survived as a backwater empire, close to the Indian frontier. It subsisted as a minor administrative and military post, servicing a growing trade in **hides** and dried/salted **meat** and later as a transshipment point for smuggled goods—legally, overseas commerce had to be routed via **Peru**, the Pacific coast of South America, and the Caribbean. Modern development dates from the late colonial era, when the city became the capital of the new **Viceroyalty of the River Plate** formed in 1776, including Upper Peru (present-day **Bolivia**), Paraguay, **Uruguay**, and part of what had been colonial **Chile**, as well as Argentina. There was considerable growth in the military and administrative establishment. Related reforms allowing direct trade with **Spain** and other Spanish imperial territories further boosted economic activity and prosperity.

Between 1777 and 1809, the population of the city virtually quadrupled, rising from 22,500 to 92,000 inhabitants. A further boost occurred with the **May Revolution of 1810**, when the city aspired to become the capital of an independent country that included all regions of the former viceroyalty—that is, capital of the **United Provinces of South America**. This was not to be, as peripheral regions spun off. In 1826, the city was declared de jure capital of the **United Provinces of the River Plate**, though relegated to the status of de facto capital of the **Argentine Confederation** during the Rosas period (1829–1852)—Buenos Aires Provincial Governor **Juan Manuel de Rosas** was charged with the conduct of foreign affairs by the autonomous provinces of the Confederation. Briefly, in 1852, Buenos Aires once again became the national capital, only to revert to the status of provincial capital when the province seceded from the Confederation between 1854 and 1861—when the city of **Paraná**, province of **Entre Ríos**, was designated national capital. When the province rejoined the Confederation, the city functioned as both provincial and national capital until 1880, when it was federalized and a new provincial capital commissioned at **La Plata**.

In 1869, the population of the city was over 180,000. By now the modern city was taking shape, benefiting from **immigration** from Europe associated with the emergence of new export **commodities** like **wool** and a flow of foreign investment. New city blocks were being laid out, particularly to the north and west, and government and other public buildings being constructed. In 1720, the city grid extended to about 13 blocks from south to north and nine from east to west; in 1869, around 40 south to north and 25 east to west. *Saladeros* were concentrated on the south side of the city, with various workshops and factories developing elsewhere. Urban facilities like street lighting, water, and drainage were extended and improved, but not sufficiently to prevent an outbreak of cholera in 1868 and yellow fever in 1870, triggering an exodus of the elite from the old colonial center around San Telmo to more salubrious northern districts, present-day Barrio Norte. The city was not immune to the political turbulence of the time, though the major upheaval would come after the election of **Julio A. Roca** to the presidency in 1880 and the federalization of the city. Notwithstanding local opposition to the separation of province and city, the city benefited from its new unequivocal status as federal capital, even if administered directly by the national government—the president nominated the city mayor (*intendente*). The mayor was assisted by a city council that was directly elected but whose powers were limited. By the end of the 1880s, the former colonial dimensions of Buenos Aires had been extended to include the districts of Flores and Belgrano, more or less establishing the current city limits. Toward the end of the 19th century, the population was about 650,000, of which more than half were immigrants.

Urban beautification around 1900 in preparation for the centenary of **independence** earned for the city the title the "Paris of South America." Many immigrant national associations raised funds to embellish the city to mark the event. For example, the French community financed the remodeling of Plaza

Francia. Buenos Aires became a European-style metropolis, one of the great cities of the world endowed with broad avenues, parks, and public spaces. There were iconic buildings like the **Colón** opera house, opened in 1908; an extended and refurbished presidential palace, the **Casa Rosada**; as well as grand private houses, palatial bank headquarters, elegant shops, well-endowed museums, numerous places of worship, and office buildings. There were modern docks and railway termini; by 1914, the city boasted one of the most extensive tramway networks in the world and one of the first underground railway systems. With a population of over 1,000,000, there were other manifestations of urban modernity associated with mass immigration, rapid population growth, and economic expansion—slums, prostitution, and crime. The centenary was also the age of *tango* and *conventillos*, and of emergent *villas miseria*. Social and political violence—strikes and street protest—became a pronounced feature of city life, leading to reform projects as much at the municipal level as at the national level. It was at this time that **Alfredo Palacios** was elected to the provincial legislature and later the National **Congress** by voters in the capital. He served in the Chamber of Deputies from 1912 to 1915, the first socialist to be elected in the Americas.

During the 20th century, major national political events were played out in the city. The most high-profile included the swearing in of the first fully democratically elected president, **Hipólito Yrigoyen**, in 1916 following electoral reform a few years earlier; **the military coup of 1930**; demonstrations in support of future president, then colonel, **Juan Domingo Perón** in 1945, which brought hundreds of thousands of workers from outlying districts into the center of the city; the funeral of **Eva Perón** years later; armed conflict during the years of political instability in the 1960s and 1970s; and public protest at moments of economic crisis such as the unraveling of the **Austral Plan** in 1985 and the collapse of the **Convertibility Plan** in 2001. The largest gatherings invariable occurred in the Plaza de Mayo and surrounding streets, the biggest being in 1982, first when President General **Leopoldo Fortunato Galtieri** announced the invasion/recovery of the **Falkland Islands**, and again several weeks later when the surrender to British forces was confirmed, and in 1983 with the return of democracy and the inauguration of President **Raúl Alfonsín**. Invariably, the cry would resound, "Vamos a la Plaza!"

From the 1950s to the 1970s, there was a substantial deterioration in the fabric of the city as the result of spending cuts, economic instability that triggered the emergence of the informal economy and street trading, acute pressure on accommodation, and general administrative drift. Military regimes of the **Proceso de Reorganización Nacional** proposed an authoritarian solution to these problems—building urban highways and slum clearance, which mainly entailed relocating shantytown dwellers to the province. There was a major overhaul of the urban transport system during the presidency of **Carlos Saúl Menem**, along with several prestige projects, many provoking charges of **corruption**. Successive popularly elected mayors (now titled head of government of the city), such as **Fernando de la Rúa**, **Aníbal Ibarra**, and **Mauricio Macri**, were given more credit for upgrading the physical and social environment of the city and for running fairly efficient administrations—De la Rúa and Macri would use the office as a stepping stone to become national president. Ambitious plans for infrastructure improvement and social spending continue—notably, schemes to enhance rail and underground services, improve the water supply and drainage system, and address deficiencies in educational and social facilities. Despite recent improvements, the current city administration acknowledges the poor quality of much of the housing stock, lack of access to basic public services, scarcity of green spaces, traffic congestion, and similar problems that have a negative impact on the quality of urban life. Residents are the first to highlight these problems and, in recent years, have proved to be extremely vocal in demanding solutions—and transparency—from city authorities.

In 2017, the population of the city was around 3,000,000, a figure that has changed little since the middle of the 20th century, while the population of greater Buenos Aires (including neighboring districts of the province) is well above 13,000,000, making the metropolitan area one of the largest conurbations in the world. The city economy is overwhelmingly dominated by services and administration; the city financial sector and information technology firms account for 70 percent of total national output in these sectors, and the port handles by far the largest share of international trade, though manufacturing accounts for around 20 percent of the local gross domestic product, and international **tourism** is enjoying something of a boom, while the city is by a large measure the cultural capital of the country. *See also* AGUAS ARGENTINAS; ANGLO–ARGENTINE TRAMWAYS COMPANY; BARING CRISIS; CACCIATORE, OSVALDO (1924–2007); *COLECTIVOS*; CONQUEST OF THE DESERT/DESERT CAMPAIGN; INDUSTRY; REVOLUTION OF 1890; SEMANA TRÁGICA; TRANSPORTATION.

BUENOS AIRES (PROVINCE). The most important province in the republic, accounting for about 40 percent of the total national population, and a slightly larger percentage of voters—by far the largest electoral district in the country—and almost half the national gross domestic product. To the east, it is bounded by the Atlantic; to the north, the **River Plate**, the **Paraná** Delta, and province of **Santa Fe**; to the west, **Córdoba**, **La Pampa**, and **Río Negro**.

The city of **Buenos Aires** was first founded in 1536, then abandoned and refounded in 1580. For most of the colonial period and until the 1830s, much of the present-day territory of the province was unsettled, the preserve of nomadic Indians and wild cattle. The effective frontier of settlement was the

Salado River, though there were regular expeditions beyond the river to round up, brand, and slaughter wild cattle and horses—*vaquerías*—licensed by the Crown. Dried and salted **meat** and salted hides were the principal export **commodities** produced on the **pampas** before mass **immigration** after the middle of the 19th century. By the 1820s, cattle ranching had become more organized and settled, with new salting plants, *saladeros*, being established around the city of Buenos Aires and *estancias* taking form. **Independence** in May 1810, followed by the virtual disintegration of the country into several competing, virtually autonomous jurisdictions, gave the province added importance. Not only was the government in the city of Buenos Aires charged with representing the interior overseas, but the national customs house was established there, virtually making the provincial authorities national tax collectors. Products from interior provinces, as well as from the interior of the province, were taxed there before being exported, and import duties were similarly applied. Largely representing *estancia* and *saladero* interests, when **Juan Manuel de Rosas** was chosen as governor in 1829, the hegemony of the province was virtually complete. A ruthless **caudillo**, Rosas set about expanding the frontier. His campaign against Indian settlements in 1833 and 1834 marked the beginning of what would become the **Conquest of the Desert**. His expeditions pushed the boundaries of the province farther west than present-day limits. With the frontier secured through military might and treaties with compliant tribes, the interior of the province was opened to settlement and ranching. By the 1840s, modern **sheep** stations were being set up in the north and east of the province, and creole cattle occupied regions in the center and south. The fall of Rosas in 1852 brought instability on the frontier, but the desert campaign was renewed during the presidency of **Domingo Faustino Sarmiento** in 1872, and again in 1875 during the presidency of **Nicolás Avellaneda**, with the definitive campaign of 1879 being led by General (soon-to-be-President) **Julio A. Roca**.

Roca's ascent to the presidency in 1880 marked a turning point in the history of the province, which was lukewarm about his presidential ambitions. Following talk of a new round of civil conflict, Roca acted decisively: the city of Buenos Aires was separated from the province and declare national capital—since the early 1860s, both the federal and provincial governments had sat in the city. The **federalization of the city of Buenos Aires** led to the construction of a new provincial capital at **La Plata**. Economic expansion continued apace, first as more land was brought into cultivation to produce cereals—mainly wheat and **maize**—and later turned over to pedigree cattle. Modern meatpacking plants (*frigoríficos*) displaced *saladeros*. More than the country, the province became the breadbasket of the world. By 1910, the province was crisscrossed with railway lines radiating from port cities like Buenos Aires, **Bahía Blanca**, **San Nicolás**, and **Zárate**, with important commercial and distribution centers such as Azul, **Campana**, Coronel Suárez, San Pedro, and Tres Arroyos developed in the interior of the province. By the 1930s, some of these cities were beginning to emerge as centers of manufacturing—for example, San Nicolás and Zárate. From the 1930s, road construction and later the development of modern highways overwhelmingly favored the province. A new wave of industrialization in the 1960s ensured that **Avellaneda**, **La Matanza**, and Bahía Blanca and their surrounding districts became significant zones of manufacturing and heavy **industry**. Not all survived the **privatization** of state enterprises in the 1990s and deindustrialization during **economic crises** of the early 21st century. Some of these former centers of manufacturing are now among the most deprived in the country, notwithstanding the wealth of the province and a tendency for social indicators to be better than the national average. *See also* AGRICULTURE; BUENOS AYRES & PACIFIC RAILWAY COMPANY (BA&P); BUENOS AYRES & ROSARIO RAILWAY COMPANY (BA& R); BUENOS AYRES WESTERN RAILWAY COMPANY (BAW); ECONOMY; FOREIGN TRADE; INDUSTRY; STATE-OWNED ENTERPRISES (SOEs); TRANSPORTATION.

BUENOS AIRES CENTRAL RAILWAY COMPANY (BAC). Sometimes Buenos Ayres Central Railway Company and Ferrocarril Central de Buenos Aires. *See* ARGENTINE NORTH EASTERN RAILWAY COMPANY (ANE).

BUENOS AIRES HERALD. Originally *Buenos Ayres Herald*, English-language daily published between 1876 and 2017. First owned by a Scottish immigrant, the paper changed hands several times over the decades but was always regarded as the newspaper of the British Argentine community. In addition to covering national and regional economic and political matters, the *Herald*, as it was generally known, devoted much space to community sporting and cultural matters as well as featuring topics of special interest to a British readership—at least until the 1950s, when it began to address subjects that appealed to broader English-speaking expatriate business and commercial interests. The paper was particularly applauded for the fearless publication of information about state terrorism during the **Proceso de Reorganización Nacional**—including the names of those "disappeared" by the regime that came to power with the **military coup of 1976**. It was one of the few newspapers to cover such topics consistently. *La Opinión* had done so until the kidnapping of editor **Jacobo Timerman** and repeated closures by the regime, while *La Prensa* also reported on acts of state violence, despite having supported the coup. It was argued at the time that the *Herald* was able to write about such matters and feature critical articles on the economic policies of the government because it published in English and because of its circulation among the resident foreign business community. This did not prevent the detention of British editor Robert Cox and death threats against his family. The Coxes were compelled to leave the country in 1979. Feature writer Andrew Graham-Yooll was forced into exile when he continued to write about disappearances, torture, and state terror. During the **Falklands War** of 1982, as a "patriotic gesture" many newsstands refused to sell the paper. In 2015, the paper broke the story of the death of state prosecutor **Alberto Nisman**, which caused friction with the government of President **Cristina Fernández de Kirchner**. There were rumors of death threats issued against the journalist who covered the story, and the withdrawal of official advertising compounded the title's financial difficulties. The paper switched from daily to weekly publication in November 2016, months before closure. *See also* DESAPARECIDOS; DIRTY WAR; MARTÍNEZ DE HOZ, JOSÉ ALFREDO (1925–2013); WAR TO ANNIHILATE SUBVERSION.

BUENOS AYRES & PACIFIC RAILWAY COMPANY (BA&P). Sometimes known as the Buenos Aires Pacific Railway and the Ferrocarril Buenos Aires al Pacífico (FCBAP) in Spanish, the BA&P and associated companies formed the principal rail link between the port of **Buenos Aires** and the **Cuyo** region bordering **Chile**. The name derives from the original concession that envisaged a line connecting the eastern and western seaboards of South America, running from Buenos Aires to Valparaíso on the Pacific Ocean. Although never built as planned, at **Mendoza** the broad-gauge network connected with the meter-gauge Transandine Railway, which ran through the **Andes** via the Uspallata Pass and Cumbre Tunnel to Santa Rosa de los Andes in Chile, where it joined the Chilean State Railway.

The Argentine concession was issued in 1872, yet it was another 10 years before the BA&P was registered in London and construction began on the section between Mercedes in the province of Buenos Aires and Villa Mercedes in the province of **San Luis**. At Mercedes, the BA&P connected with the province of Buenos Aires state railway, the Ferrocarril Oeste (FCO). (The FCO would later be sold to the London-registered **Buenos Ayres Western Railway Company** [BAW]) The BA&P had running rights over FCO track to its terminal in Plaza Once. On completion of the first section in 1886, the BA&P applied for a franchise to construct independent access to Buenos Aires. The line to Palermo on the then outskirts of the city center was opened in 1888; it would not be until 1912 that the railhead reached the center of Buenos Aires when the company opened a "temporary" terminus at Retiro.

Between the late 1880s and the early 1920s, the company pursued an aggressive expansion policy, building new lines and incorporating other companies, acquiring in succession the Villa Maria & Rufino Railway Company, the Argentine Great Western Railway Company (AGW), and the Bahia Blanca & North-Western Railway Company (BB&NW). Some of these companies were acquired by share swaps, others by dividend guarantees. For example, the agreement with the AGW guaranteed its shareholders a basic dividend that was above that often paid to BA&P ordinary stockholders. Such arrangements led to a rapid inflation in nominal capitalization and reduced flexibility to respond to **economic crises**. Of the so-called big four British-owned railways—the other three were the **Buenos Ayres Great Southern Railway Company** (BAGS), the BAW, and the **Central Argentine Railway Company** (CAR)—the BA&P had the most inflated capital account, provoking claims that the company had "watered" stock to escape limits on dividend payments.

In 1928, the Argentine minister of public works accused the BA&P, along the other broad-gauge lines, of exceeding prescribed profit limits. An investigation was ordered and the companies threatened with enforced tariff reductions. In 1933, the Pacific was again at the center of a political storm when the chairman of the board claimed that the company was facing unfair competition from state railways. Later in the decade, he charged that the British government was negotiating the sale of British-owned companies to the Argentine authorities behind the backs of shareholders. The administration of President **Agustín P. Justo** was at the time in discussion with the **Cordoba Central Railway** (CCR) for the transfer of the company and announced toward the end of 1936 a willingness to purchase all foreign-owned railways. The shrill stance of the BAP board was due to higher operating costs and a more precarious financial position compared to other major railways.

Rail nationalization came in 1948, when the BA&P formed the core of the newly designated Ferrocarril Nacional General San Martín (FCNGSM), named for General **José de San Martín**, liberator of much of southern South America, becoming part of the state railway system Empresa de Ferrocarriles del Estado Argentino (EFEA), later **Ferrocarriles Argentinos** (FFAA). With **privatization** in the 1990s, a variant of the original company name was reused, Buenos Aires al Pacífico S.A. *See also* ARGENTINE NORTH EASTERN RAILWAY COMPANY (ANE); CONCORDANCIA; ECONOMY; FOREIGN DEBT/FOREIGN INVESTMENT; FOREIGN TRADE; GREAT BRITAIN; STATE-OWNED ENTERPRISES (SOEs); TRANSPORTATION.

BUENOS AYRES & ROSARIO RAILWAY COMPANY (BA&R). One of the former British-owned broad-gauge railways, and one of the most dynamic. The company dates from the 1870s and traces its origin to two distinct firms, the Buenos Ayres Northern (BAN)—sometimes known as the Buenos Ayres & San Fernando—and a concession to build a railway between the city of **Buenos Aires** and **Campana**, intended as a terminal to connect with river ferries serving up-delta ports such as **Rosario**. Access to the center of Buenos Aires would be over BAN tracks. Both the BAN and the Campana were franchised by the province of Buenos Aires, which insisted that the Campana railway establish a junction with the provincially owned Ferrocarril Oeste (FCO). When the line to Campana was inaugurated in 1876, the company applied for a federal concession to build on to Rosario, transferring its assets to the BA&R, which had been registered in London and which had acquired a profit guarantee from the national government. The section to Rosario was completed in 1886, thereby establishing a direct connection between the hitherto separate rail networks centered respectively on the cities of Buenos Aires and Rosario, whereupon the BA&R applied for another concession to construct on to **Tucumán** through the province of **Santa Fe**, agreeing to abandon the federal profit guarantee to gain the concession. This brought the company into competition with the **Central Argentine Railway Company** (CAR), which operated a broad-gauge line between Rosario and the city of **Córdoba**, where it joined the state-owned meter-gauge network that ran to Tucumán and the northwest. In response, the CAR applied for a concession to build to Buenos Aires and acquired the BAN both to gain access to the city and to constrain the expansion of the BA&R.

Around 1900, the BA&R took over various meter-gauge routes and extended others, becoming the second largest network in the country after the **Buenos Ayres Great Southern Railway Company** (BAGS), and broke the stranglehold of the CAR on traffic to and from the northwest. Competition between the BA&R and the CAR was particularly damaging to the latter. Discussion about rationalization gave way to amalgamation negotiations, which resulted in a takeover by the BA&R. This required government approval, one of the conditions of which was that the merged company should retain the name of the historic line. The new CAR became the largest rail network in the country and remained so until rail nationalization in 1948, when the line was renamed the Ferrocarril Nacional General Bartolomé Mitre.

The significance of the BAR derives from the fact that it integrated what had been two separate rail networks, that it was prepared to embark on a large rail construction program without a state profit guarantee, and because rivalry between it and the CAR demonstrated that there was often competition among British Argentine railways—and not always the collusion argued by nationalists. *See also* ARGENTINE NORTH EASTERN RAILWAY COMPANY (ANE); BUENOS AYRES & PACIFIC RAILWAY COMPANY (BA&P); BUENOS AYRES WESTERN RAILWAY COMPANY (BAW); CORDOBA CENTRAL RAILWAY COMPANY (CCR); ECONOMY; FERROCARRILES ARGENTINOS (FFAA); FOREIGN DEBT/ FOREIGN INVESTMENT; FOREIGN TRADE; GREAT BRITAIN; PRIVATIZATION; STATE-OWNED ENTERPRISES (SOEs); TRANSPORTATION.

BUENOS AYRES GREAT SOUTHERN RAILWAY COMPANY (BAGS). The premier British-owned railway—a blue-chip company. The concession was published by the province of **Buenos Aires** in 1862; construction started two years later. The contract required that the line be built to the same gauge as the then provincially owned Ferrocarril Oeste (FCO). The BAGS was organized by a group of *estancieros* and resident merchants, who took the project to London, where the enterprise was registered. Like many contemporary railways, the company enjoyed a profit guarantee from the province. The company abandoned the guarantee in 1870, the first railway to do so.

In the early years, there was significant local investment in the line. This proportion was diluted as equity was raised in **Great Britain**, yet until the 1890s the business was largely managed by local groups, notably "British" landed and commercial interests, many of whom are commemorated in the names of railway stations. Local engagement ensured good political cover and ability to identify economic opportunity. The network expanded steadily across the south and west of the province as new territory was incorporated with the **Conquest of the Desert**. In part, network growth was driven by competition with the FCO, which was also pushing railheads west. In 1884, the main line reached **Bahía Blanca**, soon to be a major port in the southwest of the province. With other Pampean towns like Chascomús, Azul, Dolores, Maipú, Ayacucho, Olavarría, and Tandil already served by the company, the BAGS operated the largest network in the country. By the early 20th century, lines were being pushed farther across the **pampas** and into northern **Patagonia**. In addition to handling a rising volume of freight traffic—mainly **grains**, **wool**, and cattle—the company was also developing substantial long-distance and commuter passenger traffic as well as seasonal holiday traffic to such resorts as Mar del Plata, Miramar, and Necochea. The main commuter stations were Banfield, **La Plata**, Lomas, and Temperley.

To cope with growth in freight and passenger traffic, the main workshops and repair facilities were modernized in 1901. At the time, they were the largest in Latin America and constituted the biggest integrated manufacturing complex in the country and probably the continent. Sections of the line out of the main Buenos Aires terminus at Constitución were quadrupled and busy long-distance routes doubled. Commuter services were dieselized to improve speed and frequency. Investment in permanent way improvement also included bridge replacement and the construction of branches, passing loops, "high-speed" crossovers, and signaling. Around 1900, minor London-registered companies were incorporated in the network, but the major acquisition was in 1925 with the purchase of the Bahia Blanca North Western Railway Company from the **Buenos Ayres & Pacific Railway Company** (BA&P). This ensured that BAGS would remain by far the biggest network in Argentina. Following the acquisition, the BAGS network totaled more than 4,450 route miles; the **Central Argentine Railway Company** (CAR) network 3,300; the BA&P 2,650; **Buenos Ayres Western Railway Company** 1,880. At **nationalization** in 1948, the BAGS network was in excess of 5,000 route miles.

In the 1920s, there was further growth, diversification, and innovation. Passenger traffic represented about a quarter of gross revenue, and the operation of dockyards, tramways, grain elevators, and hotels generated additional revenue streams—the company claimed that as much as 15 percent of net revenue derived from activities not directly related to railway operations. With traditional freight under pressure, like many other premier railways the BAGS invested in agricultural research stations to encourage farmers to plant pedigree grains and experiment with new crops. Unusually, in the 1930s, the BAGS was exploring the possibility of developing industrial parks to encourage yet other new lines of business. The BAGS sought to project the image of a modern, dynamic corporation that was efficient and contributed greatly to the national economy, mainly due to its freight and passenger services, but also as an employer of a workforce in excess of 30,000 and the industrial scale of plants and workshops. Yet commuter revenues were threatened by the expanding bus system and freight income squeezed by rising operating costs, including wages, and road competition. With nationalization, the company was renamed the Ferrocarril Nacional General Roca (FCNGR) after the hero of the desert campaign and twice president of the republic **Julio A. Roca**. The BAGS accounted for by far the greater part of the FCNGR, the other components being the formerly French-owned Rosario–Puerto Belgrano railway and the state-owned broad-gauge Patagonia system, parts of which had been operated by the BAGS. *See also* ARGENTINE NORTH EASTERN RAILWAY COMPANY (ANE); *COLECTIVOS*; CONCORDANCIA; CORDOBA CENTRAL RAILWAY COMPANY (CCR); ECONOMIC CRISES; ECONOMY; FERROCARRILES ARGENTINOS (FFAA); FOREIGN DEBT/FOREIGN INVESTMENT; FOREIGN TRADE; PRIVATIZATION; STATE-OWNED ENTERPRISES (SOEs); TRANSPORTATION.

BUENOS AYRES WESTERN RAILWAY COMPANY (BAW). The line incorporated the first railway launched in the country, the Sociedad Anónima Camino Ferrocarril al Oeste, also known as the Ferocarril Oeste (FCO). Inaugurated in 1857 with much pomp and circumstance, including the blessing of the locomotive *La Porteña* by the bishop of **Buenos Aires**, the FCO was franchised as a private firm by the province of Buenos Aires at a time when the province had separated from the **Argentine Confederation**.

As the pioneer railway, the FCO established what was to become the "national" gauge for many of the broad-gauge railways of the **pampas**—5 feet, 6 inches (1.676 m). The province had taken an early stake in the line, and when further loans were requested in 1862, the government bought out private shareholders. Over the next couple of decades, the line was operated by the province: the network expanded, and the company initially maintained a reputation for effective management and efficient services. In 1868, it was proposed that the line should be built to the frontier with **Chile**. The railway sometimes served as security for provincial loans, and funds were borrowed overseas to extend the network. By 1889, the FCO operated the second largest railway in the country—the **Buenos Ayres Great Southern Railway Company** (BAGS) was larger. During the boom of the 1880s, the reputation of the administration began to slip; new routes were determined as much by politics as economics. The enterprise—and the province—was caught by the **Baring Crisis**. To settle outstanding liabilities, the line was sold to the BAW, which had been registered in London. The new company assumed responsibility for provincial debts secured on the railway. Part of the network was sold to established London companies. The **Central Argentine Railway Company** (CAR) acquired the largest chunk of former FCO track, with the BAGS another sizeable portion, and there were other minor disposals. The result was that the BAW operated barely one-half the former FCO network. What London companies saw as rationalization, local interests viewed as a carve up designed to limit competition. Sandwiched between the **Buenos Ayres & Pacific Railway Company** (BA&P) and the BAGS, the BAW gradually extended its network through the center-west of the province, opening fertile new land to pasture and cereal production. Its rails crossed some of the best land in the country. The network was dense and integrated. By the 1920s, the company was profitable and innovative: the main commuter line was electrified and linked into the underground railway, Subterráneo de Buenos Aires (Subte); a tunnel was constructed to give direct access to the main docks and grain elevators built in the port and at principal up-country stations. Closely associated with the BAGS, when financial conditions deteriorated during the 1930s, there was discussion about integrating the operations of the two companies. Nothing came of the project—which was opposed by the governing **Concordancia**. The separate identity of the line was preserved at **nationalization** in 1948 when it became the Ferrocarril Nacional Domingo Sarmiento, named for the statesman-president. The entity now operates as the Ferrocarril Domingo Faustino Sarmiento. *See also* ARGENTINE NORTH EASTERN RAILWAY COMPANY (ANE); *COLECTIVOS*; ECONOMIC CRISES; ECONOMY; FERROCARRILES ARGENTINOS (FFAA); FOREIGN DEBT/FOREIGN INVESTMENT; FOREIGN TRADE; GREAT BRITAIN; PRIVATIZATION; SARMIENTO, DOMINGO FAUSTINO (1811–1888); STATE-OWNED ENTERPRISES (SOEs); TRANSPORTATION.

BULLRICH, ESTEBAN JOSÉ (1969–). Politician and sometimes minister and federal deputy, descendant of the aristocratic Bullrich family, second cousin of **Patricia Bullrich**. He served as President **Mauricio Macri**'s first minister of **education** from 2015 to 2017, having held the same portfolio in the city of **Buenos Aires** government from between 2010 and 2015—a position to which he had also been appointed by Macri. Bullrich was a member of the political party **Recrear para el Crecimiento** (commonly Recrear), of which he was elected head in 2008, displacing **Ricardo López Murphy**, having previously led the youth wing of the party. He was elected several times to the federal Chamber of Deputies with the support of Macri's party, **Propuesta Republicana** (PRO). Trained in information technology in Argentina and management at the Kellogg School of Management in the **United States**, Bullrich has been a strong advocate of making computers widely available in schools and colleges. His achievements as a minister were mixed, and he has been accused of using public office to further party political objectives, and of sometimes failing to differentiate with sufficient care between his public role and private business initiatives. He is a young, ambitious politician. *See also* MINISTRY OF EDUCATION.

BULLRICH, PATRICIA (1956–). Depending on source, a center-right or right-of-center politician; one of the first **women** to hold high ministerial office. Her political affiliations have changed considerably over time. A member of a traditional family, in her student days she was associated with the youth wing of the Peronist party—**Juventud Peronista**—and, allegedly, closely involved with the left-wing **Montoneros**, especially **Rodolfo Galimberti**, whom her sister had married. Later a senior official in the **Partido Justicialista** (PJ), she was elected to the national Chamber of Deputies in 1993. By the end of the decade, she had broken with Peronism. She was an active member of the renewalist branch of the PJ that was attempting to democratize and modernize it. When the project failed, she left in disgust and created the right-of-center grouping that ultimately joined the coalition that brought to power the **Alianza** administration headed by President **Fernando de la Rúa** of the **Unión Cívica Radical** (UCR). She served successively as minister of labor and minister of social security in the ill-fated De la Rúa government, leaving office when the president resigned during the economic and political crisis at the end of 2001. Following the collapse of the De la Rúa government, she founded Unión por la Libertad (Union for Liberty), in effect the city **Buenos Aires** branch of **Recrear para el Crecimiento**, the political party set up by **Ricardo López Murphy**. In 2007, she led her political grouping into the **Coalición Cívica**, joining forces with **Elisa Carrió** of the **Afirmación para una República Igualitaria** (ARI)—again being elected to the Chamber of Deputies for her new party in the **congressional** and **presidential elections of 2007**. (The two women would later fall out.) In the **congressional** and **presidential elections of 2015**, she was close-ly associated with the center-right **Mauricio Macri**. When Macri was elected president, she was rewarded with the security portfolio. Bullrich's political journey is not untypical of many radical intellectuals of the 1970s, while the groupings and parties that she has been associated with, or formed, highlight the fluidity of party structures and party politics in the 21st century. Bullrich is a controversial figure, not only for the ideological flexibility or indepen-dence of mind that she has manifested, but also for appointing close rela-tions—including her son—to positions in the ministries she has headed. There have also been accusations that branches of the security services, which fall within her area of ministerial responsibility, have used excessive force—and that Bullrich should be held to account. Given the recent history of the country, notably the **Proceso de Reorganización Nacional**, this is a sensitive issue. *See also* MINISTRY OF LABOR; MINISTRY OF SECUR-ITY; MINISTRY OF SOCIAL DEVELOPMENT; MOVIMIENTO RE-NOVADOR PERONISTA (MRP).

BUNGE & BORN. Argentine multinational corporation that during the 20th century was considered the most powerful and influential in the country. Created by Ernst Bunge and Jorge Born in 1884, the company had a focus on cereal exports and estate ownership—the initial landholding was a 60,000-hectare rural property. In 1897, two European immigrants, Jorge Oster and Alfredo Hirsch, joined the partnership. Oster specialized in grain commer-cialization; Hirsch had a key role in the industrial diversification of the group. In 1899, Bunge & Born acquired a metallurgical workshop, which became the firm Centenera and the main producer of tinplate for food can-ning. This encouraged the group to diversify into processing its main prod-uct, wheat, and install a flour mill under the name of **Molinos Río de la Plata**. The enterprise conquered the Argentine market by purchasing wheat at high prices and selling the cheapest flour, which ruined small- and me-dium-scale rivals, thereafter diversifying into **Uruguay** and **Brazil**, where new mills were set up—in Brazil the firm was also engaged in cotton produc-tion.

Economic difficulties caused by the First World War, and later the world depression, led to further diversification. In the 1920s and 1930s, La Fabril was established to process raw cotton; Grafa to manufacture textiles; Alba to enter the market for paint; and Compañía Química, specializing in the pro-duction of household chemicals and cleaning products. In effect, several of these firms processed by-products deriving from the main cereal business, while Molinos itself became the vehicle to dominate food processing. Moli-nos first expanded into sunflower, rice, **yerba mate**, and vegetable oils. After the Second World War, it entered the production of branded foodstuffs with more aggregate value, some of which became household names. Expansion by Molinos would continue throughout the second half of the 20th century, to the point that it controlled 44 food-producing firms by the 1980s.

Bunge & Born entered a period of upheaval starting in the 1970s. The first shock would be the **kidnapping of the Born brothers** carried out by the **Montoneros** in 1974. It created great strain for the group, not least because the release of the brothers only took place the following year at a cost of 60 million US dollars—the highest ransom ever paid. Bunge & Born then moved its headquarters to São Paulo, the economic powerhouse of Brazil, and also expanded its activities into countries such as Australia. The group faced many difficulties in the 1990s, ranging from disputes among the key shareholding families to production problems in its many firms, which resulted in a major restructuring.

The Bermuda-registered holding company Bunge International was established in 1994. Bunge & Born only retained that name in Argentina, and in 1998 divested itself of food processing in order to concentrate on its activities in the world grain market. *See also* AGRICULTURE; BORN BROTHERS, KIDNAPPING OF THE (1974–1975); COMMODITIES; ECONOMIC CRISES; ECONOMY; FOREIGN TRADE; GRAINS; INDUSTRY.

BUSTILLO, ALEJANDRO (1889–1982). Prominent architect responsible for major private buildings and national landmarks. His first professional experience was work on *estancia* residences, the best known of these being the *estancia* "La Primavera" in the province of **Neuquén**, constructed in 1918.

Bustillo was subsequently commissioned to undertake key public projects. His most famous included several in the city of **Buenos Aires**, for example, the headquarters of the **Banco Tornquist** (1927–1929), the remodeling of the Palais de Glace (1931), the conversion of a pumping station into the Museo Nacional de Bellas Artes (1932), and the massive headquarters of the **Banco de la Nación Argentina** (1944–1955). Outside the capital, he designed the Hotel Llao Llao (1935–1939) in the Parque Nacional Nahuel Huapi in the province of **Río Negro**; the Hotel Provincial, Casino, and La Rambla (1937–1939) in the seaside resort of Mar del Plata; and the Monumento a la Bandera (1957) in the city of **Rosario**.

C

CABECITA NEGRA. Term of racial abuse that became current after the 1950s, applied partly to internal migrants from the north and northwest of the country, though mainly to immigrants from **Bolivia**, **Paraguay**, **Peru**, and **Chile**, moving to large cities of the **Littoral**, especially **Buenos Aires**, in search of jobs and better conditions. Between the 1850s and 1950s, massive **immigration** from Europe had transformed the country. After the mid-20th century, as the number of immigrants from Europe declined, the balance of migrant flows shifted to people arriving from neighboring republics. Such new immigrants were seen as depressing the wages of unionized formal-sector workers, leading to the expansion of the informal sector and slums and shanty towns—*villas miseria* or *villas de emergencia*—and political cannon fodder for populist regimes. Meaning "little blackhead," the term alluded to the ethnicity of these migrants—relatively small stature, black hair, and dark appearance. It has similar connotations to the *n* word in the **United States**, *Paki* in Great Britain, or *islander* in Australia and New Zealand.

CABEZAS AFFAIR. A notorious case of crime, **corruption**, and politics. José Luis Cabezas (1961–1997), a photojournalist working for the highly regarded weekly current affairs magazine *Noticias*, was found murdered on 25 January 1997. Cabezas's body was discovered on the beach at Pinamar, an exclusive resort on the coast of the province of **Buenos Aires**.

The case had implications for the then governor of the province, **Eduardo Duhalde**, and sitting president **Carlos Saúl Menem**. Duhalde's presidential ambitions had been frustrated in 1994 when Menem had secured a change in the constitution that allowed him to stand for a consecutive term; Menem was known to harbor a desire to secure a third term, something that might have required further constitutional amendment. Cabezas had been investigating the activities of gangs operating in coastal resorts, involved in organized crime and money laundering—activities connected with **Alfredo Yabrán**, a businessman close to Menem. Cabezas had taken a photograph of publicity-shy Yabrán and some of his henchmen. The corpse was found badly burnt in Cabezas's hired car. Court documents revealed that he had been handcuffed, badly beaten, and shot through the head before being set alight. When the police were called to the scene of the crime, observers formed the opinion that the officers were more intent on destroying evidence than gathering material that might identify the killer or killers, action that was entirely consistent with the reputation of the Buenos Aires provincial police as corrupt and in the pay of the gangs. For journalists, the murder represented an attack on the freedom of the press, which chimed with the public at large and the prevailing sense of impunity enjoyed by figures close to the regime. Aware of the potential damage to his presidential ambitions, Duhalde demanded that the police deliver results that would secure a conviction.

Two investigations developed in parallel, one into the murder of Cabezas, another into Yabrán. As these investigations proceeded, *Noticias* published a series of articles about provincial police practices, depicted as inefficient, violent, and corrupt, detailing involvement in prostitution, drug trafficking, and unlicensed gambling. There were also exposés of the involvement of Buenos Aires police officials in the death squads of the 1970s. When a police officer and some police informants were taken into custody, they were seen as scapegoats whose arrest was designed to deflect attention from the force and from Duhalde. Investigations into Yabrán revealed that a number of journalists who had attempted to run stories on his business activities had been threatened and attacked, and that Yabrán frequently boasted of his connections with the government and had used strong-arm tactics against commercial competitors. The trial came to court in February 2000; eight members of the Los Horneros gang were charged, several of whom were serving uniformed and plain-clothes police officers. Court proceedings detailed contacts between gang members and the provincial and federal administrations. All eight were convicted, though most were released before completing their sentences or had sentences commuted to house arrest, mainly on grounds of ill health, remission, and other technicalities, some going on to find employment with private security firms; one died in prison. The affair and legal investigations leading to the trial damaged both Duhalde and Menem politically, and probably contributed to the victory of the **Alianza** in the **presidential election of 1999**.

CABILDO. The town council, *cabildo*, was the principal institution of local government in colonial Spanish America and the only part of the administration to which local-born white males (of appropriate status) had access. *Cabildos* held legal, administrative, economic, and military power within their respective urban jurisdictions. They were responsible for administering local justice, policing the streets, maintaining order, and enforcing market standards and prices. Over time, they became the principal interface between local elites and the imperial bureaucracy. The *cabildo* of **Buenos Aires** rapidly gained moral and political authority in the backwater empire, located close to the Indian frontier. As such, matters of local defense and economic and political organization were exercised by the council, usually composed of about half a dozen councilors and one or two mayors or magistrates. Local influence in the *cabildo* was somewhat reduced with the creation of the **Viceroyalty of the River Plate** in 1776 when Buenos Aires was declared the viceregal capital and the cohort of Spanish administrative and military officials mushroomed, though the status of the Buenos Aires council as primus inter pares increased vis-à-vis *cabildos* of the interior.

CABILDO ABIERTO. As primus inter pares, the *cabildo* of **Buenos Aires** assumed particular prominence during the **independence** period, first coordinating resistance to the **British invasions** of 1806 and 1807 and later serving as a focus for debates about the future organization of the republic. Such functions often entailed the calling of a *cabildo abierto*, a town hall meeting to which prominent figures were invited to deliberate policy.

A *cabildo abierto* was called in 1806 to deal with the first British invasion, which ultimately acclaimed **Santiago de Liniers**, the hero of the hour, viceroy, a move subsequently recognized by Madrid. The *cabildo* became a center of patriotic and revolutionary fervor, and also a place where interests loyal to Spain retained a voice. When news of the French invasion of **Spain**, and the deposition of the Bourbon monarchy reached Buenos Aires, the *cabildo* met to determine the local response and consider the position of the colony. Buenos Aires accepted the viceroy, **Baltasar Hidalgo de Cisneros**, dispatched in 1809 by the Patriotic Junta formed in Seville to organize resistance to the French. Various options were being considered by contending groups in the **River Plate**: declaration of fealty to the deposed Bourbons; the establishment of an independent monarchy headed by a Bourbon prince or princess (the sister of Ferdinand VII, married to the heir to the Portuguese throne was already in Rio de Janeiro, to which the Portuguese court had fled); independence, though this was not explicitly mooted. The situation changed when, in May 1810, news arrived that French forces had taken Seville. There was now no legitimate government in Spain. Viceregal officials and Spanish merchants argued that the status quo should be maintained until the situation in Spain stabilized—anticipating a restoration of the Bourbons. Others, especially those favoring a looser relationship with Spain and the ending of colonial restrictions on trade and the participation of local interests in the administration, argued that with the collapse of legitimate government, sovereignty reverted to the people.

Cisneros was prevailed upon to call a *cabildo abierto*. Resistant at first, he agreed to call an open meeting on 22 May 1810. This was the most famous *cabildo abierto* in the history of the city and led directly to the **May Revolution of 1810**. Some 450 invitations were sent to notables, including landowners, merchants, naval and military officers, and senior clerics. Those favoring the status quo were in a minority, but a compromise was hammered out on 24 May whereby a small junta would be formed headed by Cisneros. Submitted to popular consideration on 25 May, the compromise was rejected and a national junta consisting entirely of local interests was acclaimed. According to differing accounts, Cisneros resigned or was deposed, and rule from Spain effectively ended. Popular decisions endorsed by the *cabildo abierto* on 25 May 1810 set the country on the path to independence. Some 11 years later, by which time independence had been more or less secured, the Buenos Aires *cabildo* was abolished as an institution of government by **Bernardino Rivadavia**, then minister of interior of the province of Buenos Aires.

CACCIATORE, OSVALDO (1924–2007). Air force brigadier and de facto mayor of the city of **Buenos Aires** during the **Proceso de Reorganización Nacional** (1976–1982); he was able to pursue reforms to the character of the city without opposition. When Cacciatore took the helm, Argentina was preparing to host the football World Cup in 1978 and two stadiums were made available in Buenos Aires for scheduled matches. However, the city suffered from two major logistical problems. First, the rapid growth in road traffic after the 1950s, reaching 1,500,000 vehicles daily in 1976, had not been met by appropriate infrastructure improvements. Secondly, unrelenting migrant flows from northern Argentina, **Bolivia**, and **Paraguay** had resulted in the mushrooming of more than 30 *villas miseria*. These shantytowns, with varying degrees of squalor and illegally built on derelict land, were believed to house 200,000 people or 6 percent of the city's population in 1976.

Cacciatore moved quickly to deal with these problems, with no regard to the economic or social costs. He executed plans that dated from the beginning of the 20th century to widen stretches of the streets Independencia, San Juan, Juan de Garay, Jujuy, Brasil, and Caseros and turn them into avenues. The mayor then announced a controversial Plan de Autopistas Urbanas in 1977, which foresaw the eventual construction of nine city freeways and improvements to existing roads. Properties along the proposed routes were expropriated, with credits for rehousing provided for the owners and the use of force applied against those who refused to cede their properties. The construction of the first two freeways, which cost 1,000 million US dollars of **foreign debt** guaranteed by the National Treasury, began in 1978 and was completed in 1980. They were the only ones completed during the tenure of Cacciatore, and to this day operate as toll roads. In later decades, three more sections of projected freeways were completed—but it is a far cry from the original project.

Cacciatore also tried to change the face of Buenos Aires by eradicating the *villas miseria* in areas near the stadiums hosting the World Cup and where such settlements were not tolerated. The plan was to relocate them in Greater

Buenos Aires, mainly in the district of **La Matanza**—legally, slum clearance could not begin until suitable housing had been arranged for those affected. Between late 1977 and early 1978, the Villa de Bajo Belgrano was removed from the vicinity of one of the stadiums and nearby parks. This was followed by the virtual elimination of the Villa 31 near the Retiro railway terminus and the beginning of the destruction of the Villa de Bajo Flores—the largest illegal settlement in the city—in 1979. In December of that year, a court of appeals issued an injunction against further removals as many *villa* inhabitants were unwilling to relocate, which had led to violence and numerous injuries and deaths, and the eradications did not comply with the legal requirement of providing alternative accommodation—and there had been scant regard for the **human rights** of residents. In the long term, the removals of *villas miseria* did not work. The Villa de Bajo Belgrano was permanently eradicated, but in time Villa 31 and Villa de Bajo Flores reemerged bigger than ever in their original locations; moreover, new *villas* continue to spring up in the city.

Largely remembered for his *autopistas* project and the eradication of the *villas* plan, Cacciatore also built numerous parks and launched the Plan 60 Escuelas. Although the latter only managed to complete 24 schools by the end of the mayor's tenure, it is noteworthy because it was the last plan to build primary schools in Buenos Aires. He resigned after a huge march and protests against the ruling dictatorship organized by the **trade unions** and **political parties** on the eve of the **Falklands War**. *See also* DIRTY WAR; GALTIERI, LEOPOLDO FORTUNATO (1926–2003); IMMIGRATION; INDUSTRY; MILITARY COUP OF 1976; TRANSPORTATION; WAR TO ANNIHILATE SUBVERSION.

CAFIERO, ANTONIO FRANCISCO (1922–2014). Prominent Peronist politician and a graduate of the **University of Buenos Aires**, first reading accountancy in 1944 and then becoming a doctor in economic sciences in 1948. Cafiero was first active in the Peronist movement in October 1945, participating in protests against the **military** for arresting **Juan Domingo Perón** in a futile attempt to contain Perón's political ambitions. One of the few student leaders to back Perón, he began his political career thanks to the support of **Eva Perón**, who valued his capacity for work. Cafiero went on to hold several posts in the Foreign Ministry between 1948 and 1951 and then served as minister of **foreign trade** from 1952 to 1955. In the period extending from the **military coup of 1955** until 1972, he was an active militant in the "Peronist resistance" against both military and civilian governments. After the Peronists won the general elections of 1973, he was appointed secretary of trade.

During the presidency of **Isabel Perón**, Cafiero was first interventor in the province of **Mendoza** from August 1974 to May 1975 and then served as minister of economy between August 1975 and February 1976. His appointment to the latter post was supported by the **Confederación General del Trabajo** and its political arm, the 62 Organizaciones. Together with **Alfredo Gómez Morales**, Cafiero gained a reputation as one of the chief economists of the **Partido Justicialista** (PJ). He grappled with the aftermath of the **Rodrigazo**, having to contain the spiraling inflation without affecting the unions' interests and secure external lines of credit overseas. He had few options to tackle these problems, even though he brought to the ministry a technical team that included **Guido Di Tella**, **Javier Villanueva**, and **Juan Vital Sourrouille**, all of whom had experience in the **Consejo Nacional de Desarrollo** (CONADE) and would feature prominently in the **Ministry of Economy**.

Cafiero confronted the inflationary spiral with a general and gradual indexation of wages, prices, and the exchange rate. But periodic corrections of the official US dollar exchange rate, price adjustments, and salary compensations only served to dictate the pace at which the inflation rate increased. In contrast, he had some success in securing external lines of credit. As the state of public finances prevented the country from meeting its international obligations, he had urgent negotiations with the International Monetary Fund and private foreign banks and managed to obtain a modest but crucial amount of short-term loans. But these were holding policies, unlikely to succeed in the long term; Cafiero knew that he had to take much harsher action. But he was opposed by Mrs. Perón and the unions; he was dismissed and replaced by **Emilio Mondelli** one month before the **military coup of 1976**.

Following the return of democracy in 1983, Cafiero served as president of the PJ from 1985 until 1990 while having an active political career. He represented the province of **Buenos Aires** in a number of capacities: as a national deputy between 1985 and 1987, as governor from 1987 to 1991, and as a member of the convention that crafted the **Constitution of 1994**. Finally, Cafiero was national senator for Buenos Aires from 1993 to 2005, except for a brief interruption when he served as cabinet chief (aka prime minister) in the two-day presidency of **Eduardo Camaño** during the economic and political collapse of 2001–2002. *See also* CONGRESS; CURRENCY; ECONOMIC CRISES; ECONOMY; MINISTRY OF FOREIGN RELATIONS AND RELIGION; MOVIMIENTO RENOVADOR PERONISTA (MRP); TRADE UNIONS.

CAHEN D'ANVERS, MÓNICA (1934–). A highly respected journalist and television news anchor, the daughter of the French aristocrat Louis Cahen d'Anvers, who held the title of count and whose family had founded numerous banks, such as the Banque de Paris et des Pays-Bas (now Paribas). The bank financed several infrastructure projects and industrial enterprises in Argentina around the First World War. The journalistic career of Cahen d'Anvers is intimately linked with the television station **Canal 13**. Her career started in 1966 when she became one of the presenters of *Telenoche*, the broadcaster's flagship prime-time news program; she remained in that role until 1973. She was awarded her own journalistic show in 1977: *Mónica presenta*, which involved extensive overseas travel, in part to avoid antagonizing the authorities of the **Proceso de Reorganización Nacional**. It began as a weekly broadcast but was such a hit that it was then televised daily. Not only did Cahen d'Anvers interview celebrities, but she directly covered major international events such as the US embassy hostage crisis in Iran. *Mónica presenta* came to an end in 1980. The program had an excellent team of journalists, one of whom was César Maschetti. He became her life partner in 1978, and the pair became the news anchors of *Telenoche* in 1990. Cahen d'Anvers and Maschetti were widely respected for their professionalism, and until 2003 they were the face of the flagship evening news broadcast, which became the most watched in prime time and received a considerable number of awards.

CAJA DE CONVERSIÓN. In English, the (Gold) Conversion Office, responsible for establishing the peso on a gold basis and managing money supply. The office was set up in 1890, following the **Baring Crisis**, and was charged with returning the country to the gold standard, convertibility having been "temporarily suspended" in 1885.

The first national **currency** was created in 1881, early in the presidency of **Julio A. Roca**, when the predecessor of the Caja was formed to determine the gold basis of the peso and accumulate sufficient gold to back the currency. By 1883, when sufficient reserves had been built up, new "gold" paper peso notes were printed and gold peso coins entered into circulation on a one-to-one basis. This arrangement lasted barely two years: the increase in gold stocks failed to match the volume of notes issued. The first task of the Caja after 1890 was to retire paper, an operation backed by a sterling loan floated by the government. Although note supply was gradually reduced, and gold stocks increased, reserves were insufficient to return to gold at the old parity. Thus, in 1899, a new parity was determined. Imaginatively dividing the volume of paper in circulation by Caja reserves, the par value of the gold peso was set at 2.27 paper (m$n). This meant an exchange value of $2.35 m$n to the gold US dollar and $11.23 m$n to the pound sterling.

The new system held until 1914, when convertibility was again suspended. Yet careful management of money supply by the Caja, coupled with substantial trade surpluses, ensured that the paper peso fluctuated close to its historic par value to the gold peso. Indeed, the paper peso appreciated against many foreign currencies. Convertibility, at the old gold–paper parity, was restored in 1927. The Wall Street crash of 1929, and onset of the world crisis, resulted in a hemorrhage of gold, the "temporary" closure of the Conversion Office, and suspension of convertibility. By 1933, any pretense of a return to gold had been abandoned—as in most parts of the world. In 1935, with the creation of the Central Bank (**Banco Central de la República Argentina**— BCRA), the functions and gold reserves of the Caja were transferred to the bank. Symbolic of the new order, the BCRA opened in the old headquarters of the Caja and continued to apply the conservative policies of its predecessor, promoting economic growth and monetary order during the 1930s and Second World War.

The largely orthodox approach of the Caja and the bank, rooted in the chaos of the Baring Crisis, ensured that the country enjoyed a period of remarkable monetary stability during the first half of the 20th century, notwithstanding profound global shocks. Only after 1946, when the bank was nationalized, was there a major policy shift in the direction of **developmentalism**. *See also* CONCORDANCIA; CONVERTIBILITY PLAN; ECONOMIC CRISES; PERÓN, JUAN DOMINGO (1895–1974); PREBISCH, RAÚL (1901–1986); ROCA–RUNCIMAN PACT (1933).

CALVO, CARLOS (1822–1906). International jurist, author, and diplomat; regarded at home as an important figure on the world stage; viewed from Washington, DC, as an irritant and impediment to **United States** hegemony in Latin America; recipient of numerous international awards. Trained in law at the **University of Buenos Aires**, Calvo originally hailed from Montevideo. He spent most of his adult life abroad in the diplomatic service of his adopted country in missions in Berlin, Brussels, Paris, Rome, Vienna, and Washington, DC. He also served as Paraguayan minister in London and Paris before breaking with the then strongman of **Paraguay**, Francisco Solano López, a few years before the outbreak of the **War of the Triple Alliance**.

Calvo published extensively on international law, diplomatic protocol, and international treaties and is best known for the enunciation of the Calvo Doctrine, elaborated in a multivolume study, *Derecho internacional teórico y práctico de Europa y América* (The Theory and Practice of International Law in Europe and the Americas), first published in Paris in 1863. He also produced an 11-volume compendium of diplomatic agreements among the states of Latin America, and a five-volume analysis of revolutions in Latin America—mainly from the perspective of international claims arising from civil conflict. The Calvo Doctrine derives from his study of revolutions and relations among Latin American countries—and the imbalance in power between the fledgling nations of Latin America and European states. It is rooted in two basic premises: that independent states have the right to be free from external interventions, and that nationals and foreigners should enjoy equal right in domestic courts and have equal rights of redress. The main tenets of the doctrine are that domestic courts are sovereign in disputes involving foreign interests (particularly investors and agents making financial claims for the damage and destruction of life and property), and that only when all local forms of redress have been exhausted should claimants appeal to international tribunals. It explicitly prohibits the use of armed force (gunboat diplomacy) in the prosecution of claims. So-called Calvo Clauses have been inserted into agreements made by Latin American governments with foreign consortia and individuals, that is, clauses giving local courts jurisdiction over aliens in host countries. Such clauses often require foreign parties to renounce seeking the diplomatic assistance of their respective home government.

The Calvo Doctrine was later refined by another Argentine lawyer and diplomat, Luis María Drago, sometime minister of foreign relations—the Drago Doctrine. Many modern constitutions in Latin America contain a Calvo Clause. The United States fiercely resisted both the Calvo and Drago Doctrines in Panamerican Conferences and elsewhere, regarding them as limiting its influence and an affront to the Monroe Doctrine. Although the Calvo Doctrine is now a well-established element of legal traditions in Latin America, its principles are far from universally accepted in other jurisdiction—especially due to the accepted practice that no individual can be made to forfeit the right to diplomatic protection. *See also* CUBA; FOREIGN DEBT/FOREIGN INVESTMENT; MINISTRY OF FOREIGN RELATIONS AND RELIGION; SPAIN; VENEZUELA.

CALVO DOCTRINE. *See* CALVO, CARLOS (1822–1906).

CAMAÑO, EDUARDO (1946–). Career politician, member of the **Partido Justicialista** (PJ), and two-day president of the republic at the height of the political and economic crisis that followed the resignation of President **Fernando de la Rúa** on 20 December 2001. Sometime provincial deputy in the **Buenos Aires** legislature and mayor of Quilmes, Camaño was elected to the national Chamber of Deputies in 1991 and returned on four consecutive occasions. He served as president of the chamber from 2001 to 2005. It was in this capacity that he became interim president. When **Ramón Puerta**, president of the National Senate, resigned the presidency for the second time on 30 December 2001, as president of the chamber Camaño was next in the line of succession. His principal achievement was to organize the assembly that elected **Eduardo Duhalde** president on 2 January 2002 to serve out the remainder of De la Rúa's term. Although on the anti-**Kirchner** wing of the party, supporting the candidature of **Roberto Lavagna** in the **presidential election of 2007**, Camaño was appointed minister of interior of the province of Buenos Aires by Governor **Daniel Scioli** in 2009, a post he held for two years before becoming the head of the institutional coordination secretariat of the province. His principal claim to fame is as one of five presidents to have held office between 20 December 2001 and 2 January 2002 following the collapse of the De la Rúa administration. *See also* CONVERTIBILITY PLAN; ECONOMIC CRISES.

CAMBIEMOS. A centrist coalition composed of several **political parties**, some of which are themselves coalitions. Generally translated as "Let's Change" (alternative meaning "We Can Change"), Cambiemos sought to capitalize on the groundswell for political renewal after the 12-year dominance of national politics by the Kirchners, a period that had begun with the presidency of **Néstor Kirchner** in 2003. Formed on the eve of the **congressional** and **presidential elections of 2015**, the grouping signaled recognition by diverse political interests of the need for unity if the administration of **Cristina Fernández de Kirchner** was to be successfully confronted at the polls. The main components of the coalition are **Propuesta Republicana (PRO)**, **Unión Cívica Radical (UCR)**, and **Coalición Cívica (CC)**, headed respectively by **Mauricio Macri**, **Ernesto Sanz**, and **Elisa Carrió**. Following primary elections held in August 2015, Macri emerged as the candidate who would represent the coalition in the **presidential election of 2015**, in which he was ultimately victorious on the November second round, defeating the Kirchner nominee, **Daniel Scioli**, who had topped the polls in the October first round. Described by its opponents as a probusiness grouping, or as a party of the elite, the electoral victory of Cambiemos in 2015 marked the end of the *kirchnerato*. It must hold together to survive. The midterm **congressional elections of October 2017** demonstrated that the party and the administration still enjoyed the support of the electorate. Cambiemos is now looking to the congressional and presidential elections of 2019 to secure a second term for President Macri and its representation in **Congress**.

CAMPANA. Located in the northwest of the province of **Buenos Aires** on the **Paraná** Delta, with the adjacent jurisdiction (*partido*) of **Zárate**, Campana is one of the largest industrial complexes in the province and is developing as a center of modern manufacturing. Both enjoy good regional and national communications, including the federal capital 50 miles (75 kilometers) away.

Although the city and district trace their origins to the 1750s, their modern history dates from the arrival of the railways and mass **immigration** (largely from Italy and Spain) in the 1870s. Today, the district continues to experience rapid population growth, largely due to immigration attracted by new industries. Initially, the **economy** was dominated by **agriculture**—the first meatpacking plant opened at the beginning of the 20th century—but **indus-**

try was always important: the first motor vehicle factory in the republic was set up between 1903 and 1907, while kerosene production began around 1906 at the national oil refinery, which was acquired five years later by Standard Oil. By this time, there were already major railway workshops—in the 1920s, Campana had one of the largest factories for the repair and manufacture of railway equipment in the country. The railway workshops closed in the 1990s. Techint, the Italian–Argentine conglomerate, set up operation in the late 1940s, attracted by the industrialization drive sponsored by president **Juan Domingo Perón**; other metal-working plants followed in the 1950s; the district is now a manufacturing hub for tubes and parts for the energy, motor vehicle, and agro-industry sectors.

Recently, "new" industries have come to the fore. **Bunge & Born** opened an agrochemical plant in 2004. Other important modern industries include an Esso oil refinery, one of the largest and most up to date in the region. Honda inaugurated a factory in 2011, following Toyota, which had opened in Zárate a few years before. Much of the output of these firms is exported. *See also* BUENOS AYRES & ROSARIO RAILWAY COMPANY (BA&R); CENTRAL ARGENTINE RAILWAY COMPANY (CAR); FOREIGN DEBT/ FOREIGN INVESTMENT; FOREIGN TRADE; *FRIGORÍFICOS*; TRANSPORTATION; UNITED STATES OF AMERICA.

CÁMPORA, HÉCTOR JOSÉ (1909–1980). President of Argentina (May–July 1973), known as "El Tío" (uncle) to his inner circle. A dentist from San Andrés de Giles, province of **Buenos Aires**, Cámpora met then minister of labor **Juan Domingo Perón** in 1944. Following the **presidential election of 1946**, Cámpora won a seat in the Chamber of Deputies—he was president of the chamber from 1948 until 1952. He rapidly emerged as a "super loyalist" to the ousted Perón.

In exile in 1971, Perón chose Cámpora as his "personal delegate" in Argentina. The following year, when Perón was prevented by the outgoing **military** regime from contesting the scheduled **presidential election of March 1973**, he appointed Cámpora as the candidate of the **Frente Justicialista de Liberacion** (FREJULI). Although Cámpora won the election, Perón was determined to take charge himself as he was dissatisfied with the leftist stance adopted by Cámpora from the moment he took office on 25 May 1973. Cámpora's inauguration had been marred by serious disorder from guerrilla organizations, whose jailed members were released under a promised amnesty and changes in antisubversion legislation. The government itself was infiltrated by the left, and the cabinet included some people very disagreeable to Perón, most notably Minister of Interior **Esteban Righi**. The country was riven by social conflict, notably, disarray in the universities, strikes, and factory occupations. The FREJULI did not deliver platform promises, other than the amnestying of political prisoners and the establishment of diplomatic relations with **Cuba**, North Vietnam, and North Korea.

Journeying to Madrid as part of the delegation that would accompany Perón for his final return from exile on 20 June 1973, Cámpora was treated with total disdain by the former head of state. Matters only worsened when a rally organized near the international airport of Buenos Aires to welcome Perón turned into carnage. The so-called **Ezeiza Massacre** caused the aircraft bringing Perón to be diverted to a military air base. The day after the Ezeiza Massacre, the decision was taken that Cámpora and Vice President **Vicente Solano Lima** would resign, thus initiating a process that would enable Perón to take power by constitutional means. The resignations were scheduled for 14 July 1973 but were brought forward by one day as Cámpora preferred to jump before being pushed. With the next successor in line (the provisional head of the Senate) conveniently dispatched on a trip abroad, President of the Chamber of Deputies **Raul Lastiri** became interim president, and a new presidential election was called for September 1973.

Cámpora was president for 49 chaotic, bloody days. Following the **military coup of 1976**, he took refuge in the Mexican embassy in Buenos Aires. Three years later, having been diagnosed terminally ill with cancer, he was allowed to fly to Mexico. *See also* LA CÁMPORA.

CANAL 13. Known by its current brand name El Trece, it is a television network whose flagship station of the same name is located in **Buenos Aires**. The channel was tendered to the company Río de la Plata S.A. TV—set up by Cuban immigrant Goar Mestre, the US network CBS, and the Time-Life company—and began broadcasting in October 1960. Editorial Atlántida and Mestre's wife bought the shares of the company in the mid-1960s, and since then Canal 13 began to compete with the other two open private channels— Canal 9 and Canal 11 (present-day Telefe). The government of **Isabel Perón** nationalized all three private broadcasters in 1974. During the **Proceso de Reorganización Nacional**, the administration of Canal 13 was handed over to the Argentine navy, which helped the station in its transition to color broadcasts in 1980. It remained under government ownership after the return of democracy in 1983 and underwent **privatization** in December 1989.

Artear, a company that was part of the multimedia conglomerate owned by the *Clarín* newspaper, officially took over the management of Canal 13. Since then, the station has been a market leader and achieved great ratings. The Clarín Group faced an onslaught from the administration headed by President **Cristina Fernández de Kirchner** and opposed the latter. This was reflected in the often justified negative coverage of the government in the prime-time newscast *Telenoche* and other high-profile journalistic programs broadcast by Canal 13. *See also* CAHEN D'ANVERS, MÓNICA (1934–); LANATA, JORGE (1960–); MEDIA.

CANITROT, ADOLFO PRUDENCIO MARTÍN (1928–2012). An academic economist and policy maker, Adolfo Canitrot was trained in the **University of Buenos Aires**, where he read civil engineering, and at Stanford University in the **United States**, where he obtained a PhD in economics. Best remembered as one of the architects of the **Austral Plan**, along with then minister of economy **Juan Vital Sourroulle**, and head of the Central Bank (**Banco Central de la República Argentina**—BCRA), he served as planning secretary in the presidential office of **Raúl Alfonsín** from 1983 to 1985 and as deputy economics minister between 1985 and 1989. During the **Alianza** administration of President **Fernando de la Rúa**, he was deputy head of the **Banco de la Nación Argentina** and appointed to the board of the national pension agency. He also acted as advisor to the World Bank and to the governments of **Chile** and **Peru** and was a distinguished research professor at such academic organizations as the **Instituto Torcuato Di Tella** and the Centro de Estudios de Estado y Sociedad (CEDES)—a research center partly funded by the Ford Foundation during the bloody military dictatorship of the **Proceso de Reorganización Nacional**. An exponent of **developmentalism**, he is known for his theoretical and empirical contributions about the economics of populism, tariffs and protectionism, income policy and wages, and the labor market.

CAPITAL FEDERAL. *See* FEDERAL CAPITAL.

CAPITANICH, JORGE MILTON (1964). Businessman, academic, and politician who has held various public offices, most notably serving as head of the cabinet of ministers during the second presidency of **Cristina Fernández de Kirchner**. He held this prime ministerial post from 2013 until almost the end of her second administration in 2015.

  Born to a family that originated in the Balkans and had settled in the **Chaco** region, Capitanich studied accountancy, economics, and public administration. He founded several companies specializing in finance and business consultancy. As such, he was involved in bank liquidations and acted as financial advisor to the government of the province of **Formosa**. Among his associates was **Axel Kicillof**, who would later become Cristina Kirchner's economic guru and minister of economy. Capitanich first came to national attention during the turbulent year of 2001 when elected national senator for his native province. He was briefly appointed interim minister of economy by interim president **Ramón Puerta** and then head of the cabinet by interim president **Eduardo Duhalde** at the beginning of 2002. Although he retained the Senate seat, the nomination as chief of the cabinet required that he divest himself of his business assets. It is unclear whether he did so, being subsequently charged with arranging government loans through agencies in which he retained a financial interest.

Described as a loyal *kirchnerista*, he was elected governor of Chaco in 2007 in a closely fought contest, narrowly defeating the sitting **Unión Cívica Radical** (UCR) incumbent who had roundly beaten him in 2003. In 2011, Capitanich was reelected with a very large majority. Scandals continued. As governor, he appointed his wife to head the provincial Heath Department—the couple fell out and divorced after he sacked her—and arranged special pensions for his parents. During his term, the provincial authorities were accused of taking a lax approach to drug smuggling. He was investigated for siphoning funds from housing schemes and creaming off resources from other projects. Capitanich denied all charges of wrongdoing, as he had rebutted earlier complaints, and the scandals did not prevent him from being reappointed to head the cabinet of ministers by Cristina Fernández.

Capitanich was brought in to lead the cabinet after the poor showing of the governing **Frente para la Victoria/Partido Justicialista** (FpV/PJ) in the **congressional elections of 2013**, partly because he had been favored by the president's late husband, former president **Néstor Kirchner**. Kicillof was promoted minister of economy at much the same time; although technically number two at the ministry, he had been the main political force there for some time. The idea was that together Capitanich and Kicillof would work as a team to steady the ship. Around two meters tall, Capitanich appeared to overshadow Kicillof at 2013 press conferences, physically and politically, yet it soon emerged that the boyish Kicillof was the key figure in the administration. Despite their former collaboration, tension soon emerged about the conduct of **economic policy**, though both adapted a pronounced nationalist stance in foreign economic policy—especially continuing negotiations with holders of overseas debt who had not settled in 2005. It was rumored that they were rivals for the attention of Mrs. Kirchner, with whom both were allegedly romantically linked. If the intention had been that they would relaunch the administration, they failed to do so. Kicillof soon adopted a pronouncedly radical approach to rebooting the economy, favoring great government control and statization, while Capitanich appeared to prefer a business-friendly stance.

In and out of government, investigations about the misuse of public funds and **corruption** plagued Capitanich. Despite continuing investigations on charges of corruption and a turbulent relationship with the press, he remains active in political life. Currently mayor of **Resistencia**, provincial capital of Chaco, he is reputed still to have national political ambitions. *See also* ECONOMIC CRISES; LA CÁMPORA; MINISTRY OF ECONOMY.

CAPUTO, DANTE (1943–). Politician and diplomat trained in political science in Argentina, international relations in the **United States**, and sociology in France. Having been associated with **Raúl Alfonsín** since the early 1970s, he was appointed minister of foreign relations by Alfonsín in 1983, exceptionally holding office for almost the whole of the presidency. The terms of his ministerial colleagues were considerably shorter. Before being appointed minister, he had held posts at the Organization of American States (OAS). After stepping down from the ministry, Caputo acted in various capacities at the **United Nations**, serving as president of the General Assembly, heading the UN mission to Haiti, and acting as the special representative of the UN secretary general. He was elected a national deputy, becoming deputy leader of the Foreign Affairs Committee of the Chamber of Deputies. His domestic political ambitions were less successful. A member of the **Unión Cívica Radical** (UCR), he endorsed the **Frente País Solidario** (FREPASO) in the **presidential** and **congressional elections of 1995**, seeking the FREPASO nomination in the 1999 mayoral elections for the city of **Buenos Aires** government—he was knocked out on the first round. However, he became secretary of science and technology under President **Fernando de la Ruá** of the UCR, who headed the ill-fated **Alianza** administration: appointed in 2000, Caputo resigned when the regime collapsed at the end of 2001.

Caputo's greatest achievement as minister of foreign affairs was negotiating the Treaty of Peace and Friendship with **Chile** in 1984 and successfully heading the campaign to have the treaty endorsed in a national referendum. He was honored by the UN for this achievement. He also played a significant role in negotiations with **Brazil** and **Uruguay**, leading to the formation of **MERCOSUR**, the South American Common Market. He was less successful in reaching agreement with **Great Britain** over the **Falkland Islands**—according to some, due to his intransigence, though he has since become more pragmatic. His association with the OAS continues—he has headed electoral observation missions—and he served on several Argentine agencies active in the areas of **human rights** and international relations. *See also* MINISTRY OF FOREIGN RELATIONS AND RELIGION.

CARACAS PACT. Deal concluded between **Arturo Frondizi** and exiled **Juan Domingo Perón** in the run-up to the **presidential election of 1958**. Frondizi needed the Peronist vote in order to win the election; Perón needed an arrangement with a non-Peronist force that would enable him to reorganize his party and the **trade unions**. The pact was negotiated by **Rogelio Julio Frigerio** on behalf of Frondizi and by **John William Cooke** for Perón and carried their four signatures. That of Frondizi was forged, enabling the latter to deny the existence of the deal.

Under the Caracas Pact, Frondizi agreed to normalize the unions and the **Confederación General del Trabajo**, return the property of the **Fundación Eva Perón**, award the Partido Peronista the status of a juridical person, reorganize the Supreme Court, call elections for a constitutional convention, and clear the ground for a new general election. In exchange, Perón offered to create a peaceful climate that was essential for the plan and to keep the deal secret until August 1958. The pact ensured the election of Frondizi as president, but it soon became clear that neither he nor Perón would adhere to its terms. Moreover, there was a financial side to the transaction. Perón received a government stipend through intermediaries, which enabled him to buy his Madrid residence in 1960—by the time the **military coup of 1962** struck, Perón had gained 27 million pesos from the arrangement. *See also* SPAIN.

CARAPINTADAS. The term, which means "painted faces," refers to a series of barrack revolts that occurred in the late 1980s, led by middle-ranking officers wearing camouflage paint on their faces—hence "painted faces"— and dressed in **military** fatigues.

The revolts, usually involving several scores of officers and junior ranks, were not attempted coups, nor dress rehearsals designed to provoke an uprising by the armed forces—though at the time there was concern that this might result. Nominally, the protests were organized to defend the dignity of the forces. Rebels expressed concern that the prosecution of senior members of the de facto governments of the **Proceso de Reorganización Nacional** might spread to lower ranks who were "simply obeying orders." The resignation of the army chief of staff, General José Caridi, along with other senior officers was also demanded on the grounds that they had failed to defend the honor of the army and protect the armed forces from budget cuts imposed by the government.

The first revolts occurred in April 1987 and January 1988, led by Lieutenant Colonel **Aldo Rico**. On both occasions, there were massive, spontaneous peaceful popular protests. Crowds of civilians surrounded the Campo de Mayo base in **Buenos Aires** to remonstrate with the mutineers, and took to the streets of other cities in support of the civilian government of President **Raúl Alfonsín** elected in 1983. Alfonsín demanded an immediate end to the April revolt. Although all the main figures were seized, only two were formally charged, though several senior military figures were forced to retire. The January revolt was more serious, though again provoking popular outrage. After a three-day standoff, 2,000 loyal troops led by Caridi stormed the Monte Caseros camp in the province of **Corrientes**, where Rico was held under house arrest. Short-lived demonstrations in support of Rico took place at bases in **San Juan**, **San Luis**, and **Tucumán**, and there was a three-hour protest by members of the armed forces stationed near the airport in the city of **Buenos Aires**. Around 300 mutineers were arrested.

Another potentially serious revolt occurred in December 1988. Led by Colonel **Mohamed Alí Seineldín**, special forces units seized the Villa Martelli base on the edge of the federal capital. Caridi acted decisively to put down the rebellion. Seineldín and other ringleaders were taken into custody. In October 1989, months after taking office, Alfonsín's successor, **Carlos Saúl Menem**, issued a series of pardons to figures prosecuted for abuses of **human rights** during the Proceso, including in the pardon a number of *carapintadas*. This did not, however, placate Seineldín, who staged a further revolt in December 1990, which resulted in several deaths. Held responsible for the deaths, Seineldín was sentenced to life imprisonment. He was pardoned by President **Eduardo Duhalde** in 2003.

The leaders of the *carapintadas* presented themselves as patriots, nationalists, and heroes of the **Falklands War** who were defending the honor of the country and the military. During the prosecutions of Rico, Seineldín, and their associates, it emerged that many had been active participants in the human rights abuses perpetrated during the Proceso, responsible for murder, torture, and the trafficking of children and property of the **Desaparecidos**— people "disappeared" during the state terrorism of the period. After the revolts, Rico attempted to build a political career for himself, standing in the **presidential election of 1995**. *See also* DIRTY WAR; MILITARY COUP OF 1976; WAR TO ANNIHILATE SUBVERSION.

CARRIÓ, ELISA MARÍA AVELINA "LILITA" (1956–). Lawyer, academic, politician, and prominent public figure. From beauty contest winner—she is a former Miss **Chaco**—to political pinup, Carrió has had a colorful, flamboyant career. Elected to the federal Chamber of Deputies on several occasions, representing her home province and the city of **Buenos Aires**, she has been a consistent champion of **human rights** and transparency in government and unafraid of controversy.

A native of **Resistencia**, the provincial capital, Carrió's career began in the legal office of the Chaco government in 1979. She was rapidly promoted to head the agency. The mid-1980s found her teaching in the law faculty of the **University of Buenos Aires** and an active member of the then governing party, the **Unión Cívica Radical** (UCR), which had surprisingly gained power in the **presidential election of 1983**. In the 1980s and 1990s, she campaigned assiduously for the UCR, representing the party in the lower chamber of **Congress**, becoming a prominent figure in the **Alianza** that gained the presidency for **Fernando de la Rúa** in the **congressional** and **presidential elections of 1999**. When the Alianza began to crumble in 2000 with the resignation of Vice President **Carlos "Chacho" Álvarez**, who left office on learning that De la Rúa had been bribing opposition senators to secure the passage of legislation, Carrió began to distance herself from the UCR. With other like-minded center-left politicians, she formed an ephemeral coalition, Argentinos por una República de Iguales (ARI). The grouping hardly lasted a year before morphing into another coalition using the same acronym, **Afirmación para una República Igualitaria** (ARI), which was composed of many of the same individuals though somewhat further left. The second ARI proved rather more durable as part of yet another coalition, **Coalición Cívica para la Afirmación de una República Igualitaria** (CC-ARI), which formed part of the alliance that delivered the presidency to **Mauricio Macri** in 2015.

Carrió stood as ARI candidate in the **presidential election of 2003**, and for CC-ARI in the **presidential election of 2007**. On the second occasion, she obtained a respectable 23 percent of the vote, though coming a long way behind **Cristina Fernández de Kirchner**, who romped to victory. The disparate performance of different elements of the coalition in the **congressional elections of 2007** held at the same time as the presidential contest caused disagreement within CC-ARI, leading Carrió to reconsider her position. She dithered about whether to run in the **presidential election of 2011**. Changing her mind late in the campaign, she obtained less than 2 percent, coming last of a long list of candidates. So began a journey to the right that saw her moving closer to former associates in the UCR. In 2013, she helped organize the **Frente Amplio UNEN** (FAUNEN)—a progressive social-democratic coalition fiercely opposed to the "ideology" and policies of the *kirchnerato*. Running on the FAUNEN ticket in the midterm **congressional elections of 2013**, Carrió was returned as a deputy for Buenos Aires to Congress. She was reelected in 2017 and sits with the **Cambiemos** bloc. Her term will expire in 2021. During recent years in the chamber, Carrió has been an unstinting critic of the Kirchner years, exposing its **corruption** and malpractices. Her exposure of shortcomings that contributed to the sinking of the submarine **ARA *San Juan*** received much attention and acclaim.

In a relatively long and eventful career, Carrió has made many enemies and several errors of judgment and been criticized for ideological inconsistency and a poor attendance record in Congress. She has, however, been consistent in a commitment to democracy and transparency in political life. *See also* ALIANZA PARA EL TRABAJO, LA JUSTICIA Y LA EDUCACIÓN.

CARTAGENA GROUP. A debtors' cartel, or debtors' club, composed of 11 Latin American countries that campaigned for a more sympathetic response by creditors to the debt/loan crisis of the early 1980s. In June 1984, following unrest in several countries at the imposition of austerity measures proposed by the International Monetary Fund, foreign and finance ministers of the founder countries met in Cartagena, Colombia, to set out a joint approach to institutional and private creditors. In part, the move was a response to expressions of creditor anxiety about "punishing" debtors, given the return to democracy in several debtor countries, and that much of the debt had been run up by authoritarian regimes—as was the Argentine case. By the early 1980s, expressed in terms of the relation of debt service payments to export earning, Argentina was the second most indebted country after **Brazil**.

The crisis derived in part from the scale of borrowing, but the principal drivers were the sharp decline in export earnings and the rise in interest rates, and because much of the borrowing had not been invested productively. After the collapse of the **military** regime of the **Proceso de Reorganización Nacional**, it was discovered that a quarter of the public debt could not be accounted for and that much of the balance had been squandered on the purchase of military equipment. On election, President **Raúl Alfonsín** had anticipated a "democratic dividend" from international banks and international financial agencies. When this was not forthcoming, Argentina became one of the principal forces pressing for collective action by debtors. Little was achieved by the group. Frustration in Argentina at the lack of progress, as well as what was regarded as the intransigence of international financiers, led directly to the launch of the heterodox **Austral Plan** in June 1985. *See also* FOREIGN DEBT/FOREIGN INVESTMENT; FOREIGN TRADE.

CARTONEROS/AS. The term, deriving from the Spanish for cardboard, *cartón*, was coined around 2000, used to describe people who make a precarious living by sorting through rubbish in bins and skips to separate cardboard, paper, plastic, and other recyclable materials. These activities were on the rise in the late 1990s but exploded with the economic crisis of 2001–2002, becoming a pronounced feature of daily life in central districts of the city of **Buenos Aires** and other major urban areas. Initially, *cartoneros* worked individually or in family groups, later as members of cooperatives. Such "institutionalization" of informal rubbish sifting dated from efforts by the Buenos Aires authorities to ban haphazard waste collection in 2002, the provision of a special late-night train (the famous *tren blanco*) from the city center to the main rubbish disposal plant, the 2005 Zero Rubbish ordinance designed to reduce landfill waste disposal, and later "green" campaigns. These measures were accompanied by the provision of receptacles for recycling waste in strategic locations every few blocks and official encouragement of collective action by *cartoneros*. By the second presidency of **Cristina Fernández de Kirchner** (2011–2015), many *cartoneros* had become politically organized. As cooperatives collaborated with private waste disposal companies and the municipal authorities, organization meant a regular (if extremely low) income and a slightly less precarious existence. *See also* CONVERTIBILITY PLAN; DE LA RÚA, FERNANDO (1937–); ECONOMIC CRISES; ECONOMY.

CASA ROSADA. The presidential palace, located on the east side of the Plaza de Mayo, which commemorated the **May Revolution of 1810**, facing the town hall, the **Cabildo**, scene of the meeting that led to **independence**. Established on the site of the colonial fort, the present building dates from the 1880s; it was commissioned by constitutional President **Julio A. Roca** in 1882 and completed in 1884, though not officially inaugurated until 1898. Most recently remodeled for the bicentenary of independence in 2010. The pink color is supposed to represent a fusion of the favors of contending factions of the early independence period: white for the **Unitarians**, red for the **Federalists**. The palace includes several sumptuous reception rooms and offices like the Salón Blanco and Presidential Office (Despacho del Presidente). One of its most famous external features is the balcony from which **Eva Perón** made a final speech to the nation months before her death. Following inauguration, newly elected presidents greet the nation from the balcony. The palace is now used mainly for ceremonial events, as the official residence is the **Quinta de Olivos**, located in the Buenos Aires suburb of the same name. *See also* CABILDO ABIERTO; OLIVOS PACT.

CASTILLO, RAMÓN S. (1873–1944). Argentine vice president (1938–1942), and acting president (1940–1942), and president (1942–1943). An unreconstructed conservative from **Catamarca** province, he entered politics after 1930 and was elected vice president on the **Concordancia** ticket headed by **Roberto M. Ortiz** in the fraudulent **presidential election of 1937**.

Ortiz was forced to take a leave of absence in July 1940, which became permanent and put an end to his efforts to restore democracy. Castillo consolidated his position by resorting to the worst political practices. Elections held in 1940–1941 in the provinces of **Santa Fe, Mendoza**, and most notoriously **Buenos Aires** were marred by all sorts of fraud and violence against the opposition, and the results enabled a kind of political equilibrium in **Congress**. He also got rid of ministers and placed his own men in key posts. Despite the terrible political costs incurred, Castillo carried on regardless. He paid a heavy price: when he nominated Robustiano Patrón Costas to succeed him, he was overthrown. *See also* MILITARY COUP OF 1943.

CATAMARCA (CITY). Capital of the province of the same name, formally San Fernando del Valle de Catamarca, the city was officially chartered in 1683, several decades after other districts had been settled and cities founded.

Dedicated to administration and finance—there is also some **industry**—the city benefits from **tourism**. It has well-preserved colonial architecture and is a place of national pilgrimage (the cult of the Virgin of the Valley dates from the late 17th century). The current population, including the suburbs, exceeds 200,000. *See also* CATAMARCA (PROVINCE).

CATAMARCA (PROVINCE). Located in the northeast, the international frontier with **Chile** marks the western border of the province; from the north to the east to the south, the province is bordered by **Salta, Tucumán, Santiago del Estero, Córdoba**, and **La Rioja**. Incorporated into the Inca Empire in the latter part of the 15th century, the western areas of the region that was to become the province were first settled by Europeans around 1554, as Spanish forces pushed east across the **Andes**. Decades later, further groups of Spaniards pushed south into the region from **Peru**. At this point, in the late 16th century, the region composed part of the Gobernación de Tucumán, a dependency of the Charcas (present-day **Bolivia**) district of the Viceroyalty of Peru. Subsequently incorporated into the new **Viceroyalty of the River Plate**, set up in 1776, as part of the intendency of **San Miguel de Tucumán**, and then the short-lived Republic of Tucumán, Catamarca acceded to the **Argentine Confederation** in 1821, enjoying a great deal of local autonomy, like other founder provinces, promulgating its own constitution in 1823. The decades between the 1820s and 1840s were ones of considerable political upheaval, though the province enjoyed a degree of prosperity—largely self-sufficient, the provincial economy was based on **agriculture** (cotton was an important crop, along with maize and sugarcane) and substantial cottage woolen textile production.

With the arrival of the railway in 1888, domestic textile production declined. The focus of economic activity shifted to agriculture, though the province benefited from the process of **national organization** when schools were established and banks formed, and there was investment in public buildings as well as public services, including irrigation projects. In 1943, the province gained from the suppression of the national territory of **Los Andes**; districts transferred from Los Andes represent about one-third of the province. The modern **economy** is based on mining, particularly precious and nonferrous metals (there are extensive reserves of tin), plus small-scale farming. By regional standards, the province is reasonably prosperous. The total population is approaching 400,000 (2015) and, according to the 2010 national census, has one of the lowest illiteracy rates in the republic, with health statistics equally positive. *See also* CATAMARCA (CITY); CORDOBA CENTRAL RAILWAY COMPANY (CCR); TRANSPORTATION.

CATHOLIC CHURCH. According to data produced by the **Ministry of Foreign Relations and Religion**, the country is around 90 percent Catholic, though less than a quarter of communicants regularly attend religious services.

During the colonial period, the church had a dominant religious presence in the country and provided a wide range of charitable services in such fields as **education**, palliative health care, and poverty relief. Following the **May Revolution of 1810**, there were sharp disagreements within the ruling elite over the degree of influence to be exercised by the religious orders and hierarchy in the new country. Debate intensified when, not wanting to offend **Spain**, the papacy condemned the revolutions for **independence** sweeping across Spanish America.

Although the **Constitution of 1853** ordered the separation of church and state and established religious freedom, it reserved a special place for the Catholic Church: the head of state had to be a Catholic, and the state would provide the church with financial support. Nonetheless, church–state relations in the 19th century were characterized by a series of conflicts over civil marriage, compulsory secular education, and the governmental appointment of religious authorities. In the 1880s, Argentina and the Holy See broke off diplomatic relations over these issues; almost 20 years passed before they were restored. Relations improved during the early 20th century as various conservative administrations worked with the Vatican to create a mutually acceptable relationship. **Buenos Aires** even hosted the International Eucharistic Congress in 1934; the papal legate was Cardinal Eugenio Pacelli, who became Pope Pius XII in 1939.

During the second presidency of **Juan Domingo Perón**, relations with the Catholic Church became confrontational. It was the one institution—arguably the most powerful—that his regime did not control. In addition, the church had considerable influence among sections of the middle class and the rural and urban working class—key social and political groups that Peronism claimed to "represent." Having first been inclined to collaborate with the hierarchy in such areas as education and welfare, Perón determined to reinforce the presence of the government in these fields. Among measures designed to reduce the social and political influence of the Catholic Church, Perón reinforced constitutional provisions establishing the separation of church and state and sponsored divorce legislation. The hierarchy, for its part, organized public demonstrations in support of traditional family values. The confrontation between Perón and the church, coupled with attacks on church property orchestrated by the government, proved an important catalyst for the **military coup of 1955**. For much of the 1950s and the 1960s, **military** administrations granted the Catholic Church a considerable indirect role in education policy. This role would cloud future relations between the Catholic hierarchy and laity and more secularly inclined civilian administrations. Future church–state relations would also be marked by conflict over economic measures implemented by both military and civilian regimes that sections of the religious establishment regarded as exacerbating poverty and inequality.

In 1966, the de facto government of **Juan Carlos Onganía** (through its foreign minister, **Nicanor Costa Méndez**) signed a concordat that attempted to recalibrate church–state relations and formalize the relationship between Argentina and the Holy See. Among other measures, the concordat accepted Vatican control over clerical appointments and oversight of the religious authorities. Following the **military coup of 1966**, the timing of the concordat chimed with the increasingly hard-line stance of the Onganía regime in social and cultural matters. This found expression in an emphasis on "Christian values," the importance of "family" and "morality" in the face of perceived threats to national, traditional values by radical groups on the left, especially the influence of such groups in the arts, the **media**, and the universities.

The ethical record of the church regarding the **Proceso de Reorganización Nacional** is best described as "mixed," owing to ambivalent attitudes toward the **Dirty War** and abuses of **human rights** that were the hallmark of the regime, as was subsequently accepted by Cardinal Archbishop Jorge Mario Bergoglio of **Buenos Aires**, the future **Pope Francis**. Following the restoration of democracy in 1983, President **Raúl Alfonsín** had a difficult relationship with the Vatican. Before 1987, the Civil Code recognized the de facto separation of husband and wife but did not allow remarriage. When the Chamber of Deputies approved a law of divorce in 1986, the church unsuccessfully pressured the National Senate to block it; the legislation was passed in March 1987 shortly before Pope John Paul II was due to visit Argentina. During his stay in the country, his holiness publicly criticized the recently sanctioned divorce bill.

Church–government relations were fraught during the *kirchnerato*. President **Néstor Kirchner** chastised the church as an institution for its record during the Proceso. It was claimed that elements of the hierarchy "sanctified" the regime. Mrs. **Cristina Fernández de Kirchner** was equally critical. It was rumored that she actively pursued such projects as same-sex marriage legislation in 2010 to provoke the religious establishment. This and similar challenges to traditional family values were protested by Bergoglio. He was similarly vocal about economic measures associated with the Kirchner administrations that he saw as leading to an increase in social distress and the confrontational stance of government—he pressed for greater political tolerance and cooperation to deal with problems confronting the country. The current issue generating differences between church and state relate to abortion, which is opposed by the hierarchy and Vatican. Yet public attitudes appear to be changing, arguably meaning that the church is losing the battle to sustain traditional attitudes. For example, while President **Carlos Saúl**

Menem closely followed the Vatican line on abortion and contraception in 1998, current president **Mauricio Macri**, who is a pro-life supporter, has announced that he will not veto an abortion bill presented to **Congress** in 2018 if sanctioned by legislators. *See also* INSTITUTO TORCUATO DI TELLA; RELIGION; REVOLUCIÓN ARGENTINA (1966–1973); UNIVERSIDAD DE TUCUMÁN; UNIVERSITY OF BUENOS AIRES (UBA); UNIVERSITY OF CÓRDOBA (UC).

CATTLE. Livestock production—particularly cattle raising—is the oldest economic activity in the country, and for long was the most important. Cattle were first introduced in the mid-16th century. The open, unfenced **pampas** quickly became home to millions of wild cattle, where animals that had escaped from early settlements multiplied. Until the 1840s, **meat** was a by-product of the hides and tallow trade; within a few decades, the relationship was inverted. Modern ranching dates from the late 19th century when the opening of fertile new territory and the use of barbed wire permitted the introduction of imported European bloodstock and the upgrading of herds. The principal breeds introduced at the time were Shorthorn, Hereford, Aberdeen Angus, and Frisian (Holando-Argentino); recent additions include Brahman and Brahman crossbreeds. The development of high-quality meat production was facilitated first by advances in freezing technology and later chilling, which allowed the export of a valued-added commodity produced in capital-intensive industrial-style *frigoríficos*. The 1888 cattle census recorded the national herd at almost 22,000,000 head; in 1914, the figure was about 26,000,000; in 1930, 32,000,000; in 1947, 41,000,000; in 1960, 43,500,000; in 1974, 55,400,000. From around this time, the size of the herd declined, but it started to increase again toward the end of the century. It reached 49,000,000 in 2001 and 60,000,000 in 2007, when decline set in once again. By 2010, the national herd had fallen to 48,000,000, the lowest level since 1964. Cattle stocks increased once more around 2014 to reach almost 53,400,000 head in 2017.

The reduction in cattle stock in the late 1960s through the 1970s can be attributed to an outbreak of foot-and-mouth disease in **Great Britain** in 1967–1968 that was blamed on Argentina, though it may have originated in **Uruguay**, and to underinvestment in meatpacking facilities. Foot-and-mouth caused a suspension of beef exports. This, and **developmentalist** programs designed to promote domestic manufacturing, discouraged the modernization of *frigoríficos*. Meat was increasingly directed toward the local market, but prices were subject to regulation. Contraction after 2007 was due to export taxes, which increased greatly during the administrations of President **Cristina Fernández de Kirchner**, and the growth in international demand for soya. Pasture was plowed and land switched from a **commodity** that was highly taxed and subject to price control in the home market to one that generated income for landowners and revenue and foreign exchange for the government. A change in the tax regime and official support for the country to recover its place in world meat productions accounts for the recent recovery is the size of the national herd, coupled with a desire to diversify. Now the emphasis is once again on raising high-quality fatstock and adjusting to changing market preferences, such as demand for organic meat. This is resulting in a substantial recapitalization of the cattle and meat-processing sectors. *See also* AGRICULTURE; CONCORDANCIA; CONQUEST OF THE DESERT/DESERT CAMPAIGN; ECONOMY; *ESTANCIA* COMPANIES; FARM PROTESTS; FOREIGN TRADE; GAUCHO; ROCA–RUNCIMAN PACT (1933); *SALADEROS*; SOCIEDAD RURAL ARGENTINA (SRA); TRANSPORTATION; *VAQUERÍAS*.

CAUDILLO. Leader or military strongman. The term originated around the time of **independence** and was applied to charismatic figures who headed irregular forces, often composed of **gauchos**, pampean Indians, free blacks, and *peones*—rural workers dependent on the owners of large estates. Such irregular forces played a large role in the revolutionary wars and civil wars that followed. All caudillos of this period were not necessarily owners of massive *estancias* or leaders of informal guerrilla forces; some were lawyers and urban professionals—but all acquired a reputation for leadership and decisive military action. Sometimes portrayed as heroic champions of the cause of independence or regional autonomy, at other times they are depicted as ruthless, violent, and barbarous. **Domingo Faustino Sarmiento**, sometime national president, educationalist, and philosopher, wrote a particularly scathing account of one such caudillo, **Juan Facundo Quiroga**, castigating **Juan Manuel de Rosas** and **Justo José de Urquiza** in similar mode. **Julio A. Roca** and other decisive military and political leaders of his generation are similarly described as caudillos. By the 1950s, the term was being applied mainly to populist, charismatic leaders like **Juan Domingo Perón**. Later figures such as **Carlos Saúl Menem** and **Eduardo Duhalde** have cultivated an image of strong, popular leadership, with an emphasis on nationalism and authority, resulting in an association with authoritarianism. A more common present-day usage, however, is for a local or regional party boss or **trade union** leader—someone who delivers votes by dispensing largesse and granting favors—and established patron–client relationships, reinforcing the connection with **populism**, clientelism, and the politics of **corruption**. During the interwar period, when Adolf Hitler and Benito Mussolini in Europe were titling themselves *führer* and *duce*, in **Spain** Generalissimo Francisco Franco appropriated the term: his image appeared on coins and in the press with the tag "El Caudillo," something that would have been appreciated by Perón when living in his exile in Madrid.

CAVALLO, DOMINGO FELIPE (1946–).

Academic, statesman, technocrat, and technopol—a technocrat turned politician. Twice minister of economy, first in the **Partido Justicialista** (PJ) government of **Carlos Saúl Menem**, then in the government headed by **Fernando de la Rúa** of the **Unión Cívica Radical** (UCR), Cavallo is sometimes known as "Mingo" and "El Brujo" (The Wizard) due to his economic wizardry as author of the **Convertibility Plan**.

Trained in Argentina and the **United States**—he holds a first degree in public finance from the National University of **Córdoba** and a PhD in economics, and a PhD in economics from Harvard, where he also completed a masters degree—"Mingo" Cavallo held several ministerial and subministerial posts from the late 1960s yet is best known for stints at the Economics Ministry. Active in student politics in the economics faculty at the **University of Córdoba** (UC) while an undergraduate, he first obtained public office as deputy head of the Development Secretariat of the provincial government, serving from 1969 to 1970, around the time of the **Cordobazo**. Later, he ran the provincial bank and was appointed vice minister of the interior in the federal government during the de facto presidency of General **Alejandro Agustín Lanusse**, head of the last administration of the **Revolución Argentina**.

For much of the 1970s, Cavallo was based in the United States, working on his second doctorate about credit and commodity production and teaching courses on macroeconomics, finance, and the economic history of Latin America. This period would inform his subsequent approaches to the economic dilemmas facing Argentina, and his policy solutions to them. He became a vocal critic of the rent-seeking behavior that had emerged during **developmentalist** phases of state-led industrialization marked by fiscal indiscipline, stagflation, and the growth of informality. Yet he was also critical of the monetarist approach of many **military** regimes of the period, including the **Proceso de Reorganización Nacional**, maintaining that conventional solutions to inflation—freezing wages while failing to balance the budget—were doomed to fail. This was a prescient critique of the outcome of policies applied by **José Alfredo Martínez de Hoz**, who headed the **Ministry of Economy** for much of the Proceso period. Martínez de Hoz recognized the logic of the analysis advanced by Cavallo but was unable to curb the profligacy of his masters, who refused to moderate spending on loss-making **state-owned enterprises** run by the armed forces and deal with mushrooming expenditure on military materiel in anticipation of conflict with **Chile** and adventurism in the South Atlantic. While Cavallo despaired of the bloated, kleptocratic state that intervened and centralized—the hallmark of crony capitalism—he advocated the need for a small, efficient, fiscally responsible state, able to act when necessary and strong enough to resist capture. The Cavallo model state was the antithesis of the state that had emerged in Argentina from the 1940s to the 1970s.

Before the return of democracy in 1983, Cavallo was back in Argentina, based at the Fundación Mediterránea in his native Córdoba, which went on to fund the Instituto de Estudios Económicos sobre la Realidad Argentina y América Latina (IEERAL). The think tank became the training ground of a small group of young, highly motivated, technically bright, collegial, internationally orientated economists. The so-called Cavallo boys were messianic in their enthusiasm and zeal, confident of their ability to transform the country. This cadre of shock troops would accompany Cavallo on his mission. The mission statement, *Volver a crecer*, an accessible short book, was published in 1984, the title becoming the slogan of the campaign. The first opportunity to put his ideas into effect came at the fag end of the military regime of the Proceso: he was appointed to head the Central Bank (**Banco Central de la República Argentina**[BCRA]) in 1982. Although in post for barely two months, he rescinded one of the key policies of economics minister, Martínez de Hoz, namely debt indexation—loans and interest payments were linked to the US dollar. The move saved millions of businesses, and families with mortgages, from financial collapse and generated considerable public gratitude for Cavallo. He also exposed the "statization" of private debt, something that had occurred before Cavallo was appointed and would continue after he left the bank. His opposition to the conversion of private debt into public obligations, which was a factor in his resignation, earned him few friends among business but was regarded as a mark of principle and in keeping with his research and writing about the structural problems bedeviling the country.

In 1987, Cavallo accepted an invitation to run for **Congress** on the PJ ticket, joining the party. The decision surprised many, given that Peronism was regarded as the progenitor of the bloated, ineffective state. Yet, having been defeated in the **congressional** and **presidential elections of 1983** and the midterm **congressional elections of 1985**, the **Renovación** wing of the party embraced modernization, democratization, and fiscal responsibility. These were people with whom Cavallo could work. Elected to the Chamber of Deputies, he gained valuable insights into the real world of politics. It proved an unhappy but vital learning experience, perhaps preparing him for the 1988 PJ party primaries when Menem defeated the Renovación candidate, **Antonio Cafiero**, though pledging to modernize the party. Cavallo actively supported Menem's presidential campaign and was offered the foreign affairs portfolio when Menem became president, not the Economics Ministry. He accepted, holding the post for approximately 18 months. Not until February 1991 did Cavallo obtain the economy portfolio: he was Menem's fourth minister of economy. Immediately, he introduced the Convertibility Plan, the project with which he and Menem are most associated. The principal elements of the plan—the dual monetary system, which granted the US dollar joint legal tender status and exchangeable on a one-to-one basis with the peso, balanced budgets, **privatization**, and the liberalization of markets, with transitional support from the state, and reinsertion into the international economy—were consistent with the ideas that Cavallo had been developing over the previous 20 years.

The Ministry of Economy over which Cavallo presided became a super-ministry, reflected in its official designation—Ministry of Economy, Public Works, and Public Services. During Cavallo's tenure, the ministry established subagencies in virtually all the other principal offices of state, staffed by Cavallo boys. Despite painful structural adjustment, the plan worked. There was currency stability with growth, the fiscal account improved, as did international reserves—not least due to a massive inflow of foreign capital; confidence in the plan and the country returned. Yet the relationship with Menem was stormy, partly due to personality clashes, though increasingly to what Cavallo saw as political resistance to the economic logic of his model, which was compromised by cronyism. The drive for fiscal discipline and macroeconomic efficiency were being undermined by "corrupt mafias" inside and outside the administration, to use Cavallo's words on leaving office. **Corruption** would ultimately bring Menem down, even though the public was at first prepared to accept a lack of political transparency as the price of macroeconomic stability. Perhaps success in the **presidential election of 1995**, following hard on the **Olivos Pact** of 1994 with the UCR, which facilitated the constitutional change that allowed him to stand for a second consecutive term, gave Menem a heightened sense of impunity. Whatever, having campaigned together in the elections, Cavallo and Menem parted company within months of Menem's second inauguration. The only question is whether Cavallo jumped or was pushed: Menem maintains that he demanded Cavallo's resignation, Cavallo that he was determined to go given the step up in corruption.

Having broken with Menem, Cavallo founded a center-right political party, **Acción por la República** (AR), which gained him a seat in the national Chamber of Deputies, representing the city of **Buenos Aires**, in the midterm **congressional elections of 1997**. Support for Menem slipped considerably in the midterms, which probably encouraged Cavallo to stand as candidate for the AR in the **presidential election of 1999**—he came in a poor third, behind the victor, **Fernando de la Rúa** of the UCR, and **Eduardo Duhalde**, standing for the PJ. In 2000, he stood in the mayoral elections for the city of Buenos Aires, being beaten by **Aníbal Ibarra** in the first round. Cavallo's political and ministerial life appeared to be at an end.

Fate intervened. The victory of De la Rúa in 1999 was attributed to the endorsement of convertibility by the **Alianza** electoral coalition that he headed and public disgust at the corruption of the Menem administration. As the plan began to founder, De la Rúa offered Cavallo his old portfolio in March 2001: Cavallo became the third and last minister of economy appointed by De la Rúa. At first, the return of "The Wizard" was greeted with popular enthusiasm: if anyone could save convertibility, it was Cavallo. But it was already too late. Failure to tackle the fiscal deficit had led to an exponential increase in public borrowing, much of it since Cavallo left office in 1996. There were no more state assets to be privatized. The inflow of private investment had dried up, replaced by capital flight, and institutional lenders were getting cold feet. The room for maneuver was limited. Having granted the Central Bank independence in 1991, Cavallo restricted its autonomy. Successively, he ordered government institutions and privatized pension funds to buy government bonds—to make up the dearth in overseas loans, imposed steep tax increases and sharp expenditure cuts to balance the budget—which was expected to achieve equilibrium monthly under the Zero Deficit Law—and, finally, imposed restriction on withdrawals from private bank accounts—the notorious *corralito*—in an effort to stem the hemorrhage of funds from the banking system. All to little avail.

At the beginning of December, when the IMF announced that it would not release the next tranche of anticipated aid, default loomed. Cavallo ordered fixed-term deposits in the banking system to be converted into public bonds—both to shore up government finances and to stabilize the banking system. By the middle of the month, Argentina was seeking to defer payments on the overseas debt, and the 2002 budget proposed another round of eye-watering tax cuts. Almost immediately, Congress revoked the special powers awarded to Cavallo. He resigned. The government declared a state of siege—martial law. The cabinet resigned. On 21 December, De la Rúa resigned as public disorder mounted. The banks closed. Convertibility was the next casualty.

Within months of the crisis, Cavallo was charged with engaging in illegal arms deals during the Menem presidency. He denied the charges. Jailed, he was later exonerated. By 2003, he was back in the United States, teaching at Harvard and later at Yale. Back in Argentina, he stood in the midterm **congressional elections of 2013**, performing abysmally. More criminal charges followed in 2015, and he was banned from holding public office for life. Although he remains a controversial figure, Cavallo is consulted for his views on the **economic crisis** of 2001–2002 and for his comments on the problems confronting the country. Vilified and applauded, he is still regarded as the man who might have saved Argentina, had his project been applied coherently and consistently. *See also* FOREIGN DEBT/FOREIGN INVESTMENT; YABRÁN CASE.

CÉDULAS. A financial instrument intended to finance *estancia* modernization. Launched in 1872, *cédulas hipotecarias* (state-guaranteed mortgage
bonds) came into their own in the 1880s. The overissue of bonds, coupled
with plummeting confidence in the administration of the system and **currency** depreciation, contributed to the **Baring Crisis**.

At a time when the flow of direct investment into **agriculture** from overseas was limited and local long-term credit scarce, mortgage bonds were
devised as a mechanism to improve liquidity and generate funds for land
improvement. The objective was understandable when international demand
for temperate agricultural products was growing rapidly, large tracts of territory had become available following the **Conquest of the Desert**, and a
surge in trunk line railway construction brought fertile, frontier zones within
the margin of profitable cultivation. In theory, the mortgage scheme was easy
to understand and administer, in practice far from transparent. *Cédulas* were
negotiable bonds, endorsed by an official mortgage bank, usually carrying
interest at 7 or 8 percent. They were issued to landowners for sale on the
open market to enable mortgagees to secure capital. The Banco Hipotecario
de la Provincia de Buenos Aires was set up in 1871 to handle mortgage paper
variously known as *cédulas hipotecarias* or *cédulas de crédito*. Several years
later, in 1886, the Banco Hipotecario Nacional was created as part of a
general project for more effective central government control of money,
credit, and banking. Guaranteed respectively by the provincial and federal
governments, the banks were in effect intermediaries between would-be borrowers and potential lenders. They were required to assess the value of a
property and to ensure that the 50 percent mortgage limit was not exceeded;
according to their charters, the banks were only permitted to issue *cédulas* up
to 50 percent of the value of land offered as security. Banks were expected to
ensure that the property was unencumbered by any prior lien and that the
estate was capable of yielding an income sufficient to meet annual interest
and amortization charges. In addition, the banks were responsible for dis-
charging the debt and honoring coupons payable to the bearer. It was assumed that *cédulas* would become readily transferable pieces of paper, easily
placeable by mortgagees and renegotiable by creditors. For their part, *estancieros* undertook to redeem the loan within the period specified and to meet
quarterly or half-yearly interest payments (usually at the rate of 10 percent
per annum, that is, at a rate that covered interest payments and amortization
charges payable by the bank, plus a small commission). Landowners could
cancel the debt at any time during the currency of the contract by paying off
the balance of the loan, but the action would in no way affect the rights of the
bondholder, as *cédulas* could only be extinguished by the relevant bank.

The scheme proved immediately popular with *estancieros*, though European investors were initially more cautious. But *cédulas* gained in acceptabil-
ity later and were readily placed abroad during the 1880s boom. Between

1872 and 1885, the **Buenos Aires** mortgage bank issued bonds to the value of $76,557,000 (paper pesos), of which approximately $26 million had been extinguished by December 1885. By the end of 1890, the bank had issued several further series of *cédulas* bringing post-1872 emission totals to about $370 million paper. Over the same period, $5 million in gold bonds had also been printed. Between 1886 and 1890, the Banco Hipotecario Nacional placed *cédulas* to the value of $90 million paper and $20 million gold. It was contemplating a further emission of $40 million paper authorized in November 1889 when operations were brought to a close by the crisis. London became the most important overseas secondary market for "paper" *cédulas*; Berlin virtually monopolized dealing in mortgage bonds denominated in gold pesos. Although placed on the market as secure, semiofficial paper designed to attract rentier capital, the bonds soon became synonymous with unbridled speculation and **corruption**. Official investigations undertaken after the Baring Crisis revealed that the banks had paid scant regard to regulations that established maximum limits for any individual loan and even less to the 50 percent ceiling. Furthermore, little had been done to ascertain the real value of properties. Clandestine emissions, favoritism, and various other corrupt practices surfaced in the postcrisis official inquiry. Mortgage bank officials had been suborned by credit-hungry landowners who had little to lose.

When the first mortgage bonds were launched, Argentina was on a bimetallic standard, and although the short-lived experiment with the gold standard had already been abandoned by the time the federal bank was set up, the administration then in power was at least nominally committed to a speedy return to convertibility. But the temptation to inflate proved irresistible to the **Miguel Júarez Celman** government. As the vast majority of the bonds were denominated in paper pesos and largely held overseas, while landowner interests were paramount in the Argentine, perhaps it is unsurprising that the late 1880s was a period of rapid inflation, currency depreciation, and spiraling land values—a debtor's paradise. By the end of the decade, the real cost of borrowing on *cédulas* was nominal and possibly negative as *estancieros* could cancel debt by purchasing heavily discounted bonds on the open market. Moreover, as interest charges were fixed and denominated in paper pesos, other than for gold issues, most borrowers had little difficulty meeting interest charges and so maintaining their "credit" with the endorsing bank. Little wonder that *cédulas* denominated in paper pesos found such favor among politically powerful landowners. Foreign bondholders, particularly those who held paper peso bonds, took a very different view.

The behavior of the provincial and federal mortgage banks prefigured that of state banks in the latter part of the 20th century and later—institutions of the state were transformed into mechanisms for the enrichment of the political elite and its patrons and associates. *See also* AGRICULTURAL COLONIZATION; *ESTANCIA* COMPANIES; FOREIGN DEBT/FOREIGN INVESTMENT; FOREIGN TRADE.

CENTRAL ARGENTINE RAILWAY COMPANY (CAR). Sometimes regarded as a maverick by other premier British broad-gauge lines, the CAR was one of the first railways to be projected but the last of the original schemes to be realized. It was unique among Argentine railways in being awarded an extensive land grant, similar to that of near contemporary railways in the **United States**.

Mooted in 1854, the concession for a line from **Rosario** to **Córdoba** and the northwest was published in 1855. The line was actively promoted by **Justo José de Urquiza**, sometime **caudillo** of **Entre Ríos** and then president of the fragile **Argentine Confederation**. The province of **Buenos Aires** had seceded from the Confederation, and Urquiza viewed the project as a vehicle to unify the country. The railway was associated with engineers and promoters from the United States. After several modifications in 1862 and 1863, the concession was awarded to US railway pioneer William Wheelwright, who looked to London for funding. Construction began in 1863. Rail services between Rosario to Córdoba started in 1870. When the government pressed the company to build on to **Tucumán** as envisaged in the 1854 survey, the directors of the company refused. They argued that funds were scarce and time was needed to develop traffic along the existing route but promised that the land grant would be put to good use by promoting **agricultural colonization**. In response, the federal government decided to construct a meter-gauge line to the northwest—first to Tucumán and then into neighboring provinces like **Catamarca, Santiago del Estero, Salta**, and **Jujuy**. Part of this network would subsequently be acquired by the **Cordoba Central Railway Company** (CCR).

The fitful progress of the CAR and its reluctance to build beyond Córdoba can be attributed to the political uncertainty of the 1860s and unrealistic costing. Construction estimates in the 1855 concession assumed that the railway could be built for around half the cost per mile of what was then the actual cost of railway building in Buenos Aires. The land grant was an insufficient sweetener. Only when construction estimates were revised and a government profit guarantee granted was Wheelwright able to take the project to London. Yet management may have been overcautious. The company strategy appeared to be to allow others to do the heavy lifting, building meter-gauge lines north and west of Córdoba, while the CAR retained control of the broad-gauge railway from the city to the port of Rosario. The extensive land grant precluded the construction of a close, competitive line so that it could retain a stronghold on freight flowing down to the port. For 18 years, the company did not lay a single mile of track. Such complacency was overturned first by the **Buenos Ayres & Rosario Railway Company** (BA&R) and later the CCR, the former building up from Buenos Aires and the latter down from Córdoba to the federal capital via Rosario. The principal and greater challenge came from the BA&R, which reached Rosario in 1886 and then built on to Tucumán, as well as buying up local feeder networks. This forced the CAR into a competitive program of acquisitions and extensions.

Notwithstanding boom conditions of the time and rising profits, the CAR was forced to consider a buyout by the BA&R. First mooted in 1892, congressional approval for the merger was granted in 1908. In effect, the BA&R took over the CAR, but **Congress** required that the new entity should preserve the historic name. The zone covered by the new CAR was one of the most fertile in Argentina, and it served densely settled parts of the north of the province of Buenos Aires and major cities in the central **Littoral**. Despite the impact of the First World War, the CAR entered a "golden" era after the merger. Network integration and rationalization were accompanied by modest extension building and permanent way upgrading to ease freight congestion. An ambitious program of grain elevator construction was completed before 1914 and continued after the war. In the 1920s, the company sponsored a new wave of agricultural colonization and promoted crop diversification. Perhaps the largest financial commitment assumed at this time was the modernization of commuter services and passenger station refurbishment. The main terminus in Buenos Aires was completely rebuilt in grand style— Retiro reputedly rivaled major US termini in scale and opulence. Commuter services to the suburbs and resorts along the **Paraná** Delta were electrified, becoming the first fully electrified commuter system in Latin America. There was a parallel upgrading of station facilities at principal destinations in the interior and the introduction of crack express trains to Rosario, Córdoba, and Tucumán.

The CAR established a reputation for the quality of long-distance passenger trains. Its most iconic service was *La Estrella del Norte*, running between Buenos Aires and Tucumán. Introduced in 1914, it ran as a weekly deluxe sleeper express until 1930, when the name was used for a daily conventional service on the same route. The express journey time was 23 hours. In 1896, when the BA&R launched a weekly express on the route, the running time was 26 hours; the daily stopping train took 36 hours. *El Panamericano* was introduced on the Buenos Aires–Tucumán route in 1929, substituting for the *Estrella* express a year later. It became one of the classic long-distance expresses of South America. *El Panamericano* took its name from connecting services available. At Tucumán, passengers transferred to the meter-gauge system and *La Veloz del Norte*, which ran to the frontier to combine with trains to **Bolivia** and **Chile** and on to **Peru**. Finally, in 1939, the CAR launched *El Tucumano*, which made the trip in 16 hours and 15 minutes; a similar service to Córdoba, *El Cordobés*, started a year earlier. The fastest scheduled running time achieved on the Buenos Aires–Tucumán route was 15 hours—the famous air-conditioned night *Expreso Buenos Aires–Tucumán*, which boasted luxurious services; it was equipped with a cinema car, sleeper carriages, a dining car, and carriages with reclining airline seats. This was the showpiece train launched in 1969 to highlight the project of technical modernization promoted by the military regime of the **Revolución Argentina**.

With nationalization in 1948, the CAR was renamed the Ferrocarril Nacional General Bartolomé Mitre (FCNGBM), absorbing sections of connecting formerly French-owned broad-gauge companies. *See also* ARGENTINE NORTH EASTERN RAILWAY COMPANY (ANE); BUENOS AYRES & PACIFIC RAILWAY COMPANY (BA&P); BUENOS AYRES GREAT SOUTHERN RAILWAY COMPANY (BAGS); BUENOS AYRES WESTERN RAILWAY COMPANY (BAW); ECONOMIC CRISES; ECONOMY; FERROCARRILES ARGENTINOS (FFAA); FOREIGN DEBT/FOREIGN INVESTMENT; GREAT BRITAIN; PRIVATIZATION; STATE-OWNED ENTERPRISES (SOEs); TRANSPORTATION.

CENTRO DE ESTUDIOS DEL ESTADO Y SOCIEDAD (CEDES). A research center specializing in the applied social sciences founded in 1975. It is a well-regarded school of advanced studies that is home to a network of scholars and part of a regional consortium of similarly prestigious research and teaching institutions, with academic partners in **Brazil, Chile**, Mexico, and elsewhere.

The center was particularly influential in the difficult years immediately before and after the **Proceso de Reorganización Nacional**. Increasing political violence in the last year of the administration of President **Isabel Perón** and following the **military coup of 1976** had a dramatic impact on the universities, as on society at large. The universities were intervened. Academics and students were kidnapped and murdered by shadowy paramilitary organizations of the left and the right, and later by state organizations. The intellectual environment became crabbed and sterile. The social sciences were a particularly "dangerous" field of research and study, regarded as subversive and a breeding ground for undesirable thinking. Pluralism and reasoned argument were crowded out by a rising tide of radicalism and nationalism. "History" also became a dangerous subject—whose history and what history? For a small group of social scientists—those who were forced out of the universities, or who did not feel safe in established seats of learning, or who were not murdered and had not fled abroad—CEDES became an institutional and intellectual base where research and writing could continue and independent thinking flourish. Scholars associated with the center were productive, though most of the research was only available in working-document format, not being published until after 1983. It produced critical documents in various fields of public policy. In addition, CEDES was important because it provided space—usually a shared office or teaching room—for small, less well-endowed research groups.

During the Proceso years, CEDES received funding from Canadian, Swedish, and US foundations, including the Mellon Foundation and the Ford Foundation. The Ford Foundation was particularly generous. In 1983, instead of providing grants to cover running costs and fund individual research projects, the Ford Foundation made a substantial donation that allowed CEDES to purchase a building. This secured the future of the center. The building now houses the administrative offices, a library and document collection, and space for researchers. In recent years, the center has benefited from state funds allocated to research projects based there and continues to receive grants from national and international private foundations. It is now an accredited center of higher education. Its mission statement reiterates the role of promoting work in such areas as macroeconomics, social policy, social movements and civil society, history, and the theory and practice of governance—all with an emphasis on public policy. During and after the 1980s, many scholars associated with the institution were reintegrated into the public universities. Academics connected with the center have served as advisors and policy consultants in several government ministries. CEDES researchers played a critical role in the administration of President **Raúl Alfonsín**. *See also* DESAPARECIDOS; EDUCATION; TRIPLE A (ALIANZA ANTICOMUNISTA ARGENTINA); UNIVERSITY OF BUENOS AIRES (UBA).

CENTRO DE ESTUDIOS MACROECONÓMICOS DE ARGENTINA (CEMA/UCEMA). A private institution—an economics and business school, founded in 1978 as the Center for the Study of Macroeconomics of Argentina, in 1995 reformed as a university, hence UCEMA. The institution specializes in the areas of economics, finance, management, and political science, offering undergraduate and postgraduate courses in these disciplines and executive programs in corporate finance, capital markets, and investment strategy. It promotes research and policy analyses and is particularly associated with advancing a free-market approach to economics and neoliberal perspectives. Well-known faculty and alumni include such political figures and ministers and officials as **Amado Boudou** and **Roque Fernández**. *See also* EDUCATION.

CERVECERÍA Y MALTERÍA QUILMES. Argentine brewery founded by the Bemberg family in 1888 in Quilmes, outside the city of **Buenos Aires**, by German immigrant Otto Bemberg. Initially engaged in the import of textiles and export of **grains**, the family diversified into beer production as well as consolidating its position as one of the main cereal export houses. Brewery operations expanded rapidly, and Quilmes was already the most popular beer in Buenos Aires in the 1920s. By the 1940s, until it fell out of favor with the government of President **Juan Domingo Perón**, the company had established a virtual monopoly on the local market, buying up smaller breweries. The family conglomerate was nationalized in the early 1950s—by this time, the Bemberg group controlled 33 industrial companies and owned several *estancias*. The nationalization made headlines across the world. Group assets were returned to the family after the **military coup of 1955**. The brewery has since become something of a national symbol: it not only has 75 percent of the market share in Argentina, but it is also widely exported. In the early 21st century, the company was taken over by the international drinks group AmBev. *See also* BEMBERG, MARÍA LUISA (1922–1995); INDUSTRY; STATE-OWNED ENTERPRISES (SOEs).

CHACO. Province in the northeast of the country, located in the **Grand Chaco** region that straddles Argentina, **Paraguay**, and **Bolivia**. Chaco is bordered by **Santa Fe** to the south, by **Salta** and **Santiago del Estero** to the west, and by **Formosa** to the north. To the east, the rivers **Paraguay** and **Paraná** separate the province from Paraguay and **Corrientes**, respectively.

What is the present-day Chaco province remained largely unexplored and uninhabited until the region was contested by Argentina and Paraguay during the **War of the Triple Alliance** (1865–1870). Paraguay was defeated, and Argentina set up the Territorio Nacional del Gran Chaco in 1872. **Resistencia** was established on the site of a long-abandoned 17th-century Spanish military outpost in 1876 and became the territorial capital two years later. The Territorio Nacional del Gran Chaco, which included the current province of Formosa, was administratively divided in 1884 and turned into the Territorio Nacional del Chaco. In 1951, the territory became a province: it was named Provincia Presidente Perón until the **military coup of 1955** and thereafter changed back to its historic name.

The current population of Chaco is approximately 1,200,000, and the provincial **economy** is predominantly associated with the commercial growing of quebracho wood and cotton. The province generates 60 percent of Argentine output of cotton. Other crops such as sunflower are grown, and production of livestock has benefited from the introduction of Brahman **cattle** (which are well suited to the geography and climate of the area). *See also* AGRICULTURE; FORESTAL ARGENTINA S.A; INDUSTRY.

CHACO WAR. The most significant **military** conflict in South America in the 20th century, the war was fought between **Bolivia** and **Paraguay** from 1932 to 1935, with a treaty brokered by the **United States** signed in 1938.

The antecedents of the conflict originate in indistinct colonial boundaries—Spanish forces barely penetrated the northern Chaco (Chaco Boreal)—and Bolivian ambitions to secure a river outlet to the Atlantic following the loss of Pacific coast territory to **Chile** after the **War of the Pacific**. Paraguayan sensitivities to Bolivian claims were heightened by massive territorial losses suffered following the **War of the Triple Alliance**, a factor that made Argentina an interested party. The discovery of oil in the Chaco in 1928 was a complication, giving the region greater economic importance. Neighboring countries were drawn into the fray: a German military mission arrived in Bolivia in 1911 to train the army, triggering concerns in Chile and **Peru** and overseas. At the beginning of the conflict, Bolivian forces were led by General Hans Kundt and received equipment from Germany. The Paraguayan army was French-trained, and White Russians fought for the country. In 1932, all four neighboring countries attempted to mediate—Argentina, **Brazil**, Chile, and Peru—sometimes in concert, sometimes not. At various points, Chile and Peru were accused of facilitating the supply of arms to the belligerents. **Carlos Saavedra Lamas**, Argentine minister of foreign affairs in the **Concordancia** government headed by General **Agustín P. Justo**, was one of the main mediators, earning the Nobel Peace Prize in 1936 for his efforts to end the conflict. After massive losses on both sides, political turmoil in both countries, and virtual stalemate on the battlefield, a peace protocol was signed in Buenos Aires in 1935. The settlement required both sides to modify territorial claims, though Paraguay is generally considered to have won the war. *See also* GRAND CHACO.

CHACRA. Originally a small estate or farm, derived from the Quechua, particularly common in the colonial period in the northwest of the country. Later, it was a smallholding on the **pampas** used to raise products for the market. Present-day usage includes, particularly if located on the outskirts of a city, a market garden or truck farm specializing in the production of vegetables, or a "country cottage"—rustic weekend holiday home. *Chacarero/a* means "smallholder."

CHE. Common form of address, peculiar to Argentina and **Uruguay**, applied to either sex. Used in place of *tu* (second person singular), or as an exclamation or greeting, it roughly translates as "chum," "mate," "cobber," or "buddy." The word gained international recognition when applied to the iconic revolutionary **Ernesto "Che" Guevara**, the Argentine national who participated in the Cuban Revolution and whose frequent use of the expression when in **Cuba** led fellow revolutionaries to dub him "Che." The expression is said to have been developed by **gauchos** in the 18th century and in common usage at the end of the 19th.

CHILE. The "sister republic" on the other side of the **Andes** has not always enjoyed cordial relations with Argentina, notwithstanding Argentine contributions to the liberation of the country in the 1810s, though the debt to General **José de San Martín** and the **Army of the Andes** is widely acknowledged.

In the 19th century, the countries collaborated periodically to exterminate "troublesome" Indian tribes located on both sides of the mountains, recognizing that, with a porous border, a push on one side would result in the temporary displacement of hostile tribes from one side to the other. There was a particularly closely coordinated campaign during the latter stages of the **Conquest of the Desert** in the 1870s. Yet the conquest and occupation of Indian territory in **Patagonia** were also a cause of future boundary disputes, with Chile laying claim to an Atlantic coast. The principal border disputes occurred in the Andes and Straits of Magellan. Frontier disputes, which had been simmering for decades—the countries had agreed in principle in 1881 to fix the border along the watershed—were resolved by arbitration in 1902, nominally overseen by King Edward VII of **Great Britain**. British arbitration was again sought in the 1960s to resolve a disagreement about the location of a section of the frontier in western **Chubut**. The most serious dispute, in terms of potential consequence, occurred over the Beagle Channel in the 1970s, bringing the countries to the brink of war. Having initially accepted continued British arbitration, Argentina rejected the award and vetoed any possible further British involvement in 1978. Even as the de facto governments headed by General Augusto Pinochet in Chile and General **Jorge Rafael Videla** in Argentina were collaborating in the kidnapping and rendition of their respective citizen through **Operación Condor**, the Argentine **military** was preparing for conflict. The junta signed the order to invade on 21 December 1978: the invasion was stopped by Videla at the last minute. Only after concerted papal action—later resulting in papal arbitration—was Operación Soberania aborted by the Argentine generals. Unlike the invasion of the **Falkland Islands**, launched years later, Operación Soberania was carefully crafted: there would be a three-pronged invasion of Chile along central and southern sections of the frontier, with defensive positions adopted elsewhere, and a joint army and navy operation in **Tierra del Fuego**. Defensive positions along the river frontier with **Brazil** also formed part of the plan. It is claimed that the Argentine military wrongly assumed that **Peru** would take advantage of their action to launch an attack on northern Chile. Had the Falklands debacle ended differently, there is no doubt that the Argentine military would have returned to the Chilean theater.

Since the return of democracy in Chile and Argentina, conflict between the two nations has been confined to the sports field. A definitive settlement to the **Beagle Channel Dispute** was reached in 1984, and since then trade has increased, as has economic collaboration—in the main. Both governments and militaries have sought to collaborate to defuse any possibility of border tensions. This does not mean that the frontier has been the only source of potential conflict. During the 1910s and 1920s, the authorities in Chile protested against the treatment of Chilean workers in Patagonia. In 2005, when Argentina was facing an energy crisis, President **Néstor Kirchner** unilaterally and abruptly abrogated a gas supply contract signed in 1996, much to the annoyance and inconvenience of Chile. There is considerable regional cross-border trade and **tourism** between the two countries. *See also* CUYO; FOREIGN TRADE; MENDOZA (PROVINCE); MERCOSUR.

CHINA. Term widely used in the 19th and early 20th century, the female equivalent of **gaucho**—*china*, not *gaucha*. Hence *el gaucho y la china*: the gaucho and his woman. It is largely derogatory, implying darker skinned, uneducated people from the interior. *See also CABECITA NEGRA.*

CHINA. As with many Latin American and African economies, modern engagement with China is largely a 21st-century phenomenon closely linked to the **commodities** boom triggered by Asian demand. Argentina did not recognize the People's Republic until 1972. Early in the 21st century, the Argentine–China relationship could be summed up in one word—soya. Since then, the relationship has been much more diverse and complex. It now involves finance as much as trade. In addition, for Argentina, the China connection also involves **immigration.**

Immigration from East Asia has risen significantly since around 2000 and involves settlers rather than expatriates. The first waves of Asian immigration followed the Second World War and the Korean War, consisting of Japanese and Korean migration, respectively. Now immigration from Asia is massively from China. Although still relatively small at around 200,000 in 2018, the Chinese community represents one of the fastest-growing ethnic groups in the country. The community is mainly concentrated in large urban centers, particularly Greater **Buenos Aires**, where Asians dominate the small-scale independent trading sector. In residential districts, about one-third of mom-and-pop-type convenience stores are Chinese run.

The trade relationship is focused on soya and soya-related products. In the early period, commodity exports to China generated a huge trade surplus for Argentina, since when China has been anxious to promote exports of goods and services to close its trade deficit. Exports of soya products declined after 2008 as China applied measures to protect the home soy-product sector, leading to a refocusing on the raw commodity. Currently, China exports a wide range of manufactures to Argentina, including consumer durables and electronic equipment like computers. Argentina now has a trade deficit with China, importing more than twice as much as the value of exports. This imbalance is unlikely to be much reduced by a recent rise in demand for **meat** in China. The commercial relationship with China is doubly important. First, China–Argentina trade is a critical factor in domestic export-led growth; secondly, as **Brazil** is Argentina's major trading partner, a significant component of the Argentina–Brazil commercial dynamic results from a spillover effect from the Brazil–China relationship.

The administration of President **Cristina Fernández de Kirchner** was particularly assiduous in its cultivation of China, especially as a source of capital, negotiating some very large loans. Although President **Mauricio Macri** has been critical of several of the China deals signed by his predecessor, charging a lack of transparency and **corruption**, he too has been keen to encourage the flow of investment. Over the last two decades, Chinese direct investment has targeted motor vehicle assembly, mining, banking, and ports. Loans estimated around US$40,000,000,000 have been made available for infrastructure projects, including railways, hydroelectricity generation, and nuclear energy. Chinese corporate investment in land has been a source of dispute between the two countries.

For much of the 2002–2015 period, China was the main—often the only—source of foreign capital available to Argentina, a dependence that led to financial asset swaps. In the 2016–2018 period, Brazil was Argentina's main market and source of imports; China was the third most important destination for exports and the second most significant source of imports; the **United States** was the second export market and the third supplier of imports. Some have compared the Sino–Argentine commercial and financial relationship of the 21st century with that of **Great Britain** and Argentina in the decades around 1900. *See also* AGRICULTURE; ECONOMIC CRISES; ECONOMY; FOREIGN DEBT/FOREIGN INVESTMENT; FOREIGN TRADE; INDUSTRY; TRANSPORTATION.

CHRISTIAN DEMOCRATIC PARTY. *See* PARTIDO DEMÓCRATA CRISTIANO (PDC).

CHUBUT. Province in the southern Argentine region of **Patagonia**, bordered by **Santa Cruz** to the south, **Chile** to the west, **Río Negro** to the north, and the Atlantic to the east. The **Tehuelches** were the original inhabitants of the area, to which Spanish missionaries came in the 17th and 18th centuries. In 1865, Welsh settlers arrived in the Chubut Valley; they founded **Rawson**, which would become the capital of Chubut. Following the **Conquest of the Desert**, the region was organized as the Territorio Nacional de Chubut in 1884. It acquired provincial status in 1955 and, along with Spanish, recognizes Welsh as an official language. The current population exceeds 510,000, and the economy is one of the least diversified in the country. It largely depends on the oil sector, which is centered around Comodoro Rivadavia—the largest city in Chubut. Oil refining is the principal activity of the province, which generates 13 percent of national oil production. **Sheep** ranching remains important at the local level, and Chubut produces 21 percent of the nation's fish catch. **Tourism** is a growing industry, the main attraction being the Valdés Peninsula with its whales, elephant seals, penguins, and many other animals.

CHURCH. *See* CATHOLIC CHURCH.

CISNEROS, BALTASAR HIDALGO DE (1756–1829). Last Spanish viceroy of the **River Plate**. A career naval officer who rose to the rank of admiral, following the French invasion of Spain and the imposition of Napoleon Bonaparte's brother as king he joined the resistance. Named viceroy of the River Plate by the Patriotic Junta of Seville, he replaced **Santiago de Liniers**, who had led local forces successfully confronting the invading British in 1806. Of French origin, Liniers's loyalty to the Spanish cause was called into question in Seville and the River Plate, though events would prove him faithful to his adopted country. It was largely due to Liniers's efforts that Cisneros was able to assume his post in **Buenos Aires**. Cisneros arrived in a city on the verge of revolution, riven by divisions between royalists and would-be revolutionaries—those who wished to preserve the Spanish monopoly of trade and political power, and those who favored free trade and a looser relationship with Spain—and there were tensions between Buenos Aires and Montevideo. Cisneros was aware that the **British invasions** of 1806 and 1807, defeated largely by local forces, had generated patriotic fervor and changed the balance of military power. He sought to steer a middle course while ensuring the integrity of the viceroyalty—he attempted to organize an expeditionary force to suppress revolution in what is now **Bolivia**. However, when news that Seville had fallen to French forces reached the River Plate, proponents of **independence** argued that as there was no longer a legitimate government in Spain, sovereignty reverted to the people. The demise of the Seville junta, which had appointed him, was a significant blow to Cisneros's authority. He responded cautiously to demands for the calling of an open town council meeting, the **Cabildo Abierto**. When he finally acceded, it was to propose a junta representing various factions with himself as head. On 25 May 1810, this solution was rejected. He resigned but soon became a focus for loyalist groups—he had sent a request to Liniers, then based in **Córdoba**, to support the royalist cause. As the situation became more delicate, Cisneros was advised to leave the River Plate. He sailed to the Canary Islands on a Royal Navy ship in July 1810. There would be no more viceroys of the River Plate.

CLARÍN. *Clarín* has the largest print run in Argentine, despite the general decline in print media sales in recent years. It is one of the most influential daily newspapers in Argentina, and the Sunday edition is, arguably, the widest selling Spanish-language newspaper in the world. Founded in 1945 by a **Buenos Aires** politician Roberto Noble, it pioneered a number of innovations in the industry and has proved to be commercially successful. It was the first title to be published in tabloid format in Argentine. With *La Nación* and *La Razón*, *Clarín* formed Papel Prensa, a newsprint company, in 1977; the federal government retained a 27.5 percent holding in the company. It was one of the first newspapers in the country to offer an online service in 1996. When changes in the law in 1999 facilitated diversification, Grupo Clarín was created as a multimedia organization combining radio, television, newspapers, and magazines and digital news services. Circulation of the daily peaked at 500,000 in 1983, on the return of democracy, when it accounted for over one-third of all daily newspaper sales. Current circulation (2015) hovers just below 300,000 for the daily. The *Clarín* website is among the top 10 most visited in the country; the company television channel, **Canal 13**, is the market leader. The group dominates the cable television sector and accounts for around a third of the internet market. Praised for the quality and coverage of its reporting, some of the country's most prominent current affairs and cultural commentators have written for *Clarín*—and continue to do so.

Initially fairly close to the Kirchners, after 2008 the group became embroiled in several disputes with the government. Relations with the administration deteriorated sharply when the paper came out strongly in favor of the rural sector during the 2008 tax dispute. A year later, reportedly under pressure from the government, the Argentine Football Association terminated the Clarín Group contract to broadcast matches, since when league fixtures have been shown on a government-leaning sports channel. Injunctions claiming unpaid taxes were issued against the group, which also became a target of 2009 **media** antitrust legislation, and the newspaper offices raided.

The owners of *Clarín* have been slated for their support of the 1976–1983 military dictatorship, and favors obtained from that regime—notably when setting up Papel Prensa. There is also a widely held conviction among some civil rights groups that the Noble-Herrera children, adopted in 1976, may have been born to parents kidnapped and murdered during the **Proceso de Reorganizació Nacional**. It is undeniable that the Grupo Clarín is one of the largest and most influential media companies in Latin America and has been fiercely critical of the government. Supporters of *Clarín* maintain that it has exposed government wrongdoing and **corruption**. *See also ÁMBITO FINANCIERO*; *CRONISTA COMERCIAL*; KIRCHNER, CRISTINA ELISABET FERNÁNDEZ DE (1953–); KIRCHNER, NÉSTOR CARLOS (1950–2010); *LA PRENSA*; MADRES DE PLAZA DE MAYO; MILITARY COUP OF 1976; WAR TO ANNIHILATE SUBVERSION.

COALICIÓN CÍVICA (CC). Originally a political association founded by **Elisa Carrió** in 2002 to support a new left-of-center political party, **Afirmación para una República Igualitaria** (ARI). Although the CC was initially the junior partner, splits within the ARI and the general state of economic chaos and political flux in the country at the beginning of the 21st century soon contributed to the greater electoral appeal of the CC, which in effect absorbed the ARI. Hence the party adopted the title Coalición Cívica para la Afirmación de una República Igualitaria (CC-ARI). In 2015, CC-ARI merged with other political organizations to form **Cambiemos**, which delivered the presidency to **Mauricio Macri** in the **presidential election of 2015**.

ARI had been formed as a left-of-center grouping by dissidents disillusioned with the **Alianza** government of President **Fernando de la Rúa** around 2000, on the eve of the collapse of the **Convertibility Plan**, in protest at what they saw as a lurch to the right by the government. A former member of De la Rúa's **Unión Cívica Radical** (UCR), Carrió had broken with the president in 1999, a couple of years later forming the Coalición Cívica to support the ARI—hence the conscious incorporation of "Cívica" in the title of the new movement. The CC registered as an official political party in 2002. The current name of the party (CC-ARI) was registered in 2009 and continued until the construction of Cambiemos. ARI performed modestly in the **congressional elections of 2001** and the **presidential election of 2003**. Its breakthrough came when fielding Carrió as its presidential candidate to challenge **Cristina Fernández de Kirchner** in 2007. Although Cristina Kirchner topped the poll, with 23 percent of the vote Carrió did unexpectedly well, particularly in the cities of **Buenos Aires** and **Rosario**.

Following this strong showing, Carrió sought to broaden the appeal of the party, approaching such figures of the center-right as **Patricia Bullrich** and Alfonso Prat Gay, sometime governor of the **Banco Central de la República Argentina** and a future Cambiemos minister of economy. This caused a split in ARI and the consolidation of the CC-ARI in 2009. The split damaged the electoral performance of the party, which saw its share of the vote decline considerably in 2009 and 2011. In 2011, party members criticized Carrió for her leadership style and strategic miscalculations; she stepped down as head of the party and ceded the leadership of the CC-ARI bloc in the Chamber of Deputies to Prat Gay. The resulting internal reorganization, coupled with the emergence of new national and regional political groupings, prepared the ground for the formation of Cambiemos, and CC-ARI's adhesion to it. The CC-ARI bloc maintains a modest representation in **Congress**.

COBOS, JULIO CÉSAR CLETO (1955–). Politician and academic, trained as a civil engineer at the National Technical University. He taught at the Technical University, serving as one of the faculty deans between 1997 and 2003, and at the National University of **Cuyo.** His shifting party allegiances, and offices held, neatly capture the ideological flexibility of prominent figures and the fluidity of political party groupings since the 1990s.

Already a member of the **Unión Cívica Radical** (UCR), he was successively appointed to positions in the town planning and public works offices of the provincial government of **Mendoza** during the 1990s, becoming minister for environment and public works in 2000. In 2003, he was elected governor of the province, heading a coalition of the UCR and **Recrear.** Regarded as an effective administrator, Julio Cobos was soon at loggerheads with his predecessor as governor, Roberto Iglesias of the UCR. Recognizing the way the wind was blowing, Cobos sought an accommodation with President **Néstor Kirchner.** Iglesias, who went on to head the party, argued that the UCR should take a hard line with Radicals who gravitated toward the Kirchners. When Cobos agreed to serve as vice presidential running mate to **Cristina Fernández de Kirchner** in the **presidential election of 2007,** largely due to the intervention of her husband, he was expelled from the UCR. The Fernández de Kirchner–Cobos ticket triumphed, yet as **farm protests** grew in the face of export taxes hikes, and as he became disillusioned by the statization program favored by other associates of the president, Cobos distanced himself from Cristina Fernández. In 2008, when a new bill to increase export taxes came before the Senate and resulted in a tie, Cobos cast his vote with the opposition. (As vice president, Cobos was ex officio chairman of the Senate.) An infuriated Cristina Fernández demanded his resignation. Cobos declined, maintaining that he had an obligation to perform the duties of the post to which he had been elected. Despite a crescendo of abuse orchestrated by members of the government, Cobos held his ground and continued to vote against the government in the event of tied votes in the Senate.

The spat with Fernández de Kirchner did not harm Cobos's political career. Quite the contrary. Although he dithered about standing for the presidency in the **presidential election of 2011**—he was readmitted to the UCR in 2010—he declared that he would stand neither for the presidency nor the governorship of Mendoza in 2011. He was elected national deputy for the province of Mendoza in the midterm **congressional elections of 2013** and senator for the province in the **congressional elections of 2015.** Cobos currently heads the **Cambiemos** bloc in the National Senate, which supports President **Mauricio Macri.** His term is due to end in 2021.

COLECTIVOS. Term used for local buses in urban areas: long-distance buses are *micros*. The word derives from the "collective" taxis that plied on fixed routes, stopping en route to pick up and drop off passengers. *Colectivo* buses emerged in the 1920s as an answer to the rapid growth of major cities like **Buenos Aires** and an exponential increase in demand for cheap, flexible rapid city transport that could not be met by existing providers, notably tramways. In Buenos Aires, urban beautification, particularly the widening of streets and the construction of broad avenues linking the center with outlying districts, facilitated the emergence of bus routes.

The first *colectivos* were small vehicles, consisting of locally made bodies attached to imported lorry chassis, with seats for up to 15, although considerably more passengers would be squeezed into the far-from-generous standing space. Usually highly decorated, the buses were operated as mini cooperatives, owned by between three and five individuals who would work in shifts around the clock driving and collecting fares. Arrangements like routes were haphazard and unregulated. The chaotic development of *colectivos* provoked demands from vested interests like the **Anglo-Argentine Tramways Company** and railways operating commuter services for municipal supervision and regulation. During the **Concordancia** period, this resulted in the notorious transport coordination scheme for the city of Buenos Aires—the formation of a mixed entity composed of the Anglo-Argentine (its tram and bus services), the underground railway, and the *colectivos. Colectivo* drivers/owners were required to join the scheme. The scheme was seen to favor foreign interests as the organization of the mixed corporation would be determined by the valuation of capital assets, a mechanism weighted toward the tramway and underground railways. There were fare protests and riots leading to the burning of trams. *Colectivos* were presented as a national solution to transport problems of the day, the tramways as obsolete and grasping. The result was expropriation of the Anglo-Argentine; transport was municipalized and *colectivos* licensed.

Today, *colectivos* form the backbone of urban transport in all major cities. Although services are now provided by modern buses—more than half the national fleet is manufactured locally by Mercedes-Benz—that ply fixed routes, are equipped with automatic fare machines, are painted in standard route colors, and are operated by major franchisees, the term *colectivo* survives. Residual individualism of the early era is to be found in the way that drivers decorate cabs, which are bedecked with family photographs, charms, and trinkets and garishly illuminated. *See also* BUENOS AYRES & PACIFIC RAILWAY COMPANY (BA&P); BUENOS AYRES GREAT SOUTHERN RAILWAY COMPANY (BAGS); BUENOS AYRES WESTERN RAILWAY COMPANY (BAW); CENTRAL ARGENTINE RAILWAY COMPANY (CAR); ECONOMIC CRISES; FERROCARRILES ARGEN-

TINOS (FFAA); FOREIGN DEBT/FOREIGN INVESTMENT; GREAT BRITAIN; PRIVATIZATION; STATE-OWNED ENTERPRISES (SOEs); TRANSPORTATION.

COLÓN. *See* TEATRO COLÓN.

COLONIZATION. *See* AGRICULTURAL COLONIZATION.

COMISIÓN ECONÓMICA PARA AMÉRICA LATINA (Y EL CARIBE) (CEPAL). *See* ECONOMIC COMMISSION FOR LATIN AMERICA (ECLA).

COMISIÓN NACIONAL SOBRE LA DESAPARACIÓN DE PERSONAS (CONADEP). Set up by President **Raúl Alfonsín** in December 1983 shortly after his inauguration in fulfillment of a campaign promise, the National Commission for Disappeared People was given the brief to assemble data on those who had been "disappeared" during the **Proceso de Reorganización Nacional**. A lawyer who had acted for families seeking redress during the Proceso, Alfonsín saw the work of the commission and related measures that he enacted as a means of arraigning those who had perpetrated the worst **human rights** violations, and as a means of drawing a line over the past. Closure would facilitate the consolidation of civil society and the reconstruction of democratic institutions. It would also serve to reincorporate the armed forces into national life—itself a crucial mechanism of democratic institution building.

Alfonsín argued that in carrying out an investigation of what had occurred, it was critical that the commission identified those who had issued the orders to kidnap, detain, and kill; those who had carried out instruction precisely; and those who had exceeded orders—and to differentiate among these categories. Initially, Alfonsín proposed that the evidence assembled by the commission should be passed to **military** courts, which would be responsible for legal procedures and sentencing. Both these positions were challenged by human rights organizations and those acting for families of the "disappeared"—the **Desaparecidos**. The commission was given six months to collect evidence. The principal report was published by CONADEP in 1984— *Nunca Más* (*Never Again*), sometimes known as the Sábato Report after the president of the commission, **Ernesto Sábato**. Reviewing events of 1976–1977, the report identified several hundred illicit detention centers, documented the deaths of almost 9,000 people and the manner of their death, listed the names of the perpetrators of murder and torture and detailed the organizational and operational structure of the agencies of death, provided information on complicit individuals and organizations, attempted to calculate the "profits of terror" (assets stolen from victims and taken during searches of their property), and reported on the conduct of state bodies during the terror—notably, official responses to demands by families of the victims for information. The report also contained information about possible burial sites. The commission recognized that its investigations may not have identified all the victims.

Nunca Más was widely distributed and widely read. The report and the process became something of a model for similar truth commissions established elsewhere. For some, the work of the CONADEP and its report was the conclusion to a dark period in Argentine history, for others the starting point in a quest for justice and punishment. *Nunca Más* remains in print. *See also* BIGNONE, REYNALDO BENITO (1928–2018); BONAFINI, HEBE PASTOR DE (1928–); DIRTY WAR; DISPOSICIÓN FINAL; ESCUELA SUPERIOR DE MECÁNICA DE LA ARMADA (ESMA); FERNÁNDEZ MEIJIDE, GRACIELA (1931–); GALTIERI, LEOPOLDO FORTUNATO (1926–2003); MASSERA, EMILIO EDUARDO (1925–2010); MILITARY JUNTAS, TRIALS OF THE; PRESIDENTIAL ELECTION OF 1983; VIDELA, JORGE RAFAEL (1925–2013); VIOLA, ROBERTO EDUARDO (1924–1994); WAR TO ANNIHILATE SUBVERSION.

COMMODITIES. The geography and size of Argentina ensure that a diverse range of commodities are produced, many of which have featured significantly in **foreign trade** as well as satisfying domestic needs. Commodity exports were a critical factor driving growth and economic diversification for much of the 19th century. Their relative importance declined in the middle third of the 20th century but recovered their dynamic around 2000. In 2010, one-quarter of total exports by value consisted of unprocessed commodities, and another third processed or semiprocessed commodities. These proportions are likely to increase further. The principal agro-pastoral commodities groups produced in the country are cereals, oilseeds, **meat** and dairy products, fruits (including grapes, citrus, and hard and stone fruit), fibers (principally **wool**, cotton, and flax), vegetables, and fish and seafood; the main minerals groups include aluminum, copper, gold, iron, lithium, silver, and zinc, plus oil and natural gas. With motor vehicles and components and industrial chemicals accounting for little more than 15 percent of total exports by value, commodities—largely agro-pastoral items—dominate exports.

The prodigiously fertile **pampas** in particular are renowned for a capacity to raise most temperate and subtropical agricultural commodities, including wheat, **maize**, and linseed, as well as other cereals like barley, sorghum, and oats—rice is grown in the northeast. In addition to linseed, grown for fiber and oil, crops like sunflowers and peanuts are raised for oil (and as feed), as is soya. Yet from the late 19th century until the mid-20th, the principal arable commodities produced in the central grasslands were wheat, maize, and alfalfa (*Medicago sativa* or lucerne used to fatten **cattle**). Cattle and **sheep** were similarly significant across the region. In the 1920s, Argentina was the principal world exporter of maize and one of the top four exporters of wheat. During the decade, Canada, Argentina, Australia, and the **United States** supplied 90 percent of world demand. Wheat was the top export of Canada and Argentina, with both countries exporting about two-thirds of their respective total national output. In the interwar years, Canada accounted for one-third of total world wheat exports and Argentina around one-fifth. By 2017, Argentina no longer featured in the world's top 10 producers of wheat, and only just made the top 10 exporters, supplying 5 percent of global demand compared with 15 percent for US exports, 12 percent for Canadian, and 10 percent for Australian. The country has recovered its position as a maize exporter in recent years, in 2017 accounting for about 15 percent of world exports, second to the United States, which supplied 36 percent. Previously used almost exclusively for food and animal feed, maize is increasingly demanded to produce renewable energy—ethanol.

For much of its modern history, Argentina has been a major importer of energy; until the 1930s, this was coal, but by the 1950s oil had become the main fuel. Yet Argentina could become a major regional and world fuel supplier. In addition to maize/ethanol and other vegetable-oil-based renewable energies, discoveries of oil in various parts of the county since the early 20th century—and later natural gas deposits—point to potential as a producer and supplier of petroleum and gas. Hydroelectricity, developed in the north and west from the late 19th century, is now generated mainly along the **Andes** in western **Patagonia** and in the northeast in the upper **Paraná** Basin, and again indicates the possibility of producing and exporting yet another energy "commodity." In 2017, Argentina accounted for around 0.1 percent of world proven oil reserves and 0.2 percent of natural gas—corresponding figures for the United States are 2.8 percent and 4.7 percent. Considerable opportunities for hydroelectricity generation remain untapped. Although hardly a notable player, the country could become a supplier in the international fossil fuel market, as well as that for renewable energy. This has not been realized, largely due to underinvestment, which has led to bottlenecks in exploration and production, and because of the reputation of the country as an unreliable partner. Around 2003–2004, President **Néstor Kirchner** froze energy tariffs, which led to a dramatic decline in investment in the energy sector, precipitating a domestic energy crisis and unilateral cuts on gas exports to **Chile**—at the time, imports of gas from Argentina fueled a quarter of the electricity generated and consumed in central Chile. Recent years have witnessed increases in gas and oil capacity, production, and energy swaps across the Andes. *See also* AGRICULTURAL COLONIZATION; AGRICULTURE; CONQUEST OF THE DESERT/DESERT CAMPAIGN; ECO-

NOMIC CRISES; ECONOMY; *ESTANCIA*; *ESTANCIA* COMPANIES; FORESTAL ARGENTINA S.A; *FRIGORÍFICOS*; GRAINS; INSTITUTO ARGENTINO DE PROMOCIÓN DEL INTERCAMBIO (IAPI); ITAIPÚ DAM; SALTO GRANDE; YACIMIENTOS PETROLÍFEROS FISCALES (YPF); YACYRETÁ-APIPÉ; YERBA MATE.

COMPROMISO PARA EL CAMBIO. A center-right political party formed in 2005 by **Mauricio Macri**. As soon as the party was registered, Macri entered into an electoral alliance with **Ricardo López Murphy** of **Recrear** to contest the midterm **congressional elections of 2005**. The alliance was known as the **Propuesta Republicana** (PRO). When the PRO was constituted as a political party in 2008, it became Macri's political-party-cum-electoral-machine.

The Compromiso was itself an amalgamation of parties, having initially surfaced in 2003 as the Frente Compromiso para el Cambio, the bloc that supported Macri's campaign for the mayoral elections in the city of **Buenos Aires**: Macri topped the poll on the first round but came in second to **Aníbal Ibarra** in a runoff, Ibarra picking up most of the votes of the candidates knocked out after the first round. The Frente brought together dissident Peronists, the **Partido Demócrata Progresista**, and others. Having superseded the Frente, when displaced by the PRO in 2008, the short-lived Compromiso was consigned to the dustbin of history, like many other electoral groupings and temporary alliances constructed during the early years of the *kirchnerato*. PRO is now part of the governing coalition, **Cambiemos**, that delivered the presidency to Macri in 2015 and performed well in the **congressional elections of 2017**.

CONCORDANCIA. Political coalition that governed Argentina in 1932–1943. It comprised the *antipersonalista* Radicals, who provided Presidents **Agustin P. Justo** and **Roberto M. Ortiz**; the **Partido Demócrata Nacional**, the old-time Conservatives, who supplied Vice Presidents **Julio A. Roca Jr.**and **Ramon S. Castillo**; and the Independent Socialists.

Although the Concordancia has usually been accused of pandering to agricultural interests, not least because of the **Roca–Runciman Pact**, its economic policies were more pragmatic than has been acknowledged. The **Plan de Acción Económica**, launched in 1933, led to a speedy recovery from the Depression. Two years later the government created the **Banco Central de la República Argentina**, modeled on the Bank of England. Contrary to the popular belief that state intervention was a creature of Peronism, it was the Concordancia that first resorted to increasing the role of the state, namely providing price support for **commodity** producers, managing the exchange rate, and experimenting with Keynesian-style interventionist measures, including investing substantially in physical infrastructure, while broadly committed to balancing the federal budget.

However, the regime lost its legitimacy as well as its moral authority. It relied on political violence and electoral fraud (the so-called *fraude patriótico*) to maintain power, though there was a short-lived attempt to remedy this deficiency during the Ortiz presidency, with moves to reestablish free and fair elections. Growing dissatisfaction with this state of affairs resulted in the political defeat of the **Pinedo Plan**, which was a bold attempt to deal with the impact of the Second World War and more crucially a tacit acknowledgment that the country had to change economic direction. The Concordancia was brought to an abrupt end by the **military coup of 1943**.

CONDOR MISSILE PROGRAM. A multinational space research program initiated in the 1970s by the Dirección General de Desarrollos Espaciales of the air force. It involved significant contract work being performed by the German company MBB (now a group within Daimler AG) and later developed into a ballistic missile program.

The original Condor I rocket had little military capability, but it helped build expertise for the Alacrán program of 1978. The Alacrán short-range ballistic missile was derived from the Condor IAIII prototype; nonetheless, it had shorter stabilization fins, an inertial guidance system, and a cluster munition warhead. During and after the **Falklands War** of 1982, France ceased to be a missile supplier as a consequence of an arms embargo against Argentina. This led the air force to develop its own medium-range ballistic missile, the Condor II. The program was undertaken in close collaboration with Egypt and then Iraq; the latter's version was called BADR-2000. The Condor II, which was developed in Falda del Carmen in the province of **Córdoba**, had a range of 800 to 1,000 kilometers and a 500 kilogram cluster munition warhead.

The missile program was discontinued in the early 1990s, not least because President **Carlos Menem** sided with the **United States** during the first Gulf War that liberated Kuwait from brutal Iraqi occupation.

CONDUCCIÓN POLÍTICA. Coined by **Juan Domingo Perón** in 1951, the term provided a unique glimpse into the thought processes and values that guided him throughout his political career. Perón borrowed from **military** concepts to construct an approach to civilian leadership. The base element of his notion of leadership was the proposition that the *conductor* (leader) was born, not made. For Perón, politics—like warfare—meant conflict; its goal was to impose one's will upon the "enemy." His definition of leadership applied equally to the military and political spheres: the leader was to be judged by results alone. Another idea Perón borrowed from the military model was the need for centralized control in the hands of the *conductor*. In politics as well as the military, the essential component of leadership was the availability of a group of people capable of being led. The prerequisite for political leadership was the formation of what Perón called the mass; that is, a citizenry not merely willing but ready and able to be led. The relationship between the *conductor* and the mass was of crucial importance. The first task of the leader was to locate his mass—in Perón's case, this was the working class. He then had to train his mass by inculcating them with doctrine, so that "everybody kicks toward the same goal." The leader had to organize his followers in a simple structure, yet one cohesive enough to ensure stability. And finally, an indoctrinated, organized mass was transformed into a people or community conscious of its rights and duties.

Conducción política exposed the amorality underlying Perón's approach to politics: what succeeded was good, and success justified the mantle of leadership. As a result, the strategic goals—as elaborated by **Justicialismo**— had to remain elastic and loosely defined to ensure that they could be reached. This elasticity was clearly visible in the contradictions of the "Twenty Truths" of the Justicialista doctrine. Truth 1 was "True democracy is the system where the government carries out the will of the people defending a single objective: the interests of the people," which begged the question of how the will of the people was to be ascertained. Truth 4, which stated that "There is only one class of men for the Peronist cause: the workers," contradicted truth 11, which determined that "Peronism desires the establishment of national unity" (i.e., a multiclass alliance)—this never ceased to cause bedevilment. But since the achievement of the (changeable) goal was the measure of success, doctrinal flexibility primarily benefited the leader and not the mass. *See also* PARTIDO JUSTICIALISTA (PJ).

CONFEDERACIÓN GENERAL DEL TRABAJO (CGT). Established in its present form in late September 1930, three weeks after the **military coup of 1930**, it was the largest and most influential body representing organized labor in Latin America around the 1950s and 1960s. Initially, the organization was dominated by **trade unions** representing railway and utility workers, headed by immigrants influenced by European socialism and models of unionism, and later represented industrial worker unions dominated by Peronists.

The CGT was created following agreement among reformist socialists, anarcho-syndicalists, and Marxists, previously influential in different sections of the labor movement. The first trade unions had been formed in the late 19th century. Many of these were closely associated with such contemporary political currents as anarchism, which sought to overthrow the state, and revolutionary socialists opposed to capitalism. Anarchism and **anarcho-**

syndicalism were the predominant ideologies. Fragmented along ideological lines, and depicted as agents of foreign subversion by nationalists, the labor movement was weak and largely ineffective. Worker protest and strike action was usually met with violent repression, as during the **Semana Trágica** of January 1919. Gradually, two factors effected change. First, democratic socialism gained influence in the labor movement and established a political presence. Secondly, concern increased among sections of the governing elite about social conditions and an acceptance of the need for social reform. Advocating political participation, reformist socialists favored a "historic compromise" with capitalism and the state. Proponents of social and political reform presented social legislation and electoral reform as a mechanism to incorporate workers and the lower middle classes within the system. Such measures as social welfare and employment regulations sponsored by the likes of **Juan B. Justo**, founder of the **Partido Socialista**, and political reform such as electoral changes promoted by President **Roque Sáenz Peña** signaled new attitudes that enhanced the influence of socialists within the labor movement, and a focus on wages, employment conditions, and worker rights. The coup of 1930 also helped forge unity among worker organizations, who recognized the need for a single representative body. The principal unions affiliated with the CGT at this point were those representing railway, tramway, telephone, and port workers, along with some public-sector workers and employees. The confederation was first headquartered in the offices of the craft railway union, **Unión Ferroviaria** (UF). In the 1930s, the CGT was led by the heads of railway unions and **Ángel Borlenghi** of the shop workers. Later, especially around midcentury, industrial unions (workers in the iron and steel, chemical and pharmaceutical, textile, motor vehicle, energy, and print sectors) would dominate. Later still, service-sector unions such as those representing school teachers, bank workers, and the expanding state sector would assume a significant role. Of course, these groupings were not mutually exclusive, particularly as the role of the state grew through nationalization and bureaucratic expansion—to its critics, featherbedding and *empleomanía*.

Unity proved problematic. In 1935, a spat between the socialists and syndicalists led to a split—the CGT-Independencia and CGT-Catamarca, the socialist- and syndicalist-dominated factions named after the streets on which their offices were based. There was a further split in 1942: the CGT-1 (anticommunist socialists) and CGT-2 (communists and fellow travelers). The organization was reunified in 1943, largely due to the efforts of Colonel and later General and President **Juan Domingo Perón**, who served as head of the labor secretariat set up following the **military coup of 1943**. Perón's prolabor program and industrial growth resulted in the rapid expansion of CGT membership, along with the influence of the organization. By the end of the 1940s, the CGT counted around 2.5 million members and played an active role in supporting the political ambitions of Perón. The CGT formed the **Partido Laborista** (PL) to contest the **congressional** and **presidential elections of 1946**, nominating Perón as presidential candidate. The CGT was rewarded with two important portfolios in Perón's first cabinet—Borlenghi was appointed minister of interior and **Juan Atilio Bramuglia** minister of foreign relations. The CGT acquired considerable political influence during the first two Perón presidencies but was rapidly Peronized, falling under state control: independent union leaders were weeded out, and unions that continued to elect socialists or non-Peronists were marginalized or lost legal recognition, substituted by compliant new unions that were accorded official recognition. After 1943, and particularly after 1946, the CGT secured new rights for workers, including retirement pensions and a broad range of social benefits and improved wages and working conditions, though at the cost of near complete subordination to the state. When the railway union attempted to organize a strike in the early 1950s, the leadership and workers were made to toe the official line.

Elements within the CGT attempted to use the ouster of Perón following the **military coup of 1955** to reestablish its autonomy, supporting the **Unión Popular** (UP), an alternative to the **Partido Justicialista** (PJ), an arrangement favored by groups within the **military** administration of the **Revolución Libertadora**. These efforts were thwarted by Perón, then in exile in **Spain.** The result was an ongoing struggle within the CGT between those who argued for an accommodation with military governments of the 1950s and 1960s or who favored **"Peronism without Perón,"** and revolutionary Peronists who regarded violent opposition to the regime as the only way of safeguarding worker rights.

Despite factionalism and government intervention, the CGT grew in importance, its finances sustained by compulsory deductions from workers' wages. By the 1960s, the CGT was channeling resources into property development—including housing and social facilities for workers—ran an investment bank, and acquired additional income from running worker social insurances schemes and medical facilities (*obras sociales*). Union and CGT officials were also accused of soliciting funds from employers, or demanding bribes, using the threat of calling strikes or organizing shop floor go-slows as a means of extortion. With hindsight, the 1960s probably represented a high point in the importance and influence of the CGT. Subsequently, factionalism, political repression, **economic crisis**, and the growth of the informal sector—unregistered workers were not unionized (and so did not pay compulsory dues)—reduced its economic relevance and political clout.

Internal conflict over how to deal with the military and Perón came to a head in 1968, following the **military coup of 1966**. The CGT split: the CGT-Azopardo, led by **Augusto Vandor** of the steel workers' union, **José Alonso** of the textile workers' union, and **José Ignacio Rucci** also of the steelworkers, prepared to collaborate with the military regime, and the **Confederación General del Trabajo de los Argentinos** (CGTA), which remained loyal to Perón, headed by **Raimundo Ongaro**. Factionalism—often associated with rigged internal elections and bloody conflict—within the CGT, as well as **corruption**, characterized the deterioration in public life during the period. Vandor was assassinated in 1969 and Alonso a year later. Rucci was murdered by the left-wing **Montonero** group in 1973, again underlining personal rivalry and ideological infighting within the labor movement. Further bloodletting in the labor movement, and directed against it by external agents, would only increase after 1975—namely, the reign of terror associated with the **Triple A** (Alianza Anticomunista Argentina) that epitomized the descent into violence during the presidency of **Isabel Perón** and, above all, the military regime of the **Proceso de Reorganización Nacional**.

Briefly reunited in the early 1970s, the CGT divided again in 1975. Named after the streets on which they were headquartered, and echoing what had transpired in 1966, the CGT-Azopardo and the CGT-Brasil respectively favored doing a deal with the armed forces after the **military coup of 1976** and opposed any such arrangement. The CGT-Azopardo was tolerated by regimes of the Proceso; the CGT-Brasil was banned yet operated clandestinely. The labor movement paid a heavy price during the **War to Annihilate Subversion**. More than 2,500 unionists were "disappeared" and murdered—union leaders, shop-floor activists, and ordinary members. And the movement suffered as a result of austerity measures applied by Minister of Economy **José Alfredo Martínez de Hoz** and factory closures triggered by the economic crisis of 1981. Following unsuccessful attempts at reunification at the beginning of the decade, the CGT was reunited again in 1983 under **Saúl Ubaldini** of the beer workers' union, formerly head of the CGT-Brasil. Ubaldini resisted efforts by President **Raúl Alfonsín** to democratize and normalize the union movement, a stance that further damaged the organization. It was viewed by large sections of the public as corrupt and tainted by the willingness of some union leaders to do deals with administrations of the Proceso.

The election of President **Carlos Saúl Menem** of the Peronist PJ in 1989 brought expectations of renewed close contacts between the CGT and the government. These efforts were dashed as Menem opted for neoliberal economic policies that included deregulation of the labor market and social policy changes that impacted worker pensions and social benefits. The 1990s was another period of splits within the movement and alternating moments of distance from and proximity to the government of the day. Elements within the CGT broke with Menem in 1989, while others offered conditional support. Yet others organized a general strike in 1992. Most of the movement endorsed Menem's reelection campaign in 1995. By this stage, however, the government's **privatization** program had weakened the influence of the labor movement, a trend that would continue during the economic crisis of 2001–2002. The influence of the central body suffered further during the early 21st century, again notwithstanding expectations (and initially the substance) of better relations with the Peronist administrations of **Néstor Kirchner** and his wife, **Cristina Fernández de Kirchner**. Factionalism within the PJ was mirrored by factionalism in the CGT, coupled with personal conflict among heads of the main unions jockeying for power in the organization. In addition to factionalism and sequences of splinters, the political influence of the CGT has been further eroded by the proliferation of grassroots movements and direct-action groups like *piqueteros*, answerable to individuals and groups associated with the Kirchners: CGT leaders had no monopoly of direct action or capacity to mobilize *piqueteros*.

Although the main factions of the CGT came together in 2016 in opposition to the economic policies of President **Maurico Macri**, elected the previous year, promising to develop an agenda that would facilitate reunification, there is little likelihood that more than token consolidation will result. Changes in the labor market, as well as economic crises, have had a prejudicial impact on the confederation. Corruption and violence in the movement have reduced its prestige and standing. It is unlikely that the national labor organization will ever again achieved the status and influence that it had from the 1940s to the 1960s. *See also* ARAMBURAZO (29 MAY–1 JUNE 1970); CORDOBAZO (29 MAY–3 JUNE 1969); IMMIGRATION.

CONFEDERACIÓN GENERAL DEL TRABAJO DE LOS ARGENTINOS (CGTA). An offshoot of the **Confederación General del Trabajo** (CGT) created in May 1968 and which subsisted until 1972, officially known as the CGT de los Argentinos. The origins of the CGTA lie in a split within the CGT over how to deal with the de facto government of General **Juan Carlos Onganía**. **Raimundo Ongaro**, who opposed collaboration with the regime, engineered the removal of the leader of his union, the Federación de Gráficos Bonaerenses (FGB). This pitted him against **José Alonso**, the head of the CGT, and **Augusto Vandor**, leader of the powerful Unión Obrera Metalúrgica (UOM), two men who found common cause in "participationism." This was a euphemism for collaboration, favoring negotiations with the dictatorship rather than outright opposition to it.

Authorized by the government, the CGT held a normalization congress in March 1968. An election was held for a new secretary general, in which Vandor lost to Ongaro (who was backed by the exiled **Juan Domingo Perón** and many radical elements). The regime promptly annulled the election, preventing Ongaro from taking office, with the "participationists" retaining control of the CGT headquarters, Ongaro headed a splinter movement that led to the formation of the CGTA. While the latter was outlawed immediately, the CGT was only "temporarily suspended" by the **military** government.

The CGTA brought together branches of major radical unions, including those representing port, oil, and sugar **industry** workers. The CGTA epitomized the revolutionary brand of Peronism and **trade unionism**, a stance associated with **John William Cooke**. The organization was also close to the **Movimiento de Sacerdotes para el Tercer Mundo** (MSTM). The CGTA participated actively in the **Cordobazo**, which earned it the support of workers while further antagonizing the Onganía administration, but its fate was sealed by the reconciliation between Vandor and Perón in 1969 and the "normalization" of the CGT in 1970. At this point, the CGTA witnessed the defection of many of its affiliated unions to the 62 Organizaciones, the political arm of the CGT. Nominally, the CGTA remained in existence until 1972, when it became clear that Peronism would participate in the general election scheduled for 1973. *See also* RUCCI, JOSÉ IGNACIO (1924–1973).

CONFEDERACIÓN GENERAL ECONÓMICA (CGE). Set up in 1950 to represent the interests of small- and medium-sized national industrial and commercial enterprises. From inception, CGE reports and propaganda emphasized the national origin of firms represented, as distinct from the established Unión Industrial Argentina (UIA), which dates from the 1870s and which the Confederación depicted as dominated by agribusinesses and large-scale enterprises, many of which were foreign owned or based overseas. Its declared mission was to press the case for official support of small, national firms that, up to the point, had no voice and to influence government policy. The timing of the formation of the CGE was no accident. It reflected a contemporary stress on development and national industrialization, which by then had become pronounced features of Peronist **economic policy**. Indeed, critics maintained that it was attempting to capitalize on the corporatist drift in government thinking and that the organization and growth of the CGE was actively promoted by President **Juan Domingo Perón** himself. This probably explains why the Confederación was "intervened" following the **military coup of 1955**. In 1958, large-scale firms opposed to emerging interventionist ideology set up a lobby group, the Asociación Coordinadora de Instituciones Empresarias Libres (ACIEL), to argue the case for liberal economics while attempting to eliminate the CGE altogether. As a result, the CGE moderated criticism of the liberal model applied by successive administrations in the late 1950s and early 1960s and concentrated on the representation of small firms located in the interior of the country. A national role again appeared possible in 1962 when the CGE collaborated with the **Confederación General del Trabajo** (CGT), the body representing **trade unions**, advocating a social pact to confront a severe **economic crisis**: salary increases, aid for small interior businesses, and the development of the local market were the central elements.

The idea of a popular, national development strategy was promoted again in the late 1960s, when the CGE campaigned vociferously against the project of **privatization** and denationalization advocated by **Adalbert Krieger Vasena**, appointed minister of economy by de facto president General **Juan Carlos Onganía** soon after the **military coup of 1966**. This was also the period when the Confederación built bridges to **political parties** thought to share its approach to national development, for example, **Partido Demócrata Cristiano (PDC)** and both branches of the Radical Party—the **Unión Cívica Radical del Pueblo** (UCRP) and the **Unión Cívica Radical Intransigente** (UCRI). When General **Alejandro Agustín Lanusse** displaced his colleague, General **Roberto Levingston**, as president in 1971, it seemed that the hour of the CGE had come, even more so with the return of democracy in 1973 and the election in rapid succession of Presidents **Héctor Cámpora** and Perón. Once again in association with the CGT, the CGE proposed a joint plan of action with the government to reactivate the economy and promote social justice and national liberation—action that also entailed close links with the Soviet bloc.

With the **military coup of 1976**, the CGE was once again intervened. It was formally dissolved a year later and the assets of the organization seized by the state. The restitution of assets and the refounding of the Confederación occurred in 1984 after the return of democracy in the **presidential election of 1983**. Since then, the CGE has functioned mainly as a business lobby and coordinator, continuing to represent small- and medium-size firms. It was instrumental in establishing the Day of the National Entrepreneur and collaborates with other business organizations, notably regional associations and minor sectoral federations, for which it provides a national platform. *See also* BER GELBARD, JOSÉ (1917–1977).

CONGRESS. The national legislature, Congreso de la Nación Argentina, is a bicameral body composed of the National Senate (Senado de la Nación Argentina) and the Chamber of Deputies (Cámara de Diputados de la Nación Argentina). Congress is located in the Palacio del Congreso de la Nación Argentina, at the western end of the Avenida de Mayo, 15 blocks (approximately a mile) from the presidential palace, the **Casa Rosada**, situated at the eastern end of the avenue.

Congress is the supreme lawmaking institution of the country. A peculiar feature of Argentina is that for lengthy periods during the second-half of the 20th century, the activities of Congress have been suspended—most recently for several years following the **military coup of 1976**. With Congress suspended, de facto administrations rule by decree, which technically had full legal force, though laws were not subject to normal constitutional procedure and parliamentary scrutiny.

There are currently 72 senators, three for each province and the autonomous city of **Buenos Aires**, and 257 deputies. The number of deputies is subject to change, being determined by population. Districts are subject to revision following national censuses held every 10 years, based on one deputy for every 33,000 inhabitants. Election to both chambers is by the d'Hondt system of proportional representation with "closed" party lists, though there are slight differences for each house. For the Senate, the party topping the poll in each electoral district (that is, each province and the city of Buenos Aires) is allocated two seats (the "majority" seats) and the principal runner-up one (the "minority" seat). For the chamber, each electoral district is divided into multiseat constituencies, with seats being allocated in accordance with the proportion of votes obtained. The province of Buenos Aires currently accounts for 70 seats in the Chamber of Deputies; the city of Buenos Aires, the next largest electoral district, has 25; the province of **Santa Fe**, the third largest electoral district, 19; the province of **Córdoba**, 18; the province of **Mendoza**, 10; the provinces of **Entre Ríos** and **Tucumán**, nine each; the number of seats allocated to the remaining provinces ranges from seven to five. In theory, deputies directly represent citizens, senators the provinces (and the city of Buenos Aires) that elect them.

Deputies sit for four years, senators for six. Every two years, one-half of the chamber and one-third of the Senate is renewed in rotation. Renewal arrangements are slightly different for each house. For the chamber, one-half the seats in each multiconstituency electoral district are renewed at midterm. In the case of the Senate, all three seats in one-third of the electoral districts are renewed. Every four years, presidential elections coincide with the cycle of congressional midterm renewals. These arrangements have been in force since the promulgation of the **Constitution of 1994**, which increased the number of senators per district from two to three and, among other features, reduced the term of senators from nine to six years and permitted the immediate reelections of a sitting president and provincial governors. The four-year term served by deputies was not changed. Other new electoral arrangements introduced in 1994 provided for the direct election of the president and senators—previously, presidents had been indirectly elected by an electoral college and senators by provincial legislatures. Another change was the creation of the post of chief of the cabinet, in effect a prime minister, a move intended to constrain the excessive presidentialism that had previously characterized the Argentine system by conferring additional power of scrutiny on Congress.

Congress has the power to initiate, debate, and sanction new laws and to modify existing legislation. Congress also has the power to hold the president and administration to account and to initiate investigation and call for information about matters consistent with its legislative, deliberating, and scrutiny functions. Specific powers reserved for each house include, for the chamber, to receive and debate new laws initiated by the public, consider proposals sent to it by the executive, and initiate investigations into the conduct of the president, vice president, prime minister, ministers, and members of the Supreme Court for reference to the Senate; for the Senate, to judge cases referred to it by the chamber, authorize the president to declare a state of siege in the case of an attack from abroad, supervise revenue-sharing agreements between the executive and provincial administrations, adjudicate in the case of disputes among local jurisdictions (for example, among provinces and lower levels of government and between branches of the administration), and approve the appointment of such public officials as senior judges, ambassadors, and senior members of the **military**.

Legislation proceeds through Congress in the following manner: first, project laws are tabled; secondly, they are assessed by relevant advisory committees of the house; thirdly, they are debated and passed to the other house. If laws are approved by both houses, they are sent to the executive for signature and promulgation. The president has 10 working days in which to sign; should he or she fail to do so within the required period, a law is applied automatically. Presidents also have the power to veto—partially or completely—a law. In the case of a partial veto, a law returns to Congress, which may (or may not) accept presidential modifications. A two-thirds majority in both houses is required to overturn a veto. When legislation is introduced into the Chamber of Deputies, the chamber becomes the house of origin and the Senate the house of revision, and vice versa. If legislation is passed by the house of origin but rejected by the house of revision, it may not be reintroduced in the same legislative session.

Following the 1994 constitution, presidents have the power to promulgate special decrees—Decrees of Necessity and Urgency—in exceptional circumstances. Such decrees must be signed by all ministers and have immediate force of law, but they are subject to scrutiny by Congress within 10 days of promulgation and may be overturned.

Members of Congress sit in party blocs or coalitions arranged around the horseshoe houses. Bloc and subbloc presidents wield considerable power and are responsible for maintaining discipline. Legislators enjoy parliamentary immunity: they may not be subject to judicial process when in office. Such immunity may be suspended, or a member expelled, by a two-thirds majority of the house in which the legislator sits. Congress normally sits between 1 March and 30 November in ordinary session. The executive has the authority to call for extraordinary sessions, should they be deemed necessary, while the houses have the capacity to prorogue ordinary sessions. *See also* CONGRESSIONAL ELECTIONS; CONSTITUTION OF 1853; *LISTA SÁBANA*; MILITARY COUPS; OLIVOS PACT; PRESIDENTIAL ELECTIONS.

CONGRESS OF TUCUMÁN. Historians dispute the importance of the Constituent Congress of the **United Provinces of the River Plate** (or the **United Provinces of South America**, another contemporary variant) held in the capital of the province of the same name. The Congress sat between 1816 and 1820, declaring **independence** on 9 July 1816, recognizing the reality of the separation from **Spain** that had occurred years earlier. All existing provinces were represented, save **Corrientes, Entre Ríos**, and **Santa Fe**. Also represented were four provinces of present-day **Bolivia**. At the time, Upper Peru (Bolvia today) was considered by **Buenos Aires** to be part of the United Provinces, the successor entity of the **Viceroyalty of the River Plate**. While the Congress was sitting, the fate of the country and its extent was still far from determined. Spanish armies occupied Lower Peru (**Peru**) and **Chile**. Contemporaneously, the Uruguayan patriot Artigas seemed intent on carving out a new political entity composed of **Uruguay** and the neighboring Argentine provinces of Entre Ríos and Corrientes, hence their decision not to send delegates to Tucumán.

Although little progress was made establishing the definitive constitutional and political framework of the country, and many of the objectives of the congress were overtaken by events, the bold assertion of independence at a time of uncertainly gave considerable impulse to the patriot cause: 9 July is celebrated as one of the key dates on the national calendar. *See also* SAN MIGUEL DE TUCUMÁN (CITY).

CONGRESSIONAL ELECTIONS OF 1854 TO 1910. Congressional elections were held at regular two-yearly intervals, as prescribed by the **Constitution of 1853**, usually coinciding with the **presidential election** every six years, as for example in 1854, 1860, 1874, 1880, 1886, 1892, and so forth—exceptionally, presidential elections were held in 1862 and 1868. On each occasion, one-half of the lower house of **Congress**, the Chamber of Deputies, was renewed, and one-third of the Senate. Deputies sat for four years, Senators for nine. Before the passage of the **Sáenz Peña Law** of 1912, which among other reforms introduced the secret ballot—previously electors marked their vote in an open book—elections were "managed," generally ensuring victory and working majorities in Congress for the Partido Autonomista Nacional (PAN). This arrangement resulted in abstentionism, mainly by the **Unión Cívica Radical** (UCR), which did not contest elections between 1892 and 1912, and campaigns for electoral reform headed by the UCR, the **Partido Socialista** (PS), and the Liga del Sur. Some of these parties participated in local and provincial elections, for example, in the province of **Santa Fe** and the city of **Buenos Aires**, but rarely in national elections. *See also* ALEM, LEANDRO NICEBRO (1842–1896); CRY OF ALCORTA; JUSTO, JUAN BAUTISTA (1865–1928); PALACIOS, AL-

FREDO LORENZO RAMÓN (1880–1965); REVOLUTION OF 1890; SÁENZ PEÑA, ROQUE (1851–1914); YRIGOYEN, HIPÓLITO (1852–1933).

CONGRESSIONAL ELECTIONS OF 1912 AND 1913. Elections for the Chamber of Deputies, the lower house of **Congress**, were held on 7 April. Their importance lies in the fact that they were the first fair and free national elections to be held hard on the heels of the introduction of the secret ballot, a reform instituted by the **Sáenz Peña Law** of 1912, and because the **Unión Cívica Radical** (UCR), which had long campaigned for the change, agreed to participate, abandoning abstentionism. Perhaps in recognition of the greater transparency and democratic accountability signaled by the reform, voter turnout was an unprecedented 68.5 percent, around double that of many previous elections. Of the 60 seats in the 120-member chamber up for renewal, the UCR won 11. Elections for the National Senate were held on 7 April 1912 and 30 March 1913; one-third of the seats in the 30-member upper house were renewed. Doubting the reliability of procedures in many districts—Senate elections were controlled by provincial governments and senators elected by provincial legislatures—the UCR did not field candidates across the country. The party obtained only one seat, in the province of **Santa Fe**, which returned its first ever senator; in the city of **Buenos Aires**, the UCR was defeated by the candidate of the **Partido Socialista** (PS). The main loser in the elections was the conservative Partido Atonomista National (PAN); while retaining control of the Senate, the PAN lost its overall majority in the chamber. The 1912–1913 elections marked the beginning of the end of the PAN; as a national organization, it disintegrated shortly afterward.

CONGRESSIONAL ELECTIONS OF 1914. Taking place on 22 March, the congressional and gubernatorial elections of 1914 are significant because they were the second nationwide contest held following the introduction of the secret ballot, a reform instituted by the **Sáenz Peña Law** of 1912, and because the **Unión Cívica Radical** (UCR) contested the elections, thereby confirming the position adopted in the **congressional elections of 1912** and **1913**, namely that it had abandoned its historic stance of abstaining from elections. Although the UCR only contested seats for the lower house of **Congress**, doubting the fairness of elections for the National Senate, which were ordered by provincial governments, the party obtained one-third of the popular vote and gained 19 of the 60 seats in the 120-member Chamber of Deputies due for renewal. In addition to seats already held, this gave the UCR a total of 28 seats, making it the largest party in the chamber.

CONGRESSIONAL ELECTIONS OF 1916. Held on 2 April at the same time as the presidential election, these were the first simultaneous presidential and congressional elections to be held following the **Sáenz Peña Law** of 1912 that introduced the secret ballot. Voter turnout was almost 63 percent, double that of the previous general elections six years earlier. The presidential contest was won by **Hipólito Yrigoyen** of the **Unión Cívica Radical** (UCR), ending the hegemony of the Partido Autonomista Nacional (PAN), which had dominated national politics since the 1870s by means of "managed" elections. Of the 120-member Chamber of Deputies, one-half the seats were up for renewal; the UCR gained 16, bringing its total to 44, still far short of a majority. One-third of the seats in the National Senate were renewed. Although the Radicals remained in the minority in both houses, the elections are important as they marked the beginnings of modern democracy in the country. *See also* PRESIDENTIAL ELECTION OF 1916.

CONGRESSIONAL ELECTIONS OF 1918. Midterm elections for the lower house of **Congress**, the Chamber of Deputies, were held on 3 March, and for the upper house, the National Senate, a year later in April 1919. With one-half of the chamber up for renewal, the governing **Unión Cívica Radical** (UCR) gained 12 of the 60 seats contested, taking its representation in the lower house to 56. The party also performed well in the gubernatorial elections, notably in the province of **Buenos Aires**, which elected its first UCR governor. Across the country, the party obtained almost half the popular vote. Of the 10 seats in the National Senate due for renewal—one-third—the UCR took seven, increasing its representation in the upper house to eight. With the aid of other parties, the elections enabled the UCR to command a majority in the chamber to secure legislation, though far short of controlling the Senate. The 1918 and 1919 elections were marred by interventions in several provinces ordered by President **Hipólito Yrigoyen**, which damaged the UCR, and also by social unrest that favored the conservatives in some areas and the socialists in others.

CONGRESSIONAL ELECTIONS OF 1920. Congressional and gubernatorial elections took place on 7 March and were regarded as a victory for the **Unión Cívica Radical** (UCR), giving it a working majority in **Congress**. One-half of the 158 seats in the Chamber of Deputies and one-third in the 30-member National Senate were renewed. (The number of seats in the chamber had been increased by 38 in 1920 to reflect the growth in population registered by the national census taken in 1914.) The UCR gained 28 of the seats up for renewal in the chamber, giving it a total of 84, the first time that the party achieved an absolute majority in the lower house. UCR gains in the National Senate were distinctly modest, though it performed well in gubernatorial contests. Other progressive parties like the **Partido Socialista** (PS) and **Partido Demócrata Progresista** (PDP) made gains. The principal losers were the conservatives—regional parties and the Partido Autonomista Nacional (PAN). Although the UCR was threatened with splits and voter turnout had been declining since 1916, commanding around 44 percent of the popular vote, the party's showing in 1920 was seen as a good omen for the upcoming **presidential election of 1922**, not least because it appeared to have contained the threat from the democratic left, especially in the city and province of **Buenos Aires**, where most of the newly created seats had fallen to the Radicals.

CONGRESSIONAL ELECTIONS OF 1922. Held on 2 April at the same time as the **presidential election of 1922**. The congressional and presidential elections of 1922 are important because the governing party, the **Unión Cívica Radical** (UCR), obtained almost 50 percent of the popular vote. In addition to retaining the presidency, with **Marcelo T. de Alvear** replacing **Hipólito Yrigoyen**, the congressional contest saw the UCR increase its majority in the 158-seat Chamber of Deputies to 91—the third successive increase since 1916—and make gains in the National Senate, where its tally of seats rose to 15 in the 30-member upper house. Thus, in 1922, the Radicals commanded the presidency and both houses of **Congress**. This dominance, however, would soon be undermined by splits in the party—the *antipersonalista* wing headed by Alvear and the *personalistas* by Yrigoyen—and by a growing threat from the right.

CONGRESSIONAL ELECTIONS OF 1924. Held on 7 March, the midterms marked a significant moment in the modern political history of the country. For the first time since the introduction of the secret ballot instituted by the **Sáenz Peña Law** of 1912, voter turnout was less than 50 percent—it had been falling steadily in previous elections. Another critical factor was the decline in the share of votes obtained by the governing **Unión Cívica Radical** (UCR); for the first time since 1912, when the UCR abandoned abstentionism, it lost seats in the Chamber of Deputies. The officialist wing of the party lost 19 seats, reducing its representation to 72 in the 158-member lower house. Some of these losses were to dissident factions of the party, others to the **Partido Socialista** (PS) (which almost doubled its seats in the chamber to 18), and yet others to conservative national and regional parties. The officialist wing of the party, *personalistas* controlled by former president **Hipólito Yrigoyen**, also lost ground in the National Senate. Splits within the UCR would become more pronounced thereafter, limiting the ability of the party to respond to the **military coup of 1930** and fraudulent elections under the **Concordancia**.

CONGRESSIONAL ELECTIONS OF 1926. Voter turnout increased by a few percentage points in the midterm elections held on 7 March compared with the 1924 midterms—49 percent against 44 percent—yet continued to reflect disenchantment with the democratic process. The *personalista* wing of the **Unión Cívica Radical** (UCR) headed by ex-president **Hipólito Yrigoyen** continued to lose ground; its representation in the Chamber of Deputies falling by 15 seats, after registering a substantial decline in the **congressional elections of 1924**. Dissident factions of the party increased their representation, possibly strengthening the influence of sitting UCR president **Marcelo T. de Alvear**. The fragmentation of the UCR, as well as voter antipathy and the failure of other parties to form a credible alternative to the Radicals, boded ill for the future—beyond the **congressional** and **presidential elections of 1928**.

CONGRESSIONAL ELECTIONS OF 1928. Held on 1 April, at the same time as the presidential election, the congressional and gubernatorial elections of 1928 were one of the most hotly contested elections in modern Argentine political history, which was partly reflected in voter participation. At near 81 percent, voter turnout was almost double that of the **congressional elections of 1924** and substantially higher than in the **congressional elections of 1926**, setting a record since the introduction of the secret ballot implemented by the **Sáenz Peña Law** of 1912. Enthusiasm for former president **Hipólito Yrigoyen**, who commanded almost 62 percent of the popular vote in the presidential contest, propelled officialist **Unión Cívica Radical** (UCR) candidates to power in **Congress** and the provinces. Taking 53 of the 79 seats at stake in the 158-member Chamber of Deputies, *personalista* pro-Yrigoyen Radicals regained a majority in the lower house with a total of 92 seats. In the National Senate, where one-third of the 30 seats were up for renewal, Yrigoyenistas won five, half the places available, taking their total to eight. This matched the postelection representation of outgoing *antipersonalista* UCR president **Marcelo T. de Alvear**—a one seat gain meant that Alvear also controlled eight senators. Yrigoyen's sweeping victory was attributed to his charisma and populist stance on **foreign debt/foreign investment**. He was also aided by divisions among the socialists, who had often performed well in the city of **Buenos Aires**. The 1928 elections were a high point in Yrigoyen's political career. He would be 78 years old on taking office and in declining health. In government, he would prove indecisive, incapable of dealing with the economic and political problems buffeting the country, including the world depression of 1930, factors that contributed to the **military coup of 1930**. *See also* ECONOMIC CRISES; PRESIDENTIAL ELECTION OF 1928.

CONGRESSIONAL ELECTIONS OF 1931 TO 1940. The legislative elections of the 1930s were marred by rigging (the rather cynically so-called *fraude patriótico*) designed to favor the conservative **Partido Demócrata Nacional** (PDN), the leading party in the **Concordancia** coalition with *antipersonalista* Radicals and the Independent Socialists.

In 1931, the *personalista* Radicals abstained from participating in the congressional elections in protest at their overthrow in the **military coup of 1930**. Out of the 158 seats in the Chamber of Deputies, the PDN secured 58 with just over 43 percent of the vote, *antipersonalistas* obtained 17 with 4 percent of ballots cast, while the Independent Socialists garnered 11 with a little more than 6 percent of the vote. Electoral fraud became even more blatant in subsequent elections. In 1934, the PDN secured 60 out of a total of 158 deputies with 29 percent of ballots cast, while *antipersonalista* Radicals won 16 seats with 1.5 percent of the vote, and the Independent Socialists obtained six seats with a minimal number of votes. In 1935, the then formally reunified **Unión Cívica Radical** (UCR) reentered the political arena and, fearing fraud in forthcoming elections, unsuccessfully petitioned the government to make them fair. In 1936, the UCR secured 40 out of 158 seats in the Chamber of Deputies with 44 percent of the vote, while the PDN obtained 55 with just under 23 percent of ballots cast. *Antipersonalistas* won 11 seats with 2.5 percent of votes cast, while the Independent Socialists garnered two with just over 0.5 percent.

The legislative elections of 1938 cannot be taken seriously, as every electoral district in the country reported widespread fraud. Notwithstanding the fraudulent win by **Roberto M. Ortiz** in the **presidential election of 1937**, the new president brought some hope as he was determined to clean up the system. The congressional elections of 1940 resulted in significant gains by the opposition, but fate intervened. Ortiz had to take what became a permanent leave of absence on health grounds and was replaced by Vice President **Ramón S. Castillo**, an unreconstructed conservative who undid the redemocratization measures undertaken by Ortiz and resorted to the worst political practices of the past.

Following the rigging of several gubernatorial elections in 1940, the opposition in the Chamber of Deputies claimed a major scalp. It blocked the **Pinedo Plan**, a program that was not only designed to deal with the impact of the Second World War but also tacitly acknowledged that the existing economic model no longer worked. Yet the UCR was unable to turn its opposition to the Concordancia into an advantage. There was severe criticism of party leader **Marcelo T. de Alvear**, who had been the presidential candidate in 1937 in an election he knew he could not win and had thereby legitimized a regime that prevented his accession to government. Matters were aggravated by the legislative elections of 1942. These were the last held before the **military coup of 1943**, and one of the most anodyne in Argentine electoral history with little need to resort to fraud: the UCR lost several districts, including the **federal capital**, which was won by the **Partido Socialista** (PS). *See also* ECONOMY; INDUSTRY; JUSTO, AGUSTÍN PEDRO (1876–1943); ROCA–RUNCIMAN PACT (1933).

CONGRESSIONAL ELECTIONS OF 1946. Held on 24 February, simultaneously with the presidential contest in which **Juan Domingo Perón** was victorious. With a voter turnout of more than 83 percent, Perón won the **presidential election** by a substantial margin over the main opposition, sweeping supporters in the **Partido Laborista** (PL) into **Congress**. The PL obtained 43.5 percent of the popular vote and secured 101 out of 158 seats available in the Chamber of Deputies. The **Unión Cívica Radical** (UCR) garnered 27.5 percent of the vote, gaining 44 seats, and the anti-Peronist **Union Democrática** (UD) with 14 percent got a mere five seats. Remaining seats were distributed among minor regional parties.

CONGRESSIONAL ELECTIONS OF 1948. Called for 7 March, these were the last congressional and gubernatorial elections in which only men could vote. The franchise was extended to **women** by the **Constitution of 1949**. The **Partido Peronista** (PP) obtained 64 percent of the vote and ended up with 109 of the 158 seats in the Chamber of Deputies, increasing the representation gained by the **Partido Laborista** (PL) in the preceding **congressional** and **presidential elections of 1946**; the **Unión Cívica Radical** (UCR) got 28 percent and the remaining 49 seats, increasing its number of seats at the expense of minor parties.

CONGRESSIONAL ELECTIONS OF 1951. Held on 24 November under the terms of the **Constitution of 1949** and the electoral law of 1951, they were won overwhelmingly by the **Partido Peronista** (PP)—not least thanks to a clever redistricting system that reduced the number of seats in the Chamber of Deputies from 158 to 149. The PP secured 63.5 percent of the vote and 135 seats, while the **Unión Cívica Radical** (UCR) obtained 32 percent and the remaining 14 seats.

CONGRESSIONAL ELECTIONS OF 1958. Took place on 23 February, simultaneously with the presidential contest that got **Arturo Frondizi** of the **Unión Cívica Radical Intransigente** (UCRI) elected. Reversing an amendment made during the *peronato*, the contest was governed once again by the 1912 electoral law and a new statute of **political parties** that replaced the one enacted in 1949. Voter turnout for the elections was almost 91 percent, the highest in national history, reflecting the desire among the electorate to make a statement in support of democratic institutions following the return of the armed forces to the barracks after the **military coup of 1955**.

However, the election was restricted, not least because of the proscription of the **Partido Peronista** (PP). Rather than allow a neo-Peronist party (**"Peronism without Perón"**) to contest the election, exiled former president **Juan Domingo Perón** struck the infamous **Caracas Pact** with Frondizi and ordered his supporters to back the UCRI. For Frondizi, it paid handsomely. Of the 187 seats up for grabs in the Chamber of Deputies, the UCRI secured 133 with 49.5 percent of the popular vote. The **Unión Cívica Radical del Pueblo** (UCRP) garnered 32 percent of votes cast and 52 seats, while the Partido Liberal de Corrientes got 0.5 percent and the remaining two seats. *See also* PRESIDENTIAL ELECTION OF 1958.

CONGRESSIONAL ELECTIONS OF 1960. Held on 27 March, it was restricted as Peronism was proscribed. Out of the 192 seats of the Chamber of Deputies, the **Unión Cívica Radical Intransigente** (UCRI) of President **Arturo Frondizi** obtained 109 with 27 percent of the vote, while the **Unión Cívica Radical del Pueblo** (UCRP) led by **Ricardo Balbín** garnered 74 with 31 percent of ballots cast. Notwithstanding the percentage of votes obtained, the UCRI retained the majority since its loss of seats went mostly to the UCRP.

It is noteworthy that the proscription of Peronism did not prevent exiled former president **Juan Domingo Perón** from interfering in the election. He deprived Frondizi of anti-Peronist support by revealing the infamous **Caracas Pact** between the two men in the run-up to the **presidential election of 1958** and urged his own supporters to cast blank ballots. The latter totaled 25 percent of the vote, which was one of the highest such incidences in Argentine electoral history.

CONGRESSIONAL ELECTIONS OF 1962. Held on 18 March, they were the trigger for the overthrow of President **Arturo Frondizi** 11 days later. Buoyed by the victory of his **Unión Cívica Radical Intransigente** (UCRI) party in provincial elections in **Santa Fe** in December 1961, and in the hope of still garnering Peronist votes, Frondizi convinced the **military** to permit candidates from neo-Peronist groups to stand in congressional and provincial elections. Fronzidi argued that the parties in question would not win enough seats to do any harm and that allowing them to take part would serve to destroy the myth of **Juan Domingo Perón**'s power and hold over voters. The strategy failed disastrously. Neo-Peronists obtained almost 32 percent of the votes, with a total of 2,530,000, against 2,454,000 for the UCRI and 1,886,000 for the **Unión Cívica Radical del Pueblo** (UCRP). As a result, the

Peronists obtained 45 of the 96 seats up for renewal in the Chamber of Deputies. In simultaneous provincial elections, they won nine out of 14 governorships—most spectacularly in the province of **Buenos Aires**. These election victories served to legitimize Peronism but did not pave the way for the legalization of the **Partido Justicialista** (PJ). If anything, the results signaled the beginning of the end of Frondizi. *See also* MILITARY COUP OF 1962.

CONGRESSIONAL ELECTIONS OF 1963. They were held on 7 July, simultaneously with the **presidential election of 1963**. Out of 192 seats, the **Unión Cívica Radical del Pueblo** (UCRP) secured 73 seats with 28.5 percent of the vote, the **Unión Cívica Radical Intransigente** (UCRI) won 40 seats with 16.4 percent of ballots cast, and the Unión del Pueblo Argentino (UDELPA) obtained 14 seats with 7.5 percent of the vote. Although the Frente Nacional y Popular—which comprised the neo-Peronist **Unión Popular** (UP), the **Partido Conservador Popular** (PCP), and the **Movimiento de Integración y Desarrollo** (MID)—was proscribed during this election, an array of minor neo-Peronist groups garnered a total of 16 seats.

CONGRESSIONAL ELECTIONS OF 1965. Held on 14 March, several features marked the importance of these midterm elections. First, that the successful participation of neo-Peronism did not trigger the immediate overthrow of President **Arturo Illia**, as had happened to President **Arturo Frondizi** after the **congressional elections of 1962**; secondly, the strong performance of groupings supporting the concept of **"Peronism without Perón"**; and thirdly, the further splintering of the Radical vote. At 83.5 percent, voter participation demonstrated continuing strong commitment for the democratic process on the part of the electorate in the face of increasing "supervision" by the armed forces.

Illia refused to bow to pressure from the **military** and other anti-Peronists to bar the neo-Peronist **Unión Popular** (UP) from fielding candidates. **Augusto Vandor,** secretary general of the Unión de Obreros Metalúrgicos (UOM), took up the mantle of the UP in direct defiance of the call of exiled **Juan Domingo Perón** for open conflict with the government, a move that divided Vandor and his allies in the **Confederacion General del Trabajo** (CGT) from **José Alonso,** leader of the CGT. Nevertheless, Vandor set up a coalition of trade unionists and neo-Peronist parties with the UP at its center. These maneuvers transformed Vandor into a national electable political figure, raising the public profile and viability of the campaign for "Peronism without Perón."

The Vandorista coalition defeated the governing **Unión Cívica Radical del Pueblo** (UCRP) by gaining 30 percent of the vote to its 28.5 percent. However, this did not translate into a similarly proportionate number of seats in the Chamber of Deputies (192 members). While the UP and its partners obtained 52 seats, the UCRP secured 68. The size of the Vandorista vote also frustrated the political ambitions of former de facto president **Pedro Eugenio Aramburu**. The anti-Peronist organization, Unión del Pueblo Argentino (UDELPA), that he had set up and which he assumed would benefit from efforts to frustrate the return of Perón, saw its number of seats halved to seven, garnering only 2 percent of the vote. Another loser was the **Unión Cívica Radical Intransigente** (UCRI), which lost 29 seats, retaining only 11, on taking 5 percent of the vote. The UCRI was beaten by its splinter group, the **Movimiento de Integración y Desarrollo** (MID), formed in 1963. This was the first electoral test of the MID, as it had been barred from standing in the elections of 1963: it gained 16 seats with 6.5 percent of the vote.

While in 1962 congressional elections were held simultaneously with those for governors, this was not the case in 1965. The next gubernatorial contests, due to be held in 1967, boded ill for the government as the armed forces were bound to prevent a repeat of March 1962. The matter would become purely academic, as Illia was ousted in the **military coup of 1966**. *See also* TRADE UNIONS.

CONGRESSIONAL ELECTIONS OF 1973. Held on 11 March, the contest delivered a similar result to the presidential election held simultaneously—a substantial victory for Peronism. The Chamber of Deputies comprised 243 members at the time. The Peroinist-dominated **Frente Justicialista de Liberación** (FREJULI) garnered 50 percent of the vote, which translated into 145 seats, split as follows among its components: **Partido Justicialista (PJ)**, 131; **Monvimiento de Integración y Desarrollo** (MID), 12; and **Partido Conservador Popular** (PCP), 2. The **Unión Cívica Radical** (UCR) obtained 21 percent of the vote and 51 seats; the Alianza Popular Federalista obtained 15 percent of the vote and 20 seats. Remaining seats were divided among many small parties. *See also* PRESIDENTIAL ELECTION OF MARCH 1973.

CONGRESSIONAL ELECTIONS OF 1985. The first midterm elections to be held after the return to democracy two years earlier, which had resulted in the unexpected victory of **Raúl Alfonsín** of the **Unión Cívica Radical** (UCR) in the **presidential election of 1983**. The 1985 elections for **Congress** were a critical test for the government, which had inherited a broken **economy** from the departing **military** regime of the **Proceso de**

Reorganización Nacional and had to confront a recalcitrant military and deal with high public expectations. Held on 3 November, the elections were a strong endorsement of Alfonsín's approach to the problems confronting the country, in the face of considerable antagonism from the **Partido Justicialista** (PJ) and its close allies in the labor movement, the **Confederación General del Trabajo**. With a turnout of almost 84 percent, and one-half of the Chamber of Deputies up for renewal—127 of 254 seats—the UCR retained control of the lower house, gaining one additional seat to take its tally to 130, with a shade under 44 percent of the poll. The divided PJ lost eight seats with 34 percent of the vote. Alfonsín's victory was widely attributed to his handling of the military and, even more so, to the initial success of the heterodox growth package, the **Austral Plan**, introduced in June of that year.

CONGRESSIONAL ELECTIONS OF 1987. Taking place on 6 September, the midterm elections were significant because the governing **Unión Cívica Radical** (UCR) lost control of the Chamber of Deputies, the lower house of **Congress**, while victories in the gubernatorial contests by the opposition **Partido Justcialista** (PJ) meant that it came to control 17 of the 23 provinces. Of the seven governorships won in the **presidential** and **congressional elections of 1983**, all but two were lost by the UCR—including that of the crucial province of **Buenos Aires**. The PJ strengthened its grip on the National Senate. Occurring as the government was losing control of the economy, the midterms signaled that UCR President **Raúl Alfonsín** would head a lame-duck administration for the final two years of his mandate.

CONGRESSIONAL ELECTIONS OF 1989. The general elections were held on 14 May—congressional and presidential elections being held simultaneously at a time of political and **economic crises** as inflation accelerated and social disorder threatened. Turnout was over 85 percent. **Carlos Saúl Menem** and his **Partido Justicialista** (PJ) swept to power, gaining control of both house of **Congress**. One-half of the seats in the 254-member Chamber of Deputies were renewed, as was one-third of the 48-seat National Senate. Of the seats contested in the lower house, the **Unión Cívica Radical** (UCR) had held 65 but lost 23; the PJ gained 12 to take 65; the representation of the conservative **Unión del Centro Democrático** (UCeDé) rose by two, taking its tally in the new Chamber to 11—the UCeDe would subsequently align with the PJ. In the new chamber, the PJ held 126 seats and the UCR 89; in the Senate, 28 to 12. Commanding comfortable majorities with allies in each house, the PJ would go on to secure the passage of controversial legislation proposed by incoming president Menem. See also CONVERTIBILITY PLAN; OLIVOS PACT; PRESIDENTIAL ELECTION OF 1989; PRIVATIZATION.

CONGRESSIONAL ELECTIONS OF 1991. The timing of the midterm elections varied across the country, but most provinces voted on 8 September. Although the governing party of President **Carlos Saúl Menem**, the **Partido Justicialista** (PJ), lost three of the 17 provincial governorship held in 1987 and the opposition **Unión Cívica Radical** (UCR) gained two, the elections were a resounding endorsement of the neoliberal **Convertibility Plan** introduced by Menem and his minister of economy, **Domingo Cavallo**, earlier in the year. The UCR lost seats in the lower house of **Congress**, particularly in the province of **Buenos Aires**, most of which were picked up by fringe parties that would collaborate with the PJ. The elections showed that the UCR was still being castigated by voters for the **economic crises** that plagued the last years of the administration of former president **Raúl Alfonsín** and that the indictment of associates of Menem on charges of **corruption** had little impact.

CONGRESSIONAL ELECTIONS OF 1993. Held on 3 October, the elections strengthened the grip on power of President **Carlos Saúl Menem** as the governing **Partido Justicialista** (PJ) increased its control of **Congress**. Topping the poll in the city of **Buenos Aires** and 16 of the 23 provinces, the PJ was the main victor, although the opposition **Unión Cívica Radical** (UCR) made some modest, surprising gains. In the 257-member lower house, the Chamber of Deputies, almost half the seats were up for renewal. After the election, the PJ held 127 seats and could count on the support of many minor parties; the UCR, 84. The elections signaled enduring voter support for Menem's economic strategy and enabled him to engineer constitutional reform that would allow him to stand for immediate reelection in 1995—the **Constitution of 1853** proscribed immediate reelection. *See also* CONSTITUTION OF 1994; CONVERTIBILITY PLAN; OLIVOS PACT; PRIVATIZATION.

CONGRESSIONAL ELECTIONS OF 1995. The general elections (presidential and congressional elections were held at the same time) took place on 14 May. They are significant because they were the first to take place following the adoption of the **Constitution of 1994**. In the congressional contest, one-half of the seats in the Chamber of Deputies were renewed and one-third in the National Senate, the number of seats in the Senate being increased from two to three per province and for the city of **Buenos Aires**. Other noteworthy features include the challenge to sitting president **Carlos Saúl Menem** and the **Partido Justicialista** (PJ) mounted by dissident factions of the party, which coalesced around **José Octavio Bordón** and **Carlos "Chacho" Álvarez**, founders of the **Frente País Solidario** (FREPASO), who campaigned against the increasing **corruption** of the regime. Such splits would become more pronounced in the future. The elections are also important because voter turnout increased marginally to 82 percent—turnout had declined over previous midterm congressional elections (around 80 percent in 1993 and 1991, down from 85 percent in 1989). Despite challenges, the PJ was victorious, topping the poll in 19 out of 24 congressional electoral districts to win 68 of the 130 seats renewed. The **Unión Cívica Radical** (UCR)—the historic opposition to the PJ—took 28 seats and FREPASO 20. In the newly enlarged Senate, PJ and UCR gains were more evenly balanced: after the elections, the PJ held 39 seats in the 72-member upper house, the UCR 20, and the FREPASO 3, others being held by regional electoral alliances. In gubernatorial contests, the PJ won 14 governorships and the UCR 5; elsewhere, regional parties won. These victories, and Menem's reelection as president, once again signaled voter endorsement of the **Convertibility Plan** and the economic growth associated with it, notwithstanding turmoil in international **currency** markets around the time of the elections. *See also* CAVALLO, DOMINGO FELIPE (1946–); OLIVOS PACT; PRESIDENTIAL ELECTION OF 1995; PRIVATIZATION.

CONGRESSIONAL ELECTIONS OF 1997. Some 127 seats in the 257-member Chamber of Deputies, the lower house of **Congress**, were contested in the midterm elections held on 26 October, along with one-third of the National Senate. The elections are notable because they witnessed the emergence of the **Alianza** composed of the **Unión Cívica Radical** (UCR) and the **Frente País Solidario** (FREPASO), and because it was the first time since 1985 that the ruling **Partido Justicialista** (PJ) had been defeated. The Alianza gained 18 deputies; the PJ lost 13.

The elections took place amid mounting criticism of President **Carlos Saúl Menem** and an economic slowdown. Menem's wizard minister of economy, **Domingo Cavallo**, had resigned more than a year earlier, protesting **corruption**. The national **trade unions** movement, the **Confederación General del Trabajo** (CGT), had organized a series of general strikes—only the second time that the CGT had acted against a PJ administration. Political scandals included the murder of journalist **José Luis Cabezas** and the implication of a close associate of Menem, **Alfredo Yabrán**. On a turnout of 80 percent, the Alianza gained almost 46 percent of the votes and the PJ 36 percent, going on to win the **presidential election of 1999**.

CONGRESSIONAL ELECTIONS OF 1999. Simultaneous with the presidential election on 24 October; gubernatorial elections in 21 provinces were also held on the same day—the exceptions were **Córdoba** and **Corrientes** and the city of **Buenos Aires**. After the elections, the **Partido Justicialista** (PJ) composed the largest bloc in the 257-seat Chamber of Deputies with 100 seats, despite sustaining losses. The **Alianza**, which delivered the presidency to **Fernando de la Ruá**, held 121 seats—85 for the **Unión Cívica Radical** (UCR), the senior partner in the Alliance, and 36 for the **Frente País Solidario** (FREPASO). Other seats were distributed among minor parties and regional groupings. Although the Alianza lacked a majority in the lower house of **Congress**, it was able to assemble a working majority. The Senate, however, was dominated by the PJ, a situation that destabilized a coalition government confronting internal divisions and acute economic challenges as the **Convertibility Plan** launched at the beginning of the decade by former president **Carlos Saúl Menem** began to unravel. Of the 21 provincial governorships, 12 were won by the (PJ), including the province of **Buenos Aires**, and six by the Alianza, mainly the UCR; the remainder were won by small provincial groupings.

Although the elections had taken place in a mood of political optimism—as the electorate voted in favor of "clean" democratic politics and against the **corruption** that mired the last years of the Menem administration—with the economy stalling, the outcome meant that the administration and the governing class were ill prepared for looming political and **economic crises**. *See also* ÁLVAREZ, CARLOS ALBERTO "CHACHO" (1948–); CAVALLO, DOMINGO FELIPE (1946–); CONGRESSIONAL ELECTIONS OF 2001; DUHALDE, EDUARDO ALBERTO (1941–); KIRCHNER, NÉSTOR CARLOS (1950–2010); PRESIDENTIAL ELECTION OF 1999; PRESIDENTIAL ELECTION OF 2003.

CONGRESSIONAL ELECTIONS OF 2001. Called for the 14 October, midway through the term of President **Fernando de la Ruá**, at a time of profound institutional crisis that would culminate weeks later in the resignation of De la Ruá and **default**—the largest in international financial history. In the lower house of **Congress**, the 257-seat Chamber of Deputies, 127 members faced the electorate. Exceptionally, all seats in the 72-member National Senate were renewed following the **Constitution of 1994**, which had reduced the term of Senators from nine to six years—an arrangement designed to facilitate future partial renewals every two years, when one-third of seats would be contested.

Voter disillusionment with the prevailing order was reflected in a low turnout of 75 percent, down almost seven points on the **presidential** and **congressional elections of 1999**, and the fact that 25 percent of those who voted cast blank ballots or spoilt their papers. The opposition **Partido Justicialista** (PJ) was the victor in terms of overall gains, yet the total number of votes received was more than 12 points down on 1999. The principal loser was the governing **Alianza**; it received almost 60 percent fewer votes. After the elections, the PJ and its allies held 40 seats in the new Senate, and the Alianza 25; in the chamber, the PJ 121 seats and the Alianza 80—of the seats contested, the PJ obtained almost two seats for each garnered by the Alianza;

other seats were held by minor parties and provincial alliances. With unemployment and poverty rising, and its mandate seriously impaired, the weakened administration did not survive until the end of the year, collapsing in the wake of street protests, bank closures, and the looting of supermarkets. *See also* CAVALLO, DOMINGO FELIPE (1946–); CONVERTIBILITY PLAN; DUHALDE, EDUARDO ALBERTO (1941–); ECONOMIC CRISES; LÓPEZ MURPHY, RICARDO HIPÓLITO (1951–); PRESIDENTIAL ELECTION OF 2003.

CONGRESSIONAL ELECTIONS OF 2003. Taking place at the same time as the presidential contest, the elections of 27 April castigated the **Unión Cívica Radical** (UCR) for the shambolic demise of the administration of President **Fernando de la Rúa** in December 2001, putting into question the survival of the party as a national political force. Subsequent elections would show that the way forward for the UCR would lie in alliances with provincial parties and diverse coalitions. The elections also marked increasing factionalism within the **Partido Justicialista** (PJ). For the legislative elections, voter turnout was three points higher than in the **congressional elections of 2001**, though four points down on the previous presidential elections. After the elections, the PJ held 129 seats in the 257-seat Chamber of Deputies, and 41 in the 72-member National Senate. With 54 seats in the chamber and 16 in the Senate, UCR representation in **Congress** was at its lowest since the mid-1950s. The PJ also gained two governorships. *See also* CONVERTIBILITY PLAN; DUHALDE, EDUARDO ALBERTO (1941–); ECONOMIC CRISES; KIRCHNER, NÉSTOR CARLOS (1950–2010); MENEM, CARLOS SAÚL (1930–); PRESIDENTIAL ELECTION OF 2003.

CONGRESSIONAL ELECTIONS OF 2005. First midterm elections held after **Néstor Kirchner** gained the presidency in 2003 following the chaos generated by the political and **economic crises** of 2001–2002. These midterm elections were important because of the inconclusive nature of the **presidential election of 2003**; former president **Carlos Saúl Menem** had topped the poll on the first round, beating Kirchner by a few points, but then pulled out before the second round. Kirchner took the presidency by default. It was argued that Menem consciously sought to undermine the legitimacy of Kirchner by refusing to contest the second round. In the event, the strategy failed. Held on 23 October, the midterm elections were a resounding endorsement of the Kirchner presidency. Of the 127 seats contested in the 257-member Chamber of Deputies, the Kirchner faction of the Peronist party the **Frente para la Victoria/Partido Justicialista** (FpV/PJ) and its allies took 69, the Menem faction nine. One-third of the National Senate was renewed; of the 24 seats contested, the FpV/PJ and allies claimed 17. The most telling Senate election results were in the province of **Buenos Aires**, where Mrs. **Cristina Fernández de Kirchner** topped the poll by a very large margin, trouncing the official **Partido Justicialista** (PJ) candidate, and in the province of **La Rioja**, where Menem was awarded the "minority" seat. Other significant features of the elections included the strong showing of the **Partido Socialista** (PS) in the province of **Santa Fe** and the consolidation of such new center and center-right groupings as **Afirmación para una República Igualitaria** (ARI) and **Propuesta Republicana** (PRO), which had emerged during and after the **congressional elections of 2001**. Gains made by these parties can be explained by PJ factionalism and continuing voter disillusionment with the **Unión Cívica Radical** (UCR) following the collapse of the **Fernando de la Rúa** presidency. *See also* CARRIÓ, ELISA MARÍA AVELINA "LILITA" (1956–); DUHALDE, EDUARDO ALBERTO (1941–); DUHALDE, HILDA BEATRIZ "CHICHE" GONZÁLEZ DE (1946–); MACRI, MAURICIO (1959–).

CONGRESSIONAL ELECTIONS OF 2007. Held at the same time as the **presidential election of 2007**, they may be seen as confirming the ascendency of the Kirchner husband-and-wife team—**Néstor Kirchner** and **Cristina Fernández de Kirchner**. On 27 October, 130 seats in the 257-member Chamber of Deputies were contested; one-third of the 72-member National Senate was renewed—all three Senate seats in eight of the senatorial districts. Turnout was relatively low at 76 percent. The Kirchnerist faction of the **Partido Justicialista** (PJ), **Frente para la Victoria/Partido Justicialista** (FpV/PJ), gained 78 of the seats up for renewal in the chamber, increasing its representation by 13 to give a total of 153—a substantial majority. In the Senate, the FpV/PJ increased its majority by three seats, taking its tally to 44 senators—again a substantial majority. Other winners were electoral coalitions like the **Coalición Cívica/Afirmación para una República Igualitaria** (CC-ARI) and regional groupings. The principal losers were anti-Kirchner PJ factions and the **Unión Cívica Radical** (UCR).

CONGRESSIONAL ELECTIONS OF 2009. The elections were scheduled for October—two years after the previous midterm **congressional** and **presidential elections of 2007**. Due to political maneuvering on the part of **Mauricio Macri**, then mayor of the city of **Buenos Aires**, and President **Cristina Fernández de Kirchner**, the legislative elections were brought forward to 28 June. Questionable practices by the ruling faction of the **Partido Justicialista** (PJ), the Kirchnerist **Frente para la Victoria/Partido Justicialista** (FpV/PJ), cost it dear. With almost one-half of the seats in the Chamber of Deputies (127 out of 257) and one-third of the seats in the National Senate (24 of 72) up for renewal, the FpV/PJ lost its absolute majority in both houses of **Congress**, though it was still able to cobble together voting alliances with minor parties. Of the seats previously held and up for renewal in the chamber, the FpV/PJ lost 19 and suffered losses in the Senate. The main winners were centrist and right-of-center groups like the **Coalición Cívica/Afirmación para una República Igualitaria** (CC-ARI) and **Propuesta Republicana** (PRO), and PJ dissidents. Particularly galling for the Kirchners was the defeat of the FpV/PJ list in the province of **Buenos Ares**, headed by former president **Néstor Kirchner**. Government losses were mainly attributed to its handling of **farm protests** and general discontent over its agricultural policies. *See also* COBOS, JULIO CÉSAR CLETO (1955–); ECONOMIC CRISES; *RETENCIONES*; REUTEMANN, CARLOS ALBERTO (1942–).

CONGRESSIONAL ELECTIONS OF 2011. Coinciding with the **presidential election of 2011**, in retrospect the congressional and gubernatorial elections of 23 October may be regarded as the high point of Kirchnerismo. In the presidential contest, Mrs. **Cristina Fernández de Kirchner** was returned for a second term and her faction of the **Partido Justicialista** (PJ)— the **Frente para la Victoria/Partido Justicialista** (FpV/PJ)—triumphed. Of the 130 seats in the 257-member Chamber of Deputies due for renewal, the FpV/PJ took 86, increasing its representation; in the National Senate, 16 of the 24 seats renewed—one-third of the seats were contested. In the gubernatorial elections, the FpV/PJ and its allies elected 21 governors, nearly all of the 23 provincial governorships that were contested on 23 October. These results overturned the poor showing of the government in the **congressional elections of 2009** and appeared to stall previous advances made by new centrist parties and dissident factions of the PJ. Voter turnout was almost 80 percent, several points higher than in immediately preceding elections. Along with the presidential elections, these legislative and gubernatorial contests were preceded by the holding of compulsory **primary elections**, the first occasion that Primarias Abiertas Simultáneas y Obligatorias (PASO) had been held. *See also* AFIRMACIÓN PARA UNA REPÚBLICA IGUALITARIA (ARI); COALICIÓN CÍVICA (CC); DUHALDE, EDUARDO ALBERTO (1941–); PROPUESTA REPUBLICANA (PRO); RODRÍGUEZ SAÁ, ADOLFO (1947–).

CONGRESSIONAL ELECTIONS OF 2013. The midterm congressional elections held on 27 October are significant because the outcome ended any possibility of effecting a change to the **Constitution of 1994** that would have allowed President **Cristina Fernández de Kirchner** to stand for a third consecutive term. They are also important because of the contrast with the **presidential election of 2011**, when the share of the vote taken by Mrs.

Kirchner was the largest recorded by the victor in modern Argentine political history—54 percent. In the 2013 midterm elections, the ruling **Frente para la Victoria/Partido Justicialista** (FpV/PJ) share of the vote fell to 33 percent. Another noteworthy feature of the elections is that they were only the second time that the system of compulsory **primary elections** operated. Primaries (Primarias Abiertas Simultáneas y Obligatorias—PASO) had been introduced in 2011. One-third of the National Senate—all three seats in eight districts—were renewed along with 127 seats in the 257-constituency Chamber of Deputies, that is, approximately half the seats in every province.

Changes in the composition of each house of **Congress** were marginal, yet the government had failed to make the breakthrough that it had anticipated. Due to an opposition surge in the **congressional elections of 2009**, the government was defending fewer seats in 2013 than its opponents and assumed that its share of votes obtained in the 2011 presidential contest augured well for 2013. In the event, the FpV/PJ did not secure the two-thirds majority that would have allowed passage of a constitutional amendment to permit a sitting president to seek a third consecutive term. Moreover, the contraction in its share of the vote represented a moral defeat that emboldened both dissident Peronists, particularly the **Frente Renovador/Partido Justicialista** (FpV/PJ) headed by **Sergio Massa**, and center and center-right groupings such as the **Coalición Cívica/Afirmación para una República Igualitaria** (CC-ARI) and **Propuesta Republicana** (PRO). In the all-important province of **Buenos Aires**, Massa and the FR/PJ obtained almost 44 percent of the vote, compared with the FpV/PJ's 32 percent; in the city of Buenos Aires, the main opposition groups took 39 percent and 28 percent of the vote, respectively, compared with 23 percent for the FpV/PJ. Elsewhere, erstwhile allies of Mrs. Kirchner like **José Manuel de la Sota** broke ranks. These results encouraged Massa to harbor presidential ambitions for elections due in 2015, and center and center-right parties to forge closer alliances that would convince voters of their preparedness for government. In retrospect, the elections marked the beginning of the end of the *kirchnerato*. See also CARRIÓ, ELISA MARÍA AVELINA "LILITA" (1956–); CONGRESSIONAL ELECTIONS OF 2015; MACRI, MAURICIO (1959–); PRESIDENTIAL ELECTION OF 2015.

CONGRESSIONAL ELECTIONS OF 2015. Held simultaneously with the gubernatorial and presidential elections on 25 October, the congressional elections were a shock for the outgoing administration of President **Cristina Fernández de Kirchner**. Yet there are several ways of reading the congressional contest. In addition to retaining a large majority in the Senate, Mrs. Kirchner assumed that she would control the largest party in the Chamber of Deputies, despite sustaining a considerable loss of seats. The composition of the new **Congress** was as follows: Chamber of Deputies (total of 257 seats),

Kirchnerists and allies 117 seats (down 26), incoming **Mauricio Macri** administration including allies 91; National Senate (72 seats), Kirchnerists and allies 42 seats, the new administration 15.

Arguably, a greater blow to the prestige of the retiring president was the loss of the province of **Buenos Aires** in the gubernatorial elections. **Daniel Scioli**, official candidate of the ruling **Frente para la Victoria**/Partido Justicialista (FpV/PJ) for the presidency, had stepped down from the governorship, expecting to pass power to his designated successor, **Aníbal Fernández**, a close associate of the president. Fernández was defeated by **María Eugenia Vidal** of the **Cambiemos/Propuesta Republicana** (PRO). For Macri, elected on the second round of the **presidential election of 2015** in November, victory in the province and city of Buenos Aires meant control of the second and third most important administrations in the country after the presidency itself. And Macristas topped the poll in other important provinces, or finished a very close second—for example, in **Entre Ríos**, where the FpV/PJ garnered 42 percent of the vote and Cambiemos 41 percent. After the elections, Cambiemos and PRO held four governorships, including the position of mayor of the city Buenos Aires, the FpV and allies 11, dissident Peronists five, with the balance accounted for by regional groupings and minor national parties.

The 2015 congressional and gubernatorial elections, coupled with the outcome of the presidential contest, would virtually destroy the FpV/PJ faction of the Peronist party—Mrs. Kirchner would go on to create the **Unidad Ciudadana** to sustain her political ambitions, and possibly signaled the revival of the historic **Unión Cívica Radical** (UCR) as a national political force, albeit as a pale shadow of its former self. FpV/PJ setbacks were attributed to public perceptions of **corruption** within the Fernández de Kirchner administration and factionalism within the Peronist party, as well as the appeal of former opposition groupings. *See also* BOUDOU, AMADO (1962–); CONGRESSIONAL ELECTIONS OF 2017; *KIRCHNERATO*; MASSA, SERGIO TOMÁS (1972–); RODRÍGUEZ SAÁ, ADOLFO (1947–).

CONGRESSIONAL ELECTIONS OF 2017. Held on 22 October. One-third of seats in the National Senate were contested—that is, all three seats in one-third of the electoral districts (provinces), or 24 seats; and approximately one-half of the seats—127 out of 257—in the Chamber of Deputies. President **Mauricio Macri** and the governing coalition, **Cambiemos**, is generally regarded to have won the election, and former president **Cristina Fernández de Kirchner**, heading her new party **Unidad Ciudadana** (UC), to have lost. Although the government failed to gain a majority in either house of **Congress**, it substantially increased its representation in both. Capturing more than 40 percent of the popular vote, Cambiemos and its allies topped the poll in 13 out of 23 provinces and in the capital, critically in the principal provinces. Mrs. Kirchner even lost ground in her home province of **Santa Cruz**. In the chamber, Cambiemos increased its representation from 90 to 109 seats, becoming by far the largest grouping; having lost 25 seats, the **Partido Justicialista** (PJ) is the second largest party with 78 seats; UC representation rose from five to 30 seats. In the National Senate, Cambiemos increased its representation from 17 to 26; the PJ's fell from 39 to 28; the UC's grew from three to six.

The result was an endorsement of Macri's economic and political strategy and is attributed to what he had delivered since the **presidential election of 2015**—falling inflation, a managed devaluation of the **peso**, economic recovery, and a controversial settlement of the outstanding **foreign debt**. The victory is also attributed to the performance of Governor of the Province of **Buenos Aires María Eugenia Vidal**, a close ally of Macri and widely viewed as an efficient and personable administrator, and to **corruption** scandals surrounding the former president and a number of her closest associates—some of whom would be arrested and jailed. The midterm election strengthened Macri's mandate and encouraged him to consider a second term in the **presidential election of 2019**—unless he decides to step aside in favor of Governor Vidal. *See also* BOUDOU, AMADO (1962–); DE VIDO, JULIO (1949–).

CONQUEST OF THE DESERT/DESERT CAMPAIGN. A pivotal moment in national history, the **"desert"** refers to "unsettled" territory, rather than Sahara-like expanses of sand, and alludes to the final phase of military campaigns against pampean and Patagonian Indians from around 1875 to 1881, including the last onslaught headed by General **Julio A. Roca** in 1878–1879. As a result, vast regions in the southwest and south of the country were opened to permanent settlement in a process that paralleled similar programs of extermination of indigenous peoples in the **United States**. The massive increase in national territory—the area brought under the control of the federal government virtually doubled the size of the country—facilitated the export boom that made Argentina the 10th largest economy in the world by 1910 and the third most populous country in Latin America. The desert campaign also, apart from minor adjustments made at the beginning of the 20th century and in the 1970s, defined the frontier with **Chile**.

As late as the 1820s, the southern boundary of European colonization in Argentina lay hardly 100 miles southwest of the city of **Buenos Aires**, demarcated by the **Río Salado**. Although subject to sporadic raids in the late colonial period, licensed by the authorities to round up wild cattle, the territory on the south bank of the river was firmly under Indian control. It was not until after 1829, when **Juan Manuel de Rosas** became governor of the province of **Buenos Aires**, that determined efforts were made to secure the frontier. This was achieved in two phases. First, through negotiations with "civilized" Indians, who were granted subsidies and supplies in exchange for promises to protect the area from hostile action and to refrain from raiding settlements. Secondly, by punitive **military** action and the construction of a line of forts where mobile defensive forces were garrison. This carrot-and-stick approach was perfected by Rosas in 1833 when, following a well-executed aggressive campaign that largely established the present-day boundary of the province, peace was secured for approximately 20 years. During the Rosas governorship, treaty obligations were honored; subsidies were delivered promptly, strengthening defensive alliances, though the regime always maintained a strong military presence in the region.

With the fall of Rosas in 1852, and during the ensuing civil wars, despite several punitive expeditions and rearguard actions, frontier defense was neglected, fortifications fell into disrepair, and promised subsidies were delivered less regularly, processes that accelerated during the **War of the Triple Alliance**, when the regular army was fully committed in the north. Events in Chile also conspired to destabilize the Argentine Indian frontier. There the southern frontier was successively—and permanently—extended as the regular army systematically destroyed Indian encampments during successive campaign seasons, constructing defensive positions and securing supply lines. Chilean military action in the west triggered the migration of tribes across the **Andes** and competition for resources among indigenous nomadic communities, just as European colonists were encroaching from the east, often settling in areas close to or beyond the recognized (if ill-policed) Indian frontier. Exposed settlements offered easy pickings. Indian raids increased in frequency and ferocity; local militias were no match for well-armed, superbly skilled Indian cavalry. Incursions and cattle raids intensified in the late 1860s and early 1870s, with tales of kidnappings and massacres widely reported in the national and international press.

There was outrage (and anxiety) in many settlements. The notorious incursion of 1872 resulted in the slaughter of many hundreds of settlers, the razing of homesteads and towns, the capture of around 300 women and children, and the rustling of over 300,000 head of cattle, and in diplomatic action by European governments. Instability on the frontier threatened to derail the **immigration** project then gathering steam. There was another massive incursion in 1875–1876. Something had to be done, namely a campaign of occupation and pacification—or extermination. **Adolfo Alsina, Nicolás Avellaneda's** minister of war, proposed the construction of a series of defensive positions, aping Chilean policy. The construction of a 250-mile-long ditch and palisade, punctuated with major forts at strategic locations and intermediate blockhouses, all linked by telegraph, signaled the intention to establish peace and order. On the death of Alsina in 1877, Roca assumed command.

Careful planning and substantial funding ensured that in 1878 and 1879 Roca led a force of 6,000 well-provisioned solders on an extended campaign of coordinated sweeps through the southern and western **pampas**. Crossing the river Colorado, the army advanced to the **Negro** River, and then on to the confluence of the Neuquén and Limay, where defensive outposts were established before driving farther south. Some 1,300 Indians were killed and a further 14,000 captured, most of whom were forcibly resettled or conscripted. By the end of the 1878–1879 campaign season, northern **Patagonia** and the western pampas had been secured, laying the ground for the occupation of southern Patagonia during Roca's presidency. Peace and security, complemented by the modernization project of the period, ensured that newly acquired territory was soon brought into productive use. Within a decade or so, trunk railways had been driven across the pampas and contiguous regions of Patagonia. Settlers flowed in—a population of just under two million in 1869 had reached around eight million by 1914, a half of whom consisted of immigrants. **Foreign trade** increased exponentially—the value of exports, which doubled between the late 1870s and late 1880s, had more than doubled again by 1900, and doubled yet again by 1914. Other consequences of the sudden incorporation of land were a shift from arable farming to ranching and a change in the pattern of land ownership—from the 1850s to the 1870s, cereal cultivation and **sheep** raising, and inheritance laws, had produced a "democratization" of land ownership in eastern and central parts of the country; after 1880, large estates tended to predominate in newly open regions, reversing the earlier trend. Economic, social, and demographic structures, as well as politics, were all profoundly reshaped by the Conquest of the Desert. *See also* AGRICULTURAL COLONIZATION; AGRICULTURE; CATTLE; COMMODITIES; *ESTANCIA*; *ESTANCIA* COMPANIES; FOREIGN DEBT/FOREIGN INVESTMENT; MEAT; TRANSPORTATION; WOOL.

CONSEJO NACIONAL DE DESARROLLO (CONADE). Created in 1961, during the final months of the administration of **Arturo Frondizi**, CONADE reflected the contemporary thinking about **developmentalism**, notably state-led industrialization as a mechanism to promote structural change, economic modernization, and sustained growth. Its action was also shaped by ideas about economic independence and the need for national development inherited from the 1940s and 1950s as well as the developmentalist agenda. Beginning with analyses of macroeconomic problems, with working groups focused on data gathering, theory and methodology, investment and finance, the agency produced studies on public finances, trade, and investment. Emphasizing the need for public investment, the agency became the principal planning body in the country, stressing the importance of regional development and the promotion of national business, including support for the private sector. By 1966, CONADE was charged with developing four-year plans, the first such exercise since the first presidencies of **Juan Domingo Perón**. During the 1970s, the agency was headed by internationally recognized academic economists like **Eduardo Zalduendo, Javier Villanueva, Adolfo Canitrot**, and Héctor Diéguez. CONADE was most influential during the 1960s and 1970s, the heyday of developmentalism. *See also* ALSOGARAY, ÁLVARO (1913–2005); KRIEGER VASENA, ADALBERT (1920–2000).

CONSEJO NACIONAL DE POSGUERRA. Sometimes regarded as a parallel government set up by **Juan Domingo Perón** during the de facto presidency of **Edelmiro Farrell**, it was established in 1944 with the purpose of shaping Argentine policy in the period following the Second World War. According to its secretary general, **José Figuerola**, the Consejo had two fundamental goals. The first was to prevent difficulties that could arise from the state's transition from war to peace in the world order; the second was to coordinate planning for a distinct national economic future. With these aims, the Consejo prepared a socioeconomic blueprint calling for intensified rural and industrial output, and established which manufacturing activities needed state protection. In a similar vein, it took measures to tackle inflation, stabilize prices, and set both a minimum wage and salary scales for different occupations. *See also* COMMODITIES; ECONOMIC CRISES; ECONOMY; FOREIGN DEBT/FOREIGN INVESTMENT; FOREIGN TRADE.

CONSTITUENT ASSEMBLY OF 1813. In Spanish, the Asamblea del Año XIII, an early attempt to establish the legal framework of the fledgling republic, the **United Provinces of the River Plate** (sometimes the **United Provinces of South America**). Representatives were invited from regions of the **Viceroyalty of the River Plate** (Virreinato del Río de la Plata) that today form **Bolivia** and **Uruguay**, as well as interior provinces of Argentina. Among other actions, the Assembly declared the **independence** of the region from **Spain**; debated the institutional organization of the country, including the powers of the executive; reformed the legal code (for example, ending torture); introduced the Free Womb Law, in which children born to slave mothers were declared free, though slavery itself was not abolished; devised a national coat of arms; established a national **currency**; declared free trade; deliberated educational reforms; and ended censorship. The assembly met at a time of crisis. Attempts to define the legal status of the new state following the **May Revolution of 1810** had produced more uncertainly than resolution. The Army of the North, headed by **Manuel Belgrano**, dispatched to secure the adhesion of Bolivia to the United Provinces and confront royalist forces in northern provinces still loyal to Spain, had been defeated. Interim administrations formed after 1810 had proved ephemeral and unpopular. Yet there were grounds for optimism. At the end of 1812, the United Provinces constituted the only part of Spanish America where patriots remained in control of the government, and the return to Buenos Aires of such future key figures as **José de San Martín** augured well. The assembly failed to devise a national constitution, and the organization of the country that it was supposed to secure was overtaken by internal divisions and conflict. The collapse of the assembly and the authorities responsible for convening it highlighted the problems of **national organization**. But declarations promulgated in 1813 prefigured later constitutional charters and efforts to prosecute independence constituted the groundwork for future successful military action. *See also* ARMY OF THE ANDES; CONGRESS OF TUCUMÁN; CONSTITUTION OF 1819; CONSTITUTION OF 1826; CONSTITUTION OF 1853.

CONSTITUTION OF 1819. The first formal constitution of the country, preliminary work on which started at the **Congress of Tucumán** in 1816, though it was not completed until 1819 in the city of **Buenos Aires**. The drafting committee considered other written constitutions of the period, including those of the **United States**, early republican France, and the liberal Spanish constitution enacted at the Cádiz in 1812, and took account of the achievements and failures of the **Constituent Assembly of 1813**. It proposed a strong executive (supreme director) indirectly elected by **Congress** and a centralized state. Congress would be composed of two houses, the lower house consisting of representatives sent by the provinces and an upper house selected by a council of notables who would chose candidates from lists provided by provincial administrations. The upper house would also include representatives of the armed forces, the **Catholic Church**, and the universities; former supreme directors would also sit in the upper house. These arrangements owed much to the monarchical leanings of the drafting committee—around 1816 there was discussion about inviting a Bourbon prince or princess to serve as head of state.

The constitution of the **United Provinces of South America** was approved by **Congress** on 22 May and popularly acclaimed in Buenos Aires, which supported the **Unitarian** sentiments that it reflected. The constitution was rejected by the provinces, some of which opposed what were regarded as aristocratic and authoritarian traits and others by the emphasis on centralization viewed as reflecting the interests of Buenos Aires. The provinces were strongly **Federalist** in inclination. The ensuing conflict led to civil war (the so-called years of anarchy), the resignation of Supreme Director **Juan Martín de Pueyrredón**, another abortive charter (the **Constitution of 1826**) that led to the appointment of **Bernardino Rivadavia** as president, and, ultimately, the rise of the **caudillo** governor of the province of Buenos Aires **Juan Manuel de Rosas**. *See also* CABILDO ABIERTO; MAY REVOLUTION OF 1810; UNITED PROVINCES OF THE RIVER PLATE.

CONSTITUTION OF 1826. As opposition to the **Constitution of 1819** mounted, notably in the interior, the government of the province of **Buenos Aires** suggested convening a constituent assembly to devise a new charter. In 1824, letters were sent to the provinces asking for opinions about the future organization of the country, along with invitations to participate in the assembly. Administrations in **Córdoba, Entre Ríos, Mendoza, Santa Fe, Santiago del Estero**, and **San Juan** expressed strong preferences for a loose confederation composed of autonomous provinces. **Jujuy, La Rioja, Salta,** and **Tucumán** indicated a firm interest in a centralist, **Unitarian** arrangement. Yet other administrations, including governments in **Uruguay** and regions that now form part of **Bolivia** who were also invited to send delegates, expressed a willingness to follow the decision of the majority. Delegates began to arrive in the city of Buenos Aires in 1825 to debate the new constitution, and the assembly began to function almost immediately as a national legislature—to the surprise of many. While the constitution was being discussed, the legislature created the national executive power of the **United Provinces of the River Plate**, choosing **Bernardino Rivadavia** as its head, and federalized the resources of the province of Buenos Aires, essentially the revenues of the Buenos Aires customs house, and set about framing a Unitarian constitution under the influence of Rivadavia. Centralism was opposed by representatives from several provinces and by Buenos Aires federalists led by **Manuel Moreno**. Nevertheless, the views of Rivadavia prevailed: the new constitution was completed on 24 December 1826 and sent to the provinces for ratification. It was rejected by all. Federalist sentiments had increased markedly in the interior between the calling of the constituent assembly and the end of 1826, partly driven by liberal, secular opinions expressed by Unitarians, and among Buenos Aires Federalists who resented the redirection of provincial resources. Disputes triggered by the constitution would result in civil war and anarchy. *See also* CONSTITUTION OF 1853; FEDERALIZATION OF THE CITY OF BUENOS AIRES; NATIONAL ORGANIZATION; ROCA, JULIO ARGENTINO (1843–1914); ROSAS, JUAN MANUEL DE (1793–1877); UNITED PROVINCES OF SOUTH AMERICA; URQUIZA, JUSTO JOSÉ DE (1801–1870).

CONSTITUTION OF 1853. The first formal, national constitution was adopted in May 1853. It defined the country as the Argentine Republic (la República Argentina) and the Argentine Nation (la Nación Argentina), dispensing with such terms as the **United Provinces of the River Plate** and the **Argentine Confederation** that had been used in earlier charters, and remained in force until 1994, though temporarily displaced by the so-called Peronist **Constitution of 1949**.

Following the fall of **Juan Manuel de Rosas**, a constituent assembly had been called to deliberate the political future of what had been until then a very loose confederation of provinces that often acted as independent territories. Indeed, the province of Buenos Aires remained outside the new arrangement until 1859. The constitution was strongly influenced by that of the **United States**, to such an extent that for decades in the late 19th and early 20th centuries, the Argentine Supreme Court often referred to action by the US Supreme Court when dealing with jurisdictional disputes between the federal government and the provinces. It was also strongly influenced by prevailing liberal ideas, as reflected in the writing of **Juan Bautista Alberdi** and other influential figures of the 1830s opposed to Rosas, and by early unsuccessful attempts at crafting a viable constitutional settlement that reconciled the interests of interior provinces with those of Buenos Aires.

The constitution established the country as a federal republic, with specific powers exercised independently by the executive. There was, however, an effort to blend federalism and centralism—a sentiment manifest in the award of special powers to the presidency, for example, the right to intervene in the internal affairs of provinces if national order was threatened, provincial constitutions were subject to federal scrutiny, and subsoil rights were vested in the federal government. The legislature was bicameral: the National Senate, composed of two representatives for each province, and the Chamber of Deputies, whose members were elected by districts based proportionally on population size—one deputy per 20,000 inhabitants. The Supreme Court, initially composed of nine judges, was to guarantee a national system of justice through the establishment of offices and appellate courts in provincial capitals. The presidential term was set at six years, with no immediate reelection—that is, an incumbent could not serve two consecutive terms but was eligible to stand for election again after a lapse of six years. The senatorial term was nine years, with a third of the National Senate (chosen by lot) being renewed every three years. Deputies served four years, subject to the renewal of half the chamber every two years. This made for an extended electoral cycle that was designed to ensure stability. Deputies were elected directly, on the first-past-the-post basis, the president, vice president, and senators indirectly by national and provincial electoral colleges, respectively. Roman Catholicism was declared the state religion, and the president and vice president had to be Roman Catholics, though liberty of conscience was enshrined in the constitution, along with other basic freedoms—of association and the press. A near unique aspect of the constitution was that the vote was accorded to all native-born males without being subject to a literacy or property test. The franchise was not extended to **women** until 1949. Foreigners were accorded the same civil rights as nationals—there was to be no discrimination before the law on grounds of gender, nationality, or ethnicity. Other liberal features included declarations of the inviolability of private property and free navigation of the rivers; in addition, the government was specifically charged with the promotion of **immigration**. Reflecting the spirit of the times, another unique aspect of the constitution, set out in the preamble, instructed the government to foster railway construction. Although far from perfect, and far from perfectly applied, the 1853 constitution was widely embraced as a national symbol—a mark of statehood and modernity, and an aspiration of what the nation could become.

CONSTITUTION OF 1949. Whereas the 1853 constitution was shaped largely by liberal ideals, the new charter was framed by equally contemporary views about social justice and political economy, earning it the title of the Peronist Constitution (Constitución Peronista, or Constitución Justicialista), as it supposedly reflected new social and economic realities. The preamble emphasized social justice, economic independence, and political sovereignty, terms that resonated with the language of the regime and the period. The main practical and conceptual differences with the 1853 constitution were the extension of the franchise to **women**; increased centralization, including enhanced presidential power (the executive now became the dominant branch of government with considerable influence over **Congress** and the judiciary); immediate reelection of a sitting president; the abolition of electoral colleges for the presidency and senatorial contests (as with deputies, all would be directly elected); a substantial increase in state economic influence (utilities were declared government monopolies and the federal state granted control of internal and **foreign trade**, while the inviolability of private property was conditional on the demonstration of social value); and worker rights, most notably employment law and social protection. Designed to institutionalize the Peronist system, and allow **Juan Domingo Perón** to stand for a second successive term, the 1949 charter lasted only as long as the man himself. It was suspended after the **military coup of 1955** and formally repealed in 1956. The **Constitutional Convention of 1957** was convoked to reinstate and reform the Constitution of 1853. It rejected all changes introduced in 1949, save some social measures, including the right to strike. Other social provisions from 1949 would be reincorporated in the **Constitution of 1994**. While it may be argued that many constitutions represent a particularist project, the Argentine Constitution of 1949 was notably partisan.

CONSTITUTION OF 1994. The 1994 charter followed an agreement between sitting president **Carlos Saúl Menem** and his immediate predecessor, **Raúl Alfonsín**, known as the **Olivos Pact** of 1993, and was sanctioned by a constituent assembly convened a year later. The main, novel aspects of this constitution were allowing a sitting president to stand for immediate reelection (candidates who secured two consecutive terms were excluded from standing for the presidency again); the requirement that the president had to be a Roman Catholic was removed; the creation of the post of cabinet secretary, in effect a prime minister, a move that was regarded as countering an excessive presidentialism that had characterized previous structures and, possibly, permitting future shifts toward a prime ministerial form of government; reductions in terms—presidential terms were reduced from six to four years, and that of national senators from nine to six (Deputies continued to be elected for four years), with one-third of the National Senate being renewed every two years; the formation of an independent council of justice composed of representatives from both houses of **Congress**, to oversee appointments and regulation of the judiciary, a move that reduced the functions of the Supreme Court and **Ministry of Justice**; changes in the legal status of the city of **Buenos Aires**—no longer designated the **federal capital**, it became the autonomous city of Buenos Aires, in effect enjoying the same constitutional status as a province; electoral reform in the shape of ballotage, which replaced the electoral college arrangement—in the event of no candidate achieving 50 percent of the vote, the two candidates heading the poll would face a second-round runoff; echoing 1949, the inclusion of worker and social rights, along with the incorporation of human rights legislation deriving from international treaties to which the country already subscribed; citizen protection was strengthened by technical changes to habeas corpus; the appointment of an independent ombudsman and explicit rights to resist coups d'état or threats to the constitutional order, with explicit penalties for perpetrators of **military** insurrection.

Proponents of the constitution insisted that key changes were required to ensure political and institutional continuity, essential prerequisites for the survival and success of the new economic system, basically the **Convertibility Plan**. Critics argued that measures like the increase in the number of national senators meant that small interior provinces, with a history of political manipulation, were overrepresented. Certainly, the arrangement contributed to the "excessive" representation of Argentine politics, where the ratio of politicians to electors became one of the highest in the world. The creation of the Council of Justice may also have yielded greater influence to the executive and scope for manipulation. The advantages of the 1994 charter for serving President Menem and the Peronists are clear, but why did the Radicals support the project? The argument at the time was that the opposition perceived it as the only way of containing Menem, who would now be limited to two terms, the second of which was shorter than would have been possible had immediate reelection been permitted by a plebiscite and more limited reform. Similarly, raising the number of national senators to three per province created more space for the opposition. The emphasis on citizen and human rights owed much to the dark history of the 1976–1983 period of military rule and threats to democratic consolidation during the early years of the Alfonsín presidency.

CONSTITUTIONAL CONVENTION ELECTION OF 1957. Held on 26 July to choose delegates for a convention to modify the **Constitution of 1853**, 8,706,206 ballots were cast. Although the **Unión Cívica Radical del Pueblo** (UCRP) performed brilliantly in the provinces of **Buenos Aires** and **Córdoba** and won with 2,106,524 votes, this total was surpassed by 2,115,864 Peronist blank votes and abstentions. **Santiago del Estero, Tucumán**, and **Santa Fe** were the provinces with most Peronist electors, while in the **federal capital** they constituted only 18 percent. The **Unión Cívica Radical Intransigente** (UCRI) obtained 1,850,603 votes and triumphed in **Mendoza, Entre Ríos, La Rioja, Salta**, and the **Patagonian** provinces. A number of minor parties also succeeded, benefiting from the application of a proportional system for the first time in these elections. The 119 delegates elected on behalf of parties supporting the government constituted the majority, against the 85 opposed to the convention being called by a de facto administration.

CONSTITUTIONAL CONVENTION OF 1957. Held in the city of **Santa Fe** between 30 August and 14 November, its convocation by the de facto government of General **Pedro Eugenio Aramburu** was validated despite the withdrawal of the **Unión Cívica Radical Intransigente** (UCRI) delegates. The principal business at hand was to repeal the so-called Constitución Peronista, adopted in 1949, which had allowed sitting president **Juan Domingo Perón** to stand for immediate reelection, something prohibited by the **Constitution of 1853**.

The 1853 constitution (with the reforms of 1860, 1866, and 1898) was declared to be in force and certain articles subject to reform. This was in order to guarantee individual freedoms and the federal system and the judiciary and to establish the electoral regime and the ownership of energy sources. But deadlock ensued owing to the bickering between **political parties**, and after two and a half months the convention wound up due to the lack of a quorum. Nevertheless, the Constitutional Convention of 1957 had a major achievement on the subject of labor. The topic was discussed in mid-October, at a time when the authorities were repressing a wave of strikes. The regime had issued a decree restricting the right to strike without notifying the convention members, all of whom opposed the move. In a rare display of political consensus, the social rights of workers and social security, deriving from the **Constitution of 1949**, were incorporated into the 1853 constitution in an addendum known as article 14 bis. *See also* CONSTITUTIONAL CONVENTION ELECTION OF 1957.

CONVENTILLOS. Deriving from the word *convento* (convent), the English translation is "tenement." Not to be confused with *villas miseria*, though they often degenerated into slum housing, *conventillos* were former elite residences converted into multiple-occupancy buildings during the period of mass **immigration**, notably in the San Telmo and **La Boca** districts of the city of **Buenos Aires**. These had been districts favored by the elite, located on the south side of the Plaza de Mayo, close the presidential palace, the **Casa Rosada**. Typically, the one- and two-story houses had a narrow street frontage but gave way to a series of inner courtyards—usually three—around which rooms were grouped with balconies or patios. The courtyards provided air and light; there was usually a well in the rear courtyard, with a small garden and space for a few animals. Servants lived in the rear courtyards, the family were accommodated in the middle, with reception rooms located around the courtyard closest to the street.

A sequence of cholera and yellow fever epidemics in the 1870s caused wealthy families to abandon the historic parishes south of the Plaza de Mayo. They moved to salubrious areas to the north and to Palermo—what would become fashionable Barrio Norte. There families of the rural and commercial oligarchy constructed new townhouses. With large numbers of Italian and Spanish migrants arriving in the last decades of the 19th century, speculators bought up the colonial residences of the elite, divided houses laterally, and roofed over some courtyards with timber and corrugated iron. Some basic services were also provided by landlords. Families would usually rent one room, in which they lived, slept, and ate, though sometimes more than one family would be housed in one room. Occupancy rates of five to eight people per room was not unusual, though a figure of 10 or 12 was sometimes recorded. By 1900, speculative builders were constructing two-story tenements with rooms giving onto a single large courtyard, a design largely modeled on subdivided colonial courtyard houses. *Conventillos* became synonymous with poverty, squalor, disease, and exorbitant rents.

By the early 20th century, following rent strikes, protest, and action by social reformers, there were campaigns for better housing and the provision of modern services for slum dwellers—housing that included latrines and separate areas for washing and cooking. In reality, urban improvement—the widening of roads, the construction of grand avenues, and the laying out of public parks—may have resulted in the displacement of most of the poor, not the provision of better housing. Romantic accounts have presented *conventillos* as the origins of popular culture, including **tango** and the emergence of realism in poetry and novels.

CONVERTIBILITY PLAN. The plan, designed to inaugurate an era of macroeconomic stability and growth, was given legislative backing by Convertibility Law 23.928, promulgated on 27 March 1991. **Congress** legally fixed the rate of exchange and approved a raft of ancillary measures and related policies. In short, the plan was not simply an administrative measure adopted by the government but a formally constituted law. A new **currency**—the peso convertible—was introduced at the beginning of 1992 following nine months of stability in the exchange rate. The arrangement lasted nearly 10 years; it was formally abandoned on 3 January 2002.

The immediate context of the plan was several bouts of **hyperinflation** in an 18-month period between the end of the administration of President **Raúl Alfonsín** and the first year of the government of President **Carlos Saul Menem**. Long-term explanations relate to a history of monetary instability and price volatility over preceding decades: there had been five currency units or monetary regimes between December 1969 and January 1992, including the peso convertible. Most of these were introduced by government fiat during periods of military rule. Hence the emphasis on a democratic legislative backing for the new order, which was also intended to differentiate it from earlier ephemeral monetary experiments. Embedding the new currency in law would demonstrate democratic accountability and permanence. Theoretically, the arrangement proposed by Economy Minister **Domingo Cavallo**—he always referred to it as a new monetary system—was based on the self-regulating 19th-century gold standard. The main difference was that the system was anchored on the US dollar not gold. Chiming with the prevailing neoliberal orthodoxy of deregulation, fiscal responsibility, and the market, the success of the plan depended on the ability of the Argentine monetary authority, the **Banco Central de la República Argentina** (BCRA), to accumulate dollars. According to Law 23.928, the BCRA was required to maintain dollar reserved equal to the monetary base. In reality, during the convertibility era around one-third of the backing was in dollar-denominated debt, not dollar bills.

In advance of the introduction of the peso convertible—scheduled to take place several months later—at the end of March 1991 the austral was massively devalued, providing a substantial "cushion" to defend the new rate of ₳10,000 to US$1. In January 1992, the new currency was fixed at a rate of ₳10,000 per $1, or one Argentine peso to one dollar—and the monetary base was (supposedly) 100 percent dollar backed. The principal features of the system involved the dual circulation, and interchangeability, of dollars and pesos. The peso and the dollar enjoyed equal status as legal tender: parties could specify contracts in either currency; bank deposits and withdrawals could be made (or demanded) in each currency. The government, however, required that all payments to it should be made in pesos. There were important corollaries. The fiscal accounts should be in balance—ideally, there should be a modest surplus. The financial sector needed to be robust and well regulated, with strong reserves and liquidity, and capable of taking effective corrective action at moments of crisis. Given that Argentina was operating as an open economy, macroeconomic efficiency and international competitiveness were equally essential, and the ability of the authorities to respond to sharp changes in the external accounts critical.

Initially, the **privatization** of **state-owned enterprises** strengthened the fiscal accounts and eased budgetary pressure. Both features were intrinsic to the plan and served to encourage an inflow of foreign capital, an important mechanism in stabilizing the external accounts, though at a cost. Yet the government was unable to balance the budget due to rising levels of provincial public debt, even after the forced privatization of provincial state banks that had run up substantial debts. Social security payments were another drain on the exchequer, despite efforts to privatize social insurance schemes. During the period of the Convertibility Plan, from 1991 to 2001, the annual fiscal deficit averaged 2 percent. And an overvaluation of the peso, partly due to the inflow of hot money, reduced international competitiveness. Currency crises in Russia, Asia, and Brazil also damaged confidence in the arrangement and led to a decline in economic growth toward the end of the decade, with a negative knock-on effect on government income and the trade balance. The resignation of Cavallo in 1996—he complained of **corruption** in official circles and an unwillingness to accept the necessary fiscal discipline—also undermined confidence.

By 1998, with the economy slipping into recession, room for maneuver was becoming increasingly limited, though the election of President **Fernando de la Rúa** in 1999 seemed to hint at clean government and greater discipline. But as the recession deepened, the new administration was caught in a Keynesian trap: as fiscal income fell, the government raised taxes, but increases in taxes depressed economic activity, triggering additional tax hikes that in turn pushed the economy further into recession. In the face of declining income, the government resorted to borrowing overseas. Rising debt had a negative impact: in 1993, the ratio of debt to GDP was 30 percent; in 1999, 50 percent. In 1993, the debt service to exports ratio was 22 percent; in 1999, 35 percent. Reappointed minister of economy in March 2001, Cavallo embarked on a series of emergency measures. He promulgated the Zero Fiscal Deficit Law (requiring the fiscal account to balance on a monthly basis); curtailed the autonomy of the BCRA, having sponsored it several years earlier; required domestic banks and the social insurance fund to buy dollar-denominated government bonds as overseas creditors were increasingly reluctant to do so; and on 3 December 2001, announced a freeze on bank deposits, the notorious *corralito*. All failed to stem the tide. The economic crisis had become a political crisis as street protest erupted: De la Rúa and his cabinet resigned on 21 December. The plan would only survive a few more days, abandoned as interim president **Eduardo Duhalde** was inaugurated.

Had convertibility been anchored to a trade-weighted basket of currencies, the system would have had greater chances of success, as was recognized by Cavallo. He several times mooted the advantages of moving in this direction, but popular attachment to the sanctity of the peso–dollar dual system frustrated any such rationality. Had there been less corruption, the outcome might also have been different. Had there not been currency crises in Asia in 1997, in Russia in 1998, and in Brazil in 1999, the outcome might again have been different—even financial wizards like Cavallo need luck. For many Argentines, the two searing events of recent decades are the **Proceso de Reorganización Nacional** (the last bloody military regime) and the collapse of convertibility. *See also* AUSTRAL PLAN; BARING CRISIS; ECONOMIC CRISES; ECONOMY; MINISTRY OF ECONOMY.

COOKE, JOHN WILLIAM (1920–1968). Peronist revolutionary and leading figure of the Peronist left. A descendant of Irish immigrants elected to the Chamber of Deputies in 1946, he only attained a major political role after the **military coup in 1955**. The ousted and exiled **Juan Domingo Perón** named him as his delegate in Argentina and leader of the Peronist resistance.

Cooke promoted two methods of struggle: direct industrial action, and sabotage activities. In 1959, he headed the strike at the Lisandro de la Torre municipal meatpacking plant in **Buenos Aires,** unsuccessfully aiming to turn it into a general revolutionary strike. He was jailed by the government and abandoned by Perón when the strike ended. Cooke was allowed to leave the country in 1960 and did not return until 1963. For the remainder of his life, his influence was mainly ideological. He had spent his three-year exile in **Cuba**, which heavily influenced his political writings. He advocated national liberation and social revolution, which became the cornerstones of the more revolutionary thinking of the Peronist left, and he supported all forms of direct action (general strikes, insurrection, guerrilla warfare).

CORACH, CARLOS VLADIMIRO (1935–). Politician and lawyer who was the right-hand man of President **Carlos Saúl Menem**, commonly regarded as Menem's fixer-in-chief. He held the crucially important portfolio of the **Ministry of Interior** during Menem's second term from 1995 to 1999, having previously served as assistant secretary of the presidential office and as deputy minister in the Departments of Foreign Affairs, Social Action, and the Justice. One of his key roles was to manage the passage of the **Constitu-**

tion of **1994** through the constituent assembly convened that year. The new constitution allowed Menem to stand for election for a second consecutive term as president.

It is acknowledged that the appointment of Corach to the Ministry of Interior was a contributory factor to the resignation of **Domingo Cavallo**, Menem's minister of economy and economic wizard of the **Convertibility Plan**. After he left office in 1996, Cavallo denounced Corach as manipulating judges hearing cases involving Menem—several judges were named as being in the pay of the president, and being associated with the "mafias" who surrounded the president. During his stint at the Interior Ministry, Corach was accused of soliciting and receiving bribes for the awarding of contracts to computerize agencies within his purview—criminal investigations in the **United States** and Germany cited Siemens. Tens of millions of US dollars were reported as being paid to Menem, Corach, and their associates via accounts in the Bahamas, **China**, Dubai, and **Uruguay**. In 2012, his younger brother Jorge Eduardo committed suicide in a small public square in the fashionable Recoleta district of **Buenos Aires**. Jorge Eduardo had benefited from several public concessions and contracts, though there is little evidence to suggest that the family tragedy was business related. Charges against Corach continue to be heard in Argentine courts. *See also* CABEZAS AFFAIR; CORRUPTION; OLIVOS PACT; YABRÁN CASE.

CÓRDOBA (CITY). Capital of the province of the same name, founded in 1573 by Jerónimo Luis de Cabrera, named Córdoba de la Nueva Andalucia. It is an important seat of learning—the **University of Córdoba** was established in 1613, the fourth oldest in the Americas—as well as an important administrative center—an internal customs house (*aduana seca*) was set up in the city in 1622, making it the fiscal frontier between the interior and the coast in an attempt to curb smuggling. Its strategic central location was further confirmed by being named temporary capital on two occasions: in 1806, the time of the **British invasion** of the **River Plate**, and again at the beginning of the **military coup of 1955**. The national significance of the city is also marked by the events of 1918—it was at the center of the **university reform movement**, which spread to the rest of the country—and of 1969, when popular protest by students and workers, known as the **Cordobazo**, triggered the beginning of the end of the de facto presidency of **Juan Carlos Onganía**.

An important administrative and religious city by the 17th century—in addition to the university, the Jesuits had founded several seminaries and mission stations—Córdoba became capital of a new intendancy in 1776, when the **Viceroyalty of the River Plate** was created. The decades following **independence** in 1810 were politically turbulent, with the city and the province a battleground, metaphorically and physically, for powers based in the interior and **Littoral**. Independence undermined the importance of the city as a staging post between the coast and mining districts in **Bolivia** (Upper Peru), which the region had supplied with draft animals and manufactures, a factor that contributed to the chaos of the period. The modern history of the city dates from the early 1870s, when it was the interior terminus of the **Central Argentine Railway Company** (CAR), being constructed from **Rosario**. Further railway development followed in the 1880s, by which time immigrants were populating the countryside and the city regained its importance as a major commercial center. By the early 20th century, the city had reconfirmed its position as the most important political center outside the Littoral. As farming and ranching developed in the countryside, manufacturing took off in the city. Aircraft production began in the 1920s and expanded over the next couple of decades. The principal stimulus to industrialization, however, came later when the city was declared the industrial pole of the interior. **Industrias Kaiser Argentina** (IKA) opened a motor vehicle plant in 1955. Other US and European multinationals followed, including FIAT and Renault, which absorbed the IKA factory. Industrial growth forged an industrial working class (many of the workers were part-time students), who played a prominent role in the Cordobazo, which in part also explains the degree of vengeance visited on the city following the **military coup of 1976**. From 1975 to 1979, the head of the Third Army Group, centered on Córdoba, was **Luciano Benjamín Menéndez**, responsible for putting down the **Ejército Revolucionario del Pueblo** (ERP) campaign of urban insurrection in the city in 1975–1976.

Civil society and the industrial sector recovered with the return of democracy, and the city maintains a tradition of political and economic innovation. The development of the soya economy in the province has brought prosperity to the city, largely due to the production of agricultural machinery and as a service center. Motor vehicle production has rebounded since 2004, though subject to the situation in **Brazil**, an important market. And there is now a development technology sector, thanks to research and training at the university, and the promotion of a new industrial park. Córdoba wishes to project the image of a "green" industrial city. The current population of the city is approaching 1,500,000, making it the third largest city in the country. *See also* CÓRDOBA (PROVINCE); FOREIGN DEBT/FOREIGN INVESTMENT.

CÓRDOBA (PROVINCE). A pivotal province, "neither of the interior, nor the **Littoral**," as the saying goes; sometimes conservative, both with a small *c* and a large *C*, and sometimes radical, both with a small *r* and a large *R*, though rarely Peronist; and sometimes a political bellwether, certainly since the mid-20th century—the province was instrumental in **Unión Cívica Radical (UCR)** victories in the **presidential elections 1983** and **1999** and delivered the presidency to **Mauricio Macri** in 2015.

Situated in the middle of the country, the province is bordered to the north by **Catamarca** and **Santiago del Estero**, to the east by **Santa Fe**, to the southeast by **Buenos Aires**, to the south by **La Pampa**, and to the east by **San Luis** and **La Rioja**. As with regions to the north and west, Córdoba was first settled by Europeans arriving from **Chile**, and later from the **River Plate**, though large-scale European migration did not occur until the mass **immigration** of the late 19th century. As with the rest of the future republic, the area formed part of the Viceroyalty of Peru, latterly as part of the Gobernación del Tucumán. Years after the formation of the new **Viceroyalty of the River Plate** in 1776, the province achieved the status of *gobernación* in its own right, in association with provinces to the north and west. Part of the provincial elite was lukewarm about **independence** in 1810, partly due to rivalry with Buenos Aires, for which it paid a price. Over the next few years, governors were appointed by Buenos Aires. Although the province participated in the **Congress of Tucumán** in 1816, which declared the definitive independence of the country, Córdoba declared independence and autonomy in 1820. By this time, the province was already a battleground between **Unitarians** and **Federalists**, and remained so for the next couple of decades, not always choosing sides carefully. When **Justo José de Urquiza**, strongman of **Entre Ríos**, declared against his erstwhile patron **Juan Manuel de Rosas** in 1852 and called for other provinces to join him, Córdoba decided to remain loyal to the Buenos Aires **caudillo**, causing yet more turmoil after Rosas fell.

Circumstances began to improve during the presidency of **Domingo Faustino Sarmiento**, a modernizer who recognized the importance of developing the provinces. Federal support in the 1870s ensured that the province became an important hub in the developing rail network, which brought immigrants and agricultural development—the province, together with Santa Fe, became an area of rural colonization promoted by land and railway companies and by the state. Irrigation was improved, and by the 1880s the province was boasting the earliest hydroelectricity plant in the country. In addition to the development of intensive farming and the improvement of **cattle** and **sheep** breeds, fundamental to the growth of the new pastoral sector, manufacturing expanded around the provincial capital. Around 1900, the vast majority of the population claimed European ancestry, with the workforce—urban and rural—clamoring for better working conditions and political rights. The city and province became a hotbed of agitation for reform, in **education** and the franchise. The labor movement was well established before the presidency of **Juan Domingo Perón**. There were robust challenges to authoritarian regimes in the 1960s and 1970s—and bloody reprisals and federal interventions. This tradition continues. Just as industrialization from the 1950s to the 1970s fostered the development of a labor movement and demands for workers' rights, so the return of rural prosperity in the 1990s, associated with substantial reinvestment, and the "soya revolution" in the 21st century have triggered political activism. Córdoba was a major area of rural agitation and opposition to the farm policies of **Néstor Kirchner** and **Cristina Fernández de Kirchner**.

Recent demographic data (rates of population growth, fertility, infant mortality, and life expectancy) are very close to the national average. In 2015, provincial economic growth was also close to the national average and comparable with rates among OECD countries. The province has lower levels of socioeconomic inequality than most other provinces, and these have declined over the last 10 years or so. Literacy rates are among the best in Argentina. Youth unemployment is relatively high, and parts of the housing stock are deficient, but health insurance coverage has improved. Political engagement—measured in terms of voter turnout—is almost at the national average, which is very high by OECD levels. *See also* CENTRAL ARGENTINE RAILWAY COMPANY (CAR); CÓRDOBA (CITY); CORDOBA CENTRAL RAILWAY COMPANY (CCR); CORDOBAZO (29 MAY–3 JUNE 1969).

CORDOBA CENTRAL RAILWAY COMPANY (CCR). Once one of the major rail networks in the country, originating from several distinct lines that merged to form a meter-gauge regional grouping connecting the northwest and center of the country with ports of the **Littoral**—notably **Buenos Aires** and **Rosario**. The first section of what became the CCR was the Ferrocarril Central Norte (FCCN), a trunk line financed by the federal government in 1868; construction started in 1873 and was completed three years later. The original project was designed to link the city of **Córdoba**, then the railhead of the British-owned broad-gauge **Central Argentine Railway Company** (CAR) that was being built from Rosario, and the city of **San Miguel de Tucumán**, via the provinces of **Catamarca** and **Jujuy**. At around 340 miles (550 kilometers), the original line was the longest in South America. Subsequent branch and main-line construction soon established connections with the provinces of **Salta** and **Santiago del Estero**. In 1887, most of the network, which was then 550 miles (885 kilometers), was acquired by the CCR. The CCR was itself a creature of the railway mania of the 1880s, going on to acquire other lines after the **Baring Crisis**, among them the London-registered Cordoba & Rosario Railway, which partly duplicated the CAR broad-gauge route between the two cities. By the early 1900s, the company operated an extensive meter-gauge network centered on the city of Córdoba when it obtained a federal franchise to build between Rosario and Buenos Aires—the

extension opened in 1914. The onset of the First World War impacted consolidation, but the company appeared to prosper in the 1920s with the recovery of exports and further investment.

The significance of the CCR derives from its gauge and process of expansion. It purported to demonstrate the efficacy of an integrated "economical"
network—the meter gauge was presented at lower cost than broad gauge—
and because it adopted a corporate model more associated with the **United
States**, financing acquisition and much construction by bond issues. Highly
geared, and increasingly unable to service debt during the 1930s, the company was threatened with bankruptcy. In 1939, the railway was taken over by
the federal government. This gave the company's trajectory added significance. Arguably, the fate of the CCR served as a model for the nationalization of other foreign-owned lines after the Second World War. Some in
British railway circles viewed government acquisition of the CCR as a threat
to neighboring better-managed lines—large parts of the CCR network duplicated other routes—raising the possibility of "unfair competition" that might
result in forced sales to the state. This threat did not materialize, but the fear
underlined the paranoia of the time as the economic crisis deepened and
economic nationalism gained traction. The CCR network formed the basis of
the subsequent state railway, Ferrocarril General Manuel Belgrano
(FCGMB), named after one of the heroes of the **independence** period. *See
also* ARGENTINE NORTH EASTERN RAILWAY COMPANY (ANE);
BUENOS AYRES & PACIFIC RAILWAY COMPANY (BA&P); BUE-
NOS AYRES GREAT SOUTHERN RAILWAY COMPANY (BAGS);
BUENOS AYRES WESTERN RAILWAY COMPANY (BAW); CON-
CORDANCIA; ECONOMIC CRISES; ECONOMY; FERROCARRILES
ARGENTINOS (FFAA); FOREIGN DEBT/FOREIGN INVESTMENT;
GREAT BRITAIN; PRIVATIZATION; STATE-OWNED ENTERPRISES
(SOEs); TRANSPORTATION.

CORDOBAZO (29 MAY–3 JUNE 1969). Uprising in **Córdoba** that arose
from a combination of worker discontent and social tensions. The immediate
trigger was the withdrawal of various benefits enjoyed by industrial workers
in the city, which was then the country's second largest urban area and also
the main site of classist unionism. It began on the morning of 29 May 1969
with marches of industrial and public-sector workers toward the city center,
which were joined by students and ordinary citizens. The death of an automotive plant worker during a confrontation between the police and the
marchers turned the mobilization into a spontaneous urban revolt.

The entire community, including the residents of middle-class neighborhoods and major organized groups with mainly political and revolutionary
objectives, joined the insurrection. There was massive destruction of property, not least of that associated with transnational corporations, the govern-

ment, and the **military**. The police force was overwhelmed, and the army intervened on the afternoon of 29 May. It took several days to bring the city under control, and the entire episode left 12 dead and 93 wounded.

The Cordobazo, which was an ominous harbinger of the problems that would soon rack the country, fatally weakened the ruling military regime. It obliterated the myth of authority and exposed the government's inability to maintain order, particularly in the face of the sudden eruption of an opposition of formidable strength and scope. In fact, it led the head of the army, General **Alejandro Agustín Lanusse**, to begin searching for a way to extricate the armed forces from government.

CORRALITO. Term applied to an emergency measure restricting withdrawals from bank accounts in a last-ditch attempt to save the **Convertibility Plan**. The measure, which limited cash withdrawals from bank accounts to 1,000 pesos a month (then equal to US$1,000), was announced by Minister of Economy **Domingo Cavallo** to an expectant nation in a televised broadcast from the ministry on the evening of Saturday, 1 December 2001. The broadcast, initially advertised for the previous day, was delayed several times. Intended to last for 90 days, the *corralito* applied only to cash withdrawals. Other transactions, such as standing orders and purchases made on debit and credit cards linked to the accounts, were not affected, other than by the usual limits applied by bank and card companies. The move was intended to ensure that cash remained within the banking system and to halt a run on the banks, which had seen massive withdrawals in the days preceding the announcement. A secondary objective was to shore up tax revenues—tax was paid automatically on electronic transactions. It was the last in a series of measures introduced by Cavallo since returning to the **Ministry of Economy** earlier in the year. The move caused outrage, triggered legal challenges, and failed to stem the demand for cash—and US dollars. Following massive street demonstrations, Cavallo resigned along with other members of the cabinet on 20 December. By 21 December, President **Fernando de la Rúa** himself had gone.

The response of the administration of interim president **Eduardo Duhalde**, which took office on 2 January 2002, was to extend and deepen the *corralito*—which thus became known as the *corralón*: *corralito* means little corral, *corralón* big corral. The *corralón* involved the forced conversion of all accounts and bonds into nonconvertible pesos (the so-called *pesificación*)—under the Convertibility Plan, cash could have been withdrawn in either dollars or pesos, irrespective of the **currency** in which deposits had been made. Most public anger was vented on the political class and the banks, which kept their doors closed for many days. It took several years, including debt restructuring and continuing support from the **Banco Central de la República Argentina**, to restore a degree of stability to the banking system and resolve legal challenges.

CORREO ARGENTINO. *See* ENCOTEL.

CORRIENTES (CITY). Capital of the province of the same name. Founded by Spanish settlers from Asunción in 1588 led by Juan Torres de Vera y Aragón, from whom the settlement took its original name, San Juan de Vera de las Siete Corrientes, which also referred to its location at a bend on the **Paraná** River and surrounding streams. For much of the colonial period, it was a defensive frontier town, subject to repeated attacks from unpacified Tupí Indians. With the establishment of Jesuit missions in neighboring **Paraguay**, the threat from this quarter abated, only to be replaced by insecurity triggered by slaving expeditions from **Brazil**. Defense taxation, much resisted, produced further problems, as did jurisdictional changes. With the declaration of **independence** in May 1810, residents of Corrientes supported the junta in Buenos Aires; in 1852, they sided with **Justo José de Urquiza**, **caudillo** of neighboring **Entre Ríos**, when he declared against **Juan Manuel de Rosas** in 1852. In 1865, at the outset of the **War of the Triple Alliance**, Corrientes was invaded and briefly occupied by the Paraguay army, the only city in the country to suffer foreign invasion in modern times. Like the province, the city acquired a reputation for its turbulent politics, experiencing repeated interventions by the federal government. The most remembered uprising was in 1969, the Correntinazo, a student-led protest violently repressed by the government headed by de facto president **Juan Carlos Onganía**. The scale of the protest and severity of the repression that followed has been compared to the **Cordobazo**. Despite further tumult in the 1990s and early 21st century, the city is now seeking to cultivate its image as a **tourist** destination, a historic center endowed with parks and handsome public building and an abundance of rural activities. The city has been linked by the General Belgrano Bridge across the Paraná River to **Resistencia** since 1973, and its current population is approaching 400,000. *See also* CORRIENTES (PROVINCE).

CORRIENTES (PROVINCE). The second largest province in **Mesopotamia**, located in the northeast of the country. The **Paraná** River marks the northern and western boundary of the province: to the north, the river separates it from **Paraguay**, to the west, from the Argentine provinces of **Chaco** and **Santa Fe**. To the northeast, Corrientes is bordered by the province of **Misiones**, while to the east, the **Uruguay River** separates the province from **Brazil** and **Uruguay**. The province of **Entre Ríos** lies to the south. One of the 14 original provinces of the **Argentine Confederation**, its name alludes to the many rivers and streams that flow through the territory. A distinct feature of the province is that it recognizes more than one official language, Guaraní in addition to Spanish; the only other province to do so is **Chubut**, which recognizes Welsh.

Settlements spread from the capital, founded in 1588, slowly at first but accelerating with the establishment of Jesuit missions in the north of the province, which helped pacify the native Guaraní. Yet pressure from Portuguese Brazilian slavers continued, contributing to a sense of self-identity and spirit of independence, sentiments that gave the province a reputation for political turbulence. In 1732 and 1764, there were protests at arbitrary government action—initially successful but brutally repressed—which served further to instill a sense of separateness and injustice. The province enthusiastically supported the **May Revolution of 1810** and later declaration of national **independence** by **Buenos Aires**, patriotic loyalty that resulted in the awarding of provincial status in 1820—hitherto, Corrientes had formed part of a single jurisdiction with Entre Ríos, subject to Buenos Aires. Nevertheless, the decades following independence were turbulent: it was unclear whether the province would remain part of the Argentine Confederation or opt for independence. At distinct times, Corrientes formed part of the Republic of Entre Ríos and appeared to consider an association with Paraguay or Uruguay. The 1850s brought stability and modernization: there were improvements in **education** and transport and economic growth centered on logging and ranching. Thereafter, the province continued to cultivate a reputation for turbulent and troublesome politics. It is one of the most intervened-in provinces in the republic: between the adoption of the **Constitution of 1853** and the **military coup of 1976**, the federal authorities intervened on 16 occasions. Since the return of democracy in 1983, further interventions have occurred. Barely one-third of governors have completed their constitutional term.

Interventions have had an impact on economic and social indicators, despite reasonable economic progress. Although it is not the most fertile part of the country, the agricultural sector is diverse. **Cattle** and timber were the main colonial products, and during the 19th century Corrientes became renowned for the quality of its **yerba mate** (Paraguayan tea). Citrus fruit developed as a staple in the interwar decades. In the south of the province, modern ranching (cattle and **sheep**) consolidated fairly consistently from the early 20th century. Transport has been much improved in recent years, and the provincial economy has grown strongly over the last 10 years or so. Yet population is massively clustered around the provincial capital, and largely young (almost half the population is under 25) and poorly educated. The province has some of the highest rates of poverty and indigence in the country, and the lowest household incomes. The capital city currently holds the title of the poorest provincial capital in the country. Homicide rates in the province are almost three times the national average and eightfold greater than provinces with the lowest rates, further evidencing the lack of security and poverty. The current population is approximately 1,000,000.

CORRUPTION. Since the colonial era, bribery and corruption have been distinct features of the political system. A convention, established during the Spanish period, influenced practice into the 19th century, namely that payments designed to expedite bureaucratic decision making were acceptable, but not gifts intended to change official adjudications: in short, it was acceptable to offer an inducement to a government official to do his job (and the official was almost invariably male) but not to act in ways not established by law and custom. As the state grew, engaging in a wider range of activities, the scope for illicit and discretionary payments increased—to secure a contract or obtain a concession (for example, to supply goods to a state enterprise or obtain a public utility concession). Such payments were illegal but prosecutions rare. Arguably, around the middle third of the 20th century, with the opening of politics and the development of a strong and independent **media**, public awareness of corruption and criticism of it grew. Economic mismanagement and corruption were charges levied against democratically elected administrations by those organizing coups, such as those staged by General **José Félix Uriburu** to overturn the administration of **Hipólito Yrigyen** in 1930 and the ouster of **Juan Domingo Perón** by General **Eduardo Lonardi** in 1955. Prominent figures in **military** regimes of the 1950s, 1960s, and 1970s were not immune from charges of receiving kickbacks and the embezzlement of public money, though convictions were highly unusual.

Charges of graft and corruption were rife during the presidencies of **Carlos Saúl Menem** and included both minor officials and those holding high office. Menem was accused of accepting gifts from investors seeking to acquire state assets that were privatized cheaply, and **privatization** payments were siphoned off by members of Menem's inner circle. There were also charges of money laundering and drug dealing, and illicit deals brokered by customs officials. In 2000, IBM was required to pay a civil penalty by the US Securities and Exchange Commission in connection with bribes paid to Argentine government agencies in order to gain contracts. Later, staff at the **Ministries of Defense** and **Foreign Affairs** were prosecuted for selling arms illegally to Ecuador at a time when Buenos Aires was mediating in a border dispute between Ecuador and **Peru**. **María Julia Alsogaray**, Menem's environment secretary was convicted in 2004 for the misappropriation of public funds, becoming the only member of the president's entourage to serve a jail sentence. Public antagonism at the scale of corruption was a major factor in the victory of the opposition in the **presidential** and **congressional elections of 1999**, when **Fernando de la Rúa** of the **Unión Cívica Radical** (UCR) defeated **Eduardo Duhalde** of the **Partido Justicialista** (PJ). Yet De la Rúa was soon accused of bribing opposition national senators to secure the passage of government legislation and was subsequently charged with malfeasance and financial irregularities involving foreign banks, along with other members of his administration.

There was a step change in the scale and nature of corruption during the presidencies of **Néstor Kirchner** and **Cristina Fernández de Kirchner**, notably after the midterm **congressional elections of 2005**. What had been endemic became systemic, intrinsic to the mechanics of government. As governor of the province of **Santa Cruz**, before being elected president, Néstor Kirchner had acquired a reputation for adopting a cavalier attitude to official funds, tending to regard them as his own and using government resources to further his political career and those of members of his family. No longer a mechanism for personal gain, illicit financial deals were institutionalized: while the Kirchners and their cronies derived great wealth through the diversion of state resources and the collection of illicit cash payments, bribery and the soliciting and awarding of extralegal payments became instruments of policy. As business, in particular, was subject to tightening regulation, and viewed as subservient to the needs of the state, the day-to-day operation of enterprises were subject to official scrutiny; the allocation of contracts as well as the adjustment of operating terms and conditions became increasingly discretionary. The awarding of import permits, access to lines of credit and strategic supplies, and adjustments of wages and prices required ministerial authorization—often withheld or granted depending on the payment of a bribe or provision of goods and services to politicians and officials. Corruption generated a flow of funds and resources that could be allocated to strengthen the regime and cement new alliances; the payment of a bribe or receipt of a favor compromised the individuals and organizations involved, integrating them into the governing apparatus or making them increasingly beholden to it.

For example, following a legal investigation, it was found that clandestine funds from **Venezuela**, possibly the result of money laundering and contraband trade, were used to fund Cristina Kirchner's 2007 election campaign. Key figures in the administration and prominent politicians in the governing party were charged with involvement in criminal deals and the under- or nonpayment of taxes, charges that were usually overturned in court by compliant judges. In 2010, Minister of Economy **Amado Boudou**, who was a close associate of Mrs. Fernández de Kirchner, was indicted for engineering the bankruptcy of a major printing firm so that it could be acquired cheaply by friends of the regime. Other government associates were charged with embezzlement. Since leaving office, Mrs. Kirchner has been indicted on charges of fraud and corruption involving public works and the misappropriation of government funds by businesses controlled by her family, charges that she denies. As in 1999, public disgust at corruption was a factor in opposition victories in the **presidential** and **congressional elections of 2015** and in the midterm **congressional elections of 2017**. Within days of the October 2017 midterms, Mrs. Kirchner's former minister of planning and public investment, **Julio De Vido**, was arrested, and Boudou a few days later.

In 2016, Transparency International ranked Argentina 107 out of 175 in its Corruption Index, calculating that between 1990 and 2013 corruption had cost the country US$6.2 billion, and argued that such catastrophes as the 2012 rail crash in which 52 people were killed was the result of contract irregularities and inadequate supervision due to the bribery of officials. *See also* ECONOMIC CRISES; YABRÁN CASE

CORTÁZAR, JULIO (1914–1984). Argentine writer and intellectual. He was born the son of an Argentine diplomat then posted in Belgium and returned with the family to Argentina in 1919. His father abandoned the family in 1920, and Cortázar lived with his mother, sister, and aunt in Banfield, to the south of Greater **Buenos Aires**. As a child, he was frequently ill and spent much time in bed doing inordinate amounts of reading (including that of a whole dictionary), which eventually led to his writing career. Cortázar studied at the Faculty of Philosophy and Letters of the **University of Buenos Aires** and in 1951, deeply unhappy with the government of **Juan Domingo Perón**, immigrated to France, settling in Paris. He lived and worked there for the rest of his life, though he took a few trips in Europe and to Latin America, and in 1981 opted for French nationality in protest to the brutal **Proceso de Reorganización Nacional** regime.

Cortázar is considered one of the most innovative and original authors of his time, a master of the brief narrative and poetic prose, and the creator of important novels that inaugurated a new way of making literature in the Hispanic world. He broke classic molds, and the content of his work is on the edge between the real and the fantastic—a style known as magic realism. The novels by Cortázar are *Los premios* (1960), *Rayuela* (1963), *62/Modelo para armar* (1968), and *Libro de Manuel* (1973). His collections of stories include *Bestiario* (1951), *Final del juego* (1956), *Las armas secretas* (1959), *Todos los fuegos al fuego* (1966), *Octaedro* (1974), *Alguien anda por ahí* (1977), *Queremos tanto a Glenda* (1980), and *Deshoras* (1982). Other works by Cortázar include *Historia de cronopios y de famas* (1962), *La vuelta al día en ochenta mundos* (1967), *Último round* (1969), *Prosa del Observatorio* (1972), *Un tal Lucas* (1979), and *Los autonautas de la cosmopista* (1983). Encouraged by **Victoria Ocampo**, he was a regular contributor to the literary magazine *Sur*; his work was regularly reviewed in the magazine.

CORTES DE RUTA. See PIQUETERO/PIQUETEROS.

COSTA MÉNDEZ, NICANOR (1922–1992). Diplomat from a privileged background who served as minister of foreign relations on two occasions, from 1966 to 1969 and, highly controversially, from December 1981 until June 1982. Costa Méndez had served as ambassador to **Chile** from 1962 to 1964, and then as chargé d'affaires and ambassador to Taiwan from 1965 to 1966, before his appointment to head the **Ministry of Foreign Relations**. He was appointed minister by de facto president **Juan Carlos Onganía**. During his first tenure, negotiations between Buenos Aires and London regarding the **Falklands Dispute** led to the Memorandum of Understanding of August 1968. This document stated that the friendly resolution of the dispute should take into account the interests of the islanders, that measures would be taken to improve freedom of movement and communications between the mainland and the **Falkland Islands**, and that **Great Britain** would recognize Argentine sovereignty over the archipelago starting on a date to be agreed. Despite the significance of the memorandum, the Onganía government made no decision for four months. It finally accepted the document in December 1968, but the British had been frustrated by the delay and were no longer interested.

Costa Méndez has never accounted for the delay in accepting a proposal that would have solved the dispute and instead attempted to exonerate his conduct. He met Michael Stewart, his British counterpart, when attending the **United Nations** (UN) General Assembly in New York one month after the document had been finalized. Costa Méndez claimed that he was asked not to make any declaration on the memorandum until Stewart had done so, and that the British parliament raised objections that killed off the proposal. Yet this cannot be entirely true for two reasons. First, because the Argentine Foreign Ministry did accept the proposal, despite sitting on it for four months. Second, because Britain had initiated its withdrawal from east of Suez, which would have required parliamentary approval, and the offer eventually to return the Falklands was made in good faith.

A victim of the political fallout from the **Cordobazo**, Costa Méndez's first term as foreign minister ended in 1969. In December 1981, he was again appointed foreign minister, this time by de facto president General **Leopoldo Fortunato Galtieri**, on the condition that he became an accomplice in the military's designs on the Falklands. While the ruling junta in Buenos Aires proceeded to plan the invasion, a new round of negotiations was held in New York on 26 and 27 February 1982. Britain accepted the Argentine proposal for the establishment of a permanent negotiating commission, but this modest progress was officially rejected by Costa Méndez.

Argentina occupied the Falkland Islands on 2 April 1982 and, in an attempt to maintain secrecy around the operation, made no preparations for the diplomatic consequences of the invasion. In an attempt to exonerate himself, Costa Méndez has claimed that the idea behind the occupation was to internationalize the conflict and trigger the intervention of the UN. This is totally untrue, as the military resolution of the Falklands Dispute had been devised by the Argentine navy as a means of rallying a public highly disgruntled with the **Proceso de Reorganización Nacional**. It was a last-ditch attempt to save the de facto regime. While Costa Méndez on the eve of the invasion told one of his members of staff at the Foreign Ministry that the British would never send the Royal Navy—not least on financial grounds—the British instead responded on 5 April by dispatching a task force to the archipelago. US Secretary of State Alexander Haig embarked unsuccessfully on a diplomatic shuttle mission between London and **Buenos Aires** in a bid to stave off the looming war. Hostilities began on 1 May 1982, while there was an unsuccessful proposal from President Fernando Belaúnde Terry of **Peru** to resolve the dispute definitively and further futile bids at the UN to try to bring about a cease-fire.

With Argentine diplomacy adrift, Galtieri decided to strengthen links with **Cuba**. Costa Méndez was dispatched to the Caribbean island, with the Argentine president ludicrously saying, "Bueno, ahora irán a La Habana con mi amigo Fidel Castro y haremos poner de rodillas a la Thatcher" (Well, you'll go to Havana with my friend Fidel Castro and we'll get Thatcher on her knees). He was suggesting an alliance with the Cuban dictator, the same man who since the late 1960s had trained and armed the terrorist organizations that racked Argentina in the early and mid-1970s, who held and administered funds obtained through the kidnapping and death of Argentines, and who had given sanctuary to the leadership of the **Montoneros** in 1978. Even more notorious was that the foreign minister, one of the more rancid exponents of the intellectual establishment of the Argentine right, accepted the mission to Havana.

Costa Méndez arrived in Cuba on 2 June and hugged Castro at the airport. The foreign minister, who only a few months earlier had declared that Argentina did not belong to the Third World, attended the Non-Aligned summit and stated that the movement had been a great support for Argentina in international negotiations. Without even blushing, Costa Méndez compared the war against the British in the Falklands with the liberation struggles for independence in Algeria, India, Cuba, and Vietnam. The visit to Havana caused such uproar back in Argentina that the foreign minister, during a stop in Caracas on the way home, was forced to state that there would not be a socialist fatherland in his country.

Argentina was by then facing defeat in the Falkland Islands—Argentine forces surrendered on 14 June 1982. The president and the minister were forced to resign, but still Costa Méndez attempted to position himself to succeed Galtieri. His maneuvering was unsuccessful; it was well known that he had mishandled diplomatic aspects of the **Falklands War**. Costa Méndez spent the rest of his life trying to exonerate himself from his highly controversial actions. *See also* FOREIGN RELATIONS; MILITARY.

CRONISTA COMERCIAL. Officially founded in 1908, though previously operating as an agency providing information about credit, money, and production, *El Cronista Comercial* was the first business daily published in Argentina. Known since 1989 as *Cronista*, it was also the first newspaper in the country to be made available via the internet—the online version went live in 1994. Given the niche market, *Cronista* did circulate widely and was generally only available by subscription. It is an important title because for much of the 20th century it was the only newspaper that explicitly and consistently supported business, for which it campaigned zealously, describing commercial enterprises as the "living forces of the country." The early focus was on the commercial code and legal framework regulating business; later, it sought to counter the indifferent approach of established papers to commerce and economic affairs, which tended to be given a low priority, or presented in partisan fashion—either uncritically probusiness or antagonistic. *Cronista* promised an informed and balanced approach in the face of a generally unsympathetic political environment. The position adopted by the **Unión Cívica Radical** (UCR) to business was often equivocal, sometimes unsympathetic, sometimes hostile. The early rhetoric of **Juan Domingo Perón** was antagonistic—conflating "big business" with antinational forces. Later Peronist administrations and the **Partido Justicialista** (PJ) would adopt a pro-small-firm stance, while advancing a statist and prolabor agenda. Statism, economic nationalism, and **developmentalism** were the main features of the economy for much of the 1930s–1960s, constraining opportunities for private initiative. *Cronista* sought to represent business and cater to its needs in this unfavorable context. By the 1960s, the newspaper had become the virtual house magazine of the national business elite, well connected commercially and politically.

At precisely the moment when the environment began to change, that is with the avowedly probusiness position taken by **military** regimes of the **Proceso de Reorganización Nacional**, which came to power with the **military coup of 1976**, the subsequent emergence of an explicitly probusiness political party—the **Unión del Centro Democrático** (UCeDe) created by **Álvaro Alsogaray**—and above all the consolidation of the regime of President **Carlos Saúl Menem**, *Cronista* was confronted by profound challenges. In 1977, Rafael Perrotta the proprietor whose family had acquired the title almost 60 years earlier, was arrested and "disappeared," along with journalists and workers at the paper; most of the bodies were never recovered. A year before, *El Ámbito Financiero* had been launched, a daily that would rapidly displace *Cronista* to become the go-to read of the financial and business community, and which retained this position for the next 30 years or so. Changes in ownership followed the murder of Perrotta; others occurred as the journal lost circulation, partly due to competition, the **economic crises** of the period, and technical challenges. Ownership passed among various consortia, some involving multimedia international conglomerates. There were frequent changes of editor and editorial policy—and format. In 2006, the title was acquired by the Grupo de Narváez, since then the fortunes of the paper have revived, notwithstanding an uneasy relationship between government and the **media**. The company was recapitalized, journalistic style and coverage modified to provide greater context on business, financial, and economic affairs, as well as highlighting broader events that impact on core subjects. Content became lively and credible. *See also CLARÍN*; CONFEDERACIÓN GENERAL ECONÓMICA (CGE); KIRCHNER, CRISTINA ELISABET FERNÁNDEZ DE (1953–); KIRCHNER, NÉSTOR CARLOS (1950–2010); *LA NACIÓN*; *LA PRENSA*; MARTÍNEZ DE HOZ, JOSÉ ALFREDO (1925–2013); SOCIEDAD RURAL ARGENTINA (SRA); STATE-OWNED ENTERPRISES (SOEs).

CRUZADA JUSTICIALISTA DE LA SOLIDARIDAD. Public entity set up in 1973 intended to replicate the **Fundación Eva Perón**; chaired by **Isabel Perón**, it was supposed to fund social projects and help the poor. The board of directors included **José López Rega**, his daughter Norma, his son-in-law **Raúl Lastiri, Celestino Rodrigo**, and Carlos Villone (chief administrator at the Ministry of Social Welfare). Funds were to come from the collection of takings from the *Quiniela*, a recently legalized form of gambling, and from contributions by companies and private individuals. Though the Cruzada was meant to emulate the Fundación Eva Perón in its charitable work, this did not happen. The original foundation, for all the **corruption** that surrounded it, actually assisted the poor through monetary gifts and social action. The same cannot be said of its poor reincarnation in the 1970s.

The first bank account of the Cruzada was opened in Mrs. Perón's name (she personally issued and signed the cheques), and then a further two accounts were opened in the names of **José Ber Gelbard** and López Rega to handle the government's *fondos reservados* for discretionary expenditure that did not require congressional approval. The result was that, rather than helping the poor, the Cruzada became the source of easy funds for Isabel's intimate circle. Cheques issued by the entity covered the cost of repairing and refurbishing the **Casa Rosada**, trips by members of the **Juventud Peronista** (JP), IBM cards for playing the *Quiniela* in the Ministry of Social Welfare, Peronist party propaganda, and the like.

The misuse of funds would land Isabel Perón herself in trouble. Badly advised, she issued a cheque covered by funds from the Cruzada to pay off claims by the sisters of **Eva Perón** on the estate of **Juan Domingo Perón**. The cheque amounted to 3,100 million pesos and, once it became clear that this was a scandalous attempt to use public funds for private matters, she attempted to repair the damage by reimbursing the Cruzada with funds she had obtained from the restitution of Perón's property seized by the **military**. The mishandling of Cruzada funds would come back to haunt Isabel after her downfall.

CRY OF ALCORTA. In Spanish, El Grito de Alcorta, variously described as a rural rebellion, an agrarian protest movement, and an immigrant uprising. Initially centered on the Alcorta district in the province of **Santa Fe**, it spread rapidly across large areas of the **pampas**. Mainly involving sharecroppers and tenant farmers, proprietors of small farms and rural laborers were also caught up—that is, many of those who were involved in the project to make Argentina the granary of the world. The immediate cause of the crisis was the almost total failure of the **maize** harvest in 1911 and a bumper **grain** harvest in 1912, which precipitated a dramatic fall in prices. Encumbered by debt, high rents, and short contracts or leases, tenant farmers and sharecroppers faced destitution. The Grito occurred on 25 June 1912, when protesters gathered at the Italian Social Club in Alcorta and declared an immediate and open-ended strike. This led to the formation of the Agrarian Federation, **Federación Agraria Argentina**, founded seven weeks later at the Italian Club in **Rosario**, the principal port city in the grain zone. Most of the farmers were Italian and Spanish immigrants, and their ability to organize was initially constrained by ethnic and regional rivalry, and by fear of deportation—the residency law (**Ley de Residencia**) of 1902 had been designed to facilitate the removal of "troublemakers."

Among demands articulated in June 1912 were reductions in rents, freedom to sell grain on the open market, and a minimum period of four years for leasehold and sharecropping contracts. Farmers and workers also complained of high prices for basic goods and freight charges levied by merchants and rail companies. Such demands and complaints were not so different from those articulated at the end of the 19th century by the Granger Movement in the **United States**. The initial response of the authorities, egged on by nervous landowners, was violence. Two anarchists credited with organizing demonstrations were assassinated. This only served to encourage solidarity among protestors, and support from other political organizations like the Socialists, and support from professionals and workers living in rural townships.

Little changed in the countryside in the short term, but there were substantial rent rebates in 1913. Protests subsided as cereal prices picked up, yet the events of 1912 are important because they were the first major rural challenge to the oligarchic order associated with General (then President) **Julio A. Roca** in 1880—earlier protests such as the **revolution of 1890** had been principally urban based. They were also significant because regional **political parties**, which grew in significance during the interwar decades, emerged from the Grito. Despite obvious differences in their scale and intensity, the events of 1912 prefigured major rural protest movements of the early 21st century, particularly during the presidency of **Cristina Fernández de Kirchner**, owing to deteriorating conditions in the countryside and government indifference or, in the case of the latter period, a rural economic and financial crisis driven by official policy. *See also* COBOS, JULIO CÉSAR CLETO (1955–); FARM PROTESTS; KIRCHNER, NÉSTOR CARLOS (1950–2010).

CUBA. Caribbean island under Communist rule that attempted to export its revolution to other Latin American countries, including Argentina, during the 1960s and 1970s. **Ernesto "Che" Guevara**, an Argentine-born leading figure of the Cuban Revolution, was already thinking as early as January 1960 about a revolution in Argentina. But he did not consider three adverse factors: it would be attempting to overthrow the elected government of **Arturo Frondizi**, the Argentine **military** were not mercenaries, and the roots of the working class were Peronist and therefore anti-Communist. Argentina may not have been ripe for a Cuban-style revolution, but its government made Cuba an issue by pursuing an "independent" policy toward Havana.

Frondizi decided in August 1961 to take advantage of Guevara's attendance of a meeting of the Inter-American Economic and Social Council in **Uruguay** and hold a secret meeting with him. The necessary arrangements were made for "Che" to travel in a private small aircraft, which cost 25,000 pesos paid with a loan from the Consejo Federal de Inversiones. The meeting was held in the **Quinta de Olivos** (the presidential residence), in which the visitor was dishonest. As soon as it finished the meeting became public knowledge. Frondizi had to explain himself to the military, who were keeping a close watch on him owing to mistrust. The president argued that he was entitled to meet a minister from a country with which Argentina had diplomatic relations and was backed by important commanders who limited their criticism to the secrecy surrounding the meeting.

The issue of Cuba next surfaced in January 1962, at the summit of foreign ministers of the Organization of American States (OAS) in Uruguay. One of the decisions of the meeting was to exclude Havana from the Inter-American Defense Board. But the more important one was to approve a Colombian proposal to expel Cuba from the OAS, which required a two-thirds majority. The resolution was passed, although Argentina and five other countries abstained. The abstention caused such furor in **Buenos Aires**, not least among the military, that ties with Havana were severed in February. This measure was seen as too little and too late for Frondizi's political survival. His handling of the Cuban question, and the Peronist victories in the **congressional elections of 1962**, resulted in the **military coup of 1962**.

The Cuban Missile Crisis of October 1962, which pitted the **United States** against Moscow over the placement of Soviet offensive weapons on the island, had the Argentine government firmly in the Washington camp. The United States imposed a blockade on shipping to Cuba and gave a legal basis to its enforcement through a resolution passed in the OAS, which was supported by Argentina. The resolution demanded the immediate dismantling and withdrawal of the offensive weapons and, invoking Articles 7 and 8 of the Inter-American Treaty of Reciprocal Assistance, recommended that OAS member states take individual and collective measures (including the use of armed force) to prevent Cuba from continuing to threaten the peace and security of the continent. The Argentine contribution to the newly created 137th US–Latin American Combined Task Force comprised the leadership of a rear admiral, a battle cruiser, two destructors, and aircraft and pilots.

The Cuban Missile Crisis was resolved, with Havana left more isolated than ever. But this did not stop "Che" from thinking concretely about exporting revolution to Argentina. He aimed to send a "vanguard" of Argentines and Cubans to create a revolutionary *foco*, in the belief that they could attract the populace's discontent on the basis of "objective conditions" in the country: the government of **Jose María Guido** confronted economic and social difficulties, Peronism was proscribed, and the military (the power behind the throne) was deeply split and might prevent the holding of presidential elections.

The plan, named Operación Penélope, envisaged the penetration of the north of Argentina from **Bolivia** and the opening of a guerrilla front that would end up provoking a Cuban-style revolution in the country. The Ejército Guerrillero del Pueblo (EGP) was established on 21 June 1963 and immediately began a reconnaissance mission that lasted a few days. On 7 July, the feasibility of the scheme came into question as one of the necessary "objective conditions" changed: **Arturo Illia** was chosen in a presidential election, which meant that the struggle would be against a constitutional government and not a dictatorship. Nevertheless, it was decided to proceed and not return to Bolivia, which severed ties with Cuba on 22 August. Operación Penélope began in late September 1963, and despite pressure from the military to take charge of its repression, the government decided that the Gendarmería Nacional would deal with the EGP. The subversive initiative failed, and it was all over by May 1964.

But Che was still determined to export the Cuban revolution. In late 1966, he returned to South America, and by March 1967 guerrilla activity was detected in the Ñancahuazú district of Bolivia. Guevara commanded the Ejército de Liberación Nacional (ELN), which aimed to integrate with Bolivian subversives in 1969 and organize a rural guerrilla front that would operate simultaneously in the north of Argentina. The scheme was unsuccessful, not least because Che was captured by the Bolivian Army and executed in October 1967.

Nevertheless, the fracturing of the ELN meant that many of its Argentine members would become part of three major terrorist groups that emerged in Argentina: the **Fuerzas Armadas Revolucionarias** (FAR), the **Fuerzas Armadas Peronistas** (FAP), and the **Montoneros**. In fact, the two former organizations would merge with the latter in 1973. This was in order to challenge **Juan Domingo Perón**, who was once again elected president and determined to put an end to Castroist infiltration of his movement.

Cuba played a duplicitous game. On one hand, it was accepting Argentine help in breaking the economic embargo to which the island was being subjected by the United States. Buenos Aires had restored diplomatic relations with Havana during the short-lived presidency of **Héctor J. Cámpora** and in February 1974 had provided Cuba a credit of 1,600 million US dollars for the purchase of Argentine products such as automobiles, trucks, auto parts, and food. On the other hand, with Argentina now racked by an undeclared civil war, Cuba was training and arming the terrorists, which gave the Argentine armed forces the one argument that enabled the **military coup of 1976** and the **Proceso de Reorganización Nacional**: to finish with Marxist subversion. Those who had wanted to transform Argentina into another Cuba lost, but the consequences of their actions scarred the country.

CURRENCY. For most of the period since **independence**, the national currency has been the peso ($); the main exception was between 1985 and 1991, when the austral (A) was issued. However, there have been many series of pesos, reflecting the checkered financial history of the country—notably, periodic bouts of inflation and currency depreciation that culminated in stabilization packages centered on a new currency unit.

The first national currency was not issued until 1881, the *peso moneda nacional* (m$n). Paper notes, exchanged on a one-to-one basis with gold coins, were known as *moneda corriente* (m$c), a reference to a nonconvertible series of notes in circulation since 1826 when the link between paper and silver was nominally "suspended." Established early in the presidency of

Julio A. Roca, the new nationwide circulating medium was intended to symbolize the definitive political and economic organization of the country. Legally, the m$n survived until the end of 1969; it was substituted on 1 January 1970 by the Peso Ley 18.188 ($ley) at the rate of 1 $ley to m$n 100. A new series was introduced in 1983, following the **Falklands War** debacle that terminated the **military** regime of the **Proceso de Reorganización Nacional**. The printing of the *peso argentino* ($) reflected currency collapse in the final days of the regime: $1 was exchanged for 10,000 $ley. Yet another bout of macroeconomic instability triggered yet another new currency: on 14 June 1985, the austral displaced the *peso argentino* at the rate of ₳1 to $1,000. Early in the presidency of **Carlos Saúl Menem**, the *peso convertible* ($) was introduced as part of the **Convertibility Plan**: in 1992, $1 equaled ₳10,000. Although the law requiring the **Banco Central de la República Argentina** (BCRA) to exchange pesos and US dollars on a one-to-one basis was canceled at the beginning of 2002, the 1992 series remains in circulation. The current $1 is the equivalent to m$n10,000,000,000,000,000.

The early monetary history of the republic was one of confusion and chaos, foreshadowing subsequent moments of currency collapse punctuated by the quest for monetary stability. Different currencies circulated in various parts of the country: competitive (or complementary) monetary regimes flagged the weakness of the central administration and pretensions to statehood on the part of provinces (many provinces claimed monetary sovereignty). Multiple monies also signaled a general want of coinage. After independence, several regional currency "zones" emerged: a number of provinces minted their own coinage, and coins from neighboring countries enjoyed the status of legal tender. In the province of **Buenos Aires**, the provincial paper peso was the principal medium of exchange and accepted elsewhere. The Argentine silver peso (*peso fuerte*) was rarely seen, serving largely as a unit of account, even more so when convertibility of the Buenos Aires paper peso was "suspended" in 1826: convertibility would not be restored (briefly) until 1866. From 1867 to 1874, Argentina was officially a member of the gold club, though in modified from. The country operated a "limping" mixed metallic and paper standard, a system based on fractionary reserves. Despite efforts to establish the currency on a metallic base, "monetary anarchy" continued until the late 1870s. Even the introduction of the *peso moneda nacional* in 1881, when national notes and coins went into circulation, did not end monetary confusion. Although the legal tender status of the m$n survived until 1969, there were a number of iterations.

In circumstances similar to the monetary disorder of the first part of the 19th century, the collapse of convertibility at the end of the 20th was foreshadowed by the printing of provincial "monies," something that was proscribed by the constitution. Fairly early in the Menem presidency, minor interior provinces started to issue promissory notes, technically provincial treasury bills or bonds, used to settle government accounts and pay the wages of provincial officials. Such bills were designed to look like, and circulated as, money within the issuing province. Unlike *pesos convertibles*, these notes were not backed by US dollars yet represented little threat to convertibility given the small significance of issuing provinces in the national economy. This was not the case when, in 2001, the province of Buenos Aires began to issue notes and the city government of Buenos Aires announced that it intended to do the same. While *patacones*, as the Buenos Aires provincial bills were known, were widely accepted, initially circulating at par value alongside the *peso convertible* and US dollar, the writing was on the wall. The retirement of these provincial issues came to represent a substantial charge on the national treasury, but a necessary step in the restoration of monetary stability.

Monetary reform, enacted in July 1881, creating the first national monetary system, broke new ground in several respects. Gold coins and notes denominated in *pesos moneda nacional* circulated alongside each other and alone enjoyed legal-tender status. The reform took almost two years to implement, partly due to the need to mint and print sufficient currency to meet national needs, and in part due to the complexity of retiring series of notes issued when convertibility had been again suspended in 1876. Yet the convertibility of the m$n was again "suspended" in 1884. Convertibility would not be restored until 1899. The rate at which convertibility was restored was imaginative. Whereas in 1881 the par value of 1 paper peso was set at 1 gold peso, the 1899 arrangement set the par value of $1.00 gold at $2.27 paper, giving the m$n1.00 paper a value of 44 gold cents. The new gold/paper parity represented a 56 percent devaluation of the 1881 paper peso, which had enjoyed a one-to-one relationship with the *peso oro*. For almost half a century following the return to gold in 1899, the republic experienced a period of remarkable monetary and exchange-rate stability. Indeed, the longest period of monetary order occurred during the first half of the 20th century, lasting from 1899 to the 1940s, when money supply was controlled by the Conversion Office (**Caja de Conversión**), which accumulated gold to back the paper peso and exchanged gold for paper and vice versa, and later by the BCRA, a mixed state–private entity modeled on the Bank of England, established in 1935 to manage money supply and maintain the exchange rate.

The nationalization of the BCRA in 1946 marked a definitive rupture. Monetary creation and cheap credit was the new ideology and would remain so for virtually the next four decades, notwithstanding the implementation of periodic stabilization programs. Government intervention spelled the nationalization of money, credit, and foreign exchange markets. From the mid-1940s until the end of the 1980s, the country experienced acute macroeconomic instability that was captured by the incidence of price changes and the exchange rate. For almost the whole of the first half of the 20th century, rates of inflation annualized by presidential term never exceeded 5.6 percent and were usually two or three points lower. After 1946, average rates of inflation were always in double figures, often with considerable volatility within two- to three-year periods. And there were bouts of **hyperinflation** (or near hyper- inflation): hence the new currencies launched in 1970, 1983, 1985, and 1992.

In December 1946, one US dollar was worth around m$n4.20; when re- tired in December 1969, the rate was m$n352 to the dollar. Monetary crea- tion and exchange-rate slippage was initially a pronounced feature of the *peronato* and subsequently featured largely in **developmentalist** programs sponsored by civilian and military regimes in the 1950s and 1960s. Intro- duced at 3.50$ley to the US dollar in January 1970, when discontinued in May 1983 the rate was 98,500$ley to the dollar. The *peso argentino* opened at $11.50 to the dollar in June 1983 and closed at $673 in May 1985. When launched in June 1985, the austral bought around US$1.20; on retirement in December 1991, the monthly average rate was ₳10,028 to the dollar. The *peso convertible* remained at one US dollar between January 1992 and late 2001; by December 2002, the rate was $3.40 to the dollar. Careful manage- ment by the BCRA sustained this rate until approximately late 2008. At the end of December 2016, the rate was $15.80 on the dollar, slippage accelerat- ing in 2014 and 2015, the final years of the *kirchnerato*.

Nevertheless, despite the formal ending of the Convertibility Plan at the beginning of 2002, the arrangement initiated in January 1992 produced the second longest period of monetary stability in modern Argentine history. Even after 2002, careful management of money supply ensured that there was no precipitate depreciation, notwithstanding an implicit devaluation at the beginning of 2014 and substantial slippage thereafter. When the Convert- ibility Plan was introduced, the strategy consciously echoed that of 1899, employing much the same language, save that the US dollar was substituted for gold as the currency anchor. It is ironic that the trajectory of the peso since 1992 mirrored that of its predecessor. That is, stability until late 2001, followed by relative stability thereafter, in much the same manner as the earlier variant maintained its external value for more than a decade following the closure of the Caja de Conversión. *See also* AUSTRAL PLAN; ECO- NOMIC CRISES.

CUYO. Deriving from the indigenous word for sandy soil, the term applies to the center-west, comprising the provinces of **Mendoza, San Juan**, and **San Luis**—the principal wine-producing region of the country. In colonial times, the area was an important provisioning area on the **Buenos Aires–Chile** trade route and supplied **cattle** and draught animals for the silver mines of Upper Peru (present-day **Bolivia**). A short-lived intendancy during the early national period, Cuyo became the supply center for **military**

operations headed by General **José de San Martín** to liberate Chile and **Peru**. The region was splitting into its constituent provinces by the 1820s, though inhabitants of the area continue to acknowledge a shared heritage.

DE LA PLAZA, VICTORINO (1840–1919). Vice president of Argentina (1910–1914) and president (1914–1916). A native of **Salta** of relatively humble origins, he studied law at the **University of Buenos Aires** and enlisted to fight in the **War of the Triple Alliance**. He collaborated with **Dalmacio Vélez Sarsfield**, the renowned national jurist, to write the commercial code of the province of **Buenos Aires**, which was subsequently adopted by the federal government and was instrumental in the project of monetary reform that that led to the creation of the first national **currency** in 1881. He held ministerial office under **Nicolás Avellaneda** and **Julio A. Roca**, including the portfolios of finance and foreign affairs, and headed the Argentine delegation that went to London in 1890 to negotiate the settlement of Argentine debts following the **Baring Crisis**. In 1910, he was elected vice president on the ticket with **Roque Sáenz Peña**. He served as acting president during Sáenz Peña's repeated bouts of ill health and, upon the death of the latter in 1914, succeeded to the presidency to complete Sáenz Peña's term in 1916. As such, he was responsible for implementing the electoral reform bill sponsored by Sáenz Peña in 1912, the **Sáenz Peña Law**, thereby becoming the last "oligarchic" president of the republic prior to the introduction of the secret ballot, which was first applied in the **presidential** and **congressional elections of 1916**.

DE LA RÚA, FERNANDO (1937–). Lawyer and politician who was president of the republic between 1999 and 2001; his mandate, which should have ended in 2003, collapsed amid economic crisis. Born to a middle-class **Córdoba** family of Spanish and Italian immigrant origin, he was a member of the **Unión Cívica Radical** (UCR). He served in a minor capacity in the administration of **Arturo Illia** in the 1960s, but first came to national prominence in the **presidential** and **congressional elections of March 1973**. He was elected national senator for the city of **Buenos Aires**, possibly the most important victory secured by the UCR, an achievement that led to his nomination as vice presidential running mate of **Ricardo Balbín** on the UCR ticket for the **presidential election of September 1973**. He continued as senator until the **military coup of 1976**, when he withdrew from political life, working as a lawyer for the Argentine multinational **Bunge & Born**.

With the announcement by de facto president General **Reynaldo Bignone** in 1982 that elections would be held the following year, at a meeting of representatives of the principal political grouping called to establish a common front in the face of conditions imposed by the **military** for the projected return to democracy a number of views were expressed. Moralists argued that the parties should not countenance any deal with the generals and admirals, given the **human rights** violations perpetrated by the administrations of the **Proceso de Reorganización Nacional**. Pragmatists maintained that the military were so discredited that no deal was necessary—the military had no alternative but to return to the barracks, and negotiation would taint any democratically elected government.

It is rumored that only De la Rúa spoke in favor of a deal. Perhaps this explains why, when represented the Balbín wing of the party in the UCR primaries, he lost to **Raúl Alfonsín** by a substantial margin. Alfonsín was vehemently and publicly opposed to efforts by the generals and admirals to amnesty themselves and preempt an investigation of abuse of power. In the **presidential** and **congressional elections of 1983**, De la Rúa stood for his old Buenos Aires senate seat, topping the poll above Peronist candidate **Carlos Ruckauf**. Following changes introduced by the **Constitution of 1994**, which granted the **federal capital** autonomy, that is provincial status, he was victorious in the 1996 city elections, becoming the first elected head of the new city government.

As head of the city of Buenos Aires government, De la Rúa oversaw major public works programs: there was substantial investment in transport infrastructure; parks and public spaces were extended and modernized; there was a general improvement in urban amenities. Despite reported irregularities in the awarding of some contracts, the administration was popular, furthering De la Rúa's ambition to stand for the presidency. But it was clear that the UCR would need to form an alliance with other progressive groups. The result was the **Alianza**, an electoral coalition that nominated De la Rúa presidential candidate and **Carlos "Chacho" Álvarez** of the **Frente País Solidaro** (FREPASO) for vice president. It proved to be a winning formula for the **presidential** and **congressional elections of 1999**.

The **economy** was already in recession when De la Rúa assumed the presidency: output was falling, unemployment rising, poverty on the increase, and debt mushrooming, problems in part inherited from the outgoing Peronist administration of **Carlos Saúl Menem**. Efforts to stabilize the public finances failed, but major problems confronting the administration soon became political. Vice President Álvarez resigned on learning that De la Rúa had been bribing members of the National Senate to secure the passage of legislation. Social unrest, partly organized by the Peronist opposition, and an unsympathetic attitude by the International Monetary Fund contributed to the government's problems, yet the major difficulties arose from its incapacity to regain control of the economy or make the hard decisions needed to stabilize the situation. The government lost its moral authority. There was spontaneous violence on the streets, mainly involving middle-class professionals protesting against the freezing of bank accounts—subsequent looting of supermarkets was attributed to goon squads organized by Peronist **caudillos**, particularly in the province of Buenos Aires. In the final days of the administration, 30 people were killed, supposedly as the result of police action ordered by the president. At the height of the turmoil, De la Rúa instructed the armed forces to maintain order. Mindful of the reputation of the forces and of the prosecution of the heads of the military juntas of the Proceso, the chief of the Joint General Staff and head of each branch of the services reminded the president of changes to the law that prohibited the deployment of the armed forces at home without congressional authorization, declining to comply without such authorization. Government losses in the midterm **congressional elections of 2001** precluded approval for the use of troops on domestic security detail. De la Rúa resigned and abandoned the **Casa Rosada**, being flown out by helicopter. Another UCR president left office before the end of his mandate amid a massive **economic crisis** and fears (though not the reality) of **hyperinflation**.

Since leaving office, De la Rúa has largely maintained a low profile. He has been subject to several legal investigations arising from his time in office, including charges of authorizing excessive action in response to public protest, mismanagement of public affairs, and misuse of public funds. Cleared of most of these charges, the enduring image of De la Rúa is of a weak, indecisive politician, not up to the final job to which he was elected. *See also* ECONOMIC CRISES; FOREIGN DEBT/FOREIGN INVESTMENT.

DE LA SOTA, JOSÉ MANUEL (1949–2018). Lawyer and career politician, sometime member of the **Partido Justicialista** (PJ) and governor of the province of **Córdoba**, briefly in the running to become interim president following the collapse of the **Convertibility Plan** and the resignation of President **Fernando De la Rúa**. A native of Córdoba, De la Sota read law at the **University of Córdoba**, where he met and married his first wife, the daughter of a former governor of the province, and was active in student politics. At the time, the province was regarded as a stronghold of the **Unión Cívica Radical** (UCR). This was amply demonstrated when De la Sota was roundly defeated in attempts to run for governor of the province and mayor of the city. However, he narrowly managed to secure a seat in the national Chamber of Deputies in the midterm **congressional elections of 1985**. At this point, he was identified with the modernizing (*renovadora*) wing of the PJ. This, and repeated failures to secure the governorship of the province, not least during the gubernatorial and **congressional elections of 1991** when the PJ virtually swept the board, cost De la Sota support within the provincial party and aroused the ire of President **Carlos Saúl Menem**. In the midterm **congressional elections of 1993**, he even lost his seat in the Chamber of Deputies. However, running for the National Senate in the **congressional** and **presidential elections of 1995**, he gained the "minority" seat for the PJ—the two majority Senate seats went to the UCR. Time in the Senate allowed him to rebuild his political career; he acquired a reputation as a fiscal reformer and voice of moderation. He won the governorship of the province in 1999 and was reelected in 2003, rolling out an ambitious program of public works and social spending—especially on **education**. Some of these projects triggered rumors of kickbacks and **corruption**.

Despite an equivocal relationship with President **Néstor Kirchner**, De la Sota endorsed the presidential candidature of **Cristina Fernández de Kirchner** in the **presidential election of 2011** and obtained her support for another tilt at the governorship in the same year. He defeated rivals in the PJ, as well as the UCR candidate, and returned to the governor's mansion. A year later, he broke with Cristina Fernández to join the anti-K federalist wing of the PJ. De la Sota became associated with "federal Peronism" and placied himself on the social-democratic-cum-Christian-socialist end of the political spectrum, he was known to harbor presidential ambitions. Yet he is remembered as a president-who-might-have-been. When De la Rúa resigned on 20 December 2001, as there was no vice president—**Carlos "Chaco" Álvarez** had resigned and not been replaced in October 2000—the acting president of the National Senate, **Ramón Puerta**, assumed office. When Puerta resigned after a few days, it fell to a cabal of PJ governors to nominate a successor, one of whom was De la Sota. As sitting governor of Córdoba, a pivotal province, De la Sota was a strong contender to replace Puerta. Wisely, he declined; he and other members of the cabal nominated **Adolfo Rodríguez Saá**, who in turn survived barely a week. De la Sota died in a motor accident in September 2018. *See also* CONGRESSIONAL ELECTIONS OF 1999; FRENTE RENOVADOR (FR/PJ); PRESIDENTIAL ELECTION OF 1999.

DE VIDO, JULIO (1949–). Politician and former minister of planning; he read architecture at the **University of Buenos Aires** (UBA) and was jailed for **corruption**. Born in the city of **Buenos Aires**, De Vido spent most of his early professional life in the province of **Santa Cruz**, in the far south of the country. There he served the provincial administration in various capacities, successively working for the housing and urban planning unit and the highway agency and was appointed provincial minister of economy in 1991. In this post, he was responsible for overseeing a massive program of public investment, funded by the state oil company, **Yacimientos Petrolíferos Fiscales** (YPF), and came to the attention of recently elected governor of the province **Néstor Kirchner**. Kirchner had negotiated a deal with President **Carlos Saúl Menem** for the transfer of funds to the province when YPF was privatized in 1993. Although De Vido was elected to the National Congress in 1997, he resigned the seat after two years on appointment as minister of interior of the province by Kirchner. He became a close associate of the governor and his wife, **Cristina Fernández de Kirchner**. When Kirchner became president in 2003, De Vido followed the Kirchners to Buenos Aires. He was offered the position of minister of planning and public investment. He held this cabinet post for 12 years during the presidency of Néstor and the two subsequent terms of Cristina. Under De Vido, the responsibilities of the department grew; it became a "super" ministry, and its budget mushroomed as he became one of the longest-serving cabinet ministers continuously in post in the modern history of the country.

As planning minister, De Vido was responsible for massive expenditure. Among other projects, he oversaw plans for the construction of a high-speed rail link between Buenos Aires and **Córdoba**—the project was canceled after considerable sums had been disbursed—and upgrading the country's energy infrastructure at a time when the country was experiencing a serious energy deficit. In 2012, while continuing to hold the ministerial portfolio, he was placed at the head of a renationalized YPF. For part of the time that he administered huge public capital investment schemes, De Vido enjoyed a cozy relationship with the head of the Public Audit Office, who was his wife. This arrangement raised many eyebrows and would lead to charges of cronyism and abuse of office. The net assets of husband and wife grew exponentially during their time in government; they were subject to several criminal investigations. In a particularly bizarre instance, one of De Vido's underlings was found tossing bags stuffed with millions of US dollars into the grounds of a convent: De Vido was charged and convicted of skimming funds intended for road projects, obtaining kickbacks from oil and gas contracts, and embezzlement. Other charges are pending.

In addition to the scale of corruption, De Vido will be remembered as the first senior member of the Kirchner team to be jailed. In 2017, while a national deputy, the chamber voted to lift his immunity from imprisonment. He turned himself in to the judicial authorities on 25 October, the day immunity was lifted, and was taken directly to jail. Critics view him as a symbol of the endemic corruption that plagues the country and dubbed him the "Minister of Corruption." His conviction and imprisonment posed problems for Cristina Fernández. De Vido was Mrs. Kirchner's right-hand man: he knows where the bodies are buried and is unlikely to remain silent, particularly if he remains in prison. In 2018, a court sentenced De Vido to a further term in jail for his role in a major rail accident in 2012: funds skimmed from public works projects were held to have contributed to the accident.

DEFAULT. *See* BARING CRISIS; CAVALLO, DOMINGO FELIPE (1946–); CONGRESSIONAL ELECTIONS OF 2001; CONVERTIBILITY PLAN; DE LA RÚA, FERNANDO (1937–); DUHALDE, EDUARDO ALBERTO (1941–); ECONOMIC CRISES; KIRCHNER, NÉSTOR CARLOS (1950–2010); PRESIDENTIAL ELECTION OF 2003; RODRÍGUEZ SAÁ, ADOLFO (1947–).

DEL VALLE, ARISTÓBULO (1845–1896). Journalist and lawyer—trained at the **University of Buenos Aires**; a major figure in the **Revolution of 1890**, he served in the **Buenos Aires** provincial legislature and in the National Senate and was sometime minister in the federal administration. In the language of the time, he was a radical and progressive democrat.

Closely associated with **Adolfo Alsina** and **Leandro Alem**, he was a consistent advocate of reforms that would "pacify" and institutionalize politics. A constitutional lawyer, he was particularly concerned with federal intervention in the province, which he regarded as undermining constitutional democracy. He was also a strong advocate of reform projects likely to democratize politics and strengthen constitutionalism, notably legislation that culminated in the 1912 **Sáenz Peña Law**, though he died long before it was enacted. Having already served in the provincial legislature, he was first elected to the National Senate in 1876, becoming provisional president of the Senate in 1880—the position was normally held by the vice president of the nation. He played an active role in the Revolution of 1890, which forced the resignation of constitutional president **Miguel Júarez Celman**, and in the formation of the **Unión Cívica Radical** (UCR). He resigned as senator to organize the 1890 revolution but was immediately reelected. Anticipating political and electoral reform, and to facilitate the integration of the UCR into constitutional politics, he agreed to serve in the cabinet of President **Luis Sáenz Peña**, father of the author of the 1912 Law. He briefly held the war portfolio and acted as de facto head of the cabinet. *See also* IRIGOYEN, BERNARDO DE (1822–1906).

DERQUI, SANTIAGO RAFAEL LUIS MANUEL JOSÉ MARÍA (1809–1867). A lawyer, academic, newspaper editor, and politician from **Córdoba** who served as constitutional president for 18 months in 1860–1861. He studied at the **University of Córdoba**, of which he became vice rector. An opponent of **Juan Manuel de Rosas** who was active in the civil conflicts of the time, he spent time in exile in **Brazil** and **Uruguay**. He was one of the signatories of the **Constitution of 1853**, having served as vice president of the constituent assembly held in **Santa Fe** to draw up the constitution of the **Argentine Confederation**. He followed **military** strongman **Justo José de Urquiza** as president of the Confederation. Although on election he attempted to reintegrate the province of **Buenos Aires** into the Confederation, and appeared to enjoy positive relations with **Bartolomé Mitre**, who was elected governor of the province at the same time, the two men soon fell out, making Derqui dependent on Urquiza, who remained head of the army. When conflict broke out, Confederation forces failed to secure the day at the indecisive battle of Pavón, Derqui resigned. He became the "forgotten president," succeeded by his nemesis Mitre. Yet he was the president who formally decreed in 1860 that the official name of the country was to be La República Argentina, no longer La Confederación Argentina or La Nación Argentina, terms that had prevailed hitherto.

DESAPARECIDOS. The term, "The Disappeared," was coined during the military dictatorship of 1976–1983 and applied to victims kidnapped and murdered. Many were literally "disappeared" from their homes or the streets. The bodies of almost 9,000 victims of the military dictatorship were never recovered. Disappearances began with kidnapping and detention, followed by interrogation at a secret location; detainees were left at the mercy of their captors before they were summarily executed. The process was then completed by the gruesome disposal of the bodies. There were three means of doing so: dumping them in the sea, dam reservoirs, or rivers; burning them in ovens or piles of car tires; or burying them in unmarked individual or common graves.

Before his death in 2013, former de facto president **Jorge Rafael Videla** admitted that most of the Desaparecidos were killed during the first two years after he took power in 1976 and that each disappearance was the definite masking of a death. *See also* DIRTY WAR; DISPOSICIÓN FINAL; MADRES DE PLAZA DE MAYO; WAR TO ANNIHILATE SUBVERSION.

DESARROLLISMO. *See* DEVELOPMENTALISM/DEVELOPMENTALIST.

DESCAMISADOS. Literally "shirtless ones," or "those without shirts," a term used by the political elite and members of the ruling class to describe working-class supporters of **Juan Domingo Perón** who came onto the streets to protest when he was incarcerated by the **military** in October 1945. Later voting for him in the **presidential election of 1946**, the *descamisados* came to form the core of his electoral base and were fanatically loyal to him and his wife **Eva Perón**—who mobilized them and claimed to bring dignity to rural and urban workers hitherto marginal to the political process. As with the put-down *sans-culottes* during the French Revolution, the term was appropriated by those it was meant to disparage and used as a badge of honor. The term is still acknowledged by organized labor and rank-and-file members of the **Partido Justicialista** (PJ). *See also* CONVENTILLOS; ECONOMY; INDUSTRY; KIRCHNER, CRISTINA ELISABET FERNÁNDEZ DE (1953–); KIRCHNER, NÉSTOR CARLOS (1950–2010); *PERONATO*; TRADE UNIONS.

DESERT. A misnomer: the term *the desert* was used to describe the grasslands to the west and south of the capital, an "unpopulated," deserted region. Settling the desert with immigrants was central to the 19th-century project of nation building envisioned by statesmen such as **Bartolomé Mitre** and **Domingo Faustino Sarmiento**, among others. They viewed Argentina as the **United States** of South America, populated by immigrants from Europe who would "civilize" the **pampas**, spreading from the coast to the distant interior. *See also* CONQUEST OF THE DESERT/DESERT CAMPAIGN; NATIONAL ORGANIZATION; ROCA, JULIO ARGENTINO (1843–1914).

DEVELOPMENTALISM/DEVELOPMENTALIST. A branch of economics (and theory of economic development) pioneered by **Raúl Prebisch** and initially associated with the analyses and policy prescriptions of the **Economic Commission for Latin America** (ECLA). ECLA was created in 1948 as one of five regional economic bodies set up by the **United Nations**. In Spanish, Comisión Económica para América Latina (CEPAL), the agency now includes the Caribbean, hence Economic Commission for Latin America and the Caribbean (ECLAC). Under the direction of Prebisch, the commission became associated with a diagnosis of contemporary Latin American development problems that offered state-sponsored industrialization as a solution. The result was the formulation of a strategy of state-supported import-substituting industrialization (ISI), or *cepalismo*, a term deriving from the Spanish and Portuguese acronym for the commission.

Conceived as a theory of applied economics in the "economic periphery for the economic periphery," developmentalism would ultimately consolidate as development economics, challenging conventional economics, particularly in the fields of trade theory and state-sponsored structural change. In addition to innovative concepts resulting from the work of Prebisch, development economics incorporates theories and approaches about "unequal exchange" and the utility of state-promoted countercyclical growth associated with ideas espoused by such near contemporaries as Hans Singer and John Maynard Keynes. Developmentalism (*desarrollismo* in Spanish and *desen-*

volvimentismo in Portuguese) or development economics emerged as a robust challenge to prevailing economic orthodoxy, being viewed as particularly relevant to the emergent economies of Latin America and Asia in the post–Second World War period. The high point of *desarrollismo* is associated with Prebish's early connection with the United Nations: he served as executive secretary of ECLA from 1950 to 1963 and was founding secretary general of the United Nations Conference on Trade and Development (UNCTAD), set up in 1964—a post he held for five years.

Known in English also as structuralism as well as developmentalism, the ideas advanced by Prebish to explain the economic predicament of Latin America had a profound influence across the continent and beyond from the 1950s to the 1970s, and would again resonate in the early 21st century, the years of the "Pink Tide," when democratic left-of-center governments were elected in many part of the continent following a rejection of market-orientated strategies associated with the Washington Consensus. In Argentina, the presidencies of **Néstor Kirchner** and **Cristina Fernández de Kirchner** are regarded as epitomizing a particular brand of Pink Tide political economy.

Prebisch based his pessimistic assessment of the position of Latin America on a rejection of traditional trade theory and an evaluation of structural imbalances in the international economy. He observed that since the late 19th century there had been a secular decline in the terms of trade of primary exporting economies (the periphery)—that is, the unit costs of imports relative to exports. This meant that over time, a greater volume of commodities (say agricultural goods like cereals or coffee or **wool**, or minerals like copper or tin) had to be exported in order to import a given amount of manufactures from industrialized economies (the center). He explained this deterioration in the terms of trade of primary-commodity exporting economies by reference to the differing income elasticities of demand for distinct items and producer responses to the trade cycle. As individuals and households became more affluent, they tended to spend a smaller proportion of each income increment on basic items like food and clothing, and more on consumer durables such as household appliances or motor vehicles and intangibles like leisure, and would save a relatively larger share of income. As with households, so with economies: over time, primary producing economies would have a high propensity to consume manufactured imports, while predominantly industrial economies would have a declining propensity to consume imported commodities, coupled with a rising propensity to consume domestically produced manufactures. Hence, over time, demand for commodities would increase at a slower rate than the demand for manufactured goods and modern services, meaning that commodity-exporting peripheral economies would experience a deterioration in their terms of trade relative to economies of the center that specialized in the production and export of manufactures and modern services. In short, the gains from international trade were distributed unequally, not equitably as predicted by classical trade theory.

And there were structural-cum-cyclical imbalances in the system such as distinct competitive practices and the impact of technological change that intensified the income effect of the terms of trade. An upturn in the world trade cycle was likely to see a relatively rapid response by commodity production as prices rose, though a sluggish response by manufacturers, given the longer lead-in period required to increase industrial output. A downturn in the cycle would induce "perverse" responses by commodity producers, that is, effort to produce and export more to protect overall incomes from a fall in unit prices; manufacturers, on the other hand, would seek to restrain output to "protect" prices. Thus, commodities prices would rise more slowly than the price of manufactures during an upturn in the global economy but fall more rapidly during a downturn, thereby intensifying the long-run deterioration in the terms of trade of the periphery. Prebisch developed this unorthodox theory of international trade by observing trends in international trade and prices from the late 19th century, and particularly during the 1920s and 1930s. In addition, there was the impact of technology, which was both practical and structural. Technological change tended to economize the use of commodities: for example, a smaller volume of steel was required to produce vehicles and appliances, engines became more fuel-efficient and require less petroleum, rayon could be substituted for cotton—again meaning sluggish growth in the demand for commodities. Distinct structural factors also limited the international distribution of the gains from technological change. In industrialized economies, organized labor and manufacturing firms conspired to "capture" a disproportionate share of the gains from technical change in the form of higher wages and profits. In commodity-exporting economies, labor was unorganized and producers less inclined to collaborate. Classical trade theory, based on assumptions of perfect competition, argued that cost-reducing technical change would produce a fall in prices. Prebisch found to the contrary, once again arguing that prices of manufactures were "sticky" while those of commodities more susceptible to downward pressures.

In sum, Prebisch overturned traditional trade theory and questioned the gains from comparative advantage, economic specialization, and international trade. His analysis has been questioned, notably the reliability of his terms of trade data (was there a secular decline in the terms of trade of commodity exporters, or were there long swings in relative prices, trends that sometimes favor commodities and other times manufactured goods and services) and for a failure to recognize that changes in quality explain differentials in relative price movements—a grain of cereal today is hardly different from a grain of cereal decades ago, but a motor vehicle or electronic appliance is qualitatively different. Although the ideas and analyses of Prebisch about unequal exchange were later hijacked by dependency theorists, who accepted his analyses of the predicament of Latin America (and other parts of the "Third World"), though not the solutions proposed, and rejected by neoclassical economists, who repudiated both his diagnoses and his solutions, much of his analysis has stood the test of time.

Prebisch's diagnosis and solutions proposed were particularly influential in shaping **economic policy** across Latin America during the immediate post–Second World War decades, notably a body of policies that coalesced into state-induced import-substituting industrialization, agrarian reform, and regional economic integration. Although detractors of *desarrollismo* sometimes argue otherwise, economic solutions proposed by Prebisch to problems confronting the Latin American economies were not anti–international trade, anti–foreign investment, or anti–private sector, notwithstanding that a distorted interpretation of Prebisch's theory and misapplication of ECLA policy recommendations sometimes gave this impression. Prebisch argued that governments in Latin America should foster industrial growth and that, given the structural imbalances within these economies and the international economy, industrialization in peripheral economies was impossible without state support. He also acknowledged that, in the early stages of state-induced industrialization, there would be a relative increase in manufactured imports before newly industrializing economies were in a position to supply domestic demand and, indeed, yield a surplus for export. He also recognized that imported technology and capital would play a vital role in such "forced" industrialization, as might foreign firms. Regional economic integration was not a substitute for engagement in world trade but a springboard for greater engagement and beneficial association with the global economy. Lower "internal" tariffs (and a higher external tariff wall) proposed by regional economic integration implied "infant industry protection" and a level playing field for regional firms. For example, Brazilian and Argentine industrial businesses would compete in the regional marketplace, protected in the short to medium term against unequal competition from international conglomerates who might flood the market and destroy local enterprises. Agrarian reform was viewed as a mechanism of promoting more efficient production and expanding local output, thus economizing on imports and reducing inflationary pressure—given the disproportionate impact for food costs in the budgets of low-income families who typified much of the continent—as well as raising rural incomes and hence overall demand for (local) manufactures.

Aspiring politicians were not slow to recognize the legitimizing effect of ISI strategies—namely, opportunities provided to local business elites and the urban bourgeoisie; better employment prospects for the burgeoning, organizing working class; and the ideological appeal to nationalists who favored economic modernization and industrial self-sufficiency. Such politicians may have been less sanguine about other components of the ECLA model, namely regional economic integration and agrarian reform. The theory was palatable, all the policy implication less so. Nevertheless, although later hijacked by dependency theorists and rejected by neoliberal economists, the analysis of Prebisch and the policy recommendations of ECLA had a notable impact on economic policy, especially during the presidencies of **Arturo Frondizi, Juan Carlos Onganía,** and **Raúl Alfonsín**; in the Peronist governments of the mid-1970s; and, in attenuated from, for the administrations of **Juan Domingo Perón** in the late 1940s as well as the Kirchners. *See also* ALEMANN, ROBERTO TEODORO (1922–); ALSOGARAY, ÁLVARO (1913–2005); BER GELBARD, JOSÉ (1917–1977); CAFIERO, ANTONIO FRANCISCO (1922–2014); CONCORDANCIA; ECONOMY; FERRER, ALDO (1927–2016); FOREIGN DEBT/FOREIGN INVESTMENT; GRINSPUN, BERNARDO (1925–1996); INDUSTRY; KICILLOF, AXEL (1971–); KRIEGER VASENA, ADALBERT (1920–2000); MACHINEA, JOSÉ LUIS (1946–); SOURROUILLE, JUAN VITAL (1940–).

DI TELLA, GUIDO JOSÉ MARIO (1931–2001). The younger son of **Torcuato Di Tella** senior, Guido was a statesman and academic. He held various ministerial posts and official positions and devoted a considerable part of his political and academic career to improving relations with **Great Britain** and the image of the country abroad. Urbane and endowed with considerable charm, he was an approachable man who seemed equally at ease attending Peronist political rallies, engaging with colleagues and students at Oxford, and hosting diplomatic receptions in Washington, DC.

Guido followed the family tradition by reading engineering at the **University of Buenos Aires** (UBA) and appeared destined to run **Sección Industrial Amasadoras Mecánicas** (SIAM Di Tella), the business founded by his father. However, from the first, he displayed an interest in politics and **education**—he would later teach at the UBA and at the Roman Catholic university, **Universidad Católica Argentina** (UCA). In 1954, one year before graduating from the UBA, he helped form the center-right **Partido Demócrata Cristiano** (PDC). Modeled on similar European parties and associated with a trend to establish confessional parties and groupings in the Americas, the PDC was inaugurated as relations between the **Juan Domingo Perón** government and the **Catholic Church** were deteriorating. On completing the engineering degree in 1955, Guido studied for a doctorate in economics at the Massachusetts Institute of Technology, awarded in 1959, a change of discipline that would have a profound impact on his future intellectual development and career. In his doctoral research and related early publications, he developed theories about indirect development and late industrialization, subsequently writing about macroeconomic instability and comparative growth. These ideas influenced his political action and activities in government. By the 1960s, he was a strong supporter of Peronism, viewing the movement as a vehicle to facilitate the incorporation of the working class into mainstream politics and for national economic development, advocating also the return of Perón. These views got him into trouble with the **Revolución Argentina** military regime and led to his exile in the early 1970s, a time spent at the Latin America Centre, St Antony's College, Oxford, of which he became a fellow. In 1972, he accompanied Perón on the latter's brief visit to Argentina, and in 1974 was appointed deputy minister of economy by Perón's widow and successor as president, **Isabel Perón**, though in effect he ran the ministry. The **military coup of 1976** saw him arrested along with other key Peronists, including future president **Carlos Saúl Menem**, though he was soon freed following lobbying by prominent economists, including soon-to-be-minister **José Alfredo Martínez de Hoz**. Another spell of exile in Oxford followed.

The return of democracy in 1983 found Guido back in Argentina and a PJ member of **Congress** and, when Menem was elected in 1989, back as deputy at the **Ministry of Economy** for a short period. He held several positions under Menem: ambassador in Washington, minister of defense (for six days only), and then minister of foreign affairs, a post for which he was eminently suited and held from 1991 to 1999, becoming one of Menem's longest-serving cabinet members. It was in this position that he sought to improve relations with Britain and woo Falkland Islanders—unsuccessfully—a charm offensive that entailed sending Christmas cards to the islanders, while there was also a resettlement scheme: each family would be offered £1 million to set up home elsewhere. Concrete achievements included the resumption of limited flights between the mainland and the islands following a meeting with the British foreign secretary and representatives of the islanders, and a significant realignment in foreign policy, notably rapprochement with the **United States**. Argentina sent naval vessels to support the US-led coalition in the First Gulf War and voted consistently with the United States in the **United Nations**, in contrast to earlier decades when the country had identified with the "Third World" and generally opposed US initiatives in international fora. In a phrase that he probably came to regret, Foreign Minister Di Tella stated that he favored "carnal relations" with the United States, yet this was consistent with his support for the Menem project, which he argued would make Argentina "a normal country again." His last months in office were clouded by ill health and the charge, for which he was arraigned before the courts, that he was involved in an illicit arms deal—the sale of equipment to Ecuador that was intended for Croatia during the Yugoslav conflict. It is likely that he knew nothing about the deal, yet it occurred on his watch. His principal publications included *Las etapas del desarrollo económico argentino* (coauthored with Miguel Zymelman in 1961)—a modified version of the Rostow stages of economic growth theory—and *La estrategia del desarrollo* *indirecto* (1973), works that informed much of his **economic policy** recommendations; jointly edited compilations with various colleagues on the Argentine economy, several of which contained comparative perspectives on Australia and Canada, pointing to the relative decline of the country; and studies of Peronism. *See also* DI TELLA, TORCUATO SALVADOR FRANCISCO NICOLÁS (1929–2016).

DI TELLA, TORCUATO (1882–1948). Born in Italy, he moved to Argentina with his parents in 1905. An entrepreneur and academic, Di Tella became a prominent figure in the world of business and finance, having trained as an engineer. Best known as an industrialist, he founded **Sección Industrial Amasadoras Mecánicas** (SIAM Di Tella) in 1910 and oversaw its expansion and diversification from the manufacture of bread-making equipment to the production of household appliances and motor vehicles; he headed the company until his death. In addition, he served on the board of the Unión Industrial Argentina, the principal body representing manufacturing and commercial interests, and held a chair in the Faculty of Natural and Exact Sciences at the **University of Buenos Aires**. He sat on the directorates of commercial and philanthropic organizations such as the Banco Popular, the Argentina–Chile Chamber of Commerce, and the Argentine Committee of the Red Cross. An antifascist social reformer and promoter of labor legislation, he was also an important patron of the arts and sponsor of **education**, through the family charitable trust founded in his honor, the **Centro Torcuato Di Tella**, and the social science research center, the **Instituto Torcuato Di Tella**, which later became a private university, the **Universidad Torcuato Di Tella**. *See also* DI TELLA, GUIDO JOSÉ MARIO (1931–2001); DI TELLA, TORCUATO SALVADOR FRANCISCO NICOLÁS (1929–2016).

DI TELLA, TORCUATO SALVADOR FRANCISCO NICOLÁS (1929–2016). The elder son of **Torcuato Di Tella**, like his brother Guido, Torcuato ("Hijo") Junior was a prominent public figure. Also like his brother, he seemed destined for the family manufacturing business, **Sección Industrial Amasadoras Mecánicas** (SIAM Di Tella), created by his father, but preferred and academic career. He obtained a first degree in engineering from the **University of Buenos Aires** in 1951, and two years later an MA in sociology at Columbia University, New York. Political sociology became his principal field of research and writing, mainly studies of the working class and labor movement. During his academic career, he held various visiting professorships, including at the University of Chile, the University of California, and the University of Oxford. He and Guido were joint founders—and funders—of the social science research and teaching center the **Instituto Torcuato Di Tella** in 1958, later the **University Torcuato Di Tella**, named after their father. He was also instrumental in the creation of the Instituto de Desarrollo Económico y Social two years later. Often critical of official cultural policy, he was unafraid to irritate the cultural establishment while aspiring to the status of a public intellectual. He was briefly minister of culture during the **Néstor Kirchner** presidency: appointed in May 2003, he resigned in November 2004. In 2010, he was appointed Argentine ambassador in Rome by President **Cristina Fernández de Kirchner**: he held this post until his death in 2016; he was also resident in Italy, he was also named ambassador to Albania in 2011. He is most recognized for such publications as *El sistema politico argentino y la clase obrera* (1964), *Sindicato y comunidad: dos tipos de estructura sindical latinoamericana* (1967), *Sociología de los procesos politicos* (1986), and *Historia de los partidos politicos de América Latina* (1994). *See also* DI TELLA, GUIDO JOSÉ MARIO (1931–2001).

DIRECCIÓN GENERAL DE FERROCARRILES (DGF). A regulatory-body-cum-administrator-of-federal-government-railway-lines, the State Railway Executive was a dependency of the **Ministry of Public Works** created in the late 19th century and was the principal body overseeing rail transport for around 60 years. Initially charged with enforcing regulations governing the operations of railways, gathering data, and advising the government on rail policy, the Administración General de los Ferrocarriles del Estado was absorbed in 1910 by the DGF. As such, it became responsible for the operation of federal government lines, which were located mainly in the national territories on the fringes of the **pampas**. The regulatory brief of the DGF had been refocused and codified with the **Mitre Law** of 1907 that effectively refranchised and harmonized the concessions of private railway companies operating in the country. Around 1910, and particularly during the first presidency of **Hipólito Yrigoyen**, the DGF pursued a dynamic program of construction—mainly by building branch lines that integrated semi-isolated regional systems into the national rail network. The 1920s saw the agency assume a more interventionist position regarding regulation, and there was an acrimonious dispute about rail tariffs and corporate profits. During the 1920s and 1930s, the DGF took control of ailing London companies. These actions were viewed in some British Argentine rail circles as aggressive and challenging the hitherto dominant position of London-registered companies in the sector. Yet others applauded what was depicted as a patriotic stance. Between 1909 and 1930, the rail network operated by the DGF grew 250 percent so that it came to control more than a fifth of the national rail network. By the late 1930s, all new investment in the rail sector was being undertaken by the DGF, and officials there were charged by President **Agustín P. Justo** with preparing plans to negotiate the purchase of British-

and French-owned railway companies. Skeptical British rail officials complained that there was a clear conflict of interest. The agency was a regulator and a competitor and had access to sensitive commercial data.

Action taken by the DGF is significant because the interventionist and nationalist stance adopted in the 1930s contradicts the perceived image of the **Concordancia** as a supine *vendepatria* administration and because it prefigured and influenced the railway strategy of President **Juan Domingo Perón**. With the nationalization of all private railways in 1948, the agency was dissolved and its functions transferred to the newly constituted state rail authority **Ferrocarriles Argentinos** (FFAA). *See also* BUENOS AYRES & PACIFIC RAILWAY COMPANY (BA&P); BUENOS AYRES & ROSARIO RAILWAY COMPANY (BA&R); BUENOS AYRES GREAT SOUTHERN RAILWAY COMPANY (BAGS); BUENOS AYRES WESTERN RAILWAY COMPANY (BAW); CENTRAL ARGENTINE RAILWAY COMPANY (CAR); CORDOBA CENTRAL RAILWAY COMPANY (CCR); ECONOMIC CRISES; ECONOMY; FOREIGN DEBT/ FOREIGN INVESTMENT; GREAT BRITAIN; ROCA–RUNCIMAN PACT (1933); TRANSPORTATION.

DIRTY WAR. English term for the Guerra Sucia, waged by the **military** regime of the **Proceso de Reorganización Nacional**. *See also* DESAPARECIDOS; DISPOSICIÓN FINAL; WAR TO ANNIHILATE SUBVERSION.

DISPOSICIÓN FINAL. Military jargon, which commonly means to dispose of something that no longer has any use (e.g., old clothes), used by the armed forces to describe what took place in the **War to Annihilate Subversion**. To understand the military reasoning behind this process, there is the deposition of former de facto president **Jorge Rafael Videla** before his death in 2013. Convinced to the end that he had done the right thing, Videla maintained that the war against terrorism could not have been won without the deaths of 7,000 or 8,000 people. However, he indicated that at the time of the 1976 coup the military had no idea of how they would deal with all those thousands of prisoners deemed "unrecoverable" and who could not be executed publicly or condemned judicially. These prisoners could not be freed as they were likely to combat or challenge the dictatorship, not least because of its wide, elastic, and discretional definition of "subversion" (it was not restricted to those who had taken up arms).

The Military Junta, the supreme authority in the country comprising the three armed forces, never met to discuss the fate of all these detainees. In fact, Videla has taken responsibility for reaching the decision that the victims of state terror had to be "disappeared," arguing that it was "the best solution" in the context of the time, and for authorizing the disappearances tacitly and not in writing. It has to be stressed that the **Desaparecidos** included the remains of both "unrecoverable" prisoners and of guerrillas killed in shootouts—the latter included **Mário Roberto Santucho**, the leader of the **Ejército Revolucionario del Pueblo** (ERP).

The junta concealed its decision not to respect due legal process or fundamental human rights. It gave the security forces the green light to deal with internal security by any available means, with the condition that the government should be in a position of "possible denial" of all responsibility. By eliminating those picked up by military, police, and paramilitary snatch squads "without society noticing," the regime aimed to prevent both domestic and international protests. It was particularly aware that the US government was not well disposed toward "friendly" governments that violated **human rights**. Public opinion in the **United States** had shifted thanks to overt Republican backing for the 1973 coup in **Chile** and the ensuing brutal dictatorship of General Augusto Pinochet. This was followed in late 1976 by the election of Democratic candidate Jimmy Carter to the White House; one of his flagship policies was the application of principles of human rights to US diplomacy, particularly the condemnation of illegal repression in the Soviet Union, Eastern Europe, and military regimes in southern South America—the new ethical foreign policy.

General **Albano Harguindeguy**, the minister of interior during Videla's presidency, has stated that the problem of the disappeared became unresolvable. Not least, this was due to the method employed. The country was divided into five zones in order to tackle subversion, with their commanders deciding what to do with each detainee without having to inform the junta. Harguindeguy added that the military made the mistake of not changing the method of the Disposición Final, namely enacting specific legislation to establish special tribunals to deal with guerrilla organizations, as done during the de facto presidency of General **Alejandro Agustín Lanusse**.

It seems that the military realized their error too late, when campaigns over the Desaparecidos began to mushroom globally in the late 1970s. Between 1979 and 1981, the last two years of Videla's tenure, the disappearances became the major political topic. When the regime called for "political dialogue" with all sectors, leaders of **political parties** and civic organization pressed the junta for information about the disappeared. In fact, the subject continues to provoke debate. Ever since democracy returned with the **presidential election of 1983**, efforts have continued to bring former members of the military government to book, notwithstanding the statute of limitations enacted during the presidency of **Raúl Alfonsín**, most recently during the presidencies of **Néstor Kirchner** and **Cristina Fernández de Kirchner**.

DORREGO, MANUEL (1787–1828). Democratic **Federalist** from **Buenos Aires** who played a major role in the wars of **independence**. A republican who challenged monarchist projects, he was elected governor of the province of Buenos Aires in August 1828, a proxy national president given the loose federal arrangements of the time. He was opposed by centralists championing the national project represented by **Bernardino Rivadavia**. Defeated at the battle of Navarro in November 1829 by **Unitarian** forces led by General Juan Gallo Lavalle, he escaped. When captured the following month, his execution was ordered by Lavalle. The execution of Dorrego, who was widely regarded as a man of principle and an advocate of political accommodation who might have brought unity to the new republic, triggered a blood feud between Federalists and centralist Unitarians. The former claimed him as a martyr, pursuing a war to the death with centralists that ultimately led to the long, authoritarian rule of **Juan Manuel de Rosas**.

DUARTE, MARÍA EVA. The future **Eva Perón**.

DUHALDE, EDUARDO ALBERTO (1941–). Lawyer, career politician, and president of Argentina (2002–2003). First active in politics in the early 1970s, he joined the **Partido Justicialista** (PJ), rapidly rising through the ranks from small-town branch secretary to **Buenos Aires** provincial **caudillo**. In addition to serving as interim president to complete the term of **Fernando de la Rúa**, who resigned on 20 December 2001, Duhalde occupied a wide range of political posts, including mayor of his hometown of Lomas de Zamora in the province of Buenos Aires, positions in the provincial legislature, governorship of the province, and the vice presidency of the nation.

His started in political life was as a centrist member of the party, which allowed him to stand as a compromise candidate, as in his election as mayor of Lomas. In the PJ party primaries held before the **presidential** and **congressional elections of 1989**, largely a contest between **Antonio Cafiero**, governor of Buenos Aires, and **Carlos Saúl Menem**, governor of **La Rioja**, Duhalde threw his weight behind Menem, agreeing to stand as his vice president. The resounding victory of the Menem–Duhalde ticket destroyed the influence of Cafiero in the province and ensured Duhalde's dominance of the party there. Relations between Menem and Duhalde soured as Menem centralized power in his own hands, and there was a rumored drug turf war between them. A compromise was reached in 1991: Duhalde stepped down as vice president in order to contest midterm elections for the governorship of the province of Buenos Aires, and Menem promised to throw money behind the campaign and to ensure an increase in federal transfers to the province. Peace between the two men, however, was short lived. Duhalde was incensed when it became clear that Menem was intent on changing the constitution in order to stand for immediate reelection in 1995, claiming that Menem had agreed to support his bid for the presidency. Unable to prevent the constitutional amendment, agreed on in principle between Menem and his predecessor **Raúl Alfonsín** in the **Olivos Pact** of 1994, and unable to defeat Menem in the 1995 PJ presidential primaries, Duhalde engineered an amendment to the provincial constitution to allowed him to stand for immediate reelection as governor. Reelected governor, Duhalde upped his criticism of Menem, maintaining that the latter's neoliberal program was un-Peronist and socially destructive. From 1995, immediately after reelection as governor, when Duhalde announced his decision to stand for the presidency in 1999, there was an intense struggle for control of the PJ, a struggle that became even more destructive when Menem advanced his own intention of standing again in 1999. Employing traditional Peronist tactics, Menem endeavored to promote rivals to Duhalde within the party while still advancing his own case for reelection. In the event, the fortunes of the PJ were in decline, as illustrated by losses in the midterm **congressional elections of 1997** and defeat in the **presidential election of 1999**—the PJ ticket of Duhalde and **Ramón "Palito" Ortega** was defeated by the **Alianza** ticket composed of Fernando de la Rúa and **Carlos "Chacho" Álvarez**.

Fate was to intervene yet again in January 2002 when, following the collapse of the presidency of De la Ruá, Duhalde was selected president by a special legislative assembly to serve out the remainder of De la Rúa's term—notwithstanding strong opposition by Menem, who still controlled a sizeable bloc of supporters in **Congress**, though with the support of Alfonsín, who instructed **Unión Cívica Radical** (UCR) members to back Duhalde. It was argued that, as the runner-up in 1999, and having been endorsed by the Buenos Aires electorate in the 2011 elections, of all national politicians, Duhalde enjoyed the most legitimacy, not that any politician was held in high regard at that point. Yet Duhalde's short presidency was a success. He held the country together, stabilizing the **economy**, preventing social meltdown, and preparing the way for new elections in 2003. He oversaw an orderly devaluation of the peso, brought some stability to the banking system, nationalized the provincial debt, managed a primary surplus on the fiscal accounts (helped by debt default), and presided over the beginnings of economic recovery. As a result, the feared **hyperinflation** did not materialize. Perhaps the major initiative of his presidency was the introduction of an emergency system of family income support, an innovative arrangement funded by the federal government that halted the descent into poverty—almost half the population was recorded as living below the poverty line at the height of the crisis. The country survived. Luck also played a part. Commodity prices began to pick up, ensuring a supply of foreign exchange and rebuilding of the **currency** reserves. The political elite, shocked by the scale of social protest seen in December 2001, pulled together, providing Duhalde with the political clout needed to order the PJ and command support across society—from business, the labor movement, and the **Catholic Church**. Alfonsín was unstinting in his assistance.

Despite these achievements, Duhalde was unable to advance his political career much further. He failed to thwart Menem's efforts to stand in the **presidential election of 2003**. Although his chosen nominee, **Néstor Kirchner**, ultimately gained the presidency, Duhalde soon found Kirchner less compliant than he had imagined and was outmaneuvered by the new president and his increasingly influential wife, **Cristina Fernández de Kirchner**. His waning influence was reflected in a proxy contest for a National Senate seat for Buenos Aires province in the midterm **congressional elections of 2005**: Duhalde's wife, **Hilda "Chiche" González de Duhalde**, went head-to-head against Fernández de Kirchner, representing different wings of the PJ. Fernández de Kirchner won. Organizing his own bloc within the PJ to contest the **presidential election of 2011**, he obtained a shade under 6 percent of the vote. Since then, he has largely retired from public life, though there has been a much-publicized reconciliation with Menem.

Duhalde's decline can be attributed to the unsavory reputation acquired in his ascent to the governorship of Buenos Aires, captured in a phrase common at the time: "Menem roba; Duhalde mata"—Menem steals, Duhalde kills. Already ensnared in corruption scandals, he was rumored to have orchestrated the murder of photojournalist José Luis Cabezas in 1997, who was investigating illicit deals by the Duhalde clique—deals that included money laundering, drug dealing, and kickbacks for official contracts. The Buenos Aires police were said to have had a hand in the murder and cover-up that followed. In 2001, Duhalde was reputed to have instigated the looting of supermarkets—which resulted in several deaths—intended to bring down De la Rúa. Once again, Buenos Aires police connivance was asserted. Duhalde rejects all such assertions. Perhaps the event that most tarnished his image was the **Avellaneda Massacre** in June 2002. Sections of the provincial force were said to have worked closely with PJ regional caudillos answerable to Duhalde and engaged in illegal acts that included intimidating political opponents and murder.

History will most remember Duhalde for his appointment in 2002 that marked the conclusion of the revolving-door presidencies of the period between 20 December 2001 and 2 January 2002; there were five presidents in two weeks—technically six presidencies, given that **Ramón Puerta** held office twice, albeit only for minutes on the second occasion. He will also be remembered as the man who stabilized polity, society, and economy in 2002. And his reputation for involvement with the darker side of Argentine politics will not be forgotten. It is ironic that Duhalde, having been defeated by De la

Rúa in the presidential election of 1999, should have ended the instability triggered by the resignation of De la Rúa in 2001. *See also* CABEZAS AFFAIR.

DUHALDE, HILDA BEATRIZ "CHICHE" GONZÁLEZ DE (1946–). Politician, minister, and briefly first lady of Argentina when her husband **Eduardo Duhalde**, a former governor of the province of **Buenos Aires**, was appointed interim president by **Congress** in January 2002. He appointed her to head the Ministry of Social Welfare. Trained as a teacher, Chiche first came to national prominence when Eduardo ran on the **Partido Justicialista** (PJ) ticket with **Carlos Saúl Menem** in the **congressional** and **presidential elections of 1989**—he for the vice presidency, Menem for the presidency. Chiche featured prominently in the campaign. Although the two men soon fell out, Eduardo retained control of the PJ in the all-important province of Buenos Aires. Chiche was elected to the National Congress as a deputy for the province in the midterm **congressional elections of 1997** and reelected in the significant **congressional elections of 2003**, held simultaneously with the presidential election of that year, the first to be held following the collapse of the **Convertibility Plan**. Her stint at the Social Welfare Ministry, which played an important role in coping with the social fallout of the 2001–2002 **economic crisis**, added considerably to her national political profile. Chiche is best remembered, however, for the campaign for the **congressional elections of 2005**, when she went head-to-head with **Cristina Fernández de Kirchner**, wife of sitting president **Néstor Kirchner**. The contest highlighted the factionalism then splitting the PJ. Both **women** were fighting for a province of Buenos Aires seat in the National Senate at a time when Néstor was seeking to distance himself from Eduardo Duhalde. Eduardo had supported Néstor's bid for the presidency in 2003, anticipating that he would be the power behind the throne. Given Duhalde's control of the official PJ machine in the province, Chiche was expected to win easily. In the event, Cristina topped the poll. She gained 44 percent of the vote for the **Frente para la Victoria/Partido Justicialista** (FpV/PJ) to Chiche's 19 percent for the mainstream PJ. Although both women gained a Senate seat—Chiche took the "minority" seat—Cristina's victory was a fatal blow to the political ambitions of the Duhaldes and marked the transition of power in the province from them to the Kirchners. Both Duhaldes remain in the public eye and continue to harbor national political aspirations. *See also* MINISTRY OF SOCIAL DEVELOPMENT; PRESIDENTIAL ELECTION OF 2003.

ECONOMIC COMMISSION FOR LATIN AMERICA (ECLA). Now the Economic Commission for Latin America and the Caribbean (ECLAC). A United Nations Organization (UNO) regional commission—there were four others—founded in 1948. The name was changed to include the Caribbean in 1984, reflecting the fact that many colonial territories in the region had become independent by the latter date. The commission is widely known by the Spanish and Portuguese acronym CEPAL, which was not modified in 1984. The regional headquarters of the agency is in Santiago de Chile.

The commission is important for Argentina for several reasons. The second executive secretary of the agency was **Raúl Prebisch**, its longest serving executive secretary to date. He was in post from 1950 to 1963 and, arguably, contributed most to the organization and prominence of the commission and its impact well beyond the region. The commission and Prebisch played a critical role in the emergence of development economics as a distinct discipline. **Developmentalism** (or structuralism) challenged the prevailing orthodoxy in economics, formulating what was described as a "theory of development from the third world for the third world." This argued that there was no single or uniform pattern of economic growth. Structural heterogeneity among economies necessitated distinct policy solutions and programs of development—though always with a stress on state action.

Developmentalism influenced post–Second World War **economic policy**. The advice of Prebisch was sought by Argentine administrations, most notably the de facto regime headed by President General **Pedro Eugenio Aramburu** and democratically elected president **Raúl Alfonsín**. Featuring in the curriculum of several universities in the country, developmentalism shaped the thinking of a generation of scholars and public figures, some of the academics who pioneered the teaching of the new discipline going on to hold high ministerial office. Others, challenging the theoretical assumptions that underpinned state-led programs of industrialization pioneered by Prebisch and ECLA, also gained prominence. Structuralist paradigms and policies have been most associated with specific regimes—though, Prebisch might claim, applied in a distorted or partial manner—namely, the first presidency of **Juan Domingo Perón**, the **military** regimes of the **Revolución Argentina**, the short-lived chaotic presidency of **Isabel Perón**, and the presidencies of **Cristina Fernández de Kirchner**. Regimes reacting against ideas and analyses identified with CEPAL statism include those of the **Proceso de Reorganización Nacional**. *See also* AGRICULTURE; ALEMANN, ROBERTO TEODORO (1922–); ALSOGARAY, ÁLVARO (1913–2005); BER GELBARD, JOSÉ (1917–1977); CAFIERO, ANTONIO FRANCISCO (1922–2014); CONSEJO NACIONAL DE DESARROLLO (CONADE); CONSEJO NACIONAL DE POSGUERRA; COMMODITIES; DI TELLA, GUIDO JOSÉ MARIO (1931–2001); ECONOMIC CRISES; ECONOMY; FERRER, ALDO (1927–2016); FRONDIZI, ARTURO (1908–1995); GÓMEZ MORALES, ALFREDO (1908–1990); INDUSTRY; INSTITUTO ARGENTINO DE PROMOCIÓN DEL INTERCAMBIO (IAPI); KICILLOF, AXEL (1971–); KRIEGER VASENA, ADALBERT (1920–2000); MARTÍNEZ DE HOZ, JOSÉ ALFREDO (1925–2013); MINISTRY OF ECONOMY; MIRANDA, MIGUEL (1891–1953); ONGANÍA, JUAN CARLOS (1914–1995); PINEDO, FEDERICO (1895–1971); PINEDO PLAN; PRIVATIZATION; RODRIGAZO; RODRIGO, CELESTINO (1915–1987); SALIMEI, JORGE NÉSTOR (1926–1975); STATE-OWNED ENTERPRISES (SOEs).

ECONOMIC CRISES. Since **independence**, crises have been a pronounced feature of the economic history of the country. Until approximately the late 1940s, the causes of financial and commercial shocks were external; since then, they have been internal and structural. (Argentina was hardly impacted by the 2007–2008 global financial crisis because it had been largely excluded from international capital markets.) By the 1980s, the country had acquired the reputation of an economic basket case, and by the early 21st century as a serial defaulter.

In 1824, the London merchant bank Barings underwrote a loan for the province of **Buenos Aires**. The loan was costly: real rates of interest were high, and a substantial part of the loan was retained in London to service the first coupon payments. The South American independence bubble burst in 1825: outflows of investment from London dried up; in the ensuing commercial crisis, the price and volume of exports from the **River Plate** declined dramatically, as did foreign exchange earnings and the tax receipts of the government of Buenos Aires. By the end of the decade, the loan was in default, establishing a pattern that would be repeated several times over coming decades. Sporadic negotiations to settle were frustrated by domestic and regional wars, and the unwillingness of the administration of General **Juan Manuel de Rosas** to acknowledge a debt contracted by the government of **Bernardino Rivadavia**, which he regarded as anathema, despite an improvement in the commercial and fiscal position in the 1840s. Following the fall of Rosas, the government of the province agreed to repay the 1824 loan in 1857. Growth was subsequently brought to a halt with the financial panic in London in 1866 caused by the failure of the discount house Overend, Gurney & Company. By 1870, another cycle was well underway; direct private investment flowed in, and the federal and several provincial governments raised loans overseas. Again, the process was brought to a sudden end; on this occasion following the Vienna Stock Market crash on Black Friday, 9 May 1873. Arguably, this was the first global financial crisis, the so-called Long Depression, as panic spread rapidly from Austria-Hungary to Berlin, Paris, St. Petersburg, New York, and beyond. By the early 1880s, yet another boom was underway in Argentina, associated with the rapid expansion of the frontier, **immigration**, railway building, and a rising tide of investment and debt. This cycle ended with the **Baring Crisis** and the **Revolution of 1890**. The government in Buenos Aires announced that it would settle gold obligations in depreciating paper pesos; Barings was unable to offload Argentine paper in London; for a moment, even the Bank of England wobbled, requiring assistance from the Bank of France. The crisis was due to excess borrowing (or lending), and the long gestation period required by some development projects, though principally to waste and **corruption**. Cuts in government expenditure, debt rescheduling, and **currency** stabilization ultimately calmed the markets; commodity price rises and dramatic export growth underwrote recovery and growth, leading to the long pre–First World War boom when Argentina was the principal beneficiary of capital outflows from London, capturing also a substantial share of overseas investment channeled through Paris.

Three exogenous shocks in fairly rapid succession changed the global environment that had largely made the Argentine **economy**: the First World War, the Great Depression, and the Second World War. Yet it was the crisis of 1930 that brought a definitive end to the Belle Epoque, associated with post-1870s exponential growth in foreign trade, rapid frontier expansion, mass immigration, and a sequence of surges in capital inflows. War in the Balkans destabilized European money markets in the run-up to the First World War. New investment flows faltered, official lines of credit dried up, and with the declaration of war in Europe, loans were called in. Between 1913 and 1916, Argentina experienced its most severe crisis to date, and one that would prove to be more profound than that associated with the 1929 Wall Street Crash. Recovery from the turmoil of the opening years of the First World War was again associated with an improvement in commodity prices—after 1915, volume growth in such strategic commodity exports as **grain**, **wool**, and canned and frozen **meat**; Allied demand compensating for a loss of markets in central Europe; and the suspension of the gold standard. From 1916, official short-term borrowing at home compensated for the dearth of capital imports—in part—while tariff adjustments and government spending also fostered domestic demand. Instability in the 1920s was similarly associated with the post–First World War boom and international deflationary cycle, as well as the speculative bubble of the Roaring Twenties. Although international commodity prices had been softening since around 1928, and foreign capital inflows had faltered, it was events on Wall Street that occasioned another sharp economic downturn. Export demand collapsed and, with the contraction of overseas trade, government revenue, which was largely dependent on import duties, threatened a fiscal crisis. Unemployment grew, as did social unrest. As in 1890, economic crisis in 1930 triggered a political crisis—the **military coup of 1930**. Compared with the North Atlantic economies, however, Argentina suffered a less severe contraction, with recovery and renewed growth starting considerably earlier, around 1933–1935. This was largely due to imaginative economic intervention. The gold standard, which had been restored in 1927, was again "suspended," protecting the reserves, which had been hemorrhaging. Debt consolidation and government borrowing, coupled with innovative fiscal measures—income tax was introduced—facilitated borrowing. Intervention in exchange markets stabilized the currency and yielded a further stream of government revenue that was used to support commodity prices and rural-sector incomes. Measures were also taken to protect export markets, most significantly the **Roca–Runciman Pact** signed with **Great Britain**. Together, these and others measures underpinned a successful program of economic reactivation that may be described as semi-Keynesian. The declaration of war in Europe in 1939 represented the last major exogenous shock, and a sequence of events that initially reflected those of 1914 in the foreign trade and domestic sectors, though the external financial and investment positions were obviously quite different.

Since the 1940s, macroeconomic instability has been largely driven by internal processes—namely, distributional conflict (struggles among sectors, social groups, and ideologies over resource allocation) and profound disagreement about **economic policy** ("closed" or open economy; proindustry, or proagriculture). Domestic distributional and structural problems have manifested themselves in fiscal deficits, inflation, balance-of-payments crises, and foreign exchange scarcity. Such economic shocks frequently ended in **military** coups between 1955 and 1976. For example, the dramatic decline in rural output after 1952, as the Second Five-Year Plan was being launched by the government of **Juan Domingo Perón**, reduced exports, fueled inflation, and caused a sharp contraction in the economy, contributing to the **military coup of 1955**. The IMF, called in by the military government in 1957, advocated the standard liberal panaceas of the time: reduction of the fiscal deficit, devaluation and stabilization of the exchange rate, phasing out of protectionism and industrial subsidies, wage freeze, increased investment (from overseas), and debt reduction. These measures were applied for a time, resulting in a recession and reduction in real wages. Shortening economic cycles—a further sharp downturn between 1961 and 1963, with recovery in 1964—and the start of another recession in 1965 led to the **military coup of 1966**. Economics Minister **Adalbert Krieger Vasena**, appointed by the incoming military administration, launched a state-led productivity and investment drive that favored big businesses (many of which were foreign owned); low inflation, wage control, tight money supply, and government allocation of credit were related features of the program. Between 1966 and 1970, growth averaged 5 percent, but while unemployment remained low, real wages were compressed. After 1969, the government began to lose control of the economy and the streets: there was a series of large-scale protests against wage compression and failure of small businesses; the overvalued exchange rate led to a flood of imports; inflation rocketed; the currency was devalued—the decimal point was moved two places to the right, 100 old pesos became one *peso ley*. A sequence of internal military coups followed: in 1970, General **Juan Carlos Onganía** was replaced as president by General **Roberto Levingston**, and in 1971 Levingston by General **Alejandro Agustín Lanusse**. Unable to stabilize the economy, Lanusse called elections; 1973 became the year of the three presidents and two presidential elections.

When Perón returned to power in September 1973, the government embarked on an expansionary monetary program and salary hikes designed to promote domestic **industry**, in part financed by the short-lived 1973–1974 commodity boom. Real wages increased by almost 25 percent between 1972 and 1973. The plan was unsustainable and followed in quick succession by economic shock therapy, known as the **Rodrigazo**, in 1975 and the **military coup of 1976**. When **José Alfredo Martínez de Hoz**, the incoming minister of economy, took office in March, the monthly rate of inflation was 50 percent—that is, almost 1,000 for the previous 12, or a projected annualized rate of 16,000 percent. Regarding the contemporary crisis of near **hyperinflation** as a symptom of acute structural problems caused by the "closed" economy model associated with import-substituting industrialization, Martínez de Hoz determined on a strategy of stabilization and growth predicated on economic liberalization, an approach applauded at the time by the IMF. He proposed to eliminate price regulation, remove exchange controls, generally liberalize the foreign trade regime by phasing out restrictions on export and import licenses and quotas, reduce and eradicate subsidies and protection, and free labor and capital markets. Arguably internally coherent—possibly optimistic—the minister was frustrated in the implementation of this strategy by prointerventionist factions of the military, especially those who profited from running state–military corporations like **Fabricaciones Militares**; an unregulated inflow of hot money; overhasty deregulation, particularly in the financial sector; and the continuation of an initial wage freeze, on which he had insisted notwithstanding a supposed commitment to free collective bargaining. Wage earners suffered a substantial cut in purchasing power, which discouraged productive investment. Capital inflows resulted in an overvalued exchange rate. High interest rates encouraged speculation and borrowing, not least to finance consumer expenditure. As the economy began to overheat, various controls were reintroduced, running counter to the ethos of Martínez de Hoz's avowed strategy, and generated bottlenecks in the economy. The experiment culminated in the banking crisis of 1980, the largest financial collapse in Argentine history when several banks failed, and the end of the minister's career the following year. With the military in power, there was an echo of 1970–1971. As the economy unraveled, general succeeded general until de facto president General **Leopoldo Fortunato Galtieri** fixed on the **Falklands War** as a way to save the regime and salvage its reputation. He failed in both respects. When General **Reynaldo Bignone** announced that elections would be held in October 1983, the war in the South Atlantic had been lost and the economy was in free fall. The indicators of mismanagement were spectacular: the external debt had almost tripled under the military—with interest charges standing at approximately 17 percent of gross domestic product in 1983; industrial employment had contracted by about a third; the number of families living in poverty had increased by a factor of five.

With the election of President **Raúl Alfonsín** of the **Unión Cívica Radical** (UCR) and the return of democracy, expectations were high. The economy began to recover and grow. An adventurous heterodox program, the **Austral Plan**, introduced by Minister of Economy **Juan Vital Sourrouille** in 1985, promised stabilization through growth, instead of stabilization through contraction. Again, the plan was initially successful: the monthly rate of inflation fell to around 2 percent and the economy grew by 7 percent in 1986. Debt overhang from the military period, an equivocal response by the international financial community, but above all an uncooperative stance by the Peronist opposition in **Congress**, which encouraged antagonistic action by the **Confederación General del Trabajo**, coupled with an ill-managed deregulation of wages and prices that alienated the business sector, undermined the stimulus package. Distributional conflict destabilized economy and polity. In July 1989, the monthly rate of inflation peaked around 200 percent, or 5,000 percent for the year. When launched in June 1985, the new unit of currency, the austral, bought US$1.4; in December 1991, when it was retired, US$1 bought 10,000 australes. Hyperinflation and currency collapse set the scene for the election of President **Carlos Saúl Menem** and subsequently the launch of the **Convertibility Plan**, engineered by Minister of Economy **Domingo Cavallo**. The Menem–Cavallo project delivered **privatization**, economic opening, deregulation, and growth, with the new dual currency arrangement, whereby US dollars and Argentine pesos circulated freely in the domestic market at a one-to-one conversion, the hallmark of the system.

Convertibility delivered almost a decade of growth and macroeconomic stability. Though lacking sufficient flexibility, and initially regarded with some skepticism by the IMF, the plan was brought down by an unwillingness (or inability) to control government spending or curb borrowing, and significantly by corruption. With the economy contracting and the government seemingly incapable of action, in the face of mounting social protest, the plan was abandoned in January 2002, accompanied by the repudiation of the **foreign debt**, triggering the largest default in international financial history up to that point and the effective exclusion of the country from global capital markets for several years. Crisis and default were accompanied by a deep recession: after several years of slow or negative growth, GDP fell by a further 10 percentage points in 2002; at the end of that year, nearly 60 percent of the urban population was living in poverty.

Recovery from economic collapse in 2002 was due to efficacious economic management and progressive social expenditure and, above all, the beginning of a commodity boom driven by the **China** effect. Between 2003 and 2011, GDP growth averaged nearly 8 percent per annum; absolute poverty fell, but inequality rose. After 2011, there was greater volatility, partly due to the weakening commodity boom, though principally due to government policy—the fiscal deficit grew, inflation increased, and corruption became institutionalized. In 2014, when the government failed to pay interest on bonds issued in connection with the 2005 debt restructuring, the country was once again in default, a technical default that had long been anticipated by the markets. While the economy continued to contract or grew fitfully, there was no hard landing. A deep crisis, which many had predicted for 2015–2016, did not materialize: rising government spending kept the economy afloat, at the cost of postponing an overdue structural adjustment. By 2017, global financial and commercial links were reviving following promises by the **Mauricio Macri** administration elected at the end of 2015. *See also* AGRICULTURE; COMMODITIES; DEVELOPMENTALISM/DEVELOPMENTALIST; FOREIGN TRADE; STATE-OWNED ENTERPRISES (SOEs); TRANSPORTATION.

ECONOMIC POLICY. *See* AGRICULTURAL COLONIZATION; AGRICULTURE; ALEMANN, ROBERTO TEODORO (1922–); ALSOGARAY, ÁLVARO (1913–2005); AUSTRAL PLAN; BER GELBARD, JOSÉ (1917–1977); CAFIERO, ANTONIO FRANCISCO (1922–2014); CAVALLO, DOMINGO FELIPE (1946–); COMMODITIES; CONSEJO NACIONAL DE DESARROLLO (CONADE); CONVERTIBILITY PLAN; CORRUPTION; DEVELOPMENTALISM/DEVELOPMENTALIST; ECONOMIC CRISES; ECONOMY; FARM PROTESTS; FERRER, ALDO (1927–2016); FOREIGN DEBT/FOREIGN INVESTMENT; FOREIGN TRADE; FRIGERIO, ROGELIO (1970–); GÓMEZ MORALES, ALFRE-

DO (1908–1990); GRINSPUN, BERNARDO (1925–1996); INDUSTRY; KICILLOF, AXEL (1971–); KRIEGER VASENA, ADALBERT (1920–2000); MACHINEA, JOSÉ LUIS (1946–); MARTÍNEZ DE HOZ, JOSÉ ALFREDO (1925–2013); MIRANDA, MIGUEL (1891–1953); MONDELLI, EMILIO (1914–1993); PINEDO, FEDERICO (1895–1971); PINEDO PLAN; PREBISCH, RAÚL (1901–1986); PREBISCH PLAN; PRIVATIZATION; ROCA–RUNCIMAN PACT (1933); RODRIGAZO; RODRIGO, CELESTINO (1915–1987); SALIMEI, JORGE NÉSTOR (1926–1975); SIGAUT, LORENZO (1933–); SOURROUILLE, JUAN VITAL (1940–); STATE-OWNED ENTERPRISES (SOEs).

ECONOMY. Argentina is an upper middle-income economy that experienced extreme macroeconomic volatility during the last third of the 20th century and the early years of the 21st century. The system is capitalist, but there have been periods of considerable state intervention, sometimes on a scale approaching that of former command economies of Eastern Europe. Before 1930, economic vulnerability was a feature of economic openness—crises were generated by commodity price falls and sharp contractions in the flow of foreign investment. Since then, crises have been largely internally driven, a function of fiscal indiscipline, inflation, and balance-of-payments shocks.

Around 1900, Argentina was one of the 10 most important economies in the world. It accounted for more than one-half of South American gross domestic product (GDP) and a similar proportion of the continent's international trade. By the end of the century, the Argentine economy was about the same size as that of the Brazilian state of São Paulo. For around two decades before the First World War, annual average Argentine growth rates were the highest in the world, setting a record that was only exceeded by **China** 100 years later. In the years immediately prior to 1913, more portfolio and direct **foreign investment** flowed from the London capital market to Argentina than to any other country, including the **United States** and parts of the British Empire. After the 2002 economic crisis, when the economy contracted by about 30 percent, Argentina ranked around 82 in the world. In 2017, based on nominal GDP, Argentina ranked 21—other calculations would place the country lower, but nevertheless in a position broadly similar to that held for much of the latter decades of the 20th century. Critics date the beginnings of international divergence from the first presidencies of **Juan Domingo Perón** (1946–1955), though this may underestimate the national and global challenges facing the regime.

The principal economic growth periods, which are broadly coterminous with policy cycles, are trade-led growth based on commodity exports, mass **immigration**, and foreign investment, from approximately the 1840s to the 1920s; a period of accelerating industrial expansion, first characterized by "natural" industrial growth and then state-led import-substituting industrialization, from around 1930 to the 1960s; a phase of hesitant and abrupt opening to the international economy from the 1960s to the end of the century; a period of renewed state macroeconomic management and partial statization of the economy, from around 2004 to 2015; and a retreat from interventionism, coupled with continuing social intervention, since 2015. In the 1840s, Argentina was described as one of the most open economies in the world, notwithstanding a reliance on customs revenue to finance the state, a condition that prevailed for much of the rest of the century. By the early 20th century, policy was gradually shifting in favor of greater government support for activities that would internalize growth and reduce dependence on foreign markets as sources of demand and supply. The shocks of the two world wars and the international depression of the 1930s caused these policies to morph into more overtly nationalist programs: autarky, and possibly autarchy, was on the agenda. Proindustry programs were advanced by **Raúl Prebisch**, the academic economist and official who was primarily responsible for the **Pinedo Plan**. At the time, Prebisch advocated measured support for manufacturing to meet domestic demand and diversify exports. Later, these ideas would underpin programs of import substitution and neo-Keynesian demand stimulation that were subject to capture by advocates of state control and economic nationalism. Such ideas were popularized and predominated in national business and policy-making circles from the 1940s to the 1970s, when they were challenged by the neoliberal Washington Consensus as the import-substituting model became exhausted intellectually and economic performance faltered. **Military** regimes of the **Proceso de Reorganización Nacional** implemented the crudest from of neoliberalism. Although the Debt Crisis of the 1980s interrupted the neoliberal experiment, by the 1990s Washington Consensus ideas had gained renewed vigor and shaped **economic policy** until the collapse of 2001–2002, a shock that revitalized statism. Emphasis on internalizing growth was a feature of the *kirchnerato*, with a focus on reindustrialization and deprivatization—avowedly echoing strategies of the *peronato* essayed in the late 1940s and early 1950s. Yet there was a difference with the phase of import-substituting industrialization. Then, the state assumed a large role in the manufacturing sector; under the Kirchners, utilities were taken back under state control, but manufacturing and related productive activities were left to business—usually entrepreneurs closely associated with the regime.

Agriculture was the main source of economic activity until the 1920s. Around the 1840s, traditional pastoral by-products like hides, dried salted **meat**, and tallow were challenged by **wool**, a new lucrative, dynamic item as imported breeds of **sheep** displaced criollo **cattle** in settled parts of the **pampas**. By the end of the century, while sheep, wool, and traditional commodities continued to be produced—the former predominating in **Patagonia** and the latter in **Mesopotamia** and **Chaco**—**grains** and improved breeds of cattle dominated the pampas. By the 1920s, quality meat was the "new" highly profitable commodity: the fatstock sector focused increasingly on the production of chilled beef for the export market as lower-grade cattle supplied domestic demand. Oilseed plantings also increased, destined for the home and overseas markets, as fruit production expanded for the domestic market—hard and stone fruit in northern Patagonia and citrus in the northeast. Notwithstanding the dominance of agriculture, by the 1910s **industry** was significant, accounting for about 16 percent of GDP, and grew in relative importance thereafter.

In the 1940s, industry provided a shade over 24 percent of GDP, and by the 1960s over 28 percent of GDP—one of the highest participation rates of the 20th century. During this period, there were marked changes in the composition of industrial output. Until the 1940s, basic wage goods like foodstuffs, beverages, clothing, and tobacco were the main items—supplying around 60 percent of total industrial output, though subsectors like chemicals, iron and steel, and oil were of growing importance. By 1975, on the eve of the **military coup of 1976**, there had been a major shift in the composition of manufacturing. Traditional items like food, beverages, textiles, and tobacco represented less that 30 percent of output, while petrochemicals accounted for 19 percent; household goods, motor vehicles, equipment and machinery almost 33 percent; and iron and steel production not quite 7 percent. Between the 1940s and the mid-1970s, there had been significant developments in the scale of production: firms became larger and more capital intensive in most sectors—nondurables, consumer durables, and capital goods—with transnational corporations dominating modern and dynamic branches of manufacturing, the latter trait provoking much anguish among nationalists, who complained of the "transnationalization" of "industria argentina." From the mid-1930s to the late 1970s, manufacturing was the sector driving economic expansion. For some, such structural changes and growth represented the achievements of import-substituting industrialization. By the early 1970s, agriculture provided little more than 11 percent of GDP.

Manufacturing accounted for 30 percent of GDP at the end of the 1980s, declining thereafter to about 17 percent by the end of the century. The participation of agriculture declined from approximately 10 percent to 5 percent during the same period. Services grew from a shade under 49 percent to a little over 62 percent. There was a huge recapitalization of agriculture during the 1990s—**maize**, sunflower, and soya output increased massively, with more modest growth for wheat, due to new production techniques and mechanization. There was substantial investment in industry—motor vehicles and parts, plus tires, registering the highest rates of growth, with household appliances, agrochemicals, and iron and steel also expanding significantly. Ranching was the only activity not to grow as prime pampean land was devoted to grains and oilseed, while cattle and sheep were displaced to marginal areas in the northeast and northwest; the decline in wool production was especially dramatic.

A marked feature of the 1960s and 1970s was growth in the weight of the tertiary sector, and informality. The growing importance of such services as finance, entertainment, **education**, and the hospitality subsector partly represented the maturity of the economy; the growth of informality and the black economy did not, pointing to a deepening structural crisis. An increasing proportion of the workforce was engaged in precarious employment, unregulated work, and activities not covered by social protection. The most obvious manifestations were a surge in street trading; backyard production based on recycling plastic, wood, and metals for household use; personal services; and rubbish sifting—though the *cartoneros* would not be so much in evidence until the end of the century. Informality increased in the late 1990s as unemployment rose and experienced exponential growth following economic collapse in 2001–2002.

From the late 1960s to the early 1990s, volatility was an important characteristic. The 1980s was a period of persistent and profound deterioration unrivaled in Argentina's economic history; notwithstanding short bursts of growth, the decade registered some of the greatest annual declines in GDP and real incomes, especially during the final years of the 1976–1983 military government and the presidency of **Raúl Alfonsín** (1983–1989). Despite recurrent crises, notably that of 2001–2002, growth was less volatile between the early 1990s and 2010, permitting some convergence with the developed world. Between 2011 and 2015, growth was virtually zero as confidence was undermined by a widening fiscal deficit (despite high rates of taxation) and inflation. Modest recovery began in late 2016 and is forecast to continue. Market-friendly reforms introduced at the beginning of the administration of President **Mauricio Macri** (2015–) have helped stability return to the financial sector—savings and investment picked up, levels of corporate debt are relatively low, consumer confidence returned—partly due to declining levels of unemployment and falling rates of inflation.

Before the 1930s, changes in the relative weight of industry in the economy, and changes in the structure of the sector, were associated with modest, selective tariff protection, some measures prompting complaints from agricultural and pastoral interests, who feared retaliations from overseas markets where Argentine exports were consumed, and bodies representing organized labor, who argued that tariffs raised the cost of basic goods for workers. Protectionism and promanufacturing strategies became the norm thereafter. From the 1940s to the 1960s, industry was favored by access to easy credit, subsidies, and policies designed to promote income growth, strategies largely funded by taxes on the rural sector—and inflation. Industrialization and intervention were the principal economic ideas of this period, yet manufacturing proved incapable of servicing its own import requirements. And although there was a considerable restructuring of the economy, aggregate growth from the 1950s to the 1980s was sluggish. Manufacturing and agriculture competed for resources: increases in investment in industry were accompanied by a decline in investment in agriculture, and vice versa, while labor drained from the countryside to the cities, finding employment in manufacturing and informal activities. The appointment of **José Martínez de Hoz** as minister of economy by the 1976 military government marked the end of the import-substituting model, at least until the economic reactivation plans of President **Néstor Kirchner** (2003–2007), of the post-1975 years. Both military and civilian administrations now stressed the importance of increasing productivity and international competitiveness—technical modernization that would facilitate export-led recovery and growth. The only debate was whether this would be accomplished by an abrupt or measured opening of the economy, and by regional economic integration or global reinsertion. Since then, except for the 2005–2015 decade, policy has been generally market friendly, cautiously so under Alfonsín and Macri, more avowedly so during the **Convertibility Plan** presidencies of **Carlos Saúl Menem** (1989–1999), though tempered by **corruption**.

Until the 1960s, Argentines enjoyed living standards on a par with Western European countries, the United States, and such places as Australia, Canada, and New Zealand. Traditionally, the country had a more equal distribution of incomes than other Latin America countries and a larger middle class. Since the 1970s, levels of inequality have approximated those of Latin America, though levels of poverty and inequality declined around 2010. Corruption has been a significant feature of the Argentine economy in recent years and was particularly pronounced for much of the 1990s, a period of growth and stability, and between approximately 2007 and 2015, a period of growth and then stagnation and contraction when corruption constrained productive economic activity. *See also* AUSTRAL PLAN; CONSEJO NACIONAL DE DESARROLLO (CONADE); DEVELOPMENTALISM/DEVELOPMENTALIST; ECONOMIC CRISES; MERCOSUR; PRIVATIZATION; STATE-OWNED ENTERPRISES (SOEs).

EDUCATION. Literacy rates (the proportion of the population over the age of 15 who can read and write) stood at 98 percent in 2017, one percentage point less than the **United States**; the figure was 94 percent in 1980, five points below the United States.

Responsibility for education is divided between the federal government and the provinces. Basic guidelines about standards, evaluating attainment, curriculum objectives, and so forth are established by the national **Ministry of Education**; the provinces are responsible for curriculum content and implementing federal policies. The modern educational system dates from the mid-19th century. The first attempt to create a national system of basic education began during the presidency of **Justo José de Urquiza**, though major advances did not occur until the administration of President **Domingo Faustino Sarmiento**. Sarmiento was alarmed by the 22 percent literacy rates recorded by the 1869 National Census. By the time of the second census in 1895, literacy rates had risen to 46 percent, and to 65 percent by the third taken in 1914. A recodification of 1884 made basic education compulsory, free, and secular.

During the 20th century, the expansion of educational facilities was driven by population growth, especially demands from immigrants, and the emergent urban working and middle classes for better provision, and by educational reformers. Intellectual and popular pressures led to curriculum developments such as the provision of teaching in the exact and social sciences and in technical subjects—hitherto, the focus had been on traditional classical and humanistic fields, with medicine and law the elite disciplines in the tertiary sector. There was also debate about the role of the **Catholic Church**. The 1930s saw the church seek to enhance its influence on education, notwithstanding the separation of church and state ordained by the **Constitution of 1853** and its stress on secularism. Following the **military coup of 1943**, there was an emphasis on nationalism and Catholicism and a distinctly antiliberal and antisecular tone in the debate about education and education policy. In 1947, compulsory religious education was reinstated in the school curriculum, with the support of President **Juan Domingo Perón**, though opposed by significant sections of the ruling party. However, when Perón and the church fell out in 1954, the law requiring compulsory religious education was rescinded. The clash with the church over education was a factor in the **military coup of 1955**. For much of the period from the mid-1950s to the 1970s, especially during periods of **military** rule, the church was said to have exercised a veto over education policy, particularly regarding the role of **religion** in the private sector. There was a close relationship between sections of the military and the hierarchy during the de facto presidencies of Generals **Juan Carlos Onganía** and **Jorge Rafael Videla**. The pendulum swung back toward the secular with the return of democracy in 1983; there was renewed stress on the classic late-19th-century proposition that education should be compulsory, free, and laic. Although these principles continue to shape public education policy, the expansion of private provision means that fee-paying education at all levels has grown considerably in recent years.

Basic (elementary) schooling, usually preceded by a preschool year, starts at the age of six (grade 1) and continues to the age of 10 or 11 (grades 6 and 7), depending on province, at which point secondary education begins. By law, all pupils are now required to complete 13 years of schooling, including the preschool year. According to a recent official survey, there are around

20,000 preschool establishments in the country enrolling children between the ages of three and five, 23,000 primary schools, and 12,000 secondary schools. Around 7 percent of elementary establishments and 30 percent of secondary schools are private or semiprivate, most of which receive some form of state funding. There are around 11,000,000 pupils and 700,000 teachers in the education system; 73 percent of the pupils and 75 percent of teachers are in the state sector. These figures vary significantly across the country. In the city of **Buenos Aires**, around 40 percent of pupils attend private schools, in the provinces of Buenos Aires and **Córdoba** just over 30 percent; in **Chubut**, 13 percent; and in **Santa Cruz** 14 percent. Private education, which has always existed alongside the state sector, grew during the latter part of the 1950s and in the 1960s. Private provision continued to grow steadily thereafter. The growth in private education was particularly pronounced in the 1990s following the decentralization of state elementary and secondary education under President **Carlos Saúl Menem**, when school administration and funding was devolved to the provinces and additional state funding made available to the private sector. According to recent estimates, around a quarter of all primary and secondary children are privately educated, about two-thirds of whom attend Catholic schools.

There is continuing debate about the quality of education. While 98 percent of the age cohort is enrolled in elementary education, the figure for secondary schooling is 72 percent. Some 70 percent of pupils in the state sector do not complete secondary education within the prescribed number of years, a figure that includes a dropout rate of almost 16 percent. Barely a half of all pupils leave secondary school with a formal qualification. These figures are among the worst in the region.

With the **university reform** of 1918, higher education became formally autonomous; the system grew, and universities became accessible to a broader social spectrum. Before 1918, there were only five universities in the country. These were the **University of Córdoba**, which dated from the colonial period; the **University of Buenos Aires**, established by **Bernardino Rivadavia** in 1821; the **Universidad de Tucumán**, officially set up in 1913 but dating from an institution that began admitting students in 1875; the **Universidad Nacional de La Plata**, which was organized shortly after the foundation of **La Plata** as the new capital of the province of Buenos Aires; and the **Universidad de Santa Fe**, founded by the then governor of the province of **Santa Fe**, José de Gálvez, in 1889. The Universidad Popular de la Boca, founded in 1917 by Tomás le Bretón, functioned largely as a center of technical education, training students in such fields as mechanical engineering, electronics, and avionics. In the decades immediately following the reform of 1918, several new public universities were founded, the **Universi-**

dad del Litoral in 1919 (which displaced the Universidad de Santa Fe), the Universidad Nacional de Cuyo in 1939, the Universidad del Sur in the city of Bahía Blanca in 1946, and the Universidad del Nordeste in 1956. The next wave of university expansion took place in the 1950s and featured mainly private—often confessional—establishments. Degree-awarding private universities were first authorized in 1955, early in the de facto presidency of General Pedro Eugenio Aramburu, a measure that reflected the close relationship between some members of the Revolución Libertadora and the Catholic Church—it was correctly assumed that the church would be among the first organizations to set up private universities. Among the first centers to be established was the Universidad Católica de Buenos Aires, set up in 1958 (later renamed the Pontificia Universidad Católica Argentina—UCA), and the Universidad Católica de Córdoba, founded a year later. The church would have a similarly influential role on educational policy following the military coup of 1966, which ushered in the Revolución Argentina, notably during the administration headed by General Onganía. Yet not all new private foundations around this time were confessional: for example, the Universidad de Morón, founded in 1960, and the Universidad Belgrano, in 1964, both located in greater Buenos Aires, were not. And public universities continued to be created; for example, the Universidad Nacional de Mar del Plata opened in 1962.

The third quarter of the 20th century was a particularly troubled time for the universities—they were hardly untouched by the situation in the country beyond the campus as the republic drifted into political and economic chaos. Despite vociferous opposition by students in 1948 and 1954, Perón ordered intervention in the universities: non-Peronist academics, or faculty considered unsympathetic to the government, were purged, and university administrations thoroughly Peronized. Following the 1955 coup, the universities were de-Peronized and a degree of autonomy reinstated. Many on the campuses who had opposed the coup that ousted Perón also protested proposals to permit the foundation of private universities. By the mid-1960s, the universities were in financial crisis: unrestricted admissions had led to a mushrooming of the student body and severe overcrowding; faculties were underequipped and staff underpaid, ill trained, and often incompetent. Categorizing the universities as hotbeds of Communist subversion, de facto president General Juan Carlos Onganía ordered the police and military onto the campuses immediately following the 1966 coup, an intervention that became notorious as the "night of the long canes," a reference to the truncheons used by the police to clear lecture halls. Several deaths and many injuries resulted. Senior academics fled abroad.

Yet unrest continued. Students were active in many demonstrations and protests of the period, such as uprisings in the cities of Corrientes and Tucumán, and the Cordobazo. Student participation in the worker–student uprising against the military government was most pronounced in the city of Córdoba—many students worked part time in the motor vehicle factories of the city to fund studies. The violent response of the government to such protests would lead some students to join guerrilla groups and radical organization like the **Ejército Revolucionario del Pueblo** (ERP) and the **Montoneros**, which were committed to armed struggle. Most student groups welcomed the return of Perón in 1973. In response to support from students, university entry requirements were further relaxed, course attendance requirements eased, and student representatives placed on academic appointment and curriculum development committees. There was also a major expansion in the number of national universities around this time. New campuses were set up in virtually every provincial capital, save the provinces of **Patagonia**. For example, the Universidad Nacional of La Rioja was founded in 1972, as was the Universidad Nacional de Salta. The following year, national universities were opened in **Entre Ríos, Misiones, La Pampa, San Juan, San Luis**, and **Santiago del Estero**. New public universities also appeared in some of the larger provincial cities, for example, the Universidad Nacional de Río Cuarto (province of Córdoba), founded in 1971; the Universidad Nacional de Lomas de Zamora (province of Buenos Aires), in 1972; and the Universidad Nacional del Centro (province of Buenos Aires), in 1974.

The **military coup of 1976** and the **Proceso de Reorganización Nacional** saw violence return to campuses and another exodus of students and faculty, many who could do so fleeing abroad. Intellectual debate was stifled, and research, particularly in the social sciences and "dangerous" subjects like history, plummeted. Limited new initiatives in teaching were largely confined to private universities and research to externally funded centers like the **Centro de Estudios del Estado y Sociedad** (CEDES). New academic institutions created around this time tended to be business schools like the **Centro de Estudios Macroeconómicos de Argentina** (CEMA/UCEMA).

On the campuses, as in other levels of education, the Alfonsín administration sought to reestablish liberal, secular, and democratic values and promote free academic discussion and access. Considerable autonomy was again granted to the universities and efforts made to increased funding and modernize teaching and research, objectives that were in part assisted by the return of faculty who had fled abroad and students who had completed higher degrees in the United States and Europe and elsewhere in Latin America. A significant change made in 1983 was the introduction of entrance examinations, designed to give greater credibility to courses taught at public institutions. Over the next three years, the number of students enrolled at state institutions nearly doubled. Yet Alfonsín's objectives were only partly realized. Less than 10 percent of the student body is composed of those from the poorest strata of society. Funding was a continuing problem, exacerbated by the unraveling of the **Austral Plan** and recurrent **economic crises**. Academic salaries in the public universities remained low, and facilities that had been underfunded for years required years to be refurbished. Most academics survived by taking multiple jobs or combining teaching at university with other regular, more lucrative employment. Only a handful of private universities aspired to offer salaries comparable with overseas institutions that enabled faculty to work full time as researchers and teachers.

The 1990s witnessed another massive expansion in tertiary education provision, in both the state and private sectors. Many of the new state universities were located in the *conurbano*, parts of Greater Buenos Aires lying adjacent to the city in the province. The Universidad Nacional de Lanús, the Universidad Nacional de General San Martín, the Universidad Nacional de General Sarmiento, and the Universidad Nacional de Tres de Febrero were founded or opened between 1992 and 1995; such institutions were usually located in the *partido* (county) of the province in which they were founded. There were similar foundations elsewhere in the country; for example, the Universidad Nacional de la Patagonia Austral inaugurated several campuses in the province of **Santa Cruz** around 1995. Focusing mainly on undergraduate teaching, many of these new national universities were intended to remain small establishments, admitting no more than 10,000 students, though some were larger. Private universities also appeared around this time, for example, the **Universidad Torcuato Di Tella** (UTDT) in 1991 and the Universidad Austral in 1992. The most recent round of university expansion took place during the presidencies of **Néstor Kirchner** and **Cristina Fernández de Kirchner**. In addition to new private foundations, this is when national universities were created in provincial capitals still lacking centers of tertiary education: the Universidad Nacional de Río Negro was inaugurated in 2007 and the Universidad Nacional de Tierra del Fuego in 2010.

While some recently established universities have gained a positive reputation—the Universidad de Quilmes, which focuses on distance learning, is ranked 13th nationally and 125th in Latin America—most have not. Cynics describe many of the most recent foundations as *fábricas de títulos* (degree factories) or *fábricas de peronistas* (manufactories of Peronists). Funding remains an acute problem for public universities, and many (state and private) offer low-quality education. According to the 2017 QS World University Ranking, only the UBA features in the top 100, at 75th, and only 27 Argentine universities feature in the top 200. In the 2017 QS review of business schools, the highest placed Argentine institution was the Business School of the Universidad Austral, coming in at joint 121–130.

There are around 100 recognized centers of higher education in the country, with virtually an equal number of public and private institutions; public universities account for by far the greater proportion of students. Currently, there are around 1,500,000 students in higher education, about half the demographic cohort. The basic undergraduate degree, the *profesorado*, requires students to complete a specified number of units and usually takes three or four years. The more prestigious *licenciatura*, which is regarded as the equivalent of a bachelor degree, takes a year or so longer and requires the submission of a dissertation in addition to the course units accumulated for the *profesorado*. It is unusual for students to complete a *licenciatura* in less than five years. Indeed, given that the vast majority of students study part time, it can take considerably longer to complete the requirements for either title.

Argentina is a literary culture: the print **media** is healthy, publishing thrives, literacy levels are high. Yet at all levels, debate continues about education quality, dropout rates, and the labor-market relevance of higher education programs. There has been no improvement in school pupil attainment levels since 2000; many state schools only function for four days a week. This is not necessarily due to a lack of funding: the 2006 education law mandated school spending at 6 percent of gross domestic product. The problem seems to be allocation and efficiency; expenditure levels appear to have little impact on outcomes. The maturing crisis in public education partly explains the growth of the private sector at all levels, given that until the mid-20th century the reputation of the state system was the highest in Latin America and Argentine state schools and public universities were held in great esteem. *See also* CORRUPTION; ECONOMY; MINISTRY OF EDUCATION; TRADE UNIONS; UNIVERSITIES.

EJÉRCITO REVOLUCIONARIO DEL PUEBLO (ERP). Founded as the armed wing of the Partido Revolucionario de los Trabajadores (PRT) but never officially acknowledged as such, it became the country's largest non-Peronist Marxist guerrilla group. The ERP was established under the leadership of **Mario Roberto Santucho** in 1969 and began a campaign against the de facto **Revolución Argentina** regime. It started by employing targeted urban guerrilla warfare methods, such as kidnapping and assassinating government officials and foreign company executives. The most notorious instance occurred in 1972 and involved Fiat executive Oberdan Sallustro. He was abducted by an ERP cell on 21 March, held in a so-called *cárcel del pueblo* (people's prison) in the Villa Lugano district of **Buenos Aires**, and murdered by some of his jailers on 10 April when the federal police discovered the hideout. The group continued its campaign of violence after Argentina returned to civilian rule in 1973, with the avowed aim of promoting a communist revolution in pursuit of "proletarian rule." It attacked **military** facilities, police stations, and convoys and, using the Cuban revolutionary *foco* as a model, then shifted more toward a rural strategy designed to secure a large area of territory as a base for military operations against the state. As a rural base, the ERP chose **Tucumán** in the impoverished northwest of the country, which it believed to be fertile ground for revolutionary activity. Soon the ERP was in control of one-third of the province and organized a base of approximately 2,500 sympathizers.

In February 1975, President **Isabel Perón** signed a decree ordering the military operations deemed necessary to "neutralize or annihilate" subversive actives in Tucumán. Acdel Vilas, a general with Peronist and nationalist sympathies, was put in charge of Operativo Independencia, and over 5,000 troops were deployed in the province. The pattern of the war was mostly dictated by the nature of the terrain—mountains, rivers, and extensive jungle, which denied both sides easy movement; the air force too had a leading role. In May 1975, the army had a major breakthrough. ERP figure Amilcar Santucho was captured trying to cross into **Paraguay** and, to save himself, provided information about the organization to the Secretaría de Inteligencia (SIDE). This enabled the security services to infiltrate the group and finish it off. While fighting in the jungle and the mountains, the army also concentrated on ERP support networks in the towns. By July, commandos were mounting search-and-destroy operations; the base camp of Mario Santucho was found the following month, and the group's urban headquarters in **San Miguel de Tucumán** were raided in September 1975. Although the ERP was decimated, pockets of guerrillas continued to operate in the forested mountains of the province for many months. Being encircled in Tucumán did not prevent the group from operating elsewhere; it still remained strong in the national capital. On 23 December 1975, Mario Santucho launched a failed Christmas offensive. ERP units mounted a large-scale assault against the army supply base in the suburb of Monte Chingolo to the south of Buenos Aires. The attackers were defeated and driven off. They then attempted to seize bridges across the river Riachuelo giving accesses to the neighborhoods of **La Boca** and **Avellaneda**.

The armed forces were legally enabled to carry out a nationalwide **War to Annihilate Subversion** by decrees issued by civilian acting president **Ítalo Luder** in October 1975, authorization that the military continued to invoke following the **military coup of 1976**. The ERP leadership lost 12 members in a gun battle in downtown Buenos Aires on 29 March 1976, only five days after the coup, and 300 militants supporting ERP operations in the province of **Córdoba** were killed about a fortnight later. By mid-1976, the army had destroyed the group's "Elite Squad," and as the ERP was negotiating a merger with the **Montoneros**, Mario Santucho was killed in July of that year. The organization continued to exist formally for a while, but the truth is that by late 1977 it no longer posed a serious threat and had gone underground. The ERP would claim to have lost 5,000 members, combatants killed in action and **Desaparecidos** who were detained and killed by the military. *See also* DISPOSICIÓN FINAL; VIDELA, JORGE RAFAEL (1925–2013).

EL CHOCÓN. The third most important dam in the country, it is one of five built on the Limay River in the province of **Neuquén**. It is utilized for regulating the flow of the Limay, irrigation, and the generation of hydroelectricity.

The power station of El Chocón is the largest hydroelectric power plant in **Patagonia**, with a capacity of 1,260 megawatts (1,690,000 horsepower). It was built by the **state-owned enterprise** Hidronor, started operating in 1973, attained full capacity in 1978, and underwent **privatization** in 1993, with an exploitation concession granted to Hidroeléctrica El Chocón. *See also* ECONOMY.

EL GAUCHITO GIL. Sometimes known as El Gaucho Antonio Gil or El Gauchito Antonio Gil, a romanticized, semimythical Robin Hood–type figure and folk-religion-occult-catholic "saint." According to legend, Gil was a farm laborer in rural **Corrientes** around the mid-19th century and a devotee of San Muerte (Saint Death), a figure probably derived from a mix of beliefs drawn from indigenous practices and African slave religions as well as Roman Catholicism. A hero of regional conflicts and the **War of the Triple Alliance**, Gil was conscripted by **Federalists** to fight in the civil wars of the period. He deserted, became an outlaw, and developed a reputation as a protector of the poor and oppressed, defending them against the exactions of rapacious authorities. He was also credited with healing powers and immunity from bullets. Captured, Gil's throat was cut and his body placed on public display. Before execution, he foretold several events, including the impending death of the child of his executioner—the child would only be saved if the father venerated Gil.

Shrines to Gil are found in rural areas all over the country but are particularly prominent in his native **Mesopotamia** and the **Chaco**. Festooned with red ribbons or flags—the color of Corrientes autonomists and the **caudillo Juan Manuel de Rosas**—the shrines contain votive offerings of food, alcohol, and cigarettes, as well as statuettes of the Gaucho and other "saints," along with crucifixes and rosaries. Adherents attribute to Gil the power to bring good fortune and health, cure illnesses, and confer courage and a fruitful love life. His image is also used to venerate the **gaucho** tradition and rural virtues of self-reliance and independence. *See also CHINA; MARTÍN FIERRO.*

ELECTIONS. *See* CONGRESSIONAL ELECTIONS; PRESIDENTIAL ELECTIONS.

ELECTORAL SYSTEM. *See LISTA SÁBANA.*

ELOY MARTÍNEZ, TOMÁS (1934–2010). Writer and journalist regarded as one of the most distinguished and prolific Argentine novelists of his generation. He was a pioneer of the "new" journalism of the 1970s, a style that was more direct, investigative, and analytical than earlier forms, which tended toward the rhetorical and formulaic. Noted contributor to the newspaper *La Opinión*, edited by **Jacobo Timerman**, Eloy Martínez later became an international columnist and critic. With the Colombian author Gabriel García Márquez, he established the Foundation for New Journalism in Bogotá in 1995, which has had a large impact across the continent.

Born in the city of **San Miguel de Tucumán**, Eloy Martínez studied at the university there and at the Sorbonne in Paris. He started his career in journalism as an arts and film critic writing for *La Nación* in the 1960s. He also worked on *Primera Plana*, a weekly developed by Timerman. Having already received death threats from the **Triple A** (Alianza Anticomunista Argentina) as the result of his writing during the chaotic presidency of **Isabel Perón**, he fled into exile following the **military coup of 1976**, settling first in **Venezuela**. He also lived in Mexico and the **United States**. He taught at the University of Maryland in the mid-1980s and was appointed professor of Spanish literature at Rutgers University in 1995, where he headed the Center for Latin American Studies. By the 1990s, pieces he wrote for *La Nación* and the *New York Times* were widely reprinted in the English- and Spanish-language international press. He returned to live permanently in Argentina in 2006.

Many of his novels were imagined accounts based on real events, for example, *La Pasión Según Trelew* (The Passion of Trelew), an account of the **Trelew Massacre**. Similar later works include *El vuelo de la reina* (The Flight of the Queen) and *El cantor de tango* (The Tango Singer), both set around the time of economic and political meltdown that marked the collapse of the presidency of **Fernando de la Rúa** in 2001. He is probably best known abroad for his surrealist (semi-fact-based) novels about Perón and Peronism, notably *La novela de Perón* (The Perón Novel)—he met **Juan Domingo Perón** many times when the latter was living in Madrid—and *Santa Evita* (Saint Evita), about the cult that developed around Perón's second wife. Often portrayed as a supporter of Perón, Eloy Martínez was highly critical of the regime of President **Néstor Kirchner**, which sought to capitalize on the legacy of Perón and Evita by frequent use of their images and rhetoric. *See also* CONVERTIBILITY PLAN; ECONOMIC CRISES; KIRCHNER, CRISTINA ELISABET FERNÁNDEZ DE (1953–); PERÓN, EVA (1919–1952).

ENCOTEL. The formal title of the state postal and telecommunications monopoly adopted in 1972, derived from Empresa Nacional de Correos y Telégrafos. The current shorthand is Correo Argentino, the marketing name of Correo Oficial de la República Argentina Sociedad Anónima (CORASA). The modern postal and telecommunications entity dates from the 1850s, when it was successively a dependency of the Finance Ministry (now **Ministry of Economy**) and **Ministry of Interior**. The national telegraph started in the 1870s, telephone services a decade or so later. Like the domestic mail, the internal telegraph was state owned, though some railway companies ran their own systems in connection with train operations. The early telephone companies were privately run, initially financed from Europe; by 1929, most private operators had been acquired by **United States** conglomerate International Telephone and Telegraph Corporation (IT&T). IT&T Argentina was nationalized in 1948, which partly explains organizational and administrative changes during the decade. In the 1940s, the autonomous Directorate of Post and Telecommunications was created, subsequently becoming the Secretariat of Post and Telecommunications and later still the State Secretariat of Communications. For most of the 20th century, the service was headquartered in the splendid neoclassical Palacio de Correos y Telecomunicaciones, generally known as the Correo Central, inaugurated by President **Marcelo T. de Alvear** in 1928. In 1997, the building was declared a national monument, becoming in 2010 the Cultural Center of the Bicentenary of **Independence**. During the second administration of President **Cristina Fernández de Kirchner**, the center was redesignated first as the Centro Cultural **Néstor Kirchner** and then as the Centro Cultural Kirchner.

The original entity has experienced several institutional transformations, paralleling that of other **state-owned enterprises**. Partial **privatization** occurred under the **military** regimes of the **Proceso de Reorganización Nacional** following the neoliberal agenda advanced by Minister of Economy **José Alfredo Martínez de Hoz**. The sale of the business took place under President **Carlos Saúl Menem**. Preparatory to sale, the enterprise was restructured as Empresa Nacional de Correo y Telégrafos S.A. (ENCOTESA) in 1992; full privatization came in 1997, when operations were transferred to the Macri Group on 30-year lease. The group coined the operating title Correo Argentino. The terms of the lease were murky and triggered rumors of **corruption**. At the time, the Macri Group was headed by the father of future president **Mauricio Macri**. Within weeks of assuming office in 2003, President Néstor Kirchner took Correo Argentino back into state ownership. This is the current situation, an arrangement that is unlikely to be changed by President Macri. *See also* CAVALLO, DOMINGO FELIPE (1946–).

ENTRE RÍOS (PROVINCE). Located on the east bank of the **Paraná River**, Entre Ríos is the second largest province in **Mesopotamia** after **Corrientes**, which borders it to the north, yet it is the most populous. The river also marks the boundary with **Santa Fe** to the west and **Buenos Aires** to the south. **Uruguay** lies to the east, on the opposite bank of the river of the same name.

Spanish settlers began to arrive in the late 16th century, entering from Buenos Aires and Santa Fe, but everywhere encountering resistance by the Guaraní, who had a fierce reputation, slowing European occupation. The threat lasted until Jesuit priests managed to encourage Indians to adopt a sedentary life in missions—the famous *reducciones* to the north. Military expeditions were launched in the mid-18th century against tribes in the north, and across the Uruguay, that resisted proselytization, action that continued after the expulsion of the Jesuits in 1767. Several prominent families trace their origins back to **cattle** estates carved out of conquered territory and seized from the Jesuits around this time. At **independence**, most of the provincial elite supported the **May Revolution of 1810** and was initially anxious to preserve the integrity of the former **Viceroyalty of the River Plate** (which included present-day **Bolivia, Paraguay**, and Uruguay) for the successor republic. This sentiment changed as Uruguay sought separation. Opposition to Buenos Aires's vision for the future of the country grew, and an autonomous—possibly an independent—existence for Entre Ríos was contemplated, possibly in association with Uruguay or Santa Fe. The province did not send representatives to the **Congress of Tucumán**, which formally declared independence in 1816. Representatives had been sent a year earlier to the Congress of the East, a distinct project of national organization from that being considered at Tucumán—the League of Free Peoples—and which included deputies from **Misiones, Córdoba**, Corrientes, Santa Fe, and Uruguay in addition to Entre Ríos. In 1820, however, the province signed a treaty of association with Buenos Aires and Santa Fe. In addition to outlining the distinct "national" options contemplated by the Entrerriano elite, such congresses and associations demonstrated how fluid boundaries were and that the emergence of Argentina as it became was not a given.

For much of the 1820s and 1830s, the province was ruled by a succession of **caudillos**; provincial status is usually dated from 1820, when the then caudillo declared the territory the Republic of Entre Ríos, a title retained for the next 10 years. By 1841, **Justo José de Urquiza**, an associate of **Juan Manuel de Rosas**, caudillo of Buenos Aires, had become the dominant force in the province and ruled it as if it were his personal estate until he was assassinated in 1870. Urquiza proved to be a modernizing caudillo. During his reign, **education** was promoted—primary schools for girls and boys were opened in every department—a printing press was set up, **immigration** was encouraged and **agricultural colonies** founded, transport was upgraded—

Urquiza promoted river steam navigation and inaugurated the first railway in Mesopotamia. The modern growth of the province is usually dated from this period, when it was regarded as socially and economically liberal compared with the Buenos Aires of Rosas and many interior provinces, even if its political system was not. The assassination of Urquiza was followed by federal intervention and several years of civil war. Growth recurred in the 1880s and 1890s, with the construction of a provincial railway system, the improvement of river ports, the development of urban centers, and above all rural colonization. **Sheep** raising and **wool** production took off. Farming was a major activity by 1900. The upgrading of cattle herds meant that *frigoríficos* were operating in the main Paraná River ports by the 1920s.

Economic and social modernization were also features of the second half of the 20th century, in which infrastructure upgrading played an important part. Since the early 1970s, three modern bridges link the province with Uruguay, complemented by the Salto Grande Dam, which includes a railway line. There have been similar improvements on the other side of the province, beginning with a road tunnel to Santa Fe opened in 1969 and a high-span road bridge opened in 2003: a road bridge across to Buenos Aires was opened in 1977. These improvements have encouraged industries to locate in the province, with access to local, regional, and international markets in **MERCOSUR**, most engaged in the processing of agricultural **commodities** and logging. The more economically dynamic areas of the province are those enjoying good communications across the rivers. With the deterioration of the rail system, interior districts have fared less well. Most social indicators are at or below the national average, while poverty has tended to increase faster in Entre Ríos than in neighboring **Littoral** provinces in recent years. The current population of the province is approaching 1,500,000.

ENTRE RIOS RAILWAY COMPANY (ER). *See* ARGENTINE NORTH EASTERN RAILWAY COMPANY (ANE).

ERMAN GONZÁLEZ, ANTONIO (1935–2007). Politician, parliamentarian, minister, and diplomat; he began his public career as treasury secretary of the capital city of **La Rioja** province before being appointed to head various provincial and federal agencies and ministries. Generally known as Erman González, he was a childhood friend and longtime associate of President **Carlos Saúl Menem**—both hailed from the small interior province. He served Menem in various capacities when the latter was governor of La Rioja and president of the republic, being appointed vice president of the **Banco Central de la República Argentina** and to head such ministries as Health and Social Action, Economy, Defense, and Labor. His most prominent positions were as minister of economy and minister of defense. He held the economy portfolio from December 1989 to February 1991. This was a period of **hyperinflation**, which he attempted to resolve by a forced conversion of short-term high-interest savings accounts into long-term low-interest bonds, the so-called Plan Bonex. Designed to reduce liquidity and inflationary pressure, the plan was unsuccessful. González was replaced by **Domingo Cavallo**, architect of the **Convertibility Plan**. On leaving economy, González was offered the **Ministry of Defense**. He retained the post for approximately two years and was caught up in the scandal of illicit arms sales to **Ecuador** and Croatia. It was the cause célèbre of the Menem regime. He was the first of Menem's ministers to be arrested on charges of **corruption**, briefly serving time in preventative detention with Menem himself. In the midterm **congressional elections of 1993**, he headed the governing **Partido Justicialista** (PJ) Chamber of Deputies list for the city of **Buenos Aires**—one of the electoral high points in Menem's political career and the last time the PJ would win in the capital until the **congressional** and **presidential elections of 2011**.

To his friends, he was "Sup-Erman," a capable politician who struggled to serve his country in difficult times; to his critics, a crook who typified the cabal of cronies connected to Menem—his personal wealth increased by a factor of between eight and 10 during the time he held federal appointments. *See also* ALFONSÍN, RAÚL RICARDO (1927–2009); AUSTRAL PLAN; DI TELLA, GUIDO JOSÉ MARIO (1931–2001); ECONOMIC CRISES; PRIVATIZATION.

ESCUELA SUPERIOR DE MECÁNICA DE LA ARMADA (ESMA). The building that formerly housed the Navy Engineering School, responsible for training officers and artificers, is probably the most notorious of the 400 to 500 clandestine detention centers set up during the **War to Annihilate Subversion** in the 1970s. It was built in neoclassical style in the 1920s as a club for navy officers on a large site in Nuñez, an affluent northern suburb of the city of **Buenos Aires**. For some time, the ESMA enjoyed a high reputation for the quality of its technical and defense training, receiving naval cadets are well as career officers and engineers. At various times, the site accommodated a cadet school, officer induction center, advanced technical training workshops, and a strategic planning think tank. By 1975, various buildings on the site had been converted into barracks, prison blocks, and torture chambers. Some 5,000 victims were said to have been "processed" at the center, though precise figures will never be known. Much of what was done there was said to have been directly ordered by Admiral **Emilio Massera**. The ESMA became the base of operations of the notorious Task Force 3.3.2, a section of the Naval Intelligence Service. Some of the principal torturers included **Jorge Acosta** ("The Tiger"), **Alfredo Astiz** ("The Blond Angel of Death"), and Raúl Scheller ("The Penguin"). Since 2004, the building has functioned as a museum dedicated to the memory of those "disappeared" during the 1976–1983 **military** government and for the promotion of **human rights**, the Espacio para la Memoria y para la Promoción y la Defensa de los Derechos Humanos. In 2014, part of the complex was occupied by the **Falklands War** Museum (Museo Malvinas e Islas del Atlántico Sur). The building was declared a national historic monument by President **Cristina Fernández de Kirchner** in 2008. The ESMA, now known as the Escuela de Suboficiales de la Amada (ESSA), has relocated to the Puerto Belgrano Naval Base. For most Argentines, the building is the symbol of state terrorism; it is still commonly known by the acronym ESMA, or the Escuela Mecánica. *See also* DESAPARECIDOS; DISPOSICIÓN FINAL.

ESTANCIA. Large rural estate, a dominant feature of the political economy from the late colonial period to the early 20th century. Hence *estanciero*— the owner of a large estate. Before **independence**, when land was held by the Crown, licenses were awarded to hunt and herd wild **cattle** and horses, activities that led to the production of staple exports like dried **meat** and hides. Gradually, such licenses morphed into usufruct rights for the land itself. After independence, during the presidency of **Bernardino Rivadavia**, the state briefly experimented with a derivative of the colonial system, emphyteusis, awarding rights to enjoy the use of land on long leases. Holders of leases would pay rent to the government, and, in theory, when leases were renewed, rents would be adjusted to reflect increases in the value of land, ensuring that the state captured a share in capital growth. When **Juan Manuel de Rosas** converted leases into titles, the main beneficiaries were existing landowners, established creole families and merchants, the principal supporters of Rosas, who would form the future ruling *estanciero*, land-owning oligarchy. As the Indian frontier was pushed south and west from the 1830s to the 1880s during the **Conquest of the Desert**, vast territories were open to settlement and development. Originally the preserve of creole cattle, *estancias* were soon stocked with European breeds of **sheep** and cattle, such as Merino, Lincoln, Rambouillet, Corridale, and Romney Marsh and various crosses, and Shorthorn, Hereford, and Aberdeen Angus—and very recently Brahman. Cereals and fodder were also raised. It was at this stage that the great landed estates, some the size of small European countries, were consolidated and the popular image of Argentina as a country of huge *estancias* and fabulously wealthy landed families emerged—by 1910, the phrase coined in Paris "wealthy as an Argentine" was widely used. Families like the **Anchorena**, Alvear, Alzaga Unzué, Cárcano, Devoto, Dorrego, Gibson, Martínez de Hoz, Moyano, Ramos Mejía, and Roca spent part of the year on their estates in houses built in the style of Loire châteaux, baronial castles, or Tudor manor houses, as well as in Buenos Aires town palaces and London or Paris residences. Those days are long gone, though the image remains. Once vaunted as modernizing entrepreneurs responsible for the transformation of the country, *estanciero* oligarchs suffered a bad press after the 1930s. The political climate had changed, as had economic conditions. Large estates have been broken up as the result of inheritance laws that divide property equally among heirs, sale, and poor management. Productive estates now tend to be medium in size (yet still large by European standards) engaged in mixed farming, while in place of estate-owning cattle barons there are now soya magnates who lease small estates or own the vast parks of equipment contracted to plant and harvest soya. *See also* AGRICULTURAL COLONIZATION; AGRICULTURE; BUENOS AIRES (PROVINCE); COMMODITIES; ECONOMY; *ESTANCIA* COMPANIES; FOREIGN TRADE; *FRIGORÍFICOS*; GRAINS; MAIZE; PAMPAS; PATAGONIA; SOCIEDAD RURAL ARGENTINA (SRA); *VAQUERÍAS*; WOOL.

ESTANCIA COMPANIES. Mainly associated with frontier development around the end of the 19th century, following the **Conquest of the Desert**. *Estancia* companies represented institutional modernization and became a key vehicle for channeling investment—mainly overseas investment—to the rural sector. The emergence of "impersonal" land enterprises was a function of broader changes occurring in Argentina and in the international economy around the 1870s. Capturing efficiency gains and profit opportunities generated by externalities such as deepening capital markets and railway expansion explains the rise of joint stock farming enterprises after the 1850s and 1860s, as does greater political stability associated with the reintegration of the province of **Buenos Aires** into the **Argentine Confederation** in 1862 and the **federalization of the City of Buenos Aires** in 1880. The outward movement of the frontier resulted in successive surges in the supply of land and reshaped the organization of rural enterprises engaged in the production of a shifting basket of commodities—from hides and dried **meat**, to **wool**, to **grains**, and finally to the raising of prime livestock. Greater security of property rights, rising property values, and buoyant international markets provided the general context within which specific Argentine factors operated. Some estates were converted into private joint stock companies for administrative convenience—to circumvent inheritance laws that required the division of a property among all heirs—others to raise the very substantial funds required for land and stock improvement.

The life history of one such *estancia* company illustrates the larger process. The landholding of La Germania Estancia Company originated in a massive estate of 100 square leagues acquired by the Gunther family from the province of Buenos Aires in 1883, originally designed for colonization under the auspices of the Western Buenos Aires Land Company. The Gunthers were a Belgian family resident in Argentina and London who would later be associated with two of the largest land companies to operate in Argentina—**Liebig Extract of Meat Company** and the Forestal Land, Timber, and

Railway Company (now known as **Forestal Argentina**). With interests in land, **commodity** processing, and finance, and enjoying connections with capital markets in London and continental Europe, the Gunthers were well placed to raise cheap capital overseas and at home. La Germania was formed as a stand-alone company in 1899, endowed with 13 squares leagues from the original holding. Capitalized at £150,000 (US$727,500), the company issued £50,000 in 5.5 percent debentures. Virtually all equity was held by the Gunther brothers, and the estate was placed in the hands of a manager and team trained in rural economics and husbandry. Located in the northwest of the province of Buenos Aires, close to the **Buenos Ayres & Pacific Railway** (BA&P), the estate experienced a tremendous increase in land values, allowing modest sale to finance further development. A large part of the original estate was under cereals, cultivated by Italian colonists, with several acres devoted to market gardening and fruit production. By the 1910s, the estate was producing cereals and prime beef **cattle** and endowed with a township, telephones, railway station, outlying pastures, and a population of many hundreds. It was a heavily capitalized estate. La Germania was not untypical of many joint-stock *estancia* companies established between the 1840s and 1880s.

The formation of *estancia* companies was a key institutional innovation and represented a further stage in the institutionality of the *estancia* as a system of production. The 19th century witnessed waves of organizational innovation as land was broken in by criollo cattle, improved to carry new breeds of **sheep**, and reshaped to the requirements of prime beef production. The improvement of bloodstock, scientific breeding techniques, and information dissemination was another aspect of institutional innovation. *Estancia* companies also reflected a changed external reality that facilitated a shift from a personal to a more institutional form of economic organization once access to institutional finance became a practical proposition. They were Schumpeterian profit-orientated firms focused on the preparation and stocking of land, the identification of market opportunities, and the switch from the production of one commodity to another as market opportunities changed and developed. Successful corporate *estancias* popularized the limited liability model among landowners and served further to institutionalize rural businesses. *See also* AGRICULTURAL COLONIZATION; AGRICULTURE; *CÉDULAS*; ECONOMY; FOREIGN DEBT/FOREIGN INVESTMENT; FOREIGN TRADE; IMMIGRATION; TRANSPORTATION.

EXECUTIONS OF JUNE 1956. The most difficult moment faced by the de facto regime headed by General **Pedro Eugenio Aramburu**: a botched countercoup by Peronist military, followed by the imposition of martial law and the execution of 27 people (10 of whom were civilians). The executions, carried out within the framework of martial law, contravened the **Constitution of 1853**, which had just been reinstated by the government.

The conspiracy of 9 June was headed by Generals Juan José Valle and Raúl D. Tanco, both of whom had remained loyal to the government ousted in the **military coup of 1955**. Their insurrectional proclamation complained about imprisonments, lack of freedoms, political proscriptions, the economic program, and the destruction of **trade union** structures. It listed the traditional Justicialista slogans (social justice, economic independence, political sovereignty), though at no point mentioned **Juan Domingo Perón**, who in fact did not support the conspirators.

The conspirators had assumed that they would not face the death penalty in the event of failure since the legislation of internal state of war of 1951 had been rescinded. They were wrong: hard-line **military** elements prevailed after 1955, seeking the harshest punishment for any counterrevolution and casting aside the article in the constitution that abolished the death penalty for political reasons. The government was well aware of the countercoup and the day before secretly prepared the decrees imposing martial law and the formation of military tribunals. Although they were signed by both Aramburu and vice president Admiral **Isaac Rojas**, it was the former who ordered their implementation on 9 June.

The countercoup failed from the outset, and Aramburu claimed the attempt was financed with funds from Panama and had been part of a conspiracy with continental dimensions arranged by a foreign Communist organization. There was no evidence whatsoever for this claim, which only served to justify the decree imposing martial law. Sentencing by military tribunals led to the infamous executions, including those of civilians. General Valle turned himself in on 12 June, and martial law was lifted after his execution the following day. In what appears as an act of cowardice, General Tanco sought refuge in the Haitian embassy and eventually left the country.

The executions of June 1956 merit attention for a number of reasons. First, notwithstanding that Aramburu took full responsibility and that they prevented further rebellions during the remainder of his presidency, the executions were a grave punishment that broke with the tradition of tolerating the defeated as applied after the civil wars of the 19th century. Second, the tragic outcome was unexpected, as the conspiracy was undertaken under the assumption that there would be no martial law, which the government imposed in the most underhand manner. Third, the use of the death penalty in a military rebellion against a de facto regime was a disproportionate punishment. Finally, the government never explained the alleged continental terrorist plan and limited itself to expelling the Soviet naval attaché.

The tragic episode is a terrible stain on the **Revolución Libertadora** and widened the abyss in an already fractured society. Fourteen years later, it became one of the justifications for the **Aramburazo**, which opened the violent decade of the 1970s. With the advantage of hindsight, it is possible to view the executions of June 1956 as marking the onset of a new and bloody phase in Argentine political life, as the country embarked on a two-decade cycle of alternating military and civilian administrations that culminated in the **military coup of 1976**.

EZEIZA MASSACRE (20 JUNE 1973). The carnage resulting from a shoot-out that marred the rally to welcome **Juan Domingo Perón** back from exile on the access road to Ezeiza International Airport near **Buenos Aires**. Around 2,000,000 people gathered close to the airport, including members of armed groups such as the **Triple A**, the **Montoneros**, the **Fuerzas Armadas Revolucionarias** (FAR), and even the **Ejercito Revolucionario del Pueblo** (ERP), who were positioned near the stage where Perón was due to speak. Who started the firing of weapons has always been a matter of debate, but besides the shoot-out between the Peronist left and right there were all manner of incidents such as lynchings, castrations, and people being strung up from trees. Statements published at the time referred to 13 bodies, though the total death count was probably nearer 400, with countless more wounded.

The aircraft bringing Perón back from Madrid had to be diverted to the Morón Air Base, not least because of the probability of an attempt on his life. Until his death the following year, Perón remained convinced that left-wing groups had tried to kill him in Ezeiza. No official inquiry into the events of 20 June 1973 was ever held.

F

FÁBRICA ARGENTINA DE AVIONES (FAdeA). The main Argentine aircraft manufacturer, it is located in the city of **Córdoba**. Founded in 1927, for most of its existence it was known as the Fábrica Militar de Aviones (FMA), until privatized in 1995 as a concession to the US defense contractor Lockheed Martin. In 2009, the concession was terminated, and the plant is now wholly owned by the Argentine government.

The FMA is best known for having produced the first jet fighter aircraft in Latin America: the Pulqui I and the Pulqui II, under the direction of engineers Emile Dewotine (French) and Kurt Tank (German), respectively. Only one prototype of the Pulqui I was ever built, which made its maiden flight in 1947 and was powered by a Rolls Royce Derwent V turbine. The Pulqui II was a more innovative design, with a pioneering layout of the wings in the shape of an arrow that allowed it to attain very high subsonic speed levels. Powered by a Rolls Royce Nene II turbine, only five prototypes of the Pulqui II were ever built—and their history was checkered. The first prototype faced static trials and was tested to destruction. The second one flew in 1950 and, notwithstanding significant modifications, suffered a fatal accident after it had been officially presented to the public in 1951. After some redesigning, the third prototype fared no better, with another fatal accident two days before a scheduled demonstration in the presence of President **Juan Domingo Perón** in 1952. The fourth prototype was built in 1953 and was the most tested. It still had problems, but series production was planned. Following the **military coup of 1955**, the new authorities had no interest in continuing with the expensive project. In an attempt to gain political backing, a new demonstration was held in 1956 and ended in a nonfatal accident. A fifth prototype was built and made its maiden flight in 1959. But the aircraft was technologically outdated, and the Argentine air force instead purchased North American F-86 Sabre fighters.

During this arguably "golden age" of state-sponsored **developmentalism** and of the FMA, there were other daring projects such as wing-shaped aircraft, but little came of them, not least due to costs and technical issues. The 1960s saw the launch of the light transport Guaraní and the counterinsurgency light attack aircraft Pucará. In the mid-1970s, the 120 Pucará that were built played a key role in combating the **Ejército Revolucionario del Pueblo** (ERP) in the province of **Tucumán**.

In 1995, the FMA was privatized by the government of President **Carlos Saúl Menem**. From that year until March 2009, it was leased out to Lockheed Martin Aircraft Argentina, a subsidiary of the Lockheed Martin Corporation. Under the terms of the **privatization** agreement, Lockheed Martin Aircraft Argentina would have the concession for 25 years—with the option of renewal for two 10-year periods. The factory merely serviced and maintained aircraft during that quarter of a century, and as the lease was ending, it was nationalized by the government of President **Cristina Fernández de Kirchner**. Her administration paid 67 million pesos for the plant in August 2009, and in December of that year the name was changed to Fábrica Argentina de Aviones. *See also* INDUSTRIAS AERONÁUTICAS Y MECÁNICAS DEL ESTADO (IAME); STATE-OWNED ENTERPRISES (SOEs).

FÁBRICA MILITAR DE AVIONES (FMA). *See* FÁBRICA ARGENTINA DE AVIONES (FAdeA).

FABRICACIONES MILITARES (FM). This military-industrial complex, which is formally named the Dirección General de Fabricaciones Militares, was created in 1941 with the purpose of domestically supplying war materiél. FM owned 14 military plants and was the key shareholder in base-industry enterprises such as the **Sociedad Mixta Siderúrgica Argentina** (SOMISA) and Atanor–Compañía Nacional para la Industria Química. Most of the establishments it owned were privatized starting in the 1980s, not least because they were economically inefficient. The SOMISA steelworks lacked economies of scale and was overmanned. It had a workforce of 12,000, which was halved by forced dismissals in the run-up to **privatization**. Once the company was sold to the Techint group, it became a success story. Atanor, which in 1988 was sold to **Bunge & Born** and then on to Iowa-based Albaugh in 1997, became one of the leading manufacturers of chemicals, petrochemicals, and polymers in Argentina and the largest producer and exporter of agrochemicals—especially herbicides—in Latin America.

The current activity of FM is concentrated in three factories: the Fábrica Militar Fray Luis Beltrán located in the province of **Santa Fe**, which manufactures armaments and munitions; the Fábrica Militar Villa María in the province of **Córdoba**, specializing in gunpowder and explosives; and the Fábrica Militar Río Tercero, which is also situated in Córdoba and produces chemical and metal-mechanic goods. The latter include rolling stock and urban commuter trains for **Ferrocarriles Argentinos**, as well as trains for the underground system in **Buenos Aires**.

Fabricaciones Militares acquired international notoriety owing to an arms trafficking scandal involving the illegal shipment of 6,500 tons of weapons and ammunition to Croatia and Ecuador between 1991 and 1995. At the time, Croatia was under a **United Nations** arms embargo, and Argentina was prohibited from selling weapons to Ecuador as it was one of the four official guarantors of the peace treaty of 1942 between **Peru** and Ecuador. Matters were aggravated by the fact that President **Carlos Saúl Menem** himself had signed the secret decrees that enabled the sales, which were covered by military equipment initially assigned for other purposes. The scandal became public when that equipment was discovered missing, and the cover-up was botched. In November 1995, a massive explosion at the Fábrica Militar Río Tercero not only killed seven people and injured over 300 but also devastated the town. Subsequently, it became known that the plant had been destroyed deliberately to hide the missing war materiél relating to the illegal sales to Croatia and Ecuador.

In more recent years, during the second presidency of **Cristina Fernández de Kirchner**, FM was milked by **La Cámpora**—its placement controlled the state-owned entity and its budget, from which money was siphoned off in **corruption** as well as to finance the federal government. A lack of public oversight over the finances of Fabricaciones Militares was not exclusive to the *kirchnerato* but had been a constant in the company's history, as the **military** was particularly secretive about its activities. *See also* ECONOMIC CRISES; ECONOMY; DEVELOPMENTALISM/DEVELOPMENTALIST; DI TELLA, GUIDO JOSÉ MARIO (1931–2001); INDUSTRY; STATE-OWNED ENTERPRISES (SOEs).

FACULTAD LATINOAMERICANA DE CIENCIAS SOCIALES (FLACSO). This Buenos Aires center is one of a confederation of similar institutions of higher learning in Latin America. Each institution is autonomous, though there is an emphasis on cooperation across the network and a commitment to interdisciplinarity and methodological pluralism within the social sciences. The first institution in the network was established in 1957. FLACSO-Argentina was founded in 1974, initially functioning as a center of teaching and research, offering specific programs, becoming an accredited institution of higher education in 1992. The network sees itself as engaged in the training of academics and civil servants with a brief to contribute to democratic institution building.

In addition to Argentina, major FLACSO centers are located in **Brazil**, **Chile**, Costa Rica, Mexico, and **Uruguay**; there are also centers in other countries. Most centers focus on the social sciences, and there is a degree of disciplinary specialization, with provision for an exchange of students and academics and collaborative teaching programs. For example, the center in Buenos Aires specializes in international relations, social policy, and **education**. During periods of authoritarian rule in a particular country, centers in other countries have attempted to provide an institutional haven for academics expelled—or forced to flee—from their home institutions. Researchers based in Buenos Aires have made signal contributions to the study of the theory and practice of international relations and the operation of the global economic system, the study of social policy and social policy outcomes—especially issues of equity and poverty in the functioning of social security and social insurance regimes—and education and human development. Individual associates have had a significant impact on policy formation in the **Ministry of Foreign Relations and Religion**, the **Ministry of Education**, and the **Ministry of Social Development**, some acting as advisors, others holding official positions.

FALKLAND ISLANDS. Known in Spanish as the Islas Malvinas, the archipelago is located on the Patagonian shelf in the south Atlantic Ocean. It comprises East Falkland (Gran Malvina), West Falkland (Soledad), and 776 smaller islands.

The Falklands were uninhabited until the 18th century, when French captain Louis Antoine de Bougainville established Port Louis on East Falkland in 1764 and British captain John MacBride set up Port Egmont on Saunders Island in 1766. In the latter year, France surrendered its claim to the islands to **Spain**. Problems began when the Spaniards discovered and captured Port Egmont in 1770, with war narrowly being avoided when the outpost was returned to **Great Britain** the following year.

Both British and Spanish settlements coexisted in the islands until 1774. Britain then withdrew out of new strategic and economic considerations, but left a plaque claiming the archipelago for the Crown. The **Viceroyalty of the River Plate** therefore retained the only government and military presence in the Falklands, but that came to an end with the **British invasions** and the subsequent collapse of Spanish authority on the mainland. Only **gauchos** and fishermen stayed there voluntarily.

The archipelago was claimed by the newly independent **United Provinces of the River Plate** after 1816. In 1823, the authorities in Buenos Aires granted German-born merchant Luis Vernet permission to conduct fishing activities and exploit feral **cattle** in the Falklands. He accumulated resources on the islands until the venture was secure enough to bring permanent settlers. Vernet was named civilian and military commander in 1829 but faced serious difficulties when trying to regulate fishing and whale and seal hunting. This led to a raid in 1831 by the US warship USS *Lexington*, whose commander, Silas Duncan, then dissolved the islands' government. Buenos Aires attempted to retain some influence over the settlement by installing a garrison, which the following year mutinied.

In 1833, Britain sent forces that reasserted its rule over the islands. The Falklands became a Crown Colony in 1840, and Scottish settlers subsequently established a pastoral community there. Although Argentina has registered protests with Britain ever since, the **Falklands Dispute** did not become acute until the second half of the 20th century, resulting in the **Falklands War** of 1982. Although diplomatic relations between Buenos Aires and London were restored during the presidency of **Carlos Saúl Menem**—they had been cut off in 1982—there appears to be no resolution in sight to the dispute.

As for the islands' economy, growth only began when in 1851 the Falkland Islands Company successfully introduced Cheviot **sheep** for **wool** farming; this spurred other farms to follow suit. A sheep monoculture ensued, with the stock expanded with the introduction of other breeds such as Corriedale and Polwarth. However, following the Falklands War, some diversification came with the establishment of an exclusive economic zone. The fishing industry now accounts for 50–60 percent of the annual GDP of the islands. However, there are concerns over dependence on fishing licenses, threats from overfishing, illegal fishing, and fish market price fluctuations. This has increased interest in offshore oil drilling, but exploration has not yet led to viable finds.

Since becoming a Crown Colony in the 19th century, the Falkland Islands have had their status modified twice: they became a British Dependent Territory in 1981 and then a British Overseas Territory in 2002. The current population is almost 3,400, and the capital is Port Stanley.

FALKLANDS DISPUTE. From 1833, when **Great Britain** took the **Falkland Islands**, until the second half of the 20th century, the main consequence was that Buenos Aires simply addressed repeated protests to London. The problem became more acute starting in December 1960. The **United Nations** (UN) passed Resolution 1514 on decolonization, establishing that the organization would annually examine progress on the subject. This provided Argentina with the opportunity to raise the Falklands question at a multilateral level. In 1964, the relevant UN committee unanimously approved—with a British abstention—a report inviting both interested parties to negotiate the conflict over sovereignty of the islands. In December 1965, this became a formal requirement when the UN General Assembly passed Resolution 2065.

Negotiations began in January 1966, during the presidency of **Arturo Illia**, but achieved little as both Buenos Aires and London stuck to their positions on the subject. Following the **military coup of 1966**, further meetings were held, and a memorandum of understanding was reached in August 1968. It was decided that the peaceful solution to the conflict should take into account "the interests of the islanders" and that concrete measures should be taken to promote freedom of movement and communications between the archipelago and the mainland. More importantly, Britain intended to recognize Argentine sovereignty after a date to be agreed on.

Although the memorandum of understanding explicitly involved the transfer of the Falklands to Argentina, the de facto government of **Juan Carlos Onganía** did not act on the document for four months. In December 1968, it finally decided that the memorandum should become an official agreement between the two parties. However, London refused to sign as it had taken offense at the delay in the Argentine response. The hiatus in negotiations lasted for three years, which then resumed during the de facto presidency of **Alejandro Agustín Lanusse**. The result was the **Agreement between Argentina and Great Britain concerning the Falkland Islands** of 1971, which did not deal with the issue of sovereignty. It established communications between the mainland and archipelago and also freedom of movement in both directions and came into effect the following year.

In 1974, following confidential conversations, Britain proposed a form of condominium over the Falklands. President **Juan Domingo Perón** authorized a counterproposal that in many ways coincided with the British one, but after his death the agreement was allowed to founder by both sides. Tensions increased in 1975 after the British government announced an economic mission to the islands headed by Lord Shackleton, to the point that his ship was fired at in February 1976 as it approached Argentine territorial waters.

Following the **military coup of 1976**, negotiations recommenced but led nowhere as Britain was only interested in subjects such as joint cooperation in oil exploration and fishing. In November 1976, the Argentine navy set up an observation post on Thule in the South Sandwich Islands; it drew a protest from London and then a discreet British military presence in the area when in late 1977 it appeared that a second Argentine contingent would land. By this time, the navy—under the command of **Emilio Eduardo Massera** and the direction of **Jorge Isaac Anaya**—was pushing for a military solution to the Falklands Dispute. In June 1978, Massera was successfully confronted over his plans by **Jorge Rafael Videla** (the head of the army and de facto president of Argentina) and **Orlando Agosti** (commander-in-chief of the air force).

In July 1980, Argentina wasted the greatest opportunity to get the contested archipelago back. During a visit to Britain, Minister of Economy **José Alfredo Martínez de Hoz** met Undersecretary of State Nicholas Ridley. The latter was interested in resolving the Falklands Dispute and proposed a leaseback arrangement whereby Britain would transfer sovereignty but continue to administer the islands for a period of 30 years, after which they would be returned to Argentina. Since it was not in his remit, Martínez de Hoz informed the **Ministry of Foreign Relations** in Buenos Aires of the proposal;

he received no reply. Also in 1980, and crucial considering events two years later, four senior naval officers presented an accurate report on the diplomatic and military implications of an Argentine attack on the Falklands. Their key recommendation was to continue negotiations, especially at a multilateral level in the UN. Unfortunately, the report was ignored by the ruling junta and the Foreign Ministry when they launched the **Falklands War** in 1982. As transpired, the report correctly predicted how Britain would react to an invasion and accurately gauged the response of the **United States**—namely, that it would support Britain.

Videla was succeeded in March 1981 as de facto president by **Roberto Viola**, who retired from active service and was replaced as head of the army by **Leopoldo Fortunato Galtieri**. In turn, in December 1981, Viola was ousted as president by the commander-in-chief of the army. But Galtieri paid a heavy price for his palace coup: Anaya, by now the head of the navy, gave his support on the condition that the Falklands issue was resolved militarily. On 2 April 1982, Argentina invaded the archipelago. The military junta mishandled the ensuing conflict. Argentine troops consisted of poorly trained and ill-equipped conscripts who were no match for the highly professional British task force sent to retake the islands, and the Argentine public were misled by their government on the actual situation in the theater of war. Argentina surrendered on 14 June 1982, and the debacle spelled the beginning of the end of the **Proceso de Reorganización Nacional**.

Following the election of **Raúl Alfonsín** to the presidency in late 1983, Foreign Minister **Dante Caputo** remained totally intransigent on the subject of the Falklands. Things changed somewhat after **Carlos Saúl Menem** won the **presidential election of 1989**. Menem restored diplomatic relations with London in 1990, and the positions of both parties in relation to their rights over the disputed islands were frozen. Anglophile Minister of Foreign Relations **Guido Di Tella** engaged in a charm offensive to woo islanders. There were imaginative (possibly bizarre) proposals, including a suggestion that each Falklands family might be offered £1,000,000 to emigrate—New Zealand and Scotland were mentioned as possible destinations. Nevertheless, unsuccessful negotiations were undertaken on two economic issues of joint interest concerning the Falklands—fishing and oil exploration. Yet by the end of the Menem presidency, Argentina had a success of sorts: a monthly air link between the mainland and the archipelago resumed, Argentines once again were allowed to visit the islands, and a monument would be built in the cemetery in the Falklands for the Argentine fallen during the conflict in 1982.

In the early 21st century, President **Cristina Fernández de Kirchner** engaged in saber rattling over the Falklands. But it amounted to no more than that, since the armed forces were in no real position to undertake an invasion. The Argentine pursuit of sovereignty over the archipelago was dealt further blows during the presidency of Mrs. Kirchner. In 2009, she met with then British prime minister Gordon Brown, who informed her that sovereignty was an issue no longer to be discussed, and the Falkland Islands held a referendum on its political status in March 2013. The outcome was that almost 100 percent of voters favored remaining under British rule.

Argentine handling of the dispute since 1960 has been one of missed opportunities. The British submitted proposals in 1968 and 1980 that would have satisfactorily resolved the conflict but were ignored respectively by the de facto administrations of Generals Onganía and Videla. This reflects the narrow thinking of recent Argentine military regimes, which thought they had all the answers to the country's problems. And General Galtieri—yet another dictator—made matters worse by going to war over the islands. The 1982 invasion and brief occupation proved to be a major setback to Argentine ambitions to recover the island by diplomatic means. The islanders bitterly resent the occupation of the archipelago. They remember slights experienced—the immediate change of signage from English to Spanish and traffic circulation (continuing to drive on the left became an act of defiance), the arrogance of some Argentine officials, and the mood of fear. Islander intransigence—and self-confidence—has been strengthened by economic growth. Post-1982 land reform (until the early 1980s, most land was owned by the Falkland Islands Company) has given inhabitants a greater stake. Growth and prosperity have been generated by the issue of fishing licenses, revenue has been applied to infrastructure and social projects, and there is the promise of oil. Economic prosperity has stimulated population growth; the number of inhabitants has increased by more than 50 percent since the invasion due to natural growth, return migration, and new settlement, not counting the large military presence. A spirit of independence (under the Crown) and self-sufficiency have put pay to any prospect of a settlement, about which the islands now have a veto. The resolution of the Falklands Dispute appears to be far off.

FALKLANDS WAR (2 APRIL–14 JUNE 1982). La Guerra de las Malvinas in Spanish, it was the gravest moment of the long-running **Falklands Dispute** between Argentina and **Great Britain**. The **military** solution to the problem of the **Falkland Islands** was devised by the Argentine navy as a means of uniting the public and salvaging the by then extremely unpopular **Proceso de Reorganización Nacional**, but its failure instead accelerated the collapse of the dictatorship and permanently damaged the reputation of the armed forces.

When de facto president General **Roberto Eduardo Viola** was replaced by Army Commander-in-Chief **Leopoldo Fortunato Galtieri** in a palace coup on 11 December 1981, head of the navy **Jorge Isaac Anaya** exacted a heavy price for backing the move: the Falklands Dispute would be resolved by force. Galtieri assumed the presidency on 22 December and appointed **Nicanor Costa Méndez** as foreign minister on condition that he became an accomplice in the military designs on the Falkland Islands. Planning for the invasion of the archipelago proceeded apace during January and February 1982, based on plans that dated back to the 1960s. A round of negotiations between Buenos Aires and London was held in New York on 26 and 27 February, but the little progress made was officially rejected by Costa Méndez.

The first Argentine move was on the South Georgia Islands—which were also claimed by Argentina—in late March 1982. This was followed by the Argentine fleet setting sail on 28 March toward the Falklands, and due to weather conditions the landing was set for the first minute of 2 April. Both Britain and the **United States** detected the movements of the Argentine fleet, and Prime Minister Margaret Thatcher asked President Ronald Reagan to contact Galtieri to try to stop the invasion. Late on 1 April, when the point of no return had been reached, the Argentine de facto president deigned himself to take the call from his US counterpart. For 40 minutes, Reagan warned Galtieri of the determination of Mrs. Thatcher and that she would respond militarily; Galtieri would have none of it.

The invasion, which took place three days after severe clashes between demonstrators protesting against the military dictatorship and the police in the center of **Buenos Aires**, did attain its goal of rallying the public—and even political figures—behind the cause, albeit temporarily. Diplomatic relations between Britain and Argentina were severed, and on 3 April Argentina suffered a major diplomatic defeat at the **United Nations** (UN) Security Council. On 5 April, a British task force, rapidly assembled as London had contingency plans for such an emergency, set sail for the Falklands, with the advantage that on the way it was authorized to organize itself and resupply at the US military facilities in the British outpost of Ascension Island in the South Atlantic. This contradicted the comment that Costa Méndez had made a few days earlier to a member of his staff at the Foreign Ministry, namely, that the British would never send their fleet, not least on financial grounds.

Mario Benjamín Menéndez was sworn in with great fanfare as governor of the Malvinas on 7 April, while London declared a maritime exclusion zone around the Falklands within which any Argentine warship or naval auxiliary could be attacked by British nuclear-powered submarines. On 23 April, Her Majesty's Government clarified that Argentine ships or aircraft deemed a threat to British forces would be attacked, and a week later the exclusion zone was upgraded from military to total, the purpose having been to reduce the amount of time needed to determine if any vessel in the zone was hostile or not, thereby extending the scope of military action by the British. Argentina was made aware of these decisions, which would lead to the tragedy of the battle cruiser **ARA *General Belgrano*** on 2 May.

US Secretary of State Alexander Haig undertook a shuttle diplomacy mission between Buenos Aires and London throughout April 1982, which failed as Argentina was making the US choose between it and Britain—the Reagan administration chose the latter. A recalcitrant Costa Méndez then made the ludicrous threat that Argentina might seek Soviet assistance—the European Economic Community (EEC) had imposed sanctions, as would the United States. This left Haig unimpressed, as Washington, DC, and Moscow had already discussed the Falklands crisis on the "hot line." The US secretary of state warned his Argentine counterpart that, in the event of war, Britain would be supported by the United States and Western Europe. On 29 April, Galtieri telephoned Costa Méndez in New York and informed him that he was removing the occupying troops from the islands; however, for unknown reasons, nothing happened.

Hostilities began on 1 May with a British bombing raid on the Port Stanley airfield, and the next day the ARA *General Belgrano* was sunk by the HMS *Conqueror*. Also on 2 May, President Fernando Belaúnde Terry of **Peru** produced the only major—but unsuccessful—peace proposal to resolve the crisis. First, it requested the immediate cessation of hostilities and the mutual withdrawal of forces. Second, that representatives unconnected to either party involved in the conflict would temporarily administer the archipelago. Third, that the governments in London and **Buenos Aires** would mutually recognized the existence of conflicting claims on the Falklands and that the aspirations and interests of the islanders would have to be taken into account in any definitive solution to the problem. Fourth, that the contact group that would intervene immediately to implement this deal would be composed of several countries designated by common agreement. And finally, that under the responsibility of those countries, a definitive agreement was to be reached by 30 April 1983. The unfortunate failure of this proposal, due to the intransigence of the parties as the conflict on the ground worsened, was another wasted opportunity to resolve the Falklands Dispute.

Following the sinking of the ARA *General Belgrano*, the Argentine navy—which had been the proponent of the military takeover of the islands—withdrew back to bases on the mainland in an act of cowardice. This left the air force and army to do the bulk of the fighting, and the former was unquestionably the better performer. The air force sank the destroyer HMS *Sheffield* on 4 May 1982 and, after the British landed in the Falklands on 21 May, had destroyed the transport HMS *Atlantic Conveyor*, the destroyer HMS *Coventry*, and the frigates HMS *Antelope* and HMS *Ardent* by 1 June. The British fleet suffered even further on 8 June, when the HMS *Tristram* was damaged, and it lost a frigate (the HMS *Plymouth*) and the HMS *Sir Galahad*. The latter exploded, and shrapnel caused severe casualties. Futile negotiations had been in the meantime continuing at the UN to bring about a cease-fire and an end to the conflict, but the material and human losses on the

HMS *Sir Galahad* prompted Mrs. Thatcher to reject the possibility of a diplomatic solution. She went for broke—with the full backing of President Reagan.

While the Argentine air force had performed reasonably, the same cannot be said of the army, as clearly shown during the British retaking of the islands. Galtieri had famously said "Si quieren venir que vengan, les presentaremos batalla" (If they [the British] want to come they can, and we'll battle them), but the bulk of troops consisted of ill-trained conscripts who were poorly equipped to deal with the professionally and technologically superior British forces, let alone the harsh weather and environment. The Argentines were overwhelmed in fighting at locations such as Darwin and Goose Green, and the British made their way to Port Stanley. All along, the Argentine public was misled about the war situation by both the government and the **media**. Military communiqués and press headlines were overly triumphalist; the most memorable cover title of a weekly was "Estamos ganando" (We're winning). When Port Stanley was retaken and Governor Menéndez surrendered on 14 June, most of the country was in shock. The following evening there was rioting in front of the **Casa Rosada**, the presidential palace in downtown Buenos Aires.

Argentine casualties totaled 649 deaths and 1,188 injured, while British ones amounted to 258 deaths (including three female islanders killed when an Argentine mortar misfired in Port Stanley) and 777 injured. The Argentine armed forces were permanently discredited by their failure, and the military adventure did not prevent the collapse of the Proceso. It also put paid to the access that Argentines had to the archipelago under the terms of the **Agreement between Argentina and Great Britain concerning the Falkland Islands** (1971). The commanders-in-chief of the army, navy, and air force would have been wise not to ignore a report from 1980 in which four naval officers accurately assessed the consequences of a military operation in the Falklands and advised the continuation of negotiations at the UN. *See also* ASTIZ, ALFREDO IGNACIO (1951–); FOREIGN RELATIONS.

FANGIO, JUAN MANUEL (1911–1995). Racing car driver who dominated the first decade of Formula One racing. He won the World Championship of Drivers five times (1951, 1954, 1955, 1956, and 1957)—a record that stood unbroken for 47 years—with four different teams (Alfa Romeo, Ferrari, Mercedes Benz, and Maserati), a feat that has not been repeated. He holds the highest winning percentage in Formula One, having won 24 of the 53 races he entered.

FARM PROTESTS. Term applied to a series of events in the countryside—with parallel action in some large cities—in the first presidency of **Cristina Fernández de Kirchner**. The immediate cause of the protests was hikes in export taxes, coupled with a long-standing sense of grievance that the government was using the farm sector as a cash cow. At best, the government was seen as being ignorant of the needs of **agriculture**, at worst antifarm (*anti-ganadero*).

Taxes on agricultural exports—*retenciones*—were abolished in the 1990s but reintroduced as a "temporary" measure following the 2002 crisis to fund emergency social assistance schemes implemented by President **Eduardo Duhalde**. Export taxes were additional to conventional payroll, business, and income taxes. Capitalizing on rising soya prices, in 2008 the government raised export taxes on soya from 35 percent to 44 percent, demanding partial payment in advance. The hike was justified on the grounds that farmers were reaping windfall profits and that funds were needed to finance ambitious social projects. The increase may also have been intended to encourage a switch back to the production of food staples that would have a knock-on effect on living costs—the government was struggling to curb inflation. Farmers responded by staging marches, blocking roads, and going on strike, refusing to send **commodities** to market.

The importance of the protests is due to the political fallout. The campaign against export tax increases unified all four bodies representing agriculture—a disparate set of organizations that shared little in common and were often at loggerheads. The campaign also brought together rural and urban groups opposed to the government; consumers in the cities (many of whom could have expected to benefit from lower food prices or proposed social projects) sided with small farmers, large *estancieros*, and agribusinesses. For several days in middle-class districts of **Buenos Aires**, householders organized nightly *cacerolazos*—beating on pots and pans—while in the center of the city there was a series of huge gatherings that easily dwarfed counterdemonstrations mobilized by the government. There were similar antigovernment protests in major towns and cities across the main agricultural districts, for example, **Córdoba, Rosario**, and **Tucumán**. Although President Fernández plowed on and submitted the tax bill to **Congress**, it fell when her vice president, **Julio Cobos**, cast a tiebreaking vote against it in the National Senate. As chair of the Senate, the vice president only votes in the event of a tie. The government was forced to back down. Due to the crisis, Mrs. Kirchner's opinion poll rating plummeted, falling from an approval rate of 58 percent to 23 percent. The protests are comparable to popular mobilizations that animated the countryside and transformed the politics of several provinces a century earlier.

Honoring a campaign pledge to eliminate and reduce export taxes, in December 2015 President **Maurico Macri** abolished export taxes on **meat, maize,** and wheat and reduced taxes on soya from 35 percent to 30 percent. Following the abolition of *retenciones*, grain exports increased by 25 percent in 2016. Taxes on soya were reduced again in 2018 to 27 percent, but promised further, gradual reductions are only likely to be phased in over a very long period as taxes on soya cover about a third of total government expenditure. *See also* CONGRESSIONAL ELECTIONS OF 2009; CRY OF ALCORTA; ECONOMIC CRISES; KIRCHNER, NÉSTOR CARLOS (1950–2010); *PIQUETERO/PIQUETEROS*; SOCIEDAD RURAL ARGENTINA (SRA).

FARRELL, EDELMIRO JULIÁN (1887–1980). De facto president of Argentina (1944–1946). Commander of a detachment of mountain troops in **Mendoza,** he met Colonel **Juan Domingo Perón** in 1941 and developed personal ties with him. In 1942, Farrell became commander of the inspectorate of mountain troops in **Buenos Aires,** where the colonel remained his subordinate. Following the **military coup of 1943,** he became minister of war and was appointed vice president in October of that year. He became president in February 1944 after overthrowing General **Pedro Pablo Ramírez** in a palace coup. However, Farrell had little interest in affairs of state; his tenure was beset by the continuing power struggle within the regime and the relentless rise of Perón.

Perón held the posts of vice president, minister of war, and secretary of labor. He used his government positions to build up dominance within the army and to construct a political apparatus to ensure victory in a future election. He also took the lead in **economic policy,** promoting industrial development and the establishment of **military**-related industries, and creating the **Banco de Crédito Industrial** and the Secretariat of Industry and Commerce.

Civilian opposition to the Farrell regime in general and Perón in particular reached new heights, leading the president to opt for harsh repression. Pressure to return to constitutional rule from most civilian sectors was unsuccessful, and the malaise spread through military ranks. There were no signs of Perón resigning despite assurances from Farrell; if anything, he acted more and more as an election candidate. Perón reacted to his opponents with actions designed to whip up support from the laboring masses and more repression against his foes. Matters came to a head in October 1945, when the Campo de Mayo garrison in the vicinity of Buenos Aires prepared to move against Perón. He was forced to resign all his public posts and detained. Thousands of workers poured into the capital to demonstrate in favor of Perón; the army was the only force that could control the situation but was not used, and Perón returned. Farrell reshuffled his cabinet with ministers from Perón's camp and became more than ever a lame-duck president.

The main objective of the Farrell government after the events of October 1945 was to end military rule. It committed itself to holding free and fair elections and supported the candidacy of Perón in the knowledge that he could genuinely win. Voting took place in February 1946, and the final act of the outgoing administration was to decree the restoration of Perón to active duty and his promotion to the rank of general. *See also* PRESIDENTIAL ELECTION OF 1946.

FEDERACIÓN AGRARIA ARGENTINA (FAA). Formed in 1912 during the rural protest movement that became known as the **Cry of Alcorta** (Grito de Alcorta). Initially set up to articulate the demands of sharecroppers and tenant farmers in zones of **agricultural colonization** in the **pampas** who were campaigning for fixed-term contracts and lower rents, the organization now represents small- and medium-sized farm owners in the provinces of **Córdoba** and **Santa Fe**.

The Grito resulted in the mass mobilization of small-scale farmers and some rural laborers and a determination to establish a representative body, possibly reflecting the much more powerful and prestigious **Sociedad Rural Argentina** founded in 1866 to represent the proprietors of large-scale modernizing *estancias*. The FAA was especially active soon after its foundation and during the interwar decades, coordinating representations to government, landlords, and business interests like grain dealers, suppliers, and transport companies. Now an umbrella organization, it was most recently prominent during the **farm protests** of the early 21st century and campaigns for such things as rural credit and the diffusion of new rural technology, as well as offering advice and support directed at small family farms.

FEDERAL CAPITAL. Official designation of the city of **Buenos Aires** from 1880 to 1995. *See* FEDERALIZATION OF THE CITY OF BUENOS AIRES.

FEDERAL INTERVENTION. Authority granted to the executive power to intervene in the affairs of the provinces, first established by the **Constitution of 1853**. Grounds for intervention include the preservation of the republican order and political integrity of the country, in response to a request by provincial authorities for assistance, and to comply with a request for such from **Congress**. In order to effect an intervention, the president is required to appoint an interventor and provide him (or her) with the necessary powers, including **military** or police capabilities, should such be required. During the oligarchic republic (1880–1916), when politics were circumscribed and elections "directed," the power was little used. The Radical ascendancy (1916–1930) witnessed several interventions, usually on the grounds of rectifying electoral irregularities and of opposition victories. All but two of the provinces were intervened to secure the acceptance of the **military coup of 1930**, and subsequently the **Concordancia** (1932–1943) intervened in specific provinces to secure a necessary majority in the electoral college. Following the **presidential** and **congressional elections of 1946**, the administration of **Juan Domingo Perón** used its majority in Congress to invoke intervention where election results proved inconvenient. Following most military coups of the 1950s and 1960s, the power of federal intervention was the legal device by which democratically elected provincial administrations were turned out and generals or admirals appointed to head them. With the restoration of democracy in 1983, there were no interventions during the presidency of **Raúl Alfonsín**. **Carlos Saúl Menem** was only marginally less abstemious; in his 10-year presidency there were three interventions, largely due to the inability of provincial administrations to deal with local crises. There was one intervention during the truncated presidency of **Fernando de la Rúa**, and another during the presidency of **Néstor Kirchner**. Although the system is open to abuse, and was abused before and after 1916, since 1983 interventions have been considerably less frequent and more in keeping with the spirit and letter of the constitution.

FEDERALISM/FEDERALISTS. A term from the **independence** and early national periods, used by proponents of a project for nation building that envisaged a would-be Argentina composed of a loose confederation of provinces, possibly even of autonomous states. This form of postindependence nationhood was the antithesis of the highly centralized, secular, liberal model proposed by **Unitarians**. Federalism was particularly influenced by the chaos of the independence period, especially following the **May Revolution of 1810** and ensuing civil war and regional conflicts. Federalists also regarded the Unitarian project as ill suited to the needs of the country and the nature of the times, as well as objecting to the politics of liberalism and secularism. The Federalist cause was particularly associated with **Juan Manuel de Rosas**, **caudillo** of the province of **Buenos Aires**, who served as governor of the province for much of the period between 1829 and 1852 and, in effect, head of state, as many interior provinces delegated the conduct of foreign affairs to the province of Buenos Aires.

Rosas governed without a constitution, defended the interests of Buenos Aires against other provinces and states, maintaining order by constructing loose alliances with caudillos in the interior. Most Federalists did not recognize the idea of a nation-state developed in Europe and then taking form in other parts of Latin America. While Unitarians had been prepared to devote the resources of Buenos Aires to constructing a nation, Rosas was an aggressive defender of Buenos Aires self-interest, a stance that critics depicted as economically exploiting the interior in order to subordinate provinces to dominance from Buenos Aires. Regardless, the rhetoric of Federalism and provincial autonomy was sustained through the Rosas ascendancy. European liberal ideals were rejected. Roman Catholicism was defended and integrated into the system of government. In place of constitutionalism and elections, the Rosas system favored mass demonstration of public support, an identification with the regime by means of symbols and slogans—red was the official color, with tokens worn by virtually all. Aspects of the regime prefigured elements of 20th-century **populism**. In the early 21st century, Peronist organizations in the interior reminted the term *Federalist* to signal opposition to Buenos Aires–dominated factions of the party. Present-day conflicts between the federal government and provincial administrations over the distribution of fiscal resources would be recognized by early 19th-century Federalists and Unitarians.

FEDERALIZATION OF THE CITY OF BUENOS AIRES. The federalization of **Buenos Aires** in 1880, on the eve of the presidency of former general **Julio A. Roca,** marked the end of the process of **national organization** underway for decades. The principal features of the federalization, officially implemented on 6 December, were the separation of the city from the jurisdiction of the province, which would construct a new provincial capital in **La Plata**; the creation of the federal district (**federal capital**) in place of the former municipality of Buenos Aires, which would be directly administered by the central government; and the declaration of the city as the national capital, the exclusive seat of the national government. The new federal district was considerably larger than the old municipality. Parts of the province were included in the new capital: the *partidos* of Belgrano and Flores were almost totally incorporated, as was a section of the *partido* of San Martín.

The status and jurisdiction of the city of Buenos Aires changed considerably during the 19th century. At the beginning of the century, it was the center of the **Viceroyalty of the River Plate**, an administrative unit of the Spanish Empire formed in 1776 and which included present-day **Bolivia, Paraguay,** and **Uruguay** in addition to Argentina. As such, the fiscal resources of the territory—principally taxes on the production of silver—flowed to Buenos Aires, deployed to cover the costs of administration and defense and, sometimes, fund transfers to other parts of the empire. At **independence**, aspirant authorities in Buenos Aires were committed to maintaining the territorial and fiscal integrity of the former colony. **Bernardino Rivadavia,** first national constitutional president, who favored a strong, centralized state, proposed the "nationalization" of the city, meaning that the resources of the city should be placed at the disposal of the new republic. With regions of the former viceroyalty seeking their own independence—a process that resulted in a loss of control of silver production in Upper Peru/Bolivia—this meant revenue generated at the port of Buenos Aires, the center for **foreign trade**. As the principal source of government revenue shifted from taxes on silver production to tariffs on exports and imports, Buenos Aires **Federalists** violently opposed the "federalization" of the Buenos Aires customs house. During the Federalist ascendancy, epitomized by the rule of the **caudillo Juan Manuel de Rosas**, governor of the province of Buenos Aires, what would become Argentina consisted of a group of autonomous jurisdictions. While several interior provinces conferred on Rosas authority to handle their **foreign relations**, from 1829 to 1852 there was no nation-state, and no national capital. The city of Buenos Aires was the capital of the province—that was the limit of its formal jurisdiction. With the fall of Rosas, the province and city maintained this arrangement, refusing to participate in the project of national consolidation enshrined in the **Constitution of 1853**. Between 1852 and 1862, the city of **Paraná** was designated the "national" capital, the city of Buenos Aires continuing solely as the seat of government of the autonomous state of Buenos Aires.

When the province agreed to rejoin the other provinces, and until 1880, the city served as both the provincial and national capital. It was an uneasy arrangement: as "guests" in the provincial capital, members of the federal administration were, in effect, dependent on handouts from the province. Disputes about revenue sharing and about the presidential succession in 1874 and 1880 brought matters to a head. As skirmishes threatened full-blown civil war, Roca, fresh from a victorious Indian campaign in the south—the final stage of the **Conquest of the Desert**—exerted his authority and pushed through the federalization project sponsored by constitutional president **Nicolás Avellaneda** at the end of his term. Economic growth associated with the export boom that followed resulted in the beautification of Buenos Aires and its emergence as a great metropolis, in keeping with its status as the capital of what, until the 1940s, was one of the most dynamic economies in the world. Since 1880, Buenos Aires's status as federal capital was challenged only once, during the presidency of **Raúl Alfonsín**, when there was a project to move the capital to **Viedma**.

There have, however, been significant changes in the governance of the city. Until 1996, the head of the city administration, the mayor, was appointed by the president of the republic, assisted by a deliberative council, also nominated. Gradually, elections to the council were democratized. More significant were changes implemented with the new **Constitution of 1994**, which conferred on the city provincial status. Now officially designated the Autonomous City of Buenos Aires (Ciudad Autónoma de Buenos Aires), it is no longer the Capital Federal. Since 1996, city mayors have been directly elected; the city Legislative Council enjoys the same status as provincial assemblies; the city returns three senators to the National Senate, as does each province. **Fernando de la Rúa**, the future president, was the first directly, democratically elected mayor.

FERNÁNDEZ, ALBERTO ÁNGEL (1959–). Lawyer and politician trained at the **University of Buenos Aires** in criminal law. Fernández subsequently became an expert in finance and insurance, serving in this capacity on various national and international official bodies as well as in private business associations. His political career entailed periods as an elected member of the legislative council of the city of **Buenos Aires** and the federal **Congress**. His political affiliations and contacts-cum-sponsors have shifted considerably over time, perhaps reflecting an intellectual journey and contacts with the worlds of business and insurance in addition to politics. Initially closely connected with **Eduardo Duhalde** when the latter was governor of the province of **Buenos Aires**, Fernández served in the **Ministry of Economy** during the presidency of **Carlos Saúl Menem** under **Domingo Cavallo**, where he handled trade negotiations. At this time, he was a member of the governing **Partido Justicialista** (PJ). In 2000, he was elected to the Buenos Aires city legislature for **Acción por la República**, the party created by Cavallo, who had by then broken with Menem. A few years later, he was associated with the Kirchnerist **Frente para la Victoria/Partido Justicialista** (FpV/PJ) and obtained his most prominent national role. In 2003, he was chosen by President **Néstor Kirchner** as chief of the cabinet of ministers, a position akin to that of prime minister created by the **Constitution of 1994**. He held this position for the whole Néstor Kirchner presidency and retained it for several months at the beginning of the presidency of **Cristina Fernández de Kirchner**. Having been in post from 2003 to 2008, he remains the longest serving cabinet chief since the post was created. As cabinet secretary, he headed the government team responsible for negotiations with the rural sector during the **farm protests** of 2007–2008, when farmers complained about penal taxation. The negotiations were unsuccessful. Fernández was reported to be a lukewarm supporter of Cristina Fernández, although finally endorsing her bid for the presidency; the course of negotiations with farmers may have further damaged his reputation with the incoming president.

From time to time, Fernández has been connected with the probusiness **Unión del Centro Democrático** (UCeDe), though he was rumored to harbor presidential ambitions and attempted to obtain the endorsement of the PJ for the **presidential election of 2011**. By then, he was aligned with the anti-Kirchner wing of the PJ, the **Frente Renovador/Partido Justicialista** (FV/PJ) and headed the political campaign of **Sergio Massa** in the **presidential election of 2015**. He remains a prominent figure among PJ factions and has further distanced himself from the former *presidenta*, describing her as a barrier to the renewal of the PJ and to the emergence of new, credible leaders. He should not be confused with **Aníbal Fernández**, a more prominent member of the Kirchner coterie, who is no relation. *See also* COBOS, JULIO CÉSAR CLETO (1955–).

FERNÁNDEZ, ANÍBAL DOMINGO (1957–). A career politician from the province of **Buenos Aires**, he trained as an accountant at the National University of Lomas de Zamora, a municipality in the Greater Buenos Aires conurbation. Fernández emerged as a "super loyalist" of the Kirchners and, for some, an éminence grise of the Kirchner era.

Initially embarking on an administrative career as a provincial civil servant, like many others Fernández soon entered politics, rising to become one of the most powerful figures in the administrations of **Néstor Kirchner** and **Cristina Fernández de Kirchner** (no relation), holding several of the highest offices of state. Beginning in the early 1980s as an *asesor* (advisor) of the Budget Committee of the provincial senate, and serving the municipalities of Quilmes and Lomas de Zamora in a similar capacity, by 1985 he had been appointed secretary to the powerful Peronist block in the Buenos Aires senate. The line between his administrative functions and political activities became increasingly blurred, and in 1991 he was elected mayor of Quilmes. By 1994, he was a member of the provincial constituent assembly, chairing the electoral commission; in 1995, he was elected to the provincial senate; and, by 1999, was head of the Quilmes branch of the **Partido Justicialista** (PJ), when Governor **Carlos Ruckauf** appointed him secretary of labor, becoming minister in 2001. Fernández's first federal appointments came during the interim administration of **Eduardo Duhalde**, who first appointed him secretary to the presidency, early in 2002, and then minister of production. He was elected to the National **Congress** in 2003 but resigned later that year on appointment as minister of interior by President Néstor Kirchner, a position he held until 2007, going on to serve as minister of justice from 2007 to 2009 and as head of the cabinet (roughly prime minister) from 2009 to 2011 in the first administration of President Fernández de Kirchner. He resigned from the latter post on election to the National Senate to represent his home province in late 2011, until appointed once more as secretary to the presidency in December 2014, a position he held for three months until being promoted to head of the cabinet again, a position he held until the end of the Kirchner regime in December 2015.

Fernández's whole political career was dogged by controversy and scandal, including multiple charges of **corruption**, beginning with his election as mayor of Quilmes. He was charged with misappropriating public funds in 1994 and, while at the Justice Ministry, seeking to influence court decisions in cases dealing with corruption and crimes involving murder and drug dealing—indeed, there were several instances in which he was rumored to be directly involved in assassinations and money laundering. Unsparing in his defense of the Kirchners, Fernández antagonized fellow politicians inside and outside the PJ and was involved in several public confrontations with figures he regarded as critical of the regime, including prominent intellectuals and media personalities. He harbored ambitions to become governor of the province of Buenos Aires in 2007 and was disappointed when **Daniel Scioli** was nominated by the PJ.

By 2014, he was canvasing support to succeed Cristina Fernández de Kirchner in the 2015 presidential election, but he was again pipped at the post by Scioli, who received Fernández de Kirchner's backing to head the **Frente para la Victoria/Partido Justicialista** (FpV/PJ) ticket. Fernández instead stood for the governorship of the province of Buenos Aires. He was roundly defeated by the opposition candidate, **María Eugenia Vidal**, despite being in control of the formidable FpV/PJ party machine in the province. Fernández's rejection by voters was largely attributed to his unsavory reputation. *See also* CONGRESSIONAL ELECTIONS OF 2015.

FERNÁNDEZ, ROQUE BENJAMIN (1947–). Academic economist and civil servant; former head of the **Banco Central de la República Argentina** (BCRA) and minister of economy. Trained in economics at the Universities of **Córdoba** and Chicago, sometimes described as one of the Chicago Boys, Fernández was founder of the **Centro de Estudios Macroeconomocs de Argentina** (CEMA), now a university (hence UCEMA).

With the CEMA dedicated to research and teaching in the field of market economics, it was unsurprising that Fernández was the first choice of then minister of economy **Domingo Cavallo** to head the BCRA when the **Convertibility Plan** was introduced—among other elements, the plan instituted the autonomy of the central bank and charged it with maintaining the dual **currency** arrangement that involved the US dollar and the Argentina peso circulating alongside each other at a parity of one to one. When Cavallo and President **Carlos Saúl Menem** parted company in 1996, Menem appointed Fernández to replace Cavallo. As such, Fernández was one of the key figures of the Cavallo–Menem economic project from 1991 until 1999, first as central bank head and then as minister of economy. During this time, he maintained the stability of the currency, notwithstanding several external shocks such as those provoked by the currency devaluation in Mexico and financial market crises in **Brazil**, Russia, and the Far East.

He has held visiting professorships at universities in **Chile** and the **United States** and has worked as a consultant in Washington at the International Monetary Fund and World Bank. He continues to publish academic papers in the fields of theoretical and applied economics and has written about his experiences in office.

FERNÁNDEZ MEIJIDE, GRACIELA (1931–). Human rights activist and politician whose family suffered during the **Dirty War**—a son was "disappeared." When her son became a "statistic" among the **Desaparecidos** in 1976, Fernández Meijide embarked on an investigative campaign to ascertain the fate of those taken during the bloody dictatorship of the **Proceso de Reorganización Nacional**. She argued that families had the right to know what had happened to loved ones, and that the perpetrators of abduction, torture, and murder should be brought to justice. Her tireless efforts attracted public attention. Following the return of democracy with the victory of **Raúl Alfonsín** in the **presidential election of 1983**, she was offered a position on the **Comision Nacional sobre la Desaparición de Personas** (CONADEP)—the National Commission for Disappeared People—set up by Alfonsín. Approached by several **political parties** who wished to capitalize on the esteem that she enjoyed, she finally became a member of the **Frente País Solidario** (FREPASO) in the early 1990s, a newly formed left-of-center coalition. Her decision to assume a political career was influenced by the passage of legislation—the **Ley de Punto Final** and **Ley de Obediencia Debida**—intended to bring closure to the issue of the disappearances and prosecution of the heads of the military juntas that governed the country from 1976 to 1983. She was successively elected to the Chamber of Deputies and the National Senate on the FREPASO ticket and served as minister of social development and the environment for about 15 months in the short-lived **Alianza** government headed by President **Fernando de la Rúa**. She had stood against De la Rúa in the Alianza primaries. Having been defeated by him, she declined to run as his vice president in the **congressional** and **presidential elections of 1999**, deferring to her FREPASO colleague **Carlos "Chacho" Álvarez**, but was prevailed upon to accept the ministerial appointment after the elections. When the Alianza government collapsed at the end of 2001, she retired from political life.

Although she has since done much to reestablish a positive public image, Fernández Meijide's reputation was seriously damaged during her short ministerial career. First, she appointed her sister to head the **Programa de Atención Médica Integrada** (PAMI), a dependency of the ministry with a very large budget. Her sister was charged with misusing officials funds; at the time, the sister's husband (that is Fernández Meijide's brother-in-law) was the chief financial officer of the agency. The brother-in-law was the first political appointee of the De la Rúa administration to be charged with **corruption**, seriously damaging one of the main campaign planks during the election that it would be a clean government. Secondly, Fernández Meijide was discovered to have placed her tennis coach on the ministerial payroll. The scandals had an immediate and dramatic impact on her reputation, which plummeted.

Fernández Meijide's engagement with the CONADEP, coupled with the institutionalist stance that she adopted, caused difficulties with some of the other groups campaigning for justice for the families of the disappeared, for example, **Hebe de Bonafini** of the **Madres de Plaza de Mayo**. Fernández Meijide has also been critical of the position on human rights taken by the administrations of Presidents **Néstor Kirchner** and **Cristina Fernández de Kirchner**, accusing them of making political capital out of the issue. Despite the damage to her reputation suffered at the end of her ministerial career, Fernández Meijide's views are widely noticed, much to the annoyance of those she upbraids. *See also* BIGNONE, REYNALDO BENITO (1928–2018); DISPOSICIÓN FINAL; ESCUELA SUPERIOR DE MECÁNICA DE LA ARMADA (ESMA); GALTIERI, LEOPOLDO FORTUNATO (1926–2003); MASSERA, EMILIO EDUARDO (1925–2010); MILITARY JUNTAS, TRIALS OF THE; MINISTRY OF SOCIAL DEVELOPMENT; VIDELA, JORGE RAFAEL (1925–2013); VIOLA, ROBERTO EDUARDO (1924–1994); WAR TO ANNIHILATE SUBVERSION.

FERNÁNDEZ MEIJIDE, ROSA GRACIELA CASTAGNOLA DE. *See* FERNÁNDEZ MEIJIDE, GRACIELA (1931–).

FERRER, ALDO (1927–2016). Economist and leading proponent of economic nationalism in Argentina; minister of economy (1970–1971). He is best known for his now classic work *La Economíia Argentina*, which was first published in 1963, translated into English, and revised numerous times, most recently in 2004.

Ferrer was appointed to head the **Ministry of Economy** in October 1970 by de facto president General **Roberto Levingston**, pursuing a policy of *Argentinización*, with explicit support for national capital and private national firms to enter sectors of vanguard technology and basic **industry** and for a moderate redistribution of income to boost consumption. However, the project did not question the goal of an "open" economy or Argentina's insertion into the world economy, simply demanding a renegotiated dependency and a greater role for the state and national capital in the industrialization process.

Argentinización aimed to redirect and redistribute credit in favor of domestically owned firms. Growth in liquidity was achieved by lowering the reserve requirements restricting loan operations, and it was given a nationalist tinge by mandating that new loans go specifically to enterprises with predominantly national capital. In addition, the *Argentinización* of credit was designed to force transnational corporations to increase their reliance on external loans and new investment from parent companies in order to bolster the foreign exchange position of the **Banco Central de la República Argen-**

tina (BCRA). The nationalist Ley de Compre Nacional (Buy National Law) was passed in December 1970. It obligated government agencies and companies to channel purchases away from imported goods toward local basic industries using national technologies, and therefore attempted to make it possible for domestic industry to compete on an equal footing with transnationals.

Ferrer's project soon ran into difficulties. The *Argentinización* of credit increased the country's growing **foreign debt** and placed new burdens on the balance of payments, and it enabled transnationals to take advantage of the situation by extending payment schedules to local suppliers and by increasing the prices of vital inputs consumed by domestic buyers. The Ley de Compre Nacional was extremely hard to implement and made ineffective by the microeconomic needs of individual government-owned corporations and the macroeconomic limitations of the state budget.

Matters were aggravated by worsening social tensions and mounting economic problems that resulted in a full-blown fiscal crisis and accelerating inflation. To contain the latter, new legislation created the Comisión Nacional de Precios and empowered the secretary of industry and commerce to fix prices for both strategic industrial goods and items of popular mass consumption. Supplementary legislation awarded the state expanded powers to regulate prices and supply by overseeing commercialization and distribution, and the authority to set maximum prices and profit margins. Ferrer's final price control measure, the imposition of a *veda* banning the domestic sale of beef on certain days so as to increase supplies for export, was the most notorious and generated such furor that it laid bare the opposition of the private sector to Ferrer and his policies.

General **Alejandro Agustin Lanusse** replaced Levingston as de facto president in March 1971 and initially retained Ferrer as minister of economy. However, the minister's days were numbered. With the *Argentinización* project no longer viable and in the absence of a coherent alternative, Ferrer was dismissed in May 1971. *See also* DEVELOPMENTALISM/DEVELOPMENTALIST; ECONOMIC CRISES; ECONOMY; FOREIGN TRADE.

FERROCARRILES ARGENTINOS (FFAA). Formed as Empresa de Ferrocarriles del Estado Argentino (EFEA) in 1948 and rebranded in 1949, for much of the second half of the 20th century FFAA was the official name of the state-owned railway network, an amalgam of formerly foreign-owned and government regional lines. At the time, it was one of the largest state-owned businesses in Latin America. Currently, the operational name of passenger services is Trenes Argentinos.

The first railway was opened in 1857, the Sociedad Anónima Camino Ferrocarril al Oeste, later known as the Ferrocarril Oeste (FO). Franchised by the **Buenos Aires** provincial government, the company was privately owned, financed by a group of merchants and landowners, but was soon purchased by the province. Around the same time, the federal government was negotiating with foreign consortia to build a line from **Rosario** to the interior—what would become the **Central Argentine Railway Company** (CAR). Railway development in Argentina was late and slow—railways were already operating in other parts of Latin America. The delay is explained by the political uncertainly of the period, epitomized by the regime of the Buenos Aires **caudillo Juan Manuel de Rosas**. With **national organization**, rail expansion accelerated. The two processes were mutually reinforcing: political consolidation delivered order, order encouraged the financing of rail construction, railways consolidated order. **Foreign trade**, investment, and **immigration** grew.

There was modest yet steady growth in the network in the late 1860s and the mid-1870s, but the first major boom did not occur until the 1880s—the railway mania that followed the conclusion of the **Conquest of the Desert** and the political settlement secured during the presidency of **Julio A. Roca**. Many early private companies were beneficiaries of federal and provincial government profit guarantees; there was an exponential growth in the number of companies with guarantees in the late 1880s, along with considerable government construction financed by foreign borrowing. This was when the main trunk lines were built or projected. The boom came to an end with the **Baring Crisis**—indeed, the mania played an important role in triggering the crisis and led to the **privatization** of several state railways. Another massive rail construction boom occurred in the 10 years preceding the First World War, with modest network expansion in the mid- to late 1920s. Between 1893 and 1930, network consolidation and growth were almost entirely accounted for by foreign-owned enterprises, mainly British though with substantial French participation. Thereafter, state-owned companies were responsible for network expansion. Government investment in infrastructure was a feature of the **Concordancia** period, especially during the administration of President **Agustín P. Justo**. Justo had been trained as a military engineer, and his regime viewed public works projects as a means of generating political support and fostering economic recovery. Already in 1915, Argentina had the 10th largest rail system in the world, a ranking that was consolidated during the interwar decades. In the 1930s, the government also began a program of road building that would ultimately undermine the viability of the railways. Road building, which featured in the **Pinedo Plan**, fostered the growth of motor vehicle import and assembly, principally from the **United States**.

In the late 1930s, as private operators faced increased economic and financial difficulties—rail freight fell by almost a quarter during the first half of the decade, operating profits by an even larger proportion, and overseas profit remittance virtually ceased—the authorities assumed a larger presence in railway management and operation. Some British-owned lines were taken into state administration, which prepared the ground for nationalization. In 1946, the project for a mixed state–private consortium was outlined, with the gradual transfer of ownership from the private to the state sector phased over time, during which operation would remain in private (largely British) hands. There was protracted discussion about the valuation of private lines and the level of state financing. The formation of a mixed corporation was opposed by Washington, which viewed it as likely to favor **Great Britain**, the assumption being that the corporation would preference British equipment imports. These difficulties were short-circuited by outright government purchase of the railways and associated enterprises. In 1948, EFEA took over British- and French-owned companies; at this point, British companies accounted for about 60 percent of the network and French another 12 percent. Five new regional groupings were formed, largely based on former London-registered enterprises: Ferrocarril Nacional General Mitre (FCNGM), Ferrocarril Nacional General Roca (FCNGR), Ferrocarril Nacional General San Martín (FCNGSM), Ferrocarril Nacional Sarmiento, and Ferrocarril Nacional General Urquiza (FCNGU). The ex-British **Cordoba Central Railway Company** (CCR), which had been taken into government administration in 1938, was renamed the Ferrocarril Nacional General Belgrano (FCNGB). Most of the former Paris-registered lines were absorbed into these groupings. President **Juan Domingo Perón** signed the nationalization decree on 1 March 1948, declaring that the country had gained its economic independence. Accompanied by such slogans as "Perón Delivers" and "Already They [the railways] Are Argentine," a glorious future was promised. Patriotic projects included a national locomotive construction program—the first engine was name *La Justicialista* after the ruling party. Little else was delivered, though employment on the railways doubled over the next 10 years while traffic declined; highway construction in the 1950s led to further declines in rail cargo and passenger traffic.

By the 1960s, the operating deficit of FFAA was the single largest item in the federal budget and driving the fiscal deficit. Despite periodic attempts at reorganization and "rationalization," accompanied by proposals to upgrade parts of the network, the efficiency and quality of services plummeted. With little new investment and rail services deteriorating, freight traffic virtually halved between 1970 and 1990. By this time, the operating deficit was running at one million US dollars a day. Modern rail **privatization** was initiated in 1993 by President **Saúl Carlos Menem**: 30-year freight operating contracts were awarded to consortia of national and foreign operators for most lines, save FCNGB freight, which continued to be operated by a state-owned company. Most long-distance passenger services were suspended, except those taken over by the provinces. The principal commuter routes, mainly in greater Buenos Aires, were also franchised. Agreement with the

World Bank secured funds for the upgrading of some sections of the network, and there was a major recapitalization of Buenos Aires commuter services. Yet large-scale upgrading of long-distance freight routes had to wait until the early 21st century, when Chinese capital was promised, lured by the explosion in soya production.

Trenes Argentinos was officially set up in 2008 as a dependency of FFAA but only started to function in 2010, gradually absorbing services that had been privatized. Some freight and passenger operators were taken back into state hands when contracts lapsed; others were bought out. The process of renationalization was virtually completed in 2015, by which time virtually all long-distance and commuter trains operated under government control, as well as freight. Renationalization chimed with the political rhetoric and economic policy stance of the *kirchnerato*, notably that of President **Cristina Fernández de Kirchner**. The final nationalization law was tabled in **Congress** on 1 March 2015, the anniversary of the Perón decree. Ferrocarriles Argentinos Sociedad del Estado (FCASE) was launched under the banner Nuevos Ferrocarriles Argentinos, once again to much patriotic applause and promises of a new era in rail transport. The agency would take charge of renegotiating outstanding private rail contracts. In 2012 and between 2014 and 2015, some long-distance passenger services were relaunched, with regional passenger service assumed by the state entity between 2011 and 2012. (Some of these services have since been discontinued.) Flagship luxury passenger services from Buenos Aires to such cities as Mar del Plata, Rosario, **Tucumán**, and **Córdoba** were rolled out progressively. Discussions with Chinese capitalists continued through this period. In 2013, an outline document proposed investment of around US$2.5 billion in freight network refurbishment, most provided by **China**. An agreement was signed in 2014 by the two governments; it was ratified two years later. By 2017, these agreements had begun to bear fruit in long-distance freight line reconstruction. There was also investment in new passenger rolling stock, mainly imported from China, with the promise of the construction of Chinese-funded locomotive and rolling stock assembly and manufacturing plant, projects endorsed by President **Mauricio Macri**. When the first luxury, semi-Pullman passenger trains began to operate around 2015 with new rolling stock imported from China, humorists argued that Trenes Argentinos should be rebranded as "Trenes Chinos." *See also* ARGENTINE NORTH EASTERN RAILWAY COMPANY (ANE); BUENOS AYRES & PACIFIC RAILWAY COMPANY (BA& P); BUENOS AYRES WESTERN RAILWAY COMPANY (BAW); ECONOMIC CRISES; ECONOMY; FOREIGN DEBT/FOREIGN INVESTMENT; INDUSTRY; MIRANDA, MIGUEL (1891–1953); MIRANDA–EADY AGREEMENT; STATE-OWNED ENTERPRISES (SOEs); TRANSPORTATION.

FIGUEROA ALCORTA, JOSÉ MARÍA CORNELIO (1860–1931). Elected as vice president to **Manuel Quintana** in 1904, he succeeded to the presidency on the death of Quintana in 1906, serving out his term until 1910. A native of the city of **Córdoba**, he was a journalist, politician, and Freemason. He held several posts in the province, serving in the Córdoba senate, before appointment to several positions in the federal government. Although held hostage during the 1905 revolt organized by the **Unión Cívica Radical** (UCR), he recognized that the system of oligarchic rule required change. He broke with the strongman of the old order, **Julio A. Roca**, adopting a less hard-line response to social protests of the period, and facilitated the election of **Roque Sáenz Peña** in 1910, who went on to promote electoral reform—the **Sáenz Peña Law** of 1912.

FIGUEROLA, JOSÉ MIGUEL FRANCISCO LUIS (1897–1970). A leading Peronist figure and secretary of technical affairs (1946–1949). Born in Catalonia, he became a specialist in labor relations and social statistics. Figuerola served in the Labor Ministry in Spain during the dictatorship of General Primo de Rivera and achieved international recognition due to his interest in statistics and expertise on social legislation. For a time, he represented Spain in the International Labour Organization in Geneva and had been sent to Italy to study the structure of Mussolini's labor programs.

Figuerola migrated to Argentina following the downfall of Primo de Rivera in 1930 and joined the National Department of Labor as both head of its statistics division and chief of professional organization. Although this department had been created in 1907, it had little clout until Colonel **Juan Domingo Perón** arrived on the scene in 1943. Figuerola quickly earned Perón's trust, as he had ample knowledge of social and labor legislation, management, and statistics. The demographic data he showed Perón persuaded the latter that the potential power of the urban working class was the key to political success. Perón was also influenced by Figuerola's book *La colaboración social en Hispanoamérica*, which appeared in 1943 and advocated the formal integration of apolitical **trade unions** into the state structure and control of their activity in accordance with state guidelines.

Figuerola and **Juan Atilio Bramuglia** helped Perón transform the Labor Department into a secretariat with ministerial status, which became the springboard to his career in civilian politics. Perón made Figuerola secretary general of the **Consejo Nacional de Posguerra** in 1944 and, after he won the **presidential election of 1946**, appointed him secretary of technical affairs. This was a ministerial portfolio with responsibility for coordinating relations between government offices and all the organizations connected to the national government.

As secretary of technical affairs, Figuerola drafted a great deal of legisla-tion and wrote several policy documents for the **Partido Peronista** (PP) as well as major speeches for the president. He is regarded as the architect of the Five-Year Plan of development and modernization that was implemented in 1947. The plan envisaged a gradual progression toward industrial develop-ment: first, to collect precise information on Argentine requirements, particu-larly in the energy, transport, and equipment sectors; second, to assess the capacity of various industries to produce the relevant goods and services and advance a strategy to raise productivity; third, to create industrial zones, which would be established in the interior so that all regions of the country could enjoy a similar degree of modernization, an objective that meant build-ing new roads and energy distribution grids. Perón and Figuerola successful-ly presented the Five-Year Plan to **Congress** in October 1946 in two volumes detailing government priorities. Nevertheless, for reasons that were totally unrelated to planning by the secretary of technical affairs, the highly ambi-tious Five-Year Plan was not very successful.

In late 1948, the president awarded Figuerola the job of drafting a new constitution to replace the **Constitution of 1853**. But his work was deemed unsatisfactory by a number of Peronist leaders and Perón himself. A congres-sional committee subsequently laid the bases for the definitive version passed in 1949. Moreover, by this time, Figuerola's influence was deeply resented, not least by the first lady, who wanted him out of the president's inner circle.

A clause in the **Constitution of 1949** determined that only native Argen-tines could serve as federal government ministers, forcing Figuerola to re-sign. Yet he remained loyal to Perón and Peronism, and for this he was imprisoned by the de facto administration that governed Argentina between 1955 and 1958. In 1963, Figuerola was named secretary general of the Insti-tuto Superior de Investigaciones Sociales and technical adviser to the Federación Gremial de la Carne and the Sindicatos Unidos Petroleros del Estado; he also served as parliamentary secretary to the Chamber of Deputies in the years 1965–1966.

FIRMENICH, MARIO EDUARDO (1948–). One of the founders of the **Montoneros** and one of its main leaders from 1970 until the guerrilla group's formal dissolution in the early 1980s. A graduate of the Colegio Nacional Buenos Aires, he joined the Juventud Estudiantil Católica (JEC) together with **Fernando Abal Medina** and **Carlos Gustavo Ramus** in 1964. There the group met Father **Carlos Mugica**, who eventually parted company with them. In early 1967, Firmenich joined the Comando Camilo Torres, named after the Marxist Colombian priest, which had been set up by **Juan García Elorrio**. After the latter broke with Abal Medina, he became one of the founders of the Montoneros in 1968.

Firmenich participated in the **Aramburazo** and, following the deaths of both Abal Medina and Ramus in September 1970, rose to the leadership of the organization. He was secretary general of the Montoneros, becoming its political ideologue, and is frequently considered a representative of the more militarist wing of the organization.

From exile, **Juan Domingo Perón**, who was manipulating both the right and left within his movement, actively encouraged the Montoneros. That would change, especially after his return to Argentina and victory in the **presidential election of September 1973**. The **Frente Justicialista de Liberación** (FREJULI) was barely savoring its electoral triumph when **José Ignacio Rucci**, secretary general of the **Confederación General del Trabajo**, was assassinated. In early 1974, Perón pressed the "Montonero deputies" in Congress to back a harsh antisubversion law or resign their seats; they resigned and were expelled from the party, which prompted Firmenich to distance himself from the government. After Perón very publicly broke with the Montoneros on Labor Day 1974, the guerrilla group resumed the armed struggle under Firmenich's direction.

Attempting to destabilize the government, the Montoneros assassinated former minister of interior **Arturo Mor Roig** in July 1974. In September 1974, the organization went underground and organized the kidnapping of the **Born brothers**, for whom the guerrilla group was paid a record ransom. One year later, the ill-fated government of **Isabel Perón** declared the Montoneros illegal.

Following the **military coup of 1976**, the organization was virtually wiped out in the **War to Annihilate Subversion**. But it refused to accept defeat and, totally disconnected from the Peronists, created the Partido Montonero Peronista (MPM) in April 1977. A misnamed "counteroffensive" was launched by the guerrillas in 1979, which ended in disaster. That same year, Firmenich went to Nicaragua, where he collaborated with the new revolutionary Sandinista government.

During the tenure of President **Raúl Alfonsín** in the second half of the 1980s, Firmenich was captured in **Brazil**. He was extradited, judged, and condemned to 30 years in prison but then pardoned by President **Carlos Saúl Menem** in December 1990. Firmenich went on to graduate in economics from the **University of Buenos Aires** (UBA) in 1996 and then completed a doctorate in Barcelona. He lives in **Spain**.

FONTENLA, NORMA (1930–1971). Renowned Argentine prima ballerina. As a child, she attended the Conservatorio Nacional de Música in **Buenos Aires** and was later accepted into the dance school of the **Teatro Colón**, the country's premier opera house. Fontenla became a member of its ballet company and was eventually named its prima ballerina.

She joined the Rio de Janeiro Ballet in the early 1960s, and with them made her first European tours. Once she returned to Argentina, Fontenla led the Colón ballet in major productions. Most notable was her 1967 performance in Adolphe Adam's *Giselle*, in which she collaborated with Margot Fonteyn and Rudolph Nureyev. In 1970, Fontenla was invited to direct the ballet company at the famed La Scala Opera House in Milan. Her previous collaboration with Nureyev led him to choose the Teatro Colón to perform Peter Tchaikovsky's *The Nutcracker* for the 1971 season. Its success was followed by a series of performances by Nureyev for Argentine television alongside Fontenla. Together with seven other fellow members of the ballet company, she died in an aviation accident on route to perform in the Patagonian city of **Trelew**.

FOREIGN DEBT/FOREIGN INVESTMENT. Overseas borrowing and direct foreign investment have played a prominent role in the Argentine **economy** since **independence**. Sometimes the process has proved sustainable, other times not.

The first foreign loan, the famous **Baring** Loan, was floated in 1824 for the government of the province of **Buenos Aires**, arranged by the then finance minister **Bernardino Rivadavia** to cover the costs of independence and fund such public projects as the modernization of the port of Buenos Aires and road construction. Nominally £1 million, little more than half that sum reached the government, the difference being swallowed by commissions and the retention in London of funds to cover the first coupon and amortization payments. The loan was soon in default, triggering a series of protracted negotiations with foreign bondholders that prefigured similar defaults like those around 1890 and 2001/2.

An agreement with Barings in 1857 permitted a return to foreign capital markets, stimulating a revival of foreign investment in the 1860s and new state borrowing in the 1870s. Notwithstanding external shocks, increased confidence facilitated a massive foreign credit and investment boom from the 1880s to the 1920s, funded by an agro-export surge driven by **immigration** and infrastructure modernization. Commodity exports and increasing fiscal resources ensured that debt-led growth was largely sustainable. Later periods of debt-led growth proved less sustainable.

Unusually among debtor economies, Argentina was able to borrow during the 1930s, though public opinion was turning against foreign investment, questioning its cost and utility. In part, this was due to the politics and the economics of **Concordancia** administrations. Economic nationalism was in the ascendant. During the first presidency of **Juan Domingo Perón**, the government paid off the foreign debt and repatriated much direct foreign investment, using funds accumulated during the Second World War by supplying **commodities** to the Allies. Around 1949, the country was virtually debt free and had become a net creditor. Nationalist sentiments apart, some administrations of the late 1950s and 1960s sought to encourage foreign direct investment to promote national **industry** and established relations with the Washington agencies to facilitate institutional borrowing. The experience proved less than positive: exports were insufficient to service the flow of foreign capital. Another period of debt-led growth followed during the **Proceso de Reorganización Nacional** under the auspices of Minister of Economy **José Alfredo Martínez de Hoz**: foreign investment and overseas borrowing were intended to stimulate economic modernization and market discipline. While there was some lending by the Washington agencies, by far the greatest proportion of public debt was handled by international banks operating in the eurodollar market. Excess borrowing—and the application of funds to nonproductive actives resulted in another crash.

Despite the so-called lost decade that followed the debt/loan crisis of the 1980s and difficult relations with overseas lenders during the administration of President **Raúl Alfonsín**, foreign borrowing and the promotion of direct foreign investment became the hallmark of the presidencies of **Carlos Saúl Menem** under the **Convertibility Plan**. In addition to inflows of hot money and much needed long-term capital investment, the volume of government domestic and overseas loans soared as the administration borrowed to cover a shortfall in fiscal receipts. By 2001, the level of borrowing was out of control, precipitating the resignation of the government of President **Fernando de la Rúa** and default on the public debt—the largest public default in international financial history. The debt then stood at US$132,000 million. President **Néstor Kirchner** came to an agreement with most foreign creditors in 2005, but the country remained a pariah, and its reputation suffered further as a result of nationalist rhetoric during the administrations of President **Cristina Fernández de Kirchner**. Sustained new government borrowing on overseas capital markets only became feasible again during the government of President **Mauricio Macri**, who reached an agreement with foreign bondholders who had not settled in 2005 and consciously sought to cultivate foreign investors.

At the end of 2017, the level of foreign debt stood at approximately US$210,000 million, equal to about a third of gross domestic product (GDP), that is, down from over 100 percent of GDP at the time of the 2001 default, and down from 60 percent following the 2005 settlement with bondholders. *See also* ARAMBURU, PEDRO EUGENIO (1903–1970); BARING CRISIS; ECONOMIC CRISES; FRONDIZI, ARTURO (1908–1995); GRAINS; ILLIA, ARTURO UMBERTO (1900–1983); MEAT; RODRÍGUEZ SAÁ, ADOLFO (1947–); *VENDEPATRIA(S)*; WOOL.

FOREIGN RELATIONS. Diplomatic affairs are handled by the **Ministry of Foreign Relations and Religion**, one of the historic ministries established by the **Constitution of 1853**. Relations with neighboring countries have been relatively peaceful since **independence**, save for conflict with **Brazil** in the 1820s and the devastating **War of the Triple Alliance**, when Argentina, Brazil, and **Uruguay** were arranged against **Paraguay**. At distinct moments in the late 19th century and during the 1970s, relations with **Chile** have been strained by border disputes, sometimes almost resulting in open conflict. Relations with Brazil have been generally cordial since the 1820s, despite a brief moment of naval rivalry in the 1920s, resulting in a mini arms race, and aspirations of continental leadership harbored by both countries—Argentina has taken a distinctly jaundiced view of periodic discussions at the **United Nations Organization** (UN) to award Brazil a permanent seat on the Security Council as "regional" representative.

A long-standing issue in Argentine–British relations has been the dispute over the sovereignty of the **Falkland Islands** (las Islas Malvinas in Spanish). These date from British occupation of the islands in 1833. The dispute surfaced several times in the 20th century, resulting in an Argentine invasion of the islands in 1982, and generated considerable hot air during the second presidency of **Cristina Fernández de Kirchner**—both at the United Nations and in other international fora. The dispute now includes counterclaims to the British overseas territories of the South Georgia and South Sandwich Islands and overlapping claims to administrative jurisdiction in part of Antarctica. This aspect of the bilateral relationship was further soured by a claim registered with the UN in 2009 to a large part of the continental shelf in the South Atlantic. Argentine claims to the continental shelf, and to jurisdiction in Antarctica, also infringe on Chilean claims in these areas. Having been disrupted in 1982, full diplomatic relations between Argentina and **Great Britain** were restored in 1990 and improved substantially in 2015 with the election of President **Mauricio Macri**.

Argentine relations with the **United States** have been generally friendly, despite moments of considerable tension. Closely associated economically with Great Britain for almost a century after the 1840s, Argentina was suspicious of what Buenos Aires regarded as US projects for continental hegemony dressed up as continental solidarity ranging from the Pan-Americanism to the Good Neighbor Policy. This suspicion has also included such US initiatives as the creation of the Organization of American States and negotiations to establish the Free Trade Area of the Americas. In part, such tensions were underwritten by Argentine pretentions to continental leadership or primacy in Latin America.

Relations with the United States were especially strained during the 1940s, partly because of what Washington, DC, regarded as active support for Nazi Germany during the Second World War. The United States was also skeptical about domestic economic policy in Argentina during the first administration of **Juan Domingo Perón**, which it regarded as statist and unsustainable and which, given the strength of the Argentine labor movement, might have encouraged adventurism by the Soviet Union during the early years of the Cold War. Argentine antagonism to the United States was again manifest in international fora from the 1950s to the 1970s, often connected with disagreement over loans and investment and US intervention in South America and the Caribbean. Around this time, Argentina's "worldview" was shaped by membership in the Non-Aligned Movement.

US–Argentine relations were particularly cordial in the 1990s following the election of President **Carlos Saúl Menem**, only to sour once more with economic meltdown in 2001–2002, when Washington was thought to have influenced an unsympathetic response by the International Monetary Fund to requests for help. This suspicion intensified during **foreign debt** negotiations in the presidencies of **Néstor Kirchner** and Cristina Fernández de Kirchner. Mrs. Kirchner was particularly vocal in her criticism of Washington and New York in her dealings with the so-called vulture funds, that is, bankers who had acquired the bonds of creditors who had not settled in 2005 and were blocking Argentine access to overseas credit. Relations between the two countries have warmed under Macri. *See also* AGREEMENT BETWEEN ARGENTINA AND CHILE ACCEPTING PAPAL MEDIATION IN THE BEAGLE CHANNEL DISPUTE (1979); AGREEMENT BETWEEN ARGENTINA AND GREAT BRITAIN CONCERNING THE FALKLAND ISLANDS (1971); AGUIRRE LANARI, JUAN RAMÓN (1920–2017); BEAGLE CHANNEL DISPUTE; BOLIVIA; CALVO, CARLOS (1822–1906); CAPUTO, DANTE (1943–); CHACO WAR; CHINA; CONDOR MISSILE PROGRAM; COSTA MÉNDEZ, NICANOR (1922–1992); CUBA; DI TELLA, GUIDO JOSÉ MARIO (1931–2001); FALKLANDS DISPUTE; FALKLANDS WAR (2 APRIL–14 JUNE 1982); MILITARY COUP OF 1943; MIRANDA–EADY AGREEMENT; OPERACIÓN CONDOR; PERU; ROCA–RUNCIMAN PACT (1933); SPAIN; VENEZUELA.

FOREIGN TRADE. In the 1840s, Argentina—or rather, the province of **Buenos Aires**—was described as the most open **economy** in the world, notwithstanding that tariffs were the main source of government income. Around 1910, Argentina was counted among the 10 top trading nations of the world, and foreign commerce probably accounted for approximately a quarter of gross domestic product (GDP). During the early decades of the 20th century, Argentina's main trading partners were **Great Britain** and the **United States**. This situation changed after the Second World War, partly due to structural changes in the global economy and partly due to the influence of **developmentalism** and related strategies of import-substituting industrialization. Internal development, focused on promoting manufacturing, rather than export-led growth associated with the production of **commodities** for overseas markets, became the order of the day, dominating the economic policy agenda from the 1940s to the 1970s, resurfacing again as a persuasive economic ideology in official circles at the beginning of the 21st century. For much of the third quarter of the 20th century, the United States remained a key supplier of imports, while Europe was an important destination of exports—the countries of the Soviet bloc were briefly significant buyers of Argentine commodities in the 1970s. During the last decade or so of the 20th century, Argentine trade with **MERCOSUR** (mainly **Brazil**) grew rapidly, and trade with **China** proved to be particularly dynamic after around 2007.

According to World Trade Organization data, in 2016 international trade (exports and imports) accounted for almost 13 percent of GDP. The value of exports was US$57,700,000,000, ranking the country 38th in terms of global exports; the value of imports was US$55,600,000,000, ranking 43rd. The principal categories of exports were agricultural commodities and related products, 61 percent; manufactures, 28 percent; fuels, 5 percent; and miscellaneous, 6 percent. The main imports: agricultural products, 4 percent; manufactures, 82 percent; fuels, mining products, and miscellaneous items, 14 percent. The principal destinations of exports were Brazil at approximately 16 percent; the European Union, 15 percent; the United States, 8 percent; China, 8 percent; the most important sources of imports were Brazil at around 25 percent; China, 19 percent; the European Union, 18 percent; the United States, 13 percent. *See also* AGRICULTURAL COLONIZATION; AGRICULTURE; CATTLE; ECONOMIC CRISES; ECONOMY; *FRIGORÍFICOS*; GRAINS; INSTITUTO ARGENTINO DE PROMOCIÓN DEL INTERCAMBIO (IAPI); MAIZE; MEAT; MIRANDA–EADY AGREEMENT; PINEDO PLAN; ROCA–RUNCIMAN PACT (1933); *SALADEROS*; SHEEP; WOOL.

FORESTAL ARGENTINA S.A. A branch of the international conglomerate Forestal Tornegaleones since 2007. The company was established in its current form in 1995, though it originates in a national logging and tanning enterprise that became one of the country's pioneer global corporations.

First located in the **Chaco** region of Argentina and geared to logging and the production of quebracho or tannin extract, Forestal came to own or operate timber plantations in neighboring countries as well as overseas. Its history illustrates how, with access to international finance, the firm fostered consolidation within the sector though amalgamation and acquisitions to become a dominant world player, later diversifying into related activities. At the beginning of the 20th century, Forestal began to exhibit proto–transnational corporation characteristics, expanding horizontally and vertically from a core activity to consolidate a global position.

Logging in Argentina was a comparatively late developer; although the Chaco was known to contained large stands of timber, and the properties of the local red quebracho were highly valued (the wood was extremely hard, and the percentage of tannin yielded by Chaco reds was significantly higher than average), development in the area was hindered by its isolation. Until the turn of the century, logging was largely a by-product of land clearing for **agricultural colonization** in the province of **Santa Fe**. In addition to locational disadvantages, at this point the lumber business was further constrained by a shortage of labor and faced competition from southern **Brazil** and North America. Producers in these and other areas enjoyed lower domestic transport costs and were closer to the principal markets in Germany and the **United States**. Lack of an extract processing plant also raised transport costs, reducing access to overseas markets. Nevertheless, by the late 1900s, between 250,000 and 300,000 tons of quebracho balks were exported annually. The steady growth of timber encouraged several small firms to engage in extract production. By 1908, the volume of tannin extract exported reached 68,625 tons, compared with 291,423 tons of timber. Extract production was stimulated by the First World War. After the conflict, extract output increased while timber exports fell away, but not before the growth of the industry had been checked by the imposition in Germany of differential tariffs on timber and extract to protect domestic tannin processing plants. There was intense competition among the multitude of local Argentine producers to secure a larger share of a declining market, which drove down prices still further. Before the war, the industry was highly fragmented, characterized by small firms scattered along the upper reaches of the **Paraná** River. The typical firm was capitalized at around £30,000–£60,000 (US$145,500–291,000) and operated a single plant that yielded between 200 and 450 tons of extract per month. Distilleries were served by private narrow-gauge railways. Some firms enjoyed a connection with the national railway network; others did not. Many operations were very small, depending on outside contractors to supply logs. At the beginning of the century, there were only two large firms: the Formosa, which had £200,000 (c. US$1 million) invested in land and a refinery capable of delivering more than 1,000 tons of extract per month, and the Compañía Industrial del Chaco (sometimes reported as the Compañía Forestal del Chaco), capitalized at £348,000 (c. US$1.7 million) and which operated two processing plants with a joint output of 1,600 tons per month. Enter Forestal.

Established in 1901 and floated in 1906 to take over the land and plant of the Argentine enterprise of the same name, Forestal displaced local capital, raising funds in Berlin and London to finance the modernization, expansion, and centralization of distilling and the upgrade of transport. In addition, the process represented a substitution of capital for scarce labor in the Chaco. Later, the firm established an international system of production and distribution. The business was originally capitalized at £1 million (US$4.85 million) but rapidly issued further scrip. The board of directors included prominent local businessmen like Charles Gunther, who had investments in *estancia* **companies**, and international financiers like Baron Emile d'Erlanger. The company was registered in London, but operations were controlled from Argentina and international distribution rights for the sale of extract vested in a Hamburg-based firm.

On the outbreak of war in 1914, Forestal abandoned the Hamburg agency, setting up its own international sales division. Stimulated by opportunities for expansion provided by the First World War and the need to adjust during the postwar collapse, the company bought out or merged with surviving single-plant operators and aggressively established an unassailable position. The company gradually gained a lead position in the Chaco quebracho business, absorbing other firms or purchasing distribution rights to their extract. By the late 1920s, Forestal accounted for over two-thirds of the capital invested in the Argentine industry and over two-fifths of extract production, a position of strength that enabled it to establish the international quebracho extract pool. Besides internalizing marketing and securing control of Argentine extract production, restructuring also entailed a refocusing on logging and extract—Argentine **cattle** ranches were sold, a distillery and distribution company in the United States acquired, and estates, a processing plant, and distribution agencies purchased in southern and eastern Africa. By the early 1930s, Forestal in London had become a holding company, in effect an international marketing organization with wholly owned locally registered subsidiaries operating estates and distilleries in Argentina and Africa. By the end of the decade, the Forestal Group held an almost unassailable position in the global tannin extract business, with marketing agreements in virtually all the main centers of consumption.

La Forestal Argentina, Sociedad Anónima de Tierras, Maderas y Explotaciones Comerciales e Industriales was incorporated in Buenos Aires in 1931, an arrangement that enabled Forestal (London) to circumvent Argentine antitrust legislation. By the 1930s, the company possessed three million acres of forests and several processing plants in Argentina, almost 350 miles of railways, and a fleet of river tugs and barges channeling timber from logging camps to processing stations. "Model" townships were laid out, equipped with hospitals, schools, churches, and social and sporting clubs, at the principal stations. Chaco distilleries alone could deliver 80 percent of world consumption. Business boomed during the Second World War and again during the Korean War, but the local company was adversely affected by the operations of the state monopoly **Instituto Argentino Promoción del Intercambio** and by exchange controls, which limited the remittance of profits to Britain and discouraged new investment. Some distilleries were closed, the Argentine business was gradually run down between 1948 and 1963, and the group became dependent for international operations on African estates and plants. The Argentine company was formally dissolved in 1966, its assets being acquired by the British firm Slater Walker, which focused operation on estates in East Africa before selling the company on. The Argentine business revived toward the end of the 20th century, benefiting from **economic policy** changes in the 1990s as well as technological innovation. Regional (mainly Chilean) and international capital revived the operations of Forestal Argentina in Chaco and neighboring **Mesopotamia**. Renewed investment in the 1990s resulted in the rapid recovery of the local business and its thorough integration into the operations of the Tornegaleones conglomerate.

The history of Forestal, as with **Bunge & Born**, illustrates how local enterprises were transformed by access to international capital during the late 19th and early 20th centuries, emerging as international businesses with a global outreach. This trend was brought to an end by domestic economic policy changes in the post–Second World War period, along with shifting patterns of international trade. *See also* AGRICULTURE; COMMODITIES; ECONOMY; FOREIGN DEBT/FOREIGN INVESTMENT; FOREIGN TRADE; INDUSTRY; TRANSPORTATION.

FORESTAL, LAND, TIMBER AND RAILWAY COMPANY. *See* FORESTAL ARGENTINA S.A.

FORJA. *See* FUERZA DE ORIENTACIÓN RADICAL DE LA JOVEN ARGENTINA (FORJA).

FORMOSA (CITY). Capital city of the province of **Formosa**, it was founded in 1879 on the banks of the **Paraguay** River. With a current population of approximately 240,000, it is the hub of industries processing the natural products of the province. Facing Paraguay on the east bank of the Paraguay River, the port is a key transport hub for the province and the region.

FORMOSA (PROVINCE). Situated in the northeast of the country, it is bordered by **Chaco** to the south, **Salta** to the west, and **Paraguay** to the north and east.

The area was contested by Argentina and Paraguay in the 19th century, and the matter was only resolved with the **War of the Triple Alliance** (1865–1870). From 1872 to 1884, it formed part of the Territorio Nacional del Gran Chaco, which was then divided into the national territories of Chaco and Formosa. The latter acquired the status of province in 1955, during the short-lived second presidency of **Juan Domingo Perón**. The current population is around 550,000.

Formosa suffers from an inhospitable geography and climate, which in turn has made the local **economy** one of the poorest in the country. The mainstay of the province has long been **cattle**, and half of its agricultural wealth is represented by cotton. Other natural products from Formosa include soya, **maize**, timber, and bananas. *See also* AGRICULTURE; COMMODITIES.

FRENTE AMPLIO UNEN (FAUNEN). Broad-based center-center-left social-democratic coalition formed in 2013 and wound up in 2015. The principal components of the front varied across the country but generally included representations of social-democratic and socialist parties along with regional parties, plus dissident members of the **Unión Cívica Radical** (UCR). The initial impetus derived from an amendment to national electoral law sanctioned in 2009 that required all parties to hold **primary elections**, first applied in advance of the **presidential** and **congressional elections of 2011**. In addition to the legal requirement to hold primaries, smaller parties saw financial advantages in forging campaign coalitions; official funds were available to parties or groupings attracting 1.5 percent of registered voters. FAUNEN was particularly active in advance of the midterm **congressional elections of 2013**. Subsequently, it sought to collaborate with other similarly minded alliances like **Propuesta Republicana** (PRO), which propelled **Mauricio Macri** to the mayorship of the city of **Buenos Aires**. Key figures in the Frente include Hermes Binner, **Elisa Carrió**, and **Julio Cobos**. FAUNEN disintegrated in the early months of 2015 as various individuals migrated to other electoral coalitions or rejoined parties with which they had previously been associated. The brief history of the Frente captures the fluidity of Argentine party politics at the time and the problems—personal and ideological—of forging an electorally credible party of the center.

FRENTE GRANDE. *See* FRENTE PAÍS SOLIDARIO (FREPASO).

FRENTE JUSTICIALISTA DE LIBERACIÓN (FREJULI). It was both an electoral alliance and a front for the **Partido Justicialista** (PJ) formed in 1972 in advance of the projected return to civilian rule orchestrated by President General **Alejandro Agustín Lanusse**. Besides the PJ, the only other significant party involved was the **Movimiento de Integración y Desarrollo** (MID), led by **Arturo Frondizi** and **Rogelio Julio Frigerio**; it joined in the forlorn hope of having a say in **economic policy** once the FREJULI was in power. An array of minor parties completed the lineup, but a number of them rapidly withdrew in protest at both the allocation of 75 percent of congressional seats to the PJ and the front's program. The latter promised the establishment of diplomatic relations with **Cuba**, North Vietnam, and North Korea; a general wage increase; an amnesty for political prisoners; the nationalization of bank deposits and of **foreign trade**; support measures for **industry**; land reform; and an extensive socialization of the economy.

Electoral ground rules set by the outgoing **military** government precluded **Juan Domingo Perón** from standing in what became the first presidential election of 1973, held in March of that year. Thus, **Héctor Cámpora** headed the FREJULI election ticket, which campaigned under the banner "Freedom and Amnesty." *See also* PRESIDENTIAL ELECTION OF MARCH 1973.

FRENTE PAÍS SOLIDARIO (FREPASO). Various acronyms have been used, including FrePaSo and FrepaSO. A progressive political party formed in 1994, FREPASO emerged from the Frente Grande, a broad grouping of dissident members of the **Partido Justicialista** (PJ) that had come together in 1993. They were appalled by the **corruption** of the administration of President **Carlos Saúl Menem**, elected four years earlier, and questioned the rightist lurch in economic and social policy represented by the **Convertibility Plan**. The Frente Grande combined with other dissident Peronists and politicians from some small left-wing parties to form the FREPASO. The principal figures were **José Octavio Bordón, Carlos "Chacho" Álvarez**, and **Graciela Fernández Meijide**. It was a promising political alliance that gained considerable popular support and achieved high office, only to prove ephemeral.

The imperative in 1994 was to establish a credible party able to challenge Menem in the upcoming 1995 elections. Menem had engineered the **Olivos Pact** with predecessor **Raúl Alfonsín** of the **Unión Cívica Radical** (UCR), which paved the way for constitutional change—the **Constitution of 1994**—that allowed him to stand for a second consecutive presidential term. In the **presidential election of 1995**, Bordón headed the FREPASO ticket; Álvarez was his vice presidential running mate. For a recently formed party, the ticket and the platform (clean government and a questioning of economic liberalism) proved surprisingly popular. The party took a third of the vote in the presidential race; Menem and his vice presidential partner **Carlos Ruckauf** obtained virtually half. FREPASO also did well in the congressional contest, becoming the third largest party in the Chamber of Deputies. For the first time in modern history, the UCR came in third in terms of share of the vote.

In **Congress**, FREPASO built bridges with other parties in an effort to establish a viable opposition, but there was disagreement as to whether the grouping should remain a loose confederation or function as an integrated, disciplined body. Bordón resigned—he would later return to the PJ. This paved the way for Álvarez to take FREPASO into an electoral alliance with the UCR in 1997 ahead of the **presidential** and **congressional elections of 1999**—the **Alianza para el Trabajo, la Justicia y la Educación** (Alianza). It was an uneasy alliance. Fernández Meijide, who had won a seat in the

National Senate for the city of **Buenos Aires** in the **congressional elections of 1995**, challenged **Fernando de la Rúa** (UCR) in the Alianza primaries to head the ticket in the 1999 presidential contest; she lost. In 1996, De la Rúa had defeated the FREPASO candidate in the mayoral contest in the city of Buenos Aires to become the first directly elected mayor of the city. In the event, De la Rúa headed the 1999 Alianza ticket with Álvarez slated for the vice presidency. They won with a shade over 48 percent of the popular vote; **Eduardo Duhalde**, Menem's former vice president, came in second with 38 percent. But it was a mixed success as Fernández Meijide failed to take the governorship of the province of Buenos Aires, which had been widely anticipated; she lost to Ruckauf.

In government, the Alianza had to cope with difficult parliamentary arithmetic and a deepening economic crisis as the Convertibility Plan, which it was by now pledged to maintain, began to unravel. In 2000, Álvarez resigned as vice president when he discovered that De la Rúa had been bribing opposition senators to secure the passage of vital legislation. Although there was continued electoral success—in 2000, **Aníbal Ibarra** from the FREPASO wing of the Alliance took the mayorship of the city of Buenos Aires—the writing was on the wall. In the midterm **congressional elections of 2001**, the Alianza vote fell by around 60 percent; it ended with less than a quarter of the popular vote. The De la Rúa administration collapsed on 20 December 2001; FREPASO was dissolved the same day. Most of the principal figures of the party retired from public life, though some sustained a political profile and were subsequently reelected to office for political groupings contesting the near hegemony of the husband-and-wife presidential team **Néstor Kirchner** and **Cristina Fernández de Kirchner**.

The trajectory of FREPASO is instructive. Its rise marked the end of the political duopoly of the UCR and PJ that had characterized much of the second half of the 20th century and prefigured the splintering of those parties. A coalition of coalitions, its painful emergence and abrupt implosion signaled the growing factionalism of the political system and the problematic of constructing credible, disciplined "normal" political organizations in the fraught aftermath of the **Proceso de la Reorganización Nacional** and **economic crises**. Although FREPASO may have been unfortunate in the timing of its emergence, the circumstances of its rise highlighted another factor: the demand of the electorate for macroeconomic stability—a "normal" **economy**. The electorate had been prepared to tolerate the corruption of the Menem administrations when it promised and delivered economic stability, prioritizing "normal" economics over "normal" politics. Only when FREPASO endorsed the Convertibility Plan did it become electable. But the economy was in crisis, and only by compromising its stance on corruption could FREPASO conduct the business of government. Political fragmentation had helped to institutionalize corruption. *See also* AUSTRAL PLAN.

FRENTE PARA LA VICTORIA (FpV/PJ). A wing of the **Partido Justicialista** (PJ) formed in 2003 by **Néstor Kirchner** to contest the upcoming presidential and congressional elections. The party became a vehicle to realize the political ambitions of the Kirchners, husband and wife, delivering for them three successive electoral victories in the **presidential elections of 2003, 2007,** and **2011.** Although constituting the majoritarian branch of the PJ, the FpV was opposed by various dissident Peronist groupings. It served the Kirchners well as a means of forging coalitions with minor national and regional parties, in addition to factions of historic national parties, thereby delivering some historic victories, notably in 2011 when **Cristina Fernández de Kirchner** obtained over 54 percent of the popular vote, a record exceeded only by **Hipólito Yrigoyen** and **Juan Domingo Perón** in the **presidential elections of 1928** and **September 1973,** when they received 62 percent and 60 percent of the popular vote, respectively. The dominance of the FpV among Peronist factions was not seriously challenged until 2013, when the **Frente Renovador** (FR/PJ) was set up in 2013 by anti-Kirchner groups, a challenge that cost Fernández de Kirchner dear in 2015. *See also* CONGRESSIONAL ELECTIONS OF 2015; PRESIDENTIAL ELECTION OF 2015.

FRENTE RENOVADOR (FR/PJ). Set up in 2013 to contest midterm congressional elections, largely by factions of the **Partido Justicialista** (PJ) in the province of **Buenos Aires** opposed to the continuing presidential ambitions of **Cristina Fernández de Kirchner**—a motivation reflected in its name, Front for Renewal. The grouping was headed by **Sergio Massa**, a former mayor of the municipality of Tigre, an affluent residential suburb of Greater Buenos Aires. Massa had served as a provincial deputy in the Buenos Aires assembly, and also as representative of the province in the national Chamber of Deputies. He was appointed head of the cabinet, virtual prime minister, by Fernández de Kirchner in 2008, a position he held until breaking with the president to form the FR in 2013. The FR performed particularly well in the **congressional elections of 2013**; it topped the poll in the province of Buenos Aries, where it gained 44 percent of the votes to 32 percent obtained by the Kirchnerist faction, **Frente para la Victoria** (FpV/PJ). This achievement, and associated gains at the national level, thwarted any ambitions that Mrs. Kirchner might have had to stand for a third term, denying her the number of votes in the National Congress required to change the constitution. Campaigning under the designation **Unidos por una Nueva Alternativa** (UNA), although the UNA/FR did not do so well in the **presidential** and **congressional elections of 2015**, its performance at the polls was sufficient to deny the FpV candidate, **Daniel Scioli**, victory in the first round of the presidential contest, ensuring a second-round runoff between Scioli and **Mauricio Macri**, candidate of the center-right **Cambiemos** coalition, which

338 • FRIGERIO, ROGELIO (1970–)

Macri won. Following the 2015 elections, the future of the UNA/FR is unclear. Much will depend on the likely reorganization of the PJ. Moves to unify Peronism could see Massa and other figures associated with the former FR reintegrate into the party.

FRIGERIO, ROGELIO (1970–). Grandson of **Rogelio Julio Frigerio**; academic economist and politician. A member of the **Propuesta Republicana** (PRO) political party, part of the ruling **Cambiemos** coalition, Frigerio was appointed minister of interior, public works, and housing in 2015 by President **Mauricio Macri**. Trained at the **University of Buenos Aires**, where he specialized in development and planning, like his grandfather he is an advocate of **developmentalism**. He has taught at various universities in Argentina and held a visiting professorship at Carlos III University in Madrid, as well as heading several think tanks and consultancy firms, mainly working in the fields of planning and regional development. His political career began during the second administration of President **Carlos Saúl Menem**, most prominently as secretary of planning at the **Ministry of Economy** under **Roque Fernández**, a position to which he was appointed in 1998. Before being selected to head the **Ministry of Interior**, he was elected to the legislative assembly of the city of **Buenos Aires** in 2011 and appointed chair of the Budget Committee. He resigned from the assembly seat two years later when named president of the Bank of the City of Buenos Aires. At the time, Macri was head of the city administration. While directing the bank, Frigerio was involved in a controversial plan to promote home ownership and support the rented sector—substantial sums were set aside, but not many families benefited—and an equally controversial land deal involving **Boca Juniors**, President Macri's soccer club.

FRIGERIO, ROGELIO JULIO (1914–2006). Politician, promoter of **developmentalism**, and close associate of **Arturo Frondizi**. Frigerio met Frondizi in 1956, when the **Unión Cívica Radical** (UCR) split into the **Unión Cívica Radical del Pueblo** (UCRP) led by **Ricardo Balbín** and the **Unión Cívica Radical Intransigente** (UCRI) headed by Frondizi. Frigerio engineered Frondizi's victory in the **presidential election of 1958** by arranging the notorious **Caracas Pact** with exiled former president **Juan Domingo Perón**, who got the supporters of his proscribed party to vote for the UCRI.

Frigerio was appointed secretary of socioeconomic relations by Frondizi but by the end of 1958 was forced to resign under pressure from the **military**. Nonetheless, he remained Frondizi's leading collaborator and adviser and cofounded the **Movimiento de Integración y Desarrollo** (MID) in 1963. Given the minor position of the new party, Frigerio sought to cooperate with other political groups: the MID joined the **Frente Justicialista de**

Liberación (FREJULI) in 1972 and endorsed **Carlos Saúl Menem** of the **Partido Justicialista** (PJ) in the **presidential election of 1989**. Frigerio unsuccessfully contested the **presidential election of 1983** and replaced Frondizi as leader of the MID in 1986.

FRIGORÍFICOS. Meatpacking plants, initially freezing facilities, now predominantly chilling preserved **meat**. Frozen meat is shipped at around 5.5 degrees C, chilled a fraction above freezing—1 degree C. The technology was developed in France. In 1870, the **Sociedad Rural Argentina** (SRA) created a prize to advance the technology.

Frigoríficos were set up in the 1880s—the first in 1882: Frigorífico Anglo, founded by a consortium of British *estancerios* at **Zárate** and Eugenio Terrasón at **San Nicolás**, who converted a *saladero* to a freezing factory. Others soon followed: the River Plate Fresh Meat Company opened at **Campana** in 1883, the Compañía Sansinena de Carnes Congeladas at **Avellaneda** in 1885, and James Nelson & Sons opened Frigorífico Las Palmas in **Zárate** in 1886. This flurry of innovative activity demonstrated the appeal of the new technology, which promised to deliver a higher-value product to the rapidly expanding markets for imported fresh meat in western Europe, particularly **Great Britain**, hitherto supplied from the **United States**. Two features characterize the early phase of the industry: all firms were locally funded, either by nationals or long-term foreign residents; the business largely froze **sheep** as the carcass was small and froze rapidly.

The next phase of the industry began around 1907 with the arrival of US meatpackers. Swift acquired the La Plata Cold Storage Plant; a year later Swift, Armour, and Morris bought the La Blanca factory in Avellaneda. The arrival of US packing houses changed fundamentally the nature of the business. While established packers had begun to process more **cattle**, converting from frozen lamb and mutton to beef, the new arrivals focused mainly on chilled beef: they invested massively in the more expensive technology, expanded the scale of production, and integrated the business—engaging in transport, distribution, and marketing in addition to packing. Chilling also required a different type of animal from freezing: a freezer plant handled animals little different from creole cattle processed by *saladeros*; chilling was better suited to a carcass that was leaner and heavier, requiring investment by *estancieros* in breed improvement and the importing of European bloodstock. This resulted in the transformation of the **pampas** and the cattle industry: new breeds such as Herefords and Aberdeen Angus dominated the countryside; new grasses and alfalfa—for fattening—were planted; prestige cattle studs appeared as *estancieros* completed for prizes awarded at the annual fatstock show organized by the SRA; cattlemen became rich, *frigoíficos* expanded and multiplied—employing thousands of workers; the country became rich, acquiring the reputation of being the granary and cattle ranch of the world.

For more than three decades, Argentina was the principal prime meat exporter. Rising demand in Europe and declining North American meat export surpluses set the scene for this dominance, yet it is principally explained by domestic factors. It was a function of large-scale investment at all stages of the process of transforming cattle into high-quality **meat** from estate to table, the natural fertility of the land, and the integration of the industry. It was also a function of the limits of chilling technology of the time: chilled meat could only be maintained in tip-top condition for about three weeks: Argentina lay on the right side of this time frontier. Packing in the **River Plate**, transporting to Europe in meat boats especially constructed for the trade, and distributing from Liverpool, La Havre, or Hamburg to the main centers of consumption was just possible within the time frame. Until the late 1930s, other potential suppliers in southern Africa, Australia, and New Zealand could not. Argentina was to be the top world beef exporter. The environment for *frigoríficos* began to change thereafter. A move from multilateral to bilateral trade reduced market access. The industrialization drive during and after the 1940s meant increased taxation on the rural sector, while the promotion of a cheap food policy at home deflected supplies toward the home market. The domestic political environment became harsher—*estancieros* were no longer depicted as dynamic and entrepreneurial but as exploitative oligarchs and *vendepatrias*. The features may have been exaggerated during the middle years of the first two presidencies of **Juan Domingo Perón** but were by no means confined to it. **Military** governments of the 1960s and 1970s, supposedly inclined to favor business groups, did little to ease the burden imposed on the rural sector or encourage long-term investment: interventionist regulations were largely maintained, the fiscal burden was not materially reduced, and the exchange regime remained penal.

From the 1950s, there was little new investment in Argentine meatpacking: technology and practice became obsolescent. By the early 1960s, older firms began to close, with closures accelerating between 1967 and 1983, but not all plants were old or obsolete. Underinvestment gave way to disinvestment: foreign packers began to pull out, and production was focused more on the domestic market. The situation became even worse during the presidencies of **Néstor Kirchner** and **Cristina Fernández de Kirchner**, accused of pursuing an *antiganadería* (anticattle) policy: taxes rose, beef exports were banned to keep prices down in domestic markets, and the allure of soya, which enjoyed a more favorable tax regime, led to destocking. In 2005, Argentina was the third largest exporter of beef in the world, and in 2015 the 30th. **Brazil** had become the world's largest exporter of meat products and the main supplier of beef in MERCOSUR. *See also* AGRICULTURE; CON-

CORDANCIA; ECONOMIC CRISES; ECONOMY; FOREIGN DEBT/ FOREIGN INVESTMENT; FOREIGN TRADE; INDUSTRY; ROCA–RUNCIMAN PACT (1933).

FRONDIZI, ARTURO (1908–1995). Lawyer, journalist, and politician; president of Argentina (1958–1962). Active in the **Unión Cívica Radical** (UCR), he was elected national deputy for the city of **Buenos Aires** in 1946 and was the running mate of **Ricardo Balbín** in the **presidential election of 1951**. In 1956, Frondizi's inability to cooperate with Balbín resulted in the UCR splintering into the **Unión Cívica Radical del Pueblo** (UCRP) and the **Unión Cívica Radical Intransigente** (UCRI).

Frondizi was a duplicitous character, and this was apparent more than once. In the **presidential election of 1958**, he secured victory as the UCRI candidate thanks to the **Caracas Pact**, a deal reached with exiled former president **Juan Domingo Perón** (whose party was proscribed) and which neither man intended to uphold. Even more spectacular was Frondizi's volte-face on oil policy once he assumed the presidency, which is undoubtedly the single most remembered issue of his administration. Before the **military coup of 1955**, Frondizi had been an oil nationalist and strongly opposed to Perón's decision to negotiate contracts with Standard Oil of California; Perón had rigorously followed procedure by presenting his project to **Congress**, where it was then shelved. In 1958, Frondizi undertook to sign direct contracts with various private companies, claiming that an international tender "would have entailed considerable delays" and that the "emergency situation" in which he found the country warranted immediate action. By not dealing with the legislative power on this matter, he had acted unconstitutionally.

Frondizi had become convinced of the need for foreign capital in oil exploration in order to supplement the resources of the state-owned **Yacimientos Petrolíferos Fiscales** (YPF) and reduce the balance-of-payments cost of oil imports, which in 1957 represented approximately 21 percent of all Argentine imports. Upon becoming president, he moved very quickly to sign contracts with various private companies. These were of three kinds. The first and most controversial were those signed with Amoco, Cities Service, and Tennessee Gas, which provided for the drilling of wells in areas where oil had already been discovered and in some cases partially developed by YPF. These companies were to be paid cash for oil produced, at prices significantly below international prices. The second type were specifically drilling contracts with payments per meter drilled or per hour spent drilling in areas selected by YPF. Finally, pure exploration contracts were concluded with Esso, Shell, and Union Oil, with payment also to be in cash per cubic meter of oil or gas discovered, with the exception of the Shell contract, which was more of the profit-sharing kind.

The policy proved to be highly successful in its primary goal, which was to get the oil industry moving again. Output tripled in five years, and by 1962 Argentina was effectively self-sufficient. This had been achieved without any reduction in proven reserve levels, and most of the increased production came from YPF itself. The contracts for development drilling, while important, were thereby secondary in economic terms but politically toxic. They were subsequently canceled by President **Arturo Illia** in 1963.

Although Frondizi was an advocate of state-induced **developmentalism**—in 1960, he finally inaugurated the long-delayed **Sociedad Mixta Siderúrgica Argentina** (SOMISA) steelworks in **San Nicolás**—he wanted to attract foreign capital. The Ley de Radicación de Capitales was passed in 1959, by which foreign capital was granted the same rights as domestic capital, including tax exemptions where applicable. By 1962, the location of 254 foreign firms was authorized, and though they covered the whole industrial spectrum, 90 percent were concentrated in the chemical, petrochemical, transport, metallurgy, and machinery sectors.

Regarding foreign policy, Frondizi contradictorily sought both to get close to the administration of John F. Kennedy in the **United States** and take an "independent" line. He traveled to major Non-Aligned nations such as India and Indonesia, and his policy toward **Cuba** was to become a factor in the **military coup of 1962**. Frondizi met Jânio Quadros, the eccentric and mercurial president of **Brazil**, in April 1961 in a bid to cooperate in international relations and economic projects. This resulted in the signature of the Acuerdo de Amistad y Consulta, but nothing came of it as Quadros resigned in August 1961; when Frondizi subsequently submitted the agreement to the National Senate for ratification, it was met with stony silence.

Throughout Frondizi's presidential mandate, the armed forces kept a close eye on him. The government's economic stabilization program generated severe labor unrest, prompting the **military** to get more involved in repressing the disorder. In January 1959, troops and tanks ended the occupation of the *frigorífico* Lisandro de la Torre. The Peronists resorted to increased sabotage and terrorism, especially after Perón publicly denounced the Caracas Pact in June 1959. Frondizi, out of character with his previous record but albeit in line with his occasional paranoia of internal and external conspiracies, responded by swiftly declaring a state of siege and followed that in March 1960 with the Plan CONINTES (Conmoción Interna del Estado). This was the most controversial piece of repressive legislation, sanctioning a state of emergency in which the armed forces were given direct control of the repression of terrorism, as well as subordinating provincial police forces to the army's authority. The contentious element about CONINTES was the setting up of military tribunals, given the constitutional requirement that the population be mobilized militarily before a civilian could be subjected to military justice.

Frondizi faced innumerable *planteos*, that is, repeated challenges by the military and their questioning of his ministerial appointments. Notwithstanding these problems, he convinced the armed forces that the Peronists could be defeated electorally and that they should be allowed to stand in the **congressional elections of 1962**. It was a gamble that failed spectacularly and, combined with the government's handling of Cuba, resulted in the overthrow of Frondizi.

Frondizi broke with the UCRI and its leader **Oscar Alende** in the run-up to the **congressional** and **presidential elections of 1963** and formed the **Movimiento de Integración y Desarrollo** (MID)—yet another party. He supported a national front that included Peronism, the ulterior motive being that his new political outfit would be part of a possible winning coalition in future elections. The MID joined the Frente Nacional y Popular, an alliance that also comprised the **Unión Popular** (UP) and the **Partido Conservador Popular** (PCP) and was set up with Perón's blessing to contest the general elections scheduled for July 1963. Frondizi's party and its allies were proscribed and unable to field candidates in the electoral contest, owing to pressure from the armed forces and conservative elements. A decade later, when de facto president **Alejandro Agustín Lanusse** called the **congressional** and **presidential elections of March 1973**, the MID joined the Peronist-led **Frente Justicialista de Liberación** (FREJULI). Aware that the latter could win, Frondizi hoped that by participating in the coalition he would have a say in **economic policy**, but his hopes never materialized. Toward the end of his life, Frondizi got his party to endorse the successful Peronist candidacy of **Carlos Saúl Menem** in the **presidential election of 1989**, which landed the MID two ministerial posts during the decade-long Menem presidency. Though Frondizi thereby achieved a long-sought goal, the truth was that since the **presidential election of 1983** the MID had been effectively a minor party. *See also* GUEVARA, ERNESTO "CHE" (1928–1967); GUIDO, JOSÉ MARÍA (1910–1975); PRESIDENTIAL SUCCESSION OF 1962.

FUERZA DE ORIENTACIÓN RADICAL DE LA JOVEN ARGENTINA (FORJA). Established by Arturo Jauretche in 1934, this splinter faction of the **Unión Cívica Radical** (UCR) would eventually combine with Peronism as a result of the doctrine it espoused. FORJA stood for what it called "radical nationalism." Jauretche differentiated this concept from Italian Fascism, which he saw as "making man an instrument of the State," and from German National Socialism, as making man an instrument of race, while Soviet Communism made man the subject of dialectical materialism. FORJA aimed "to make a State the defender of the freedom of man," by ensuring that the owners of the **economy** were unable to "infringe on the freedom of man."

Given these aims, it is little wonder that FORJA pursued what became the Peronist mantra: "social justice, economic independence, and national sovereignty." It identified social justice with nationalism, stating that there could be no possible conception of nationalism in a country that did not have an implicit demand for social justice. Jauretche believed that a nationalist state owed to its people the "fair distribution" of goods, otherwise the country would remain under colonial status and not have control over its resources; these were references to the British role in the Argentine economy, and Argentine groups, especially rural interests, regarded as closely associated with British financial and commercial interests—the so-called *vendepatrias*.

FORJA advocated the nationalization of the **Banco Central de la República Argentina** (BCRA), control of **foreign trade**, foreign exchange regulation, the redistribution of income, the consolidation of the domestic market, the nationalization of public services, and industrial development. Since these objectives neatly dovetailed with those of **Juan Domingo Perón**, FORJA aligned itself behind him in the **presidential election of 1946** and Jauretche himself would serve as president of the newly nationalized **Banco de la Provincia de Buenos Aires** from 1946 to 1951.

FUERZAS ARMADAS PERONISTAS (FAP). Created in 1968 to carry out rural and urban guerrilla warfare, the FAP included experienced Peronist militants. Having failed in its rural ambitions, the group concentrated on the urban struggle from 1969 and carried out a sustained campaign in 1970. In addition, several FAP guerrillas assisted veteran trade unionists in the creation of a revolutionary organization (Peronismo de Base [PB]) to operate at the factory level.

Having managed to save other left-wing armed groups (the **Montoneros** and the **Fuerzas Armadas Revolucionarias** [FAR]) from annihilation, the FAP itself suffered various setbacks. Its leadership was jailed in 1971 and would remain so until 1973. In 1974, it splintered into two factions: the FAP Comando Nacional, which tilted to the far left and merged with the **Ejercito Revolucionario del Pueblo** (ERP), and the FAP 17 de Octubre, which merged with the Montoneros.

FUERZAS ARMADAS REVOLUCIONARIAS (FAR). Armed left-wing group created in 1966 in the hope of becoming the Argentine appendage of **Ernesto "Che" Guevara**'s *foco* in **Bolivia**. With the death of Che and the collapse of his Bolivian scheme in 1967, the FAR became politically and socially isolated.

The FAR turned to urban struggle in 1969 and, as a means to end its isolation, successfully embarked on a process of Peronization. Its most notable early action was the occupation of the town of Garín, outside the city of

Buenos Aires, in 1970. Subsequently, the FAR suffered major setbacks and was saved from annihilation by the **Fuerzas Armadas Peronistas** (FAP). From the start of 1972, and especially in the months before and after the **Trelew Massacre**, the FAR and the **Montoneros** debated merging the former with the latter. In October 1973, the merger of the two armed groups was announced.

FUNDACIÓN EVA PERÓN. Set up initially as the Fundación de Ayuda Social María Eva Duarte by First Lady **Eva Perón** in 1948, the foundation had four aims. First, loaning money, providing tools, and establishing scholarships for deserving people lacking resources; second, building housing for needy families as well as recreational facilities, educational establishments, hospitals, and any other edifice that the Fundación deemed necessary; third, constructing buildings for the common good that could be transferred with or without charge to national, provincial, or municipal authorities; and finally, contributing and collaborating by any means available to the realization of works constructed for the common good and that helped meet the basic needs of the least favored social classes.

The Fundación was established with 10,000 pesos from the first lady's own savings and financed by "voluntary" contributions from the **trade unions**, 20 percent of the proceeds from the Lotería Nacional, grants in aid from **Congress**, as well as compulsory private donations. Notwithstanding its useful work in charity and social programs, the organization had a major negative aspect. Only Eva Perón controlled the funds and determined how they would be spent. The foundation therefore became a source of considerable political patronage and tainted with **corruption**. More importantly, she used her Fundación to funnel vast sums of money into Swiss bank accounts—perhaps as much as 700 million US dollars.

Following the death of Eva Perón in 1952, President **Juan Domingo Perón** took over the running of the foundation. He headed a nine-member council composed of five workers and four state delegates, which met every 15 days. Following the **military coup of 1955**, the Fundación was liquidated. *See also* EDUCATION.

FUNDACIÓN MADRES DE PLAZA DE MAYO. Charitable-cum-funding organization established by and for the faction of the **Madres de Plaza de Mayo** associated with **Hebe Pastore de Bonafini**. It is currently under scrutiny for misuse of public money. An investigating magistrate has declared the foundation bankrupt, lacking sufficient funds to pay staff and sustain the projects for which it is responsible—notably, the construction of low-cost housing. Investigations began in 2016, and as of June 2017 Bonafini, who has been accused of fraud, is prohibited from leaving the country until the case is completed.

G

GALIMBERTI, RODOLFO (1947–2002). A leader of the **Montoneros** guerrilla group. In 1961, he joined the **Movimiento Nacionalista Tacuara**, which was outlawed four years later. Galimberti founded the Juventud Argentina por la Emancipación Nacional (JAEN) in 1967 and was appointed by exiled former president **Juan Domingo Perón** as a youth representative in the Consejo Superior of the Movimiento Justicialista Nacional in 1971.

Galimberti was recruited by the Montoneros in 1972. He became the leader of its so-called North Column, which stretched between the suburbs of Vicente López and Tigre to the northwest of the city of **Buenos Aires** and participated in numerous guerrilla operations, including the notorious kidnapping of the **Born brothers**. Following the **military coup of 1976** and the virtual annihilation of the North Column by the armed forces, Galimberti went into exile. He broke with the Montoneros over their failed "counteroffensive" in 1979. He returned to Argentina after the restoration of democracy and, in a bizarre twist, in the 1990s got involved in business with Jorge Born, whom he had kidnapped in 1974. Their dealings came under investigation for fraud.

GALTIERI, LEOPOLDO FORTUNATO (1926–2003). The less-than-fortunate failed dictator with a penchant for Scotch whisky. He was responsible for the **Falklands War** as de facto president of Argentina in 1981–1982. He was interested in **military** engineering when he joined the army as a young man, and given what would happen in the future, that should perhaps have been the limit of his ambitions. But Galtieri was born into a poor family and wanted to do better. While a lieutenant, he was noticed by American advisers to the Argentine army and in 1949 attended the US Army's School of the Americas in Panama, where a number of future Latin American dictators received training in anti-Communism and counterinsurgency. Galtieri is reputedly the only student in the history of the school to have failed the course. Nevertheless, he continued to be promoted—all the way to the top.

In December 1981, he ousted de facto president **Roberto Eduardo Viola** and replaced him as head of state; the navy's support for the palace coup came at a heavy price: Galtieri would have to embark on a military adventure to recover the **Falkland Islands**. He had no understanding of the consequences of taking such a course of action, and Argentina invaded the archipelago on 2 April 1982. He may have understood this as a last-ditch maneuver to generate popularity in the dying days of the dictatorship—days before the invasion was announced, there had been massive protests in Plaza de Mayo, in front of the presidential palace, organized by the **Confederación General del Trabajo**. As the invasion showed, Argentine troops were largely made up of poorly trained and poorly-equipped conscripts, who were no match for the professional British task force dispatched by Prime Minister Margaret Thatcher to retake the islands. The Argentines surrendered on 14 June 1982; Galtieri was forced to resign and succeeded by **Reynaldo Bignone**.

Galtieri was acquitted over charges of **human rights** abuses in the trials of the military juntas in 1985, but the following year was sentenced by a military tribunal for misconduct relating to the Falklands War—he received a 12-year prison sentence. He was among the senior officers pardoned by President **Carlos Saúl Menem**, but in 2002 new charges were brought against him over human rights abuses. Galtieri was allowed to remain under house arrest owing to his ill health; he died several months later. *See also* ALEMANN, ROBERTO TEODORO (1922–); FALKLANDS DISPUTE; MILITARY JUNTAS, TRIALS OF THE.

GARCÍA ELORRIO, JUAN (1938–1970). Politician and a mentor of the founders of the **Montoneros**. He established the Comando Camilo Torres (CCT) in early 1967, with the aim of setting up a Cuban-style rural guerrilla force in either the province of **Santa Fe** or **Tucumán**. The CCT had 30 militants, including **Fernando Abal Medina**, **Norma Arrostito**, and **Carlos Gustavo Ramus**. These three individuals trained in **Cuba** and upon their return to Argentina questioned García Elorrio over his leadership and his delay in starting guerrilla activity. This resulted in Abal Medina, Arrostito, and Ramus breaking with the CCT leader and moving on to found the Montoneros, which made a spectacular public debut with the **Aramburazo** in 1970. García Elorrio replaced the CCT with the short-lived Comandos Peronistas de Liberación (CPL); he was killed in a hit-and-run incident.

GARDEL, CARLOS (1890–1935). Claimed by both Argentina and **Uruguay**, but born Charles Romuald Gardès in Toulouse, he was a French Argentine singer, songwriter, composer, and actor and the most prominent figure in the history of the **tango**. To avoid the social stigma of having a child out of wedlock, his mother and he sailed to **Buenos Aires** in early 1893. On arrival, she registered herself as a widow, which is why Gardel throughout his life remained ambiguous about his birthplace. Toulouse was only confirmed as his place of birth in 2012 when his birth certificate was discovered.

Gardel began his singing career in bars and at private parties and created the *tango-canción* in 1917 with his rendition of "Mi noche triste"; the recording became a hit throughout Latin America. He toured Argentina, Uruguay, **Chile**, **Brazil**, Puerto Rico, **Venezuela**, and Colombia, as well as making appearances in Paris, New York, Barcelona, and Madrid. As his popularity grew, Gardel made a number of films in the 1920s and 1930s. While sentimental pictures such as *Cuesta abajo* (1934) and *El día que me quieras* (1935) lack lasting dramatic value, they were outstanding showcases of his tremendous singing talents and movie star looks. In addition, Gardel composed numerous well-known tangos; one of them is "Mi Buenos Aires querido," released in 1934. He also recorded a famous version of "La cumparsita," which was written in 1916 and is among the most recognizable tangos of all time. Gardel died in an airplane crash in Medellín in 1935, at the height of his career. Thousands came to pay their respects as his body was taken from Colombia to Buenos Aires by way of New York, Rio de Janeiro, and Montevideo.

GARRÉ, NILDA CECILIA (1945–). Lawyer and politician who held two ministerial posts. She also served briefly as ambassador to **Venezuela** and has been elected several times to the lower house of **Congress**, the Chamber of Deputies, most recently in 2015.

Arguably, most famous as the first woman to serve as minister of defense in the history of the country, she was appointed by President **Néstor Kirchner** in 2005 and continued to hold the post until 2010 during the presidency of **Cristina Fernández de Kirchner**, who then offered her the equally sensitive portfolio of minister of national security, a position that she held until 2013. One of the longest serving ministers of the *kirchnerato*, she was a close ideological fellow traveler of the presidential couple. She is married to Juan Manuel Abal Medina, an important figure of the left-leaning **Juventud Peronista** (JP) who accompanied former president **Juan Domingo Perón** on his short-lived return to the country in 1972 before the **presidential election of March 1973**. Reputed to have been an active member of the **Montoneros**, she is an influential figure on the Peronist left in her own right, campaigning against **human rights** abuses committed by members of the armed forces during the **Proceso de Reorganización Nacional**, and an outspoken nationalist. (Abal Medina is sometimes described as one of the best-known Montoneros and his wife as the "minister of terrorism" when she accepted the ministerial portfolio for national security.)

Garré was also elected national deputy for the **Frente País Solidario** (FREPASO), of which she was also an active member, and held subministerial positions in the **Alianza** government of President **Fernando de la Rúa** of the **Unión Cívica Radical** (UCR). In 2003, representing one of the left-wing parties in the grouping, she headed the rump FREPASO bloc in the chamber. She resigned her seat in the chamber on being appointed minister of defense.

During her tenure at Defense, she is most remembered for reviving policies first essayed during the UCR presidency of **Raúl Alfonsín** to democratize the armed forces—a policy that she regarded as an extension of her human rights campaigning—for the prosecution on charges of **corruption** of several middle- and lower-ranking officers, and for the recovery of "national sovereignty" in the field of **military** technology and the procurement of defense equipment—she renationalized a plant privatized during the administration of Peronist president **Carlos Saúl Menem**. At National Security, she is credited with efforts to enhance the technical capacity and professionalization of the service. As minister of both defense and national security, she is also credited with attempts to improve the working and living conditions of personnel and to promote gender equality, as well as relations between the forces and the public. However, Garré has been accused of coordinating a government crackdown on the press, failing sufficiently to safeguard the rights of citizens, turning a blind eye to the diversion of funds to party-political projects, and presiding over a reduction in expenditure that compromised the efficiency of the armed forces. The latter charge resurfaced in 2017 with the disappearance of the submarine **ARA** *San Juan*. *See also* FABRICACIONES MILITARES (FM); PRIVATIZATION; STATE-OWNED ENTERPRISES (SOEs).

GAUCHO. Sometimes compared to the cowboy in the **United States** as a national icon, the image of the gaucho as a free-spirited, resourceful, skilled horseman of the plains (**pampas**) is even more celebrated in Argentina than his US counterpart in his country, and even more of a contemporary political reference.

Today celebrated for his hardy individualism, prowess as a ranch hand, independence, loyalty, and valor in cultural events that commemorate the crafts, music, and literature of the *estancia* and rural life, the figure of the gaucho emerged in the colonial period. Then he was regarded as an outsider or a vagrant, someone who existed beyond the law and outside society, leading a nomadic life. Living off the land, the gaucho's prime (possibly sole) possessions consisted of his horse, saddle, poncho, knife, bolas (or *boleadoras*)—used for capturing wild cattle—and lasso. His diet consisted of dried **meat** and **yerba mate**—and alcohol—trading animal hides and meat for necessities that he could not obtain from hunting. Usually of European stock, but also of mixed race, gauchos by the late colonial period were valued for their skills by urban merchants and *estancieros* who held licenses from the Crown to organize roundups of wild **cattle** and horses—*vaquerías*. As the *estancia* economy developed, gauchos would find seasonal employment herding cattle but never considered themselves to be bound to the estate like the *peón*, who in exchange for the right to farm a small plot of land was tied to the *estancia*. The military reputation of the gaucho—as a skilled lancer and fierce fighter—came to the fore during the struggle for **independence**; gauchos also featured prominently in the campaigns of **Juan Manuel de Rosas**, **caudillo** and sometimes governor of the province of **Buenos Aires**, and during the **Conquest of the Desert**. Yet the gaucho rejected discipline and authority, traits that contributed to the reputation of the gaucho as a vagrant and outlaw. This was the *gaucho malo* or *gaucho malentendido* depicted by such modernizers as **Domingo Faustino Sarmiento** as blood-thirsty, barbarous, and uncivilized—a symbol of the past rather than the future.

By the 1870s, the gaucho was disappearing as the open frontier gave way to modern *estancias* stocked with European breeds of sheep and cattle; barbed wire, **immigrants**, and railways put pay to the gaucho. But it was precisely at this time that the myth of the heroic gaucho was created, celebrated in literature and later film. By 1900, it became fashionable in the countryside for members of the landed elite to effect gaucho dress, while many immigrants adopted the tools and techniques of the gaucho—but not his nomadic habits. Thus, there were "Jewish gauchos" in the colonies of the province of **Santa Fe**; "Italian gauchos" predominated in the agricultural colonies of **Córdoba**; there were even "Welsh gauchos" in **Patagonia**. In the late 1930s, the Day of Tradition or the Day of the Gaucho was established as a festival to display gaucho equestrian skills, music, and storytelling, and it is not uncommon for urban politicians on campaign in the countryside in the 21st century to present themselves as heirs of the noble gaucho. *See also* *CHINA*; DUHALDE, EDUARDO ALBERTO (1941–); *MARTÍN FIERRO*; MENEM, CARLOS SAÚL (1930–).

GAY, LUIS (1903–1988). Leader of the telecommunications workers union in its various incarnations between the late 1920s and early 1940s and major supporter of the alliance of **trade unions** with **Juan Domingo Perón** following the **military coup of 1943**. Together with union leader **Cipriano Reyes**, he founded the **Partido Laborista** (PL) in 1945 and became the party's president. The PL was the political vehicle that propelled Perón to victory in the **presidential election of 1946**, and was then dissolved to give way to the **Partido Peronista** (PP).

Gay was elected secretary general of the **Confederación General del Trabajo** in 1946 and then displaced when he challenged other union leaders and Perón himself. Following the **military coup of 1955**, he went into exile. Gay briefly ran the Mutual de Telefónicos in the mid-1960s but was ousted following the **military coup of 1966**. He became affiliated with the **Unión Cívica Radical** (UCR) in 1971 but never again held posts in trade unions or politics.

GENERATION OF THE 1880s (GENERACIÓN DEL OCHENTA). Term applied to a group of public intellectuals, idealists, and reformers who played a critical role in national life following the process of **national organization** concluded around 1880, after the **Conquest of the Desert**, the **Federalization of the City of Buenos Aires**, and the first presidency of **Julio A. Roca**. Influenced by European positivism, they regarded the oligarchic political system consolidated by Roca as suited to the needs of the country. It would deliver order and progress—disciplined politics, economic modernization, and social advance. Advocating such contemporary liberal values as freedom of conscience, freedom of expression—in speech and the press—equality before the law, and personal rights, while also supporting economic liberal values—free trade and a small, noninterventionist state—they nevertheless endorsed the principle of "guided" democracy until **education** and societal progress had forged an informed and responsible citizenry and electorate. The Generation of the 1880s saw the decades immediately following the 1880 settlement as a progressive interregnum between the chaos and disorder of the past—the age of the **caudillo** and "barbarism"—and the emergence of a modern nation. The future would be better than the past: the country would be pacified and centralized; **immigration**, investment, and modern technology would promote growth; Argentina would be the **United States** of the southern hemisphere, a utopia of progress.

Economic liberalism and ordered politics would ultimately deliver a dynamic capitalist economy and fully fledged democracy, ideally by the centenary of **independence** in 1910. This was the republic that could be—or might have been. Events such as electoral reform encapsulated in the **Sáenz Peña Law** of 1912 and the election of President **Hipólito Yrigoyen** in 1916 can be regarded as benchmarks on the road to modernity envisaged by the Generation of the 1880s, the violent repression of social protest around 1910, the **military coup of 1930**, and the **Concordancia** regimes that followed as setbacks. *See also* CONGRESSIONAL ELECTIONS OF 1916; ECONOMIC CRISES; ECONOMY; FOREIGN DEBT/FOREIGN INVESTMENT; FOREIGN TRADE; PRESIDENTIAL ELECTION OF 1916; REVOLUTION OF 1890; SEMANA TRÁGICA; TRADE UNIONS.

GIL, ANTONIO. *See* EL GAUCHITO GIL.

GÓMEZ MORALES, ALFREDO (1908–1990). Economist who held the posts of minister of economic affairs (1952–1955) and minister of economy (1974–1975). President of the **Banco Central de la República Argentina** (BCRA) between 1949 and 1952, Gómez Morales then headed what would become the **Ministry of Economy** during the truncated second presidency of **Juan Domingo Perón**. During his tenure, he had to deal with a decline in industrial—and more particularly—rural production as credit became scarce. To remedy this problem, he increased interest rates. While this reduced inflationary pressures and halted the rapid growth of wage participation in total output, it failed to address structural problems. In a bid to repair the damage done to the economy during Perón's first presidency, Gómez Morales then implemented the Plan Económico de Coyuntura. This looked to foreign investment to kick-start production, recapitalize the economy, and ease the foreign exchange position. He was again appointed president of the BCRA in May 1973 and held the post until September 1974. In this short period, he served no less than four administrations, those of **Héctor Cámpora**, **Raúl Lastiri**, Juan Domingo Perón—in his final mandate—and **Isabel Perón**.

In October 1974, Gómez Morales succeeded **José Ber Gelbard** as minister of economy. He implemented a liberal economic program, which both curtailed the purchasing power of wages and reduced the share of wages in national income; he also devalued the **currency**. But the expected results were not attained; economic activity was not reinvigorated, while the pressure for wage increases from the **Confederación General del Trabajo** became more pronounced. At the end of May 1975, Gómez Morales was forced to resign by **José López Rega**, the all-too-powerful minister of social welfare, and replaced by **Celestino Rodrigo**. *See also* ECONOMIC CRISES; ECONOMY; FOREIGN DEBT/FOREIGN INVESTMENT; FOREIGN TRADE; MINISTRY OF ECONOMY; RODRIGAZO.

GOROSTIZA, CARLOS (1920–2016). Leading playwright, theater director, and novelist of the second half of the 20th century and early 21st century; well-regarded secretary of culture. Gorostiza both wrote and directed his own plays. His stage debut was *El puente* (1949), which revolutionized Argentine theater. The ambience of the *conventillo* was left behind and the reality of class surfaced in a potent metaphor—"los que están de un lado y del otro del puente en cuestión" (those on opposite sides of the bridge in question, or those on opposite sides of the said bridge). Commenting on emergent social tensions, the play was exceptionally successful; it was quickly translated and even performed in the **United States**. The second major theatrical success as author-director was *El pan de la locura* (1958). His other significant plays, many of which were critical allegories of contemporary social and political reality, are *El fabricante de piolín* (1950), *El caso del hombre de la valija negra* (1951), *El reloj de Baltasar* (1956), *Los prójimos* (1966), *La ira* (1969), *Los cinco sentidos capitales* (1973), *Juana y Pedro* (1976), *Los cuartos oscuros* (1976), *Los hermanos queridos* (1978), *El acompañamiento* (1981), *Matar el tiempo* (1982), *Hay que apagar el fuego* (1982), *Papi* (1983), *El frac rojo* (1988), *Aeroplanos* (1990), *El patio de atrás* (1994), *Los otros papeles* (1996), *A propósito del tiempo* (1997), *Vuelo a Capistrano* (2011), and *Distracciones* (2015). Gorostiza penned a few novels: *Los cuartos oscuros* (1976), *Cuerpos presentes* (1981), *El basural* (1988), *Vuelan las palomas* (1999), and *La buena gente* (2001). Two other narrative works are worthy of mention: *El merodeador enmascarado* (2004)—his memoirs—and *De Narciso a las selfies* (2016), which was published not long after his death.

Gorostiza is credited with coining the campaign slogan "¡Ahora, Alfonsín!" which contributed to the landslide victory of **Raúl Alfonsín** in the **presidential election of 1983**. Appointed to head the **Ministry of Culture** by Alfonsín, he served for a little more than two years from the end of 1983 to early 1986, where he is remembered for dismantling the apparatus of censorship reinforced by successive **military** regimes and encouraging the reemergence of a vibrant theater and film scene after the artistically crabbed years of the **Proceso de Reorganización Nacional**—his own works had been banned by the regime. He left the ministry, frustrated by the constraints of office and the inability of the government to deliver on its ambitious cultural project due to financial cuts. He and Alfonsín parted company on good terms, and Gorostiza returned to writing and publishing.

GRAFFIGNA, OMAR DOMINGO RUBENS (1926–). Commander-in-chief of the air force and member of the **military** juntas headed by **Jorge Rafael Videla** (1979–1981) and **Roberto Eduardo Viola** (1981). A graduate of the Escuela Militar de Aviación, Graffigna became chief of staff of the air force following the **military coup of 1976** and initiated the **Condor missile program** during his tenure. He succeeded **Orlando Agosti** as head of the air force in January 1979 and served in this capacity until December 1981. Although Graffigna continued his predecessor's policy of serving as a moderating counterweight to the hard-line navy stance, he was a vocal advocate of the **War to Annihilate Subversion**. Following the restoration of democracy, Graffigna was acquitted of charges of **human rights** violations in the **trials of the military juntas** in 1985.

In 2016, aged 90, he and two former subordinates were put on trial over the abduction and disappearance of José Manuel Pérez Rojo and Patricia Roisinblit, an activist left-wing couple, in 1978. The abduction was carried out by the Regional Intelligence Centre of **Buenos Aires** (RIBA), which was under the control of the air force; at the time, 25-year-old Roisinblit was eight months pregnant. She was kept alive by her captors for several weeks at the notorious **Escuela Superior de Mecánica de la Armada** (ESMA) and then murdered after she gave birth. Her newborn son was handed over to air force intelligence operative Francisco Gómez and his wife to raise as their own. The boy, Guillermo Pérez Roisinblit, only found out his true identity at the age of 21 and was a plaintiff in the trial. Graffigna and the former head of the RIBA were sentenced to 25 years in prison for the murder and Gómez to 12 years for his part in the affair.

GRAINS. Cereals and seeds have been major staple **commodities** in Argentina since the opening of the **pampas** to modern **agriculture** in the mid-19th century, though wheat and flour were regularly imported until the 1870s. Changes in the commodity mix have been market/price led, conditioned by government policy, and shaped by domestic structural change. Soil and weather conditions on the pampas allow virtually any type of temperate and subtropical cereal to be produced profitably, with a degree of regional specialization observed in the planting of others.

The boom in production—and export—began in the final stages of the **Conquest of the Desert** and was underwritten by mass **immigration** and the growth of the rail network. Land was broken by sharecroppers and tenant farmers, usually working on three- to five-year contracts. They sowed mainly wheat and **maize** to start, and then planted European grasses and alfalfa (lucerne) in the final season before moving on. This arrangement facilitated the improvement of *estancias*, allowing them to be restocked with pedigree breeds of **sheep** and **cattle** for the **wool** and **meat** trades. Initially, wheat was the principal grain produced in Argentina. Large-scale maize planting began around 1900 and would soon rival wheat in terms of volume of production and export. Before the First World War, Argentina and Canada vied for the position of principal supplier of wheat to the international market, yet by the 1920s Canada had far outstripped Argentina and the **United States**, often selling more wheat on the world market than the other two countries combined. The United States remained the largest producer of grains but not the most important exporter. Canada dominated the international wheat market in the 1920s and 1930s; it was the largest global supplier in 16 out of the 18 seasons between 1921–1922 and 1938–1939.

In the 1920s, maize production in Argentina began to outstrip wheat planting, only to decline during the crisis of the 1930s. Maize made a comeback in the 1940s, by which time the volume of output of the two cereals was similar. (During the First and Second World Wars, grain production had been cut back as *estancieros* switched to higher-value items like meat.) Also, by the interwar decades, linseed (flax) was being planted extensively, raised for both fiber and seeds. Linseed never rivaled the other two grains in terms of total volume of production or export, though the country was ranked as a major world exporter of flax and oilseed. Barley and oats were also grown across the pampas—though in considerably lower quantities and rarely exported. Rice, initially planted in the province of **Tucumán**, was another grain that took off during the interwar period, by which time the center of production had shifted to the subtropical wetlands of **Mesopotamia** and riverine regions of nearby **Santa Fe**. These have been the main rice-producing areas since the 1950s. Although not a major item of trade, substantial volumes of rice have been exported since the early 1990s, but exports fluctuate dramatically from year to year. Diverse, large-scale oilseed production was another phenomenon that dates from the interwar decades. In addition to linseed, sunflowers became an important crop, again representing attempts at commodity diversification during the difficult 1930s as well as a growth in industrial demand for oil. Between the 1950s and the 1970s, grain production was particularly impacted by the vagaries of government agricultural policy, while the volume of exports was constrained by rising domestic demand, a function of population growth and industrialization.

Having grown massively during the first half of the 20th century, the total volume of grain production tended to stagnate during the second half, with an adverse impact on the surplus available for export. State intervention, in the form of price controls and the operation of government monopoly commodity buying agencies, was a distinct feature of the first administration of President **Juan Domingo Perón**. Thereafter, successive **military** and civilian governments of the 1960s and 1970s sought access to fiscal income and foreign exchange by taxing cereals and other rural exports. This fiscal regime was relaxed in the 1990s during the government of President **Carlos Saúl Menem** but reintroduced after the crisis of 2001 and tightened by President **Cristina Fernández de Kirchner**. After around 2000, land available for grain production was also constrained by a massive shift into soya, a change explained by rising demand in **China**.

While the production of individual grains varies from year to year, maize accounts for about 50 percent of total current production, wheat for around 30 percent, sorghum 7 percent, and barley and rice a little above 5 percent each. In recent years, grain production and export have been stimulated by the abolition of export taxes (*retenciones*). For example, the 23 percent tax on wheat was removed in December 2015, along with the 20 percent levy on maize exports. Barley has been making a comeback, but the removal of *retenciones* may halt this process as farmers switch back to other grains. The area under barley was about a third less in the 2016–2017 and 2017–2018 seasons than in 2015–2016; the area planted with maize and wheat rose substantially in the two latter seasons. Grain production is expected to reach an all-time high in 2017–2018, with maize exports forecast to hit record levels. *See also* AGRICULTURAL COLONIZATION; BUENOS AYRES & PACIFIC RAILWAY COMPANY (BA&P); BUENOS AYRES & ROSA-

RIO RAILWAY COMPANY (BA&R); BUENOS AYRES GREAT SOUTHERN RAILWAY COMPANY (BAGS); BUENOS AYRES WESTERN RAILWAY COMPANY (BAW); CENTRAL ARGENTINE RAILWAY COMPANY (CAR); CORDOBA CENTRAL RAILWAY COMPANY (CCR); ECONOMIC CRISES; ECONOMY; FARM PROTESTS; FERROCARRILES ARGENTINOS (FFAA); FOREIGN TRADE; INSTITUTO ARGENTINO DE PROMOCIÓN DEL INTERCAMBIO (IAPI); TRANSPORTATION.

GRANADEROS A CABALLO GENERAL SAN MARTÍN. A historic unit formed by General **José de San Martín** in 1812 as the Regimiento de Granaderos a Caballo (mounted grenadiers). Disbanded in the 1820s, the regiment took San Martín's name in 1903, when it was reformed; four years later, it was officially designated the Presidential Honor Guard, a duty that it continues to perform.

The corps was one of the first formally trained and organized units in the Argentine army. It was created by San Martín specifically to confront regular royalist forces in the wars of **independence** in place of poorly disciplined provincial militias and irregular bands of horsemen, hitherto the core of the insurgent army. San Martín regarded the formation of a regular army as the best means of liberating Argentina and neighboring countries, a task that could not be left to untrained, ill-equipped, ephemeral bands. Military technology and strategy had been transformed by the French Revolutionary and Napoleonic Wars in Europe, of which San Martín had firsthand experience. Officers were recruited from aristocratic families, and the regiment remains the elite unit of the Argentine army. All recruits had to be tall, first-class horsemen, and expert in the use of sabers and rifles. During the revolutionary period, the regiment saw service in areas that are now **Bolivia, Chile**, Ecuador, **Peru**, and **Uruguay**, in addition to Argentina itself. The regiment fought in many of the major conflicts of the period and particularly distinguished itself at the battles of San Lorenzo, Riobamba (considered to be the classic cavalry victory of the independence wars), and Ayacucho. In modern times, the regiment fought in the **Falklands War**.

The distinctive ceremonial uniform is modeled on that of French and Spanish grenadiers of the early 19th century and includes a dark blue shako adorned with gold cap badges and red pompoms, high-waisted dark blue jacket and trousers, with a white cavalry sabre belt and sash and black knee-length boots. *See also* ARMY OF THE ANDES; MILITARY; PATRICIOS.

GRAND CHACO. In Spanish, Gran Chaco; an elevated forested plateau in central South America, covering around 250,000 square miles (650,000 square kilometers): hot and dry in the north; humid in the south. At its

358 • GREAT BRITAIN

widest, the region stretches 450 miles (720 kilometers) from east to west; from north to south, 700 miles (1,100 kilometers), including semiarid southeastern **Bolivia**, as well as parts of the Brazilian states of Mato Grosso and Mato Grosso do Sul, western **Paraguay**, and center-north Argentina. Around two-thirds of the region is to be found in Argentina, a subdivision generally known as the Southern Chaco (Chaco Austral), which merges into the northern **pampas** (the *pampa seca*) at its southern tip. At the time of **independence**, around 1810, the region was contested by Bolivia, Paraguay, and Argentina, in the 20th century becoming the theater of one of South America's bloodies modern conflicts, the **Chaco War** between Bolivia and Paraguay. Once an important logging center, the Chaco Austral has recently been subject to massive deforestation. After the 1900s, land was cleared to grow such **grains** as sorghum; now soya is the main crop, leading to further rapid deforestation over a much larger area, a subject that has resulted in political protest and rising concern about environmental degradation and loss of biodiversity. Current development is having a catastrophic impact on indigenous peoples in all countries of the region and on flora and fauna. Around 2010, some 5 percent of the forest was being lost each year; the current rate is likely to be much larger. *See also* CHACO; FORESTAL ARGENTINA S.A; FORMOSA (PROVINCE).

GREAT BRITAIN. Britain and Argentina enjoy a complex relationship that may be summed up in a number of keywords—invasion, investment, **immigration**, imperialism. The **British Invasions** of the **River Plate** in 1806 and 1807 during the Napoleonic Wars contributed to the struggle for **independence**. The attack on **Buenos Aires** in 1806 exposed the weakness of Spanish imperial power—the viceroy fled to the interior, leaving the city and its inhabitants to their own devices. The subsequent recapture of the city and surrender of British regiments, defeated largely by local militia and irregulars, generated a sense of pride and confidence. The following year, when a British naval and military expedition returned, Montevideo was taken, but the assault on Buenos Aires failed, again routed largely by patriotic forces. British survivors were allowed to retreat to Montevideo, which was abandoned shortly afterward. These events contributed directly to the **May Revolution of 1810**, which deposed the viceroy and established a patriotic junta to rule until events in **Spain**, which had been invaded by France, with Napoleon Bonaparte's brother Joseph appointed king, became clearer. With the opening of the ports, the British returned—British merchants had been active in the region for many decades, but not bearing arms. Independence was declared in 1816, recognized by Britain in 1825, with the signing of a treaty of friendship, commerce, and navigation.

Trade prospects and investment opportunities were not as buoyant as anticipated. The notorious Baring Loan of 1825 was soon in default. Yet by the 1840s, as **wool** exports picked up—largely due to the migration of Scots and Irish shepherds, as well as Basques—trade expanded. Between the 1850s and 1870, there was a hesitant growth in investment: many early railways, tramways, and urban utilities, whether registered in Buenos Aires or London, involved British and British Argentine capital. The 1870s and 1880s saw London financing new railway construction, by the state and private companies. There was an investment boom in the 1880s, until terminated by the **Baring Crisis** of 1890. Yet as frontier of settlement expanded after the **Conquest of the Desert**, by the end of the 1890s trade grew rapidly, notably between the two countries. In the 1810s and from the 1830s, Britain had been the principal source of Argentine imports; now it was also the major market for exports. In the years immediately before the First World War, Argentina was the single most important destination of overseas investment from London.

The British community in Argentina (including second- and third-generation immigrants and expatriates) remained large—estimates for the interwar period range between 100,000 and 250,000, the larger figure probably including Irish immigrants. Although this community hardly compared with the German and French, and was dwarfed by the Italian and Spanish, who constituted around 80 percent of mass immigration, it was socially and culturally significant as well as economically important. Many of the early sports clubs had been set up by Britons, or by London-registered banks, railways, and utilities; there were British schools, attended by children from Spanish- and English-speaking families; there were "English" department stores, including a branch of Harrods (where taking afternoon tea became an institution); "English"-style architecture could be observed in residential districts, banks, railway stations (as well as station names), and *estancia* houses. It was this type of connection that had led to Argentina being described as the "Sixth Dominion" in the 1920s, that is, enjoying links with Britain similar to Australia, Canada, India, South Africa, and New Zealand.

Yet British–Argentine relations soured, partly due to the trade deal struck in 1930s—the **Roca–Runciman Pact**—and haggling over blocked sterling balances, credits to Argentina that had accumulated during the Second World War in the Bank of England when Britain had bought Argentine exports on tick. With the rise of economic nationalism and anti-imperialism, while the **United States** was the butt of antiforeign sentiments elsewhere in Latin America, in Argentina it was Britain that figured in this role, at least until the 1950s. At the end of the Second World War, the stock of British investment in Argentina was greater than that of the United States, though only marginally so. It would shrink dramatically during the first presidency of **Juan Domingo Perón** due to debt repatriation and the nationalization of the railways and utilities. What had been a symbiotic trade relationship faltered at much the same time, as the export performance of Argentina became more volatile and Britain was not capable of providing the new types of imports required, which now came largely from the United States and later continental Europe and Japan.

Efforts to revive the commercial relationship were doomed by economic and political conditions in the two countries and aggravated by intermittent disputes that culminated in the **Falklands War** of 1982—the last throw of the dice of the regime that had come to power as a result of the **military coup of 1976**. British business played only a marginal role in the **privatizations** of the presidencies of **Carlos Saúl Menem** (1989–1999). Investment and trade have picked up since the beginning of the 21st century, but British investment in the country lags behind that of France, Germany, Italy, and Spain; Britain is well behind western European countries, not to mention **Brazil**, **China**, and the United States, in the current commercial relationship. *See also* ANGLO–ARGENTINE TRAMWAYS COMPANY; BUENOS AYRES & PACIFIC RAILWAY COMPANY (BA&P); BUENOS AYRES & ROSARIO RAILWAY COMPANY (BA&R); BUENOS AYRES GREAT SOUTHERN RAILWAY COMPANY (BAGS); BUENOS AYRES WESTERN RAILWAY COMPANY (BAW); CENTRAL ARGENTINE RAILWAY COMPANY (CAR); COMMODITIES; CORDOBA CENTRAL RAILWAY COMPANY (CCR); ECONOMY; FALKLANDS DISPUTE; FERROCARRILES ARGENTINOS (FFAA); FOREIGN DEBT/FOREIGN INVESTMENT; FOREIGN TRADE; MIRANDA–EADY AGREEMENT; STATE-OWNED ENTERPRISES (SOEs); TRANSPORTATION.

GRINSPUN, BERNARDO (1925–1996). Politician, short-lived reformist minister of economy, lifelong member of the **Unión Cívica Radical** (UCR), and adherent to its modernization wing, the **Movimiento de Renovación y Cambio** (MRC), in which he was closely associated with **Raúl Alfonsín**. Trained in economics at the **University of Buenos Aires** (UBA), where he had been active in student politics, Grinspun was much influenced by the writings of **Raúl Prebisch**. He became a strong advocate of **developmentalism**, ideas that he attempted to implement when a member of the economic team during the presidency of **Arturo Illia**. When Illia was ejected from office by the **military coup of 1966**, he redoubled efforts to make the UCR electable, siding with Alfonsín in the struggle against the old guard headed by **Ricardo Balbín**. Convinced of the efficacy of a social-democratic, state-market economic project, he advanced these ideas during the dark days of the **Proceso de Reorganización Nacional**. When the UCR unexpectedly gained power following the **congressional** and **presidential elections of 1983**, he was the logical choice as Alfonsín's first minister of economy and charged with stabilizing the economy. The outgoing **military** regime left the country encumbered with massive **foreign debt** and in a deep recession, as well as the disaster of the **Falklands War**. Grinspun's solution to the multifaceted economic crisis was a neo-Keynesian developmentalist program to reboot the economy and address the related social crisis by stimulating domestic demand. Confronted by an unsympathetic International Monetary Fund and a banking community insistent that Argentina honor obligations accumulated by post-1976 military administrations, he had little chance of success. After 14 months in office, with **hyperinflation** threatening, Grinspun was replaced by **Juan Vital Sourrouille** at the **Ministry of Economy**.

Upon leaving office, he was appointed to a position at the **United Nations**, where he continued to argue for international understanding of difficulties confronting developing economies, while recognizing the need for greater productivity on the part of national business, increased public-sector efficiency, and the importance of raising national savings and investment. His reputation is that of a committed democrat, convinced of the need for economic and political modernization.

GRUPO DE OFICIALES UNIDOS (GOU). Secret **military** society frequently credited with masterminding the **military coup of 1943**. It was the brainchild of Colonel **Juan Domingo Perón**; in addition to him, the original nucleus consisted of seven officers. In their effort to persuade their fellow officers of the need for a special organization, Perón and his associates of this inner group played on a variety of themes: distaste for a political system based on fraud, the loss of prestige the army would suffer if it became identified with that system (former president General **Agustín P. Justo** was dead and Robustiano Patrón Costas was the nominated presidential candidate), the need to guard against a Communist upsurge, fear of involvement in the Second World War as a result of external (mainly US) pressure, and a sense of solidarity within the officer corps. To cast aside any suspicion of ulterior motives, the promoters of the secret society insisted on their absolute lack of personal ambitions. There would be no leader but an executive body working anonymously. They claimed that their only interest was the welfare of the army and the Fatherland (*la Patria*).

The society was formally established in March 1943: the name Grupo de Oficiales Unidos (GOU) was adopted, the draft charter prepared by Perón was accepted with modifications, and its executive body (*grupo directivo*) was constituted. The directorate came to consist of 20 officers, all of them stationed in **Buenos Aires** or the neighboring garrison. When General **Pedro Pablo Ramírez** became de facto president in the aftermath of the June 1943 coup, he opened the door to GOU influence. Lieutenant Colonel Enrique P. González, his chief of the Presidential Secretariat, was a close friend and a leading GOU figure. General **Edelmiro Farrell** (Perón's chief) was placed in the crucial post of minister of war. Perón became his deputy by heading the War Ministry Secretariat and used his ministerial position to build himself up into a major political force, and flagrantly promote the GOU and his own prestige. He created an internal espionage network to keep tabs on the officer corps and spread his web into the presidential palace itself.

Ramírez was ambivalent about the need to get rid of the two key figures in the War Ministry, and his failure to do so led to a major political shake-up in October 1943. Farrell added the vice presidency to his portfolio; Perón also became head of the National Labor Department, which he transformed into the Secretariat of Labor and Welfare. In time, this would lead him to create a broad personal following among labor rank and file. **Trade union** leaders had positions in the new agency, the powers of the latter were placed behind union demands and to promote the unionization of the unskilled, and labor grievances were treated as legitimate concerns of the government.

Not all GOU leaders viewed Perón's activities with sympathy. He was seeking to convert the society into an instrument of his political ambitions, and they had pledged not to seek public office. As a result, the members of the executive body dissolved the GOU in February 1944.

GÜEMES GOYECHEA, MARTÍN MIGUEL JUAN DE MATA DE (1875–1821). Charismatic hero of the **independence** period, sometime governor of the province of **Salta**, and archetypical **caudillo**, generally known as Martín Güemes. He was born into an aristocratic family of Spanish origin that had become one of the most prominent families of the region—many still-powerful political clans in the Argentine northwest trace their origins from Güemes. He entered the **military** at an early age, training as a cadet in **Buenos Aires** before serving in his native region. He played an active role in confronting the **British invasions** of 1806 and 1807, and particularly distinguished himself as an aide to Viceroy **Santiago de Liniers**. Back in Salta when the **May Revolution of 1810** occurred, he became an enthusiastic supporter of independence, forming cavalry and irregular units to protect the country against royalist administrations firmly established to the north. One of his most prominent roles was commanding **gaucho** groups, whose respect he earned and who were immensely loyal to him. He proved to be an adroit, strategic, and effective defender of the frontier, notwithstanding reverses suffered by the insurgent cause. In addition to containing the royalist threat, he liaised with the authorities in Buenos Aires and was nominated governor of his province. He endorsed the Continental Plan of General **José de San Martín**, who argued that the survival of Argentina as an independent polity required taking the revolutionary struggle to surrounding areas still under Spanish control. While San Martín crossed the **Andes** to campaign in **Chile**, he left Güemes in charge of prosecuting the war in the northern theater. Here Güemes's contributions were multifaceted: he reorganized the provincial administration, stabilized the region, raised funds to finance the war, attempted to promote unity among local factions, and harried Spanish garrisons. He repeatedly repulsed royalist efforts to reconquer the area and advance on Buenos Aires. His contributions to political change included a commitment to democratic principles—as understood at the time—land reform, and the modernization of the tax structure. These offended traditional families, who had regarded Güemes as one of their own. He was also an advocate of provincial rights, a stance that brought him into conflict with centralizers in Buenos Aires.

Güemes died as a result of injuries sustained in a skirmish with royalist troops who had temporarily retaken the city of Salta. He is remembered as an indomitable fighter and strategist whose defense of the north tied down royalists, allowing the successful execution of the Continental Plan in Chile and **Peru**, and as a modernizing patriot and proponent of provincial rights. He is also idealized as a gaucho commander, an icon of guerrilla resistance. He was declared a national hero in 2006 and has a public holiday dedicated to his memory, 17 June, the anniversary of his death. *See also* ARMY OF THE ANDES; MILITARY.

GUERRA SUCIA. *See* DESAPARECIDOS; DIRTY WAR; DISPOSICIÓN FINAL; WAR TO ANNIHILATE SUBVERSION.

GUEVARA, ERNESTO "CHE" (1928–1967). Born in Argentina and died in **Bolivia**; an icon of the revolutionary left who advocated armed struggle; a symbol of youth counterculture. Arguably, with **Eva Perón**, Guevara is the most instantly internationally recognized Argentine. Guevara was born to a well-read, politically aware middle-class family in **Rosario** of Basque, Italian, and Irish origin. The last might explain his passion for rugby, which provided his second nickname. He was "Fuser," a reference to his aggressive style as a fly-half, before he became Che. He acquired the latter nickname in **Cuba** due to his frequent use of the Argentine figure of speech *che*, meaning chum or buddy. In early life, he had been called "Ernestito" as his father was also named Ernesto. When a medical student at the **University of Buenos Aires**, he traveled in the interior of Argentina and later and more extensively in South and Central America. It was during these travels that he encountered levels of poverty, squalor, and malnutrition among rural and industrial workers that he had not observed in prosperous Rosario and **Buenos Aires**. He contributed to the program of social and agrarian reforms attempted in Guatemala in the early 1950s—the reformist regime was subsequently overthrown by a **United States**–inspired coup. These journeys convinced him that the social and economic plight of the poor were a function of the capitalist system and inculcated a belief that the only remedy lay in revolution.

Guevara was a multifaceted individual. He helped formulate the strategy of guerrilla warfare applied in Cuba, which he later attempted to export to Africa and mainland South America. During the years immediately following the victory of the Cuban Revolution in 1959, he devised an innovative and adventurous program of emergency measures designed to stabilize and kick-start the Cuban economy, serving as minister for industries and president of the central bank. His theory of the "new man" (the antithesis of *homos economicus*) envisaged individuals responding to moral rather than material incentives that would foster growth with equity. He also acted as a roving ambassador for Cuba, in which capacity he promoted closer economic and diplomatic relations with the Soviet Union and the countries of Eastern Europe to counter threats posed by the United States and overcome economic constraints arising from Washington's embargo on trade with the island. He represented Cuba at various international fora, including the **United Nations** headquarters in New York and at several gatherings of "Third World leaders," where he was considered a passionate and persuasive speaker. It was in this capacity that he held secret meetings with President **Arturo Frondizi** in 1961, an event said to have contributed to the **military coup of 1962**.

Accounts differ about the factors that led Guevara to leave Cuba in 1965—disagreement with Fidel Castro, or a determination to promote armed struggle elsewhere. He was reported to have been in Central and East Africa at various times in 1965 and 1966. What is not in doubt is that he was in Bolivia by the end of 1966, where he soon established a guerrilla *foco* intended to spread revolution across the country and the continent. He was captured by Bolivian special forces at the beginning of October 1967 and executed a few days later.

By some, Guevara is lauded for his incisive analysis of the social and economic predicament of Latin America, for his courage and skill as a fearless guerrilla leader and fighter, for his achievements as a key figure in the Cuban Revolution and his contributions to its success and legacy, and for his steadfast practical and intellectual commitment to revolution. Others point to his ruthlessness, namely the treatment meted out to deserters when commanding guerrilla forces in Cuba and his organization of summary executions of supporters of the defeated regime, whom Guevara and other revolutionaries accused of torture and themselves paying scant regard to due process, and for a broader application of "revolutionary justice" to counterrevolutionaries and economic saboteurs. He is also remembered for his view that social progress was impossible under democracy.

GUIDO, JOSÉ MARÍA (1910–1975). President of Argentina from 1962 to 1963. In the **congressional elections of 1958**, he was elected national senator for the province of **Río Negro** on behalf of the **Unión Cívica Radical**

Intransigente (UCRI). Following the resignation of Vice President Alejandro Gómez, Guido was elected provisional president of the Senate and became first in line to the presidency.

President **Arturo Frondizi** was overthrown in the **military coup of 1962**, and squabbling among the armed forces resulted in an immediate power vacuum. As a result, the Supreme Court used the Ley de Acefalía en el Poder Ejecutivo to swear Guido in as Frondizi's successor. He became the only civilian to take power in Argentina in a **military** coup, which is why he is sometimes considered a de facto president. The armed forces reluctantly accepted the decision of the Supreme Court but did reserve the right to remove him from office. Guido assumed both the executive and legislative powers; **Congress** was dissolved after it annulled the **congressional elections of 1962** and declared all the country's provinces intervened in.

The Guido administration endured numerous military rebellions, plus the confrontation of the *azul* and *colorado* factions of the armed forces. This split exposed the inability of the military to deal with the fact that Peronism was there to stay and can be traced back to the **Revolución Libertadora** (1955–1958). The *azules* sought institutional normalization, while the *colorados* wanted the complete eradication of Peronism. The former won when the open struggle reached its climax in April 1963, leaving 24 dead and 87 injured on both sides.

Guido's commitment to holding general elections was finally realized in July 1963, though as a result of pressure from the armed forces and conservative elements they were restricted by the proscription of the Frente Nacional y Popular, an electoral alliance set up with the blessing of exiled former president **Juan Domingo Perón** and which comprised the **Unión Popular** (UP), the **Partido Conservador Popular** (PCP), and the **Movimiento de Integración y Desarrollo** (MID). Guido was succeeded by **Arturo Illia** of the **Unión Cívica Radical del Pueblo** (UCRP). *See also* CONGRESSIONAL ELECTIONS OF 1963; PRESIDENTIAL ELECTION OF 1963; PRESIDENTIAL SUCCESSION OF 1962.

GÜIRALDES, RICARDO (1886–1927). A novelist and poet, he was one of the most significant writers of his era. He was born into a wealthy landed family, whose ranch "La Porteña" was located near the town of San Antonio de Areco in the province of **Buenos Aires**. Here Güiraldes came into contact with the world of the **gauchos**, which figured prominently in two of his novels, *Raucho* (1917) and the more famous *Don Segundo Sombra* (1926). As with **Martín Fierro**, *Don Segundo Sombra* has a main protagonist. But unlike in the former work, the character is not fictional but loosely inspired on Segundo Ramírez, a native of San Antonio de Areco. *Don Segundo Sombra* does not romanticize the gaucho but simply examines the character as a shadow (*sombra*) cast across Argentine history. Excepting *El cencerro de* *cristal* (1915), Güiraldes' poetry was published posthumously: *Poemas místicos* (1928), *Poemas solitarios* (1928), *El libro bravo* (1936), and *El pájaro blanco* (1952).

H

HARGUINDEGUY, ALBANO EDUARDO (1927–2012). Minister of interior during the de facto presidency of **Jorge Rafael Videla**. Implicated in the **human rights** abuses of the **Proceso de Reorganización Nacional**—during his ministerial tenure, Harguindeguy held the list of the almost 9,000 **Desaparecidos**—he was one of the senior **military** officers pardoned by President **Carlos Saúl Menem**. In 2004, Harguindeguy refused to testify before a judge investigating illegal detentions and killings under **Operación Condor** and was placed under house arrest. He remained there for the rest of his life since in 2006 the Supreme Court had declared the pardons issued by Menem unconstitutional. *See also* DISPOSICIÓN FINAL; MINISTRY OF INTERIOR, PUBLIC WORKS, AND HOUSING; WAR TO ANNIHILATE SUBVERSION.

HIJO DEL PAÍS. Patronizing term meaning "son of the country" (or "child of the country," that is, from the countryside), applied to residents of the interior by Argentines living in the **Littoral**. The country was transformed demographically between the 1850s and 1950s as the result of mass **immigration** from Europe: 97 percent of Argentines claim European descent. Although forming a small proportion of total population, in the north and northeast of the country there were relatively small clusters of people claiming mestizo (mixed race) and Indian descent. The term *hijo del país* was widely used in the early 20th century, especially in the decades after 1930 when **economic crises** triggered the movement of people from the interior to pampean and coastal cities. Ethnically determined, the phrase was not necessarily a term of racial abuse. It was later displaced by the phrase *cabecita negra*, which was.

HUMAN RIGHTS. In Argentina, the issue of human rights—the violation of human rights—is particularly associated with the last **military** dictatorship, the self-designated **Proceso de Reorganización Nacional** brought to power by the **military coup of 1976**. This is understandable but ignores abuses that occurred earlier, though the term *human rights* was not widely used. Rather, such terms as *violence* and the "suspension" of civil, constitutional, and political rights tended to circulate, but these sentiments approximated those set out in the Universal Declaration of Human Rights adopted by the **United Nations** in 1948 and the European Convention on Human Rights signed by member states of the Council of Europe in Rome in 1950. These rights include the right to life and to enjoy a private and family life; the right to liberty, which embraces freedom from slavery and nonjudicial detention; freedom of thought, conscious, expression, association, and religion; the right to a fair trial, not to be punished for something that is not against the law, and not to be subject to unjust punishment by the state; freedom from discrimination on grounds of opinion, faith, gender, or race; the right to basic **education**; the right to hold private property; and the right to participate in free elections.

It is a commonplace that the level of violence associated with *golpes de estado* and related violation of human rights increased over time. The **military coup of 1930**, which was broadly supported by many sectors of society, involved injuries and led to imprisonments. Shots were fired, **political parties** were banned, and the **Constitution of 1853** suspended. Political life was constrained and elections rigged, but efforts to establish a fascist state failed. The **military coup of 1943**, which brought an end to the "directed democracy" of the **Concordancia** years, was not violence free nor immediately democratic. Estimates of casualties vary, but there were probably around 30 deaths and 100 injuries arising from several skirmishes. Imprisonments and purges followed, and there was no significant improvement in what would be regarded as human rights. Yet the *golpe* led to the calling of fair and free elections in 1946, which brought the restoration of democracy. Around 1951, as the administration of President **Juan Domingo Perón** became more authoritarian, political freedoms were circumscribed. Members of opposition political parties and dissidents within the government-dominated labor movement were harassed and imprisoned—instances of torture were reported. Press freedom was restricted: parts of the **media** were censored or closed. Again, although the term was not used, there was an abuse of human rights.

The **military coup of 1955** that ousted Perón was associated with much greater violence. In June, some months before the *golpe*, navy and air force aircraft bombed the center of the city of **Buenos Aires**, allegedly in an attempt to murder Perón. There was little respect of the right to life—approximately 300 were killed and many more were injured. Shortly after the coup proper, which took place in September, the **Constitution of 1949** was suspended, in preparation for revision. Although the military junta headed by Generals **Eduardo Lonardi** and **Pedro Eugenio Aramburu** and Admiral **Isaac Rojas** appointed a council of civilians drawn from the main political parties opposed to Perón to advise them, the military was firmly in command. There were skirmished in the cities of Buenos Aires, **Córdoba**, and **Bahía Blanca** and in the province of **Corrientes**. The city of Mar del Plata was subjected to a naval bombardment, and warships blockaded the Río de la Plata while the air force patrolled the skies above. Much of the fighting, and many of the casualties, was between units supporting the coup and those loyal to the government. Aramburu, who soon emerged as the dominant figure, set about de-Peronizing the body politic. Some military personnel loyal to Perón were summarily executed. Prominent Peronists were imprisoned, tortured, and murdered. Prisons were packed with political prisoners. When elections were finally called in 1958, Peronists were prevented from standing. These events constituted a clear breach of human rights, prefiguring what would occur in 1966.

In addition to the level of violence associated with the **military coup of 1966**, once more partly due to infighting among the **military** itself, distinct features included the intervention in the **University of Buenos Aires** (UBA) ordered by General **Juan Carlos Onganía** and the lack of a speedy return to civilian rule. The mission statement delivered by the ruling junta envisaged the armed forces remaining in control for at least 15 years—there would be a five-year phase of economic reconstruction, followed by a phase of social reconstruction that would facilitate the final phase of gradual political reconstruction, after which democracy would be restored. The constitution was suspended, political parties banned, the media controlled, and cultural life made to conform to a moral template established by the regime, which was Catholic and nationalistic in tone. In short, human rights were violated and restricted. Yet even worse was to come.

The **military coup of 1976** remains the benchmark event in the story of human rights abuses in Argentina, associated with mass murder, torture, and imprisonment—all without due process. Civil, political, and legal rights specified in the Constitution of 1853 were suspended. Like their counterparts in 1966, the instigators of the 1976 *golpe* envisaged a regime that would remain in power for some time, deploying state violence to transform society, polity, and **economy**. Yet there was one distinct feature. Hitherto, most of the violence and violation of human rights associated with military intervention in politics had followed a coup. Unusually in 1976, much violence had been perpetrated before the actual coup, during the last year or so of the presidency of **Isabel Perón** when the military had been given a virtual free hand to curb internal subversion, and radical groups on the left and right engaged in a killing and kidnapping spree. Abuses of the period have been well recorded and reported, for example, in the trials of the military juntas, the work of the **Comisión Nacional sobre la Desaparición de Personas** (CONADEP) and its report *Nunca Más*, and the writing and journalism of **Jacobo Timerman**.

It would be a mistake to assume that human rights were ignored only around the time of *golpes de estado* or did not occur before the middle of the 20th century. Basic freedoms and rights expressed in the Universal Declaration and European Convention would have been enjoyed by few in the 19th century. The **Trelew Massacre** of 1972 showed as little regard for the human rights of escaping *guerrilleros* as many of them had those of their victims. Yet it is abuses of the Proceso period that are mostly known abroad and which have seared themselves on the national conscience. The legacy is understandable and continues. There is particular sensitivity to any action by the police, military, and security services that may echo—or be portrayed as similar to—what occurred in the mid- and late 1970s, for example, the **Avellaneda Massacre** of 2002. Memories of the Proceso years have also been used for political purposes by various groups and interests. Critics were not slow to lambast President **Cristina Fernández de Kirchner** for seeking to make political capital out of the issue of human rights, families of the victims less so. Human rights campaigns have also moved beyond the Proceso in recent years to embrace the rights of indigenous people. The **Conquest of the Desert** in the late 19th century, which decimated the native populations of the **pampas**, has triggered similar demands for recognition as abuses committed by forces of the state during the so-called Indian Wars of the **United States**, though much lower in key. Greater momentum has been generated by human rights campaigners fighting against the material conditions of surviving indigenous communities in the north and west of the country where poverty is greater, access to such public services as basic education much less, and social deprivation much higher than the national norm.

Notwithstanding the enormity of violations committed during the 1970s, there have been several instances in recent Argentine history when human rights have been little respected. No one regime or period has had a monopoly on violations and abuses. As the democratically elected government headed by President **Raúl Alfonsín** recognized, democracy—and the consolidation of democratic institutions—requires a respect for human dignity and the defense and preservation of basic freedoms. In a society traumatized by government terror and violence perpetrated by nonstate organizations, it is important to acknowledge the past, bring to account the perpetrators and instigators of the worst excesses, and secure justice for victims and their families so as to be able to move on. *See also* ACOSTA, JORGE EDUARDO (1941–); ANAYA, JORGE ISAAC (1926–2008); ARAMBURAZO (29 MAY–1 JUNE 1970); ASTIZ, ALFREDO IGNACIO (1951–); BIGNONE, REYNALDO BENITO (1928–2018); BONAFINI, HEBE PASTOR DE (1928–); CARRIÓ, ELISA MARÍA AVELINA "LILITA" (1956–); CONGRESSIONAL ELECTIONS OF 1946; DESAPARECIDOS; DISPOSICIÓN FINAL; ESCUELA SUPERIOR DE MECÁNICA DE LA ARMADA (ESMA); EJÉRCITO REVOLUCIONARIO DEL PUEBLO

(ERP); FERNÁNDEZ MEIJIDE, GRACIELA (1931–); GALTIERI, LEO-
POLDO FORTUNATO (1926–2003); GRAFFIGNA, OMAR DOMINGO
RUBENS (1926–); HARGUINDEGUY, ALBANO EDUARDO
(1927–2012); INSTITUTO TORCUATO DI TELLA; JUSTO, ALICIA MO-
REAU DE (1885–1986); KIRCHNER, NÉSTOR CARLOS (1950–2010);
LA PRENSA; LAMBRUSCHINI, ARMANDO (1924–2004); LEY DE OBE-
DIENCIA DEBIDA; LEY DE PUNTO FINAL; LUDER, ÍTALO ARGEN-
TINO (1916–2008); MADRES DE PLAZA DE MAYO; MENEM, CAR-
LOS SAÚL (1930–); MILITARY COUP OF 1951 (FAILED); MILITARY
JUNTAS, TRIALS OF THE; MONTONEROS; PRESIDENTIAL ELEC-
TION OF 1946; SÁBATO, ERNESTO (1911–2011); SALA, MILAGRO
AMALIA ÁNGELA (1964–); SEINELDÍN, MOHAMED ALÍ (1933–2009);
TRADE UNIONS; VIDELA, JORGE RAFAEL (1925–2013); WAR TO
ANNIHILATE SUBVERSION.

HYPERINFLATION. Technically, hyperinflation occurs when prices rise
by more than 50 percent per month, meaning that money becomes worthless
and prices cease to function as economic indicators. During periods of inflation, some producers and consumers can adjust to changes in prices and may
hedge against it. While inflation damages the functioning of an **economy**, it
also creates "winners" as well as "losers." That is, those who hold assets that
may retain or increase in value in real terms gain; those who do not—
typically wage earners whose salaries are not adjusted and those who hold
cash savings—lose. In the chaos of hyperinflation, there are no winners—all
lose. Hence the argument that while inflation may be tolerated or welcomed
by some, hyperinflation brings its own solutions; because all are losers, a
new political economy will result—it has a cathartic affect. The main causes
of hyperinflation include an accelerating public-sector deficit as government
expenditure exceeds fiscal receipts and the nominal level of taxes is eroded
by inflation, by excessive emissions of paper money, and by shocks exogenous to the system, or combinations of these.

Exceptional among modern economies, Argentina has experienced several
periods of hyperinflation. The first occurred during the last year of the presidency of **Raúl Alfonsín** in 1989, when the annualized monthly peak of price
rises threatened to top 6,000 percent, and the first year of the administration
of President **Carlos Saúl Menem**, when a figure of around 12,000 percent
loomed. In additions, there were other occasions when the country appeared
on the verge of hyperinflation and general economic meltdown, for example,
during the presidency of **Isabel Perón**, when the average annual rate of
inflation reached over 300 percent and the annualized highest monthly rate
almost touched 1,000 percent, and around 1980–1981 as the bloody **military**
regime of the **Proceso de Reorganización Nacional** was in its death throws
and a run on the banks and Falklands debacle triggered price rises in excess

of 1,000 percent. There was fear of hyperinflation, which did not materialize, as the administration of **Fernando de la Rúa** collapsed at the end of 2001. *See also* AUSTRAL PLAN; CAVALLO, DOMINGO FELIPE (1946–); CONVERTIBILITY PLAN; CURRENCY; ECONOMIC CRISES; MARTÍNEZ DE HOZ, JOSÉ ALFREDO (1925–2013); MENEM, CARLOS SAÚL (1930–); RODRIGAZO; RODRIGO, CELESTINO (1915–1987); SOURROUILLE, JUAN VITAL (1940–).

I

IBARRA, ANÍBAL (1958–). Lawyer trained at the **University of Buenos Aires** (UBA); center-left politician and mayor of **Buenos Aires** (2000–2005). Becoming a prominent, modernizing influence in the judiciary, Ibarra served in various capacities and acquired a reputation as a strong campaigner against **corruption**. Objecting to the pardons granted by President **Carlos Saúl Menem** to members of the **military** juntas of the **Proceso de Reorganizacón Nacional** convicted of **human rights** abuses, he was forced to resign as a public prosecutor. He was one of the architects of the **Constitution of 1994**, which permitted the immediate reelection of a sitting president (reducing the term from six to four years), increased the number of senators per province from two to three, and in effect granted provincial status to the city of Buenos Aires. He was elected to the Buenos Aires city council in 1991 and 1993, before the constitutional change, for the **Frente País Solidario** (FREPASO). Following the midterm **congressional elections of 1997**, he obtained a seat on the recently formed legislative assembly of the city of Buenos Aires, becoming vice president. Elected mayor in 2000, he was returned in 2003 with the support of President **Néstor Kirchner**, who was at the time anxious to construct alliances with political groupings beyond the **Partido Justicialista** (PJ) in order to consolidate his hold on power. Ibarra was forced to step down in 2005 following a fire in the **República Cromañón** nightclub in which almost 200 people died—city officials were accused of a dereliction of duty for not enforcing safety regulations, for which Ibarra was impeached.

Ibarra's period as mayor is remembered for substantial investment in public works, including the modernization and extension of the underground rail system, the improvement of flood defenses and public parks, as well as major initiatives in **education**, health, and the arts. Since being forced to step down as mayor, he has been several times reelected to the city legislature. He continues to be associated with Kirchnerismo and harbors national political ambitions, though his earlier reputation as a fearless opponent of corruption in official circles is somewhat tarnished.

IGUAZÚ FALLS. Described as one of the wonders of the world, the falls at Iguazú, in the province of **Misiones**, are one of the largest in the world. In Spanish, the name is Cataratas del Iguazú; Foz do Iguaçu in Portuguese. The Iguazú/Iguaçu River forms the boundary between Argentina and **Brazil**, though the greater part of the falls is located on the Argentine side, 14 miles before the river drains into the **Paraná** River, just below the **Itaipú Dam**. The areas on both sides of the river enjoy national park status. The span of the falls is greater than Niagara in the **United States** and Canada, while the drop is somewhat shorter than at Victoria Falls in southern Africa.

ILLIA, ARTURO UMBERTO (1900–1983). Doctor and politician; president of Argentina from 1963 to 1966. Affiliated with the **Unión Cívica Radical** (UCR) in 1918, he settled in the railway town of Cruz del Eje in the province of **Córdoba**. There Illia worked as a doctor between 1929 and 1963, excepting the period 1940–1943, when he was the elected provincial vice governor. As a national deputy from 1948 to 1952, he served on two congressional committees that dealt with major issues pertaining to his profession. Illia went on to be elected governor of Córdoba in the gubernatorial elections held simultaneously with the **congressional elections of 1962**, but the **military** ousted President **Arturo Frondizi** of the **Unión Cívica Radical Intransigente** (UCRI) shortly afterward and prevented Illia from taking office.

Illia contested the **presidential election of 1963** as the candidate of the **Unión Cívica Radical del Pueblo** (UCRP). Although he obtained only 25 percent of the vote, he secured the necessary majority in the electoral college with the support of several minor parties. An honest man, Illia turned out to be an inept president. By relying on the UCRI and not expanding his political base, he was perceived as weak. Moreover, his policies irked important sectors that ultimately came to view him with contempt. In November 1963, Illia annulled the oil contracts with US companies signed by Frondizi five years earlier. The US State Department got the corporations to negotiate with the Argentine government, which agreed to return money, interest, and an allowance for the rate of return on capital. Given the amount of work that some of the firms had put in, this represented an excellent bargain for Argentina. While the **United States** had not reacted as harshly as might have been expected, the rescinding of the contracts and Illia's attitude toward foreign capital instilled fear in potential foreign investors and thereby weakened the country's international position.

The government, challenged by the **Confederación General del Trabajo** (CGT) with a series of demands, responded in June 1964 with the passage of the Ley del Salario Mínimo, Vital y Móvil, which established a national minimum wage in order to ensure an adequate minimum income and improve the salaries of the poorest workers. In the same vein, a Ley de Abastecimiento was approved, which aimed to control the prices of basic foodstuffs and set minimum standards for pensions. Yet the legislation satisfied nobody. For a start, the CGT was not prepared to be indulgent with an administration elected thanks to the proscription of Peronism and resorted to massive disruption. The **Unión Industrial Argentina** (UIA) and the **Sociedad Rural Argentina** (SRA) were also openly opposed to the Ley de Salario Mínimo, Vital y Móvil on the grounds of its inflationary effects.

Also contentious was the Ley de Medicamentos sanctioned in August 1964. A government study had indicated that a considerable part of medicines commercialized in Argentina were different in quality and composition to that declared by the laboratories. On the other hand, there was no relation between costs and final sales prices, thereby generating extraordinary revenues for the manufacturers. The administration passed a Ley de Medicamentos establishing a policy of price and quality controls for pharmaceuticals, freezing the prices of patented medicines, and setting limits to expenditures on advertising and to the amount of money remitted abroad for royalties and related payments. Since many pharmaceutical laboratories were transnational, they lobbied the governments in their countries of origin. The results were tense relations with the United States and a veto by Switzerland at a meeting of the Paris Club to renegotiate Argentine debt.

Finally and crucially, Illia managed to displease the military, which had kept a watchful eye on civilian administrations since 1958, on two issues in 1965. First was the question of Peronism. Although he had foiled the return of exiled former president **Juan Domingo Perón** in December 1964, he was adamant that the Peronists participate in the **congressional elections of 1965**. Various neo-Peronist groups performed well, which boded ill for the gubernatorial elections due in 1967. And the second issue was a matter of prestige. In the aftermath of US intervention in the Dominican Republic, the Argentine government had acceded to a request to join but then withdrew from the proposed inter-American force to bring the country under control. The force was then commanded by a Brazilian general, which was considered a loss of face.

The inept Illia gradually lost support from all quarters and was overthrown in the **military coup of 1966**. Few lamented his departure, and when he was ousted he was literally ejected from the **Casa Rosada**. *See also* FALKLANDS DISPUTE.

IMMIGRATION. Like Australia, Canada, and the **United States**, Argentina is a country of recent settlement. Arguably, the country is even more a country of immigrants than the United States. In 1914, the national census recorded 30.3 percent of the population as born overseas. This was double the highest equivalent ever registered in the United States, which was in 1890 when the national census of that year recorded the foreign-born proportion of the total population as 14.8 percent.

The period of mass immigration occurred between the 1870s and 1910s, with substantial inflows of people during the interwar decades and again in the late 1940s and early 1950s. These early waves of settlers came overwhelmingly from Europe. Immigrants from neighboring countries formed the main source of new arrivals since approximately the 1950s, though there had been significant seasonal migration from around the beginning of the century. For example, rural workers from **Chile** worked on **sheep** estates in **Patagonia** during the **wool** clip; gangs of workers, mainly from **Bolivia** and **Peru**, migrated to sugar-producing regions of the northwest during the cane-cutting season. Since around 2000, East Asia has constituted the main new source of intercontinental migrants.

Immigration and settlement were actively promoted at the time of **independence**. **Agricultural colonization** was encouraged by **Bernardino Rivadavia** as part of a larger program of modernization. A government immigration agency was set up in 1824. Although the agency was abolished years later by **Juan Manuel de Rosas**, governor of the province of **Buenos Aires**, the resident foreign merchant community continued to expand, and settlers, mainly Basque, Scots, and Irish shepherds, were attracted by the boom in wool production that was well underway by the 1840s. Following the fall of Rosas, an article of the **Constitution of 1853** specifically charged the federal government with the task of encouraging European immigration, an obligation that was embraced by General **Justo José de Urquiza**, elected president in 1854. The Immigration Law of 1876 reestablished the Department of Immigration and provided funding for the appointment of agents overseas and payment of assisted passages for immigrants. By the 1880s, commercial organizations like *estancia* **companies**, colonization companies, and railway companies had entered the business of promoting settlement. Many such schemes were encouraged by provincial administrations such as the governments of **Córdoba**, **Entre Ríos**, and **Santa Fe**. The official language of the time referred to settling and acclimatizing the English spirit of liberty, French culture, and the industriousness of residents of Europe and the United States on the banks of the **River Plate** as part of a mission to "civilize the country": "to govern is to populate" became the slogan of the day.

Pro-migration attitudes and policies began to change around 1900, sentiments that found expression in new legislation. The Residency Law of 1902 (**Ley de Residencia**), followed by the Ley de Defensa Social a few years later, signaled a more cautious approach to mass immigration and reflected similar contemporary shifts in the United States. In part triggered by a wave of strikes and unrest among urban and rural workers, these measures did little to halt the flow of immigrants yet signaled a new mood among the elite.

Immigration legislation sought to be more selective, weeding out "agitators" and the "ideologically" suspect from "industrious settlers." Social attitudes would harden further after the Second World War as the principal source of immigrants shifted from Europe to neighboring republics. While Europeans arriving before the 1950s had been regarded as "settlers," intracontinental immigrants tended to be described as "economic migrants," a term that was increasingly used after the 1980s.

Between 1869 and 1914, the total population grew from 1,800,000 to 7,900,000: immigrants accounted for almost 60 percent of the increase. However, of the 6,500,000 arrivals between 1857 and 1940, only half that number settled, reflecting the so-called *golondrina* (swallow) phenomenon of seasonal migration. Although net immigration recovered quickly after the end of the First World War, the flow of settlers was not as substantial as before. Argentina remained a significant destination for international immigrants until the 1980s, even as the principal source of immigrants shifted from Europe to neighboring countries. Yet the foreign-born proportion of the population had declined continuously from the 1914 peak. The 1947 National Census recorded 15.3 percent of the total population as foreign born, the 1960 census as 13.0 percent and the 1970 as 9.5 percent. The 2000 census recorded the foreign-born proportion of the total population as 4.1 percent, of whom 60 percent were from Latin American countries.

A country of immigrants, Argentina has experienced bouts of political and economic emigration. In the mid-1970s, there was an exodus of those fleeing the violence chaos of the last year or so of the administration of President **Isabel Perón** and the terror of the **Proceso de Reorganización Nacional** instigated after the **military coup of 1976**. There was a significant brain drain at the time of **hyperinflation** and successive **economic crises** in the late 1980s toward the end of the presidency of **Raúl Alfonsín** and again around 2001 with the collapse of the **Convertibility Plan**. On both occasions, there was a very heavy demand for Spanish and Italian passports.

About 47 percent of Argentines claim Italian descent, and a further 35 percent Spanish origin—the Basque and Galician communities are disproportionately large; there are sizable German, French, Jewish, and Irish communities. In addition, there are more modest but nonetheless significant immigrant communities from the Levant (present-day Syria and Lebanon). Commonly referred to as *turcos* (Turks), immigrants from the Levant came from both Christian and Muslim communities. In the 1920s, the British community numbered around 250,000, supposedly the largest "outside the empire," ignoring those who had emigrated from the British Isles to the United States. A unique feature of Argentine immigration history is the story of the Welsh community, largely a function of official sponsorship by the Argentine government. The community is largely concentrated in the province of **Chubut**. Although there were considerably larger numbers of emigrants from Wales to North America and Australasia, the Welsh community in Argentina is exceptional in the way that it has preserved its identity and secured cultural recognition. Uniquely, Chubut is the only jurisdiction other than Wales where Welsh has the status of an official language.

Immigrants have contributed to all walks of life. Migrants arriving in the mid-19th century—notably, French Basques, Scots, and Irish—were well-represented among the landowning elite by 1900. A couple of decades later, two-thirds of industrial establishments were owned by foreign-born entrepreneurs. There was a substantial immigrant representation in national finance and commerce. Many **trade unions** and sociocultural clubs were pioneered by immigrants. Of the present-day population estimated at approximately 44,600,000, 97 percent self-describes as being of European or mainly European descent. *See also* BOCA JUNIORS FOOTBALL CLUB (CABJ); *CABECITA NEGRA*; CENTRAL ARGENTINE RAILWAY COMPANY (CAR); RIVER PLATE FOOTBALL CLUB.

INDEPENDENCE. Argentines celebrate two Independence Days, 25 May and 9 July. The first commemorates the **May Revolution of 1810**, the second the formal declaration of independence made at the **Congress of Tucumán** in 1816.

When news of the French invasion of the Iberian Peninsula reached **Buenos Aires**, early in May 1810, announcing the abdication of Charles IV, the succession of his son Ferdinand VII, and the capture of both monarchs by Napoleon Bonaparte, who substituted his brother Joseph as king of **Spain**, local notables clamored for Viceroy **Baltasar Hidalgo de Cisneros** to call a *cabildo abierto*, which he did for 22 May. Over the next days, the council debated how best to respond to news from Spain. With autonomist sentiments on the rise since the **British invasions** of 1806 and 1807, there was disagreement about how to proceed. Initially, it was agreed to establish a patriotic junta, headed by Cisneros, composed of various factions representing pro-Spanish, promonarchy, proautonomy, and proindependence groups. Creole political and military leaders refused to accept Cisneros as president of the junta and, backed by local public opinion, voted against his appointment on 25 May. Cisneros resigned and retired from public life, though continuing to occupy the viceregal residence. On the same day, **Cornelio Saavedra** was appointed head of the junta. At first, the junta continued to rule in the name of the deposed Bourbons but has since come to be regarded as the earliest expression of an independent national administration, marking the end of the colonial era.

Events moved rapidly after May as the junta attempted to maintain the integrity of the **Viceroyalty of the River Plate**, facing down demands for autonomy and independence from peripheral regions of the colony in addition to secessionist movements in what would become Argentina. There was also disagreement about forms of government, centralist or federalist, monarchical or republican. As the region spiraled into conflict, and with royalist authority firmly entrenched in **Peru** and restored in **Chile**, patriots called the Congress of Tucumán to determine future political arrangements and defend what was now called the **United Provinces of the River Plate**. Meeting from 1816 to 1820, one of the first acts of the congress was to declare independence on 9 July 1816. **Juan Martín de Pueyrredón** was appointed supreme director, in effect the first president of the country. He in turn nominated General **José de San Martín** to take charge of the defense of the fledgling state and secure its complete liberation.

In recognition of the distinct nature of the events of 1810 and 1816, different regimes have tended to place distinct emphases on the two dates: 25 May is officially celebrated as Independence Day, yet **military** governments of the 1950s, 1960s, and 1970s placed greater emphasis on 9 July. With the return of democracy in 1983, more attention has been devoted to 25 May, marking popular participation in the formation of democratic institutions, and the extensive parades that were staged on 9 July by de facto administrations scaled back. *See also* ALFONSÍN, RAÚL RICARDO (1927–2009); BELGRANO, MANUEL JOSÉ JOAQUIN DEL CORAZÓN DE JESÚS (1770–1820); LINIERS, SANTIAGO ANTONIO MARÍA DE (1753–1810); MORENO, MARIANO (1778–1811); NATIONAL ORGANIZATION.

INDIO/A. Meaning "Indian," a widely used term, sometimes conflated with *indigena*, though the words should not be used interchangeably. It can be a term of racial abuse, though more commonly it is used as an endearment when addressing family or friends, for example, as in the case of a mother referring to her dark-haired baby son as "mi indiecito" (my little Indian) or someone referring to a female relation or friends as "mi indiecita."

INDUSTRIAS AERONÁUTICAS Y MECÁNICAS DEL ESTADO (IAME). Founded in 1951, this state-owned autarkic conglomerate was established to manufacture aircraft and related materials (jet engines, propellers, engine parts, and parachutes), machines and tools, automobiles, tractors, and motorbikes. IAME relied on the existing **Fábrica Militar de Aviones** (FMA) and set up a further nine plants to achieve its purposes. The enterprise was financed by a 53-million-peso loan guaranteed by the government. At the height of production, the firm employed 12,000 workers and managers. The foray into automobile manufacturing led to an array of projects, many of which were highly influenced by models produced overseas. The resultant range of 21 models, including one called Justicialista, was unsuccessful, and IAME pulled out of direct involvement in the sector. Instead, it became a partner in **Industrias Kaiser Argentina** (IKA). Following the **military coup**

of **1955**, IAME became the Dirección Nacional de Fabricación e Investigación Aeronáutica (DINFIA) in 1956. *See also* INDUSTRY; PRIVATIZATION; STATE-OWNED ENTERPRISES (SOEs).

INDUSTRIAS KAISER ARGENTINA (IKA). The first large automobile manufacturer set up in Argentina, under an agreement between the Argentine government and Kaiser Motors concluded in January 1955. The US automaker Kaiser was facing problems in its domestic market, and in 1955 had also taken out of production the Willys Aero. With two sets of redundant vehicle production lines, it decided to enter the two largest South American markets. Kaiser shipped its auto manufacturing equipment to Argentina, while the Willys equipment formed the automaker's contribution to establish a new company in **Brazil**. Kaiser created a wholly owned subsidiary, the holding company Kaiser Automotores, that owned part of the newly created IKA—its manufacturing and marketing arm. Other partners in this venture included the state-owned **Industrias Aeronáuticas y Mecánicas del Estado** (IAME) as well as private investors.

IKA opened its factory in **Córdoba** province in 1956 and produced a variety of Jeep models like the Estanciera as well as sedans such as the Carabela and Manhattan. IKA accounted for 81 percent of total Argentine vehicle production in 1958 and agreed to manufacture Renault cars locally the following year. It entered into a further agreement with the American Motors Corporation (AMC) in 1962. IKA ceased production of its old sedan types and produced AMC models like those of the Rambler vehicle range.

By the middle of the 1960s, Kaiser wanted to exit the auto business in South America; the disengagement began in 1967. Willys merged with Ford in Brazil, and the Régie Nationale des Usines Renault assumed control of IKA by purchasing a large percentage of the shares; it renamed the company IKA-Renault. Kaiser sold the remainder of its IKA holdings to its French partner in 1970, and the firm acquired the name Renault Argentina. *See also* CORDOBAZO (29 MAY–3 JUNE 1969); DEVELOPMENTALISM/DEVELOPMENTALIST; ECONOMY; FOREIGN DEBT/FOREIGN INVESTMENT; INDUSTRY; TRANSPORTATION.

INDUSTRY. For Argentine policy makers, as for many Argentines, industrialization has long been an aspiration and the driving force of state action. The meaning of the word *industry* has changed markedly over time. In the mid-19th century, contemporaries spoke of the "**wool** industry" and the "**meat** industry," referring to the production of wool and dried/salted meat for overseas markets; later of the "cereal industry," namely the boom in wheat and **maize** exports, and the "**cattle** industry"—a reference to *estancia* modernization and selective improvement of cattle prefiguring the production of high-quality meat that took off around the 1890s. Modern manufacturing also dates from the latter decade, associated with the appearance of capital-intensive factories producing a range of wage goods like textiles and beverages, and the industrialization of commodity production—for example, the processing of products like frozen and chilled meat for the world market in highly mechanized, large-scale, technically sophisticated meatpacking *frigoríficos*.

After the 1890s, there was a tendency for modern factory production to displace craft "industries" and sweatshops that had previously characterized production for the domestic market. There was not necessarily a significant increase in total production; rather, the composition of manufactured output became more "industrial." During periods of economic boom, factories imported capital equipment, mechanized production lines, and switched to new forms of power like electricity. Nevertheless, many enterprises were relatively small, organized as family businesses and partnerships. Most such firms were owned and run by immigrants (or settlers). In 1914, approximately three-quarters of the industrial entrepreneuriat were immigrants, a not dissimilar proportion to the composition of the working class of the city of **Buenos Aires**, where the bulk of industrial firms were concentrated. Impersonal finance associated with corporate capitalism and access to institutional credit via the stock exchange were largely to be found in plants processing **commodities** for overseas markets. **Cervecería y Maltería Quilmes** is an early example of a locally owned capital-intensive corporate business "processing" for the national market. Sugar refining was another sector where big business predominated and was largely nationally (or settler) owned. By the early 20th century, Quilmes, as the brand became known, was one of the largest breweries in the world and one of the largest nationally owned corporations in the country—this at a time when such entities were largely concentrated in export processing, the likes of **Forestal**, the *frigoríficos*, and **Molinos Río de la Plata**. Gradually, export-commodity-producing enterprises began to supply the domestic, as well as the overseas, market.

According to some estimates, industry accounted for around 15 percent of gross domestic product (GDP) by the early 20th century, as the composition of output diversified. By 1910, Argentina was the most "industrialized" country in Latin America. In some branches of manufacturing, domestically produced wage goods represented between a half and two-thirds of total national consumption, notably in sectors like clothing, footwear, and foodstuffs. Some capital goods were also produced nationally, for example, windmills and pumps used in the countryside and small industrial motors, along with metal processing in general, and construction material. Increasing local production in these areas was reflected in a decline in imports. The growth of national industry was aided by tariff protection but was mainly caused by increasing home demand and the availability of capital and imported technology associated with the boom in primary exports.

Following an economic shock that began around 1913 and was compounded by the First World War, there was little change in the volume of domestic industrial output in the 1920s, though there was change in the scale and quality of production. Output recovered around the middle of the decade, leading to a modest increase in the participation of industry in GDP. Major changes occurred from the 1930s to the 1960s, especially during and after the 1940s. This was the period of **developmentalism**, economic nationalism, and **populism**, the latter being distinct features of the 1940s and early 1950s, with policy becoming explicitly proindustry and prodomestic manufacture in the 1950s and 1960s. Import-substituting industrialization was promoted by policy makers and captured the public imagination. Various business organizations competed for government attention. For example, the **Confederación General Económica** (CGE), representing small "national" firms, and the more established lobby, the **Unión Industrial Argentina** (UIA), competed for official attention.

By the end of the 1920s, industry accounted for around 18 percent of GDP; by the end of the 1930s, 23 percent; by the end of the 1940s, 25 percent; by the end of the 1960s, the participation of industry in GDP reached a high point of about 28 percent. More important than the growing participation of industry in GDP were structural changes. On average, firms got bigger. Production became more diverse—growth was especially marked in such subsectors as motor vehicle production and the manufacture of domestic appliances. Ownership changed: hitherto, firms producing for the home market were largely locally owned, whether by immigrant settlers or nationals; now there was a "transnationalization" of ownership. While national capital tended to predominate in areas like clothing and textiles, beverages, footwear, and some subsectors of food products, dynamic, heavily capitalized corporations involved in the motor-mechanical, electrical, and appliance subsectors tended to be foreign owned. There were exceptions like **Sección Industrial Amasadoras Mecánicas Di Tella** (SIAM Di Tella), which manufactured motor vehicles and domestic appliances under license, but most technically advanced companies producing consumer durables were foreign owned. The state also assumed a larger role in manufacturing, a role that was epitomized by enterprises like the government oil corporation **Yacimientos Petrolíferos Fiscales** (YPF) and **Fabricaciones Militares** (FM), which produced transport equipment as well as **military** hardware. As transnational and state production in such sectors as metal goods, machinery, chemicals, and oil products increased, so the participation of established traditional subsectors like foodstuffs and beverages, textiles and clothing, and cement and construction material in total industrial output declined relatively.

Growth in the scale and complexity of industrial output was accompanied by the emergence of an urban, factory-based industrial workforce, increasingly employed in large plants. Transnationalization and statization of the ownership of industrial establishments, along with the consolidation of larger firms in more sophisticated branches of industry, facilitated the organization of workers and the growth of **trade unions**. Perhaps because they were technically advanced and profitable, foreign-owned firms tended to offer higher wages and better working conditions than nationally owned companies. Nevertheless, worker organization and the articulation of demands for improvement in material conditions was strongest and more vociferous in the "transnationalized" sectors of industry. Organization and mobilization was supported by the state, notably during the first administration of President **Juan Domingo Perón** and during his third presidency in the mid-1970s, when there were large wage hikes and the share of wages in national income increased significantly. During periods of military rule, for example, following the **military coup of 1966** and the **military coup of 1976**, there were squeezes on wages. Wage compression was frequently associated with a drive to increase industrial productivity and facilitate manufactured exports. By the late 1950s, policy makers came to regard domestic industry as overreliant on imports and unable to compete in world markets. In the late 1950s and early 1960s, there was a concerted effort to transform national industry and promote the development of an integrated industrial complex. There was an emphasis on the production of basic goods, the intensive exploitation of natural resources, and the modernization of the production of energy, steel, industrial chemicals, equipment, and machinery that would support firms already producing motor vehicles and household goods and enable them to export, reducing the "import deficit" of the industrial sector.

The growth and diversification of industrial output through the middle third of the 20th century was impressive. Yet industrial inputs (including capital and technology) continued to be financed by commodity exports that also funded subsidies and fiscal transfers enjoyed by manufacturers. The flow of labor, credit, and foreign exchange earnings to industry caused much sectional tension. The poor productivity record of the industrial sector in the 1960s and 1970s was a contributory factor to the political and economic instability of the period, as were the remedies attempted. By the 1970s, the drive to industrialize was also losing political support and popular appeal, among sections of the public as well as the policy-making community. The proindustry *desarrollista* consensus that had existed (despite ideological and political differences) since the late 1940s, and which included manufacturers, trade unions, and sections of the military, was breaking down. By the mid-1970s, it appeared clear to many policy makers and theoreticians that attempts at industrial deepening during the civilian and de facto presidencies of **Arturo Frondizi** and General **Juan Carlos Onganía** were not delivering.

Import-substituting industrialization was a strategy that could have succeeded. That it did not was due to flawed application, particularly the timing and sequencing of the shift from "easy" horizontal industrialization (producing more of the same, especially in the light industrial sector) to "difficult" capital-intensive industrial deepening (backward linking into the manufacture of capital goods and intermediate products) and to political "capture" and manipulation. The crisis of the strategy was highlighted by macroeconomic instability and descent into political violence during the chaotic presidency of **Isabel Perón**. Despite determined efforts to promote industrial exports between 1973 and 1975, manufactures made up less than one-fifth of total exports by value; commodities accounted for two-fifths, the remainder made up of processed agricultural products. One of the few success stories during this period was the preferential export of motor vehicles to **Cuba**, some of which were produced by Argentine affiliates of **United States** corporations, much to the annoyance of Washington. It was time to change the economic model. That change came with the **military coup of 1976**.

Minister of Economy **José Alfredo Martínez de Hoz** opened the **economy** in an attempt to promote efficiency. Martínez de Hoz's tenure at the **Ministry of Economy** marked the end of import-substituting industrialization, at least until the beginning of the 21st century. Martínez de Hoz promised that rents creamed off **agriculture** would no longer be used to subsidize manufacturing industry; they would be ploughed into value-adding agroindustries. The wage repression that accompanied subsidy cuts and the liberalization of credit was intended to ease the transition to market realism— among industrial firms as well as other sectors of the economy. The plan did not work, at least for manufactures. Imports and reduced domestic purchasing power resulted in a 20 percent contraction in national industrial production during the early 1980s. Employment in manufacturing fell by more than one-third. Deindustrialization became a pronounced feature of the **Proceso de Reorganización Nacional**. Even when the economy began to bounce back from the 1982 economic crisis, manufacturing did not rebound, hampered by a scarcity of imported inputs. During the 1980s, the share of industry in GDP had fallen to around 24 percent; at the beginning of the 1990s, the participation of industry in GDP was at the level it had been in the early 1940s. Small enterprises and firms clustered in such traditional areas as foodstuff and clothing were especially adversely affected by **economic crises** of the period.

Local businesses benefited from the **privatization** of **state-owned enterprises** during the administrations of President **Carlos Saúl Menem**: between 1988 and 1998, industrial output grew by an average of 3.6 percent per annum, and there was a pickup in manufactured exports, especially to **Brazil**. Structural change in the industrial sector around this time included a decline in employment in manufacturing, which fell by about one-third between

1991 and 2001 (taken by some to signal increased productivity and by others as a mark of further deindustrialization); a consolidation of the presence of transnational corporate capital and industrial deepening in such sectors as the manufacture of transport equipment and spare parts; and the production of agricultural equipment and industrial and agricultural chemicals. In the crisis year of 2001, as the **Convertibility Plan** was collapsing and the economy spiraling out of control, industry accounted for 16 percent of GDP and 31 percent of total exports. The export performance of industry occurred despite an overvalued **currency**; this was not all down to increased international competitiveness—it was aided by tax breaks.

The contribution of industry to GDP grew during the *kirchnerato*, according to some estimates touching 20 percent. Growth was partly explained by "natural" bounce back after the crisis that followed the collapse of convertibility and by the commodity-led boom that followed. Manufacturers benefited from emergency distributionist measures introduced by interim president **Eduardo Duhalde** and continued by President **Néstor Kirchner** that helped sustain domestic demand for basic wage goods. The devaluation of the peso also helped initially by restricting competitive imports. The main factor, however, was a dramatic reversal of the policy regime. Echoing autarchic and promanufacturing measures of the mid-1940s to the mid-1970s, taxes on agro-exports funded transfers to industry, particularly firms close to the regime. The crucial difference between the Kirchner approach and earlier periods of import-substituting industrialization was that the state did not intervene directly in production, save in a few reserved areas like oil and transport. Government structured the market and set priorities but left entrepreneurial responses to the market—or strategically placed businesses. The export boom underwrote an impressive growth in GDP per capita that fueled household and government consumption, while increasingly sophisticated controls ensured that rising foreign exchange earnings were channeled into projects favored by the regime, especially during the two administrations headed by President **Cristina Fernández de Kirchner**. Protection increased; unemployment declined; employment in manufacturing rose; real wages grew despite the return of inflation after 2007. The regulatory regime became more stringent and social expenditure more targeted, especially between 2004 and 2013. All these factors explain the boom in manufacturing. These measures disproportionately benefited firms close to the regime, as did the exit of foreign corporations. "National industrialization" was delivered by the government, though at a cost that would become clearer as the commodity boom weakened, foreign exchange reserves were run down, and inflationary pressure mounted. Policy-induced stagnation in other parts of the economy may also have magnified the relative performance of industry, but absolute expansion was real enough.

Today, the major industries are food and beverage production, motor vehicles and components, textiles, chemicals and petrochemicals, pharmaceuticals, industrial and agricultural machinery, household goods, and building material. The principal agroprocessing industries include milling, biofuels, meat and meat products, wine, sugar refining, and semi-elaborated forestry products. The current (2018) participation of industry in GDP is about 28 percent—including agroprocessing and construction—compared with 11 percent for agriculture; services account for 61 percent of GDP, including finance and insurance, telecommunications, transport, and a sizeable informal sector. In addition to Greater Buenos Aires, the principal centers of manufacturing are **Bahía Blanca**, **Córdoba**, and **Rosario**. *See also* BANCO DE CRÉDITO INDUSTRIAL ARGENTINO (BCIA); BER GELBARD, JOSÉ (1917–1977); BUNGE & BORN; CAMPANA; DI TELLA, TORCUATO (1882–1948); FARM PROTESTS; GÓMEZ MORALES, ALFREDO (1908–1990); INDUSTRIAS AERONÁUTICAS Y MECÁNICAS DEL ESTADO (IAME); INDUSTRIAS KAISER ARGENTINA (IKA); INSTITUTO ARGENTINO DE PROMOCIÓN DEL INTERCAMBIO (IAPI); KRIEGER VASENA, ADALBERT (1920–2000); LA MATANZA; PREBISCH, RAÚL (1901–1986); RODRIGAZO; SECCIÓN INDUSTRIAL AMASADORAS MECÁNICAS (SIAM Di Tella); SOCIEDAD MIXTA SIDERURGICA ARGENTINA (SOMISA); TORNQUIST, ERNESTO CARLOS (1842–1908); ZÁRATE.

INSTITUTO ARGENTINO DE PROMOCIÓN DEL INTERCAMBIO (IAPI). One of the pillars of Peronist **economic policy**, especially in the 1946–1949 period. Established in May 1946 during the final days of the lame-duck de facto administration of **Edelmiro Farrell**, its key functions were the buying and selling of **commodities** at home, trading exports in foreign markets, and financing essential imports. At home, IAPI operated as a monopoly state buying agency—producers were obliged to sell to it, though commodity production as such was not nationalized. It became the main channel for overseas trade, handling the greater part of exports and a substantial proportion of imports.

IAPI became the leading instrument to control **foreign trade**, with a monopoly over practically all exports. These included **grains** and **meat**, which were handled by commodity boards set up by the **Concordancia**, as well as linseed and leather, but not **wool**. It was the sole buyer of rural goods from local producers, in order to ensure cheap/subsidized sales in the domestic market while securing the highest possible price for exports and favorable terms for purchases of imports. The low prices paid to domestic producers—lower than prevailing world prices—were designed to ensure low-cost foodstuffs for households and low-cost inputs for firms manufacturing and processing goods for the national market.

The government set the basic prices for rural products at the time of planting. In terms of the home market, it distributed wheat to flour mills and on a number of occasions subsidized the price of bread—it was considered an essential mass consumption good. As for the international market, IAPI purchased the grain at the established basic prices and exported it at prices set in Chicago, Winnipeg, and Australia. It made enormous profits for a time by buying commodities cheaply from farmers and selling dear abroad. Profits earned from the differentials in prices were allocated as follows: purchasing foreign-owned utilities; subsidizing imports; financing the acquisition of capital goods, fuel, and supplies for public companies and the **military**; and for *obras de bien común* (works for the public good) of Peronist urban and welfare programs. In the language of the time, IAPI bought (and sold) cheap at home and sold dear abroad.

This system worked well until 1949, the year in which the **economy** ran into severe difficulties as a result of government policy. Rural producers, who had been squeezed by IAPI, responded to disadvantageous prices by switching production from grain to livestock, reducing the export surplus. Commodity production was further reduced by a number of droughts in the early 1950s. The country's export earnings fell sharply, owing to competition from the **United States**, Canada, and Australia in the grain trade and due to decline in international agricultural commodity prices. Moreover, wastage during the first three years in which **Juan Domingo Perón** was president—a period that Argentine historian **Félix Luna** has described as "una fiesta" (a party)—led to severe mismanagement of the public accounts and the country's foreign exchange reserves. As a result, the IAPI went into decline and its economic role diminished as Perón was forced to change course and attempt to repair the damage done by his policy mistakes. *See also* AGRICULTURE; BANCO DE CRÉDITO INDUSTRIAL ARGENTINO (BCIA); CURRENCY; ECONOMIC CRISES; FOREIGN DEBT/FOREIGN INVESTMENT; GÓMEZ MORALES, ALFREDO (1908–1990); INDUSTRY.

INSTITUTO TORCUATO DI TELLA. An arts and cultural center set up by the brothers **Torcuato** and **Guido Di Tella** in 1958, the institute was named in honor of their industrialist father **Torcuato** senior, who established the industrial conglomerate **Sección Industrial Amasadoras Mecánicas Di Tella**, by then known as SIAM Di Tella. It was founded on the 10th anniversary of his death. The center was endowed with 10 percent of SIAM shares, along with donations from local and overseas sources, including the US Ford and Rockefeller Foundations. The project was influenced by corporate-sponsored arts and educational foundations such as those in the **United States** and, probably, the British Nuffield Trust: SIAM manufactured Morris and Austin cars under license, and the trust was endowed by the Morris family. (When William Morris was elevated to the peerage in 1934, he took the title

Viscount Nuffield.) Initially, the Instituto focused on the arts and was a vehicle for the display of mainly Impressionist works acquired by the family, though it soon became the most important private cultural venue in Argentina. By the 1960s, it acquired a reputation for the avant-garde in its spacious theater and gallery in fashionable Calle Florida in central **Buenos Aires**. Pioneering exotic, often erotic, works, along with politically contentious material meant that the Instituto fell foul of the 1966 **military** regime; General President **Juan Carlos Onganía**, a traditionalist influenced by Opus Dei, was said to have been particularly offended by events like "experience theater" and experimental "political" poetry readings and seminar discussions organized at the Instituto. Like other cutting-edge artistic venues at the time, the Instituto was raided by the federal police. Whether due to political pressure or deteriorating finances as SIAM Di Tella profits fell, activities were scaled back and the Instituto held its last event in 1970. Remaining assets were used to fund a social science research institute, which continued under the same name. The course of events, and the history of the Instituto during the 1960s, prefigured much darker days for arts and culture during the **Proceso de Reorganización Nacional**. *See also* EDUCATION; UNIVERSIDAD TORCUATO DI TELLA (UTDT).

INTRANSIGENT RADICAL CIVIC UNION. *See* UNIÓN CÍVICA RADICAL (UCR); UNIÓN CÍVICA RADICAL INTRANSIGENTE (UCRI).

IRIGOYEN, BERNARDO DE (1822–1906). Lawyer, diplomat, minister, and parliamentarian; one of the key intellectuals of the 19th century. Having read law at the **University of Buenos Aires** (UBA), his earliest political attachments were to **Federalism** as an autonomist who favored a substantial degree of provincial autonomy, particularly for his native province of **Buenos Aires**, later advocating the cause of Radicalism.

Appointed by Governor of Buenos Aires **Juan Manuel de Rosas** to a commission adjudicating the border with **Chile** in the early 1840s, following the **caudillo**'s Indian campaigns, Irigoyen would subsequently continue this work, preparing the justification for Argentine claims to disputed channels in the Straits of Magellan. These activities shaped his view of foreign affairs and intra–South American relations, fostering an advocacy of the peaceful resolution of border disputes. Following the **War of the Triple Alliance**, he helped establish the international frontier between **Brazil** and **Paraguay**.

In the late 1840s, he was sent by Rosas to the province of **Mendoza**, where he initiated a series of legislative and administrative reforms that helped bring order to the region. He went on to participate in the **San Nicolás** Convention of 1852, which prepared the ground for the **Constitution of**

1853. This, and his earlier activities in Mendoza, resulted in commissions to review various provincial constitutions and legal codes. In the early 1870s, he was elected successively to the lower house and senate of the province of Buenos Aires. During the presidency of **Nicolás Avellaneda**, he served first as minister of foreign affairs and then as minister of interior. He was reappointed to head the Foreign Ministry by Avellaneda's successor, President **Julio A. Roca**, in 1880, serving for two years. Despite being a close confident of Roca, in the presidential election of 1886 he stood against Roca's preferred candidate, **Miguel Juárez Celman**, and opposed the officialist candidate again in 1892; he was defeated on both occasions.

In 1894, Irigoyen was elected to the National Senate by the city of Buenos Aires, and he was reelected the following year. He would return to the federal Senate in 1902, representing the province. By the late 1890s, Irigoyen had become one of the leading figures in the Radical movement campaigning for fair elections. He was successively associated with the Radical Youth Movement, the Unión Cívica, and the **Unión Cívica Radical** (UCR)—it was as UCR candidate that he stood in the 1892 presidential race. In 1898, he was elected governor of the province of Buenos Aires, administering the province from the new capital of **La Plata**—he had assisted Roca in the **federalization of the city of Buenos Aires**.

A member of the ruling oligarchy, Irigoyen argued the case for political reform and accepted the need for fair elections, which he regarded as conducive to political peace. Abroad, he argued the case for the peaceful resolution of territorial disputes, which he saw as fostering South American solidarity, though he was suspicious of claims by the **United States** to regional leadership. He is remembered for his work in the areas of legal and administrative reform, including efforts to professionalize the Argentine diplomatic service, and as one of the leading thinkers of the age. *See also* ALEM, LEANDRO NICEBRO (1842–1896); BEAGLE CHANNEL DISPUTE; DEL VALLE, ARISTÓBULO (1845–1896); MINISTRY OF FOREIGN RELATIONS AND RELIGION; MINISTRY OF INTERIOR, PUBLIC WORKS, AND HOUSING; MITRE, BARTOLOMÉ (1821–1906); SÁENZ PEÑA LAW.

ITAIPÚ DAM. Hydroelectricity dam on the river **Paraná** on the **Brazil–Paraguay** border and a subject of dispute between Argentina and Brazil. The dam currently holds the world record for energy production. Most of the energy produced is consumed in Brazil. The treaty to construct the dam was signed in 1966; construction work started in 1975; electricity started to be generated in 1984; full capacity was reached in 2007, when the last of the 20 generators to be installed became operational. As work started, the de facto government headed by General **Jorge Rafael Videla** protested. Illustrative of the paranoia of the regime, and the parlous state of relations with neighboring authoritarian governments, notwithstanding **Operación Condor** collaboration, the Argentine **military** feared that in the event of a conflict with Brazil the dam might become an instrument of war—opening the flood gates could damage the **Yacyretá** dam or flood **Buenos Aires**. A tripartite agreement was reached in 1979 to regulate the flow of water.

J

JAURETCHE, ARTURO MARTÍN (1901–1974). *See* FUERZA DE ORIENTACIÓN RADICAL DE LA JOVEN ARGENTINA (FORJA).

JUÁREZ CELMAN, MIGUEL ÁNGEL (1844–1909). Lawyer, politician, governor of his native province of **Córdoba**, one of the leading liberals of his day committed to the promotion of secular **education**; constitutional president of the republic between 1886 and 1890. He was the brother-in-law of **Julio A. Roca**, who preceded him as president and from whose influence he was unable to escape. His presidency collapsed in the chaos of the **Baring Crisis** of 1890.

As governor, Juárez Celman had favored the civil registration of marriage and secularization in other areas of social life. In addition, he promoted administrative reform, including the devolution of functions to municipalities, in part reflecting population growth resulting from **immigration**. As president, his administration was characterized by a debt-fueled expansion of public works—notably, railways and port improvements, land speculation involving the development of areas opened up by Roca's **Conquest of the Desert**, and a lax banking regime that resulted in a massive expansion of money supply and credit, much of it channeled to friends of the regime. The boom engineered by Juárez Celman was partly designed to cement the political arrangement associated with the Partido Autonomista Nacional (PAN), a system devised largely by the governors of interior provinces to ensure that their respective areas benefited from economic expansion, and partly to head off opposition from new political forces that would coalesce around the future **Unión Cívica Radical** (UCR). While many of the projects initiated during his presidency would ultimately prove productive, other ventures were of little economic value or entirely speculative. Popular discontent grew as inflation accelerated. Mounting political protest alarmed sections of the elite that had already become antagonized by the narrowness of the circle of financiers with whom Juárez Celman had surrounded himself, thereby undermining the system of a distribution of rewards and favors essential to the functioning of the PAN. Elsewhere, disquiet was engendered by the specter of default and an end to cheap foreign credit. An uprising in the center of the city of **Buenos Aires** in July 1890 was the last straw. This event, and the resulting casualties, shocked the establishment and foreign observers alike. Castigated by the press, when his vice president, **Carlos Pellegrini**, and brother-in-law Roca publicly withdrew support, Juárez Celman resigned. He was the first constitutionally elected president not to complete his term, and his period in office became a byword for **corruption** and speculation.

JUJUY. A province located in the far northwest of the country, bordered to the west by **Chile**, to the north by **Bolivia**, and surrounded to the east and south by the province of **Salta**. Spanish occupation began in the last decade of the 1590s. With the formation of the **Viceroyalty of the River Plate** in 1776, the province enjoyed a strategic position on the boundary of the new jurisdiction but suffered economic decline as traditional trade links to the north and west were severed. In the late colonial period, the region was incorporated within the new intendancy of Salta but gained provincial status with the republic when declaring its autonomy as a separate jurisdiction from Salta in 1834. During the **independence** period, it was a major theater of war and the northern bastion of insurgent Argentina against royalist forces in Bolivia and **Peru**. As a sensitive frontier, it was invaded in 1836 during hostilities between Argentina and the Bolivia–Peru Confederation. Part of the territory of the province remained in dispute until the end of the 19th century, when settlements were reached with Bolivia and Chile in 1900. Internal boundary adjustments in 1943 meant that the province absorbed part of the former national territory of **Los Andes**. The province is one of the poorest in the country. It was not connected to the national rail network until 1900 and attracted few immigrants. The current population is around 700,000; literacy rates are several percentage points below the national average, and inequality and poverty higher, as are school dropout rates. The economy is overwhelmingly agricultural—sugar and tropical fruit—with a large service sector (mainly government) and not insignificant subsistence sector. *See also* SALA, MILAGRO AMALIA ÁNGELA (1964–).

JUSTICIALISMO. "Justicialism" in English, derived from the name of the Peronist party, **Partido Justicialista** (PJ). More a pragmatic set of policies that evolved over time than a political ideology, Justicialismo proposed a **Tercera Posición**, a middle way between capitalism and communism—*ni capitalismo ni comunismo*, to employ an early slogan. It combined the interests of the state, business, and labor, promising economic independence, social justice, and participatory democracy, orchestrated by "El Lider," namely **Juan Domingo Perón**. The PJ emerged from the **Labor Party**, organized by the **Confederación General del Trabajo** to support Perón's candidacy in the **presidential election of 1946**, which was superseded by the **Partido Peronista** (PP) and subsequently by the PJ itself. During Perón's first two terms in office (1946–1955), until ousted by the **Revolución Libertadora**, Justicialismo was associated with state intervention, manifest though large-scale nationalization; credit and exchange control; the regulation of **foreign trade**; wage and price control; the expansion of social insurance and worker rights; the promotion of "corporate blocs" representing business, workers, and other social groups; and the persecution of opposition **political parties** and so-called antinational sectors, notably large landowners, foreign consortia, and independent organizations. Interventionism and controls were eased following **economic crises** around 1951, and there was the promise of political liberalization, yet in practice Justisialismo remained essentially **populist**, nationalist, and authoritarian. During the 1950s and 1960s, when Peronism was proscribed, the PJ was fronted by neo-Peronist parties, though invariably seeking a dominant role. Many of the original features and rhetoric of Justicialismo were revived during the *kirchnerato* in 2003–2015. *See also* CÁMPORA, HÉCTOR JOSÉ (1909–1980); FRENTE JUSTICIALISTA DE LIBERACIÓN (FREJULI); FRONDIZI, ARTURO (1908–1995); KIRCHNER, CRISTINA ELISABET FERNÁNDEZ DE (1953–); KIRCHNER, NÉSTOR CARLOS (1950–2010); MENEM, CARLOS SAÚL (1930–); "PERONISM WITHOUT PERÓN".

JUSTICIALIST LIBERATION FRONT. *See* FRENTE JUSTICIALISTA DE LIBERACIÓN (FREJULI).

JUSTO, AGUSTÍN PEDRO (1876–1943). President of Argentina from 1932 to 1938. He entered the Colegio Militar de la Nación at age 11 and began active service in earnest in 1892. Without abandoning his **military** career, he also studied engineering at the **University of Buenos Aires** (UBA). Justo was director of the Colegio Militar from 1915 to 1922, which earned him an extremely high professional reputation among his fellow officers and high regard in aristocratic civilian circles due to his family background. Justo's father had been a governor of **Corrientes** and a friend of **Bartolomé Mitre**, the liberal statesman and political leader, and his father-in-law had been the proprietor of extensive landholdings as well as governor of **Río Negro**. Justo himself was a member of the Círculo de Armas, the most exclusive men's club in **Buenos Aires**; its members were well aware of his disapproval of President **Hipólito Yrigoyen**, leader of the **Unión Cívica Radical** (UCR).

Justo served as minister of war from 1922 to 1928 under President **Marcelo T. de Alvear** (another Radical) and aligned himself with the *antipersonalista* branch of the UCR when the party split in 1924. He was vehemently opposed to Yrigoyen's return to the presidency in 1928, and his faction in the army conspired with that led by General **José Félix Uriburu**, who overthrew Yrigoyen in the **military coup of 1930**. Justo was not part of the provisional government but was an ambitious man biding his time to construct an *anti-yrigoyenista* coalition to get him elected president. The unpopularity of the Uriburu regime enabled Justo to force the calling of a presidential election, which the UCR boycotted. Justo won the **presidential election of 1931** as candidate of the **Concordancia**. He was the first professional officer to be elected president since **Julio A. Roca** and only the second to hold the office since Mitre. Considered the heir of the preceding de facto government, Justo aimed to emphasize the civilian side of his character. He retired from active duty and appointed civilians rather than military men to most ministries.

The Justo administration inherited serious economic problems derived from both the Great Depression and domestic financial mismanagement. It responded to the possibility of losing its key export market by concluding the highly controversial **Roca–Runciman Pact** with **Great Britain** in 1933. This **foreign trade** agreement crucially included the so-called Roca Funding Loan, which was secured through a government bond offering and contributed to the success of the **Plan de Acción Económica** and the country's economic recovery. Fiscal issues were dealt with through the modernization of the taxation system and the creation of the **Banco Central de la República Argentina** (BCRA) in 1935. In addition, Justo acknowledged the needs of the Argentine interior for better communications, and his administration developed a national highway program at breakneck pace.

Whatever the economic successes, Justo's government was marred by its questionable legitimacy. When the UCR resumed electoral politics in 1935, he faced the possible loss of various provinces, especially **Buenos Aires** with its large representation in **Congress** and its key role in the next presidential election. To prevent this, he allowed Buenos Aires conservatives to rig the gubernatorial election of November 1935. Electoral theft (known as *fraude patriótico*) followed in the March 1936 congressional elections in several provinces, and again in spectacular fashion in the **presidential election of 1937**.

Justo had handpicked **Roberto M. Ortiz** as his successor in the hope that he would continue his economic policies, protect the reputation of his administration, and pave the way for his return to the presidency in the election due in 1943. Instead, Ortiz was determined to end the parody of fraudulent elections and facilitate a return to democratic politics. However, he was forced by ill health to take what became a permanent leave of absence, being replaced by Vice President **Ramón S. Castillo**. The latter was not prepared to be the instrument of Justo's ambitions, let alone respect UCR demands for honest elections. Therefore, Castillo tried to build up his own political power and prestige to the point where he would be in a position to dictate the political succession. Justo then worked with some success to persuade civilian politicians that his was the only candidacy capable of thwarting Castillo and winning an election. The deaths of both Alvear and Ortiz in 1942 thinned out the ranks of national leaders, and Justo hoped to win support from the Radicals and Socialists. To those politicians with a practical mind, he offered the possibility of their gaining power in the forthcoming elections, and this prospect encouraged them to forget his dubious democratic record.

Fate ended Justo's ambitions: he died suddenly in January 1943. With the passing of Justo—the last of the three living ex-presidents to die within 10 months—no opposition leader of comparable stature remained to rival Castillo. The latter nominated his chosen successor, thereby triggering the **military coup of 1943**.

JUSTO, ALICIA MOREAU DE (1885–1986). Born in London to a French émigré family—her father was an **anarcho-syndicalist** who had participated in the Paris Commune—Justo and her family settled in **Buenos Aires** around 1890. Trained as a medic, she became a lifelong educationalist, socialist, internationalist, and pacifist, and a prominent advocate of **women**'s rights—what would become gender equality and **human rights**. These were subjects on which she would publish extensively. The principal influences on her life and thinking appear to have been the ideological commitment of her parents and the experience of growing up in Argentina during the age of mass **immigration**—she was a keen observer of the precarious living and working conditions of families crowded into slum housing and *conventillos*. She was one of the founder members of the Women's Movement and the **Partido Socialista** (PS) and a major influence at international gatherings associated with these organizations. In 1921, she married fellow medic and advocate of social reform **Juan B. Justo**. Following his early death years later, she redoubled efforts to promote the causes in which they had been jointly influential.

Strongly opposed to militarization, which she viewed as a consequence of the First World War, she acknowledged that the war had created opportunities for the spread of socialism—notably, revolution in Russia. A supporter of the Second Spanish Republic, she was alarmed by the violence that ensued, adopting a similarly critical approach to **Peronism** years later. Welcoming progressive social reforms and the extension of the franchise essayed during the early years of the first presidency of **Juan Domingo Perón**—many of which had long been advocated by the PS—she condemned the nondemocratic and authoritarian tendencies of the regime. She was equally critical of the **military** governments that followed the overthrow of Perón, though willing to collaborate with those within the **Partido Justicialista** (PJ) who sought to democratize Peronism. Throughout her life, she struggled to preserve the unity of the PS and make it an effective vehicle for social change.

In her early 90s, she campaigned against human rights abuses committed by military administrations of the **Proceso de Reorganización Nacional**. A cofounder of the Argentine Human Rights Movement, along with future president **Raúl Alfonsín** and others, she participated in demonstrations organized by the **Mothers of the Plaza de Mayo**. In recognition of her support, the Mothers presented her with a white headscarf, the emblem of the organization, on her 99th birthday. At the age of 100, she was honored by the city of Buenos Aires for her work as an educationalist and valiant social campaigner. *See also* EDUCATION.

JUSTO, JUAN BAUTISTA (1865–1928). Surgeon and general practitioner; democratic socialist and political reformer; important thinker and author; invariably known as Juan B. Justo. A native of the city of **Buenos Aires**, he studied medicine at the **University of Buenos Aires** (UBA). Graduating at the top of his class, he went on to study in Europe, where he developed his ideas about socialism and social justice. On returning to Argentina, he devoted his life to advancing new techniques in medicine and campaigning for an enlightened approach to social issues of the day. His political thinking was disseminated via writing and journalism and promulgated during a distinguished political career. He set up the socialist newspaper *La Vanguardia*, for which he wrote regularly; he was a frequent contributor to the established newspaper *La Prensa*, widely read by the traditional landed elite. In addition, he published books and pamphlets on the history of social theory and the history of political ideas, and about labor issues and economic policy, particularly measures affecting the working class. He regarded one of his principal achievements as the founding of a workers' circulating library and cultural center. Opened in 1897 and renamed in his honor after his death, the Casa del Pueblo and the Biblioteca Obrera Juan B. Justo were torched by Peronist mobs in 1953. The library was reestablished in 1957 and relaunched in 1961. It continues as a center for research and teaching, offering cultural and practical courses.

Justo's political career involved engagement with precursors of the **Unión Cívica Radical** (UCR) and the founding of the **Partido Socialista** (PS), which he established with the likes of **Alfredo Palacios**. He was first elected to **Congress** in 1912 by voters of the city of Buenos Aires and repeatedly reelected to the Chamber of Deputies until 1924, when he was sent to the National Senate by city voters. His term in the Senate was cut short by his death. As a deputy and senator, Justo sponsored legislation intended to ameliorate social conditions, improve worker housing, promote literacy, and curb alcohol abuse. Justo's endeavors in these fields were ably abetted by his wife, **Alicia Moreau de Justo**, also a medical doctor and possibly better known outside Argentina than he. Justo's practical and intellectual contributions to social and political progress during the period are widely acknowledged, as is his place in the development of worker rights and the labor movement, and the consolidation of democracy—before the intervention of the **military** in politics. What he would have made of the role played by the PS in national politics during the **Concordancia** years is a moot point. *See also* MILITARY COUP OF 1930; TRADE UNIONS.

JUVENTUD PERONISTA (JP). Encompassing the youth section of the Peronist movement, it initially emerged as the Movimiento de la Juventud Peronista (MJP) in 1951 and ceased to exist after the Partido Peronista (PP) was dissolved by de facto president General **Pedro Eugenio Aramburu** following the **military coup of 1955**. The JP was refounded in 1957 and initiated armed resistance under the name Ejército Peronista de Liberación Nacional (EPLN). Most of its leadership was captured under the repression of the Plan CONINTES (Conmoción Interna del Estado) during the presidency of **Arturo Frondizi**. In July 1963, the government of **Arturo Illia** released all political prisoners, and the JP vowed to reorganize itself.

The first national congress of the JP was held in October 1963 and issued a declaration with the following demands: the revoking of all repressive legislation, a general amnesty for political and social prisoners; the return of the exiled **Juan Domingo Perón** to Argentina and the restitution of the remains of **Eva Perón**—they had been taken and hidden by the Aramburu government; state control over means of production and **foreign trade**; the nationalization of the banking system; the expropriation of latifundia without compensation; the total nationalization of the oil, steel, electricity, and meatpacking industries; bans on imports competing with domestic manufactures and on the export of capital; the annulment of the **foreign debt** and international obligations; worker control of the means of production; the denunciation of international treaties that affected sovereignty; respect for the self-determination of peoples and nations; and solidarity with the peoples of the world that were struggling for liberation.

Even though the declaration was approved unanimously, the patently left-wing JP was heavily factionalized. During the 1960s, no less than 25 groupings were part of the JP, including the Juventud Argentina por la Emancipación Nacional (JAEN) headed by **Rodolfo Galimberti** and financed by **Diego Muniz Barreto**. Between 1970 and 1972, many of the smaller organizations merged into bigger structures within the JP, such as the JP de las Regionales and the Juventud Universitaria Peronista (JUP).

By that time, the JP was totally infiltrated by the **Montoneros**. In the **congressional elections of March 1973**, the JP got eight of its Montonero-supporting members elected to the Chamber of Deputies under the banner of the **Frente Justicialista de Liberación** (FREJULI)—one of them was Muniz Barreto. These so-called Montonero deputies increasingly refused to toe the party line, and in January 1974 they were forced to resign from **Congress** and expelled from the **Partido Justicialista** (PJ). Reflecting the implosion of Peronism, the JP fractured and on 1 May 1974 Perón broke with the Montoneros. The latter became a clandestine organization and were declared illegal by the government of **Isabel Perón**.

Following the **military coup of 1976**, the Montoneros (and by extension the JP) were subjected to the murderousness of the **War to Annihilate Subversion**. In the two decades following the return of democracy at the end of 1983, there were unsuccessful attempts to relaunch the JP. The latter then got a new lease on life during the *kirchnerato*. The Peronist youth was restructured into a number of groups that includes **La Cámpora**, headed by **Máximo Kirchner**, and JP Evita, linked to the **Frente para la Victoria/ Partido Justicialista** (FpV/PJ) faction of **Néstor Kirchner** and **Cristina Fernández de Kirchner**.

K

KICILLOF, AXEL (1971–). An academic, sometime government official, and politician, the youthful Kicillof had considerable ideological influence on President **Cristina Fernández de Kirchner**, especially during her second term in office. She appointed him minister of economy in 2013, and he remained in that post until 2015.

Born and raised in the city of **Buenos Aires**, he studied economics at the **University of Buenos Aires** (UBA), first as an undergraduate between 1990 and 1995 and then going on to complete a PhD from 1997 to 2005, writing a doctoral dissertation on Keynes's general theory. While at the UBA, he was active in student politics, heading the student group Tontos pero No Tanto (Stupid but Not So Stupid), and joined the youth wing of the Kirchnerist branch of the Peronist party, **La Cámpora**. He served as assistant professor at the UBA between 1998 and 2010 and held positions at the National University of Quilmes and the National University of General San Martín and in the **Facultad Latinoamericana de Ciencias Sociales** (Latin American Social Science Faculty—FLACSO), as well as being appointed researcher at the National Research Council (CONICET). At these institutions, he taught economics, political economy, and the history of economic thought, usually with a focus on Argentine development and institutions, publishing various articles and working papers in these fields. His research and writing tended toward the applied, though with a strong theoretical component. A controversial figure, scourge of global vulture capitalism and critical of "establishment" economists (domestic and foreign), he is an advocate of neo-Marxian-cum-neo-Keynesian economics.

Kicillof made little secret of a desire to engineer a new order through creative destruction, that is, viewing economic collapse as likely to produce a social upheaval from which a new political system would emerge. He relished the role of head of the Argentine **foreign debt** negotiating team. He came to this task having served in several official and semiofficial capacities. These included acting as advisor to a number of companies and to scientific, educational, and regional development agencies. In the mid-1990s, he was appointed undersecretary of technical affairs at the Secretariat of Social Development, which later became a ministry. Arguably, by the early 21st century, his principal official and semiofficial positions were as one of the key intellectuals of La Cámpora and as holder of a succession of appointments at the renationalized state airline, **Aerolíneas Argentinas** (AA)—he was appointed deputy general manager of the company in 2011. The airline was to become a significant political and economic resource for La Cámpora. At the same time, he held a directorship on the board of the mixed (state and private) steel conglomerate—technically, he represented the government on the board. He was subsequently appointed secretary for policy and planning at the **Ministry of Economy**, where he was widely regarded as de facto head, an arrangement that was formalized in 2013 when he was appointed minister.

Close to Cristina Fernández—she often referred to him by his nickname "Kichi" in public, a form of address that some viewed as maternal and others interpreted as signaling a romantic attachment—during the last years of her presidency, it became increasingly clear that he was one of the key and possibly the key figure in the cabinet, someone from whom President Kirchner sought political and economic advice. There were reports of clashes between Kicillof and **Jorge Capitanich**, chief of the cabinet of ministers (aka prime minister). The principal clashes were over economic strategy, especially how to deal with the so-called holdouts (small foreign holders of the national debt who had not settled in 2005). By this stage, most of the bonds had been acquired by hedge funds, who were actively pressing claims through courts in the **United States**. As head of the mission to New York to present the Argentine government case in the dispute with the "vulture funds," Kicillof took a robust line and came to international attention. His approach to the bondholders was intellectually consistent with his economic philosophy and strategy at the ministry.

Since the end of the Kirchner era, Kicillof has been accused of abuse of power, insider dealing, and mismanagement, charges that he dismisses as politically motivated. Elected to the federal Chamber of Deputies for the city of Buenos Aires in the **congressional elections of 2015**, where he is an active participant in debates. Kicillof is a bright, determined, charismatic, and self-confident individual who has built for himself a significant base on the left of the political spectrum. He has a project; he has support; he has a political future. *See also* CONVERTIBILITY PLAN; ECONOMIC CRISES; MINISTRY OF SOCIAL DEVELOPMENT.

KIDNAPPING OF THE BORN BROTHERS. *See* BORN BROTHERS, KIDNAPPING OF THE (1974–1975)

KIRCHNER, ALICIA MARGARITA (1946–). Politician and a former schoolteacher and social worker who trained in social policy; she owes her preferment to family connections. The sister of President **Néstor Kirchner**, she served as his minister of social affairs when he was governor of the province of **Santa Cruz**. He later appointed Alicia to the federal portfolio in 2006; she continued in post during the subsequent presidencies of his wife, **Cristina Fernández de Kirchner**, until 2015.

In 2015, she was elected governor of Santa Cruz, experiencing a very short honeymoon. Financial mismanagement, arguably a polite term for the plundering of the province by the Kirchner family, produced a budget crisis in lightly populated, resource-rich Santa Cruz that revealed the bankruptcy of the Kirchner "model." On several occasions in the first half of 2017, Governor Kirchner was trapped for many hours in her office by protesting unpaid state officials and pensioners—on one occasion for around 10 hours and on another when being visited by her sister-in-law, the former president. And this despite the province receiving more transfers from the federal government than any other between 2003 and 2015. During the latter stages of the *kirchnerato*, around 90 percent of the inflated provincial budget was spent on running costs, including the payment of salaries and pensions. By this stage, such was the vilification of the Kirchner family in their home province that Governor Alicia Kirchner was unable to appear without a strong security presence.

The level of public hostility to the family was confirmed by the result of the midterm **congressional elections of October 2017** in the province. The governing coalition headed by President **Mauricio Macri** took almost 44 percent of the popular vote, the Kirchnerist **Frente para la Victoria/Partido Justicialista** (FpV/PJ) almost 32 percent. This was a resounding defeat for the family in their home province.

KIRCHNER, CRISTINA ELISABET FERNÁNDEZ DE (1953–). Politician, member of the husband-and-wife team that dominated Argentine politics for much of the early 21st century. She served two terms as president: 2007–2011 and 2011–2015. She was the first woman to be directly elected president and only the second to hold the position, being preceded by **Isabel Perón**, who as vice president succeeded her husband, **Juan Domingo Perón**, on his death. One of the most divisive figures in Argentine politics, she is loved and loathed in equal portions.

Born in the city of **La Plata** in the province of **Buenos Aires**, she went to the national university there, first reading philosophy and then switching to law. Two controversies surround her student years in La Plata: first, whether or not she was an active member of the **Montoneros**, a left-wing Peronist group committed to armed struggle, or simply a fellow traveler; second, whether she completed the law degree—if she did not, she practiced illegally.

Beyond doubt, her political ideas—populist, left-wing, and anti-imperialist—were forged at this point, possibly influenced by her soon-to-be husband **Néstor Kirchner**. With the **military coup of 1976**, the Kirchners—they married the previous year—headed south to **Río Gallegos**, the provincial capital of **Santa Cruz** and Néstor's hometown, where he opened a law practice. There the Kirchners began to build an impressive property portfolio, possibly due to insider knowledge: the practice dealt in evictions resulting from mortgage arears. The practice also represented labor organizations and minor **military** figures accused of **human rights** violations during the **Proceso de Reorganización Nacional**. With the return of democracy, the husband was elected mayor of Río Gallegos and the wife to the provincial assembly, positions that enabled them to prepare Nestor's campaign for the governorship. Her political rise was impressive: she was elected to the constituent assembly that drafted the new **Constitution of 1994** and a year later to the National Senate, representing the province of Buenos Aires. In **Congress**, she manifested her radicalism by challenging aspects of the neoliberal program of President **Carlos Saúl Menem**, later serving on a commission investigating illicit arms deals, **corruption**, and money laundering. The confrontation with Menem led to her expulsion from the **Partido Justicialista** (PJ) in 1997. She resigned her Senate seat and stood as an independent for the Chamber of Deputies in the midterm **congressional elections of 1997**, which were a disaster for Menem and marked the beginning of the end of his presidency. It was at this time that Fernández de Kirchner acquired a reputation for being uncollegial and easy to take offense.

When Néstor was elected president with the support of **Eduardo Duhalde**, PJ **caudillo** of the province of Buenos Aires, Cristina entered the **Casa Rosada** and began to look to the refurbishment of her own political career. By the midterm **congressional elections of 2005**, the Kirchners had fallen out with Duhalde. The dispute, which led to the splintering of the PJ, was blamed by their opponents on the Kirchners. When the PJ failed to produce a single list for the elections, the Kirchners formed their own grouping within the party, the **Frente para la Victoria** (FpV/PJ). Cristina headed the FpV/PJ list, and Duhalde's wife, **Hilda "Chiche" González de Duhalde**, the officialist list. Cristina won the National Senate seat. With the **economy** performing well and the administration strengthening its grip on the state, she was well placed to stand to replace her husband in the **presidential** and **congressional elections of 2007**. The only doubt was whether she would win in the first round—she did, avoiding the need for a second-round runoff. Reappointing approximately half the cabinet of her husband, the first presidency of Cristina Fernández promised continuity with the policies of her husband, who remained a powerful influence. Yet, from the start, the new administration was beset with problems: there was a simmering dispute with the rural sector over taxation, inflation was on the rise, inequality was increasing, the energy and transport infrastructure was deteriorating, and crime and personal security were becoming a critical factor undermining public confidence in the regime. Government handling of rural-sector export taxes brought about a rupture between the president and her vice president, **Julio Cobos**, in 2008 when he voted against the administration in a tie-breaking vote in the National Senate. Challenges multiplied, leading to a poor performance in the midterm **congressional elections of 2009**, a result largely attributed to government mishandling of the rural sector and public concern about corruption and cronyism. The response of the government was to seek to centralize power and silence the opposition. The state statistical agency had been intervened in 2007, before Cristina took over; she further undermined the credibility of the agency. On her watch, the assets of private pension funds were nationalized (sequestered, according to opponents), and the president of the **Banco Central de la República Argentina** (BCRA) resigned as he refused to use the bank's foreign exchange reserves to pay off the foreign institutional debt. As the economic language and policy of the regime became more radical, foreign consortia, especially those involved in **privatization** deals of the 1990s, began to scale back operations, while other firms were renationalized. And there were corruption scandals. The most spectacular related to slush funds established by President Hugo Chávez of **Venezuela** to finance Kirchner's 2007 election campaign—the so-called suitcase affair, when a Venezuela business associate of Chávez was stopped in the main domestic airport of Buenos Aires and found to be carrying US$800,000 in cash. Other revelations of illicit funding of the 2007 campaign came to light later.

Notwithstanding these scandals and poor showing in the 2009 midterms, Cristina Fernández de Kirchner triumphed spectacularly in the **presidential election of 2011**. She obtained one of the largest shares of votes in modern Argentine political history, a proportion exceeded only by that of the PJ ticket in the **presidential election of September 1973**. The result in 2011 was influenced by a sympathy vote resulting from the death of her husband. And she also benefited from the introduction of universal child benefit in 2009, an imaginative policy and a first for the country that, in time, would have a positive impact on the social condition of millions of families. The policy was a response to charges that the poorest sections of society had not benefited from growth during the presidency of Néstor and had been adversely affected by macroeconomic instability during Cristina's first term. In the 2011 election campaign, and following reelection, Fernández de Kirchner tightened her control on the government and the party—she is said to have selected most candidates on the FpV/JP list personally, and handpicked her running mate, **Amado Boudou**, her former youthful minister of economy with whom she was romantically linked. Boudou would later be subject to several criminal investigations. The style and rhetoric of the administration became more populist and personalist, consciously echoing the language and policy of the first administration of Juan Domingo Perón. A personality cult was assiduously manufactured: the now deceased Néstor was compared to Perón and Cristina to **Eva Perón**. FpV/PJ propaganda depicted images of both couples, material that was also used in official publications. The widowed *presidenta* claimed to be inspired by the Peróns and her husband, whose legacy she sought to burnish, frequently referring to him as "El," as if he was still alive. (Later, this behavior would occasion rumors about her mental health.)

During the second administration, as the economy stalled, the president passed control of policy to a group of young radical intellectuals associated with **La Cámpora**, an organization that took its name from Peronist president **Héctor Cámpora**. Although he was not named minister of economy until 2013—he had been number two at the ministry since 2011—**Axel Kicillof** was the economic guru running policy. Sometimes described as a neo-Keynesian, at others as a Marxist economist, Kicillof is another youthful minister of economy romantically associated with the *presidenta*, much being made of his nickname, "Kichi," derived from the **River Plate** Spanish pronunciation of his surname. Kicillof is credited with the renationalization of the former state oil corporation **Yacimientos Petrolíferos Fiscales**, at the time the largest expropriation in Argentine history; the refusal to negotiate with bondholders who had not accepted the 2005 debt settlement negotiated by Néstor Kirchner and his minister of economy, **Roberto Lavagna**; the 2014 devaluation of the peso; and tightening control of the foreign exchange market to curb capital flight.

In the last years of the second presidency, street protests proliferated—spontaneous demonstrations against economic mismanagement, which was characterized by accelerating inflation, empty supermarket shelves, and rising crime. There were also vociferous protests against government efforts to control the **media**, the deterioration of public services reflected in rail disasters and catastrophic floods that claimed scores of lives, government measures to control the judiciary, and the mysterious death of public prosecutor **Alberto Nisman**. There were marches and demonstrations in favor of the government—according to critics, events organized by La Cámpora featuring rent-a-mobs. And there were multiple corruption scandals involving the presidential family and high-ranking officials, accused of siphoning funds from public works contracts, extralegal acquisition of businesses, money laundering, and illicit transfers to foreign bank accounts.

Cristina Fernández's worldview was formed during her student days and the work of **Ernesto Laclau**, a political theorist and public intellectual who wrote about Marxism and **populism**. It was radical and anti-imperialist; she continued the line in foreign policy developed by her husband. There was a particularly close relationship with Venezuela, **Bolivia**, and **Ecuador**, though relations with **Brazil**, **Chile**, **Paraguay**, and **Uruguay** were less cordial, partly due to measures designed to curb imports, and disagreement about regional approaches to foreign investment and international capital markets, and a spat about admitting Venezuela to **MERCOSUR** (the South American Common Market)—Paraguay objected. At home and abroad, Cristina Fernández used the dispute with **Great Britain** over the **Falkland Islands** to drum up support and often pursued anti-Americanism to similar effect.

Since leaving the Casa Rosada, Cristina Fernández de Kirchner has shown little desire to retire from public life. She maintains a large public profile, having organized rallies and expressed an interest in continuing to play a role in politics, notwithstanding the splintering of the FpV/JP after the **presidential** and **congressional elections of 2015**. Cynics maintain that she needs to secure election to public office in order to escape jail. She is under investigation for the misuse of public funds, notably deals relating to the sale of BCRA stocks of US dollars and kickbacks from public works contracts. The courts have ordered the freezing of some of her assets. She has also been cited in the investigation into the death of Nisman, which is particularly threatening. She denies all charges and involvement.

Mrs. Fernández de Kirchner stood for election to the National Senate for the province of Buenos Aires in the midterm **congressional elections of 2017** at the head of her newly formed coalition **Unidad/Unión Ciudadana** (UC). Expecting that the UC would gain the two "majority" seats at stake, Mrs. Kirchner in fact secured the single "minority" seat available to the runner-up party. Unless Congress removes her immunity from prosecution while in office, she will escape jail, yet her political future remains uncertain. Perhaps even more ignominious was the defeat suffered in the family's home province of Santa Cruz, where the governing coalition topped the poll with 44 percent of the vote, Mrs. Kirchner's party coming in a distant second with 32 percent. The family had come to regard the province as their fiefdom—and had treated it as such.

The Kirchners demonstrated the factious nature of Argentine politics—not least within the PJ—and how corruption was institutionalized, becoming intrinsic and strategic to the system of government as much as a mechanism for personal gain. Perhaps this is their most significant legacy. This, and imaginative social policy initiatives like family assistance inherited from Duhalde, which helped stabilize the country during the early years of Néstor's presidency, and the universal child benefit, which had a dramatic impact on inequality during Cristina's second. *See also* FOREIGN DEBT/ FOREIGN INVESTMENT; KIRCHNER, ALICIA MARGARITA (1946–); KIRCHNER, MÁXIMO CARLOS (1977–); MINISTRY OF ECONOMY; STATE-OWNED ENTERPRISES (SOEs); UNIVERSIDAD NACIONAL DE LA PLATA (UNLP).

KIRCHNER, MÁXIMO CARLOS (1977–). Would-be politician; son of Presidents **Néstor Kirchner** and **Cristina Fernández de Kirchner**; elected national deputy for his native province of **Santa Cruz** in the federal **congressional elections of 2015**. Although the Kirchners regarded the province as their own and ran local politics virtually as a family business, the **Frente para la Victoria/Partido Justicialista** (FpV/PJ) list headed by Máximo came in second, losing first place to the **Unión Cívica Radical** (UCR) list. While the margin between the two lists was just a little over three percentage points, the result was a humiliation for the Kirchners, driven by popular discontent triggered by evidence of **corruption** surrounding their administration of the province and, indeed, at the national level. Máximo is a founding member of **La Cámpora**, a left-of-center organization that served as the youth wing of the FpV/PJ. Nominally head of La Cámpora, the day-to-day administration of the movement was ordered by others, as was its strategy and ideological perspective. In mid-2017, he was investigated for tax fraud and illegal money transfers, charges he denies.

KIRCHNER, NÉSTOR CARLOS (1950–2010). Student activist, lawyer, and politician; president of the republic between 2003 and 2007, following the economic crisis of 2001–2002. Born in **Río Gallegos**, capital of the southernmost province of **Santa Cruz**, Kirchner's family was of German Swiss and Chilean Croat origin. He studied law at the national university of **La Plata** in the province of **Buenos Aires**, where he met his future wife, Cristina Fernández. At university, he was a member of the militant Juventud Universitaria Peronista (JUP); La Plata was then the city most associated with the radical, revolutionary wing of Peronism, engaged in confronting the regime headed by de facto president **Juan Carlos Onganía**. According to some accounts, this is where the Kirchners first became involved with the **Montoneros**, a left-wing Peronist organization committed to armed struggle. Following the **military coup of 1976**, the newly wed Kirchners relocated to Río Gallegos, where they established a law practice, though Cristina had not completed her degree. While friends were tortured and disappeared, the Kirchners appear to have been protected by their families. They kept a low profile and, notwithstanding economic challenges, appeared to have prospered, developing the practice and investing in property. They did not entirely escape the attention of the authorities. In the final days of the **military** regime of the **Proceso de Reoganización Nacional**, Kirchner was a member of one of the Peronist organization that became close to the regime. However, the return of democracy in 1983 found him active in the **Movimiento Renovador Peronista** (MRP), which would later challenge **Carlos Saúl Menem**, future president.

In 1987, Kirchner was elected mayor of Río Gallegos; two years later, his wife obtained a seat in the provincial legislature. Kirchner had already appointed his wife and sister **Alicia Kirchner** to positions in the city government. Yet he acquired a reputation for efficiency and gradually built up a political base that resulted in his election as governor of the province in 1991 by a large majority. In all, he was elected governor on three successive occasions, serving until 2003. During his 12-year tenure, provincial finances improved, partly by securing provincial participation in revenue generated by the local operations of **Yacimientos Petrolíferos Fiscales** (YPF), partly by negotiating fiscal transfers from the federal government, and partly through careful management of the budget. Increased fiscal resources facilitated infrastructure investment and social expenditure that had a dramatic impact on poverty and inequality in the province. At this stage, Kirchner enjoyed a warm relationship with by-now president Menem. As governor, Kirchner continued the practice he had developed as mayor of Río Gallegos, appointing family and friends to senior—and lucrative—positions in the administration. Relations with Menem deteriorated after 1994, but by then Kirchner was sufficiently well established to secure reelection as governor. He also acquired greater national prominence, building links with reformist and anti-Menem sections of the **Partido Justicialista** (PJ). Relations with Menem improved during Kirchner's third term as governor, though he appeared to be developing presidential ambitions as the end of the *menemato* approached.

When the presidency of **Fernando de la Rúa** collapsed at the end of 2001, Kirchner was well placed to advance his cause, actively cultivating PJ **caudillos** like **Alberto Fernández** (no relation of his wife) in the province of **Buenos Aires**. When President **Eduardo Duhalde**, PJ strongman who had been selected president by **Congress** in 2002 to serve out the remainder of De la Rúa's term, was casting around for a compliant PJ candidate to stand in the **presidential** and **congressional elections of 2003**, in the expectation of ensuring his own election to the presidency in 2007, his attention alighted on Kirchner, though Kirchner was not his first choice. Kirchner and his vice presidential running mate, **Daniel Scioli**, campaigned under the banner of the **Frente para La Victoria/Partido Justicialista** (FpV/PJ). Although Kirchner was beaten in the first round of the presidential election by Menem, who claimed to represent the PJ mainstream, Kirchner became president by default when Menem pulled out days before the scheduled second-round run-off.

Kirchner's first years in office were marked by social progress and economic recovery. He maintained the system of family support introduced by Duhalde at the height of the crisis and retained his minister of economy, **Roberto Lavagna**. Such constructive continuity was politically astute and enabled Kirchner to embark on a strategy of *transversalismo* (transversalism), constructing alliances within the PJ and establishing pacts with other parties so as to reinforce his authority—Menem's withdrawal from the second round of the 2003 presidential election may have been intended to weaken the legitimacy of Kirchner's mandate. Cabinet posts were offered to reformist Peronists, and in another manifestation of continuity, his sister was appointed minister of social development while other ministries were packed with cronies. Debt default brought a fiscal windfall, later sustained by the commodity boom, while Lavagna's strategy of ensuring a fiscal and trade surplus delivered funds and foreign exchange—and a large increase in foreign reserves. The economy grew by an average of almost 9 percent annually during Kirchner's presidency: investment in economic and social projects increased dramatically. Incomes rose, unemployment and poverty fell sharply to near historic lows, and Kirchner increased his control of the PJ and the administration. There were other dividends: agreement was reached with the majority of foreign bondholders in 2005, and obligations to the IMF were canceled in 2006. After 2003, the government also began to reverse Menem's program of **privatization**, taking back into state control such corporations as **Aerolíneas Argentinas**. Controversially, the government reopened investigations into **human rights** abuses during the Proceso, setting aside limiting legislation like the **Ley de Punto Final** and **Ley de Obediencia Debida**, which were introduced during the presidency of **Raúl Alfonsín** and intended to draw a line over the past and reintegrate the military into society. The prosecutions that resulted were broadly supported by civil society, gaining further kudos for Kirchner. In 2004, in a former navy clandestine detention and torture center, the **Escuela Superior de Mecánica de la Armada** (ESMA), he inaugurated a center-cum-museum of remembrance and an agency for the promotion and defense of human rights. The move that was well received by the families of the **Desaparecidos** as necessary for the process of national reconciliation. These programs and policies contributed to electoral gains in the midterm **congressional elections of 2005**—gains that further increased his grip on the party and politics.

Economic and political success at home may have encouraged an adventurous international policy, an alignment that became increasingly radical, echoing the rhetoric and worldview of Kirchner's student days. Although he promised to maintain a strong commitment to **MERCOSUR**, the government was soon closely associated with countries like **Venezuela** and **Ecuador** that espoused a distinctly anti-US position. This was an alliance with the radical left, not the reformist, democratic left typified by the then governments of **Brazil**, **Chile**, and **Uruguay**. Relations with Uruguay were soured in 2006 due to overseas investment in a cellulose plant there; soon relations with Chile cooled when Argentina reneged on an energy deal. The so-called Pink Tide sweeping across Latin America during the early 21st century consisted of two currents, the pluralistic, social-market economic internationalism epitomized by Chile, and the authoritarian, neopopulist, statist model represented by Venezuela. After 2007, Argentina would be increasingly identified with the latter.

Although there was considerable speculation at the time that he would stand for reelection in 2007, Kirchner promoted the candidature of his wife. It was argued that, had he stood and been successful in 2007, with a limit of two terms, he would have been unable to stand for the presidency again. By deferring to **Cristina Fernández de Kirchner** in 2007, he would qualify to seek reelection in 2011, and she again in 2015, resulting in an interminable **tango** of the Kirchners. Kirchner determined, however, to control the PJ, becoming president of the party in questionable elections that reflected divisions within the movement that had splintered in 2005 when Kirchner confronted the hitherto dominant faction headed by Duhalde. He retained this post until his death, notwithstanding his poor showing in the midterm **congressional elections of 2009**, when the Chamber of Deputies list that he headed came in second. Some months before his death in 2010, he was elected secretary general of **Unión de Naciones Sudamericanas** (Union of South American Nations—UNASUR), a Venezuela-inspired grouping opposed to the **United States**.

Before becoming president, Kirchner had run an anticorruption campaign, though little was delivered. During his time as governor and president, the Kirchner family and several of its associates became extremely wealthy. Provincial assets were deposited in a Swiss bank account in his name, and despite promises to repatriate the cash, substantial sums went missing. Yet during his presidency, the sharp rise in poverty and unemployment triggered by the collapse of the **Convertibility Plan** was reversed. Infant mortality and malnutrition fell. Wages and living standards rose. Whether due to design or luck, he remains as much remembered for these achievements as for **corruption** and the deterioration of democratic accountability—perhaps because his misdemeanors were dwarfed by those of his wife. *See also* FOREIGN DEBT/FOREIGN INVESTMENT; KIRCHNER, MÁXIMO CARLOS (1977–); MINISTRY OF ECONOMY; MINISTRY OF SOCIAL DEVELOPMENT; UNIVERSIDAD NACIONAL DE LA PLATA (UNLP).

KIRCHNERATO. Applied to the period of rule by the husband-and-wife presidential team **Néstor Kirchner**, president from 2003 to 2007, and **Cristina Fernández de Kirchner**, president from 2007 to 2015. Derived from *peronato*, the first two presidencies of **Juan Domingo Perón** (1946–1955), the term is used to describe a system of government characterized by personalism and authoritarianism—a political arrangement that embraces "electoral democracy" and top–down government rather than fully functioning, open democratic processes. *See also MENEMATO*; MENEM, CARLOS SAÚL (1930–).

KRIEGER VASENA, ADALBERT (1920–2000). Internationally recognized academic economist; public official and minister of economy (1967–1969). Trained in economics at the **University of Buenos Aires** (UBA), Krieger Vasena taught and conducted research there, mainly about contemporary economic problems and development theory. In 1957, he was appointed to head the **Ministry of Economy** by General **Pedro Eugenio Aramburu**, de facto president installed soon after the **Revolución Libertadora**. Krieger Vasena was Aramburu's third minister of economy and, aged 37 at the time, one of the youngest ever to be appointed to the portfolio; he had previously been director of the **Banco Central de la República Argentina** (BCRA). It was at this point that Argentina applied for membership in the International Monetary Fund, of which he became president in 1958. In 1967, he returned to the Ministry of Economy; he was the second economics minister appointed by de facto president **Juan Carlos Onganía**, a hard-line anti-Peronist and instigator of the **Revolución Argentina**. As minister, Krieger Vasena was charged with supervising the critical first phase of the project envisaged by the **military** administration, namely economic reform, social stabilization, and a supervised return to democracy. He proposed a two-prong strategy: first, an orthodox stabilization program involving devaluation, a wage freeze, partial deregulation of prices accompanied by windfall taxes on exports, followed by a program of state-supported industrialization that drew on **developmentalist** theory, that is, investment in infrastructure (energy and transport) and heavy **industry** (iron and steel)—a strategy financed largely by foreign capital. With wages tightly controlled, the exchange rate stabilizing, and overseas investors favorably disposed, the project was initially successful. However, by 1968, the program began to unravel. Inflation picked up; the trade balance deteriorated; worker demands for wage hikes grew, notwithstanding continuing political repression; sections of the military and national business sector questioned the role accorded to foreign corporations. The resulting social explosion, the **Cordobazo**, spelled the end of Krieger Vasena's strategy—he stepped down in June 1969.

On leaving office for the last time, Krieger Vasena continued to publish, his international reputation enhanced by his research and, possibly, by what he had attempted while in government. In 1973, he was appointed to the World Bank as vice president for Latin America, a post he held until 1978, and subsequently accepted positions on various national and international commissions and councils. *See also* ECONOMIC CRISES; FOREIGN DEBT/FOREIGN INVESTMENT.

L

LA BOCA. Now a popular tourist destination, at the southeastern edge of the city of **Buenos Aires**, noted for art galleries, museums, restaurants, markets, and street theater, and iconic, brightly decorated corrugated iron architecture, the locality was once the principal port of the city, situated on the estuary of the Riachuelo River (*la boca* is the Spanish term for "mouth" and "estuary"), which provided a safe, natural harbor. Modern development began in the mid-19th century with the arrival of Italian **immigrants**, the construction of one of the first railway lines in the country, and the canalization of the Riachuelo in the 1870s, which facilitated the expansion and modernization of the harbor. Historically, the district is noted for returning **Alfredo Palacios** to **Congress** in 1904, the first socialist representative to be elected in the Americas, and as one of the places were **tango** first emerged. Arguably, La Boca is even more famous as the original location of two world-class soccer clubs, **Boca Juniors** (Club Atlético Boca Juniors) and **River Plate** (Club Atlético River Plate)—River Plate is now based in the north of Buenos Aires. Boca Juniors is the most popular club in the country in terms of fan base, and its renowned La Bombonera stadium is recognized around the world, though River Plate has won more national and international trophies.

LA CÁMPORA. A political youth movement, nominally associated with the Peronist **Partido Justicialista** (PJ). Its origins date from the 2003 presidential electoral campaign of **Néstor Kirchner**, but it came to prominence after 2006, becoming particularly active during the second presidency of **Cristina Fernández de Kirchner**. Originally, the movement provided campaign "shock troops"—a function that it still performs—though it is increasingly responsible for the intellectual and ideological underpinning of what became the late Kirchner economic and political project.

La Cámpora takes its name from **Héctor Cámpora**, the super-loyalist anointed by **Juan Domingo Perón**, then in exile in **Spain**, to contest the **presidential election of March 1973**. Cámpora was close to the **Montoneros**, a semiclandestine movement on the left of the PJ active in the universities, and he stepped down after only seven weeks in office, triggering the **presidential election of September 1973**, which resulted in Perón's return to the **Casa Rosada**.

Although the nominal head of La Cámpora is **Máximo Kirchner**, son of Néstor and Cristina, effective leadership lies with former student activists. Many are graduates of the **University of Buenos Aires** (UBA), where they had read economics and other social sciences, forging their political ideas and skills in student politics in the 1990s. Several were born during the period of the **Proceso de Reorganización Nacional**, or the chaotic years that preceded it, and their views were shaped by Peronist resistance to the **Revolución Libertadora** and the **Revolución Argentina** as well as disappointment with the achievements of Peronism in power between 1973 and 1976. In addition, the Camporistas were opposed to the neoliberal economic model applied during the *menemato*. The influence of La Cámpora within government grew exponentially after 2011. By this stage, it was arguably the most active component of the political grouping **Frente para la Victoria/ Partido Justicialista** (FpV/PJ), established to further the political and electoral ambitions of the Kirchners. By the second presidency of Mrs. Fernández de Kirchner, the movement had displaced the **trade unions** and the PJ party apparatus, previously the most powerful factions within Peronism.

The agenda advanced by La Cámpora is anticapitalist and "antiglobalization." It seeks to promote greater state involvement in the **economy** and favors mass, or direct, democracy rather than conventional parliamentary democracy. Many key figures in the group formed their ideas about economics and politics in student movements of the 1990s opposed to the Menemist program and the cosy relationship between the state and domestic and foreign business. And there is an acknowledgment of the influence of notions of armed struggle forged during the chaos of the 1960s and 1970s, when Marxist activists on the fringe of the PJ fought to secure a more prominent position in the Peronist movement and government, efforts and elements with whom the Kirchners engaged. Whether this worldview was formed by assessments of events in the 1970s, or experiences of the 1990s, the Kirchner-cum-La-Cámpora model is presented by its proponents as a mechanism to forge a new future. Until his death in 2014, the intellectual guru of the administration was **Ernesto Laclau**, a distinguished Argentine political sociologist who had taught in Europe and the **United States**.

La Cámpora acknowledges its support for revolutionary Peronism and applauds the actions of the Montoneros, recognizing their achievements and seeking to learn from their failures. It also views the traditional establishment, including the **media**, as inhibiting the transformation of the country, blocking political progress, and preventing a social revolution. It used modern forms of technology associated with social media to combat views expressed in the traditional media and to mobilize support in ways that prefigured such youthful political organizations as Podemos in Spain and Syriza in Greece and, indeed, young supporters of Bernie Sanders in the 2016 presidential primaries in the United States and Corbynistas in **Great Britain** the following year. Key figures in La Cámpora were determined to wrest control of the PJ from the traditional leadership and, possibly, size control of the state itself. It is a moot point whether the Kirchners had created La Cámpora to serve their own political imperative, or the regime of Cristina Fernández was captured by it. Arguably, the group favors a strategy of creative destruction, engineering economic meltdown to destroy the old political and economic order to facilitate the emergence of a new, radically different country and society.

After 2011, prominent members of La Cámpora were appointed to significant positions in strategic ministries and to run state entities, as well as to critical embassies. Around 2012, Camporistas controlled the budgets of 15 state agencies and government subministries, totaling $6.2 million pesos. The agencies and subministries included **Aerolíneas Argentinas**, **Fabricaciones Militares**, the television company Canal 7, the Administración de Bienes del Estado, the Secretariat of Justice, and the Secretariat of Economic Policy. In addition, La Cámpora placed people on the boards of the **Banco de la Nación Argentina** and **Yaciminetos Petrolíferos Fiscales** (YPF). Furthermore, Camporistas were to be found in the Cabinet Office and such **ministries** as **Agriculture**, **Justice**, **Interior and Transport**, and **Planning**. Notoriously, they milked Aerolíneas Argentinas to fund political activities and pet projects.

During the declining months of the second presidency of Mrs. Kirchner, preceding the inauguration of President **Mauricio Macri**, who defeated Cristina Fernández de Kirchner's nominee in the **presidential election of 2015**, the outgoing president attempted to pack several state bodies and agencies with Camporistas. Although La Cámpora lacks a broad political base, beyond youth and university organizations, it has secured a presence in **Congress**. In the **congressional elections of 2015**, adherents of La Cámpora secured three seats (out of 72) in the National Senate and 24 seats (out of 257) in the Chamber of Deputies. *See also* KICILLOF, AXEL (1971–).

"LA HORA DEL PUEBLO". Joint statement issued by the Peronists, the Radicals, the Progressive Democrats, the Popular Conservatives, the Argentine Socialists, and regional *bloquistas* in November 1970. It called for the immediate recognition of **political parties**, the promulgation of a political party statute after a consultation with politicians, a speedy return to democracy, and elections with neither vetoes nor proscriptions. The signatories pledged themselves to promote the establishment of a government with three characteristics. First, it would be based on cooperation between the parties and an agreement on basic points of national policy (i.e., defense of the internal market and of national capital, income redistribution by means of wage increases). Second, it would have the participation of the best men in the country. And third, it would respect the rights of minority parties.

The declaration's significance was that the two largest parties (the Peronists and the Radicals) put aside their differences and united to demand the opening up of the political process. This was the result of widespread disillusionment with an exhausted **military** regime, the intransigence of President **Roberto Levingston** in maintaining the ban on political party activities, and his vague commitment to general elections four or five years down the road. When **Alejandro Agustín Lanusse** acceded to the presidency in March 1971, his sole objective was to extricate the armed forces from government, and he envisaged the "La Hora del Pueblo" statement as the starting point for ultimately unsuccessful negotiations for a grand accord leading to the election of a transitional "unity" government.

LA MATANZA. One of the largest administrative subdivisions (*partidos*) of the province of **Buenos Aires**, abutting the southwest of the **federal capital**. Although geographically large, it is also the most populous in the province, and also one of the most historic, tracing its origin back to the early 17th century. Population grew rapidly in the 1930s. Many factories were built there during the industrialization drive of the 1940s, attracted by cheap land, proximity to the capital, and availability of labor. As a heavily unionized, working-class industrial district, it was badly affected by major political developments in the late 20th century: first, the state terror of the **Proceso de Reorganización Nacional** of the mid-1970s; second, **privatization** in the 1990s. Indeed, though exaggerated, its experience was typical of similar districts. During the Proceso, kidnapping, disappearances, and torture were rife, no doubt in part due to its reputation for militancy. La Matanza lived up to its name—slaughter. During the 1990s, main manufacturing firms and large industrial plants closed, as did small and medium-sized workshops. The promised new industries were slow to appear. Some recovery took place under the reactivation plans of **Néstor Kirchner** and his wife, **Cristina Fernández de Kirchner**, particularly of small, labor-intensive firms. The only large company is a Mercedes-Benz axel plant, one of the few geared to the export market. Plastics, textiles, and shoes are the main sectors. Whether this progress can be maintained is a moot point. A substantial part of the housing stock is substandard, and around 40 percent of the population does not have adequate health coverage, notwithstanding sums thrown at the district by the Kirchners. The current federal and provincial administrations, headed respectively by President **Mauricio Macri** and Governor **María Eugenia Vidal**, have also targeted the area. Large sums have been plowed into infrastructure projects, and the district is being presented a pilot scheme in urban renewal. Macri claims that the benefits will be direct and immediate because funds will not be siphoned off due to **corruption** as during the Kirchner era. *See also* INDUSTRY; TRADE UNIONS.

LA NACIÓN. One of the historic daily newspapers of Argentina and Latin America, founded in 1870 by **Bartolomé Mitre**, a couple of years after he had completed his term as president, to advance liberal principles for the modernization of the country. Mitre had earlier published *La Nación Argentina*. The daily appeared in broadsheet format; the weekend editions were tabloid. Often the leading newspaper in terms of circulation, *La Nación* is still considered one of the most prestigious titles in the country and remains in the hands of the Mitre family.

The paper has frequently ruffled the feathers of the government of the day. It first closed in 1874 and again in 1875 due to Mitre's support for autonomist sentiments in the city and province of **Buenos Aires**. Publication was again suspended during the **Revolution of 1890**. Although closure did not result, the **Concordancia** administration was highly critical of editorial policy in 1937. Regarded as an organ of the establishment, *La Nación* escaped intervention during the first two presidencies of **Juan Domingo Perón**, unlike some titles, by adopting a cautious editorial stance on **Peronism**. As with many **media** companies, *La Nación* did not enjoy an easy relationship with the administration of **Cristina Fernández de Kirchner**. The newspaper complained that the government was attempting to curb press freedom; the administration retorted that *La Nación* had taken a "soft" (or pro-official) line during the **Proceso de Reorganización Nacional** and that it has consistently supported military coups d'état from 1930 to 1976. The paper claimed that this was a smear intended to deflect attention from the charge of attempting to limit journalistic freedom and that the title had reported impartially about state terrorism and acts of violence committed by guerrilla groups during the 1970s. With *Clarín*, *La Nación* was caught up in a spat with Cristina Kirchner over its acquisition of shares in Papel Prensa, the state–private newsprint producer originally organized during the national-industrialization/import-substituting drive orchestrated by the administration of de facto president General **Juan Carlos Onganía**.

From inception, *La Nación* consistently argued the case for liberalism (or liberal conservatism), which it sought to promote while declaring itself free of any party-political affiliations. By the mid-20th century, critics of its editorial stance regarded its take on liberalism as dated, more attuned to views of pro-rural, pro-international-trade interests than the needs of a modern **economy**. This did not prevent daily sales of more than a third of a million copies at its peak; it was the largest-circulating daily in the country and the most widely read daily in Latin America in the 1930s. Challenged by such popular newspapers as *La Razón* around midcentury, *La Nación* began to lose ground to serious titles like *La Opinón* and *Clarín* in the 1970s and 1980s, dailies that published in tabloid format and offered more incisive journalism and analysis. By this stage, *La Nación* was seen as staid and old-fashioned in content as well as layout, despite having been an early pioneer of technological advances and design in newspaper publishing. It had been one of the first to use telegraphic news services in 1870, had introduced linotype in 1900, and was among the pioneers of color a few years later. By the early 21st century, the La Nación group was beginning to recover some of its former dynamism, acquiring Spanish-language publications elsewhere in the Americas, investing in popular and sensationalist titles, and diversifying into other branches of the media, including cable television. In 2012, the daily went tabloid. Its website is one of the most visited in Argentina and the daily edition the second most widely read newspaper. *See also* MONTONEROS; MILITARY COUP OF 1930; MILITARY COUP OF 1955; MILITARY COUP OF 1962; MILITARY COUP OF 1966; MILITARY COUP OF 1976; PERÓN, ISABEL (1931–); TRIPLE A (ALIANZA ANTICOMUNISTA ARGENTINA); WAR TO ANNIHILATE SUBVERSION.

LA OPINIÓN. Founded in 1971 by **Jacobo Timerman**, a daily newspaper modeled on *Le Monde* in masthead, tabloid format, dense print style, ideological stance, and emphasis on reportage with comment. Timerman's other near contemporary title was *Primera Plana*, a weekly that ran from 1962 to 1972 and was envisaged as the Argentine equivalent of *Newsweek* or *Time*, covering contemporary political, economic, and cultural affairs. Reputedly initially close to left/reformist sections of the armed forces, both the daily and weekly were subject to censorship and temporary closure by **military** regimes of the period. Timerman only remained in control of the newspaper until April 1977, when he was kidnapped, but by that stage *La Opinión* had already acquired a reputation for cutting-edge reporting and balanced analysis.

Like *Le Monde*, *La Opinión* devoted much attention to international and regional politics, the Non-Aligned Movement, global conflict, and the rise of socialism in postcolonial Africa and Asia. Coverage and approach were politically centrist, economically liberal, and culturally left leaning. Some of the prominent cultural figures of the day like **Tomás Eloy Martínez** and **Ernesto Sábato** served the paper as editor, feature writers, or regular contributors. As the country descended into violence, *La Opinión* devoted considerable attention to such topics as state terrorism and the actions of guerrilla groups like the **Montoneros**, reporting impartially and without fear. This provoked the ire of the administration of President **Isabel Perón** and the de facto regime that came to power with the **military coup of 1976**. Timerman and others at *La Opinión* received death threats from right- and left-wing terrorist organizations, and several were "disappeared" during the **Proceso** de **Reorganización Nacional**. Timerman was tortured and survived; others did not—their bodies were never discovered. Before he was kidnapped, Timerman was active overseas in focusing attention on the horrors of the **Dirty War**. During the latter part of 1976 and early 1977, the paper was subjected to the seizure of print runs and temporary closures.

With the disappearance of journalists, workers, and production staff in 1977, the paper struggled on for a few years under federal intervention, finally closing in 1980. By this stage, the regime had charged Timerman with complicity with the Montoneros—one of *La Opinión*'s major financial backers was associated with the movement. The matter of the disposal of residual assets of the newspaper by the military would resurface years later in a dispute between *Clarín*—sometimes regarded as a latter-day version of *La Opinión*—and the government of President **Cristina Fernández de Kirchner**. *See also* LA RAZÓN; LÓPEZ REGA, JOSÉ (1916–1989); TRIPLE A (ALIANZA ANTICOMUNISTA ARGENTINA); VIDELA, JORGE RAFAEL (1925–2013); WAR TO ANNIHILATE SUBVERSION.

LA PAMPA. Sparsely populated province located in the center of the country, bordered by **Río Negro** to the south, **Mendoza** to the west and northwest, **San Luis** and **Córdoba** to the north, and **Buenos Aires** to the east. It was not until the 18th century that Spanish colonists established settlements, but resistance by the local indigenous people prevented much expansion until the government of **Juan Manuel de Rosas** and did not cease until the **Conquest of the Desert**. In 1884, the area was organized as the Territorio Nacional de la Pampa Central, and in 1952 it was turned into a province. It was named Provincia Eva Perón until the **military coup of 1955**, when it was renamed La Pampa.

The provincial economy is centered on rural production, with the most important activity being **cattle** ranching. In the northeast and east of the province, there is cultivation of cereals such as wheat, sunflower, **maize**, and barley. La Pampa generates 10 percent of the national output of wheat and 13 percent of sunflower oilseeds. The province has a population of approximately 350,000, and its capital is **Santa Rosa**.

LA PLATA. Modern, planned "garden city," designed as the new capital of the province of **Buenos Aires** following the **federalization of the city of Buenos Aires** in 1880. Officially founded in 1882 and planned according to contemporary thinking about "rational urban living," La Plata was intended by its promoters to rival the former provincial and national capital, now exclusively the seat of the federal government. The "rational" lines of the city design combined broad diagonal avenues with a standard grid system, though most streets were wider than those of town and city centers dating from the colonial period, with parks and squares every half a dozen blocks. Most streets and avenues were designed to be tree lined, and in addition to setting aside spaces for public parks, the original plan featured elegant buildings located at strategic intervals in parks and squares and at major street/avenue intersections. Many public buildings are situated at such intersections. In addition to the provincial parliament and government offices, these include the opera house (the original building destroyed by fire in 1977 was second only to the **Colón** in the city of Buenos Aires), the cathedral (which is considerably larger than its colonial counterpart in the **federal capital**), the university complex (the main university enjoys a national and international reputation second to none in the country), as well as numerous other public buildings, places of worship, museums, and important corporate offices and private residences.

Initially based around government and the service sector, the city is now the fourth or fifth largest conurbation in the country and boasts such industries as a major oil refinery—the largest in the country—around which a substantial petrochemical complex is based. The port, at Ensenada, is the second largest in the country. Formerly, there were major meatpacking plants, the sites of which are now being developed as a duty-free industrial complex. Modern, clean **industry** includes high-tech firms—the city claims to be the Silicon Valley of Argentina, drawing on skills developed at the highly regarded National University of La Plata. There are two other large universities. Now part of the Greater Buenos Aires conurbation—the two cities are about 40 miles apart—La Plata has belatedly forged its own identity. It is a decidedly green city that is pedestrian friendly. In 2018, the population of Greater La Plata was around 1,000,000. Between 1952 and 1955, the city was known as Eva Perón. *See also* UNIVERSIDAD NACIONAL DE LA PLATA (UNLP).

LA PRENSA. Commencing publication in 1869, a year earlier than its longtime rival *La Nación*, from inception *La Prensa* was regarded as the organ of the conservative rural oligarchy. The founder, José Camilo Paz, was a wealthy landowner and politician-cum-diplomat who epitomized the group whose project for the modernization of the country came to fruition after the **Conquest of the Desert** with the ascendancy of President (former general) **Julio A Roca** and the Partido Autonomista Nacional (PAN). The family's townhouse, the Palacio Paz, was and remains one of the largest and most imposing residences in **Buenos Aires**—it was sold to the army in the 1930s and is now the officers' club, the Circulo Militar.

Throughout, the newspaper advanced the cause of republican conservatism, supporting the "managed politics" that was intrinsic to the system set up by Roca and economic arrangements associated with rapid economic growth at the turn of the century. Around this time, the editorial line was skeptical about democratic opening and political reform and advocated that authorities take a strong line in the face of "agitation" as manifest during the **Semana Trágica** of 1919. The paper opposed what it saw as the demagoguery of the first popularly elected government of President **Hipólito Yrigoyen** of the **Unión Cívica Radical** (UCR). Unsurprisingly, *La Prensa* supported the **military coup of 1930** that ousted Yrigoyen and the **Concordancia** regime that emerged shortly thereafter. Adopting a high-profile anti-Peronist position in the run up to the **congressional** and **presidential elections of 1946**, it was equally unsurprising that *La Prensa* provoked **Juan Domingo Perón** when he gained the presidency. The title was soon involved in criminal and congressional investigations relating to past financial irregularities, including the nonpayment of taxes, and embroiled in labor disputes. As the regime became intolerant of opposition voices, and in advance of the **congressional** and **presidential elections of 1952**, *La Prensa* was expropriated in 1951 and handed over to the **Confederación General del Trabajo** (CGT) and the newspaper sellers' trade union. A year after the **military coup of 1955**, the de facto administration of President **Pedro Eugenio Aramburu** returned the title to the Gainza Paz family.

The return of ownership to the family did not produce a material change in the fortunes of the newspaper, which had lost circulation to other titles like *Clarín* when run by the CGT, a situation compounded by its continued virulent hostility to Peronism and perceived association with the **military** during the 1960s and 1970s. Although *La Prensa* supported the **military coup of 1976**, it was one of the few titles to publish information about those who had been "disappeared" by the armed forces, police, and security services during the **Dirty War**. The return of democracy in 1983 did not bring better times for *La Prensa*. It was quick to highlight the shortcomings of the government of President **Raúl Alfonsín** and failed to shake off the reputation of being especially close to the 1976 military regime, struggling with rising debts and shrinking circulation. To cut costs, the prestigious head office in the center of Buenos Aires was sold in 1988 and the administration installed in the print works, which had been modernized in 1935. Refinancing in the early 1990s and a major revamp of format and content in 1994 accompanied by an aggressive advertising campaign failed to resolve the company's problems. The newspaper ceased publication by the end of the decade. The title is now formally part of the Multimedios consortium, which owns several regional newspapers, radio stations, and television channels. *See also* DESAPARECIDOS; WAR TO ANNIHILATE SUBVERSION.

LA RAZÓN. Began publishing in 1905 as a popular evening broadsheet, initially circulating mainly in the province of **Buenos Aires**. The first newspaper in the country to be owned by a journalist, *La Razón* rapidly built a reputation for reporting the leading stories of the day: by the interwar period, it had become famous for its scoops. It was an early publisher of regular cartoon strips and pioneered the heavy use of photographs, all of which contributed to its popularity and rising circulation. The significance of the title also derives from its checkered ownership. In 1939, it was bought by the aristocratic Peralta Ramos family. Expropriated by the government of President **Juan Domingo Perón** in 1947, the president's wife **Eva Perón** was put in charge, further enhancing its popular appeal and circulation. By the early 1950s, *La Razón* was the largest-circulating newspaper in the country and Latin America, a position formerly held by *La Nación*. Inclined to retain control of the title, the de facto regime that came to power following the **military coup of 1955** was forced to return the paper to the Peralta Ramos family after a protracted legal battle. Still an important paper in the 1960s, the title never regained its former poll position, which had been taken by *Clarín*. When he returned from exile in 1984, the editor-proprietor of *La Opinión* and victim of the **Proceso de Reorganización Nacional Jacobo Timerman** was appointed editor. Timerman attempted to replicate the success that he had achieved with *La Opinión* by relaunching *La Razón* as a morning daily in tabloid format; he failed. The paper declared bankruptcy in 1987, beset with labor disputes at a time of increasing economic uncertainty, and was acquired by the Buenos Aires city administration, which attempted another relaunch—as a free newspaper. Bought by the Clarín Group in 2000, *La Razón* is now the most widely read free-distribution paper in the country. *See also LA PRENSA.*

LA RIOJA (CITY). Capital of the province of the same name; founded by Spanish conquistadores in 1591 in the face of considerable resistance. They named the city after their home region in **Spain**, hence the first title of the settlement—Todos los Santos de la Nueva Rioja. Originally a significant jurisdiction and center of missionary activity by the Franciscan and Dominican Orders, the status of the city was downgraded when the province was incorporated into larger administrations. The city featured in the political turmoil of the postindependence period and was the sometime seat of the **caudillo** and guerrilla leader **Juan Facundo Quiroga**. For much of the 19th century, the city and province languished, generally regarded as a backwater even in a region renowned for its poverty. Almost half the population of the province lives in the greater metropolitan area—approximately 180,000. One of the smallest provincial capitals in the country, the city economy is based largely on administration, though now it is promoted as a center for **tourism** and adventure sports. *See also* LA RIOJA (PROVINCE).

LA RIOJA (PROVINCE). Situated in the west-northwest of the country—an area subject to earthquakes—on the border with **Chile**, the province is bordered to the north by **Catamarca**, to the east by **Córdoba**, and to the south-southeast by **San Luis** and **San Juan**. For most of the colonial period, the territory formed part of the Gobernación de Tucumán, a substantial subdivision within the Viceroyalty of **Peru**, passing to the **Viceroyalty of the River Plate** when the new jurisdiction was created in 1776. At the beginning of the national period in 1810, the area was a dependency of the intendancy of Córdoba, acquiring provincial status a decade later. European settlement began in the late 16th century, largely due to the garrison sent from Peru to quell Indian rebellions. During the 17th century, slaves from Africa were imported to work on the latifundia. The region attracted few migrants during the period of mass **immigration** in the decades around 1900 but experienced significant immigration from the Levant in the mid-20th century. The province is one of the least densely populated parts of the republic and has one of the smallest populations, currently around one-third of a million.

The semiarid, mountainous nature of the terrain has shaped the **economy**, which is largely devoted to **agriculture**—grapes, dates, and semitropical fruits are the principal products marketed; hydroelectricity is being developed, mainly by foreign consortia; there is some **tourism**. As a son of the province, President **Carlos Saúl Menem** was a generous benefactor, having also served as provincial governor and senator, as well as a national senator. **Isabel Perón** also hails from the province.

LABOR PARTY. *See* PARTIDO LABORISTA.

LACLAU, ERNESTO (1935–2014). Academic, public intellectual, and original thinker. Laclau was trained in history at the **University of Buenos Aires** (UBA) and in political theory at the University of Essex, **Great Britain**, where he obtained a doctorate. For many years, he taught at Essex, where he became an advocate of discourse analysis and radical democracy, though he was also associated with prestigious institutions in France, **Spain**, and the **United States**. His principal writing involved the study of Antonio Gramsci, the Italian Marxist theorist and politician, which developed into analyses of hegemony and **populism**. This led him to challenge Marxist orthodoxy and socialist nationalism, work that melded ideas from history, philosophy, and political science. In later years, in his writing and thinking he revisited early work through an optic that integrated post-Marxism and post**developmentalism**, an intellectual fusion from which he forged ideas about politics and economics. From this philosophical fusion emerged distinct views about society and the state and strategies of political and economic action. He viewed the emergence of Podemos in Spain and Syriza in

Greece, and their antiausterity economic philosophy and policy, as a practical expression of his theories of radical democracy. This was a line of thought that made him the thinker of choice of **Néstor Kirchner** and, particularly, **Cristina Fernández de Kirchner**. He became their "organic intellectual," or guru, defending the Kirchner brand of populism and the economic policies associated with it. In turn, his ideas were used by the regime to justify its actions.

LACOSTE, ALBERTO CARLOS (1929–2004). Admiral Carlos Lacoste served as de facto interim president for 10 days in December 1981 following the ousting of General **Roberto Viola** by fellow officers and before the selection of General **Leopoldo Galtieri** as Viola's agreed successor. He is most remembered for organizing the 1978 Soccer World Cup hosted by Argentina and engineering the country's victory. *See also* DIRTY WAR: HUMAN RIGHTS; MILITARY COUP OF 1976; PROCESO DE REORGANIZACIÓN NACIONAL.

LAMBRUSCHINI, ARMANDO (1924–2004). Commander-in-chief of the navy (1978–1981) during the de facto presidencies of **Jorge Rafael Videla** and **Roberto Viola**. He became chief of staff of the navy in 1975 and succeeded **Emilio Eduardo Massera** as navy head in 1978. He remained as commander of the navy until 1981, when he was succeeded by **Jorge Isaac Anaya**.

Lambruschini was one of the defendants in the **trials of the military juntas** in 1985 over **human rights** violations during the **Proceso de Reorganización Nacional**. He was found guilty of 35 proven cases of kidnapping and 10 of reiterated torture and condemned to eight years in prison. He only served two-thirds of his sentence, as he was one of the senior military commanders who benefited from the pardons issued by President **Carlos Saúl Menem**. Lambruschini was tried again on charges of genocide, terrorism, and torture in 1996 and placed under house arrest as he was over 70 years old. *See also* DESAPARECIDOS; DIRTY WAR; DISPOSICIÓN FINAL; WAR TO ANNIHILATE SUBVERSION.

LAMI DOZO, BASILIO ARTURO IGNACIO (1929–2017). Commander-in-chief of the air force and member of the **military** junta headed by **Leopoldo Fortunato Galtieri** (1981–1982). In 2009–2010, Lami Dozo talked publicly for the first time about the **Falklands War**. He claimed that, when he became a member of the junta with Galtieri and **Jorge Isaac Anaya** in December 1981, he was unaware of the navy's plans to recover the islands militarily. Even so, Lami Dozo correctly blamed Anaya and the navy for having abandoned the war and left the army and air force to do the fighting.

The most startling revelation of Lami Dozo was that, in the event of a victory in the Falklands, the Argentine military was going to launch a war against **Chile**—they had already pulled back from the brink of one in 1978. According to the plan, following successful action in the Falklands, Argentina would move on to take islands that were central to the **Beagle Channel Dispute**—Lami Dozo claimed that the air force never endorsed the belligerent position of radical "hawks" in the army and navy.

Following the return of democracy in 1983, Lami Dozo was one of the defendants in the **trials of the military juntas** in 1985. Accused of the kidnapping of 239 people, he was acquitted. However, he did pay a price for the Falklands debacle. The Rattenbach Report of 1983, an official inquiry into the 1982 war, was a scathing testimony to military ineptitude. When the junta was court-martialed by the Supreme Council of the Armed Forces, Lami Dozo received the most lenient sentence. He was sentenced to only eight years in jail, perhaps because the air force had been the best performer out of the three services during the Falklands War. Nevertheless, a civilian court of appeals later ruled that all three former heads of the armed forces should serve 12 years, as they bore equal responsibility for the fiasco. In 1990, President **Carlos Saúl Menem** pardoned Lami Dozo along with other top officers. *See also* DESAPARECIDOS; DISPOSICIÓN FINAL; WAR TO ANNIHILATE SUBVERSION.

LANATA, JORGE (1960–). Award-wining journalist, broadcaster, author, and public figure, involved in the production of radio and television programs while writing for newspapers and magazines. Founder and editor of *Pagina/12*, a left-leaning daily, in 1987 and *Crítica de la Argentina* in 2008—the title echoed that of a paper widely read in the 1920s and 1930—Lanata's association with both was relatively short-lived; *Crítica* survived for only a couple of years, but *Pagina/12* soon established a reputation for snappy radical journalism, attracting some of the principal cultural figures and commentators of the day to write for it, as well as a relatively young, affluent readership. It was supportive of the administrations of Presidents **Néstor Kirchner** and **Cristina Fernández de Kirchner** when most of the mainstream press became increasingly hostile to the couple.

Lanata is best known for investigative journalism and anchoring topical programs, especially *Lanata Sin Filtro* (Lanata Unedited) for Radio Mitre and *Periodismo para Todos* (News for Everyone) for **Canal 13**, a popular television channel. Researching his own material and presenting, he made a name for himself as a critical analyst of current affairs—and scourge of the Kirchners, especially the administrations of President Cristina Fernández, exposing official **corruption** and publicizing the misdeeds of key figures in the regime and their associates. Several of Lanata's productions for *Periodismo para Todos* were the most-watched programs in Argentine television history. Particularly notable were such documentaries as *La ruta de dinero K* and *Las propriedades que los K compraron en la Dictadura*, which investigated the origins of the wealth of the Kirchners, and programs about drug trafficking and money laundering that shed a light on murky developments during the Kirchner presidencies. The government and friends of the regime questioned data and evidence broadcast, threatened Lanata and the program makers with legal injunctions and attempted to limit the distribution of the programs. *See also* MEDIA.

LANUSSE, ALEJANDRO AGUSTÍN (1918–1996). President of Argentina from 1971 to 1973. Born in **Buenos Aires** to an upper-middle-class family, Lanusse graduated from the Colegio Militar de la Nación in 1938. He joined the cavalry, going on to command the **Granaderos a Caballo General San Martín**, the presidential escort. Lanusse was sentenced to life imprisonment in 1951 for participating in a failed attempt to depose **Juan Domingo Perón**, and following the downfall of the latter was released in 1955. He was ambassador to the Holy See on behalf of the **military** government of **Pedro Eugenio Aramburu**, and in 1962 he took part in the overthrow of **Arturo Frondizi**. He rose to become part of the army's high command and supported **Juan Carlos Onganía** in the **military coup of 1966**, which ousted **Arturo Illia**.

Lanusse was named commander-in-chief of the army in 1968. When the military regime became fatally weakened by the **Cordobazo** and increasing violence, he favored a return to constitutional rule and in 1970 backed the removal of Onganía. When the latter's successor, **Roberto Levingston**, attempted to extend the regime's lifespan, Lanusse mounted a palace coup and took power in March 1971. His sole priority was the restoration of a government elected by a majority that the military could support and would be transitional in nature; Lanusse believed that a four-year period was required for testing and adjustment before a return to fully competitive politics. In order to achieve this, the Radicals, the Peronists, and all other interested parties would be called on to agree not only on a set of principles and program goals for that government but also on a common presidential candidate, which would have to be acceptable to the armed forces in order to ensure the stability of the future administration. This project was named the Gran Acuerdo Nacional (GAN) or Grand National Accord.

The simultaneous elections for president and **Congress** were set for March 1973, and the new government would take office two months later. A series of constitutional amendments would take effect for this election, and a complex electoral system was devised under **Law No. 19.862**. There were three major constitutional changes. The president and vice president were to be elected directly by a majority vote for four-year terms and eligible for a single reelection. National senators and deputies were to be elected for four-year terms and eligible for reelection without limitation. There were also to be three national senators instead of two for each province and the **federal capital**. The opening up of the political process proved irreversible, even though the GAN failed to materialize, as the two main parties would not cooperate with the government. The **Unión Cívica Radical** (UCR) was anathema to this type of arrangement and strongly antimilitary—not least because three coups had ousted presidents representing Radical Party factions. The even greater problem was exiled former president Perón, who interfered in the politics of both his party and the country.

Lanusse was determined to keep Peronists within the consensus required to hold truly free elections while eliminating the candidacy of their exiled leader. He thus found himself engaged in a personal contest with Perón, which he ultimately lost. By placing 25 August 1972 as the deadline for prospective presidential candidates to have resigned from any government posts or be resident in the country, Lanusse ruled himself out and in effect proscribed the candidacy of Perón. But the latter was determined to return to Argentina on his own terms and made a successful one-month visit to the country at the end of 1972. He and not Lanusse achieved a national accord; he met with the representatives of most **political parties**, who went out of their way to express support for democratization without exclusions and to announce a commitment to "national" and "popular" policies. Before returning to **Spain**, Perón formed the **Frente Justicialista de Liberación** (FREJU-LI) coalition and nominated its presidential ticket.

The run-up to the elections was marred by instability and serious concerns over the tone of the FREJULI campaign. Yet at this juncture, Lanusse had no options left, and in May 1973 he completed the process of democratization he had initiated, but very differently from what had been intended at the start. He clearly knew that the military had to extricate themselves from government, failed to achieve an accord for an elected transitional "unity" administration, and was forced to proceed with a fully competitive election while fearing the consequences of the likely and actual outcome (a FREJULI victory). Arguably, Lanusse left a constitutional legacy: though his reforms were later rescinded, the **Constitution of 1994** enshrined some of the amendments he had introduced two decades earlier (direct elections for president for four-year terms with eligibility for a single reelection, and the increase in the number of national senators from two to three per province and the national capital). *See also* MOR ROIG, ARTURO (1914–1974).

LASTIRI, RAÚL ALBERTO (1915–1978). Interim president of Argentina from July to October 1973. A truly committed nationalist and Peronist all his life, he was a playboy and great lover of the **Buenos Aires** nightlife and trendy locales. In 1972, he married the daughter of **José López Rega**, an artist 30 years his junior. Lastiri was elected in March 1973 to the Chamber of Deputies, of which he was president between May 1973 and July 1975 thanks to his family ties. Following the resignation of President **Héctor Cámpora** and the vice president on 13 July 1973, and in the absence of the speaker of the National Senate, who had conveniently been dispatched abroad, he became interim president of the country for three months until **Juan Domingo Perón** took office. Lastiri's brief tenure as head of state is only remembered for his boast that he owned 300 neckties and a notorious photograph of him and his wife in their gaudy boudoir.

LAVAGNA, ROBERTO (1942–). Economist, civil servant, and politician; sometime head of various government agencies and minister of economy. Lavagna read economics at the **University of Buenos Aires** (UBA), continuing postgraduate studies in Belgium. During the short-lived presidency of **Héctor Cámpora** in 1973, he obtained his first prominent public position as head of the National Price Commission, shortly moving to head the related, but more significant, National Income Commission, where he was instrumental in drafting the Social Pact devised by Economics Minister **Jóse Ber Gelbard** to stabilize the economy. The tripartite pact, involving government, labor—represented by the **Confederación General del Trabajo**—and business—the **Confederación General Económica**—began to unravel in the chaos following the death of President **Juan Domingo Perón** in 1974. Lavagna left government, joining the board of directors of La Cantábrica, the now defunct but once pioneering national iron and steel producer, as well as returning to academia and setting up an economics research think tank. Having served in the Peronist **Partido Justicialista** (PJ) administrations of Cámpora and Perón, he reentered public office to head the Secretariat of Industry and Trade in the **Unión Cívica Radical** (UCR) administration of President **Raúl Alfonsín**. During his tenure of this post from 1985 to 1987, he was a prominent advocate of establishing the South American Common Market, **MERCOSUR**, the establishment of which he regards as one of his major achievements. He left the Alfonsín administration before the collapse of the heterodox **Austral Plan** and the **hyperinflation** of 1989. His next major public position was as minister of economy from 2002 to 2005, first appointed to the portfolio by interim president **Eduardo Duhalde** and retained in the position by **Néstor Kirchner**, elected president in 2003—both PJ presidents. He proved to be a safe pair of hands. Lavanga and his team were responsible for solving the mess left by the departing **Alianza** administration of **Fernando de la Rúa**. By ensuring a primary surplus in the fiscal accounts and securing a positive balance to trade, he stabilized the **currency**, preventing a feared free fall of the peso and ensuing inflation; ended the freeze on bank accounts, thereby bringing a sense of normality to the financial sector; and negotiated the restructuring of the domestic and **foreign debt**

in 2005. Lavanga is regarded as responsible for saving the country from economic meltdown in 2002 and laying the basis for the economic boom that followed 2005.

Despite these achievements, Lavagna was forced to resign; he objected to the cosy deals the government was doing with private firms and challenged Kirchner to curb **corruption**. This challenge became pronounced when, for the **congressional** and **presidential elections of 2007**, Lavagna formed his own party, **Una Nación Avanzada** (UNA), to contest the presidency—he stood against the outgoing president's wife, **Cristina Fernández de Kirchner**. Supported by the UCR, which endorsed Lavagna rather than field its own candidate (the disaster of the De la Rúa administration was still raw in the public mind), and by dissident Peronists, Lavagna came in a poor third in the presidential contest. Although there were rumors of a rapprochement with the Kirchners, nothing of substance materialized. Lavagna became a sharp critic of the Kirchner economic model, which he saw as unsustainable and likely to jeopardize his legacy. With dissident Peronists, he founded yet another party—Unidos Para Cambiar—to contest the midterm **congressional elections of 2013**. The **congressional** and **presidential elections of 2015** found Lavagna associated with the main dissident Peronist grouping headed by **Sergio Massa**, **Frente Renovador/Partido Jusaticialista** (FR/PJ). There was talk of Lavagna returning to the Economics Ministry should Massa get elected—he was not. Lavagna has now passed the mantle to his son, Marco, elected to a seat in the national Chamber of Deputies for the city of **Buenos Aires**, representing the FR/PJ. Lavagna continues to be seen as one of the foremost academic and practicing economists of his generation. *See also* MINISTRY OF ECONOMY.

LAW NO. 19.862 (OCTOBER 1972). Legislation enacted by the de facto government of General **Alejandro Agustín Lanusse** that introduced a complex new system for the **congressional** and **presidential elections of March 1973**. It provided for the direct election of president and vice president, running together on a single ticket. However, in a provision aimed at preventing a minority head of state, the law enabled a runoff election if no one party or alliance obtained an absolute majority of the votes cast. The runoff would be restricted to the two top parties if they together had received at least two-thirds of valid ballots. Otherwise, the parties receiving at least 15 percent of the votes could also participate by forming a joint ticket with one another or with one of the two top parties. Party conventions had to approve a common platform and the candidates of the joint ticket, but the presidential candidate had to always be someone who stood for that position in the first round.

The National **Congress** was also to be elected directly. For the National Senate, each recognized party or alliance was to put forward a slate of two candidates for the three vacancies allotted to each province and the **federal capital**. If no party obtained an absolute majority, a runoff election would be necessary. The victorious party would get two National Senate seats, while the third would go to the candidate whose name headed the slate of the runner-up party. For the Chamber of Deputies, the number of seats assigned to each province and the federal capital was to be based on population: one for every 135,000 inhabitants or a major fraction. Voters would choose from among rival slates, and the parties would be allocated seats in proportion to their share of the total votes cast in the provinces, after the elimination of blank ballots and the votes of parties obtaining less than 8 percent of the total. This provision aimed to limit the number of parties in the chamber and discourage political fragmentation.

When the March 1973 elections were held, the outgoing **military** government hoped that the complex electoral system could prevent the Peronist-led **Frente Justicialista de Liberación** (FREJULI) from winning the presidency by forcing it into a runoff that it would lose. But too many minor parties contested the position, and the FREJULI obtained almost 50 percent of the vote in the first round; their nearest rivals trailed so far behind that the second round became unnecessary. This outcome once again demonstrated that no matter what attempts were made to contain Peronism, it remained the key political force to be reckoned with.

LEVINGSTON, ROBERTO MARCELO (1920–2015). De facto president of Argentina (1970–1971). An obscure general who represented Argentina on the Inter-American Defense Board in Washington, DC, Levingston was chosen by Commander-in-Chief General **Alejandro Agustín Lanusse** to replace de facto president General **Juan Carlos Onganía** in June 1970. This was based on the assumption that he would be pliant, and thereby would not repeat Onganía's attempt to perpetuate himself in power nor challenge Lanusse's leadership of the army. Yet this is precisely what Levingston did.

Levingston tried to resurrect Onganía's doctrine of the *tres tiempos*, arguing that economic and social changes were still prerequisites for institutional normalization, and even surpassed Onganía by insisting on fundamental political changes before liberalization could be contemplated. An ambiguous promise to hold elections at a future unspecified date further clouded the situation. This strategy to extend authoritarian rule was based on the premise that traditional parties and their leaders were incapable of imposing national discipline and modernizing the country. Levingston therefore sought to co-opt lower-ranking party figures by offering official patronage in exchange for joining a pro-regime political grouping.

It soon became clear that Levingston was out of touch and alienating just about everybody. In September 1970, he rather disturbingly announced that he intended to remain in office for four or five more years, and the following month embarked on the *Argentinización* project devised by Minister of Economy **Aldo Ferrer**. **Political parties** reacted in November 1970 with the **"La Hora del Pueblo"** declaration, which called for immediate elections without exclusions, while the private sector simply opposed the economic program. Matters were made worse by an image of social disintegration and political subversion resultant from working-class militancy and guerrilla activity. By early 1971, the president faced growing isolation. Even the armed forces turned against him, and Levingston's unsuccessful attempt to remove Lanusse as commander-in-chief led to his own ouster in March of that year. *See also* MINISTRY OF ECONOMY.

LEY DE OBEDIENCIA DEBIDA. Under the **Ley de Punto Final** of 30 December 1986, **military** officers who held junior rank at the time of the **Proceso de Reorganización Nacional** and were "only obeying orders" found themselves liable to prosecution for **human rights** violations committed between 1976 and 1982. This grievance, which contributed directly to the rebellion of the *carapintadas* in April 1987, was resolved by President **Raúl Alfonsín** in the most controversial fashion. Alfonsín pressed **Congress** to enact legislation absolving all military personnel below the level of zone commander from criminal liability for their conduct during the **War to Annihilate Subversion**. Known as the Ley de Obediencia Debida, this amnesty in effect exempted all but 20 retired generals and admirals from further prosecution. In 2005, during the presidency of **Néstor Kirchner**, the Ley de Obediencia Debida was declared to be unconstitutional by the Supreme Court. *See also* COMISIÓN NACIONAL SOBRE LA DESAPARACIÓN DE PERSONAS (CONADEP); LEY DE PUNTO FINAL; MILITARY COUP OF 1976; MILITARY JUNTAS, TRIALS OF THE; *NUNCA MÁS*.

LEY DE PUNTO FINAL. Following the restoration of democracy in 1983, President **Raúl Alfonsín** aimed to increase the opportunities for national reconciliation and integration of the armed forces into the constitutional framework. He hoped to achieve this by limiting the trials for **human rights** abuses during the preceding **military** regime to a number of senior officers and to have those trials completed as quickly as possible, but he would be frustrated by the existence of an independent judiciary.

Victims or relatives of victims of the **War to Annihilate Subversion** had submitted around 2,000 denunciations against members of the armed forces, and judges were summoning serving officers for questioning in many parts of Argentina. Concerned at the effect that an indefinite prolongation of trials could have on his project for civil–military relations, Alfonsín asked **Congress** to legislate a terminal date for the start of new trials. Notwithstanding the protestations of human rights groups, on 23 December 1986 Congress approved a law that placed a 60-day limit on civilian courts for questioning military personnel about their participation in the repression. Anyone not summoned by the deadline was to be exempted from further prosecution, except in cases involving children or where the accused had absconded.

This legislation, known as the Ley de Punto Final, designed the 60-day grace period to coincide with the annual one-month vacation of the federal courts, thereby reducing by half the time for processing new cases. Nevertheless, federal prosecutors were defiant, waiving their vacations and working frantically to summon military personnel who had been named in denunciations. As a result, between 200 and 300 officers found themselves still liable to prosecution rather than the handful that the government had expected. Furthermore, the Ley de Punto Final had an unintended outcome. The burden of responsibility for human rights violations committed between 1976 and 1982 was placed on a group of officers with junior ranks at that time, rather than on the middle-level and senior officers from whom they had received their orders and who were now legally exempt from prosecution. Targeted officers, including captains in active service, saw in this situation a violation of the military code they were taught to obey. These grievances were a contributing factor to the rebellion of the *carapintadas* in April 1987.

In 2005, during the presidency of **Néstor Kirchner**, the Ley de Punto Final was declared to be unconstitutional by the Supreme Court. *See also* COMISIÓN NACIONAL SOBRE LA DESAPARACIÓN DE PERSONAS (CONADEP); LEY DE OBEDIENCIA DEBIDA; MILITARY JUNTAS, TRIALS OF THE.

LEY DE RESIDENCIA. Law 4.144 of 1902, sometimes known as the Cané Law, named after its principal proponent, Miguel Cané, a journalist and politician who has served briefly as minister of interior under President **Luis Saénz Peña** in the mid-1890s. The law was the first measure introduced in Argentina to curb **immigration**—or rather, to facilitate the removal of "undesirables"—as such representing a reconsideration of the open-door approach that had applied for much of the 19th century. The law was passed mainly in response to pressure from business organizations alarmed by the rise in **trade union** activity—labor disputes attributed to anarchist and socialist agitators who imported "antinational" ideologies. In 1910, the Ley de Residencia was reinforced by the Ley de Defensa Social following a series of worker protests, strikes, and bombings. The mood change was not peculiar to Argentina, resonating with similar near-contemporary action in the **United States** that demonized specific categories of immigrants as violent agitators and social degenerates. The individuals and the ideologies associated with them were equally suspect. In Argentina, the legislation was most invoked to deport trade union leaders and political activists. *See also* AGRICULTURAL COLONIZATION; CONFEDERACIÓN GENERAL DEL TRABAJO (CGT); CRY OF ALCORTA; MINISTRY OF INTERIOR, PUBLIC WORKS, AND HOUSING; PAMPAS.

LIEBIG EXTRACT OF MEAT COMPANY. Pioneering firm in a "low grade" sector of the ranching-cum-**meat** industry, namely corned or canned beef and beef extract. Once a significant player in Argentina and internationally, Liebig was responsible for production and managerial innovation as well as the marketing of branded food products.

Corned beef, which had a long shelf life, was produced by boiling carcasses, removing by-products like skin and bones, then compressing and canning the remaining meat. Meat extract, a popular "health" product in the second half of the 19th century, was made by "reducing" beef carcasses into a thick liquid, marketed in jars, or in dried form, packed in blocks. The extract process was devised by Justus von Liebig in the 1840s, entering mass production by the 1860s, hence the name of the company. Canned beef went into production in the 1870s. Around 1914, Liebig operated estates and plants in Argentina and neighboring republics, with extensive interests in **Paraguay**, **Uruguay**, and southern **Brazil**. Its operations focused on **cattle** raising and the processing and marketing of meat and meat products. Its niche products were largely the result of the restructuring of the international meat trade during the early decades of the 20th century. Between the 1900s and the 1920s, international trade in meat products was transformed by three key developments. First, on the supply side, US export surpluses contracted, creating opportunities for Argentina and other "new" producers. Second, demand for meat in the main centers of consumption grew and became more discriminating, shifting from low-grade products like canned and frozen meat toward higher-quality chilled meat, and from pork and mutton to beef. Third, technical developments enabled the trade to deal with larger beef carcasses—previously, only freezing ensured that larger animals could be stored for any length of time: the chilling business was confined to lambs. Location and the integrated nature of the business delivered a competitive advantage to Argentina.

Such market and technical development encouraged relocation as land values rose and supplies of animals that could be bought in from neighboring estates declined. The extract business used low-grade animals or inferior cuts. In addition to ensuring supplies of appropriate animals at competitive prices, the firm depended on branding to differentiate their products from lower-grade generic commodities like dried or salt beef and to protect their market from competition by higher-quality "fresh" chilled meat produced by meat packers. Oxo was an important, carefully marketed, Liebig branded product; Fray Bentos meat products, initially marked as "compressed, cooked, corned beef," was another key brand—the brand was named after the factory in Uruguay. Location was critical to a successful realization of these strategies. With good riverine and rail communications, and adequate supplies of "second quality" land, **Mesopotamia** and the northern **Littoral** provinces and territories were ideal for the raising of low-grade stock. The land and climate were not suitable for prime beef cattle, while transport costs weighed less heavily on low-bulk items like corned beef and meat extract. Liebig moved its regional headquarters from Fray Bentos to Colón in **Entre Ríos**.

Liebig was able to meet market and financial challenges of the interwar period because it ran parallel, interlocking operations in several areas and had established brand leadership. Responding to changes in demand, Liebig switched some plants from canning to freezing and transferred the extract business to outlying areas. Operating its own estates, Liebig could ensure adequate supplies of the correct type of animal required for extract and canning. Functioning in several regions (and countries) across the **River Plate**, it increased output at certain plants while reducing operations elsewhere in accordance with variations in local production costs and input availability. Running operations in different countries also spread political risk. Given extensive landholdings, relatively flexible plants, and established brand reputation, Liebig was also able to develop demand for higher-value lines, moving the market from proprietary extract products, corned beef, and tinned sausages to canned pies and "ready-made" meals. Above all, as a large, integrated corporation, it was able to offset losses in one sector with profits from another and take a long-term approach to profit generation. Liebig attempted to diversify operations by maximizing the comparative advantage of estates in **Corrientes** and **Misiones** for growing plantation crops like **yerba mate**, tea, and tung trees; the company even dabbled in the **agricultural colonization** business. Liebig operations and brands were acquired by the Vestey group meat and butchery chain in 1924 and subsequently merged with Brooke Bond in 1968. The firms became part of Unilever in 1984 and since 2006 operated as Premier Food, moves that illustrate the transnationalization of the food business, as well as the critical importance of brands and the internationalization of Argentine and South American regional businesses in the sector. *See also* AGRICULTURE; ECONOMY; FOREIGN DEBT/FOREIGN INVESTMENT; FOREIGN TRADE; INDUSTRY.

LINIERS, SANTIAGO ANTONIO MARÍA DE (1753–1810). A naval officer and the penultimate viceroy of the **River Plate**, he led resistance to the **British invasions** of 1806 and 1807. He served as viceroy between 1807 and 1809 and was granted the title of count of **Buenos Aires** in recognition of his contribution to the defense of the city. Of French origin, Santiago de Liniers had seen service in France and **Spain** before being sent to the River Plate to improve the fortifications of Montevideo and naval defenses in the area, primarily in response to threats from Portuguese **Brazil**. Having held administrative positions in the interior, he was appointed head of the Buenos Aires squadron in 1804, a post that he held at the time of the first invasion. When Viceroy **Rafael de Sobremonte** abandoned the city, Liniers was the most senior office on station; he first organized the local resistance and then the defeat of the British. He was the hero of the hour. The Buenos Aires council acclaimed him viceroy in place of the disgraced Sobremonte, an appointment endorsed by Madrid. Liniers was less successful confronting the British in 1807, misjudging the scale of the invasion and positioning his forces poorly. His reputation already tarnished, Liniers was further compromised by his French background when Napoleon Bonaparte invaded the Iberian Peninsula. Although Liniers was a local patriot and enjoyed support from the local merchant community and some conservative interests, he was also committed to Spain. He accepted his replacement as viceroy by **Baltasar Hidalgo de Cisneros**, appointed by the Patriotic Junta of Seville, and was instrumental in ensuring that Cisneros was able to land in Buenos Aires, which was already a hotbed of revolution. Liniers retired to the interior but refused to endorse the **May Revolution of 1810** and, with others, attempted to organize royalist resistance. He was captured and executed as a counter-revolutionary by forces sent from Buenos Aires, despite widespread demands that his services to the country be recognized and that he be spared. He is now seen as a key figure of the **independence** period and a patriotic son of his adopted country.

LISTA SÁBANA. A "closed list," proportional electoral system in which electors vote for a "bloc" of candidates—as distinct from an "open" list arrangement, which may contained the names of some candidates with space to write in the names of others. In Argentina, lists of candidates are drawn up by officially recognized parties for multiseat electoral districts. Lists are usually headed by high-profile candidates, with lesser-known figures appearing at the bottom. The number of candidates elected for each party is determined by the share of the vote obtained. If a party obtains a large share of the votes cast in the electoral district, a substantial proportion of listed candidates will be elected. Parties garnering a small proportion of votes will obtain few seats, meaning that only candidates at the top of the list are likely to be elected. In the National Senate, each province constitutes an electoral district with three seats: the party that tops the poll is awarded two seats—the "majority" seats, with the first runner-up awarded one seat, the "minority" seat. For the Chamber of Deputies, the number of seats is determined by population. For example, the province of **Buenos Aires**, the most populous electoral district, currently accounts for 70 seats in the 257-seat chamber; the least populous provinces, like **Catamarca**, **San Luis**, and **Santa Cruz** have five seats each.

In theory, the system is designed to ensure party discipline and facilitate ease of voting. In practice, a closed list system, particularly one that does not allow electors to "split" their vote among different party lists, promotes clientelism and cronyism. Power lies in the hands of party bosses, who determine where individual candidates are placed on the list—even when a party obtains a large share of the vote, candidates at the bottom of a list are unlikely to gain a seat. Periodically, there have been campaigns for the reform of the system.

LITTORAL. In Spanish, *litoral*, the term has a geopolitical meaning. In colonial times, the term was used to distinguish **Buenos Aries** and its hinterland above the **Salado** River from interior territories of the northwest that had been settled earlier from **Chile** and **Peru**, and included present-day **Paraguay** and **Uruguay**. For much of the 19th and early 20th centuries, the term was applied to the Argentine provinces of **Corrientes**, **Entre Ríos**, and **Santa Fe**, which border the lower **Paraná** River to the north of Buenos Aires. Today, it is used to describe provinces bordering the right bank of the Paraná. Sometimes, the modern provinces of **Chaco** and **Formosa** are described as being in the Littoral. The provinces of Entre Ríos, Corrientes, and **Misiones**, which constitute modern **Mesopotamia**, are included and sometimes not. It is one of the most productive and diverse regions of the country, home to large conurbations, nature reserves, and forested areas that are only now being exploited: in the south, farming and ranching have long been the main staples; in the north, logging and fruit production predominated; soya is now one of the principal **commodities**, even in heavily wooded areas once regarded as marginal.

LONARDI, EDUARDO ERNESTO (1896–1956). Provisional president of Argentina from September to November 1955. Lonardi was born in **Buenos Aires**, the son of an Italian immigrant who was music bandleader for the Argentine army. He graduated from the Colegio Militar de la Nación in 1916 and proceeded to climb up the **military** ladder. He was sent as a military attaché to **Chile** in 1938 and represented his country on the Inter-American Defense Board in Washington, DC, from 1942 to 1948. Named commander of the major garrison in **Rosario** upon his return to Argentina, he was deeply implicated in the failed September 1951 conspiracy against President **Juan Domingo Perón**. He resigned from the army and was imprisoned until December 1953. His release after being deemed harmless proved fatal for the regime, as he spearheaded the successful **military coup of 1955**.

As provisional president, Lonardi pursued a policy of national reconciliation embodied in the slogan "Ni vencedores ni vencidos" (Neither victors nor vanquished). Since pressing the issue of Peronism would create major difficulties, he decided the movement had to be decapitated but not uprooted. He cooperated with the Peronist leaders of the **Confederación General del Trabajo** (CGT), understanding that the preceding government had won real social gains for the working masses and these had to be respected. However, Lonardi's policy of national reconciliation was ultimately shattered by political fractures, especially within the military. The armed forces were seriously divided over how to deal with Peronism, and this turned into a major internal struggle over the next decade. But at the time anti-Peronist hard-liners, backed by various minor democratic actors (the Socialists, Progressive Democrats, and Conservatives), held the upper hand. Only two months after taking office, Lonardi was forced to resign and succeeded by General **Pedro Eugenio Aramburu**. Terminally ill with cancer, he died a few months after his ouster.

LOOTING. *See SAQUEOS.*

LÓPEZ MURPHY, RICARDO HIPÓLITO (1951–). Fifteen-day minister of economy in the ill-fated administration of President **Fernando de la Rúa** in 2001—one of the shortest tenures of the post. Born into a family that had long supported the **Unión Cívica Radical** (UCR), he was named after its first democratically elected president, **Hipólito Yrigoyen**.

López Murphy read economics at the National University of **La Plata**, where he took a first degree, going on to obtain a master's in economics at the University of Chicago. He first held office in the De la Rúa cabinet as minister of defense, being appointed in 1999, before moving briefly to the Economics Ministry. The **Convertibility Plan** was already collapsing when he assumed charge of the **economy** portfolio. Arguably, his program of swinging fiscal austerity was the only viable solution to the crisis in the short term. However, it triggered massive public protest, and De la Rúa did not have the courage to support him. He was replaced by **Domingo Cavallo**. After the political and financial turmoil that led to the economic crisis of 2001 and the departure of De la Rúa and Cavallo, López Murphy attempted to rebuild a political career. Abandoning the UCR in 2002, he founded **Recrear para el Crecimiento** (Recrear), standing in the **presidential election of 2003** on a platform centered on economic orthodoxy. He came in a respectable third with around 16 percent of the vote after **Carlos Saúl Menem** and **Néstor Kirchner**. This was the high point of his presidential ambitions. In the **presidential election of 2007**, he teamed up with **Mauricio Macri** and the **Propuesta Republicana** (PRO): he obtained the endorsement of 1 percent of the electorate. He abandoned Recrear a year later. López Murphy remains a public figure despite these political setbacks and continues to argue for the importance of balanced budgets and liberal economics. *See also* ECONOMIC CRISES; MINISTRY OF ECONOMY; UNIVERSIDAD NACIONAL DE LA PLATA (UNLP).

LÓPEZ REGA, JOSÉ (1916–1989). The all-too-powerful minister of social welfare from May 1973 to July 1975. Born in **Buenos Aires**, he joined the federal police in 1942, from which he retired 20 years later as a very junior officer. During a trip to **Brazil** in 1960, he became initiated in the occult, astrology, and other esoteric practices. Following his return to Buenos Aires, he joined the Logia Anael, which had been founded in 1954 by Presidents **Juan Domingo Perón** and Getúlio Vargas of Brazil.

During a visit by **Isabel Perón** to Argentina on behalf of her husband in 1965–1966, López Rega was placed as her collaborator; this was the result of a direct request from Perón to the Logia Anael. He returned to **Spain** with her and became the key figure in the household. Having been valet, butler, nurse, bodyguard, and private secretary to the exiled former president, by 1971 he participated in his employers' most private matters.

When the elected government of **Héctor Cámpora** took office in May 1973, he became minister of social welfare. He retained the post during the presidencies of **Raúl Lastiri** and Juan Domingo Perón; the latter also appointed him private secretary of the presidency. López Rega was a constant shadow at the president's side, and he devoted inordinate time and energy to his pet project and personal brainchild, the Altar de la Patria (Altar of the Fatherland), a vast necrophiliac monument whose construction was authorized by **Congress** in 1974 but never built. Following the death of Perón on 1 July 1974 and the accession of his widow Isabel to the presidency, López Rega used his ministerial and personal positions to wield real power. He moved into the presidential residence, isolated Isabel from the political class, and held such a complete sway over her that he became known as "El Brujo" (the Wizard). He had influence in Congress as his son-in-law was the president of the Chamber of Deputies, and he intervened in all the ministries besides running his own of social welfare. He also headed the **Triple A**, which he himself had created in 1973 as an armed wing of his ministry. It had a substantial infrastructure and impunity for planning and committing terrorist attacks; these were in fact clandestine acts of repression against the revolutionary subversion afflicting Argentina.

Strong opposition to López Rega finally forced his resignation in July 1975, and he left the country in disgrace. While charges against him kept accumulating back home, he simply vanished. He became the most wanted man by Argentine justice, and an international warrant for his arrest was issued before the **military coup of 1976**. López Rega was eventually tracked down in Miami and extradited to Argentina in July 1986, where he spent his final years detained in a maximum security prison. *See also* CRUZADA JUSTICIALISTA DE LA SOLIDARIDAD; MINISTRY OF SOCIAL DEVELOPMENT.

LÓPEZ Y PLANES, VICENTE (1785–1856). Titular national caretaker president (1827–1828) following the collapse of the **Bernardino Rivadavia** administration and the election of **Manuel Dorrego** as governor of the province of **Buenos Aires**. A native of Buenos Aires, he played a role in the **independence** movement, serving in the infantry regiment Los **Patricios**, which was considered the origin of the regular national army, and participated in the **Cabildo Abierto** of 1810 and the **Constituent Assembly of 1813**. López y Planes acted twice as interim head of state, first as national president between the administrations of Rivadavia and Dorrego and later as interim governor of Buenos Aires for a few months in 1852 after the fall of **Juan Manuel de Rosas**. He is best remembered as a poet of the independence period, composing the lyrics of a popular march that became the national anthem.

LOS ANDES (NATIONAL TERRITORY). Situated in the northwest, along the border with **Chile**, surrounded by the provinces of **Jujuy**, **Salta**, and **Catamarca**. In the late colonial period, following administrative reforms, in 1782 the region formed part of the Atacama Partido (present-day Chile) of the intendancy of Potosí, a key silver-producing area of the newly constituted **Viceroyalty of the River Plate**. During the wars of **independence**, in 1816 Atacama was incorporated into the Salta-Tucumán intendancy, briefly providing the emergent **United Provinces of the River Plate** with a Pacific coast. In 1825, when Atacama was incorporated within the newly formed Republic of **Bolivia**, the area that was to become Los Andes was hived off and transferred to Argentina. Following the **War of the Pacific**, when the Bolivian province of Atacama was annexed by Chile, an Argentine–Bolivian Treaty of 1890 recognized Argentine sovereignty. The demarcation was accepted by Chile in 1900. As an Argentine national territory, Los Andes existed from 1899 to 1943. The local economy was and remains based on **mining**, mainly gold, tin, and copper. Mining interests pressed the federal government to construct an international railway line between the cities of Salta (Argentina) and Antofagasta (Chile), intended to promote the development of Los Andes. The fitful progress of the line did little to stimulate growth, though a section of the line is now a major tourist attraction—the Tren a las Nubes (the Train to the Clouds). In 1943, the districts that had constituted the territory were divided broadly equally among the two neighboring provinces. *See also* TOURISM; TRANSPORTATION.

LUDER, ÍTALO ARGENTINO (1916–2008). Prominent Peronist politician. A supporter of President **Juan Domingo Perón**, who had taken office in 1946, he was elected as representative of the **Partido Peronista** (PP) to the convention that drafted the **Constitution of 1949**. Luder was elected on behalf of the **Frente Justicialista de Liberación** (FREJULI) as national senator for the province of **Santa Fe** in March 1973. Perón, who had again been elected as head of state in the **presidential election of September 1973**, died in office on 1 July 1974 and was succeeded by the vice president, his wife **Isabel Perón**. This prompted Alejandro Díaz Bialet to resign as president of the Senate, and Luder succeeded him. Between mid-September and mid-October 1975, Mrs. Perón took a leave of absence on health grounds and (in the absence of a vice president) Lúder became acting president. While holding this post, he undertook his most important and controversial action by signing the decrees that facilitated the **War to Annihilate Subversion**. The **Proceso de Reorganización Nacional** regime that came to power in the **military coup of 1976** used the decrees to legitimate its actions, which resulted in approximately 9,000 deaths.

Following the downfall of the dictatorship, Lúder contested the **presidential election of 1983** as the candidate of the **Partido Justicialista** (PJ); **Deolindo Bittel** was his running mate. Although he obtained 40 percent of the vote, he was unexpectedly defeated by **Raúl Alfonsín** of the **Unión Cívica Radical** (UCR).

LUNA, FÉLIX (1925–2009). An acclaimed historian and cultural figure, he was a lifelong supporter of the **Unión Cívica Radical** (UCR). This is unsurprising, as his grandfather founded the UCR chapter in the province of **La Rioja** and his uncle Pelagio Luna served as vice president during the first presidency of **Hipólito Yrigoyen**.

His works on Argentine history include *Yrigoyen* (1954), *Alvear* (1958), *Diálogos con Frondizi* (1962), *El 45* (1968), *Argentina de Perón a Lanusse* (1973), *Ortiz* (1978), *Buenos Aires y el país* (1982), *Golpes militares y salidas electorales* (1983), *Soy Roca* (1989), *Perón y su tiempo* (1993), and *Breve historia de los argentinos* (1993). Luna's works have withstood the test of time; they have been reprinted well beyond their original date of publication. With the aim of popularizing Argentine history, Luna founded the monthly periodical *Todo es Historia* in 1967. He was its director until his death, and it was published without interruption even during the dictatorial regimes of the **Revolución Argentina** (1966–1973) and the **Proceso de Reorganización Nacional** (1976–1983). Luna was also known as a lyricist and collaborated with Argentine composer **Ariel Ramírez**; their best-known work is *Misa Criolla* (1964).

Toward the end of his life, Luna was a sharp critic of the project of **Néstor Kirchner** and his wife, **Cristina Fernández de Kirchner**. When the Kirchners sent a wreath to Luna's funeral, the family returned it.

M

MACHINEA, JOSÉ LUIS (1946–). An economist and policy maker, his principal public offices include the presidency of the **Banco Central de la República Argentina** (BCRA) from 1986 to 1989 and as minister of economy between 1999 and 2001. Trained in economics at the **Universidad Católica Argentina** (UCA) and at the University of Minnesota in the **United States**, where he was awarded a PhD, Machinea was named deputy head of the Planning Office of the Presidency when the democratically elected government of President **Raúl Alfonsín** of the **Unión Cívica Radical** (UCR) took office in 1983.

As head of the BCRA, he was a key player in the economic team led by the architect of the **Austral Plan**, Minister of Economy **Juan Vital Sourrouille**, and had to pick up the pieces as the plan unraveled. He declared a moratorium on foreign debt payments in April 1988 and a 48-hour bank holiday in February 1989 during a run on the US dollar as the **currency** collapsed. When the UCR returned to power 10 years later, as part of the **Alianza** government headed by President **Fernando de la Rúa**, Machinea was named as De la Rúa's first minister of economy—there would be two others during the short-lived presidency. At the time, it was said that Machinea was not the president's preferred candidate for the position. In post for 15 months, Machinea had to cope with the unwinding of the **Convertibility Plan** that ended in the banking and **economic crises** of 2001. His efforts to balance the budget by raising taxes and cutting outgoings were unsuccessful, as were desperate negotiations with overseas creditors. Machinea was unfortunate in being associated with economic meltdown toward the end of two UCR administrations. He headed the UN **Economic Commission for Latin America and the Caribbean** between 2003 and 2008 and remains a prominent commentator on economic affairs while pursuing an academic career. *See also* MINISTRY OF ECONOMY

MACHISMO. Latin American term for "manliness" or "masculinity" especially associated with Argentina. The expression was initially associated with **gauchos**, who displayed a prowess for horsemanship, herding wild **cattle**,

441

the ability to survive in the desolate **pampas**, and skill with a knife. In time, the term came to encompass such virtues as courage, virility, independence, self-reliance, and pride in oneself. But machismo has also come to encompass such negative terms as cruelty and condescension toward **women**, sanctioning domestic violence, childlike petulance, and disregard of others. In the 19th century, such figures as **Juan Manuel de Rosas**, **Martín Güemes**, and **Justo José de Urquiza** forged the image of the fearless warrior, skilled with a lance and a lasso, as good a horseman as the troops he led—and as a popular leader, the **caudillo**. This image was revived and cultivated by populist politicians in the 20th century, notably **Juan Domingo Perón**, **Carlos Saúl Menem**, and **Eduardo Duhalde**.

MACRI, MAURICIO (1959–). Successful businessman and politician. Sometime deputy in the lower house of the National **Congress**, he was elected mayor of the city of **Buenos Aires** in 2007 and reelected in 2011; he was elected president of the republic in 2015.

A second-generation immigrant, Macri was born into a wealthy family of Italian origin. His father, Franco, founded what became one of the largest conglomerates in the country—the Macri Group. The holding company controls firms in **Brazil**, Panama, and **Uruguay**, with a wide range of interests in sectors such as construction, finance, food processing and meatpacking, manufacturing, postal services, rubbish collection, and transport and telecommunications. The group appears to have prospered in periods of **military** rule, growing exponentially during the de facto regime headed by General **Juan Carlos Onganía** and the administrations of the **Proceso de Reorganización Nacional**. From the late 1960s to the early 1980s, the number of firms controlled by the family increased from seven to 47. Benefiting from government contracts, Macri Group enterprises in property and construction, finance and insurance, and electronics and electromechanical engineering were associated with high-profile projects like the **Yacyretá-Apipé** dam and the Posadas–Encarnación bridge across the river **Paraná**, which connects Argentina and **Paraguay**, and construct-and-operate toll roads in the province of Buenos Aires. The group participated in the program of **privatization** launched by President **Carlos Saúl Menem** in the 1990s. Although the Macri Group experienced several setbacks, notwithstanding its achievements, it provided the resources that enhanced Mauricio Macri's public profile and launched his political career. Association with the group was, however, a mixed blessing due to its rapid rise during periods of military rule and legal disputes involving the financing of bids to acquire **state-owned enterprises** in the 1990s. The father was also sometimes less than complementary about his son's abilities.

Mauricio Macri trained as a civil engine at the **Universidad Católica Argentina** (UCA) and went on to read business at the **Universidad del CEMA** and enrolled for a short course at prestigious business schools in the **United States**. At the UCA, he formed friendships that would later mature into close political relationships. His early business career involved spells at Macri Group enterprises and stints at Citibank and local affiliates of European motor vehicle manufacturers like Fiat and Peugeot. Two events in the early 1990s had a critical impact on Macri's political formation and public image. First, in 1991, he was kidnapped by rogue elements of the federal police and held for ransom. The family reportedly paid US$6,000,000 to secure his release. Macri later stated that the experience convinced him of the rotten condition of parts of the state apparatus and triggered a determination to enter politics. The second event occurred in 1995 when, with the help of his father, he secured the chairmanship of **Boca Juniors**, one of the premier football clubs in the country. After a sticky start, under Macri's chairmanship the Boca stadium was refurbished and the club was soon winning titles. During his 12 years in post, the club won 11 international titles, or 17 prestige awards, including national titles. This gained Macri national recognition and guaranteed a considerable public presence in the city of Buenos Aires just as he was beginning his political career.

The collapse of the **Convertibility Plan** in 2001, and ensuing institutional crisis discredited existing **political parties**, mainly the **Unión Cívica Radical** (UCR) and the mainstream of the **Partido Justicialista** (PJ). Macri launched **Compromiso para el Cambio**, a new political party promising new faces and a new politics to contest the gubernatorial and **congressional** and **presidential elections of 2003**. He stood for the mayorship of the city of Buenos Aires. Although Macri came in at the top of the poll in the first round, he was defeated in the runoff by sitting mayor **Aníbal Ibarra**. Ibarra was supported by **Néstor Kirchner**, who assumed the presidency of the republic in 2003. Undeterred, Macri formed an alliance with **Ricardo López Murphy** of **Recrear para el Crecimiento** (Recrear). The alliance became known as **Propuesta Republicana** (PRO), fielding candidates across the country. Macri was elected to the Chamber of Deputies on the Compromiso–Recrear/PRO ticket in the **congressional elections of 2005**. It appeared a neat alliance: Recrear had a national presence while Compromiso had a strong base in the city of Buenos Aires. When the two men fell out, Macri used the PRO to further his political ambitions. He again contested the mayorship of the city of Buenos Aires in the gubernatorial and **congressional** and **presidential elections of 2007**. He did much better than in 2003: Macri came close to winning on the first round and scored an impressive 22-point victory in the runoff against Daniel Filmus of the Kirchnerist **Frente Para la Victoria/Partido Justicialista** (FpV/PJ). Filmus had been actively promoted by **Cristina Fernández de Kirchner**, who took the presidency. This first (proxy) contest between Macri and Fernández de Kirchner would resonate in the years ahead. Macri's running mate in the 2007 mayoral contest, Gabriela Michetti, would become a close ally, serving as his vice president when he gained the presidency of the republic in 2015. With Macri's backing, Michetti stepped down as deputy mayor to stand in the midterm **congressional elections of 2009**. Heading the PRO list in the province of Buenos Aires, she gained a seat in the Chamber of Deputies in another electoral contest that was seen as a snub for Mrs. Kirchner.

When opinion polls showed a recovery in the fortunes of Cristina Fernández in advance of the **presidential election of 2011**, Macri decided not to stand for the presidency but have a second stab at the mayoralty of the city. In the first round, Macri exceeded his share of the vote obtained in 2007, and did even better on the second round, once again roundly defeating Filmus. The result encouraged Macri to look to the presidential race scheduled for 2015. As mayor of Buenos Aires, Macri is credited with making major improvements to public transport—enhancing the quality and safety of bus, metro, and suburban rail services. The urban environment was also improved by creating more green spaces and upgrading public parks, and by pedestrianization and the construction of bicycle lanes. Macri also attempted to restructure the city police force, seeking to transfer control from the federal to the city government. He was unsuccessful but instituted a small municipal force to work alongside the federal police. Macri acquired a reputation as a capable city administrator—a man who was able to get things done, notwithstanding political problems with the national government. His efforts at police reform, and his personal backstory of kidnapping by the police, similarly generated public support.

Despite his record governing the city of Buenos Aires, Macri's ability to deliver in the **congressional** and **presidential elections of 2015** was by no means a foregone conclusion. Initially, Mrs. Fernández de Kirchner was known to want to stand again—this ambition, which would have required constitutional change, was scotched by the poor showing of the FpV/PJ in the midterm **congressional elections of 2013**. But the anti-Kirchner opposition was divided, and others, particularly dissident Peronists like **Sergio Massa**, sometimes appeared better placed to challenge Mrs. Fernández's likely nominee for the presidency. Macri made strategic decisions about the construction of an alliance capable of fielding candidates across the country, welcoming some possible associates while resisting the embrace of others. The result was the **Cambiemos** coalition. Macri also took strategic decisions about who to support to succeed him as mayor of Buenos Aires and about candidates to head lists in different parts of the country—notably the key contest for the governorship of the province of Buenos Aires—he backed **María Eugenia Vidal** and was determined to have Gabriela Michetti as his vice presidential running mate. These decisions delivered significant Cambiemos victories in several provinces. Macri's victory in the 2015 presidential contest was probably due as much to Mrs. Kirchner's dithering—late, lukewarm support for **Daniel Scioli**—as to his own calculations and reputation. Whatever, Macri beat Scioli by a tight but sufficient margin in the second round of the presidential contest in November, despite efforts by the outgoing administration to smear his reputation, highlighting his background in business, association with foreign corporations, and raising fears of a sellout of national interests to international business and finance.

The incoming Macri administration inherited a raft of problems—economic and institutional—from the outgoing Fernández de Kirchner administration, including sizeable current account and budget deficits. During her last days in office, Mrs. Kirchner seemed intent on undermining the legitimacy of Macri's victory, even seeking to sabotage his inauguration. At around two and a half percentage points, the margin in November 2015 was considerably narrower than the six-point difference forecast in late opinion polls, yet the election of Macri ended the 12-year reign of the Kirchners. His victory, as well as the campaign and initial cabinet appointments, signaled a new direction for the country. Early members of the Macri cabinet included, unsurprisingly, those with experience of national and international business—not least finance, **agriculture**, and state enterprises. There was a high proportion of economists, many partially trained abroad. Several nominees had political and administrative experience, some having served with Macri in the city of Buenos Aires government. And there was pluralism—a broad representation of distinct strands in the winning coalition, including members of the UCR and smaller parties, as well as independents, plus key figures from Macri's PRO. Following the inauguration, the administration delivered on campaign promises and the expectations of business interests and the urban and rural middle class that there would be a rapid change in the rules of the economic game, namely a speedy liberalization of the exchange rate, an easing of capital controls, and an agreement with hedge funds—the so-called vultures funds—holding debt certificates acquired on secondary markets from bondholders who had not settled in 2005. Opinion polls in 2015 and 2016 showed that the public held that the government was morally in the right to resist the demands of the funds, but that it was in the interests of the country to settle.

Highlights of the Macri presidency to date include the reestablishment of the international reputation of the country, only partly due to agreement with the vulture funds; the rolling back of interventionist measures implemented during the *kitchnerato*, including the easing of price controls; the partial removal of export taxes; the restoration of independence to the national statistical office (which had been intervened in during the *kirchnerato* and ordered to publish figures on inflation and growth that corresponded with official targets; Argentine official data is once again regarded as reliable); and the promotion of investment in public services. The international reputation of the country has also improved, with a warming of relations with the United States and alliance-building within the G20 and across Latin America as the country moves away from the close relationship with **Venezuela** established during the presidencies of Néstor Kirchner and Cristina Fernández de Kirchner. While maintaining Argentine claims to the islands, Macri has also abandoned the belligerent tone used by Mrs. Kirchner in dealings with **Great Britain** about the **Falkland Islands**. The Macri administration maintains that it is improving the efficiency of the state, rebuilding confidence in the apparatus of government, and putting an end to **corruption**—the latter claim somewhat undermined by former activities of the Macri Group. All these measures featured in campaign pledges and contributed to another highlight, the performance of the governing coalition in the midterm **congressional elections of 2017**. Following these elections, for the first time in modern Argentine political history, representatives of the same party came to hold the three most important offices in the country when, in addition to the presidency, candidates fielded by Cambiemos took the maroyalty of the city of Buenos Aires and the governorship of the province of Buenos Aires.

A less positive landmark was the **currency** crisis of May 2018, when the administration appealed to the International Monetary Fund for a standby loan to avert a hemorrhage of reserves from the **Banco Central de la República Argentina** (BCRA). For several days, the central bank had been refinancing government debt and throwing dollars at the market to stem the depreciation of the currency. Going to the IMF is a high-risk strategy. Many Argentines blame the fund for the 2001 crisis and the huge surge in poverty and unemployment that followed the end of convertibility and the resignation of President **Fernando de la Rúa**. Yet the Macri administration had few options left if it was to calm the situation at a moment of transition in economic policy—moving from the prioritizing of growth (a key feature of the first two years of government) to targeting macroeconomic stability. The calculated risk is that stability in the short term will stimulate investment-led growth in the medium term that will allow Macri to stand for a second term in 2019. The alternative is that he steps aside for Vidal to head the Cambiemos ticket, something that is already mooted.

The **Ministry of Economy** and BCRA appeared to have regained control of the **economy** by mid-2018. The initial approach to the fund was thought to have been for a loan of around US\$30,000,000,000. In the event, the IMF agreed to US\$50,000,000,000. It is likely that the fund will not demand a speedy dismantling of remaining controls, nor insist on targeted reductions to bring down the fiscal deficit or defend a specific rate for the peso, instead supporting the "gradualist" approach announced by the government. But the IMF will press for an early restoration of central bank independence—something to which the government maintains it is committed—and for less intervention in the currency market. The jury remains out on the Macri administration. It is too early to call whether he will consider it worthwhile to contest the upcoming presidential election. *See also* CACCIATORE, OSVALDO (1924–2007); ECONOMIC CRISES; ENCOTEL; FOREIGN DEBT/ FOREIGN INVESTMENT; IMMIGRATION; INDUSTRY; MILITARY COUP OF 1966; MILITARY COUP OF 1976; POSADAS; TRANSPORTATION.

MACRI GROUP. *See* MACRI, MAURICIO (1959–).

MADRES DE PLAZA DE MAYO. In English, Mothers of the Plaza de Mayo; sometimes simply "the Mothers," given the domestic and international profile of the organization, globally recognized by the emblematic white headscarves worn by members when demonstrating in the Plaza de Mayo in front of the presidential palace, the **Casa Rosada**. These protests brought attention to demands of the mothers (and grandmothers) for information about children seized by agencies of the government and semiclandestine parastate bodies.

Demonstrations started in 1977, soon after the **military coup of 1976** that instituted the **Proceso de Reorganización Nacional**, a campaign of state terror that led to the "disappearance" of many thousands. In the early days, the mothers would enter the square in groups of two and three, with headscarves hidden in bags and pockets. Once assembled, they would don the scarves and begin a dignified, silent demonstration, usually walking in a circle. For long, the Mothers were the only group drawing attention to **human rights** violations perpetrated by regimes of the Proceso. Demonstrators often had to deal with rough handling by the police and public apathy—sometimes public hostility—yet remained steadfast in the campaign for information about "disappeared" loved ones, the **Desaparecidos**. The demonstrations were initiated and led by Azucena Villaflor. When one of Villaflor's sons was kidnapped, she visited various government offices in search of information about him, searches that brought her into contact with others engaged in similarly painful attempts to ascertain what had happened to those "disappeared." Failing to obtain details or redress, the **women** decided to demonstrate in the plaza. On doing so, they were told to move on by the police. It was then that they began a slow circuit of the square. This became their form of weekly protest on Thursdays. Villaflor died in December 1977, but the demonstrations continued. Her role and mantle were assumed by others, notably María Adela Gard de Antokoletz, **Hebe de Bonafini**, Nora Cortiñas, and Taty Almeida.

Antokoletz and Bonafini soon emerged as leaders of the movement. Antokoletz was the intellectual and strategist, Bonafini, the younger of the two, the activist. The two women traveled to the **United States** and Europe, bringing attention to the violations of human rights that were occurring in Argentina. Through their actions, and that of colleagues who remained at home and continued the weekly demonstrations, the Mothers were widely applauded for their courage and steadfastness in the face of a brutal regime. By this stage, often unbeknown to them, several of the mothers had become grandmothers—their grandchildren delivered in illicit detention centers and handed to childless couples close to the regime. Mothers of the babies were murdered shortly after they had given birth. During these dark days, the Mothers were held together by hopes of redress and the resolve of the leadership, and the knowledge that their quest for information and justice was gaining traction. Paradoxically, the return of democracy in 1983, following the election of President **Raúl Alfonsín**, brought internal differences within the movement to the surface—that is, between those pressing for immediate justice and those willing to subscribe to Alfonsín's gradualist, contained approach.

Antokoletz, Cortiñas, and Almeida formed the Madres de Plaza de Mayo Línea Fundadora, which they regarded as an authentic expression of the founding principles of the movement. They were politically inclusive, emphasizing the need for information about loved ones, while focusing on broader issues of human rights and the campaign for justice. Heading the Asociación Madres de Plaza de Mayo, Bonafini favored a more radical stand, seeking to make the organization more political. Initially, following a split around 1985, the two wings of the movement continued to cooperate, but they gradually diverged, especially when Bonafini became associated with the *kirchnerato*, regimes headed successively by **Néstor Kirchner** and his wife, **Cristina Fernández de Kirchner**. Bonafini was especially close to Cristina Fernández and was given an office in the presidential palace and access to government money. To her critics, after 2003 Bonafini was converting the Mothers into an instrument of the ruling party rather than developing as a broader champion of human rights as the quest for justice for the "disappeared" was being realized. "Capture" of protest groups was a feature of the governing strategy of the Kirchners. This view appeared to be vindicated when Bonafini declared that the Mothers would become "Las Cristinas," a woman's group dedicated to supporting the political project of Fernández de Kirchner. Bonafini's critics also accused her of self-aggrandizement and self-enrichment at the expense of the movement, a charge that appeared vindicated when she was arraigned for misappropriating public money.

The splintering of the movement and charges against Bonafini do not detract from the courage of the Mothers manifest in years of struggle during the Proceso and what has been achieved in advancing the cause of human rights in Argentina and internationally. The fortitude of many individual members of the organization and the painful details about the death of loved ones—and grandchildren stolen—uncovered as the result of their action is also testimony to their fortitude and resilience. *See also* BIGNONE, REYNALDO BENITO (1928–2018); DIRTY WAR; DISPOSICIÓN FINAL; ESCUELA SUPERIOR DE MECÁNICA DE LA ARMADA (ESMA); FUNDACIÓN MADRES DE PLAZA DE MAYO; GALTIERI, LEOPOLDO FORTUNATO (1926–2003); LEY DE OBEDIENCIA DEBIDA; LEY DE PUNTO FINAL; MASSERA, EMILIO EDUARDO (1925–2010); VIDELA, JORGE RAFAEL (1925–2013); VIOLA, ROBERTO EDUARDO (1924–1994); WAR TO ANNIHILATE SUBVERSION.

MADRES DE PLAZA DE MAYO LÍNEA FUNDADORA. *See* BONAFINI, HEBE PASTOR DE (1928–); DIRTY WAR; FUNDACIÓN MADRES DE PLAZA DE MAYO; MADRES DE PLAZA DE MAYO; WAR TO ANNIHILATE SUBVERSION.

MAGALDI, AUGUSTÍN (1898–1938). Musician and composer, best known during his lifetime as a **tango** singer—and to posterity for a rumored relationship with **María Eva Duarte**, who later married **Juan Domingo Perón**, becoming the first lady of Argentina as María Eva Duarte de Perón, or "Evita" to contemporary admirers and later generations.

Popularly known as the "Sentimental Voice of Buenos Aires," with near contemporary **Carlos Gardel**, Magaldi was the face—and voice—of tango during its interwar heyday. The development of radio helped make his career and contributed to record sales; his main hits were "Levanta la frente," "Nieve," "No quiero verte llorar," and "Libertad," among many others. His career was already in decline when he began a fleeting affair with Evita, then 15 years old, while on a tour of the interior. The encounter featured prominently in the world-hit musical drama *Evita* by Andrew Lloyd Webber and Tim Rice. In the 1996 award-winning film of the stage version, Evita is played by Madonna and Magaldi by Jimmy Nail. When the film was shot partly on location in **Buenos Aires**, allegedly with the initial encouragement of President **Carlos Saúl Menem**, it provoked controversy. Critics objected to the portrayal of the affair with Magaldi, which is depicted as the first of several liaisons engineered by Evita, and another plot line that suggested that the presidential couple plundered the country. *See also* CORRUPTION; FUNDACIÓN EVA PERÓN; MEDIA; MILITARY COUP OF 1943; MILITARY COUP OF 1955; PRESIDENTIAL ELECTION OF 1946; PRESIDENTIAL ELECTION OF 1951.

MAIZE. Also known as corn and Indian corn, a cereal that is indigenous to the Americas. In pre-Columbian times, it is thought to have been cultivated in the north of the country, mainly in the present-day provinces of **Tucumán**

and **Santiago del Estero** and the **Chaco** region. Modern exploitation began in the late 19th century; the rapid growth in its popularity, and diffusion of planting to various regions of the country, prefigured that of soya in the early 21st.

First grown commercially in the area around **Rosario**, cultivation spread quickly to surrounding districts of the provinces of **Córdoba** and **Santa Fe**, and to the northwest of the province of **Buenos Aires**, largely following the routes of the **Central Argentine Railway**, the **Buenos Ayres and Pacific Railway**, and neighboring lines. Later, the frontier of production included southern provinces of **Mesopotamia**. The humid, subtropical climate of these areas seemed particularly to suit maize. By the early 20th century, the area sown with maize was beginning to challenge the primacy of wheat in the **pampas**. Maize was especially favored in the 1920s, only to fall back in the 1930s and early 1940s. However, by this stage, it was well established as one of the two main **grains** cultivated and exported by the country. The areas under wheat and maize were broadly similar by the early 1970s. Decades later, maize output was almost double that of wheat. In 2016–2017 maize production stood above 31,000,000 tons to 14,000,000 tons for wheat; the forecasts of 2017–2018 were for 39,000,000 and 17,000,000 tons, respectively, changes largely due to the removal of export taxes (*retenciones*) on the two **commodities** in 2015.

At the beginning of the 21st century, the main producing areas were the provinces of Córdoba, Buenos Aires, and Santa Fe: Córdoba accounts for well over a third of national output, Buenos Aires somewhat less, and Santa Fe around a seventh. Together, these provinces usually supply considerably more than 80 percent of national production, yet changes in farming techniques have meant that maize is also produced in some western provinces and the northwest, though in much smaller quantities. Maize production also continues in Mesopotamia. More exhaustive of the land than other cereals like wheat, maize is a much more versatile commodity. When first grown commercially, it was used both as a food staple and as a feed and fattening agent for **cattle** and poultry. By the 1920s and 1930s, industrial demand for maize was on the increase; maize starch and maize cellulose are bases for plastics and various chemicals. By around 2000, maize was established as a biofuel, used in the production of ethanol, a source of "renewal oil" and petrol additive, and as an input in biogas fermentation plants. The timing of the harvest also favors maize: starting in the north, the harvest begins to come in toward the end of February, permitting an early planting of other commodities. *See also* AGRICULTURAL COLONIZATION; AGRICULTURE; ECONOMIC CRISES; ECONOMY; *ESTANCIA* COMPANIES; FOREIGN TRADE; IMMIGRATION; INDUSTRY.

MANRIQUE, FRANCISCO (1919–1988). Naval officer, journalist, policy maker, and presidential candidate. Manrique was jailed as an opponent of President **Juan Domingo Perón** in the early 1950s, served as head of the Casa Militar during the **Revolución Libertadora** period, and then moved into journalism. In 1965, he successfully launched the *Correo de la Semana*, which became known for its advocacy of support for senior citizens, and remained involved with the paper until his death over two decades later.

During the de facto presidency of **Alejandro Agustín Lanusse**, Manrique served as minister of social welfare from March 1971 until August 1972. In that capacity, he organized a myriad of federal and provincial health insurance programs into the **Programa de Atención Médica Integrada** (PAMI) and housing assistance programs into the Fondo Nacional de la Vivienda (FONAVI). These reforms contributed to a marked reduction in infant mortality in Argentina during the 1970s.

He contested the **presidential election of March 1973** on the ticket of the Alianza Popular Federalista, a grouping of small, moderately conservative parties. He came in third with 15 percent of the vote, which was then the most received by a third-party candidate in Argentina. *See also* MINISTRY OF SOCIAL DEVELOPMENT.

MARADONA, DIEGO ARMANDO (1960–). Legendary retired professional footballer, an advanced playmaker who operated in the number 10 position. During his club career, he played for domestic teams Argentinos Juniors, **Boca Juniors Football Club** (CABJ), and Newell's Old Boys, and European teams Barcelona, Napoli, and Sevilla. In his international career, with Argentina he earned 91 caps and scored 34 goals. Maradona's vision, passing, ball control, dribbling skills, speed, reflexes, and reaction time were combined with a small/compact physique, enabling him to maneuver better than most other players; he would often dribble past multiple opposing players on a single run.

Maradona played in four FIFA World Cups (1982, 1986, 1990, 1994). In the tournament held in Mexico in 1986, he captained Argentina and led it to victory in the final but is more remembered for an incident in a match against England in which he scored a goal that had an unpenalized handing foul. On Maradona's denial of the hand foul, it became known the "Hand of God." In the tournament held in the **United States** in 1994, he was sent home after playing only two matches on failing a drug test for ephedrine doping. Maradona's expulsion from that FIFA World Cup put an end to his international career, and also confirmed a dark side within the great footballer.

Maradona has struggled with drug abuse and ill health. From the mid-1980s until 2004, he was addicted to cocaine. He also has a tendency to put on weight, and increasingly suffered from obesity from the end of his playing career until undergoing gastric bypass surgery in 2005. In 2007, Maradona was treated for hepatitis and the effects of alcohol abuse.

Notwithstanding these problems, Maradona is regarded as one of the two greatest professional footballers of the 20th century—the other being Pelé of **Brazil**. He is considered a sporting hero in Argentina, and ever since 1986 it is common for Argentines abroad to hear Maradona's name as a token of recognition even in remote places.

MARTÍN FIERRO. Written by José Hernández in two stages in the 1870s, this epic poem forms part of the national myth, eulogizes and idealizing **gaucho** life at precisely the moment when the untrammeled open spaces on which the lifestyle of the gaucho depended were being transformed by railways and *estancia* modernization. Martín Fierro, the protagonist, is portrayed as a free spirit, surviving—more than surviving, rising above—the privation and injustice experienced by such landless seminomads. Sometimes finding employment on *estancias*—though not bound to the estate like the *peón*—sometimes existing by hunting wild **cattle**, the gaucho made the poem an immediate literary success and was later referenced as iconic of a society and way of life that typified the country before it was transformed by **immigration**, overseas investment, and the national project associated with figures like **Domingo Faustino Sarmiento** and **Julio A. Roca**.

The principal elements of the poem relate how Fierro is conscripted into the army and forced to serve on the Indian frontier during early campaigns of the **Conquest of the Desert**. After three years, he returns to his smallholding to find it deserted—his wife and children gone. Regarded by the authorities as a deserter, he flees to the countryside, frequenting local stores and drinking dens, where he gets involved in scuffles and kills. Pursued by a patrol, he is captured and impresses the head of the patrol Cruz with his stoicism. Cruz engineers Fierro's escape, and the two flee to seek sanctuary beyond the frontier in Indian encampments. The poem relates the life of Fierro and Cruz among the Indians, detailing their customs. Cruz dies of fever. Fierro kills an Indian, liberating a white captive; he and the women flee back across the frontier. At a fiesta on an *estancia*, Fierro narrates or sings the story of his life, as is the tradition at such events. His children are present at the fiesta and, listening to the story, realize that Fierro is their father. They greet their father and recount their own stories of injustice. Other figures also appear: the son of Cruz and the brother of a man murdered by Fierro. There is tension as the man wishes to avenge the death of his brother. Through the intervention of others, they reconcile. Fierro leaves, accompanied by his sons and the son of Cruz. They reflect on their circumstances, and Fierro advised the boys that they must learn more about their condition, the moral being that the world needs to recognize the rights of the people of the **pampa**. The poem presents the main characters as the embodiment of individualism, liberty, and common sense who are reduced to violence by circumstances. *See also* AGRICULTURAL COLONIZATION; AGRICULTURE; CAUDILLO; ECONOMY; EL GAUCHITO GIL; FOREIGN DEBT/FOREIGN INVESTMENT; NATIONAL ORGANIZATION; ROSAS, JUAN MANUEL DE (1793–1877);

MARTÍNEZ DE HOZ, JOSÉ ALFREDO (1925–2013). Sometime head of the **Ministry of Economy** under President **José María Guido** (1962-1963) and highly controversial minister of economy from 1976 to 1981. A businessman and academic lawyer, he was the scion of a landed family and one of several people asked by the heads of the armed forces to present an economic proposal in the run-up to the **military coup of 1976**. With the selection of his project, Martínez de Hoz was appointed to the economy portfolio by de facto President General **Jorge Rafael Videla**. He proposed a radical "New Political Economy," which would dismantle many state controls and public enterprises through forced liberalization and reinsert Argentina into the world economy with a far-reaching opening.

A number of features were essential to the implementation of the "New Political Economy." First was compressing real wages by about 40 percent below the average for the preceding five years—after all, wage and price hikes during the chaotic presidency of **Isabel Perón** had fuelled **hyperinflation**. Second, the removal of export taxes on rural **commodities**, the latter being the key source of hard currency. Third, the opening of the domestic market by progressively reducing import duties with the aim of ending artificial protection for local manufacturers and raising the competitiveness and overall efficiency of **industry**. Fourth, the elimination of a many subsidies instituted to promote non-traditional manufactured exports. Fifth, financial reform and liberalization of foreign exchange markets, together with the domestic sale of government bonds to finance public sector deficits and investments. Finally, measures would be taken to improve the performance of **state-owned enterprises** (SOEs)—including the imposition of limits on state activities.

The economic project might have made sense on paper, but it ultimately failed. Martínez de Hoz stuck to its original over-arching principles during his tenure, but policies evolved through four distinct phases with short-term changes in direction motivated by failures to meet objectives. The first stage (April 1976–May 1977) was one of orthodox stabilization. To tackle hyperinflation, Martínez de Hoz sought to manipulate relative prices and impose drastic deflation. He generally eliminated price controls while enforcing wage controls, but the drastic reduction in real wages failed to curb inflation.

The foreign debt was renegotiated with the International Monetary Fund (IMF) as a matter of urgency. Even **Emilio Mondelli**, while serving as the last minister of economy under Mrs. Perón, had understood that the country was on the verge of defaulting on the debt and had to turn to the IMF. In an attempt to deal with the fiscal crisis, Martínez de Hoz curbed government expenditure, increased taxes, and announced a crackdown on tax evasion. In addition, he made explicit his intention to open the economy and enacted a new foreign investment law.

Although the IMF approved and many international banks provided loans to help Argentina sort out the economy, by early 1977 it was clear that the initial stabilization measures had not been successful. The second phase of the economic project (June 1977–April 1978) can be termed as one of ortho-dox monetarist stabilization. Its centrepiece was an ambitious financial re-form that freed interest rates, decentralized control of bank deposits, and instituted a new law regulating financial institutions. The purpose was to free the economy by linking the banking system to short-term capital markets (while lifting most controls over interest rates) and to force state companies to turn to the money market to meet their financial requirements.

Unfortunately, the consequent boom in interest rates further fuelled infla-tion and led to all manner of financial speculation. Moreover, success in attracting loans and foreign capital had a highly inflationary impact on do-mestic money supply, which subsequently led to the imposition of controls in September 1977. Efforts to curb the supply of money and credit failed. Mon-etarism was gradually abandoned and was followed by a third stage of poli-cymaking (May–November 1978). Its key component was *desindexación*, by which future exchange rate devaluations and modifications in public sector prices would be systematically adjusted below the rate of private sector price rises. This was meant to push inflation downward, but again the *desindexación* stage ended in failure.

The fourth and final policy phase implemented by Martínez de Hoz (De-cember 1978–February 1981) was the lengthiest and by far the most contro-versial. Although it retained certain vital components of preceding phases and policies, this stage was guided by the theory of *convergencia*. With a *tablita* setting out a schedule of predetermined devaluations, the government announced that the value of the currency would continue to be held consider-ably below the general level of price rises, thereby forcing a fall in inflation. It was argued that in this way the exchange rate would cease to reflect the inflationary spiral and turn into a real instrument of anti-inflationary policy. In theory, the rate of inflation would be forced to converge toward a level equivalent to international inflation plus domestic devaluation.

The policy of *convergencia*, which was based on the overriding need to create a relative price structure to provide the correct signals required to direct local and foreign investment into priority areas enjoying comparative advantages, had differential effects across the economy. The rural sector faced few problems, as it was export oriented and followed price movements on the international market closely. On the other hand, industry was severely hit by the policy. Protective tariffs were further reduced, and traditionally high-cost nationally owned companies and local subsidiaries of transnational corporations had to face the consequences of stiff competition from cheap imports and the possibility of serious financial difficulties or outright bankruptcy. A third sector of the economy, that producing goods and services unconnected to foreign trade, was dealt with by using traditional anti-inflationary measures. Demand was managed through wage controls and credit restrictions, and efforts to contain prices were stepped up.

Economic agents did not respond to the measures as anticipated, and a deep crisis ensued. In March 1980, the large private-owned Banco de Intercambio Regional (BIR) was forced into liquidation by the **Banco Central de la República Argentina** (BCRA) owing to irregularities in its operations. Panic spread, and 72 financial institutions had folded by March 1981. Two months earlier, the **Sasetru** conglomerate, which was the largest Argentine agricultural exporter, collapsed and left billions of dollars in debt. Growing uncertainty and the rapidly deepening financial crisis precipitated a massive wave of capital flight.

The "New Political Economy" had crash landed by the time Videla and his minister of the economy left office. However, it can be argued that the blame for its failure does not entirely rest with Martinez de Hoz, as fault can be found with the dictatorial regime, the public and some sections of industry. The ruling military were obstructionist and interfered. Regarding the sale of state assets, they prevented (not unsurprisingly) the **privatization** of the sprawling and highly uneconomic **Fabricaciones Militares** empire. In terms of the financial reform, Martinez de Hoz claimed in his memoirs that some existing financial legislation had to be scrapped for his policies to work, yet the de facto government refused to countenance the necessary changes. The public bore some responsibility through its response to the boom in interest rates that followed the financial reform. As indicated earlier, large segments of the population reacted by engaging in all sorts of speculation geared to maximum short-term profits. This was the so-called *bicicleta*—moving cash from one bank or financial institution to another in pursuit of higher interest. The game was very damaging as banks competed by jacking up deposit rates—notably weaker institutions in a desperate attempt to secure or retain cash deposits. Some sections of industry simply failed to adapt to the opening of the economy. The closure of many factories could not be avoided with the lowering of artificially high tariffs and a flood of cheap imports. Nevertheless, there are two examples that show that some sectors did respond to the economic medicine as Martínez de Hoz had anticipated, demonstrating what the reforms might have achieved. The textile industry took advantage of tariff-free imports of capital goods and equipment to modernize plants, and the automotive industry was successfully given incentives to improve efficiency and competitiveness through the Ley de Reconversión de la Industria Automotriz of 1979.

Even if Martínez de Hoz may not be entirely to blame for the failure of his "New Political Economy," two outstanding issues remain. First, his economic project was controversial and ultimately did not deliver. Second, he tainted his excellent reputation by having served a particularly brutal dictatorship. *See also* AGRICULTURE; ECONOMIC CRISES; FOREIGN DEBT/ FOREIGN INVESTMENT; STATE-OWNED ENTERPRISES (SOEs).

MASSA, SERGIO TOMÁS (1972–). Second-generation immigrant born to Italian parents who settled in the province of **Buenos Aires**. Something of a political butterfly, Massa was a successful mayor who harbored ambitions to become president—ambitions that undermined the position of sitting president Cristina **Fernández de Kirchner** toward the end of her second presidency.

At the outset of his political career, Massa was a member of the probusiness center-right **Unión del Centro Democrático** (UCEDE, sometimes UCeDe) founded by **Álvaro Alsogaray**—Massa headed the youth wing of the party. Around 1989, when newly elected president **Carlos Saúl Menem** of the **Partido Justicialista** (PJ) was flirting with neoliberalism, the UCeDé entered into a political alliance with him. Massa joined the PJ when the UCEDE endorsed Menem's decision to seek reelection for a second term in the upcoming **presidential election of 1995**. By 2001, Massa was associated with the traditional wing of the PJ, which had been instrumental in appointing **Eduardo Duhalde**, Menem's former vice president but now arch enemy, interim president of the republic after the economic crisis of 2001–2002. Duhalde appointed Massa to head the state pension and social security agency. Four years later, Massa was working with President **Néstor Kirchner**, sometime protégé of Duhalde who had become president when Menem pulled out of the second round of the presidential race in 2003, and was seeking to distance himself from Duhalde. By now, Massa was affiliated with the **Frente para la Victoria/Partido Justicialista** (FpV/PJ), the Kirchnerista wing of the PJ. He stood for the FpV/PJ in the midterm **congressional elections of 2005** but did not take up a seat in the federal Chamber of Deputies, remaining at the pension agency. Two years later, Massa was elected on the FpV/PJ ticket as mayor of Tigre, an affluent suburb in the north of the Greater Buenos Aires metropolitan area. He now enjoyed the support of Cristina Fernández, who had succeeded her husband following the **presidential election of 2007**. Within less than a year, Massa had been talent spotted by Mrs. Kirchner and appointed head of the cabinet of ministers (prime minister) to steady the ship as she encountered the first major crisis of her presidency due to **farm protests**. At 36, Massa was the youngest to hold the post, which had been created by the **Constitution of 1994**. Obtaining such a powerful position at such a young age, Massa's political future seemed assured. This was not to be. The poor showing of the Frente para la Victoria in the midterm **congressional elections of 2009** and charges of **corruption** arising from his time at the pensions and social security agency caused Massa to step down as cabinet head.

Returning to the mayor's office in Tigre—he had appointed a substitute to run the city when he took up the post of prime minister—Massa set about rebuilding his reputation as a reformist, efficient administrator. In 2011, he was reelected mayor of Tigre in a landslide victory, gaining almost three-quarters of the votes, a result that encouraged presidential ambitions. With opinion polls showing the approval rating of President Fernández de Kirchner slipping, Massa decided to form a dissident wing of the PJ—the **Frente Renovador/Partido Justicialista** (FR/PJ). The wisdom of this judgment appeared to be confirmed by the results of the midterm **congressional elections of 2013** when the FR/PJ comfortably pushed the FpV/PJ into second place in the all-important province of Buenos Aires, the largest electoral district in the country. Massa obtained a seat in the federal Chamber of Deputies. Mrs. Kirchner was furious; Massa looked confidently to the **presidential election of 2015**. The contest did not go as had been predicted at the beginning of the presidential campaign. Massa was knocked out in the first round of the presidential race in October 2015; Mrs. Kirchner's nominee, **Daniel Scioli**, and **Mauricio Macri** went on to contest the second round in November, which Macri won. Having divided the PJ vote, Massa was castigated for delivering victory to Macri. With his term as deputy expiring, Massa stood for the National Senate in the midterm **congressional elections of 2017**. He failed to get elected but remains head of the FR/PJ. Massa has announced that he intends to stand in the presidential election of 2019, though whether as head of the Frente Renovador in alliance with other anti-Kirchner faction of the PJ or in coalition with other groups remains unclear. *See also* COBOS, JULIO CÉSAR CLETO (1955–); PRESIDENTIAL ELECTION OF 2003.

MASSERA, EMILIO EDUARDO (1925–2010). A key participant in the **military coup of 1976**, he is considered the architect of the **War to Annihilate Subversion**. Massera became the commander-in-chief of the navy in 1974, during the third presidency of **Juan Domingo Perón**, and together with **Jorge Rafael Videla** and **Orlando Ramón Agosti** formed the three-man military junta that toppled **Isabel Perón** in March 1976.

Massera turned the navy into a criminal organization. He was in charge of the **Escuela Superior de Mecánica de la Armada** (ESMA), where a notorious clandestine detention center functioned and thousands of political detainees were "disappeared." The only voice in Argentina at the time to report on the crimes of the **Proceso de Reorganización Nacional** was the *Buenos Aires Herald*, the English-language newspaper; its editor was threatened by Massera on a number of occasions and finally forced to flee the country in 1979.

The ambition of Massera was to become a new Perón, and to promote his bid he set up his own newspaper. This earned him enemies in the armed forces, and he failed to scale the political heights to which he aspired. He stepped down as commander-in-chief of the navy in 1978 and was replaced by **Armando Lambruschini**. Following the collapse of the dictatorship, Massera was one of the defendants in the trials of the military juntas in 1985. He was sentenced to life imprisonment for crimes against humanity but five years later benefited from the pardons granted to senior officers by President **Carlos Saúl Menem**. In 1998, Massera was arrested on charges of stealing babies born to detainees at the ESMA. The pardons granted by Menem were overturned in the early 21st century, and officers of the Proceso began to be sent back to jail, but Massera had suffered a stroke and his failing health excused him from further prosecution. *See also* ACOSTA, JORGE EDUARDO (1941–); ASTIZ, ALFREDO IGNACIO (1951–); COMISIÓN NACIONAL SOBRE LA DESAPARACIÓN DE PERSONAS (CONADEP); DESAPARECIDOS; DIRTY WAR; DISPOSICIÓN FINAL; MILITARY JUNTAS, TRIALS OF THE; *NUNCA MÁS*.

MATE. *See* YERBA MATE.

MAY REVOLUTION OF 1810. In Spanish, Revolución de Mayo; so famous a moment in Argentine history that it is simply referred to as the "May Revolution," without reference to the year. The term refers to a series of events in mid-May culminating in the formation of the first revolutionary junta (Primera Junta) on 25 May. Although **independence** was not declared formally until 9 July 1816 at the **Congress of Tucumán**, 25 May 1810 is celebrated as Independence Day. Following the **British invasions** of 1806 and 1807, when the defense and recapture of the city of **Buenos Aires** had been due mainly to local efforts, various factions formed, some committed to independence, others to continuing association with **Spain**, though possibly in modified from. It was the series of events in Spain between 1808 and 1810 that finally precipitated the formation of the Revolutionary Junta, namely the Napoleonic invasion of the Iberian Peninsula, the abdication of Charles IV; the succession of his son, Ferdinand VII, who was captured and deposed by the French; and the imposition of Napoleon Bonaparte's brother, Joseph, as king of Spain. Buenos Aires initially recognized the viceroy, **Baltasar Hidalgo de Cisneros**, dispatched by the patriotic Spanish junta formed in Seville to resist the French and welcomed economic reforms by him, such as the opening of the port to free trade with all friendly nations. When news of the fall of Seville reached the **River Plate**, a group of notables called for an open town hall meeting, the **Cabildo Abierto**, to address the future governance of the colony. While various options were considered—loyalty to Spain or the formation of a constitutional monarchy headed by a Spanish prince or princess—forces favoring independence were in the ascendant. Ideas and forces unleashed in Buenos Aires in May rapidly spread throughout the interior. Of all the revolutionary juntas created in Spanish America around 1810, the Buenos Aires junta was the only one not to be suppressed by royalists. This contributed to the aura of popular revolutionary patriotism surrounding the events of May 1810 that ultimately led to the formation of the modern state and nation.

MEAT. "Meat" in Argentina means beef, and "meat" eating is embedded in the national culture. That said, the flesh of other animals is consumed, and the country raises a variety of meat-producing birds. **Cattle, sheep** (though lamb does not loom large in the national diet except in **Patagonia**), pigs, and goats are raised commercially across the country for meat and by-products, with llamas to be found along the **Andes**. Poultry is also produced nationwide. Less common, the rhea (the South American ostrich) is farmed for its feathers and meat; in the wetlands of the northeast, the capybara (related to the beaver) is widely distributed and sometimes encountered on restaurant menus. In times past, **gauchos** reputedly regarded armadillo as a delicacy.

Current fresh meat consumption per capita is around 120 kilos a year (c. 264 pounds), of which "meat" represents 54 percent, chicken 36 percent, and pork 10 percent. Total meat consumption has remained fairly stable since 1950, despite cyclical variation ranging between 90 and 120 kilos. However, product distribution has changed markedly. In 1950, beef represented about 85 percent of total meat consumption per capita—beef consumption peaked in 1956 at 100 kilos per capita. The change is attributed to late 20th-century health concerns about red meat, but more to economic circumstances and the policy regime.

From around 1900 until the 1930s, high-quality beef was traditionally produced from grass-fed cattle, fattened on alfalfa pasture before being shipped to slaughterhouses for domestic consumption and modern *frigoríficos* specializing in the production of chilled beef for export. Estates in the southern **pampas** and parts of **Mesopotamia** raised sheep for meat as well as **wool** at least until the 1920s; mutton and lamb tended to be exported frozen. **Great Britain** was the main consumer; before 1939, Argentina supplied 40 percent of total British meat imports. In 1914, 59 percent of meat production was consumed domestically and 41 percent exported. In 1938, home consumption absorbed 68 percent of total output; in 1951, 86 percent. Since the 1960s, the proportion of total meat output consumed domestically has remained at this high level, with a tendency to increase. In the first decade of the 21st century, well above 85 percent of beef was directed toward the domestic market. This long-term trend is partly explained by volatility in overseas demand but mainly due to government policy. The principal factors accounting for a decline in the beef exports since the 1930s are stagnation in the national cattle stock and rising domestic demand, which have squeezed the surplus available for export—both a function of government action.

Although as recently as 2005, Argentina was the third largest world exporter of beef, by 2012 it was eleventh—Mexico and New Zealand exported more. Only in 2017 did the country once again became one of the top 10 suppliers to the international market—just. During the presidencies of **Néstor Kirchner** and **Cristina Fernández de Kirchner**, government policy became distinctly *antiganadera* (antiranching). This was reflected in rising export taxes on "meat" and a 180-day ban on beef exports in 2006, measures designed to massage inflation data, given the importance of beef consumption and meat prices in the official index. (This contrasted with periodic bans on domestic consumption in the early 1970s to promote beef exports—despite the promanufacturing, **developmentalist** stance in **economic policy**, traditional exports remain the principal source of foreign exchange.) By 2010, Argentina was failing to meet its Hilton quota—the amount of beef that could be exported to the European Union (EU)—with countries like **Chile** and New Zealand bidding for a share of the unfilled Argentine quota.

The rural-sector response to high export taxes was to shift from pasture to arable, with a pronounced preference for soya, which attracted a less penal tax regime. A consequence of the switch to soya was more intensive meat production: corn-fed cattle and feedlot cattle production became more common, displacing open-range, grass-fed beef. The situation began to change in 2016, with the national stock of cattle starting to recover. Total beef production increased 5 percent in 2018, while exports rose by 25 percent to a nine-year high. Argentina still retains a substantial competitive advantage in the productions of high-quality "meat," with beef sold as grass fed enjoying a considerable premium, despite the strength of the peso inhibiting sales in some markets. In 2018, the EU was the main market by value, **China** by volume; other key markets are Israel and Chile. *See also* CONCORDANCIA; ROCA–RUNCIMAN PACT (1933); *SALADEROS*; *VAQUERÍAS*.

MEDIA. Buenos Aires is a major Spanish-language publishing center—one of the largest in the world—and the country has a prolific media industry. Argentines are widely read and have traditionally been served by a diverse range of dailies and weeklies, radio stations, and television channels. There are around 150 national and regional newspapers, a few hundred radio stations, and a dozen television channels; with 30 million users, internet coverage is about 70 percent. The principal media consortia are the Clarín Group (the largest) followed by the La Nación organization; Atlántida, Crónica, and Ámbito are also important multimedia companies. Most consortia are centered around, or emerged from, well-regarded daily newspapers. Following deregulation and **privatization** in the 1990s, ownership in the sector is highly concentrated.

Constitutionally, there is freedom of the press and expression, but this was often compromised during periods of **military** rule, characterized by censorship and self-censorship. De facto president General **José Félix Uriburu** curtailed the freedom of the press shortly after the **military coup of 1930** that brought him to power. The media was subject to government control during the **Concordancia** administration of President (formerly General) **Agustín Pedro Justo** in 1932. The administration that came to power with the **military coup of 1943** tightly regulated in the media; restrictions were only lifted in the run-up to the **congressional** and **presidential elections of 1946**. Military regimes of the 1960s and 1970s closely monitored the press; even when not subject to direct intervention, open criticism of de facto governments was not tolerated; in 1972, the government prohibited the use of foreign news services; for a few days at the outset of the **military coup of 1976**, there was virtual national media censorship, soon to be followed by self-censorship as editors, journalists, and technical staff were subject to death threats and "disappeared." In the late 20th and early 21st centuries, there was a resurgence of violence directed against investigative journalists, who were subject to physical abuse by gangs associated with criminal organization and prominent politicians.

Curbs were also placed on the media by democratically elected governments. During the first presidencies of **Juan Domingo Perón**, there was a systematic campaign against press freedom. Newspapers were intervened in and expropriated; opposition titles were closely monitored, as were radio stations. Tactics to bring critical media outlets to heel included restricting supplies of newsprint and criminal investigation for supposed breaches of tax, labor, and sanitary regulations. In 1949, the law of "disrespect" made it an offence to offend the dignity of public officials. A year later, several interior newspapers were closed for failing to display official slogans. The administration of President **Cristina Fernández de Kirchner** had a frayed relationship with the media, especially the Clarín Group, giving rise to complaints that the government was seeking to curb journalistic freedom. The media regulatory regime changed dramatically in 2009. Arguing the case for competition and greater diversity, the government introduced legislation to restructure broadcasting. The new law, rushed through **Congress** within months of the devastating defeat suffered by the government in the midterm **congressional elections of 2009**, had several controversial features. A new body was formed to adjudicate on the number of outlets a media group could own—essentially geared to television—limiting each consortium to the ownership of one cable or one broadcast channel. There would be a tripartite division of the airwaves: one-third of licenses to be allocated to the private sector, by competitive bidding; one-third to state broadcasters; one-third to not-for-profit organizations. Quotas were established to ensure the national content of programing. Media consortia refuted official claims that the legislation, which overhauled statutes enacted by military regimes of the **Proceso de Reorganización Nacional**, was designed to break up monopolies that had consolidated during the dictatorship, maintaining that government action was designed to intimidate opposition broadcasters, notably by intervening in the awarding of licenses, and by fostering the emergence of smaller, compliant players. Such charges were widely recorded in the national opposition media and covered extensively by foreign media groups. President Fernández de Kirchner rebutted these complaints as attempts to smear a popularly elected government. The law was upheld by the Supreme Court in 2013 as consistent with the constitution, though judges noted that its application might leave media companies open to an abuse of power by the government. Following victory in the **presidential election of 2015**, **Mauricio Macri** ordered a review of the legislation. In 2016, much of the Fernández de Kirchner legislation was overturned. Regulatory arrangements were simplified; the limit on the number of broadcast licenses a media group could own was lifted; television broadcast networks may now operate cable services. It is predicted that as the new legislation comes into force, and licenses come up for renewal, ownership in the sector is likely to become even more concentrated.

Two prestigious Buenos Aires–based daily newspapers feature among the earliest to be established in Latin America: *La Prensa* founded in 1869 and *La Nación* a year later; *La Prensa* ceased publication at the end of the 20th century. These titles enjoyed a national circulation, distributed by the expanding rail network to provincial capitals and principal interior cities, most of which supported at least one local paper. Well-regarded provincial titles include *Diario de Cuyo* (**San Juan**), *El Litoral* (**Santa Fe**), *La Capital* (**Rosario**), *La Nueva Provincia* (**Bahia Blanca**), and *Los Andes* (**Mendoza**); most were firmly established around 1900. By this time, there was also a flourishing foreign-language daily and weekly press catering to immigrant and expatriate commercial communities. For example, the *Argentinisches Tageblatt*, the **Buenos Aires Herald**, *I'Italia del Popolo*, and the *Review of the River Plate*. The emergences of **trade unions**, new **political parties**, and social and sporting clubs added further diversity. For example, the socialist *La Vanguardia*, which first appeared in 1894 and continues; *Caras y Caretas*, a popular satirical weekly that made extensive use of color and political cartoons that was first produced in Buenos Aires in 1898; *El Hogar*, an illustrated fortnightly geared to a middle-class female readership that covered cultural and social affairs and fashions and began in 1904. The number of specialist newspapers and magazines grew exponentially between the 1920s and 1940s, while radio broadcasting also took off. Many present-day stations date from the golden age of radio, for example, Radio Argentina, founded in 1920, and Radio Mitre, which began transmitting in the same year, and Radio Nacional, which opened in 1937. Well before the Second World War, many Buenos Aires–based stations were informing prospective advertisers of their national outreach and the licensing of popular programs to partners in the provinces. Before she met and married soon-to-be president Juan Domingo Perón, **María Eva Duarte**, as she then was, had become a popular radio and film actress; the plays and dramas in which she performed attracted advertising, as did concerts by popular **tango** singers like **Carlos Gardel** and **Agustín Magaldi**.

Radio had little negative impact on the print media, but from the 1940s to the 1980s, the status and circulation of prestige, historic broadsheets would be challenged. Several contenders, among whom were *Clarín*, *La Opinión*, *La Razón*, and *Página/12*, adopted a tabloid format and promised livelier features, more comment, and impartial analysis. The 1980s was the peak decade for newspaper circulation, which declined thereafter. In 2010, *Clarín* was the top circulating newspaper, with an average production of around 315,000 copies daily; *La Nación* was next with 155,000. Total circulation of dailies was just above 1,000,000 copies.

Unlike radio broadcasting, television services came relatively late to Argentina. Transmission did not begin until 1951, pioneered by the government-run Canal 7. Color broadcasting was even more delayed, not beginning until 1978, when it was promoted by the de facto regime of General **Jorge Rafael Videla** for the Soccer World Cup, which was hosted that year by Argentina. Although games were transmitted in color overseas, at that stage Argentines could only view matches in black and white as there were few color sets in the country—only the final was available nationally in color, and then only on a few sets located mainly in the studios of Canal 7. It would be years before there was nationwide color transmission. This, and the poor quality of state-run television programing, explains the popularity of cable television, which started in 1965; the country now has a cable coverage of almost 80 percent of households, the third highest in the world. The main national television networks are Televisión América, Televisión Pública Argentina, Canal 9, **Canal 13** (El Trece), and Telefe, Telefe and Canal 13 being the most popular. *See also* *ÁMBITO FINANCIERO*; CABEZAS AFFAIR; *CRONISTA COMERCIAL*; DESAPARECIDOS; DIRTY WAR; LANATA, JORGE (1960–); MENEM, CARLOS SAÚL (1930–); MILITARY COUP OF 1955; MILITARY COUP OF 1962; MILITARY COUP OF 1966; NISMAN CASE.

MENDOZA (CITY). When Spanish forces arrived from **Chile** in 1551, they found the site of the present-day city was already settled and fortified by Indians with well-developed agriculture and ceramic production, skills reflecting the influence of the Inca. After first contact, the Spaniards retreated but returned in 1562. They maintained amicable contact with established Indian communities and founded the city, which was named after the then governor of Chile, García Hurtado de Mendoza, son of the third viceroy of **Peru**. The governor of Mendoza was named captain-general of **Cuyo**, giving the city jurisdiction over the current territories of **San Luis** and **San Juan** in addition to Mendoza, that is, a subdivision of Chile within the Viceroyalty of Peru. For much of the 17th and 18th centuries, Mendoza remained a modest settlement, a staging post on the route between Santiago de Chile and **Buenos Aires**, open to attack by pampean Indians. As the local population declined, slaves were imported and irrigation improved to provide supplies for east–west traders: grapes were planted, and wine production began around the 1660s. With the creation of the **Viceroyalty of the River Plate** in 1776, the city and provinces were transferred to the jurisdiction of Buenos Aires. In May 1810, the city and province declared **independence**, a process in which it played a major role. **General José de San Martín** and his **Army of the Andes** were based there. San Martín was appointed governor intendent of Cuyo in 1814, a position that enabled him to finance and provision operations for the liberation of Chile and Peru. During and after independence, the city maintained close economic and political relations with Chile, intensifying the anarchy of the period. Urban development was further interrupted by an earthquake in 1861 that devastated much of the colonial center.

Modern expansion predates the coming of the railways in the 1880s, marked by the arrival of the **Buenos Ayres & Pacific Railway**, part of the transandean rail link between Buenos Aires on the Atlantic and Valparaíso on the Pacific, but was shaped by it. **Education** was expanded in the 1870s, and the first bank opened at much the same time as piped water and street lighting were installed. The population grew; wine production and **agriculture** drew settlers from Italy, **Spain**, and surrounding areas, as well as the French capital. Enjoying good communications to the north and south, by 1900 the city was emerging as a regional commercial and financial center; most foreign banks had opened there, and the city counted an architecturally handsome branch of the **Banco de la Nación Argentina**. Parks were laid out and boulevards beautified. The regional importance of the city was underscored with the founding of the University of Cuyo in 1939—later the **Universidad Nacional del Cuyo**. Further beautification followed in the 1940s, when Mendoza benefited from Peronist largesse. The **Fundación Eva Perón** financed the construction of the Parque General San Martín, a planned "model" district with worker housing, schools, hospitals, and recreation areas. Another wave of modernization and growth occurred in the 1960s, largely entailing road construction and the "organization of urban space" designed to bring order to the haphazard expansion experienced in the immediately preceding years.

Enlightened local government in the 21st century has done much to improve the urban environment. City authorities have pursued a program of environmentally friendly development, greening parks, avenues, and residential districts. Consistent with such efforts, in 2005 the city was described as (relatively) the most digitized in Latin America and a city of technology. A 2014 survey found that the city had the best quality of life in the country. The city is youthful, with an educated workforce. There is substantial expenditure on the arts and culture. Rates of population growth are around the national average but rates of infant mortality lower. These features attract clean industries and tourists. The 2010 census records the population of the metropolitan district as a little more than 1,000,000. *See also* MENDOZA (PROVINCE).

MENDOZA (PROVINCE). A founding province of the **Argentine Confederation**, to the west the province shares a border with **Chile**, to the north the province of **San Juan**, to the east **San Luis**, to the southeast **La Pampa**, and to the south **Neuquén**. The city of Mendoza was sometime colonial capital of the **Cuyo** region, an area initially settled by Europeans arriving from Chile in the 16th century. Although never fully incorporated within the Inca Empire, northern parts of the future province reflected its powerful influences. While Indian communities to the north were sedentary, based on the growing of **maize**, squashes, and **grains**, those to the south were nomadic and warlike. Today, the province is a major center of wine production, noted for the quality of its Malbec.

For much of the colonial period, towns and cities founded by the Spanish were subject to Indian attack, a threat not fully resolved until the **Conquest of the Desert**, which determined the southern boundary of the province, adding territory to it. Controlled from Chile and on the fringe of empire, the province was left much to its own devices though was already developing as a center of wine production: snow-fed streams and irrigation facilitated the steady expansion and diversification of **agriculture**. With the creation of the **Viceroyalty of the River Plate** in 1776, Cuyo was detached from Chile and transferred to the new jurisdiction. It was in the early 1810s that the area played a dramatic role in national and regional affairs. General **José de San Martín** and his **Army of the Andes** were based there. San Martín was named governor intendent by the revolutionary junta in **Buenos Aires** in 1814 and launched his campaign to liberate Chile and **Peru**. The cost of San Martín's campaign was largely financed by the province—a campaign that did not end until 1821, when San Martín proclaimed the independence of Peru in Lima.

The liberation of Chile and Peru did not bring peace to the province, which was formally created in 1820. Economic activities were more focused on Chile than Buenos Aires: even today, the city is only six hours by road from Santiago, 14 from Buenos Aires. Distinctly **Federalist** in the late 1820s and 1830s, the local elite were more inclined to autonomy than national integration. In the 1840s, the province was caught up in renewed conflict between Federalists and **Unitarians**. By the time of the fall of **Juan Manuel de Rosas** in 1852, the province was peaceful and beginning to prosper. A provincial constitution was adopted in 1854, and there was the promise of order. Yet underlying sentiments remained Federalist, opposed to the liberal persuasions of the federal government in Buenos Aires, especially during the presidency of **Bartolomé Mitre**. The **War of the Triple Alliance** against **Paraguay** was particularly unpopular: provincial sentiment opposed the conflict in principle and resented the taxes and conscription demanded by Buenos Aires. Mendoza was involved, with others, in a revolt against the national government in 1874, which was put down by soon-to-be national president **Julio A. Roca**. But modernization was already in process: the wine **industry** established a national reputation, agricultural colonies were being set up, and the provincial government sought to improve public services, building hospitals and schools. These trends would be strengthened with the coming of the railways. By 1910, the province stood at the center of an extensive rail system—extensive for the interior—which facilitated production for regional and national markets and **foreign trade** with the Pacific.

The population of the province doubled between the mid-1860s and mid-1890s, doubled again by 1914, and again by 1947, and yet again by 1980. At a little under two million today, Mendoza is one of the more populous interior provinces. Good transport and irrigation contributed to the growth of the province and economic diversification. Although Mendoza is known for the quality of its wine—it accounts for around two-thirds of total national production, and its Malbec enjoys an international reputation—other sectors are economically important. Quality is not confined to grapes and wine: the production of stone fruits has increased since the 1960s; today, market gardening is thriving, growing **commodities** as diverse as tomatoes, garlic, and potatoes, with vines producing wine and tables grapes. Minerals and energy are also important—the province accounted for around 15 percent of total national **petroleum** production in 2010. Manufacturing has had a distinct presence since the 1980s. **Tourism** is important, associated with adventure sports, including skiing, and the now internationally famous wine trail. Western valleys are noted for lakes, rivers, and spectacular views of the **Andes**. Inward investment has been attracted from overseas.

Since the 1980s, Mendoza has acquired the reputation of being a well-governed province. Hitherto it was subject to repeated interventions. Recent governors have included members of the **Partido Justicialista** (PJ) and

Unión Cívica Radical (UCR), among whom have been reformist Peronists, such as José Octavio Bordón, who switched from the PJ to the then newly formed Frente País Solidario (FREPASO) during the first presidency of Carlos Saúl Menem, objecting to corruption and a lack of internal democracy within the PJ, as well as to Menem's neoliberal economic policies. Julio Cobos moved in the opposite direction: having served as UCR governor of the province from 2003 to 2007, he agreed to be running mate of Cristina Fernández de Kirchner of the Frente para la Victoria/Partido Justicialista (FpV/PJ) in the presidential election of 2007, resulting in his expulsion from the party. In contrast to what has occurred elsewhere, PJ and UCR governors have been inclined to consult with opponents. Such pluralism and dialogue is not usual and is neatly epitomized by the recent political and diplomatic career of Bordón; having broken with Menem, he was subsequently appointed to the prestige post of ambassador in Washington, DC, by Néstor Kirchner and later to ambassador in the strategically important post of ambassador in Santiago de Chile by Mauricio Macri. Although one of the most socially developed and economically dynamic provinces in the republic, this does not mean that the province is exempt from such problems as low-quality housing and underemployment. *See also* MENDOZA (CITY); TRANSPORTATION.

MENEM, CARLOS SAÚL (1930–). Politician and lawyer; president of Argentina from 1989 to 1999, the last president to serve a six-year term under the Constitution of 1853 and the first president elected for four years under the Constitution of 1994, which permitted immediate reelection of an incumbent. Menem was born in the province of La Rioja to Muslim immigrants from the former Ottoman Empire, in what is now Syria, where the family still has relatives. This background led to various rumors that Menem was not born in the republic and not baptized as a Catholic, both of which would have barred him from standing for the presidency under the 1853 constitution. A member of the Partido Justicialista (PJ), he founded the provincial branch of the party's youth wing, Juventud Peronista (JP), and initially identified with the revolutionary branch of the movement. He was incarcerated on a number of occasions for his political affiliation and actions; Menem acted as lawyer for trade unions and the regional office of the Confederación General del Trabajo (CGT). He was first detained in 1956, during the administration of de facto president General Pedro Eugenio Aramburu, and the second time following the military coup of 1976. On the latter occasion, he was held for five years. It was during this period that he is on record as converting to Christianity, a move that caused division within his family. His first wife, Zulema Yoma de Menem, refused to accept his conversion from Islam. Menem met Zulema in Syria, the marriage being arranged by the two families, who had connections in La Rioja and the Middle East. The couple divorced in 1991.

Before becoming president, he was twice elected governor of his province, in 1973—the term was cut short in 1976—and again in 1983. In the 1988 PJ party primaries, Menem defeated the favorite, **Antonio Cafiero**, sitting governor of the province of **Buenos Aires** and a former minister in the first administration of **Juan Domingo Perón**. Cafiero headed the reformist, renewal wing of the party, seeking to modernize and democratize it. Menem presented a traditional, populist platform, a stance that he continued on the campaign trail for the **presidential** and **congressional elections of 1989**. The strategy served him well. During the chaos of the last year of the presidency of **Raúl Alfonsín**, the opinion polls were moving firmly in Menem's direction, notwithstanding the vagueness of his campaign promises and association with some particularly unsavory figures from the administration of **Isabel Perón**, including members of the **Triple A**, the **Montoneros**, and trade union officials compromised by deals with regimes of the **Proceso de Reorganización Nacional**.

Despite the populist stance during the campaign, which promised a productivity revolution involving a compromise between business and labor that echoed the rhetoric of the **Tercera Posición** of the first Peronist administration, such was the economic crisis confronting Menem that he was gradually persuaded to embrace the Washington Consensus. The model, then in the ascendant, emphasized trade liberalization, **privatization**, and market economics; these policies had been tentatively essayed during the latter part of the Alfonsín presidency but blocked by Peroinist trade unions and scuppered by the PJ majority in **Congress**. Menem approached the business community, appointing an economic team associated with the Argentine multinational conglomerate **Bunge & Born**, and appointed conservative politicians from the **Unión del Centro Democrático** (UCEDE, sometimes UCeDe), for example, **Álvaro Alsogaray** and his daughter **María Julia Alsogaray**, to his cabinet. Despite the passage of emergency legislation designed to shrink the state, increase taxes, and end subsidies, the economic crisis deepened and there was another bout of **hyperinflation**. Renewed economic and political chaos paved the way in 1991 for his fourth minister of economy, **Domingo Cavallo**, and the **Convertibility Plan**, a fully fledged neoliberal package that included the introduction of a new **currency** system and a commitment to balance the budget; there would be no monetizing of the fiscal deficit. At first, the arrangement worked. Order was restored to the fiscal accounts, though a balanced budget eluded Cavallo and his successors. Privatization facilitated debt reduction and financed current expenditure. Resources were passed to the provinces as a sweetener to pursue structural reform and fund social projects. Foreign capital flowed in, despite initial reservations by the

International Monetary Fund (IMF) about convertibility; the economy stabilized and boomed. Public confidence in the administration and political support grew; the PJ increased its majority in the **congressional elections of 1993**, and with the **Olivos Pact**, Menem engineered constitutional change. The **Constitution of 1994** enabled him to stand for immediate reelection in 1995. Menem endeavored to finesse constitutional change to stand again in 1999 but was prevented from doing so.

Despite a number of challenges, including a late 1994 currency crisis in Mexico, the resignation of Cavallo in 1996, financial panic in Asia in 1997, and again in Russia the following year, the Argentine economy appeared stable, notwithstanding a steady accumulation of debt. Such apparent economic achievements were matched by developments on the world stage. There was a rapprochement with the **United States** orchestrated by Menem's Anglophile minister of foreign affairs, **Guido Di Tella**. Argentina participated in **United Nations** peacekeeping operations and sent forces to the Middle East during the First Gulf War. Relations with **Great Britain** improved as the two countries agreed to differ about the sovereignty of the **Falkland Islands** while collaborating in other areas. The world image of the country, which had begun to improve under Alfonsín, was further enhanced. If the image of the administration improved overseas, it deteriorated domestically. On the pretext of strengthening the Supreme Court in order to cope with anticipated legal challenges arising from government economic policy, especially privatization and the appointment of regulators intended to oversee privatized public utilities, the court was packed. Changes introduced by the 1994 constitution also facilitated manipulation, for example, an increase from two to three in the number of national senators allotted each province and the immediate reelection of provincial governors. Menem's efforts at national reconciliation—intended to continue what had been achieved by his predecessor—were also flawed: pardons handed out to convicted members of the Proceso juntas were unpopular. Despite the pardons, however, Menem reacted firmly when threatened with barrack revolts similar to those that had occurred during the Alfonsín term. With the support of the high command, renewed *carapintada* protest led by Colonel **Mohamed Alí Seineldín** was rapidly scotched. Menem's efforts to control the PJ were less successful, resulting in an exodus from the party, particularly ambitious young reformers, and a strengthening of anti-Menem traditionalists headed by **Eduardo Duhalde**, Menem's former vice president and governor of the province of Buenos Aires. True to Peronist traditions, Menem had encouraged talent only to constrain and exclude when rising stars posed a threat. Arguably, the most delicate event that confronted the regime was the terrorist attack on the Israeli embassy in 1992, claimed by Hezbollah in reprisal for the country's participation in the First Gulf War, and a similar attack on the Jewish Mutual Aid Society headquarters two years later that left 85 dead and many injured.

Yet it was **corruption**, which contributed to the unraveling of convertibility, that remains Menem's principal legacy. As early as 1993, **Gustavo Béliz**, Menem's youthful and well-regarded interior minister, had resigned, claiming that the president was surrounded by crooks. Three years later, Cavallo resigned, denouncing mafias who were frustrating economic reform, presumably cronies protected by the president. The principal charges of corruption during Menem's presidencies involved various devices employed to cream off funds from privatization deals, bribes demanded by his entourage for the awarding of state contracts, drug trafficking and money laundering, shady business deals with associates who enjoyed police protection and immunity from prosecution—notably, **Alfredo Yabrán**. Many scams were said to involve the family of his first wife, while the mysterious death of their son in a helicopter crash in 1995 was attributed to a money-laundering deal gone wrong with Colombian drug barons. The frequency of such scandals and the proliferation of charges of corruption caused public disgust and defeat for the administration in the **congressional elections of 1997**, a defeat that emboldened the opposition and dissident factions within the PJ and put pay to any chance of a presidential comeback in 2003.

Since leaving the **Casa Rosada**, a number of charges have been brought against Menem, including illicit arms dealing, the embezzlement of public funds, and benefiting from kickbacks. In 2001, he was briefly held under house arrest. To date, he is the only president to have received a custodial sentence. He was elected national senator for his province in 2005, a position that he currently holds. Apart from rampant corruption, Menem is most remembered for the Convertibility Plan and the waves of privatization associated with it, for dubious contacts with key **military** figures of the Proceso (despite being incarcerated by the generals), and for a colorful private life. In 2013, following a ruling by the Court of Appeal, Menem was sentenced to a seven-year jail term. However, while he holds public office, he is protected from imprisonment. At the moment, as a sitting national senator, only the Senate can remove his immunity from imprisonment even though the conviction stands. The Menem presidencies are regarded as the second most venal in modern Argentine political history, trumped only by the Kirchners. *See also* CORACH, CARLOS VLADIMIRO (1935–); ECONOMIC CRISES; FOREIGN DEBT/FOREIGN INVESTMENT; FOREIGN TRADE; MENEM, EDUARDO (1938–); MENEM, ZULEMA FÁTIMA YOMA DE (1942–).

MENEM, EDUARDO (1938–). Politician, senior member of the **Partido Justicialista** (PJ) elected four times to the national senate to represent his home province of **La Rioja**; younger brother of former president **Carlos Saúl Menem**.

While **Carlos Corach** was Carlos Menem's main political fixer and confidant, Eduardo was the member of the family trusted to look after their interests in La Rioja, a province that they regarded as their own. He served four consecutive terms as senator for La Rioja between 1983 and 2005, the year that he gave way to older brother Carlos Saúl. Carlos Saúl's election as senator for La Rioja in 2005 ensured that he would be immune from imprisonment on charges of **corruption** while holding high political office. When **Eduardo Duhalde** resigned as Carlos Menem's vice president in 1991, Eduardo Menem became acting president of the Senate, second in the line of presidential succession, a position that meant that he represented his brother as head of state during the latter's frequent official visits overseas. In 1994, Eduardo chaired the constituent assembly that drew up the **Constitution of 1994**. The adoption of the new constitution allowed Carlos Saúl Menem to run for a second consecutive term in the **presidential election of 1995**. When the PJ split during the administration of President **Néstor Kirchner**, Eduardo joined the anti-Kirchner wing of the party, becoming a thorn in the side of Néstor and his wife and successor as president, **Cristina Fernández de Kirchner**. Eduardo remains a stalwart defender of brother Carlos and continues as a prominent political figure despite not holding any public office. *See also* OLIVOS PACT.

MENEM, ZULEMA FÁTIMA YOMA DE (1942–). Born in the province of **La Rioja** to a family of Syrian origin; first wife of President **Carlos Saúl Menem** and first lady of the republic until the couple divorced. The marriage had been arranged by the couple's respective parents in 1966; they separated in 1991—their daughter Zulema ("Zulemita") María Eva Menem acted as first lady from 1991 until 1999.

It is said that Zulema never fully accepted her husband's conversion to Roman Catholicism. Years after the separation, further strain was put on the relationship between the former couple after the death of their son Carlos Saúl Facundo Menem in an air crash in 1995—the crash was declared an accident, but some argued that the death was politically motivated. President Menem refused to initiate further investigation. Relations between the former couple became even more tense when Menem married former Chilean beauty queen and winner of the 1987 Miss Universe contest Cecilia Bolocco in 2001. At the time, he was 70 and she 36. The couple later had a son, Máximo Saúl Menem Bolocco, in 2003; they separated in 2007 and divorced in 2011. Reputedly the power behind the throne, Zulema had kept a fairly low profile for most of her marriage, largely confining herself to performing official duties when her husband held various offices. Modeling public appearances on **Eva Perón**, she cut a glamorous image. Despite reports that the marriage was in difficulty, and had been for years, Zulema was always resolute in her support for Menem in public. She campaigned for him in advance of the

presidential election of 1989 and defended his changing political agenda when in office, notwithstanding political differences between them. She was equally vociferous in rebutting charges of **corruption** leveled against his administration. However, following the death of Carlos Saúl Facundo and Menem's second marriage, Zulema assumed a less supportive public profile, a position that was often interpreted as critical of her former husband, including his attitude to abortion and dealings with the army. *See also* SEINELDÍN, MOHAMED ALÍ (1933–2009).

MENEMATO. Derived from *peronato*, the word applies to the presidencies of **Carlos Saúl Menem** (1989–1999) and his system of government, which echoed the personalist style of **Juan Domingo Perón** and which became increasingly corrupt and, according to critics, undemocratic. *See also* *KIRCHNERATO.*

MENÉNDEZ, LUCIANO BENJAMÍN (1927–2018). As head of the Third Army Corps (1975–1979), he played a prominent part during the **War to Annihilate Subversion**. The youngest general in recent Argentine military history; when promoted in 1972 by de facto president **Alejandro Agustín Lanusse**, he was only 45 years old.

He was in charge of La Perla, the most important clandestine detention center in the province of **Córdoba**. In terms of size, character, and capacity, La Perla was comparable only to the **Escuela Superior de Mecánica de la Armada** (ESMA); it is estimated that over 2,200 people passed through it between the **military coup of 1976** and the end of 1979. La Perla coordinated illegal repressive activity in Córdoba, with disappearances hundreds of kilometers away being planned and ordered there, and it also handled links with the other clandestine detention centers in the rest of the country. This enabled Menéndez to direct repressive actions in 10 provinces and earned him the sobriquet "La Hiena de La Perla" (the Hyena of the Pearl).

Following the return of democracy, Menéndez was detained over various cases of repression by the Third Army Corps. However, days before his trial was due to begin, he became one of the senior **military** officers pardoned by President **Carlos Saúl Menem**. In 2006, the Supreme Court declared his pardon unconstitutional, and in 2008 Menéndez faced the first of many trials. He took responsibility for all actions that occurred under his jurisdiction and was sentenced to life imprisonment. He was again condemned to life imprisonment in trials held in 2009, 2010, 2014, and 2016. Stripped of his military titles, Menéndez spent virtually the rest of his life in prison; he died in the military hospital in Córdoba, to which he had been transferred a few days before his death. *See also* COMISIÓN NACIONAL SOBRE LA DESAPARACIÓN DE PERSONAS (CONADEP); DESAPARECIDOS; DIRTY WAR; DISPOSICIÓN FINAL; HUMAN RIGHTS; *NUNCA MÁS*.

MENÉNDEZ, MARIO BENJAMÍN (1927–2018). Cousin of notorious general **Luciano Benjamín Menéndez**; appointed governor of the **Falkland Islands** by de facto president **Leopoldo Galtieri**, who described him as the best general in the army. He served as governor between 3 April and 14 June 1982, when he surrendered to British forces, defying final telephone instruction from Galtieri. *See also* FALKLANDS DISPUTE; FALKLANDS WAR (2 APRIL–14 JUNE 1982); GREAT BRITAIN; MILITARY.

MERCANTE, DOMINGO ALFREDO (1898–1976). A leading Peronist figure and governor of the province of **Buenos Aires** (1946–1952). He was a **military** officer who developed a deep bond with **Juan Domingo Perón** from 1941, with both men being stationed in **Mendoza** and subsequently in the inspectorate of mountain troops in Buenos Aires. A key figure in the **Grupo de Oficiales Unidos** (GOU), Mercante was Perón's main ally in promoting prolabor policies following the **military coup of 1943**. After the failed attempt to contain Perón in October 1945, Mercante was rewarded with the post of secretary of labor and social welfare. The Secretariat of Labor had a primary role in the creation of the **Partido Laborista** (PL), which became the vehicle behind Perón in the **presidential election of 1946** and backed Mercante's candidacy for governorship of the province of Buenos Aires. Winning the election, Mercante served as governor during Perón's first presidency. His administration is regarded as one of the most effective the province has ever had and promoted numerous necessary public works. He always sought consensus with the opposition in the provincial legislature and often found himself at odds with the national government. Differences arose from the 1946 financial reform and its implications for the autonomy of both the **Banco de la Provincia de Buenos Aires** and the province itself, and from the encouragement of **agriculture** at a time when the central government was focusing on the promotion of **industry**.

The year 1949 marked the high point of Mercante's career: he presided over the constituent assembly convened to reform the **Constitution of 1853**. Nevertheless, he incurred the wrath of the president and First Lady **Eva Perón** by not supporting a change to the article that prohibited presidential reelection. The change was made, and Mercante and Perón quickly parted ways once the new constitution was approved. Mercante lost the internal support of the **Partido Peronista** (PP) but at no point considered openly confronting the president. He was expelled from the party in 1953 for alleged obstructionism, disloyalty, and unethical conduct.

Mercante went into self-imposed exiled in **Uruguay** during the de facto regime of 1955–1958, unsuccessfully attempting to return to politics in the ranks of the neo-Peronist **Unión Popular** (UP) in the 1960s. He died one month before the **military coup of 1976**. *See also* CONSTITUTION OF 1949; MINISTRY OF SOCIAL DEVELOPMENT.

MERCOSUR. In Spanish, Mercado Común del Sur; in Portuguese, Mercado Comun do Sul; always known as MERCOSUR, or as the South American Common Market, in English. The name reflects an ambitious objective, consciously modeled on the European Common Market. The organization originates in a project for Argentine–Brazilian economic cooperation and integration devised by President **Raúl Alfonsín** and his Brazilian counterpart, José Sarney. Both countries were emerging from periods of **military** rule during the debt crisis of the 1980s. Alfonsín viewed the project as a means of consolidating democracy though mutual political and economic support. Although for Alfonsín the original purpose was largely politically driven, he recognized the importance of the economic imperative. With the two countries heavily in debt and the global economy stagnating, regional collaboration was seen as an alternative route to recovery and growth—a necessity even. As the world economy was flatlining, there was little to lose from closer regional economic integration. Collaboration and regional growth might compensate for the lack of dynamism in the international system. If the regional project could reboot the Argentine and Brazilian economies, such growth would also help sustain democracy. Supporters of the project with longer-term perspectives argued that successful regional integration would better prepare the countries for a stronger insertion into the world economy when the global system recovered. A dynamic bloc would be more attractive to foreign investors and be better able to negotiate trade deals. Regional economic integration was a stepping stone to more effective participation in the international economy. This was designed to silence critics who argued that regional integration and global economic engagement were alternatives, not substitutes, and that openness to the world economy offered the best prospects for growth in the long run rather than regional projects.

While the arrangement was conceived as a bilateral agreement between the two largest South American countries, **Uruguay** requested inclusion, initiating the transition to a larger regional bloc. MERCOSUR was formally established by the Treaty of Asuncíon, signed in 1991, complimented by the Protocol of Ouro Preto, effected three years later. The founding members were Argentina, **Brazil, Paraguay**, and Uruguay. The emphasis on economic integration was sustained by the emergence of Washington Consensus–style market liberalization in member countries, by the Europe model, and by the perceived lack of success of earlier experiments at closer economic cooperation in Latin America narrowly based on free trade. The Latin American Free

Trade Association (LAFTA), formed in 1960, which had appeared successful in its earlier years, hit the buffers around 1970 and was diluted 10 years later. By tackling issues of economic harmonization from the outset, supporters of MERCOSUR hoped that it would avoid the same fate. There have been problems with economic integration among member countries, but the project has delivered a substantial growth in trade among the original members, the integration of production chains in key sectors, such as motor vehicle production, and substantial collaborations in educational and cultural fields. In part, this has been due to political commitment among domestic political and business elites.

There have been problems. One early difficulty arose in harmonizing internal tariffs in what had been reserved areas—special-interest sectors were granted additional time to adjust to the timetable for the creation of a common internal tariff and reduction in internal tariffs. The time frame for harmonization was extended in such areas as motor vehicles and components, sugar, and other **commodities**. Argentina has been in dispute with Uruguay about the siting of a cellulose plant, which disrupted cross-border trade between the two countries—a simmering dispute that began during the presidency of **Néstor Kirchner** and lasted for much of the second administration of President **Cristina Fernández de Kirchner**. As with the European project, membership was only open to democracies, a condition that has also caused difficulties. Paraguay was briefly suspended in 2012 following the impeachment and removal of the president. Even more problematic has been **Venezuela**. The country, which applied to join in 2006 yet was only formally admitted in 2012, was suspended in 2016 when the administration of President Nicolás Maduro was accused of **human rights** violations. In 2017, the suspension was made indefinite. **Bolivia** became a full member in 2015, having been an associate member for several years.

The achievements of MERCOSUR are reflected in agreements with other countries and blocs. In 1999, the European Union (EU) and MERCOSUR signed a framework agreement for interregional cooperation designed to harmonize existing bilateral trade arrangements between member countries of the two blocs. Viewed as potentially prefiguring a comprehensive free trade agreement, negotiations stalled. Relaunched in 2010, paused in 2012, there was progress by 2016. At that point, the EU was the most important trading partner of MERCOSUR, accounting for around 22 percent of total **foreign trade** (imports and exports). The EU was the principal source of foreign investment in the bloc, but this is not a one-way street; MERCOSUR companies have substantial investments in Europe. While outline agreements exist in several areas, major problems have to be resolved before the full implementation of free trade between the blocs. European producers of animal products and biofuels (especially those derived from sugar) complain of unfair competition by MERCOSUR suppliers; motor vehicle manufacturers in South America lobby against granting easier access to European firms. Although outstanding areas of difference involve more than beef and cars, in 2018 there was optimism that problems could be resolved and that freer trade and trade growth follow. In 2005, MERCOSUR signed an accord with the Andean Community, giving member countries virtual associated status. **Chile** was invited by MERCOSUR to enter an arrangement proximate to associate status in 1991; Chile declined, arguing that this would limit the country's ability to arrange trade and financial deals with other countries, yet had negotiated a special arrangement by 1996. MERCOSUR and Mexico agreed in 2002 to an arrangement that would facilitate trade deals between Mexico and individual member countries—deals now cover a range of items and virtually all countries of the bloc. Several Caribbean and trans-Pacific countries have observer status.

Notwithstanding continuing political differences among member states, a clamor for special treatment by commodity producers and strategic industries in the larger economies, and periodic imposition of "antidumping" bans and "temporary" tariff hikes, MERCOSUR is a successful trade bloc in the process of becoming a functioning customs union. There have been important moves to integrate the transport infrastructure, especially in the River Plate basin, southern Brazil, and Argentine **Mesopotamia**. And there have been achievements in coordinating **agriculture** and industrial policy and collaborating in such areas as energy supply and technology. The organization has a permanent headquarters in the Uruguayan capital, Montevideo. There are functioning subcommittees charged with facilitating closer integration. The organization is supported by a political structure, notably a parliament that has been functioning since 2004. There have also been limited discussions about establishing a common **currency**. Trade integration, however, has been the principal success and has developed apace. While Brazil is an outlier, with the bloc only accounting for about 10 percent of total trade, there is a much higher degree of bloc integration among other members. In recent years, between one-third and one-half of all Uruguayan trade is intrabloc, between a third and two-fifths of Paraguayan, and between a quarter and a third of Argentine. *See also* ECONOMY; INDUSTRY; TRANSPORTATION; UNIÓN DE NACIONES SURAMERICANAS (UNASUR); UNITED STATES OF AMERICA.

MESOPOTAMIA. Named as such by a 19th-century explorer, Argentine Mesopotamia lies between the **Paraná** and **Uruguay** Rivers and is composed of the provinces of **Entre Ríos**, **Corrientes**, and **Misiones**. It is a well-watered, rich agricultural region, comprising rolling **pampas**, temperate in the south and subtropical in the north. The region has a well-developed pastoral sector and a modern fruit producing industry, renowned for the quality of its citrus, stone fruit, and fruit juices. The production of **yerba**

mate (Paraguayan tea) is centered on Mesopotamia. In the early 19th century, from time to time, the area functioned as a semiseparate political entity, sometimes associated with **Uruguay** or neighboring Argentine provinces on the west bank of the Paraná. *See also* AGRICULTURE; COMMODITIES; FOREIGN TRADE; INDUSTRY.

MESSI, LIONEL ANDRÉS (1987–). Known as Lionel Messi, or simply Messi—nicknamed "La Pulga" or "El Pulgarcito" (the Flea or the Little Flea) due to of his diminutive stature. Born in the city of **Rosario**, Messi is reputed to be the richest and best soccer player in the world—claims that might be challenged by Portuguese player Cristiano Ronaldo. Undeniably the most internationally recognized Argentine footballer, outshining even **Diego Maradona**, he has become a "brand" and style icon, endorsing such products as Adidas, Dolce & Gabbana, and Pepsi. He plays for Barcelona. He signed for the club in 2001, when he was 13, joining the Barcelona Youth Academy (La Masia). His first appearance for the senior team was in 2004. He has appeared frequently for the Argentine national soccer team—he is the national team's leading all-time goal scorer and has represented his country at all major international tournaments. He has captained the national side since 2011 and received innumerable national and international awards, a frequent recipient of such trophies as the Ballon d'Or and Golden Shoe and titles like World Player of the Year, World Young Player of the Year, Best Soccer Player of the Year, Best Forward of the Year, and Best Team Player of the Year. Reputed to be worth US$340,000,000 in 2018, his financial affairs were subject to an official investigation in 2013; three years later, he and his father, who is his manager, were convicted of tax evasion. He is likely to retire from international football in 2018 but is expected to remain a leading club player for years.

MESTIZO. Word coined in colonial Latin America referring to a person of mixed race—European and Indian—a racial category established in the "sistema de castas," a table detailing racial hierarchy, with distinct legal and social implications. At **independence**, equality before the law was declared for all nonslaves. Subsequently, it has been used as a derogatory descriptor.

MIGUEL, LORENZO MARCELO (1927–2002). Prominent labor leader closely linked to the Unión Obrera Metalúrgica (UOM). Having joined the workforce of the metallurgical firm CAMEA in 1945, he was elected shop steward by his coworkers seven years later and brought to the attention of the leadership of the UOM, a **trade union** with increasing clout within the **Confederación General del Trabajo** (CGT).

Union activity was suspended following the **military coup of 1955**, which overthrew **Juan Domingo Perón**. Once the CGT was relegalized by President **Arturo Frondizi** in 1961, the UOM elected **Augusto Vandor** as leader and Miguel as treasurer. Following the assassination of Vandor in 1969 and an acrimonious power struggle, Miguel became secretary general of the UOM in March 1970. He used this victory to advance his rival **José Ignacio Rucci** as secretary general of the CGT, thereby preventing a leftist takeover of the organization and gaining a new ally in the process.

Opposition to leftists within the Peronist movement intensified after the **presidential election of March 1973**. Miguel found common cause with the all-too-powerful minister of social welfare **Jose López Rega** and his newly established death squad **Triple A**. Their ties were exposed on 20 June 1973, when UOM heavies reportedly assisted the Triple A in the **Ezeiza Massacre**. Miguel then helped persuade an aging President Perón to promote a personal friend, the right-wing admiral **Emilio Massera**, head of the navy, as well as to break with the Peronist left—which Perón did two months before his death in July 1974. Miguel's alliance with López Rega became strained when President **Isabel Perón** appointed **Celestino Rodrigo** as minister of economy in June 1975. The introduction of a highly controversial massive economic adjustment program (the **Rodrigazo**) led both the UOM and the CGT to call a general strike—for the first time ever against a Peronist government—thereby triggering the downfall of both Rodrigo and López Rega in July 1975.

Following the **military coup of 1976**, Miguel was arrested together with the president and thousands of others. His friendship with Massera, now the second-highest ranking man in the new Argentine leadership, protected him from torture. Nevertheless, Miguel had his accounts frozen and spent three years in prison and another under house arrest. He emerged from his reclusion in 1980 and severed his ties with Massera.

Miguel became a vocal opponent of the **military** regime, which was mired in severe economic difficulties and collapsed in the aftermath of the **Falklands War**, and backed the nomination of former National Senate leader **Ítalo Luder** as the candidate in the failed Peronist attempt to win the **presidential election of 1983**. Miguel then supported the candidacy of **Carlos Saúl Menem** in the successful Peronist bid to win the **presidential election of 1989**. He soon found himself at odds with Menem's policies, but his influence was waning. Industrial action at the **Sociedad Mixta Siderúrgica Argentina** (SOMISA) steelworks in 1991 failed to prevent the complex's scheduled **privatization**. *See also* DIRTY WAR; MINISTRY OF SOCIAL DEVELOPMENT; PROCESO DE REORGANIZACIÓN NACIONAL; STATE-OWNED ENTERPRISES (SOEs); WAR TO ANNIHILATE SUBVERSION.

MILITARY. The armed forces (in Spanish, *fuerzas armadas*) trace their origin to the **independence** period, beginning with the **British invasions**, the **May Revolution of 1810**, and efforts to preserve the territorial integrity of the successor state to the **Viceroyalty of the River Plate**. The earliest formations of the army were the **Patricios**, the first line regiment formed in 1806, and the mounted grenadiers created by General **José de San Martín** in 1812, later known as the **Granaderos a Caballo General San Martín**. The navy originates from a squadron formed in 1811, essentially a small force cobbled together to protect the port of **Buenos Aires** from attack by Spanish military and naval units based in Montevideo and to disrupt communications between Montevideo and upriver royalist garrisons.

The armed forces were further shaped by the civil wars of the early national period. In 1829, **Juan Manuel de Rosas**—who commanded **gaucho** militias—disbanded the regular army after his victory in the civil conflict of the time. He regarded the army as a hotbed of **Unitarian**, centralist sentiment. Until the 1850s, land forces consisted of irregular units nominally organized by provincial governments, in reality loyal to the local **caudillos**. The navy also suffered under Rosas, and it was insufficiently powerful to challenge Anglo-French blockades between 1838 and 1840. The fortunes of both services changed when **Justo José de Urquiza** ousted Rosas in 1852. The army was reconstituted in the 1850s, and with Urquiza keen to strengthen Argentine command of upriver territories, money was ploughed into the navy. Argentina successfully fought against **Paraguay** in the **War of the Triple Alliance**.

The army and navy did not assume modern shape until the end of the 19th century; the air force was not formed until 1945. Although a Military Academy was established in 1870, modernization and professionalization did not take place until the 1880s, under the auspices of **Julio A. Roca**. Both services benefited from investment in new technology. The influence of the 1899 Prussian military mission on the army was particularly important, as was conscription (introduced in 1901 and abolished in 1995) and the creation of the Superior War School in 1900. Both the army and the navy continued to modernize as the 20th century progressed, with purchases in **Great Britain** and elsewhere, but increasingly from the **United States**. This would also be true of the air force when it came into being after the Second World War.

The military became notorious for intervening in politics during the 20th century, initially claiming that such action was taken as the result of an abuse of power by civilian administrations and later in order to "reconstruct" society in the wake of economic chaos caused by politicians. Yet for almost a century following independence, the armed forces were firmly under civilian control. Although many key politicians of the pre-1930 period performed prominent military roles (for example, **Manuel Belgrano**, **Bartolomé Mitre**, and **Domingo Faustino Sarmiento**), these were more intellectuals and political thinkers who took up arms to advance a particular project than generals turned politicians. Even Rosas and Roca, who are often depicted as the principal military men of their respective ages, would have considered themselves primarily as statesmen and political strategists. Much the same could be said of **Juan Domingo Perón**. The tradition of civilian control of the military derived from San Martín, who argued that the forces should not intervene in politics, a philosophy that was enshrined in the **Constitution of 1853**.

The **military coup of 1930** was the start of more than a half a century of military intervention in Argentine politics. Five subsequent successful coups took place in that period, with the nature of the interventions changing over time. In 1930, as was the case with the **military coup of 1943** and the **military coup of 1955**, it was claimed that the military acted as a result of an abuse of power by the civilian governments headed respectively by **Hipólito Yrigoyen**, **Ramón S. Castillo**, and Perón himself. Thereafter, the stated objective of military intervention was to transform economy and society in order to stabilize politics. Perón's success in politics derived from his control of the labor movement; support by the **trade unions** contributed to his triumph in the **presidential election of 1946**. This had major consequences for Argentina in the second half of the 20th century: Peronism deeply polarized the country. In addition to the principal military interventions of 1930, 1943, 1955, 1966, and 1976, there were repeated "palace coups" as one faction of the military ousted a fellow officer installed by a different group, or as a sitting de facto president lost the confidence of officers who had initially supported him. In the main, such "coups within coups" reflected disagreement about how to deal with Perón and Peronism.

Following the overthrow of Perón in 1955, alternating military and civilian administrations—the latter closely watched by the army—proved incapable of handling Peronism and the fact that it was there to stay. Notwithstanding the restoration of restricted democracy and a degree of tolerance toward neo-Peronist parties (a **"Peronism without Perón"**), Perón still managed to exert political influence while in exile. When it called general elections for 1958, the de facto regime of **Pedro Eugenio Aramburu** hoped that **Ricardo Balbín** and his **Unión Cívica Radical del Pueblo** (UCRP) would win and that allowing neo-Peronists to participate would fragment the Peronist vote. Perón did not fall into that trap and, as a result of the **Caracas Pact**, succeeded in getting his supporters to vote for **Arturo Frondizi** and the **Unión Cívica Radical Intransigente** (UCRI). Frondizi was mistrusted by the ever-watchful military, yet he misguidedly managed to convince them to permit candidates from neo-Peronist parties to contest the gubernatorial and **congressional elections of 1962** on the grounds that such parties would not triumph and that the electoral failure of neo-Peronist parties would serve to destroy the myth of Perón's power. The gamble backfired spectacularly, triggering the **military coup of 1962**.

During the presidency of **José María Guido**, the military was deeply divided, splitting into the *azules* and *colorados* factions—divisions that resulted on open warfare. The *azules* favored institutional normalization; the *colorados* demanded the total eradication of Peronism. *Azules* maintained that a "tamed" (or contained) Peronism would act as a bulwark against the extreme left. Open confrontation in April 1963 resulted in the victory of the *azules*, at the cost of 24 dead and 87 injured on both sides, and the nomination of **Juan Carlos Onganía** as head of the army. General elections were held in 1963; Peronism was proscribed, and **Arturo Illia** of the UCRP was elected president. By this time, Perón was facing a severe challenge for the leadership of his movement from trade union boss **Augusto Vandor**, and Illia successfully resisted pressure from the military and anti-Peronists to prevent the neo-Peronist **Unión Popular** (UP) and its Vandorista allies from fielding candidates in the **congressional elections of 1965**. The UP performed strongly, and the struggle between Perón and Vandor had been resolved in favor of the former by early 1966.

In the mid-1960s, Argentina was threatened by internal subversion supported by revolutionary **Cuba**. With cold war tension on the increase, the doctrine of national security gained traction in Argentina and elsewhere in the Americas, identifying subversive "youth culture" and leftist proponents of armed struggle as the "threat from within." In this climate, the military saw itself as the only actor capable of saving the country. Onganía resigned as commander-in-chief of the army in 1965 and became the main proponent of the ethos of national security. He stated that the principal mission of the military was "the preservation of the moral and spiritual values of the Western and Christian civilization" and that if "democracy does not guarantee those objectives," the armed forces should displace popularly elected governments and take power. Despite having been part of the *azules* faction of the army that had sought institutional normalization in 1963, Onganía prepared a "national revolution" project as disillusionment with the Illia government, and civilian politicians in general, grew. The result was the **military coup of 1966**.

The de facto **Revolución Argentina** regime (1966–1973) was the forerunner of the more extreme **Proceso de Reorganización Nacional** that followed the **military coup of 1976**. Both projects did not have time limits and had transformative aims. The Revolución Argentina stressed *tres tiempos*, a three-phase program dealing first with the **economy**, then with social issues, and finally with political institutional stabilization. This compartmentalization proved unworkable, and to make matters worse the country was beginning to be racked by terrorism—particularly from the **Montoneros** and **Ejér-**

cito Revolucionario del Pueblo. The de facto government was forced to find an electoral exit and allow Peronists to contest the general elections held in March 1973. At the same time, the regime tried to deal with subversion by setting up military tribunals to try those charged with crimes of subversion and terrorism, arguing that due process was essential but that the regular courts were not up to the job. Many were tried, convicted, and jailed. In addition, in an attempt to forestall a Peronist landslide in the upcoming **congressional** and **presidential elections of March 1973**, the electoral system was changed by **Law No. 19.862** of October 1972. The principal innovations included the introduction of a two-round arrangement for the presidential contest (should no candidate obtain half the total votes cast, the top two candidates would proceed to a runoff); the introduction of direct elections for the National Senate (previously senators had been elected by provincial legislatures); and the establishment of a single list system, meaning that voters had to cast their ballot for a single party or alliance, thereby being prevented from splitting there votes for candidates of different parties in distinct electoral contests. In the event, the Peronist alliance, the **Frente Justicialista de Liberación** (FREJULI), triumphed: President **Héctor Cámpora** took office in May 1973. His first act was to free all those jailed by military tribunals.

After the collapse of the 1966 regime, the crisis of constitutional government, the insufficiency of politicians, the challenge of terrorism, and popular fears of a descent into chaos enabled the military to accumulate enormous power. Though the overthrow of **Isabel Perón** in 1976 was initially greeted with relief by large sections of society, public support for the Proceso would not last. The military argued that only they were able to resolve the evils besetting the country once and for all and were convinced that they could do practically anything they wanted without having to establish a consensus. Here lay the fundamental flaws of their project.

The Proceso imposed top-down solutions by force. It aimed to free Argentina from its "scourges" by "disciplining an anarchized society" and founding a "new economic model" that would allow the country to achieve its manifest destiny. The specific objectives were to move beyond the "demagogic populism" of Peronism, which was unbeatable at the ballot box; to discipline labor organizations, which were perceived as an "exacerbated and irrational" power factor; to move toward a liberal, market economy, epitomized and implemented by Minister of Economy **José Alfredo Martínez de Hoz**; and to extirpate the virus of the left, including radical influences in the arts and culture. The successful implementation of the program required popular acquiescence to its elements and objectives, and this ultimately contributed to the undoing of the project and the Proceso. The brutally murderous **War to Annihilate Subversion** would be the backdrop to adjustments in the economy, though austerity measures were tempered by the need to avoid alienating the population at large, whose continuing support or passivity the military understood to be crucial. Yet within a few years, the regime had become unpopular, largely because of dislocation caused by economic reform and the violation of **human rights**. Matters were aggravated by the foreign policy of the dictatorship. Rivalry with **Brazil** resulted in periodic arms races and disputes over hydroelectric power use on the **Paraná** River; Argentina and **Chile** got to the brink of war over the **Beagle Channel Dispute** in 1978. Having avoided one war with a neighboring country, the regime then embarked on the disastrous **Falklands War** in 1982. This led to the undignified end of the Proceso and, following the return of democracy in 1983, the military was put in their place and decimated. Although the air force acquitted itself well in the Falklands War, the navy scuttled back to port after the sinking of the **ARA** *General Belgrano* and the army was held to have performed disastrously, and heroic action by individual pilots did little to protect the reputation of the air force in particular or the armed forces in general. The reputation of the military was further tarnished by the treatment of war veterans, most of whom were conscripts.

The elected government of **Raúl Alfonsín** undertook the **trials of the military juntas**, though it also imposed time limits on legal processes and sought to protect lower ranks through the **Ley de Punto Final** and **Ley de Obediencia Debida**. Alfonsín's successor, **Carlos Saúl Menem**, granted pardons to the senior officers, but cases against the military began to be reopened toward the end of his administration. Justice over the issue of human rights was brought to the fore thereafter. **Néstor Kirchner** overturned the limits and pardons arranged by Alfonsín and Menem on constitutional grounds; major new trials and retrials took place during his presidency and that of his wife and successor, **Cristina Fernández de Kirchner**, resulting in the conviction of senior figures of the Proceso years.

Successive civilian administrations since 1983 have curtailed military spending. It has fallen from 3.5 percent of GDP in 1978 to less than 1 percent in 2016. Little of the money goes toward arms and equipment. The **Ministry of Defense** spends around 70 percent of its budget on wages and pensions. Argentina compounds stinginess with inefficiency—each branch of the armed services runs a separate base in Antarctica—and austerity has often caused embarrassment. In 2013, the destroyer ARA *Santísima Trinidad* keeled over in harbor. The following year, lacking resources, the submarine fleet spent just 19 hours underwater. And in 2015, aging fighter aircraft could not fly on cloudy days because of problems with their instruments. The **ARA** *San Juan*, the most modern of the navy's three submarines, disappeared with 44 crew on board in November 2017. It was refitted during the presidency of Mrs. Kirchner, but there is evidence that the bidding process for a contract to replace batteries contained "irregularities" in order to favor certain suppliers. Faulty batteries are thought to have caused explosions detected around the time and place of the disappearance of the submarine.

The role of the armed forces, which are currently 105,000 strong, has come into question. Their cold war–era weaponry is designed to counter conventional threats that no longer exist; the country is on good terms with its neighbors. As the eighth largest nation in the world, Argentina needs fighter jets, ships, and submarines to deter potential enemies and protect extensive land and sea frontiers, yet the armed forces also need to be equipped to deal with modern threats to national sovereignty and security like international terrorism and drug trafficking, and even mundane matters such as illegal fishing in territorial waters. The modern Argentine military is ill equipped for such tasks. Moreover, a change in the law would be required in order for the armed forces to be mobilized in support of civil authorities to combat threats from international terrorists or drug traffickers on Argentine soil. In 2006, Néstor Kirchner decreed that the armed forces could only be used to confront "external aggression," supposedly in an attempt to prevent another military coup. Although President **Mauricio Macri** (elected in 2015) has argued that the Kirchner decree is too restrictive, any change in the law is unlikely for the moment. See also ACOSTA, JORGE EDUARDO (1941–); AGOSTI, ORLANDO RAMÓN (1924–1997); ALSOGARAY, ÁLVARO (1913–2005); ALSOGARAY, JULIO RODOLFO (1918–1994); ANAYA, JORGE ISAAC (1926–2008); ARAMBURAZO (29 MAY–1 JUNE 1970); ARMY OF THE ANDES; ASTIZ, ALFREDO IGNACIO (1951–); BELGRANO, MANUEL JOSÉ JOAQUIN DEL CORAZÓN DE JESÚS (1770–1820); BIGNONE, REYNALDO BENITO (1928–2018); CACCIATORE, OSVALDO (1924–2007); CONQUEST OF THE DESERT/DESERT CAMPAIGN; CORDOBAZO (29 MAY–3 JUNE 1969); COSTA MÉNDEZ, NICANOR (1922–1992); DESAPARECIDOS; DIRTY WAR; DISPOSICIÓN FINAL; ESCUELA SUPERIOR DE MECÁNICA DE LA ARMADA (ESMA); EXECUTIONS OF JUNE 1956; FARRELL, EDELMIRO JULIÁN (1887–1980); GALTIERI, LEOPOLDO FORTUNATO (1926–2003); GRAFFIGNA, OMAR DOMINGO RUBENS (1926–); GRUPO DE OFICIALES UNIDOS (GOU); HARGUINDEGUY, ALBANO EDUARDO (1927–2012); LACOSTE, ALBERTO CARLOS (1929–2004); LAMBRUSCHINI, ARMANDO (1924–2004); LAMI DOZO, BASILIO ARTURO IGNACIO (1929–2017); LANUSSE, ALEJANDRO AGUSTÍN (1918–1996); LEVINGSTON, ROBERTO MARCELO (1920–2015); LONARDI, EDUARDO ERNESTO (1896–1956); MASSERA, EMILIO EDUARDO (1925–2010); MENÉNDEZ, LUCIANO BENJAMÍN (1927–2018); MENÉNDEZ, MARIO BENJAMÍN (1927–2018); PUEYRREDÓN, JUAN MARTÍN DE (1777–1850); RAMÍREZ, PEDRO PABLO (1884–1962); RAWSON, ARTURO (1885–1952); REVOLUCIÓN LIBERTADORA (1955–1958); ROJAS, ISAAC FRANCISCO (1903–1993); SAINT-JEAN, ALFREDO OSCAR (1926–1987); SUÁREZ MASON, CARLOS GUIL-

LERMO (1924–2005); URIBURU, JOSÉ FÉLIX (1864–1932); VIDELA, JORGE RAFAEL (1925–2013); VIOLA, ROBERTO EDUARDO (1924–1994).

MILITARY COUP OF 1930. Struck on 6 September, it ousted President **Hipólito Yrigoyen**, who had been elected at the age of 76 for a second term in 1928. His removal resulted from factors related to his performance as president.

Yrigoyen had done little to tackle the worsening economic crisis caused by the onset of the Great Depression. This was symptomatic of the overall incompetence of his government and resulted in popular discontent and a wish by his own supporters to displace him. Yrigoyen had focused entirely on oil nationalization, a policy aimed at strengthening his party machine and patronage powers. It could only succeed if the Radicals obtained a majority in the National Senate, which required the use of troops in federal interventions in provinces controlled by the opposition. Such a practice alienated the armed forces, which bitterly resented being frequently used for this purpose, and the elites and the opposition parties, who argued that Yrigoyen was attempting to establish a dictatorship. The oil nationalization policy thereby contributed to a serious legitimacy crisis by challenging the federal system and constitutional rights of the provinces and paved the way for the breakdown of the Argentine political system. The coup that ensued would be the first of six, and the one that followed it in 1943 would have momentous consequences. *See also* ECONOMIC CRISES; URIBURU, JOSÉ FÉLIX (1864–1932).

MILITARY COUP OF 1943. Staged on 4 June, it ousted President **Ramón S. Castillo**. The latter triggered it by nominating Robustiano Patrón Costas, the conservative sugar baron of **Salta** province who presided over the National Senate, to succeed him in the elections due in September 1943.

The motives of the **Grupo de Oficiales Unidos** (GOU), the secret military society usually associated with the coup, were purely political. The **Concordancia** had not only lost all moral authority and legitimacy but continued to promote an anachronistic economic model. The GOU disliked a political system based on fraud and feared the loss of prestige the army would suffer if identified with that system; General **Agustin P. Justo**, a former president, had died suddenly in 1943 before he could stand again for election. There was also the issue of Argentine neutrality in the Second World War. Split into pro-Allies and pro-Axis camps, the army supported Castillo's neutrality policy. The fear was a change of course under Patrón Costas. The latter was pro-Allies, and the country could end up involved in the war, not least because of pressure from the **United States**.

The coup terminated the prospect of a Patrón Costas presidency, and the de facto regime that followed had momentous consequences. From its ranks would emerge **Juan Domingo Perón**, founder of the most prominent and enduring modern Argentine political movement. *See also* RAWSON, ARTURO (1885–1952).

MILITARY COUP OF 1951 (FAILED). Somewhat uncoordinated, often referred to as a military putsch and sometimes a military revolt, the main events of the attempted coup occurred toward the end of the first term of President **Juan Domingo Perón**, about six weeks before the **congressional** and **presidential elections of 1951**, scheduled for 11 November.

The immediate context to the failed coup was a sharp economic contraction triggered by declining exports, rising inflation, and labor agitation—notably, a strike by the all-important railway workers—and curbs on press freedom and on opposition parties, coupled with the growing authoritarianism of the regime as Perón prepared to seek reelection. Reelection was permitted by the so-called Peronist **Constitution of 1949**; the **Constitution of 1853**, superseded by the 1949 charter, prohibited the immediate reelection of a sitting president. Toward the end of September, members of the **Unión Cívica Radical** (UCR) marched on **Congress** demanding the restoration of freedom of the press. The government responded by declaring a state of siege on 29 September, followed by martial law and an announcement that any member of the armed forces participating in the revolt would be summarily shot. The **Confederación General del Trabajo** (CGT) called on workers to take to the streets to defend the government. Several members of the UCR and **Partido Socialista** (PS) were arrested, and Navy Minister Enrique García resigned. The government claimed that there was a plot to assassinate Perón and his wife, **Eva Perón**, who was seriously ill and had been prevented by the **military** from standing as vice president in the forthcoming elections. In a radio broadcast from her deathbed, Eva Perón made an impassioned call for workers to defend the regime.

The principal military men associated with the revolt were Army Generals **Eduardo Leonardi**, **Luciano Benjamín Menéndez**, and **Arturo Rawson** and Air Force Generals Samuel Guaycoechea and Guillermo Zinny. Military aircraft dropped leaflets over the center of Buenos Aires signed by Menéndez announcing that the army had risen against the government. Menéndez's premature action on 28 September—he attempted to lead a military column from the Army base at Campo de Mayo to the center of **Buenos Aires** along the lines of that which had initiated the **military coup of 1930**—backfired when it was thwarted by loyalist noncommissioned officers who alerted the government. By 30 September, the revolt had petered out and Perón was firmly in control. Following the putsch, several generals were forcibly retired and around 300 officers imprisoned—some reportedly tortured—and the government reinforced the security apparatus. In addition to the main ringleaders, others who received prison sentences for their involvement in the attempted *golpe* included **Julio Rodolfo Alsogaray** and **Alejandro Agustín Lanusse**.

The 1951 revolt is seen as a precursor of anti-Perón action taken by the navy four years later, when navy aeroplanes bombed the center of Buenos Aires, and the **military coup of 1955**. *See also* ECONOMIC CRISES; FOREIGN TRADE; HUMAN RIGHTS; TRADE UNIONS; UNIÓN FERROVIARIA (UF).

MILITARY COUP OF 1955. It struck on 16 September and ousted **Juan Domingo Perón**, who was serving a second term as president. The issue that proved the catalyst was his decision to challenge the **Catholic Church**, the one institution the regime did not control.

Rooted in a belief that the church was shielding the creation of a new opposition party, the first severe attack was launched in October 1954. Perón accused "some" priests and bishops of sabotaging the government's work. The Peronist majority in **Congress** ensured rapid action—or retaliation: the religious **education** law passed in 1946 was derogated; legislation enacted establishing absolute divorce and according equal legal status to legitimate children and those born out of wedlock; brothels were legalized. Finally, in May 1955, Congress approved a law calling for a constituent assembly to enact the separation of church and state. By then, political opposition coalesced around organizations supporting the church. Fighting for what it regarded as its survival—and the defense of traditional Catholic family values—the church was able to exert considerable influence in a socially conservative country like Argentina and also provided a powerful infrastructure for all those who detested Perón and his system.

On 11 June 1955, the usually innocuous Corpus Christi procession in **Buenos Aires** turned into the largest opposition march since 1946. The burning of the curia and several churches by Peronist mobs in response, with the connivance of the security forces, was followed by a failed bloody putsch by the navy five days later. In an abrupt turn of events, Perón unsuccessfully launched a conciliatory policy toward his opponents on 6 July. Sensing weakness, the opposition hardened its stance. On 27 July, **Arturo Frondizi** of the **Unión Cívica Radical** (UCR) delivered a radio broadcast denouncing the regime's transgressions and implicitly outlining a government program.

At the same time, the armed forces were conspiring under the leadership of General **Pedro Eugenio Aramburu**. With Perón himself now suddenly threatening to annihilate all his enemies, it became a race against time. Fearing tragic consequences, Aramburu declined to commit himself. In stepped General **Eduardo Lonardi**, who accurately foresaw that a strong rebellion anywhere in the country would lead to the regime's collapse. The revolt began in **Córdoba** and ultimately led Perón to head into exile. *See also* MILITARY COUP OF 1951 (FAILED).

MILITARY COUP OF 1962. It struck on 29 March and ousted President **Arturo Frondizi**. The last straw for the armed forces had been his views on **Cuba** and the question of how to deal with Peronism.

The issue of Cuba arose two months before the coup, when Argentina abstained in the vote to expel the island from the Inter-American system at a conference of foreign ministers. This irritated both the **military**, who interpreted it as a shameful display of pro-Castroism, and the **United States**. President John F. Kennedy was intolerant of Argentina's constant refusal to share his own vision of the dangers of the cold war for the continent and accept the dictates of Washington, DC, which only fueled the opposition to Frondizi's Cuban policy in Argentine military circles. So when Buenos Aires did sever relations with Havana in February, the measure was seen as too little and too late for the president's political survival.

More crucial to Frondizi's fate was his handling of Peronism. He had managed to convince senior officers of the armed forces to permit candidates from neo-Peronist parties to contest the legislative and provincial elections to be held on 18 March, on the basis that these outfits would not triumph and thereby serve to destroy the myth of Perón's power. The gamble failed drastically; the military then refused to accept the results, annulled the election, and had interventors installed in most of the provinces where Peronism had won. No one by now was willing to offer the president any support, and he was deposed. *See also* CONGRESSIONAL ELECTIONS OF 1962; GUEVARA, ERNESTO "CHE" (1928–1967); GUIDO, JOSÉ MARÍA (1910–1975); PRESIDENTIAL SUCCESSION OF 1962.

MILITARY COUP OF 1966. It occurred on 28 June and ejected **Arturo Illia**, elected president in 1963. He was perceived as weak and unsuited to the task of preserving "the moral and spiritual values of Western and Christian civilization." In addition, some of his decisions in government were a factor.

As in 1962, there was the question of Peronist participation in politics. In the **congressional elections of 1965**, various neo-Peronist groups had performed well. This boded ill for the gubernatorial elections due in March 1967, with the renewed specter of a Peronist victory in the province of **Buenos Aires** hanging over a government that did nothing to expand its political base.

More crucially, the government made two major mistakes in 1965 when handling matters pertaining to the armed forces. In the aftermath of **United States** intervention in the Dominican Republic, the Argentine government first acceded to a request to join but then withdrew from the proposed inter-American force to bring that country under control. That force was then commanded by a Brazilian general, which irked the army. Illia followed this with the designation of a new secretary of war, notwithstanding objections from Commander-in-Chief General **Juan Carlos Onganía**. In protest, Onganía insisted on stepping down.

Freed from formal military duties, Onganía involved himself in a "national revolution" project that promised a conjunction of the army and the people— in other words, a repeat of 1945 minus **Juan Doming Perón**. This sealed the fate of the Illia government, which was generally perceived as ineffectual and viewed with contempt.

MILITARY COUP OF 1976. It struck on 24 March and ousted **Isabel Perón**, who had become president following the death in office of her husband in 1974—she had been elected vice president.

Given the general chaos that characterized her tenure of the presidency, the armed forces had already sought to increase their power and say in affairs of state in late 1975. Unable to combat the terrorism racking the country, the government empowered the **military** in October 1975 to undertake a **War to Annihilate Subversion**. Although this move, which would have terrible consequences later in the decade, enabled the armed forces to operate autonomously, they deemed it insufficient. Commander-in-Chief General **Jorge Rafael Videla** issued an ultimatum in his Christmas message: if the government did not get a grip on mounting economic and political problems in the next 90 days, the military would act.

As the deadline approached, the commanders consulted numerous specialists, and they chose the proposal by **Jose Alfredo Martínez de Hoz**, who had been assured that his project would be imposed on the president as a price for continuing military support. He was duped. Although the proposal was formally submitted on 15 March 1976, the army had already decided to overthrow Mrs. Perón. The coup took place on the date set by Videla three months earlier and with some justification was greeted with relief by a majority of Argentines. However, what came next would be one of the darkest chapters in the history of the country, and as a result, the 1976 coup was the last in the history of the country. *See also* PROCESO DE REORGANIZACIÓN NACIONAL.

MILITARY JUNTAS, TRIALS OF THE. In the run-up to the **presidential election of 1983**, the outgoing dictatorial regime was looking for ways to secure a general amnesty for members of the **military** who had committed illegal acts of repression during the **Proceso de Reorganización Nacional.** It did not even object to the **Partido Justicialista** (PJ) candidacy of **Ítalo Luder,** who as acting president in 1975 signed the decrees enabling the **War to Annihilate Subversion**, in the expectation of a PJ victory and a subsequent pardon. **Raúl Alfonsín**, presidential candidate of the **Unión Cívica Radical** (UCR), determined that in the event of his victory those responsible for **human rights** violations should be brought to justice. Rather than a wholesale condemnation of the military, he was looking for speedy trials in order to increase the prospects of national reconciliation and the integration of the armed forces into the constitutional framework.

Alfonsín unexpectedly won the presidential election and within days of taking office ordered the Supreme Council of the Armed Forces, the standing military court whose membership was made up of retired senior officers, to proceed with the trial of the nine army, navy, and air force commanders who led the three military juntas of 1976–1982 on charges of murder, kidnapping, and torture. However, Alfonsín simultaneously requested **Congress** to back this action through an amendment to the Code of Military Justice that would allow prosecutors and defendants to refer sentences issued by military courts to a civilian court of appeal. The law produced by Congress went beyond the original request: it authorized the Federal Court of Appeal of **Buenos Aires** to take over the trials if the Supreme Council was negligent or procrastinated.

The Supreme Council of the Armed Forces was not keen on expeditious trials and indeed procrastinated. After almost a year of scant progress, the trials of the nine commanders were transferred from the secrecy of the military court to the public chambers of the Federal Court of Appeal—this was unprecedented in Argentina or elsewhere in Latin America. On 9 December 1985, the court issued individual sentences for each of the defendants. General **Jorge Rafael Videla** and Admiral **Emilio Massera** were imprisoned for life, General **Roberto Viola** for 17 years, Admiral **Armando Lambruschini** for eight years, and Air Force General **Orlando Agosti** for four and a half years. Nonetheless, the court rejected the prosecutor's claim of shared responsibility by all nine commanders and acquitted General **Leopoldo Fortunato Galtieri**, Air Force Generals **Omar Graffigna** and **Basilio Lami Dozo**, and Admiral **Jorge Isaac Anaya** of the charges brought against them.

Appeals to the Supreme Court by both prosecution and defense led to a ruling on 30 December 1986 that in the main upheld the sentences of the lower court. More than half of Alfonsín's term in office had passed by the time the cases of the nine senior commanders were resolved, but the issue of human rights abuses by the armed forces would not fade away despite the hopes of the president. *See also* DESAPARECIDOS; KIRCHNER, CRISTI-

NA ELISABET FERNÁNDEZ DE (1953–); KIRCHNER, NÉSTOR CAR-LOS (1950–2010); LEY DE OBEDIENCIA DEBIDA; LEY DE PUNTO FINAL; MADRES DE PLAZA DE MAYO; MENEM, CARLOS SAÚL (1930–).

MINISTRIES. The **Constitution of 1853** established that there should be eight ministries, of which five were named: Interior, Foreign Relations, Treasury (Hacienda), Justice and Education (Public Instruction), Defense (Army and Navy). By the late 19th century, Ministries of Public Works and Agriculture had become established cabinet posts. Ministerial briefs and titles changed over time: for example, Religion (Culto) was added to the Foreign Relations portfolio; Finance became Economy or Economy and Labor; there were sometimes separate ministries for the army and the navy. By the mid-20th century, important secretariats were granted ministerial status—ministries in all but name—thus conforming with constitutional provision. A paradox of some periods of **military** rule—when the constitution was suspended and **political parties** banned—was that de facto regimes maintained the constitutional limit on the number of ministries. However, when the army, navy, and air force each claimed a ministry, other branches of the administration were compressed into remaining ministries. The **Constitution of 1994** created the new post of head of cabinet (aka prime minister) but does not set a limit on the number of ministries, nor specify ministerial briefs. In addition to the Office of the Head of Cabinet, the administration of President **Mauricio Macri** consists of the following ministries: Interior, Public Works, and Housing; Foreign Relations and Religion; Defense; Treasury; Public Finance; Production; Tourism; Modernization; Security; Justice and Human Rights; Labor, Employment, and Social Security; Health; Social Development; Education and Sport; Science, Technology, and Innovation; Culture; Agroindustry; Transport; Energy and Mining; Environment and Sustainable Development; Communications. There is also a secretary general to the president responsible for assisting in the design of public policy and presentation, a post not to be confused with that of head of the cabinet. Ministerial portfolios are subject to change; for example, treasury and public finance were combined in a single ministry at the beginning of the Macri presidency.

MINISTRY OF AGROINDUSTRY. Originally established as the Ministry of Agriculture in 1898, during the second presidency of **Julio A. Roca**, it was dissolved 60 years later during the de facto presidency of **Pedro Eugenio Aramburu**. It then functioned largely as a secretariat dependent on the **Ministry of Economy**, although its ministerial status was restored on three occasions: by de facto president **Alejandro Agustín Lanusse** in 1972, only to be revoked by President **Héctor J. Cámpora** on the day he took office in May

1973; during the de facto presidency of **Roberto Viola** (March–December 1981); and definitively by President **Cristina Fernández de Kirchner** in 2009.

The ministry took its current name when **Mauricio Macri** was sworn in as president in 2015 and designed plans of production, commercialization, and sanitation in the rural, fisheries, forestry, and agroindustrial sectors. The current designation of the ministry—and its range of responsibilities—in part reflects the structure of the **economy** and the composition of production and **foreign trade**. Argentine exports, for example, are classified as agricultural products (aka **commodities**), industrial products of agricultural origin (for example, processed commodities like processed **meat**, packed and prepared foods, vegetable oils and fats, wines, and dairy products), and manufactured goods. This is also reflected in the organization of the ministry, which includes sections responsible for agroindustrial machinery; farming, ranching, and fisheries; food, beverages, and biotechnology; machinery; and agroindustrial goods. The ministry is responsible for trade promotion, providing producers and suppliers with market information, commercial assistance, and general advice about commercial opportunities abroad. *See also* AGRICULTURE; CATTLE; FARM PROTESTS; *FRIGORÍFICOS*; GRAINS; INSTITUTO ARGENTINO DE PROMOCIÓN DEL INTERCAMBIO (IAPI); MAIZE; *RETENCIONES*; SHEEP; SOCIEDAD RURAL ARGENTINA (SRA); WOOL.

MINISTRY OF COMMUNICATIONS. First set up as a ministry in 1949 by President **Juan Domingo Perón**, at a time when the government was nationalizing formerly privately owned telephone companies and attempting to expand radio services and promote television. Television broadcasts started in 1951. Postal services and later satellite and cable broadcasting also came within the remit of the agency, though by then it had lost the status of a ministry, its functions being variously absorbed by the Ministry of Planning and Public Investment and the Treasury. There was no Ministry of Communications between 1958 and 2015, when the ministry was reformed by President **Mauricio Macri**, signaling a determination to enhance investment and modernization in the sector. The subdivisions of the ministry indicate its scope and importance. They are (1) sector investment promotion and (2) information and communication technology diffusion. *See also* MINISTRY OF PUBLIC WORKS.

MINISTRY OF CULTURE. One of the newest ministries, formed in 2014—for years cultural affairs had been directed by the Secretariat of Culture, which had operated as part of the Presidential Office. Bizarrely, a Ministry of Culture had functioned for a few weeks in 1973 and in 2001, and for months in 1981. Few other ministries could claim such an ephemeral existence or heritage. The ministry is charged with promoting all forms of artistic expression and democratizing access to the arts. The ministry directly funds several cultural centers and museums such as the National History Museum, the Fines Arts Museum, the Evita Museum, and the Center of Popular Culture. Before the revival of the ministry, some prominent figures from the world of literature and the arts had headed the secretariat. *See also* GOROSTIZA, CARLOS (1920–2016).

MINISTRY OF DEFENSE. Founded originally as the Ministry of War in the 19th century, the current name was adopted in 1948. For much of the 19th century, the responsibilities of the minister and ministry were limited, as strategic and operational matters were undertaken by the heads of the respective services, later by the coordinating office of the Joint Chiefs of Staff of the Armed Forces. Since the early 1940s, the ministry and the Office of the Joint Chiefs of Staff have been located in a huge, multistory block a couple of hundred meters from the presidential palace. The main wings have 21 levels (three below ground), and the central block several additional floors. Surrounded by an impressive park, the War Office contained separate wings for the army and navy. Officially inaugurated a few months before the **military coup of 1943**, the building overlooked and overshadowed the **Casa Rosada**, a situation, location, and proximity that came to represent the relationship between the **military** and civilian politicians.

Although the **Constitution of 1853** had enshrined the principle of civilian control over the military, by the second quarter of the 20th century this was clearly not the case. The first direct interference by the armed forces in politics came with the **military coup of 1930** and continued over the next five decades. It was only after the collapse of the final and extreme de facto regime of the **Proceso de Reorganización Nacional** that civilian control of the military would be restored. Legislation to that effect was passed in 1988 but not implemented by successive governments until 2006. President **Néstor Kirchner** restricted the role of the armed forces to acting against external aggression and reduced the powers of the chiefs of the three services. All operational decisions and acquisitions came under the control of the minister of defense, now a civilian; the function of the Joint Chiefs of Staff was reduced to that of implementing ministerial decisions.

The Ministry of Defense assists the president and head of the cabinet of ministers in matters of national defense and relations with the armed forces, and also has a number of dependent **state-owned enterprises** and agencies—including **Fabricaciones Militares** and the **Fábrica Argentina de Aviones**. *See also* AGREEMENT BETWEEN ARGENTINA AND CHILE ACCEPTING PAPAL MEDIATION IN THE BEAGLE CHANNEL DISPUTE (1979); BEAGLE CHANNEL DISPUTE; BRAZIL; CHACO WAR;

CHILE; FALKLANDS DISPUTE; FALKLANDS WAR (2 APRIL–14 JUNE 1982); GARRÉ, NILDA CECILIA (1945–); JUSTO, AGUSTÍN PEDRO (1876–1943); MINISTRY OF FOREIGN RELATIONS AND RELIGION; URUGUAY; WAR OF THE PACIFIC; WAR OF THE TRIPLE ALLIANCE.

MINISTRY OF ECONOMY. The official title of the ministry changed many times after the mid-20th century, yet the building in which the ministry is housed is still called the Palacio de Hacienda, located on the south side of the Plaza de Mayo, where it takes up a whole block, adjacent to the **Casa Rosada**.

Set up in 1854 as one of the branches of the executive authority named in the **Constitution of 1853**, the ministry was known as Hacienda (Treasury) until 1952. Its principal functions until the early 20th century were largely those of a ministry of finance. Gradually, the agency assumed responsibility for areas that would foreshadow those of an economy ministry. The institutional stability suggested by the near 100-year use of the title "Ministerio de Hacienda" contrasts with subsequent changes in nomenclature and areas of ministerial responsibility (sometimes frequent) that reflect the shifting political environment and economic objectives of post-mid-20th-century decades. At the beginning of the second presidency of **Juan Domingo Perón**, the ministry was retitled Treasury and Finance; the designation Ministry of Economy was first used at the swearing in of the cabinet of President **Arturo Frondizi**, marking the new government's commitment to **developmentalism**. For much of the **Revolución Argentina** period, labor was included in the remit of the ministry, flagging the economic priorities and political concerns of the regime. From 1971 to 1973, the ministry was named Treasury and Finance, reverting to Economy between 1973 and 1981, only to become Economy, Treasury, and Finance for nine months in 1981. At the end of that year, Treasury and Finance were dropped, and the agency remained simply Economy for the next 10 years. When **Domingo Cavallo** was appointed head in 1991, on the eve of the launching of the **Convertibility Plan**, the ministry became Economy and Public Works and Services—in effect, a super-ministry giving Cavallo massive outreach. Cavallo established suboffices of the ministry in virtually every other major branch of the administration. The super-ministry concept was dropped by President **Fernando de la Rúa** in 1999, even when Cavallo returned as head. Between 2003 and 2009 titled Ministry of Economy and Production, the ministry was rebranded Economy and Public Finance after the disastrous showing of the government in the midterm **congressional elections of 2009**. President **Cristina Fernández de Kirchner** named her close confidant **Amado Boudou** minister: he survived for less than two-and-a-half years, the designation until the end of 2015. Under President **Mauricio Macri**, the ministry began as Treasury and Public

Finance, only to be separated into two distinct ministries responsible for each area. The current principal areas of responsibility are taxation and tax policy, preparing and managing the budget, ensuring compliance with fiscal and commercial legislation, and managing and monitoring public investment. The ministry has oversight of the mint, the National Audit Office, the Office of Statistics and Censuses (INDEC), the Tax Tribunal, and the **Banco Central de la República Argentina**. *See also* AGRICULTURE; ALEMANN, ROBERTO TEODORO (1922–); ALSOGARAY, ÁLVARO (1913–2005); AUSTRAL PLAN; BER GELBARD, JOSÉ (1917–1977); CAFIERO, ANTONIO FRANCISCO (1922–2014); CAPITANICH, JORGE MILTON (1964); ECONOMIC CRISES; ECONOMY; ERMAN GONZÁLEZ, ANTONIO (1935–2007); FERNÁNDEZ, ROQUE BENJAMIN (1947–); FERRER, ALDO (1927–2016); FOREIGN DEBT/FOREIGN INVESTMENT; FOREIGN TRADE; GÓMEZ MORALES, ALFREDO (1908–1990); GRINSPUN, BERNARDO (1925–1996); INDUSTRY; KICILLOF, AXEL (1971–); KRIEGER VASENA, ADALBERT (1920–2000); LAVAGNA, ROBERTO (1942–); LÓPEZ MURPHY, RICARDO HIPÓLITO (1951–); MACHINEA, JOSÉ LUIS (1946–); MARTÍNEZ DE HOZ, JOSÉ ALFREDO (1925–2013); PINEDO, FEDERICO (1895–1971); RODRIGO, CELESTINO (1915–1987); SALIMEI, JORGE NÉSTOR (1926–1975); SOURROUILLE, JUAN VITAL (1940–).

MINISTRY OF EDUCATION. A long-standing ministry—originally part of the Justice Ministry as Public Instruction—this branch of the administration gained importance during the 20th century as the secondary and higher education sectors expanded. A specific Ministry of Education was first created in 1949. At various times since, the portfolio has been several times reconnected with Justice, and linked to Culture as well as Science and Technology, and Sport. The ministry is responsible for determining the objectives of the educational system at all levels and liaising with its provincial counterparts and for supervising teacher training. The sensitivity of the portfolio is enhanced by the fact that teaching unions are highly organized and because of the autonomy legally granted to universities. The main subdivisions are primary and secondary education, education policy, university policy, and sport. Arguably, the most prominent recent head was Jorge Federico Sabato, who served as minister of education and justice during the latter part of the presidency of **Raúl Alfonsín**. *See also* EDUCATION.

MINISTRY OF ENVIRONMENT AND SUSTAINABLE DEVELOPMENT. New ministry created by President **Mauricio Macri** in 2015; previously, there had been a Secretariat for the Environment and Sustainable Development attached to the Office of the Prime Minister (head of the cabinet of ministers). The main function of the ministry is planning coordination—assessing the environmental impact of the activities of other ministries and state organizations—and advisory. It has oversight of national parks, the federal forests, and nature reserves.

MINISTRY OF FOREIGN RELATIONS AND RELIGION. One of the original ministries created by the **Constitution of 1853**, initially as the Ministry of Foreign Relations. It assumed its current name in 1898 and added **foreign trade** to its portfolio in 1992. The foreign minister is often known as the chancellor—*el canciller argentino/la cancillera argentina*.

Though the ministry operates autonomously, some aspects of foreign policy are conditioned by the **Constitution of 1994**—it obliges the federal government to strengthen peaceful and commercial relations with foreign powers and ratifies sovereignty over the Islas Malvinas (**Falkland Islands**). The principal subdivisions of the ministry include diplomatic missions and consular affairs; South American trade and relations; international cooperation and cultural relations; **human rights**; foreign economic relations; agency for the promotion of foreign trade and investment; and religious affairs— the religious affairs section has two subdivisions, one for Roman Catholics and another for the registrations of religious organizations. The new constitution also requires the foreign minister to collaborate with his colleague at the **Ministry of Defense** in those areas where their interests coincide, without compromising the respective areas of competence of the two ministries. Since 1936, the ministry has been located in the Palacio San Martín, the former townhouse of the **Anchorena Family**, a splendid Belle Epoque mansion that stretches for virtually a whole block on the north side of the prestigious square of the same name. *See also* AGREEMENT BETWEEN ARGENTINA AND CHILE ACCEPTING PAPAL MEDIATION IN THE BEAGLE CHANNEL DISPUTE (1979); AGREEMENT BETWEEN ARGENTINA AND GREAT BRITAIN CONCERNING THE FALKLAND ISLANDS (1971); AGUIRRE LANARI, JUAN RAMÓN (1920–2017); ANAYA, JORGE ISAAC (1926–2008); ARA *GENERAL BELGRANO*; BEAGLE CHANNEL DISPUTE; BOLIVIA; BRAMUGLIA, JUAN ATILIO (1903–1962); BRAZIL; CALVO, CARLOS (1822–1906); CAPUTO, DANTE (1943–); CAVALLO, DOMINGO FELIPE (1946–); CHILE; CHINA; COSTA MÉNDEZ, NICANOR (1922–1992); CUBA; DI TELLA, GUIDO JOSÉ MARIO (1931–2001); FALKLANDS DISPUTE; FALKLANDS WAR (2 APRIL–14 JUNE 1982); FOREIGN DEBT/FOREIGN INVESTMENT; FOREIGN RELATIONS; GALTIERI, LEOPOLDO FORTUNATO (1926–2003); GREAT BRITAIN; ITAIPÚ DAM; PARAGUAY; PERU; SAAVEDRA LAMAS, CARLOS (1878–1959); SPAIN; TERCERA POSICIÓN; UNITED STATES OF AMERICA; URUGUAY; VENEZUELA; WAR OF THE TRIPLE ALLIANCE; YACYRETÁ-APIPÉ.

MINISTRY OF HEALTH. Health-related facilities are mainly operated by the provinces; the federal ministry is largely concerned with coordination and planning. Nonetheless, from time to time, the national authorities have established and operated hospitals and clinics, as have the **military** and the **trade unions**. There are also private hospitals. The Health Ministry dates from the Secretariat of Public Health, created in 1946—ministerial status was achieved in 1949; both initiatives occurred during the first presidency of **Juan Domingo Perón**. In 1958, with the election of President **Arturo Frondizi**, the agency became the Ministry of Social Assistance and Public Health. Over the following decades, responsibility for health was often combined with other areas of welfare or social intervention until 1983, when President **Raúl Alfonsín** set up the Ministry of Health and Social Action, reestablishing health as a priority area. The ministry survived in this format until 2001. Between 2002 and 2007, health was part of the Ministry of Health and the Environment. The present arrangement and title, Ministry of Health, was determined by President **Cristina Fernández de Kirchner**. In addition to inspection and policy formulation, the ministry is responsible for community health programs. It also has oversight of important federal facilities like the national medical research laboratories and inspection and validation of drugs and medicines agency, rehabilitation clinics, the human organs bank. *See also* ERMAN GONZÁLEZ, ANTONIO (1935–2007).

MINISTRY OF INTERIOR, PUBLIC WORKS, AND HOUSING. The current designation was established by President **Mauricio Macri**. Interior was one of the early ministries named in the **Constitution of 1853**. For 100 years from 1854, the ministry was simply Interior, being combined with Justice for about a year and a half before reverting to Interior in 1955, remaining as such until 2012, when Transportation was added. The present designation dates from 2015.

Arguably one of the most politically sensitive ministries and a key portfolio during periods of political change, the ministry was headed by many former presidents before or after serving as president of the republic. The remit of the ministry was also economically and politically important during the period of mass **immigration** in the decades around 1900; the sensitivity of the functions of Interior were heightened during periods of **military** rule. The ministry is responsible for the administration of a state of siege—the temporary suspension of political and civic rights during an emergency.

Interior deals with citizenship—the registration of citizens, the administration of the constitutional rights of citizens, and matters pertaining to nationality—areas of crucial significance at moments of franchise reform; it handles voter registration and is responsible for the supervision of elections. Relations between the federal government and the provinces are handled by the ministry, as well as relations among the provinces—historically, the ministry has organized **federal interventions** of the provinces. Now its oversight is principally fiscal and financial. Similar functions are exercised with regard to municipalities. The ministry deals with the implementation and policing of regulations relating to public services, including the franchising of such services, competition policy, sanitary and consumer standards, and the use of natural resources and matters generally relating to the civic and commercial codes. In addition to separate Secretariats for Public Works and Housing, the core subdivisions of Interior are the Municipal Affairs Office, the Provincial Relations Office, and the Center For National Documentation. The ministry also manages the national archive—the Archivo General de la Nación. *See also* BELIZ, GUSTAVO (1962–); CORACH, CARLOS VLADIMIRO (1935–); DERQUI, SANTIAGO RAFAEL LUIS MANUEL JOSÉ MARÍA (1809–1867); FERNÁNDEZ, ANÍBAL DOMINGO (1957–); FRIGERIO, ROGELIO (1970–); HARGUINDEGUY, ALBANO EDUARDO (1927–2012); LEY DE RESIDENCIA; MILITARY COUP OF 1930; MILITARY COUP OF 1955; MILITARY COUP OF 1962; MILITARY COUP OF 1966; MILITARY COUP OF 1976; MOR ROIG, ARTURO (1914–1974); QUINTANA, MANUEL (1835–1906); RANDAZZO, ANÍBAL FLORENCIO (1964–); ROCA, JULIO ARGENTINO (1843–1914); RUCKAUF, CARLOS FEDERICO (1944–); SARMIENTO, DOMINGO FAUSTINO (1811–1888).

MINISTRY OF JUSTICE AND HUMAN RIGHTS. Originally set up as the Ministry of Justice and Instruction during the presidency of **Justo José de Urquiza,** when the **Constitution of 1853** stipulated a maximum limit of eight ministries. When that limitation was abolished by the **Constitution of 1949,** a separate Ministry of Justice was created. Although the de facto **Revolución Libertadora** regime abolished the constitutional reform, the ministry remained separate until **Arturo Frondizi** merged it with the **education** portfolio in 1958. Following the **military coup of 1966,** President **Juan Carlos Onganía** reestablished the Ministry of Justice, which remained as such until 1983. The ministry was dissolved by President **Raúl Alfonsín** and reinstated by his successor, **Carlos Saúl Menem. Cristina Fernández de Kirchner** renamed it the Ministry of Justice, Security, and **Human Rights** in 2007, only to split security into a new separate ministerial portfolio three years later.

The ministry assists the president and head of the cabinet of ministers in relations with the judiciary and the updating of national legislation; it has a number of dependencies that include the Office of the Attorney General and the registries of property, vehicles, firearms, and author copyrights. *See also* BELIZ, GUSTAVO (1962–); BORLENGHI, ÁNGEL GABRIEL (1906–1962); FERNÁNDEZ, ANÍBAL DOMINGO (1957–).

MINISTRY OF LABOR. The Labor Ministry traces its origins from the National Labor Department (NLD), formed in 1907 following social unrest and protests for worker rights organized by **trade unions**, and from the Secretariat for Labor and Social Protection, established in 1944. Before the 1940s, the NLD was a dependency of the **Ministry of Interior**. Ministerial status was achieved in 1949, since when the labor portfolio has become an established and important cabinet post. The formation of a separate Labor Ministry during the first presidency of **Juan Domingo Perón** signaled the importance of workers and the labor movement to the regime as the **Partido Laborista** morphed into the **Partido Peronista**. Often linked with Social Protection or Social Security, the longest period when the ministry was known simply as Labor was between 1973 and 1989. During the de facto presidencies of **Juan Carlos Onganía** and **Roberto Marcelo Levingston** following the **military coup of 1966**, Labor was attached to the **Ministry of Economy**, reflecting the regime's emphasis on economic modernization and social discipline. During periods of **military** rule, the ministry has been as much concerned with policing the labor movement as with the routine functions of the ministry. Routine responsibilities include the implementation of the labor code, overseeing labor and employment regulation, and enforcing legislation related to wages and collective bargaining (or the administration of social pacts as and when they operated), training, and workplace surveys. When linked to Social Welfare or Social Protection, the ministry has also been responsible for overseeing retirement pension schemes and social projects. During its relatively brief existence, the **Fundación Eva Perón** was housed in the ministry. Unsurprisingly, given the current title of the ministry, the main secretariats are Labor, Employment, and Social Security. The two autonomous agencies are the National Social Security Department and the Office of Employment Risk and Accident at Work. *See also* BULLRICH, PATRICIA (1956–); CONFEDERACIÓN GENERAL DEL TRABAJO (CGT); CONFEDERACIÓN GENERAL DEL TRABAJO DE LOS ARGENTINOS (CGTA); ERMAN GONZÁLEZ, ANTONIO (1935–2007); RUCKAUF, CARLOS FEDERICO (1944–); SEMANA TRÁGICA.

MINISTRY OF MODERNIZATION. One of the new ministries created by President **Mauricio Macri** in 2015, intended to demonstrate the commitment of the incoming administration to technical and scientific modernization, notably as regards the effectiveness of the administration of government and the implementation of public policy. In addition, the ministry was expected to facilitate transparency and the use of modern information technology in the conduct of government business. The main responsibilities of the ministry are oversights of the Digitalized Nation program, the Innovation Planning and Development Office, and the Information and Communications Technology Office.

MINISTRY OF PRODUCTION. A Ministry of Industry in all but name, established in its present form by President **Mauricio Macri** in 2015, intended to demonstrate the determination of the incoming government to promote economic modernization. Essentially, the newly designated ministry absorbed the functions previously associated with such earlier incarnations as the Ministry of Industry and Commerce.

A Ministry of Industry and Commerce was first set up by President **Juan Domingo Perón** in 1949 as part of a program of federal planning and development—notably, the promotion of national **industry** in an attempted to shift the focus of the **economy** from **agriculture** and exports to manufacturing. The emphasis on planned industrialization was reflected in a name change in 1952; the agency was rebranded as the Ministry of Industry. With the ouster of Perón in 1955, there were briefly separate tandem Ministries of Industry and Commerce, with the Ministry of Industry and Commerce being reformed in 1956. This ministry was suppressed in 1958. When revived in 1971 by de facto president General **Alejandro Agustín Lanusse**, it was as the Ministry of Commerce. The ministry was suppressed again in 1973 when the military regime of the **Revolución Argentina** handed it over to the democratically elected administration of President **Héctor Cámpora**. Although Cámpora soon transferred power to Perón, who triumphed in the **presidential election of September 1973**, the ministry was not revived. "Commerce" and "Industry" resurfaced briefly in 1981 during the de facto presidency of General **Roberto Viola**, as part of a larger ministry, only to disappear again until 2002. That year, President **Eduardo Duhalde** established the Ministry of Production, the first time that title was used, but the ministry was short lived.

From 2003 to 2008, there was no Ministry of Production nor of Industry. The Ministry of Industry was revived by President **Cristina Fernández de Kirchner** in 2008, only for Macri to revert to Production in 2015. The Minister of Production is charged with assisting manufacturing and elaborating policies that are supportive of the industrial sector and business bodies in general—special emphasis is placed on programs and actions that assist small- and medium-sized firms. See also ALSOGARAY, ÁLVARO (1913–2005); ASOCIACIÓN EMPRESARIA ARGENTINA (AEA); CONFEDERACIÓN GENERAL ECONÓMICA (CGE); DEVELOPMEN-TALISM/DEVELOPMENTALIST; ECONOMY; FERNÁNDEZ, ANÍBAL DOMINGO (1957–); INDUSTRY; UNIÓN INDUSTRIAL ARGENTINA (UIA).

MINISTRY OF PUBLIC WORKS. Now part of the **Ministry of Interior**, though merged with the **Ministry of Economy** in 1991, for much of the 19th and early 20th century, Public Works as possibly the most important "economic" agency of the administration—at the time, what would become the Ministry of Economy (the Treasury) was mainly concerned with public finance and taxation.

The Public Works Ministry was created in 1898—there had previously been a Department of Public Works, part of the **Ministry of Interior**. The ministry was responsible for the development of highways, ports, irrigation, and communications generally. For many decades, it was headed by civil engineers. Major projects overseen by the ministry included development projects in the national territories of **Patagonia**—principally rail construction—and the city of **Buenos Aires** water and sewage system. Many ministers, like aristocrat Ezequiel Ramos Mejía and **Roberto M. Ortiz**, assumed a high profile promoting projects designed to facilitate the development of **agriculture** and **foreign trade**. The historic ministry is now best known for its iconic building, Edificio del Ministerio de Obras Públicas, located in the center of the city of Buenos Aires. Work on the 22-story structure began in 1934 and was completed two years later, with extensions being added in 1947 and 1980. Observable from most of the central area, the north and south facades are adorned with massive profiles of **Eva Perón**. The images were decreed by President **Cristina Fernández de Kirchner** in 2011; the building was declared a national monument and a homage to "Evita" and the governing **Partido Justicialista** (PJ). The building has historic references for Peronists. It was from a platform erected in front of the building that Evita announced to massive crowds in 1951 that she would not be the party's vice presidential candidate in the upcoming presidential election. The first national television broadcast was made from the building soon after Evita's "resignation speech" in the presence of her husband, **Juan Domingo Perón**. Months before the **military coup of 1955**, which ousted Perón, navy warplanes bombarded the building and the Plaza de Mayo in an attempt to kill Perón and key aides—380 died, including 40 schoolchildren. Today known as Edificio de Evita, the building houses the **Ministry of Health** and the **Ministry of Social Development**.

MINISTRY OF SCIENCE, TECHNOLOGY, AND PRODUCTIVE IN-NOVATION. First established by President **Cristina Fernández de Kirchner** in 2007, its remit was and is to promote technology that contributes to economic efficiency and to support the diffusion of such technology as is consistent with the objectives of macroeconomic planning. With the election of President **Mauricio Macri** in 2015, this was one of the few ministerial portfolios not to be restructured. Macri also retained in place the original minister appointed by Mrs. Kirchner, **Lino Barañao**.

MINISTRY OF SECURITY. Created by a decree issued by President **Cristina Fernández de Kirchner** in 2010, it is in charge of the federal police, the Airports Security Police, the Naval Prefecture, and the National Gendarmerie. The ministry is charged with ensuring the security of the international frontiers of the country, including protection against the operation of international criminal networks; guaranteeing internal security; the preservation of liberty, life, and property; and vigilance in the defense of domestic democratic institutions. The ministry has restructured the security forces and carried out several security operations. *See also* BULLRICH, PATRICIA (1956–); GARRÉ, NILDA CECILIA (1945–); MILITARY; MINISTRY OF JUSTICE AND HUMAN RIGHTS.

MINISTRY OF SOCIAL DEVELOPMENT. The ministry has existed in its present form since 1999, set up at the beginning of the administration of **Fernando de la Rúa** and initially headed by **Graciela Fernández Meijide**. A separate ministry for social affairs was originally created by General **Eduardo Lonardi**, the first president of the **Revolución Libertadora** that followed the **military coup of 1955**. Attempting to extirpate Peronism, the **military** government recognized that the emphasis placed on welfare and social citizenship by ousted president **Juan Domingo Perón** could not be ignored. Some sections of the regime viewed the promotion of welfare policy as a route to political power, as had Perón himself. Under Lonardi, the ministry was named Social Assistance; under civilian regimes of the 1958–1966 period, as Social Assistance and Public Health. Following the **Revolución Argentina**, installed by the **military coup of 1966**, the ministry became Social Welfare, a designation that survived until 1981, when the Ministry of Social Action was created. In 1983, with the return of democracy, President **Raúl Alfonsín** brought health back into the remit of the ministry; it remained Health and Social Action until 1999 and the appointment of Fernández Meijide. As the longer-surviving titles of the ministry imply, it has been mainly responsible for the administration of an expanding range of social programs, from contributory social insurance and mutual assistance schemes to broader social interventions. There has been sizable budget expansion as the ministry took on responsibility for old-age pensions—still overseen by the ministry when the funds themselves were privatized under President **Carlos Saúl Menem**—and social safety nets that were rolled out for families, the elderly, and children following the collapse of the **Convertibility Plan** in 2001. Important agencies of the ministry include the Office for Community Affairs and the Agency for Children and the Family. The ministry also oversees the National Lottery and the Microcredit Commission. *See also* DUHALDE, EDUARDO ALBERTO (1941–); DUHALDE, HILDA BEATRIZ "CHICHE" GONZÁLEZ DE (1946–); ECONOMIC CRISES; ERMAN GONZÁLEZ, ANTONIO (1935–2007); KIRCHNER, ALI-

CIA MARGARITA (1946–); KIRCHNER, CRISTINA ELISABET FERNÁNDEZ DE (1953–); KIRCHNER, NÉSTOR CARLOS (1950–2010); LÓPEZ REGA, JOSÉ (1916–1989); PRIVATIZATION.

MINISTRY OF TOURISM. Originally a secretariat, the ministry was created under a decree issued by President **Cristina Fernández de Kirchner** in 2010. Its mission is to promote optimal competitive conditions that lead to the balanced and sustainable development of **tourism** as well as improvements in the quality of life of Argentine nationals and visitors and aims to transform Argentina into the top South American destination for international tourists.

MINISTRY OF TRANSPORT. Transport became a separate ministry again in 2015, reformed as such by President **Mauricio Macri**. The first Ministry of Transport was created in 1949 by President **Juan Domingo Perón**; formed a year after the nationalization of the railways, the ministry gave the sector a high priority in the government's economic program. The ministry survived until 1958, abolished by the incoming democratically elected president **Arturo Frondizi**. Between 1958 and 2015, transport was demoted to the status of a secretariat dependent variously on the **Ministry of the Interior**, the Ministry of Planning, and the **Ministry of Public Works**, among others. The reestablishment of the ministry by Macri signals the importance attached by the new president to the modernization of infrastructure and concern about the impact of years of underinvestment in the sector on economic efficiency, not least production and **foreign trade**. The brief includes the regulation of charges and conditions of transport services, the supervision of franchises awarded to private concessionaires—an area that grew significantly with **privatization** in the 1990s—the inspection of transport services and facilities, and the integration of land, water, and air transport—there are separate secretariats for rail, road, river, and air transport and the ports. *See also* BUENOS AYRES & PACIFIC RAILWAY COMPANY (BA&P); BUENOS AYRES GREAT SOUTHERN RAILWAY COMPANY (BAGS); BUENOS AYRES WESTERN RAILWAY COMPANY (BAW); CENTRAL ARGENTINE RAILWAY COMPANY (CAR); CORDOBA CENTRAL RAILWAY COMPANY (CCR); FERROCARRILES ARGENTINOS (FFAA); KIRCHNER, CRISTINA ELISABET FERNÁNDEZ DE (1953–); MENEM, CARLOS SAÚL (1930–); STATE-OWNED ENTERPRISES (SOEs); TRANSPORTATION.

MIRANDA, MIGUEL (1891–1953). A leading Peronist figure and the chief architect of **economic policy** (1946–1948). A self-made man, his entrepreneurial career began when he opened a small metalworking factory. This business allowed him to accumulate capital, which he reinvested in different businesses. He gradually diversified from sheet metal production and became proprietor of substantial interests in fishing and canned food companies as well as the rapidly developing airline industry. By the time of the **military coup of 1943**, Miranda had become a very powerful and influential industrialist and was a member of the board of the **Unión Industrial Argentina** (UIA). Miranda's vision was an industrialized Argentina able to supply most of its own needs and exporting industrial products to compete in world markets. This dovetailed with the ideas of **Juan Domingo Perón**, who was rapidly becoming the leading figure of a **military** government that favored industrial development. Miranda first met Perón in 1944 and was invited to join the **Consejo Nacional de Posguerra**, which was established to define economic development priorities.

Once Perón won the **presidential election of 1946**, he granted Miranda wide powers and authority on the mistaken assumption that a person who had successfully managed his own business affairs would be competent to handle the nation's finances. Miranda was appointed president of the newly nationalized **Banco Central de la República Argentina** (BCRA) in March 1946 and two months later took charge of the newly created **Instituto Argentino de Promoción del Intercambio** (IAPI). The IAPI bought local agricultural products cheaply and sold them abroad at much higher prices, channeling the profits into industrial development and Perón's social projects. For a couple of years, this system delivered. Full employment was achieved, the situation of the working class improved, industrial production accelerated, and air transport and a merchant navy were developed. But difficulties rapidly emerged. Expected export levels failed to materialize, foreign exchange reserves were depleted by their use in the nationalization of public services, and the industrial strategy did not go far enough.

Under fire from different economic actors, Miranda resigned as head of both the BCRA and the IAPI in July 1947. Nevertheless, he retained the confidence of Perón and was appointed as president of the Consejo Económico Nacional, a job of recent creation and ministerial rank. Miranda faced numerous setbacks, not least in terms of attracting overseas investment to modernize the railways and oil production.

When renegotiating the Anglo-Argentine relationship in the **Miranda–Eady Agreement**, he did not propose buying the mainly British-owned railways—he regarded the network as undercapitalized and operating largely obsolete equipment. Miranda had favored the establishment of a joint corporation that would assume control of the existing companies; the latter would in turn receive shares in the new enterprise. The idea was rejected by parties of all hues, and the president could not be seen as backtracking on promises of "economic independence," so the deal was renegotiated and the railways nationalized. Perón received a short-term political dividend, but the opposition would accuse the government and Miranda more specifically of having paid an exorbitant price for infrastructure that would require substantial investment to be modernized. In fact, the purchase of the railways triggered a steady and enormous drain on the national budget as a result of operating deficits.

Miranda also failed to attract foreign investment for the exploration and exploitation of local oil reserves. Foreign Minister **Juan Atilio Bramuglia** also favored this idea, but more nationalist members of the cabinet objected and defended the position of the state-owned oil company **Yacimientos Petrolíferos Fiscales**. These failed attempts to encourage foreign investment did not mean that Miranda was keen on good relations with the **United States**, which found his policies "dangerous" and from 1948 worked to get him removed from office. Miranda was forced to resign in January 1949, but this was due entirely to the dire condition of the Argentine **economy** at the time. Pushed out of the Peronist leadership and fearing arrest, he went into self-imposed exiled in **Uruguay**. *See also* DEVELOPMENTALISM/DE-VELOPMENTALIST; FERROCARRILES ARGENTINOS (FFAA); FOREIGN DEBT/FOREIGN INVESTMENT; FOREIGN TRADE; INDUSTRY; PINEDO PLAN; TRANSPORTATION.

MIRANDA–EADY AGREEMENT. Signed in 1946, the agreement may be presented as the final chapter in a series of commercial and financial understandings between Argentina and **Great Britain** that began with the 1933 **Roca–Runciman Pact** and continued under the Anglo–Argentine Commercial Treaty of 1936. Its was named after the principal negotiators, Miguel Miranda, then president of the **Banco Central de la República Argentina** (BCRA), and Sir Wilfred Eady, a senior official at the British Treasury who had been born in Argentina. Described at the time as a meat-for-oil deal—Great Britain undertook to ensure oil supplies to Argentina and Argentina critical **meat** exports to Great Britain—the agreement is significant because it prepared the way for the nationalization of British-owned railway companies and the liquidation of Argentina's sterling balances at the Bank of England. The blocked sterling balances had been run up during the Second World War when Argentina had agreed to export strategic **commodities** to Britain on credit. The railway deal envisaged by Miranda and Eady involved the formation of a mixed corporation, jointly owned by the Argentine state and shareholders of the privately owned British Argentine Railways, with a gradual transfer of ownership over time as the Argentine government increased its capital stake in the join enterprise. In the event, the blocked balances were used to repatriate Argentina's sterling debt and finance the outright purchase of the railways.

The 1946 agreement is important because it marked the end of the close commercial and financial relations that had existed between the two countries since the early 19th century. The purchase of the railways also signaled a substantial expansion of the role of the state in the Argentine economy, chiming with the nationalist development strategy of the incoming administration of President **Juan Domingo Perón**. *See also* ARGENTINE NORTH EASTERN RAILWAY COMPANY (ANE); BUENOS AYRES & PACIFIC RAILWAY COMPANY (BA&P); BUENOS AYRES GREAT SOUTHERN RAILWAY COMPANY (BAGS); BUENOS AYRES WESTERN RAILWAY COMPANY (BAW); CENTRAL ARGENTINE RAILWAY COMPANY (CAR); CORDOBA CENTRAL RAILWAY COMPANY (CCR); DEVELOPMENTALISM/DEVELOPMENTALIST; ECONOMY; FERROCARRILES ARGENTINOS (FFAA); INSTITUTO ARGENTINO DE PROMOCIÓN DEL INTERCAMBIO (IAPI); MITRE, EMILIO EDILMIRO (1853–1909); STATE-OWNED ENTERPRISES (SOEs); TRANSPORTATION.

MISIONES. Province of **Mesopotamia** located in the northeast corner of the country. The second smallest province after **Tucumán** and home of the spectacular **Iguazú Falls**, it is surrounded by **Paraguay** to the northwest; by **Brazil** to the north, east, and south; and by the province of **Corrientes** to the southwest.

Indigenous peoples of various cultures inhabited the area of the future province before the first Europeans arrived in the 16th century. Members of the Jesuit Order came to the region as missionaries in the 17th century, establishing approximately 30 settlements (*reducciones*) and giving the area its name. With the Jesuits operating as a "state within a state," the Portuguese and Spanish (the colonial powers in the region) forced the pope to suppress the order in 1759. The **United Provinces of the River Plate** incorporated Misiones in 1814, but their control was merely nominal as the area was contested with Paraguay. With the defeat of the latter in the **War of the Triple Alliance**, Argentina incorporated Misiones as a national territory. The passage of the **Immigration** and Colonization Law during the presidency of **Nicolás Avellaneda** fostered the establishment of several **agricultural colonization** companies and the arrival of European immigrants.

Misiones gained the status of province in 1953, and its capital is the city of **Posadas**. The population exceeds one million; the mainstay of the **economy** is **agriculture**, particularly the cultivation of **yerba mate**. Forestry, light manufacturing, and **tourism** also make a contribution.

MITRE, BARTOLOMÉ (1821–1906). Author, statesman, and public intellectual. Mitre was one of the outstanding politicians of his age—and an adversary of General and President **Julio A. Roca**. He served as constitutional president between 1862 and 1869, wrote the definitive history of the **independence** period (which informed his contribution to **national organization**), and founded *La Nación*, one of the most prominent liberal newspapers published in Latin America.

Descended from established families in **Buenos Aires** and Montevideo, he was born in Carmen de Patagones, a small coastal settlement in the southwest of the province of Buenos Aires close to the Indian frontier. Bookish and largely self-educated, as a youth he was sent to learn the *estancia* business on one of the estates of **Juan Manuel de Rosas**. It was not a success. He went on to study mathematics at the Montevideo military academy, graduating as an artillery officer. He saw action in **Uruguay** and **Mesopotamia**, fighting against the forces of Rosas in the late 1830s and early 1840s. Later, forced to leave Montevideo along with other Argentine exiles, Mitre traveled to **Bolivia** and **Peru**, where he pursued a career in journalism and associated with anti-Rosas exiles. In 1852, when **Justo José de Urquiza** rose against Rosas, he joined the Ejército Grande as an artillery commander. When Buenos Aires rejected the **Constitution of 1853**, objecting to the federalization of the customs house and the ascendency of Urquiza, it seceded from the **Argentine Confederation**. Mitre was appointed to various portfolios in the provincial administration, including foreign affairs, interior, and war. He fought in several campaigns, in defense of provincial independence, and was elected to the Buenos Aires assembly. His first major work, *Historia del General Belgrano*, appeared in 1857—it was both a study of the man and the period and a treatise on the organization of the country, ideas that would later be developed in his other historical writing and journalism.

Heading Buenos Aires forces, Mitre was soundly defeated by Urquiza at the battle of Cepeda in 1859. However, he had favored reconciliation with the interior provinces and, elected governor of the province in 1860, worked to this end, while strengthening the military capacity of Buenos Aires. In 1861, at the hard-fought battle of Pavón, Buenos Aires forces led by Mitre reversed the result of Cepeda. Pavón was even more a political than a military defeat for Urquiza, as the province prepared to rejoin the Confederation, largely on its own terms. **Santiago Derqui**, who had succeeded Urquiza as Confederation president, resigned, preparing the ground for the election of Mitre as constitutional president of the reunited Confederation, now renamed the **Argentine Republic**, in 1862. In effect, Mitre became the first president of the republic. Through a combination of compromise and reconciliation, and by attracting talent from the interior, Mitre sought to make the new arrangement work, ensuring that federal resources were used to develop the interior, partly by a program of public works that included profit guarantees for **railways**. The city of Buenos Aires was declared the national and provincial capital.

In addition to establishing domestic order, one of the greatest political, diplomatic, and military challenges to confront Mitre was the **War of the Triple Alliance** against **Paraguay**, seen by many contemporaries as a conflict that would determine the future direction of the country. The war was controversial in the interior; some provincial elites regarded the attack on Paraguay as a proxy for an attack on the claims of their provinces for greater autonomy. As president, Mitre assumed command of allied forces and was responsible for strategy and the early prosecution of the war. His strategy and campaign were not a great success. The death of Mitre's vice president, to whom he had handed over the day-to-day running of the country, required Mitre to step down, passing the leadership of allied forces to the head of the Brazilian army. In his final year as president, Mitre prepared the ground for his successor, **Domingo Faustino Sarmiento**. He was elected national senator for Buenos Aires in the 1868 presidential and congressional elections. For much of the rest of his life, he served as an elder statesman, presenting his views about the future direction of the country through the columns of *La Nación*, which he bought and transformed in 1869. In 1874, Mitre again stood for the presidency but was defeated by **Nicolás Avellaneda**, a candidate from the interior. Mitre protested against electoral fraud and organized a rebellion, which was put down by then colonel **Julio A. Roca**. Mitre was imprisoned for several months as a result, time that he devoted to writing his second major book, *Historia de San Martín y de la Independencia Sudamericana*. Although stripped of his rank and offices at a court-martial and sentenced to exile, Mitre was pardoned by Avellaneda.

Mitre's experience in 1874 informed his action in 1880 and 1890. In 1880, when elements of the Buenos Aires elite challenged the election of Roca to the presidency and threatened revolt, he refused to join them. Opposed to the flagrant **corruption** and political bankruptcy of the regime headed by **Miguel Juárez Celman**, with **Leandro Alem** he founded the Unión Cívica (UC), predecessor of the **Unión Cívica Radical** (UCR), but Mitre did not participate in the **revolution of 1890**. Having caught a sense of events and not wishing to be associated with the coming turmoil, he left the country, a move that caused a breach with erstwhile UC associates. On returning to Buenos Aires, his negotiations with Roca were instrumental in securing the administration of **Carlos Pellegrini**, who served out Juárez Celman's term. In 1883, Mitre was reinstated into the army and promoted to lieutenant general, though he had long ceased active service. Mitre declined to stand for the presidency in the 1892 elections. Elected national senator in the 1894 midterm congressional elections, he was appointed president of the Senate, the third most important political position in the republic after the president and vice president.

His passing in 1906 was marked by national commemoration, his life and work being seen as coterminous with the emergence of the country from the chaos of the 1820s to its formation as a modern state—a transformation to which he contributed substantially. The republic consolidated during the Mitre presidency. Civil disorder was contained, internal peace established, and political life institutionalized—new civil and commercial codes were enacted during Mitre's presidency and the judicial system revised. The **economy** grew, fueled by the expansion of **agriculture**, exports, and **immigration**. Government revenue mushroomed, financing investment in **education** and the beginnings of urban modernization. Confidence in the country at home and overseas increased.

MITRE, EMILIO EDILMIRO (1853–1909). Parliamentarian, journalist, son of **Bartolomé Mitre**; named after his father's younger brother Emilio; succeeded Bartolomé as editor of the newspaper *La Nación*. Trained as a civil engineer, he was responsible for, or oversaw, a number of projects, including port works and river improvement. He was also a member of the board of the directors of the province of **Buenos Aires** state railway, which later became the **Buenos Ayres Western Railway Company** (BAW). His political career included terms in the provincial legislature and the National **Congress**, where he represented both the province and city of **Buenos Aires** at different times. It was while serving in the National Senate that he sponsored an important piece of legislation that took his name and drew on his experience as a civil engineer and engagement with public works projects.

Law 5315, or the Mitre Law, was significant because it codified and regulated concessions governing private—mainly British-owned—railway companies. The Mitre Law did not supersede the general railway statute but applied several novel features, the principal of which were the consolidation of various concessions acquired over time by individual companies, extending them for a period of 40 years, and the introduction of a tax on the profits of railways and mechanisms for the regulation of profits. The expiry of the 40-year period on 1 January 1947 was a key factor leading to the nationalization of foreign-owned railways the following year. The 40-year concession extension was the sweetener that persuaded rail companies to accept the 3 percent tax, the proceeds of which were to be spent on improving road access to railway stations. The concessions originally awarded rail companies had exempted them from all forms of taxation. Another unique feature of the Mitre Law was the setting out of a formula for calculating operating profits and fixing a ceiling on them—the limit was set at 6.8 percent. This clause was both threatened and invoked during the 1920s, resulting in some companies reducing freight charges and passenger fares. The taxation and profit-limit provisions of the Mitre Law were regarded as innovative at the time they were devised and as marking the beginning a new era in relations between the state and foreign corporations. *See also* ARGENTINE NORTH EASTERN RAILWAY COMPANY (ANE); BUENOS AYRES & PACIFIC RAILWAY COMPANY (BA&P); BUENOS AYRES GREAT SOUTHERN RAILWAY COMPANY (BAGS); CENTRAL ARGENTINE RAILWAY COMPANY (CAR); CORDOBA CENTRAL RAILWAY COMPANY (CCR); FERROCARRILES ARGENTINOS (FFAA); MIRANDA–EADY AGREEMENT; TRANSPORTATION.

MITRE LAW (LEY 5315). *See* MITRE, EMILIO EDILMIRO (1853–1909).

MOLINOS RÍO DE LA PLATA. Founded in 1902 by the **Bunge & Born** group, which retained ownership until 1998, Molinos is the largest food brand in Argentina. It produces a wide range of packaged foods for the domestic market, particularly bottled oil, margarine, pasta, premixes, packaged flours, **yerba mate**, rice, cold cuts, and frozen foods. It is also the largest exporter of sunflower oil and one of the country's main exporters of bottled oil. Molinos operates 20 manufacturing plants, 10 distribution centers, and 600 trucks, among other facilities, and owns 75,000 hectares of prime **pampas** land for wheat production.

MONDELLI, EMILIO (1914–1993). Minister of economy from February to March 1976. A banker born in Lincoln, province of **Buenos Aires**, he worked in the private sector until 1975. In June of that year, he became a member of the board of the **Banco Central de la República Argentina** (BCRA), and the following month was appointed the bank's president.

In February 1976, one month before **Isabel Perón** was toppled, Mondelli replaced **Antonio Cafiero** as minister of economy. In an attempt to halt the unstoppable race of prices and wages unleashed by the **Rodrigazo** (the mega-adjustment introduced by **Celestino Rodrigo** in mid-1975), he announced a Plan de Emergencia Económica. The main measures were a 22 percent devaluation of the main commercial exchange rate, a 12 percent wage increase, a 100 percent rise in utility rates, and new maximum prices for bread, pasta, cheese, and other basic foodstuffs. Although these measures were seen by many as just another Rodrigazo, Mondelli displayed greater understanding of the problems with the Argentine balance of payments and its key components. He was highly critical of the government's foreign investment laws and the proposed *Argentinización* of companies and banks, for which there were no funds. Moreover, with no international credit available and the country heading for an imminent default, the minister saw no alternative but to turn to the International Monetary Fund (IMF).

Mondelli may have had the best of intentions, but it was too little and too late. Following the **military coup of 1976**, he retired from public life. *See also* ECONOMIC CRISES; ECONOMY; FOREIGN DEBT/FOREIGN INVESTMENT; MINISTRY OF ECONOMY.

MONTONEROS. The largest Peronist leftist guerrilla movement of its time, it was based on a lie. Constituted initially by left-wing elements who had nothing to do with **Peronism**, they became aware that they would not succeed unless able to connect with the leading mass movement in the country, namely Peronism. The Montoneros thus dressed themselves up as Peronists and slowly appropriated what appeared to be the **Justicialista** truth. They were a deadly group that controlled the **Juventud Peronista** (JP) and were at the heart of power briefly in 1973. With their violent methods, the Montoneros could not have met any other fate than that which befell them.

Founded in 1968 by **Fernando Abal Medina** (who became leader), **Carlos Gustavo Ramus**, **Mario Firmenich**, and **Norma Arrostito**, the Montoneros made a spectacular public debut with the **Aramburazo** (29 May–1 June 1970). Several major setbacks followed, the most important being the decapitation of the leadership in September 1970: Abal Medina and Ramus were killed in a shoot-out with the police; Firmenich became the group's secretary general and the author of its policy line. Between then and the end of 1970, the main activity of the Montoneros—which consisted of 20 militants—was robberies. The avowed aim was to accumulate financial, military, and logistical resources to enable the group to further its project and ideology. The group was careful not to attack the **military** or the police and thereby protected its image. Foreign companies and executives were particularly targeted as objects of punishment, but it was their property and not people that were the targets. The Montoneros were saved from extinction by the help and protection of the **Fuerzas Armadas Peronistas** (FAP) and also popular support from the **Movimiento de Sacerdotes para el Tercer Mundo** as well as ample sections of Peronism and its youth groups. By 1971, the Montoneros were a national organization.

The fundamental vehicle for Montonero orientation toward mass movements was the JP, which comprised 25 youth organizations that between 1970 and 1972 were fused into larger structures that served as a uniting and mobilizing force. In a dangerous political dance with exiled leader **Juan Domingo Perón**, the Montoneros became the leading Peronist "fuerza especial." While the Montoneros needed the former president to advance their cause, Perón sponsored them to strike at the embattled de facto government of **Alejandro Agustín Lanusse**. At the same time, four guerrilla groups—the

FAP, the **Fuerzas Armadas Revolucionarias** (FAR), the minnow Comando Descamisado, and the Montoneros—were converging toward unity. This would result in the Montoneros becoming the most visible and most powerful left-wing youth organization. The arrangements were completed in late 1972 with the Descamisados, in October 1973 with the FAR, and in June 1974 with a small group of the FAP.

The Montoneros were briefly close to the heart of power during the chaotic and bloody 49-day tenure of left-leaning **Héctor Cámpora** (25 May–13 July 1973), who had won the **presidential election of March 1973** as the candidate of the Peronist-run **Frente Justicialista de Liberación** (FREJULI). The Montoneros saw their guerrilla colleagues freed from prison under an amnesty enacted by Cámpora on his first day in office. They took advantage of the moment to extend political influence through legal activities. **Esteban Righi** was the cabinet minister closest to the group, which also had influence through governors and in **Congress**—the JP had eight Montonero deputies, including **Diego Muniz Barreto**. Nevertheless, having submitted themselves to party discipline, the eight failed to get the more radical promises of the FREJULI electoral platform enacted.

Perón returned to Argentina definitively on 20 June 1973—although unable to land at the main international airport in **Buenos Aires** as the event to welcome him back degenerated into the **Ezeiza Massacre**. Perón forced Cámpora to resign in July and took charge of national affairs after winning the snap **presidential election of September 1973**. By then, the Montoneros had served their purpose. Perón had used the Montoneros and the JP as spearheads in his battle against the **Revolución Argentina** regime and to drive electoral campaigns in March and September 1973. With his election in September, Perón no longer required the services of the Montoneros. Moreover, he could not control them—they were trying to take over the Peronist movement and transform Peronism into a radical leftist organization—something it never was. Congress introduced legislation restoring provisions in the penal code that had been abolished by former minister of interior Righi to secure the amnesty promised by the FREJULI in 1973; it was a tough anti-subversion law so broad in scope that it could be employed to repress any dissent, including from the Peronist left. The eight Montonero deputies of the JP objected to this "repressive legislation" and, already under pressure from the president, resigned when the law was passed in January 1974; they were immediately expelled from the **Partido Justicialista** (PJ). This clearly demonstrated that Perón was concerned not with maintaining a fictitious unity but with expelling the left from his movement. The Montoneros faced a definitive break with Perón on May Day 1974, with a speech by the president that is best remembered for the Montoneros being called "esos estúpidos imberbes." The Montoneros also experienced lethal attacks from the **Triple A**—the death squad set up by the all-powerful minister of social welfare **José López Rega**.

Yet even at the time of Perón's death in office on 1 July 1974, the Montoneros remained active. Two of their most notorious assassinations were those of **José Ignacio Rucci**, the head of the **Confederación General del Trabajo** (CGT), and of former interior minister **Arturo Mor Roig**. Following the accession of **Isabel Perón** to the presidency, the Montoneros returned to clandestinity. In early September 1974, they decided to resume the armed struggle; this time it would be full scale, with an authentic guerrilla army. The creation of such an apparatus required a good information service and abundant economic resources, as well as arms. The highly effective Servicio de Informaciones Montonero was set up, and toward the end of September 1974 the financial problem was resolved with the kidnapping of the **Born brothers**, who headed the leading Argentine multinational **Bunge & Born**. The company eventually caved in on the ransom demand of 60 million US dollars, which was paid in June 1975 and set a still unmatched world record. A Montoneros incursion into the Halcón arms factory outside Buenos Aires at the end of 1975 spared them financial outlays on weapons. Its production chief was a Montonero, so the assailants emptied the plant of arms, parts, machinery, and even accessories—this enabled the guerrilla group to begin their own weapons manufacturing.

In the meantime, the Montoneros had wasted no time in resuming their violent campaign. They caused public revulsion in mid-October 1974 when they seized the remains of **Pedro Eugenio Aramburu**, their very first victim back in 1970, hiding the body for a month. In November 1974, they assassinated **Alberto Villar**, the chief of the Federal Police and one of the founders of the Triple A; he was only one of the victims of a persistent campaign against the Triple A, which affected policemen and staff of the Ministry of Social Welfare. Having reached a tactical agreement with the **Ejército Revolucionario del Pueblo** (ERP) that left the latter exclusively in charge of attacks against the military, the Montoneros concentrated their firepower on the police, business firms, and the Peronist right. With the ERP increasingly weakened by the armed forces in their *foco* in **Tucumán**, in August 1975 the Montoneros decided to take their guerrilla struggle to new heights. They launched major operations against the three branches of the armed services: the most elaborate and best executed one was against the garrison of a powerful infantry regiment in the province of **Formosa** on 5 October 1975.

The immediate consequences of the Formosa attack would prove fatal for the Montoneros, who were now declared illegal. While Mrs. Perón was on medical leave, acting president **Ítalo Luder** signed the decrees giving the armed forces carte blanche to undertake a **War to Annihilate Subversion** nationally. Simultaneously, as the challenge of terrorism was combined with the crisis of constitutional government and the inefficiency of politicians, the military began to prepare for a coup. Nonetheless, the Montoneros continued to concentrate their firepower on the three armed services and their sponsors in the elite. In his Christmas message of 1975, Commander-in-Chief of the Army **Jorge Rafael Videla** warned the government that, if in 90 days it did not get a grip on things, the military would act. Sure enough, the **military coup of 1976** struck when the threatened deadline was reached.

The Montoneros continued their campaign throughout 1976 and 1977 but ended up defeated by state terrorism. The methods employed by the armed forces to eradicate subversion took them completely by surprise: officially authorized but nevertheless clandestine concentration camps, torture centers, and special units based in the three armed services and the police whose mission was to kidnap, interrogate, torture, and kill. It was the kidnappings and their consequences that proved fatal for the guerrilla group. Captured Montoneros betrayed their former companions by denouncing them, and thereby more guerrillas were felled. Because of its violent methods, the Montoneros could not have met any other fate. However, this in no way justifies the terrible abuses of **human rights** committed by the brutally murderous de facto **Proceso de Reorganización Nacional** regime. While the approximately 9,000 victims of state terrorism are frequently mentioned, the same cannot be said about the victims of both the Montoneros and the ERP. *See also* ACOSTA, JORGE EDUARDO (1941–); ASTIZ, ALFREDO IGNACIO (1951–); BIGNONE, REYNALDO BENITO (1928–2018); DESAPARECIDOS; DISPOSICIÓN FINAL; ESCUELA SUPERIOR DE MECÁNICA DE LA ARMADA (ESMA); GALIMBERTI, RODOLFO (1947–2002); GARCÍA ELORRIO, JUAN (1938–1970); HARGUINDEGUY, ALBANO EDUARDO (1927–2012); MASSERA, EMILIO EDUARDO (1925–2010); MENÉNDEZ, LUCIANO BENJAMÍN (1927–2018); MINISTRY OF INTERIOR, PUBLIC WORKS, AND HOUSING; MINISTRY OF SOCIAL DEVELOPMENT; MUGICA, CARLOS FRANCISCO SERGIO (1930–1974); SUÁREZ MASON, CARLOS GUILLERMO (1924–2005); TRELEW MASSACRE (22 AUGUST 1972).

MOR ROIG, ARTURO (1914–1974). Minister of interior from 1971 to 1973. Born in **Spain**, he immigrated with his parents to Argentina. Mor Roig joined the **Union Civica Radical** (UCR) in 1939 and was provincial senator for **Buenos Aires** between 1953 and 1955.

When the UCR split, he joined the **Union Cívica Radical del Pueblo** (UCRP). Elected to the Chamber of Deputies in 1958, Mor Roig remained a member until the army ousted President **Arturo Frondizi** and closed **Congress** in 1962. Elections held in 1963 returned him to the Chamber of Deputies, over which he presided until the **military coup of 1966**. With the faltering **military** regime remaining intransigent, he became one of the architects of a multiparty declaration setting forth a political program; this statement was **"La Hora del Pueblo"** and was issued in November 1970.

When General **Alejandro Agustín Lanusse** became de facto president in 1971 with the aim of extricating the armed forces from government, he crucially appointed Mor Roig to the post of minister of interior. The signatories of "La Hora del Pueblo" backed the appointment as the best way to guarantee the opening of the political process. Before taking office, Mor Roig resigned from the UCRP in order to take up his new duties without party ties. He lifted the ban on the activities of **political parties** and returned them their property, and he wholeheartedly supported Lanusse's endeavors by promoting the constitutional changes and legislation governing the **congressional** and **presidential elections of March 1973**.

Mor Roig retired from politics at the end of his ministerial stint and was assassinated by the **Montoneros** the following year. *See also* MINISTRY OF INTERIOR, PUBLIC WORKS, AND HOUSING.

MORA Y ARAUJO, MANUEL (1937–2017). Political sociologist—he read law and sociology at the **University of Buenos Aires** (UBA) and studied in France, **Chile**, and Norway. Awarded research fellowships by foundations in **Great Britain** and the **United States**, he was a successful businessman, distinguished academic, and opinion shaper.

In addition to his academic positions—Mora y Araujo led the **Universidad Torcuato Di Tella** at a difficult time, as well as teaching there and at other institutions—he is best known publicly for his work in the fields of market research and opinion polling. In 1984, he founded the market analysis firm Mora y Araujo & Asociados, and in 1990 the public relations consultancy Comunicación Institucional SA, a business he headed for many years. These were, arguably, the first companies in the country to undertake serious market analysis based on modern scientific principles. It is said that his businesses conducted many official surveys during the 1990s that helped shape policy and public opinion—sometimes described as the pollster of choice of President **Carlos Saúl Menem**. Mora y Araujo's principal academic works include *El voto peronista* (1980) (The Peronist Vote), *Liberalismo y democracia* (1988) (Liberalism and Democracy), *Democracias desafiantes* (2005) (Discordant Democracies), and *La Argentina bipolar* (2011) (Bipolar Argentina).

MORENO, GUILLERMO (1955–). Career politician who acquired a reputation for militancy when a student—there is debate as to whether his ideas and actions were drawn from the revolutionary left or nationalistic right;

served as secretary for domestic commerce between 2005 and 2013. Appointed by President **Nèstor Kirchner**, Moreno was retained in post by President **Cristina Fernández de Kirchner** until forced to resign.

Before appointment, Moreno was closely associated with the left wing of the labor movement and subsequently a key figure in the group surrounding the Kirchners who pressed hard for the reversal of neoliberal economics associated with President **Carlos Saúl Menem** and Minister of Economy **Domingo Cavallo** that they argued brought the country to its knees in 2001 when the **Convertibility Plan** crashed. Taking up his position at the secretariat as urbane minister of economy **Roberto Lavagna**, who had been appointed by interim president **Eduardo Duhalde** and whom Néstor Kirchner had kept on, was leaving office, Moreno soon came to be regarded as the real minister of economy as various holders of that position came and went during the latter part of Néstor's presidency. Moreno also enjoyed a stormy relationship with the first, youthful minister of economy, Martín Lousteau, appointed by Cristina Kirchner. On appointment one of the youngest to have held the office, Lousteau was in post for barely four months.

Moreno is most remembered as an ardent advocate of the Kirchner economic model and the individual who enforced the official line on price control. Although he had read management at the **Universidad Argentina de la Empresa** (UADE), Moreno was loathed by business leaders because of the way he dealt with firms during the battle to control inflation and massage prices. Praised by associates for a robust, pugilistic approach to political debate, he was depicted as a bully and a thug by opponents. He was accused of intimidating businesses when implementing price control—mobilizing labor groups and **La Cámpora** to confront businesses, company shareholders, and individual entrepreneurs considered to be reluctant to toe the official line. He was also instrumental in the removal of the head of the government statistical office when the agency attempted to publish real data on inflation—the agency was intervened and key personnel dismissed.

Moreno was brought down by his role in the intervention in the statistical office and crude efforts to massage prices. He was charged with dereliction of duty and abuse of office. The charges were upheld in court. It was observed at the time that Moreno's personal assets had grown substantially while he held public office. On leaving the secretariat, Moreno was offered a job at the Argentine Embassy in Rome. As the newspaper *La Nación* observed, it was a diplomatic position for which he was ill qualified. In 2017, Moreno was convicted of a misuse of public funds while in office and given an 18-month suspended prison sentence. He subsequently complained that Cristina Kirchner has not sufficiently protected her former associates charged with **corruption**.

MORENO, MARIANO (1778–1811). Lawyer, writer, and statesmen; intellectual progenitor of the republic, sometimes referred to as the soul of the **May Revolution of 1810**. One of the ablest scholars of his generation, Moreno was born to a Spanish colonial official and a creole mother and went on to gain a reputation for questioning many aspects of the juridical justification of the system of Spanish administration in the Americas. His intellectual journey involved moving from the ideas of the Enlightenment and associated Spanish liberalism of the period to something approximating the English school of social and economic liberalism, a journey that led him to reject Spanish colonial mercantilism—he campaigned for free trade for the colonies—and the unrepresentative nature of the system of imperial administration. He did not play an active role in opposing the **British invasions** of 1806 and 1807 but was one of the patriotic, radical group clamoring for a *cabildo abierto* in response to the French invasion of the Iberian Peninsula years later. In the *cabildo*, he argued for the dismissal of the viceroy and the selection of a junta to represent the people. When the so-called First Junta (Primera Junta) was selected, headed by **Cornelio Saavedra**, Moreno was named secretary, charged with supervising military and political affairs. Although he may have flirted with the idea of home rule for the viceroyalty, he rapidly became an advocate of **independence** and republicanism, and for the formation of a centralized, constitutional state. As such, his ideas diverged from those of Saavedra, whose position he successfully attempted to undermine. A fervent advocate of root-and-branch change in the organization and governing principles of the country, some of his ideas were in advance of the time and were weakened by his tendency to rubbish the views of opponents. Indeed, opposition was a flame to his radicalism. Disillusioned, he resigned as secretary to the junta but accepted a diplomatic commission; he was on his way to London when he died at sea. His writing marks the starting point of modern Argentine political thought, as well as establishing the economic and political ideas that shaped the formation of the state.

MOSCONI, ENRIQUE CARLOS ALBERTO (1877–1940). First director general of the state-owned oil company **Yacimientos Petrolíferos Fiscales** (YPF) (1922–1930). Mosconi was born in **Buenos Aires** and, like the sons of numerous middle-class immigrants, chose a career in the **military**. He graduated from the Colegio Militar de la Nación in 1894 and received a degree in civil engineering in 1903.

Promoted to colonel in 1914, Mosconi was appointed by President **Marcelo T. de Alvear** as chief administrator of YPF in 1922. Aiming to create a vertically integrated state enterprise that would not only produce oil but refine it and market the resulting products at competitive prices, he launched an ambitious reorganization and development plan. His project had some successes. YPF obtained complete administrative autonomy in 1923 and during the late 1920s completed a major refinery in **La Plata** (near the largest market in Buenos Aires), expanded its product range, and established a distribution and sales network. However, Argentina remained heavily reliant on imported products as YPF failed to increase crude output by continuing intensive drilling on already developed oil fields. In 1928, Alvear was succeeded as president by **Hipólito Yrigoyen**, who strove to nationalize all private oil companies operating in the country and create a state monopoly that would provide an attractive source of political patronage. The new president would thus find himself pitted against Mosconi, who remained head of the state oil company and had by then been promoted to general.

The director general of YPF had always been hostile to foreign companies but regarded Yrigoyen's expropriation and state monopoly plans as ill conceived. He instead formulated a comprehensive ideology of nationalistic petroleum development that incorporated the mixed company concept and aimed both for maximum efficiency and national ownership. Basing his ideas on the British government's organization of the Anglo-Persian Oil Company, Mosconi proposed a mixed monopoly to be financed 51 percent by the government and 49 percent by private Argentine investors, with the company being administered by the private investors and the government members of the board of directors retaining veto power over major policy decisions. Yrigoyen ignored the mixed company concept but did not achieve his oil nationalization plans either as he was ousted by the **military coup of 1930**. Mosconi opposed the military takeover, for which he paid a heavy price. Shortly after General **José Félix Uriburu** became president, he was fired as director general of YPF and sent into exile in Europe. Allowed to return to Argentina after General **Agustin P. Justo** took power, he encountered official insult. All this ill treatment took a severe toll on his health during the 1930s and led to his death.

Although Mosconi failed to obtain political support for a monopolistic mixed company, his state monopoly thesis survived to form the core of modern Argentine oil nationalism. The political appeal of a YPF monopoly grew after 1930, and YPF itself is identified as the model for the state oil companies established in **Uruguay**, **Bolivia**, and **Brazil**. Mosconi's aspirations for YPF were undermined during the presidency of **Carlos Saúl Menem**, though revived during that of **Cristina Fernández de Kirchner**. *See also* COMMODITIES; ECONOMY; PRIVATIZATION; STATE-OWNED ENTERPRISES (SOEs).

MOTHERS OF THE PLAZA DE MAYO. *See* MADRES DE PLAZA DE MAYO.

MOVIMIENTO DE INTEGRACIÓN Y DESARROLLO (MID). Splinter of the **Unión Cívica Radical Intransigente** (UCRI) founded by **Arturo Frondizi** and **Rogelio Julio Frigerio** in 1963. The MID was unable to field candidates in the **congressional** and **presidential elections of 1963** due to opposition from the armed forces and conservative elements: Frondizi had been overthrown in the **military coup of 1962**. As a result, the MID joined the Frente Nacional y Popular, an electoral alliance set up with the blessing of the exiled **Juan Domingo Perón** that also comprised the **Unión Popular** (UP) and the **Partido Conservador Popular** (PCP). When the Frente was proscribed under pressure from the military, the MID leadership endorsed a "blank vote" in the election, a move that was opposed by the rump UCRI led by **Oscar Alende**, which was determined to contest the election rather than, in effect, abstain.

President **Arturo Illia** allowed the MID to contest the **congressional elections of 1965**. The party secured 16 seats and vigorously opposed Illia in the National **Congress**, principally because he had canceled Frondizi-era risk contracts awarded to US oil companies. Following the **Revolución Argentina**, the MID joined the Peronist-dominated **Frente Justicialista de Liberación** (FREJULI) to contest the **presidential election of March 1973** in an unsuccessful bid to exert influence over Peronist **economic policy**. Thereafter, the MID survived as a fringe grouping, fielding Frigerio as a candidate in the **presidential election of 1983**. It was a longshot candidacy and suffered from the failure of the MID to condemn **human rights** atrocities committed by the outgoing **military** regime: Frigerio obtained a shade over 1 percent of the popular vote. Three years later, Frigerio succeeded the ailing Frondizi as party leader. The MID then endorsed successful Peronist candidate **Carlos Saúl Menem** in the **presidential election of 1989**, providing Antonio Salonia as minister of **education** and later Oscar Camilión as minister of defense.

Frondizi died in 1995, and Frigerio passed away in 2006. Since then, the MID has behaved like many other minor **political parties**, constantly switching allegiances in order to exert influence or maintain a representation in Congress. It backed the candidacy of **Roberto Lavagna** in the **presidential election of 2007**, **Eduardo Duhalde** in the **presidential election of 2011**, and **Sergio Massa** during the **presidential election of 2015**, consistently failing to back the winning candidate. *See also* MINISTRY OF EDUCATION; PROCESO DE REORGANIZACIÓN NACIONAL.

MOVIMIENTO DE RENOVACIÓN Y CAMBIO. The Movement for Renewal and Change was organized in 1972 to promote the modernization of the **Unión Cívica Radical** (UCR) at a time when the electoral future of the party appeared threatened by the rise of Peronism and the **Partido Justicialista** (PJ). The group was headed by future president **Raúl Alfonsín** and included such key figures as **Bernardo Grinspun**. Its political approach was social democratic, favoring a mixed state–market **developmentalist** economic model. The Renovación group opposed the traditional Línea Nacional associated with **Ricardo Balbín**. As well as the threat posed by Peronism, Renewalists were exercised by splits in the party in the 1960s. The imperative for change was reinforced by the **Proceso de Reorganización Nacional** that followed the **military coup of 1976**; reformists argued that politics as usual was no longer an option. In the face of the terror of the Proceso, members of the movement protested against the violation of **human rights** and courageously opposed the **Falklands War**. When, in late 1982, the **military** government announced that elections would be held the following year, the Movimiento campaigned in party primaries for Alfonsín, who stood against the Balbinista faction. Although Balbín died in 1981, his equivocal approach to the military regimes of the Proceso had discredited the Línea Nacional, within the party and the country. The campaign secured the UCR nomination for Alfonsín and subsequently the presidency of the nation. The grouping barely survived the Alfonsín government. It split and virtually disappeared in 1992, yet it had played a crucial role in driving the modernization of the party and strengthening internal democracy. It also provided a model for near contemporary—but ultimately unsuccessful—groupings within the PJ.

MOVIMIENTO DE SACERDOTES PARA EL TERCER MUNDO (MSTM). A tendency among the **Catholic Church** in Argentina aimed at combining reform that followed the Second Vatican Council with a strong political and social participation. The movement, sometimes abbreviated as MSTM, was formed mainly by priests active in shantytowns and workers' neighborhoods. It was an important vehicle for social action between 1967 and 1976, close to the Peronist left and occasionally Marxism. It was also close to the **Confederación General del Trabajo de los Argentinos** (CGTA), which was heavily involved in the **Cordobazo**.

Having declared its support for Socialist revolutionary movements and for the abolition of private ownership of the means of production, the MSTM was condemned by the Catholic hierarchy in **Buenos Aires** in December 1969. Within four years, the movement had ruptured over a conflict between members supporting Peronism and those supporting Guevarism. It lost any capacity for action and became a victim of repression during the **War to Annihilate Subversion**, which led to its dissolution. *See also* MUGICA, CARLOS FRANCISCO SERGIO (1930–1974).

MOVIMIENTO NACIONALISTA TACUARA (MNT). Founded in 1957, it is sometimes considered the first urban guerrilla group in Argentina. Its first model being the Falange in **Spain**, the movement defended nationalist, Catholic, anti-Communist, anti-Semitic, and antidemocratic ideas. There were three major ideological splits in the early 1960s, and the police cracked down on all factions in March 1964. The entire MNT was outlawed by President **Arturo Illia** in 1965.

MOVIMIENTO POPULAR NEUQUINO (MPN). Provincial party founded in **Neuquén** in 1961 that, created at the time of Peronism's proscription, remains the only neo-Peronist political entity that survives to date. The dominant figure in the MPN during its first three decades of existence was **Felipe Sapag**, a member of a family clan of Lebanese origin that wielded political and economic clout in Neuquén. He was six-time governor of the province, though most of his tenures occurred in exceptional circumstances. First elected in March 1962, Sapag was promptly removed in the coup that overthrew President **Arturo Frondizi**. Again elected in 1963, he remained in office until the **military coup of 1966**. Sapag was then paradoxically appointed governor by de facto president **Juan Carlos Onganía** in February 1970; it was an extraordinary appointment arising from mutual needs. The Sapag family and the MPN backed the technocratic and **developmentalist** approach of the **military** regime, despite being strongly in favor of the restoration of democracy. Onganía required the cooperation of the MPN, whose experienced and efficient leadership could run Neuquén. Sapag remained governor of the province until early 1972.

The MPN and the other neo-Peronist parties would then reiterate their adherence to Peronism and recognized the leadership of exiled leader **Juan Domingo Perón**. But the goodwill did not last. When they were instructed in December 1972 to join the **Frente Justicialista de Liberación** (FREJULI), these parties objected owing to major ideological and strategic differences. Following the elections held in March 1973, the MPN remained the only neo-Peronist party that did not fade away. In fact, it had performed reasonably well in the electoral contest; the MPN won the governorship of Neuquén and provided half of the national deputies and two of the three national senators allotted to the province.

Sapag was once again ousted as governor in the **military coup of 1976**. With the return of democracy in 1983, the MPN won the gubernatorial elections in Neuquén held that year as well as all the subsequent ones. Although Sapag served as governor for full four-year terms in 1983–1987 and 1995–1999, his influence was reduced by old age and the rise of competing factions within the party. Yet his family remained determined to control the MPN. Jorge Augusto Sapag, the nephew of the former governor, was elected to that post in 2007 and 2011. *See also* MILITARY COUP OF 1962.

MOVIMIENTO RENOVADOR PERONISTA (MRP). Founded following the shock defeat of the **Partido Justicialista** (PJ) in the **congressional and presidential elections of 1983**, the MRP was intended to recapture the electoral dominance of the party by renewing the leadership and reconnecting with voters and the **trade unions**. For some, it signaled an attempt to make the PJ a "normal" **political party** with greater internal democracy and formal organizational structures. In some respects, the MRP echoed the **Movimiento de Renovación y Cambio** set up by younger members of the **Unión Cívica Radical** (UCR).

Various factions of the PJ had been struggling to control the party apparatus following the death of **Juan Domingo Perón** in 1974, internal schisms contributed to the chaos of the last years of the administration of President **Isabel Perón**—as vice president, she had succeeded on the death of her husband—and to the **military coup of 1976**. This turmoil, and the collaboration of figures in the PJ and trade union leadership with de facto regimes during the **Proceso de Reorganización Nacional**, was seen as contributing to electoral defeat in 1983. In the run-up to the **congressional elections of 1985**, the MRP emerged, bringing together factions of the historical leadership of Peronism and modernizers intent on reform. Modernizers, or *renovadores* as they were know, assumed that it would be relatively easy to transform the movement and make Peronism electorally triumphant again. They were wrong. With the refusal of traditionalists to cede power, and failing to agree on a common list of candidates, for the first time in its history the PJ submitted two lists of candidates to voters in the key electoral district of the province of **Buenos Aires**. The *renovadora* list was headed by **Antonio Francisco Cafiero**, the official party list by Herminio Iglesias. The "split list" in 1985 set a precedent for how internal division within the PJ would be handled during the *kirchnerato*, when the PJ regularly presented voters with separate lists of candidates.

The list headed by Cafiero triumphed in the 1985 elections—Cafiero was elected governor of the province of Buenos Aires—but internal rivalries continued. With the **congressional** and **presidential elections of 1989** looming, and once again failing to agree, the PJ held internal primary elections, another first in its history. Cafiero was expected to win the PJ presidential nomination. In the event, he was defeated by **Carlos Saúl Menem**, who went on to win the presidential election of 1989. Menem's victory in the primaries was attributed to his broad-church approach. He promised to take on demands of modernizers for greater transparency and internal democracy while also appealing to traditionalists—he was not from the *renovadora* wing. The promise of internal renewal and modernization appealed to many. In addition to explaining Menem's victory in the 1989 presidential contest, it attracted the support of a younger generation of Peronists like **José Octavio Bordón**, **Carlos Alberto "Chacho" Álvarez** (Álvarez was one of the founders of the

MRP), and **Gustavo Beliz**. The dream of PJ modernizers was never realized. In office, Menem resorted to traditional Peronist tactics of patronage politics and divide and rule; he proved adept at identifying and promoting talent only to destroy it when individuals became a threat—a device perfected by Juan Domingo Perón and some of his successors. **Corruption** and patronage were reinforced as mechanisms of leadership and control, as was the promotion of competing factions.

The MRP is important because it represents an attempt—possibly the last opportunity—to transform the PJ into a "normal" political organization. Although an ephemeral organization, the mantle of the MRP has been claimed by successive factions of the PJ. Competing with **Cristina Fernández de Kirchner** for control of the PJ, the name devised by Sergio Massa for his electoral coalition—**Frente Renovador/Partido Justicialista** (FR/PJ)—consciously echoed that of the MRP. As with the other grouping before, Massa advocated reform and democratic accountability within the party. While Mrs. Fernández de Kirchner seeks to retain control of the PJ, many others like Massa echo the language and aspirations of the founders of the MRP. *See also* FRENTE PARA LA VICTORIA (FpV/PJ); KIRCHNER, NÉSTOR CARLOS (1950–2010); "PERONISM WITHOUT PERÓN".

MOYANO, HUGO (1944–). Powerful **trade union** leader; lifelong activist on the right of **Partido Justicialista** (PJ)—viscerally opposed to the Peronist left. Born and raised in the province of **Buenos Aires**, Moyano was employed by his late teens in a small removal firm based in the affluent seaside city of Mar del Plata. Elected shop steward by fellow workers in 1962, he was soon head of the local branch of the powerful road haulers union, the Sindicato de Choferes de Camiones, the *camioneros*. Some 10 years later, he was reputed to be close to the éminence grise of the recently reelected President **Juan Domingo Perón**, **José López Rega**, and the **Triple A**. López Rega was responsible for the "disappearance" and murder of left-wing trade unionists and others deemed to be subversive. It is unclear whether contacts with the **military** and police established at this time kept Moyano "safe" after the **military coup of 1976**. Although trade union activities were either banned or rigorously controlled during the **Proceso de Reorganización Nacional**, Moyano remained active in trade union politics and was responsible for organizing demonstrations against the regime when it began to unravel after 1980—he was arrested several times.

With the return of democracy in 1983, Moyano was elected head of the Mar del Plata branch of the PJ, and within a few years he was a major national figure in the *camioneros* union—he headed the union's social welfare division, in charge of a substantial budget. Around this time, he was elected to **Congress**, serving as a deputy in the lower chamber. The 1990s saw Moyano ascend the union hierarchy, giving him a role in the national trade union organization, the **Confederación General del Trabajo** (CGT) and prominence in the international labor movement—he represented the *camioneros* at union gatherings in Europe and the Americas. Like many senior figures in the labor movement, Moyano was ambivalent about **privatization** strategies pursued by President **Carlos Saúl Menem**. Moyano and dissident factions of the CGT organized strikes against Menem in 1996 while clamoring for PJ unity, notwithstanding splits within the CGT.

Moyano gained further national prominence after the collapse of the **Convertibility Plan** and the administration of President **Fernando de la Rúa**. Moyano and the CGT played a key role in ensuring political stability during the interim presidency of **Eduardo Duhalde**. In 2004, Moyano was elected secretary general of the recently reunited CGT, a post that ensured him considerable influence in the administration of President **Néstor Kirchner**, which had assumed office the previous year. Moyano remained a crucial force in the first administration of President **Cristina Fernández de Kirchner**. He held senior posts within the administration and was a powerful defender of it at moments of crisis such as during the **farm protests** and conflicts with the **media**, which beset the government around 2008 and 2009. Moyano helped organize counterdemonstrations when the opposition appeared to be gaining popular support, and the *camioneros*—then headed by his son Pablo—embargoed the distribution networks of critical newspapers. It was around this time that Moyano was subject to death threats and he and members of his family charged with **corruption** and money laundering—charges that are still under investigation.

Moyano broke with Cristina Fernández around 2011, reputedly because she refused to accord the CGT greater prominence in government and Congress. By 2012, Pablo Moyano was leading strikes by *camioneros* against the government, blockading oil refineries and disrupting traffic. The government responded with fines and legal proceedings against the union. Hugo Moyano organized a split in the CGT, taking anti-Kirchner unions out of the organization. Despite this break with Mrs. Kirchner and the defeat of the PJ in the presidential election of 2015, Moyano remains a force in the labor movement and national politics. Beset by ill health, in 2018 he was described as the most powerful union leader in the country, his influence compared with that of Jimmy Hoffa, the notorious former head of the Teamsters union in the **United States**. *See also* CONFEDERACIÓN GENERAL DEL TRABAJO DE LOS ARGENTINOS (CGTA).

MUGICA, CARLOS FRANCISCO SERGIO (1930–1974). Catholic priest and activist. He was born into a well-off family, with his father Adolfo having been one of the founders of the **Partido Demócrata Nacional** (PDN). Mugica entered the priesthood in 1952 and four years later became a Peronist out of enormous guilt over the church's support for the overthrow of **Juan**

Domingo Perón in the **military coup of 1955** and the consequent identification of the church with the oligarchy and the de facto provisional government by various sectors of the working class. This guilt was paralleled by that experienced by students turning to Peronism as a consequence of the anti-Peronism of their predecessors. If anything, this "rebelliousness" demonstrated an incredibly naïve attitude toward Peronism.

By the time Mugica was ordained as a priest of the Jesuit Order in 1959, the **Catholic Church** had veered to the left in order to compete with Marxism in Latin America, giving rise to liberation theology, which inspired many young Catholics, who became increasingly radicalized. The more radical advocated political violence as a response to repressive governments, and their two leading Argentine examples are Mugica and **Juan García Elorrio**.

Mugica became a regular guest at the leftist Juventud Estudiantil Católica (JEC), where in 1964 he met **Fernando Abal Medina, Carlos Gustavo Ramus**, and **Mario Firmenich**. But he eventually distanced himself from them as there were limits to his espousal of violence. In 1968, he joined the **Movimiento de Sacerdotes para el Tercer Mundo** (MSTM), an outfit that was close to the Peronist left and at times Marxist. From then on, Mugica engaged in social action in the Villa 31, an increasingly sprawling *villa miseria* located behind the railway tracks at the Retiro terminus in the city of **Buenos Aires**.

Mugica was heavily criticized by the Catholic hierarchy in Buenos Aires for his involvement with the MSTM, a movement the church had condemned in December 1969. Vehemently opposed to the church's support for the **Revolución Libertadora**, he caused even greater controversy when he defended Abal Medina, Ramus, and Firmenich over the **Aramburazo**. Mugica only made matters worse by officiating at the funerals of Abal Medina and Ramus, who were killed in a shoot-out with police in September 1970.

Within Peronism, Father Mugica was closest to **Héctor Cámpora**. Following the victory of the **Frente Justicialista de Liberación** (FREJULI) in the **presidential election of March 1973**, and with the consent of a highly manipulative Perón, Mugica was appointed as an unpaid, senior consultant to the all-too-powerful **José López Rega**. The latter, who was the minister of social welfare, used his position and control of 30 percent of the national budget to organize and arm the **Triple A**. The spate of revenge killings between the Triple A and the far left, and Perón's victory in the **presidential election of September 1973**, led Mugica to leave his government post as well as definitively break with the **Montoneros**.

With mounting threats to his life, Mugica went to see López Rega. At this meeting, he argued that he was a Peronist and that he had thought that so were the Montoneros, that he was anti-Marxist, and would always work for his *"villero"* brothers. This last-ditch bid by Mugica to save his life had no effect; he was murdered by the Triple A in May 1974. *See also* MINISTRY OF SOCIAL DEVELOPMENT.

MUNIZ BARRETO, DIEGO (1934–1977). A member of **Congress** from May 1973 to January 1974; one of the eight **Montoneros** elected to the Chamber of Deputies. Muniz Barreto's political origins, however, were far removed from the left, and over time his trajectory spanned the whole political spectrum.

Muniz Barreto was born into a landed, strongly anti-Peronist family. During the first half of the 1950s, his activities opposing President **Juan Domingo Perón** resulted in him having to flee the country. Under the de facto regime of **Juan Carlos Onganía** in the late 1960s, he worked in the Secretariat of Legal and Technical Affairs of the Presidential Office, which prepared speeches as well as policy and legislative initiatives for the president.

As with many young people at the time, Muniz Barreto took "the road to Damascus" and converted to the Peronist left. He espoused a popular revolutionary nationalism and contacted the Juventud Argentina por la Emancipación Nacional (JAEN), an outfit to which he provided funds and which was led by **Rodolfo Galimberti**. The latter was then recruited by the Montoneros in 1972, and Muniz Barreto also drew close to the terrorist group.

Muniz Barreto was one of the financiers of the Peronist campaign for the general elections held in March 1973 and was himself elected as a deputy for the **Frente Justicialista de Liberación** (FREJULI). Like the other Montoneros, in the chamber he made radical speeches advocating the FREJULI platform. Yet, having submitted to party discipline, they failed to achieve the implementation of the electoral promises regarding land reform and extensive economic socialization. Muniz Barreto and his seven colleagues were forced to confront the president in January 1974, when they were asked to vote for legislation to restore provisions in the penal code that former minister of interior **Esteban Righi** had abolished in order to secure the political amnesty promised by the FREJULI in 1973. The eight Montonero congressmen objected to the "repressive legislation" and, already under pressure from Perón himself, resigned when it was passed; they were immediately expelled from the **Partido Justicialista** (PJ).

Muniz Barreto placed himself in great danger with his subsequent activities, especially after the Montoneros went underground. He was a more than likely target for the **Triple A**, and matters came to a head following the **military coup of 1976**. Muniz Barreto was captured in February 1977 and held and tortured at the clandestine detention center "El Campito," which was run by **Reynaldo Bignone** in Campo de Mayo, the main **military** base outside the city of **Buenos Aires**. A month later, his body was found in the province of **Entre Ríos**, the victim of the old trick of being "killed in a car crash while attempting to escape." *See also* CONGRESSIONAL ELECTIONS OF 1973; PRESIDENTIAL ELECTION OF MARCH 1973.

N

NATIONAL COMMISSION FOR DISAPPEARED PEOPLE/PERSONS. *See* COMISIÓN NACIONAL SOBRE LA DESAPARACIÓN DE PERSONAS (CONADEP).

NATIONAL ORGANIZATION. Term applied to the definitive formation of the state and the nation between 1852, when **Juan Manuel de Rosas** was ousted, and the installation of General **Julio A. Roca** as national president in 1880 after the successful conclusion of the **Conquest of the Desert**. Sometimes referred to as national consolidation.

Following the **May Revolution of 1810**, taken as marking the end of the colonial era, and the **Congress of Tucumán**, which began deliberating in 1816, various projects for the organization of the country emerged. The earliest envisaged an independent, centralized polity based on the **Viceroyalty of the River Plate** (Virreinato de Río de la Plata) formed in 1776. Such an arrangement, the **United Provinces of the River Plate** (Provincias Unidas de Río de la Plata), was favored by the **Buenos Aires** commercial elite and an emergent liberal urban class intent on modernization, for example, **Cornelio Saavedra, Manuel Belgrano, Juan Martín de Pueyrredón**, and **Bernardino Rivadavia**. The principal point at issue for these groups was whether the form of government should be a constitutional monarchy or a republic. The project was soon challenged. With **independence** from Spain, elites in such regions of the former viceroyalty as present-day **Bolivia, Paraguay**, and **Uruguay** saw little advantage in rule from Buenos Aires. Within what would become Argentina, there was reluctance to accept the hegemony of Buenos Aires. In areas like **Córdoba, Cuyo, Mesopotamia**, and the northwest, regional sentiments prevailed with demands for autonomy or independence—boundaries and identities were fluid. Challenged from many quarters, the centralist **Unitarian** project faltered and was displaced by **Federalism**, epitomized in its most extreme form by the loose association of provinces, with each displaying many aspects of statehood, during the Rosas period. The years between the mid-1820s and early 1850s were notoriously a period of anarchy—intermittent civil war and regional conflict. There was no national state during the **Argentine Confederation** (Confederación Argentina) period (1831–1852) and no functioning national constitution.

When Rosas was removed by erstwhile ally **Justo José de Urquiza**, at the head of an army of provincial and regional troops largely financed by **Brazil**, it was by no means clear that a unified nation-state would result. The fall of Rosas, and the struggle that preceded it, cast doubt on the prevailing informal settlement that he oversaw, an arrangement that had resulted in instability in the interior and near continuous civil conflict. The events of 1852 triggered renewed demands for a definitive national organization and highlighted the problems involved in securing such a settlement. Would a strong unitary state emerge, or would multiple states result as former provinces aspired to statehood? Although the **Constitution of 1853** envisioned a strong nation-state, the rejection by the province of Buenos Aires of key provisions of the constitution highlighted the fragility of the project. From 1852 to 1862, the State of Buenos Aires operated as an independent polity, separate from the now-reduced Argentina Confederation. Buenos Aires rejoined the Confederation in 1862, but relations between it and other provinces remained fraught; and there was continued resistance to the "national arrangement" in the interior as provincial factions jockeyed for position among themselves while united in suspicion of Buenos Aires. Unitarian and Federalist sentiments remained strong, as did antagonism between them. Tension continued through the 1870s with disagreement about taxation and funding of the state, the distribution of resources, state rights and the power of the presidency, and state–church relations.

National unity was only achieved by a combination of consensus and repression encapsulated in the **federalization of the City of Buenos Aires** in 1880. The definitive settlement was underwritten by the rapid economic growth associated with mass **immigration** and foreign investment, though it remains debatable whether national consolidation per se triggered the boom, or the boom fostered consolidation. *See also* AVELLANEDA, NICOLÁS REMIGIO AURELIO (1836–1885); CAUDILLO; CONSTITUENT ASSEMBLY OF 1813; CONSTITUTION OF 1819; DERQUI, SANTIAGO RAFAEL LUIS MANUEL JOSÉ MARÍA (1809–1867); FOREIGN DEBT/ FOREIGN INVESTMENT; MITRE, BARTOLOMÉ (1821–1906); SAN NICOLÁS; SARMIENTO, DOMINGO FAUSTINO (1811–1888); WAR OF THE TRIPLE ALLIANCE.

NEGRO (RIVER). Large river in northern **Patagonia**, which gives its name to the province, formed by the confluence of the rivers Neuquén (to the northwest) and Limay (to the southwest) at the city of **Neuquén**, where the name changes to Río Negro, just as the river enters the province. Flows southeastward across the province to reach the Atlantic miles below the provincial capital (and sometime projected national capital) **Viedma**. Approximately 12 miles (20 kilometers) wide in the upper reaches, the river irrigates the fruit-growing region. The irrigation system was completed in the 1930s, since when the upper and middle sections of the valley have produced around two-thirds of the apples and pears consumed in the country. In some districts, vines are now displacing hard fruit as wine production takes off. Dams generate hydroelectricity. During the later stages of the **Conquest of the Desert**, the campaign against nomadic pampean Indians in the 19th century, the river served as the frontier between civilized Argentina and "barbarous" territory to the south. *See also* RÍO NEGRO (PROVINCE).

NEUQUÉN (CITY). Founded in 1904, it is the newest provincial capital in the country and the capital of the province of **Neuquén**. Located at the confluence of the Limay and Neuquén Rivers, where the **Río Negro** forms. It is an important agricultural center located in a fruit-growing area and a key location for the petrochemical industry, receiving petroleum extracted in different parts of the province. The current population of the city is approximately 230,000. *See also* AGRICULTURE; INDUSTRY; YACIMIENTOS PETROLÍFEROS FISCALES (YPF).

NEUQUÉN (PROVINCE). Province located at the northern end of **Patagonia**, bordered by **Río Negro** to the southeast, **Mendoza** to the north, and **Chile** to the west. In the late 16th and early 17th centuries, Jesuits established in southern Chile attempted to set up missions in the area but largely failed as the native **Tehuelches** resisted. Aboriginal resistance was only broken with the **Conquest of the Desert**, and in 1884 the area became the Territorio de Neuquén. At the beginning of the 20th century, a new irrigation system was completed and the railway reached the recently founded city of **Neuquén**, which facilitated the production and later transportation of crops. Oil was first discovered in Plaza Huincul in 1918, and further major discoveries would come in the 1960s. The territory was made a province in 1955.

The provincial **economy** is heavily dependent on the mining and extractive sector. Around half of its output is accounted for by its massive gas and oil production. The province generates a significant amount of Patagonia's electric power through a number of hydroelectric plants such as **El Chocón** and is also an important fruit producer. The current population of the province of Neuquén is around 560,000. *See also* AGRICULTURE; BUENOS AYRES GREAT SOUTHERN RAILWAY COMPANY (BAGS); FERROCARRILES ARGENTINOS (FFAA); INDUSTRY; TRANSPORTATION; YACIMIENTOS PETROLÍFEROS FISCALES (YPF).

NISMAN, NATALIO ALBERTO (1963–2015). *See* NISMAN CASE.

NISMAN CASE. Natalio Alberto Nisman (1963–2015) was a lawyer and prosecuting magistrate found dead in mysterious circumstances on the eve of the publication of his report into the bombing of the Israeli–Argentine Mutual Association (AMIA), a devastating terrorist attack in central **Buenos Aires** in 1994 in which 85 people were killed and hundreds injured. The perpetrators have never been brought to justice. Over the years, amid charges of incompetence and cover-up, the outrage has been subject to several investigations, most recently the one headed by Nisman.

Trained at the **University of Buenos Aires** (UBA), Nisman was a bright, personable young lawyer born into a middle-class immigrant family of Jewish origin. He rapidly made a name for himself as a tenacious investigating magistrate. He was appointed special investigator into the AMIA bombing in 2004, some 10 years after the outrage and following several earlier inconclusive inquiries. By the end of 2006, Nisman concluded that there was sufficient information to charge the government of Iran with planning the bombing and Hezbollah with carrying it out. As the investigation proceeded, there were complaints that Nisman may have been too close to the **United States** Embassy in Buenos Aires—the United States was seeking to enforce trade embargoes on Tehran and prevent Iranian access to Argentine nuclear technology—and that he was using the case to advance his own legal and political career. Nevertheless, his investigation was regarded as thorough, and he acquired a reputation for dogged persistence. Although at one point thought to be a protégé of President **Cristina Fernández de Kirchner**, within a few years Nisman had become convinced of an official cover-up. First, he requested the arraignment of former president **Carlos Saúl Menem** (on whose watch the AMIA bombing had occurred), claiming that there was evidence that Menem had accepted a bribe from Tehran to stall or sideline earlier investigations. By 2013, he was further convinced that officials in the Fernández de Kirchner administration were attempting to thwart the course of justice, a conviction that was strengthened when President Fernández signed a memorandum of understanding with Tehran to establish an Argentine–Iranian truth commission to ascertain the fact of the AMIA bombing.

On the eve of his death, Nisman was about to publish a report that implicated President Fernández de Kirchner in the cover-up and of accepting bribes from Tehran. Nisman's investigation and his charges were overtaken by his death. First reported as suicide, his death provoked public outrage, particularly as rumors soon began to circulate of official collusion in his death—possibly by rogue elements of the security services. The most recent reports of the investigation into Nisman's death suggest that he was murdered, possibly as he entered the building in which his flat was located, and the body then moved to his apartment. Latest court documents state that Nisman was murdered as the direct result of his assessment that former president Fernández de Kirchner instigated a cover-up of Iran's role in the

AMIA bombing. Evidence suggests that the murder was ordered by high officials in the Fernández de Kirchner administration—possibly even the president herself. The case is far from complete, and may never be concluded, though there is considerable circumstantial evidence to point to the involvement of the presidential office in the death of Nisman. *See also* ASOCIACIÓN MUTUAL ISRAELITA ARGENTINA (AMIA); CABEZAS AFFAIR; CORRUPTION; YABRÁN CASE.

NOTICIAS. Widely considered the leading Spanish-language newsmagazine in the world; founded as *Noticias de la Semana* in 1976. Published in a similar format to US publications such as *Time* and *Newsweek*, it took its current name in 1989. In addition to the high standards of its reporting and quality of production, *Noticias* is also known in Argentina for the loss of its photojournalist José Luis Cabezas in the so-called **Cabezas Affair**. The editorials are currently written by James Neilson, a former editor of the *Buenos Aires Herald*. The magazine became a thorn in the side of Presidents **Néstor Kirchner** and **Cristina Fernández de Kirchner**, noted and respected for its highly critical coverage of the husband-and-wife team. In the face of considerable pressure, it has proved unafraid to report on political maneuvers of the regime; its investigative journalists have uncovered a number of **corruption** scandals.

NUEVA FUERZA. Center-right political party set up by **Álvaro Alsogaray** to contest the **presidential election of March 1973**. Although it performed dismally and did not survive the **military coup of 1976**, its noteworthiness lies in its electoral platform.

The program of Nueva Fuerza emphasized the transfer of pension funds to interested parties, the sale of state-owned enterprises and land, and free competition in the markets as the condition for an economic system based on private initiative, risk, private ownership of the means of production, and **trade union** freedom. Such an agenda was ahead of its time but made Nueva Fuerza the direct forerunner of the **Unión del Centro Democrático** (UCEDE/UCeDe), which incorporated many of the Nueva Fuerza proposals. The latter party was also set up by Alsogaray with the return of democracy in 1983, and its platform would be implemented in the 1990s following the co-option of the UCEDE by the Peronist government of **Carlos Saúl Menem**.

NUNCA MÁS. Often referred to as the Informe Sábato (Sábato Report) named after **Ernesto Sábato**, chair of the truth-style commission that investigated "disappearances" during the **Proceso de Reorganización Nacional**. Produced by the **Comisión Nacional sobre la Disaparición de Personas** (CONADEP), *Nunca Más* was first published in 1984. Running to around

50,000 pages and alluding to 30,000 cases, the report contains detailed testimonies relating to 8,961 individuals who were "disappeared" and murdered by the **military**, security services, and police during the 1976–1983 military dictatorships, notably during the presidency of General **Jorge Rafael Videla**. The investigation was commissioned by President **Raúl Alfonsín**, who was elected in 1983, in fulfillment of a campaign promise during the **congressional** and **presidential elections of 1983**. The report also mentions disappearances and murders that had occurred between 1973 and 1976, that is, immediately before the coup under the presidencies of **Juan Domingo Perón** and **Isabel Perón**, which were attributed to the **Triple A** (Alianza Anticomunista Argentina) and shadowy organizations connected to the police and security apparatus. Various sections of the report contain statements by survivors, information presented by relatives of the "disappeared," an assessment of the organization of state terror, and accounts of the treatment of prisoners and the behavior of the security forces. The report states that around one-third of the victims were **women** and that 200 children were kidnapped. Since publication, *Nunca Más* has never been out of print in Argentina. *See also* ASTIZ, ALFREDO IGNACIO (1951–); BIGNONE, REYNALDO BENITO (1928–2018); DIRTY WAR; DISPOSICIÓN FINAL; ESCUELA SUPERIOR DE MECÁNICA DE LA ARMADA (ESMA); GALTIERI, LEOPOLDO FORTUNATO (1926–2003); MASSERA, EMILIO EDUARDO (1925–2010); MILITARY JUNTAS, TRIALS OF THE; VIOLA, ROBERTO EDUARDO (1924–1994); WAR TO ANNIHILATE SUBVERSION.

OBREGÓN CANO, RICARDO (1917–2016). A left-wing Peronist close to **Héctor Cámpora**, he was elected governor of the province of **Córdoba** for the **Frente Justicialista de Liberación** (FREJULI) in March 1973. Although elected with the support of the Peronist left and the **Montoneros**, Obregón Cano later tacked toward the center and allied himself with the **Unión Cívica Radical** (UCR) and some Christian democrats. This shift led to his administration being reviled by both the Peronist left and right, and the governor quickly lost the support of **Juan Domingo Perón**. On 28 February 1974, Obregón Cano was toppled in a coup headed by the provincial chief of police. A week later, on 7 March, both the governor and the elected vice governor, Hipólito Atilio López of the Unión Tranviaria Automotor (UTA), formally resigned. López was subsequently assassinated by the **Triple A** in September 1974. The ouster of Obregón Cano clearly showed the tendency of the Peronists to use the security services to resolve internal problems of their movement.

OCAMPO, RAMONA VICTORIA EPIFANÍA RUFINA. *See* OCAMPO, VICTORIA (1891–1979).

OCAMPO, VICTORIA (1891–1979). Always called Victoria, notwithstanding her baptismal name; author, essayist, social commentator, and socialite; one of the most distinguished cultural and intellectual figures of her generation. She was born into the landed oligarchy—the family owned extensive estates in the province of **Buenos Aires**; Villa Ocampo, the family townhouse, was renowned for glittering social and cultural events that she organized there. Graham Greene dedicated one of his novels to her in recognition of hospitality received at Villa Ocampo and on the family's country estates. Partly educated in France, which she visited frequently, she also traveled extensively in Europe and the **United States**. Sometimes enamored with Italian Fascism, she was nevertheless a strong advocate of parliamentary democracy and served on League of Nations cultural commissions. In 1953, she was briefly arrested following protests against the government of President **Juan Domingo Perón**.

Her principal works (often written in French and English) include *De Francesca a Beatrice* (1924) (Letters from Francesca to Beatrice), *Domingos en Hyde Park* (1936) (Sundays in Hyde Park), *Lawrence of Arabia* (1947), and critical works on various authors, including those of her day—for example, **Jorge Luis Borges**, Emily Brontë, Virginia Wolfe, and T. E. Lawrence. She popularized contemporary foreign literature by translating into Spanish novels and poetry by the likes of Mahatma Gandhi, Greene, and Dylan Thomas. She is particularly remembered for editing the iconic literary review *Sur*, in which such figures as Borges, Albert Camus, Waldo Frank, Ezequiel Martínez Estrada, and Ernesto Sábato published regularly. In addition to her literary output and publishing, Ocampo was a pioneer of what would now be described as the women's movement. She founded the Unión Argentina de Mujeres (Women's Union) in 1936, serving as its first president until 1938 and again in 1953. Among other things, the union sought to advance the role of **women** in politics and the arts.

Her work received international recognition: she was awarded an honorary doctorate by Harvard University and a gold medal by the Académie Française and was made an honorary Commander of the Order of the British Empire. In 1976, she was the first woman to be admitted to the Argentine National Literary Academy. In a typically astute reference to the internationalism and aspirations of her class, she observed that when in Argentina, we feel European, when in Europe, Argentine.

O'DONNELL, GUILLERMO (1936–2011). Distinguished, internationally recognized political scientist. He read law at the **University of Buenos Aires** (UBA), practicing briefly as a lawyer before enrolling for a postgraduate degree in political science at Yale University—it would be many years before he completed the thesis. Associated with some of the most prestigious academic institutions in the world, he held teaching posts at Harvard University, the University of Notre Dame—with which he enjoyed a long connection—and the Woodrow Wilson Center in the **United States**; was awarded visiting professorships at research centers in **Brazil**, **Great Britain**, **Spain**, and the United States; and was connected with many universities and think tanks in his native Argentina.

Much of O'Donnell's work analyses political and economic problems of the periods through which he lived; his analysis was often comparative, combined theory with practical observation, and always drew on political economy. His major works explored the difficulties of economic modernization in fragile polities—his analysis of industrialization in the 1960s and 1970s led him to coin the phrase "bureaucratic authoritarianism," the problematic of transitioning from authoritarian regimes—analysis that used game theory to explore/assess/predict the positions and actions of distinct interest groups, and the nature of democracy—he devised a typology to classify and asses the quality of institutions and their functionality. Although he did not argue that authoritarian polities were a prerequisite for economic modernization, his critics often misinterpreted his position. Similarly, his work arguing the plurality of routes to democracy and the distinct nature of different types of democracy—he coined another important phrase, "delegative democracy"—has led to his position and line of reasoning being misunderstood or misapplied. None, however, would doubt the prescience of his analysis of key periods in the recent political history of Argentina and Latin America, notably the political and economic strategies applied following the **military coup of 1966** and during the **Proceso de Reorganización Nacional**, the nature of the constraints on democratic reconstruction encountered by President **Raúl Alfonsín**, the interaction of economics and politics during the presidencies of **Carlos Saúl Menem**, and the politics of the presidencies of **Néstor Kirchner** and **Cristina Fernández de Kirchner**.

Some of O'Donnell's most influential works include *Modernization and Bureaucratic Authoritarianism* (1973), *Transitions from Authoritarian Rule: Tentative Conclusions about Uncertain Democracies* (coauthored) (1986), *Counterpoints: Selected Essays on Authoritarianism and Democracy* (1999), *Dissonances: Democratic Critiques of Democracy* (2007), and *Democracy, Agency and the State: Theory with Comparative Intent* (2010), as well as numerous edited volumes and many seminal articles. *See also* DEVELOPMENTALISM/DEVELOPMENTALIST; ECONOMY; KRIEGER VASENA, ADALBERT (1920–2000); INDUSTRY; MARTÍNEZ DE HOZ, JOSÉ ALFREDO (1925–2013).

OLIVOS PACT. In Spanish, Pacto de Olivos; named after the official residence of the president of the republic, the **Quinta de Olivos**. Sitting president **Carlos Saúl Menem** and his predecessor, **Raúl Alfonsín**, met at the residence in 1993 and agreed on the pact, which prepared the ground for the adoption of the **Constitution of 1994**.

Menem and Alfonsín initially met secretly at the Quinta in early November 1993 and hammered out the main changes that would feature in the new constitution. Of these, the principal one of immediate concern to Menem was an amendment that would allow a sitting president to stand for immediate reelection. Other changes included a reduction in the presidential term from six to four years; an increase in the number of senators allocated to each province in the National Senate from two to three (the third seat, the so-called minority seat, would be awarded to the party coming in second in the election); the creation of the post of head of the cabinet of ministers (prime minister); granting representation to the opposition on the judicial council responsible for the appointment of senior judges; and conferring virtual provincial status on the city of **Buenos Aires** (hitherto the mayor of the city had been appointed by the president; henceforth, the post would be directly elected and the city redesignated the Autonomous City of Buenos Aires). Alfonsín agreed to instruct members of his party, the **Unión Cívica Radical** (UCR), to support these changes and enable the necessary legislation to be passed by **Congress**.

The immediate background to the proposed constitutional change included a messy transfer of power from Alfonsín to Menem in 1989 amid **hyperinflation**, street protest, and rising poverty, and the **Convertibility Plan** introduced a couple of years later by Menem's fourth minister of economy, **Domingo Cavallo**. By the end of 1993, the plan had stabilized the economy and was becoming increasingly popular with the electorate. Formally, the pact and the constitutional reforms that flowed from it were presented as measures designed to promote the political continuity necessary to ensure economic stability, thereby facilitating institutional reconstruction following the **Proceso de Reorganización Nacional** amid fears that the **military** might again stage a coup. Alfonsín was much criticized by some colleagues and others for the deal struck with Menem. He and his supporters defended the pact by restating a commitment to democratic institution building and, pragmatically, argued that the measures would limit the ambitions of Menem and a resurgent **Partido Justicialista** (PJ), which was beginning to register surges in electoral support with the Convertibility Plan as the UCR languished in the polls. Menem would be limited to one more term of four years only. The establishment of the post of prime minister, direct elections for the head of the government of Buenos Aires, and arrangements for the appointment of judges would limit the excessive presidentialism of the existing structure. The creation of additional senators would guarantee the UCR minimum levels of representation in the National Senate. The new status of the city of Buenos Aires—the city electorate was considered to be pro-UCR—would strengthen the party's political representation and serve as a base for recovery nationally. In addition, Alfonsín argued that with the PJ in the ascendant, Menem might be able to engineer immediate reelection without the safeguards proposed in the pact.

Alfonsín was in no doubt that Menem would be reelected in 1995—he was—though may have been a little naïve in his assumptions of the robustness of the curbs on presidentialism. He might also have trusted Menem less. Although during the 1993 negotiations and when standing for reelection in 1995, Menem had stated that he would not seek more than two terms, by the time of the **presidential election of 1999** he began to claim that he was entitled to stand for two terms under arrangements introduced in 1994. As his first term as president from 1989 to 1995 had been served in accordance with the **Constitution of 1853**, Menem maintained that he was constitutionally entitled to stand for reelection in 1999, given that he had only completed one term under the Constitution of 1994. The electorate, and his colleagues in the PJ who wanted their own stab at the presidency, took a different view. *See also* AUSTRAL PLAN; *CARAPINTADAS*; CONGRESSIONAL ELEC-TIONS OF 1991; CONGRESSIONAL ELECTIONS OF 1993; DUHALDE, EDUARDO ALBERTO (1941–); MINISTRY OF ECONOMY; PRESI-DENTIAL ELECTION OF 1995.

OMBÚ. Often described as the only indigenous tree of the **pampas**, techni-cally the ombú (*Phytolacca*) is not a tree but a shrub as it does not have a defined trunk. Branches can sprout from the exposed root system, though more commonly the canopy develops from fused lower branches. There are four different subspecies, of which the *Ph. dioica* is the largest, attaining a height of approximately 60 feet (20 meters), with a similar diameter spread of branches. The wood is soft and spongy and of little commercial value. According to popular belief, individual shrubs can live for up to 600 years. An iconic national symbol, the ombú has featured prominently in art and history, especially images of rural life, portrayed as providing shelter from the elements for both man and beast. Particularly fine examples are to be found in the Plaza San Martín, city of **Buenos Aires**, and San Isidro, Buenos Aires province, though classic paintings of the 19th century depict the ombú as a majestic feature of the broad-horizoned pampa. *See also* PUEYRREDÓN, PRILIDIANO (1823–1870).

ONGANÍA, JUAN CARLOS (1914–1995). De facto president of Argentina (1966–1970). A cavalryman and commander-in-chief of the army during the presidency of **Arturo Illia**, he came to power in the **military coup of 1966**. Onganía headed the **Revolución Argentina**, a project that aimed to establish a new political and social order opposed to liberal democracy and Commu-nism, thereby giving the armed forces a leading political and economic role. The transformation was to be carried out in three distinct stages: the first dealing with the **economy**, the next with society, and the final one with politics. Until the final phase was reached, the government would tolerate no opposition; this made the Onganía administration particularly aggressive and would lead to its downfall.

    Congress was dissolved and all political groupings declared illegal. The judges of the Supreme Court were replaced, **trade unions** were curbed, and the press and arts came under government censorship. Onganía imposed a centralized system of university governance, which was opposed by the deans and rectors of the **University of Buenos Aires** (UBA). Barely a month into his tenure, the president decided to end university autonomy and became responsible for the so-called La Noche de los Bastones Largos: he ordered the police to invade the Faculty of Exact Sciences of the UBA—students and professors were beaten up and arrested.

Onganía also repressed all forms of "immoralism," proscribing miniskirts, long hair for boys, and all avant-garde artistic movements. This moral campaign only exacerbated the situation in the universities, where the middle class was overrepresented and became increasingly radicalized. The president's aggressiveness generated growing resentment among Argentines, especially as more students, union leaders, and civilian political figures were jailed.

The government's heavy-handedness created the illusion of law and order, but this was shattered in 1969. A number of cities suffered serious bouts of disorder, the most notorious of all being the **Cordobazo**. In the wake of the unrest, **Alejandro Agustín Lanusse**, the commander-in-chief of the army, decided that the **military** had to extricate themselves from government through an electoral solution. He understood that Onganía's transformative project was unworkable and that the lack of a time limit on the presidential term was a major problem.

A plot to unseat Onganía got underway, and crucially involved former de facto head of state **Pedro Eugenio Aramburu**. It was finally clear to the conspirators that moderate Peronist elements would have to be incorporated into the democratic process. Exactly one year after the Cordobazo came the **Aramburazo**, which shocked the country and sealed Onganía's fate. A palace coup was engineered by Lanusse, and the obscure (and hopefully pliant) **Roberto M. Levingston** was put in power. But Levingston, as with Onganía, wanted to perpetuate himself in power and was in turn ousted in a further palace coup by Lanusse. After two years in which Lanusse unsuccessfully tried to engineer an electoral solution to his liking, in 1973 the military extricated themselves from government by calling elections. *See also* CONGRESSIONAL ELECTIONS OF 1973; KRIEGER VASENA, ADALBERT (1920–2000); PRESIDENTIAL ELECTION OF MARCH 1973; SALIMEI, JORGE NÉSTOR (1926–1975).

ONGARO, RAIMUNDO JOSÉ (1924–2016). Prominent Peronist labor leader. An apprenticed print worker born in Mar del Plata, he worked for the large publishing cooperative COGTAL and became active in the Federación de Gráficos Bonaerenses (FGB). The **military coup of 1966** and its resultant antilabor policies led to Ongaro ousting the FGB head in November of that year. The FGB was one of the 62 unions in the all-encompassing **Confederación General del Trabajo** (CGT), whose leading figures **Augusto Vandor** and **José Alonso** disapproved of Ongaro's move. Ongaro opposed the conciliatory strategy of Vandor and Alonso toward the **military** regime and traveled to **Cuba** in early 1968. He went on to Madrid, where he was introduced to exiled former president **Juan Domingo Perón**. The latter subscribed to Ongaro's view that efforts by the CGT leadership to negotiate with the de facto government would be in vain.

The internal CGT elections of March 1968 pitted Vandor against Ongaro, who was backed by Perón. Ongaro was elected secretary general of the CGT, and the regime swiftly annulled the election, preventing him from taking office. As a result, he was joined by journalist Rodolfo Walsh, numerous CGT supporters, and adherents of the **Movimiento de Sacerdotes para el Tercer Mundo** in the splinter **Confederación General del Trabajo de los Argentinos** (CGTA), formed in May 1968.

Following the **congressional** and **presidential elections of March 1973**, and for having an independent union and leftist stance, Ongaro became a target for both the CGT and the far-right **Triple A** death squad headed by **José López Rega**. Arrested in March 1975 and released five months later, he was promptly deported. He returned to Argentina in March 1984, sometime after the restoration of democracy that resulted from the **congressional** and **presidential elections of 1983**. Ongaro once again got involved with the FGB, enjoying a stint as secretary general, and even acquiesced in the neoliberal policies of Peronist president **Carlos Saúl Menem**, who triumphed in the **presidential election of 1989**. *See also* ECONOMY; PRIVATIZATION; TRADE UNIONS.

OPERACIÓN CONDOR. A clandestine operation that entailed political repression, torture, and murder, based on collaboration among several **military** regimes in South America. At various times, the military and security services of Argentina, **Bolivia**, **Brazil**, **Chile**, **Paraguay**, and **Uruguay** were involved; less prominently, Ecuador and **Peru**. In Argentina, it morphed into the Guerra Sucia, which it prefigured. The Washington-inspired doctrine of national security, which stressed the threat from the "enemy within," had particular resonance for sections of the Argentine military opposed to **Juan Domingo Perón** and **Peronism**, concerned about labor unrest and Marxist infiltration of the powerful labor movement, and the emergence of radical groups like the **Montoneros** and the **Ejército Revolucionario del Pueblo** committed to violent insurgency. Within the context of the cold war, the doctrine of national security was developed at the US Army School of the Americas, Panama, founded in 1946. By the 1960s, the school was offering anticommunist counterinsurgency training to military personnel from across the continent. As well as providing technical and logistical support, the school stressed the importance of intelligence sharing while also teaching courses on Marxist ideology and doctrine. Information sharing and counterinsurgency training were mainly coordinated by the Central Intelligence Agency. The school served to instill a common worldview among key players in the South American armed forces. **Leopoldo Fortunato Galtieri, Emilio Massera, Jorge Rafael Videla**, and **Roberto Viola** were Argentine "graduates" of the Panama school.

With the onset of right-wing military regimes in the **Southern Cone** in the mid-1960s and early 1970s, for example, the de facto administration of **Juan Carlos Onganía**, security services began to monitor the activities of exiles and dissidents from neighboring countries, with host governments sharing information with home governments. The practice soon gave way to kidnapping and torture, victims often being returned to their countries of origin. Key events in the development of Condor included a meeting in **Buenos Aires** in 1974 convened by **Alberto Villar** (deputy head of the federal police and founding member of the **Triple A**), with police delegations from Bolivia, Chile, and Uruguay attending, and a meeting of senior figures in the Argentine, Bolivian, Chilean, Paraguayan, and Uruguayan military intelligence services a year later in Santiago de Chile. Argentine military intelligence officer General Rivero was one of the main protagonists of the Plan Condor, precursor of the Operación, which emphasized the physical extermination of so-called treacherous subversives.

Although officials of the armed forces, including members of the 1976–1983 juntas, were charged and convicted of atrocities committed during the **War to Annihilate Subversion**, only in 2016 were cases involving Operación Condor brought before the courts. Sentences were handed down on 15 former officers, including Uruguayan Colonel Manuel Cordero and General **Reynaldo Bignone**, head of the last junta before the return of democracy in 1983. *See also* DIRTY WAR; DISPOSICIÓN FINAL; PROCESO DE REORGANIZACIÓN NACIONAL.

ORTEGA, RAMÓN BAUTISTA "PALITO" (1941–). Actor and crooner turned politician; one-term governor of his native province of **Tucumán** from 1991 to 1995 and one-term national senator for the province between 1990 and 2000. Before entering politics, Ortega had a successful career in the arts and **media**; he was also a businessman. Of humble origin—his parents were sugarcane cutters—and born into what became a large family, Ortega had little formal schooling as he was sent out to work at an early age by his parents. He worked in the informal sector as a shoe-shine boy, newspaper seller, and street trader. As he grew older, he found employment as a gardener, cleaner, and waiter. When the family broke up—he was barely in his teens—he moved to **Buenos Aires**, eking out a living in a similar way. By this time, he was also singing on the streets, impersonating international stars like Elvis Presley; he had taught himself to play the guitar and had joined a group. His big break came when he was spotted by a local television and radio station where he had been working as a general factotum. By the early 1960s, he had secured a recording contract and was broadcasting regularly.

In addition to making popular recordings, he was also appearing in films, all of which increased his popularity and public recognition. By the 1980s, he was appearing with international stars of radio and television on visits to Buenos Aires, some of whom he brought to Argentina as a budding impresario. It was a risky business, but he survived. International contacts enabled him to establish a career in the **United States**, where he worked as the producer and presenter of an arts-cum-music program.

Ortega returned to Argentina at the end of the 1980s and was "spotted" a second time, on this occasion by President **Carlos Saúl Menem**. Menem persuaded Ortega to stand for the **Partido Justicialist** (PJ) in the gubernatorial elections of 1991, which he won. Ortega's campaign for governor helped raise the profile of the PJ in the provincial and national midterm **congressional elections of 1991**. Perhaps the high point in his political career came in 1999, when he joined **Eduardo Duhalde** on the PJ ticket for the **presidential election of 1999**, Ortega standing for the vice presidency. They lost. The defeat caused Ortega to abandon politics and return to recording and filming. He continues to enjoy a successful career as a singer and performer and still gains international recognition, earning national and international awards. He has cut around 50 original albums and directed over half a dozen films and appeared in many, many more. He remains an important cultural figure. Ortega's trajectory is significant as it illustrates the openness of Argentine society and a tendency that became particularly marked in the 1990s of personalities from the sporting and artistic worlds entering politics. *See also* REUTEMANN, CARLOS ALBERTO (1942–).

ORTIZ, ROBERTO MARCELINO (1886–1942). President of Argentina from 1938 to 1942, on leave from 1940 to 1942. His complete name is Jaime Gerardo Roberto Marcelino María Ortiz. Invariably known to friends and family as Roberto, his official signature was "Roberto M. Ortiz," which was sometimes expanded to "Roberto Marcelino Ortiz" and occasionally (confusingly) to "Roberto Mária Ortiz."

An *antipersonalista* Radical, Ortiz headed the **Concordancia** ticket that won the fraudulent **presidential election of 1937**. However, once in office, he vigorously worked to make politics open and more democratic. Elections in 1940 strengthened the presence of the opposition in **Congress**. Ortiz was forced to take leave from his office for health reasons. His replacement, acting president **Ramón S. Castillo**, undid all that Ortiz had achieved in terms of redemocratizing electoral politics. As a result, the opposition was in no mood to collaborate with the government. The first victim of the new climate was the **Pinedo Plan**, an imaginative project devised to deal with the impact of the Second World War; it became bogged down in Congress. Ortiz resigned from office a few weeks before his death; the actions of his successor led to the **military coup of 1943**.

P

PALACIOS, ALFREDO LORENZO RAMÓN (1880–1965). Known as Alfredo Palacios; academic, social reformer, and educationalist; democrat, parliamentarian, and major public figure of the early 20th century. Born in **Buenos Aires**, he read law at the **University of Buenos Aires** (UBA) and went on to teach there. A pragmatic, reformist socialist, Palacios was one of the founders of the **Partido Socialista** (PS), on whose ticket he was elected to the Buenos Aires provincial legislature in 1902 by the voters of **La Boca**. Two years later, he was elected to the National Chamber of Deputies, representing the city of Buenos Aires. He was returned to the chamber on several occasions and elected to the National Senate in 1935, where he served until 1943. He was the first member of the PS to sit in **Congress** and the first socialist parliamentarian to be elected in the Americas. In Congress, he rapidly acquired a progressive reputation, sponsoring reforms in such areas as labor legislation, including the regulation of child and female labor, establishing limits on the working week and laying the bases for social insurance and worker compensation. Despite participating in elections during the **Concordancia**—the regime was renowned for electoral fraud and gerrymandering—from the benches of Congress he campaigned for fair elections and spoke against **corruption**. His reputation as a legislator was equaled by his standing as an academic and legal expert. In addition to holding prestigious positions in law and social sciences at the UBA, Palacios went on to head the **Universidad Nacional de La Plata** (UNLP), where he held a chair and was dean of the Social Science Faculty. He was the first holder of the chair in labor and social security law at the UNLP, a position that had been created for him—he published prolifically in these fields.

Palacios's interest in social reform is partly explained by his early academic training; his thesis was about poverty and the condition of the working poor. He was a strong supporter of the **University Reform Movement**. His legislative initiatives had an important impact on the development of the **trade union** movement and the emergence of state welfare. Opposed to the regime of President **Juan Domingo Perón**, which he saw as antidemocratic, he resigned in protest again the Peronization of the universities and was briefly arrested by the regime in 1951. Palacios stood unsuccessfully for the PS in the **presidential election of 1958** and was last elected to the Chamber of Deputies in 1963, dying in the middle of the four-year term.

PAMPAS. The grasslands of South America and the principal geographical feature of Argentina, defining its history and shaping its reputation abroad. Derived from the Quechua word for flat, featureless grassy plain or meadow, the pampas stretch from the Atlantic seaboard to the foothills of the **Andes**, and from northern **Patagonia** to the formerly heavily forested subtropical **Grand Chaco** in the north. The area includes the provinces of **Buenos Aires**, **Córdoba**, **Entre Ríos**, **La Pampa**, and **Santa Fe** in Argentina, extending also into **Uruguay** and southern **Brazil**. Sometimes described as the southern pampas, the northern Patagonian provinces of **Río Negro** and **Neuquén**, and part of **Chubut**, constitute a drier, rolling landscape, giving way to tundra farther south. East to west, the pampa proper rises from sea level to around 1,600 feet (500 meters) over a distance of approximately 800 miles. It is conventionally divided into two zones, the black earth *pampa húmeda* in the east, and the drier *pampa seca* in the west-northwest. Extremely fertile, capable of raising a wide range of temperate **commodities**, by the early 20th century the pampas had earned for the country the titles of the **United States of South America** and Granary of the World; wheat and **maize** were then the principal **grains**, as well as supplying the European market with large quantities of **meat** (**cattle** and **sheep**) and **wool**. Most of the area had been opened up in the second half of the 19th century following the **Conquest of the Desert** and settlement by European immigrants, the majority of whom were sharecroppers and tenant farmers, except for parts of the north and center of the province of Buenos Aires, where a significant proportion of early immigrants became *estancieros*, and parts of Santa Fe and Córdoba, where agricultural colonies were established. Today, mixed farming tends to predominate, though soya became the principal commodity during the presidencies of **Néstor Kirchner** and his wife, **Cristina Fernández de Kirchner** (2003–2015), when export bans and taxes favored a concentration on soya. *See also* AGRICULTURAL COLONIZATION; *ESTANCIA*; *ESTANCIA* COMPANIES.

PARAGUAY. First part of the **River Plate** region to be permanently settled by Europeans, who arrived around 1537; Asunción was capital of the whole region until 1617. When the city of **Buenos Aires** was abandoned in 1541, settlers moved to Asunción; Buenos Aires was refounded from Asunción in 1580. For much of the 17th and 18th centuries, when the area was given over to Jesuit missionary activities among Guaraní Indians and involving the creation of permanent self-sufficient agricultural settlements (*reducciones de in-*

dios), Paraguay and neighboring parts of present-day Argentina, **Bolivia**, and **Brazil**, functioned as a separate jurisdiction-cum-theocracy. When the Jesuits were expelled in 1767, the missions fell under the jurisdiction of Buenos Aires, and Paraguay was incorporated into the **Viceroyalty of the River Plate**, created in 1776. In May 1810, when Buenos Aires declared **independence** from **Spain**, Paraguay declared its own independence, defeating an army sent from Buenos Aires to bring it to heel in 1811–1812. Although Buenos Aires accepted the separation of Paraguay, border incidents were not infrequent, playing a part in the **War of the Triple Alliance**, as did a project of nation building (involving rearmament) under the rule of father and son **caudillos** Carlos Antonio López and Francisco Solano López. The war decimated the population and devastated the country. For years thereafter, Paraguay functioned as a virtual dependency of Brazil—a source of disquiet in Buenos Aires. By the early 20th century, with river and rail communication between the two countries improving, Paraguay gravitated toward Argentina. The **Chaco War** once again took a heavy toll on society and economy, resulting in around 20 years of political instability; Argentina and Brazil were not disinterested bystanders. In 1954, Alfredo Stroessner seized power. His authoritarian and often tyrannical rule resulted in some modernization. During the reign of Stroessner, Paraguay participated in **Operación Condor**—Paraguay was a founding member and active participant in this regional arrangement of state terror. At much the same time, Argentina and Paraguay completed studies to construct the **Yacyretá-Apipé** Dam. With democracy came plans to develop **tourism** and **foreign trade**, also involving Brazil, but the Paraguayan frontier remains lawless. Contraband trade, involving arms and drugs, along with more mundane items, probably dwarfs legitimate commerce. Taxes and controls in Brazil and Argentina mean that lucrative **commodities** like soya are smuggled—Paraguay exports a great deal more soya than it is reckoned to produce—again making for cool relations among the republics.

PARAGUAY (RIVER). One of the main rivers of South America, and an important tributary of the river **Paraná**, into which it flows after crossing the southern border of **Paraguay**. Rising in **Brazil**, it is over 1,500 miles (2,600 kilometers) long, fed by the river Pilcomayo; it cuts through the center of Paraguay. Navigable for the greater part of its length, the river is the principal geographical feature of the country and a major means of communication with the outside world; Asunción, the capital of Paraguay, is located on the river. The Paraguay–Paraná basin is the second largest in South America.

PARAGUAYAN WAR. *See* WAR OF THE TRIPLE ALLIANCE.

PARANÁ (CITY). Major river port on the left bank of the **Paraná** River, capital of the province of **Entre Ríos**, and sometime national capital. Originally named La Bajada del Paraná, the city was founded in 1730 by settlers from **Santa Fe**, on the other side of the river, as a defensive position again Indian tribes unsubdued by Spanish colonial forces and to open fertile land to ranching. Named provincial capital in 1822, the city began to prosper in the 1840s as local **caudillo Justo José de Urquiza** consolidated his control of the area. One of the first newspapers to be published in the Republic, *El Federal Entre-riano*, appeared there around the middle of the decade, and a state primary school was established at much the same time, becoming a model for such schools established elsewhere in the province and nation. When the province of **Buenos Aires** seceded from the **Argentine Confederation** in 1853, the city was declared the national capital and remained so until 1861, when Buenos Aires rejoined the Confederation. Despite losing the status of national capital, the city prospered from the 1880s as the interior of the province was opened to ranching and farming. The city was beautified around 1900, with parks, avenues, and public buildings, and was maturing as a regional center of banking and commerce. In 1919, a branch of the National University of the Littoral opened, and the urban **economy** benefited from the construction of *frigoríficos* and flour mills, attracted by its strategic location on the river and port improvements. Further transport improvements, notably the inauguration of the tunnel under the river connecting the city with the provincial capital of Santa Fe in 1969, encouraged further growth. Today, with a population approaching 300,000, it is one of the most important urban centers of the **Littoral** and **Mesopotamia**. *See also* UNIVERSIDAD DEL LITORAL

PARANÁ (RIVER). One of the largest river systems in the world, covering more than one million square miles (approximately 2.8 square kilometers), the **Paraguay**–Paraná basin is the second largest in South America after the Amazon. It drains much of the southeast of the continent; the Paraná Delta reaches the sea at the **River Plate**. Part of the Upper Paraná (Alto Paraná) forms the boundary between **Brazil** and **Paraguay** and Paraguay and Argentina; the river also marks the northern and western boundary of Argentine **Mesopotamia**. Some 3,000 miles (c. 5,000 kilometers) long, the river is navigable for much of its length and a strategic means of communications among Paraguay, southern Brazil, and eastern Argentina, a factor that contributed to the **War of the Triple Alliance** in the 1860s. Since the 1960s, several dams have been constructed, making the river a major source of hydroelectricity. *See also* ITAIPÚ DAM; YACYRETÁ-APIPÉ.

PARTIDO CONSERVADOR POPULAR (PCP). Founded by **Vicente Solano Lima** in 1958, it was one of multiple **political parties** that arose from the dissolution and splintering of the conservative **Partido Demócrata Nacional** (PDN). Its founder had major concerns with social and labor issues, so it comes as no surprise that the PCP would maintain a position of closeness with the Peronists.

To contest the **presidential election of 1963**, the party joined the Frente Nacional y Popular, which also included the neo-Peronist **Unión Popular** (UP) and the **Movimiento de Integración y Desarrollo** (MID). In an attempt to circumvent **military** restrictions of Peronism, the front nominated Solano Lima as presidential candidate and Carlos Sylvestre Begnis (a Frondizista) as his running mate. The army would have none of it. Not only was the UP proscribed, but so were its allies in the Frente Nacional, as they could be used to channel Peronist votes in the coming election.

Given widespread disillusion with the **Revolución Argentina** military regime that came to power in 1966, the PCP was one of the signatories of the **"La Hora del Pueblo"** declaration in 1970, which called for a quick restoration of democracy. The party aligned itself in the **Frente Justicialista de Liberación** (FREJULI) two years later and provided Solano Lima as its vice presidential candidate in the **presidential election of March 1973**.

The PCP resurfaced with the restoration of democracy in 1983, after seven years of brutal dictatorship, and restored its connection with Peronism in the early 21st century. It was part of the **Frente para la Victoria/Partido Justicialista** (FpV/PJ) in the presidential contests of 2003, 2007, and 2011, which successfully brought **Nestor Kirchner** and **Cristina Fernández de Kirchner** to power. However, in a bizarre twist, the PCP changed course for the **presidential election of 2015**. It switched its allegiance to the opposition **Cambiemos** coalition fronted by **Mauricio Macri**, which unexpectedly triumphed at the ballot box. *See also* FRONDIZI, ARTURO (1908–1995).

PARTIDO DEMÓCRATA CRISTIANO (PDC). Founded in 1954, the center-right Christian Democratic Party was associated with the Christian Democrat Organization of America and modeled on similar confessional parties then achieving power in parts of continental Europe, notably Italy and Germany. The PDC was set up as relations between the **Juan Domingo Perón** government and the **Catholic Church** were deteriorating sharply. The party split in the early 1970s, paradoxically with some members entering the Peronist-dominated **Frente Justicialísta de Liberación** (FREJULI) that propelled **Héctor Cámpora** briefly to the presidency in 1973, though most minor parties abandoned the FREJULI almost immediately. The party reunited in 1983 with the return of democracy. The 1989 election once again found the PDC supporting the Peronists, this time resulting in the election of **Carlos Saúl Menem**. There was another split, which meant that the PDC left the coalition shortly after the election. The 1990s found the party in the **Frente País Solidario** (FREPASO), a grouping of dissident Peronists and minor parties that entered an alliance with the **Unión Cívica Radical** (UCR) for the 1999 elections, facilitating the victory of **Fernando de la Rúa**. The collapse of the Alianza, and the demise of the De la Rúa administration in 2001, found the PDC once again throwing its support behind mainstream Peronist factions: in the 2003 election, it favored **Néstor Kirchner**, not Menem, and in 2007 **Cristina Fernández de Kirchner**. Yet in 2011, it backed **Eduardo Duhalde**, who lost to Cristina Fernández. In the **presidential election of 2015**, it supported **José Manuel de la Sota**, another minority PJ candidate who was defeated on the first round and lost to **Mauricio Macri**. The political journey of the PDC, to-ing and fro-ing across the center ground, is indicative of Argentine politics in the second half of the 20th century, notably the "rupture" of Peronism, and factionalism within the PJ, which denies space to more ideological or policy-driven groups. *See also* ALIANZA PARA EL TRABAJO, LA JUSTICIA Y LA EDUCACIÓN; CONGRESSIONAL ELECTIONS OF 1999; DI TELLA, GUIDO JOSÉ MARIO (1931–2001); PRESIDENTIAL ELECTION OF MARCH 1973; PRESIDENTIAL ELECTION OF SEPTEMBER 1973; PRESIDENTIAL ELECTION OF 1999; PRESIDENTIAL ELECTION OF 2003; PRESIDENTIAL ELECTION OF 2007; PRESIDENTIAL ELECTION OF 2011.

PARTIDO DEMÓCRATA NACIONAL (PDN). Conservative party created in July 1931, usually regarded as the successor to the Partido Autonomista Nacional (PAN). The party was a confederation of provincial conservative parties, and together with the *antipersonalista* Radicals and the Independent Socialists formed the **Concordancia** alliance that governed Argentina from 1932 to 1943. The PDN had little room for maneuver within this coalition, at least until Vice President **Ramón S. Castillo** took over from ailing president **Roberto M. Ortiz** in 1940.

Following the **military coup of 1943** and the suppression of political activity, the PDN was left in disarray. It was further weakened when the **Unión Cívica Radical** (UCR) blocked its participation in the **Unión Democrática** (UD) that unsuccessfully challenged **Juan Domingo Perón** in the fateful **presidential election of 1946**. With the **military coup of 1955**, the PDN found itself severely divided over how to deal with Peronism. In November 1958, it splintered into various parties, the best known of which became the **Partido Conservador Popular** (PCP).

PARTIDO DEMÓCRATA PROGRESISTA (PDP). Largely a regional party representing small landowners and tenant farmers in the province of **Santa Fe**, the PDP played a disproportionally important role in Argentine political history, often constituting a significant, coherent opposition group to a succession of ruling parties. Formed in 1914, it emerged from the Liga del Sur, established by Lisandro de la Torre in 1908, and other smaller organizations. The formation and growth of the party was largely due to political openings created by the **Saénz Peña Law** of 1912. Centrist and liberal, its support came largely from the rural middle class and, to a lesser extent, urban professionals closely associated with the agro-export sector. After the **military coup of 1930**, the PDP entered an electoral alliance with the **Partido Socialista** (PS); together, they constituted the principal opposition to the **Concordancia**, which was sustained in power between 1932 and 1943 by electoral fraud. By participating in elections during this period, the PDP–Socialist alliance was criticized for providing credence to an essentially nondemocratic arrangement. In the general elections of 1946, the Progressive Democrats were part of the anti-Peronist **Unión Democrática** (UD) and in the **presidential election of 1963** endorsed the candidature of anti-Peronist general **Pedro Eugenio Aramburu**, supplying Aramburu's vice presidential running mate, Horacio Thedy. In a volte-face, still represented by Thedy, the PDP entered the pro-Perón **"La Hora del Pueblo"** agreement of 1970. The 1973 presidential election found the party once again aligned with anti-Peronists. During the 1976–1983 **military** dictatorship, several prominent members of the PDP served the regime in various capacities, for which the party issued an official apology with the return to democracy in 1983. While between the mid-1950s and the mid-1970s the PDP managed to elect a handful of deputies to **Congress**—principally for the province of Santa Fe—and to field presidential or vice presidential candidates in elections during the 1980s and 1990s, by 2013 the party was no longer represented at the national level, though staging countrywide events to celebrate its centenary in December 2014.

PARTIDO INTRANSIGENTE (PI). Founded by **Oscar Alende** in 1972, its membership came from the rump **Unión Cívica Radical Intransigente** (UCRI), a faction into which the **Union Civica Radical** (UCR) had divided in 1956, and itself subsequently splintered in 1962 thanks to **Arturo Frondizi**.

A nationalist, populist, and center-left outfit, the PI unsuccessfully contested elections in 1973 and 1983 and became part of the **Frente País Solidario** (FREPASO) coalition in the 1990s. It first entered government as part of the **Alianza para el Trabajo, la Justicia y la Educación**, which was set up by the FREPASO and the UCR and got **Fernando de la Rúa** elected to the presidency in 1999. When the Alianza collapsed in 2001 and the FREPASO disappeared, the PI allied itself to the **Afirmación para una República Igualitaria** (ARI) and supported its candidate, **Elisa Carrió**, in the presi-

dential election of 2003. Four years later, the PI backed **Cristina Fernández de Kirchner** of the **Frente para la Victoria/Partido Justicialista** (FpV/PJ) faction as candidate in the **presidential election of 2007.**

Electoral coalitions with which the PI affiliated, and its endorsement of distinct presidential candidates, highlighted the fluidity and opportunism of the Argentina politics of the period, and the limited influence of ideology or governing principles among political groupings. *See also* UNIÓN CÍVICA RADICAL DEL PUEBLO (UCRP)

PARTIDO JUSTICIALISTA (PJ). The Peronist party, which assumed its present form between 1947 and 1949, though the official title—Partido Justicialista—was not widely used until after 1955, following the **Revolución Libertadora.** While there was disagreement within the armed forces about how to deal with ousted president **Juan Domingo Perón**, the dominant figure in the de facto administration, General and President **Pedro Eugenio Aramburu**, was determined to excise Peronism. All references to the former president and his movement were proscribed, hence increased usage of the designation Partido Justicialista.

The PJ emerged from an electoral alliance formed to campaign for then colonel Perón in the **presidential election of 1946.** The alliance was composed of the **Partido Laborista** (PL); a dissident faction of the **Unión Cívica Radical** (UCR), the **Unión Cívica Radical Junta Renovadora** (UCRJR); and the conservative Partido Independiente. The PL, which had been established by the **trade union** movement, the **Confederación General del Trabajo** (CGT), and adopted Perón as its presidential candidate, was the dominant force in the electoral coalition. At one point, it appeared that the PL would become the governing party, though sections of the CGT leadership were keen to preserve the independence of the party and project it as the exclusive representative of organized workers. This approach clashed with Perón's ambition to centralize political power. Following his election, Perón ordered the three parties that had supported him in 1946 to merge to form the Partido Único de la Revolución (PUR). Despite the resistance of sections of the labor movement, the PUR was formed in 1947 and previously independent parties officially dissolved. The PUR changed its name to the Partido Peronista (PP), acknowledging the dominant position in the movement of Perón and his wife **Eva Perón**, who headed the **women**'s branch of the organization, **Partido Peronista Feminino** (PPF). In government, the PP/PJ introduced a program of nationalization and state control, further advanced worker rights, and increased political control. Gradually, the regime developed a distinct ideology—**Justicialismo**—which pledged economic independence, social justice, and mass democracy. Proscribed for much of the 1950s and 1960s, the PJ entered electoral alliances with other parties and was the dominant element of the **Frente Justicialista de Liberación** (FREJULI). In

1973, the PJ delivered the presidency first to **Héctor Cámpora** and then Perón himself, in 1989 to **Carlos Saúl Menem**, and in 2003 to **Néstor Kirchner**.

Although technically a political party, the PJ functions more as a political movement. Since the 1940s, it has been tightly controlled by the leadership—first **Perón**, then his successors, most of whom have attempted to emulate Perón. In and out of office from the 1940s to the 1970s, Perón's dominance of the PJ was absolute—all potential challengers were dealt with ruthlessly. Following the death of Perón, the PJ has been controlled by regional **caudillos** like **Eduardo Duhalde**, sometime governor of the province of **Buenos Aires** and president of the republic. Factionalism has been particularly acute when the party has been forced into opposition; none of Perón's successors have been able to exercise his measure of control when out of office, though many have tried. The conflicting pressures of centralization and factionalism have led to defections and splits, particularly since the return to democracy in 1983. Arguably, the greatest divisions occurred during the *kirchnerato*: the **Frente para la Victoria**/PJ (FpV/PJ), controlled by Kirchner and his wife, **Cristina Fernández de Kirchner**, and the dissident **Frente Renovador**/PJ (FR/PJ).

Several attempts have been made to institutionalize and democratize the PJ. When campaigning for the PJ nomination in the run-up to the **presidential election of 1989**, **Carlos Saúl Menem** appeared to favor internal democratic reform, an idea that he rapidly abandoned on gaining the presidency. Others, like **José Octavio Bordón**, who subsequently advocated internal reform and democratization have been marginalized, leaving the movement permanently or temporarily. Given the shock result in the **presidential election of 2015**, when the FpV/PJ failed to win the presidency, demands for change have resurfaced.

Over time, the electoral base of the PJ has evolved but remains solidly rooted in the urban working class and organized elements of rural labor, especially in the far north and far south of the country. From time to time, it has also attracted support from sections of the middle class but has always struggled to secure an electoral base in the city of **Buenos Aires**, despite marshaling votes in depressed industrial zones of Greater Buenos Aires, principally those parts of the province closest to the **federal capital**. The PJ remains the largest political party/movement in the country, notwithstanding factionalism and desertions, and has been the governing party for much of the second half of the 20th century and the early 21st. Almost exclusively, it has been responsible for the incorporation of the working class within the political system, despite a questionable commitment to democratic politics. *See also* "PERONISM WITHOUT PERÓN".

PARTIDO LABORISTA. Partly modeled on the British Labor Party, the Partido Laborista was set up by the **trade union** movement, the **Confederación General del Trabajo** (CGT), to support the candidacy of Colonel **Juan Domingo Perón** in the **presidential election of 1946**. As secretary of labor in the de facto administration resulting from the **military coup of 1943**, Perón had been an advocate of worker rights and forged links with key figures in the CGT such as **Cipriano Reyes**. Like its British counterpart, the PL advocated nationalization of key industries, active state management of the **economy**, and the construction of a welfare state. In addition, the PL campaigned for electoral reform, that is, the extension of the franchise to **women**. Although the party campaigned actively for Perón in 1946, much of the PL leadership envisaged the party as the party of labor, independent of government. Having experienced official repression in the past, sections of the CGT leadership also maintained that the labor movement should be equally independent of government interference, and for similar reasons supported the freedom of the press along with broader political rights.

Following the elections, as Perón sought to centralize political power and increase his control, he attempted for forge a new political party out of the 1946 electoral alliance. This, in addition to the PL, had included a dissident faction of the **Unión Cívica Radical** (UCR)—the **Unión Cívica Radical Junta Renovadora** (UCRJR)—and the conservative Partido Independiente. Although the PL had been the dominant element of the 1946 coalition, it was agreed that the PL would supply only half the number of nominees for electoral lists and public positions. In office, Perón tended to favor the UCRJR and the Partido Independiente, especially for cabinet appointments and to head strategic public agencies. This, along with a desire to preserve the independence of the PL and the labor movement, may explain why prominent sections of the PL leadership were reluctant to join the projected new political organization, the Partido Único de la Revolución (PUR). As a result, the likes of Reyes suffered considerably at the hands of Perón—persecution that included imprisonment. By 1947, the PL accepted the inevitable, agreed to disband itself, and advised the membership to join what would become the **Partido Justicialista** (PJ), to establish a strong worker bloc within the official movement. It remains a matter of debate whether the original objective of the PL—an independent party representing the organized labor movement—would have delivered a different future from that which transpired under the dominance of Perón and the PJ.

PARTIDO PERONISTA (PP). *See* PARTIDO JUSTICIALISTA (PJ).

PARTIDO PERONISTA FEMENINO (PPF). Formed in 1949 as the **women**'s branch of the then **Partido Peronista** (PP), it was officially dissolved after the **military coup of 1955** and never revived. The franchise was not extended to women until the **Constitution of 1949**, a reform that was credited to the influence of First Lady **Eva Perón**, who entered the **Casa Rosada** when her husband, **Juan Domingo Perón**, was elected president in 1946. In guaranteeing women's representation in **Congress** and other public organizations, the PPF was regarded as particularly progressive—one-third of the places on the PP electoral lists were allocated to women. Eva Perón was elected to head the organization, which opened branches in key towns and districts, successfully mobilizing the female vote. Viewed as a vehicle for the advancement of the political career of Mrs. Perón, the PPF orchestrated a campaign with the **trade unions**, the **Confederación General del Trabajo** (CGT), to nominate Evita as her husband's running mate in the **presidential election of 1951**. This move was opposed by conservative sections of society, and by others—including some of Perón's colleagues in the **military**—who regarded the husband-and-wife ticket as concentrating too much power in the hands of the Peróns. By 1951, the regime had acquired a reputation for authoritarianism, curbing the freedom of the press and persecuting opposition groups. It is ironic that, even had she been elected, Eva Perón would not have served long as vice president; she died a few months after what might have been her inauguration. Indeed, ill health was given as the explanation for her declining to accept the nomination.

PARTIDO SOCIALISTA (PS). It was founded in 1896 by prominent left-wing reformers **Juan B. Justo**, **Alfredo Palacios**, and **Nicolás Repetto**. Arguably, the most internationally recognized supporter of the party was **Raúl Prebisch**, heterodox economist and key figure in the United Nations **Economic Commission for Latin America** (ECLA). Committed to democratic politics, the party campaigned for social reform while accepting the liberal economic orthodoxy of the period. Justo was the intellectual and ideologue, while Palacios and Repetto became distinguished parliamentarians and political commentators. Palacios was the first Socialist to be elected in the whole of the Americas, being sent by the **La Boca** district to the National Chamber of Deputies in 1904; Repetto following in his footsteps in 1912. **Women** played an important role in the organization, with **Alicia Moreau de Justo**, wife of Juan B., editing the party newspaper, *La Vanguardia*. Repetto was instrumental in negotiating an electoral pact with the **Partido Demócrata Progresista** (PDP) after the **military coup of 1930**, standing for the vice presidency with PDP presidential candidate, Lisandro de la Torre, in 1931 and accepting the PS nomination for the presidency in 1937. During the period of *fraude patriótico* of the **Concordancia**, the party secured substantial representation in **Congress**, though when unrestricted elections were held in the mid-1940s and elections were supervised by the **military** in the 1950s and 1960s, the PS was eclipsed by the Peronists and factions of the UCR, respectively.

From inception, the party was subject to splits, factionalism being especially pronounced in the 1910s and 1960s. At the beginning of the 21st century, the party regularly obtained a significant share of the votes in the city of **Buenos Aires** and other major urban centers. The PS also rebuilt a solid base in the province of **Santa Fe**, especially (though not exclusively) in the port city of **Rosario**. In the modern period, its greatest success was the election of Hermes Binner to the governorship of Santa Fe in 2007; having previously served two terms as mayor of Rosario, Binner was the first Socialist to secure a governorship in the country. He was runner-up in the **presidential election of 2011** and elected to head the party in 2012. On the center-left of the political spectrum, the party remains committed to democratic socialism and espoused progressive social democracy.

PATAGONIA. Southern hemisphere steppes at the tip of South America, lying below the Colorado River; the region is shared by Argentina and **Chile**, with the greater part in Argentine territory. Representing approximately one-third of the country, Argentine Patagonia contains the present-day provinces of **Chubut**, **Neuquén**, **Río Negro**, **Santa Cruz**, and **Tierra del Fuego** and remains sparsely populated. Although earlier explorers may have touched on the coast before, Ferdinand Magellan was the first European to plot the Atlantic seaboard in 1520. Thorough surveys were undertaken in the 19th century, most famously by HMS *Beagle*, captained by Robert FitzRoy, with Charles Darwin heading the scientific team. Darwin formed his ideas about the origin of species during these voyages. European colonization in the north and along the coast began in the 1840s, following campaigns against nomadic Indians headed from the east by **Juan Manuel de Rosas** and the west by Manuel Bulnes, president of Chile. **Sheep** were introduced in the 1860s, giving the region greater economic significance and occasioning further rivalry between Argentina and Chile. Both countries were also alarmed at the prospect of European intervention; French adventurer Orélie-Antoine de Tounens, self-styled king of Aracania and Patagonia, attempted to raise funds in Europe in the 1860s to support his ambitions. Welsh colonization in the 1860s helped establish Argentine claims to the interior on the eastern side of the **Andes**, notwithstanding Chilean pretentions to an Atlantic coast.

Argentine **military** expeditions against pampean Indians in the 1870s produced further tensions, particularly during the final stages of the **Conquest of the Desert**, which finally opened the southern **pampas** to large-scale settlement and development. In 1881, both countries agreed to fix the border along the watershed of the Andes, determined by the highest mountains. Sections of the frontier remained contested, with further agreements reached in 1902.

There were disagreements in the 1960s, but the most serious conflict was the **Beagle Channel Dispute**, which brought the countries to the brink of war in 1978. Contesting Chilean claims to strategically located islets in the Beagle Channel, the de facto government headed by General **Jorge Rafael Videla** seriously contemplated military action against Chile—Operación Soberanía. Only papal intervention and arbitration prevented open warfare. A definitive settlement in 1984, during the presidency of **Raúl Alfonsín**, brought the territorial dispute to an end.

PATRICIOS. Elite regiment founded by **Cornelio Saavedra** to confront the first **British invasion** in 1806. Composed of young patriots drawn largely from elite families, the regiment assumed a prominent role in the defense and recapture of the city of **Buenos Aires** and is regarded as the origins of the Argentine army. Although active in 1806 and 1807, the regiment assumed even greater important after the **May Revolution of 1810**. Suppressed by the last Spanish viceroy, **Baltasar Hidalgo de Cisneros**, the regiment was subsequently revived and fought valiantly in the **independence** campaign. The color of the national flag is reputedly taken from the blue-and-white plumes worn by the Patricios. The regiment saw service in the civil wars of the period and was engaged in campaigns in **Uruguay**, in conflicts against **Brazil** in the 1820s, and in the **War of the Triple Alliance** against **Paraguay**. Today, while fully incorporated in the national army, the regiment is most seen performing ceremonial duties in the city of Buenos Aires in original 19th-century uniforms composed of a black top hat with a white plume, blue swallow-tailed jacket, white breeches, and black knee-length boots. *See also* ARMY OF THE ANDES; MILITARY.

PELLEGRINI, CARLOS ENRIQUE JOSÉ (1846–1906). Businessman, economist, economic nationalist, and statesman; served as vice president to **Miguel Juárez Celman**, whom he succeeded when the latter resigned as president in 1890, completing the term in 1892. Pellegrini was something of an outsider, though a member of the elite. He was known as "El Gringo" because of his foreign parentage—his father was French–Italian and his mother Welsh—and regarded as a maverick due to his successful business career and championing of reform. Yet his career was fairly typical: he was elected national congressman for **Buenos Aires**, had served as minister of interior in the provincial government, and he held portfolios in the federal government before becoming Juárez Celman's running mate in 1886. Charged with cleaning up the mess left by his predecessor, he oversaw the renegotiation of the **foreign debt**, began the process of restoring confidence in the **currency**, and reformed the banking system, measures that helped stabilize the **economy** and prepare for sustainable growth thereafter. These achievements earned him public respect, as did a later campaign against **corruption**. He was unafraid to highlight shortcomings of the prevailing oligarchic system or to identify with critics of it, notably the socialist campaigner and later congressman **Alfredo Palacios**. The events of 1890 shaped Pellegrini's view on the corruption of the prevailing order and influenced his subsequent belief in the need for political reform, views that influenced like-minded members of the elite who would later support the electoral reform measures introduced by **Roque Sáenz Peña**.

PEÓN. Free estate worker: in many parts of the continent, a *peón* would be a rural worker bound to a hacienda or *estancia*—that is, debt peonage (*peonaje*). Traditionally, in Argentina such workers tended their own plots, working on estates as required, though often enjoying the protection of a landowner or **caudillo**. The term is not interchangeable with **gaucho**. Nowadays, virtually any rural worker may be described as a *peón*.

PERÓN, EVA (1919–1952). Second wife of **Juan Domingo Perón**, commonly referred to as Evita; all-too-powerful first lady of Argentina (1946–1952). Born María Eva Duarte in the small town of Los Toldos, province of **Buenos Aires**, she was a film and radio actress with a dubious past and high ambitions.

Evita met Perón at a charity gala for the victims of a massive earthquake in **San Juan** in January 1944 and became his mistress. Their relationship irked Perón's comrades in arms; it was very overt, and she attended his meetings with civilian and **military** friends as he steadily rose to power. They married in late October 1945, when it was clear that in the forthcoming election Perón would be elected president. Following his inauguration in June 1946, Evita was transformed into the second most powerful political personality in the country. She became the link between the masses and Perón, who did not have personal time for them. From an office in the old Secretariat of Labor, Evita dealt with workers' delegations that came with problems and requests or simply wanted to greet her husband. She gradually concentrated on the ever-rising number of appeals for personal help and finally established the **Fundación Eva Perón** in July 1948.

The Fundación was set up with 10,000 pesos from her own savings and financed by "voluntary" contributions from the **trade unions**, 20 percent of the proceeds from the Lotería Nacional, grants in aid from **Congress**, as well as compulsory private donations. Only Evita controlled the funds and determined how they would be spent. Therefore, the foundation, notwithstanding its useful work in charity and social programs, was a source of considerable political patronage and became tainted with **corruption**. The construction of a massive and extravagant headquarters for the organization was begun on

Paseo Colón in the national capital; not fully completed before the **military coup of 1955**, it now belongs to the Engineering Faculty of the **University of Buenos Aires** (UBA). More crucially, Evita used her Fundación to funnel vast sums of money into Swiss bank accounts—perhaps as much as 700 million US dollars.

Evita embarked on a solo "Rainbow Tour" of Europe from June to August 1947, not only to continue carving out a political role but also to attain social success; she wanted to best the middle and upper classes, whom she bitterly resented. She triumphed in **Spain**, fared far less well in Italy, failed to obtain a formal invitation to **Great Britain** as a result of postwar austerity, and handled herself adeptly in France. At home, the trip was deemed a success, having generated an enormous amount of publicity for Argentina and demonstrated that Evita was a political figure in her own right.

She occupied an exceptional position within government, which was formalized in October 1948, as she moved to expand her power even further. The opportunity arose from legislation enabling female suffrage already passed in 1947, which was certainly necessary but seen by Evita as a means to extend the base of support for both **Peronism** and herself. In July 1949, she set up the **Partido Peronista Femenino** (PPF), a gender-based branch of the ruling party. It became her personal fief, with no party bigwigs allowed to interfere except Perón himself. The PPF served as the launchpad for her boldest and most ambitious political move: a bid to become vice president. Yet Evita was unsuccessful in the bid to become her husband's running mate in the **presidential election of 1951**. The main objections to her candidacy came from the military, who continued to be irked by her intervention in politics and totally rejected the possibility of her becoming commander-in-chief in the event of Perón's death in office.

Gravely ill by late 1951, she died in July 1952. Although her achievements as a woman were considerable for that time and for what she accomplished in the last six years of her short life, there was a dark side. Evita's dubious past and naked ambition remain an issue. She was a ruthless and mercurial character whose venomous speeches to the masses could send the mob into a frenzy and instill deep fear in her opponents. More hypocritically, while championing the poor, Evita had a penchant for luxurious clothing and jewelry. She also encouraged a cult of adulation, which ranged from her being considered a saint to her autobiography *La razón de mi vida* becoming a mandatory school text. And finally, there was the matter of corruption, exemplified by Evita's handling of the finances of her own foundation.

Because Evita had such a multifaceted personality, she has remained an extremely divisive figure from her heyday in power to the present. *See also* ELOY MARTÍNEZ, TOMÁS (1934–2010); MAGALDI, AUGUSTÍN (1898–1938); MINISTRY OF PUBLIC WORKS; PARTIDO JUSTICIALISTA (PJ); PRESIDENTIAL ELECTION OF 1946.

PERÓN, ISABEL (1931–). Third wife of **Juan Domingo Perón**; president of Argentina (1974–1976). Born Maria Estela Martínez Cartas in **La Rioja**, she moved with her family at the age of three to a well-off **Buenos Aires** neighborhood. Starting in 1953, she danced for numerous ensembles in various Latin American countries under the artistic name Isabel, which is most commonly used when referring to her. During a Caribbean tour with the dancing troupe of Joe Herald in 1955, in which she performed at the notorious Happy Land cabaret in Panama, she met Perón in extremely dubious circumstances. She accompanied him throughout his exile in several countries until they settled in **Spain**, where they got married in 1961.

After Perón finally returned from exile to Argentina, Isabel became the vice presidential candidate on her husband's ticket for the **presidential election of September 1973**. They took office in October 1973, and as vice president, she failed to perform her duties as head of the National Senate. Following the death of her husband on 1 July 1974, she succeeded him as president. She was under the spell of **José López Rega**, the key figure in the Perón household and all-too-powerful minister of social welfare, until strong opposition to him forced his resignation in July 1975.

Isabel proved incapable of dealing with the mounting challenges facing Argentina. Although a steady hand was needed to run the **economy**, she had a whole string of unsuccessful ministers—**José Ber Gelbard, Alfredo Gómez Morales, Celestino Rodrigo, Antonio Cafiero**, and **Emilio Mondelli**. Not only was the economy out of control by the middle of 1975, but the country had also descended into what was becoming an undeclared civil war. The **Montoneros** and the **Ejército Revolucionario del Pueblo** (ERP) had stepped up the number of kidnappings, robberies, and terrorist attacks. Moreover, the ERP attempted to set up a liberated zone for operating, obtaining supplies and receiving reinforcements, and establishing contact with neighboring countries.

The government's initial response to escalating terrorism, which was to decree a state of siege in November 1974, was inconsequential. In February 1975, the army was authorized to begin what became successful military operations against the ERP in its refuges in the province of **Tucumán**. A subsequent decree in October 1975, enacted by acting president **Ítalo Luder** while Isabel took a leave of absence on medical grounds, empowered the army to carry out a **War to Annihilate Subversion** in the whole of the country. This had major consequences. It made the armed forces autonomous and would be used as the legal basis for the state terror carried out by the military dictatorship that would follow Isabel.

By the end of 1975, Argentina was careening toward disaster. With society deeply fractured and the government paralyzed, the armed forces decided to resolve the institutional crisis by taking charge. In what was probably the most anticipated coup ever, the military struck on 24 March 1976 and ousted

Isabel. She was detained for five years, and after her release in 1981 she traveled to Spain. Unlike what happened during her late husband's exile in the 1960s, Isabel did not turn her residence in Madrid into a springboard of Peronist agitation. In fact, she remains a recluse. *See also* CRUZADA JUS-TICIALISTA DE LA SOLIDARIDAD; MINISTRY OF SOCIAL DEVEL-OPMENT; MILITARY COUP OF 1976.

PERÓN, JUAN DOMINGO (1895–1974). Founder of the most prominent modern Argentine political movement; president of Argentina in 1946–1955 and 1973–1974. Perón was born in the town of Lobos, province of **Buenos Aires**. He began his **military** career in 1911 and married Aurelia Tizón in 1929. Following the death of his wife in 1938, he attended a school for mountain warfare in Italy and served with various Italian army units in the Alps between July 1939 and May 1940. This commission would lead Perón to admire some traits of Mussolini's Fascist Italy, which he would replicate later in his political career: providing a major role to **trade unions**, using mass spectacle as a political tool, espousing a virulent anti-Communism, and carrying out repression.

In 1941, he became commanding officer of a detachment of mountain troops in **Mendoza**. It was here that Perón developed close personal ties with General **Edelmiro Farrell**, which were to be of great use at a later date. In 1942, he was shifted to the inspectorate of mountain troops in Buenos Aires, which was under Farrell's command. His political career began in earnest the following year, when he established the **Grupo de Oficiales Unidos**. This secret military lodge was heavily involved in the **military coup of 1943**, which was triggered by the nomination of the archconservative sugar baron Robustiano Patrón Costas as presidential candidate for the **Concordancia**. Perón acquired real power during the de facto presidencies of **Pedro Pablo Ramírez** and Farrell, and the latter was particularly influenced by him.

A widower since 1938, Perón had a weakness for young girls and younger women. This is of more than passing interest as two of these relationships would substantially affect both his career and the course of Argentine history. In 1944, during a charity gala for the victims of a massive earthquake in **San Juan**, he met actress María Eva Duarte. She became his mistress, then married him in 1945, and transformed herself into the famous **Eva Perón**.

Narrowly elected president in February 1946, Perón gained overwhelming control of both houses of **Congress** and the governorships of all provinces bar one. Perón displayed his authoritarian tendencies from early on. He terminated the independence of the Supreme Court, dissolved the **political parties** that had served as his election vehicle and replaced them with the **Partido Peronista**, secured government control of the trade unions, and from 1948 enacted legislation hobbling dissent and opposition. A new constitution was approved in March 1949, which aimed at institutionalizing the regime.

In the beginning, Perón's economic policy was heavily skewed toward his working-class base. Rather than focusing on a much-needed restructuring of the **economy**, it concentrated on increasing income, health care, **education**, and housing for the workers. The state sector, which was vastly expanded through nationalizations, was also used for the featherbedding of government supporters. Perón's policies were financed by the newly nationalized **Banco Central de la República Argentina** (BCRA) and by squeezing the rural sector through the state-owned **Instituto Argentino de Promoción del Intercambio** (IAPI). By 1949, the strategy was in crisis, and Perón had to revert to more traditional economic policies by the early 1950s.

In November 1951, Perón stood for reelection under the provisions of the **Constitution of 1949**, which made him eligible to do so and instituted direct presidential elections. His wife Eva failed to place herself on the ticket as vice presidential candidate, not least because of the army's opposition to her candidacy. The election posed severe problems for the opposition in terms of access to mass media and the ability to campaign without intimidation. Moreover, a new election law made multiparty coalitions impossible; the failure to run a presidential candidate would cause a party to lose its legal status. The Peronists faced an array of opponents and won handsomely.

Perón lost the connection between himself and the masses with the death of his wife in July 1952 and confronted severe economic problems with measures that were mostly too little, too late. He displayed contempt for the law and for established norms, as demonstrated by the scandal involving teenager **Nelly Rivas**. In 1954, he decided to go against a new enemy—the **Catholic Church**. Congress was considering bills to legalize prostitution and divorce and to grant illegitimate children the same rights as those of legitimate ones. In addition, an anticlerical campaign was launched. The decision to confront the church was a colossal blunder, almost certainly the worst of Perón's career. It united his political enemies and perplexed many Peronists who were also devout Catholics. In May 1955, there was a call for a constitutional convention to separate church and state, a move that was far too progressive for the time.

A failed putsch by the anti-Peronist navy in June 1955 resulted in the deaths of 355 civilians, who were avenged instantly with the burning of churches in the center of Buenos Aires. Belated efforts by Perón to be conciliatory to his opponents failed, as the tide was against him. In fact, his call for violence at the end of August sealed the fate of his presidency. Perón was ousted by a military rebellion in September 1955, and his exile took him to **Paraguay**, Panama, **Venezuela**, and the Dominican Republic before he finally settled in **Spain** in 1960. Along the way, he met an Argentine dancer, whom he married in 1961; she became simply known as **Isabel Perón**.

Perón remained very much a factor in Argentine politics and retained control of the Peronist movement. In December 1964, an attempt by Perón to return to Argentina on an Iberia commercial flight was foiled during a scheduled stop in Rio de Janeiro with the help of the Brazilian military government; he was dispatched back to Spain on the return leg of the flight that brought him to South America. In 1967, Perón took advantage of the expansion of a radicalized youth to counter challenges to him from within and without the movement. This *trasvasamiento generacional* would be a "true revolution inside Peronism" to be carried out by young supporters. Instead, what he called "esa juventud maravillosa" became a nightmare. Unwittingly, he had opened a Pandora's box. Guerrilla groups, including Peronist organizations, committed to armed struggle emerged and became a vehicle to spread radicalism within the working class. This was a problem that would dog administrations from then on, including Perón's elected third and final presidency, which began on 12 October 1973.

Perón initially insisted that all guerrillas, including Peronist ones, were bandits and ordered their repression by the police; he wished to avoid military participation at all costs, probably understanding the consequences this would entail. In the face of objection from opposition parties, Congress passed the Ley de Asociaciones Profesionales in November 1973. As intended, left-wing activists in factories and public entities had little room to maneuver.

Following an attack by the **Ejército Revolucionario del Pueblo** (ERP) on the military garrison in Azul (province of Buenos Aires) in January 1974, Perón addressed the nation in a live televised broadcast dressed in a military uniform. He strongly criticized the ERP; the **Montoneros**; the latter's spearhead in the Buenos Aires provincial government, Oscar Bidegain; and implicitly **Cuba**, as it was accused of arming the guerrillas. The attack on the Azul garrison coincided with a debate in Congress about changes to the penal code. These restored sanctions and definitions of criminal offences, especially those related to acts of subversion, which had been abolished the day after **Héctor Campora** became president. Eight "Montonero" deputies in Congress objected to the "repressive legislation" and, already under pressure from Perón, resigned when it was passed; they were immediately expelled from the **Partido Justicialista** (PJ).

Thereafter, events moved fast. **Alberto Villar** returned to the federal police as deputy head and became a founder of the **Triple A**; Bidegain resigned as Buenos Aires governor and was replaced by his deputy, Victorio Calabró; and **Ricardo Obregón Cano** was ejected as governor of **Córdoba** and the province came under **federal intervention**. The president was aware of the activities of the Triple A but not directly involved. Perón grew further and further apart from the Montoneros. There had been no real dialogue since February 1974, and the definitive break came while the president made a speech from the balcony of the **Casa Rosada** at a major rally on 1 May 1974. Grouped in a corner of the Plaza de Mayo, the Montoneros jeered and left the square. Perón's last public appearance was on 12 June that year, and he died on 1 July.

In office and in exile, Perón displayed a ruthless determination to remain in control of the party and the movement. He established precedents that were emulated by many of his successors. For example, a tendency to identify and co-opt potential rivals in order to destroy them, and to create competing groups within the movement and administration: divide and rule was an axiom that might have been coined with Perón and Peronism in mind. This was a device that facilitated *verticalismo*—namely, direction and control by "El Líder." Other enduring features of Perón were charismatic leadership and an understanding of the political aspirations of his fellow citizens far better than his contemporaries. Notwithstanding an emphasis on "ideology," pragmatism, rhetoric, and iconic symbols were the main characteristics of the man and the movement. On the issue of whether Perón was radical or conservative, his treatment of the **Partido Laborista** (PL) in the 1940s and the Montoneros in the 1970s suggests that he saw independent leftist popular organizations as critical threats, notwithstanding attacks on the Catholic Church in the 1950s. Peronism appealed to factions on the right and the left, some of whom thought that they could control it—or use it as a vehicle for advancing their own agenda. To the end, Perón almost invariably succeeded in destroying what he could not control. *See also* BER GELBARD, JOSÉ (1917–1977); BORLENGHI, ÁNGEL GABRIEL (1906–1962); BRAMUGLIA, JUAN ATILIO (1903–1962); *CONDUCCIÓN POLÍTICA*; FIGUEROLA, JOSÉ MIGUEL FRANCISCO LUIS (1897–1970); FRENTE JUSTICIALISTA DE LIBERACIÓN (FREJULI); FUERZA DE ORIENTACIÓN RADICAL DE LA JOVEN ARGENTINA (FORJA); GÓMEZ MORALES, ALFREDO (1908–1990); JUSTICIALISMO; LÓPEZ REGA, JOSÉ (1916–1989); MERCANTE, DOMINGO ALFREDO (1898–1976); MIGUEL, LORENZO MARCELO (1927–2002); MIRANDA, MIGUEL (1891–1953); MUNIZ BARRETO, DIEGO (1934–1977); "PERONISM WITHOUT PERÓN"; POPULISM; STATE-OWNED ENTERPRISES (SOEs); TERCERA POSICIÓN.

PERÓN, MARÍA ESTELA MARTÍNEZ CARTAS DE. *See* PERÓN, ISABEL (1931–).

PERÓN, MARÍA EVA DUARTE DE. *See* PERÓN, EVA (1919–1952).

PERÓN AND PERONISM. *See* CÁMPORA, HÉCTOR JOSÉ (1909–1980); *CONDUCCIÓN POLÍTICA*; DUHALDE, EDUARDO ALBERTO (1941–); FRENTE JUSTICIALISTA DE LIBERACIÓN (FREJULI); FRONDIZI, ARTURO (1908–1995); ILLIA, ARTURO UMBERTO (1900–1983); JUSTICIALISMO; KIRCHNER, CRISTINA ELISABET FERNÁNDEZ DE (1953–); KIRCHNER, NÉSTOR CARLOS (1950–2010); MENEM, CARLOS SAÚL (1930–); MILITARY; MILITARY COUP OF 1943; MILITARY COUP OF 1955; MILITARY COUP OF 1962; MILITARY COUP OF 1966; MILITARY COUP OF 1976; MONTONEROS; MOVIMIENTO RENOVADOR PERONISTA (MRP); PARTIDO JUSTICIALISTA (PJ); PARTIDO LABORISTA; PARTIDO PERONISTA FEMENINO (PPF); PERÓN, EVA (1919–1952); PERÓN, ISABEL (1931–); PERÓN, JUAN DOMINGO (1895–1974); *PERONATO*; "PERONISM WITHOUT PERÓN"; POPULISM; STATE-OWNED ENTERPRISES (SOEs); TERCERA POSICIÓN; TRADE UNIONS.

PERONATO. Term applied to the administrations of **Juan Domingo Perón**, particularly the first two presidencies in 1946–1955. In part, it alludes to efforts by Perón to establish a guiding ideology for the regime—**Justicialismo**—a concept embracing political theory and the practice of governance, and the policies derived from the ideology: economic interventionism, social justice, and mass democracy. By extension, the term became applied to the regime as a whole and the system of government practiced by Perón—personalist, **populist**, and authoritarian. Although used by the regime itself and by its opponents, the term generally has negative connotations. In Spanish, the suffix *-ato* refers to a period or system, and when applied to a political period or process includes the attributes of decisiveness, authoritarianism, and a regime or ideology associated with a particular individual.

PERONISM. *See* JUSTICIALISMO. *See also* CÁMPORA, HÉCTOR JOSÉ (1909–1980); *CONDUCCIÓN POLÍTICA*; DUHALDE, EDUARDO ALBERTO (1941–); FRENTE JUSTICIALISTA DE LIBERACIÓN (FREJULI); FRONDIZI, ARTURO (1908–1995); ILLIA, ARTURO UMBERTO (1900–1983); JUSTICIALISMO; KIRCHNER, CRISTINA ELISABET FERNÁNDEZ DE (1953–); KIRCHNER, NÉSTOR CARLOS (1950–2010); MENEM, CARLOS SAÚL (1930–); MILITARY; MILITARY COUP OF 1943; MILITARY COUP OF 1955; MILITARY COUP OF 1962; MILITARY COUP OF 1966; MILITARY COUP OF 1976; MONTONEROS; MOVIMIENTO RENOVADOR PERONISTA (MRP); PARTIDO JUSTICIALISTA (PJ); PARTIDO LABORISTA; PARTIDO PERONISTA FEMENINO (PPF); PERÓN, EVA (1919–1952); PERÓN, ISABEL (1931–);

PERÓN, JUAN DOMINGO (1895–1974); *PERONATO*; "PERONISM WITHOUT PERÓN"; POPULISM; STATE-OWNED ENTERPRISES (SOEs); TERCERA POSICIÓN; TRADE UNIONS.

"PERONISM WITHOUT PERÓN". Following the **military coup of 1955**, which resulted in ousted president **Juan Domingo Perón** being exiled and his party proscribed, local Peronist leaders began to organize a so-called Peronism without Perón or neo-Peronism to keep the flag flying and have some political participation. This phenomenon became a significant component of Argentine politics. "Peronism without Perón" was an additional strand to the conflict between the Peronists and anti-Peronists—as well as among Peronists—and contributed to the survival and restoration of Peronism.

The de facto **Revolución Libertadora** regime that came to power in September 1955 was itself divided over how to deal with Peronism. President **Eduardo Lonardi** criticized the leadership of Perón but allowed the **Confederación General del Trabajo** (CGT) to remain in Peronist hands, allowed the **Partido Peronista** (PP) to reorganize itself under new leaders, and preserved the social and labor legislation enacted by Perón. In November 1955, Lonardi was ousted in a palace coup by **Pedro Eugenio Aramburu**, a hard-line anti-Peronist who took a far more radical course, including purging the **military** of suspected Peronist sympathizers, the prohibition of the use of Peronist slogans and symbols, the outlawing of the PP, and taking over of the CGT. In 1956, the government decreed a new statute of **political parties** that contained provisions that made it illegal for Perón or his immediate collaborators to form a new party controlled by the exiled leader; an implicit military veto put teeth into the legislation.

Unlike Lonardi, Aramburu failed to grasp that Peronism was here to stay. By banning the PP and prohibiting the formation of new parties under Perón's direct control, Aramburu paved the way for the rise of neo-Peronist parties. These groupings gave broad support to Perón's doctrine and policies but did not put themselves under the former president's guidance or supervision, thereby complying with the statute of political parties. Neo-Peronist parties—of which the most important was the **Unión Popular** (UP)—were tolerated by Aramburu as a means of fragmenting the Peronist vote, while Perón saw them as a direct challenge to his authority. By 1958, Peronist political and union leaders had come to favor participating in elections through neo-Peronist parties, and this raised the specter of an irreversible move to a "Peronism without Perón." Therefore, in order to preserve his influence over the movement, the exiled leader made the **Caracas Pact** in the run-up to the **presidential election of 1958** with candidate **Arturo Frondizi** of the **Unión Cívica Radical Intransigente** (UCRI). The election deal secured the backing of Perón's supporters for Frondizi, enabling him to become president.

In the 1960s, **Augusto Vandor**, leader of the Unión Obrera Metalúrgica (UOM), the largest of the CGT's 62 **trade unions**, overtly challenged Perón's influence, giving even more substance to the possibility of a "Peronism without Perón." The open conflict between Vandor and Perón became explicit as the provincial and **congressional elections of 1962** approached. Frondizi allowed the participation of Peronists in the polls; a coalition of neo-Peronist groupings decided to contest the elections, opening the way for Vandor. With his enormous and tightly controlled organization, his legendary negotiating skills behind the scenes, and his proven capacity to mobilize thousands of workers in a matter of hours, Vandor extended his influence over the political wing of Peronism. The Vandoristas agreed to place their powerful machine at the disposal of the UP in exchange for securing key candidacies. This raised the prospect of a victory by a UP dominated by Vandor, with Perón being reduced to a symbolic role. Needing the UP with its legal status to contest the elections and unforgiving toward attempts at independence by the party leadership, Perón resolved the quandary by imposing his own candidates. The subsequent victory of the UP and other neo-Peronist parties at the ballot box triggered the **military coup of 1962**.

Neo-Peronists and Vandoristas displayed considerable moderation during the presidency of **José María Guido**, and thereby the UP was allowed to participate in the **presidential election of 1963**. The UP set up the Frente Nacional y Popular (FNP) with the **Movimiento de Integración y Desarrollo** (MID) and the **Partido Conservador Popular** (PCP); **Vicente Solano Lima**, the leader of the latter grouping, was imposed by Perón as the presidential candidate of the coalition. It is assumed that the exiled leader had chosen Solano Lima because if elected he would be totally beholden to him and did not constitute a rival for the control of the Peronist movement. Solano Lima announced that if he won he would allow the return of Perón to Argentina. As a result, the ever-watchful military—the real power behind Guido—secured the proscription of the FNP two weeks before the election was held.

During the presidency of **Arturo Illia** of the **Unión Cívica Radical del Pueblo** (UCRP), Vandor headed an initiative by Peronist union leaders and neo-Peronist politicians to set up a party to represent Peronism without its exiled leader. Behind Vandor's advance on the political branch of Peronism was a loosening of electoral restrictions on the movement. Some military leaders had become more flexible, and by early 1964 most of the UCRP leadership was in favor of relaxing the proscription on Peronism. Proponents of ending proscription assumed that it would vastly increase the patronage powers of Vandor and neo-Peronist politicians and further undermine the influenced of Perón. As a result, Perón sought to promote an extreme version of Peronism in order the get the party banned once again. Hence, he reorganized and promoted the **Partido Justicialista** (PJ), packing it with extremists just as the party appeared to be on the verge of obtaining legal political status. The move backfired due to the power of the UOM, and as Perón still needed Vandor's organizational support, he accepted the placement of allies of the union leader on the proposed PJ reorganizing committee. To adapt to the legislation requiring internal democracy in political parties, the reorganization of the PJ would be led "from below," depriving Perón of a say in the selection of party leaders. A membership drive was undertaken, and in June 1964 internal elections were held for delegates to a congress that would choose the party leaders. Vandor scored a decisive victory, and one of his allies took charge of the party, even though Perón formally remained head of the PJ.

The stature of Vandor within the trade union movement had also increased with the campaign to occupy factories in May and June 1964, which was supported by factory owners as it was aimed at the unpopular and weak Illia government. Nevertheless, the conflict between the exiled former president and the UOM leadership began to tilt against the latter. The first instance was "Operativo Retorno," the unsuccessful attempt by Perón to return to Argentina in December 1964, in which both men had competing agendas. Vandor participated in the operation's planning and then made it public in a bid to foil the return of the exiled leader. The commercial flight bringing Perón from Madrid had a scheduled stop in Rio de Janeiro, where—at the request of the Illia government—the Brazilian authorities prevented him from continuing the trip, and he was dispatched back to **Spain** on the return leg of the flight. While Vandor claimed that the former president would never be allowed back, Perón succeeded in conveying to his supporters the view that the attempted return had been thwarted as much by factions within "Peronism without Perón" as by the government and the military.

Matters were worsened by the **congressional elections of 1965**. One month before the electoral contest, the PJ was proscribed on the grounds that the party was still controlled by Perón. This led Vandor to set up a coalition with the UP, again providing his electoral machine in exchange for key candidacies. The UP garnered 31 percent of ballots cast, a success that seemed to suggest that the electoral future of Peronism depended on both mass support for Perón and the organization of Vandor. The latter's advance in the political arm of Peronism was strengthened by the election of an ally as head of the Peronist block in the Chamber of Deputies, which prompted disgruntled PJ politicians to demand that Vandoristas resign from the leadership of their party. Vandor then pushed for a legal, unified party dominated by the trade unions and independent of Perón, echoing the original position of the **Partido Laborista**. In July 1965, Vandor proposed that the UP unite under a single banner with eight other neo-Peronist parties. Prefiguring a proposal that the **Movimiento Renovador Peronista** (MRP) made in 1987, the charter of the new party replaced the system of thirds for each branch of the Peronist movement (male section, **women**'s section, and the trade unions) by direct or indirect elections for the governing body. As the system of thirds had never been used in reality, Vandor's project to dismantle it symbolically defied the "corporatist" nature of the movement. (The system of thirds had enabled Perón to maintain control of the party leadership by promoting conflict among the different branches.) In October 1965, the exiled leader responded by sending his wife **Isabel Perón** to Argentina on a mission of "peace and reconciliation" whose real aim was to destroy the project. The rupture between Perón and Vandor became public, and although Vandor was weakened, he still controlled the UOM and many of the Peronists in the Chamber of Deputies owed their election to him. The delicate balance of forces within the Peronist leadership meant that the struggle would be resolved at the ballot box.

The gubernatorial election in the province of **Jujuy** in January 1966 was the first opportunity for a show of strength. Vandor backed José Humberto Martiarena, the incumbent governor and leader of the neo-Peronist Partido Blanco de los Trabajadores, while Perón supported José Nasif, the provincial leader of the PJ, which had been allowed to put up candidates in Jujuy. The easy reelection of Martiarena was followed by the rebellion of most trade union leaders against Vandor. The real test of strength came in the gubernatorial election in the province of **Mendoza** in April 1966. Emilio Jofré, the candidate of the ruling Partido Demócrata, was the favorite to win, yet the more interesting contest was that between the two Peronist candidates: Alberto Serú of the neo-Peronist Movimiento Popular Mendocino (MPM), who was supported by Vandor, and Ernesto Corvalán of the PJ, who was backed by Perón and had been allowed to stand by the national government. The latter was alarmed that a victory for Serú in Mendoza would presage the results of gubernatorial elections in three major provinces (**Buenos Aires**, **Santa Fe**, and **Córdoba**) due in March 1967; allowing a PJ candidate to participate in the elections was intended to split the Peronist vote. Ignoring a ban on Peronist propaganda, the government then authorized the transmission on radio and television in Mendoza of a recorded message from Perón calling on his supporters to vote for Corvalán. In spite of the superior organization of the MPM, the exhortation of the exiled former president worked. Jofré won the election as expected, but Corvalán came in a strong second. The project of a "Peronism without Perón" was being undermined; the Vandoristas announced that they would no longer interfere in the political wing of Peronism.

The **military coup of 1966** brought to power the de facto administrations of the **Revolución Argentina**. Within a few years, the military was forced to extricate themselves from power and allow Peronism to reenter the political arena. Although unable to stand himself, in November 1972 Perón set up the **Frente Justicialista de Liberación** (FREJULI) to contest the general election called for March 1973. Owing to strategic and ideological differences, the neo-Peronist parties refused to join this front dominated by the PJ. With the sole exception of the **Movimiento Popular Neuquino** (MPN), which survives to this day, all neo-Peronist parties faded away in the aftermath of the electoral contest. Perón returned to Argentina in June 1973 and took charge of the country following the snap **presidential election of September 1973**.

Although "Peronism without Perón" is the term used to describe the attempts to institutionalize the party independently from its exiled leader, in recent times it has also been employed to depict the PJ after the death of Perón. He was succeeded as president by his vice president and wife, Isabel, on 1 July 1974. Her presidency was spectacularly chaotic, not least because Peronism was at war with itself, and terminated by the **military coup of 1976**. When democracy returned, the PJ failed to win the **presidential election of 1983**, in part because of the memory of their last term in government. The party attempted to "modernize" itself but has not really succeeded. It remains a movement riven by factions that compete against each other in national elections, as clearly demonstrated in the **presidential election of 2015**, which pitted the **Frente para la Victoria**/PJ against the **Frente Renovador**/PJ. *See also* ARAMBURAZO (29 MAY–1 JUNE 1970); BRAMUGLIA, JUAN ATILIO (1903–1962); CÁMPORA, HÉCTOR JOSÉ (1909–1980); CONGRESSIONAL ELECTIONS OF 1973; DUHALDE, EDUARDO ALBERTO (1941–); EZEIZA MASSACRE (20 JUNE 1973); JUVENTUD PERONISTA (JP); KIRCHNER, CRISTINA ELISABET FERNÁNDEZ DE (1953–); KIRCHNER, NÉSTOR CARLOS (1950–2010); "LA HORA DEL PUEBLO"; LANUSSE, ALEJANDRO AGUSTÍN (1918–1996); LASTIRI, RAÚL ALBERTO (1915–1978); LÓPEZ REGA, JOSÉ (1916–1989); MASSA, SERGIO TOMÁS (1972–); MENEM, CARLOS SAÚL (1930–); MONTONEROS; ONGARO, RAIMUNDO JOSÉ (1924–2016); PRESIDENTIAL ELECTION OF MARCH 1973; SAPAG, FELIPE (1917–2010); TRIPLE A (ALIANZA ANTICOMUNISTA ARGENTINA).

PERU. For much of the colonial period, Argentina along with **Bolivia** (Upper Peru), **Chile**, **Paraguay**, and **Uruguay** formed part of the Viceroyalty of Peru. When created in the 16th century, the viceroyalty included all Spanish territory in South America, below and including Panama. Chile was relatively soon established as a separate jurisdiction, as a capitancy general.

Administrative changes in the 18th century resulted in subdivisions and the creation of new viceroyalties, for example, the **Viceroyalty of the River Plate** in 1776, which included Upper Peru, Paraguay, and Uruguay in addition to Argentina. With **independence**, the administration in the city of **Buenos Aires**, the viceregal capital, claimed authority over the whole territory, despite the fact that insurgents in Upper Peru had already declared independence from Madrid, Lima, and Buenos Aires. With royalist authority secure in Peru and Upper Peru and threatening the north of Argentina, insurgents in the latter saw exporting the revolution to Peru as the only means of securing their own independence. The result was the formation of the **Army of the Andes**, led by General **José de San Martín**, and the liberation of much of southern South America as separate political entities. Relations between the two countries since have been largely cordial, mainly determined by their approach to third parties. For example, Argentina tended to favor Peru during the **War of the Pacific**.

PESIFICACIÓN. Term applied to the forced conversion of bank accounts and financial instruments following the economic crisis of 2001–2002 that saw the end of the **Convertibility Plan** and debt default at the turn of the year. Convertibility was a legal instrument approved by **Congress** that, among other features, established a monetary order whereby pesos and US dollars circulated side by side on a one-to-one basis; both had the status of legal tender. When convertibility was abandoned and the peso plummeted, an arrangement had to be found to normalize bank accounts, as well as debt and credit contracts denominated in formerly convertible pesos and dollars. "Pesoization" also had to cope with the "emergency 90-day" part freezing of bank accounts in December 2001, the *corralito*. The *corralito* was extended, becoming the so-called *corralón*, an interim arrangement that could not be sustained indefinitely. It was clear that a long-term solution would be required to normalize the banking system and the financial sector, and to resolve multiple legal challenges provoked by the *corralito* and the mess that had resulted when the banks had closed their doors at the height of the crisis. *Pesificación* was that solution.

When convertibility was abandoned, there was a sharp rise in the US dollar and in nonperforming loans. Bankruptcy threatened households and businesses, and the banks. Applied in February 2002, the *corralón* and "pesoization" were intended to begin the process of normalization. Conditions of term deposits were extended and accounts "pesoized" at asymmetrical rates—assets at a rate of one peso per dollar, and liabilities at AR$1.40 per US$1.00. In May 2002, an adjustment was made: assets were indexed at a rate based on inflation and a wage indicator, and liabilities were linked to inflation alone. Later came a mechanism for indexing government bonds and loans that would permit a gradual conversion with market value. Intended to protect businesses and households from liabilities denominated in dollars (or "convertible pesos"), pesoization merely shifted the burden of the ensuing devaluation onto the banks, in the first instance, and, ultimately, the tax payer as the government had to bail out the banks. In the medium term, *pesificación* did little to restore confidence or liquidity, though it decidedly prevented a total collapse. Difficulties for the banking sector were compounded by the asymmetrical nature of assets and liability pesoization and, because as the extended limits on term deposits expired, the public withdrew cash. Between 2002 and 2006, depositors and asset holders had claims to the value of around 10 billion pesos recognized by the courts. The banking system did not fully stabilize until the recovery program initiated by Minister of Economy **Roberto Lavagna**, who reached a settlement with a majority of foreign bondholders in 2005, and the subsequent commodity boom. *See also* BANCO CENTRAL DE LA REPÚBLICA ARGENTINA (BCRA); CAVALLO, DOMINGO FELIPE (1946–); ECONOMIC CRISES; FOREIGN DEBT/FOREIGN INVESTMENT.

PESO. *See* CURRENCY.

PETROLEUM. *See* COMMODITIES; FRONDIZI, ARTURO (1908–1995); ILLIA, ARTURO UMBERTO (1900–1983); LA PLATA; MOSCONI, ENRIQUE CARLOS ALBERTO (1877–1940); MENDOZA (PROVINCE); NEUQUÉN (CITY); NEUQUÉN (PROVINCE); PREBISCH PLAN; SANTA CRUZ; STATE-OWNED ENTERPRISES (SOEs); YACIMIENTOS PETROLÍFEROS FISCALES (YPF).

PETTORUTI, EMILIO (1892–1971). One of the most influential painters in Argentina in the 20th century, he is remembered for his unique style and vision. Influenced by Cubism, Futurism, Constructivism, and Abstraction, Pettoruti did not claim to paint in any particular style. He exhibited in Argentina—even causing a scandal with his avant-garde Cubist exhibition in **Buenos Aires** in 1924—as well as the **United States** and all over Europe. His most significant works include *La Grotta Azzurra di Capri, Pensierosa, Arlequín, El Improvisador, La Última Serenata, Sol Argentino, Invierno en París*, and *Farfalla*.

PIAZZOLLA, ASTOR PANTALEÓN (1921–1992). Musician and **tango** composer; virtuoso player of the bandoneon, a type of concertina popular in Argentina and **Uruguay**—an essential instrument in tango ensembles. Piazzolla revolutionized traditional tango. He established a new individual style known as *nuevo tango*, which incorporated elements from jazz, used intricate harmonies and dissonance as well as counterpoint, and ventured into extended compositional forms. Among other forms, this led to the development of orchestrated tango, which formed the basis of tango shows that he helped to promote in Argentina and overseas. This was quite distinct from the traditional tango sung by iconic figures such as **Carlos Gardel** and **Agustín Magaldi**.

Piazzolla regularly performed his own compositions with a variety of tango ensembles. Having broadcast and recorded in **Buenos Aires** in the 1940s and 1950s, he entered a particularly prolific period in the 1970s and 1980s, living and working in France and Italy and performing elsewhere. He toured the **United States** and Canada, where he broadcast from prestigious venues—as he had in Europe. One of his most famous works was *Libertango*, recorded and published in 1974. He earned many awards for his compositions, recordings, and film scores.

PINEDO, FEDERICO (1895–1971). Minister of finance (minister of economy) during the presidencies of **Agustín P. Justo** and **Roberto M. Ortiz**. An Independent Socialist, he joined the **Concordancia** alliance together with the **Partido Demócrata Nacional** (PDN) and the *antipersonalista* faction of the **Unión Cívica Radical** (UCR).

As minister, Pinedo had **Raúl Prebisch** as adviser and they worked closely. During the Justo presidency, their main economic measure was the **Plan de Acción Económica** of 1933, which successfully overcame the effects of the Great Depression. After an interlude, Pinedo returned to the Ministry of Finance in 1940. Not only had by then president Ortiz taken medical leave and been temporarily replaced by vice president **Ramón S. Castillo**, but the Second World War was raging. Once again with the assistance of Prebisch, Pinedo presented to **Congress** the Plan de Reactivación Económica (better known as the **Pinedo Plan**). Although it was rejected in a hostile political environment and the minister of finance resigned in early 1941, it is worth pointing out that elements of the Pinedo Plan were implemented in modified form by President **Juan Domingo Perón** after 1946. See also ECONOMIC CRISES; ECONOMY; MINISTRY OF ECONOMY.

PINEDO PLAN. Named for Minister of Hacienda (a.k.a. economy) **Federico Pinedo**; formally called the Plan de Reactivación Económica, this project aimed to address challenges arising from the Second World War. Presented to **Congress** by the ruling **Concordancia** in November 1940 and debated for two months, the plan was rejected in January 1941 for political reasons. Yet it remains a landmark for being the most daring, comprehensive effort at state economic planning and intervention in Argentina to that date.

The government had a two-pronged strategy. On the one hand, it sought to alleviate immediate difficulties. Since **agriculture** remained the "great master wheel" of the Argentine **economy**, the government committed itself to supporting the sector with a new state agency that would purchase unsold products, sell them overseas, and use the resulting profits to acquire necessary industrial imports. In urban areas, it proposed a massive public and private housing program for low- and middle-income earners, thereby stimulating employment and the reinvigoration of the whole economy. On the other hand, more interestingly, the government tacitly recognized that the existing economic framework was no longer functioning and proposed long-term changes. Arguing that the "master wheel" had spokes and smaller wheels, the plan fostered a strategy of industrial development—but not at any price. It proposed the creation of a new industrial credit bank, aimed at export competitiveness in the **United States** and the **Southern Cone**, and called for trade agreements with other Latin American countries to create markets for Argentine products. Finally, in a sign of the times, the Pinedo Plan included provisions regarding the nationalization of the mostly British-owned railways.

Notwithstanding political failure, it must be noted that elements of the plan are reflected in the post-1943 policies of both the **military** regime and its Peronist successors. *See also* ECONOMIC CRISES; FERROCARRILES ARGENTINOS (FFAA); FOREIGN TRADE; MILITARY COUP OF 1943; MINISTRY OF ECONOMY; PERÓN, JUAN DOMINGO (1895–1974); PLAN DE ACCIÓN ECONÓMICA; PREBISCH PLAN; TRANSPORTATION.

PIQUETERO/PIQUETEROS. The *piquetero* movement (derived from the English "to picket") began during the 1990s, though it assumed considerable prominence after the turn of the century. It was initially associated with spontaneous demonstrations against the **Convertibility Plan** introduced by President **Carlos Saúl Menem** of the **Partido Justicialista** (PJ) and Minister of Economy **Domingo Cavallo**. **Privatization** and budget cuts resulted in a substantial rise in unemployment and heightened concerns about inequality and social exclusion. Blocking major highways was the hallmark of the resulting protests. If the main focus was originally aimed at economic and social policies of the day, there was soon a political dimension—namely, rising disillusion with conventional party politics and the stance of the mainstream labor organization, the **Confederación General del Trabajo** (CGT), traditionally closely aligned with the PJ. The organized labor movement had paid scant regard to workers in the informal sector. The economic crisis at the end of 2001, which left 50 percent of the population of greater **Buenos Aires** living below the poverty line and around two-thirds of the urban workforce officially unemployed, gave the movement renewed momentum, bringing together laid-off formal-sector workers, the mass of unregistered laborers in the black **economy**, and the newly impoverished middle class. *Cortes de ruta*, erecting barricades to disrupt traffic and trade, were intended to bring to attention the plight of the poor in government and society at large. Despite the diversity of groups involved—their differing ideologies and objectives—there was a great deal of common ground and coordination during the early years of the 21st century. Among the most active organizers and coordinators were radicalized district committees composed of local residents. When the administration of interim president **Eduardo Duhalde** unfolded an innovative family allowance program, Planes Jefes de Hogar, which undoubtedly prevented social collapse and halted the decline into poverty, handouts were often arranged by such local committees. However, the device also facilitated capture by the state.

As the system of Planes was advanced under President **Néstor Kirchner**, who also announced his determination to maintain order as well as to promote social harmony, the allocation of family grants was used to divide and rule the movement. Kirchner's strategy was consistent with traditional PJ policy of attempting to absorb new social actors within Peronism. With distinct factions of the PJ, its regional affiliates, and groups within the CGT involved in the distributions of funds, the cohesion of the movement was diluted. *Piquetero* organizations were co-opted by political and union bosses. Solidarity was also undermined by economic recovery after 2005. Middle-class support for the movement, which had been strong, dissipated with the proliferation of *cortes de ruta*, which became regarded as unnecessary, inconvenient, a mechanism of extortion or intimidation, and a reflection of internal divisions—especially as the violence of protests increased and *piqueteros* took to wearing face masks. During the presidency of **Cristina Fernández de Kirchner**, one of the largest and most active *piquetero* groups was coordinated by **La Cámpora**, nominally headed by **Máximo Kirchner**. It was used to orchestrate demonstrations in support of the regime, provide protection for *la Presidenta*, and intimidate opponents—in short, functioning as a rent-a-mob.

PLAN DE ACCIÓN ECONÓMICA. Presented to **Congress** by Minister of Economy **Federico Pinedo** of the ruling **Concordancia** in November 1933, it was an emergency response to the Great Depression and succeeded not least due to the so-called Roca Funding Loan, which was secured through the issue of a major government bond offering and was part of the highly controversial **Roca–Runciman Pact** between Argentina and **Great Britain**.

The plan supported productive activity in the private sector by stimulating agricultural output. The government would purchase the principal crops at minimum guaranteed prices, which required an improvement in the country's exchange position and hence the importance of the Roca Funding Loan. This unblocked the remittances of foreign obligations, thereby relieving pressure on the peso, allowing a controlled devaluation to support exports, and the reform of the exchange control system to aid the rural sector. The state Junta Reguladora de Granos purchased wheat, **maize**, and linseed crops whenever the international quotations of those staples fell below a stipulated minimum. To obtain the funds to subsidize cereal prices, the system of exchange control was modified so as to yield a profit, which derived from the difference between the rate at which the government bought and sold foreign exchange. Other elements of the plan, or schemes deriving from it that were connected to efforts to stabilize and stimulate the **economy**, included public works projects—road building and railway construction—and the establishment of a central bank, **Banco Central de la República Argentina** (BCRA).

Given the importance of agricultural production in the national economy, the price guarantee not only afforded relief to farmers badly hit by the Depression but also led to a general improvement in the returns of commerce and trade. Devised as a temporary measure, it put Argentina firmly on the path to recovery and was terminated when international **grain** prices recovered in late 1936. Arrangements for commodity support and the management of the exchange rate in the 1930s were much more sophisticated, transparent, and effective than those essayed later in the 20th century and during the presidencies of **Néstor Kirchner** and **Cristina Fernández de Kirchner**. See also AGRICULTURE; COMMODITIES; CURRENCY; ECONOMIC CRISES; FOREIGN DEBT/FOREIGN INVESTMENT; FOREIGN TRADE; PREBISCH, RAÚL (1901–1986); PREBISCH PLAN; TRANSPORTATION.

PLAN DE REACTIVACIÓN ECONÓMICA. *See* PINEDO PLAN.

POLITICAL PARTIES. Argentina has a dynamic political party culture, often highly personalistic, sometimes ideologically based. Embryonic, proto-party groupings were observable from **independence**, clearly identifiable at the time of the **May Revolution of 1810**, when political debate centered on the form of **national organization**—a constitutional monarchy or representative republic, a state organized along federalist or centralist lines—as well as about the position of the **Catholic Church** and about free trade. By the 1820s, what would become the **Unitarian** and **Federalist** positions were sharply defined even if there were no formally constituted political parties or organizations.

Recognizably modern political parties date from the late 19th century, several identified with the main ideologies of the period. The **Unión Cívica Radical** (UCR) was established at this time—one of the oldest surviving political parties to be founded in Latin America. Electoral reform—the

Sáenz Peña Law of 1912—gave a further boost to the creation of political parties, as did public funding of parties, first available in limited form in 1959. For much of the 20th century, and notwithstanding frequent periods of **military** rule between 1930 and 1983, politics was dominated by two parties, the UCR and the **Peronist Party**, now the **Partido Justicialista**. The two parties usually commanded well above 80 percent of the popular vote in general elections. This dualistic structure fragmented around the turn of the 20th century as distinct factions emerged within and outside the two main parties. Party fragmentation and the proliferation of political parties is associated with current arrangements for the public funding of parties, introduced in 2002 following a **corruption** scandal that surfaced during the administration of President **Fernando de la Rúa** when it was revealed that he had been bribing members of the National Senate to secure the passage of vital legislation. The 2002 law provides annual public funding for registered political parties: 80 percent of the total fund is allocated based on the number of seats held in the federal **Congress**, with 20 percent divided equally among all parties. In addition, special funds are distributed for election campaigning, 70 percent of which is allocated to parties based on seats in Congress, with 30 percent being divided among all parties. Currently, over 40 parties are recognized at the federal level, with more than 650 registered at the provincial level. *See also* ACCIÓN POR LA REPÚBLICA (AR); AFIRMACIÓN PARA UNA REPÚBLICA IGUALITARIA (ARI); CAMBIEMOS; COALICIÓN CÍVICA (CC); FRENTE AMPLIO UNEN (FAUNEN); FRENTE JUSTICIALISTA DE LIBERACIÓN (FREJULI); FRENTE PAÍS SOLIDARIO (FREPASO); FRENTE PARA LA VICTORIA (FpV/PJ); FRENTE RENOVADOR (FR/PJ); MOVIMIENTO DE INTEGRACIÓN Y DESARROLLO (MID); MOVIMIENTO DE SACERDOTES PARA EL TERCER MUNDO (MSTM); MOVIMIENTO NACIONALISTA TACUARA (MNT); MOVIMIENTO POPULAR NEUQUINO (MPN); MOVIMIENTO RENOVADOR PERONISTA (MRP); PARTIDO CONSERVADOR POPULAR (PCP); PARTIDO DEMÓCRATA CRISTIANO (PDC); PARTIDO DEMÓCRATA NACIONAL (PDN); PARTIDO DEMÓCRATA PROGRESISTA (PDP); PARTIDO INTRANSIGENTE (PI); PARTIDO JUSTICIALISTA (PJ); PARTIDO PERONISTA FEMENINO (PPF); PROPUESTA REPUBLICANA (PRO); PARTIDO SOCIALISTA (PS); UNA NACIÓN AVANZADA (UNA); UNIDAD/UNIÓN CIUDADANA (UC); UNIDOS POR UNA NUEVA ALTERNATIVA (UNA); UNIÓN CÍVICA RADICAL DEL PUEBLO (UCRP); UNIÓN CÍVICA RADICAL INTRANSIGENTE (UCRI); UNIÓN DEL CENTRO DEMOCRÁTICO (UCEDE); UNIÓN DEMOCRÁTICA (UD); UNIÓN POPULAR (UP).

POPE FRANCIS (1936–). Elected to the papal throne in 2013, Jorge Mario Bergoglio is arguably set to become the most famous Argentine of the 21st century. Renowned for his piety and modesty—he maintains a simple life-style notwithstanding the office—when elected Bergoglio was regarded as a traditionalist. His views on abortion, marriage, the ordination of **women**, and priestly celibacy remain staunchly conservative, but he is seen as socially progressive—in some areas. He has spoken out against poverty and social injustice and argued that the church should be more open and approachable to communicants and less concerned with pomp and ceremony and that a greater role should be accorded to the laity. As pope, Bergoglio has empha-sized a commitment to ecumenism and interfaith dialogue. He has been particularly supportive of embattled Christians in the Near East, while strengthening ties with Orthodox churches, the Anglican Church, and various Protestant denominations. His outreach to Judaism and Islam is widely rec-ognized, in part based on individual relationships established when he was a priest in **Buenos Aires**.

Named cardinal by Pope John Paul II in 2001, Bergoglio held a number of influential positions in the Argentine church before succeeding to the papacy. He became principal superior of the Jesuit Order in Argentina in 1973, a position he held until 1979. His relations with fellow Jesuits were not always harmonious—there were differences over doctrine and mission and what he saw as the excessive influence of liberation theology among some fellow priests. Appointed an auxiliary bishop of Buenos Aires in 1992; six years later, he became archbishop of Buenos Aires and so head of the church in Argentina. From 2005 until 2011, he chaired the Argentine Bishops Confer-ence. As archbishop, he proved to be a reformer and an efficient administra-tor. He established new parishes, streamedlined the administration, and in-creased the presence of the church in *villas miseria*—he became known as the Bishop of the Slums. In part this was due to a sense of moral outrage at the growth of inequality during the 1990s, in part due to the rising influence of evangelical Protestant sects among the poor. Bergoglio spoke out against fiscal austerity in 2000 and protested against police handling of popular protests in 2001, as the **Convertibility Plan** was collapsing. He often had a less than cordial relationship with Presidents **Néstor Kirchner** and **Cristina Fernández de Kirchner**. Bergoglio's calls for political tolerance and plural-ism, his veiled criticisms of **populism** and stress on democratic institution building, did not go down well with Néstor, who like President **Juan Domin-go Perón** appears to have regarded the church as a political rival, competing for the attention of the masses. Bergoglio's support for the rural sector during **farm protests** around 2008, and continuing emphasis on tolerance and politi-cal dialogue, similarly offended Cristina, whose promotion of same-sex mar-riage some saw as an act of political revenge. Relations between Mrs. Kirch-ner and Pope Francis improved following his election.

The election of Bergoglio marked a number of firsts. Of Italian extraction—his father left Italy in 1929 and his mother was of Italian origin but born in Argentina—he is sometimes described as the first non-European pope. He is certainly the first pope from the Americas. He is also the first pope to succeed while his predecessor was still alive—his predecessor, Pope Benedict XVI (now Pope Emeritus Benedict), had abdicated. Bergoglio is also the first Jesuit to be elected pope. His appointment was not without controversy, mainly due to accusations of ambivalence to the last **military** regime—the **Proceso de Reoganización Nacional**—that came to power with the **military coup of 1976**. Two Jesuit priests were kidnapped and tortured while he was head of the order; Bergoglio was said to have done little to save them, possibly because he disagreed with their endorsement of liberation theology. Bergoglio maintains that he interceded with de facto president General **Jorge Rafael Videla** on behalf of the priests, an intervention that saved them from death at the hands of their torturers but not from torture itself. Around 2000, Bergoglio acknowledged that the local hierarchy could have done more during the reign of terror instituted during the Proceso—the church had "sinned." When head of the Bishops Conference, he issued a statement admitting that the church had been insufficiently diligent in protecting society from the worst excesses of the period. Perhaps these were sins of omission rather than commission. There is no evidence that, unlike some members of the hierarchy, Bergoglio collaborated with regimes of the Proceso. Critics have also pointed to the irony of Pope Francis's emphasis on traditional family values and clerical celibacy and his stance on historic cases of child sexual abuse by priests and princes of the church. *See also* DIRTY WAR; HUMAN RIGHTS; IMMIGRATION; WAR TO ANNIHILATE SUBVERSION.

POPULAR CONSERVATIVE PARTY. *See* PARTIDO CONSERVADOR POPULAR (PCP).

POPULAR RADICAL CIVIC UNION. *See* UNIÓN CÍVICA RADICAL (UCR); UNIÓN CÍVICA RADICAL DEL PUEBLO (UCRP); UNIÓN CÍVICA RADICAL INTRANSIGENTE (UCRI).

POPULISM. The defining feature of Argentine political history since at least the 1940s. Its opponents viewed populism as antidemocratic and economically illiterate and associated it with fiscal indiscipline, inflation and balance-of-payments shocks, and macroeconomic instability leading to crises that destabilized political life. Proponents of populism maintain that it has broadened participation in electoral politics though policies directed at those lacking political voice and an economic stake in society. Conventional definitions present populism as a multiclass movement that eschews ideology and institutionalized politics, headed by a charismatic leader who interprets the will and needs of the masses. Other defining features would be antipluralism and a project that is "neither capitalism nor communism." These aspects are neatly reflected in Argentine manifestations of the phenomenon, notably Peronist governments from the time of the first presidency of **Juan Domingo Perón**. While all subsequent **Partido Justicialista** (PJ) administrations at national and provincial level would honor the memories and achievements of Perón and his second wife, **Eva Perón**, none demonstrated the same style of leadership, though borrowing many of their methods and language.

Following Perón, later manifestations of populism, notably the two presidencies of **Carlos Saúl Menem** and the **Néstor Kirchner** and **Cristina Fernández de Kirchner** presidencies, adopted a "big tent" approach to politics, claiming that there was room within Peronism for all—often seeking to co-opt the opposition or build alliances with representative bodies that might mount a challenge. There was also a tendency to demonize those who were not Peronist as anti-Peronist and antinational.

A critical political failure of Peronist populism was the inability to deal with the problem of leadership renewal and the succession. This was exemplified by Perón himself in office and in exile, as well as in the Menem period and particularly in the second Fernández de Kirchner presidency. Distinct currents were (and are) encouraged within the movement—there were usually several quite distinct factions, with a number of potential future leaders seeming to emerge. This served the party leader well as a divide-and-rule mechanism, and as a means to identify and emasculate serious leadership contenders. Menem famously fell out with his vice president, **Eduardo Duhalde**, when he became a threat to Menem's ambition to be reelected. Mrs. Kirchner notoriously refused to nominate a successor when she herself was unable to seek a third term until very late in the campaign for the **presidential election of 2015**. The favored method seems to have been to keep the succession within the family. In the run-up to the **presidential election of 1951**, Perón contemplated nominating his wife Eva as his presidential running mate, a move that was scotched by the **military**. He was more successful in 1973, when **Isabel Perón** was put on the ticket and succeeded to the presidency on his death in 1974. But most successful of all were the Kirchners, who around 2006 appeared to contemplate husband and wife alternating in office. In the end, while Néstor Kirchner ensured the succession of his wife in the **presidential election of 2007**, his death a few years later ended prospects of this perpetual **tango**, though Mrs. Fernández de Kirchner was able to ensure a second term in office in 2011. The nemesis of Peronist regimes was usually **economic crisis** and **corruption**. *See also*

"PERONISM WITHOUT PERÓN"; PROCESO DE REORGANIZACIÓN NACIONAL; REVOLUCIÓN LIBERTADORA (1955–1958); VANDOR, AUGUSTO TIMOTEO (1923–1969).

POSADAS. Capital city of **Misiones**, which is situated at the south end of the province on the shores of the **Paraná** River. Established as a Jesuit missionary settlement (*reducción*) in the 17th century, across from Encarnación in what is now **Paraguay**, Posadas became the capital of the then national territory of Misiones in 1884. The population of the city is around 340,000. The leading industries of the city are furniture, tobacco, food, textiles, and construction, together with commerce and services. Posadas has been home to the Universidad Nacional de Misiones since 1973 and is also culturally and economically linked to Encarnación; a bridge connects the cities.

PREBISCH, RAÚL (1901–1986). Although best known for his roles in the **United Nations** Organization (UNO) as secretary general of the **Economic Commission for Latin America** (ECLA) and of the Conference on Trade and Development (UNCTAD), he was a key Argentine policy maker in the period 1930–1943.

Prebisch was named director of the newly created Office of Economic Research of the **Banco de la Nación Argentina** in 1927 and then appointed undersecretary of finance by the de facto provisional government that came to power following the **military coup of 1930**. He launched a huge modernization program at the ministry and shouldered responsibility for tackling the crisis triggered by the worldwide depression. When orthodox measures failed to revive the **economy**, he devised alternative strategies. In order to stem the outflow of gold and facilitate payments of Argentine hard **currency** debt, Prebisch convinced the government to introduce exchange controls in October 1931. He also proposed import duties and explored the possibility of setting up a central bank. But his major achievement was the overhaul of taxation policy: emergency legislation was enacted in January 1932 establishing a progressive income tax, which has been renewed annually to this day.

Following the accession of **Agustín P. Justo** to the presidency in February 1932, Prebisch resigned as undersecretary of finance. He retained his post at the Banco Nación, which got the Argentine government to nominate him to work with the League of Nations' Preparatory Commission for the World Economic Conference scheduled for 1933, intended to revive international trade and stabilize the global financial system. From Geneva, he was summoned by the Argentine vice president to join a mission to **Great Britain** and became one of the negotiators of the controversial **Roca–Runciman**

Pact, and then attended the League of Nations London Monetary and Economic Conference, which signally failed to secure agreement on a raft of measures intended to combat the world depression, largely due to opposition from Washington.

Upon his return to Argentina, Prebisch became adviser to both the ministers of finance and **agriculture**. He worked full time on the **Plan de Acción Económica**, which was presented to **Congress** in November 1933. The success of this economic program depended in part on dealing with a major banking crisis. Several private banks in Argentina were on the verge of bankruptcy, and the Banco Nación had insufficient powers to deal with the emergency, which made the creation of a central bank unavoidable. Prebisch prepared the legislation that was introduced to Congress in early 1935 and in May of that year became the general manager of the **Banco Central de la República Argentina** (BCRA) that resulted from the legislation. He controlled the bank for seven years, directing its policy and administration.

The economic advice of Prebisch was sought again in 1940, and he prepared the politically doomed **Pinedo Plan**. Following the **military coup of 1943**, the new de facto regime sacked him as general manager of the BCRA. In later years, the counsel of Prebisch was sought on two occasions, but it turned out to be a waste of his efforts. The first time was at the request of the provisional government that came to power with the **military coup of 1955**; he produced the **Prebisch Plan**, which could not be implemented owing to the furor it generated across the political spectrum. The second time followed the **presidential election of 1983**, when President-Elect **Raúl Alfonsín** sought but then ignored Prebisch's advice. *See also* DEVELOPMENTAL-ISM/DEVELOPMENTALIST.

PREBISCH PLAN. Economic blueprint prepared by **Raúl Prebisch** at the request of provisional president **Eduardo Lonardi** and submitted in its final form to his successor, General **Pedro Eugenio Aramburu**, in January 1956. Although the plan supported a wage increase of 10 percent, it proposed an austerity program and liberal reforms. The principal measures included government staff and budget cuts; the **privatization** of inefficient state enterprises like **Aerolíneas Argentinas**; reductions in public expenditure to curb the fiscal deficit; the removal of price controls; a devaluation and freeing of the exchange rate in order to weed out inefficient firms; taxation reform to increase revenue and prevent evasion; the promotion of rural production and exports, including the establishment of the Instituto Nacional de Tecnología Agropecuaria; immediate investment in basic industries such as the petroleum and steel sectors; attracting foreign capital, except in the oil industry; and joining multilateral international institutions.

The Prebisch Plan caused such furor across the political spectrum that it became largely academic. The government increased wages by 30 percent, intensified price controls, did not privatize Aerolíneas Argentinas, postponed taxation reform, and was unable to reform the state (which consumed 42 percent of gross domestic product). However, Argentina did join the International Monetary Fund (IMF), the World Bank, and the General Agreement on Tariffs and Trade (GATT). *See also* AGRICULTURE; DEVELOPMENTALISM/DEVELOPMENTALIST; ECONOMIC CRISES; ECONOMY; FOREIGN DEBT/FOREIGN INVESTMENT; FOREIGN TRADE; INDUSTRY.

PRESIDENCY/PRESIDENTIALISM. Nominally a federal arrangement and with power theoretically apportioned among the executive, legislative, and judicial branches, the modern Argentine political system is highly centralized and highly presidential. Since the **Constitution of 1994**, presidents serve a four-year term and may stand for immediate reelection, though a president who has served two consecutive terms may not stand again. Previously, following the **Constitution of 1853**, presidents served for six years and were barred from seeking immediate reelection. The president is head of state, head of the government, and head of the armed forces—commander-in-chief. Presidents have to be native-born citizens, or the offspring of native-born citizens if born abroad, and 30 years of age.

If the president is unable to complete a term, the line of succession moves to the vice president, who may perform the duties of president until the expiry of the term. In the absence or incapacity of both president and vice president, the next in line of succession is the interim president of the National Senate—interim president because the vice president chairs the Senate. Thereafter, the succession moves to the president of the Chamber of Deputies and the president of the Supreme Court, though these may not use the title of president. While performing the duties of a president, their main function is to organize new presidential and vice presidential elections.

Constitutional presidents do not have the power to legislate unilaterally, though they are required to participate in the lawmaking process and may rule by decree. They are also empowered to declare a state of siege. Decrees of Necessity and Urgency may be issued by a president in exceptional circumstances. Technically, such decree laws are subject to review by a joint committee of both houses of **Congress**—the National Senate and Chamber of Deputies—within 10 days. Should both houses reject a decree law, it becomes invalid. In practice, such measures can remain in force for some time. President **Carlos Saúl Menem** conducted a considerable amount of government business under the provisions of such decrees.

As head of the nation, the president is responsible for ensuring that the constitution is enforced and for signing and applying legislation passed by Congress, including laws submitted for its consideration by the executive. He or she appoints judges to the Supreme Court and ambassadors, subject to the approval of the Senate; selects ministers and is responsible for the administration of the government; is expected to attend Congress to explain the conduct of the administration; and may grant pardons or commute criminal sentences, subject to judicial review, and bestow grants and pensions.

Partly to address the recognized problem of excessive presidentialism, the 1994 constitution created the office of chief of cabinet (*jefe del gabinete de ministros de la Nación Argentino*), a.k.a. prime minister, a position not to be confused with the post of cabinet secretary. In practice, little was achieved. Centralization is long standing and embedded: the 1853 constitution envisaged a strong executive as critical for the preservation of order and maintenance of national unity—in part a solution to the long tradition of civil wars and rule by **military** strongmen. Centralization and presidentialism derive from the concentration of political power and fiscal resources in the hands of the federal government. Most provinces have only limited capacity to raise revenue and are dependent on transfers from the center. This ensures that provincial governors have considerable power within their respective provinces and on provincial representatives in Congress, while also making them beholden to the president. Only once during the recent political history of the country did the system become more parliamentary rather than presidential, during the political and **economic crises** of 2001–2002, when the task of nominating a replacement for President **Fernando de la Rúa** fell to Congress. *See also* ALFONSÍN, RAÚL RICARDO (1927–2009); CAMAÑO, EDUARDO (1946–); CAUDILLO; CONSTITUTION OF 1949; DUHALDE, EDUARDO ALBERTO (1941–); KIRCHNER, CRISTINA ELISABET FERNÁNDEZ DE (1953–); KIRCHNER, NÉSTOR CARLOS (1950–2010); *KIRCHNERATO*; MACRI, MAURICIO (1959–); *MENEMATO*; NATIONAL ORGANIZATION; OLIVOS PACT; PERÓN, JUAN DOMINGO (1895–1974); *PERONATO*; POPULISM; PUERTA, RAMÓN (1951–); ROCA, JULIO ARGENTINO (1843–1914); RODRÍGUEZ SAÁ, ADOLFO (1947–); ROSAS, JUAN MANUEL DE (1793–1877).

PRESIDENTIAL ELECTION OF 1916. Electoral reform in 1912, sponsored by President **Roque Sáenz Peña** (1910–13), led to the first free and fair presidential and congressional elections in Argentine political history in 1916. The presidential contest, held on 2 April, was won by **Hipólito Yrigoyen** of the **Unión Cívica Radical** (UCR) with 46 percent of the popular vote; the conservative coalition, dominated by the Partido Autonomista Nacional (PAN), headed by Ángel Rojas, was runner-up, gaining 20 percent; the **Partido Demócrata Progresista** (PDP) came in third with 8 percent; the

Partida Socialista (PS) fourth with 7 percent. The principal features of the election, in addition to the size of the UCR victory, was the turnout rate—at 63 percent, it was more than double that of previous elections—and the clear rejection of the PAN, which had governed the country since the 1880s. The 1916 elections also prefigured the Radical ascendancy of 1916–1930. Pro-electoral-reform elements in the PAN had assumed that voter gratitude and a nationalist platform would facilitate a continuation of conservative rule, tame the opposition, and, perhaps, head off revolution—the years immediately prior to the 1912 settlement had witness increasingly violent challenges to the legitimacy of the political and electoral system.

PRESIDENTIAL ELECTION OF 1922. Marcelo Torcuato de Alvear won the elections, held on 2 April, gaining 48 percent of the vote; the runner-up was Norberto Piñero of the conservative Concentración Nacional with 23 percent. Although they would later split, Alvear was strongly supported by outgoing president **Hipólito Yrigoyen**. His triumph confirmed the continuing appeal of the **Unión Cívica Radical** (UCR) and its hold on power, as well as appearing to represent the consolidation of democratic politics.

PRESIDENTIAL ELECTION OF 1928. Having stepped down in 1922— the **Constitution of 1853** did not permit immediate reelection—former president **Hipólito Yrigoyen** of the **Unión Cívica Radical** (UCR) was elected on 1 April with 57 percent of the popular vote; he was opposed by Leopoldo Melo of the *antipersonalista* Radicals, who secured 30 percent. A third successive win for the Radicals, and an ascending share of the vote that had increased from 46 percent in 1916 and 48 percent in 1922, dismayed the democratic opposition and alarmed sections of the elite that had challenged electoral reform in 1912. Indeed, with the two branches of the Radicals achieving around 88 percent of the vote, it appeared that the UCR could not be defeated in fair elections and that the party had secured a monopoly on the presidency and looked to be consolidating its grip on **Congress**.

PRESIDENTIAL ELECTION OF 1931. Held on 8 November, a little more than a year after the overthrow of President **Hipólito Yrigoyen**, they were contested by the **Concordancia** (comprising the conservative **Partido Demócrata Nacional** [PDN], the *antipersonalista* Radicals, and the Independent Socialists) and the Alianza Civil (composed of the **Partido Socialista** [PS] and the Partido Demócrata Progresista [PDP]). The *personalista* **Union Civica Radical** (UCR) boycotted the election, but many of its supporters voted for Concordancia party lists. The level of abstentions was low, and there were no instances of major fraud excepting that which took place in the provinces of **Buenos Aires** and **Mendoza**.

This enabled an easy if somewhat fraudulent victory for the Concordancia. Its presidential ticket headed by General **Agustin P. Justo** obtained 234 electors in the electoral college against the 124 of the Alianza Civil, and it secured a majority in **Congress** and eight provinces. The resulting government met the immediate challenges of the day but would soon lose its moral authority as it increasingly relied on electoral fraud to remain in power. *See also* URIBURU, JOSÉ FÉLIX (1864–1932).

PRESIDENTIAL ELECTION OF 1937. Held on 5 September and won by **Roberto M. Ortiz**, the candidate of the ruling **Concordancia** coalition. The contest was totally fraudulent, not least due to legislation passed in 1936 that changed the electoral law, stacking the odds in favor of the government ticket. Previously, the electoral college, responsible for naming the president, had been composed of delegates determined by the share of the vote obtained by candidates; following the 1936 modification, delegates were allocated to the party topping the poll in each electoral district. This enabled the regime to win in key conservative provinces such as **Buenos Aires** and **Santa Fe**, engineered victories that offset losses in other areas. The Concordancia obtained 240 electors, against the 127 gained by the opposition **Unión Cívica Radical** (UCR). The officially recognized national percentages were respectively 54 and 40. Efforts of outgoing president **Agustin P. Justo** to cover up electoral malfeasance were met by an unsuccessful public outcry.

PRESIDENTIAL ELECTION OF 1946. Held on 24 February, it was the culmination of **Juan Domingo Perón**'s efforts to become president. Having utterly failed to contain Perón in October 1945, the government of General **Edelmiro Farrell** decided to call elections and bring **military** rule to an end. However, it pursued two seemingly contradictory goals: to maintain or create conditions that would favor the victory of its erstwhile colleague Perón, who was no longer on active duty; and to guarantee that the election would be free of the fraud and violence of immediately previous contests. Farrell had pledged the honor of the armed forces to ensuring an honest vote.

The regime was divided over which of the two objectives should be pursued more vigorously. The Secretariat of Labor continued to serve the interests of Perón, providing him with a bureaucratic apparatus throughout the country and substantial funding to make the recently created **Partido Laborista** (PL) viable. Supporters of Perón in the provinces paralleled the secretariat's activities. The Ministry of War was committed to a free election in the belief that Perón could win, while the **Ministry of Interior** worked for equitable ground rules for campaigning that would deliver a level playing field to all parties.

The candidacy of Perón was backed in the main by the PL, the **Unión Cívica Radical Junta Renovadora** (UCRJR), and the Alianza Libertadora Nacional. A single slate was put forward against Perón: the José Tamborini–Enrique Mosca ticket of the **Unión Democrática** (UD), which comprised the Radical, Socialist, Progressive Democrat, and Communist Parties. These parties were again legal, and their representatives were authorized to apply for the return of their property and papers. The Ministry of Interior curtailed post office interference with the circulation of anti-Perón press and the handling of political party mail and issued a decree endorsed by the whole cabinet setting out the rules of behavior for federal civil servants. It had some success in establishing equitable arrangements for radio broadcasting but failed to eliminate the partisan use of public office to support Perón. Moreover, a state of siege was still in effect, and therefore the application of constitutional guarantees of rights of expression and assembly and against arbitrary arrest depended on the government.

On 11 February 1946, the US State Department overtly interfered in the election campaign with the publication of the "Argentine Blue Book." The latter charged numerous members of the administration (mostly Perón) with being Nazi sympathizers during the Second World War and wishing to create a Nazi–Fascist state in Argentina. The "Blue Book" also documented the protection given to Nazi espionage and economic interests, the totalitarian character of the Farrell regime, and the threat it posed to neighboring countries. The "Blue Book" overshadowed the remainder of the campaign and became a factor in the electoral outcome.

The election was one of the cleanest in Argentine history: the military guaranteed fairness by ensuring access to the polls and the free exercise of the right to vote and by securing ballot boxes so they could not be tampered with. Perón won the presidency narrowly. He received 1,487,886 votes, or 52 percent of the 2,839,507 cast, and had a margin of only 280,806 over Tamborini. Nevertheless, he triumphed in the simultaneous congressional and provincial elections, gaining overwhelming control of both chambers of **Congress** and all governorships but one. *See also* CONGRESSIONAL ELECTIONS OF 1946

PRESIDENTIAL ELECTION OF 1951. Held on 24 November under the terms of the **Constitution of 1949** and the electoral law of 1951; **Juan Domingo Perón** was reelected with over 60 percent of the vote. Elections were held simultaneously for the whole Chamber of Deputies, as the mandate of its members had been extended from four to six years by the new legal framework. The elections for deputies were also won overwhelmingly by the Peronists, not least owing to a clever redistricting system.

The significance of these elections was that they were held in an increasingly totalitarian climate. The opposition was hard hit as deputies from **Unión Cívica Radical** (UCR) were being imprisoned or forced into exile, 70 **media** outlets were shut down, official media banned the presence of non-Peronist politicians, and the vociferous newspaper *La Prensa* was closed and confiscated. Moreover, three major reforms to the statute of **political parties** had been enacted in 1949. First, political parties were recognized if they had been in existence for the preceding three years. Secondly, an alliance of parties was deemed to be a new party and therefore deemed to be ineligible, thereby safeguarding Peronism against any possible agreement between its opponents. Thirdly, any party advocating abstention in elections would lose its legal status. In these circumstances, the elections of 1951 can only be seen as a crude attempt to give Peronism, and its inevitable electoral victory, a veneer of legitimacy. *See also* CONGRESSIONAL ELECTIONS OF 1951

PRESIDENTIAL ELECTION OF 1958. Held on 23 February, it was a contest between 19 parties governed once again by the 1912 electoral law and a new statute of **political parties** that replaced the one enacted in 1949. The election was won by the **Unión Civica Radical Intransigente** (UCRI) ticket headed by **Arturo Frondizi** and Alejandro Gómez.

There were two highly significant features in this election. First, two of the major parties of the past had suffered major splits during the **Revolución Libertadora** period, and second, there was the response of Peronism to its proscription. The **Unión Cívica Radical** (UCR) had fractured into the **Unión Cívica Radical del Pueblo** (UCRP) and the UCRI. The conservative **Partido Demócrata Nacional** (PDN) had also splintered, with one of its best known successor parties being the **Partido Conservador Popular** (PCP). In the meantime, a number of neo-Peronist groupings had been established to circumvent the proscription of Peronism, of which the **Unión Popular** (UP) was the most notable. Perón, who was pulling strings even in exile, forced them not to participate in the ballot. Instead, he ordered his supporters to back Frondizi under a deal reached with the latter; this was the infamous **Caracas Pact**.

The Frondizi–Gómez ticket garnered 4,090,840 votes, and in simultaneous congressional elections the UCRI obtained 3,761,250; this represented over 40 percent of ballots cast. Blank votes, totaling 836,658, represented 9 percent, which meant Peronist supporters had followed their leader's instruction. The new ruling party had an ample majority in both Chambers of **Congress**, and in simultaneously held provincial elections had taken virtually all the governorships. *See also* CONGRESSIONAL ELECTIONS OF 1958.

PRESIDENTIAL ELECTION OF 1963. Held on 7 July, it was won by **Arturo Illia** of the **Unión Cívica Radical del Pueblo** (UCRP). The election had two significant features. Peronism was once again proscribed despite its attempt to stand in a cleverly devised coalition, and a complex proportional representation system introduced by the government of **José María Guido** was applied.

With the blessing of an interfering and exiled **Juan Domingo Perón**, the Frente Nacional y Popular was formed by the neo-Peronist **Union Popular** (UP), the **Movimiento de Integración y Desarrollo** (MID), and the **Partido Conservador Popular** (PCP). In an attempt to make the coalition acceptable to the authorities, **Vicente Solano Lima** of the PCP and Carlos Sylvestre Begnis of the MID were announced as the candidates on its ticket. But the **military** would have none of it, and the front was proscribed.

Of great importance to the outcome of the election were the fragmentation of politics and the use of a complex proportional system, which enabled 49 parties to compete nationally. The UCRP garnered 2,500,000 votes or barely 26 percent of the total. Blank votes totaled 1,700,000 and came in second, reflecting the destroyed Frente Nacional y Popular. **Oscar Alende**, the official UCRI candidate, gained 1,600,000 votes. Despite having obtained only 168 out of the necessary 270 electors, Illia was propelled to the presidency with the support of minor parties in the absence of any coherent opposition force. *See also* CONGRESSIONAL ELECTIONS OF 1963.

PRESIDENTIAL ELECTION OF MARCH 1973. Held on 11 March, it was the first since the **military coup of 1955** that the Peronists were allowed to contest freely, though **Juan Domingo Perón** himself was proscribed. It was also the first direct presidential election, regulated by **Law No. 19.862**. This legislation, passed by the outgoing **military** government in October 1972, stipulated a two-round election in the misplaced hope that the Peronist-dominated **Frente Justicialista de Liberación** (FREJULI) would lose in the runoff.

In fact, the *ballotage* became unnecessary, not least because too many small parties (such as **Nueva Fuerza**) contested the election. The FREJULI ticket, fronted by **Héctor Cámpora** and **Vicente Solano Lima**, obtained 5,907,464 ballots or virtually 50 percent of the vote. Its nearest rival, the **Ricardo Balbín**–Eduardo Gamond ticket of the **Unión Cívica Radical** (UCR), got 2,537,605 votes or 21 percent of the total. A third-party ticket headed by **Francisco Manrique** and Rafael Martínez Raymonda of the Alianza Popular Federalista garnered 15 percent with 1,775,867 votes.

Nevertheless, there would be a second electoral contest, though not in the form originally intended by the military. Perón returned from exile to take charge of affairs himself, forcing Cámpora and Solano Lima to resign only

49 days after they had been sworn in. This triggered the **presidential election of September 1973**. *See also* CONGRESSIONAL ELECTIONS OF 1973.

PRESIDENTIAL ELECTION OF SEPTEMBER 1973. Held on 23 September, it enabled **Juan Domingo Perón** to assume the presidency for a third term. This was the second election to be held in 1973, following the resignations of President **Héctor Cámpora** and Vice President **Vicente Solano Lima** on 13 July of that year—they had been elected in March.

The possibility of a joint ticket between the **Frente Justicialista de Liberacion** (FREJULI) and the **Unión Cívica Radical** (UCR) headed by Perón with **Ricardo Balbín** as running mate was mooted but proved unfeasible. The internal politics of both Peronism and Radicalism undermined the prospect; moreover, Perón had to paper over the cracks in his movement. On 26 July, the **federal capital** branch of the **Partido Justicialista** (PJ) proposed a ticket fronted by Perón with his wife, **Isabel Perón**, as running mate. Given the issue of his age and health, Perón was initially adamant that she could not be the vice presidential candidate. He was aware that he might not complete his mandate and did not want her exposed to the consequences. Nevertheless, Isabel decided to impose her candidacy on him, and on 4 August the national party congress backed the Perón–Perón ticket.

Both the FREJULI and the UCR campaigned on the promise to find "national liberation," but there was never any question that Perón would win. The FREJULI obtained 7,359,252 votes or 60 percent of the total, which exceeded Cámpora's tally in the **presidential election of March 1973** by just over 10 percent. Its nearest rival, the UCR ticket fronted by Balbín and **Fernando de la Rúa**, garnered 2,905,719 votes or 24 percent.

Two days after the election, **José Ignacio Rucci**, the head of the **Confederación General del Trabajo** (CGT), was assassinated by the **Montoneros**. This was a clear warning to Perón that the election result did not change their aim of establishing the *patria socialista* through violence. It was at this point that Perón determined to break with the subversive groups, initiating a campaign against the left that was pursued with vigor by the associates of his wife when she succeeded to the presidency.

PRESIDENTIAL ELECTION OF 1983. Held on 30 October, when the **military** regime of the **Proceso de Reorganización Nacional** scuttled back to the barracks, simultaneously with elections for all seats in both houses of **Congress**, as well as for provincial and municipal branches of government. Leading the **Unión Cívica Radical** (UCR), **Raúl Alfonsín** campaigned on a platform of democratic renewal and the reconstruction of civil society, and holding the military to account while recognizing that the military had to be reintegrated into society and subject to civilian control. Some other political leaders took a less robust position and were prepared to negotiate with the heads of the outgoing regime, to facilitate a "dignified" exit from office by the armed forces. Indeed, Alfonsín's principled stand contrasted with that of Peroinsts known to be negotiating with the military, and who were held by many to have provoked the chaos that had contributed to the **military coup of 1976**. Alfonsín topped the presidential poll with 52 percent of the vote, and runner-up **Ítalo Luder** of the **Partido Justicialista** (PJ) obtained 41 percent. The voter turnout rate of over 85 percent further confirmed the scale of the Radical victory, as well as commitment to democratic politics.

These were the elections that the UCR did not expect to win; the party was as surprised by the victory as their political opponents. On taking office, Alfonsín was confronted with an expectant electorate, a recalcitrant and uncooperative opposition, and a discredited yet disgruntled military, still smarting from defeat in the **Falklands War**. In addition to coping with unrealistic voter expectations of what could be feasibly delivered by the incoming administration, the government also had to cope with the economic mess left by the military, including massive international debt—there would be little in the way of a democratic dividend from the international financial community. Nevertheless, Alfonsín's victory was a watershed in Argentine political history: it was the first time that the PJ had been defeated in free, fully democratic elections. *See also* CONGRESSIONAL ELECTIONS OF 1985.

PRESIDENTIAL ELECTION OF 1989. Held on 14 May, the 1989 elections took place at a moment of profound economic chaos marked by **hyperinflation** triggered by the failure of the **Austral Plan** and international debt crisis. Hoping to succeed Alfonsín, **Eduardo Angeloz**, a distinguished national senator from **Córdoba**, represented the **Unión Cívica Radical** (UCR). His principal opponent was **Carlos Saúl Menem** of the **Partido Justicialista** (PJ), sometime governor of **La Rioja**. An outsider in Peronist politics, Menem had defeated **Antonio Cafiero** in party primaries to head the PJ ticket. His running mate was **Eduardo Duhalde**. Unsurprisingly, given political turmoil and economic meltdown in the run-up to the elections, the Menem–Duhalde formula triumphed, obtaining 47.5 percent of the popular vote, 15 points above the 32 percent taken by the UCR. Voter turnout was again high at 85 percent. Menem campaigned on a fairly conventional Peronist platform, promising massive wage hikes, support for national business, and a "productive revolution," designed to attract traditional supporters. In the event, as the crisis deepened, he jettisoned this economic program and opted for a neoliberal strategy, the **Convertibility Plan** devised by Economics Minister **Domingo Cavallo**. Indeed, so acute was the crisis that Menem was sworn in early. Menem should have taken office on 10 December but was inaugurated on 8 July 1989.

Despite the turmoil surrounding Menem's accession to office, the handover in 1989 marked the first peaceful transfer of power from a democratically elected civilian head of state representing one political party to a candidate of another political party who had secured a mandate in free, unrestricted elections. In addition, the transfer of power in 1989 was remarkable because there was no **military** coup: on previous moments of near political or economic collapse, the armed forces had invariably intervened. *See also* CONGRESSIONAL ELECTIONS OF 1989; ECONOMIC CRISES.

PRESIDENTIAL ELECTION OF 1995. Although the **Constitution of 1853** proscribed immediate reelection, **Carlos Saúl Menem** secured the agreement of former president **Raúl Alfonsín** to stage a constituent convention to draw up a new constitution—the so-call **Olivos Pact.** Among other changes, the new **Constitution of 1994** permitted immediate reelection, while reducing the presidential term from six to four years.

With a new running mate, **Carlos Ruckauf,** in the 14 May election, the Menem–Ruckauf ticket took almost 50 percent of the vote; the runners-up were the **Frente País Solidario** (FREPASO), a new grouping headed by former Peronist **Octavio Bordón** and **Carlos "Chacho" Álvarez,** with 28 percent; the **Unión Cívica Radical** (UCR) ticket obtained 17 percent.

Menem campaigned on a platform of continuity, claiming that only he could guarantee the success of the **Convertibility Plan,** which was beginning to deliver recovery and growth plus stability and hope, despite some painful economic medicine associated with shrinking the state sector. The neoliberal model, which had served the PJ well in the 1991 and 1993 midterm congressional elections, resonated with voters, who continued to endorse the economic program, as well as the internationalist position pursued by the government—prosperity at home and peace abroad. *See also* CONGRESSIONAL ELECTIONS OF 1995.

PRESIDENTIAL ELECTION OF 1999. The election was won by the **Alianza,** an electoral coalition painfully put together by the **Unión Cívica Radical** (UCR) and **Frente País Solidario** (FREPASO), with **Fernando de la Rúa** representing the UCR and **Carlos "Chacho" Álvarez** the FREPASO.

With the election held on 24 October, the De la Rúa–Álvarez team gained 48 percent of the vote; heading the **Partido Justicialista** (PJ) list, **Eduardo Duhalde** obtained 38 percent; in third place was the **Acción por la República** (AR), represented by **Domingo Cavallo.** Menem refused to endorse his former running-mate Duhalde, with whom he had split several years earlier; Cavallo, Menem's former minister of economy who had resigned in protest against the **corruption** of the regime, claimed to represent the continuity. The Alianza victory can be attributed to a pledge to retain the fundamentals of the **Convertibility Plan** while promising targeted social expenditure and an end to corruption.

By 1999, voters had become alienated by the excesses of the Menem government; corruption and impunity had become particularly pronounced during the second administration. Corruption had been tolerated by voters when the main concern was economic stability; once that objective appeared to be achieved, the electorate demanded economic stability and political transparency—"clean politics and clean economics." Efforts by Menem to engineer a third term also contributed to the rejection of the PJ. Menem claimed that he was entitled to stand for immediate reelection under the **Constitution of 1994** as his first period in office under the **Constitution of 1853** did not constitute a barrier to standing for a second (or third) term. *See also* CONGRESSIONAL ELECTIONS OF 1999.

PRESIDENTIAL ELECTION OF 2003. It was held on 27 April, in the aftermath of the 2001–2002 economic crisis that threatened social upheaval and institutional collapse: between the resignation of **Fernando de la Rúa** in December 2001 and the nomination of **Eduardo Duhalde** as president by **Congress** in January 2002, the presidency had changed hands five times.

Duhalde, who was chosen as interim president to serve out the remainder of the De la Rúa's term, had ambitions to seek election in his own right. This was scotched by sections of the **Partido Justicialista** (PJ) representing the interior, despite the fact that the PJ was unable to decide on a single nominee. As a result, the electorate was presented with a choice of PJ candidates, **Carlos Saúl Menem** and **Néstor Kirchner**, who was endorsed by Duhalde, in addition to several other hopefuls. In the first round, Menem came in at the top of the poll with 24 percent, closely followed by Kirchner with 22 percent. In third place, **Ricardo López Murphy**, who had briefly served as De la Rúa's economics minister, obtained 16 percent; Peronist **Adolfo Rodríguez Saá**, who held the presidency for a few days in December 2001, took 14 percent; **Elisa Carrió** of **Afirmación para una República Igualitaria** (ARI) also garnered 14 percent.

As neither of the top two candidates obtained 45 percent of the vote, or 40 percent with a margin of 10 percent over the second most voted candidate, the election was scheduled to go to a second round. However, four days before the runoff was due to take place on 18 May, Menem withdrew his candidature; Kirchner became president by default. Critics attributed the sudden withdrawal of Menem to the assumption that the mass of voters who had favored third parties in the first round would switch to Kirchner in the second. By standing down, Menem could claim that he had never lost an election and hoped to weaken Kirchner's mandate, thus generating instability that might yet result in a return to the presidency. **Daniel Scioli** was Kirchner's vice president. *See also* CONGRESSIONAL ELECTIONS OF 2003; CONVERTIBILITY PLAN; ECONOMIC CRISES.

PRESIDENTIAL ELECTION OF 2007. Until a few months before the election, it was widely assumed that **Néstor Kirchner** would stand for a second term, capitalizing on a successful first term that had witnessed economic recovery, an imaginative social program that had generated employment and reduced poverty, and a scheme of alliance building that had delivered considerable cross-party and cross-sector support as well as a concentration of power in the hands of the president. Confounding pundits, Kirchner passed the baton to his wife, **Cristina Fernández de Kirchner**, who stood for the **Frente para la Victoria** faction of the **Partido Justicialista** (PJ), created as their electoral vehicle.

Held on 28 October, with **Julio Cobos** as vice president, Fernández de Kirchner obtained 45 percent of the vote; **Elisa Carrió**, now representing the **Coalición Cívica** (CC), gained 23 percent; **Roberto Lavagna**, minister of economy under Duhalde and Kirchner, got 17 percent; dissident Peronist **Adolfo Rodríguez Saá** garnered almost 8 percent. Having secured 45 percent of the poll, with more than 10 percentage points separating the top two candidates, Cristina Fernández de Kirchner was elected in the first round. Cynics attributed Kirchner's decision not to stand to a long-term electoral ruse to capture the presidency for himself and his wife indefinitely. Had he stood and won a second consecutive term in 2007, Kirchner would have been barred from seeking a third term. With the husband deferring to the wife, the Kirchners could alternate "forever." Not entirely fanciful, this scenario was not realized: Kirchner died in 2010. *See also* CONGRESSIONAL ELECTIONS OF 2007.

PRESIDENTIAL ELECTION OF 2011. Presenting herself for reelection with **Amado Boudou** as vice president, **Cristina Fernández de Kirchner** triumphed in the 23 October elections, gaining 54 percent of the vote—the highest proportion in recent Argentine electoral history. The Fernández de Kirchner–Boudou ticket also won with a massive margin over runner-up Hermes Binner, a Socialist and former governor of the province of **Santa Fe** heading the progressive grouping **Frente Amplio Progresista** (FAP), who obtained 17 percent. **Ricardo Alfonsín**, son of former president **Raúl Alfonsín**, came in third heading the **Unión para el Desarrollo Social** (UDESO) coalition, in which the **Unión Cívica Radical** (UCR) predominated.

Mrs. Kirchner campaigned on a record of innovative social policy, which was beginning to reduce inequality—this was an important electoral issue—economic growth, and an increasingly combative international program—

there were disputes with **Brazil** and the **United States**, as well as saber rattling over the **Falkland Islands** and criticism of foreign investment funds and multinational business. Fernández de Kirchner also drew heavily on Peronist mythology, portraying herself as a second **Eva Perón**. She may also have benefited from a sympathy vote following the death of her husband. *See also* CONGRESSIONAL ELECTIONS OF 2011; ECONOMIC CRISES; FOREIGN DEBT/FOREIGN INVESTMENT.

PRESIDENTIAL ELECTION OF 2015. The first round was held on 25 October, delivering a shock for **Cristina Fernández de Kirchner**. Her preferred candidate failed to secure a substantial margin over opponents in the first round and lost in the second. The elections are important because they marked the end of the Kirchner project and challenged the electoral hegemony of the **Partido Justicialista** (PJ). They are also significant because the elections went to a second round—the first time that a runoff occurred since the adoption of the **Constitution of 1994**. The importance attached to the elections by the public was marked by the high turnout—around 81 percent in October and November.

Daniel Scioli, who had stepped down as governor of the province of **Buenos Aires** to stand as the **Frente para la Victoria**/Partido Justicialista (FpV/PJ) presidential candidate, was expected to face **Sergio Massa** of the **Frente Renovador/Partido Justicialista** (FR/PJ) in the second round. Unexpectedly, Scioli obtained 37 percent of the vote and **Mauricio Macri** of the **Cambiemos** coalition 34 percent; Massa came in third with 21 percent. The narrow 2.5 percentage point difference between Scioli and Macri resulted in the second round on 22 November. Macri captured 51 percent of the vote in the runoff, with under 49 percent going to Scioli. The result was considerably narrower than suggested by polls conducted several days before the vote that gave Macri a nine-point lead, yet the result was enough to mark a moment of change. In the October congressional elections, Cambiemos had taken control of the province and city of **Buenos Aires**, so Macri could count on the allegiance of these two key electoral districts. In the runoff, he carried important provinces such as **Córdoba**, **Entre Ríos**, **Mendoza**, and **Santa Fe**, along with others.

To varying degrees, the main presidential hopefuls had charged the outgoing regime with authoritarianism and **corruption**. Campaign slogans epitomized this consensus: "Continuity and Change" for the FpV/PJ, "We Can Change" for Cambiemos, and "Fair Change" and "We Are Change" for the FR/PJ. The outcome of the first round showed that "change" had triumphed over "continuity." By the second round, Mrs. Kirchner's lukewarm endorsement of Scioli had damaged his campaign, making it difficult for him to establish a distinct and credible position. In addition, the government failed to convince voters about the sustainability of the Kirchner project, or to scare them when disparaging Macri's proposals as unbridled neoliberalism, likely to result in social and economic collapse and foreign exploitation. Macri had a good campaign, which was well organized, enhancing his stature. He had momentum and captured the mood for change, particularly among young and new voters, anti-Kirchner factions of the PJ, and others who had never benefited from the Kirchner model. *See also* CONGRESSIONAL ELECTIONS OF 2015.

PRESIDENTIAL SUCCESSION OF 1962. José María Guido of the **Unión Cívica Radical Intransigente** (UCRI), who had been elected national senator for the province of **Río Negro** in 1958, was elected provisional president of the Senate on the resignation of Vice President Alejandro Gómez, who had been forced out of office on expulsion from the UCRI. When the armed forces ousted President **Arturo Frondizi** in the **military coup of 1962**, factions within them squabbled over which general should assume the presidency. In the interval, the Supreme Court acted and declared Guido head of state. As acting president of the National Senate, he was constitutionally the next in line to succeed to the presidency. The succession was opposed by some **military** groups, but the decision of the judges held. Guido became president under the watchful eye of the armed forces.

PRIMARIAS, ABIERTAS, SIMULTÁNEAS Y OBLIGATORIAS (PASO). *See* PRIMARY ELECTIONS.

PRIMARY ELECTIONS. First discussed by **Congress** earlier in the year as part of legislation governing **political parties**, the system of open, compulsory primary elections (in Spanish, Primarias Abiertas Simultáneas y Obligatorias—PASO) were instituted by Law 26.571 passed on 2 December 2009, and first applied in the **congressional** and **presidential elections of 2011**. The law requires that all political parties hold primaries and that all the party primaries should be held on the same day. As with elections, voting is compulsory, hence the Spanish acronym—primaries are simultaneous and compulsory—and open to all citizens, who may vote for any candidate of any party—though they can only vote once, not in multiple party primaries. Parties need to obtain at least 1.5 percent of total votes cast to be allowed to contest upcoming elections. Called several months in advance of the main elections, primaries have become a good predictor of the likely outcome of national and provincial elections. Although the law states that primaries should take place on the same day across the country, in recent years there has been a tendency for provinces to hold primaries at slightly different times—in this sense, they are no longer "simultaneous."

PRIVATIZATION. The flagship economic program of the late 20th century, privatization was central to the stabilization project associated with President **Carlos Saúl Menem** and Economy Minister **Domingo Cavallo** known as the **Convertibility Plan**. Neoliberal macroeconomic stabilization would deliver growth and structural change: markets would be deregulated, the **economy** opened, the external and fiscal accounts balanced, inflation conquered, and exchange rate volatility consigned to the dustbin of history. Privatization touched many of these objectives. Disposing of loss-making **state-owned enterprises** (SOEs) would ease current and future pressure on the budget and generate cash for the Treasury. Assets sold overseas signaled inward investment and renewed engagement with international capital markets. Well-run private firms would generate income and investment flows and, particularly in the case of the transport, communications, and financial sectors, would promote efficiency and competitiveness by reducing transaction costs (the price of doing business). This was the theory peddled by its proponents, endorsed by many politicians and policy makers, and accepted by aggrieved consumers. Large sections of popular opinion held that international conglomerates would deliver better-quality, low-cost services than state companies. With access to international finance, new technology, and highly trained professional management, large corporations were vaunted as vehicles for the modernization of creaky government-run infrastructure monopolies that had failed consumers and users.

Privatization as a means of promoting stability and growth had been considered during the presidency of **Arturo Frondizi** but was not seriously and systematically addressed until **José Alfredo Martínez de Hoz** was appointed minister of economy at the outset of the **Proceso de Reorganización Nacional**. Despite arguing a strong, cogent case, Martínez de Hoz lacked sufficient political clout to implement the strategy, which was thwarted by an alliance of nationalist generals, managers of SOEs, key state firm suppliers and consumers, and labor leaders. General Diego Urricarriet, chief of **Fabricaciones Militares**, a huge, multisector, **military**-owned industrial and services complex, was particularly vociferous. Martínez de Hoz succeeded in closing or selling no more than 120 firms between 1976 and 1981, largely bankrupt service-sector businesses that had been acquired by official banks. Indeed, during his tenure, the size of the state industrial sector grew. With the return of democracy in 1983, modernization and deficit reduction were advanced as the principal reasons for privatization by President **Raúl Alfonsín**, with the latter pragmatic emphasis on budget savings taking precedence over strategic or ideological considerations. Public sentiment, congressional opposition, legal challenges, and perhaps insufficient commitment to the policy frustrated key, symbolic sales—notably, of **Aerolíneas Argentinas**, the country flag carrier, and **ENTel**, the state telephone monopoly. The Peronist bloc in Congress stymied government attempts to partially privatize both firms in 1988, despite the fact that 51 percent of voting shares would be retained by the government, with 9 percent being distributed among the workforce and only 40 percent allocated to the private partner–manager. Of the 305 state-owned firms inherited by Alfonsín, only four companies were privatized, including a white goods manufacturer and a regional airline, raising US$32 million for the government. All were relatively small businesses, acquired by the state through bankruptcy; they were not substantial or strategic enterprises long in government hands.

The crown jewels of the state were sold or franchised in the Menem presidencies. A rapid, far-reaching program of privatization was essayed between 1990 and 1994; 117 SOEs were disposed of. By the end of Menem's first term in 1995, few major businesses remained in government ownership. While direct negotiations with partner-operators or purchasers had been favored under Alfonsín, public auctions were the norm under Menem, involving the outright sale of shares and assets, or the tendering of fixed-term operating contracts. Early large privatizations were offered to consortia composed of transnational corporations, minority domestic stakeholders, and banks and were paid for by a mix of cash, equity, and government bonds— mainly **foreign debt** accepted at nominal value. As debt-equity swaps undervalued assets, later sales were effected by cash and bonds at contemporary market value. Most electricity generating and supply firms were sold, along with the natural gas company, petrochemical firms, steelworks and shipyards, and radio and television channels; railways, toll roads, and ports were leased, complemented by build-and-operate schemes, as was as was water supply and sanitation. In power, Peronist majorities in **Congress** now approved the disposal of Aerolíneas Argentinas and ENTel, and the iconic state oil fields, **Yacimientos Petrolíferos Fiscales** (YPF). Subsequently, following the disposal of industrial businesses, transport and communications firms, and utilities, several official banks were privatized along with pension funds. Given the speed and nature of the process, and the opacity of many deals, estimates of the total value of privatization vary enormously. By the end of 1994, privatization had earned the Treasury at least US$27,000 million, of which about US$15,000 million was composed of bonds retired at face value, though the net worth of assets transferred from the public to the private sector must have been considerably larger.

Initially, privatization was popular. Polls conducted when Menem assumed office showed that only 16 percent of those surveyed actively opposed the sale of SOEs in principle. By late 1993, the approval rating had risen to around 66 percent. There was less agreement about the actual conduct of the process; depending on sector and public awareness of sale details, by late 1993 only 47 percent approved of the manner in which television and radio stations had been privatized, with only 20 percent support for the manner in which Aerolineas Argentinas had been sold. Mounting antagonism to the way privatization had been carried out, coupled with outcomes that were less than promised, led approval rates to drop sharply. The collapse of the Convertibility Plan and **economic crises** further undermined public support for privatization, paving the way for the policy reversal by the Kirchners. Renationalization was a pronounced feature of the second administration of President **Cristina Fernández de Kirchner**. Confronted by a very different environment, manifested in antagonistic rhetoric and problematic contract revision or renewal (for example, adjusting charges), some corporations quietly sought local buyers; others pursued a vociferous, antagonistic, and legalistic course in national tribunals, at the same time threatening recourse to international courts, while yet others simply abandoned the country. YPF (at that point a subsidiary of Spanish-owned Repsol) was seized by the government in 2012, joining public utilities and private pension funds that had been previously restatized. The main beneficiaries of this process were national firms close to the regime and suppliers and contractors dependent on businesses operated directly by the government. The closeness of many firms to the Kirchners triggered the charge of favoritism and **corruption**—the epitome of crony capitalism. The election of business-friendly **Mauricio Macri** to the presidency in November 2015 is unlikely to lead to reprivatization in the short-term, notwithstanding promises of greater transparency and an improvement in relations with international business and finance. It is ironic that many of the utilities privatized or franchised to overseas consortia by Menem had been foreign-owned utilities nationalized during the first administration of **Juan Domingo Perón** and that the Kirchners gained popularity by reversing a strategy that had once secured reelection victories for Menem—three different regimes, all Peronist. *See also* INDUSTRY.

PROCESO DE REORGANIZACIÓN NACIONAL. The project of the **military** regime of 1976–1983, whose radical nature originated in the self-belief of the armed forces that they were more capable of formulating a new economic project and "reforming" society to deliver political stability than civilian politicians, whom they accused of mismanagement. Less susceptible to the pressure of interest groups—special pleading that had led to the abandonment of previous stabilization projects—the military argued that only they were able to resolve the evils besetting the country once and for all.

A precedent for the transformative project of the Proceso had been set by the **Revolución Argentina** (1966–1973), which had stressed a three-phase program dealing first with the **economy**, then with social issues, and finally with political institution stabilization. The program proved unworkable and ultimately failed, but the armed forces learned from the mistakes of 1966 and were better prepared in terms of economic strategy in 1976. After the collapse of the 1966 military government, the crisis of constitutional government, the inefficiency of politicians, the challenge of terrorism, and people's fears enabled the armed forces to accumulate enormous power. As a result, the military was convinced that it could do practically anything it wanted without having to await for the necessary consensus.

The Proceso imposed top-down solutions by force, and not only regarding subversion. It aimed to free the country from its "scourges" by "disciplining an anarchized society" and founding a "new economic model" that would allow Argentina to reach its manifest destiny. The specific objectives were to move beyond the "demagogic **populism**" of **Peronism**, which was unbeatable at the ballot box; to discipline labor organizations, which were perceived as an "exacerbated and irrational" power factor; to move toward a liberal, market economy, epitomized and implemented by Minister of Economy **José Alfredo Martínez de Hoz**; and to destroy the virus of the left, even in culture.

Other than the intensity of violence, the principal difference between 1966 and 1976 was that the economic project of the former was structuralist and the latter neoliberal. The successful implementation of the Proceso program required simultaneous popular acquiescence to its elements and objectives, and this ultimately contributed to its undoing. The war against subversion would be the backdrop to adjustments in the economy, so the latter could not be too harsh and alienate people whose backing was crucial to both. Yet within a few years the regime had become unpopular, largely because of dislocation caused by economic reforms and the issue of **human rights**.

Matters were aggravated when the dictatorship got to the brink of war with **Chile** over the **Beagle Channel Dispute** in 1978. Having avoided one war with a neighboring country, the regime then embarked on the disastrous **Falklands War** in 1982. This led to the undignified downfall of the regime, which then claimed that it had always intended to call elections in 1983 even though the Proceso had never had a time limit. With the return of democracy, the military would be put in their place and decimated. *See also* AGOSTI, ORLANDO RAMÓN (1924–1997); ANAYA, JORGE ISAAC (1926–2008); BIGNONE, REYNALDO BENITO (1928–2018); DESAPARECIDOS; DIRTY WAR; DISPOSICIÓN FINAL; GALTIERI, LEOPOLDO FORTUNATO (1926–2003); GRAFFIGNA, OMAR DOMINGO RUBENS (1926–); LAMBRUSCHINI, ARMANDO (1924–2004); LAMI DOZO, BASILIO ARTURO IGNACIO (1929–2017); MASSERA, EMILIO EDUARDO (1925–2010); VIDELA, JORGE RAFAEL (1925–2013); VIOLA, ROBERTO EDUARDO (1924–1994); WAR TO ANNIHILATE SUBVERSION.

PROGRAMA DE ATENCIÓN MÉDICA INTEGRADA (PAMI). Established as a dependency of the Health Ministry by Law 19.032 of 13 May 1971, signed by President **Alejandro Agustín Lanusse**, with the official designation of Instituto Nacional de Servicios Sociales para Jubilados y Pensionados (INSSJP). The 1971 law was designed to integrate medical and social services targeting senior citizens (a group subsequently designated as the "third age") and the indigent, under the aegis of the institute. Following the **Falklands War**, the agency assumed responsibility for the provision of veteran care. Law 23.660 of 5 January 1989 was issued by President **Raúl Alfonsín** and provided for a 6 percent payroll tax and made affiliation to PAMI compulsory for all employees. By 2009, the scope of services had expanded to include housing benefits, cultural and recreational facilities, and other services designed to improve the quality of life of older citizens, as recognized by the mission statement issued that year: "Por una Argentina con Mayores Integrados." Originally operating only in the **federal capital**, the agency now operates countrywide; it has around 650 branches, located in virtually all major urban centers, serving well over 4.6 million affiliates, covering hospital and medical costs, including doctor visits. It is the largest health- and social-care institution in Latin America, and one of the largest such social security agencies in the country.

Recent decades have seen the agency bedeviled by deficits, fraud, and mismanagement and subject to several **corruption** investigations. It was intervened during the early years of the Alfonsín presidency, when efforts were made to reorganize finances. Members of the board appointed by President **Carlos Saúl Menem** were charged with corruption over the allocation of contracts between 1992 and 1994. The agency was also beset by corruption scandals during the presidency of **Fernando de la Rúa**. Income declined sharply in the 1995 economic downturn and the 2002 crisis. There were cost overruns, and those affiliates who were able to do so often sought alternative forms of social protection. Chronic deficits—partly attributed to waste and corruption—became endemic until funding was stabilized and increased during the Kirchner presidencies, at least until around 2010. Further corruption investigations were instigated by the incoming **Mauricio Macri** administration in 2016: officials were said to have made payments to fictitious suppliers and bogus affiliates, diverting enough resources each year to fund a new hospital. *See also* FERNÁNDEZ MEIJIDE, GRACIELA (1931–); MINISTRY OF HEALTH.

PROGRESSIVE DEMOCRAT PARTY. *See* PARTIDO DEMÓCRATA PROGRESISTA (PDP).

PROPUESTA REPUBLICANA (PRO). A center-right or right-of-center organization, depending on opinion, the PRO began as an electoral alliance in 2005 and was formally registered as a **political party** in 2010. The 2005 electoral alliance was cobbled together by **Mauricio Macri** and **Ricardo López Murphy** to contest the midterm **congressional elections of 2005**, bringing together Macri's **Compromiso para el Cambio** and López Murphy's **Recrear para el Crecimiento** (Recrear). In addition to a shared center-right ideology, the logic of the alliance derived from the fact that Compromiso was strong in the city of **Buenos Aires** while Recrear boasted a national presence. While the performance of the PRO was modest in 2005, two years later in the gubernatorial and **congressional** and **presidential elections of 2007** it did much better, especially in the gubernatorial election in Buenos Aries, held some months before the congressional and presidential contests. Macri won the mayoralty of the city of Buenos Aires decisively. Nationally, the alliance's performance was less strong, leading López Murphy to complain that he had been let down. Within two years, a year before the formal registration of the PRO as a political party, the rump of Recrear agreed to merger—for dissidents, it was a "takeover." Since then, the PRO has become the national vehicle of Macri, participating in the **Cambiemos** alliance that delivered to him the presidency in 2015. The emergence of the PRO and its metamorphosis from a fractured (possibly fractious) alliance into a political party reflects both the fluid nature of political structures and allegiances in Argentina as well as the quest to establish a center-right/right-of-center political organization capable of holding together and winning elections.

PUERTA, RAMÓN (1951–). Businessman and politician, twice president of the republic during the turbulent two-week period that ensued after the resignation of **Fernando de la Rúa** on 20 December 2001. A longtime member of the **Partido Justicialista** (PJ), Puerta served as governor of his native province of **Misiones** between 1991 and 1999 and, at various times, was elected to the provincial legislature and the Chamber of Deputies and National Senate. He was elected acting president of the Senate in 2001 when **Carlos "Chacho" Álvarez** resigned as vice president. Thus, when De la Rúa himself resigned, as acting president of the Senate, Puerta became interim president of the republic. On the first occasion, he lasted a couple of days, the time prescribed to convene an assembly to elect a new president to serve out the balance of De la Rúa's term. He stepped down when **Adolfo Rodríguez Saá** was selected. Ten days later, when Rodríguez Saá resigned, technically Puerta again became interim president, but he refused to act for a second time. Within minutes he passed the baton to the president of the Chamber of Deputies, **Eduardo Camaño**. Thereby, Puerta became the shortest serving president in the history of the republic, breaking the two-day record set by **Arturo Rawson** in June 1943.

In 2003, Puerta stood once more for the governorship of Misiones with the support of **Eduardo Duhalde**, who had succeeded Camaño as president of the republic, but was defeated by the candidate favored by **Néstor Kirchner**. On the dissident, anti-Kirchner wing of the party, he was a national deputy between 2009 and 2013 and stood in the **congressional elections of 2015** for the **Frente Renovador/Partido Justicialista** (FR/PJ) headed by **Sergio Massa**. He was named ambassador to **Spain** by President **Mauricio Macri** in 2015; he and Macri have several mutual business associates and friends, and Puerta had spoken in support of the Macri program. Puerta will go down in history as one of the five presidents to have held office between 20 December 2001 and 2 January 2002.

PUEYRREDÓN, JUAN MARTÍN DE (1777–1850). Of French Basque and Irish origin—his father was a merchant; born in **Buenos Aires** and partly educated in Paris. Acclaimed as supreme director of the **United Provinces of the River Plate** at the **Congress of Tucumán** in 1816, Pueyrredón was the first head of state of the new nation. He was the towering figure of the age, arguably second only to **José de San Martín** in making **independence** possible.

Pueyrredón first entered the family business, working in France and **Spain**. He was already a prominent figure in the *cabildo* at the time of the **British invasions**, events that effected a career change from businessman to politician and **military** leader. When a British expeditionary force took the city of Buenos Aires in 1806, he was at first inclined to cooperate with the British, possibly assuming their support for independence. He liaised between the military government and the *cabildo*. However, when it became clear that the British had other plans, he joined the patriotic cause, serving with distinction in the campaign to recapture the city led by soon-to-be-appointed viceroy **Santiago de Liniers**. Part of the delegation sent to Madrid to announce the expulsion of the British, and to seek aid (and a greater say for creoles in the administration), he became further convinced that independence was the best option after observing the moribund condition of the Bourbon monarchy.

Although he considered the creation of a constitutional monarchy of the **River Plate**—an idea that would resurface in his political thinking—he advised the *cabildo* not to recognize the authority of Viceroy **Baltasar Hidalgo de Cisneros**, dispatched by the Patriotic Junta of Seville established to coordinate resistance to the French invasion of the Iberian Peninsula and the deposition of the Bourbon monarchy—he was in Rio de Janeiro at the time of the **May Revolution of 1810**. Returning to Buenos Aires, along with the likes of **Manuel Belgrano**, he committed to the project to maintain the unity of the former viceroyalty. His vision for the future of the country was that of a **Unitarian**—a centralized state governed from Buenos Aires. In 1810 and 1811, he campaigned in the interior, including present-day **Bolivia**, confronting royalist and separatist forces. Unsuccessful in Bolivia, by seizing funds held in the Potosí mint and arranging an organized retreat to **Jujuy** and **Tucumán**, he saved the day for the patriotic cause. The Army of the North regrouped and defended what would approximate the northern boundaries of the country. Active in national politics between 1812 and 1814, he was often victim to the factionalism of the period. He became convinced of the project advanced by San Martín for the liberation of South America, that only by taking the struggle to royalist strongholds in **Chile**, Bolivia, and **Peru** could independence be secured. Elected to represent the province of **San Luis** at the Congress of Tucumán, largely due to the efforts of San Martín he was almost unanimously acclaimed supreme director as the congress went on to declare the independence of the republic.

As supreme director from 1816 to 1819, Pueyrredón had to confront rebellions in the provinces and contending ideas about the future shape of the country. He was, however, tireless in his efforts to support San Martín. Financing the campaign of the **Army of the Andes** in the liberation of Chile and Peru was his first priority—he ensured the necessary supply of men and materiel. During his time in office, national finances were stabilized, the army reorganized, institutions of the state established, and the foundation laid for constitutional government—the **Constitution of 1819** was adopted toward the end of his term. At first, **Congress** refused to accept his resignation, but he prevailed, insisting on complying with the terms of his mandate. Although occasionally active in politics in the 1820s, he was largely resident overseas, in **Brazil**, France, and **Uruguay**. He returned to Buenos Aires in 1849, about six months before his death the following year. Despite the civil wars that marked Pueyrredón's period in office, and the chaos that followed, he is regarded as central to the foundation of the modern state and a key figure of the independence period.

PUEYRREDÓN, PRILIDIANO (1823–1870). The son of **Juan Martín de Pueyrredón**, he is the leading Argentine painter of the 19th century. The 1850s and 1860s were his most prolific period, and 223 works from these years are preserved. More than half of these are portraits of society figures, but he is better known for his landscapes of the shores of the **River Plate** and of the **pampas**. A number of these paintings depict the native **ombú**, with the most notable ones being *Paisaje de la costa, Un alto en el campo, Costa del Río de la Plata, Un domingo en los suburbios de San Isidro,* and *El ombú de San Isidro. See also* QUINTA DE OLIVOS.

Q

QUIJANO, HORTENSIO JUAN (1884–1952). Lawyer, politician, public official, and vice president from 1946 to 1952; a native of the province of **Corrientes**, he read law at the **University of Buenos Aires** (UBA). Active in student politics at the beginning of the 20th century, Quijano became a distinguished member of the **Unión Cívica Radical** (UCR) and was chosen by the party to contest the elections for the governorship of his native province in 1918. He was unsuccessful but subsequently appointed to several official positions. A strong supporter of President **Hipólito Yrigoyen**, Quijano acted as lawyer for various state entities, such as the **Banco de la Nación Argentina**, and supervised public works contracts, including railway construction in the **Chaco**, where he also established a successful legal practice that represented several regional business organizations. Following the **military coup of 1930**, he became closely associated with efforts by former president **Marcelo T. de Alvear** to rebuild the fortunes of the UCR.

With the **military coup of 1943**, he recognized that change was coming and attempted to persuade colleagues in the UCR to support **Juan Domingo Perón**. In 1945, he served briefly as minster of the interior in the administration of de facto president General **Edelmiro Farrell**. When the UCR leadership opted to join the alliance of traditional parties opposed to Perón in the **presidential election of 1946**, with other dissidents he forged the breakaway faction **Unión Cívica Radical Junta Renovadora** (UCRJR), which combined with groups coordinated by the newly formed **Partido Laborista**. Quijano was selected as Perón's running mate in 1946, serving as national vice president from 1946 to 1952. Initially, it was assumed that he would step down in 1952 as the name of **Eva Perón** was being mentioned for the upcoming elections. However, when the **military** scotched the idea of Eva running alongside Perón in the **congressional** and **presidential elections of 1952**, Quijano was renominated Perón's running mate. He did not serve a second vice presidential term as he died before the inauguration.

QUINQUELA MARTÍN, BENITO (1890–1977). One of the most popular Argentine painters, his works depict the activity and daily life of the port district of **La Boca** in **Buenos Aires**. The paintings of Quinquela Martín were much admired by **Marcelo T. de Alvear**, who became a lasting friend. Upon becoming president of the republic in 1922, Alvear dispatched him to Europe and enabled the painter to promote his work. Quinquela Martín exhibited in Madrid and Paris, where a few of his paintings were acquired by the Círculo de Bellas Artes de Madrid, the Museum of Modern Art of Madrid, and the Musée du Luxembourg. In 1927, he left Europe for New York City, where two of his works wound up in the Metropolitan Museum of Art, and then returned to Argentina.

Quinquela Martín then held an exhibition on a trip to Italy in 1929. Several of his paintings were chosen by dictator Benito Mussolini from the display, which were then acquired by the Museum of Modern Art in Rome. He then made a final overseas trip in 1930, which took him to London. Following an exhibition there, several museums in **Great Britain** acquired his paintings. His most famous works include *Tormenta en el Astillero*, owned by the Musée du Luxembourg in Paris, and the *Puente de la Boca*, housed in St. James's Palace in London.

QUINTA DE OLIVOS. Official residence of the president of the republic, originally the summer residence of the president. The former presidential palace, the iconic **Casa Rosada**, located in the center of the city of **Buenos Aires**, is now used mainly for ceremonial functions and houses government offices. The Quinta—the term roughly translates as "country estate"—is located to the north, a little beyond the city limits, about 13 miles (20 kilometers) from the center.

The estate covers the equivalent of 20 city blocks—around 86 acres (35 hectares)—and includes an extensive park and formal gardens as well as the main residence and associated buildings. The original estate was designed by the 19th-century artist and painter **Prilidiano Pueyrredón**. It was bequeathed to the nation in 1913 but did not become the principal residence of presidents until the latter part of the 20th century. While it was used occasionally by some of his predecessors, **Juan Domingo Perón** was the first to spend a substantial amount of time in the Quinta. It was reputed to be the favored residence of First Lady **Eva Perón**. After her death, the site acquired some notoriety when Perón established a "gymnastic academy" for young ladies in the grounds and was reported to enjoy spending time with nubile pupils. By the late 1950s and 1960s, the Quinta was established as the presidential residence.

Several key national events have taken place at Olivos. It was a discrete location for secret meetings between President **Arturo Frondizi** and **Ernesto "Ché" Guevara**. Unfortunately for Frondizi, the location was insufficiently discrete; when news leaked, his contacts with Guevara were a factor triggering the **military coup of 1962**. **Perón** was at the Quinta when he died in 1974. It was the scene of massive demonstrations of public grief and later turned into a virtual shrine to the dead president and Eva Perón by Perón's third wife and successor, President **Isabel Perón**. In 1993, sitting president **Carlos Saúl Menem** and his predecessor, **Raúl Alfonsín**, met there and agreed on the **Olivos Pact**, which prepared the way for constitutional reform the following year, allowing Menem to stand for a second consecutive term. During **farm protests** a decade or so later, regular noisy demonstrations were held close to the Quinta, drawing residents from surrounding affluent neighborhoods. The Quinta was especially favored by Menem, who made extensive changes to the grounds, and President **Cristina Fernández de Kirchner**—it became her "bunker." Both Menem and Fernández de Kirchner saw the residence as an escape from the clamor of the city, especially at moments of protest. *See also* CONSTITUTION OF 1994.

QUINTANA, MANUEL (1835–1906). Lawyer, international jurist, and statesman. Elected constitutional president in 1904, he died in 1906 and was succeeded by Vice President **José Figueroa Alcorta**. A native of **Buenos Aires**, Quintana taught law, was dean of the Law Faculty and rector of the **University of Buenos Aires** (UBA), and represented his country at international law conferences. He served on several occasions as national deputy and senator and was briefly a minister in the **Luis Sáenz Peña** administration. When confronted with a revolt organized by the **Unión Cívica Radical** (UCR) in 1905, he took a firm line, notwithstanding the fact that Vice President Figueroa Alcorta and a son of strongman **Julio A. Roca** had been kidnapped and held hostage. Order was restored, but as illustrated by similar events during the presidency of Luis Sáenz Peña, the system of oligarchic rule was being challenged, in part as a result of economic growth and mass **immigration**: the opposition was getting stronger and more vociferous. Quintana was himself the victim of an unsuccessful assassination attempt.

QUIROGA, JUAN FACUNDO (1788–1835). Born in **La Rioja** in the northwest, of humble origins, Quiroga epitomized the charismatic **military**-political leaders who emerged during the **independence** period—the **caudillo** who commanded **gaucho** hordes. An entrepreneurial landowner and sometime governor of his native province, at one point he commanded the northern provinces from **Mendoza** to **Catamarca**, championing the **Federalist** cause and becoming the scourge of **Unitarians**. Violent and courageous, endowed with a sharp political mind, he commanded fierce loyalty among his supporters and clients and generated fear among his opponents. His assassination in 1835, widely believed to have been instigated by **Juan Manuel**

de Rosas and Estanislao López, caudillos respectively of Buenos Aires and Santa Fe, cleared the way for the hegemony of Rosas. Proponents of the federal cause regarded Quiroga as a popular leader who brought stability to the country and whose championing of Federalism with a large degree of provincial autonomy represented the type of leadership required to hold the country together. To his detractors, he represented the antithesis of centralized, democratic institutionalized government necessary for modernization. Domingo Faustino Sarmiento, public intellectual and future president, wrote a scathing account of *caudillismo* in *Facundo: Civilization and Barbarism*, which was published from exile in Chile in 1845.

RADICAL CIVIC UNION. *See* UNIÓN CÍVICA RADICAL (UCR); UNIÓN CÍVICA RADICAL DEL PUEBLO (UCRP); UNIÓN CÍVICA RADICAL INTRANSIGENTE (UCRI).

RAILWAYS. *See* BUENOS AYRES & PACIFIC RAILWAY COMPANY (BA&P); BUENOS AYRES GREAT SOUTHERN RAILWAY COMPANY (BAGS); BUENOS AYRES WESTERN RAILWAY COMPANY (BAW); CENTRAL ARGENTINE RAILWAY COMPANY (CAR); CORDOBA CENTRAL RAILWAY COMPANY (CCR); ECONOMY; FERROCAR-RILES ARGENTINOS (FFAA); FOREIGN DEBT/FOREIGN INVEST-MENT; GREAT BRITAIN; PRIVATIZATION; STATE-OWNED ENTER-PRISES (SOEs); TRANSPORTATION.

RAMÍREZ, ARIEL (1921–2010). Composer, pianist, and music director; a leading exponent of Argentine folk music. He is best known for the *Misa Criolla* (1964), whose lyrics were written by historian **Félix Luna**. The *Misa* is a 16-minute Mass for either male or female soloists, chorus, and traditional instruments and was one of the first masses not in Latin shortly after the Second Vatican Council allowed the use of the vernacular in Catholic churches.

RAMÍREZ, PEDRO PABLO (1884–1962). De facto president of Argentina (1943–1944). His tenure was characterized by a bitter power struggle and controversy over foreign policy that pitted him against General **Edelmiro Farrell**, the minister of war, and his subordinate Colonel **Juan Domingo Perón**, head of the War Ministry Secretariat.

General Ramírez was ambivalent about the need to get rid of Farrell and Perón, and his failure to do so resulted in a political shake-up in October 1943, when the regime became more right-wing and authoritarian. Farrell added the post of vice president to his portfolio, and Perón was appointed to head the National Labor Department (NLD). Perón would transform the Labor Department into the Secretariat of Labor and Welfare, which became the launchpad for his presidential ambitions.

Farrell and Perón took over the government by force on 25 February 1944, following the decision by Ramírez to break relations with Germany and Japan a month earlier. This move was the outcome of a diplomatic crisis emanating from two ventures: a mission to secure German weapons, and assistance to revolutionary movements in neighboring countries in an attempt to create a pro-Argentine, anti–**United States** bloc in South America. The Allies had documentary evidence of both cases, and the Argentine government broke relations with the Axis to prevent the publication of the documents. The rank and file of the army comprised hundreds of neutralist officers, and they supported the palace coup against the president. *see also* MINISTRY OF DEFENSE; MINISTRY OF LABOR.

RAMUS, CARLOS GUSTAVO (1947–1970). One of the founders of the **Montoneros** and a lifelong close associate of **Fernando Abal Medina**. Both men have the same life trajectory. Ramus studied in the Colegio Nacional Buenos Aires and in his teens was a member of the violent right-wing **Movimiento Nacionalista Tacuara** (MNT). As many who would take up arms as Montoneros in the late 1960s and early 1970s, Ramus had not begun his life as a Peronist and did not come from the left. This changed in 1964 when he joined the Juventud Estudiantil Católica and met Father **Carlos Mugica**, a radicalized Roman Catholic Peronist who advocated political violence as a response to repressive governments. Ramus eventually parted company with Mugica and in late 1966 took part in actions supporting sugar **industry** workers in **Tucumán**, a province where the de facto government of General **Juan Carlos Onganía** aimed to reform the archaic economic structure.

In early 1967, Ramus joined the Comando Camilo Torres set up by **Juan García Elorrio**. After the latter broke with Abal Medina, he became one of the founders of the Montoneros in 1968 and a key participant in the **Aramburazo** in May 1970. Former provisional president General **Pedro Eugenio Aramburu** was held captive and killed in the farmstead "La Celma," a Ramus family property near the township of Timote in the west of the province of **Buenos Aires**. Together with Abal Medina, Ramus subsequently lost his life in a shoot-out with the police in September 1970. *See also* TRADE UNIONS.

RANDAZZO, ANÍBAL FLORENCIO (1964–). Personable politician-cum-technocrat from the interior of the province of **Buenos Aires**; rising star of the **Partido Justicialista** (PJ) who has held various public offices; minister of interior from 2007 to 2015, and one of a handful of ministers to retain the same post for the full term of the two administrations of President **Cristina Fernández de Kirchner**. Born into a family long affiliated with the PJ, Florencio Randazzo seemed destined for a political career. Having trained as an accountant at the **University of Buenos Aires** (UBA), he moved seamlessly into the provincial administration. First appointed as an advisor to the Interior Ministry of the government of the province of Buenos Aires led by **Eduardo Duhalde** in 1991, within a year Randazzo had become the minister's right-hand man. While serving in the provincial administration, he was also mayor of his hometown of Chivilcoy, having been elected in 1993, and a deputy in the provincial assembly, to which he was elected in 1995. In 2002, he secured a ministerial appointment in the provincial government, now headed by Felipe Solá. A year later, he was appointed head of Solá's cabinet of ministers. His appointment to the federal government seemed almost inevitable when Solá's term as governor of Buenos Aires came to an end. Having learned the ropes in the provincial administration, Randazzo proved to be a capable federal minister of interior. During the second Fernández de Kirchner administration, he sponsored a major program of infrastructure renewal, the transport portfolio having been merged with the Interior Ministry by that point. He made a name for himself by pressing ahead with rail modernization, especially in the commuter belt of metropolitan Buenos Aires and strategic intercity routes. This was something that he had championed while in the provincial administration, following several rail accidents. His projects resulted in much public exposure in various parts of the province. In addition, he modernized arrangements for the production of identity documents, an established responsibility of the **Ministry of Interior**. This again chimed with his image as a modernizer and proficient technocrat.

Already in 2013, it was clear that he had presidential ambitions. By 2014, he had become one of the two vice presidents of the PJ and was organizing support for his campaign. He founded youth groups and was active on social media. His campaign was also supported by rail workers. Yet he failed to secure the backing of Mrs. Kirchner. In the final stages of the run-up to the **presidential election of 2015**, she threw her weight behind **Daniel Scioli**. Randazzo switched his ambitions to seeking the governorship of Buenos Aires. Again, he failed to secure Mrs. Kirchner's support; she nominated **Aníbal Fernández**. Perhaps she thought Randazzo too much of a threat; both Scioli and Fernández were regarded as super-loyalists. These are now regarded as the two biggest miscalculations made by Mrs. Kirchner at the end of her presidency. Scioli proved to be a lackluster choice to head the Kirchnerista **Frente para la Victoria/Partido Justicialista** (FpV/PJ) presidential ticket. Fernández was a toxic choice for the provincial governor race. It is widely held that had Randazzo secured the FpV/PJ presidential nomination, **Mauricio Macri** would not have won in November 2015, and had Fernández not stood for the FpV/PJ for the Buenos Aires governorship, **María Eugenia**

Vidal would not have taken the province for the **Cambiemos** coalition. Randazzo subsequently broke with the FpV/PJ, joining the Frente Justicialista, the anti-Kirchner rump of the PJ. He campaigned for a seat in the National Senate in the midterm **congressional elections of 2017** but failed. Despite this setback, Randazzo remains a man to watch. *See also* FERROCARRILES ARGENTINOS (FFAA); TRANSPORTATION; UNIÓN FERROVIARIA (UF).

RAWSON. Capital of the province of **Chubut**, founded in 1865. Originally called Trerawson, from the Welsh for town (*tre*), the city was named in honor of the then Argentine minister of interior, Guillermo Rawson, who had supported Welsh colonization. The region had been explored some years earlier by a Welsh merchant and rancher, Henry Jones, resident in **Buenos Aires**, who may have brought the area to the attention of the sponsors of Welsh colonization in **Patagonia**. The current population is approximately 28,000. *See also* IMMIGRATION; MINISTRY OF INTERIOR, PUBLIC WORKS, AND HOUSING.

RAWSON, ARTURO (1885–1952). De facto president of Argentina from 4 to 6 June 1943. The commanding officer of the cavalry at the Campo de Mayo garrison outside the city of **Buenos Aires**, General Rawson was contacted on 3 June 1943 by members of the **Grupo de Oficiales Unidos** (GOU) planning to overthrow the civilian administration. The GOU, lacking adequate troop numbers to succeed, knew he could provide the necessary soldiers. Rawson had been scheming to topple the government even before he was sought out by the conspirators and agreed to their plan. The following day, at the head of 10,000 troops, Rawson overthrew President **Ramón S. Castillo**.

Rawson promptly declared himself president with the expectation of ruling for a long time, thereby frustrating the presidential ambitions of fellow cavalry general **Pedro Pablo Ramírez**, founder of the fascist Guardia Nacional. However, his choices for the cabinet alienated the GOU leadership, who forced him to resign on the night of 6 June, when he was replaced by Ramírez. Rawson's tenure of only two days was the briefest for an Argentine president until the economic crisis of December 2001. *See also* MILITARY COUP OF 1943; PUERTA, RAMÓN (1951–).

RECOLETA. La Recoleta is a fashionable cemetery located in affluent Barrio Norte a little to the north of the center of the city of **Buenos Aires**. Established in its present form in 1823, it is on the site of a Franciscan monastery secularized during the modernization program launched by **Bernardino Rivadavia**. The final resting place of many of the most prominent figures of the 19th and 20th century, the cemetery is owned by the city authorities, which rents plots, most of which are leased by families of the old landed oligarchy and upper middle class. The name, which now denominates the whole district and not only the cemetery itself, derived from the Franciscan Order and means "to collect" or to "harvest" souls. The former monastic church, Nuestra Señora del Pilar, still functions; the former cloisters are now an art gallery and cultural center, fronted by a park on the south side, surrounded by cafés and restaurants. Now a national monument, the whole complex—the functioning cemetery, church, and gallery—has become a popular **tourist** destination. Visitors are attracted by the architecture of Belle Epoque mausolea (many designed in the style of mini baronial castles, French chateaux, and Italian palazzi) beautified with neoclassical statuary, as well as to honor the life and work of eminent "residents." The tombs of many former presidents, ministers, senior **military** personnel, and artists and writers are in the cemetery.

RECREAR PARA EL CRECIMIENTO (RECREAR). Political party, a splinter group of the **Unión Cívica Radical** (UCR) formed and headed by **Ricardo López Murphy** in 2002. The party was composed mainly of economically liberal members of the UCR. It was devised largely to serve the presidential ambitions of López Murphy, as well as to advance the case for socially responsible economic liberalism. An ephemeral entity, which was absorbed by the **Propuesta Republicana** (PRO) in 2009, it had limited electoral success despite entering an alliance with **Compromiso para el Cambio**, the electoral vehicle formed by **Mauricio Macri** in 2005. In the **presidential election of 2003**, Recrear gained 18 percent for López Murphy; in the midterm **congressional elections of 2005**, when López Murphy contested the National Senate seat for the city of **Buenos Aires**, his share of the votes was less than half that obtained in 2003—he came in fifth, behind the UCR nominee. In the **presidential election of 2007**, López Murphy came in a distant sixth. He lost the leadership of the party the following year and resigned in 2009. Like several other **political parties** and alliances formed during the early years of the 21st century, Recrear illustrated the increasingly fragmented nature of party politics and the tendency for new groupings, often headed by nationally recognized politicians, to rise and disappear without trace.

RELIGION. The **Constitution of 1853** provided for the separation of church and state and guaranteed freedom of religion, though it made special provisions for the **Catholic Church**. The **Constitution of 1994** removed the requirement that the head of state should be a Catholic, while reiterating freedom of religious expression and continuing to recognize Roman Catholicism as the official religion of the state. Both the 1853 and 1994 constitutions invoked the name of God.

According to data produced by the **Ministry of Foreign Relations and Religion**, the vast majority of Argentines identify as Christian. Estimates of the number of Roman Catholics range from between 70 percent and 90 percent of those acknowledging religious beliefs. There is a similar range regarding the number of Protestants, usually given as between 10 percent and 15 percent of the total population; it is generally agreed that Evangelicals or Pentecostals account for the greatest proportion of Protestants, a proportion that has increased markedly in recent years at the expense of other denominations and the Catholic Church. There are also sizable Orthodox and Greek Catholic communities. There is a diocese of the Anglican Church—the Province of the **Southern Cone**—which includes Anglican communities in **Bolivia**, **Chile**, **Paraguay**, **Peru**, and **Uruguay** in addition to Argentina. Unlike the Anglican Church elsewhere in Latin America, which is overseen by the Episcopal Church in the **United States**, the archbishop of Canterbury has oversight of the Province of the Southern Cone. Approaching 500,000, upper-bound estimates of the Muslim community would place it at around 1 percent of the total population (or around half a percent if lower figures are accepted). The community largely originates from **immigration** from the former Ottoman empire, though the vast majority of immigrants of Arab origin are Christian. The Argentine Jewish community is the largest in Latin America, and the community in **Buenos Aires** is second only to that of New York in the Americas. Calculations of the size of the community place it between 300,000 and 400,000. It is accepted that the community has shrunk in recent decades due to economic emigration, political considerations, and the appeal of settlement in Israel. Events like the bombing of the **Asociación Mutual Israelita Argentina** (AMIA) are a factor. The proportion of the total population admitting to holding no religious belief is approximately 10 percent. About a quarter of Roman Catholics attend regular religious services; the proportion is higher among Protestants, especially among fast-growing Evangelical churches.

REPÚBLICA CROMAÑÓN. One of the worst disasters to have occurred in Argentina in recent years: a fire in a nightclub that occurred on 30 December 2004, claiming almost 200 lives and left around 1,500 injured. Located in a fairly prosperous, middle-class neighborhood in the city of **Buenos Aires**, the club was a popular venue for pop concerts and similar events, attracting people from across the city.

The fire probably started when a firework was lit—it was close to New Year's Eve at the start of the Christmas and summer holiday season. Seasonal decorations and the poor quality of materials meant that the fire spread rapidly. Paper decorations, wood paneling, and polystyrene ceiling tiles quickly caught fire: many of the deaths and injuries resulted from melting tiles and the inhalation of toxic gases. The high number of deaths and injuries were also caused because fire doors had been locked. Inquiries held after the disaster revealed how regulations had been breached. In addition to poor construction material, insufficient firefighting equipment, and locked fire exits, the authorities were accused of failing to inspect the building and ensure compliance with building and operating regulations—the validity of official certification was questioned—and the police and fire services charged with not responding sufficiently quickly. As well as the owner and operator of the facility, the authorities were held to be responsible for the disaster. It was seen to reflect the poor quality of city governance and possibly the **corruption** of local officials. Families of those killed and injured organized demonstrations, marches, and a widely supported campaign for justice; some marches were roughly broken up by the police, triggering memories of police violence during the **Proceso de Reorganización Nacional**. In addition to the loss of life and injuries, the tragedy cost city mayor **Aníbal Ibarra** his political career, or at least severely curtailed it.

RESISTENCIA. The capital city of the province of **Chaco**, it was established in 1876 on the site of a long-abandoned 17th-century Spanish **military** outpost and acquired its administrative functions two years later. Resistencia is located on a tributary of the **Paraná** River opposite the city of **Corrientes**, to which it has been linked by a bridge since 1973, and its population is approximately 390,000 when the Greater Resistencia municipalities are included. The city's **economy**, which was originally based on **agriculture** and **foreign trade**, has expanded into the services sector.

RETENCIONES. Term used for taxes on exports, particularly **commodities**; functions as a withholding levy normally paid before export certificates are granted. The conventional assumption is that such taxes are "paid" by importers rather than exporters and are usually applied when commodity prices are high and rising in international markets; hence, they are also viewed as a temporary windfall tax. Sometimes-adjustable levies were related to price changes in world markets or to the exchange rate, given that many commodity prices are fixed in US dollars. In practice, *retenciones* have been a mayor plank in Argentine fiscal policy for much of the second half of the 20th century and beyond, generating a significant proportion of total federal tax revenue and foreign **currency** available to the government, whether civilian or **military**.

Legally, *retenciones* date from the **Constitution of 1853**, which authorized the federal government to raise taxes on exports, a facility that soon fell into abeyance. A variant developed during the first presidency of **Juan Domingo Perón** with the application of differential buying and selling prices operated by the state trade monopoly **Instituto Argentino de Promoción del Intercambio** (IAPA), which bought "cheap" and home and sold "dear" abroad—that is, offered lower prices to farmers than those charged to overseas buyers. Following the **military coup of 1955**, when the government implemented a large devaluation of the peso, a 25 percent export tax was levied on a wide range of commodities as a temporary expedient to raise revenue and to ensure that society at large, rather than farmers and exporters, reaped the benefit of devaluation. In 1958, commodities export taxes ranging between 10 and 20 percent were formalized; exporters were required to process two-thirds of foreign exchange earnings at the official rate and allowed to sell one-third on the open market. Despite protests by the **Sociedad Rural Argentina** (SRA) and moves by producers to withhold supplies from the market, *retenciones* remained in place for many decades, though the rates levied on individual commodities and the proportion of foreign exchange earnings channeled via the **Banco Central de la República Argentina** (BCRA) Exchange Office were subject to change. For example, following a 40 percent devaluation effected by Minister of Economy **Adalbert Krieger Vasena** in 1967, rates were raised to between 20 percent and 25 percent. There were further adjustments in the early 1970s during the democratically elected administrations of Presidents Juan Domingo Perón and **Isabel Perón**, and a substantial hike in *retenciones* in 1982, partly associated with needs to finance the **Falklands War**, during the presidency of General **Leopoldo Fortunato Galtieri**. Export taxes were also a feature of the latter part of the administration of democratically elected president **Raúl Alfonsín**, particularly as the government scrambled for revenue as the **economy** was spiraling out of control. Abolished in the 1990s by Minister of Economy **Domingo Cavallo** to promote exports, *retenciones* were reapplied in 2002 and became a cause célèbre during the first presidency of **Cristina Fernández de Kirchner**.

Retenciones were a major issue in the **presidential election of 2015**, with victorious **Mauricio Macri** campaigning on a platform to abolish or phase out export taxes. *See also* AGRICULTURE; AUSTRAL PLAN; ECONOMIC CRISES; FARM PROTESTS; FOREIGN TRADE.

REUTEMANN, CARLOS ALBERTO (1942–). Nicknamed "Lole," former racing driver turned politician for his native province of **Santa Fe**. As a racing driver, Reutemann was one of the leading Formula One protagonists between 1972 and 1982. He competed for four teams (Brabham, Ferrari,

Lotus, and Williams), scored 12 Grand Prix wins and six pole positions, and in 1981 finished second in the World Drivers' Championship by one point—he was overtaken in the last race of the season.

After retiring from racing, Reutemann's popularity led the **Partido Justicialista** (PJ) of his province to invite him to run for governor. He served as governor of Santa Fe from 1991 to 1995 and, with no immediate reelection then allowed, again from 1999 to 2003. An honest and efficient administrator, he declined to run for the presidency on numerous occasions in the early 21st century. In the **congressional elections of 2003**, Reutemann won a seat in the National Senate. By the time he successfully won reelection in 2009, he had split from the parliamentary bloc of the **Frente para la Victoria/ Partido Justicialista** (FpV/PJ) and created his own faction—Santa Fe Federal—with the intention of protecting the interests of the province. Six years later, he was again reelected as national senator, by then having become part of **Cambiemos**, which delivered the presidency to **Mauricio Macri** in the **presidential election of 2015**. Reutemann's current mandate as national senator expires in 2021.

REVOLUCIÓN ARGENTINA (1966–1973). Politically illiberal but economically liberal regime that emerged from the **military coup of 1966**, whose character was set out in the "Estatutos de la Revolución." The division of powers as prescribed in the **Constitution of 1853** were abolished. The executive and legislative powers were vested in the president, who had no limits set on his term of office. The president also appointed provincial governors, who in turn exercised executive and legislative powers in the provinces. New judges were designated for the Supreme Court, who had to swear to prioritize the requirements of the Estatutos over those of the constitution.

The objectives of the "revolution" were a total transformation of the country, to be carried out in *tres tiempos* (three stages). The first of these was the *tiempo económico*: it envisaged industrial development, facilitating investment in the most modern sectors. Those sectors, as they reduced operating costs, would constitute a more efficient productive apparatus that would end inflation and recurring recessionary cycles. At this point, the *tiempo social* would begin, in which the wealth accumulated in the previous stage would be redistributed, overcoming the regressive character inevitable in the *tiempo económico* and thereby eliminate social conflicts. Finally would come the *tiempo político*, which in a distant future would allow an opening for the participation of society in an as yet unknown institutional framework that would be different to that existing before 1966. Until the arrival of the *tiempo político*, the government would not tolerate any kind of opposition; it believed that the "modernization" of Argentina could not be subject to political debate and the arbitrariness of social conflict.

Such a regimented plan soon ran into trouble. Political and social issues could not be separated from the economic project, and there was no time framework. **Juan Carlos Onganía**, who had become president after the coup, had not been precise about the duration of his term and made it understood that a decade was necessary to implement the economic and social changes that would precede the political institutionalization founded on new bases. As opposition, social unrest, and radicalization of the youth gathered pace, **Alejandro Agustín Lanusse**, the commander-in-chief of the army, reached the view that the **military** had to extricate themselves from government. He engineered a palace coup in 1970, which put the obscure **Roberto M. Levingston** in power, in the belief that he would be pliant. But Levingston had other ideas, wishing to remain in power. Lanusse himself took power in another palace coup in 1971 and, having unsuccessfully tried to engineer a political solution to his liking, called for free elections two years later.

With its transformative project, the Revolución Argentina was the direct forerunner of the **Proceso de Reorganización Nacional**. However, there were important differences. While in 1966 there had been economic drift for the first six months, in 1976 the military already had an economic plan. More crucial was the different way that the two regimes dealt with terrorism. The dictatorship from 1966 to 1973 set up military tribunals and filled the jails with subversives, only to see them released when the elected government of **Héctor J. Cámpora** took office. In 1976, the armed forces avoided due process and embarked on an extermination campaign that in a couple of years resulted in almost 9,000 deaths. But both the Revolución Argentina and the Proceso shared one common characteristic: they were unworkable transformative projects with no time frame. *See also* ARAMBURAZO (29 MAY–1 JUNE 1970); CONGRESSIONAL ELECTIONS OF 1973; CORDOBAZO (29 MAY–3 JUNE 1969); FERRER, ALDO (1927–2016); KRIEGER VASENA, ADALBERT (1920–2000); "LA HORA DEL PUEBLO"; LAW NO. 19.862 (OCTOBER 1972); MOR ROIG, ARTURO (1914–1974); PRESIDENTIAL ELECTION OF MARCH 1973; SALIMEI, JORGE NÉSTOR (1926–1975); TRELEW MASSACRE (22 AUGUST 1972).

REVOLUCIÓN LIBERTADORA (1955–1958). For having "liberated" Argentina from the "despotism" of **Juan Domingo Perón**, this is the euphemism that describes the de facto regime that came to power with the **military coup of 1955**. Although the Revolución Libertadora was greeted at the time with considerable jubilation, it has few defenders now. Those who remain its supporters had been oppressed during the *peronato*, considering the coup against Perón justified as an exercise of the right to resist oppression. With the benefit of hindsight, it is clear that the coup of September 1955 marked the start of a new, bloody phase in Argentine political life. The next three decades would be punctuated by an alternation of civilian and **military** governments and the fostering of a climate in which subversive violence and state repression would reach unprecedented levels. The blame for this turn of events lies squarely on the victors and vanquished in the Revolución Libertadora and their successors. *See also* ARAMBURAZO (29 MAY–1 JUNE 1970); ARAMBURU, PEDRO EUGENIO (1903–1970); EXECUTIONS OF JUNE 1956; LONARDI, EDUARDO ERNESTO (1896–1956); ROJAS, ISAAC FRANCISCO (1903–1993).

REVOLUTION OF MAY 1810. *See* MAY REVOLUTION OF 1810.

REVOLUTION OF 1890. The last major conflict of the 19th century—with a difference. Civil wars, a major feature of the decades around **independence**, had been fought about competing projects for **national organization** advanced by **Federalists** and **Unitarians**, as well as rivalry among regional **caudillos** struggling for national hegemony and violent conflict within individual provinces and among them. The events of 1890 represent more a demand by rising urban middle classes—especially in **Buenos Aires**—for political space. Such demands can be presented as both a struggle for accommodation within the existing system and an attempt to overthrow it.

Also known as the "Revolution in the Park," a reference to the location of the most prominent protest and armed conflict, the Plaza del Parque or Plaza Lavalle, the main events occurred in late July. The immediate context was the political crisis faced by the administration of President **Miguel Juárez Celman**, which in turn was precipitated by the profound economic and financial crisis confronting the country—the **Baring Crisis**. The rise in government indebtedness, coupled with an export squeeze and declining living standards, induced political protest, concerns that the government would lose control, and fears of a debt default. All concerns and fears were realized, coming together around the middle of 1890. In effect, there were two political crises: challenges to the regime and the political system as a whole spearheaded by new political organizations that would become the **Unión Cívica Radical** (UCR), and disagreement within the governing coalition— the Partido Autonomista Nacional (PAN)—about how to deal with the economic/debt crisis and challenges on the streets. Sections of the army and navy supported the ideals expressed by the civilian leaders of the revolution. There was intellectual support by figures such as **Bartolomé Mitre**; even former president and sometime head of the PAN **Julio A. Roca** was initially said to be supportive, or at least inclined to come to an agreement with rebel **military** units. Dissidents within the PAN were also supportive; the rebels assumed that they could count on Vice President **Carlos Pellegrini**, who was captured and then released by the rebels. Heading the rebels were such figures as **Leandro Alem, Aristóbulo Del Valle**, and **Hipólito Yrigoyen**.

By the end of hostilities, estimates of the dead and injured varied: some reports state that 300 were killed, others that up to 1,500 had been killed and injured. The figures are substantial, and the conflict was the first such major challenge to national authorities since the civil wars of a generation earlier. The short-term consequences included a government crackdown as the regime pulled together. In the medium term, Juárez Celman was forced to resign, being replaced by Pellegrini, and the events of 1890 were crucial to the consolidation of the UCR. In the longer term, the results were sustained efforts at reform from within, typified by the **Sáenz Peña Law** and electoral reform; broader political debate that facilitated the consolidation of new political parties like the **Partido Socialista** and Liga del Sur; and the formation of greater political consciousness on the part of rural and urban middle-class groups and urban labor. The 1890 revolution signaled the emergence of a new polity and **economy** associated with mass **immigration** and urban industrial growth. *See also* ANARCHO-SYNDICALISM; ECONOMIC CRISES; FOREIGN DEBT/FOREIGN INVESTMENT; INDUSTRY; POLITICAL PARTIES; SEMANA TRÁGICA; TRADE UNIONS.

REYES, CIPRIANO (1906–2001). Trade union leader and politician; one of the founders of the **Partido Laborista** (PL) and an influential figure in the birth of **Peronism**. Born in Lincoln, province of **Buenos Aires**, Reyes moved with his family to **Zárate** in 1921 and worked in *frigorífico* Armour, where he was a founder of the first trade union established in the **meat** industry in 1923. In the early 1940s, he settled on the outskirts of the national capital and, now employed at *frigorífico*, Anglo became active in the communist-dominated Federación de Obreros de la Industria de la Carne (FOIC).

Following the **military coup of 1943**, Reyes became one of the trade unionists in the alliance between a part of the workers' movement and Colonels **Juan Domingo Perón** and **Domingo Mercante** in the Secretariat of Labor, which would lead to the emergence of the Peronist movement. By the end of 1943, he was the leader of the Sindicato Autónomo de la Industria de La Carne, a splinter of the then disbanded FOIC.

Reyes participated in the mass demonstrations of October 1945, which resulted in the failure of an attempt by sections of the **military** to contain Perón. Immediately after, Reyes, **Luis Gay**, and other union leaders founded the PL to support Perón's candidacy in the **presidential election of 1946**. Once elected head of state, Perón ordered the parties that supported him to dissolve and merge into a single political entity led by himself. Reyes and Gay refused to cooperate, not out of opposition to the president but because the democratic and autonomous practices of the PL were threatened.

Reyes, elected national deputy for the province of Buenos Aires in 1946, became a constant irritant for Perón and paid dearly for it. He was seriously injured in an assassination attempt in July 1947 and imprisoned in September 1948 on trumped-up charges of being involved in a plot to assassinate the president and the first lady. Reyes was released from jail following the **military coup of 1955**. *See also* TRADE UNIONS

RICO, ALDO (1943–). Retired military officer and politician who acquired a pugilistic reputation while serving in the army and when in politics. He is best known for leading a series of barrack room mutinies during the presidency of **Raúl Alfonsín**—the revolt of the so-called *carapintadas*, who wore camouflage paint and combat uniforms when staging protests. Aldo was a key figure in the events that took place around Easter 1987 and which prefigured bloodier revolts staged the following year by **Mohamed Alí Seineldín**.

Rico and his associates claimed to be defending the honor of the **military** while protesting budget cuts and the arraignment of senior officers for deaths, "disappearances," and **human rights** violations during the **Proceso de Reorganización Nacional**. Although there was no prospect of the barrack revolts leading to a full-blown military coup, occurring less than four years after the return of democracy and at a time of economic crisis—similar crises had previously served as a pretext for intervention by the **military**—there was considerable unease. The revolts triggered massive public support for the government: streets around barracks commandeered by the mutineers were surrounded by thousands of angry civilians. Despite the public outcry against Rico and associates, Alfonsín was subsequently accused of not taking a sufficiently robust line with them. Sentenced to prison, Rico was pardoned by Alfonsín's successor, President **Carlos Saúl Menem**, in 1989.

On release, Rico pursued a fairly successful political career, founding a conservative, nationalist party, Movimiento por la Dignidad Nacional (MODIN). He was elected to various offices: he served in the constituent assembly that drew up the **Constitution of 1994** and in 1997 as mayor of the district of San Miguel, located in the northeast of the province of **Buenos Aires**. His most prominent role came two years later when he was appointed provincial police minister by Governor **Carlos Ruckauf** of the **Partido Justicialista** (PJ), a position that he held for less than four months. Some years later, he took his party into the PJ, seeking reelection as mayor of San Miguel. Initially positioning himself with the **Frente para la Victoria/Partido Justicialista** (FvP/PJ) wing of the party, he subsequently switched to the anti-Kirchner Unión Popular wing of the PJ associated with **Eduardo Duhalde**. He lost the election yet remains in the public eye and continues to aspire to a political career. *See also* AUSTRAL PLAN; ECONOMIC CRISES; KIRCHNER, CRISTINA ELISABET FERNÁNDEZ DE (1953–).

RIGHI, ESTEBAN JUSTO ANTONIO (1938–). Minister of interior (May–July 1973) and federal attorney general (2005–2012). Righi was head of the **Ministry of Interior** during the presidency of **Héctor J. Cámpora**; he was the member of the cabinet closest to the **Montoneros**. He steered through **Congress** legislation to amend specific provisions of the penal code that would amnesty those convicted of terrorist offences, as promised in the election platform of the **Frente Justicialista de Liberación** (FREJULI). As a result, political prisoners were released. Moreover, he suppressed the repressive apparatus of the state by facing down the Policía Federal. Righi dismantled the Departamento para la Información Antidemocrática, which had conducted a witch hunt against the left, and destroyed its archives. He also reprimanded police chiefs for actions against the Montoneros from 1970 and ordered them to cease torture and death-squad-type activities.

Unsurprisingly, Righi became the leading target of attacks from the Peronist right. Even **Juan Domingo Perón** himself, in a show of utter contempt for the man, described him in extremely colorful terms. Righi's tenure in office ended when Cámpora resigned. Righi had to flee the country immediately. He went into exile in Mexico, where he remained until 1983. Righi returned to national public service just over two decades later when President **Néstor Kirchner** appointed him federal attorney general. His posting lasted into the second presidency of **Cristina Fernández de Kirchner**, when Righi was forced to resign in a highly underhand move to prevent him from investigating **corruption** charges against Vice President **Amado Boudou**.

RÍO GALLEGOS. Capital and largest settlement of the province of **Santa Cruz**, with a population of over 100,000. The city was founded in 1885 as part of a drive to project Argentine power in southern **Patagonia**. It became the capital of the national territory of Santa Cruz in 1888 and retained its status when the territory became a province in 1957. Río Gallegos became the area's principal port for exporting **sheep** and their products and also developed as a major **military** base, from which the air force operated during the **Falklands War**. Arguably, the city's most famous son is **Néstor Kirchner**. He served as mayor from 1987 to 1991, then as governor of Santa Cruz between 1991 and 2003, and finally as president of Argentina from 2003 until 2007. Kirchner's mausoleum is in Río Gallegos, and a street bears his name.

RÍO NEGRO (PROVINCE). Province on the northern edge of **Patagonia**, bordered by **Chubut** to the south, **Neuquén** to the west, **La Pampa** to the north, and **Buenos Aires** and the Atlantic to the east. Following the **Conquest of the Desert**, the area was organized as the Territorio Nacional del Río Negro in 1884. It acquired the status of province in 1957; the current population is approximately 640,000, and its capital is **Viedma**. Río Negro is a mostly arid province, and its main water source is the **Negro** River, which through a system completed in the 1930s irrigates the upper and middle sections of the valley. These areas contain the fruit-growing region, which produces around two-thirds of the apples and pears consumed in the country and is diversifying into wine production. **Tourism** is another important sector: skiing and hiking are based around the Andean town of **San Carlos de Bariloche**, and whale watching is centered on the San Matías Gulf on the Atlantic coast.

RIVADAVIA, BERNARDINO (1780–1845). President of the **United Provinces of the River Plate** (1826–1827), elected by the constituent congress convened in 1824 to draw up what became the **Constitution of 1826**, the first national charter. Regarded as the first president of the republic, he was a **Unitarian** visionary whose project for the country was out of tune with contemporary political and economic reality.

Born to Spanish parents, Rivadavia played a prominent role in the defense of the city of **Buenos Aires** during the **British invasions** and in the **May Revolution of 1810**. From an established family, reflected in the splendid baptismal name of Bernardino de la Trinidad González de Rivadavia y Rodríguez de Rivadavia, and educated at the prestigious Real Colegio de San Carlos, he came to believe strongly in the liberal sentiments that were then emerging among a section of the elite. Rivadavia was sent on a diplomatic mission to Europe to secure recognition and aid. He returned convinced that the country needed a strong central, constitutional government. (In later life, Rivadavia would translate into Spanish the complete works of Jeremy Bentham, whom he had met while in London and with whom he maintained a long correspondence.) During his presidency, **independence** was recognized by **Brazil**, **Great Britain**, Portugal, and the **United States**. His principal domestic contributions included the secularization of the wealth and property of the **Catholic Church** and efforts to promote secularism. Former church wealth was applied to charitable and educational facilities—embryonic social protection administered by the **Sociedad de Beneficencia** and what would become the **University of Buenos Aires** (UBA). The special legal status enjoyed by the church and religious establishments was abolished and control of cemeteries and schools transferred to the state. The city of **Buenos Aires** was federalized—that is, separated from the province. There were projects to promote **immigration** and **education**, to modernize the port, and to prohibit the sale of state assets (especially public land on which the **Baring Loan** was secured). Many of these measures built on those that he had implemented while a minister in the government of the province of Buenos Aires, when he had been instrumental in creating a police force and established the franchise, according the vote to all male citizens. In addition to implementing such ambitious proposals, President Rivadavia prosecuted a war with Brazil to sustain Argentine claims to the east bank for the **River Plate** (**Uruguay**) and suppressed **Federalist** revolts in the interior. To his opponents, Rivadavia's program of secularization was viewed as antireligious, as well as anticlerical, while his insistence on establishing a unitary, centralized state was seen as designed to advance the hegemony of Buenos Aires. An anti-Rivadavia campaign in the interior was spearheaded by the **caudillo Juan Facundo Quiroga**, and in Buenos Aires opponents clustered around **Juan Manuel de Rosas**. Confronted by mounting opposition, Rivadavia resigned, retiring to his estates. In 1829, he left for exile in **Spain**. Attempting to return in 1834, he was denied landing: after stays in Montevideo and Rio de Janeiro, he went back to Spain. Opinion about Rivadavia and his project continue to divide: some regard his proposals as visionary and, to a considerable degree, delivered after the 1860s; others view his ideas as naïve, disconnected from contemporary reality, thus prolonging disorder and the chaos of the decades that followed. *See also* FEDERALIZATION OF THE CITY OF BUENOS AIRES.

RIVAS, NELLY (1939–2012). Teenager involved in a scandalous relationship with **Juan Domingo Perón** during his second presidency. Rivas was 14 years old when they met during a youth sports event of the Unión de Estudiantes Secundarios (UES) in 1953 and began living with him early the following year.

The affair merits attention as it indicates when president Perón felt disdain for social norms and contempt for the law. Few would consider it appropriate for a man of almost 60 years old to be cohabiting with a 14-year-old girl, an offense that was punishable by law. The matter was all the graver because he was the holder of the country's highest office, which required him to uphold the law. At least before his overthrow, Perón covered his tracks carefully. His inner circle never let anything slip, and the opposition did not detect her existence.

The **military coup of 1955** put paid to the relationship and also brought it to light. Before going into exile, Perón ensured that Rivas had something to live on by giving her some jewels and 400,000 pesos—then a fortune. Once in **Paraguay**, he wrote the girl two letters indicating that he would send for her. They were discovered, and anti-Peronists raided the Rivas household and took everything. She then tried to escape to Paraguay but was stopped at the border by the new authorities and detained at an institution for underage prostitutes.

Statutory rape was one of many charges laid against Perón by the **military** government. He ferociously denied the affair, despite the existence of proof. Her parents acknowledged the existence of the relationship in the tribunal that charged them with complicity in statutory rape. Later, Rivas sold her story to *Time* magazine in the **United States**. There are photographs of Perón and Rivas together taken at a number of UES events.

The charges of statutory rape were still in effect in 1971, when the military government of General **Alejandro Agustín Lanusse** was trying to negotiate an electoral exit strategy with the exiled former president. They were never acted upon. Perón met Rivas once after his definitive return from exile in 1973, but by that time she was married with two sons.

RIVER PLATE. The Río de la Plata is not a river but a massive delta—some 140 miles across at the entrance and around 160 miles long until narrowing—formed by the confluence of the **Paraná** and **Uruguay** rivers on the north side. It is also fed by minor rivers from the south. It was first named by Juan Díaz de Solís, who had been commissioned by Ferdinand II of Aragon (and **Spain**) to explore the southern ocean off the east coast of Latin America. Mistaking the delta for the estuary of a major river, perhaps similar to the Amazon, when he reached the area in 1516, having sailed along the coast of **Brazil**, Solís called the river the Río Santa Maria and the Mar Dulce—the low salinity of the water underpinning the assumption that it was an estuary. Some 12 years later, influenced by the legend of a Mountain of Silver located in the interior, and hoping that a river route might be discovered to this fabled land, the explorer Sebastian Cabot renamed the delta the River of Silver. The name stuck and was applied to the region as a geographical term, to the Spanish **Viceroyalty of the River Plate** created in 1776 and was subsequently adopted by the successor republic (the **United Provinces of the River Plate** and Confederation of the Río de la Plata), and to the Second World War naval battle between Royal Navy cruisers HMS *Exeter*, HMS *Ajax*, and *HMS Achilles* and the German pocket battleship *Admiral Graf Spee*—the encounter actually took place off the coast of Uruguay.

RIVER PLATE FOOTBALL CLUB. In Spanish, Club Atlético River Plate (CARP)—not Club Atlético Río de la Plata. Founded in 1901, it is the leading professional soccer club in the country in terms of championships won, games won (with least defeats, most goals scored, and least conceded), and most points accumulated. This record partly explains its nickname, "Los Millonarios" (the Millionaires), due to an ability to finance expensive transfers. The club is the fierce rival of **Boca Juniors** (CABJ). Both clubs were originally based in **La Boca**; the "River" stadium is now located in the Belgrano, an upper-middle-class district of the city of **Buenos Aires**. Boca fans know River Plate as "Las Gallinas" (the Chickens). Another nickname,

"La Máquina" (the Machine), derives from its capacity to manufacture victories. Independiente, Racing Club, and San Lorenzo de Almagro are the other premier teams.

The club has had its ups and downs but is once again at the top of its game. In addition to national awards, the club has won more regional international contests than any other Argentine team, recognized by the South American Football Confederation as the best in the region, and by the International Federation of Association Football (FIFA) as the ninth best club in the world in 2000. The main stadium has a capacity of 76,000, the biggest in Argentina, and the club an active fan base of around 8,700,000. Recent star players include Martín Demechelis, Radamel Falcao, Matias Kranevitter, Ángel Labruna, Erik Lamela, Javier Mascherano, and Daniel Passarella. The main strip consists of a white shirt emblazoned with a broad red diagonal stripe, black shorts, and white socks.

ROCA, JULIO ARGENTINO (1843–1914). General, statesman, and a key political figure from the 1880s until his death; Roca is one of only three elected presidents to serve two complete terms (1880–1886, 1898–1904), the others being **Carlos Saúl Menem** and **Cristina Fernández de Kirchner**, though in his case, as per the **Constitution of 1853**, he could not stand for immediate reelection, unlike the other two.

A native of **Tucumán**, Roca was a career soldier who cut his teeth in the civil wars of the middle third of the 19th century, during the struggle for **national organization**, and the **War of the Triple Alliance** against **Paraguay**, though he is best remembered for the **Conquest of the Desert**, a victory that propelled him into the presidency in 1880. On being elected president, the authority of Roca was immediately challenged by opponents in the province of **Buenos Aires** who refused to accept the results of the election. The rebellion was swiftly put down, resulting in the **federalization of the City of Buenos Aires**, which thereupon became exclusively the national capital—hitherto it has served as the seat of both the federal and provincial governments. This event and date is generally accepted as marking the end of the phase of national consolidation and the inauguration of a political and economic model that survived for more than a generation and resulted in the emergence of the country as it now exists. Associated with the Generación del Ochenta (the **Generation of the 1880s**), of which Roca, nicknamed the Fox (El Zorro), was the principal example and key proponent, this model was based on "guided" democracy and an open **economy**.

The political arrangement, an alliance of regional oligarchies that delivered "sound administration" and working majorities in **Congress**, was predicated on rotation in office and a distribution of power—and of the fruits of growth. In curbing the influence of Buenos Aires and ensuring the representation of the interior provinces, the system brought an end to the intermittent civil conflict that had defined the country since the fall of **Juan Manuel de Rosas**. The success of the model was in no small part due to the concurrent boom in exports and a massive inflow of immigrants and foreign investment. The period was also characterized by a broad adhesion to what would later be described as orthodox economics—a commitment to (or quest for) monetary stability, largely free trade, and a relatively small state. Luck and policy delivered the Belle Epoque of rapid growth and political order, subsequently promoted as the historic example (or laboratory) on which the economics of the **Convertibility Plan** of the 1990s were founded. Accepting the critical importance of the external environment, not least the huge expansion in trade and finance, the political and economic gains of the project of the 1880s were also a function of Roca's desert campaigns (1879–1881), which doubled the effective size of the country by securing and opening up eastern **Patagonia** and largely defining the frontier with **Chile**.

One of the dominant political figures of the age, and the most influential advocate of the conservative or oligarchic republic (*república conservadora*), Roca was frequently called upon to defend the project, as in 1890, when default triggered a panic that threatened to bring down the whole global financial order—the **Baring Crisis**—and in the early years of the 20th century, when the political system was challenged from within and without. On such occasions, he acted with vigor and a keen preference to manage change from inside the system in order to preempt clamor for radical political and social reform that would destroy the model. *See also* AGRICULTURAL COLONIZATION; AGRICULTURE; ECONOMIC CRISES; FOREIGN DEBT/FOREIGN INVESTMENT; FOREIGN TRADE; IMMIGRATION.

ROCA–RUNCIMAN PACT (1933). Trade agreement that has been highly controversial ever since it was signed by Argentina and **Great Britain**. Although the treaty was vital to protect a key export market in an age of protectionism, its many Argentine critics complain of too many concessions to the British.

In exchange for continued access to British markets for **meat** and **grain**, Buenos Aires agreed to favorable treatment for British investments in public services, to facilitate the sale of British goods in Argentina (even against competition from possible domestic suppliers), to assure preferential use of foreign exchange earnings for remittances to Britain, and to guarantee a monopoly of meat exports for foreign-owned *frigoríficos*.

Harsh as the Argentine commitments to Britain appear, the many opponents of the Roca–Runciman Pact missed three points. First is that, while critics are convinced that the deal exclusively benefited the landowning class and was done by what they call *el gobierno de las vacas*, the government of the day (known as the **Concordancia**) was a coalition of *antipersonalista* Radicals, old-time Conservatives of the **Partido Demócrata Nacional**

(PDN), and the Independent Socialists, who represented a fairly broad spectrum of society. Second, since Argentina depended on **foreign trade** and lacked alternative markets for meat and grain exports, in the short term the government had no leverage in the negotiations and little choice but to accept British terms. Third, a much ignored crucial clause in the treaty provided for the so-called Roca Funding Loan, which was secured through a government bond offering that contributed to the success of the **Plan de Acción Económica**, which restored order to the financial system, stabilized the **economy**, and facilitated recovery—in part thought noninflationary public expenditure.

The Roca–Runciman Pact lifted a threat to the entire economy and not just the interests of big landowners. Nevertheless, its terms helped generate a nationalist reaction that was to shape the politics and economics of the next decade. *See also* AGRICULTURE; COMMODITIES; FOREIGN DEBT/ FOREIGN INVESTMENT; MIRANDA–EADY AGREEMENT; PRE-BISCH, RAÚL (1901–1986).

RODRIGAZO. Stabilization package introduced on 4 June 1975 in a last-ditch effort to regain control of the **economy** and save the presidency of **Isabel Perón**. Applied without warning by Mrs. Perón's third minister of economy, **Celestino Rodrigo**, the package aimed to correct record fiscal and external trade deficits. The immediate background to Rodrigo's shock therapy was the unraveling of the Social Pact, a tripartite agreement reached in 1973 by the government, **trade unions** represented by the **Confederación General del Trabajo** (CGT), and the then favored pro-Peronist business organization the **Confederación General Económica** (CGE). The pact attempted to promote economic restructuring through state-directed growth; essential elements included a project to raise the share of wages in national income to between 40 and 50 percent and a freeze of wages and prices for two years. It was opposed by businesses not represented by the CGE and by workers who objected to the two-year ban on any further wage negotiation. The return of inflation in 1974 occasioned demands for wage increases, to which the government acceded while trying to maintain the freeze on prices—firms responded by withholding products or selling on the black market, and closing factories. Aiming to eliminate such distortions, the Rodrigazo devalued the principal commercial rate of exchange by 160 percent; the financial rate was devalued by 100 percent; fuel, utility, and transport charges were hiked by between 100 and 180 percent; wages raised by 45 percent. The result was massive protest across the country; the CGT called for a two-day general strike at the end of June, the first ever against a Peronist administration. By the end of the year, the annualized rate of inflation was heading for 800 percent. The Isabel Perón administration collapsed amid economic and political chaos. *See also* DEVELOPMENTALISM/DE-VELOPMENTALIST; ECONOMIC CRISES; MILITARY COUP OF 1976; MINISTRY OF ECONOMY.

RODRIGO, CELESTINO (1915–1987). Minister of economy (June–July 1975) appointed by **Isabel Perón** on 2 June 1975, largely owing to his close association with the all-powerful minister of social welfare, **José López Rega**. Within 48 hours of taking office, he introduced a raft of measures aimed at tackling inflation through shock therapy.

Rodrigo first increased the air fares of state-owned **Aerolíneas Argenti-nas**. This left many passengers stranded in the country's airports, as they were to be charged the increase on tickets that had been purchased earlier before being allowed to board their flights. This measure was followed by a package of economic policies that, together with their immediate aftermath, became known as the **Rodrigazo**. The main measures were massive exchange devaluations and eye-watering hikes in transport and utility charges, coupled with comparatively modest adjustments in wages and salaries. As a result, real wages (i.e., the purchasing power of salaries) fell as prices continued their relentless rise.

Blindsided by the draconian policies, the normally supportive **Confederación General del Trabajo** (CGT) called a general strike, the first called against a Peronist government. With Mrs. Perón having first conceded to the unions' demand for a 100 to 150 percent mandatory wage hike, and then withdrawing the offer, the CGT turned its ire toward López Rega and his cronies. The minister of social welfare was forced out of office, and the president removed Rodrigo on 17 July 1975. *See also* MINISTRY OF ECONOMY; MINISTRY OF SOCIAL DEVELOPMENT.

RODRÍGUEZ SAÁ, ADOLFO (1947–). Lawyer and member of the **Parti-do Justicialista** (PJ) from his youth; sometime national deputy and national senator, he was elected to five consecutive terms as governor of **San Luis** between 1983 and 2001; seven-day president of the republic during the two-week period of crisis following the resignation of **Fernando de la Rúa** on 20 December 2001—having been elected to serve for 90 days on 23 December 2001, he resigned on 30 December.

Rodríguez Saá traces his ancestry from indigenous chieftains of **Cuyo**, creole patriots, and European immigrants. Viewed as a modernizing governor of San Luis—during his terms of office, there was substantial investment in manufacturing, public works, and social services—he associated with the reformist wing of the PJ. When selected interim president, Rodríguez Saá had been charged with bringing order to the economy and establishing rules for the holding of new presidential elections. During his brief presidency, the county defaulted on the national debt—the largest default in international financial history—abandoned peso–US dollar convertibility, and began the managed depreciation of the peso. However, when it transpired that he had ambitions to serve out the balance of De la Rúa's term—and possibly more—key PJ provincial governors who harbored presidential ambitions of their own withdrew their support. He had little choice but to resign. Standing in the **presidential election of 2003**, according to early opinion polls he was initially the front-runner. However, scandals intervened and he came in third in the first round of the elections, after **Carlos Saúl Menem** and **Néstor Kirchner**. He stood again in the **presidential election of 2015**, when he came in sixth in the first round. History will remember him principally as one of five presidents to have held office between 20 December 2001 and 2 January 2002 and the one who announced that the country would default on the debt in his inaugural address to **Congress**—"Nos vamos al default"—to resounding cheers and cries of "Viva Perón!" from around the chamber. *See also* ECONOMIC CRISES; ECONOMY; FOREIGN DEBT/FOREIGN INVESTMENT; INDUSTRY.

ROJAS, ISAAC FRANCISCO (1903–1993). Provisional vice president of Argentina (1955–1958). Having joined the navy in 1920, he had numerous postings and in 1938 was sent to **Great Britain** to observe the construction of two warships purchased by Argentina. He was naval attaché in **Brazil** from 1950 to 1952 and then benefited from the forced retirement of various admirals and was named admiral at a comparatively young age.

Following the **military coup of 1955**, Rojas became vice president, serving under provisional presidents **Eduardo Lonardi** and **Pedro Eugenio Aramburu**. When the latter took office in a palace coup, the navy was placed on an equal basis with the army in the power structure. The Consejo Militar Revolucionario was created, which comprised the president, the vice president, and ministers representing all three armed forces. Yet the fact remained that Aramburu and Rojas did not get on.

Rojas played a part in dealing with the botched countercoup by Peronist **military** officers in June 1956. The government was aware that a conspiracy was afoot, and though Aramburu was away from **Buenos Aires** he had already left three legal instruments ready to scotch the rebellion: they were decrees imposing a state of siege and martial law and the creation of military tribunals to deal with the conspirators. Rojas, who had also signed the decrees, received them from the hands of **Francisco Manrique** (the head of the Casa Militar) and put them into effect under orders from Aramburu. Sentencing by the military tribunals resulted in the notorious **executions of June 1956**, which would permanently taint the **Revolución Libertadora** and widen the abyss in an already fractured society.

Following the return of civilian rule with the **presidential election of 1958**, Rojas intended to keep a close watch on **Arturo Frondizi**, on the lookout for even the smallest symptom of subversive activity in politics, **trade unions**, and universities. He therefore backed attempts to overthrow Frondizi and was detained on Martín García Island during the internal military conflict that ensued in the presidency of **José María Guido**. In later years, Rojas took a keen interest in issues concerning Argentina's international borders, for example, hydroelectric plants on the **Paraná** River and the Beagle Channel. He also collected documents and narrated his experiences in order to exalt the memory of the Revolución Libertadora, thereby providing historians and researchers with a veritable treasure trove. *See also* BEAGLE CHANNEL DISPUTE; ITAIPÚ DAM; YACYRETÁ-APIPÉ.

ROSARIO. Located in the southeast of the province of **Santa Fe**, it is the third most important city in the republic, after **Buenos Aires** and **Córdoba**— for much of the 19th and 20th centuries, it was second only to Buenos Aires and remains the second most important port complex after the capital. It is a major transport hub for the interior, located on the **Paraná** River around 190 miles (c. 300 kilometers) northwest of Buenos Aires, navigable by large seagoing vessels, and an important industrial center. The current population is around 1,400,000.

Founded in in the late 17th century, though subject to Indian attacks, the city grew steadily in the 18th. Its modern economic history dates from the 1850s due to a combination of locational and political factors. In 1852, in the final days of the hegemony of **Juan Manuel de Rosas**, the city was virtually leveled by Buenos Aires forces, defending its claim to monopolize the **foreign trade** of the **Argentine Confederation**. As reconstruction commenced, Rosario was granted city status and, when the province of Buenos Aires seceded, was declared the official port of the Confederation, open to vessels of all flags. The first bank was set up in 1854, and a "national" newspaper began publication. However, the key to future growth was the inauguration of the **Central Argentine Railway** (CAR) in 1863, a London-registered company guaranteed by the Confederation government and endowed with a large land grant, modeled on the system then being rolled out in the **United States**. By the mid-1880s, Rosario stood at the head of an extensive network of trunk lines serving the north and northwest and would soon be connected by rail to Buenos Aires. Such was the rapid expansion of the city, and continuing antagonism in interior provinces to the pretentions of Buenos Aires, that there were proposals in the late 1860s and mid-1870s to name the city the national capital.

Immigration and **agricultural colonization** in the interior, notably in the provinces of Santa Fe and Córdoba, facilitated further expansion. In the early 1920s, around half the population of the city was foreign born, and even today approximately two-thirds of Argentine **grain** exports continue to be channeled through Rosario, although the national significance of the docks began to decline after 1900 as other ports developed—for example, **Bahía Blanca**. Despite such challenges, the city prospered, benefiting from urban beautification in the early 20th century and the modernization of the docks and expansion of the banking sector. Some of the first grain elevators erected in the country were built at Rosario. Recent growth has been more focused on manufacturing, again partly dependent on its status as a regional transport hub, and the industrialization drive associated with the first presidency of **Juan Domingo Perón** in the 1940s. While exports and processing of **commodities** continue, the second half of the 20th century witnessed the growth of modern manufacturing, including the opening of plants by such multinationals as Petrobrás (the Brazilian state oil corporation), General Motors, and Unilever.

Rosario has played a role in the political history of the republic. In 1812, the national flag was first unfurled there by **Manuel Belgrano**—the city is home to the national flag monument and museum (Monumento Histórico Nacional a la Bandera), designed by **Alejandro Bustillo** and opened in 1957. The city also acquired a reputation for radicalism with the inflow of migrants and the development of a large working class and prosperous middle class. In 1905, the city was at the center of the revolution headed by **Leandro N. Alem**, sponsored by the **Unión Cívica Radical** (UCR), and would later go on to support **Hipólito Yrigogen** in the **presidential election of 1916**. In the 1930s, political and workers groups in the city organized against the renewal of the operating contract that had been awarded to the French-owned company that had built much of the port, which was declared illegal. Rosario dockworkers had acquired a reputation for militancy, and the protest was in part directed at the politics and economics of the **Concordancia**. Continuing protest resulted in the nationalization of the port in 1942 during the doomed presidency of **Ramón S. Castillo**. In 1969, students and workers protested against the austerity policies of the de facto government of General **Juan Carlos Onganía**, on a scale that approached that of the **Cordobazo**. The Rosariazo was on a smaller scale, though no less violently repressed, and had a similar impact on the military mind, which reflected the treatment of the city after the **military coup of 1976**.

Economic crises of the early 21st century, following the **privatization** of **state-owned enterprises** in the 1990s, triggered economic decline and some of the highest rates of open, urban unemployment in the country. Despite recent recovery and a dramatic decline in poverty levels, social deprivation remains: the city has one of the worst crime rates and highest murder rates in the republic, much of it drug related and focused on the *villas miseria*. These areas have been targeted by the municipal, provincial, and national authorities—and subject to a combination of social programs and police action. The municipal authorities have attempted to combat this image by redeveloping the historic district (which is well provided with Belle Epoque architecture), pedestrianizing streets, and promoting the city as a cultural and sporting center. Arguably, the city's most famous sons are **Ernesto "Che" Guevara** and **Lionel Messi**. *See also* AGRICULTURE; BUENOS AYRES & ROSARIO RAILWAY COMPANY (BA&R); FOREIGN TRADE; INDUSTRY; TRADE UNIONS; TRANSPORTATION.

ROSAS, JUAN MANUEL DE (1793–1877). *Estanciero*, **caudillo**, businessman, and **military** strongman who was twice acclaimed governor and captain general of the province of **Buenos Aires** (1829–1833 and 1835–1852). As autonomous interior provinces had conferred on the governor of Buenos Aires the right to negotiate with foreign powers, Rosas was titular head of the state that would become Argentina.

To his supporters, he was the Restorer of the Laws (Restaurador de la Leyes), a title granted in 1829 on his appointment as governor with extraordinary powers; to his opponents, he was the Bloody Tyrant (or Tiger) of the **Pampas**. Rosas remains a controversial figure, lending his name to an era in Argentine history that he dominated and of which he became a symbol. With an ability to mobilize **gauchos** and *peones*, largely due to his personality, and enthuse the urban poor—even slaves—he is seen by some as the first in a line of populists that includes **Hipólito Yrigoyen** and **Juan Domingo Perón**. Owner of extensive herds and estates, and a pioneering *saladerista*, Rosas came to epitomize the ruling class of the province of Buenos Aires, whose interests he promoted. Brought up on one of the family estates close to the **Salado River**, he was acutely aware of the threat posed by nomadic Indians of the pampas. Even before being appointed governor, he led irregular forces in advancing and securing the frontier by means of establishing forts and seeking alliances with friendly tribes, a strategy that he would institutionalize when in office. In the early 1830s, between terms as governor, he led a military campaign in the south of the province that prefigured the **Conquest of the Desert** (or marked its opening phase), securing much of the modern frontier of the province.

A **Federalist**, opposed to the **Unitarian** project of **national organization**, which he regarded as premature and ill suited to the age and the country, he fought in the interior of Buenos Aires and neighboring provinces to advance the Federalist cause, particularly in the years following the collapse of the presidency of **Bernardino Rivadavia** in 1827. Rosas's acclamation as governor two years later marked a major setback for the Unitarian project. However, defending the federal cause did not necessarily mean supporting Federalists in the interior. Rather, Rosas actively undermined rival caudillos, for example, **Juan Facundo Quiroga**, who threatened his authority and the hegemony of Buenos Aires. Noncompliant Federalist interior governors suffered almost as much at his hands as Unitarians. Rosas ruled the province and the interior through a mix of fear and the threat of armed intervention: he may have been the first to institutionalize terror as a mechanism of government. The *mazorca*, a political organization initially set up by supporters, came to function as an informal branch of the state, responsible for whipping up popular support and terrorizing those opposed to Rosas. Some of the actions of the *mazorca* prefigured that of the death squads of the **Triple A** around a century and a half later, namely kidnapping and torture. After the fall of Rosas, leading figures in the organization were brought before the courts, in procedures similar to those instituted in the 1980s after the collapse of the regime of the **Proceso de Reorganización Nacional** installed after the **military coup of 1976**. The Rosas system bore many of the hallmarks of a totalitarian regime. There were orchestrated demonstrations of public support. Opponents were castigated as enemies of the state. Publications were monitored and controlled. The cult of personality was promoted, with all being encouraged—or feeling compelled—to wear red ribbons and headbands, the colors of the regime, and mouth the slogans of the day, the most prominent being "Federation or Death" and "Death to the Savage Unitarians," which appeared on public documents and proclamations.

Buenos Aires prospered under Rosas. His campaigns to sustain the regime were mainly conducted outside the province: there was relative peace in the province, but war was exported to the interior and to **Uruguay**. Rosas may have ended anarchy in the province but not in the region. Campaigns on the frontier added productive new land. Tariff protection in 1835 is credited with supporting manufacturing, though the reality may simply have been to extract more resources from the interior. Defending the claims of Buenos Aires to control river navigation on the **Paraná**, Rosas is also credited with protecting national interests. He confronted Brazilian aspirations to hegemony in the region. He resisted the 1838–1840 French blockade and 1845–1847 Anglo-French blockade, events that secured his place in the nationalist historiography, despite that fact that Rosas generally enjoyed good relations with the British merchant community and that British interests flourished during his rule. When Rosas was overthrown in 1852, he was granted safe passage on a Royal Navy vessel and settled near Southampton, where he lived in relative obscurity for another 25 years. He was buried in the municipal cemetery in Southampton. After several aborted attempts, Rosas's remains were transferred to Argentina in 1989 during the presidency of **Carlos Saúl Menem**. *See also* AGRICULTURE; CATTLE; COMMODITIES; ECONOMY; FOREIGN TRADE; SHEEP; WOOL.

RUCCI, JOSÉ IGNACIO (1924–1973). Politician and **trade union** leader. A weapons factory worker, Rucci got involved in the Unión Obrera Metalúrgica (UOM); he progressed rapidly inside the union's hierarchy and in 1960 became press secretary of the UOM, sitting on its board alongside **Augusto Vandor** and **Lorenzo Miguel**.

Rucci opposed both the confrontational and pragmatic stances of union leaders toward the **Revolución Argentina** military regime—that is, the **Confederación General del Trabajo de los Argentinos** (CGTA), formed by **Raimundo Ongaro**, which in May 1968 had separated from the **Confederación General del Trabajo** (CGT), the main organization. Yet the views held by Rucci did not prevent his being elected secretary general of the CGT in July 1970.

Notwithstanding his opposition to the political strategy of de facto president **Alejandro Agustín Lanusse**, who had taken power in March 1971, Rucci kept private contacts with the regime. In April 1971, he hosted Lanusse at a summit with the CGT, urging him to begin negotiations with **Juan Domingo Perón** and other political leaders and to facilitate the return of the remains of **Eva Perón**. However, he privately doubted that the aging Perón would return in time to run again for office and pondered an option by which Lanusse would call elections and the CGT would back an amenable candidate from the armed forces. In the end, Lanusse called elections for March 1973, in which the Peronists were allowed to run.

Following the victory of the **Frente Justicialista de Liberación** (FREJU-LI), Rucci became isolated within the Peronist movement. He was assassinated by the **Montoneros** two days after the **presidential election of September 1973**, which had returned Perón to power. The slain CGT leader was shot 23 times, which led him to being gruesomely nicknamed "Traviata" after a brand of crackers known for having 23 holes punched through them.

RUCKAUF, CARLOS FEDERICO (1944–). Lifelong Peronist and career politician elected to various posts, including the national vice presidency and governorship of the province of **Buenos Aires**, two of the most powerful political positions in the country. Ruckauf studied at the **University of Buenos Aires** (UBA), where he was active in student politics and later the labor movement. His contacts in the **trade unions** led to an appointment in the labor division of the judiciary when the **military** returned to the barracks in 1973 and subsequently to his appointment as minister of labor in the administration of President **Isabel Perón** in 1974. As minister, he was joint signatory of a decree that, in effect, granted a blanket amnesty to military personnel engaged in action against terrorists. The campaign—the **War to Annihilate Subversion**—has since been seen as marking the beginning of the **Dirty War**. The decree was viewed by the high command as giving them carte blanche, leading inexorably to the **military coup of 1976** and the **Proceso de**

Reorganización Nacional. This earlier association with the military probably explains why he survived—he was said to have become a protégé of Admiral **Emilio Massera**, one of the leaders of the coup.

The return of democracy in 1983 found Ruckauf a well-established figure in the **Partido Justicialista** (PJ); he was chosen to head the branch of the party in the city of **Buenos Aires**. He was elected to the lower house of **Congress**, the Chamber of Deputies, in the midterm **congressional elections of 1987** and returned to the chamber after a stint in the diplomatic service following the midterm **congressional elections of 1991**. By this time, Ruckauf had already caught the eye of sitting PJ president **Carlos Saúl Menem**, who first appointed him minister of interior and then chose him as his running mate in the **presidential election of 1995**. The Menem–Ruckauf formula triumphed, taking almost 50 percent of the vote to the 30 percent gained by the **José Octavio Bordón–Carlos "Chacho" Álvarez** ticket. The vice presidency proved a stepping-stone to becoming governor of the province of Buenos Aires. It was a mixed blessing as the country was already beset by a profound economic crisis as the **Convertibility Plan** unraveled. To cope with the province's financial crisis, Ruckauf hit upon the expedient of issuing *patacones*, a provincial currency. As only the federal authorities were authorized to print money, technically *patacones* were Buenos Aires provincial bonds or promissory notes that could be used to settle tax and debt payments due the province. Modeled on peso notes printed by the **Banco Central de la República Argentina** (BCRA) yet clearly issued by the province, the Buenos Aires *patacón* circulated as **currency**. Although not convertible into **United States** dollars on demand like the peso, Buenos Aires notes were widely accepted in the province, city, and beyond, regarded as more secure than similar promissory notes issues by other jurisdictions.

Appointed minister of foreign relations by interim president **Eduardo Duhalde** in 2002, Ruckauf's political star declined subsequently. He identified with the anti-Kirchner wing of the PJ. From various quarters, there were demands for his political rights to be withdrawn, which would have barred him from standing for election and holding official appointments. Yet he managed to return to the Chamber of Deputies in the midterm **congressional elections of 2003**, serving until 2007. Today he keeps a low profile, remembered for his association with the military in the mid-1970s and for the doomed experiment of issuing a provincial "currency." *See also* ECONOMIC CRISES; KIRCHNER, CRISTINA ELISABET FERNÁNDEZ DE (1953–); KIRCHNER, NÉSTOR CARLOS (1950–2010); MINISTRY OF FOREIGN RELATIONS AND RELIGION; MINISTRY OF INTERIOR, PUBLIC WORKS, AND HOUSING; MINISTRY OF LABOR; RICO, ALDO (1943–).

S

SAADI, VICENTE LEONIDAS (1913–1988). Peronist politician; patriarch of a family of Syrian-Lebanese origin that has dominated politics in the province of **Catamarca** since the 1940s; a modern-day political **caudillo**. Initially allied with the **Unión Cívica Radical** (UCR), he switched allegiance to **populist** leader **Juan Domingo Perón** in 1945, the first of several movements between parties and across the political spectrum.

Saadi was elected national senator in 1946, serving for three years until elected as governor of Catamarca for the **Partido Peronista** (PP) in 1949. Amid allegations of **corruption** in the administration of the province, President Perón ordered his removal from the post after four months. Saadi was subsequently expelled from the PP, and served time in prison. He returned to the National Senate for the Peronist-dominated **Frente Justicialista de Liberación** (FREJULI) in 1973, serving there until the **military coup of 1976**. By this stage, Saadi had become a leading supporter of the far-left **Montoneros**: he set up the Intransigencia y Movilización faction and was a patron of future defense minister **Nilda Garré**.

When the armed forces retreated to the barracks in 1983, Saadi abandoned his earlier support for left-wing Peronists and was elected vice president of the **Partido Justicialista** (PJ). In that capacity, he worked closely with President Elect **Raúl Alfonsín**, the leader of the UCR, during the transition to democracy. In the **congressional elections of 1983**, Saadi was once again elected to the National Senate, where he led the PJ—the party had 21 seats to the 18 of the UCR. Four years later, he resigned from the Senate—a move that would enable his son successfully to contest the seat—to stand for the governorship of Catamarca. He was returned as governor in late 1987 but died seven months into his mandate. *See also* MINISTRY OF DEFENSE.

SAAVEDRA, CORNELIO (1759–1829). Statesman and significant **military** and political figure of the **independence** period; member of the creole landowning, merchant aristocracy. Born in the then Viceroyalty of **Peru**, he and his family moved to **Buenos Aires** when he was around eight years old—his father was from a prominent city family.

Educated at the Real Colegio de San Carlos, which was patronized by the local elite, he married his first cousin María Francisca Cabrera y Saavedra in 1788. Recently widowed, she brought a considerable fortune to the marriage. Ten years later, on the death of María Francisca, Cornelio married María Saturnina Bárbara de Otárola de Ribero; the second marriage brought further connections with the dominant commercial and administrative elite. Such family links ensured that Cornelio soon assumed a prominent role in the Buenos Aires *cabildo*, the city council. A magistrate before the end of the century, he was elected deputy mayor in 1801, a position that entailed the regulation of grain supplies and prices in the city. Already a prominent member of the council, after initial hesitation he helped organize resistance to the **British invasions** of 1806 and 1807, being elected leader of the **Patricios**, a local regiment that would play a prominent role in expelling the British and in the struggle for independence after the **May Revolution of 1810**. As head of the Patricios, he was instrumental in securing the position of Viceroy **Santiago de Liniers**, who led the military and naval campaign against the British and whose position had been threatened by the Spanish merchant community in early 1809.

Saavedra's political and military career after 1809 reflected the disputes and disagreements surrounding efforts to forge the new nation. In the **Cabildo Abierto** of 1810, he favored a conservative approach to independence, possibly an arrangement approximating "home rule" within the existing imperial order, perhaps based on federal principles that foreshadowed the future **Federalist** stance. He was elected president of the First Junta, charged with governing the country and considering its future. His approach was challenged by radicals such as **Mariano Moreno** and **Juan Martín de Pueyrredón**, who sought immediate independence. In 1811, when patriotic forces in the far north were defeated by royalist forces dispatched from Peru, Saavedra headed for **Salta** to take command and reorganize the army. While there, news came of a change of government in Buenos Aires and his dismissal as president of the junta and head of the army. Various charges were made against Saavedra: that he had been lukewarm in opposing the British— possibly being prepared to treat with them—and in supporting the formation of the republic. Charges against him multiplied as Moreno and his associates gained the upper hand in Buenos Aires, forcing Saavedra into exile in **Chile** in 1814. By 1818, all charges against him had been dropped and full military rank and honors restored. His return to Buenos Aires in 1819 was, however, short lived. Charges of disloyalty, possibly involving dealings with **Spain**, resurfaced. By 1820, he was in exile again in Montevideo. Following a general pardon in 1821, Saavedra returned to Buenos Aires, again with his rank and honors reinstated. Never completely absent from public life, he lived privately until his death. Gradually, his services to the state and the military were recognized. He is now regarded as a hero of the independence period, if not a republican by conviction.

SAAVEDRA LAMAS, CARLOS (1878–1959). Statesman, author, diplomat, and international jurist; member of an oligarchic family, descended from **Cornelio Saavedra**, he married a daughter of President **Roque Sáenz Peña**. He read law at the **University of Buenos Aires** (UBA)—he was rector of the university between 1941 and 1943, having taught constitutional law, labor law, and political economy there. He served two terms as a national deputy, from 1908 to 1912 representing the city of **Buenos Aires** and between 1912 and 1915 the province. His first ministerial post was as minister of justice and public instruction (1915–1916) during the presidency of **Victorino de la Plaza**, the second as minister of foreign affairs (1932–1938) in the cabinet of **Concordancia** president **Agustín P. Justo**. Although a prolific writer and active in public life through the 1940s and early 1950s—he opposed the presidential campaign of **Juan Domingo Perón**—today he is best remembered as the first Argentine Nobel laureate, being awarded the 1936 Peace Prize for his efforts to end the bloody **Chaco War** between **Bolivia** and **Paraguay**. Only five Argentines have been awarded Nobel Prizes. *See also* MINISTRY OF FOREIGN RELATIONS AND RELIGION.

SÁBATO, ERNESTO (1911–2011). Author, scientist, distinguished polymath, and public intellectual; possibly most known abroad for chairing the truth-commission-style inquiry into "disappearances" during the **Proceso de Reorganización Nacional**. He chaired the **Comisión Nacional sobre la Disaparición de Personas** (CONADEP), which delivered the report *Nunca Más*, first published in 1984.

Before being appointed to head CONADEP, Sábato had already acquired national eminence as a physicist—he had read physics and obtained a doctorate in the subject in 1938 at the National University in **La Plata**—and as a writer and commentator. He traveled extensively as a researcher and thinker, including in France, where he worked at the Institut Curie, and in the Soviet Union and the **United States**, where he was based at the Massachusetts Institute of Technology. Initially a committed communist, he became disillusioned with Stalinism after studying in Moscow. Finding his interests moving away from science, he developed a new career as a novelist and essayist; he was a prolific contributor to the important literary magazine *Sur*. His work, which was widely translated, drew him to the attention of such peers as Carlos Fuentes, Gabriel García Marquéz, and Mario Vargas Llosa. He was a key figure in the boom in Latin American literature of the 1960s.

Having studies and worked in Europe and the United States, he returned to Argentina in the early 1940s. It was at this point that his career as a writer took off. He became a respected commentator on social and political issues of the day—he was removed from a position at the University of La Plata due to opposition to President **Juan Domingo Perón**. Some of his early essays critical of the regime were published after the ouster of Perón by the **military coup of 1955**. He was noted for the metaphysical style of his novels, which reflected on the counterpoint of civilization and barbarism, and on isolation and loneliness. His work exuded a strong sense of moral purpose. Such writing had a particular resonance as the country descended into the terror of the years around the **military coup of 1976**. He became a commentator on, and former of public opinion about, Argentine reality. His training as a scientist, though more his sense of moral purpose and the defense of **human rights** in his writing, explain the invitation by President **Raúl Alfonsín** to chair CONADEP in 1983 with a brief to examine abuses committed during the first presidency of the Proceso, that of General **Jorge Rafael Videla**.

Sábato's acclaimed novels include *El túnel* (The Tunnel) (1948), *Sobre héroes y tumbas* (Heroes and Tombs) (1961), *Tres aproximaciones a la litertura de nuestro tiempo* (Three Takes on Contemporary Literature) (1974), *Antes del fin* (Before the End) (1998), and *La Resistencia* (Resistance) (2000). His contributions to Spanish literature, as well as his work in the field of human rights, have been recognized internationally, notably in France, Italy, and **Spain**. *See also* DESAPARECIDOS; DIRTY WAR; DISPOSICIÓN FINAL; ESCUELA SUPERIOR DE MECÁNICA DE LA ARMADA (ESMA); MILITARY JUNTAS, TRIALS OF THE; PRESIDENTIAL ELECTION OF 1983; UNIVERSIDAD NACIONAL DE LA PLATA (UNLP); WAR TO ANNIHILATE SUBVERSION.

SÁENZ PEÑA, LUIS (1822–1907). Lawyer and constitutional president (1892–1895) who resigned before the end of his term, being succeeded by Vice President **José Evaristo Uriburu**. He was the father of the more famous **Roque Sáenz Peña**. He served various times as a national deputy and senator. Beginning his presidency in the aftermath of the **Baring Crisis**, he was beset by political and economic problems, notably revolution orchestrated by the emergent **Unión Cívica Radical** (UCR). Under pressure from the conservative old guard, particularly strongman **Julio A. Roca**, to restore order, his administration was characterized by indecision; some doubted his capacity and competence. Faced by the resignation of his whole cabinet in 1895, he had little option but to resign himself. The tumultuous years of his time in office indicated that the old, oligarchic order was being challenged by popular forces. While many argued that the old system of controlled politics could be forcibly defended, other elite factions favored accommodation with the emergent middle and urban working classes, paving the way for the electoral reform introduced by his son in 1912, the **Sáenz Peña Law**. *See also* ANARCHO-SYNDICALISM; ECONOMIC CRISES; FOREIGN DEBT/FOREIGN INVESTMENT; INDUSTRY; POLITICAL PARTIES; TRADE UNIONS.

SÁENZ PEÑA, ROQUE (1851–1914). Lawyer, statesman, and diplomat; son of **Luis Sáenz Peña**. Constitutional president of the Republic elected in 1910, he died in office and was succeeded by **Victorino de la Plaza**. On the modernizing wing of the conservative Partido Autonomista Nacional (PAN), which administered the country from the 1880s to 1916, he is remembered as a progressive, promoting the electoral law that bears his name, the **Sáenz Peña Law**, enacted in 1912.

His baptismal name, Roque José Antonio del Sagrado Corazón de Jesús Sáenz Peña, suggests a traditional and conservative background; his family had been supporters of **Juan Manuel de Rosas**, sometime governor and **caudillo** of the province of **Buenos Aires**. In his twenties, he served as a deputy in the Buenos Aires provincial legislature. With the outbreak of the **War of the Pacific**, he resigned his seat and quietly left the country, volunteering to serve in the Peruvian army. He was wounded and taken prisoner; on release, he returned to Argentina and entered the diplomatic service, representing his country as ambassador in **Uruguay** and at various international congresses, as well as traveling extensively in Europe. A convinced internationalist, he viewed Pan-Americanism as a **United States** bid for hegemony in the Americas, a view that resonated among his generation and helped to shape the independent stance manifest in Argentine foreign policy for the rest of the century and well beyond.

As the 1892 elections approached, the reformers chose the young Sáenz Peña as presidential candidate: to finesse this move, PAN oligarchs selected Luis Sáenz Peña as their nominee. The son withdrew, and the father went on to win the presidency. Reconciled with the PAN, he was associated with the anti-Roca wing of the party, opposed to the authoritarian stance of the general and twice president **Julio A. Roca**, convinced that the PAN and the system associated with it had to be reformed. This conviction was strengthened by the **corruption** and chaos associated with the **Baring Crisis** of 1890 and the political turmoil that it had provoked, including the revolt organized by erstwhile associates of his father in the Partido Popular, **Leandro N. Alem**, **Aristóbulo del Valle**, and **Hipólito Yrigoyen**, future stalwarts of the **Unión Cívica Radical** (UCR). These sentiments underpinned his insistence on reform and efforts to ensure that the UCR participated in elections rather than abstain. He made approaches to Yrigoyen and convinced like-minded colleagues within the PAN of the need for change. And the country was changing, witnessed by rural unrest, epitomized by the **Cry of Alcorta** during Sáenz Peña's presidency, as well as agitation in urban areas by workers and professionals. His arguments presented reform or revolution as the alternatives confronting the country. His lasting legacy was the Sáenz Peña Law, which facilitated the fair and free elections that allowed Yrigoyen to assume the presidency in 1916. *See also* ANARCHO-SYNDICALISM; ECONOMIC CRISES; FOREIGN DEBT/FOREIGN INVESTMENT; INDUSTRY; POLITICAL PARTIES; REVOLUTION OF 1890; TRADE UNIONS.

SÁENZ PEÑA LAW. Enacted in 1912, this law is named after President **Roque Sáenz Peña**, who was its principal proponent. Some accounts erroneously state that the law introduced democracy to the country. It did not; the **Constitution of 1853** accorded all native-born males the right to vote. The franchise was not extended to **women** until the **Constitution of 1949**. The stated purpose of electoral reform in 1912 was to buttress the political system by promising voters *effective* representative democracy.

Almost unique for constitutions of the period, the 1853 Argentine constitution did not apply a literacy or property test to the right to vote. The 1912 law was designed to encourage broader participation in the electoral process, incorporating dissident groups that had abstained from elections or advocated revolution. The three key provisions of the law were the introduction of the secret ballot (previous voting had been "open"); allocation of one-third of seats in multiseat constituencies to the party coming in second in the poll, intended to promote competitive politics and strong two-party government; making voting compulsory, designed to foster a sense of citizenship and "ownership." Thus, the law promised an end to the fraud and **corruption** that had characterized elections up to that point, namely the system of oligarchic politics presided over by the Partido Autonomista Nacional (PAN), associated with the likes of President **Julio A. Roca**. That arrangement had been challenged by the **Revolution of 1890** and undermined by growing political abstentionism, especially by supporters of what would become the **Unión Cívica Radical** (UCR). Reform-minded members of the elite recognized that oligarchic politics was no longer an option given demographic and social changes triggered by mass **immigration** and rapid economic growth. The 1912 legislation was a compromise, a gradualist solution to problems posed by political exclusion and challenges to the existing order represented by a rapidly expanding middle class and an increasingly vociferous urban working class.

The Sáenz Peña Law is important because it succeeded in its immediate objective—there was a massive increase in voter participation in the first general election held after its passage, the **congressional** and **presidential elections of 1916**. The dramatic increase in turnout, and the result of the elections, which saw opposition groups gain power—notably, the UCR when **Hipólito Yrigoyen** was elected president—promised to deliver a structure that had greater stability because it was fairer and more representative. The law, and the new system that it promised, was flawed because it was essentially a political solution to social issues, which were barely addressed. It was also flawed because large sections of the population remained unrepresented. In addition to women, immigrants were unrepresented. In 1914, about one-third of the population was foreign born, with hardly 1 percent seeking naturalization and thus acquiring the right to vote. In the city of **Buenos Aires**, around 70 percent of workers were immigrants and so unenfranchised. Despite the optimism of reformers and the real promise of democratic consolidation, the limits of the gradualist approach were exposed by events such as the **Semana Trágica** and the **military coup of 1930**.

The Sáenz Peña Law might have delivered a political opening leading to the institutionalization of democracy and accountable, representative politics. The coup of 1930 marked the beginning of more than 50 years of institutional fragility; decades that witnessed alternating periods of democratic and authoritarian rule, the legacy of which still shapes Argentine society and politics. *See also* ANARCHO-SYNDICALISM; CONCORDANCIA; CONGRESSIONAL ELECTIONS OF 1912 AND 1913; CONGRESSIONAL ELECTIONS OF 1914; ECONOMIC CRISES; JUSTICIALISMO; PARTIDO SOCIALISTA (PS); POPULISM; TRADE UNIONS.

SAINT-JEAN, ALFREDO OSCAR (1926–1987). Penultimate de facto interim president of the **Proceso de Reorganización Nacional** that came to power with the **military coup of 1976**. Installed and removed in a palace coup, his presidency lasted barely two weeks in late June 1982. He took office when the **military** demanded the resignation of de facto president General **Leopoldo Fortunato Galtieri** as Argentine forces surrendered to the British expeditionary force at the end of the **Falklands War**, and he was in turn replaced by de facto president General **Reynaldo Bignone** when fellow officers fixed on Bignone as better placed to negotiate a return to the barracks. As minister of interior, Saint-Jean had taken a particularly hard line with mounting protests against the military junta in March 1982 organized by the **trade unions** and **political parties** as the regime was unraveling and before it sought to save itself by invading the **Falkland Islands**. *See also* CONFEDERACIÓN GENERAL DEL TRABAJO (CGT); DIRTY WAR; ECONOMIC CRISES; HUMAN RIGHTS; MINISTRY OF INTERIOR, PUBLIC WORKS, AND HOUSING; WAR TO ANNIHILATE SUBVERSION.

SALA, MILAGRO AMALIA ÁNGELA (1964–). A native of **Jujuy**, political activist, campaigner for indigenous rights, and head of a publicly funded national housing association (Organización Barrial Tupac Amaru) mainly charged with the construction of low-cost housing. Sometime deputy in the provincial legislature, Milagro Sala, as she is generally known, was elected on the ticket of the umbrella body representing local and indigenous associations, and to the parliament of the **Unión de Naciones Sudamericanas** (UNASUR) on the **Frente para la Victoria/Partido Justicialista** (FpV/PJ) slate.

The story of Milagro Sala reflects the sensitivity of charges of **human rights** abuses in the country following the **Proceso de Reorganización Nacional** and the exposure of cases of "disappearances," torture, and murder committed by agencies of the state. Sala was abandoned as an infant and brought up by a middle-class family. Around the age of 14, when she discovered that she had been adopted, she walked out of the home and took to living on the streets. For much of her teenage years during the Proceso, she led a precarious life, in and out of prison—by her own testimony, engaged in petty crime and drug dealing. Her capacity for organization and mobilization was manifest during time spent in jail. She promoted social events involving indigenous music and folk dancing, led hunger strikes, and campaigned against injustice and for prison reform. It was a formative experience that contributed to the development of a political career. She set up refuges for abandoned children and adopted many. In the 1990s, she was active in local grassroots organizations. It was about this time that she became involved with the Tupac Amaru, playing an active role in local protests as the country teetered on the edge of economic and political chaos with the collapse of the **Convertibility Plan**. She helped organize emergency food supplies for destitute children and assistance with basic **education**. By the early 21st century, headed by Sala, Tupac Amaru was probably one of the principal campaign groups in the region lobbying for the rights of minorities—**women**, gays, and indigenous communities—especially in such areas as the provision of housing, education, health care, and social benefits.

Her ability to mobilize, and the local prominence that she had gained, brought her to the attention of President **Néstor Kirchner**, who was building alliances across the country to sustain his presidency in the difficult years after 2003, and later to his wife, President **Cristina Fernández de Kirchner**. The strategy of "transversalism" and emergency economic relief devised by Néstor served neighborhood associations and lobby groups well and propelled Sala onto the national stage. In 2012, a general meeting of the Tupac Amaru decided to form a political party, Partido por la Soberanía Popular, which returned Sala into the Jujuy legislature in 2013 and two years later into the UNASUR parliament. This success and enhanced public profile was not without negative consequences. Sala had made several enemies and was a victim of death threats. Yet it was the charge of **corruption** and extortion and the exposure of her misdeeds by telejournalist **Jorge Lanata** that proved likely to bring her down. She and Tupac Amaru were charged with diverting funds intended to sustain social projects to serve her political ambitions. Much money had supposedly been spent by 32 housing cooperatives managed in the north and west of the country, but there was little concrete to show for the expenditure. Sala's response to these charges, and to her later arrest—which was condemned by Lanata as idiotic and heavy-handed—was to claim that her human rights had been abused. She took her case to the Human Rights Commission of the Organization of American States and the **United Nations Organization** (UNO). She claimed that she was a political prisoner, that her life was in danger, and that her human rights had been abused. To her supporters, she is an active social campaigner who is a thorn in the side of the government; to her detractors, a symbol of the greed and corruption—and the abuse of public funds—that characterized the reign of the Kirchners, along with the tendency of some to play the human rights card when subject to due process, having been caught with their hands in the till. *See also* COMISIÓN NACIONAL SOBRE LA DESAPARACIÓN DE PERSONAS (CONADEP); DESAPARECIDOS; DIRTY WAR; DISPOSICIÓN FINAL; MILITARY JUNTAS, TRIALS OF THE; *NUNCA MÁS*; WAR TO ANNIHILATE SUBVERSION.

SALADEROS. **Meat**-salting plant, the precursors of modern meatpacking *frigoríficos*. Like their modern equivalents, the *saladeros* were large and relatively capital-intensive processing units, employing the most up-to-date technology of the day. They displaced such early colonial practices as the *vaquerías*, from which they in part derived. The early salting plants were set up in the late 18th century, devised as a means of using the carcasses of **cattle** that were principally valued for the hides and tallow that they produced, the staple exports of the **pampas**. Although initially viewed as a means of adding value to a by-product that was otherwise of no worth, in the immediate post**independence** period salt meat exports, principally aimed at the slave markets in **Brazil** and **Cuba**, became a lucrative commodity. Most of the late colonial *saladeros* were located in **Uruguay**, but the crisis of independence there resulted in a shift in the focus of the industry to **Buenos Aires**. New plants were established to the south of the city, mainly along the coast and close to rivers and streams; water was an essential ingredient for processing and access to small ports necessary to reduce transport costs. By the 1840s, *saladeros* were substantial industrial complexes. Capital was invested in brick-built boiler houses, massive caldrons and steam power, iron cart tracks, stockyards, and drying racks. Scores of workers were employed at the largest establishments, which could process over 1,000 animals a day. **Juan Manuel de Rosas**, the Buenos Aires **caudillo** and governor, was a *saladerista* (owner of a *saladero*). Such was the scale and intensity of operations that, when the wind blew toward the city, residents of Buenos Aires complained about the stench. Like Rosas, many landowners and merchants connected with the business were **Federalists**, anxious to retain the monopoly on the trade enjoyed by the province. When refrigeration developed later in the century, several established *saladeristas*, notably European landowners and financiers, converted plants to *frigoríficos*, becoming pioneers of a new technology that promised a more valuable commodity and larger international markets. *See also* AGRICULTURE; COMMODITIES; ECONOMY; INDUSTRY; SHEEP; WOOL.

SALADO RIVER (BUENOS AIRES PROVINCE). Relatively short river confined almost entirely to the province of **Buenos Aires**, where it enters the sea at the Bay of Samborombón, rising in Chañar Lake in the south of the province of **Santa Fe**. It is sometimes known as the Salado del Sur, to distinguish it from the more important river of the same name farther north, notwithstanding that there are other Salado Rivers in the south. Despite its short length, less than 400 miles (about 640 kilometers), flowing west to east across the northern part of the present-day province, the river is of considerable strategic significance. For much of the colonial period and until the 1830s, the river marked the boundary between European settlement and **Indian** territory. It was a porous border associated with illicit commerce and lawlessness—**cattle** rustling was common, and fugitives (vagabonds) found sanctuary on the south bank. Spanish forces had failed to subdue nomadic tribes in the central and southern **pampas**; raids were not uncommon north of the river. The frequency of incursions grew during the struggle for **independence** and postindependence civil wars of the 1810s and 1820s, when frontier defense was neglected. Frontier security was tackled by **Juan Manuel de Rosas**, governor of the province of Buenos Aires. He organized the 1833–1834 **military** campaign in the south and west of the province, a process usually regarded as marking the beginning of the **Conquest of the Desert**. The Rosas campaign of conquest and subjugation, reinforced by a system of treaties and subsidy payments to allied tribes, virtually established the current limits of the province. This arrangement pacified the frontier until the fall of Rosas in 1852, when further incursions into settled areas pushed the frontier back east, ultimately leading to the final phases of the Conquest of the Desert. Today, by means of canals and small dams, the Salado basin waters the center-east of the province, a region that contains some of the most fertile and productive land in the country.

SALADO RIVER (INTERIOR PROVINCES). An extensive system located in the center-north of the country, the Salado River and its tributaries rise in the northwest, in the province of **Salta**, where the upper reaches are also known as the Juramento River, with some tributaries also originating in **Paraguay** and **Grand Chaco** to the north-northeast. The main river runs for over 700 miles (around 1,100 kilometers), crossing or touching the provinces of **Santiago del Estero**, **Tucumán**, and **Santa Fe**, where it enters the

Paraná. Including all the principal tributaries and canals, the system probably runs to 1,400 miles (2,250 kilometers). For many of these provinces, the system is an important economic resource: it is dammed to regulate the flow, though mainly to provide irrigation and hydroelectricity. There are also several deltas. Part of the system dries out when the flow reduces, though at other times, especially when there are rapid ice melts in the **Andes,** flash flooding occurs. In recent years, efforts have been made to regulate the flow and ensure year-round irrigation, improvements that have had a significant impact on output and crop diversification.

SALAMANCA, RENÉ (1940–1976). Trade union leader and politician who became a member of the Partido Comunista Revolucionario in 1968. A metalworker in the city of **Córdoba** and member of the body of delegates of the Unión Obrera Metalúrgica, he participated in the **Cordobazo** in 1969. At the time, Salamanca worked at the IKA-Renault (formerly, **Industrias Kaiser Argentina**) plant. In 1972, he headed the triumphant electoral list put forward by his party for the Córdoba branch of the Sindicato de Mecánicos y Afines del Transporte Automotor (SMATA), becoming its secretary general.

As a leader of SMATA, the main industrial union in the Argentine interior, Salamanca pushed the idea that unions should not be just instruments to defend the interests of members but also lead the political and revolutionary struggle of the working class. Together with **Agustín Tosco** of Luz y Fuerza and Hipólito Atilio López of the Unión Tranviaria Automotor, he established the Movimiento Sindical Combativo. When the national secretary of SMATA intervened in the Córdoba branch during the presidency of **Isabel Perón,** Salamanca went underground. He was detained and "disappeared" on the day the **military coup of 1976** struck.

SALIMEI, JORGE NÉSTOR (1926–1975). Minister of economy from June to December 1966. An entrepreneur and member of the **Partido Demócrata Cristiano** (PDC), he was one of the founders and president of the **Sasetru** conglomerate. Following the **military coup of 1966**, de facto president **Juan Carlos Onganía** appointed him to the **economy** portfolio.

Salimei's economic plan was characterized by a gradualist monetary policy to bring inflation under control coupled with exchange controls. His tenure also comprised a project to restructure the economy of the province of **Tucumán,** which failed due to local rejection of the planned closure of much of the area's sugar **industry. Carlos Gustavo Ramus** was among those organizing worker resistance to the reorganization of sugar production: he would become one of the founders of the **Montoneros.** Some members of the armed forces also worked to prevent the full implementation of Salimei's economic plan. Resistance to the Salimei plan also came from the then Argentine ambassador in Washington, DC, **Álvaro Alsogaray**, who wished to sign an agreement to attract US investment in Argentina. Salimei opposed the deal. Within six months, Salimei was replaced by **Adalbert Krieger Vasena**. *See also* COMMODITIES; DEVELOPMENTALISM/DEVELOPMENTALIST; ECONOMIC CRISES; MILITARY; MINISTRY OF ECONOMY; REVOLUCIÓN ARGENTINA (1966–1973); TRADE UNIONS.

SALTA (CITY). Capital of the province of the same name, the city was an important commercial, political, and cultural center, arguably the quasi-capital of the northwest for much of the colonial period and early 19th century. It remains one of the most attractive cities in the country and is a popular **tourist** destination. Initially known as San Felipe de Salta, in honor of Phillip II of **Spain**, the city was founded on 16 April 1582 by Hernando de Lerma, an ineffective colonial official with a reputation for violence and arbitrary rule. Despite being subject to Indian attacks and experiencing earthquakes, the city grew steadily in the 17th and 18th centuries on the back of its strategic location, as the center of regional government and the development of silver mining and the production of silverware. It was an important provisioning center during the **independence** wars, on the front line between royalist **Peru** and the insurgent **United Provinces of the River Plate**. Political instability in the province and surrounding region triggered decline in the 19th century, economic recovery being associated with the arrival of the railway in the 1890s. Substantial demographic growth from around the 1950s meant that the conurbation of Greater Salta reached around 550,000 inhabitants in 2010, up from around 70,000 in 1950, making the city the eighth largest in the country. *See also* CATAMARCA (PROVINCE); CENTRAL ARGENTINE RAILWAY COMPANY (CAR); CORDOBA CENTRAL RAILWAY COMPANY (CCR); SALTA (PROVINCE); SANTIAGO DEL ESTERO (PROVINCE); TUCUMÁN (PROVINCE).

SALTA (PROVINCE). Located in the **Andes** in the northwest, the province comprises arid puna and high mountains in the west and humid, lush valleys in the east and southeast, much of which remains heavily forested. The province is bordered to the east by the provinces of **Chaco** and **Formosa**; the south by the provinces of **Catamarca, Tucumán**, and **Santiago del Estero**; and the north by **Jujuy**; the province also lies on the frontier with **Bolivia** to the north and **Chile** to the west, while also touching the frontier with **Paraguay** to the northeast. It is one of the original provinces of the **Argentine Confederation**.

Toward the end of the 15th century, the area was briefly incorporated in the Inca Empire. Spanish conquistadores appeared in the 1530s and 1540s, though it was not until between the 1560s and 1590s that permanent towns and cities began to appear. Until 1776, like much of the surrounding territory, Salta formed part of the Viceroyalty of **Peru**, administered from present-day Bolivia, when it was incorporated in the newly constituted **Viceroyalty of the River Plate** governed from the city of **Buenos Aires**. Briefly, at the time of **independence**, Bolivia challenged Argentine control. Strategically located on the main route between the **River Plate** and Lima, during the late colonial period Salta was successively part of the intendancy of San Miguel de Tucumán (1783) and subsequently of Salta del Tucumán (1792), with jurisdiction over the surrounding regions, territories that would subsequently emerge as Argentine, Chilean, and Bolivian provinces—the frontier with Bolivia was not definitively settled until 1889 and 1925, when an exchange of disputed areas was arranged and competing claims abandoned. As late as the mid-18th century, the province was subject to attack from **Grand Chaco** tribes that had resisted both the Incas and the Spaniards, a threat that was not totally eliminated until 1879–1880. During the struggle for independence, the province was invaded in 1811–1812, 1817, 1820, and 1821 by royalist forces from Peru, some occupations lasting several months despite fierce guerrilla resistance, led by the **caudillo Martín Miguel de Güemes** until his assassination in 1821. Instability continued in the early national period: **Federalists** and **Unitarians** competed for power, and there were clashes between liberal reformers and prochurch traditionalists, as well as struggles with neighboring jurisdictions, during which the province lost territory. Having lost territory as a result of colonial and national boundary changes, the province gained from the suppression of the **Los Andes** national territory in 1900. The province formally adhered to the Confederation in 1853.

Although unattractive to the mass of foreign migrants who settled in Argentina between the 1880s and 1920s, the province benefited from growth and modernization in the 1870s and 1880s that witnessed the development of a press, banks, and irrigation and the arrivals of the telegraph and railways. Economic activity centered on mining in the north and west and on the raising of **commodities** like rice, cotton, **maize**, and root vegetables in the east and south; sugarcane production was prominent in the center. Growth industries in the 21st century include oil production—there are also large known reserves of natural gas—and **tourism**. Around 2000, the population passed the 1,000,000 mark, though density is low in most districts, with almost half the population living in and around the provincial capital, the only large conurbation and eighth largest city in the country in 2007. With more than 3 percent of total national population at that point, the province contributed only 1 percent of national gross domestic product: around a quarter of the economically active population is employed in the informal sector, the fourth highest proportion in the republic. As elsewhere in the northwest, income and social disparities are marked, with much of **agriculture** characterized by "feudal" relations. Socially and politically conservative, the influence of the **Catholic Church** in the province is substantial; educational attainment is low and infant mortality high. *See also* CENTRAL ARGENTINE RAILWAY COMPANY (CAR); CORDOBA CENTRAL RAILWAY COMPANY (CCR); SALTA (CITY).

SALTO GRANDE. Hydroelectric dam on the **Uruguay** River. Located between Concordia in the Argentine province of **Entre Ríos** and Salto in **Uruguay**, it is thereby shared between the two countries. Construction of Salto Grande began in 1974 and was completed in 1979. Power is generated by 14 Kaplan turbines, which are propeller-type water turbines with adjustable blades, and the total installed capacity is 1,890 megawatts (2,530,000 horsepower). The dam passes approximately 64,000 cubic meters of water per second; running along the top of the dam is a rail and road bridge that was opened in 1982. *See also* ECONOMY; TRANSPORTATION.

SAN CARLOS DE BARILOCHE. Town in the province of **Río Negro**, commonly known as Bariloche. It was established in 1902 on the southern shore of Lake Nahuel Huapi, a large lake surrounded by the **Andes** in an area of outstanding natural beauty. Known for its Alpine-style architecture and its chocolate, Bariloche has a population of around 110,000 and is a popular base for skiing and hiking in the area. The main ski slopes are those at Cerro Catedral, which is the largest ski resort in South America. *See also* TOURISM; TRANSPORTATION.

SAN JUAN (CITY). Capital of the province of the same name, founded in 1562 by the Spanish conquistador Juan Jufré y Montesaón on the banks of the San Juan River. The city has twice been destroyed by earthquakes, in 1776 and 1944. The latter catastrophe, the worst natural disaster in Argentine history, claimed over 10,000 lives—many of the victims buried under rubble—and left around 100,000 homeless, including around 1,000 orphans. Almost the entire city was rebuilt after 1944 to a new building code that incorporated existing knowledge and technology about earthquake-proof construction. It was the first major state urban public works program in the country. Colonel **Juan Domingo Perón**, soon to be elected president, and his future wife, María Eva Duarte, met while fund raising for victims. The disaster and rebuilding program helped shape future Peronist economic and social policy. The 10th largest city in the republic, the current population is around 550,000. *See also* SAN JUAN (PROVINCE).

SAN JUAN (PROVINCE). One of the founding provinces, and the most northerly of the three provinces that compose the region of **Cuyo**; the others are **Mendoza** and **San Luis**. To the west, the province is bordered by **Chile**, to the north-northeast by the province of **Catamarca**, to the east by San Luis, and to the south by Mendoza. The region that constitutes much of the present-day province was initially settled from Chile, a military expedition being dispatched there by Governor Francisco de Villagra in 1562. In 1776, with the creation of the **Viceroyalty of the River Plate**, the area was administratively separated from Chile and included in the new viceroyalty, later forming part of the intendancy of **Córdoba**. With the **May Revolution of 1810**, the province declared in favor of **Buenos Aires**, rejecting royal authority, and contributed men, money, and arms to the revolutionary cause. Having been part of the intendancy of Cuyo, set up by the early republican administration, with Mendoza and San Luis, San Juan declared itself independent in 1820, adopting a particularly liberal constitution in 1825, one of the first provincial constitutions drafted in the country. This modernizing tradition continued: **women** were granted the vote in local elections in 1923—nationally, the franchise was only extended to women in 1949.

After a turbulent history during the first decades after **independence** when, like many others, the province functioned as a semiautonomous political unit, the 1860s saw steady progress, particularly during the governorship of **Domingo Faustino Sarmiento** (1862–1864); communications and public services were improved. By the late 19th century, the province was attracting immigrants from Italy, **Spain**, and Germany. A relatively prosperous interior province, the current population is around 750,000 and predominantly urban. **Agriculture** is the main economic activity—vines were introduced in the mid-17th century; wine production is well established and dynamic. Mining is important, attracting foreign investment. Service activities are concentrated around the provincial capital. *See also* BUENOS AYRES & PACIFIC RAILWAY COMPANY (BA&P); IMMIGRATION; SAN JUAN (CITY); TOURISM.

SAN LUIS (CITY). Capital of the province, the city stands 711 meters above sea level in the foothills of the **Andes**, in the far northeast of the province. Founded on 25 August 1594 by Luis Jufré de Loaiza y Meneses, early records refer to the city as San Luis (named for Louis of France), San Luis de Loyola (Loyola was captain general of **Chile** and had instructed Jufré de Loaiza y Meneses to establish the city), and San Luis de la Punta (a reference to the surrounding geographical features). With a population of 210,000, the city is prosperous, well endowed with public parks, and serves as a center for regional **tourism** as well as being the provincial commercial and financial center. *See also* SAN LUIS (PROVINCE).

SAN LUIS (PROVINCE). Located in the **Cuyo** region in the west of the country, the province is bordered to the north by the provinces of **San Juan**, **La Rioja**, and **Córdoba**; to the east by Córdoba and **La Pampa**, which also forms the southern border; and to the west by the province of **Mendoza**. San Luis is one of the original provinces of the country, being represented at the **Congress of Tucumán**, which declared **independence**. For much of the early colonial period—the jurisdiction originates from 1594, when it was founded on the orders of Captain-General of **Chile** Martín de Loyola—the region was sparsely settled. In part, this was due to the unprotected southern frontier where unconquered nomadic Indian tribes held sway—the much feared Ranqueles and Pehuenches. Even after independence, these tribes continued to mount successful **cattle** raids into settled parts of the future province. Yet it was cattle that secured the early prosperity of the region. *Vaquerías*, periodic roundups of wild cattle licensed by the Crown, generated public revenue and provided a source of income. When the new **Viceroyalty of the River Plate** was formed in 1776, San Luis, which had previously been administered from Santiago de Chile, was assigned to Buenos Aires, forming part of the intendancy of Córdoba. In 1813, the province was united with Mendoza to from the intendancy of Cuyo; in 1820, it declared itself to be an autonomous province of the **Argentine Confederation**. The province was affected by the turmoil of the early national period, notably from the mid-1820s to the 1840s.

San Luis gradually gained a strong reputation for good governance. Modernization in the 1840s and 1850s was associated with the opening of schools and the publication of the first newspaper. Although there were setbacks, the arrival of the railways in 1875 witnessed the creation of banks and the development of civil society associated with the formation of political clubs and organizations. The definitive closing of the Indian frontier around 1880, along with the parceling out of public lands and a slow but steady stream of immigrants, furthered growth. By 1900, the **economy** was fairly diverse, with ranching, arable farming, and mining; irrigation and hydroelectricity projects favored **agriculture** and modest industrial expansion. Road building after the 1950s also served the province well; it has one of the most extensive road networks outside the **Littoral**. The early 21st century found San Luis to be a moderately prosperous middle-ranking interior province with a relatively balanced economy that occasionally played a role in national political life, as governors such as **Adolfo Rodríguez Saá** ascended to the National Senate and took a tilt at the presidency. The current population is nearing 500,000. *See also* BUENOS AYRES & PACIFIC RAILWAY COMPANY (BA&P); IMMIGRATION; SAN LUIS (CITY).

SAN MARTÍN, JOSÉ FRANCISCO DE (1778–1850). Patriot; hero of **independence**, ranked alongside Simón Bolívar as a liberator of South America—acknowledged as such in **Bolivia, Chile, Ecuador, Peru**, and **Uruguay** as well as Argentina; one of the few national figures of the 19th century recognized by Argentines of all political persuasions as a national hero. Usually know as José de San Martín, he was born in **Corrientes** to a Spanish **military** family, spending his early years in garrison towns and mission stations in **Mesopotamia** and the city of **Buenos Aires**, before moving to **Spain** in 1783 when his father was recalled to Madrid. There San Martín entered an elite seminary before being commissioned into the army. He saw service in North Africa and in the Iberian Peninsula itself during the Napoleonic invasion. Fighting to liberate Spain from French control, he was exposed to liberal ideas and the influence of freemasonry prevalent among the **River Plate** community with whom he associated, notably in Cadiz, the only part of Spain not to be conquered. In 1811, he resigned his commission and returned to South America via **Great Britain**, where he encountered others campaigning for independence. He reached Buenos Aires in March 1812, almost two years after the outbreak of the **May Revolution of 1810**, which would ultimately trigger the break with Spain. He immediately offered his sword to the Patriotic Junta, which charged him with forming military units, one of which was a regiment of mounted grenadiers, the **Granaderos a Caballo**. By 1813, he had been given command of the Army of the North, stationed on the frontier with still royalist Chile and Peru, charged with defending the country from reconquest. Up to that point, insurgent efforts to challenge Spanish authority powerfully entrenched in Lima had proved unsuccessful. San Martín devised the "Continental Plan," a project to hold the frontier with Peru while taking the war to Chile, which would be developed as the springboard for a seaborne and land attack on Peru itself. Appointed governor and intendent of **Cuyo**, he set about raising funds to create the **Army of the Andes** and finance campaigning in Chile. The army was assembled in **Mendoza**, composed of liberated slaves, regular troops, provincial militia, and Chilean volunteers—Chile had declared independence from Spain in September 1810 but was reconquered from Peru a few years later. In January 1817, at the head of the patriotic army, San Martín began the arduous crossing of the **Andes**.

San Martín's strategy worked. Despite setbacks, Chilean independence was secured in 1818 largely due to San Martín's efforts, epitomized by the battle of Maipú, the strategic turning point in the campaign. Plans were soon underway for the projected sea and land assault on Peru, but these were disrupted by political turmoil in Buenos Aires. Despite repeated demands by **Juan Martín de Pueyrredón** that he return to Buenos Aires to defend the fragile government of the **United Provinces of the River Plate** from attack by secessionist provinces and restore order, San Martín continued to prosecute the Continental Plan. His reluctance to return to Buenos Aires may have owed as much to a desire to avoid entanglement in embryonic conflicts between **Unitarian** and **Federalist** projects for the future of the nation as to a determination to prioritize the cause of independence. By August 1820, the expedition to take the war to Lima was ready; San Martín set sail and landed in Southern Peru at the head of a joint Argentine–Chilean–Peruvian force in mid-September. Early in July 1821, he entered Lima, declaring the independence of Peru on 28 July, and was acclaimed protector of Peru. However, Spanish forces had not been completely defeated, the army was plagued by factionalism, and San Martín had fallen out with Scottish lord Thomas Cochrane, appointed admiral of the Chilean fleet; Cochrane took the fleet back to Chile. There was also resentment among prominent Lima families at the presence of Chilean and Argentine officials.

While San Martín had been active in the south of the country, Simón Bolívar was engaging royalist forces in the north of Peru, advancing from Colombia into present-day Ecuador. To determine the future shape of independent South America, San Martín met Bolívar at the famous Guayaquil Conference, held in late July 1822. There are differing accounts of what was agreed on, but the outcome was that San Martín felt betrayed by Bolívar. The men differed about territorial arrangement and governance. Critically, San Martín's view of the future role of the military differed from those of Bolívar; San Martín was firmly of the opinion that the military should not be involved in politics, Bolívar was known to harbor political ambitions and was not hesitant about using the army to secure them. It was rumored that San Martín was a crypto-monarchist—he regarded monarchy as the most effective means of securing national unity and civilian government—while Bolívar was an advocate of republicanism. To avoid conflict that might jeopardize the cause of independence, San Martín withdrew, a course of action subsequently applauded as an act of unselfish dedication to the liberation of the continent and an example of firm moral principle. Leaving Guayaquil, San Martín returned to Lima, where he resigned his commissions, and returned to Chile. By late January 1823, he was back in Mendoza, and anxious to leave for Buenos Aires, where his wife was terminally ill. Refused permission to travel to Buenos Aires by **Bernardino Rivadavia**, then the most powerful figure in government, who was suspicious of San Martín's intentions, he languished in the west. He arrived in Buenos Aires by the end of the year but set sail for Europe in February 1824 on the death of his wife. He returned to Buenos Aires at the beginning of 1829. Finding the country in turmoil, he decided not to disembark, perhaps not to be seen as favoring one faction over another, though he did receive friends and former companions in arms on board ship. Adamant that he would not take sides, he left for Europe, settling in France. He died in Boulogne-sur-Mer in 1850, where he had taken a house a few years earlier on health grounds. In his will, he bequeathed his sword to **Juan Manuel de Rosas**, then governing Argentina. It was a controversial gesture, given Rosas's reputation. After the death of Rosas, San Martín's sword was donated to the nation.

In 1880, San Martín's remains were reburied in the cathedral in Buenos Aires in a moving ceremony that recognized his contributions to the founding of the nation and cause of the independence in southern South America. (Technically, San Martín rests in a side chapel, somewhat outside the historic boundaries of the building as the church objected to his adherence to freemasonry.) He is commemorated by statues and public buildings around the country; in most towns and cities, the principal square is named the Plaza San Martín. *See also* BELGRANO, MANUEL JOSÉ JOAQUIN DEL CORAZÓN DE JESÚS (1770–1820); MORENO, MARIANO (1778–1811); NATIONAL ORGANIZATION; SAAVEDRA, CORNELIO (1759–1829).

SAN MIGUEL DE TUCUMÁN (CITY). Capital of the province of **Tucumán**; founded in 1565 by Diego de Villarroel, one of the original Spanish conquerors of **Peru**, the city was relocated to its present site in 1685. The decisive battle of Tucumán was fought close to the city on 24 September 1812, in effect determining the frontier between royalist forces in Peru and supporters of **independence**. The national significance of the city was further reinforced when the **Congress of Tucumán** was inaugurated there on 9 July 1816, declaring the country independent from **Spain**. Some 800 miles (1,300 kilometers) to the northwest of **Buenos Aires**, the city is an important regional center. Its modern development dates from the 1870s and 1880s, with the arrival of the railways and the beautification of the central district—modern avenues, public buildings, and parks were established. *See also* BUENOS AYRES & ROSARIO RAILWAY COMPANY (BA&R); CENTRAL ARGENTINE RAILWAY COMPANY (CAR).

SAN NICOLÁS. Medium-sized port on the **Paraná**, located in the northeast of the province of **Buenos Aires** on the border with the province of **Santa Fe**—140 miles (230 kilometers) from the national capital. The settlement was founded in the middle of the 18th century but is important because the first naval conflicts during the struggle for **independence** took place there in 1811 because it was the location for several peace pacts during the early national period and industrial expansion in the 20th century.

City status was conferred in 1819, and shortly afterward the city acquired the sobriquet "City of Pacts": the first one was signed there in 1820, followed by others in 1821, 1831, and 1852. The most famous were the Pact of the **Littoral** of 1831, which attempted to secure peace among the provinces of Buenos Aires, **Entre Ríos**, and Santa Fe, and the San Nicolás Accord of 1852, signed by 13 provinces except Buenos Aires, establishing the **Argen-**

tine **Confederation** and prefiguring the calling of the constituent assembly that drew up of the **Constitution of 1853**. The strategic location of the city on the river also explains why some of the first modern meatpacking plants—*frigoríficos*—set up there, as was the first integrated steel mill. The city was chosen as the location of the plant set up by the **Sociedad Mixta Siderúrgica Argentina** (SOMISA) in 1947 as part of the industrial drive associated with the first administration of **Juan Domingo Perón**. In addition to steel production, the city emerged as a center for energy production—electricity generators and oil refineries featured in the industrialization plan, a project that was supported during the presidencies of **Arturo Frondizi** and several **military** administrations. The steel plant is now owned by Techint, which continues to produce cables, wires, and tubes there, mainly for the construction and oil industries—about 60 percent of present-day output is exported, mainly to South America. The current population is about 140,000.

SAN SALVADOR DE JUJUY. With a population of around 260,000 in 2010, one of the larger cities of the north-west. It was founded and re-founded several times during the late 16th century—continuous settlement is dated from 1593. It was declared capital of the province of Jujuy in 1834. For much of the colonial period, the importance of the city derived from its location on the supply route to Upper Peru (present-day Bolivia). It was a way-station where cattle and mules were fattened for the final stage of the journey north, later developing as a center of artisanal textile production destined for the silver mines. Independence brought turbulence and de-cline—the city was attacked several times by royalist forces from the north, compounded by natural disasters—the region was subject to earthquakes. Modern development began with the arrival of the railway in 1890s—San Salvador was one of the last provincial capitals to be connected to the national rail network. The modern urban economy is largely based on services—formal employment in the city and provincial government accounts for about 70 percent of jobs, though the informal sector is significant. Tourism is developing, with visitors attracted by surviving colonial architecture, colorful religious fiestas and resorts and activities based in the Valley of Jujuy. The metropolitan district, home to almost one half of the total population of the province, remains one of the poorest in the country. *See also* CORDOBA CENTRAL RAILWAY COMPANY (CCR); SHEEP.

SANTA CRUZ. Province located in **Patagonia**, in the southern part of Argentina. It borders the province of **Chubut** to the north, **Chile** to the west and south, and the Atlantic to the east. Santa Cruz is the second largest province in the country (after the province of **Buenos Aires**) and the least densely populated in mainland Argentina.

The indigenous people of the province were the **Tehuelches**, who despite European exploration from the 16th century onward, retained independence until made practically extinct in the late 19th century. The region was set under the rule of the **Viceroyalty of the River Plate** when the latter was created in 1776. Following the **Conquest of the Desert**, the area was organized as the Territorio Nacional de Santa Cruz. In 1888, its capital was established in **Río Gallegos** and has remained there since. Santa Cruz became a province in 1957, and its current population is approximately 300,000.

The provincial **economy** is not very diversified. Fully half of its output is accounted for by the extractive sector (petroleum, gas, and the mining of gold and coal). The second most important sector is that linked to the production of **sheep wool** and **meat**, most of which is designated for export, followed by fishing, whose production is mostly frozen and also exported. KIRCHNER, ALICIA MARGARITA (1946–); KIRCHNER, CRISTINA ELISABET FERNÁNDEZ DE (1953–); KIRCHNER, NÉSTOR CARLOS (1950–2010); YACIMIENTOS PETROLÍFEROS FISCALES (YPF).

SANTA FE (CITY). Founded on the banks of the river **Paraná** as Santa Fe de la Vera Cruz by Juan de Garay in 1573, the city is the capital of the province of the same name. The settlement led a precarious existence, subject to attack by unpacified Indians, yet claims to have been the first formally organized urban center on the **River Plate**, and the "mother (founding) city" of several others in the area, including **Buenos Aires**.

Fortunes began to improve when the city was declared a *puerto preciso* in 1622, which required all shipping on the river to stop at the port, substantially improving communications with the outside world and municipal revenue. By the early 18th century, Santa Fe was an important regional administrative center, as well as a focus for regional trade. Later development was fostered by good government—the city and province were well served by energetic, forward-thinking governors. This would change in the decades following **independence** in 1810, when national and regional conflict curtailed trade and damaged the physical fabric. Around 1818–1819, the province was invaded several times and the city occupied by forces from Buenos Aires. Modest prosperity returned in the 1830s, to be followed by further anarchy. Steady improvements in the fortunes of Santa Fe only came after the 1860s, notably from the 1880s as colonists flocked to the countryside and farming and ranching generated demands for urban services, and provided the funds to develop the city. The docks were expanded and transport system improved, as were specifically urban facilities like tramways and street lighting. In 1886, plans for a regional rail network in the center and south of the province, focused on the city, were launched. Urban beautification began in earnest around 1900. Parts of the historic center were cleared, making way for parks and avenues, as befitted the capital of a prosperous province. A contract to modernize the ports was signed in 1904, and a new government house was built between 1908 and 1917. Such changes were a reflection of social as well as economic developments. By the 1920s, dockworkers in the port had acquired a well-deserved reputation for militancy. At this time, new **political parties** and labor organizations were headquartered there, where a large literate population supported a diverse press. At the beginning of the 21st century, with a population of 700,000, the city is the third largest provincial capital in Argentina and one of the most affluent. *See also* CRY OF ALCORTA; IMMIGRATION; SANTA FE (PROVINCE); TRADE UNIONS.

SANTA FE (PROVINCE). A founding province of the **Argentine Confederation**, prosperous and politically progressive, located in the **Littoral**. In terms of wealth and population, the province is second only to **Buenos Aires**, with which it shares a border to the south; the western border is shared with **Córdoba** and **Santiago del Estero**; the northern with **Chaco**; the eastern boundary is the river **Paraná**, across which lie the **Mesopotamian** provinces of **Corrientes** and **Entre Ríos**.

The territory was settled by the Spaniards in the late 16th century, with an expedition headed by the explorer Juan de Garay; the jurisdiction he established included Entre Ríos and part of the province of Buenos Aires. For much of the colonial period, the area was subject to attack by pampean Indians, a threat not finally eradicated until around 1880, despite strenuous effort at pacification in the 1770s that included the construction of forts and blockhouses and peace agreements with amenable tribes. For reasons of defense and supply, most early settlements were clustered in the southeast of the province. The province actively supported the **May Revolution of 1810**, and the new national flag was first unfurled there by **Manuel Belgrano** in 1812. (The National Flag Monument, Monumento Nacional a la Bandera, is located at **Rosario**.) Yet the provincial elite was distinctly inclined to the **Federalist** cause, rejecting **Unitarianist** sentiments (and pretentions to national leadership) that emerged in Buenos Aires in the 1820s. Like neighboring Córdoba, Santa Fe became a theater of war in the conflict between the two groups and was also threatened by regional **caudillos**, particularly the competing ambitions of Francisco Ramírez in Entre Ríos and José Artigas in **Uruguay** to forge a confederation unifying territory on both side of the Paraná. After 1818, as the *santafecino* caudillo Estanislao López consolidated his power, the autonomy of the province was confirmed and a couple of decades of relative stability followed. López held sway in the Santa Fe and extended his influence over adjacent provinces. His death in 1838 brought renewed instability.

The defeat of **Juan Manuel de Rosas** in 1852 and the organization of the constituent assembly of Santa Fe, which adopted the **Constitution of 1853**, brought renewed order and economic growth, notwithstanding the separation of Buenos Aires from the Confederation between 1853 and 1862. The 1850s saw the beginning of **agricultural colonization** with the establishment of the colony La Esperanza in 1854, for which the province would become exemplar. Other indications of modernity in the 1860s and 1870s were the development of roads and railways in the province, the expansion of the port of Rosario, the institution of civil marriage—in the face of stiff opposition from traditionalists—and the development of secular **education** in the 1880s. As the port of Rosario expanded, it was seriously considered as a likely site of the national capital until the **federalization of the city of Buenos Aires** in 1880. Such economic and social changes had an impact on political life. The province was among the first to see the emergence of the **Unión Cívica Radical** (UCR). Arguably, at the time, even more significant were the emergence of political organizations representing farmers and small utility and industrial workers: namely, Liga del Sur and the **Partido Demócrata Progresista** (PDP) and the **Federación Agraria Argentina** (FAA), specifically representing sharecroppers, tenant farmers, and small proprietor. Together, these organizations pressed for effective electoral representation and social reform—worker rights, labor legislation, and social protection. By 1910, dockworkers and railway workers had been organizing strikes in Rosario. On 25 July 1912, the FAA organized the **Cry of Alcorta** (Grito de Alcorta), the first mass protest by small-scale farmers in the history of the country. The same year also witnessed significant political change in the province. Elections held there were the first major elections to be called after the passage of the **Sáenz Peña Law**. The Radicals substantially increased their representation, paving the way for national victory in 1916.

Even in the late 19th century, the provincial government had acquired a reputation for economic activism. In addition to promoting **immigration** and agricultural colonization, and franchising railway construction, it also developed its own railway system, though most of this had passed into private hands and foreign banks by 1900. Improvements in transport and the emergence of a regional credit market played a role in the industrial growth of the province, as well as its agricultural development. Today, the province accounts for about one-third of national production of wheat and a large proportion of **commodities** like flax, oilseeds, and soya. Along with agriculture-related industries, such as oilseed production and food processing, **industry** is significant—there are heavy industries like steel and petrochemicals, and motor vehicle and electric appliance manufacturers, mainly grouped around the provincial and regional port of Rosario. Yet it is agricultural colonization that has made the province distinct, resulting in a relatively diverse pattern of land ownership that underwrote the growth and industrial diversity of its major cities. Perhaps this, and the history of provincial politics, explains the election of the first socialist governor in the history of the country: in 2007, Hermes Binner, a member of the **Partido Socialista** (PS) who was descended from a Swiss family that had moved to the colonies some generations earlier, became governor. The current population of the province is approximately 3,500,000. *See also* BUENOS AYRES & ROSARIO RAILWAY COMPANY (BA&R); CENTRAL ARGENTINE RAILWAY COMPANY (CAR); IMMIGRATION; SANTA FE (CITY); TRADE UNIONS.

SANTA ROSA. Capital of the province of **La Pampa** and home to the National University of La Pampa (UNLPam) established in 1973 at a time when universities were founded in various other provincial capitals lacking an institute of higher education up to that point—the city was created in 1892. An important transport hub, located at the western edge of the pampas proper, where the plains give way to rolling country side, the population of the metropolitan area was recorded at around 115,000 in 2010. Two major national highways intersect at the city; east-west passenger rail services were restored in 2014, but largely abandoned within a year or so. The service sector dominates the urban economy (mainly government, **education**, finance and **agriculture**-related activities), construction is also important and increasing—Santa Rosa is one of the fastest growing small cities of the pampas, admittedly growing from a small base.

SANTIAGO DEL ESTERO (CITY). The oldest continuously occupied urban center in the republic, the city was established sometime between 1550 and 1553 by Spanish forces from **Peru** headed by Juan Núñez de Prado, a conquistador responsible for founding other settlements in the Argentine northwest. The early date is officially recognized as the founding date.

The initial population was largely composed of Indians who had accompanied Núñez de Prado. Later settlements soon eclipsed the city. In 1817, much of the city was devastated by an earthquake, which further delayed growth, as did regular outbreaks of malaria. The modern history of Santiago dates from 1884 with the arrival of the **Central Argentine Railway**, which offered direct communications with **Buenos Aires** and the **Littoral**. Despite urban modernization in the early decades of the 20th century, it was not until the 1980s that such urban services as street lighting, water, and drainage covered the greater part of the city. Today, with a population of 250,000, it is the 12th most populous city in Argentina. The **economy** is largely dependent on the government and **tourism**, and the city is the commercial center for the extensive farming and **cattle** industry based in the province of the same name. *See also* SANTIAGO DEL ESTERO (PROVINCE).

SANTIAGO DEL ESTERO (PROVINCE). Located in the center-north, the province is bordered by **Salta**, **Chaco**, **Santa Fe**, **Córdoba**, **Catamarca**, and **Tucumán**. It is one of the original provinces of the **Argentine Confederation**, declaring its autonomy in 1820. The region was initially settled by the Spanish in the 1530s and 1540s, moving southeastward from present-day **Peru** and **Chile**, having already founded settlements like the city of **San Miguel de Tucumán**. Much of the province was opened up by conquistador Juan Núñez de Prado, who was allegedly searching for a route to the **River Plate**. Many of the early inhabitants were Indians resettled from parts of the Viceroyalty of Peru.

By the 17th century, Santiago was overshadowed by neighboring areas like Córdoba and Tucumán, which had already emerged as important supply centers for the silver mines of Upper Peru (present-day **Bolivia**). By the end of the 18th century, the territory had been incorporated within the intendancy of Salta. In 1810, the would-be province sided with insurgents in **Buenos Aires** and declared for **independence**. Some 10 years of anarchy followed, reflected in Santiago being variously attached administratively to jurisdictions headed by Salta, Tucumán, and Catamarca. Order was restored by **Federalist** strongman Juan Felipe Ibarra. Declaring the independence of Santiago from the Federal Republic of Tucumán, into which the province had been forcibly incorporated, Ibarra ruled the province like a typical **caudillo** until his death in 1851. The chaos of the 1810s destroyed the budding textile **industry**. There were only three minor towns besides the provincial capital. The province lapsed into subsistence. It was subject to repeated federal interventions, though usually under the control of the Taboada family—the dynasty was established by Manuel Taboada, Ibarra's nephew.

The province remained one of the most deprived parts of the republic until the mid-20th century, typified by debt peonage, squalor, and acute poverty— and outmigration to the **Littoral**, especially Buenos Aires. Economic and social conditions only began to improve with the construction of the Los Quiroga Dam and accompanying irrigation work in the 1950s. Ranching expanded, and **agriculture** diversified to include **commodities** like cotton, alfalfa, fruit, and vegetables. Now soya is the main crop, accounting for around half the total value of rural production. There is some hydroelectricity generating potential, and projects to develop **tourism** based around thermal springs. The total population is approaching one million, making the province one of the less densely settled parts of the country. Literacy rates are a couple of points below the national average, and life expectancy six years lower. *See also* SANTIAGO DEL ESTERO (CITY).

SANTUCHO, MARIO ROBERTO (1936–1976). Revolutionary and guerrilla combatant born in the city of Santiago del Estero. In the early 1960s, he was crucial in efforts to unite the Frente Revolucionario Indoamericano Popular, which he then headed, with the Trotskyite Palabra Obrera. The two groups merged on 25 May 1965 into the Partido Revolucionario de los Trabajadores (PRT), a Marxist–Leninist party combining the indigenous struggle of the former and the class-based politics of the latter.

Following the **Cordobazo** of 1969, and on Santucho's initiative, the fifth congress of the PRT voted to form the **Ejército Revolucionario del Pueblo** (ERP). It was never officially recognized as the armed wing of the party, but there is sufficient evidence that it was. The PRT served as the political and military command center of the ERP, with Santucho acting as the secretary general of the former and commanding officer of the latter. The ERP had an essentially anti-imperialist and anticapitalist political platform with the program of the PRT at its heart, and among its membership were a large group of PRT militants as well as armed combatants from diverse political and social backgrounds.

Santucho was arrested in August 1971, and on 15 August 1972 he escaped from the maximum-security prison in **Rawson** in a bold episode that culminated in the tragic **Trelew Massacre**. He returned to Argentina in November 1972 and resumed his leadership of both the PRT and the ERP. Notwithstanding the pressure on him, Santucho did not abandon the armed struggle, and the ERP became the largest (non-Peronist) Marxist guerrilla group in the country as well as a prime Argentine example of the Cuban revolutionary *foco* strategy.

Following the **military coup of 1976**, the leadership of the ERP and the **Montoneros** worked on building a unified guerrilla force. However, nothing came of the plan as Santucho was killed in a military ambush in July 1976. The de facto government of General **Jorge Rafael Videla** erased any trace of the body, as it believed that the appearance of the latter would result in homages and veneration of the slain subversive.

SANZ, ERNESTO (1956–). Academic, lawyer, and politician; he represented the **Unión Cívica Radical** (UCR) in the **Mendoza** provincial senate and the National Senate. On the eve of the **congressional** and **presidential elections of 2015**, he was a strong advocate for entering an electoral coalition with other groupings opposed to the administration of **Cristina Fernández de Kirchner**. He was successful in persuading the UCR to form what became the **Cambiemos** coalition, abandoning the **Frente Amplio UNEN** broad front to which it had previously been affiliated. *See also* POLITICAL PARTIES.

SAPAG, FELIPE (1917–2010). Six-time governor of the province of **Neuquén**, leading figure of the **Movimiento Popular Neuquino**, and member of a locally influential family. The family are of Maronite Christian, Arab origin, hailing from present-day Lebanon. Sapag first stood for governor in March 1962, but the elections were promptly annulled after a **military** coup. He was again elected governor with 60 percent of the vote in 1963 and left office following the **military coup of 1966**. His administration's achievements include the establishment of the Banco de la Provincia de Neuquén and the present-day Universidad Nacional de Comahue.

De facto president **Juan Carlos Onganía**, in a bid to improve his standing by appointing popular governors, nominated Sapag as governor of Neuquén in February 1970; he retained this post until 1972. The following year he was reelected governor but again removed after the **military coup of 1976**. With the restoration of democracy, he was returned as governor in 1983–1987 and 1995–1999. The career of Sapag neatly reflects an enduring tradition in national politics, particularly in relatively small or underpopulated provinces, namely an ability to capture and dominate local politics—by democratic means or otherwise. *See also* IMMIGRATION; MILITARY COUP OF 1962; POLITICAL PARTIES; POPULISM; RELIGION; REVOLUCIÓN ARGENTINA (1966–1973).

SAQUEOS. Looting, from the verb *sacar*, "to sack," in the sense of removing or taking away. The term has been applied to the looting of shops and supermarkets during moments of acute political and **economic crises** when poverty and inequality rose, for example, during the **hyperinflation** of the last months of the presidency of **Raúl Alfonsín** in 1989 and the collapse of the **Convertibility Plan** at the end of 2001 in the middle of the term of President **Fernando de la Rúa**. In 1989, disturbances occurred in such major conurbations as **Buenos Aires**, **Córdoba**, and **Rosario**, mainly in May and June. These events, in which up to 20 people may have been killed, shocked the public and resulted in an early transfer of power from Alfonsín to President-Elect **Carlos Saúl Menem**. While supermarkets and small grocery stores were the main targets of spontaneous action, motor vehicle sales rooms and household goods stores were also attacked, suggesting the involvement of criminal gangs. In 2001, as the government imposed controls on bank accounts to defend the exchange rate and adopted measures to increase fiscal revenue, there were massive street protest against the political class in general and about the deteriorating **economy**, which had been slowing since 1997. Almost 40 people were killed during the protests and lootings. There were demonstrations against the government in middle-class residential districts and in city centers; the labor movement, the **Confederación General del Trabajo** (CGT), called a general strike; *piquetero* groups were particularly active in Greater Buenos Aires. The government was losing control of the economy and of the streets. Although there were parallels with 1989, it was rumored that goon squads connected with the **Partido Justicialista** (PJ) in the province of Buenos Aires orchestrated looting in districts of

Greater Buenos Aires that lay within the province. This rumor was given credence by the focus of attacks on small shops and the fact that some large supermarkets appear to have had advance warning, closing shutters and recruiting extra security staff before looting occurred. Looting on a considerably smaller scale took place in some interior provinces in 2013, and in some cities in 2015, incidents that appear to have been the work of armed gangs, not the result of spontaneous popular action.

SARMIENTO, DOMINGO FAUSTINO (1811–1888). Educationalist, reformer, author and journalist, soldier, statesman, and diplomat; served as constitutional president (1868–1874) and was twice elected governor of his native province of **San Juan**, in 1862 and 1864. Of humble origin, Sarmiento was a leading **Unitarian** from the interior who was active in politics from his late teens, though he spent many years in exile in **Chile** and, to a lesser extent, **Peru**. In both countries, he was associated with advances in **education** and pursued a career as a journalist. He was sent by the Chilean government to investigate systems of education in Europe and the **United States**. He wrote prolifically, contributing articles to the press and publishing treatises and works in which he expounded ideas on government and international relations. One of his early imaginative works, *Agriópolis*, proposed a confederation of Argentina, **Paraguay**, and **Uruguay**, with a capital on the island of Martín García in the **Paraná** Delta. Another work, *Civilización I Barbarie: vida de Juan Facundo Quiroga*, remains the definitive critique of *caudillismo*, the political "system" associated with the rule of **military** strongmen—**caudillos**. In Chile, he was a member of the literary elite and an active promotor of modernization. Like many Unitarian contemporaries, he enlisted in the Grand Army (Ejército Grande) raised by *entrerriano* caudillo **Justo José de Urquiza** when he rose against former **Buenos Aires** ally **Juan Manuel de Rosas** in 1852. Critical of the **Constitution of 1853** and the scheme for **national organization** that it proposed, he returned to Chile, where he continued to advance the cause of education, though he returned to Buenos Aires in 1855 to pursue a similar course.

During the separation of the province from the **Argentine Confederation**, Sarmiento earned the curious distinction of being elected national senator in the Confederation by the voters of **Tucumán**, and by voters of Buenos Aires to the senate there. He declined to serve in either body. He did, however, accept election as governor of San Juan in the 1860s, where he promoted economic growth. He resigned from the governorship in 1865 on taking up the position of Argentine minister to Washington, DC, a post to which he had been appointed by **Bartolomé Mitre**. Sarmiento traveled extensively in the United States, recognizing the importance of modern means of communication. While there, he wrote a life of Abraham Lincoln and about the political systems of the Americas. As an internationalist, he opposed the Monroe Doctrine, which he saw as a mechanism to promote US hegemony in the continent. He was in Washington, DC, when elected president.

Sarmiento's presidency is associated with the promotion of **immigration** and education—800 primary schools were opened—and infrastructure modernization—a national telegraph system was begun, and the country connected to the international network. The first National Census was held early in his presidency, in 1869; that same year, he also established the water supply and drainage company now known as **Aguas Argentinas**. The institutionalization of political life and the modernization of the state begun under Mitre were actively pursued. On completing his term as president, Sarmiento remained active in politics: he was elected national senator for San Juan and served as minister of interior in the cabinet of **Nicolás Avellaneda** and head of the Education Council and School Board under **Julio A. Roca**. Although not universally applauded—nationalists resented his continued prosecution of the **War of the Triple Alliance** against **Paraguay**, for being overinfluenced by the United States, and for being too favorably disposed to British investors—his contributions to the promotion of education, immigration, and state building earned him the title of "Father of the Nation." *See also* BUENOS AYRES WESTERN RAILWAY COMPANY (BAW); ECONOMY; ENCOTEL; FERROCARRILES ARGENTINOS (FFAA); FOREIGN DEBT/FOREIGN INVESTMENT; GREAT BRITAIN; MINISTRY OF EDUCATION; MINISTRY OF INTERIOR, PUBLIC WORKS, AND HOUSING; TRANSPORTATION.

SASETRU. Conglomerate founded in 1948 by three partners, **Jorge Salimei**, Angel Seitun, and Fermín Trucco Aguinaga; the first letters of their surnames gave the group its name. By 1970, Sasetru was one of the largest companies financed by purely national capital, and one of the two largest Argentine producers and exporters of edible oils, the other being **Molinos Río de la Plata**. Besides oil, the firm produced flour, pasta, conserves, jams, bread, wine, and rice. Composed of around 140 businesses, the group came to command 40 percent of the domestic food market: Sasetru owned the largest mill in the country, the Banco Internacional, and a merchant fleet, and operated its own docks in Belgium and Italy. By the time of the **military coup of 1976**, the enterprise was in severe financial trouble owing to the **economic crisis** that had racked the country since the **Rodrigazo**. Sasetru went bankrupt in 1981. *See also* COMMODITIES; DEVELOPMENTALISM/DEVELOPMENTALIST; ECONOMY; INDUSTRY; MARTÍNEZ DE HOZ, JOSÉ ALFREDO (1925–2013); PROCESO DE REORGANIZACIÓN NACIONAL; SECCIÓN INDUSTRIAL AMASADORAS MECÁNICAS (SIAM Di Tella).

SCALABRINI ORTIZ, RAÚL (1898–1959). Thinker, writer, and historian who participated in the unsuccessful Yrigoyenista revolt of January 1933, which resulted in his being sent into exile in Europe. There he discovered that German and Italian newspapers referred to Argentina as a British colony, leading him to refine his views on the degree of Argentine subjection to **Great Britain**. Scalabrini Ortiz returned home in 1934 and grew close to the **Fuerza de Orientación Radical de la Jóven Argentina** (FORJA). He focused on subjects related to Argentine dependency and particularly on the British-owned railways. In 1940, Scalabrini Ortiz became a full member of the FORJA, after the grouping separated from the **Unión Cívica Radical** (UCR), and published his two best-known books: *Política británica en el Río de la Plata* and *Historia de los ferrocarriles argentinos*. He broke with the FORJA when it backed the **military coup of 1943** by the **Grupo de Oficiales Unidos**. He followed the ascent of **Juan Domingo Perón** to power and submitted to him numerous works on the nationalization of the railways. However, Scalabrini Ortiz never accepted any government posts and remained apart from and critical of Peronism. *See also* ARGENTINE NORTH EASTERN RAILWAY COMPANY (ANE); BARING CRISIS; BUENOS AYRES & PACIFIC RAILWAY COMPANY (BA&P); BUENOS AYRES & ROSARIO RAILWAY COMPANY (BA&R); BUENOS AYRES GREAT SOUTHERN RAILWAY COMPANY (BAGS); BUENOS AYRES WESTERN RAILWAY COMPANY (BAW); CENTRAL ARGENTINE RAILWAY COMPANY (CAR); CONCORDANCIA; CORDOBA CENTRAL RAILWAY COMPANY (CCR); FERROCARRILES ARGENTINOS (FFAA); FOREIGN DEBT/FOREIGN INVESTMENT; STATE-OWNED ENTERPRISES (SOEs); TRANSPORTATION; *VENDEPATRIA(S)*.

SCIOLI, DANIEL OSVALDO (1957–). Politician and sporting personality; successful businessman; longtime member of the **Partido Justicialista** (PJ), which he served as president; holder of several important public offices, including vice president of the republic and governor of the province of **Buenos Aires**. Born to a middle-class business family in the province, Scioli's formative moment in political and public life came when his brother was kidnapped and held for ransom by the **Montoneros** in 1975—the family charged him with negotiating the release of his brother. Another formative moment came when he lost an arm in a motorboat accident while racing in the **Paraná** Delta. These events confirmed a resilience of character that prepared him for later challenges. His political life began when he obtained a seat in the federal Chamber of Deputies, representing the city of Buenos Aires in the midterm **congressional elections of 1997**; he was reelected in the midterm **congressional elections of 2001** but stepped down on becoming vice president to **Néstor Kirchner** in 2003. The Kirchner–Scioli ticket came in second in the first round of the **presidential election of 2003**; they were declared victors when former president **Carlos Saúl Menem**, who had topped the poll, pulled out of the second round at the last minute. Completing the vice presidential term in 2007, Scioli stood for the governorship of the province of Buenos Aires for the Kirchnerist wing of the PJ, the **Frente para la Victoria/Partido Justicialista** (FpV/PJ). He won and was returned for a second term in the gubernatorial elections of 2011. During this time, he came to be seen as a super Kirchner loyalist. Despite this, he was distrusted by sections of the party for his business background and ill served by President **Cristina Fernández de Kirchner**, who succeeded her husband in 2007 and often appeared to treat Scioli with contempt before ultimately endorsing his candidature in the **presidential election of 2015**. Whether due to the lukewarm support of Mrs. Kirchner or because of her endorsement, despite starting as front-runner in 2015, Scioli lost on the second round to **Mauricio Macri**.

In the run-up to the elections, **Sergio Massa**, who headed the dissident wing of the PJ, had challenged Scioli. Massa's intervention divided the PJ, but instead of the runoff taking place between Scioli and Massa, on coming third in October 2015 Massa simply ensured that the November second round would feature Scioli and Macri, allowing the anti-K vote to coalesce behind Macri. Since the elections, Scioli's resilience has been tested again. Pledged to reunify the PJ, he has found few factions of the party prepared to support his vision of the way forward. He has struggled to find issues or allies to unite the PJ.

SECCIÓN INDUSTRIAL AMASADORAS MECÁNICAS (SIAM Di Tella). Commonly known as SIAM Di Tella, the company was founded in 1911 by Italian immigrant **Torcuato Di Tella**. It became one of the largest privately owned multienterprise industrial complexes in the country, specializing in the production of white goods and motor vehicles. The company failed in the 1960s and was taken over by the government.

Beginning with the production of bread-making equipment, from which the firm took its name, by the 1920s the company was manufacturing fuel pumps for the oil industry, partly due to contacts with state oil company **Yacimientos Petrolíferos Fiscales** (YPF), and was already the principal domestically owned industrial complex. During the 1930s, as the **economy** began to recover from the impact of the Depression, and with exchange control constraining imports, the firm moved into the manufacture of such household appliances as cookers and refrigerators; commercial and domestic freezers were produced under an agreement with Westinghouse of the **United States**, with SIAM's "Queen of Cold" refrigerator becoming a market leader. SIAM's new kitchen appliance factory built in **Avellaneda** that decade was the biggest and most modern plant of its kind in Latin America.

In the 1940s, Lambretta motor scooters were being manufactured under license, and by the 1950s motor cars licensed by the British Motor Corporation—the Farina and Morris Oxford saloons proving particularly popular, though utility vehicles were also produced. The company lost out in the government-promoted industrialization drive of the 1960s, when foreign firms—particularly motor manufacturers—were granted permits. SIAM motor vehicle production ceased in the 1960s: automotive assembly lines were sold to **Industrias Kaiser Argentina** (IKA) in 1966 and on to IKA partner Renault a year later. Thereafter, the company refocused on the manufacture of previous staples like domestic appliances and industrial equipment, but debts already accumulated with the government development bank meant that the state became a significant partner in the business. The new economic model applied after the **military coup of 1976** by Minister **José Alfredo Martínez de Hoz**—deregulation and economic opening—signaled the end for the company. It was unable to compete with the flood of imports and filed for bankruptcy in 1981. The manufacture of household electrical appliances and industrial goods was continued under government auspices until 1986, when production lines were sold to existing domestic manufacturers. Yet the SIAM brand continued to appeal to domestic consumers, and the refrigerator model was revived in 2014. The history of the business neatly illustrates that many similar national industrial enterprises had prospered during periods of "economic closure" and policies of import substitution, but were unable to survive the abrupt opening of the economy or a loss of government favor. *See also* DEVELOPMENTALISM/DEVELOPMENTALIST; INDUSTRY; INSTITUTO TORCUATO DI TELLA; PRIVATIZATION; SASETRU; STATE-OWNED ENTERPRISES (SOEs).

SEINELDÍN, MOHAMED ALÍ (1933–2009). Veteran of the **Falklands War** who sought to cultivate a Catholic, nationalist, patriotic image as a defender of the honor of the army. Involved in barrack protests during the presidencies of **Raúl Alfonsín** and **Carlos Saúl Menem**, he had served as a member of a shadowy unit during the **Proceso de Reorganización Nacional** responsible for intelligence gathering relating to kidnapping and the abduction of children of the **Desaparecidos**.

Born in the province of **Entre Ríos** to an immigrant family of Levantine origin, Seineldín became a Catholic in his youth and appeared destined for a distinguished career in the army. In 1987 and 1988, he participated in **military** protests against budget cuts and reforms introduced by Alfonsín, and the prosecutions of senior officers for **human rights** abuses during the Proceso. In the later year, he headed a group of *carapintadas* who seized the Villa Martelli camp. After holding out for several days in the face of massive public protests, the group surrendered and were later pardoned. At the end of 1990, Seineldín led another revolt, again demanding the resignation of the head of the army and an end to prosecutions. This revolt was more violent than earlier uprisings, resulting in several deaths when units loyal to Menem recaptured bases held by rebels. Seineldín was prosecuted and sentenced to life in prison. He was pardoned in 2003 by interim president **Eduardo Duhalde** following a vociferous campaign by his supporters, who included representatives of Falkland War veterans, radical groups on the Peronist left and nationalist right, supporters of his soccer team **Boca Juniors**, as well as **Zulema Yoma de Menem**, former wife of the president. *See also* COMISIÓN NACIONAL SOBRE LA DESAPARACIÓN DE PERSONAS (CONADEP); IMMIGRATION; *NUNCA MÁS*; RICO, ALDO (1943–).

SEMANA TRÁGICA. In English the "Tragic Week," the term is applied to a series of events around the second week of January 1919, described variously as a massacre of protesting workers, violence directed at immigrants, and an anti-Semitic pogrom. Most of the events centered on the Pedro Vasena & Sons Ironworks, a substantial industrial complex in the San Cristóbal and Nueva Pompeya districts of the **federal capital**.

Labor unrest had been growing in the previous two years, triggering concerns about the "social question" and demands for curbs on **immigration**. Inflation and economic dislocation associated with the First World War had eroded worker living standards and employment, occasioning strikes, street protests, and lockouts, many of which were seen as threats to public order and the authority of the administration of President **Hipólito Yrigoyen** of the **Unión Cívica Radical** (UCR). Having taken office in 1916, the Yrigoyen administration was the first to be elected after the **Sáenz Peña Law** of 1912 facilitated fair and free elections. The immediate context was a strike at the Vasena factory called by the metalworkers' union, an organization associated with revolutionary syndicalists and socialists, in December 1918. The owners of the company refused to accept a petition about wages and conditions submitted by workers, or recognize the union, and began to recruit strikebreakers. The trade union responded by picketing the factory and company warehouses. There were several armed confrontations around the company premises in the second half of December. The first deaths occurred around the turn of the year when workers were murdered on separate occasions by the police, and a strikebreaker (and member of the police force) was killed in a struggle to remove barricades. A pivotal event took place on 7 January 1919, when a force of armed police and firemen, accompanied by strikebreakers, confronted workers. In the ensuing violence, five people were killed and around 30 injured; many were bystanders, and none of the dead were employed at the Vasena foundry. Mass demonstrations resulted, paralyzing the center of **Buenos Aires** and other major cities like **Rosario**. Further protests occurred at the funerals of the dead. Shops were looted, business premises blockaded, and transport ground to a halt, resulting in food scarcities. Pressured to restore order, the government called out the troops, while so-called patriotic vigilante groups took to the streets. Martial law was declared in Buenos Aires, troops were brought into the city, and naval vessels sailed as close to the port as possible. The worst violence occurred on 12 and 13 January. Estimates of the number killed range from 300 to 700, and of the injured between 400 and 2,000; 50,000 arrests were made. Much was made of the participation of foreigners in the events of January 1919—many union leaders (as with the membership of workers' organizations) had been born overseas—and of allegedly "antinational sentiments" and "pernicious ideologies" manifest by protesters—anarchists, "Jews," and "maximalists" were especially targeted.

While most of the events of 1919 were centered on large cities like Buenos Aires and Rosario, there were also related protests by workers in the countryside before and after 1919. Anarchist and syndicalist groups associated with organizing strikes in the cities had been similarly active among rural workers in **Patagonia**, many of whom were migrants or seasonal workers from **Chile**, while socialists had been spearheading campaigns for better working conditions for plantation workers in the northern national territories. The powerful **Sociedad Rural Argentina** (SRA), the *estanciero* association, was particularly exercised by attempts to organize workers in the countryside. There was a particularly pronounced surge in worker protest in the countryside in 1920 and 1921.

Although some concessions were made, the Yrigoyen administration was alarmed by the prospect of a right-wing backlash and inclined to take a firm line. Some within the government argued that robust action was necessary to head off the threat of a putsch that would jeopardize hard-gained political reform. Party-political calculations also played a part: the UCR was made aware of the influence, and possible electoral appeal, of other **political parties**, thereafter adopting a nationalist stance to reassure the middle classes and woo workers who had the vote with promises of benevolent state support for patriotic citizens. The threat was real enough. Many of the figures, **military** and otherwise, associated with the restoration of order in the years around 1919 would later feature in the **military coup of 1930**, leading to the view that 1919 was a dress rehearsal for 1930. This interpretation would sustain the view that the Semana Trágica and parallel events in the countryside were as much anti-Jewish, antisocialist, and anti-immigrant as antiworker, even accepting that the vast proportion of workers were immigrants from Europe, influenced by anarchist, socialist, and communist thinking. *See also* ANARCHO-SYNDICALISM; HUMAN RIGHTS; INDUSTRY; PARTIDO SOCIALISTA (PS); TRADE UNIONS.

SHANTY TOWNS. *See* VILLAS MISERIA/VILLAS DE EMERGENCIA.

SHEEP. The Spaniards introduced sheep into **Cuyo** and the northwest in the mid-16th century. The animals probably accompanied expeditions from **Chile** and Upper Peru (**Bolivia**), or possibly via the **Chaco**—present-day **Paraguay**. Modern sheep raising, however, dates from the early 19th century, when improved breeds were imported. Initially, and for most of the second half of the century, improved flocks were confined to the province of **Buenos Aires** and southern **Mesopotamia**, thereafter spreading to **Patagonia**—now the main area of the sheep industry. This displacement occurred after the **Conquest of the Desert**.

In the colonial period, sheep were mainly kept for **wool**. In the Andean region, pre-Colombian societies had developed textile production based on the use of llama wool; techniques were rapidly adapted to sheep wool. World demand for wool also drove the early development of modern sheep production but was soon accompanied by rising consumption of **meat**. Mutton was the first meat product to be processed on an industrial scale in *frigoríficos*, established from the 1870s. Originally exported as frozen mutton, sheep meat was later sent to world markets (mainly **Great Britain**) as chilled lamb. Later refinements in technology and handling led to a preference for chilled beef. Mutton and lamb were primarily consumed overseas.

Estimates place the stock of creole sheep anywhere between 2,000,000 and 3,000,000 in 1810, pastured on marginal land. By the 1840s, improved breeds of sheep were displacing **cattle** as animals were raised for both wool and tallow—demand for sheep carcasses was triggered by the expansion of *saladeros*, and there was some commercialization of mutton for the small local market in the 1860s. By 1858, the national flock was around 14,000,000 head, probably reaching almost 40 million 10 years later. In 1888, the national flock was approaching 67,000,000 head, around 80 percent of which was still located in the province of Buenos Aires. At that point, the national cattle herd was less than 20,000,000, still largely unimproved. The national flock probably peaked in the late 1890s at around 100,000,000 head. The animal census of 1908 recorded a stock of 67,000,000 head. The following two censuses (1914 and 1930) showed the national flock stable at around 44,000,000. Demand for wool during the Second World War triggered an increase; in 1952, there were 54,000,000 head of sheep. Thereafter, numbers declined. In 1980, there were only 7,000,000, and by the end of the century around 4,000,000 head. Numbers picked up in the 21st century; the 2008 census records the national flock at 16,000,000, of which about two-thirds were in Patagonia, principally merino and merino cross.

Merinos were imported in 1825; by the 1840s, merinos and merino crosses dominated the settled northern, eastern, and central district of the province of Buenos Aires. Devoted to the production of wool for exports, sheep *estancias* were worked in half shares by Irish, Scots, and Basque shepherds. Landowners stocked estates and provided the modest basic tools and facilities (corrals, sheds, and dipping pens) needed, with *estancieros* and shepherds dividing equally the annul wool clip and increase in animals. "Halves" meant that immigrant shepherds rapidly acquired capital. With land virtually "free," livestock constituted the main form of capital and the principal vehicle of accumulation. After midcentury, shepherds tended to work for "thirds," taking one-third of the clip and one-third of the increase in stock; landowners took two-thirds. By the end of the century, shepherds were hired hands. The 1870s saw the sheep frontier move to the south and west of the province and a *desmerinización* of the flock as other breeds were imported. Herbert Gibson (later Sir Herbert), whose family had had connections with the republic since the 1820s, wrote the definitive history-cum-manual of sheep raising and early wool production in the country (*The History and Present State of the Sheep-Breeding Industry in the Argentine Republic* [Buenos Aires, 1893]), claiming that the Gibsons were among the first to import new breeds and the first to promote "dual purpose" animals capable of producing a good wool clip and meat carcass. With increased demand in Europe for frozen mutton, *saladeros* gave way to *frigoríficos* and producers turned to Lincolns, Corridales, Southdowns, and Hampshires, all of which delivered a valuable fleece and quality meat. These breeds and crosses formed the bulk of the national flock until the early 20th century, when there was renewed emphasis on wool and remerinoization (a renewed preference for merinos), a trend that accelerated in the interwar decades as meatpacking plants switched to chilled beef. As the size of the flock halved between around 1900 and the early 1950s, the proportion of merinos increased.

By the end of the 20th century, with the national flock only a 10th of what it had been in the early 1950s, three-quarters were merinos and merino crosses. Wool was again king in the 21st century, but the volume and value of production did not compare with that of 100 years earlier. *See also* AGRICULTURAL COLONIZATION; AGRICULTURE; CONQUEST OF THE DESERT/DESERT CAMPAIGN; ECONOMIC CRISES; ECONOMY; *ESTANCIA* COMPANIES; FOREIGN TRADE; IMMIGRATION; URQUIZA, JUSTO JOSÉ DE (1801–1870).

SIGAUT, LORENZO (1933–). Minister of economy from March to December 1981. Sigaut served in this capacity for de facto president General **Roberto Eduardo Viola** and distanced himself from the policies of his predecessor, **José Alfredo Martínez de Hoz**. Nevertheless, he was unable to reverse the economy's downward slide and was replaced by **Roberto Alemann**.

After taking office, Sigaut quickly announced a new package of measures designed to regain control of the **economy**. The most significant initiative was a major devaluation of the peso. In order to contain the devaluation's inflationary effects, he imposed an export tax on rural **commodities**. The export subsidy for manufactured goods remained unchanged, and thereby **industry** received the full benefit of the new exchange rate. However, these policies only provided a temporary respite. A string of financial crises between April and June 1981 soon returned the country to an atmosphere of generalized collapse. Sigaut responded ineffectually, merely issuing warnings to those responsible for capital flight and to those buying dollars in expectation of large new devaluations. He acquired notoriety for the much used mantra "el que apuesta al dólar pierde" (whoever bets on the dollar loses), on one occasion restated only days before the peso lost over 30 percent of its value. Such expressions only encouraged panic buying of the US **currency**. Under pressure from all sectors, the government was forced to allow a free float of the peso for financial transactions and also agreed to a costly scheme by which it would assume responsibility for private-sector debts on very favorable terms. This scheme led Argentine businesses to create a huge amount of fictitious "paper loans," the bulk of which left Argentina in the form of capital flight.

Sigaut unsuccessfully redoubled his efforts to impose order in the chaotic exchange market and tackle the trade deficit. He also announced plans to deal with the sources of financial speculation and to provide incentives for productive investment in the rural and industrial sectors. But before Sigaut could implement any of this, his tenure as minister ended abruptly with the palace coup that ousted Viola in December 1981. *See also* AGRICULTURE; ECONOMIC CRISES; FOREIGN DEBT/FOREIGN INVESTMENT; INDUSTRY; MINISTRY OF ECONOMY.

SLUMS. *See* CONVENTILLOS; VILLAS MISERIA/VILLAS DE EMERGENCIA.

SOBREMONTE, RAFAEL DE (1746–1827). Aristocrat, military leader, and colonial official; last viceroy of the Río de la Plata to be appointed by Bourbon monarchs. His two immediate successors, **Santiago de Liniers** and **Baltasar Hidalgo de Cisneros**, were chosen by Patriotic Juntas—Liniers by the Patriotic Junta of **Buenos Aires** and Cisneros by the Patriotic Junta of Seville.

Sobremonte had seen service in various parts of the Spanish empire, including a successful spell as governor of **Córdoba**, before being nominated viceroy—he held the post from 1804 to 1807. Previously regarded as an efficient administrator, he is remembered for an inept defense of Buenos Aires during the **British invasion** 1806—he abandoned the city and suffered further indignity when the contents of the royal treasury, which he had sent to the interior for safekeeping, were captured by the British. Sobremonte refused to organize and arm the local population to defend the city, correctly fearing "revolutionary sedition," already much in evidence. He preferred a strategic retreat to Córdoba, where he counted on greater loyalty to the Crown. These mishaps led inexorably to the **May Revolution of 1810** and **independence**. Liniers, who organized a successful counterattack in 1806 and repulsed a further British invasion in 1807, largely employing domestic forces, was acclaimed the hero of the moment. These events stirred patriotic sentiments, confounding Spanish efforts to regain control. Sobremonte was kept under guard in Buenos Aires until 1809, when he returned to **Spain** in disgrace. *See also* CABILDO ABIERTO.

SOCIALIST PARTY. *See* PARTIDO SOCIALISTA (PS).

SOCIEDAD DE BENEFICENCIA DE BUENOS AIRES. Government philanthropic association established by **Bernardino Rivadavia** in 1823, using funds obtained from the secularization of property previously owned by monastic orders and the **Catholic Church**. Along with the **Sociedad Rural Argentina** (SRA) and the Jockey Club, it was once one of the most prestigious social institutions in the country.

The society was run by **women** of the elite—La Damas de la Beneficencias. It was one of the few public roles available to women at the time. It was initially charged with managing hospitals and orphanages and providing **education** for young women. Although the educational activities of the Beneficencia, as it was generally known, were much reduced with the creation of a national system of government-funded primary schools in 1876, the importance of the society as the principal provider of assistance to the poor grew, especially during the period of mass **immigration**. By the late 19th century, it was the largest charitable organization in the country, raising funds through events and donations by aristocratic families. Invitations to participate in such events and to support the work of the society were a mark of social status. By this time, the organization was conventionally headed by the wife of the president. It was this convention that led to the winding up of the Beneficencia.

When former general **Juan Domingo Perón** was elected president in 1946, his wife **Eva Perón** anticipated an invitation from the Ladies of the Beneficencia to preside. The invitation was not forthcoming. La Damas politely suggested that Mrs. Perón was too young to take on such an onerous responsibility. The ploy did not work: Eva responded that she would nominate her mother instead. The real reason was distain: Evita's social background and colorful past did not appeal to the ladies. As her memoir reveals, Evita was incandescent. The upshot was the closure of the Beneficencia and the establishment of the **Fundación Eva Perón**, which would be headed by the first lady and was now intended to be the principal charitable organization in the country. Following the **military coup of 1955**, which ousted Perón, unlike many other institutions that had been intervened or modified during the Peronist years, the Beneficencia was not revived.

SOCIEDAD MIXTA SIDERURGICA ARGENTINA (SOMISA). Corporation set up in 1947 at the behest of **Fabricaciones Militares** (FM) to develop large-scale iron and steel production in the country. It was initially intended to be a joint venture between FM and private-sector small-scale steel producers, with the former gradually reducing its stake to a basic minimum. This proved unrealistic and politically unacceptable. Moreover, the major role of ARMCO Argentina (the local subsidiary of US firm ARMCO) in the project was questioned thoroughly in the National **Congress** given the fashionableness of the idea of "economic independence," though it did remain involved.

During the first presidential term of **Juan Domingo Perón** (1946–1952), little was done to advance the project though preparatory work continued. ARMCO submitted its "Definitive Plan" to SOMISA in October 1947: a plant with an annual capacity of 500,000 tons would be built in one of the riverside ports on the **Paraná** River, which would allow for its expansion to 1,000,000 tons in the future. The main installations were to be a port for importing raw materials, a plant for coke production that could handle both national and imported coal, a blast furnace with a daily capacity to produce 1,300 tons of pig iron, a plant with six Siemens-Martin furnaces for steelmaking, a rolling mill, a thermal power plant, and auxiliary services. The last included equipment to unload ships and handle raw materials, docks, internal roads and railways, workshops, laboratories, and sewers and drainage. ARMCO would provide technical assistance for all installations except the auxiliary equipment and thermal power plant, for which no assistance was required.

The location of the plant was decided to be at Punta Argerich near **San Nicolás**, for which FM would expropriate an area covering around 3,000 hectares for the steelworks, related industries, and storage of raw materials. An area of 290 hectares was placed at the disposal of FM in order to allow for the initiation of work, which was formally acquired in May 1948. But there was no more progress as the authorized capital of SOMISA proved insufficient. It had been set at 100 million pesos, while the costs of the plant were 140 million pesos (over 20 million US dollars). Despite the necessary legislation to increase the capital being finally enacted in September 1950, the economic situation at that time forced the government not to make contributions to the augmented capital and to refuse SOMISA the right to seek foreign loans to make up for state funding deficiencies. Furthermore, the private-sector partners in the project were in no financial position to afford to contribute large amounts.

Progress was made on funding for the steelworks during Perón's short-lived second presidency (1952–1955) after he belatedly reversed his economic policies and openly strove to improve relations with the **United States**. The Argentine government made funds available for a contract signed with a French firm in 1952 for the construction of the deep-water port required for raw material deliveries. It also approved the purchase of a steel plate finishing mill manufactured in the United States for the Czech company Investa, which had been embargoed by the Americans following the Communist takeover in Prague. The impounded installations were auctioned in May 1954 by the US Treasury, which accepted an offer of nine million US dollars by FM. The title of the mill was turned over to SOMISA, and the equipment, already crated at the Port of New York, was soon on its way.

The most important Peronist reversal concerned the possibility of securing the external financing of equipment. In March 1954, SOMISA agreed in principle to award the US firm Arthur G. McKee and Company the contract for the supply, assembly, and installation of the blast furnace. This being the most expensive component of the plant, the crucial problem was financing the deal. In sharp contrast to the government attitudes during the first Perón presidency, SOMISA was authorized to approach the US Export–Import Bank directly. In March 1955, the company was notified that the bank was prepared to provide 60 million US dollars toward the cost of purchases of equipment and services in North America. Although the **military coup of 1955** resulted in further delays to the project, the progress made with SOMISA during the preceding three years enabled the completion of the steelworks in May 1961.

Nevertheless, there remained the fact that the steelworks project had been badly thought out by FM in terms of raw materials and production. Regarding the former, the SOMISA plant was not only required to employ a combination of foreign and domestic inputs but also stockpile them. Although the use of foreign raw materials cut costs, insufficient economy had been achieved owing to transport rates and the utilization of poor-quality domestic minerals. Moreover, the problem with the inland, upriver location of the steelworks was that by the time the mill became operational there had been major technical innovations with ore carriers that could not have been foreseen. The riverside location of the steelworks was increasingly disadvantaged as regards river depth, which then combined with bottlenecks in the land transport system to have an adverse effect on final delivery price of SOMISA products. As regards production, it was based on aggregate demand and a bid for national self-sufficiency. Operations were volume driven, and the plant was designed to manufacture the broadest possible assortment of iron and steel goods, even though many of these were required in small volumes and uneconomic to produce.

Three decades after the steelworks began production, the government of President **Carlos Saúl Menem** decided to carry out the **privatization** of SOMISA. **María Julia Alsogaray** became the head of the company in 1991 and charged with overseeing the sale. The process was extremely opaque, and SOMISA was sold for around 15 percent of its book value. It was acquired by Techint and took the name Siderar, and the San Nicolás steelworks became more competitive through specialization. It produces cables, wires, and tubes, mainly for the construction and oil sectors—approximately 60 percent of its present-day output is exported, mainly to other South American countries. *See also* DEVELOPMENTALISM/DEVELOPMENTALIST; ECONOMY; INDUSTRY; STATE-OWNED ENTERPRISES (SOEs); TRANSPORTATION.

SOCIEDAD RURAL ARGENTINA (SRA). Commonly referred to as the Rural; founded in 1866; until the mid-20th century, the Argentine Rural Society was the preeminent business and social institution in the country. Representing agricultural producers, it was set up by modernizing *estancieros* and in its heyday between the 1880s and 1940s was the most politically powerful nonstate entity in the country—probably more powerful than the **Ministry of Agriculture** and many other government bodies. The annual exposition held by the Rural was one of the largest and most influential agricultural shows in the world, attracting visitors, judges, and exhibitors from overseas. The show was a major event in the social calendar and usually opened by the president of the republic.

A list of founding members of the society includes such names as Agüero, Bell, Madero, Martínez de Hoz, and Pereyra. The mission statement of the Rural was and is to promote the rural sector—particularly pastoral interests—serve as a forum for discussion, encourage improvement through the dissemination of scientific knowledge—notably, about livestock breeds and animal husbandry—facilitate the development of best practices, and enhance the economic and social quality of rural life. These are areas of activity recognized by awards and categories established at the annual show. The membership and activities of the Rural grew exponentially after the **Conquest of the Desert** as the frontier moved west and south, opening enormous tracts of fertile land to farming and ranching. There were some corporate members, but the initial membership was overwhelmingly composed of individual *estancieros* and representatives of landed families. Around 1900, a list of presidents and officers of the Rural reads like a national equivalent of *Debrett's Peerage, Baronage, Knightage and Companionage* or the *Almanach de Gotha*. With the subdivision of estates, and official emphasis on promanufacturing policies during the middle third of the 20th century, the membership and influence of the Rural declined.

Clearly an elite organization, the members of the Rural was initially held in high esteem, regarded as entrepreneurial and dynamic. This public perception began to change in the 1930s, when the institution and its members were seen as the principal influence behind regimes of the **Concordancia**. As a class, landowners were now viewed as exploitative and part of the *vendepatria* clique. This image was cultivated during the first administration of **Juan Domingo Perón** and the sector loaded with taxes and controls. The organization struggled and failed to prevent the extension of social and welfare legislation to rural workers bringing pressure to bear on *peones* and organizing a lockout. The society was particularly exercised by the threat of land reform—a threat that never materialized. At the time, the Rural also had little success in the campaign against monopoly buying by the government commodity agency **Instituto Argentino de Promoción del Intercambio** (IAPI). A more positive political relationship with **military** regimes of the 1960s and 1970s had been anticipated, but with the developmentalist ideology of the period stressing the need for industrialization, this did little to relieve economic pressure on the sector, even when **José Alfredo Martínez de Hoz** was appointed minister of **economy**. He may have been a scion of an old aristocratic family, but he did agriculturalists few favors. In the face of what it regarded as government hostility and unwillingness to pay due heed to lobbying, the Rural had little to advise members other than to stage producer strikes and cut back on production. Relations with the government were particularly tense during the administration of President **Isabel Perón**.

There was not much change with the return of democracy; President Raúl Alfonsín was roundly booed by the crowd when participating in the inauguration of the 1988 exposition, an indication of impotence as much as frustration at official policy. Only in the 1990s did lobbying by the Rural and other organizations produce a change in the fiscal regime and a surge in investment in the rural sector. Speaking at the opening of the 1997 agricultural show, President **Carlos Saúl Menem** was loudly applauded. Fearing that he would receive the same treatment as Alfonsín, interim president **Eduardo Duhalde** declined to attend the 2002 annual exposition at the height of the economic crisis that accompanied the collapse of the **Convertibility Plan**. Export taxes (*retenciones*) and controls returned, and the screw was tightened during the administrations of President **Néstor Kirchner** and his wife, President **Cristina Fernández de Kirchner**. The Rural had little access to power. Deterioration in relations with the government arising from ratcheting taxes led to **farm protests** in which the Rural played a major but hardly dominant role. Members of the Rural anticipate a better relationship with the administration of President **Mauricio Macri** installed at the end of 2015. The Rural expects an end to the confrontation between the rural sector and the government that has characterized recent years, while recognizing that it has limited influence.

Today, the Rural no longer has the unique or exclusive status that it once enjoyed as the prime rural-sector lobbying organization. Now one of many such organizations, it nevertheless remains the leader in the field. *See also* AGRICULTURAL COLONIZATION; AGRICULTURE; ASOCIACIÓN EMPRESARIA ARGENTINA (AEA); CATTLE; COMMODITIES; CONFEDERACIÓN GENERAL ECONÓMICA (CGE); CRY OF ALCORTA; DEVELOPMENTALISM/DEVELOPMENTALIST; *ESTANCIA*; FOREIGN TRADE; *FRIGORÍFICOS*; MAIZE; MEAT; MINISTRY OF ECONOMY; SHEEP.

SOLANO LIMA, VICENTE (1901–1984). Founder of the **Partido Conservador Popular** (PCP); vice president of Argentina from May to July 1973. In his early career in conservative politics in the province of **Buenos Aires** and as a member of the Chamber of Deputies for the **Concordancia**, Solano Lima was noted for his major concern with social and labor affairs and acquired the sobriquet "Red Minister."

He was vice presidential candidate for the **Partido Demócrata Nacional** (PDN) in the **presidential election of 1951**. Following the **military coup of 1955**, Solano Lima became disillusioned with the anti-Peronist hard line of the party and broke away to form the PCP in 1958. Thereafter, he maintained a position of closeness with the Peronists, and his political career would peak in 1973. When the PCP joined the **Frente Justicialista de Liberación** (FREJULI), Solano Lima became its vice presidential candidate in the **presidential election of March 1973**. Successfully elected to office, he focused on helping increase university enrollment among the working and lower classes. However, his tenure lasted 49 days. President **Héctor Cámpora** and Solano Lima resigned, paving the way for a fresh election that returned **Juan Domingo Perón** to power. During the third Perón presidency, Solano Lima held two positions: first as chief of staff for the president, then as rector of the **University of Buenos Aires** (UBA) in March 1974. Following the death of Perón three months later, Solano Lima retired from public life.

SOURROUILLE, JUAN VITAL (1940–). Distinguished academic economist who became minister of **economy**; technocrat who authored the heterodox **Austral Plan**. Sourrouille read economics at the **University of Buenos Aires** (UBA), graduating in 1963, going on to study in the **United States**. There, with Richard D. Mallon, he wrote the well-received *Economic Policymaking in a Conflict Society: The Argentine Case*, published by Harvard University Press in 1975. The book challenged conventional assumptions about the rational behavior of economic agents and theories of economic policy making, arguing for the need to build political consensus to effect fundamental changes in the macroeconomy. Research for the book informed his actions as a minister. On returning to Argentina, he was appointed professor of macroeconomics at the UBA, a position he held until 1983. With the return of democracy that year, he was appointed secretary of planning at the **Ministry of Economy** by President **Raúl Alfonsín**. Two years later, he headed the ministry. Sourrouille was the second and longest serving of Alfonsín's four economics ministers, in office from 1985 until 1989.

The initial success of the Austral Plan, launched virtually out of the blue on 14 June 1985, seemed to vindicate Sourrouille's theoretical model and his approach to the practicalities of the political economy of policy making. Surprisingly, the economic team was able to sell the plan to an initially skeptical International Monetary Fund (IMF)—surprising because the plan combined Keynesian-style measures and a wage and salary hike in advance of a freeze on prices and salaries. Traditionally, the IMF advocated wage freezes combined with freeing price controls. Unfortunately, the economic cycle did not coincide with the electoral cycle. At the beginning of March 1989, Sourrouille argued that everything was under control and Alfonsín went on the record to say that there would be no change of policy nor of the economic team. Yet it was clear to most that the government had lost control of the economy; by the end of the month, Sourrouille had resigned.

On leaving office, Sourrouille returned to academic life. He has since published extensively in the fields of macroeconomics, investment, and trade and about his time in government, as well as broadcasting and writing contributions for the press. His pioneering work on heterodox economics is acknowledged, and when it appeared to be working, the Austral Plan served as a blueprint for similar contemporary experiments elsewhere in Latin America. *See also* CURRENCY; ECONOMIC CRISES; FOREIGN DEBT/ FOREIGN INVESTMENT; FOREIGN TRADE; HYPERINFLATION; MENEM, CARLOS SAÚL (1930–).

SOUTH AMERICAN COMMON MARKET. *See* MERCOSUR.

SOUTHERN CONE. Geographical and political term applied to countries at the southern tip of South America, namely Argentina, **Chile**, and **Uruguay**. By extension, occasionally **Paraguay** is included.

SPAIN. Relations with the former "mother" country have changed markedly since **independence**. While a significant proportion of the resident Spanish merchant community supported the **May Revolution of 1810**, there was disagreement among factions about the political organization of the new country—for example, whether to establish a constitutional monarchy headed by a Bourbon prince (or princess) or a republic—during which those favoring continuing links with Spain became marginalized. The Argentine–Spanish connection was at its weakest during the first half of the 19th century, revived after the 1890s, and became particularly strong around the middle of the 20th century. By the early 21st century, there was a strong association based on language, shared culture, migration between the two countries, and strengthening commercial and financial links. Both countries are members of the Organization of Ibero-American States (Organización de Estados Iberoamericanos)—the organization was founded in 1949 yet only assumed a major international profile at the end of the century. The Spanish monarch is honorary president of the organization.

Notwithstanding support for independence among some sections, by the 1820s Spain and all things Spanish were being portrayed negatively. Early 19th-century liberals like **Bernardino Rivadavia** contrasted traditional, conservative, backward Catholic Spain negatively with "enlightened," modernizing countries to the north of the Pyrenees. Spanish colonialism was similarly depicted as rapacious and the political and economic antithesis of British colonialism. Despite clashes between London and North America colonists and the War of American Independence, British colonialism was regarded as transmitting liberal ideas to the 13 colonies, fostering an emergent local democracy and dynamic agricultural, commercial, and industrial sectors. That Spain did not recognize Argentine independence until 1857 and did not establish diplomatic relations until the following year did not help. And as the country grew after the 1860s, the focus was on the **United States**, France, and **Great Britain** for political models and economic partners.

Argentine perceptions of Spain became more favorable around the 1890s. This was due in part to **immigration** flows from the Iberian Peninsula and a modest pickup in trade. Sections of the elite were drawn to *hispanismo*, an ideology or school of thought gaining traction at the time that emphasized shared cultural and social values. *Hispanismo* was also viewed as a counter to the Pan-Americanism then being peddled by the United States, which was regarded as a threat to Argentine pretentions to leadership in Latin America. The Spanish–American–Cuban War of 1898, in which the United States was seen as the aggressor and Spain the victim, helped strengthen these sentiments. By this time, there was already a steady flow of Spanish migrants to the **River Plate**. Insurgency on the island and a near full-blown civil war in the 1890s produced a shift in emigration from Spain after the 1870s from the Caribbean to the River Plate. The centenary of independence in 1910 marked the beginning of particularly cordial relations between the two countries. The principal guest of honor at ceremonies to mark the centenary was the Infanta Isabella, eldest daughter of Queen Isabella II of Spain and the most popular member of the royal family. The visit was a great success. The Spanish Civil War of 1936–1939 strengthened ties further. Although governments of the **Concordancia** were assumed to be close to General Franco and the nationalists, the country received thousands of republican refugees. Traditionally,

Mexico has been regarded as the main destination for exiles in the Americas, but recent estimates suggest that Argentina became home to between 10,000 and 20,000—the larger figure would equal the high estimates for Mexico. Republican exiles made noted contributions to **industry**, publishing, and the **media**.

The first administration of President **Juan Domingo Perón** forged particularly close economic and diplomatic contacts with Franco's Spain. Argentina was the main supplier of food aid following the civil war, and **Eva Perón** was feted by Madrid on her famous "rainbow tour" of Europe. Her reception in Spain was the warmest that she received, both by the government and the public. Later, Franco would offer refuge to Perón himself. Perón spent most of his time in exile in Spain, remaining there from 1960 to 1973, marrying his third wife, **Isabel Perón**, in Madrid in 1961. Around this time, both countries were pursuing autarchic policies of industrialization, a policy proximity that meant that they were competing for foreign investment, seeking to attract multinational corporations, notably in the motor vehicle and household appliance sectors. By the 1980s, the nature of the relationship between the countries began to shift. Until the 1960s, Argentina had been the bigger and more dynamic **economy**—the former colony had eclipsed the mother country. In the 1980s, the Spanish economy was strengthening while the Argentine was experiencing another of its periodic **economic crises**. There was a reversal in migration flows. If Argentina had been a destination of Spanish emigration from the 1870s to the 1950s, Spain became a destination for Argentine emigrants during the last years of the administration of President **Raúl Alfonsín**. The following decade, Spain emerged as a "political model" for Argentine intellectuals and policy makers: the transition in Spain from the Franco dictatorship to a fully fledged democracy, and the institutionalization of that process, was regarded in some circles as providing a map for an Argentina seeking to escape its history of repeated **military** coups and violent authoritarianism. Spain appeared to offer a blueprint for economic and political modernization at a time when Spanish business and financial corporations were seeking opportunities abroad, looking in particular to Latin America. The collapse of the **Convertibility Plan** at the beginning of the 21st century triggered another wave of emigration to Spain. Around 90,000 in 2017, the Argentine community in Spain is the largest in the world; most are of Spanish descent, able to claim a Spanish passport.

Spanish firms participated strongly in the **privatization** of Argentine **state-owned enterprises** in the 1990s. Acquisitions included the airline **Aerolíneas Argentinas**, bought by a consortium headed by the Spanish state airline Iberia in 1990, and the oil corporation **Yacimiento Petrolíferos Fiscales** (YPF), purchased by REPSOL in 1999; both were later renationalized. Spanish banks increased their presence in the country: in 1996, the Banco de Bilbao y Vizcaya bought the Banco Francés del Río de la Plata, the oldest private bank in Argentina; in 1997, Santander bought Banco del Río de la Plata (the company was renamed Banco Santander Río)—the acquisition gave the Santander group a major stake in Telecom Argentina and other former state entities that the Banco Río de la Plata had in part financed during the presidency of **Carlos Saúl Menem**. In 2017, Spain was the third largest foreign investor in Argentina in terms of total stock, after the United States and the Netherland. In recent years, Spain has often been the second most important source of new investment after the United States and regularly features in the top 10 trading partners of Argentina. More than 300 Spanish companies currently operate in Argentina, concentrated in the telecommunication, energy, and financial services sectors. Government–business relations have warmed since the inauguration of President **Mauricio Macri** in 2015, with Macri launching a charm offensive in Madrid. S*ee also* BRAMUGLIA, JUAN ATILIO (1903–1962); DEVELOPMENTALISM/DEVELOPMENTALIST; FOREIGN DEBT/FOREIGN INVESTMENT; FOREIGN TRADE; IMMIGRATION; INDUSTRY.

STATE-OWNED ENTERPRISES (SOEs). By the 1970s, Argentina was one of the most "statized" economies in the world outside the communist bloc. In addition to owning and operating public utilities, banks and insurances firms, and pension funds, the federal and provincial governments owned large industrial complexes, including heavy industries like iron and steel and petrochemicals, and mines.

Estimates of the number of firms associated with the state around 1975 range between 747 and 433, including companies owned by government banks and financial institutions and those in which the state was a minority shareholder. Official monopolies ran the railways and telecommunications; all ports were operated by government agencies; state firms were responsible for the generation and supply of all electricity and natural gas; about 80 percent of oil refining capacity was in state hands and 65 percent of petroleum production; coastal shipping was another state monopoly, while national and international sea and air transport was dominated by government carriers; a sizable chunk of the financial sector, including insurance, was run by official banks and agencies—reinsurance was yet another state monopoly. In various branches of manufacturing, government businesses were significant players—or the dominant firm. Government companies accounted for a fifth of national production, a quarter of total fixed investment. The labor force of these firms may have totaled around 500,000, when the economically active populations stood at nine million (1970 National Census), the former figure excluding those employed in the bureaucracy and other areas of government like health and **education**. Possibly 40 percent of the labor force was employed by various branches of the federal government, provincial administrations, public agencies, and SOEs. Illustrative of the *empleomania* of the period was the situation of the railways; within a few years of nationalization, the workforce had virtually doubled, while traffic and revenues declined. By 1990, SOEs accounted for half the public-sector deficit; **Ferrocarriles Argentinos** (FFAA) was the largest single drain on the national treasury, making a persuasive case for **privatization**.

Several factors account for the emergence of the modern "entrepreneurial state"; crises, economic nationalism, and economic ideology, as well as profound political changes such as those associated with **Juan Domingo Perón** and **Peronism**. The federal and some provincial governments operated railways and banks in the 19th century, yet the first modern expansion of state economic activities occurred in the 1930s and took various forms, while building on such initiatives of the 1920s as the State Oil Corporation (**Yacimientos Petrolíferos Fiscales**—YPF) formed in 1922, and the Military Aircraft Factory (Fábrica Militar de Aviones) in 1927. Following the 1929 Wall Street collapse and ensuing world depression, as in other countries, Argentine administrations instituted **commodity** boards to regulate the price of key products, mainly exports. Between 1928 and 1937, almost two dozen price-support schemes were implemented, the most important being the Junta Reguladora de Granos—later the Junta Nacional de Granos—set up in 1933, dealing in wheat, **maize**, and linseed, while the government also took over a failing *frigerífico* in order to ensure a national presence in the foreign-dominated meatpacking sector. Similar strategic consideration triggered intervention in ailing railways and utilities. Squeezed by declining traffic, rising operating costs, and a depreciating exchange rate, which decimated remittances, several minor British-owned railway companies like the **Cordoba Central** and Argentine Transandine were unable to service debentures and faced bankruptcy. After protracted negotiations with shareholders, the federal government stepped in, nationalizing companies in 1939, incorporating them into the State Railway Executive (Dirección General de Ferrocarriles del Estado), which had been formed in 1910 to administer a handful of developmental lines, located mainly in the then national territories. Profit and remittance pressures, plus mounting operating costs, similarly led to transport coordination in the city of **Buenos Aires**. Unable to respond to competition from independent bus route operators, the position of the London-registered **Anglo-Argentine Tramways** became untenable. The formation of a mixed corporation was first proposed in 1936, though only effected three years later. The municipally administered corporation took over the assets of the tramways, underground railways, and independent bus lines, awarding them shares in the new enterprise. These initiatives bailed out foreign investors and enlarged the outreach of the state. The Exchange Control Commission was established in 1931 to manage the **currency** when the peso left the gold standard, followed four years later by the central bank (**Banco Central de la República Argentina** [BCRA]), initially set up as a mixed entity composed of private (mainly foreign) and state banks. At this point, the principal clearing bank in the country, holding almost half the deposits system, was the federally owned **Banco de la Nación**.

There was a further, more marked, expansion in the economic role of the state in the 1940s, mainly though not exclusively in the first Perón presidency. Founded in 1941, the State Merchant Fleet (Flota Mercante del Estado) was initially composed of Axis vessels impounded when the country declared a state of belligerence. The fleet was expanded under Perón; by the early 1950s, the national merchant fleet was carrying more exports than any foreign flag. In 1960, the company was reorganized as Empresas Líneas Marítimas Argentina, absorbing other shipping companies, including private domestic coastal services that had already been nationalized. **Fabricaciones Militares** (FM) was also created in 1941, absorbing the aeroplane plant that had been operating since 1927 and steel rolling mill (Fábrica Militar de Aceros) authorized in 1937. Originally focusing on the production of equipment for the military, by the 1960s FM had become an important producer of motor vehicles and railway rolling stock. The government iron and steel plant, **Sociedad Mixta Siderúgica Argentina** (SOMISA), was organized in 1946. Other forays into heavy **industry** and equipment manufacture included Industrias Aeronáuticas y Mecánicas del Estado, formed in 1952, displacing the aircraft factory set up 15 years before, and the shipbuilder Astilleros y Fábricas Navales del Estado in 1953. With the nationalization of the Bemberg family group industrial holdings in 1953, the state acquired even more diverse interest. In that year, firms wholly or partly owned by government accounted for almost 10 percent of national industrial output.

Nevertheless, the greatest expansion of a government presence in the **economy** at this time occurred in the transport and utility sectors. Primitiva Compañía de Gas de Buenos Aires was taken over in 1945, subsequently expanding to become Gas del Estado. The French-owned Port of **Rosario** was nationalized at much the same time, and in 1946, on the eve of the expiry of the **Mitre Law**, the concession under which foreign-owned railways enjoyed substantial tax breaks, expropriation was initiated. Perhaps influenced by the model for transport coordination in the city of Buenos Aires, the government was first inclined toward the formation of a mixed operating concession in which London-registered companies would initially have the major representation—the British-owned Argentine Railways accounted for about two-thirds of the national network—later, outright nationalization was favored. Ferrocarriles del Estado (subsequently, **Ferrocarriles Argentinos** [FFA]) was reconstituted in 1948, absorbing British and French companies and existing state railways. By the end of the decade, the telephone service, dominated by US capital, was in state hands. Empresa Mixta Telefónica Argentina (EMTA) was the precursor of **ENCOTel**. US water and power utilities, expropriated by the 1943 **military** regime, also formed the bases of

Agua y Energía, organized in 1947. Four small airlines were converted into mixed companies in 1946; three years later, they were fused to form the wholly state-owned **Aerolíneas Argentinas** (AA). Faced with huge modernization costs to upgrade services, labor pressure for better wages and working conditions, popular demands for greater regulation, and a rising tide of economic nationalism, most of these businesses were content to pass assets to the state. Expropriation chimed with the ideology of the regime—national economic sovereignty and socially responsible capitalism. Perhaps this also explains the early stress on mixed corporations, a model assumed to meld state developmentalism and market efficiency, in addition to creating opportunities for local capitalists alongside foreign ones, while ensuring continuing access to overseas management and technology.

Advances in the utilities and industrial sectors were paralleled in banking and finance. Nationalization of the central bank came in 1946, which then assumed direct supervision of major official banking institutions like the Banco de la Nación Argentina, the **Banco de la Provincia de Buenos Aires**, the Postal Savings Bank, and the Industrial Development Bank (**Banco de Crédito Industrial Argentino** [BCIA]), set up in 1944. Hitherto, these entities had been autonomous. The Reinsurance Agency (Instituto Mixto Argentino de Reaseguros) was similarly brought under direct central bank control, as was the investment agency, the Instituto Mixto de Inversiones Mobiliarias. These measures signaled the nationalization of bank deposits and direct state control of the financial sector, paving the way for the formulation of a national investment strategy. The nationalization of investments was furthered by the formation of the National Pensions Agency, nominally designed to channel funds to development projects. Part a bailout, part cross-subsidization, definitely increasing the outreach of the state, the agency absorbed previously independent tripartite occupational pension schemes, mainly those catering to railway, tramway, and bank workers. International trade—and foreign exchange earnings—were intended to be statized with the creation of the **Instituto Argentino de Promoción del Intercambio** (IAPI), the origins of which may be traced back to commodity boards of the 1930s. The monopoly buyer of traditional arable exports, overseen by the central bank, IAPI would briefly come to control around 70 percent of exports and handle around 30 percent of imports.

Even public charity was statized. In 1948, the resources and responsibilities of the autonomous aristocratic **Sociedad de Beneficencia de Buenos Aires**, founded in 1823, were transferred to the nominally private **Fundación Eva Perón**. Intended as the centerpiece of the regime's rapidly expanding program of social welfare, funded by the government, deductions from the wages of workers, and private business "donations," the foundation rapidly expanded its areas of operation from orphanages supported by the Sociedad to hospitals, schools, day-care centers, and low-cost housing projects. Its role declined after the death of Evita in 1952. The foundation was closed by the military government in 1955.

After the overthrow of Perón, there was discussion about rolling back the frontiers of the state. Yet little was accomplished, other than the dismantling of IAPI and the investment agency, under de facto President **Pedro Eugenio Aramburu** (1955–1958), and the privatization of a handful of enterprises, the most important of which was the Buenos Aires Transport Authority, by **Frondizi** (1958–1962), as part of an International Monetary Fund stabilization package—modest achievements notwithstanding the president's nationalist and statist inclinations. Developmentalism provided the ideological underpinnings for state-directed industrialization, and as would be the case in the 1970s, the military was disinclined to divest themselves of industrial assets acquired in the 1940s and early 1950s. State economic activities were consolidated and advanced during the **Juan Carlos Onganía** presidency (1966–1970): rationalization, not privatization, was the principal objective. State corporation reorganization was most pronounced in such areas as energy generation and supply (where existing capacity in coal mines, oil wells, and gas and electricity facilities was complemented by new initiatives in hydroelectricity), petrochemicals, iron and steel, transport, and manufacturing—all the principal firms operating in these sectors had been restructured and activities expanded by the time the military stood down in 1973. These were strategic sectors and businesses, considered essential by the armed forces for national industrial development. At the same time, economic instability drove other enterprises into the arms of the government, the most important of which were the white goods and motor vehicle manufacturer **Sección Industrial Amasadoras Mecánicas Di Tella** (SIAM Di Tella), steel makers, sugar mills, and the meatpacker Swift. Some of these companies were regionally significant, others regarded as emblematic national enterprises. Military regimes of the 1966–1973 period were unwilling to allow these firms to fold, taking them into public ownership. Such sentiments would resonate with subsequent administrations, both civilian and military. **Economic crises** in 1975 and 1989 resulted in more companies being taken into state ownership, despite efforts by the **Raúl Alfonsín** government to dispose of some firms and secure private partners for others.

The most recent round of state expansion occurred under the **Kirchners**. Ideology, and opportunity dressed up as coherent policy, facilitated a particularly cozy relationship between national business and the state. Gradually, many former SOEs privatized in the 1990s were taken back into state hands, or operating concessions passed to financial-industrial groups close to the regime. The postal service was renationalized in 2003, water supply and sanitation provided by **Aguas Argentinas** in 2006, Tandanor shipyards and Fábica Militar de Aviones in 2007, Aerolíneas Argentinas in 2008, and YPF in 2012 along with a major rail franchise. The renationalization of private pension funds also began in 2008. Failure to provide adequate services and noncompliance with contractual obligations were the main reasons cited. Although not peculiar to the period, subsidies enjoyed by suppliers to and buyers of products and services from SOEs, along with sweet-deal franchises, facilitated a massive transfer of resources from the public to the private sector during the three Kirchner presidencies. **Corruption**, cronyism, and predatory behavior became a distinct feature of Argentine capitalism. *See also* AGRICULTURE; DEVELOPMENTALISM/DEVELOPMENTALIST; FOREIGN DEBT/FOREIGN INVESTMENT; FOREIGN TRADE; INDUSTRY; TRANSPORTATION.

STOCK EXCHANGE. *See* BOLSA DE COMERCIO.

STRUCTURALISM. *See* DEVELOPMENTALISM/DEVELOPMENTALIST.

SUÁREZ MASON, CARLOS GUILLERMO (1924–2005). As head of the First Army Corps (1976–1980), he was one of the main repressors during the **Proceso de Reorganización Nacional**. Under Suárez Mason's jurisdiction were four clandestine detention centers, the most notorious of which was El Olimpo. The latter functioned from August 1978 to January 1979 in an old trams and buses terminus in the city of **Buenos Aires** that had been expropriated by the de facto government of **Jorge Rafael Videla** and then legally transferred to the División de Automotores de la Policía Federal. Approximately 650 people were assassinated there, which earned Suárez Mason the sobriquet "El Carnicero del Olimpo" (the Butcher of Olympus).

After the **military** dictatorship collapsed, the former First Army Corps commander fled to the **United States** in 1984. The request for his extradition by the government of President **Raúl Alfonsín** was only met in 1988, but before the trial was completed he was one of the senior officers pardoned by then president **Carlos Saúl Menem**. Having regained his freedom, Suárez Mason returned to the United States. He was again extradited in the mid-1990s, accused of stealing children of **Desaparecidos** born in captivity in the clandestine detention centers he ran. Given his age, he was placed under house arrest. He broke the terms of the latter by celebrating his 80th birthday away from his domicile and spent the final year of his life in prison. *See also* COMISIÓN NACIONAL SOBRE LA DESAPARACIÓN DE PERSONAS (CONADEP); DIRTY WAR; DISPOSICIÓN FINAL; HUMAN RIGHTS; MADRES DE PLAZA DE MAYO; MILITARY COUP OF 1976; *NUNCA MÁS*; WAR TO ANNIHILATE SUBVERSION.

SUR. Published in **Buenos Aires**, it was the most prominent literary magazine of its time. First published in 1931, its founder and main backer was **Victoria Ocampo**. She was assisted by a multidisciplinary team of collaborators and supported intellectually by Spanish philosopher José Ortega y Gasset. Notable contributors and sometimes editors include **Jorge Luis Borges** and **Adolfo Bioy Casares**, and the last issue was published in 1970.

T

TANGO. National music of the **River Plate**, claimed equally by **Uruguay** and Argentina. Dating from the colonial era, it was first popular during the late 19th century and the early decades of the 20th, particularly from the 1920s to the 1940s. Tango declined in Argentina after the 1950s but enjoyed a major revival around the turn of the century.

The origins of tango are disputed, said to be influenced by Spanish flamenco and the rhythms of Africa brought to the region by slaves. Usually it is played by a small group of musicians, about six-to-eight, including one or two guitars, two violins, a double base, and two handheld accordions (bandoneon), not an over-the-shoulder piano accordion. Both sung and danced, the style is generally melancholic, the lyrics usually about loss and betrayal—the pain of leaving home, the death of a loved one (especially a mother) or girlfriend (an unfaithful lover), or the separation of friends. Tango criollo was played in bars and bordellos in working-class districts and precarious areas on the fringe of cities during the period of mass **immigration** around 1900. In **Buenos Aires**, it was not unusual for men to dance together, given the gender imbalance among immigrants. Tango became internationally popular (and respectable) just before the First World War when taken up in Paris. It was then "reexported" to the River Plate and embraced by the elite and middle classes as part of national culture. The golden age of traditional tango was fostered by radio: tango was orchestrated, bands became larger, as did venues—large dance halls and clubs (*milongas de tango*). The stars of this period were the likes of **Carlos Gardel** and **Agustín Magaldi**. There were few **women** exponents of tango at this time. Tango had fallen out of favor by the end of the 1950s, only to experience a spectacular comeback toward the end of the century. This was largely connected with the reworking of traditional themes and styles by **Astor Piazzolla**, notably through the development of tango ballet and a modern classical style. Argentine dance companies have taken tango spectacles to the **United States**, Europe, **China**, and Japan, where tango is immensely popular, receiving international acclaim. It is again a **tourist** attraction in Buenos Aires, staged in upmarket venues and stage shows. Locals tend to prefer *milongas de tango*, which are experiencing a similar revival.

TEATRO COLÓN. The country's premier opera house, located in **Buenos Aires** and opened in 1908. Its world rankings are as follows: it is the third best opera house, and acoustically is among the five best concert venues. The theater had a period of huge international success hosting leading singers and opera companies, but with the passage of time its decline became evident. Plans were made for massive renovations, which were carried out between 2005 and 2010. The Colón has six floors above ground and three below, and seven elevators. Its auditorium is horseshoe shaped, with a capacity for 2,487 people seated and 1,000 standing; the stage is 20 meters wide, 15 meters high, and 20 meters deep; and the large central chandelier is illuminated by 700 light bulbs. *See also* FONTENLA, NORMA (1930–1971).

TEHUELCHES. Generic name given to indigenous groups that inhabited **Patagonia** and the southern **pampas**. They were made practically extinct by the **Conquest of the Desert**.

TERCERA POSICIÓN. Slogan defining economic and foreign policy during the three presidencies of **Juan Domingo Perón** that dovetailed with the Peronist aims of political sovereignty and economic independence. Its vague message oscillated between a nationalist, anti-imperialist discourse on the one hand, and a focus on some degree of cooperation with Washington on the other.

Argentina ratified the Act of Chapultepec and the **United Nations** Charter in August 1946 and was thereby allowed to cooperate with the **United States** on defense matters at the Inter-American Conferences in Rio de Janeiro (1947), Bogotá (1948), and Washington, DC (1951). Yet it simultaneously pursued an independent line toward its neighbors and **Spain**, which aimed to diversify the country's export and import markets. Through its policy toward **Southern Cone** neighbors, Argentina tried to promote the formation of an economic bloc that would maintain the prices of raw materials and agricultural **commodities**. It hoped to buy from other Latin American states some of the components required for its industrialization project, as well as expand export markets. This strategy resulted in trade agreements with various countries and negotiations for the establishment of customs unions, which some argue prefigured the South American Common Market (**MERCOSUR**). Regarding Spain, the **Buenos Aires** government was a staunch and uncompromising ally of the Franco regime. It undertook considerable efforts to rehabilitate Spain internationally and provided economic assistance in the form of major **grain**, **meat**, and oil shipments on long-term credits, in return for which Madrid agreed to supply iron bars, sheet metal, lead, cork, and similar products. This backing was crucial to saving Spain from collapse until the United States stepped in to help in the cold war context, but it tarnished Argentina's image as Washington and Moscow concurred at this time on boycotting the Franco dictatorship.

The oscillations in Peronist foreign policy were most apparent in the country's performance at the United Nations. In the name of nonintervention in the internal affairs of a sovereign state, Argentina cast some awkward votes. It did not join in censuring South Africa for racial discrimination and opposed efforts to pressure it into granting independence to South West Africa (Namibia); it also objected to any examination of French colonialist policy in Morocco and refrained from criticizing Dutch imperialism in the Far East. Argentina even abstained in the vote supporting the partition of Palestine and the establishment of a Jewish state.

Nevertheless, Argentina handled itself very adeptly as president of the UN Security Council in October–November 1948, a position it held as part of its two-year rotating membership of that body. On Perón's orders, Foreign Minister **Juan Atilio Bramuglia** held the office rather than the head of the Argentine delegation to the UN; this was a shrewd move as the minister was highly skilled and would bolster the country's prestige. His tenure was at the height of the Berlin blockade, and a mediation attempt with sensible proposals was foiled by Moscow through a veto. Notwithstanding this failure, Argentine efforts to resolve the crisis won the backing and plaudits of the Western powers.

Shortages of US dollars and imports in 1949–1952 hindered economic plans and rendered the Tercera Posición impracticable, thereby forcing Perón to turn to both the East and the United States. Bilateral deals were concluded with Hungary, Poland, Czechoslovakia, and especially the Soviet Union by which credits paid with raw materials were used on capital and intermediate goods. The Soviet agreement also included supplying Argentina with petroleum and derivatives, coal, and oil industry equipment. The latter was inadequate and exposed the Argentine need simultaneously to improve ties with Washington. A new foreign investment law was passed in 1953 to entice North American capital but with little success. It only led to Kaiser Motors setting up its wholly owned subsidiary **Industrias Kaiser Argentina** (IKA) and above all an extremely controversial contract with Standard Oil of California to develop major oil fields during a 40-year period. This deal was signed in April 1955 but rejected by **Congress**, not least because it went against the aims of economic independence and political sovereignty.

The Tercera Posición had already faded when Perón was overthrown in 1955, but there were echoes of it after **Peronism** returned to power in 1973. The prominence of radical student organizations in the Peronist movement at this time led to an anti-imperialist stance in foreign policy. The Diplomatic relations were established with **Cuba, China,** North Korea, and North Vietnam, and the country applied for full membership of the Non-Aligned Movement on the grounds that Perón's original policy avowedly prefigured its aims. The United States was criticized, as well as irked by the expansion in commercial and financial relations with Havana. In addition, an extremely dubious trade deal was reached with Libya. The **military coup of 1976** put paid to this foreign policy. The Tercera Posición cannot be deemed as truly successful, except as a useful propaganda tool for domestic consumption. *See also* AGRICULTURE; FOREIGN DEBT/FOREIGN INVESTMENT; FOREIGN TRADE; GREAT BRITAIN; INDUSTRY; MINISTRY OF FOREIGN RELATIONS AND RELIGION.

TERRAGNO, RODOLFO HÉCTOR (1943–). Academic, writer, and politician; minister of public works and services in the cabinet of President **Raúl Alfonsín** from 1987 to 1989 and head of the cabinet of ministers (prime minister) for 11 months in 1999–2000 in the administration of President **Fernando de la Rúa**; a key figure in the modernization of the **Unión Cívica Radical** (UCR). Terragno graduated in law from the **University of Buenos Aires** (UBA) in 1967, soon afterward securing a teaching position at the university. His academic career was cut short by the **military coup of 1976**, and he spend most of the next six years in exile, around four years working as a journalist in Caracas and a couple of years in London engaged in research. Returning to Argentina, he was appointed **education** advisor to Alfonsín before moving on to head the **Ministry of Public Works**. Along with Minister of Economy **Juan Vital Sourrouille**, Terragno was responsible for tentative moves to privatize state firms. This was in keeping with a UCR campaign pledge in the **congressional** and **presidential elections of 1983**. He was a firm advocate of the case for **privatization** as a means of delivering efficient public services and macroeconomic modernization, preparing the country to participate effectively in the new global environment. In the face of concerted opposition by the **Partido Justicialista** (PJ) in **Congress**, he found it a bruising experience.

After the ignominious end of the Alfonsín presidency in 1989, Terragno campaigned to make the UCR reelectable, as a member of the Chamber of Deputies for the city of **Buenos Aires** between 1993 and 1999, and above all as president of the National Committee of the party between 1995 and 1997. With devastating honesty—though perhaps incautiously—Terragno had admitted that the UCR was ill prepared for office in 1983, not expecting to win, and that this had prevented the new government from seizing the initiative as early as it might have done during the early months of the Alfonsín presidency. Often, his fiercest battles were within the party.

Terragno left the De la Rúa administration a year before it too collapsed, a government that he had gone to considerable lengths to make electable by convincing the UCR of the need to enter into an electoral alliance with the **Frente País Solidario** (FREPASO). He secured a seat in the National Senate in the midterm **congressional elections of 2001**, in which the UCR performed badly. Holding the Senate seat until 2007, he redoubled efforts to rebuild the party. While sitting in the Senate, he wrote extensively about his time in office and about Argentine history and politics. Since retiring from political life, he has pursued a career as an academic and diplomat; his achievements have been recognized nationally and internationally—he has been decorated by the Brazilian, French, and Italian governments. *See also* STATE-OWNED ENTERPRISES (SOEs).

TESTA, CLORINDO MANUEL JOSÉ (1923–2013). Italian Argentine architect and a pioneer of the Brutalist movement in Argentina who graduated from the Faculty of Architecture of the **University of Buenos Aires** (UBA) in 1948. Although Testa worked on innumerable projects from 1950, he is most famous for two noteworthy examples of Brutalism. The first is the headquarters of the Banco de Londres y América del Sur, commissioned in 1959 and completed in 1966. Located on a street corner in the central business district of the city of **Buenos Aires**, it is one of the well-known local contributions to international architecture of the 1960s. Since 1997, the building has been owned by the Banco Hipotecario Nacional. The second is the Biblioteca Nacional Mariano Moreno, also located in the city of Buenos Aires, on the site of the former Palacio Unzué, which **Juan Domingo Perón** used as the presidential residence. The original palace was demolished in a sheer act of vandalism by order of de facto president **Pedro Eugenio Aramburu**. The Testa commission for the projected library was initiated in 1961, but repeated alternations between civilian and **military** governments as well as indifference to cultural matters delayed its implementation. Construction began in 1971, but the Biblioteca Nacional was not formally inaugurated until 1992. However, some elements of the original design were not implemented, such as the metallic blinds to shade books housed in the building from sunlight, a cause of much subsequent controversy and complaint.

THIRD POSITION. *See* TERCERA POSICIÓN.

TIERRA DEL FUEGO, ANTÁRTIDA E ISLAS DEL ATLÁNTICO SUR. The last national territory to acquire provincial status—in 1990—and the only province not located on the continental mainland even though considered a part of **Patagonia**. Its current population is approximately 130,000, and the capital is **Ushuaia**.

The province has three components. The first is the former Territorio Nacional de Tierra del Fuego, which consists of the Argentine part of the Isla Grande de Tierra del Fuego (sandwiched between **Chile** and the Atlantic) and the Isla de los Estados. The other two territories are simply nominal since they are not under national sovereignty. The largest one is known as Antártida Argentina, and the other is the disputed Islas del Atlántico Sur, comprising two self-governing British Overseas Territories: the **Falkland Islands**, and the South Georgia and South Sandwich Islands.

The Antártida Argentina overlaps with competing British and Chilean claims on Palmer Land and the Weddell Sea in the Antarctic and is uninhabited apart from the staff of scientific bases. Claims are suspended under the Antarctic Treaty, which was signed in 1959 by the 12 countries active in Antarctica during the International Geophysical Year (1957–1958) and came into force in 1961.

The Isla Grande de Tierra del Fuego (also known as Tierra del Fuego Island) was first seen by Europeans in 1520 during the expedition of Ferdinand Magellan. Like the rest of Patagonia, it came under the jurisdiction of the **Viceroyalty of the River Plate** and its successor independent state. In the early 1830s, the island and other Patagonian areas were explored by Commander Robert FitzRoy and Charles Darwin in their travels on HMS *Beagle*.

The Argentine government only took a more active interest in the area in the 1880s, asserting its sovereignty over the whole of Patagonia in order to prevent Chilean expansionism toward the Atlantic coast. The Boundary Treaty of 1881 between Argentina and Chile resolved all border issues—including the land frontier in Tierra del Fuego Island—except the **Beagle Channel**, which remained unresolved until a century later.

As two components of the province are nominal, only the former Territorio Nacional de Tierra del Fuego can be considered in terms of the **economy**. Since the 1970s, it has benefited from government subsidies to local industry and from its natural wealth. With an estimated 2006 output of 2.6 billion US dollars, Tierra del Fuego had a per capita income of US$25,720, the second highest in the country after the city of **Buenos Aires**. Manufacturing accounts for 20 percent of total output, partly due to generous tax incentives to local industry, a policy that the national government has pursued to encourage migration to the less populated areas of Argentina. A number of sizeable plants opened on Tierra del Fuego Island to take advantage of tax benefits legislated in 1972; they are mainly manufacturers of electronics and home appliances. Increasingly, they have used more Argentine components, which has raised the question of the costs of transporting them from other industrial areas of the country to such remote factories.

As in other Patagonian provinces, oil and natural gas extraction are of significance, representing 20 percent of provincial output. Agricultural income in Tierra del Fuego is modest at 5 percent, and its main source is **sheep** ranching. **Wool**, mutton, and hides are supplied throughout the province and to the wider national market. *See also* BEAGLE CHANNEL DISPUTE.

TIMERMAN, JACOBO (1923–1999). Journalist, author, political and **human rights** campaigner, and major cultural figure. Born in present-day Ukraine, he and his family moved to Argentine to escape persecution a few years after Jacobo's birth. A lifelong Zionist, Timerman was a not uncritical supporter of the state of Israel, while opposing anti-Semitism in all its manifestations.

Timerman is best known for his pioneering contributions to journalism and account of his experience as a victim of the bloody regime that came to power with the **military coup of 1976**. The innovative publications with which he was associated—or initiated—include *Primara Plana*, a short-lived glossy current-affairs weekly, and *La Opinión*, which became the outstanding newspaper of the day in Argentina. With a center-left editorial position and modeled on *Le Monde*, *La Opinión* rapidly acquired a reputation for high-quality analytical reporting. Timerman's first major clash with the authorities came as founder and editor of *Primara Plana*. The de facto administration of General **Juan Carlos Onganía** objected to the magazine's coverage of politics and economics and its take on cultural affairs, while Timerman offered a scathing criticism of the narrow cultural nationalism espoused by the regime and Onganía's effort to impose his view of Catholic morality on society. The government threatened to close the magazine and engineered the departure of Timerman, thereby ensuring the demise of the weekly. This prefigured what would occur with *La Opinión*, set up by Timerman in 1971 as the country entered a period of economic and political chaos. Reporting on state violence during the presidency of **Isabel Perón** as well as atrocities committed by guerilla groups, Timmerman was soon receiving death threats from the crypto-fascist **Triple A**, threats that would assume more concrete expression during the **Proceso de Reorganización Nacional**.

La Opinión was subject to repeated temporary closures shortly after the 1976 coup for its fearless and dispassionate coverage of "disappearances," culminating in the arrest of Timerman in 1977. His arrest and subsequent "processing" would be justified on the ground that a backer of *La Opinión* had links with the **Montoneros** terrorist group. Although condemnation was muted at the time, his case would later become a cause célèbre, partly as the result of his account of arrest and torture published (in English in 1981) as *Prisoner without a Name, Cell without a Number*. Until the return of democracy in 1983, which brought the trials of the heads of the military junta that governed the country between 1976 and 1983 and later the prosecution of notorious torturers, *Prisoner without a Name* was one of the few documentary accounts of the horrors that occurred during the Proceso.

Timerman blamed his treatment on the anti-Semitism of the regime. Others accept that while sections of the **military**, and society at large, were anti-Semitic, administrations of the Proceso were no more (or less) anti-Semitic than they were antileft, anti–organized labor, antistudent, or antidemocratic. Notwithstanding his treatment, Timerman may have been one of the lucky ones. His case was heard in various tribunals, the Supreme Court ordered his release in 1979, and he survived. On release, the regime churlishly stripped him of Argentine citizenship; he and his family were granted asylum in Israel, later taking up residence in the **United States**. He returned to **Buenos Aires** in 1984 to testify before the national commission appointed to inquire into the cases of the "disappeared." He welcomed the election of President **Raúl Alfonsín** in 1983 though was critical of Alfonsín's successor, President **Carlos Saúl Menem**, and his party, the **Partido Justicialista** (PJ)—Menem would go on to pardon key figures of the Proceso. Timerman was doubtful of the reputation of the Menem regime and was fully aware of dealing between senior figures in the PJ and the **military** and clandestine "security" groups before and after 1976. By the time of his death, Timerman had received many international awards for journalism and in recognition of a tireless campaign against human rights abuses and for justice for victims. *See also* CORRUPTION; DESAPARECIDOS; GALTIERI, LEOPOLDO FORTUNATO (1926–2003); LEY DE OBEDIENCIA DEBIDA; LEY DE PUNTO FINAL; KIRCHNER, CRISTINA ELISABET FERNÁNDEZ DE (1953–); KIRCHNER, NÉSTOR CARLOS (1950–2010); LÓPEZ REGA, JOSÉ (1916–1989); MILITARY JUNTAS, TRIALS OF THE; VIDELA, JORGE RAFAEL (1925–2013); VIOLA, ROBERTO EDUARDO (1924–1994); WAR TO ANNIHILATE SUBVERSION.

TORNQUIST, ERNESTO CARLOS (1842–1908). Banker, industrialist, agriculturalist, promoter of **agricultural colonization**, and public benefactor of Swedish–German extraction. Although originally Lutheran—Tornquist was educated at the German Evangelical School—the main branch of the family had converted to Catholicism before Tornquist was born.

One of the foremost entrepreneurs of the 19th century and champion of national **industry**, Tornquist benefited from close links with European financiers, particularly Belgian banks. Drawing on national and European funds, his initial ventures included sugar refining, the production of tannin extract, and **meat** freezing. Many of these interests were diverse, linking landownership and investment in transport, as well as processing. Around 1900, the family firm held extensive landholdings in the province of **Buenos Aires**, mainly organized as *estancia* **companies** and agricultural colonies; large sugar estates in the northwest; quebracho plantations in the **Chaco**; as well as processing plants. The principal vehicle for the development of these ventures was the holding company, Ernesto Tornquist y Cía; his descendants transformed it into the Banco Tornquist, which became one of the largest private banks in the country and had a substantial network of branches and overseas agencies. In the 1990s, the Banco Tornquist was purchased by Crédit Lyonnais; it was acquired by Banco Santander in 2000. Sometimes regarded as one of the principal financiers of national industrial enterprise, the Banco Tornquist housed one of the largest collections of documents and data relating to the growth of manufacturing in the country. That collection is now held by the **Banco Central de la República Argentina** (BCRA). *See also* AGRICULTURE; COMMODITIES; ECONOMY; FOREIGN DEBT/ FOREIGN INVESTMENT; FOREIGN TRADE.

TORRE NILSSON, LEOPOLDO (1924–1978). Film director, producer, and screenwriter. His first full-length film, *El Crimen de Oribe* (1950), was an adaptation of **Adolfo Bioy Casares**'s novel *El perjurio de la nieve*, and in 1954 he directed *Días de odio*, based on the short story "Emma Zunz" by **Jorge Luis Borges**.

Among the films directed by Torre Nilsson are a number focusing on icons of Argentine history and culture: *Martín Fierro* (1968), about the main character in Argentina's national poem; *El Santo de la Espada* (1970), about General **José de San Martín**; and *Güemes, la tierra en armas* (1971), about **Martín Miguel de Güemes**. Torre Nilsson is acknowledged as the first Argentine film director to be critically acclaimed outside the country, making Argentina's film production known at international film festivals. His 1973 film *Los siete locos* won the Silver Bear at the 23rd Berlin International Film Festival.

TOSCO, AGUSTÍN (1930–1975). Trade unionist who at the age of 27 became leader of the **Córdoba** provincial branch of Luz y Fuerza, the light and power utilities union. An anticapitalist, anti-imperialist, and antibureaucrat, he believed that labor struggles should focus on more than salary demands and fought constantly against the centralizing bureaucracy of the **trade unions**.

Tosco joined the **Confederación General del Trabajo de los Argentinos** (CGTA), a splinter of the **Confederación General del Trabajo** (CGT) formed in 1968. In addition to internal struggles particular to Luz y Fuerza, he was involved in the fight against the dictatorship of General **Juan Carlos Onganía**. Tosco actively participated in the **Cordobazo** in 1969, for which he was jailed for eight years but released after 16 months.

After his release from prison, Tosco returned to Córdoba. Following **Juan Domingo Perón**'s victory in the **presidential election of September 1973**, he began to be persecuted. The toppling of Governor **Ricardo Obregón Cano** in 1974 led to the abolition of the local branch of Luz y Fuerza, and Tosco was forced to go into hiding. He later fell gravely ill but could not go to hospital as he feared execution by the **Triple A**—the death squads were known to be monitoring the hospitals. He died aged 45.

TOURISM. Tourism is a growth sector of relatively recent origin in Argentina. The modern domestic tourist industry dates from around 1900, largely stimulated by the development of the national railway network; international tourism was largely a feature of the late 20th century.

Companies like the **Buenos Ayres Great Southern Railway Company** (BAGS) promoted beach resorts such as Mar del Plata and Necochea on the east coast of the province of **Buenos Aires** and the **Central Argentine Railway Company** (CAR) natural spas in the hills of **Córdoba**. By the 1920s, these had become major tourist attractions. The rail network brought tourists from the interior to Buenos Aires during the season: attendance at the annual fatstock show organized by the **Sociedad Rural Argentina** (SRA), opera and concerts at the **Teatro Colón**, sporting events in the **Paraná** Delta centered on the city of Tigre, prize races organized by the Jockey Club, and similar events became fixtures in the social calendar of the elite. And there were cafés, restaurants, and clubs. Above all, there was fashion and shopping. By 1914, Buenos Aires boasted some of the most glittering department stores in the world: shopping and taking tea at Harrods or Garth y Chávez was one of the few socially acceptable recreations for **women** of middle- and upper-class families. As affluence and leisure increased, sport was a well-established feature of social life for men—cycling and tennis were patronized by both men and women—or those with sufficient means. National soccer fixtures attracted spectators from across the country. Bars and bordellos catered to all classes.

In the 1930s and 1940s, when travel to Europe became difficult or impossible, regional tourism grew. Affluent Chileans and Brazilians considered the architecture and cultural life of **Buenos Aires** especially "European." Rich Argentines were attracted to the seaside towns of neighboring **Uruguay**. There was something like a boom in mass domestic tourism during the first administration of President **Juan Domingo Perón**. Real incomes rose; the state and **trade unions** built resorts and holiday facilities for workers as part the new social project. This was the time of *Argentina en fiesta*. It did not last but laid the foundations of modern recreational life for all. Economic boom (and crisis) was a feature of regional tourism. For example, around 1975,

1988, and 2002, when the peso was weak, Brazilian, Chilean, and Uruguayan tourists flocked to Argentina. When the peso was strong, as in the late 1970s and the 1990s, the flow was in the other direction, and to Miami.

While international tourism in Argentina also grew in the 1990s, it was the collapse of the **Convertibility Plan** that suddenly made Argentina a cheap and spectacular destination for intercontinental travelers, as well as for tourists from neighboring countries. While domestic tourism is the mainstay of the sector—accounting for about 80 percent of the business, international tourism grew by an average of 6.9 percent a year between 2005 and 2011, when 5,700,000 visitors were recorded. The number of foreign tourists declined in 2012 but recovered to almost 6,000,000 in 2014 before declining marginally in 2015 and 2016: 9,000,000 international visitors are anticipated in 2019. Visitors are staying longer and spending more. The direct contribution of travel and tourism to gross domestic product in 2016 and 2017 was 3.3 percent, or almost three times that figure if all ancillary services are included; approximately 10 percent of the labor force is employed in the hospitality sector. Although the categories are not mutually exclusive, particular types of tourist activities have experienced rapid growth in recent years—for instance, adventure sports like white-water rafting and hiking, notably in **Patagonia** and the northwest; gastronomical tourism featuring various wine trails in **Cuyo** and the country's world-class **meat** culture; eco- and nature tourism based around the country's spectacular scenery along the **Andes** and south Atlantic seaboard, not least the falls at **Iguazú**, "lunar" landscape of the province of **Salta**, and the Perito Moreno glacier; "tango tourism" connected to dance schools and shows. *Estancia* visits are also popular, and the city of Buenos Aires is a destination in its own right, now well established on the international cruise circuit. See also CATAMARCA (PROVINCE); CHUBUT; ECONOMIC CRISES; LA BOCA; LA RIOJA (CITY); MENDOZA (PROVINCE); MISIONES; RECOLETA; SAN LUIS (CITY); SANTIAGO DEL ESTERO (CITY); SANTIAGO DEL ESTERO (PROVINCE); TRANSPORTATION; TUCUMÁN (PROVINCE).

TRADE UNIONS. Labor organizations have been active in Argentina since the late 19th century; by the mid-20th century, the country had the largest labor movement in Latin America in terms of membership and highest proportion of the workforce enrolled in unions. Two-thirds of workers were members of a trade union by the early 1950s; today the figure is around two-fifths for formal-sector workers, and declining.

Until the 1940s, the principal unions were those representing railway and utility workers; from the 1940s to the 1970s, industrial unions constituted the fastest-growing and most powerful segment of the labor movement; while organizations in manufacturing remain influential, arguably the most powerful unions are now to be found in the tertiary sector, for example, in **educa-**

tion and health services—but above all the *camioneros*, long-distance haulage drivers. These shifts reflect changes in the structure of the **economy** and policy initiatives associated with developmentalism, statism, and **privatization**. Around 1900, the main ideological influences on the labor movement were **anarcho-syndicalism** and socialism, especially the reformist socialism espoused by the **Partido Socialista** (PS). Since the mid-20th century, **Peronism** (articulated by the **Partido Justicialista**—PJ) has been the dominant political force acting on core sections of the labor movement, despite efforts to forge independent labor organizations, as during the 1940s and 1950s, or to democratize the movement, as during the administration of President **Raúl Alfonsín**.

Initially, the labor movement was divided largely along ethnic and ideological lines. "Modern" trade unions were mainly urban and largely organized by male and immigrant workers; creoles and rural workers tended to favor the craft organizations and sociocultural clubs most observed in interior country districts. Urban labor organizations were often riven by ideological and strategic differences—notably, whether the material condition of labor would be better served by confronting the state or challenging capitalism. Socialists like **Alfredo Palacios, Juan B. Justo**, and **Ángel Gabriel Borlenghi** campaigned for such legislative initiatives as limits to the working day and to the working week, minimum wages, compulsory arbitration in labor disputes, compensation for work-related injuries, and retirement pensions. Revolutionary socialists and anarchists favored such devices as the general strike and targeted violence against organs of a repressive state. With the **Sáenz Peña Law** of 1912 and the prospect of increased worker representation in **Congress**, compromise with capitalism and the state offered a plausible legal route. Victory by the **Unión Cívica Radical** (UCR) in the **presidential election of 1916** appeared to confirm this possibility. President **Hipólito Yrigoyen** promised great freedom and legal recognition for unions. Better labor relations, however, were frustrated by disappointment at the pace of progress and the erosion of wages by inflation during the First World War. There was a dramatic increase in the number of strikes between 1913 and 1919, and the number of unions increased more than tenfold over the same period—there were over 500 trade unions by 1919, albeit many individual unions were relatively small. Although most organizations tended to be urban based, rural workers were also organizing by this time, mainly those employed by foreign-owned *estancia* **companies** and raw material processing conglomerates like **Forestal**. The level of violence and worker oppression increased: striking workers were confronted by the **military** and the police, and by right-wing "patriotic" groups seeking to expurgate "antinational" ideologies and foreign agitators. By the 1930s, partly in association with **Catholic Church**, these groups would be seeking to promote national and Catholic sentiments within the labor movement.

The 1920s witnessed the formation of unions for shopworkers, school-teachers, bank workers, civil servants, and workers in other service sectors. Reformist strands in the labor movement gained ascendency, sometimes described as "national" worker organizations. Nationalism would come to have a pronounced ideological influence within the movement. Groups of railway workers came together to form **Unión Ferroviaria** (UF) in 1922. Only locomotive footplatemen remained apart from the UF; they continued to be represented by La Fraternidad. Eight years later, the UF was instrumental in organizing the general labor organization, the **Confederación General del Trabajo** (CGT). Around this time, unions mobilizing workers in the industrial sector were also consolidating, notably in early motor vehicle assembly plants set up by **United States** companies like Ford. Since 1930, notwithstanding repeated splits (and reconsolidation), the GCT has served as the organizational force and focus of the labor movement. By the end of the decade, the CGT had become the principal political voice of urban workers, attempting to forge an alliance with progressive **political parties**, ultimately sponsoring the formation of the **Partido Laborista** (PL) in 1945. Largely at the instigation of the UF, the PL was envisaged as the political wing of the organized labor movement. Between 1930 and 1940, the number of trade unionists affiliated with the CGT grew from 124,000 to 310,000.

The CGT initially welcomed the government brought to power by the **military coup of 1943**; the UF lawyer and socialist campaigner **Juan Atilio Bramuglia** was appointed to head the social insurance agency, an appointment that promised an increase in state social welfare provision for workers, something for which the CGT had campaigned. Although the PL was largely responsible for the victory of **Juan Domingo Perón** in the **presidential election of 1946**, Perón soon curbed the independence of the PL and the CGT. By the early 1950s, both had been thoroughly Peronized—the PL became the **Partido Peronista** (PP) and ultimately the **Partido Justicialista** (PJ). Since then, the labor movement has been largely shaped by Peronism. The predominant influences are Peronism—the faction loyal to Perón or the memory of Perón; a strand advocating **"Peronism without Perón"**—that is, enjoying autonomy from the state; independent unionism—a strand that includes anti-Peronists, nationalist and confessional organizations close to the Catholic Church, and unions and union leaders associated with other political parties or none. During periods of military rule, the trade union movement has been oppressed or suppressed and factionalized as military administrations attempted to promote divisions by favoring some unions while repressing others. Civilian presidents have similarly had to live with the trade unions while seeking to co-opt or democratize. In addition to operating legally when possible—clandestinely when not—campaigning for the improvement of wages and working conditions, the labor movement has fought—and often brought an end to—austerity programs, while individual unions have organized against specific policies.

Trade unions mobilized against austerity plans implemented by President **Arturo Frondizi** in 1958, the government of President **Isabel Perón** in the early to mid-1970s, Alfonsín a decade later, President **Fernando de la Rúa** around 2000, and President **Mauricio Macri** toward the end of 2017, among others. The CGT organized against token privatization measures attempted by Frondizi and Alfonsín in the late 1950s and 1980s, respectively, and against the disposal of **state-owned enterprises** under President **Carlos Saúl Menem** of the PJ in the 1990s. Rail workers organized against the favoring of road transport under Frondizi and the de facto administration that came to power following the **military coup of 1966**. Between 1968 and 1970, the administration led by President General **Juan Carlos Onganía** both suppressed the CGT and encouraged fragmentation by favoring unions like the metalworkers' union that supported "Peronism without Perón." Members of the metalworkers' union and workers in motor vehicle factories were key actors in mass urban uprisings like the **Cordobazo**. Despite the limits on free expression, unions acted against measures by the regime of the **Proceso de Reorganización Nacional** to push back on the welfare state and social benefits that had grown—and increased massively in cost—between the 1940s and the 1970s. Go-slows, work-to-rules, and shop-floor sabotage were the principal forms of protest, though five general strikes were called and widely observed around 1980. Minister of Interior General **Albano Harguindeguy** declared that trade union solidarity was against the guiding principles of the Proceso.

Trade union politics mirrored national politics from the 1950s to the 1970s—they were violent and venal. Elections for senior posts were hotly contended and rigged. Intimidation became the norm, and disputes were settled with a bullet. Many union officials, at all levels, were the victims of violence. Bombings of union meetings and headquarters, shoot-outs, and assassinations were not infrequent. Violence was a function of ideology and personal politics. **Corruption** was a factor. By the 1960s, with membership dues deducted from wages at source and health and pension funds (*obras sociales*) operated by the major unions, union bosses controlled large budgets. Corrupt union bosses were commonly known as *los gordos*, "fatties." Corruption as much as ideology and political patronage also explain splits within individual unions and the trade union movement as a whole.

Deindustrialization in the Proceso years and privatization under Menem had a drastic impact on individual unions and union membership. Accompanied by an opening of the economy, the consequences of such processes were particularly felt by unions operating in the heavy goods and motor-mechanical sectors. **Economic crises** such as the collapse of the **Austral Plan** and the end of the **Convertibility Plan** had a similarly catastrophic effect on unions and union membership—and the material conditions of members. On the other hand, economic growth and government patronage under Presidents **Néstor Kirchner** and **Cristina Fernández de Kirchner** had a positive impact on unions and union membership, and the material condition of union bosses—at least until Cristina broke with the CGT around 2011 as she became more reliant on social movements like the **Madres de Plaza de Mayo** and ideological shock troops like **La Cámpora**. This withdrawal of official support produced a sequence of splinters within the CGT and a loss of influence by the leadership of individual unions. Having been intimately involved with groups of *piqueteros* during the early years of the *kirchnerato*, labor unions are today to be found campaigning for **human rights** as much as for worker welfare, making common cause with other organization opposed to specific lines of government policy. In part, this reflects a loss of influence by organized labor due to structural change in the economy and polity—notably, the fragmentation of traditional political parties. *See also* CONFEDERACIÓN GENERAL DEL TRABAJO DE LOS ARGENTINOS (CGTA); INDUSTRY; MIGUEL, LORENZO MARCELO (1927–2002); MOYANO, HUGO (1944–); ONGARO, RAIMUNDO JOSÉ (1924–2016); RUCCI, JOSÉ IGNACIO (1924–1973); SEMANA TRÁGICA; SECCIÓN INDUSTRIAL AMASADORAS MECÁNICAS (SIAM Di Tella); SOCIEDAD MIXTA SIDERURGICA ARGENTINA (SOMISA); TRIPLE A (ALIANZA ANTICOMUNISTA ARGENTINA); VANDOR, AUGUSTO TIMOTEO (1923–1969).

TRAMWAYS. *See* ANGLO–ARGENTINE TRAMWAYS COMPANY.

TRANSPORTATION. Argentina has an extensive system of transport, though coverage varies across the subcontinental country. Highways are the principal means of communication, but railways were important before the 1950s; air services and river and coastal shipping are well developed. About 85 percent of freight and passenger traffic is carried by road.

The national road network covered approximately 140,000 miles (c. 240,000 kilometers) in 2016, of which 49,000 miles (c. 83,000 km) was paved, with a further 25,600 miles (43,400 km) classified as all-weather; the remainder were dirt roads. About 17 percent of highways are administered by the federal government, the rest by the provinces. The main highways are generally two lane and radiate from the city of **Buenos Aires**. The principal routes are Ruta 3, which runs to the south-southwest across the province of Buenos Aires to **Bahía Blanca** and then down through coastal **Patagonia** to **Río Gallegos** and the southern frontier with **Chile** just north of **Tierra del Fuego**; Ruta 5, southwest across Buenos Aires to **Santa Rosa, La Pampa**;

Ruta 7, west to the principal cities of **Cuyo**, classified as part of the International Pan-American Highway; Ruta 8, to Río Cuarto in southern **Córdoba**; Ruta 9, northwest to **Rosario** and the city of Córdoba, where it turns north to **Santiago del Estero** and then northwest and north through **Tucumán** and **Jujuy** to the frontier with **Bolivia**. Ruta 11 begins at Rosario, leaving Ruta 9 to run north to the cities of **Santa Fe**, Reconquista, **Resistencia**, and **Formosa** and the frontier with **Paraguay**. Ruta 12 is the main highway through western **Mesopotamia**, leaving Ruta 9 at **Zárate** to run northward and then eastward to **Posadas** and the frontier with Brazil at Puerto de **Iguazú**; eastern Mesopotamia is served by Ruta 14. There are also north–south highways, for example, Ruta 33, which runs from Bahía Blanca to Rosario, and Ruta 35 from Bahía Blanca to Rio Cuarto, from where Ruta 36 runs on to Córdoba. In the west, starting close to Rio Gallegos, Ruta 40 broadly shadows the frontier with Chile for much of its length to Bolivia, though large sections are little used.

The national highway system dates from the 1930s; a planned federal network of roads was devised during the administration of President **Agustín P. Justo**. In the mid-1920s, investment in the road system was estimated to represent only 3.5 percent of that in railways. The National Road Agency was set up in 1932 to construct roads financed by a tax on fuel. By the mid-1940s, the agency had built a skeletal system of paved trunk roads connecting the main cities. Construction advanced in the 1950s and early 1960s. As part of its "economic rationalization plan," the **military** regime of the **Proceso de Reorganización Nacional** passed responsibility for highway development and maintenance to the provinces. Spending declined, and economic collapse at the end of the regime left the highway system deficient and in need of urgent refurbishment. Highway **privatization** was first mooted in 1998 during the presidency of **Raúl Alfonsín**. Minister of Transport **Rodolfo Terragno** proposed calling for tenders for the maintenance of half the main network—in the event, only 25 percent of the system was franchised, though carrying around half all traffic. The main privatization drive came in the early 1990s under President **Carlos Saúl Menem**. Concessions to operate and maintain the principal interurban highways were issued in anticipation that substantial amounts of private capital would be attracted to road improvement. The early results of toll road operation were mixed; maintenance improved, but investment was sluggish, in part attributed to a lack of transparency and **corruption** in the bidding process. By the end of the decade, toll road franchises were held by an oligopoly of concessionaires, and by 2000 the system was only kept afloat by a plethora of public subsidies to private companies. **Economic crises** and the election of President **Néstor Kirchner** brought restatization. In 2003, Kirchner launched a National Highway Plan. This resulted in large-scale investment. Between 2003 and 2014, around 770 miles (1,300 km) of new roads were built and 2,400 miles (4,100 km) paved, producing a 130 percent increase in the paved network. Tolls increased exponentially.

Although most freight is now moved by road, as recent as the 1970s about one-third was transported by rail and until the 1920s there was virtually no long-distance road freight. The rail network is currently around 23,000 miles (37,000 km), down from a maximum route mileage of over 30,000 miles in 1944. The first line was inaugurated in 1857, and the system grew rapidly in the 1880s and the 1910s, when about two-thirds of the network was British owned, with another 10th owned by French companies; much of the state system had been financed by foreign borrowing. There are three principal gauges: broad, 5'6" (1.676 m); standard, 4'8 1/2" (1.435 m); meter, 3'3 3/8". About two-thirds of the network is broad gauge, located in the economic heartland of the country—the **pampas**—as well as parts of the northwest; meter-gauge lines serve mainly the north and northeast, as well as parts of the northwest; standard gauge is largely confined to Mesopotamia. Financially, private companies were in trouble by the 1930s, and the network deteriorated rapidly after nationalization in 1948. There were periodic efforts to refurbish and rationalize the system, notably following the **military coup of 1966** and during the Proceso, to little avail. By the 1980s, the system was in crisis, leading to privatization in the 1990s—freight services were franchised, long-distance passenger services virtually abandoned, and commuter lines granted to upgrade-and-operate consortia. In the 21st century, there have been several well-publicized efforts to revive freight and long-distance passenger services by attracting investment from **China**, notably during the presidencies of **Cristina Fernández de Kirchner** and **Mauricio Macri**. Since 2010, several sections of the permanent way and signaling have been improved, and there have been some advances in passenger facilities. Much remains to be done if the system is to experience major efficiency gains and recover a fraction of its former prominence. It is accepted that rail transport is particularly suited to the movement of bulk **commodity** exports like **grains**, soya, **meat**, and **wool**.

The city of Buenos Aries underground railway, Subterráneo de Buenos Aires (Subte), is one of the oldest in the world and the oldest in Latin America. It dates from 1913, when the **Anglo-Argentine Tramways Company** inaugurated the first line, Línea A. The second line, Línea B, was opened in 1930; the first section of Línea C was opened in 1934. Until nationalization in 1939, the system was operated by three different companies. The network expanded fitfully in the late 1930s and the 1940s: existing lines were extended and new ones built. There were further extensions in the mid-1960s and early 1970s, and there was much planned growth. With privatization in 1994, operation was passed to private hands, though ownership remained vested in the government of the city of Buenos Aires. There was investment in track renewal and equipment standardization during the Menem presidency in the 1990s, while Macri attached considerable importance to improving and extending services during his terms as mayor, triggering conflict with franchisee Metrovías. Today, the system is composed of six lines (A to E and H), which continue to be operated by Metrovías; the system carries around 1,500,000 passengers a day. There are plans for news lines—F, G, and I—and the extension of existing lines. These have been under discussion, and subject to revision, for some time. No other underground railways operate in Argentina. The reintroduction of trams has been considered, to minimal effect: there is a limited tram service in the city of Mendoza and a light railway system planned for the city of Córdoba. Other than Greater Buenos Aires, commuter rail provision is extremely limited.

The country has a well-developed air transport system. Buenos Aires is served by two major airports, Ezeiza (Ministro Pistarini) and Aeroparque (Jorge Newbery)—the former is the main international airport, the latter handles mainly domestic services as well as international flights to some neighboring countries. Ezeiza is served by most major European, Latin American, and US airlines as well as a few Gulf and Asian companies. Córdoba, Mendoza, and Rosario also handle international flights. All provincial capitals have airports, as do major cities in the interior. There are over 1,000 airports and landing strips in the country. The main national carriers are **Aerolíneas Argentinas** (AA) and Austral. The country was one of the first in Latin America to develop domestic and international air services. In the 1950s, AA had one of the largest and most modern fleets in the continent, including jet aircraft, and enjoyed a good reputation for quality. This reputation slipped after the 1970s, and the company was running a substantial deficit by the 1990s—the second largest after the state railways, **Ferrocarriles Argentinos** (FFA). Having been first mooted by Alfonsín, the airline was privatized under Menem. The company was ultimately acquired by the Spanish state airline in 1991. Privatization was not a success. There were charges of corruption in the awarding of contracts—as with rail and highway services—and the carrier was loaded with debts. Already in 1999, Iberia was trying to pull out. After several changes of ownership, in 2008 President Fernández de Kirchner renationalized the company. During the Menem presidency, there was major refurbishment of Ezeiza and further extensive airport modernization under Mrs. Kirchner, when the fleets of AA and Austral were also updated—there was a big reduction in the age of the fleets. Rumors of backhanders and deals for the awarding of airport redevelopment and fleet modernization abounded. AA was restructured in 2011 and has been slow to reestablish a positive reputation. The company is not necessarily unprofitable but was milked by the Kirchner administration: Aerolíneas appeared to be regarded as the personal flight service of the regime and several of its associates, as well as a cash cow to fund favored projects. In 2012, sponsored by Delta Airlines, the company joined the Sky Track Alliance.

The principal ports are Buenos Aires and **La Plata**, which handle over 80 percent of international traffic; Rosario is also an important port for overseas trade, and there is a major port complex at Bahía Blanca, which houses the principal naval base. Most cities of any size located on the seaboard of the province of Buenos Aires and Patagonia have some port facilities. Smaller river ports like **Zárate**, **Campana**, and **San Nicolás** handle regional freight and trade with neighboring countries, as do many smaller docks and facilities located along the **Paraná** Delta and the upper reaches of the river system. Other than cross-river to **Uruguay**, there are few river and seaborn passenger services, though many small ports offer recreational and **tourist** facilities. *See also* ARGENTINE NORTH EASTERN RAILWAY COMPANY (ANE); BUENOS AYRES & PACIFIC RAILWAY COMPANY (BA&P); BUENOS AYRES GREAT SOUTHERN RAILWAY COMPANY (BAGS); BUENOS AYRES WESTERN RAILWAY COMPANY (BAW); CENTRAL ARGENTINE RAILWAY COMPANY (CAR); CONCORDANCIA; CORDOBA CENTRAL RAILWAY COMPANY (CCR); ECONOMY; FOREIGN DEBT/FOREIGN INVESTMENT; PARAGUAY (RIVER); STATE-OWNED ENTERPRISES (SOEs); URUGUAY (RIVER).

TRELEW. City founded by Welsh colonists, named after one of the promoters and pioneers of settlement, Lewis Jones (*tre* means "town"), in 1886. It was the railhead of the now defunct **Chubut** railway, to which it owed much of its initial prosperity as a commercial center. The largest city in the Chubut Valley, and one of the biggest in **Patagonia**, it is the main **wool** processing point in the country, handling over 90 percent of total output. *See also* IMMIGRATION; TRELEW MASSACRE (22 AUGUST 1972).

TRELEW MASSACRE (22 AUGUST 1972). The tragic conclusion of a bold attempt by members of left-wing armed groups to escape a Patagonian maximum-security prison and return to their subversive activities. On 15 August 1972, the **Montoneros** jailed in the prison at **Rawson** took over the facility with the assistance of imprisoned members of the **Ejército Revolucionario del Pueblo** (ERP) and the **Fuerzas Armadas Revolucionarias** (FAR) and then made a desperate bid for freedom. The fugitives were being awaited at the nearby airport in Trelew by a passenger aircraft, which had been commandeered by a guerrilla operational group. However, the scheme unraveled owing to a failure in the signal system between the prisoners and the commando outside. Although a first group of six guerrilla leaders reached Trelew on time, escaping to **Chile** on the airliner and then flying on to **Cuba**

two days later, a second group of 19 prisoners reached the airport after the aircraft had departed. They were surrounded, forced to surrender, and taken to a local military base. In the early hours of 22 August, 16 of the detainees were executed illegally; the remaining three survived with severe injuries, thanks to the arrival of some officers not involved in the killings.

TRIAL OF THE MILITARY JUNTAS. *See* MILITARY JUNTAS, TRIALS OF THE.

TRIPLE A (ALIANZA ANTICOMUNISTA ARGENTINA). Death squad founded by **José López Rega** in 1973 under the aegis of his Ministry of Social Welfare, though it did not take the name Triple A until 1974. It was a response both to left-wing militarism and against people trying to develop the left politically.

The Triple A is believed to have made its debut in the **Ezeiza Massacre** of 20 June 1973 and began its attacks on individual people in November of that year. The victims were in the main from the Peronist left but included a considerable minority of non-Peronist left-wingers and political refugees from neighboring Latin American countries. By September 1974, it had murdered 200 people.

Enjoying official protection and also tolerance if not active participation from the federal police, the Triple A was a sinister organization whose modus operandi was far dirtier than that of the most vicious subversive groups. **Montoneros** wounded in its operations were collected by doctors in the street, put into ambulances of the Ministry of Social Welfare, and would never reach a hospital: they were killed in the vehicles or taken to centers of torture before being eliminated in municipal rubbish dumps, or strung up in trees. No death squad killers or employees of the cynically called "Ministry of Death" were detained for their actions, and such impunity turned increasingly problematic. Policemen serving in regional forces such as the **Buenos Aires** provincial police became disgruntled with the connivance of the federal police in the activities of the Triple A, as it tarnished the image of the force and made them targets of left-wing armed groups. More crucially, the armed forces were hostile to the death squad, observing that the "internal security" of the country was a matter for the **military** and not the task of a private enterprise.

After López Rega was forced to resign as minister of social welfare and leave Argentina in July 1975, the military took formal control of national security. Nevertheless, the Triple A continued to operate unabated, no doubt protected by the government. By the time of the **military coup of 1976**, 1,000 people were estimated to have died at the hands of the Triple A. The organization was the forerunner of the state terror that would become the hallmark of the late 1970s. Nobody was prosecuted for Triple A crimes until 2006. *See also* DESAPARECIDOS; MINISTRY OF SOCIAL DEVELOPMENT; PROCESO DE REORGANIZACIÓN NACIONAL; VILLAR, ALBERTO (1923–1974).

TUCUMÁN (CITY). *See* SAN MIGUEL DE TUCUMÁN (CITY).

TUCUMÁN (PROVINCE). The province of Tucumán lies in the northwest, located on the western slopes of the **Andes**. Although the province boasts some of the highest peaks in the country, at around 5,500 meters, most of the population lives in intermontane valleys at around 500 meters. The current population is around 1,600,000, with about one-third in the provincial capital, **San Miguel de Tucumán**.

One of the original provinces of the **Argentine Confederation**, Tucumán is today the smallest province in the republic. The modern province took form in the later years of the 1810s. Following the dissolution of the national government in **Buenos Aires**, together with the neighboring province of **Catamarca**, in 1820–1821, Tucumán briefly constituted the Republic of Tucumán. With the secession of Catamarca, the present boundaries of the province were established. Historically, the national significance of the province is due to the **Congress of Tucumán**, held between 1816 and 1820.

The province is located in a fertile, humid region that benefits from abundant rainfall, which along with snowmelt from the Andes supplies extensive irrigation systems and hydroelectricity dams. The provincial **economy** took off after 1880, when the region was connected to the national rail network. There was some new European **immigration** and, more importantly, access to markets. Known as the "Garden of the Republic," the province's principal **commodities** include hard and citrus fruits, **grains**, and tobacco, though sugarcane was the predominant commodity from the late 19th century until the 1960s. New products such as soya and wine increased in importance around 2000. Although over 60 percent of the national crop is still produced in the province, the decline of sugarcane production triggered mass migration to the industrial cities of the **Littoral**, mainly Buenos Aires. Apart from sugarcane, which is grown on large capital-intensive estates, as is the case across the northwest, **agriculture** is small scale. Attracted by cheap energy, there is a significant manufacturing sector, mainly vehicle production, though services including finance, commerce, higher **education**, and **tourism** account for two-thirds of provincial gross domestic product. *See also* CONFEDERACIÓN GENERAL DEL TRABAJO DE LOS ARGENTINOS (CGTA); EJÉRCITO REVOLUCIONARIO DEL PUEBLO (ERP); RAMUS, CARLOS GUSTAVO (1947–1970); SALIMEI, JORGE NÉSTOR (1926–1975); VIDELA, JORGE RAFAEL (1925–2013).

U

UBALDINI, SAÚL EDÓLVER (1936–2006). Trade unionist, labor leader, and politician; generally seen as a loyalist member of the Peronist **Partido Justicialista** (PJ)—he strongly opposed doing deals with de facto administrations installed after the **military coup of 1966** and **military coup of 1976**. First working in **meat**-processing *frigoríficos*, he later became head of the relatively small beer workers' union, which he developed as a platform for a larger role in the **Confederación General del Trabajo** (CGT)—the national organization. Sometime head of the CGT, he is best remembered for his opposition to **military** regimes of the **Proceso de Reorganización Nacional** and for thwarting efforts by democratically elected president **Raúl Alfonsín** of the **Unión Cívica Radical** (UCR) to democratize the labor movement. As head of the dissident labor faction CGT-Brasil, he organized and led two protest marches against the military government in late 1981 and early 1982. The first large-scale public demonstrations of this period, they were regarded as marking a loss of control by de facto administrations of the Proceso and the beginning of the end of the regime. Once again head of a reunited CGT, he called more than a dozen general strikes during the Alfonsín presidency, challenging parts of its political reform program and economic strategies. Initially welcoming the election of President **Carlos Saúl Menem** of the PJ—Alfonsín's successor—in 1989, Ubaldini rapidly fell out with the government, opposing its neoliberal economic policies. He was ousted as head of the CGT by Menem supporters but continued to be a thorn in the side of the government, even as other labor leaders recognized the popular appeal of the **Convertibility Plan** launched by Menem. Ubaldini challenged Menem again in 1993 but secured election as a national deputy for the province of **Buenos Aires** in the **congressional elections of 1997** and was returned in 2001. *See also* TRADE UNIONS.

UNA NACIÓN AVANZADA (UNA). An ephemeral political grouping composed of dissident Peronists—elements within the **Partido Justicialista** (PJ) opposed to the dominance of the party by **Néstor Kirchner** and his wife, **Cristina Fernández de Kirchner**, and the **Movimiento de Integración y**

714 • UNIDAD/UNIÓN CIUDADANA (UC)

Desarrollo (MID). Formed to contest the **congressional** and **presidential elections of 2007**, the UNA is important because it represents an early attempt to challenge the hegemony of the Kirchners. It was created to further the political ambitions of **Roberto Lavagna**, Néstor Kirchner's well-regarded former minister of economy who had engineered the recovery from the **economic crises** of 2001–2002, and because Lavagna's candidacy for the presidency was endorsed by the **Unión Cívica Radical** (UCR), the first time in history that the Radicals did not field their own presidential candidate. It did not do so because memories of the collapse of the administration of UCR president **Fernando de la Rúa** at the end of 2001 were still raw in the public mind. Not to be confused with **Unidos por una Nueva Alternativa** (UNA), a dissident Peronist electoral coalition formed to support **Sergio Massa** of the **Frente Renovador**/Partido Justicialista (FR/PJ) at the time of the **congressional** and **presidential elections of 2015**, the acronym chosen by Una Nación Avanzada was intended to echo that of the earlier UNA and drew support from Lavagna.

UNIDAD/UNIÓN CIUDADANA (UC). Disparate electoral coalition composed of regional party groupings cobbled together by former president **Cristina Fernández de Kirchner** to sustain her political ambitions after the **Frente para la Victoria/Partido Justicialista** (FpV/PJ) disintegrated in the wake of the victory of **Mauricio Macri** in the **presidential election of 2015**. The UC was officially launched on 20 June 2017 to contest the **congressional elections of 2017** scheduled for October. It secured the "minority" seat in the National Senate for the province of **Buenos Aires** for Mrs. Kirchner; initially, the former president was expected to top the poll and so gain the two "majority" seats available for the province. Although the UC increased its representation in **Congress**, mainly at the expense of factions of the **Partido Justcialista** (PJ), its relatively poor showing and the attitude of Fernández de Kirchner places the future of the coalition in doubt. In most parts of the country, the UC campaigned as Unidad Ciudadana, in a few places as Unión Ciudadana. *See also* MINISTRY OF ECONOMY.

UNIDOS POR UNA NUEVA ALTERNATIVA (UNA). An electoral coalition formed in the April of 2015 to fight the **congressional** and **presidential elections of 2015**. A successor to the **Frente Renovador/Partido Justicialista** (FR/PJ), the grouping was composed largely of anti-Kirchner Peronists though included adherents of the **Unión Cívica Radical** (UCR), Christian Democrats, and others; it was largely a vehicle to advance the presidential ambitions of **Sergio Massa**.

Following success in the midterm **congressional elections of 2013**, especially in the province of **Buenos Aires**, Massa and some of his supporters may have anticipated an accommodation with the **Cristina Fernández de Kirchner** administration—Massa has served as her head of cabinet for a year. If so, he and they were disappointed. As the president became more intransigent, Massa broke with her and **Peronism**; the formation of UNA was a symbolic renunciation of Peronism, in part designed to broaden the appeal of the coalition, though in the public mind, the FR/JP and UNA were indistinguishable. Other principal figures in the coalition included **José Manuel de la Sota**, sometime governor of the province of **Córdoba**, and Gustavo Sáenz, Massa's vice presidential running mate in 2015 from the northwestern province of **Salta**. The intervention of UNA/FR damaged the government in 2015, with Massa coming in third in the October presidential election, the second-round runoff was between **Daniel Scioli** and **Mauricio Macri**, not between Scioli and Massa, as had been widely predicted. Macri won the November runoff. The future of UNA is unclear, though it has solid representation in the lower house of **Congress**, where it commands a bloc of around 37 deputies, known as Federal UNA, consisting of members of FR/PJ elected in October 2015 and a handful of Congress men and **women** representing minor regional parties. It is probable that, like many such coalitions, UNA will prove short lived, though it had a significant impact in 2013 and 2015.

UNIÓN CÍVICA RADICAL (UCR). The oldest **political party** in Argentina, and one of the oldest in Latin America. Often referred to as the Radical Party (or the Radicals) in English, in Spanish the acronym UCR tends to be used as the abbreviation.

Initially known as the Unión Cívica (UC), the organization was largely urban based, catering to the political aspirations of rapidly expanding middle-class professional groups disenchanted by oligarchic machine politics and the gap between the rhetoric of democracy and freedom with the cynical manipulation of elections through bribery and ballot rigging. During the 1880s and 1890s, the stance and strategy of the UC shifted from street protest, organized demonstrations, active electioneering, and a vociferous program of press and pamphlet propaganda to one of civil disobedience and armed insurrection. Electoral participation was displaced by "intransigence"—political abstention—as optimism and confidence in the system declined. The countercurrents of the period—participation and abstention, self-exclusion and proscription, *personalismo* and *antipersonalismo*, and division and factionalism—were ones that would be repeated in the subsequent history of the party.

The first major split in the party occurred around 1889, as the **Baring Crisis** marked the end of the 1880s economic boom and challenged the modernization project of the oligarchy. Young activists launched a manifesto, "Hour of the Youth" (Hora de la Juventud), which questioned the approach of the UC leadership. Campaigning for what might be described as greater transparency in the political process and ethical politics, the youth wing also espoused a program of national administrative reform (municipal autonomy and effective representation for the mass of the population). These and related demands for political change were articulated at a rally of 3,000 held in the city of **Buenos Aires** on 1 September 1889. The result was the formation of the Unión Cívica de la Juventud, which led to a split with the UC and the founding of the UCR on 26 June 1891. The main figures associated with these developments were **Leandro N. Alem** and **Aristóbulo del Valle**, previously prominent in the UC, and younger figures such as **Bernardo de Irigoyen, Hipólito Yrigoyen**, and **Marcelo T. De Alvear**—the latter two would serve as president of the republic. Prominent in the **Revolution of 1890**, the UCR sponsored unsuccessful provincial revolts in Buenos Aires and **Santa Fe** in 1893 and in Buenos Aires, Santa Fe, **Córdoba**, and **Mendoza** in 1905. Despite failing to achieve a change of government, the scale of the 1905 revolts were instrumental in provoking debate within the ruling oligarchy, a discussion that led to electoral reform in 1912—the **Saenz Peña Law**. Unsuccessful armed struggle in 1905 also triggered a rethink within the UCR and a return to electoral participation. If fair and free elections were a prospect, so might a Radical victory.

The **congressional** and **presidential elections of 1916** were the first general elections to take place following the 1912 reforms. There was a huge upsurge in political participation, and the UCR secured major triumphs. Yrigoyen took the presidency and several provinces. The party also secured the largest number of seats in the lower house of **Congress**, the Chamber of Deputies, though it failed to obtain an absolute majority and was denied a majority in the upper house, the National Senate. Following a series of federal interventions in opposition-dominated provinces, although still falling short of an outright majority after the midterm **congressional elections of 1918**, the UCR managed to put together a working majority by forming alliances with smaller parties. Further successes occurred in the 1919 Senate elections, when the party increased its representation in a branch of the legislature previously dominated by conservatives. Yet even at this time of triumph, there were splits in the party, factionalism that would intensify after 1924 as the UCR divided into pro-Yrigoyen *personalistas* (personalists) and *antipersonalistas* grouped around Alvear. Nevertheless, 1916–1918 marked the onset of the Radical Ascendancy, which lasted until 1930. Marcelo T. De Alvear was elected president in 1922, and Yrigoyen returned in 1928. While the post-1916 order was largely democratic, in office the UCR proved not to be immune from some of the practices of the old order. As in 1918, existing legislation was invoked to facilitate federal interventions in the provinces to deliver election results favorable to the UCR. Broad-based support for the Radicals, coupled with intervention, generated a fear of political exclusion among opposition groups. Hence, when the second Yrigoyen administration was unable to cope with global collapse in 1929, conservative interests associated with the rural oligarchy and the army staged the **military coup of 1930**. The so-called *década infame* of 1930–1943 was neither a decade nor quite so infamous, not least in terms of what was to follow. While the **Concordancia**, as the regime came to be known, stabilized the **economy** and promised to restore representative government, it was marked by electoral fraud (*fraude patriótico*). During this period, the "outs" of the Radical Ascendancy, the socialists and conservatives as well as dissident Radicals, sought to construct viable coalitions capable of defeating the UCR.

Dissident factions, as well as previous splits in the party, reflected the multiclass nature of the UCR, which was composed of reformist elements of the oligarchy typified by Alvear, the urban professional middle classes (Yrigoyen was a medical doctor), and the "national" working class. The party failed to attract support from immigrant workers, who tended to favor the **Partido Socialista** (PS) and **anarcho-syndicalists**, and had a correspondingly uneasy relationship with the small but active trade union movement. The UCR also neglected the rural middle class. Yet there were substantial achievements, including the opening up of higher **education**, a broadening of the political process, social legislation that prefigured later welfare reforms, and notwithstanding some backsliding, the tentative construction of a functioning democracy.

The ejection of Yrigoyen in 1930 induced a profound crisis within Radicalism, though it provided an opportunity for reconsolidation. When elections were called for late 1931, the party turned to Alvear, who attempted bridge building with Yrigoyen. Faced with the prospect of a reunified UCR, the **military** government resorted to violence. Alvear was deported and called for the boycott of elections, a strategy of abstention supported by most but not all sections of the party. The 1931 elections were characterized by intimidation and irregularities that would become the hallmark the 1930s. Given assurances that the 1937 elections would be fair and free, Alvear returned to the country in 1936 and was successful in restoring party unity and discipline, a process assisted by the death of Yrigoyen in 1933 and one that resulted in poll victories at the provincial level. In the event, the 1937 elections were neither fair not free. Notwithstanding, Alvear remained the key figure in Radicalism until his death in 1942, seeming to ensure that the party was electorally ready for any future reinstatement of democratic politics. Yet Radicalism was overtaken by events when the **Grupo de Oficiales Unidos** (GOU) staged the **military coup of 1943**, paving the way for elections in 1946.

The victory of Colonel (later General) **Juan Domingo Perón** and the trade union–sponsored **Partido Laborista** (PL) formed to support him in 1946 confounded the Radicals, who had anticipated that they would be the natural beneficiaries of a return to democracy. As the new industrial urban working class, sections of business, and nationalist military were mobilized by Perón, a perceived threat of perpetual exclusion from power confronted the Radicals and other parties. This threat was confirmed by defeat in the 1951 elections, when a Peronist victory was achieved partly due to political repression and manipulation of the **media**, but also by the enduring appeal of Perón. Confronted with this new political and electoral reality, the Radicals again split. As with earlier splits, the division was in part triggered by personality clashes and ideology, though mainly about how to handle **Peronism**—whether to seek a political accommodation with it or take a principled stand against the increasingly authoritarian populist tendencies of Perón and his movement. Although they had stood for the UCR in 1951 as, respectively, candidates for the presidency and vice presidency, **Ricardo Balbín** and **Arturo Frondizi** found it impossible to collaborate after the **military coup of 1955** that ousted Perón, even though the proscription of Peronism by the military should have favored the party. As head of the **Unión Cívica Radical del Pueblo** (UCRP), Balbín, who had suffered at the hands of Peronist goons and represented the more conservative wing of the party, was viscerally opposed to any deal with Perón. Frondizi, on the other hand, heading the **Unión Cívica Radical Intransigente** (UCRI), which drew support from left-wing professionals and intellectuals and national business, favored an informal pact with banned Peronist and pro-Peronist **trade unions**. This strategy enabled him to assume the presidency in 1958, albeit under the watchful eye of the military, who ultimately ejected him. In 1963, Frondizi broke with the UCRI and formed the **Movimiento de Integración y Desarrollo** (MID). In the run-up to the **presidential election of March 1973**, which resulted in the victory of **Héctor Cámpora**, the MID joined the Peronist electoral coalition **Frente Justicialista de Liberación** (FREJULI).

When Fronzidi was deposed, the **presidential succession of 1962** delivered the presidency to **José María Guido**. Like the ousted president, Guido belonged to the UCRI. Yet he fell into line with the coup leaders, who wished to preserve the façade of civilian government and an observance of constitutional norms, agreeing to act as interim president until new elections could be held. He also accepted that he would be closely supervised by the military. In the **presidential election of 1963**, **Arturo Illia** of the UCRP won. Widely regarded as honest and principled, if ineffective, Illia saw his mandate weakened by the omnipresent military and his poor showing in the poll. As during the Frondizi presidency, when Peronists were allowed to stand for election and campaign openly, they usually won. With the economy again faltering, partly due to policy reversals or inconsistency, and continuing popular support for the **Partido Justicialista** (PJ), Illia was soon regarded as inept. The armed forces lost patience and again intervened, deciding to govern directly, eschewing even the veneer of civilian rule maintained since 1958. Despite standing up to the platoon of middle-ranking officers sent to eject him from the presidential palace in June 1966, Illia was given his marching orders.

Personalist factionalism, ideological schism, and above all disagreement about how to deal with Peronism and the military damaged the UCR from the 1950s to the 1970s. The **presidential elections of March 1973** and **September 1973** produced sweeping victories for the Peronists and disaster for the UCR, which had regained its original name when the rump UCRI became the **Partido Intransigente** (PI). It was only with difficulty, and largely due to the efforts of **Raúl Alfonsín**, that the party was rebuilt as a disciplined organization. When another period of military rule ended in 1983 and the armed forces called elections, Alfonsín's principled stand during the dark period of the **Proceso de Reorganización Nacional** helped produce a surprise victory for the UCR and the presidency for himself.

Although the Alfonsín presidency ended in **hyperinflation** and near chaos, few doubt that the man was an honest and honorable politician—he did not amass a fortune while in office—and was a true democrat. In government, Alfonsín saw as his main tasks the embedding of civilian rule and the reconstruction of civil society, priorities that required political transparency, direct communications between politicians and the public, and an acceptance by the military of civilian control. He sponsored greater accountability and internal democracy within the UCR. The euphoria that greeted Alfonsín's inauguration in December 1983 probably generated unrealizable expectations, though it was sufficient to yield further victories for the administration in the midterm **congressional elections of 1985**. The principal difficulties confronting the government were a damaged, shrinking economy, a dramatic increase in poverty, and a society scarred by violence. Having suffered defeat in the **Falklands War**, the military was chastened but not cowed. The Peronists, who had expected to win the 1983 elections, were disinclined to cooperate in the reconstruction of political and economic life. Dominated by the PJ, most trade unions ferociously resisted government efforts to democratize the labor movement. Business was also suspicious of the UCR, an attitude that was warmly reciprocated by sections of the party. And there was the external debt: the international financial community was not prepared to accord the administration the democratic dividend that it had anticipated. The international community was also quizzical about the heterodox **Austral Plan** launched to reactivate the economy. When the plan began to unravel, public support fell away and electoral defeats generated further instability. Hyperinflation, social turmoil, and the defeat of the UCR in the 1989 elections made for a lame duck presidency, forcing Alfonsín to hand over to incoming president **Carlos Saúl Menem** of the PJ before the constitutionally determined date.

The manner of Alfonsín's retirement from the presidency left the UCR to cope with a seemingly unbeatable resurgent Peronism. Yet as the Menem administration became increasingly mired in **corruption**, it was to the Radicals, in association with the **Frente País Solidario** (FREPASO), in the form of the **Alianza** government that the electorate turned in 1999, once the UCR had signed up to the **Convertibility Plan**. Thus it was that, representing the UCR, **Fernando de la Rúa** became president, a victory that pointed to voters' trust in the party to deliver clean government, and that the electorate had forgiven the Radicals for economic failure in 1988–1989. Unfortunately, these expectations proved short lived. As the neoliberal project inherited from Menem fell apart, and De la Rúa was revealed to have bribed fellow politicians in order to secure the passage of vital legislation, the regime and party were once again diminished in public esteem. In 2001, De la Rúa resigned, leaving office amid scenes of political and economic collapse—a reprise of the events of 1988–1989, only on a more devastating scale.

In the second half of the 20th century, the UCR had to deal with Peronism and the military. It did so with little success until 1983, when the triumph of Alfonsín seemed to promise a new dawn echoing that of 1916. A telling aspect of the victories of Alfonsín and De la Rúa was that the party obtained support from beyond its traditional middle-class base, drawing votes from workers and the business community. Unfortunately, both regimes ended in shambles. Whether or not the party will fully recover is difficult to predict. In the 21st century, pundits likened the UCR to a submarine. It operates below the surface of political life yet becomes visible at strategic moments to make a mark in the polls. The party retains a national organization, if not a national electoral capability, and remains strong in some provinces. It also continues as the natural political home of substantial segments of the professional middle classes, but to achieve government the party needs to construct alliances with a plethora of different regional and sectional interests. The old duopoly of Radicalism and Peronism no longer exists; the PJ is now the dominant player in Argentine political life. This should not obscure what the UCR has achieved in recent decades—namely, the restoration of democracy, examples of principled, clean administration (despite the De la Rúa debacle), and the promotion of educational and social reforms that have stood the test of time. *See also* CONGRESSIONAL ELECTIONS OF 1951; MILITARY COUP OF 1962; OLIVOS PACT; PRESIDENTIAL ELECTION OF 1951; UNIVERSITY REFORM MOVEMENT.

UNIÓN CÍVICA RADICAL DEL PUEBLO (UCRP). When the **Unión Cívica Radical** (UCR) split in 1957, the UCRP, headed by **Ricardo Balbín**, became the larger faction, the other being the **Unión Cívica Radical Intransigente** (UCRI), led by **Arturo Fronzidi**. The principal differences between the two factions were how to deal with **Peronism**: Balbinistas viewed the Peronists as antidemocratic and a threat to democratic politics; Frondizistas argued that Peronists should be integrated into the democratic process. There were also differences about economic policy: the UCRP was inclined toward the economic liberalism of the early 20th century; the UCRI favored developmentalism, then gaining intellectual traction.

In the **congressional** and **presidential elections of 1958**, the first to be held following the **military coup of 1955**, Frondizi beat Balbín by a considerably margin, gaining over four million votes to the latter's two and a half million. However, when new elections were held in 1963—Frondizi had been forced to resign by the **military** in 1962—the UCRP topped the poll. It was a flawed victory: **Arturo Illia** of the UCRP won with 2.4 million votes, around 25 percent of the poll. **Oscar Alende**, standing for the UCRI, got just under 1.6 million votes, but 1.7 million blank ballots were cast—more than the total received by Alende. Voting "blank" was a strategy endorsed by Frondizi and his new **Movimiento de Integración y Desarrollo** (MID)—he was prevented from standing—and by the proscribed Peronists. In office, Illia and the UCRP had to confront an unstable **economy** and delicate international relations. Initially, an orthodox approach to economic policy—balancing the budget and reducing government debt—delivered a rise in living standards and employment. Yet, lacking legitimacy, the UCRP was unable to resolve the most pressing problem of the day—how to deal with Peronism. Illia was ejected by the **military coup of 1966**, the so-called **Revolución Argentina**, which promised decisive action on the economic and political fronts. The UCRP reclaimed the original name of the party in 1972, as the rump UCRI became the **Partido Intransigente** (PI). *See also* DEVELOPMENTALISM/DEVELOPMENTALIST.

UNIÓN CÍVICA RADICAL INTRANSIGENTE (UCRI). Ephemeral splinter of the historic Radical Party, the **Unión Cívica Radical** (UCR). In 1957, the UCR divided into two factions, the **Unión Cívica Radical del Pueblo** (UCRP), headed by **Ricardo Balbín**, and the UCRI, led by **Arturo Frondizi**. The UCRI was the minor grouping. It led a checkered existence, despite delivering the presidency to Frondizi in the **presidential election of 1958**: the UCRI obtained almost 48 percent of the vote to around 31 percent for the UCRP, a victory that was attributed to the last-minute endorsement of Frondizi by exiled former president **Juan Domingo Perón**. This support gained the presidency for Frondizi but compromised his relationship with the all-powerful **military**, which came to regard the UCRI as a stalking horse for the proscribed Peronists. While there was little difference in the political ideology of the two branches of the Radical Party, other than how to deal with **Peronism**, the UCRI was the more business orientated and economically internationalist. The UCRI adopted a developmentalist (*desarrollista*) stance, accepting the role of foreign capital in the promotion of national industrial growth, even participation in the oil sector. This approach was rejected by the UCRP, which was suspicious of foreign corporations, and by nationalist factions in the armed forces. Frondizi was ousted in the **military coup of 1962**, partly due to his association with US oil corporations, though mainly due to his flirting with Peronism, whereupon the UCRI fragmented. Frondizi formed the **Movimiento de Integración y Desarrollo** (MID), a title that reflected its attachment to developmentalism. The MID was prevented from fielding candidates in the **congressional** and **presidential elections of 1963**. Allowed to participate in the midterm **congressional elections of 1965**, the MID did rather better than the rump UCRI, driving it into fourth place. Barred from using the term "intransigent radicals" in its name for the elections scheduled for 1973, the rump UCRI became the **Partido Intransigente** (PI) in 1972. *See also* CARACAS PACT; DEVELOPMENTALISM/ DEVELOPMENTALIST; "LA HORA DEL PUEBLO"; UNIÓN POPULAR (UP).

UNIÓN CÍVICA RADICAL JUNTA RENOVADORA (UCRJR). Splinter of the **Unión Cívica Radical** (UCR) that, along with the **Partido Laborista** (PL) and others, formed an alliance to support the candidacy of **Juan Domingo Perón** in the **presidential election of 1946**. The mainstream of the UCR supported the **Unión Democrática** (UD), the coalition that opposed Perón. Although the recently formed PL was the dominant partner in the pro-Perón electoral coalition, such was the significance of the UCRJR that it supplied Perón's running mate **Hortensio Quijano**, several ministers in the first Perón administration, and a substantial representation in **Congress**. The grouping was dissolved in 1947, being incorporated into what became the **Partido Peronista** (PP), subsequently the **Partido Justicialista** (PJ).

UNIÓN DE NACIONES SURAMERICANAS (UNASUR). Set up in Brasilia in 2008; in English, the Union of South American Nations, sometimes the Union of the South, an economic and political organization designed to foster closer relations among member countries. The institutional structure of the UNASUR is supported by the Parlamento Sudamericano (South American Parliament). A related organization is the Banco del Sur (Bank of the South), founded in 2009 although not yet fully functioning; the bank is viewed as an alternative source of credit for member nations to the Washington international financial institutions—the International Monetary Fund

(IMF) and World Bank. At some point in the future, it is envisaged that the bank will issue a common **currency** to circulate within the bloc, a monetary unit that would displace the US dollar in regional transactions and possibly replace national currencies. The name of the currency, note and coin denominations and design, and volume of issue are as yet unknown. Cultural activities include a regional news agency and television channel, TeleSUR.

Early members were Argentina, **Bolivia**, **Brazil**, **Chile**, Ecuador, Guyana, **Peru**, Suriname, and **Venezuela**; other countries joined later. The history of the UNASUR has not been positive. Funding the organization and associate bodies has been problematic—Venezuela, formerly the principal paymaster, has been beset with financial and political crises since the death of Húgo Chávez and the fall in oil prices; there have been conflicts over the leadership and strategic objectives. Argentina, Brazil, Chile, Colombia, Paraguay, and Peru announced in 2018 that they were suspending membership until political and administrative difficulties were resolved. Critics view UNASUR variously as unrealistic (or idealistic); a brave leftist challenge to **United States** hegemony, especially proposals like the Free Trade Agreement of the Americas coupled with the primacy of the dollar; the reflection of a historic dream of political unity in South America, unrealizable due to ideological differences among members and incompatible strategic aspiration; and a Chavista vanity project that will not outlive the death of its main progenitor. Argentina's engagement with UNASUR was largely a function of the domestic political agenda of Presidents **Néstor Kirchner** and **Cristina Fernández de Kirchner**.

UNIÓN DEL CENTRO DEMOCRÁTICO (UCEDE). Sometimes UCeDe, the UCDE is a small, right-of-center, probusiness **political party** committed to advancing liberal ideas. Founded by **Álvaro Alsogaray** in 1982, it briefly enjoyed much influence when associated with the **Partido Justicialista** (PJ) during the administrations of President **Carlos Saúl Menem**.

Sometime minister of economy in the civilian administrations headed by **Arturo Frondizi** and **José Mária Guido**, Alsogaray was principally active in the 1950s and 1960s as the economic guru of **military** governments headed by de facto president Generals **Pedro Eugenio Aramburu** and **Juan Carlos Onganía**. Attempting to counter the prevailing statist-developmentalist consensus, which appealed to nationalist, proindustry sections of the military as well as the manufacturing lobby, Alsogaray became convinced of the need for a political party that could argue the case for economic liberalism in a democratic political environment. The fragility of military regimes and his frustration with the failure of their economic strategies led him to believe that a sustainable implementation of market-friendly policies could only be achieved by forging electoral support for such policies. This damascene conversion appeared to bear fruit when he was elected to the Chamber of Deputies, representing the city of **Buenos Aires**, in the **congressional elections of 1983**. As party leader, he represented the party and the city continuously between 1983 and 1999, the party's share of the vote increasing steadily in the early part of this period. In the **congressional** and **presidential elections of 1989**, Alsogaray was unsuccessful in a bid for the presidency— he came in third—but the UCEDE returned 16 deputies to **Congress**. When Menem endorsed economic liberalism, Alsogaray threw in his lot with the PJ. Alsogaray's daughter María Julia was offered a junior post in the Menem administration and the UCEDE supported Menem's bid for reelection in the **presidential election of 1995**. This proved to be a turning point in the fortunes of the party: María Julia was caught up in **corruption** scandals, and the electorate became disenchanted with the politics of the Menem administration, though not necessarily its economic model—at this point. By the beginning of the 21st century, the UCEDE was reduced to seeking alliances with other right and center-right groups, forging electoral pacts with different coalitions. In 2015, the party entered an electoral alliance with the **Propuesta Republicana** (PRO), part of the **Cambiemos** coalition that delivered the presidency to **Mauricio Macri**.

The party remains active, notably in the city of Buenos Aires and some parts of the interior, but is no longer represented in the national Congress. Its future is uncertain. The trajectory of the UCEDE validates Alsogaray's logic that a market-friendly ideology could only be popularized if championed by a democratically electable political party, but not his strategy for advancing liberal economics. *See also* ALSOGARAY, MARÍA JULIA (1942–); DEVELOPMENTALISM/DEVELOPMENTALIST; ECONOMIC CRISES; ECONOMY; MINISTRY OF ECONOMY; PRESIDENTIAL ELECTION OF 2015.

UNIÓN DEMOCRÁTICA (UD). Political alliance set up in November 1945 to challenge **Juan Domingo Perón** in the fateful **presidential election of 1946** that comprised the **Unión Cívica Radical** (UCR), the **Partido Socialista** (PS), the **Partido Demócrata Progresista** (PDP), and the Communists. The UCR was the dominant force within the coalition. It not only provided José Tamborini and Enrique Mosca as presidential and vice presidential candidates, respectively, but also excluded participation by the conservative **Partido Demócrata Nacional** (PDN). Perón's victory in the election held on 24 February 1946 led to the immediate dissolution of the UD, which altered the balance among parties opposing Perón and their strategies for dealing with **Peronism**.

UNIÓN FERROVIARIA (UF). Once the most powerful trade union in the country, due to the size of the membership and strategic location it was a force to be reckoned with by civilian administrations and **military** regimes alike. UF is significant for several reasons. First, it was an early example of an all-sector trade union. Formed in 1922, the union brought together all groups of rail workers save locomotive drivers and firemen, who continued to be represented by the "craft" union La Fraternidad. The principal groups composing the UF were station staff, signalmen, linemen, and operatives in railway workshops and depots. UF was one of the first **trade unions** to provide members with a range of social benefits, including health and medical coverage, before such were provided by the state. Thirdly, the organization is important because it was instrumental in the formation of the national labor confederation, the **Confederación General del Trabajo** (CGT). Between the 1920s and the 1940s, the UF was the largest union in the CGT and its principal source of financial support. For much of the period, the CGT was housed in the headquarters of the UF. In keeping with this dominant position, the UF was also crucial to the decision of the CGT to form the **Partido Laborista** (PL), which endorsed the candidature of General **Juan Domingo Perón** in the **presidential election of 1946**. Although the union supported Perón's political ambitions in 1946, the leadership was anxious to maintain the independence of the labor movement and the PL. Syndicalist in their ideology, the leadership viewed independence of state and employer as the best means of representing the interests of members. This is another factor underscoring the significance of the UF. It points to a countermodel of trade unionism to the one that actually emerged after the 1950s. The UF bitterly opposed the transformation of the PL into the **Partido Peronista** (PP)—later the **Partido Justicialista** (PJ). Only when the leadership was purged by groups loyal to Perón did the UF fall in line. Yet despite this forced conversion, and yet another reason why the UF is important, in 1951 the union organized a strike against the government—the first strike against a Peronist administration in the history of the country. The strike was brutally repressed. Rail workers may have benefited from rail nationalization in 1948, but there was a price to be paid. Later, the union acted against rail **privatization** during the administration of President **Carlos Saúl Menem**, who headed another PJ government.

By the 1960s, the importance of the UF in the labor movement was being undermined by the growth of unions representing industrial workers and subsequently by such white-collar unions as the teachers' union. But the final blow was the growth of road building, much associated with military governments of the 1960 and 1970s, which decimated rail freight, and rail privatization in the 1990s, which led to a massive contraction of the rail network. The institutional trajectory of the UF illustrates a recurrent theme in Argentine political history, the uneasy relationship between sections of the labor movement and **Peronism**. *See also* FERROCARRILES ARGENTINOS (FFAA); MILITARY COUP OF 1951 (FAILED); MILITARY COUP OF 1966; MILITARY COUP OF 1976; "PERONISM WITHOUT PERÓN"; STATE-OWNED ENTERPRISES (SOEs); TRANSPORTATION; VANDOR, AUGUSTO TIMOTEO (1923–1969).

UNIÓN INDUSTRIAL ARGENTINA (UIA). One of the premier, historic business organization of the country. Established in 1887 to represent manufacturing and promote the development of national industry, the origins of the UIA may be traced back to the Industrial Club set up a dozen years earlier when **Congress** was debating new tariff legislation. The Union was initially viewed as but a pale shadow of the prestigious **Sociedad Rural Argentina** (SRA) founded in 1866 by modernizing estancieros yet came to rival and supplant it.

The current UIA mission statement describes it as the principal interface between industry—at national, provincial and municipal level—and government. Encouraging the unity and integrity of the sector, it seeks to enhance the role of private business in manufacturing by shaping official policy and fostering domestic market expansion. Presently, the UIA serves as an umbrella body, coordinating the actions of sectoral and regional associations; previously, the membership was composed as much by individual firms—and individual entrepreneurs—as by corporate groupings, though key national and international businesses retain considerable prominence within the organization. The UIA collaborates with like-minded business-industrial confederations and associations in Latin America and elsewhere.

Around 1900, the membership of the Union consisted of various types of enterprises. These included small- and medium-scale family-owned industrial firms set up by immigrants—penny capitalists with knowledge and expertise who had settled in Argentina, especially the city of **Buenos Aires** during the period of mass **immigration**. Foreign-owned utility companies were counted amongst the members or associates of the UIA, as were foreign companies establishing branch factories in the country. Commercial enterprises, trading houses and financial businesses were also represented. Such diversity in scale, ownership and focus of activity tended to inhibit the formation of a common stance, especially in significant policy areas like tariffs and protection, though there was common ground regarding taxation and employment legislation. Businessman-cum-financier-cum-politician, Carlos Pellegrini, was an early supporter of the UIA, and was instrumental in advancing the case for tariff reform and national industry in the aftermath of the **Baring Crisis**. Pellegrini was something of an exception at a time when most of the political class espoused liberalism and free trade, which were endorsed by the ruling land-owning oligarchy. Although the Baring Crisis resulted in an upsurge in support for national manufacturing firms and allowed the UIA to argue that member firms generated employment as well as supplying the domestic market with essential products, such sentiments proved ephemeral. These arguments proved more convincing during the volatile inter-war decades when turbulence in international markets, the natural growth of the domestic industrial sector (along with rising employment in manufacturing) and the emergence of economic nationalism created greater receptivity to programs advocated by the Union. Not that the UIA was a passive benefici-ary of broader changes in economy and society. Major achievements during this period included substantial input into the tariff debate of 1922–1923, which resulted in a thorough overhaul of the system that featured anti-dump-ing measures, and the industrial exposition of 1924. Intended to showcase "industria argentina," the exposition was held in the grounds of the SRA in Palermo and attracted huge crowds. The UIA was consulted by government about changes to labor laws and proposed social insurance legislation es-sayed at much the same time. The administration of President **Marcelo T. de Alvear** (1922–1928) was fairly receptive to lobbying by the UIA. The **Con-cordancia** regime proved to be a mixed blessing. The **Plan de Acción Económica** of 1933 helped re-boot the economy and was especially benefi-cial to established local manufacturing businesses. Yet unintended conse-quences of the bilateral trade agreement with **Great Britain**, the **Roca–Runciman Pact**, signed the same year were less positive. Several **United States** conglomerates established subsidiaries in Argentina to circumvent commercial preferences granted to Britain, and to jump over tariff hikes introduced with the Pact and Plan. During this period, the UIA was well served by its president, Luis Colombo. Born in **Rosario** into a family of Italian immigrants, with a background in finance and industry, Colombo was elected president in 1925 and remained in post for 20 years. As president of the UIA, he was the driving force behind the first national industrial census taken in 1935.

The election of **Juan Domingo Perón** to the presidency of the republic in 1946, and the advent of Peronism, with its emphasis on national industry might have been expected to have resulted in an even more influential role for the UIA. This was not to be. Perhaps due to Colombo's cozy relationship with regimes of the Concordancia, or because of his association with the **Unión Democrática** (UD) which had campaigned against Perón in the **presi-dential election of 1946**, Colombo and the Union were regarded with suspi-cion by the incoming regime. Possibly, by this stage the UIA was considered too establishment and insufficiently attuned to the pro-labor position of the new government. The regime favored the **Confederación General Económica** (CGE), founded by **José Ber Gelbard** to represent small and medium national industrial firms, as a more suitable, compliant partner. Not-withstanding that **Miguel Miranda**, a close confidant of Perón and his some-time minister of economy, was a prominent member of the UIA board, for most of first two Perón presidencies the Union was proscribed. It was only reestablished in 1955 with the ouster of Perón. By the end of the decade, the UIA had regained the influence of earlier years, once again the principal advocate of the national industrial entrepreneuriat. It was particularly active during the 1960s and early 1970s, capitalizing on the prevailing policy emphasis on import-substituting industrialization associated with the developmentalism. The body was a strong advocate of national manufacturing enterprises at home, and an active participant in regional and international business fora—at least until 1973, when a merger with the CGE was mooted with the return of Perón. By this time, the UIA was considered the principal business organization in the country, having superseded the SRA as manufacturing displaced agriculture as the main productive sector. Although they constituted less than one-third of the membership, this was also the period when the UIA was most associated with 'big business'—large domestic corporations and transnational companies were especially influential in the organization, notwithstanding the continued representation of small- and medium-sized enterprises. Alpargatas, **Bunge & Born**, and **SIAM Di Tella** were among the most important national firms; foreign corporations included international oil companies and motor vehicle manufacturers. Membership composition resulted in the dual (or equivocal) strategy advocated by the Union—a mix of "reformist" interventionism designed to foster modernization and efficiency among national enterprises and "economic internationalism" supported by local branches of firms head-quartered overseas. All members supported campaigns intended to facilitate the growth and deepening of the home market, pro-investment measures, and the financing of infrastructure improvement.

Although some factions of the UIA regarded minister of economy **José Alfredo Martínez de Hoz**, appointed following the **military coup of 1976** as one of their own, the "New Political Economy" implemented by him was not particularly well received, especially as policies designed to make firms and households more responsive to market discipline began to bite. And abrupt economic opening resulted in the decimation of local companies in several sectors as imports flooded the market. Similarly, while companies that had to confront the threat of the kidnapping and ransoming of executives during the years preceding 1976 might have welcomed "order" promised by the **Proceso de Reorganización Nacional**, UIA firms were not immune to the regime of terror that resulted. Local businesses were decimated by the banking crisis and credit crunch of 1981 and the economic and financial chaos associated with the collapse of the Proceso. The return of democracy in 1983 found the membership of the Union equally equivocal. The inauguration of the presidency of **Raúl Alfonsín** of the **Unión Cívica Radical** (UCR) appeared to signal a return to the developmentalism and a pro-national industry stance at a time of global recession. In addition to support for domestic manufacturing, the administration also promised greater congruence in macroeconomic policymaking. Namely, harmonizing labor law, the credit and tax regimes and tariffs in order to assist industry—something for which the UIA had been pressing since the beginning of the decade. Industrialists also welcomed the promise of Keynesian-style demand stimulation contained in the **Austral Plan**—economic reactivation and "stabilizing growth"—plus an anticipated larger role for the private sector as the government toyed with **privatization**. Yet, as was the case with other major players, many private firms were not prepared to bear the costs of stabilization while enjoying it benefits. The business sector as a whole was viewed as uncooperative by the government. **Hyperinflation** at the end of the Alfonsín presidency and the opening months of the successor administration headed by President **Carlos Saal Menem** of the **Partido Justicialista** (PJ) was chastening.

The UIA endorsed the **Convertibility Plan** introduced in 1991 by Menem's fourth minister of economy, **Domingo Cavallo**. Market liberalization and de-regulation was something that most of the membership of the Union applauded, along with the promise of macroeconomic stability and easier credit. Moreover, in contrast with the neo-liberal project associated with Martínez de Hoz, Cavallo provided tax breaks, changes to employment legislation and the social security regime to cushion domestic firms against the opening of the economy and the impact of a hard/appreciating exchange rate. Privatization was pursued vigorously, generating considerably more space in the national economy for the private sector. And, there was **corruption**, which meant sweet deals and preferential tendering for government contracts. The UIA could more than live with this form of market-friendly **Peronism**. The collapse of Convertibility was a blow, but not as catastrophic for the private business sector as the chaos of 1981–1982, while efforts to stabilize the economy taken by interim PJ President **Eduardo Duhalde** and continued by his successor **Néstor Kirchner** bore fruit fairly rapidly. Careful economic management prevented the social and political implosion that some had anticipated. Pro-national developmentalism and industrial reactivation essayed by Kircher and continued by his wife, President **Cristina Fernández de Kirchner** proved to be yet another variant of Peronism with which the membership of the Union could live. Although the political economy of the Kirchners entailed greater interventionism, regulation and the imposition of exchange, credit and price controls, the government was content to "leave business to business." And de-privatization—taking back into state hands firms that had been privatized during the *menemato*—hardly impacted domestic business. Re-statization mainly affected foreign consortia. Local enterprises were granted more space in the national economy and benefitted from subsidized services and inputs supplied by renationalized firms. And there were subsidies. The **kirchnerato** was kind to firms content to toe the official line on prices, wages, and employment. The model worked well until around 2012 when inflation returned, subsidies became less generous, and the rhetoric of the administration assumed a less business-friendly tone.

The success of **Mauricio Macri** in the second round of the **presidential election of 2015** was warmly supported by most of the UIA membership. A prominent businessman, Macri was again seen as one of their own; an effective politician attuned to the needs of business and industrialists in particular. This is both his appeal and an electoral liability. He cannot be seen to be too close to business. Macri's success in the mid-term **congressional elections of 2017** was reassuring for the UIA and for those arguing the case for continued market liberalization. The current status of the UIA is flagged by the attention it receives from politicians. In recent decades, most presidents of the republic have participated in the principal annual event organized by the Union and, soon after election, presidents have found time in their diaries for an early visit to address business leaders at the UIA headquarters. *See also* ASOCIACIÓN EMPRESARIA ARGENTINA (AEA); DEVELOPMENTALISM/DEVELOPMENTALIST; ECONOMY; FRONDIZI, ARTURO (1908–1995); INDUSTRY; MONTONEROS; PELLEGRINI, CARLOS ENRIQUE JOSÉ (1846–1906); STATE-OWNED ENTERPRISES (SOEs).

UNIÓN POPULAR (UP). Leading neo-Peronist party during the exile of ousted president **Juan Domingo Perón** (1955–1973). Taking advantage of the proscription of Peronism, Perón's former foreign minister **Juan Atilio Bramuglia** established the UP in December 1955. The aim was to transform the Peronist movement into an institutionalized party, integrated into mainstream politics and upholding a Peronist social agenda. It was an overt attempt at **"Peronism without Perón,"** which the exiled president would not countenance as he saw it as a direct challenge to his authority.

Although the UP was legalized to contest the **constitutional convention election of 1957**, it followed the exiled leader's request that supporters cast blank ballots in order to show that they did not recognize the legitimacy of a political system that denied Peronists full electoral participation. Perón then stymied the chances of the UP performing successfully in the **presidential election of 1958** when he made the **Caracas Pact**, the election deal that enabled **Arturo Frondizi** of the **Unión Cívica Radical Intransigente** (UCRI) to become president. When Frondizi decided to allow Peronists to participate in various guises in the provincial and **congressional elections of 1962**, Perón recognized that he needed the UP with its legal status and powerful machine to win the elections. But, unforgiving toward the attempts at independence by the party leadership, he imposed his own candidates. The subsequent victory of the UP and other neo-Peronist groups at the ballot box triggered the **military coup of 1962**.

In order to contest the **presidential election of 1963**, and with the blessing of Perón, the UP set up the Frente Nacional y Popular with the **Movimiento de Integración y Desarrollo** (MID) and the **Partido Conservador Popular** (PCP). But the **military** objected, and the front was proscribed. *Justicialismo* remained proscribed, and attempts in December 1964 and January 1965 to form a unified neo-Peronist party to contest the **congressional elections of 1965** came to nothing. The UP then joined a coalition of trade unionists and neo-Peronist parties set up by **Augusto Vandor**, secretary general of the Unión Obrera Metalúrgica (UOM) and a leading proponent of "Peronism without Perón." At the ballot box, the Vandorista coalition defeated the governing **Unión Cívica Radical del Pueblo** (UCRP) by 30 percent to 28.5 percent of the total vote. Such a strong performance boded ill for the gubernatorial elections due in March 1967 and was a factor in the subsequent **military coup of 1966**.

When the armed forces decided to engineer a return to the barracks and allow **Peronism** to participate in the democratic process, the UP reaffirmed its loyalty to Perón and its adherence to his movement. Together with other neo-Peronist bodies, it joined the **Frente Justicialista de Liberación** (FREJULI), the electoral alliance and front for the **Partido Justicialista** (PJ) formed to contest the **presidential election of March 1973**. Such unity was short lived, as an array of parties including the UP withdrew from the FREJULI over disputes about the distribution of places on the FREJULI list of candidates (Perón insisted on 75 percent for the PJ) and about aspects of the manifesto and legislative program presented to **Congress**.

In January 1973, the UP became permanently de-Peronized and aligned itself with the Alianza Popular Federalista, a grouping of small, moderately conservative parties that supported the presidential candidacy of **Francisco Manrique**. In the congressional election held simultaneously with the presidential ballot, the UP only managed to get three national deputies elected. It later disappeared from the political stage. *See also* MINISTRY OF FOREIGN RELATIONS AND RELIGION; TRADE UNIONS.

UNITARIANISM/UNITARIANS. In Spanish, Unitarios, a term applied to those favoring a centralized, constitutional republican project for the country after **independence**. The term was first applied to those associated with **Bernardino Rivadavia**, who envisaged a unified political entity that encompassed the whole of the former **Viceroyalty of the River Plate**, with its capital in **Buenos Aires**.

Influenced by ideas of the Enlightenment and contemporary liberal economic and political thinking, the Unitarian project sought to fashion Argentina into a modern, progressive nation-state, based on principles of constitutional democracy, secularism, and market economics—the antithesis of the Spanish colonial order. Unitarians also assumed that the formation of a European-style state would be supported from Europe, in the form of funding loans and a flow of immigrants. The project found expression in the **Constitution of 1826**, under whose terms Rivadavia was elected first national president. The Unitarian project was opposed by **Federalists**, who were inclined to a looser, almost confederal arrangement that allowed the provinces considerable autonomy.

The Unitarian proposal, early practical expressions of which involved the secularization of the property of the **Catholic Church** and the "nationalization" of the resources of the Buenos Aires Customs House—tariffs were the mainstay of the Treasury in the early national period and would be applied to national use—did not prosper. Unitarian ideology and its project was opposed by clerical interests, monarchists, and Federalists, as well as those who viewed liberal ideas as anathema. Self-interest was also an important factor antagonizing such groups as Buenos Aires *estancieros*, who objected to the federalization of local resources, and provincial elites committed to protectionism, and from separatist tendencies in outlying regions of the former viceroyalty, like **Bolivia** and **Paraguay**, where dominant interests demanded independence, unwilling to submit to continuing rule from Buenos Aires. Beset by revolts in the interior and embroiled in conflict with **Brazil**, the Unitarian project foundered—defeated on the battlefield, undermined by economic and financial crises, and castigated as unfeasible and inappropriate by its opponents. **Juan Manuel de Rosas**, champion of Federalism, was the nemesis of Unitarianism, as "Death to Savage Unitarians" became the official slogan of the day from the late 1820s until the early 1850s. Yet, with the overthrow of Rosas, the **Constitution of 1853** echoed much of the original Unitarian national proposal. Between the 1860s and 1880s, economic and technical progress gave expression to much of the liberal, secular, nationally integrated polity first devised by Unitarians, though within the boundaries of present-day Argentina and not those of the Spanish viceroyalty. *See also* ECONOMIC CRISES; FOREIGN DEBT/FOREIGN INVESTMENT; IMMIGRATION.

UNITED NATIONS ORGANIZATION (UNO). Argentina is a founding member of the body, joining with other original members on 24 October 1945.

Before the UN, Argentina was also a founding member of the League of Nations from January 1920: the country left in 1921, returning to full membership in 1933. Argentina left the league in 1921 on an issue of principle, maintaining that all sovereign nations should be eligible for membership, including the Central Powers who had fought against the Allies. On rejoining the league, Argentina played an active role in the organization—**Carlos Saavedra Lamas**, the country's representative and Nobel Peace Prize laureate becoming president of the assembly of the league. Yet membership in the

UN was not a foregone conclusion. Due to the country's neutrality during the Second World War—Argentina only declared war on Germany in March 1945—and the pro-Axis stance of many members of the de facto government that came to power with the **military coup of 1943**, the Soviet Union objected to the issue of an invitation to Argentina to participate in the San Francisco Conference of April–June 1945 held to debate the formation of the UN. Participation in the conference and membership of the UN only came as a result of pressure from other Latin American countries, and with the support of the **United States**.

Argentina's role at the UN has been shaped by several factors, including an ambivalent attitude to the United States and a determination to recover sovereignty of the **Falkland Islands**. During periods of democratic rule from the 1960s to the 1980s, Argentina often voted with Non-Aligned members of the organization, often casting its vote against resolutions sponsored or favored by the United States. Argentina joined the Non-Aligned Movement a few years after its formation, first as an observer in 1964, becoming a full member in 1973 with the election of **Juan Domingo Perón** to the presidency that year. President **Carlos Saúl Menem** took the country out of the movement in 1991, around the time that Foreign Minister **Guido Di Tella** was advocating "carnal relations" with the United States. During the 1990s, Argentina indeed voted closely with the United States at the UN. With the onset of the administration of **Néstor Kirchner**, following the collapse of the **Convertibility Plan**, the country's voting pattern became more varied. President **Cristina Fernández de Kirchner** was particularly robust when speaking at UN General Assembly meetings, calling for the democratization of international institutions—especially international financial institutions— and greater international respect for the position of member countries at the UN. During the Kirchner presidencies, Argentina's voting pattern at the UN was closer to that of former Non-Aligned countries and left-of-center democratically elected governments of Latin America.

For some time, Argentina has enjoyed much success in arguing its case before the Decolonization Committee of the UN. Following the return of democracy in 1983, Minister of Foreign Relations **Dante Caputo** made a strong impression pressing the Argentine position on the Falklands, so much so that he was elected president of the General Assembly in 1988. Argentine diplomats have established that the islands are a special case and should not be treated in the same way as other colonial territories, given that the islanders consistently express overwhelming support for the status quo, which favors **Great Britain**. As the result of reasoned, efficient representation, the Argentine position on the islands is now widely appreciated and supported.

Unsurprising in view of the experience of the country during the **Proceso de Reorganización Nacional**, Argentine representatives at the UN have frequently participated in debates about **human rights**. In recent years, Argentine staffers at the organization have been well regarded and appointed to senior positions, for example, to head key agencies such as the Office of South–South Cooperation and the Disarmaments Affairs Office. Argentina currently supports UN peacekeeping operations in the Cyprus, Haiti, the Middle East, and Western Sahara. During the Second Gulf War, Argentina provided naval support, and has played a role in securing peace in Central America. *See also* ECONOMIC CRISES; FOREIGN RELATIONS; MINISTRY OF FOREIGN RELATIONS AND RELIGION.

UNITED PROVINCES OF SOUTH AMERICA. Briefly the official name of the country around the time of **independence**, the phrase features in the declaration of independence in 1816. Later, the name was superseded by the **United Provinces of the River Plate** (Provincias Unidas del Río de la Plata), **Argentine Confederation** (Confederación Argentina), and **Argentine Republic** (República Argentina). The name echoed that of the recently independent **United States**, reflecting contemporary aspirations of subcontinental status and assumptions that the territories of the **Viceroyalty of the River Plate** (Virreinato del Río de la Plata) would continue as a single, integrated polity. The phrase "United Provinces of the South" continues as a refrain in the national anthem. *See also* CONGRESS OF TUCUMÁN; CONSTITUTION OF 1819; MAY REVOLUTION OF 1810.

UNITED PROVINCES OF THE RIVER PLATE. Used for a short time after the **May Revolution of 1810**, before being displaced by **United Provinces of South America** around the enactment of the **Constitution of 1819**; revived by the **Constitution of 1826** and in use until the early 1830s. Changes in the official designation of the new nation indicate differing contemporary ideas about the ordering the country as well as reality as territories that had once constituted the late colonial entity the **Viceroyalty of the River Plate** (Virreinato del Río de la Plata) spun away from the control of **Buenos Aires** to become the separate republics of **Bolivia, Paraguay**, and **Uruguay**.

UNITED STATES OF AMERICA. Argentines have long held ambivalent opinions about the United States. Commercial relations between the two countries were established well before the independence of the United States, news of which circulated widely in the **River Plate** before the **May Revolution of 1810**. The United States was one of the first countries to recognize the **independence** of Argentina, though delayed doing so until 1822 on account of doubts about the stability of the government in **Buenos Aires** and about its capacity to defend itself from possible Spanish attempts at reconquest. The following year marked the formal beginning of official relations when the newly appointed US minister presented his credential in Buenos Aires. Distance ensured that there was initially little direct contact, though there were minor disputes and some Argentine officials were affronted when the United States was seen to be reluctant to support Argentine claims to the **Falkland Islands** in the 1830s—the government in Buenos Aires had attempted to invoke the Munroe Doctrine to secure US diplomatic and military assistance in the dispute with **Great Britain**. (Later Argentine regimes would take a more jaundiced view of US claims to continental leadership.)

Early 19th-century liberals regarded the United States as a political and economic example to be emulated while aspiring to becoming the "United States of the South." In the 1860s and for decades to come, when passing judgment in disputes between the federal authorities and provincial government and among provinces, the Argentine Supreme Court consulted decisions taken by the US Supreme Court in similar cases. The first commercial treaty between the two countries was signed in 1853, a mark of increasing commercial contacts. The United States was already an important market for Argentine **wool** exports and a source of wheat and flour imports. Yet the rise of protectionism in the United States and the development of Argentine cereal and **meat** exports limited bilateral trade and meant that the countries were becoming competitors in world markets. Nevertheless, at the turn of the century, the United States was seen as a counterweight to the increasingly dominant role of Great Britain in Argentine finance and trade. The United States was a possible source of international finance, and hopes of stronger commercial and diplomatic relations continued. Attitudes among some sections of the political elite toward the United States began to change later, notably during the First World War, when Washington, DC, exerted pressure on Buenos Aires to end its official position of neutrality and declare against the Central Powers. Even earlier, US-sponsored Pan-Americanism was regarded as an afront to Argentine pretensions to leadership in South America, a sentiment that would be strengthened when the United States was seen to be engaging in closer relations with **Brazil**. US–Argentine trade had expanded in the 1920s, but there was a more symbiotic commercial relationship between the United States and Brazil.

Paradoxically, the closer relationship with Great Britain signaled by the **Roca–Runciman Pact** of 1933 triggered a surge in US investment. Commercial preferences granted to Britain in the pact encouraged US motor vehicle manufacturers and producers of electrical goods to set up assemble plant in Argentina; there was a notable increase in US investment in Argentine **industry**. This probably helps explain why, by the late 1930s, the **Pinedo Plan** envisaged the United States as a substitute for Great Britain, not a counterbalance—a new source of finance, technology, and trade. Although, on the eve of the Second World War, the stocks of US and British investment in Argentina were approximately similar, the closer relationship with the

United States envisaged by Pinedo did not materialize. In part, this was due to domestic politics, but it had more to do with the sharp deterioration in US–Argentine relations that followed the **military coup of 1943**. Already suspicious of Buenos Aires—Argentina had resisted US efforts to persuade all Latin American countries to declare war on the Axis powers after Pearl Harbor (Argentina refused to renounce neutrality)—Washington came to regard the de facto regime headed briefly by General **Arturo Rawson** and then successively by General **Pedro Pablo Ramírez** and General **Edelmiro Julián Farrell** as pro-Nazi. (Ramírez had trained in Prussia before the First World War, and Farrell had served in Fascist Italy in the mid-1920s.) US Secretary of State Cordell Hull, who had pioneered the Good Neighbor Policy and was already offended by Argentine resistance to US hemispheric policy, was incensed by the attitude of the government in Buenos Aires. His mishandling of the situation intensified anti-US sentiment among members of the **military** junta. Diplomatic relations were formally suspended for around 14 months from early 1944.

Relations deteriorated further thereafter and hit a low point at the beginning of the first administration of President **Juan Domingo Perón**. Spruille Braden, US ambassador in Buenos Aires, campaigned actively for the **Unión Democrática** (UD) in the run-up to the **congressional** and **presidential elections of 1946**. The UD was an electoral coalition of traditional **political parties** set up to run against Perón. Braden's intervention was counterproductive. It produced the famous Peronist campaign slogan "Braden o Perón," which scuppered the UD, increasing voter support for Perón. For much of Perón's first administration, the State Department was correct and cautious. Perón's economic project was regarded with suspicion, as was his relationship with the **trade unions**. Economic policy was considered to be antibusiness and unsustainable and likely to end in a crisis that might facilitate a Communist takeover. Perón was also accused of meddling in the affairs of neighboring countries and promoting alliances inimical to US interests. Although US business and finance took a different view, pressing for closer collaboration, official relations did not become more cordial until after the **military coup of 1955** that ousted Perón. The de facto administration headed by President General **Pedro Eugenio Aramburu** cultivated close economic and financial ties with the United States, and various programs advanced by the successor civilian government of President **Arturo Frondizi** were welcomed by Washington. Frondizi's initial attempts to curb **Peronism** and his developmentalist program were cautiously applauded by official and business US representatives. Incentives for foreign investment were well received. Attempts to promote energy production and motor vehicle production were thought to offer opportunities to US firms. Argentina was still a large market. President Eisenhower visited in 1959, and Frondizi tried to mediate between the United States and **Cuba**.

Washington was concerned about political and economic turmoil in Argentina in the 1960s, and the prospect of an arms race with Brazil, notably after the 1964 coup in Brazil and the **military coup of 1966** in Argentina. And there was awareness in US official and business quarters of the opinion in Buenos Aires that the United States was more favorably disposed to Brazil. Yet US capital inflows continued, and for much of the 1960s and early 1970s the United States continued to absorb around 8 or 9 percent of Argentine exports and provide between a fifth and a quarter of Argentine imports, mainly capital equipment and intermediate goods. Pursing an ethical foreign policy, the government of President Carter was scandalized by the wanton disregard of **human rights** displayed by regimes of the **Proceso de Reorganización Nacional**. Washington was also irked by the growth in Argentine wheat and **maize** exports to the Soviet bloc during the 1970s, although the State Department had initially been supportive of the **military coup of 1976**, seeing it as likely to bring much-needed domestic political stability after the chaos of the administration of President **Isabel Perón**, which had witnessed acute macroeconomic volatility, a rise in violence, and political kidnappings and killings, including of foreign businessmen. US military aid was ratcheted up, and there was close military and security intelligence collaboration after the inauguration of President Reagan in 1981. Relations were especially cordial until the invasion of the **Falkland Islands** two years later. Arguably, the warm relationship that existed between Buenos Aires and Washington in 1981 and 1982 encouraged in de facto president General **Leopoldo Fortunato Galtieri** a belief that the United States would support the invasion, preferring Argentina as a strategic partner to Britain.

Relations between Argentina and the United States were correct rather than cordial for much of the administration of President **Raúl Alfonsín**. Washington was annoyed by the unwillingness of Buenos Aires to support Reagan's tactics in Central America, and the Argentine government was disappointed by lukewarm support for efforts to stabilize the **economy**. There was much closer proximity during the administrations of President **Carlos Saúl Menem**, when Minister of Foreign Relations **Guido Di Tella** famously announced that Buenos Aires would seek "carnal relations" with the United States. In contrast to previous decades, Argentina voted consistently with the United States in the **United Nations** (UN), sent warships to support the US-led coalition during the First Gulf War, and became a strategic partner of NATO. US businesses participated in Menem's program of **privatization**, and there was an appreciation of efforts like the **Convertibility Plan** to stabilize and grow the economy—though skepticism. Bilateral relations during the *kirchnerato* were less cordial. Even today, Argentines continue to blame Washington for the refusal of the IMF to bail out the country at the height of the 2001 debt crisis. Antagonism to the United States rose in government circles and was politically popular. Buenos Aires was cool on regional trade deals, and there was a revival of earlier opposition to anything that smacked of US-backed Pan-Americanism. President George W. Bush was given an especially hard time by his host President **Néstor Kirchner** at the Summit of the Americas in Mar del Plata in 2005.

Since then, US courts have become involved in cases involving money laundering and **corruption** by senior figures in the Argentine government and claims brought by foreign bondholders—notably, the so-called holdouts who had not settled in 2005. President **Cristina Fernández de Kirchner** was scathing about legal adjudications in favor of hedge funds that had acquired bonds in default. Argentina's proximity to **Venezuela** and **Bolivia**, the adoption of radical left-wing rhetoric, engagement with Iran, and positions taken at the UN did not go down well in Washington. President Fernández de Kirchner's endorsement of the "Bolivarian Project," intended to promote unity within Latin America, explicitly rejecting the participation of the United States, was held to epitomize anti-US attitudes and objectives. With the election of President **Mauricio Macri** in 2015, the pendulum swung in the other direction. Macri espouses a "mature" relationship with the United States that rejects the anti-US language of the 1960s and the 1970s and the Kirchner years and seeks a broad common agenda, notwithstanding the resurgence of protectionism in the United States.

Today, the United States accounts for about 14 percent of the stock of foreign capital invested in Argentina and remains the principal source of new inward investment. In 2017, more than 500 US corporations were operating in Argentina, mainly in the manufacturing, information and financial services, and commercial sectors. Absorbing between 6 and 8 percent of Argentine exports, the United States is usually the country's second most important market, though buying less than a quarter of the value of products sold to Brazil; the United States is usually Argentina's third most important source of imports, providing around 12 to 14 percent of total imports, following Brazil and **China**. Argentina buys mainly machinery, oil, and chemicals from the United States and sells energy products, **commodities**, and processed foodstuffs. *See also* BER GELBARD, JOSÉ (1917–1977); CALVO, CARLOS (1822–1906); CHILE; DEVELOPMENTALISM/DEVELOPMENTALIST; ECONOMIC CRISES; EJÉRCITO REVOLUCIONARIO DEL PUEBLO (ERP); FOREIGN DEBT/FOREIGN INVESTMENT; FOREIGN TRADE; INDUSTRIAS KAISER ARGENTINA (IKA); PRESIDENTIAL ELECTION OF 1946; SOCIEDAD MIXTA SIDERURGICA ARGENTINA (SOMISA).

UNIVERSIDAD ARGENTINA DE LA EMPRESA (UADE). Business university that dates from 1957, when the Instituto Superior de Estudios de la Empresa (School of Advanced Business Studies) was founded by a group of businessmen. The brief of the Instituto was to encourage the scientific study of management, along the lines of contemporary business schools in the **United States**, and to promote the reputation of business and the national entrepreneuriat. At the time of its foundation, the Instituto received political and material support from the government; in the early 21st century, the university signed an agreement with the state research funding body to support doctoral and postdoctoral research. In addition to management, the university now offers a mix of undergraduate and postgraduate programs in such areas as design, economics, engineering, finance, hospitality, information technology, media, and the social sciences. Its laboratories and design workshops are among the best funded in the country. In 2017, the UADE Business School was ranked fifth in the country and invariably appears within the top 10, though the overall national ranking of the college is considerably lower— the focus is on teaching not research. The institution is significant because, with the Universidad del CEMA (UCEMA), it represents an early attempt to enhance the public and political profile of national business. A later foundation, UCEMA now enjoys a much higher status than UADE. *See also* CENTRO DE ESTUDIOS MACROECONÓMICOS DE ARGENTINA (CEMA/ UCEMA); EDUCATION; INDUSTRY.

UNIVERSIDAD CATÓLICA ARGENTINA (UCA). Formally the Pontificia Universidad Católica Argentina "Santa María de los Buenos Aires," sometimes known as the Universidad Católica de Buenos Aires, the principal Roman Catholic university in the country. The modern incarnation of the university dates from 1958, when it was based around three core departments—Philosophy, Law and Political, and Social and Economic Sciences. The current mission statement describes the UCA as an Argentine Catholic institution devoted to higher **education** that seeks to achieve academic and vocational excellence through the application of Christian thinking to innovative teaching, training, and research with a commitment to the development of social and cultural knowledge centered on human dignity. In recent decades, the UCA has attracted support from traditional, mainly middle-class families appalled by the financial and administrative chaos that has beset some state universities and by the radicalization of sections of the student body on several public campuses. Notwithstanding the opening of satellite facilities in interior cities, the residential student accommodation offered by the UCA in the city of **Buenos Aires** appeals to families living in distant provinces. UCA fees are also attractive, often rather less than those charged by elite secular private universities. To such groups, the UCA offers high-quality education at reasonable cost in what the families of students regard as a secure moral environment. This has become a key marketing strategy of the university.

With the further liberalization of regulations governing private universities, the UCA expanded considerably in the 1990s. New courses and degree programs were organized, and the university moved to new premises in the prestigious redeveloped Puerto Madero docks. Most departments were relocated there, occupying four attractively refurbished interconnecting former warehouses. The university also operates four satellite campuses, three in the interior of the country in the cities of **Mendoza, Paraná**, and **Rosario** and another in the center of the province of **Buenos Aires** at Pergamino. The UCA is now a multifaculty institution with Departments of Agronomy, Art and Music, Business, Government, Journalism and Media Studies, Law, Medicine, Philosophy and Letters, Psychology and Education, Social and Economic Sciences, and Technology and Biotechnology. Most departments offer undergraduate and postgraduate programs. There is a well-equipped library, and the UCA runs its own press.

The UCA claims many former government ministers among its illustrious alumni, as well as the current president of the republic, **Mauricio Macri**, and governor of the province of Buenos Aires, **María Eugenia Vidal**. In 2018, there were almost 20,000 students and somewhat less than 4,000 members of the faculty, making the UCA the largest private university in the country, and it was ranked 36th in Latin America by an international evaluation agency. It invariably features among the top half dozen universities in Argentina and is often rated the top private university.

UNIVERSIDAD DE BUENOS AIRES (UBA). *See* UNIVERSITY OF BUENOS AIRES (UBA).

UNIVERSIDAD DE SAN ANDRÉS (UDESA). Associated with St. Andrew's Scots School, founded by the **Buenos Aires** Scottish community as a Presbyterian college in 1838, by the early 21st century the UDESA had become one of the premier private universities in the country, ranking alongside the **Universidad Torcuato Di Tella** (UTDT).

Preliminary steps to establish the university began in the mid-1980s; it was registered in 1988 and formally recognized by the **Ministry of Education** two years later as an institution of higher **education**. From the first, the university was modeled on liberal arts research and teaching institutions in **Great Britain** and the **United States**. Today the college boasts Departments of Accounting, Economics, Humanities, Law, and Mathematics and the Exact Sciences, in additions to Schools of Education and Management. It offers around a dozen undergraduate programs and 20 single and combined postgraduate degrees, including doctorates. It currently registers around 1,000 undergraduate and 500 postgraduate students. The university has one of the highest proportions of foreign students in the country. It is often ranked among the top 15 universities in Argentina. One evaluation ranked San Andrés joint 57th in Latin America in 2018, and around the 600 mark in the world. Famous alumni include figures in the arts and **media**, politicians, and members of the world of business and finance.

UNIVERSIDAD DE SANTA FE. *See* UNIVERSIDAD DEL LITORAL

UNIVERSIDAD DE TUCUMÁN. Now the Universidad Nacional de Tucumán (UNT), it is one of the historic pre-1918 universities of Argentina, located in the city of **San Miguel de Tucumán**. It derives from a program of degree courses in law offered at the National College in the 1870s; around the middle of the decade, the Faculty of Law and Political Science was set up and continued to offer courses for around 10 years, until the student body was transferred to the **University of Córdoba**. Officially refounded in 1913, the school's first students were admitted the following year, welcomed to the university by the then president of the republic **Roque Sáenz Peña**. It remained a provincial foundation until 1921, when it became a "national" university, although the process of "nationalization" was not fully completed until 1935. The number of departments and programs increased in the 1940s and 1950s, when the institution also functioned as a regional center of higher **education**, establishing institutes and schools in neighboring provinces—the Institute of Mines and Geology was opened in the province of **Jujuy** in 1946. New departments included Agronomy, Economics, Medicine, and Natural Sciences—the university engaged in pioneering research in the field of the agronomics of sugar production, the leading local industry.

The city and the campus were scenes of political agitation during the period of the **Revolución Argentina** following the **military coup of 1966**, associated with the radicalization of student politics and crisis in the sugar industry. This was a period of worker strikes and student protest. There were three major uprisings between 1969 and 1972, which were violently suppressed, prefiguring the activities of the **Ejército Revolucionario del Pueblo** (ERP) in the province around 1975. Tucumán was the principal ERP *foco*; scores died in skirmishes between army patrols and guerrilla groups in 1975 and 1976. Since the 1980s, the university has consolidated its reputation as a major regional research center in the fields of medicine, agronomy, plant biology, and the study of the environment. It is by far the largest center of higher learning in the region with over 60,000 students in 2018 enrolled in 75 degree programs across 15 departments, institutes, and centers. The UNT is also a major employer in the region, with 4,200 academic and 2,500 support staff.

UNIVERSIDAD DEL CEMA (UCEMA). *See* CENTRO DE ESTUDIOS MACROECONÓMICOS DE ARGENTINA (CEMA/UCEMA).

UNIVERSIDAD DEL LITORAL. Now the Universidad Nacional del Litoral (UNL), it originated as the Universidad de Santa Fe (sometimes the Universidad Provincial de Santa Fe), founded by the then governor of the province of **Santa Fe** José de Gálvez in 1889. The UNL was created a year after the **University Reform Movement** of 1918, the first to be established after the reform; it absorbed the Universidad de Provincial de Santa Fe to become the first "regional" university in the country, with responsibility for higher education in the neighboring provinces of **Mesopotamia** as well as its home province. In addition to the Universidad Santa Fe, the UNL also absorbed the School of **Industry**, which had been created in 1909. The foundation faculties of the UNL were Law and Industrial and Agricultural Chemistry. In addition to the historic downtown campus built in neoclassical style (now a national historical monument), the university boasts some of the most modern buildings and best-equipped laboratories of any university in Argentina. Today, the university operates institutes and centers in the cities of **Corrientes**, **Paraná**, and **Rosario**, as well as the city of **Santa Fe**. It was one of the national pioneers of distance learning in 1999. In 2018, there were 36,000 students and 4,700 academic staff. While offering a range of programs, the focus is on agronomy, biology, chemistry, engineering, medicine, the social sciences, and veterinary science, some of which are the most highly regarded programs in the country.

UNIVERSIDAD DEL NORDESTE. Now the Universidad Nacional del Nordeste (UNNE), founded in 1956 as the second regional university in the country after the **Universidad del Litoral**. Initially, some of its programs depended on the Universidad del Litoral and **Universidad de Tucumán** for validation. The university has campuses in various cities in the provinces of **Chaco** and **Corrientes**, offering courses in the arts and humanities, social sciences, and agriculture-related scientific disciplines. It was one of few new public universities founded in the 1950s, a decade that witnessed the first wave of expansion of private universities. In 2018, there were 50,000 students and 5,000 academics, supported by just under 2,000 nonteaching staff. *See also* EDUCATION.

UNIVERSIDAD DEL SUR. First established as the Instituto Tecnológico del Sur in the city of **Bahía Blanca** in 1946, functioning under its current name, Universidad Nacional del Sur [UNS]), in the same year. In 1947, the federal government and the government of the province of **Buenos Aires** signed a convention agreeing jointly to finance the university. It was only the third national university to be established after the **University Reform Movement** of 1918—the others were the **Universidad del Litoral**, set up in 1919, and the **Universidad Nacional de Cuyo** in 1939. Initially, its degrees were validated by the **Universidad Nacional de La Plata**. The university suffered a precarious existence until 1956, when it was refounded with the right to award its own degrees. The UNS is the seventh oldest university in the country. The founding departments were Accounting, Chemistry, Economics, Engineering, Geology and Geography, Humanities, Mathematics, and Physics, reflecting its origins as a technical college. The number of departments has since expanded to include Agronomy, Biology, Business, Health, and Information Technology, but the institution remains close to its core disciplines. In 2018, the university registered about 25,000 students, with around 3,000 teaching staff and 1,800 support staff, and ranked 74th in Latin America. *See also* EDUCATION.

UNIVERSIDAD NACIONAL DE CÓRDOBA. *See* UNIVERSITY OF CÓRDOBA (UC).

UNIVERSIDAD NACIONAL DE CUYO (UNCuyo). Located in the city of **Mendoza** and founded in 1939, it is the second state university to be established following the **University Reform Movement** of 1918. It too was envisaged as a regional center of higher **education**, bringing together existing educational and cultural bodies of the provinces of Mendoza, **San Juan**, and **San Luis**, integrating and upgrading them to deliver university-level teaching and investigation. The main campus in Mendoza housed the Departments of the Agronomy, Economics, the Humanities, and Medicine; Architecture and Design, Engineering, and the Sciences were located on satellite campuses elsewhere in the region. The expansion of higher education in the 1970s saw national universities set up in the provincial capitals of San Juan and San Luis, both in 1973, thus reducing the outreach of UNCuyo. Following the breakup, and especially during the 1990s, the "reduced" UNCuyo developed a full range of disciplines on the Mendoza campus and opened new satellite campuses in the province. UNCuyo remains well regarded and is better resourced than many neighboring universities, with research strengths in the fields of agronomy, engineering, biosciences, and the social sciences. According to one evaluation, in 2018, UNCuyo ranked 70th in Latin America, when it enrolled around 44,000 students and employed about 4,000 academics. The university has strong links with regional industry.

UNIVERSIDAD NACIONAL DE LA PLATA (UNLP). Projected shortly after the **federalization of the city of Buenos Aires** and the founding of the city of **La Plata**, the university opened in 1897 as the provincial Universidad de La Plata, dedicated as much to research as teaching, becoming the UNLP in 1906. The founding departments were Mechanical Engineering, Law, Pharmacology, and Quantity Surveying. A museum of natural history and associated research center was attached to the university, as was an astronomical observatory and institute of art and design. Initially, the institution struggled, but by the centenary of **independence** in 1910, it counted about 2,000 students enrolled in five departments: Agronomy and Veterinary Sciences; Architecture, Engineering, and Hydraulics; Law and Social Science; Natural History, Physical Geography, Art, and Design—home to the Museum of Natural History—and Physics, Mathematics, and Astronomy. By this stage, the observatory was also responsible for scientific research in the fields of seismology and meteorology. Adjacent to the seat of the provincial administration, the government of **Buenos Aires** kept a close eye on the campus, particularly during the **University Reform Movement** and following the **military coup of 1930**. Relations between the university and provincial authorities were tense in the interwar decades. The socialist reformer **Alfredo Palacios,** who served briefly as principal in the early 1940s, attempted to reinvigorate the original ethos of the college—an emphasis on research and scientific knowledge. Around this time, the university became an important focus of the democratic opposition to the **Concordancia** and the right-leaning de facto regime installed by the **military coup of 1943**. This was a period of expansion and new investment in the Departments of Engineering and Medicine, as well as initiatives in radio and broadcasting and the preforming arts.

From 1953 to 1955, when the city of La Plata was renamed La Ciudad Eva Perón, the university was known as La Universidad Nacional Eva Perón. Having been Peronized at this time, the university was de-Peronized following the **military coup of 1955**—4,000 faculty were expelled. There were new academic initiatives in the 1960s and 1970s, including a substantial redevelopment of the campus and opening of new research centers, but the UNLP experienced similar budgetary problems to those of other universities and student unrest. During the years of the **Proceso de Reorganización Nacional,** around 1,000 members of the university "disappeared," one of the highest proportions in the sector. There was a dramatic decline in enrollments. Student numbers increased again with the return of democracy in 1983. The 1990s saw new departments and programs, with an emphasis on the social sciences, information technology, and the **media**. This was followed by extensive campus refurbishment after the turn of the century: administrative offices were remodeled; new laboratories and teaching facilities were opened. Two additional departments followed—Social Work in 2005 and Psychology in 2006.

Composed of 17 departments offering more than 140 programs, the UNLP is now home to over 120,000 students and 13,000 teaching staff. The university is a renowned international center for paleontological and anthropological research and famous for applied work in the social sciences. Various rankings for 2017 and 2018 place the UNLP in second place nationally (after the **University of Buenos Aires** [UBA]), 27th in Latin America, and around joint 500th in the world. *See also* DESAPARECIDOS; EDUCATION.

UNIVERSIDAD TORCUATO DI TELLA (UTDT). The university derived from the **Instituto Torcuato Di Tella**, founded in 1958, largely as a cultural and exhibition center. When the institute ceased functioning as an arts venue around 1970, it was reconstituted as a social science research institute, initially financed with the residual bequests of the culture-cum-arts body and relocated from the center of the city to the suburb of Belgrano. The institute soon established an international reputation, one of its principal assets being the library. By the 1980s, the library held the most extensive collection of contemporary social sciences journals published overseas in Latin America. There was also a substantial holding of cutting-edge social science secondary material and a large holding of official material. Arguably, the institute library was the best on the continent devoted to the social sciences broadly defined. Instituto directors and faculty included some of the most distinguished Argentine academics in their respective fields, for example, Natalio Botana, Héctor Diéguez, Roberto Cortés Conde, **Guillermo O'Donnell**, Francis Korn, Ezequiel Gallo, Tulio Halperín Donghi, Rolf Mantel, and Juan Carlos Torre.

The university was set up in 1991 as changes in regulations relating to higher education facilitated the creation of fully private degree-awarding bodies. The UTDT inherited most of the assets of the institute and was similarly directed by prestigious local figures. A young, energetic Gerardo della Paolera was the first head (rector) of the university. He was responsible for an ambitious campaign of expansion involving such academic initiatives as the creation of new faculties and degree programs and the growth and relocation of the campus. The UTDT was the first private institution in Argentina to offer academic salaries that were internationally comparable, emphasizing the importance of research as well as teaching, and sought to recruit a high proportion of faculty with doctorates, many of whom had studied abroad. During Della Paolera's rectorship, innovative courses in journalism were created and the full-time faculty expanded, notably in the disciplines of economics, political science, and history. Student numbers increased and exchange agreements signed with foreign institutions. The university now boasts over 50 such exchange agreements, including with La Trobe in Australia, Dalhousie and Toronto in Canada, Humboldt in Germany, St. Gallen in Switzerland, and Emory, Georgetown, Harvard, and UCLA in the **United States**. Around the turn of the century, there were funding problems, disputes with the family, and difficulties with the government: amalgamation with other institutions of higher education was mooted. The UTDT weathered these storms. Della Paolera resigned in 2001 and was succeeded first by the economist Juan Pablo Nicolini and subsequently by the internationally renowned sociologist and political analyst **Manuel Mora y Araujo**, who was followed by the economist Ernesto Schargrodsky, the current rector. The university now houses the Business School, Law School, School of Government, and School of Architecture and Urban Studies, as well as Departments of Art, History, International Studies, and Mathematics and Statistics. It is one of the most significant centers of higher education in the country and the continent and continues to be supported financially by local and world foundations. Currently, it offers nine undergraduate programs and 24 postgraduate degrees. Since the 1970s, many senior academics associated with the institute and the university, including the Di Tella brothers, held official positions in government as advisors and ministers.

In recent years, the size of the student body has fluctuated between 4,000 and 2,500, with between a third and a half enrolled in postgraduate programs; approximately 30 percent of students receive some financial support from the university. There are around 150 regular academic staff and twice that number of part-time teachers. In 2018, according to one source, the UTDT was ranked 21st in Latin America. *See also* DI TELLA, GUIDO JOSÉ MARIO (1931–2001); DI TELLA, TORCUATO (1882–1948); DI TELLA, TORCUATO SALVADOR FRANCISCO NICOLÁS (1929–2016); EDUCATION.

UNIVERSITIES. *See* CENTRO DE ESTUDIOS MACROECONÓMICOS DE ARGENTINA (CEMA/UCEMA); EDUCATION; UNIVERSIDAD ARGENTINA DE LA EMPRESA (UADE); UNIVERSIDAD CATÓLICA ARGENTINA (UCA); UNIVERSIDAD DE SAN ANDRÉS (UDESA); UNIVERSIDAD DE TUCUMÁN; UNIVERSIDAD DEL LITORAL; UNIVERSIDAD DEL NORDESTE; UNIVERSIDAD DEL SUR; UNIVERSIDAD NACIONAL DE CUYO (UNCuyo); UNIVERSIDAD NACIONAL DE LA PLATA (UNLP); UNIVERSIDAD TORCUATO DI TELLA (UTDT); UNIVERSITY OF BUENOS AIRES (UBA); UNIVERSITY OF CÓRDOBA (UC).

UNIVERSITY OF BUENOS AIRES (UBA). The largest university in the country, and since the mid-19th century the most prestigious. Inaugurated in 1821 by **Bernardino Rivadavia**, endowed with resources generated by the secularization of property formerly belonging to the **Catholic Church**, it was only the second center of higher **education** to be established in the country. The university became a national institution in 1886, but the designation did not change to Universidad Nacional de Buenos Aires; the original name was retained.

The founding departments were General/Preparatory Studies, Humanities, Law, Science, Medicine, and Theology. In the 1860s, the Departments of Mathematics and Natural History were opened; in 1886, the Department of Social Sciences was inaugurated and the range of teaching in the humanities and the sciences expanded. With the **federalization of the city of Buenos Aires** in 1880, responsibility for the administration of the university passed to the federal government. Administrative changes followed, and around the turn of the century efforts made to professionalize teaching and research. The Faculty of Philosophy and Letters was professionalized in 1896; modern methods were applied to the teaching of classical languages, ethnography, geography, history, and sociology as well as philosophy. Similar changes followed in such areas as agronomy and veterinary science—the faculty was set up in 1909—and in economic sciences—the faculty was founded in 1913—as well as in establishing the Faculties of Law and Medicine. With the **University Reform Movement** of 1918, further efforts were made to professionalize teaching and ensure that syllabus content was tailored to vocational requirements. By the interwar decades, the UBA was recognized as a renowned international center of higher education.

The UBA struggled unsuccessfully to maintain its autonomy during the first administration of President **Juan Domingo Perón**. Several internationally respected figures in the fields of history, medicine, and science left the university. There was a large turnover in the professoriate, and the size of the student body grew exponentially—in 1955, the student body reached 72,000, placing a massive strain on the budget and infrastructure. Administrative changes saw the formation of the new Faculty of Dentistry and the Faculty of Architecture and a separate Faculty of Engineering. Despite the restructuring and financial pressures of the period, the UBA retained an enviable reputation in such fields as medicine, law, and the social sciences. A measure of autonomy was reestablished in 1955; the period between 1955 and 1958 saw a degree of normality restored with the reintegration of students and faculty who had left. The Faculty of Pharmacy and Biochemistry was created in 1957 and teaching programs revised in the Faculty of Economics and Faculty of Philosophy and Letters, and curricula subsequently updated in the Faculty of Medicine and Faculty of Exact Sciences. Funding rarely kept pace with these developments. There was growing student unrest; life and teaching at the UBA became increasingly politicized. The regime installed by the **military coup of 1966** regarded the universities in general, and the UBA in particular, as a hotbed of radical, "antinational" subversive left-wing thinking that threatened traditional values—and acted to "restore order." Further politicization of UBA campuses took place between 1973 and 1976. With the ending of formal examinations, student enrollment mushroomed: in 1974, UBA admitted 40,000 new students. Teaching standards fell; many academics failed to turn up for classes, and faculties closed for months on end. Conflict among radical groups on campus became part of the routine of university life. Students and faculty alike numbered among those assassinated by the **Triple A**.

The 10 years between the 1966 *golpe* and the **military coup of 1976** saw a steady deterioration in the physical fabric of the university and decline in the quality of teaching and research. The **military** intervenor appointed in 1976 stated that his principal task was to restore order to the UBA by "excising ideological factors." By 1977, new student enrollment had fallen by almost 60 percent. There was a hemorrhage of academics—the fortunate obtaining posts abroad. A degree of normality returned with democracy in 1983, a year that witnessed the introduction of entry examinations. New student enrollments, which had fallen to 13,000 in 1982, rose to almost 47,000 by 1987. In 1992, 170,000 students graduated. New programs were opened, and new faculties created: the Faculty of Psychology was set up in 1985 and the Faculty of Social Sciences in 1988, distinct from Economic Sciences. Once again, budgets did not keep pace with the expansion of student numbers and proliferation of programs. Salaries were squeezed, and strikes by faculty and support staff became a frequent occurrence. There was a degree of financial stability in the early 1990s, accompanied by another disruptive round of administrative change that had an impact on the UBA as on other public universities. The university was critical of government efforts to promote the formation of private universities, though more successful than most other state institutions in attracting external funding.

Around 311,000 students are currently registered at the university, making it by far the largest in the country by enrollment, and the second largest in Latin America. The dropout rate is high, with only around a third of students completing courses, or completing within time—unsurprising given that the vast majority of students study part time. There are slightly less than 30,000 academic staff, around a fifth of whom hold full-time or permanent appointments; about a third of the full-time professoriate has a PhD. In effect, the UBA is a federation of distinct faculties, a process initiated in 1874. There are now 13 faculties that function as autonomous entities. In addition, the university operates six hospitals and 10 museums; four well-regarded secondary school are connected to it.

UBA has produced five Nobel laureates—two awards each for peace and medicine, and one for chemistry—the only university to do so in Latin America; 15 former presidents of the republic graduated from the university. The QS 2018 international ranking places the UBA 75th in the world, the first university in Latin America to be included in the top 100, and ninth in Latin America; it is the top university in the country. *See also* ECONOMIC CRISES; SAAVEDRA LAMAS, CARLOS (1878–1959).

UNIVERSITY OF CÓRDOBA (UC). Founded in 1613, the oldest university in the country and one of the most prestigious, and the sixth oldest university in the Americas—already functioning 23 years before Harvard University was formed in the **United States**. Officially the Universidad Nacional de Córdoba (UNC), it is still generally referred to as the Universidad Córdoba, while being colloquially known as "Córdoba la Docta"—Córdoba, the Wise University.

The institution originates from a Jesuit seminary that first admitted students in 1610, the Collegium Maximum. Granted the status of a center of higher learning three years later, it had degree-awarding powers granted by a papal ordinance in 1621 and confirmed by a royal charter a year later. The institution remained largely focused on theology and philosophy until 1767, when the Jesuits were expelled from the Spanish Empire. Passing to the Franciscans, the curriculum was broadened: mathematics and physics were added, and a department of law and the social sciences established in 1791. By 1800, the university was known as the Royal University of San Carlos and Our Lady of Monserrat; eight years later, it was redesignated as a Royal and Pontifical University, by which time 7,000 students were graduating each year. With **independence**, the province of **Córdoba** assumed control of the institution in 1820; the university was federalized in 1854. Departments of Medicine and the Exact Sciences had been established by this time. New departments were added around 1879 and 1880, including a broader range of the humanities and the exact and natural sciences. New disciplines and new teaching methods were particularly associated with the administration of the educationalist President **Domingo Faustino Sarmiento**, who promoted the recruitment of staff from abroad. **Women** were first admitted in 1884 and now constitute half the student body. In 1886, the university was formally incorporated as the UNC. By the beginning of the 20th century, the university had become the principal center of research in the country, notably in the fields of medicine, science, technology, and engineering. Since the 1930s, the university has developed a reputation for excellence in the fields of agronomy, astronomy, chemistry, engineering, law, mathematics, medicine, and physics, areas of teaching and research that have been maintained and strengthened. Over the last 100 years or so, 36 percent of UNC students have graduated in the field of health and medicine (the largest proportion in the country), 31 percent in the social sciences, 22 percent in the applied and exact sciences (again the highest proportion nationally), and 11 percent in the humanities.

As well as being the oldest and most prestigious center of higher **education** in the country—since the 19th century second only to the **University of Buenos Aires** (UBA)—the university has frequently figured prominently in national life, most notably the **University Reform Movement** of 1918, which began on the UNC campus, and the **Cordobazo** of 1969. On a par with the Paris Spring of 1968, though considerably more violent and destructive of life and property, the student-and-worker uprising was instrumental in ending the regime of de facto president General **Juan Carlos Onganía** and effecting a return to the barracks by the **military** in 1972. The Cordobazo impacted the minds of leaders of the **military coup of 1976**, which explains the treatment of the university during the **Proceso de Reorganización Nacional**, as was recognized when autonomy was restored to the university in 1983.

In 2017, some 132,000 students were enrolled at the university, making the UNC the second largest in the country after UBA; academic staff totaled around 9,000, of which one-third was full time. There are 13 faculties offering more than 300 undergraduate and postgraduate programs. In 2017 and 2018 surveys, the university was ranked second or third nationally, joint 26th in Latin America, and joint 801st in the world. *See also* CÓRDOBA (CITY).

UNIVERSITY REFORM MOVEMENT. The University Reform Movement started at the **University of Córdoba** (UC) in 1918, beginning with student protests against the curriculum and university governance. The movement resulted in a greater role for students and academics in the governing bodies of universities and a large measure of university autonomy.

The main demands, articulated by striking students, were greater autonomy for the universities (freedom from government control and recognition of the principle of academic freedom); the representation of students, faculty, and alumni on university governing bodies (the principle of cogovernance); curriculum modernization (to include the teaching of a broader range of scientific and technical disciplines and the new social sciences, with courses drawing on modern teaching material); the selection of academic staff by means of open, competitive examination; free tuition; and an automatic right of admission to all suitably qualified school-leavers. From Córdoba, the reform movement spread rapidly to other campuses and resulted in the formation of the Argentine University Federation (Federación Universitaria Argentina) to oversee and implement the reform program across the country. Due to the reforms and the maturing of the changes introduced after 1918, by the 1930s Argentine universities were considered to be among the best in Latin

America, and premier institutions ranked with their peers in the **United States** and Europe. The movement, which democratized access to higher **education** in Argentina, had an impact across Latin America.

Despite gains made in the decades immediately following 1918, university autonomy was eroded in the 1940s and 1960s and university governance often became chaotic—and static—in the turbulent 1960s and 1970s. Problems of underfunding further undermined the principles of the reforms in the state sector, resulting in an expansion of private education during and after the 1990s. *See also* CENTRO DE ESTUDIOS MACROECONÓMICOS DE ARGENTINA (CEMA/UCEMA); UNIVERSIDAD ARGENTINA DE LA EMPRESA (UADE); UNIVERSIDAD CATÓLICA ARGENTINA (UCA); UNIVERSIDAD DE SAN ANDRÉS (UDESA); UNIVERSIDAD DEL NORDESTE; UNIVERSIDAD DEL SUR; UNIVERSIDAD NACIONAL DE CUYO (UNCuyo); UNIVERSIDAD NACIONAL DE LA PLATA (UNLP); UNIVERSIDAD TORCUATO DI TELLA (UTDT); UNIVERSITY OF BUENOS AIRES (UBA); UNIVERSITY OF CÓRDOBA (UC).

URIBURU, JOSÉ EVARISTO (1831–1914). Diplomat, statesman, lawyer, and international jurist from an aristocratic **Salta** family; he held various ministerial posts in Salta and **Buenos Aires**, representing his home province in the first national **Congress** elected after the reunification of the country in 1864. Following the **War of the Pacific**, he served on the commission to administer the truce between **Chile** and **Bolivia**, and later on the arbitration panel appointed to settle border disputes between Argentina and Chile. He became president of the nation in 1895 on the resignation of constitutionally elected president **Luis Sáenz Peña**, whose term he completed in 1898. His administration is credited with enhancing the authority of the federal government and the professionalization of the army and navy; during his term, considerable sums were spent on national defense. He brought a return to order demanded by critics of Sáenz Peña. *See also* PATAGONIA.

URIBURU, JOSÉ FÉLIX (1864–1932). Provisional president of Argentina (1930–1932). A scion of an oligarchic family of **Salta** province, he rose quickly in the **military** and ultimately attained the rank of general. By the middle of 1930, the army had two factions determined to oust President **Hipólito Yrigoyen**. One was headed by Uriburu, which took its inspiration from Mussolini; the other was led by General **Agustin P. Justo**, a former minister of war who was determined to build an *antiyrigoyenista* coalition in order to get himself elected president. Although working at cross-purposes, both camps cooperated in their common goal of toppling the government. Uriburu fronted the coup that struck on 6 September 1930 and immediately embarked on a fascist project. He aimed to close down **political parties**, replace **Congress** with an Italian-style Chamber of Corporations, and clamp down on opposition. In terms of economic policy, his government also took a number of measures in an ineffective attempt to deal with the worsening crisis. It introduced exchange controls to stem the outflow of gold and facilitate payments of Argentine hard-**currency** debt, and also import duties. But the most important and permanent measure was the overhaul of taxation policy. In January 1932, a progressive income tax was enacted in a piece of legislation that is renewed annually by Congress to this day.

Faced with rising unpopularity and increasing opposition to his political project, Uriburu called for elections in November 1931 under pressure from Justo, who had not participated in the provisional government and had been biding his time. Already gravely ill, he handed the reins of power over to his successor in February 1932. *See also* MILITARY COUP OF 1930; PRESIDENTIAL ELECTION OF 1931.

URQUIZA, JUSTO JOSÉ DE (1801–1870). Businessman, general, politician, and key figure in regional and national politics during the period of **national organization**. **Caudillo** of **Entre Ríos**, of which he was sometime governor, running the province as if it was his personal estate, he served as president of the **Argentine Confederation** from 1854 to 1860, having been "provisional director" (a.k.a. provisional head of state) since 1852.

Born in Entre Ríos, Urquiza was educated in **Buenos Aires**. Returning to the family business—which traded hides—around 1820, he was soon caught up in the turbulent politics of **Mesopotamia**. Opposed to the **Unitarian** project of national development, like other members of the provincial elite, he rejected the 1826 proposal for the creation of a centralized state. A supporter of **Federalism**, by the 1830s he was in contact with Estanislao López, caudillo of **Santa Fe**. In 1836, he met **Juan Manuel de Rosas**; the two men established a close rapport and became staunch mutual supporters. Over the next decade or so, Urquiza served as Rosas's **military** commander, heading Federalist campaigns in the interior and **Uruguay**. By the 1840s, relations between Rosas and Urquiza began to cool: Rosas viewed Urquiza's growing independence as a threat; representing *entrerriano* interests, Urquiza resented the stranglehold maintained by Buenos Aires on overseas trade, which was constraining the growth of the pastoral industry in Mesopotamia, particularly the export of hides, **sheep**, and **wool**. In 1851, Urquiza announced that the province was resuming the right to conduct an independent foreign and commercial policy. Support from other provinces was initially muted, but Urquiza signed an alliance with **Brazil** and Uruguay. Commanding his own troops, Urquiza used Brazilian gold to fund the Great Liberating Army (Ejército Grande Libertador), crossed the **Paraná**, and defeated Rosas's forces at Caseros in February 1852. Rosas resigned, leaving the organization of a new national settlement to Urquiza. He called a meeting at **San Nicolás**, which resulted in the Accord of San Nicolás, signed by most provincial governors and according to Urquiza the title of provisional director. Following the drafting of the **Constitution of 1853** at the Congress of Santa Fe, Urquiza was nominated constitutional president for six years. The province of Buenos Aires refused to adopt the constitution and withdrew from the Confederation.

Urquiza's presidency is remembered for several diplomatic achievements: **Spain** recognized Argentine independence; the Confederation recognized the independence of **Paraguay**; a treaty of free navigation was signed with Brazil. Although toward the end of his life Urquiza actively supported progressives like **Domingo Faustino Sarmiento**, he was regarded by contemporary and subsequent critics as little more than a traditional caudillo—in battle he was implacable, and unforgiving in victory. Yet Urquiza sponsored economic and social modernization, as is now accepted. **Immigration** and **agricultural colonization** were encouraged, and railways and river steam navigation promoted. **Education**, the arts, and sciences were granted official support, and a relatively free press emerged. **Agriculture** diversified and productivity was facilitated, and an embryonic manufacturing sector assisted. Perhaps these activities chimed with Urquiza's business background as an *estanciero*, merchant, and company promoter: as national president and provincial governor, he kept an entrepreneurial eye on his estates and companies—his ventures were commercially profitable. Urquiza was less successful in dealing with Buenos Aires.

As the end of his term of office approached, conflict between Buenos Aires and the Confederation loomed and Urquiza fought an indecisive campaign against **Bartolomé Mitre**. Urquiza recognized that the province of Buenos Aires was unlikely to rejoin the Confederation unless the city became the national capital. He handed over the presidency to **Santiago Derqui**, resumed the governorship of Entre Ríos, and retired to his estate, where he and his sons were assassinated by associates of Ricardo López Jordán, a rival claimant to the governorship. *See also* CATTLE; COMMODITIES; FOREIGN TRADE; MEAT; YERBA MATE.

URUGUAY. Neighboring republic, part of the former **Viceroyalty of the River Plate**, when it was known as the Banda Oriental, the East Bank (of the River Plate). The official title of the country is the Oriental Republic of Uruguay; in Spanish, La República Oriental del Uruguay. The terms *Uruguayan* and *Oriental* are used to denote citizens of the republic.

The east bank of the river had been contested by **Spain** and Portugal and subsequently Argentina and **Brazil**. Between 1816 and 1828, Uruguay was incorporated into the Portuguese Kingdom of Brazil, and later the independent Empire of Brazil, as the Cisplatine Province, notwithstanding Buenos Aires's claims to suzerainty. Uruguayan independence was secured in 1828 with British and French support as a buffer state between Argentina and

Brazil. Not that this ended foreign interference in the country. During near continuous civil wars from the 1830s to the 1860s, factions were supported by either Brazil or Argentina, or would call on support from Buenos Aires or Rio de Janeiro. Frontier violations were frequent: defeated Uruguayan forces would seek sanctuary across the frontier, or foreign forces intervened on the pretext of safeguarding often ill-defined frontiers, as was the case in the mid-1860s, when Brazilian intervention served as the immediate cause of the **War of the Triple Alliance**. Argentine **caudillo Juan Manuel de Rosas** maintained guerilla groups in the interior of Uruguay from the time of **independence** until shortly before his overthrow in 1852.

For much of the period between the early 20th century and the 1960s, Uruguay enjoyed peace and prosperity. Montevideo became the place of exile of choice of many Argentine political figures, and Montevidean banks the recipients of Argentine capital flight during the repeated **economic crises** suffered by the country since the 1930s, a feature that continues today. Indeed, Montevideo pretends to the status of a regional financial center, to which monetary authorities in Buenos Aries respond that it is merely assisting Argentines to avoid exchange and capital controls. A further cause of friction during the presidencies of **Néstor Kirchner** and **Cristina Fernández de Kirchner** was the siting of Scandinavian-financed pulp mills at Fray Bentos on the Uruguayan side of the **Uruguay** River. It was claimed that the mills would pollute the river, though the Argentine authorities had been attempting to attract overseas investment for a similar project in **Mesopotamia**. Argentina first protested against the granting of construction permits, then the building and operation of the plant. When protestors on the **Entre Ríos** side of the river blockaded the international crossing, the Kirchners were accused of tolerating the disruption. Repeated attempts by Uruguay to end the bridge blockades diplomatically and through arbitration have not ended the controversy, although the International Court in The Hague ruled in its favor in 2010. *See also* FOREIGN DEBT/FOREIGN INVESTMENT.

URUGUAY (RIVER). The river, from which the country now takes its name, rises in southern **Brazil**. It forms the border between **Mesopotamia** and Brazil and **Uruguay**. Although only suitable for navigation by oceangoing vessels in its lower reaches, the river was given international status by agreement between Argentina and Uruguay in 1975, with the two countries agreeing to collaborate on the use of the system, a treaty that was formally lodged with the **United Nations** some years later. The existence of this treaty served as a pretext for Argentine objections to the construction of pulp mills in Uruguay at the beginning of the 21st century.

USHUAIA. The southernmost city in the world, it is the capital of the province of **Tierra del Fuego, Antártida e Islas del Atlántico Sur**. Located on the shore of the Beagle Channel on the southern coast of the Isla Grande de Tierra del Fuego, its origins lie in the idea of **Julio A. Roca** to strengthen Argentine sovereignty in the area through the establishment of a penal colony.

Only after the conclusion of the Boundary Treaty of 1881 between Argentina and **Chile** did formal efforts start to establish the township and prison. Ushuaia was founded in 1884, and then recognized as the capital of the Territorio Nacional de Tierra del Fuego in 1904. Two years later, the first inmates—serious criminals and reoffenders—arrived. Life in Ushuaia centered around the prison during the first half of the 20th century, until in 1947 **Juan Domingo Perón** ordered its closure by executive decree due to reports of abuse and unsafe practices. The prisoners were relocated to jails farther north, but most of the guards remained in the city.

The current population of Ushuaia is 60,000. Electronic goods are produced in the city, owing to tax incentives and government subsidies; the other main economic activities are fishing and those associated with oil and natural gas extraction. *See also* BEAGLE CHANNEL DISPUTE.

V

VANDOR, AUGUSTO TIMOTEO (1923–1969). Peronist labor leader and politician, known as "The Wolf" (*el lobo*). Born in the province of **Entre Ríos**, he enlisted in the Argentine navy from 1940 to 1950. Vandor then joined the workforce of the new Philips factory in **Buenos Aires** and became the shop steward of the local Unión Obrera Metalúrgica (UOM) branch. He became prominent in the metalworkers' union after successfully leading a strike for better pay in 1954.

Vandor was introduced to exiled former president **Juan Domingo Perón** in 1958, and three years later elected secretary general of the UOM. Since the latter was the largest of the 62 **trade unions** in the all-encompassing **Confederación General del Trabajo** (CGT), he came to represent labor in the troika of Perón's official delegates in Argentina. As the leading CGT strategist, he helped plan Perón's failed attempt to return to Argentina in 1964. In its aftermath, Vandor became increasingly critical of Perón and his influence. Convinced that the aging leader might never return to the country, he harbored political ambitions of his own—**"Peronism without Perón."**

Having clashed increasingly with CGT Secretary General **José Alonso**, Vandor ousted the latter from his post in February 1966. Nevertheless, following the coup that brought General **Juan Carlos Onganía** to power, Vandor and Alonso found common cause in both their support for "participationism" (i.e., negotiations with the regime) and in their opposition to the more confrontational **Raimundo Ongaro**, head of the Federación de Gráficos Bonaerenses. Matters came to a head in March 1968, when both Vandor and Ongaro sought the post of CGT secretary general. Perón, in part weary of Vandor's ambitions, backed Ongaro. The latter won, and the elections were swiftly annulled by the Onganía government, leading to a schism within the CGT. Vandor was assassinated by left-wing Peronist gunmen in June 1969, but not before he had been reconciled with Perón. *See also* CONFEDERACIÓN GENERAL DEL TRABAJO DE LOS ARGENTINOS (CGTA); MILITARY COUP OF 1966; RUCCI, JOSÉ IGNACIO (1924–1973).

VAQUERÍAS. Precursor of the modern **cattle** industry. Cattle roundups licensed by the Crown, organized as **military** expeditions, were an important source of revenue and trade. Groups of cowboys (*vaqueros*) would cross the **pampas**, often entering Indian territory, to cull cattle and horses that had escaped and multiplied massively on open grasslands. The principal **commodities** were grease, tallow, and hides and some dried meat. Distinctly low-tech when compared to later manifestations of the **industry**, associated with salting plants (*saladeros*) and meatpacking (*frigoríficos*), cowboys would erect temporary corrals to contain animals, then slaughter, skin, and render fat in open cauldrons. Products would be transported to **Buenos Aires** in large, two-wheeled bullock carts, the principal means of moving goods in the countryside. At the conclusion of each roundup, the "plant" would be abandoned, though possibly reused the following season. In later generations, some holders of licenses went on to found major landowning families. Later **gaucho** culture was forged by the *vaquerías*, symbolizing a free life on the plains and living off the land.

VÉLEZ SARSFIELD, DALMACIO (1800–1875). Respected jurist, statesman, and politician; author of the first civil code and constitution of the province of **Buenos Aires**. Born in the province of **Córdoba**, a modernizing **Unitarian** politician, Vélez Sarsfield was an influential thinker and constitutionalist. A prominent advocate of the centralist project for the new nation associated with **Bernardino Rivadavia**, he remained in Argentina for much of the period when Buenos Aires **caudillo Juan Manuel de Rosas** controlled the country—and survived. Indeed, he was consulted by Rosas on several occasions about constitutional matters. Although he held various national and provincial positions, he is most remembered for drawing up the 1869 civil code, which was adopted by the national **Congress** unmodified and remained in force until 2015, and for crafting the Constitution of the State of Buenos Aires when it separated from the **Argentine Confederation** between 1852 and 1861. He collaborated closely with **Bartolomé Mitre** and **Domingo Faustino Sarmiento**.

VENDEPATRIA(S). Those who sell out their country, especially in terms of its economic interests; more broadly, those who do not consider the national interest, loosely meaning "traitor." The word was coined in the 1930s, associated with the writing of nationalists such as Arturo Jauretche and **Raúl Scalabrini Ortiz**, who attempted to shown how sections of the rural and commercial oligarchies had collaborated with foreign interests to secure their own position at the expense of those of the country at large from the time of **independence**. At the time, the label was applied to the relationship with **Great Britain**, notably the **Roca–Runciman Pact** and sweetheart deals with

British-owned railways and utility companies. The term was more widely used during the 1940s, especially during the first presidency of **Juan Domingo Perón**, when the regime argued that it was recovering economic independence and sovereignty. Perón published a book titled *Los vendepatria: las pruebas de una traición*, a treatise in defense of his first two presidencies, demonstrating how financial and commercial groups had sold the country short in collusion with external interests. Later, the concept was used to describe the relationship with the **United States**, especially deals with oil companies and transnational corporations made by civilian and **military** administrations, and applied to any who opposed the industrial development of the country. Although less widely used subsequently, it resurfaced during the presidency of **Carlos Saúl Menem**, resurrected by campaigners against the massive **privatization** of **state-owned enterprises**. To the chagrin of the Kirchners, especially President **Cristina Fernández de Kirchner**, given the association of the term with the Peronist critique of export-led growth and economic liberalism, the label was also applied by opponents to her dealings with corporate groups at home and abroad.

VENEZUELA. Located at the opposite ends of the continent, and with few common interests, close engagement between the two countries is largely a 21st-century phenomenon. As every Argentine schoolkid knows, the liberators Simón Bolívar and **José de San Martín** met in Guayaquil (present-day Ecuador) to determine the fate of postcolonial South America. Quite distinct accounts of the course and consequences of that meeting appear in Venezuelan and Argentine school textbooks, pointing to difference between the men, the projects for national development, and how the two republics viewed their place in the world in the 19th century. An incident at the beginning of the 20th century briefly focused the attention of each country on the other, namely the bombardment and blockade of the Venezuelan coast during the Venezuela Crisis of 1902–1903 by an Anglo-German fleet, supported by units of the Italian navy. Intended to force Venezuela to honor its external obligations—payments due on the foreign debt and settlement of claims by foreign businesses and investors arising from damage to property during the recent civil war—the action caused an outcry in Argentina. In the diplomatic negotiations that followed, the **United States** and Argentina supported Venezuela. US action was partly driven by an elaboration of the Monroe Doctrine, that European powers should not intervene in the Americas, though the United States might use its good offices to seek redress for European interests in dispute with Latin American governments—ideas that evolved as the Roosevelt Corollary to the Monroe Doctrine. Argentine minister of foreign relations Luis María Drago viewed this as an affront to the sovereignty of Latin American states and addressed a note to the US State Department arguing that no foreign power, including the United States, had the right to use force to settle debts, basing his arguments on ideas of national sovereignty and international relations set out by the jurist **Carlos Calvo**. The Drago Doctrine, as it became known, was rejected by the United States but was well-received elsewhere in Latin America, as had the earlier elaboration of the Calvo Doctrine.

The events of 1902 brought Venezuela to the attention of Argentines and stimulated anew Argentine national sentiments about the global importance of Argentina. There matters rested until the "Pink Tide" of the 21st century as center-left and left-wing governments were elected across the continent in response to **economic crises** and intellectual challenges to the then hegemonic neoliberal Washington Consensus model. The election of President **Néstor Kirchner** in 2003 brought Venezuela and Argentina closer together on the world stage and at international fora like the **United Nations**. Proximity to the United States, which had marked the presidencies of **Carlos Saúl Menem**, was replaced by a close association with Venezuela, particularly in regional affairs. Both Néstor and his wife and successor, President **Cristina Fernández de Kirchner**, frequently made common cause with President Húgo Chávez of Venezuela and his successor, Nicolás Maduro. At a time when Argentina was excluded from international capital markets following the 2002 default, seeking to negotiate with international financial institutions and experiencing an energy crisis, good relations with Venezuela promised access to oil and desperately needed foreign **currency**. It was to prove a convenient and lucrative, but dangerous, friendship for the Kirchners, and an expensive one for the country.

Soon after the election of Néstor, the Venezuelan authorities began to buy Argentine bonds: within five years, US$6,000,000 in bonds had been acquired, yielding precious resources that were used to pay down Argentine debts owed to the International Monetary Fund. There were energy deals, and Venezuela awarded contracts to Argentine state firms, promising jobs and support for national **industry** at a difficult time. But most financial transactions were at market rates, and according to several sources, interest rates were high. They were a good deal for Venezuela, not necessarily Argentina. In addition, individuals close to the Venezuela government were accused of illicitly funding the campaigns of Cristina Fernández in the **presidential election of 2007** and the **presidential election of 2011**. The price paid by the Kirchners was an approximation with the international position of Venezuela—closer ties with **Cuba** and support for Chávez's continental projects, namely the **Unión de Naciones Sudamericanas** (UNASUR), founded in 2008. The UNASUR was designed as an alternative to the US sponsored Free Trade Agreement of the Americas. Membership in UNASUR was also viewed in some quarters as compromising the objective of **MERCOSUR**, of which Argentina was a founding member. And there were other costs. Venezuela prevailed upon Argentina to share nuclear technology with Iran and agree to a joint Iranian–Argentine investigation of the bombing of the Jewish cultural center in Buenos Aires, an atrocity that most international observers believe had been perpetrated (or organized) by Iran. Special Investigator **Alberto Nisman** was investigating both the atrocity and the arrangements with Iran when he died in mysterious circumstances in 2015—his death has been blamed on agents of the state.

The balance between the costs and benefits of the Venezuela connection shifted over time. When international oil prices were high, Chávez was a useful friend to the Kirchners; when oil prices slumped, Venezuela was less able to support the Kirchner project. The continued association with Chávez's successor, President Nicolás Maduro, was an additional complication for Cristina Fernández. As the Venezuelan economy nose-dived, the shared economic policy rhetoric of governments in Caracas and Buenos Aires appeared to hint that the Argentine **economy** might go the same way, unlikely though this was in reality. Argentina–Venezuela relations have been correct rather than cordial since the election of President **Mauricio Macri** in 2015. Mrs. Kirchner has also begun to backtrack: continuing to express admiration for the charisma and social commitment of Chávez in 2017, she has questioned the wisdom of Maduro's actions while accepting that he faces a difficult position at home and abroad. *See also* ASOCIACIÓN MUTUAL ISRAELITA ARGENTINA (AMIA).

VICEROYALTY OF THE RIVER PLATE. In Spanish, the Virreinato del Río de la Plata. It was established in 1776 as part of a series of administrative reforms essayed in late-colonial Spanish America to improve the efficiency of royal governance and imperial defense. Up to this point, present-day Argentina had formed part of the Viceroyalty of **Peru**, one of the largest jurisdictions in the Spanish world administered from Lima. In addition to Argentina, modern **Bolivia**, **Paraguay**, **Uruguay**, and **Cuyo**, part of colonial **Chile**, were detached from the responsibility of Lima and transferred to **Buenos Aires**, which was named capital of the new viceroyalty. As a result of the changes, the new viceroyalty was legally permitted to trade directly with **Spain** and to participate in a system of "imperial free trade" that was gradually rolled out across Spanish America. Previously, the only authorized route for international trade between the River Plate and Spain had been via Lima, the west coast of South America, the Isthmus of Panama, and the Caribbean. A growth of smuggling in the 18th century had rendered this arrangement increasingly unworkable. Contraband trade reduced imperial revenue and undermined royal authority. The participation of British and French merchants in the illicit transatlantic trade with the River Plate was also seen from Madrid as likely to encourage the intervention of European powers like **Great Britain** and France in southeastern Spanish America, a fear realized with the **British invasions** of 1806 and 1807. The Portuguese presence in

Brazil, sometimes regarded as a British proxy, coupled with the ambition of Lisbon to expand its influence over the east bank for the River Plate, was also a cause for concern.

The formation of the new viceroyalty strengthened Spanish control and improved fiscal capacity. The changes also stimulated the urban and economic growth of Buenos Aires as the size of the administration grew and trade expanded. Unintended consequences were a disruption of established commercial and political relations in southern South America, a disturbance of the conventions of rule—the intricate balance of interests between royal officials and local elites—and the promotion of creole patriotic sentiment. The **May Revolution of 1810** is taken as marking the end of the viceroyalty and of Spanish rule in the region—Buenos Aires was the only part of Spanish Latin America not to be reconquered before gaining **independence**. *See also* CISNEROS, BALTASAR HIDALGO DE (1756–1829); FOREIGN TRADE; LINIERS, SANTIAGO ANTONIO MARÍA DE (1753–1810).

VIDAL, MARÍA EUGENIA (1973–). Rising star of the governing **Cambiemos** coalition; bright, personable, young, and articulate, she is representative of a coming generation of "new" politicians seeking to break the mold; elected governor of the province of **Buenos Aires** in 2015. A member of the **Propuesta Republicana** (PRO) party and educated at the **Universidad Católica Argentina** (UCA), where she read political science and international relations. After graduating she worked in social policy think tanks and acted as advisor to several government agencies and ministries as a specialist in social affairs and foreign relations. While at a think tank, she was talent spotted by **Mauricio Macri** as he was about to embark on his own political career. Elected to the city of **Buenos Aires** legislature in 2003 on the PRO list, when she was barely 30 years old, she narrowly failed to secure a seat in the lower house of the national **Congress** two years later. When Macri won the mayoral contest to become the fifth head of government of the Autonomous City of Buenos Aires in 2007, Vidal followed him into the city administration, holding ministerial posts and serving as Macri's deputy. In 2011, Macri stood for reelection and named Vidal his running mate. It was a winning combination, the pair secured almost two-thirds of the vote, roundly trouncing the Kirchnerist **Frente para la Victoria/Partido Justicialista** (FpV/PJ). Not without criticism from sections of the coalition, Macri persevered to have Vidal head the Cambiemos ticket for the province of Buenos Aires in the upcoming gubernatorial and **congressional** and **presidential** **elections of 2015**.

The dominant partners in the Cambiemos coalition for the provincial elections were the PRO and the **Unión Cívica Radical** (UCR). As Macri's minister and deputy in the city government, Vidal developed the reputation of an efficient, plain-speaking administrator who got things done, experience that served her well when she was elected governor of the province. She is becoming a powerful political figure in her own right, no longer regarded as a protégé of Macri. She has traveled widely in the province, "selling" her program to the electorate, and has a positive public profile abroad. After heading the provincial government for less than two years, she is credited with scotching an attempted Peronist comeback in Buenos Aires in the mid-term **congressional elections of 2017**, thereby contributing to the nationwide performance of Cambiemos. Since becoming governor, she has waged a hard-fought battle against **corruption**, claiming some major scalps, including those of "Mafiosi" bosses she maintains were protected by her Peronist predecessor, **Daniel Scioli**. She has also taken on the notoriously corrupt and brutal provincial police force, sacking around 7,900 rogue officers and weeding out senior officials who rarely showed up for duty. These policies are popular and risky—she has received death threats. Her often repeated mission statement is to change the political, economic, and social system that has prevailed for the past 30 years to ensure that the future will be better for "the kids." She is married and has three children.

Vidal is the first woman to be elected governor of Buenos Aires and the first non-Peronist to have been elected to the post in almost two decades. The governorship of Buenos Aires is critically important, arguably the second most important political office in the country, or the third if the vice presidency of the republic is counted; the province is the largest electoral district in the country, accounting for something under 40 percent of national voters, and is usually regarded as a Peronist stronghold. Were Argentines to elect a non-Peronist *presidenta* in the not-to-distant future, it could well be Vidal.

VIDELA, JORGE RAFAEL (1925–2013). De facto president of Argentina (1976–1981). He was appointed commander-in-chief of the army by President **Isabel Perón** in 1975. At that time, the country was in an undeclared state of civil war, racked by the terrorism of the **Montoneros** and the **Ejército Revolucionario del Pueblo**, which prompted the armed forces to intervene with the **military coup of 1976** and launch the **Proceso de Reorganización Nacional**.

The presidency of Videla is remembered for the controversial policies pursued by Minister of Economy **José Alfredo Martínez de Hoz**, but above all for the gruesome manner in which the problem of terrorism was dealt with. Using the decrees on the **War to Annihilate Subversion** of 1975 as a justification, Videla embarked on the **Disposición Final**, which can only be described as an extermination campaign. Almost 9,000 people were kidnapped, tortured, and murdered in clandestine centers, and their bodies were then disposed of away from the public eye; all of this gave rise to the term **Desaparecidos** (The Disappeared). Videla in later life claimed that this amount of people had to die for the war on terrorism to be won, which is certainly untrue. He could have set up **military** tribunals to deal with subversives, as **Alejandro Agustín Lanusse** had done during his de facto administration.

Throughout his presidency, Videla had to struggle with a public image problem. As early as 1977, he came under fire domestically from relatives of the Desaparecidos, and then the issue of gross **human rights** violations was raised internationally. Videla used the football World Cup hosted by Argentina in 1978 for political purposes. Bribes were paid to ensure that Argentina won the semifinal and reached the final, which it won. The Netherlands team, which was the other finalist, announced before the match was held that in the event of winning the tournament, the team would not accept the trophy from the hands of the Argentine president in protest at the human rights abuses committed by the military regime. Despite the success of the World Cup, the government was forced to launch a domestic publicity campaign with the slogan "Los Argentinos somos derechos y humanos" (We Argentines Are Righteous and Human) as a consequence of an extremely adverse report by the Inter-American Commission of Human Rights in 1979.

Videla stepped down from office in 1981 and was succeeded by **Roberto Viola**. Following the return of democracy, he became a defendant in the **trials of the military juntas** in 1985. Videla was sentenced to life imprisonment but was one of the senior military officers subsequently pardoned by President **Carlos Saúl Menem**. He was briefly imprisoned in 1998 when a judge convicted him of kidnapping babies during the war on terrorism, but then transferred to house arrest for health reasons. The Supreme Court declared the pardons issued by Menem unconstitutional in 2006, and a federal court restored Videla's convictions for human rights abuses the following year. Videla was put on trial for new charges of human rights violations in 2010 and sentenced once again to life imprisonment. In 2012, he was condemned to 50 years in prison for his participation in the scheme to steal babies from parents detained by the regime and have them adopted by members of the armed forces.

Despite all the evidence to the contrary, Videla was convinced until the end of his life that he had done the right thing and remained unrepentant. He died in prison and, having been stripped of his titles, was no longer entitled to a military funeral. *See also* BEAGLE CHANNEL DISPUTE; FALKLANDS DISPUTE.

VIEDMA. Capital of the province of **Río Negro**, located on the right bank of the river of the same name, 20 miles (30 kilometers) from the coast. Sometimes knows as Mercedes de Patagones, reflecting the city of Carmen de Patagones on the opposite bank of the river, the city was officially founded in 1779 by immigrants from **Spain**; the town was regarded as strategic to the defense of **Patagonia**. It remained cut off from the rest of the country and much of its hinterland until the late 19th century; access was mainly by sea from **Buenos Aires**. Terrestrial communications with the rest of the country only came in 1931, when a road-and-rail bridge across the Río Negro was finally inaugurated, a project that had been almost 80 years in the making. By around 1900, the city was already an important commercial and distribution center for **meat** and **wool**. The construction of a railway into the interior of Patagonia, begun in 1909 and completed to **San Carlos de Bariloche** sometime later, soon led to the development of fruit production, generating further wealth for the city.

Viedma enjoyed a brief moment of notoriety in the 1980s. Project Patagonia and Capital was devised by President **Raúl Alfonsín** in 1986 to develop the southern part of the country by moving the **federal capital** from Buenos Aires. A new federal district, centered on the city and neighboring Carmen de Patagones, located on the Buenos Aires bank of the Río Negro, would be carved out of the two provinces. A pet project of the president, the project was launched on an unsuspecting public in radio and television broadcasts. While the public may have been unsuspecting, some associates of the president may have got wind of the project earlier; there were accusations that members of the governing party had bought land in the area, hoping to make a financial killing should the scheme materialize. Inspiration may have come from an idea of the early **independence** period, which favored constructing a new capital in the interior, well away from the city of Buenos Aires, and various schemes to populate Patagonia following the **Conquest of the Desert**. The example of Brasília may also have been influential. The chorus of criticism was deafening: the cost of developing a new city in such a location, and the willingness of civil servants and politicians to live there were hotly debated. Nothing came of the project, other than a related measure to grant the status of province to the last surviving national territory, **Tierra del Fuego**. From time to time, there were efforts to revive the project, but the enabling legislation was finally removed from the statue books in 2014.

VILLANUEVA, JAVIER RAFAEL (1924–). Academic economist and policy maker, trained in the **United States**. He obtained his first degree at City College of New York and later a PhD from Columbia University, being appointed to visiting professorships at such institutions as Yale and Oxford and sometime head of the prestigious **Instituto Torcuato Di Tella** (now the **Universidad Torcuato Di Tella**—UTDT) in **Buenos Aires**. As head of the national development council, **Consejo Nacional de Desarrollo** (CONADE), he was a strong advocate of developmentalism, which stressed the importance of state-led industrialization and support for national businesses as a mechanism of structural modernization and sustained economic growth.

Sometimes described as the senior economic thinker of his generation, he is best known for his writing on industrialization. *See also* DEVELOPMEN-TALISM/DEVELOPMENTALIST.

VILLAR, ALBERTO (1923–1974). Senior police officer who investigated the murder of former president **Pedro Eugenio Aramburu** in 1970 and the kidnapping and subsequent murder of Fiat president Oberdan Sallustro by the **Ejército Revolucionario del Pueblo** in 1972.

Villar retired in January 1973 but was appointed deputy head of the federal police one year later. He was given a free rein to deal with subversion, as President **Juan Domingo Perón** was dedicated to combating the left by legal and extrajudicial means. The most important manifestation of the latter was the **Triple A**, a death squad established by Minister of Social Welfare **José López Rega**, and of which Villar was a founder. As a result, the federal police tolerated if not actively participated in the activities of this sinister organization. Villar was promoted to chief of the federal police in May 1974, and he set up an intelligence body of the security forces of Argentina, **Chile**, **Uruguay**, and **Bolivia** that was based in **Buenos Aires** and became a step toward **Operación Condor**. He was assassinated in November of that year by the **Montoneros**. *See also* MINISTRY OF SOCIAL DEVELOPMENT.

VILLAS MISERIA/VILLAS DE EMERGENCIA. While the terms *slum* and *shantytown* have different meanings in English—the former applied to the physical deterioration of established housing stock, possibly on being converted from single to multioccupancy, and the latter applied to temporary/ insecure improvised settlements—in Argentina the phrases have similar meanings, though period specific. *Villas miseria, villas de emergencia*, or simply *villas* describes dense settlements of precarious housing made of cardboard, corrugated steel sheets, plastic, and waste material built on waste land in the center of cities (along railway lines or derelict public land) and on the outskirts of major cities—**Buenos Aires**, **Rosario**, **Córdoba**, and other large conurbations.

Initially without title or public services, such settlements are associated with squalid living conditions, poverty, violence, crime, and drug abuse. Most residents are informal-sector workers; others, who might have had better living standards and expectations, were driven to the *villas* by unemployment during **economic crises**. In some cases, partly as the result of spontaneous organization by residents, with the assistance of nongovernmental organizations or politicians, water and sanitation are improved, roads paved, and land titles issued, resulting in the physical improvement of properties and neighborhoods. At the height of the 2001–2003 economic crisis, official estimates showed that around 7 percent of the total population of greater Buenos Aries was living in *villas*—the true percentage may have been much higher. A national estimate for 2016 places a similar percentage of the total population living in precarious conditions. Since the 1980s, agency reports and official documents tend to use the phrase *villas de emergencia* instead of *villas miseria*, though conditions remain as miserable for most.

VIOLA, ROBERTO EDUARDO (1924–1994). De facto president of Argentina in 1981. In 1978, he was promoted to commander-in-chief of the army by then de facto president **Jorge Rafael Videla**, who retired from active service but remained head of state.

Viola retired from active service and succeeded Videla as president in March 1981; **Leopoldo Fortunato Galtieri** replaced him as head of the army. Although he did not interrupt repressive actions against the remnants of subversion, Viola initiated a partial opening for career politicians and civilian technicians to reenter public service while aiming to remain in office until 1985. This enabled the **Confederación General del Trabajo** (CGT) to reorganize itself, even though it remained proscribed, and the possibility of greater freedom.

The prospective political opening, together with the failure of the economic measures taken by **Lorenzo Sigaut**, prompted hard-liner Galtieri to engineer a palace coup. In December 1981, he replaced Viola as president while remaining commander-in-chief of the army. Following the return of democracy, Viola was one of the defendants in the trials of the **military** juntas in 1985 and sentenced to 17 years in prison. He benefited from the pardons granted by President **Carlos Saúl Menem** to senior military officers in 1990; he died four years later. *See also* MILITARY COUP OF 1976; MILITARY JUNTAS, TRIALS OF THE; PROCESO DE REORGANIZACIÓN NACIONAL.

VIRGIN OF LUJÁN. The Virgin or Our Lady of Luján is the patron saint of Argentina. The image of the virgin was ordered by a family based in the north of the country in the early 17th century. Imported via the port of **Buenos Aires**, it was transported across the **pampas**. Accounts variously record that at some point the cart in which the image was being carried got stuck and could not be moved by teams of men and oxen, others that the oxen refused to pull the cart farther. This was taken as a sign that the virgin had fixed on her new home. A shrine was built at the spot. In time, the simple chapel became the Basilica of Luján, now a place of national and international pilgrimage. The image resides in the central chapel of the cathedral and is bedecked in blue and white robes, backed by a representation of the sun, motifs taken from the national flag. Copies of the virgin are to be found in public places and private homes across the republic. Over the centuries, the virgin has been credited with working many wonders and has been bestowed with several honors. Inducted into the army, due to good conduct the virgin has been duly promoted and is now one of the most senior serving officers in the armed forces.

W

WAR OF THE PACIFIC. One of two major international conflicts in South America in the 19th century that resulted in considerable boundary adjustments. The other was the **War of the Triple Alliance**.

The War of the Pacific from 1879 to 1883 saw **Peru** and **Bolivia**, who had signed a secret defensive treaty in 1873, allied against **Chile**. When Bolivia imposed sanctions on Chilean companies and workers operating in Bolivian nitrate fields, contrary to earlier agreements between the two countries, the Chilean government protested and sought arbitration. Bolivia refused, declared war, and invoked the agreement with Peru. The conflict was a turning point in naval technology, demonstrating the effectiveness of steam-powered ironclads armed with rifled cannon. The naval campaign went well for Peru at first, but the Chilean armed forces proved better organized and armed. The outcome was that Bolivia lost the mineral-rich province of Antofagasta to Chile, and its access to the sea, while Chile also acquired the Peruvian provinces of Tarapacá, Arica, and Tacna—Tacna was returned to Peru in 1929 following a plebiscite.

Alarmed at the growth of Chilean military capacity and the settlement of Chilean **Patagonia**, Argentina was not a disinterested bystander, fearing for territory claimed in eastern Patagonia and the Beagle Channel in the far south. There was a succession of disputes. A border settlement was attempted in 1881 to demarcate the international boundary in the channel and the Straits of Magellan, and again in 1904 and 1977. In 1978, the **military** government of the **Proceso de Reorganización Nacional** contemplated occupying disputed territory and drew up a plan of military action, Operación Soberanía. Conflict seemed inevitable, but the Argentine military reconsidered at the last minute. Loss of face in 1978 probably contributed to a determination among some sectors of the armed forces not to back down in 1982, when the military contemplated another confrontation had they succeeded in the **Falklands War**. Statements made by de facto president General **Leopoldo Fortunato Galtieri** and Air Force Chief Brigadier **Basilio Lami Dozo** hint at this. The boundary dispute was only resolved with the return of democracy when President **Raúl Alfonsín** signed a treaty of peace and friendship with Chile in 1984, following papal arbitration, which awarded the disputed islands to Chile. Submitted to a nonbinding national referendum, almost 83 percent approved the treaty, a massive endorsement of Alfonsín's strategy and an equally overwhelming rejection of the pretentions of the military. *See also* AGREEMENT BETWEEN ARGENTINA AND CHILE ACCEPTING PAPAL MEDIATION IN THE BEAGLE CHANNEL DISPUTE (1979); BEAGLE CHANNEL DISPUTE.

WAR OF THE TRIPLE ALLIANCE. Sometimes known as the Paraguayan War, it was the most devastating conflict experienced in South America, with **Paraguay** against Argentina, **Brazil**, and **Uruguay**.

Fought between 1864 and 1870, the immediate cause of the war was the incursion of Paraguayan forces into Argentine territory. Paraguayan dictator Francisco Solano López had requested permission from President **Bartólome Mitre** to cross **Mesopotamia** to assist clients in the Uruguayan civil war. When Mitre refused, the Paraguayan army took the city of **Corrientes**. Argentina and Brazil, in association with the new administration in Montevideo, declared war—the three allies against Paraguay. Solano López accused Argentina and Brazil of interfering in Uruguay; their response was they were attempting to restore order—Brazilian troops had been active on the frontier with Uruguay for some months. More long-term causes involved efforts by Brazil to open up its center-west provinces, notably Mato Grosso, then only accessible by the **Paraguay River**. Brazil also protested against action across its southern border by Uruguayan insurgents and sent in patrols in hot pursuit. This was the pretext for Solano López to come to the aid of the then government in Montevideo. Argentina was in the process of nation building—the province of **Buenos Aires** had only recently rejoined the **Argentine Confederation** and the government in Buenos Aires doubted the loyalty of some peripheral provinces.

All three countries—Argentina, Brazil, and Paraguay—maintained competing territorial claims in the lower reaches of the Paraguay/Paraná basin, in response to which Paraguay had been building up a large standing army in defense of its claims and independence. The British were also said to have a vested interest, seeking to open the interior of South America to trade and to undermine the statist economic model pursued by the Lópezes. The war was hard fought and an unmitigated disaster for Paraguay: around two-thirds of the population died—only one in 10 adult males survived, and the country lost approximately half its territory. Brazil was the main gainer, acquiring large swathes of what had been northern Paraguay. Argentina secured the disputed territory of **Misiones**.

WAR TO ANNIHILATE SUBVERSION. Official name of the **Dirty War**, carried out by the **military** regime of 1976–1983 and which resulted in almost 9,000 deaths. The armed forces were empowered to undertake the War to Annihilate Subversion by the government of **Isabel Perón** in two stages in 1975. In February, she declared a temporary state of emergency (which rapidly became permanent) and authorized the military to deal with the **Ejército Revolucionario del Pueblo** (ERP) only in the province of **Tucumán**, where the guerrilla group had established a territorial enclave. Then, in October, with Mrs. Perón on medical leave and following a failed terrorist attack on a military base in Formosa, acting president **Ítalo Luder** passed three decrees enabling the armed forces to "annihilate subversive elements in all the territory of the country."

The use of the word *annihilate* has been subject to different interpretations. Luder claimed he never intended repression outside the law, while General **Jorge Rafael Videla**, commander-in-chief of the army and de facto president following the **military coup of 1976**, has argued that the decrees were a "license to kill." Videla and other military chiefs insisted that the term *annihilate* in the decrees allowed them to physically eliminate all the guerrillas they found; some also say that the term authorized them to kill the guerrillas once they had surrendered or been detained. The military had such autonomy that they prepared for an unprecedented scale of repression, and the weakened Peronist government did not know, did not want to, or could not prevent them from abusing **human rights** in the struggle against terrorism.

A timetable was established to complete the task: the armed forces would significantly diminish subversive action by the end of 1975; responsibility for constraining subversion would be transferred to the police by the end of 1976; and the annihilation of residual terrorist organizations would be undertaken from 1977. This schedule, which may have been influenced by Argentina's impending hosting of the football World Cup in 1978, appears to have been met. According to Videla, the guerrillas were under control by 1977 and defeated by the time the football tournament was held. Advantage was taken of the last three and a half months of Mrs. Perón's tenure to prepare the fight against subversion. The army took "primary responsibility" and, based on plans dating back to the late 1960s, divided the country into five geographical areas defined by the distribution of the army corps; two of these were headed respectively by the notorious Generals **Carlos Guillermo Suárez Mason** and **Luciano Benjamin Menéndez**. To ensure "efficiency," each zone was in turn subdivided. The navy assumed the task of combating the **Montoneros** in the city of **Buenos Aires** and its northern suburbs, largely because of the ambitions of Admiral **Emilio Massera** to succeed Videla as president. The air force had minimal involvement.

During the process, the military established two categories of prisoners. One was of politicians, trade unionists, and public servants who would be detained immediately after the coup, in order to prevent protests and strikes against the planned detention of President Isabel Perón. Four hundred people were detained as a result, most of whom were released by June 1976. The second comprised longer lists, whose preparation was ordered and supervised by the chiefs of the five zones into which the country was divided. These lists of the **Disposición Final** catalogued the vast majority of those who would be "disappeared." The definitions of *social leaders* and *subversives* were lax and in each zone depended largely on the commanders and their political and ideological prejudices.

The centerpiece of the plan to combat subversion was the establishment of 340 clandestine detention centers spread around the country, through which thousands of prisoners were processed. Since the key was to obtain quick and definite information on the guerrillas, who tended to operate in autonomous cells, the detention centers enabled the collection of data with no regard to the methods used as long as they were "effective." This fed a savage circle of detentions, captivity, pressure through torture, information, new detentions, and so on, until each guerrilla cell was destroyed. Beyond the "efficiency" of the barbarous methods of torture, some former Montoneros later argued that cooperation by the guerrillas with the military, as a result of demoralization and defeat arising from the success of the early antisubversion campaigns, was also instrumental in the rapid dismantlement of all terrorist organizations. Cooperation was direct and indirect; besides denunciations under torture, it extended to some guerrillas devising policies and methods for a faster annihilation of the organization to which they had belonged.

Once the prisoners had served their purpose in the detention centers, their fate was decided by the zonal commanders; since the latter operated autonomously, they had no obligation to inform the ruling junta, a deliberate ploy that enabled the commanders of the armed forces to deny responsibility. The vast majority of detainees were murdered, and their bodies were disposed of gruesomely—some died under torture, others were raped, some were weighted and dropped into the sea from helicopters while still semiconscious. In a final bid to cover up the deaths, a list of 8,000 **Desaparecidos** passed by Minister of Interior General **Albano Harguindeguy** to his successor in 1981 was destroyed by decree under orders from de facto president General **Reynaldo Bignone** six months before the **presidential election of 1983**.

The methods employed in the military detention centers were based on the French doctrine of "counterrevolutionary war," which arose from the struggle against the FLN in the Algerian War of Independence and was subsequently exported. In 1960, French officials established a permanent mission at the army's headquarters in Buenos Aires. In Argentina, the doctrine dovetailed neatly with the Doctrine of National Security, then being disseminated by Washington. As early as 1964, Commander-in-Chief General **Juan Carlos Onganía** had already enunciated what later became the mantra of the dictatorship of 1976–1983: the principal mission of the military was "the preservation of the moral and spiritual values of Western and Christian civilization," and the armed forces should displace popularly elected governments and take power "if democracy does not guarantee those objectives."

With the return of democracy, a full investigation into the Desaparecidos not only revealed the extent of what the military had done but also unearthed the issue of the fate of the offspring of the detainees. Even though they accepted that "irregularities" were committed, Videla and Harguindeguy maintained that there was no systematic plan to steal the children of the detained or kidnapped, especially the babies of captive mothers who had given birth in the detention centers, and give them to couples who would change their identity and bring them up as their own. The truth is disturbing: the military government had a plan as families of the disappeared were deemed Communist and not suitable to raise infants. These children and babies were handed over to childless couples loyal to the regime, often military families. To this day, the numbers involved are not entirely certain.

The War to Annihilate Subversion is the darkest episode of modern Argentine history. Though many of the Desaparecidos were involved in subversion and terrorism, or were regarded as fellow travelers by senior figures in the armed forces, this does not justify in any way whatsoever the use of repression outside the legal framework and subsequent murder of almost 9,000 people by the military. Irrespective of their supposed crimes, the "disappeared" were denied due legal process. If anything, the brutal tragedy permanently discredited the armed forces. *See also* ACOSTA, JORGE EDUARDO (1941–); ASTIZ, ALFREDO IGNACIO (1951–); COMISIÓN NACIONAL SOBRE LA DESAPARACIÓN DE PERSONAS (CONADEP); ESCUELA SUPERIOR DE MECÁNICA DE LA ARMADA (ESMA); GALTIERI, LEOPOLDO FORTUNATO (1926–2003); MADRES DE PLAZA DE MAYO; MILITARY JUNTAS, TRIALS OF THE; MINISTRY OF INTERIOR, PUBLIC WORKS, AND HOUSING; *NUNCA MÁS*; TRADE UNIONS; VIOLA, ROBERTO EDUARDO (1924–1994).

WOMEN. The public role of women in Argentina is often assumed to be limited due to the tradition of **machismo**, for which the country is famous or notorious. Yet this view is only partially correct and misses the significant role played by many individual women and marked changes in recent decades. Women were enfranchised by the **Constitution of 1949** and granted the same voting rights as men, unrestricted by a property or literacy test. From a world perspective, this was late, but not so late. The first country to extend the franchise to women was New Zealand in 1893. Norway was the first country in Europe to do so in 1913; Uruguay the first in the Americas in 1917. All women in the **United States** did not get the vote until 1920, though some states had enfranchised women earlier. Some women were granted the vote in **Great Britain** in 1918, but all women only 10 years later. Not until 1991 did women in all Swiss cantons have the right to vote.

The changing public political role of women can be illustrated by three stories. **Eva Perón** was prevented by the **military** from standing as vice president alongside her husband, **Juan Domingo Perón**, in the **presidential election of 1951**, ostensibly on the grounds that she would succeed him as constitutional head of the armed forces in the event of his death, something senior generals would not countenance. Less than a generation later, **Isabel Perón** ran for the vice presidency alongside Juan Domingo in the **presidential election of September 1973**. The Perón–Perón formula triumphed; Isabel succeeded her husband as president in July 1974 on his death. A generation and a half later, **Cristina Fernández de Kirchner** ran for the presidency in the **congressional** and **presidential election of 2007**. She won, succeeding husband **Néstor Kirchner**. She ran again four years later and was reelected president by a massive margin. It would be trite to argue that these women were "simply wives" who owe their position and achievements to their respective husbands. She never obtained high political office, but Evita was one of the dominant personalities of the age, had a massive political support base, and played a prominent role in public and political life. She was the key interlocutor between the state and the **trade unions** and shaped social policy. Doubts had been expressed about the ability of Cristina Kirchner to govern in advance of the 2007 elections. In office, before and after the death of her husband, she proved to be an astute political operator. Whether commentators agreed or disagreed with the policies of her administrations, few doubted that she had the capacity and determination to drive through her agenda and mobilize support. It would be equally naïve to dismiss women from an earlier period such as **Alicia Moreau de Justo** as "simply a wife." She was an active campaigner for social and political reform in her own right; her reputation was well established before she married **Juan Bautista Justo**. She remained a prominent figure in organizations fighting for women's rights and **human rights** until the latter part of the 20th century.

Women now play as prominent a role in national political and cultural life as men and have done for several decades. It is instructive that when the program of emergency family assistance was set up by interim president **Eduardo Duhalde** in 2002 it was entitled the Plan Jefes y Jefas de Hogar, recognizing that households might be headed by women as much as men. There has been a significant improvement in the status of women since the return of democracy, building on what reformers like Alicia Justo achieved and the actions of campaign groups like the **Madres de Plaza de Mayo** during the bloody years of the **Proceso de Reorganización Nacional**. There is equality in the workplace; the gender pay gap is low by international standards; levels of **education** attainment are about the same (education enrollment rates for women are higher than those for men, especially in higher education); women are as well represented in the **media** as in the world of politics, at all levels. With the influence of the **Catholic Church** in decline, campaigns by women's groups in such areas as divorce and abortion have borne fruit: divorce was legalized in 1987, abortion was partially decriminalized in 2007 but remains a contentious issue. **Raúl Alfonsín**, the first democratically elected president after the Proceso, was determined to appoint a civilian to head the **Ministry of Defense**, Néstor Kirchner consciously a woman, **Nilda Cecilia Garré**.

Women make up well over half the labor force—around 70 percent of women enter the labor market at some point in their lives—and account for about 40 percent of members of **Congress**, one of the highest proportions in the world. A quota system was introduced in 1991; since then, women must make up at least 30 percent of the list of candidates in legislative elections. Women hold (and have held) important ministerial portfolios, lead (and have led) **political parties**, and have been elected to key provincial governorships like that of **Buenos Aires**. Women account for around 10 percent of the armed forces, overwhelmingly concentrated in the lower ranks and in noncombatant roles. The first woman general was appointed in 2015—María Isabel Pansa. Arguably, women remain underrepresented in the fields of business and law. *See also* ALSOGARAY, MARÍA JULIA (1942–); ARROSTITO, NORMA ESTER (1940–1978); BEMBERG, MARÍA LUISA (1922–1995); BONAFINI, HEBE PASTOR DE (1928–); BORGES, GRACIELA (1941–); BULLRICH, PATRICIA (1956–); CAHEN D'ANVERS, MÓNICA (1934–); CARRIÓ, ELISA MARÍA AVELINA "LILITA" (1956–); DUHALDE, HILDA BEATRIZ "CHICHE" GONZÁLEZ DE (1946–); FERNÁNDEZ MEIJIDE, GRACIELA (1931–); FONTENLA, NORMA (1930–1971); KIRCHNER, ALICIA MARGARITA (1946–); OCAMPO, VICTORIA (1891–1979); PRESIDENTIAL ELECTION OF 2011; SALA, MILAGRO AMALIA ÁNGELA (1964–); SOCIEDAD DE BENEFICENCIA DE BUENOS AIRES; VIDAL, MARÍA EUGENIA (1973–).

WOOL. Modern production dates from the 1840s, with the first merino **sheep** being imported in the 1820s during the administration of **Bernardino Rivadavia** in an effort to improve bloodstock. During the third quarter of the century, wool was the fastest growing export commodity, and for a while became the principal export by value. Wool represented the first modern commodity boom experienced by Argentina, blazing a trail for later "new" **commodities**.

By the 1840s, improved breeds of sheep were beginning to displace creole **cattle** in settled districts of the province of **Buenos Aires**. The stock of sheep increased massively, probably peaking at around 100,000,000 head in the 1890s, when the raising of improved sheep shifted from the central **pampas** to **Patagonia**. There was an exponential growth in wool production and wool exports as the national flock increased, and then a corresponding decline. Wool accounted for less than 1 percent of exports by value in 1822; in 1836, almost 8 percent; in 1851, 10.3 percent. Exports were shipped predominantly through the port of Buenos Aires, though wool production was increasing in the province of **Entre Ríos**. In 1865, the value of the wool clip, virtually all of which was exported, was estimated at more than 12,000,000 hard pesos or 46 percent of the value of total exports, by far outstripping traditional exports like hides and skins, salted and dried **meat**, and tallow. The highest participation of wool in exports probably occurred in the late 1880s, when it represented something above 50 percent of the total value. Thereafter, the volume and value of wool exports fell as sheep were displaced by cattle and meat and cereals in the Pampean zone. The Argentine clip also faced competition in international markets from producers in Australia and New Zealand who delivered a higher quality and cleaner fleece to the market.

During the 20th century, sheep "retreated" to Patagonia, which today produces the greater part of the national clip, mainly merino wool. By the 1960s, the value of Australian wool exports were about seven times those of Argentina, and New Zealand about double, although wool still accounted for around 7 percent of the value of total Argentine exports. Between the 1970s and the 1990s, wool production declined to less than half the immediate post–Second World War peak, continuing to fall well into the 21st century, though picking up a little recently. In 2015, wool and animal fiber represented considerably less than 1 percent of total export. Although fine grades of wool are produced, the bulk of the Argentine clip has traditionally been "carpet" quality. *See also* AGRICULTURE; CONQUEST OF THE DESERT/DESERT CAMPAIGN; ECONOMIC CRISES; ECONOMY; *ESTANCIA*; *ESTANCIA* COMPANIES; FOREIGN TRADE; *FRIGORÍFICOS*; *SALADEROS*; URQUIZA, JUSTO JOSÉ DE (1801–1870).

XUL SOLAR (1887–1963). Adopted name of Oscar Agustín Alejandro Schulz Solari; surrealist, expressionist, symbolist, and modernist painter, also inventor of imaginary languages. Xul Solar painted in relatively small formats, mainly watercolors, and in tempera using striking contrasts and bright colors. He also invented two imaginary languages, whose symbols figure in his paintings. One was Neo Criollo, which fused Spanish and Portuguese poetically, and the other was a Pan Lingua, linking mathematics, music, astrology, and the visual arts. Outside Argentina, Xul Solar may be best known for his association with **Jorge Luis Borges**.

Y

YABRÁN, ALFREDO ENRIQUE NALLIB (1944–1998). *See* YABRÁN CASE.

YABRÁN CASE. A story of murder, **corruption**, and murky politicking involving a powerful, self-made businessman, sometime close associate of President **Carlos Saúl Menem** and bête noir of **Domingo Cavallo**, Menem's minister of **economy** responsible for the **Convertibility Plan**. Alfredo Enrique Nallib Yabrán, born in Larroque, **Entre Ríos** province, to Lebanese immigrants, moved to the city of **Buenos Aires** in the 1970s, first working for the Burroughs Corporation, US manufacturer of office equipment, before setting up a courier service, Ocasa. With official encouragement during the early years of the **Proceso de Reorganización Nacional**, Yabrán expanded the courier business, competing with the grossly inefficient state postal and telecommunications former monopoly **ENCOTel**, and diversified into the delivery of **currency** and financial documents. With contacts in the government, particularly for the air force, Ocasa first signed a contract with the **Banco de la Nación Argentina** in the delivery of banknotes and subsequently became sole carrier for the distribution of all documents issued by the federal government. Later, Yabrán was awarded a contract to run cargo operations at Ezeiza, the principal airport of Buenos Aires. These lucrative contracts were obtained partly through official contracts and kickbacks, and partly though Yabrán's business "practices"—he controlled the delivery carrier trade union, and potential competitors were threatened by criminal gangs "franchised" by Ocasa that destroyed equipment and property. The courier and air freight firms were extensively involved in drug trafficking and money laundering. As the Proceso regime unraveled, Yabrán cultivated civilian politicians, using labor contacts, and was well placed to benefit from the **privatizations** of the 1980s and 1990s, particularly under Menem. Yabrán firms obtained franchises to run duty-free services at Ezeiza, as well as covering part of airport security operations, and he became the principal contributor to Menem's 1994 reelection campaign.

Yabrán now set his sights on ENCOTel, which brought him into conflict with Cavallo—the **Ministry of Economy** had become responsible for state post and telecommunications, inherited from the defunct **Ministry of Public Works**. To break Yabrán's grip on the business, Cavallo changed the management at ENCOTel and outsourced services, ensuring that contracts went to any company other than Ocasa. Cavallo also triggered investigations by the tax authority into Yabrán's companies, which were charged with tax evasion. Yabrán responded with a flurry of lawsuits and violence—the new manager of ENCOTel was beaten up, and bombs exploded at the offices and homes of newly appointed administrators. Would-be competitors of Yabrán were also warned off by members of the government, including **Carlos Corach**, sometime minister of interior, and there was a cabinet spat between Corach and Cavallo in which Cavallo accused Yabrán of deploying mafia methods to build his business empire. With the departure of Cavallo, it seemed that Yabrán had come out on top, though the scandal meant that he never obtained control of ENCOTel nor of the state airport management corporation.

With effective political protection, Yabrán's business empire appeared set to prosper. Yet the changing political climate, as Menem reached the end of his second term amid mounting public disgust at the level of official corruption and anxiety as the economy stalled, pointed to difficult times ahead. It was at this point, when he appeared most secure, that Yabrán was implicated in the **Cabezas Affair**, the murder of a journalist shortly after he had taken a photograph of the notoriously publicity-shy Yabrán. Initially, Menem was inclined to continue protecting Yabrán—an official inquiry found that there was insufficient evidence to charge him with any crimes. As the reputational damage to Menem mounted—he was then campaigning for a third term—and press investigations into the Menem–Yabrán connection were turning up a raft of unsavory detail, the president backed off. Yabrán had already been found guilty in the court of public opinion, and there was increasingly credible evidence that his business has been involved in money laundering and intimidation and that, even if he had not pulled the trigger, he was responsible for the death of Cabezas. In the face of mounting pressure, and given the collapse of his political cover, Yabrán attempted to liquidate his business and flee overseas to escape prosecution. With a warrant for his arrest issued and the involvement of Interpol, Yabrán went into hiding, taking refuge on his estate in the province of Entre Ríos. There, on the 20 May 1998, his body was discovered with his face badly mutilated, having been shot through the mouth. Rumors abounded: was it suicide; was it murder? There had been other cases of mysterious (or convenient) "suicide," when figures close to the regime had been finally brought to court. As the face was unrecognizable, many assumed that Yabrán had faked suicide and escaped, though DNA tests proved that the corpse was indeed Yabrán's.

The deaths of Cabezas and Yabrán exposed the corruption and criminality that existed at the highest levels of government and the sense of impunity of key political figures and their associates. The activities of Yabrán demonstrated how legitimate business could be used as a cover from even more lucrative illicit operations, and how such figures could infiltrate government to ensure political and judicial protection. Such immunity and impunity weakened the institutions of the state and the reputation of business. *See also* IMMIGRATION; MINISTRY OF INTERIOR, PUBLIC WORKS, AND HOUSING; NISMAN CASE; TRADE UNIONS.

YACIMIENTOS PETROLÍFEROS FISCALES (YPF). State-owned oil company founded in 1922, which took over responsibility for oil production from the **Ministry of Agriculture**—the first oil field had been discovered in Comodoro Rivadavia on the **Chubut** coast in 1907. YPF has had a checkered association with politics throughout its entire history, not least in terms of its relation vis-à-vis foreign oil companies operating in the country.

YPF was created during the presidency of **Marcelo T. de Alvear** and initially run by **Enrique Mosconi**, a **military** man. Mosconi aimed to create a vertically integrated enterprise that would not only produce oil but refine it and market the resulting products at competitive prices, and with this in mind he launched an ambitious reorganization and development plan. YPF obtained complete administrative autonomy in 1923 and during the 1920s completed a major refinery in **La Plata** (near the largest market in the city of **Buenos Aires**), expanded its product range, and established a distribution and sales network. In 1924, Alvear, who shared Mosconi's vision of oil autonomy, granted YPF monopoly drilling rights in virtually all the national territories. The only exceptions were areas where contracts had already been awarded to private companies. However, Argentina remained heavily dependent on imported products as YPF failed to increase crude output—preferring to continue intensive drilling in established oil fields, rather than to develop new areas.

Mosconi was hostile to foreign oil companies operating in the country, which included Royal Dutch/Shell and the Anglo-Persian Oil Company. Nevertheless, based on the latter enterprise, he developed the concept of a mixed corporation to be financed 51 percent by the government and 49 percent by private Argentine investors, with the company being administered by the private investors and government members of the board of directors having a veto power over major policy decisions. Such a concept was anathema to **Hipólito Yrigoyen**, who succeeded Alvear as president in 1928 and strove to nationalize all private oil companies operating in the country to create a state monopoly that would provide an attractive source of political patronage. Yrigoyen never achieved his oil nationalization aim, as he was ousted by the **military coup of 1930**, and Mosconi was fired as head of YPF for opposing the coup.

The **Concordancia** regimes of the 1930s sought to depoliticize oil by downgrading it. Private companies were barred from future expansion and forced to share the market with YPF, which was stripped of the administrative autonomy secured the previous decade. YPF was hindered by legislation passed in 1932 that brought it under tight government control and by a difficult economic situation, but it still managed to increase production as political considerations were not important to the internal running of the enterprise. However, the 1940s brought a whole new set of problems.

With the onset of the Second World War, YPF and the private companies found it impossible to import equipment, the consequence being that their existing capital stock became increasingly obsolete. The **military coup of 1943** and even more so the election of **Juan Domingo Perón** as president in 1946 resulted in the politicization of YPF. Knowledge of the industry was replaced by loyalty to the regime as a criterion for appointment: the company's subsequent reputation for inefficiency dates from this time. A limited recapitalization of YPF took place in the early 1950s, and there were several major discoveries of oil fields, particularly Campo Durán and Madrejones in **Salta**. Nonetheless, the increase in reserves was not matched by a growth in production, which exposed transport bottlenecks around the country—they affected the new finds in Salta as well as the field of Plaza Huincul, discovered in **Neuquén** in 1918.

The late 1950s produced two major volte-faces in presidential attitudes to foreign oil companies and their exploitation of Argentine petroleum, the result of the impact of oil imports on the balance of payments. The first U-turn came from Perón, who signed a contract with Standard Oil of California (SOCAL) in 1955. By then in political trouble and facing opposition from both the **Unión Cívica Radical** (UCR) and his own supporters, Perón nonetheless followed constitutional procedure and submitted the contract to **Congress**. The latter never scrutinized it as a result of the **military coup of 1955**; the contract was allowed to lapse by the new de facto regime. The second change in approach to foreign companies came from **Arturo Frondizi**, an ardent oil nationalist who was critical of the SOCAL contract and was elected president in 1958. Frondizi secretly negotiated contracts and acted unconstitutionally by presenting them as a fait accompli and not submitting them for congressional approval. The highly controversial agreements were canceled by **Arturo Illia** after he became president in 1963.

Following the **military coup of 1966**, de facto president **Juan Carlos Onganía** introduced a new oil law in 1967. This legislation allowed the government to offer oil concessions on fairly traditional terms if it wished to do so and was defended on the ground that it did not make the granting of concessions mandatory and thereby policy could be altered without further changes to the law. The legislation went through with scant opposition from within the administration or the officer corps, demonstrating once more that the army had little interest in the oil question. A number of concessions were then agreed to, while Amoco—a firm contracted by Frondizi that had not agreed on compensation terms with the Illia government—was persuaded to remain in the country. However, most of the new private exploration investment turned out to be unsuccessful.

After Onganía was replaced as de facto president by **Roberto Levingston** in 1970, the granting of new concessions to foreign oil companies was ended. Moreover, the refining sector faced a major policy alteration. Under Onganía, both YPF and the private companies had increased their refining capacity so that there was a temporary surplus. Until then, the market had been shared out according to a system that awarded YPF around 60 percent of the domestic market while the private sector held the other 40 percent. But in 1971, YPF was given exclusive rights to import crude and to take enough to cover its marketing requirements before allocating the balance to private firms; it was made transparent that YPF would run its refineries at full capacity and leave other suppliers to face the full effect of the temporary surplus. A full-scale oil nationalization may even have been briefly contemplated, but any such idea was killed off when Levingston was toppled as head of state by **Alejandro Agustín Lanusse**.

The five presidents of the period between 1971 and 1976 (Lanusse, **Héctor J. Cámpora**, **Raúl Lastiri**, Perón, and **Isabel Perón**) had little opportunity to attract foreign oil companies to sign contracts as Argentina was engulfed by chaos; national oil production declined sharply. Nonetheless, there was a noteworthy political move: in August 1974, the government of Isabel Perón, under pressure from the oil workers' union, "intervened" in private-sector marketing outlets, which was effectively a nationalization without any intent to pay compensation.

Following the **military coup of 1976**, the administration of **Jorge Rafael Videla** returned the marketing outlets to the private sector. The government also sought to attract private investment in the oil industry to the greatest extent possible, and by 1979 three major contracts had been signed for off-shore exploration, two with Royal Dutch/Shell and one with a group including Bridas, Total, and Deminex. In addition, YPF was streamlined somewhat; however, the costs of the company remained unknown as its statistics were highly inaccurate. Part of the mystery was resolved in the mid-1980s, when a unique record held by YPF became internationally known: it was the only loss-making oil company in the world as any profits it made went straight to the Treasury and were not recorded in the balance sheets.

During the presidency of **Carlos Saúl Menem**, YPF underwent **privatization**. It was acquired by Repsol of Spain, which then renamed itself Repsol-YPF; the purchase of the Argentine firm by a major Spanish group gave it favorable international exposure. After **Cristina Fernández de Kirchner** was reelected president for a second term, she renationalized YPF in 2012. When the announcement was made in Congress, the members of **La Cámpora** packing the galleries of the Chamber of Deputies threw copious amounts of confetti and unfurled a gigantic Argentine flag emblazoned with a huge face of **Néstor Kirchner**, the president's late husband and immediate predecessor. This lack of seriousness matched the occasion in 2001 when **Adolfo Rodríguez Saá** was appointed president: he instantly declared the country's default and all the deputies cheered. Although initially the administration of Mrs. Kirchner refused to pay Repsol any compensation, it eventually did so.

Campaigning in the second round of the **presidential election of 2015**, candidate **Daniel Scioli** of the **Frente para la Victoria/Partido Justicialista** (FpV/PJ) falsely accused his opponent, **Mauricio Macri** of **Cambiemos**, of planning to reprivatize YPF. In the event, Macri was elected president and did not change the status of the oil company. In other words, he steered clear of the oil question—the issues of ownership of the firm and its position in relation to foreign petroleum companies operating in Argentina. *See also* STATE-OWNED ENTERPRISES (SOEs).

YACYRETÁ-APIPÉ. Hydroelectric plant on the **Paraná** River, owned jointly by Argentina and **Paraguay**. The initial agreement to build the dam was signed in December 1973, but progress was hindered by the Paraguayans, who were dissatisfied with their share of the ownership in the Entidad Binacional Yacyretá and with the design of the project, which flooded a substantial amount of their land.

De facto president **Jorge Rafael Videla** decided to kick-start the project in August 1976, and a deal was eventually reached in April 1977 by which Argentina offered much greater financial compensation to its partner. This was followed by a formal request for financing to the Inter-American Development Bank (IADB) and the World Bank (IBRD). The IADB approved a credit for US$200,000,000 in December 1978; the IBRD then completed its technical study and in April 1979 summoned Argentine and Paraguayan representatives for the final approval of Yacyretá and its funding. Paraguay once again raised the issues of flooding compensation and design. Negotiations were suspended, and Argentina then threatened to abandon the project altogether. Argentina made some cosmetic changes to the project as a sop to Paraguay, and a deal was reached in August 1979.

Nevertheless, Yacyretá made little headway. Problems arose over World Bank financing, and there were delays in the allocation of tenders. After Videla stepped down as president in March 1981, the project remained paralyzed during the de facto governments of **Roberto Viola** and **Leopoldo Fortunato Galtieri** that followed. With the return of democracy at the end of 1983, the process of allocating tenders resumed. Costs subsequently increased substantially owing to accumulated interest on funding already received, the periodic indecision of the Entidad Binacional Yacyretá, and a renewed suspension of the project between 1988 and 1990.

The first turbine of the dam became operational in 1994. All 20 turbines were functioning in 2000, as was the lock enabling shipping to surmount a drop of over 20 meters created by the Yacyretá-Apipé Dam. Marred by so many difficulties, the project had taken almost three decades to be completed. Such delays were not uncommon. As well as technical problems, political difficulties were often more significant, particularly when **military** governments were involved in large infrastructure projects. Paraguay currently consumes about 5 percent of the electricity generated, the rest being exported to Argentina. *See also* ITAIPÚ DAM.

YERBA MATE. The national beverage, generally known simply as "mate," which derives from the gourd in which it is usually drunk. *Ilex paraguariensis* is a shrub indigenous to South America. The leaves are used to produce a tealike infusion, now commercially grown mainly in the Argentine provinces of **Misiones** and **Corrientes** close to the border with **Paraguay**, hence also known as Paraguayan Tea. First cultivated by the Guaraní and later produced commercially by the Jesuits, modern production took off in the 19th century. Mate is widely consumed in Paraguay and southern **Brazil** (where it is called *chimarrão*) in addition to Argentina, and to a much lesser extent in **Chile** and **Bolivia**, though per capita consumption is greatest in **Uruguay**. There is some cultivation in southern Brazil. Due to its reputed medicinal and health properties—it is claimed to be as effective a stimulant as tea or coffee while containing much less caffeine, and to contain 90 percent more antioxidants than green tea—mate consumption has increased in popularity in North America and western Europe. In recent years, exports to these regions and others like the Near East have also risen due to the growth of Argentine communities and return migration. In the colonial period and in the 19th century, mate was said to constitute the principal source of vitamin C for **gauchos** and *peones*, who subsisted largely on a diet of **meat**.

Argentina is the world's largest producer and exporter of yerba mate—some 10 to 15 percent of total production by volume is exported annually. Mate is one of the mainstays of the **economy** of Misiones, which accounts for about 90 percent of the national crop, where it is cultivated by small farmers. *See also* AGRICULTURE; COMMODITIES; FOREIGN TRADE.

YRIGOYEN, HIPÓLITO (1852–1933). A controversial politician—a democrat and a demagogue, joint founder of the **Unión Cívica Radical** (UCR) who served as president from 1916 to 1922 and from 1928 to 1930. The first president to be elected after the promulgation of the **Sáenz Peña Law** of 1912, in fair and free elections, his second term was cut short by the **military coup of 1930**.

Born as the regime of **Juan Manuel de Rosas** was collapsing, which resulted in the forging of the modern republic, Yrigoyen died when the system of civilian politics and increasing political participation was under threat. In his 20s and 30s, he was both a civil servant and a politician. Sometime clerk in a local government financial office, he served as a district-level head of a school board and head of the local police commission; he was elected national deputy for the province of **Buenos Aires** in 1878 and 1880. He participated in the 1874 uprising headed by **Bartolomé Mitre**, though opposed to Mitre, protesting against fraud in the elections that yielded the presidency to **Nicolás Avellaneda** that year, and may have been involved in the campaign in Buenos Aires against the election of **Julio A. Roca** as president in 1880. He was prominent in the **Revolution of 1890** and associated with his uncle **Leandro N. Alem** in the formation of the Unión Cívica (UC), precursor of the UCR, and again in the 1905 uprising organized by the UCR. For much of the 1890s, he was absent from political life, running a small estate fattening **cattle**. With the suicide of Alem in 1896, he became leader of the UCR, seeking to advance its campaign against the system of controlled elections crafted by Roca. Such was his reputation and prominence as a campaigner for voting reform—by means of armed struggle or negotiation—that he was involved in discussion with **Roque Sáenz Peña** in 1910 about electoral changes leading to the 1912 law, this despite the fact that he had previously declined appointments offered by presidents **Carlos Pellegrini** and **Luis Sáenz Peña**. Sáenz Peña convinced Yrigoyen to abandon abstentionism and participate in elections. The result was victory in 1916.

Although the UCR took the presidency, the party did not have a majority in **Congress**, which encouraged Yrigoyen to undertake provincial **interventions**, particularly if irregularities in the vote could be demonstrated, action that led to charges of an abuse of power. His major difficulties, however, derived from the international situation. Although he began his presidency after the commercial and financial turbulence triggered by the outbreak of the First World War was beginning to abate, unemployment remained high and Yrigoyen was anxious to maximize the opportunity presented by high wartime prices for **commodity** exports. He was also exercised by the influence of the **United States** in the Americas and British economic power in Argentina, concerns that shaped domestic **economic policy**: he favored the development of the national oil industry and the regulation of the activities of foreign corporations, particularly London-registered railway companies. This earned for him the reputation of a patriot and economic nationalist, and a promoter of national development, a project funded through debt. He maintained the Argentine position of neutrality during the war, though ensured that exports flowed to the Allies. Initially, he was supportive of the League of Nations.

Two major events in the latter part of Yrigoyen's first presidency were the **University Reform Movement** of 1918, to which he was sympathetic, and social unrest—the **Semana Trágica** of 1919—a mix of anti-Semitic urban violence and worker unrest, followed by protests by rural workers in 1920 and 1921. Initially seeking to negotiate in labor disputes, while proposing social reform, Yrigoyen came to regard the organization of workers by the **Partido Socialista** (PS) as an electoral threat to the UCR. The violent suppression of unrest—the government called in the army—damaged the reputation of the president and the party. The severity of Yrigoyen's response may have been shaped by awareness that sections of the traditional elite and the business community might use worker unrest, especially in the countryside, to challenge the government. And there were diplomatic dangers as many protesting rural workers in the south were Chilean. Nevertheless, the country appeared stable when Yrigoyen handed power to **Marcelo T. de Alvear**, the second democratically elected UCR president. Although no longer president, Yrigoyen remained head of the party and sought to control the new government. This led to divisions within the UCR between *antipersonalistas* (who supported an application of constitutional norms) and *personalistas*, supporters of Yrigoyen who advocated a direct, **populist** approach to government. This set the scene for his truncated second term as president. Already old, and jealous of possible rivals within the UCR, Yrigoyen proved incapable of the decisive action necessary to tackle the shock of the 1929 Wall Street Crash, which had a devastating impact on trade, investment, and the public finances. Administrative chaos was a major factor prompting the **military** coup of 1930, which enjoyed a large measure of support. A contributing factor to the coup was resentment among opposition groups at the electoral ascendancy of the UCR, not least among the traditional elite. Incarcerated after the coup, Yrigoyen first refused a "pardon" but finally left prison when he was terminally ill.

The failures of the second presidency tarnished Yrigoyen's reputation but should not detract from his legacy as the first truly democratically elected president of the republic. Attitudes were beginning to change at the time of his death in 1933—his passing was marked by public demonstrations of grief, and his funeral cortege passed through streets lined with masses of supporters. The crabbed politics of the 1930s and beyond also contributed to his rehabilitation. *See also* AGRICULTURE; CHILE; CONCORDANCIA; ECONOMIC CRISES; ECONOMY; FOREIGN DEBT/FOREIGN IN-

VESTMENT; FOREIGN TRADE; GREAT BRITAIN; INDUSTRY; STATE-OWNED ENTERPRISES (SOEs); TRADE UNIONS; YACIMIENTOS PETROLÍFEROS FISCALES (YPF).

Z

ZALDUENDO, EDUARDO A. (1928–2003). Academic economist, technocrat, civil servant, sometime president of the **Banco Central de la República Argentina** (BCRA), and secretary of the national development council, **Consejo Nacional de Desarrollo** (CONADE). A proponent of developmentalism as ideas of state-sponsored industrialization were going out of fashion, he held various positions in the 1960s and 1970s, most notably under the **military** regime of the **Revolución Argentina**. He was the architect of the 1970–1974 Development Plan, inaugurated during the de facto presidency of General **Juan Carlos Onganía**, and during the transition between the chaotic presidency of **Isabel Perón** and the de facto presidency of General **Jorge Rafael Videla**—as head of the BCRA for 48 days in 1976, he had the difficult task of negotiating with the International Monetary Fund (IMO) when the government attempted to regain control of the **economy**. He is best remembered for such books as *El empresario industrial en América Latina: Tomo 1: Argentina* (1963), *Las desigualdades económicas en las regiones de Argentina* (1973), and *Breve historia del pensamiento económico* (1998). *See also* DEVELOPMENTALISM/DEVELOPMENTALIST; INDUSTRY.

ZÁRATE. Situated in the northeast of the province of **Buenos Aires**, 56 miles (96 kilometers) from the city, and located on the **Paraná** Delta, it is a significant river port and important center of manufacturing. Founded in 1854, the district (*partido*) and town were already a center of pastoral activity—**sheep** raising and **cattle** production—before the coming of the railways. It became an important industrial center in the 1930s and 1940s, particularly paper production and meatpacking, which benefited from low-cost imports as well as land and water. With the arrival of Monsanto, plastic production began in the 1950s using agricultural by-products. Before the opening of the Zárate–Brazo Largo bridge in the late 1970s, it was an important transport hub; the main ferry port offered connections between the rest of the country and **Mcsopotamia**. Although the port is not navigable by oceangoing vessels, inward investment in the 1990s resulted in its development as a regional container terminal: there is a project to offer **Paraguay** a duty-free zone in the port. With the neighboring city of **Campana**, Zárate makes up one of the developing industrial poles of the province. *See also* AGRICULTURE; COMMODITIES; FOREIGN TRADE; *FRIGORÍFICOS*; INDUSTRY; MEAT; TRANSPORTATION.

Appendix A

Argentine Heads of State

VICEROYALTY OF THE RIVER PLATE*

May 1810   Baltasar Hidalgo de Cisneros

* Argentines date independence from the calling of the Cabildo Abierto in May 1810. The Open Town Council meeting was officially convened by the Spanish viceroy, who initially presided. Technically, he remained head of the new fledgling state until deposed after a few days.

UNITED PROVINCES OF THE RIVER PLATE

1810–1811	Cornelio Saavedra (president of the first junta and later of the grand junta)
August–September 1811	Domingo Matheu (president of the grand junta)
1811–1812	Feliciano Chiclana, Manuel de Sarratea, Juan José Paso, and Juan Martín de Pueyrredón (first collective presidency)
1812–1814	Antonio Álvarez Jonte, Juan José Paso, Gervesio Antonio de Posadas, and Nicolás Rodríguez Peña (second collective presidency)
1814–1815	Gervesio Antonio de Posadas (supreme director)
January–April 1815	Carlos María de Alvear (supreme director)
April 1815	Matías de Irigoin, José de San Martín, and Manuel de Sarratea (third collective presidency)
1815–1816	Ignacio Álvarez Thomas (acting supreme director)
1816	Antonio González de Balcarce (acting supreme director)

UNITED PROVINCES OF SOUTH AMERICA (UNITED PROVINCES OF THE RIVER PLATE; PROVINCES OF THE UNION)

1816–1819	Juan Martín de Pueyrredón (supreme director)*
1819–1820	José Rondeau (supreme director)
1820	Juan Pedro Aguirre (supreme director)
February 1820	Matías de Irigoin (interim governor of the province of Buenos Aires)**
February–March 1820	Manuel de Sarratea (governor of the province of Buenos Aires)**
March 1820	Juan Ramón González de Balcarce (interim governor of the province of Buenos Aires)**
March–May 1820	Manuel de Sarratea (governor of the province of Buenos Aires)**
May–June 1820	Ildefonso Ramos Mexía (governor of the province of Buenos Aires)**
June–September 1820	Manuel Dorrego (interim governor of the province of Buenos Aires)**
1820–1824	Martín Rodríguez (governor of the province of Buenos Aires)**
1824–1826	Juan Gregorio de Las Heras (governor of the province of Buenos Aires)**

* First head of state following the formal declaration of independence by the Congress of Tucumán, which declared the official name of the country to be the United Provinces of South America, sometimes Provinces of the Union.

** Between 1820 and 1826, the formerly centralized United Provinces functioned as a loose confederation of autonomous provinces. The conduct of foreign affairs was placed in the hands of the governor of the province of Buenos Aires, who was regarded by foreign powers as the head of the Argentine state.

ARGENTINE REPUBLIC

1826–1827	Bernardino Rivadavia*
July–August 1827	Vicente López y Planes

* First president of the reconstituted centralized republic.

ARGENTINE CONFEDERATION*

1827–1828	Manuel Dorrego (governor of the province of Buenos Aires)
1828–1829	Juan Lavelle (de facto governor of the province of Buenos Aires)
June–December 1829	Juan José Viamonte (interim governor of the province of Buenos Aires)
1829–1832	Juan Manuel de Rosas (governor of the province of Buenos Aires)
1832–1833	Juan Ramón González de Balcarce (governor of the province of Buenos Aires)
1833–1834	Juan José Viamonte (interim governor of the province of Buenos Aires)
1834–1835	Manuel Vicente Maza (interim governor of the province of Buenos Aires)
1835–1852	Juan Manuel de Rosas (governor of the province of Buenos Aires)
February–April 1852	Vicente López y Planes (interim governor of the province of Buenos Aires)
April–May 1852	Justo José de Urquiza (governor of the province of Entre Ríos and de facto president of the Confederation)

* Between 1827 and 1852, the country reverted to a loose confederation of provinces that delegated to the governor of the province of Buenos Aires the conduct of foreign relations. During this period, the country was known as the Confederation, though Republic was sometimes used.

ARGENTINE REPUBLIC*

1852–1854	Justo José de Urquiza (interim director of the Argentine Confederation and governor of the province of Buenos Aires from May to September 1852)
1854–1860	Justo José de Urquiza (president of the Argentine Confederation)
1860–1861	Santiago Derqui (president of the Argentine Republic)

November– December 1861	Juan Esteban Pedernera (Derqui's vice president; served as head of state after the resignation of the latter until the calling of new national presidential elections.)
1861–1862	Bartolomé Mitre (governor of the province of Buenos Aires and acting president of the Argentine Republic)
1862–1868	Bartolomé Mitre (president of the Argentine Republic; the election of Mitre in 1862, following the reunification of the country, is taken as marking the beginning of the modern system of constitutional, presidential government)
1868–1874	Domingo Faustino Sarmiento
1874–1880	Nicolás Avellaneda
1880–1886	Julio Argentino Roca
1886–1890	Miguel Ángel Juárez Celman
1890–1892	Carlos Pellegrini (Juárez Celman's vice president; served out the latter's term when he resigned)
1892–1895	Luis Sáenz Peña
1895–1898	José Evaristo Uruburu (Sáenz Peña's vice president; served out the latter's term when he resigned)
1898–1904	Julio Argentino Roca (second term; the first president elected twice under the Constitution of 1853)
1904–1906	Manuel Quintana
1906–1910	José Figueroa Alcorta (Manuel Quintana's vice president; served out the latter's term when he died in office)
1910–1914	Roque Sáenz Peña
1914–1916	Victorino de la Plaza (Sáenz Peña's vice president; served out the latter's term when he died in office)
1916–1922	Hpólito Yrigoyen (first president elected following the reform of the franchise in 1912 that instituted the secret ballot)
1922–1928	Marcelo Torcuato de Alvear
1928–1930	Hpólito Yrigoyen (second term; only the second president elected twice under the Constitution of 1853; his second term was terminated by the military coup of 1930)
1930–1932	José Félix Uriburu (de facto president following the ouster of Yrigoyen)

1932–1938	Agustín Pedro Justo (elected president following "managed" elections)
1938–1942	Roberto Marcelino Ortiz (elected president following "managed" elections)
1942–1943	Ramón Castillo (Ortiz's vice president; became president on the latter's death; removed by the military coup of 1943)
June 1943	Arturo Rawson (de facto president; ousted in a palace coup)
1943–1944	Pedro Pablo Ramírez (de facto president; resigned under pressure from fellow military officers)
1944–1946	Edelmiro Julián Farrell (interim de facto president; served until the calling of fair and free elections)
1946–1952	Juan Domingo Perón (elected president in the first fair and free elections to be held since 1928)
1952–1955	Juan Domingo Perón (second term; elected under the Constitution of 1949, which permitted the immediate reelection of a sitting president; ousted by the military coup of 1955)
September– November 1955	Eduardo Lonardi (de facto president following the military coup that removed Perón; ousted in a palace coup)
1955–1958	Pedro Eugenio Aramburu (de facto president following the removal of Lonardi)
1958–1962	Arturo Frondizi (elected president in restricted elections— the Peronist party was banned; ousted by the military coup of 1962)
1962–1963	José María Guido (interim president; as head of the Senate, stood in for Frondizi when the latter was ousted along with his vice president)
1963–1966	Arturo Umberto Illia (elected president in restricted elections—the Peronist party was banned; ousted by the military coup of 1966)
1966–1970	Juan Carlos Onganía (de facto president following the ouster of Illia; ousted in palace coup)
1970–1971	Roberto M. Levingston (de facto president; ousted in a palace coup)

1971–1973	Alejandro A. Lanusse (de facto president; resigned following the holding of fair and free elections, in which the ban on Peronists was lifted, though Perón himself was not allowed to run)
May–July 1973	Héctor José Cámpora (took the presidency by a comfortable margin in fair and free elections; stood down after a few weeks in office to trigger a new presidential election that Perón was able to contest)
July–October 1973	Raúl Alberto Lastiri (interim president following the resignation of Cámpora and his vice president)
1973–1974	Juan Domingo Perón
1974–1976	Isabel Perón (on the death of her husband, Isabel Perón succeeded him as vice president; unlike many former vice presidents who took office on the death of an incumbent, Isabel Perón was accorded the title of president; her term was brought to an end by the military coup of 1976)
1976–1981	Jorge Rafael Videla (de facto president; served a fixed term as agree on with fellow officers)
March–December 1981	Roberto Eduardo Viola (de facto president appointed by the military to succeed Videla when he stepped down; ousted by an internal coup)
December 1981	Carlos Alberto Lacoste (interim de facto president following the ousting of Videla by fellow officers; served until a military successor was agreed on)
1981–1982	Leopoldo Galtieri (de facto president; resigned following Argentine defeat in the Falklands/Malvinas War)
June–July 1982	Alfredo Oscar Saint-Jean (interim de facto president; ousted in a palace coup)
1982–1983	Reynaldo Bignone (de facto president, charged by the military with negotiating an orderly return to the barracks)
1983–1989	Raúl Alfonsín (first civilian president elected in free elections after the military coup of 1976; his term ended a few months prematurely amid economic chaos following the 1989 elections)
1989–1999	Carlos Saúl Menem (two-term president: first six-year term under the Constitution of 1853; second four-year term under the Constitution of 1994, which permitted the immediate reelection of a sitting president)

1999–2001	Fernando de la Rúa (resigned during the economic and political crisis of 2001)
December 2001	Ramón Puerta (interim president following the resignation of De la Rúa; succeeded as the result of his position as provisional president of the National Senate)
December 2001	Adolfo Rodríguez Saá (interim president elected by Congress following the resignation of Puerta; charged with organizing new elections within three months; resigned after a week in office)
30 Dec. 2001–2 January 2002	Eduardo Camaño (interim president; president of the Chamber of Deputies, next in the line of succession on the resignation of Rodríguez Saá)
2002–2003	Eduardo Duhalde (elected president by Congress following the resignation of Camaño to serve out the balance of De la Rúa's term)
2003–2007	Néstor Kirchner
2007–2015	Cristina Fernández de Kirchner (two-term president, 2007–2011 and 2011–2015)
2015–	Mauricio Macri

* In 1860, the name of the country was officially decreed to be the Argentine Republic. Between 1853 and 1860s, Argentine Republic and Argentine Nation had been used interchangeable. In some official documents, United Provinces continued to be used between 1853 and 1860. The province of Buenos Aires seceded from the Confederation in 1852, rejoining in 1860. During this time, Buenos Aires adopted the title State of Buenos Aires; the title of governor was retained for the head of the province/state.

Appendix B

Argentine Provinces

Province	Population	Area (km²)	Population Density (km²)
Buenos Aires	15,625,084	307,571	50.8
Catamarca	367,828	102,602	3.6
Chaco	1,055,259	99,633	10.6
Chubut	509,108	224,686	2.3
Córdoba	3,308,879	165,321	20.0
Corrientes	992,595	88.199	11.3
Entre Ríos	1,295,121	78,781	16.4
Formosa	568,331	72,066	7.9
Jujuy	673,307	53,219	12.7
La Pampa	318,951	143,440	2.2
La Rioja	333,642	89,680	3.7
Mendoza	1,738,929	148,827	11.7
Misiones	1,101,593	29,801	37.0
Neuquén	551,266	94,078	5.9
Río Negro	638,645	203,013	3.1
Salta	1,214,441	155,488	7.8
San Juan	681,055	89,651	7.6
San Luis	432,310	76,748	5.6
Santa Cruz	273,964	243,943	1.1
Santa Fe	3,194,537	133,007	24.0
Santiago del Estero	874,006	136,351	6.4
Tierra del Fuego	127,205	21,263	6.0
Tucumán	1,448,188	22,524	64.3
Autonomous City of Buenos Aires	2,890,151	200	1,4450.1

Bibliography

CONTENTS

INTRODUCTION

Writing about the modern history of Argentina originated in 19th-century contemporary works about the struggle for independence, subsequent civil wars and process of state-building, and the natural history of the region. Narratives and analyses of politics and conflict written by intellectuals and soldier-statesmen like Juan Bautista Alberdi, Bartolomé Mitre, and Domingo Faustino Sarmiento have stood the test of time, as have passages about people, places, and daily life in the River Plate and Patagonia in Charles Darwin's *Voyage of the Beagle*. By 1900, writing about history was becoming professionalized, though the focus remained largely on politics, now including such themes as the development of national political institutions, the federalization of the city of Buenos Aires, and the expansion of the frontier. Relations with neighboring republics and more general accounts of foreign affairs also appeared. Insights into social history were offered by historical studies and technical manuals on ranching and farming, debates about land tenure and colonization, and discussion about the "social question"—largely addressed within the context of immigration. What might be described as intellectual history and cultural histories was a feature of the early decades of the 20th century, partly associated with social change, including labor agitation, and demands for political reform; the study of contending ideologies of the period, social problems, and accounts of political organization were covered in monographs and essays and featured in the serious and specialist press. Much of this work was stimulated by the celebration of the centenary of independence in 1910.

Distinct schools of historical thought were beginning to appear by the 1920s. The National Academy of History diffused what might be described as an officialist view of national development since the May Revolution of 1810, associated with the prevailing liberal view of history as progress illustrated by the emergence of a unified nation-state, the ending of the tyranny of civil conflict with the politics of conciliation around 1880, the realization of the democratic and modern values enshrined in the Constitution of 1853, and economic progress—all of which were propelling the country to a significant place in the world and modernity. A counterview was offered by the revisionist school, which focused on the erosion of traditional values and constraints on national sovereignty resulting from the imperialistic design of

British commercial and financial interests, which had suborned sections of the landed elite. For this group, which included writers of the left and the right, the way forward lay in fostering a distinct national project of development that integrated society and economy through domestic industrial growth—a view of progress quite different from the internationalist, agro-export model that had dominated since the 1880s.

These different views—liberal versus nationalist—of the past, present, and the future would be sharpened as the country entered a period of economic stasis and political upheaval. A consequence of military intervention in politics in the third quarter of the 20th century would be a decline in the quality and quantity of historical production in the country, and a tendency for new approaches to the study of Argentine history to develop aboard, often pioneered by academics expelled from national universities, or who had felt constrained to emigrate. What became known as "traditional history" consolidated between the 1930s and the 1950s, placing emphasis on methodology and ideology and a reassessment of documents and established texts. This approach was particularly associated with Emiliano Ravignani, who would later give his name to the distinguished historical institute established at the University of Buenos Aires. The result was a rewriting of 19th-century history, giving a less dichotomized account of events and individuals of the period. For example, the Buenos Aires caudillo Juan Manuel de Rosas, who had been demonized by liberal historians of the 19th century, though applauded as a defender of the national interest by revisionists of the 1920s, was reintegrated into the pantheon of national figures as a proponent of federalism. For some, Rosas was a populist, for others a popular and protodemocratic leader. History was being re-presented as modern, democratic, and inclusive. There was a related vindication of traditional values as epitomized by the gaucho—hitherto, the gaucho, as with the caudillo, had been depicted as backward looking and un- if not antimodern. The issue of Britain and imperialism was revisited: for nationalists, the evils of imperialism were a function of external forces, for the left due to the attitude of the elite.

Inevitably, Peronism and populism have become a defining topic in history and the historiography since the mid-20th century. For some nationalists, there was a direct line between Juan Manuel de Rosas and Juan Domingo Perón in terms of popular mobilization and the incorporation of the masses into the democratic political life of the country. It was the liberal, internationalist project of the 19th century and international capitalism that had sold the country short. Perón and organized urban, industrial labor were the route to economic and social modernization. A narrow, crabbed view of national history and the nature of polity and society resulted with the military coups of 1966 and 1976. This, especially in the 1970s, was when post-1930 history and work on themes relating to social and economic history closed down. Authorized "history" became nationalistic and mainly 19th century in focus.

Laudatory accounts of the role of the armed forces in nation building and the defense of national sovereignty since independence became "safe" history. Writing on themes connected with demographic, socioeconomic, and modern cultural history would not emerge until the return of democracy in 1983. Only since the 1980s has there been a more balanced discussion of the place of industry and agriculture—and economic policy—in national development, and an assessment of the role of the state in economy and society, as research and publications have drawn on concepts and ideas from the social sciences as well as traditional historical methods to reappraise and reinterpret the immediate and recent past. Such new intellectual currents and themes were associated with the return of academics who had fled the country in the 1960s and 1970s and students who had been trained abroad in France, Great Britain, Mexico, the United States, and elsewhere. Argentine history is now larger and more thematically diverse than it was, though ideology and the experience of the Proceso de Reorganización Nacional continue to divide and color interpretations of history—memory remains a powerful reference point shaping approaches to the writing about past events, recent or distant. The writing of history—not only about national events, individual presidencies, Peronism, and the Proceso—is highly politicized, refracted through the prism of the present.

HISTORY

General

Bethell, Leslie, ed. *Argentina since Independence*. Cambridge: Cambridge University Press, 1993.

Cortés Conde, Roberto. *The Political Economy of Argentina in the Twentieth Century*. New York: Cambridge University Press, 2009.

Chudnovsky, Daniel. *The Elusive Quest for Growth in Argentina*. London: Routledge, 2007.

Crawley, Eduardo. *A House Divided: Argentina 1880–1980*. London: C. Hurst & Co., 1984.

Fraga, Rosendo. *¿Qué Hubiera Pasado Si . . . ? Historia Argentina Contrafáctica*. Buenos Aires: Ediciones B, 2008.

Joslin, David. *A Century of Banking in Latin America*. London: Oxford University Press, 1963.

Lewis, Colin M. *Argentina: A Short History*. Oxford: Oneworld, 2002.

Luna, Félix. *Breve historia de los argentinos*. 3rd Edition. Buenos Aires: Planeta, 1998.

Marichal, Carlos. *A Century of Debt Crises in Latin America.* Princeton, NJ: Princeton University Press, 1989.

Molano, Walter T. *In the Land of Silver: 200 Years of Argentine Political-Economic Development.* North Charleston, SC: CreateSpace, 2013.

Platt, D. C. M., ed. B*usiness Imperialism, 1840–1930: An Inquiry Based on British Experience in Latin America.* Oxford: Clarendon Press, 1977.

Rapoport, Mario. *Historia económica, política y social de la Argentina (1880–2000).* 2nd ed. Buenos Aires: Ediciones Macchi, 2003.

Rock, David. *Argentina, 1516–1987: From Spanish Colonization to Alfonsín.* Los Angeles: University of California Press, 1987.

———, ed. *Argentina in the Twentieth Century.* London: Duckworth, 1975.

Sabato, Hilda, Marcela Ternavasio, Luciano De Privitellio, and Ana Virginia Persello. *Historia de las Elecciones en la Argentina, 1805–2011.* Buenos Aires: Editorial El Ateneo, 2011.

Sarmiento, Domingo F. *Facundo: civilización y barbarie.* Garden City, NJ: Doubleday, 1961.

Solberg, Carl. *Oil and Nationalism in Argentina.* Stanford, CA: Stanford University Press, 1979.

Pre-Colombian

Bustinza, Juan Antonio, and Ciro René Lafón. *Historia precolombina, colonial y argentina hasta 1820.* Buenos Aires: A–Z Editora, 1994.

González, Rex, and José Antonio Pérez. *Historia argentina. Argentina indígena a las vísperas de la conquista.* Buenos Aires: Paidós, 1987.

Mandrini, Raúl. *La Argentina aborigen. De los primeros pobladores a 1910.* Buenos Aires: Siglo XXI, 2008.

Colonial

Assadourian, Carlos Sempat, ed. *Hisotria argentina. De la conquista a la Independencia.* Buenos Aires: Paidós, 1972.

Cicerchia, Ricardo. *Historia de la vida privada en la Argentina.* Buenos Aires: Troquel, 1998.

Fradkin, Raúl Osvaldo, ed. *La historia agrarian del Río de la Plata colonial. Los establecimientos productivos.* Buenos Aires: Centro Editor de América Latina, 1993.

Garavaglia, Juan Carlos. *Mercado interno y economía colonial.* Mexico City: Enlance-Grijalbo, 1983.

Garavaglia, Juan Carlos, and José Luis Moreno, eds. *Población, sociedad, familias y migraciones en el espacio rioplatense: siglos XVIII y XIX.* Buenos Aires: Cántaro, 1993.

806 • BIBLIOGRAPHY

Gelman, Jorge. *Campesinos y estancieros. Una region del Río de la Plata a fines de la época colonial*. Buenos Aires: Los Libros del Riel, 1998.

Lynch, John. *Spanish Colonial Administration, 1782–1810: The Intendent System in the Viceroyalty of the Río de la Plata*. London: Athlone Press, 1958.

Mayo, Carlos, ed. *La historia agraria del interior. Haciendas jesuíticas de Córdoba e el Noreste*. Buenos Aires: Centro Editor de América Latina, 1994.

Mörner, Magnus. *Las actividades políticas y económicas de los jesuitas en el Río de la Plata*. Buenos Aires: Hyspamérica, 1985.

Moutoukias, Zacarías. *Contrabando y control colonial. Buenos Aires y el espacio peruano en el siglo XVII*. Buenos Aires: Centro Editor de América Latina, 1989.

Socolow, Susan. *The Bureaucrats of Buenos Aires, 1769–1810: Amor al Real Servicio*. Durham, NC: Duke University Press, 1987.

———. *The Merchants of Buenos Aires, 1778–1810*. Cambridge: Cambridge University Press, 1978.

Independence and Early National Period

Adelman, Jeremy. "Between Order and Liberty: Juan Bautista Alberdi and the Intellectual Origins of Argentina Constitutionalism." *Latin America Research Review* 40, no. 2 (2007): 86–110.

———. *Republic of Capital: Buenos Aires and the Legal Transformation of the Atlantic World*. Stanford, CA: Stanford University Press, 1999.

Amaral, Samuel. *The Rise of Capitalism on the Pampas: The Estancias of Buenos Aires, 1785–1870.* Cambridge: Cambridge University Press, 1998.

Brown, Jonathan C. *A Socioeconomic History of Argentina, 1776–1860*. Cambridge: Cambridge University Press, 1979.

Burgin, Miron. *The Economic Aspects of Argentine Federalism, 1820–1852*. Cambridge, MA: Harvard University Press, 1946.

Bushnell, David. *Reform and Reaction in the Platine Provinces, 1810–52*. Gainesville: University Press of Florida, 1983.

Chiaramonte, José Carlos. *Ciudades, Provincias, Estado: Orígenes de la Nación Argentina (1800–1846)*. Buenos Aires: Ariel, 1997.

———. *Nacionalismo y liberalismo económicos en la Argentina, 1860–1880*. Buenos Aires: Solar/Hachette, 1971.

Ferns, Harry S. *Britain and Argentine in the Nineteenth Century*. Oxford: Clarendon Press, 1960.

Gallo, Klaus. *Great Britain and Argentina: From Invasion to Recognition, 1806–1826*. London: Palgrave/Macmillan, 2002.

Garavaglia, Juan Carlos, and Jorge Gelman. "Rural History of the Rio de la Plata, 1600–1850: Results of a Historiographical Renaissance." *Latin American Research Review* 30, no. 3 (1995): 75–105.

Garravaglia, Juan Carlos, Jorge Gelman, and Blanca Zeberio, eds. *Expansión capitalista y transformaciones regionales: Relaciones sociales y empresas agrarias en la Argentina del siglo XIX.* Buenos Aires: Editorial La Colmena, 1999.

Gelman, Jorge. "New Perspectives on an Old Problem and the Same Source: The Gaucho and the Rural History of the Colonial Rio de la Plata." *Hispanic American Historical Review* 69, no. 4 (November 1989): 715–31.

Halperín Donghi, Tulio. *De la revolución de independencia a la confederación rosista.* Buenos Aires: Paidós, 1980.

———. *Politics, Economics and Society in Argentina in the Revolutionary Period.* Cambridge: Cambridge University Press, 1975.

———. *Proyecto y construcción de una nación (1846–1880).* Caracas: Biblioteca Ayacucho, 1980.

———. *Tradición política española e ideología revolucionaria del mayo.* Buenos Aires: Centro Editor de América Latina, 1985.

Halperín Donghi, Tulio, Iván Jaksic, Gwen Kirkpatrick, and Francine Masiello. *Sarmiento: Author of a Nation.* Berkeley: University of California Press, 1994.

Irigoin, María Alejandra. "Inconvertible Paper Money, Inflation, and Economic Performance in Early Nineteenth Century Argentina." *Journal of Latin American Studies* 32, no. 2 (May 2000): 333–59.

Irigoin, María Alejandra, and Roberto Schmidt, eds. *La disintegracón de la economía colonial: comercio y moneda en el interior del espacio colonial, 1800-1850.* Buenos Aires: Editorial Biblos, 2003.

Katra, William. *The Argentine Generation of 1837: Echeverría, Alberdi, Sarmiento, Mitre.* Madison, NJ: Fairleigh Dickinson University Press, 1996.

Lynch, John. *Argentine Dictator: Juan Manuel de Rosas, 1829–1852.* Oxford: Oxford University Press, 1981.

———. "The River Plate Republics from Independence to the Paraguayan War." In *The Cambridge History of Latin America*, vol. 3: *From Independence to c. 1870*, edited by Leslie Bethel, 615–76. Cambridge: Cambridge University Press, 1985.

———. *San Martín: Argentine Soldier, American Hero.* New Haven, CT: Yale University Press, 2009.

McLean, David. *War, Diplomacy and Informal Empire: Britain and the Republics of La Plata, 1836–1853.* London: British Academic Press, 1995.

Reber, Vera Blinn. *British Mercantile Houses in Buenos Aires, 1810–1880.* Cambridge, MA: Harvard University Press, 1979.

Romero, Luis Alberto. *La feliz experiencia, 1820–1824*. Buenos Aires: La Bastilla, 1976.

Salvatore, Ricardo D. *Wandering Paysanos: State Order and Subaltern Experience in Buenos Aires during the Rosas Era*. Durham, NC: Duke University Press, 2003.

Sarmiento, Domingo Faustino. *Life in the Argentine Republic in the Days of the Tyrants; or, Civilisation versus Barbarism*. New York: Collier Books, 1961.

Szuchman, Mark. *Order, Family, and Community in Buenos Aires, 1810–1860*. Stanford, CA: Stanford University Press, 1988.

From National Consolidation to 1930

Adelman, Jeremy. "Between Order and Liberty: Juan Bautista Alberdi and the Intellectual Origins of Argentine Constitutionalism." *Latin American Research Review* 40, no. 2 (2007): 86–110.

Alonso, Paula. "Ideological Tensions in the Foundational Decade of 'Modern Argentina': Political Debates of the 1880s." *Hispanic American Historical Review* 87, no. 1 (2007): 3–42.

Botana, Natalio. *El orden conservador: la política argentina entre 1880 y 1916*. Buenos Aires: Sudamericana, 1977.

Botana, Natalio, and Ezequiel Gallo. *De la República posible a la República verdadera (1880–1910)*. Buenos Aires: Ariel, 1997.

Cortés Conde, Roberto. *El Progreso Argentino, 1880–1914*. Buenos Aires: Sudamericana, 1979.

Ferrari, Gustavo, and Ezequiel Gallo, eds. *La Argentina del ochenta al centenario*. Buenos Aires: Sudamericana, 1980.

Gallo, Ezequiel. *La pampa gringa*. Buenos Aires: Sudamericana, 1983.

Gallo, Ezequiel, and Roberto Cortés Conde. *La formación de la Argentina moderna*. Buenos Aires: Paidós, 1973.

Munck, Ronaldo. "Cycles of Class Struggle and the Mobilisation of the Working Class in Argentina, 1890–1920." *Journal of Latin American Studies* 19, no. 1 (February 1987): 19–39.

Pineda, Yovanna. *Industrial Development in a Frontier Economy: The Industrialization of Argentina, 1890–1930*. Stanford, CA: Stanford University Press, 2009.

Regalsky, Andrés. *Las inversiones extranjeras en la Argentina (1860–1914)*. Buenos Aires: Centro Editor de América Latina, 1986.

Rocchi, Fernando. *Chimneys in the Desert: Industrialization in Argentina during the Export Boom Years, 1870–1930*. Stanford, CA: Stanford University Press, 2006.

Rock, David. *Politics in Argentina 1890–1930: The Rise and Fall of Radicalism*. Cambridge: Cambridge University Press, 2009.

———. *State Building and Political Movements in Argentina, 1860–1916*. Stanford, CA: Stanford University Press, 2002.

Sabato, Hilda, and Alberto Lettieri, eds. *La vida política en la Argentina del siglo XIX: Armas, votos y voces*. Buenos Aires: Fondo de Cultura Económica, 2003.

Scobie, James R. *Revolution on the Pampas: A Social History of Argentine Wheat, 1860–1910*. Austin: University of Texas Press, 1964.

Vázquez Presedo, Vicente. *El caso argentino: migración de factores, comercio exterior y desarrollo, 1875–1914*. Buenos Aires: Eudeba, 1971.

Williams, John. *Argentine International Trade under Inconvertible Paper Currency, 1880–1900*. Westport, CT: Greenwood Press 1969.

Zimmermann, Eduardo. *Los liberales reformistas. La cuestión social en la Argentina, 1890–1916*. Buenos Aires: Sudamericana, 1995.

From the 1930 Coup to Redemocratization in 1983

Adamovsky, Ezequiel. *Historia de la clase media argentina. Apogeo y decadencia de una ilusión, 1919–2003*. Buenos Aires: Planeta, 2009.

Alen Lascano, Luis. *Yrigoyenismo y antipersonalismo*. Buenos Aires: Centro Editor de América Latina, 1986.

Alhadeff, Peter. "Dependency, Historiography and Objections to the Roca Pact." In *Latin America: Economic Imperialism and the State*, edited by Christopher Abel and Colin M. Lewis, 367–78. London: Bloomsbury, 2015.

Armus, Diego, ed. *Mundo urbano y cultura popular. Estudios de historia social argentina*. Buenos Aires: Sudamericana, 1990.

Falcoff, Mark, and Ronald H. Dolkart, eds. *Prologue to Perón: Argentina in Depression and War, 1930–1943*. Berkeley: University of California Press, 1975.

Germani, Gino. *Authoritarianism, Fascism, and National Populism*. New Brunswick, NJ: Transaction Books, 1978.

Goldwert, Marvin. *Democracy, Militarism, and Nationalism in Argentina, 1930–1966*. Austin: University of Texas Press, 1972.

Halperín Donghi, Túlio. *La república imposible (1930–1945)*. Buenos Aires: Emecé, 1995.

Horowitz, Joel. "Populism and Its Legacies in Argentina." In *Populism in Latin America*, edited by Michael L. Conniff, 22–42. Tuscaloosa: University of Alabama Press, 1999.

Lewis, Paul H. *The Crisis of Argentine Capitalism*. Chapel Hill: University of North Carolina Press, 1990.

810 • BIBLIOGRAPHY

Luna, Félix. *El 45. Crónica de un año decisivo.* Buenos Aires: Sudamericana, 1981.

———. *Golpes militares y salidas electorales.* 2nd ed. Buenos Aires: Sudamericana, 1995.

———. *La Argentina de Perón a Lanusse, 1943–1973.* Buenos Aires: Planeta, 1993.

McComb, Robert, and Carlos E. J. M. Zarazaga. "Argentina." In *The Political Economy of Latin America in the Postwar Period,* edited by Laura Randall, 149–84. Austin: University of Texas Press, 1997.

Nállim, Jorge. *Transformations and Crisis of Liberalism in Argentina, 1930–1955.* Pittsburgh: Pittsburgh University Press, 2012.

Rein, Raanan. *Peronismo, populismo, y política, Argentina 1943–1955.* Buenos Aires: Editorial de Belgrano, 1998.

Rock, David. *Authoritarian Argentina: The Nationalist Movement, Its History and Its Impact.* Berkeley: University of California Press, 1993.

Rodríguez Lamas, Daniel. *Las presidencia de Frondizi.* Buenos Aires: Centro de Editor de América Latina, 1984.

———. *La presidencia de José María Guido.* Buenos Aires: Centro de Editor de América Latina, 1990.

———. *La Revolución Libertadora.* Buenos Aires: Centro de Editor de América Latina, 1985.

Romero, Luis Alberto. *Breve Historia Contemporánea de la Argentina.* 2nd ed. Buenos Aires: Fondo de Cultura Econónomica de Argentina S.A., 2001.

Waisman, Carlos. *Reversal of Development in Argentina: Postwar Counter Revolutionary Politics and Their Structural Consequences.* Princeton, NJ: Princeton University Press, 1987.

Since 1983

Arias, María Fernanda. *Carisma y poder: El asensor de Carlos Saúl Menem a la Presidencia de la Argentina (1983–1989).* Buenos Aires: Temas, 2002.

Dzwonik, Cristian (Nik). *Nik Para Todos y Todas.* Buenos Aires: La Nación/Catapulta, 2015.

Lewis, Colin M., and Nissa Torrents, eds. *Argentina in The Crisis Years (1983–1990): From Alfonsín to Menem.* London: Institute of Latin American Studies, 1993.

Lewis, Paul H. *Agony of Argentine Capitalism: From Menem to the Kirchners.* Santa Barbara, CA: Praeger/ABC-CLIO, 2009.

Norden, Deborah Lee. *Military Rebellion in Argentina: Between Coups and Consolidation.* Lincoln: University of Nebraska Press, 1996.

GOVERNMENT AND POLITICS

General

Canitrot, Adolfo. "Crisis and Transformation of the Argentine State, 1978–1992." In *Democracy, Markets and Structural Reform in Latin America: Argentina, Bolivia, Brazil, Chile and Mexico*, edited by W. C. Smith, C. H. Acuña, and E. A. Gamarra, 75–95. New Brunswick, NJ: Transaction, 1994.

Cantón, Darío. *Elecciones y partidos políicos en la Argentina (historia, interpretación y balance: 1910–1966)*. Buenos Aires: Siglo XXI, 1973.

Devoto, Fernando, and Marcela Ferrari, eds. *La construcción de las democracias rioplatenses: proyectos institucionals y prácticas políticas, 1900–1930*. Buenos Aires: Biblos/Universidad Nacional de Mar del Plata, 1994.

Germani, Gino. *Authoritarianism, Fascism, and National Populism*. New Brunswick, NJ: Transactions Books, 1978.

Melón Pirro, Julio, and Elisa Pastoriza, eds. *Los caminos de la democracia. Alternativas y prácticas políticas, 1900–1943*. Buenos Aires: Biblos, 1996.

O'Donnell, Guillermo. *Bureaucratic Authoritarianism*. Berkeley: University of California Press, 1988.

———. "The Impossible Game: Competition and Coalitions amongst Political Parties in Argentina, 1955–1966." In *Modernization and Bureaucratic Authoritarianism: Studies in South American Politics*, edited by Guillermo O'Donnell, 166–200. Berkeley: Institute of International Studies, University of California, 1973.

———. "Modernization and Military Coups: Theory, Practice and the Argentine Case." In *Armies and Politics in Latin America*, edited by Abraham F. Lowenthal, 197–243. New York: Holmes and Meier, 1976.

———. "State and Alliances in Argentina, 1956–76." *Journal of Development Studies* (London) 15, no. 1 (1978): 3–33.

Military and Politics

Botana, Natalio, Rafael Braun, and Carlos A. Floria. *El régimen militar, 1966–1973*. Buenos Aires: Ediciones La Bastilla, 1973.

De Privitellio, Luciano. *Agustín Pedro Justo. Las armas en la política*. Buenos Aires: Fondo de Cultura Económica, 1997.

Fraga, Rosendo. *Ejército: del escarnio al poder (1973–1976)*. Buenos Aires: Planeta, 1988.

Hodges, Donald C. *Argentina's "Dirty War": An Intellectual Biography.* Austin: University of Texas Press, 1991.

Lanusse, Alejandro A. *Mi testimonio.* Buenos Aires: Lasserre Editores, 1977.

Luna, Félix. *Golpes militares y salidas electorales.* 2nd ed. Buenos Aires: Sudamericana, 1995.

Novaro, Marcos, and Vicente Palermo. *La dictadura militar, 1976–1983: del golpe de estado a la restauración de la democracia.* Buenos Aires: Paidós, 2003.

Potash, Robert A. *The Army and Politics in Argentina, 1928–1945.* Stanford, CA: Stanford University Press, 1969.

———. *The Army and Politics in Argentina, 1945–1962.* London: Athlone Press, 1980.

———. *The Army and Politics in Argentina, 1962–1973.* Stanford, CA: Stanford University Press, 1996.

———. "The Military under Alfonsín and Menem: The Search for a New Role." In *Argentina in the Crisis Years (1983–1990): From Alfonsín to Menem,* edited by Colin M. Lewis and Nissa Torrents, 53–72. London: Institute of Latin American Studies, 1993.

Rouquié, Alain. *Poder military y sociedad política en la Argentina.* 2 vols. Buenos Aires: Emecé, 1981.

Saenz Quesada, María. *La Libertadora (1955–1958). De Perón a Frondizi: Historia Pública y Secreta.* Buenos Aires: Sudamericana, 2007.

Smith, William C. *Authoritarianism and the Crisis of the Argentine Political Economy.* Stanford, CA: Stanford University Press, 1991.

Yofre, Juan B. *"Fuimos Todos": Cronologia de un fracaso, 1976–1983.* 5th ed. Buenos Aires: Sudamericana, 2007.

Zanatta, Loris. *Del Estado liberal a la nación católica. Iglesia y Ejército en los orígenes del peronismo, 1930–1943.* Buenos Aires: Universidad Nacional de Quilmes, 1999.

Political Parties and Interest Groups

Acha, Omar. *Asociaciones y política en la Argentina del siglo veinte: entre prácticas y expectativas.* Buenos Ares: Prometeo, 2015.

Adelman, Jeremy. "Socialism and Democracy in Argentina in the Age of the Second International." *Hispanic American Historical Review* 72 no. 2 (May 1992): 211–38.

Alonso, Paula. *Between Revolution and the Ballot Box: The Origins of the Argentine Radical Party in the 1890s.* Cambridge: Cambridge University Press, 2000.

Barbero, María Inés, and Fernando Devoto. *Los nacionalistas.* Buenos Aires: Centro Editor de América Latina, 1983.

Bianchi, Susana, and Norma Sanchis. *El partido peronista feminina (1949–1955)*. Buenos Aires: Centro Editor de América Latina, 1988.

Bramuglia, Juan Atilio. *Jubilaciones ferroviarias: La influencia de la acción sindical de los trabajadores en la formación de las leyes*. Buenos Aires: Unión Ferroviaria, 1941.

Brennan, James, and Marcelo Rougier. *The Politics of National Capitalism: Perón and the Argentine Bourgeoisie, 1946–1976*. University Park: Pennsylvania State University Press, 2009.

Burdick, Michael. *For God and the Fatherland: Religion and Politics in Argentina*. Albany: State University of New York Press, 1995.

Calello, Osvaldo, and Daniel Parcero. *De Vandor a Ubaldini*. Buenos Aires: Centro Editor de América Latina, 1984.

Cantón, Darío. *Elecciones y partidos políticos en la Argentina (historia, interpretación y balance: 1910–1966)*. Buenos Aires: Siglo XXI, 1973.

Castel, Pablo. *Empresariado nacional y cambios social*. Buenos Aires: El Ateneo, 1985.

Ciria, Alberto. *Parties and Power in Modern Argentina, 1930–1946*. Albany: State University of New York Press, 1974.

Clementi, Hebe. *El radicalismo. Trayectoria política*. Buenos Aires: Siglo Veinte, 1983.

Gallo, Ricardo. *Balbin, Frondizi y la division del radicalismo (1956–1958)*. Buenos Aires: Editorial de Belgrano, 1983.

Gay, Luis. *El Partido Laborista en la Argentina*. Buenos Aires: Biblos, 1999.

González Janzen, Ignacio. *La Triple A*. Buenos Aires: Contrapunto, 1986.

Hora, Roy. *Los terratenientes de la pampa argentina: Una historia social y política, 1860–1945*. Buenos Aires: Siglo XXI, 2002.

Ivereigh, Austen. *Catholicism and Politics in Argentina, 1810–1960*. New York: St. Martin's Press, 1995.

López, Mario Justo, Jr. *Entre el hegemonía y el pluralismo: Evolución del sitema de partidos políticos argentinos*. Buenos Aires: Lumiere, 2001.

Lucchini, Cristina. *Apoyo industrial en los orígenes del peronismo*. Buenos Aires: Centro Editor de América Latina, 1990.

McGee Deutsch, Sandra. *Las Derechas: The Extreme Right in Argentina, Brazil, and Chile, 1890–1939*. Stanford, CA: Stanford University Press, 1999.

McGee Deutsch, Sandra, and Ronald H. Dolkart, eds. *The Argentine Right: Its History and Intellectual Origins, 1910 to the Present*. Wilmington, DE: Scholarly Research Books, 1993.

Mignone, Emilio. *Iglesia y Dictadura*. Buenos Aires: Ediciones del Pensarmiento Nacional, 1986.

Munck, Ronaldo, Ricardo Falcón, and Bernardo Gallitelli. *Argentina from Anarchism to Peronism: Unions, Workers and Politics*. London: Zed Books, 1986.

Ostiguy, Pierre. *Argentina's Double Political Spectrum: Party Systems, Political Identities, and Strategies, 1944–2007*. Notre Dame, IN: Helen Kellogg Institute for International Studies, 2009.

Persello, Ana Virginia. *El radicalismo argentino en crisis, 1930–1943*. Rosario: Fundación Ross, 1996.

Pont, Elena Susana. *Partido Laborista: Estado y sindicatos*. Buenos Aires: Centro Editor de América Latina, 1984.

Prost, Alison E. *Foreign and Domestic Investment in Argentina: The Politics of Privatization*. New York: Cambridge University Press, 2014.

Puiggrós, Rodolfo. *Historia crítica de los partidos politicos argentinos*. Buenos Aires: Hyspanoamérica, 1986.

Rock, David. *Politics in Argentina, 1890–1930: The Rise and Fall of Radicalism*. Cambridge: Cambridge University Press, 2009.

Sabato, Jorge Federico. *La clase dominante en la formación de la Argentina*. Buenos Aires: CISEA/GEL, 1987.

Sáenz Quesada, María. *Los estancieros*. 2nd ed. Buenos Aires: Sudamericana, 1998.

Sanguinetti, Horacio. *Los socialistas independientes*. Buenos Aires: Editorial de Belgrano, 1981.

Schvarzer, Jorge. *Empresarios del pasado: La Unión Industrial Argentina*. Buenos Aires: CISEA/Imago Mundi, 1991.

Smith, Peter H. *Politics and Beef in Argentina: Patterns of Conflict and Change*. New York: Columbia University Press, 1969.

Szusterman, Celia. *Frondizi and the Politics of Developmentalism, 1955–62*. Basingstoke, UK: St. Antony's/Macmillan, 1993.

Torre, Juan Carlos, ed. *La formación del sindicalismo peronista*. Buenos Aires: Legasa, 1988.

Unión Ferroviaria. *Los 16 puntos de los ferroviarios argentinos*. Buenos Aires: 1944.

Walter, Richard. *The Socialist Party of Argentina, 1890–1930*. Austin: University of Texas Press, 1977.

Zaragoza, Gonzálo. *Anarquismo argentino (1876–1902)*. Madrid: Ediciones De la Torre, 1996.

Zanatta, Loris. *Del Estado liberal a la nación católica. Iglesia y Ejército en los orígenes del Peronismo. 1930–1943*. Buenos Aires: Universidad Nacional de Quilmes, 1996.

———. *Perón y el mito de una nación católica*. Buenos Aires: Sudamericana, 1999.

Perón and Peronism

Aizcorbe, Roberto. *Argentina, the Peronist Myth: An Essay on the Cultural Decay of Argentina after the Second World War*. Hicksville, NY: Exposition Press, 1975.

Amaral, Samuel, and Mariano Ben Plotkin, eds. *Perón del exilio al poder*. Buenos Aires: Cántaro, 1993.

Barco, Ricardo del. *El régimen peronista, 1946–1955*. Buenos Aires: Editorial de Belgrano, 1983.

Bianchi, Susana, and Norma Sanchis. *El partido peronista femenino, 1949–1955*. Buenos Aires: Centro Editor de América Latina, 1988.

Brennan, James, ed. *Peronism and Argentina*. Wilmington, DE: Scholarly Resources, 1998.

Buchruker, Cristián. *Nacionalismo y peronismo: La Argentina en las crisis ideológica mundial (1927–1955)*. Buenos Aires: Sudamericana, 1987.

Caimari, Lila. *Perón y la Iglesia Católica*. Buenos Aires: Ariel, 1995.

Camarasa, Jorge A. *La enviada: El viaje de Eva Perón a Europa*. Buenos Aires: Planeta, 1998.

Chávez, Fermín, *Eva Perón en la Historia*. Buenos Aires: Oriente, 1986.

———. *Eva Perón sin mitos*. Buenos Aires: Ediciones Teoría, 1996.

Ciria, Alberto. *Cultura y Política Popular: La Argentina Peronista, 1946–1955*. Buenos Aires: De la Flor, 1983.

Crespo, Jorge. *El coronel Perón*. Buenos Aires: Ayer y Hoy Ediciones, 1998.

Di Tella, Guido. *Argentina under Perón, 1973–1976: The Nation's Experience with a Labour-Based Government*. Basingstoke, UK: St. Antony's/Macmillan, 1983.

Eloy Martínez, Tomás. *Las Vidas del General*. Buenos Aires: Aguiar, 2004.

Gambini, Hugo. *Historia del Peronismo: El poder total (1943–1951)*. Buenos Aires: Editorial Planeta, 1999.

———. *Historia del Peronismo: La obsecuencia (1952–1955)*. Buenos Aires: Editorial Planeta, 2001.

———. *Historia del Peronismo: La violencia (1956–1983)*. Buenos Aires: Javier Vergara Editor, 2008.

Gillespie, Richard. *Soldiers of Perón: Argentina's Montoneros*. New York: Oxford University Press, 1982.

Halperín Donghi, Tulio. *Argentina en el callejón*. Buenos Aires: Ariel, 1995.

———. *La larga agonía de la Argentina peronista*. Buenos Aires: Ariel, 1994.

Horowitz, Joel. *Argentine Unions, the State, and the Rise of Peronism*. Berkeley: University of California Press, 1990.

James, Daniel. *Resistance and Integration: Peronism and the Argentine Working Class, 1946–1976*. Cambridge: Cambridge University Press, 1988.

Karush, Mathew, and Oscar Chamosa. *The New Cultural History of Peronism*. Durham, NC: Duke University Press, 2010.

Lewis, Paul H. "Was Perón a Fascist? An Inquiry into the Nature of Fascism." *Journal of Politics* 42, no. 1 (February 1980): 242–56.

Lucchini, Cristiana. *Apoyo empresarial en los origenes del peronismo*. Buenos Aires: Centro de Editor América Latina, 1990.

Luna, Félix. *Perón y su tiempo*. 2nd ed. Buenos Aires: Sudamericana, 1993.

Mackinnon, Moira. *Los años formativos del Partido Peronista (1946–1950)*. Buenos Aires: Siglo XXI, 2002.

McGuire, James W. *Peronism without Perón: Unions, Parties, and Democracy in Argentina*. Stanford, CA: Stanford University Press, 1997.

Mercante, Domingo Alfredo. *Marcante: El corazón de Perón*. Buenos Aires: De la Flor, 1995.

Mora y Araujo, Manuel, and Ignacio Llorente, eds. *El voto peronista: ensayos de sociología electoral argentina*. Buenos Aires: Sudamericana, 1980.

Murmis, Miguel, and Juan Carlos Portantiero, eds. *Estudios sobre los orígenes del peronismo*. Vol. 1. Buenos Aires: Siglo XXI, 1971.

Page, Joseph A. *Perón: A Biography*. New York: Random House, 1983.

Panaia, Marta L., Ricardo Lesser, and Pedro R. Skupch. *Estudios sobre los orígenes del peronismo*. Vol. 2. Buenos Aires: Siglo XXI, 1973.

Perón, Eva Duarte de. *Evita: Eva Duarte de Perón Tells Her Own Story*. London: Proteus, 1978.

Perón, Juan Domingo. *Perón expone su doctrina*. Buenos Aires: Ed. Nueva Argentina, 1947.

Plotkin, Mariano. *Mañana es San Perón: Propaganda, rituales políticos y educación en el régimen peronista*. Buenos Aires: Ariel, 1994.

Potash, Robert. *Perón y el GOU: Los documentos de una logia secreta*. Buenos Aires: Sudamericana, 1984.

Rein, Raanan. *In the Shadow of Perón: Juan Atilio Bramuglia and the Second Line of Argentina's Populist Movement*. Stanford, CA: Stanford University Press, 2008.

Reyes, Cipriano. *La farsa de peronismo*. Buenos Aires: Sudamericana/Planeta, 1987.

———. *Yo hice el 17 de octubre*. Buenos Aires: Centro Editor de América Latina, 1984.

Sáenz Quesada, María. *La primera presidente: Isabel Perón. Una mujer en la tormenta*. Buenos Aires: Sudamericana, 2016.

Scenna, Miguel Ángel. *FORJA: Una aventura argentina*. Buenos Aires: Editorial de Belgrano, 1972.

Sidicaro, Ricardo. *Los tres peronismos. Estado y poder económico 1946–55, 1973–76, 1989–1999*. Buenos Aires: Siglo XXI, 2005.

Tamarin, David. *The Argentine Labor Movement, 1930–1945: A Study in the Origins of Peronism*. Albuquerque: University of New Mexico Press, 1985.

Torre, Juan Carlos. *El gigante invertebrado: Los sindicatos en el gobierno, Argentina 1973–1976*. Buenos Aires: Siglo XXI, 2004.

———. *La vieja guardia sindical y Perón: Sobre los orígenes del peronismo*. Buenos Aires: Sudamericana, 1990.

Waldmann, Peter. *El peronismo*. Buenos Aires: 1981.

Yofre, Juan B. *El Escarmiento: La ofensiva de Perón contra Cámpora y los Montoneros, 1973–1974*. Buenos Aires: Sudamericana, 2010.

———. *La Trama de Madrid: Los documentos secretos sobre el retorno de Perón a la Argentina*. Buenos Aires: Sudamericana, 2013.

———. *Puerta de Hierro: Los documentos inéditos y los encuentros secretos de Perón en el exilio*. Buenos Aires: Sudamericana, 2015.

Zanatta, Loris. *Breve historia del peronismo*. Buenos Aires: Sudamericana, 2009.

Human Rights and the Mothers of the Plaza de Mayo

Brysk, Alison. *The Politics of Human Rights in Argentina: Protest, Change, and Democratization*. Stanford, CA: Stanford University Press, 1994.

Guzman Bouvard, Marguerite. *Revolutionizing Motherhood: The Mothers of the Plaza de Mayo*. Oxford: Scholarly Resources Books, 1994.

Reato, Ceferino. *Disposición Final: La confesión de Videla sobre los desaparecidos*. Buenos Aires: Editorial Sudamericana, 2012.

Dirty War/Guerra Sucia

Dinges, John. *The Condor Years: How Pinochet and His Allies Brought Terrorism to Three Continents*. New York: New Press, 2004.

Finchelstein, Federico. *The Ideological Origins of the Dirty War: Fascism, Populism and Dictatorship in Twentieth-Century Argentina*. Oxford: Oxford University Press, 2014.

Lessa, Francesca, and Vincent Druliolle, eds. *The Memory of State Terrorism in the Southern Cone: Argentina, Chile, and Uruguay*. New York: Palgrave, 2011.

Lewis, Paul H. *The Guerrilleros and Generals: The "Dirty War" in Argentina*. Westport, CT: Praeger, 2002.

Martorell, Francisco. *Operación Condor, el vuelo de muerte: La coordinación represiva en el Cono Sur*. Santiago de Chile: Lom Ediciones, 1999.

O'Donnell, Guillermo. *Catacumbas*. Buenos Aires: Prometeo, 2008.

Sheinin, David. *Consent of the Damned: Ordinary Argentinians in the Dirty War*. Gainesville: University Press of Florida, 2012.

Timerman, Jacobo. *Prisoner Without a Name, Cell Without a Number*. New York: Vintage, 1982.

FOREIGN RELATIONS

General

Ansaldi, Waldo, et al. *Argentina en la paz de dos guerras, 1914–1945*. Buenos Aires: Biblos, 1993.

Cafiero, Antonio. *La política exterior peronista, 1946–1955. El mito aislacionista*. Buenos Aires: Corregidor, 1996

Di Tella, Guido, and Donald Cameron Watt, eds. *Argentina between the Great Powers, 1939–1946*. Basingstoke, UK: St. Antony's/Macmillan, 1989.

Di Tella, Torcuato S., ed. *Argentina–Chile: ¿desarrollos paralelos?* Buenos Aires: Nuevohacer, 1997.

Dorn, Glenn J. "'Bruce Plan' and the Marshall Plan: The United States' Intervention against Peronism in Argentina, 1947–1950." *International History Review* 21, no. 2 (1999): 331–51.

———. "Peron's Gambit: The United States and the Argentine Challenge to the Inter-American Order, 1946–1948." *Diplomatic History* 26, no. 1 (2002): 1–20.

Escudé, Carlos. *Gran Bretaña, Estados Unidos y la Declinación Argentina, 1942–1949*. 4th ed. Buenos Aires: Editorial de Belgrano, 1996.

———. *La Argentina vs. las grandes potencias: El precio del desafío*. Buenos Aires: Editorial de Belgrano, 1986.

Escudé, Carlos, and Andrés Cisneros. *Historia General de las Relaciones Exteriores de la República Argentina*. Buenos Aires: Cari, 1998.

Frank, Gary. *Juan Perón vs. Spruille Braden: The Story behind the Blue Book*. Lanham, MD: University Press of America, 1980.

Fursman, Noel. "The Decline of the Anglo-Argentine Economic Connection in the Years Immediately after the Second World War: A British Perspective." D.Phil. diss., University of Oxford, 1988.

González, Martín A. *The Genesis of the Falklands (Malvinas) Conflict: Argentina, Britain and Failed Negotiations of the 1960s (Security, Conflict and Cooperation in the Contemporary World)*. London: Palgrave/Macmillan, 2013.

Graham-Yooll, Andrew. *The Forgotten Colony: A History of the English-Speaking Communities in Argentina*. London: Hutchinson, 1981.

Grenville, J. A. S., and Bernard Wasserstein. *The Major International Treaties since 1945: A History and Guide with Texts*. London: Methuen, 1987.

Hennessy, Alistair, and John King, eds. *The Land That England Lost: Argentina and Britain, a Special Relationship*. London: British Academic Press/ Tauris, 1992.

Llairó, Monserrat, Nilda Galé, and Raimundo Siepe. *Perón y las relaciones económicas con el Este*. Buenos Aires: Centro Editor de América Latina, 1994.

Llambí, Benito. *Medio siglo de política y diplomacia*. Buenos Aires: Corregidor, 1997.

MacDonald, Callum A. "The Politics of Intervention: the United States and Argentina, 1941–46." *Journal of Latin American Studies* 12, no. 2 (May 1980): 365–96.

———. "The US, the Cold War and Perón." In *Latin America: Economic Imperialism and the State*, edited by Christopher Abel and Colin M. Lewis, 405–14. London: Bloomsbury, 2015.

Monserrat Llario, María, and Raimundo Siepe. *Frondizi: Un nuevo modelo de incersión internacional*. Buenos Aires: Eudeba 2003

Peterson, Harold F. *Argentina and the United States, 1810–1960*. New York: State University of New York, 1964.

Rapoport, Mario. *¿Aliados o Neutrales? La Argentina frente a la Segunda Guerra Mundial*. Buenos Aires: Eudeba, 1988.

———. *El laberinto argentino: Política internacional en un mundo conflictivo*. Buenos Aires: Eudeba, 1997.

Rapoport, Mario, and Claudio Spiguel. *Estados Unidos y el peronismo: La política norteamericana en la Argentina, 1949–1955*. Buenos Aires: Grupo Editor Latinoamericano, 1994.

Rein, Raanan. *The Franco–Perón Alliance: Relations between Spain and Argentina, 1946–1955*. Pittsburgh: University of Pittsburgh Press, 1993.

Skupch, Pedro. "El deterioro y fin de la hegemonía británica sobre la economía argentina, 1914–47." In *Estudios sobre los orígenes del peronismo*, vol. 2, edited by L. Marta Panaia, Ricardo Lesser, and Pedro R. Skupch, 3–82. Buenos Aires: Siglo XXI, 1975.

Thompson, Andrew. "Informal Empire? An Exploration in the History of Anglo-Argentine Relations, 1810–1914." *Journal of Latin American Studies* 24, no. 2 (May 1992): 419–36.

Tulchin, Joseph S. *Argentina and the United States*. Boston: Twayne, 1990.

Vacs, Aldo César. *Discreet Partners: Argentina and the Soviet Union since 1917*. Pittsburgh: University of Pittsburgh Press, 1984.

Wood, Bryce. *The Dismantling of the Good Neighbor Policy*. Austin: University of Texas Press, 1985.

Yofre, Juan B. *Fue Cuba*. Buenos Aires: Sudamericana, 2014.

Falklands War/Guerra de la Malvinas

Argentine Army. *Informe Oficial del Ejército Argentino—Conflicto Malvinas*. 2 vols. Buenos Aires: Estado Mayor General del Ejército Argentino, 1983.

Beck, Peter J. *The Falkland Islands as an International Problem*. London: Routledge, 1988.

Boyce, D. George. *The Falklands War*. London: Palgrave, 2017.

Brands, H. W. *Reagan: The Life*. New York: Doubleday, 2015.

Debat, Alejandro, and Luis Lorenzano. *Argentina: The Malvinas and the End of Military Rule*. London: Verso, 1984.

Donaghy, Aaron. *The British Government and the Falkland Islands, 1974–79*. Basingstoke, UK: Palgrave Macmillan, 2014.

Freedman, Lawrence. *The Official History of the Falklands Campaign*. 2 vols. London: Routledge, 2005.

Thatcher, Margaret. *The Downing Street Years*. London: HarperCollins, 1993.

Yofre, Juan B. *1982: Los documentos secretos de la Guerra de Malvinas/ Falklands y el derrumbe del Proceso*. 3rd ed. Buenos Aires: Sudamericana, 2011.

ECONOMY

General

Arceo, Nicolás, Mariana González, Nuria Mendizábal, and Eduardo M. Basualde. *La economía argentina de la posconvertibilidad en tiempos de crisis mundial*. Buenos Aires: Centro de Investigación y Formación de la República Argentina/Central de Trabajadores de la Argentina, 2010.

Basualdo, Eduardo. *Concentración y centralización del capital en la Argentina durante la década del noventa*. Quilmes: Universidad Nacional de Quilmes, 2000.

———. *Estudios de historia económica argentina: desde mediados del siglo XX a la actualidad*. Buenos Aires: FLACSO/Siglo XXI, 2006.

Braun, Miguel, and Lucas Llach. *Macroeconomía argentina*. Buenos Aires: Alfaomega, 2007.

Casella, Beto, and Darío Villarruel. *La mano en la lata: Diccionario de la corrupción argentina*. Buenos Aires: Editorial Grijalbo, 2000.

Cortés Conde, Roberto. *La economía argentina en el largo plazo (siglos XIX y XX)*. Buenos Aires: Sudamericana, 1997.

Della Paolera, Gerardo, and Alan M. Taylor, eds. *A New Economic History of Argentina*. Cambridge: Cambridge University Press, 2003.

Di Tella, Guido, and Rudiger Dornbusch, eds. *The Political Economy of Argentina, 1946–83*. London: St. Antony's/Macmillan, 1989.

Di Tella, Guido, and D. C. M. Platt, eds. *The Political Economy of Argentina, 1880–1946*. London: St. Antony's/Macmillan, 1986.

Di Tella, Guido, and Miguel Zymelman. *Las etapas del desarrollo econónomico argentino*. Buenos Aires: Eudeba, 1967.

Díaz Alejandro, Carlos F. *Essays on the Economic History of the Argentine Republic*. New Haven, CT: Yale University Press, 1970.

Ferrer, Aldo. *The Argentine Economy: An Economic History of Argentina*. Berkeley: University of California Press, 1967.

———. *El capitalismo argentino*. Buenos Aires: Fondo de Cultura Económica, 1998.

———. *La Economía Argentina: Desde sus Orígenes hasta los Principios del Siglo XXI*. Buenos Aires: Fondo de Cultura Económica, 2004.

Fodor, Jorge, and Arturo O'Connell. "La Argentina y la economía atlántica en la primera mitad del siglo XX." *Desarrollo Económico* 13, no. 49 (April–June 1973): 3–65.

García Heras, Raúl. *Transportes, negocios y política: la Compañía Anglo-Argentina de Tranvías, 1870–1981*. Buenos Aires: Sudamericana, 1994.

Gerchunoff, Pablo, and Lucas Llach. *El ciclo de la ilusión y el desencanto. Un siglo de políticas económicas argentinas*. Buenos Aires: Ariel, 1998.

Halperín Donghi, Tulio. "Canción de otoño en primavera: previsions sobre la crisis de la agricultura argentina (1894–1930)." *Desarrollo Económico* 24, no. 95 (October–December 1984): 367–86.

Leuco, Alfredo, and Jorge Antonio Díaz. *El heredero del Perón: Menem entre Dios y Diablo*. Buenos Aires: Planeta, 1988.

Miller, Rory. *Britain and Latin America in the Nineteenth and Twentieth Centuries*. London: Longman, 1993.

Ortiz, Ricardo. *Historia económica de la Argentina*. Buenos Aires: Raigal, 1955.

Randall, Laura. *An Economic History of Argentina in the Twentieth Century*. New York: Columbia University Press, 1978.

Vitelli, Guillermo. *Los Dos Siglos de la Argentina. Historica Económica Comparada*. Buenos Aires: Prendergast, 1999.

Wright, Winthrop R. *British-Owned Railways in Argentina*. Austin: University of Texas Press, 1974.

Economic Crises

Blustein, Paul. *And the Money Kept Rolling In (and Out): Wall Street, the IMF, and the Bankruptcy of Argentina.* New York: Public Affairs, 2005.

Boyer, Roberto, and Julio César Neffa, eds. *Salida de crisis y estrategias alternativas de desarrollo. La experiencia argentina.* Buenos Aires: Miño y Dávila Editores, 2007.

Brailovsky, Antonio E. *1880–1982: Historia de las crisis argentinas: un sacrificio inútil.* Buenos Aires: Editorial de Belgrano, 1982.

Cohen, Michael A. *Argentina's Economic Growth and Recovery: The Economy in a Time of Default.* London: Routledge, 2012.

Di Tella, Guido, and Miguel Zymelman. *Los ciclos econónomicos argentinos.* Buenos Aires: Paidós, 1973.

García Heras, Raúl. *El Fondo Monetario y el Banco Mundial en la Argentina. Liberalismo, populismo y finanzas internacionales.* Buenos Aires: Lumiere, 2008.

Gerchunoff, Pablo, and Lucas Llach. *El ciclo de la ilusión y el desencanto: un siglo de políticas económicas argentinas.* Buenos Aires: Emecé, 2007.

———. *Entre equidad y el crecimiento. Ascenso y caída de la economía argentina, 1880–2002.* Buenos Aires: Siglo XXI, 2002.

Gerchunoff, Pablo, Fernando Rocchi, and Gastón Rossi. *Desorden y Progreso. Historia de las crisis económicas argentinas.* Buenos Aires: Editorial Edhasa, 2007.

International Monetary Fund Independent Evaluation Office. *The IMF and Argentina.* Washington, DC: International Monetary Fund, 2004.

Mussa, Michael. *Argentina y el FMI. Del triumfo a la tragedia.* Madrid: Planeta, 2002.

Sanz-Villaroya, Isabel. "Economic Cycles in Argentina, 1873–1990." *Journal of Latin American Studies* 38, no. 3 (August 2006): 549–76.

Tanzi, Vito. *Argentina: An Economic Chronicle; How One of the Richest Countries in the World Lost Its Wealth.* New York: Jorge Pinto Books, 2007.

Terragno, Rodolfo. *La simulación: Argentina y la FMI: dos décadas de mentiras y autoengaños.* Buenos Aires: Planeta, 2005.

Economic Policy

Alhadeff, Peter. "The Economic Formulae of the 1930s: A Reassessment." In *The Political Economy of Argentina, 1880–1946*, edited by Guido Di Tella and D. C. M. Platt, 95–119. London: St. Antony's/Macmillan, 1986.

Bellini, Claudio. "El grupo Bunge y la política económica del primer peronismo, 1943–1952." *Latin American Research Review* 41, no. 1 (Spring 2006): 27–50.

Canitrot, Adolfo. "La experiencia populista de redistribución de ingresos." *Desarrollo Económico* 15, no. 59 (October–December 1975): 331–51.

Cramer, Gisela. "Argentine Riddle: The Pinedo Plan of 1940 and the Political Economy of the Early War Years." *Journal of Latin American Studies* 30, no. 3 (October 1998): 519–50.

Damill, Mario, and Roberto Frankel. *Las políticas macroeconómicas en la evolución de la reciente economía argentina.* Buenos Aires: Centro de Estudios de Estado y Sociedad, 2009.

Di Tella, Guido. "Economic Controversies in Argentina from the 1920s to the 1940s." In *The Political Economy of Argentina, 1880–1946*, edited by Guido Di Tella and D. C. M. Platt, 120–32. London: St. Antony's/Macmillan, 1986.

Di Tella, Guido, and Carlos Rodríguez Braun, eds. *Argentina, 1946–83. The Economic Ministers Speak.* London: St. Antony's/Macmillan, 1989.

Elena, Eduardo. "What the People Want: State Planning and Political Participation in Peronist Argentina, 1946–1955." *Journal of Latin American Studies* 37, no. 1 (February 2005): 81–108.

Frenkel, Roberto. "Heterodox Theory and Policy: The Plan Austral in Argentina." *Journal of Development Economics* 27, nos. 1–2 (1987): 307–38.

García Heras, Raúl. "Economic Stability and Sustainable Development in Argentina." *Latin American Research Review* 44, no. 1 (2009): 278–90.

Llach, Juan José. "El Plan Pinedo de 1940, su significado histórico y los orígenes de la economía peronista." *Desarrollo Económico* 23, no. 93 (January–March 1984): 515–58.

Love, Joseph L. "Raúl Prebisch and the Origins of the Doctrine of Unequal Exchange." *Latin American Research Review* 15, no. 3 (1980): 45–72.

Mallon, Richard, and Juan V. Sourrouille. *Economic Policy-Making in a Conflict Society: The Argentine Case.* Cambridge, MA: Harvard University Press, 1975.

Margheritis, Ana. *Ajuste y reforma en Argentina (1989–1995): la economía política de las privatizaciones.* Buenos Aires: Nuevohacer/Grupo Editor Latinoamericano, 1999.

Martínez de Hoz, José Alfredo. *Más allá de los mitos: Memorias y revalaciones del ministro más polémico de la historia argentina.* Buenos Aires: Sudamericana, 2014.

Massun, Ignacio. *Menem: cirugía sin anestesia.* Buenos Aires: Editorial Métodos, 1999.

Natanson, José. *Buenos muchachos: vida y obra de los economistas del "establishment."* Buenos Aires: Mileniolibre, 2005.

Novick, Susana. *IAPI: Auge y decadencia*. Buenos Aires: Centro Editor de América Latina, 1986.

Olarra Jiménez, Rafael, and Luis García Martínez. *El derrumbe argentino: de la convertibilidad al "corralito."* Buenos Aires: Planeta, 2002.

Prebisch, Raúl. "Argentine Economic Policies since the 1930s." In *The Political Economy of Argentina, 1880–1946*, edited by Guido Di Tella and D.C.M. Platt, 133–53. London: St. Antony's/Macmillan, 1986.

Prost, Alison E. *Foreign and Domestic Investment in Argentina: The Politics of Privatization*. New York: Cambridge University Press, 2014.

Sikkink Kathryn. "The Influence of Raúl Prebisch on Economic Policy-Making in Argentina, 1950–1962." *Latin American Research Review* 23, no. 2 (1988): 91–131.

Industry

Azpiazu, Daniel, and Martín Schorr. *Hecho en Argentina. Industria y economía, 1976–2007*. Buenos Aires: Siglo XXI, 2010.

Burzaco, Ricardo. *Las alas de Perón. Aeronáutica Argentina, 1945–1960*. Buenos Aires: Editorial Da Vinci, 1995.

Dorfman, Adolfo. *Cincuenta años de industrialización en la Argentina, 1930–1980*. Buenos Aires: Solar, 1983.

————. *Historia de la industria argentina*. Buenos Aires: Solar/Hachette, 1970.

Duggan, Bernardo A. "Iron and Steel Production in Argentina c. 1920–1952: Attempts at Establishing a Strategic Industry." Ph.D. diss., University of London, 1999.

Jorge, Eduardo. *Industria y concentración económica. Desde principios de siglo hasta el peronismo*. Buenos Aires: Hyspamérica, 1986.

Katz, Jorge, and Bernardo Kosacoff. *El proceso de industrialización en la Argentina: evolución, retroceso y perspectivas*. Buenos Aires: Centro Editor de América Latina, 1989.

Schvarzer, Jorge. *La industria que supimos conseguir*. Buenos Aires: Planeta, 1996.

Schvarzer, Jorge, Teresita Gómez, and Marcelo Rougier, eds. *La empresa ayer y hoy. Nuevas Investigaciones y Debates*. Buenos Aires: UBA/FCE, 2007.

Villanueva, Javier. "El orígen de la industrialización argentina." *Desarrollo Económico* (Buenos Aires) 12, no. 47 (1972): 471–76.

DEMOGRAPHY AND SOCIETY

Immigration and Settlement

Devoto, Fernando. *Historia de la inmigración en la Argentina*. Buenos Aires: Sudamericana, 2002.

———. *Movimientos migratorios: Historiografía y problemas*. Buenos Aires: Centro Editor de América Latina, 1992.

Devoto, Fernando, and Gianfausto Rosoli, eds. *La inmigración italiana en la Argentina*. Buenos Aires: Biblos, 1985.

Korn, Francis, ed. *Los italianos en la Argentina*. Buenos Aires: Fondazione Agnelli, 1981.

Korol, Juan Carlos, and Hilda Sabato. *¿Como fue la inmigración irlandesa en la Argentina?* Buenos Aires: Editorial Plus Ultra, 1981.

Sánchez Alonso, Blanca. *La inmigración española en la Argentina. Siglos XIX y XX*. Madrid: Ediciones Júcar, 1992.

Williams, Glyn. *The Desert and the Dream: A Study of Welsh Colonization in Chubut, 1865–1915*. Aberystwyth: University of Wales Press, 1975.

Labor Movement and Labor History

Adelman, Jeremy, ed. *Essays in Argentine Labour History, 1870–1930*. London: St. Antony's/Macmillan, 1992.

Bailey, Samuel L. *Labor, Nationalism, and Politics in Argentina*. New Brunswick, NJ: Rutgers University Press, 1967.

Calello, Osvaldo, and Daniel Parcero. *De Vandor a Ubaldini*. Buenos Aires: Centro Editor de América Latina, 1984.

Del Campo, Hugo. *El sindicalismo revolucionario*. Buenos Aires: CLACSO, 1986.

Horowitz, Joel. *Argentina's Radical Party and Popular Mobilization, 1916–1930*. University Park: Pennsylvania State University Press, 2008.

———. *Argentine Unions, the State, and the Rise of Perón, 1930–1945*. Berkeley: University of California Press, 1990.

———. "Ideologías sindicales y políticas estatales en la Argentina, 1930–1943." *Desarrollo Económico* 24, no. 94 (July–September 1984): 275–96.

Falcón, Ricardo. *El mundo de trabajo urbano (1890–1914)*. Buenos Aires: Centro Editor de América Latina, 1986.

Godio, Julio. *La Semana Trágica de enero de 1919*. Buenos Aires: Hyspamérica, 1986.

Matsushita, Hiroshi. *Movimiento obrero argentino, 1930–1945: sus proyecciones en los orígenes del peronismo*. Buenos Aires: Siglo Veinte, 1983.

Munck, Ronaldo, Ricardo Falcón, and Bernardo Gallitelli. *Argentina from Anarchism to Peronism: Unions, Workers and Politics.* London: Zed Books, 1986.

Panettieri, José. *Los trabajadores en tiempos de la inmigración masiva en Argentina, 1870–1910.* La Plata: Universidad Nacional de la Plata, 1966.

Pont, Elena Susana. *Partido Laborista: Estado y sindicatos.* Buenos Aires: Centro Editor de América Latina, 1984.

Tamarin, David. *The Argentine Labor Movement, 1930–1945: A Study in the Origins of Peronism.* Albuquerque: University of New Mexico Press, 1985.

Torre, Juan Carlos, ed. *La formación del sindicalismo peronista.* Buenos Aires: Legasta, 1988.

———. *La vieja guardia sindical y Perón: Sobre los orígenes del peronismo.* Buenos Aires: Sudamericana, 1988.

Urbanization

García Heras, Raúl. *Automotores norteamericanos, caminos y modernización urbana en la Argentina, 1918–1939.* Buenos Aires: Libros de Hispanoamérica, 1985.

Gorelik, Adrián. *La grilla y el parque. Espacio público y cultural urbana en Buenos Aires, 1887–1936.* Buenos Aires: Editorial de la Universidad de Quilmes, 1998.

Gutiérrez, Leandro, and Luis Alberto Romero. *Sectores populares, cultura y política. Buenos Aires en la entreguerra.* Buenos Aires: Sudamericana, 1995.

Leragne, Catalina. *La Plata, ciudad milagro.* Buenos Aires: Corregidor, 1982.

Hardoy, Jorge E. et al. "El caso argentino (urbanización)." *Revista de la Sociedad Interamericana de Planificación* 2, nos. 5–6 (1968): 31–38.

Sarlo, Beatriz. *Una modernidad periférica: Buenos Aires, 1920 y 1930.* Buenos Aires: Nueva Visión, 1988.

Scobie, James R. *Buenos Aires: From Plaza to Suburb, 1870–1910.* New York: Oxford University Press, 1974.

———. "Changing Urban Patterns: The Porteño Case (1880–1910)." In *Urbanization in the Americas from Its Beginning to the Present,* edited by Richard P. Schaedel, Jorge E. Hardoy, and Nora Scott Kinzer, 425–42. The Hague: Mouton, 1978.

Walter, Richard. *Politics and Urban Growth in Buenos Aires, 1910–1942.* Cambridge: Cambridge University Press, 1993.

Poverty and Inequality

Altmir, Oscar. "Estimaciones de la distribución del ingreso en Argentina, 1953–1980." *Desarrollo Económico* 25, no. 100 (January–March 1986): 521–66.

Lloyd-Sherlock, Peter. *Old Age and Urban Poverty in the Developing World: The Shanty Towns of Buenos Aires*. London: Macmillan, 1997.

Lo Vuolo, Rubén. *Distribución y crecimiento. Una controversia persistente*. Madrid: CIEPP/Miño y Dávila Editores, 2009.

Powers, Nancy. "The Politics of Poverty in Argentina in the 1990s." *Journal of Inter-American Studies* 37, no. 4 (Winter 1995): 89–137.

Social Policy and Social Conditions

Alhadeff, Peter. "Social Welfare and the Slump: Argentina in the 1930s." In *Social Welfare, 1850–1950: Australia, Argentina and Canada Compared*, edited by D. C. M. Platt, 169–78. London: St. Antony's/Macmillan, 1989.

Lo Vuolo, Rubén. "Ideology and the New Social Security in the Argentine." In *Exclusion and Engagement: Social Policy in Latin America*, edited by Christopher Abel and Colin M. Lewis, 208–23. London: Institute of Latin American Studies, 2002.

Lo Vuolo, Rubén, and Alberto Barbeito. *La nueva oscuridad de la política social*. Buenos Aires: Miño y Dávila Editores, 1998.

Suriano, Juan, ed. *La cuestión social en la Argentina, 1870–1943*. Buenos Aires: La Colmena, 2000.

Zimmermann, Eduardo. "Racial Ideas and Social Reform: Argentina, 1890–1916." *Hispanic America Historical Review* 72, no. 1 (February 1992): 23–46.

Education

Ciria, Alberto, and Horacio Sanguinetti. *La Reforma Universitaria (1918–1983)*. Buenos Aires: Centro Editor de América Latina, 1983.

Puiggrós, Adriana, and Jorge Luis Bernetti, eds. *Peronismo: Cultura Política y Educación (1945–1955)*. Buenos Aires: Galerna, 2006.

Spalding, Hobart. "Education in Argentina, 1890–1914: The Limits of Oligarchic Reform." *Journal of Interdisciplinary History* 3, no. 1 (Summer 1972): 31–61.

Tedesco, Juan Carlos. *Educación y sociedad en la Argentina, 1880–1900*. Buenos Aires: Pannedille, 1970.

Health

Álvarez, Adriana and Daniel Reynoso. *Médicos e instituciones de salud. Mar del Plata, 1870–1960*. Buenos Aires: HISA/Universidad Nacional de Mar del Plata, 1995.

Armus, Diego. *La ciudad impura: salud, tuberculosis y cultura en Buenos Aires, 1870–1950*. Buenos Aires: EDHASA, 2007.

Lloyd-Sherlock, Peter. "Ambitious Plans, Modest Outcomes: The Politics of Health Care Reform in Argentina." In *Crucial Needs, Weak Incentives: Social Sector Reform, Democratization and Globalization in Latin America*, edited by Roberto R. Kaufman and Joan M. Nelson, 93–123. Baltimore, MD: Johns Hopkins University Press, 2004.

Lobato, Marta Zaida, ed. *Política, médicos y enfermedades. Lecturas de historia de la salud en la Argentina*. Buenos Aires: Biblos/Universidad Mar del Plata, 1996.

Paiva, Verónica. "Entre miasmas y microbios: la ciudad bajo la lente del higienismo, Buenos Aires, 1850–1890." *ARENA*, no. 4 (August 1996): 33–47.

Veronelli, Juan Carlos. *Medicina, gobierno y sociedad. Evolución de las instituciones de la salud en Argentina*. Buenos Aires: El Coloquio, 1975.

Religion

Ivereigh, Austen. *Catholicism and Politics in Argentina, 1810–1960*. New York: St. Martin's Press, 1995.

———. *The Great Reformer: Francis and the Making of a Radical Pope*. New York: Henry Holt, 2014.

Art and Culture

Cahen d'Anvers, Mónica. *Mónica Presenta*. Buenos Aires: Planeta, 2016.

Eloy Martínez, Tomás. "A Culture of Barbarism." In *Argentina in the Crisis Years (1983–1990): From Alfonsín to Menem*, edited by Colin M. Lewis and Nissa Torrents, 11–23. London: Institute of Latin American Studies, 1993.

Gorostiza, Carlos. *El Merodeador Enmascarado: Algunas memorias, 1920–2004*. Buenos Aires: Seix Barral, 2004.

King, John. *El Di Tella y el desarrollo cultural argentino*. Buenos Aires: Editorial Gaglianone, 1985.

———. *"Sur": A Study of the Argentine Literary Journal and Its Role in the Literary Development of a Culture, 1931–1970*. Cambridge: Cambridge University Press, 1986.

King, John, Sheila Whitaker, and Rosa Bosch, eds. *An Argentine Passion: María Luisa Bemberg and Her Films*. New York: Verso, 2000.

Lafleur, Héctor R., Sergio Provenzano, and Fernando Alonso. *Las revistas literarias argentinas, 1983–1967*. Buenos Aires: El 8vo. loco, 2006.

Romero, José Alberto. *Las ideas políticas en Argentina*. Buenos Aires: Fondo de Cultura Económica, 1986.

Saítta, Sylvia. *El escritor en el bosque de ladrillos: Una biografía de Roberto Arlt*. Buneos Aires: Sudamericana, 2000.

Sarlo, Beatriz. *Borges, un escritor en las orillas*. Buenos Aires: Ariel, 1995.

Sidicaro, Ricardo. *La política mirada desde arriba: Las ideas del diario La Nación, 1909–1989*. Buenos Aires: Sudamericana, 1993.

Torrents, Nissa. "The Cinema That Never Was." In *Argentina in the Crisis Years (1983–1990): From Alfonsín to Menem*, edited by Colin M. Lewis and Nissa Torrents, 35–51. London: Institute of Latin American Studies, 1993.

Viñas, David. *Literatura argentina y política: de Lugones a Walsh*. Buenos Aires: Sudamericana, 1996.

Wilson, Jason. *Cultural Guide to the City of Buenos Aires*. Oxford: Signal Books, 1999.

WEBSITES

A number of websites offer information about Argentina. In addition to numerous official sites, domestic and international agencies provide current and historical political, economic, and social data; several media companies also offer digital services.

The main international electronic databases are those operated by such international bodies as the International Monetary Fund (IMF), the International Bank for Reconstruction and Development (World Bank), the Economic Commission for Latin America (ECLA), and MERCOSUR. All have specific sites dedicated to Argentina containing recent and current data, with some holding substantial amounts of historical information.

Argentine Government Sources

Most official sites provide information in Spanish, English, and Portuguese. The main websites include the following:

Central Bank of the Argentine Republic: http://www.bcra.gov.ar/
National Congress of Argentina: http://www.congreso.gob.ar/
National Library: https://www.bn.gov.ar/

National Statistical Office: https://www.indec.gob.ar/
Presidential Office/Casa Rosada: https://www.casarosada.gob.ar/

Most of the principal ministries also have digital services offering current and historical information, for example:

Ministry of Economy: https://www.argentina.gob.ar/hacienda
Ministry of Foreign Relations: https://www.mrecic.gov.ar/

Similarly, many national museums operate portals that provide data and information within their respective remit, for example:

National History Museum: https://museohistoriconacional.cultura.gob.ar/
National Museum of Fine Arts: https://www.bellasartes.gob.ar/

Argentine National Organizations and Bodies

All the large political parties maintain websites, as do business organizations like the Sociedad Rural Argentina (SRA) and the Unión Industrial Argentina (UIA) and the trade union federation—the Confederación General del Trabajo (CGT).

Cambiemos: https://cambiemos.com/
Partido Justicialista: https://www.pj.org.ar (currently suspended)
Confederacion General del Trabajo: https://www.cesba.gob.ar/mas-sobre-cgt-1
Sociedad Rural Argentina: https://www.sra.org.ar/
Union Industrial Argentina: http://www.uia.org.ar/

Media

Argentina is a highly literate society and has a vibrant print media. This is partly explained by government control of radio and television during periods of authoritarian rule, when state broadcasting systems have been subject to close official scrutiny and regarded by the population at large as unreliable. Even in the current digital age, the print media is well regarded. *Clarín* is the most widely read daily newspaper, the weekend editions being among the largest circulating of the Spanish-language press. *La Nación* is the established daily. *Notícias*, published by the Perfil Group, is a weekly current affairs magazine modeled on *Time*. The main outlets are based in the city of Buenos Aires; only *La Capital*, published in Rosario, has a similar national status among newspapers published in the interior. The business press is dominated by *El Cronista*, the oldest such newspaper in the country and the first daily to appear in digital form, and *Ámbito Financiero*. Most dailies and weeklies are now available in print and digital format, some only in digital.

The main state television channel is Televisión Pública Argentina (TV Pública), formerly known as Canal 7; the most widely viewed is El Trece, which is owned by the Grupo Clarín and was previously known as Canal 13. The main 24-hour news service is provided by Todo Notícias.

The principal print and television media website are as follow:

Ámbito Financiero: http://www.ambito.com/
Clarín: https://www.clarin.com/
El Cronista: https://www.cronista.com/
La Capital: https://www.lacapital.com.ar/
La Nacion: https://www.lanacion.com.ar/
La Prensa: http://www.laprensa.com.ar/
Noticias: http://noticias.perfil.com/
El Trece: https://www.eltrecetv.com.ar/
Television Publica Argentina: http://www.tvpublica.com.ar/
Todo Noticias: https://tn.com.ar/envivo/24hs

About the Authors

Bernardo A. Duggan was born in Argentina and now lives in Australia. He studied in Argentina and Great Britain. His undergraduate degree is from the University of London; he read international history at the London School of Economics and Political Science (LSE). His doctorate is also from the University of London. His research was undertaken in the Department of Economic History at the LSE; the title of the dissertation is "Iron and Steel Production in Argentina c. 1920–1952: Attempts at Establishing a Strategic Industry" (1999).

Colin M. Lewis is professor emeritus of Latin American economic history at the London School of Economics and Political Science. He is also an honorary professorial fellow at the Institute of the Americas, University College London, and an associate fellow at the Institute for Latin American Studies, School of Advanced Studies, University of London; he has been a corresponding member of the Academia Argentina de la Historia since 1992 and a member of the Advisory Committee for the master's degree in regional policy (MERCOSUR/L, FLACSO Buenos Aires) since 1997. He has held visiting professorships at universities in Latin America, Europe, and Asia and has taught short courses at various institutions in Argentina, including the University of Buenos Aires (UBA) and the Universidad Tres de Febrero, and lectured at other centers such as the Instituto Torcuato Di Tella, the Universidad Nacional de La Plata (UNLP), the Universidad Católica Argentina (UCA), and the Universidad de San Andrés (UDESA) in Buenos Aires and at other campuses in the country. His principal books about Argentina include *British Railways in Argentina, 1857–1914: A Case Study of Foreign Investment* (2015), *Argentina: A Short History* (2002), *The Argentine: From Economic Growth to Economic Retardation (1850s–1980s)* (1996), and (with Nissa Torrents, eds.) *Argentina in the Crisis Years (1983–1990): From Alfonsín to Menem* (1993). He has written about Argentine social insurance, state formation, and industrial growth and economic imperialism, development, and economic and social policy in Latin America. He is currently working on a business history of Argentina.